CODE OF FEDERAL REGULATIONS

Title 17
Commodity and Securities Exchanges

Part 241 to End

Revised as of April 1, 2023

Containing a codification of documents
of general applicability and future effect

As of April 1, 2023

Published by the Office of the Federal Register
National Archives and Records Administration
as a Special Edition of the Federal Register

Table of Contents

	Page
Explanation	v

Title 17:

    Chapter II—Securities and Exchange Commission (Continued) 3

    Chapter IV—Department of the Treasury 583

Finding Aids:

    Table of CFR Titles and Chapters 661

    Alphabetical List of Agencies Appearing in the CFR 681

    Table of OMB Control Numbers 691

    List of CFR Sections Affected 697

Cite this Code: CFR

To cite the regulations in this volume use title, part and section number. Thus, 17 CFR 242.100 *refers to title 17, part 242, section 100.*

Explanation

The Code of Federal Regulations is a codification of the general and permanent rules published in the Federal Register by the Executive departments and agencies of the Federal Government. The Code is divided into 50 titles which represent broad areas subject to Federal regulation. Each title is divided into chapters which usually bear the name of the issuing agency. Each chapter is further subdivided into parts covering specific regulatory areas.

Each volume of the Code is revised at least once each calendar year and issued on a quarterly basis approximately as follows:

Title 1 through Title 16..as of January 1
Title 17 through Title 27 ....as of April 1
Title 28 through Title 41 ....as of July 1
Title 42 through Title 50 ....as of October 1

The appropriate revision date is printed on the cover of each volume.

LEGAL STATUS

The contents of the Federal Register are required to be judicially noticed (44 U.S.C. 1507). The Code of Federal Regulations is prima facie evidence of the text of the original documents (44 U.S.C. 1510).

HOW TO USE THE CODE OF FEDERAL REGULATIONS

The Code of Federal Regulations is kept up to date by the individual issues of the Federal Register. These two publications must be used together to determine the latest version of any given rule.

To determine whether a Code volume has been amended since its revision date (in this case, April 1, 2023), consult the "List of CFR Sections Affected (LSA)," which is issued monthly, and the "Cumulative List of Parts Affected," which appears in the Reader Aids section of the daily Federal Register. These two lists will identify the Federal Register page number of the latest amendment of any given rule.

EFFECTIVE AND EXPIRATION DATES

Each volume of the Code contains amendments published in the Federal Register since the last revision of that volume of the Code. Source citations for the regulations are referred to by volume number and page number of the Federal Register and date of publication. Publication dates and effective dates are usually not the same and care must be exercised by the user in determining the actual effective date. In instances where the effective date is beyond the cut-off date for the Code a note has been inserted to reflect the future effective date. In those instances where a regulation published in the Federal Register states a date certain for expiration, an appropriate note will be inserted following the text.

OMB CONTROL NUMBERS

The Paperwork Reduction Act of 1980 (Pub. L. 96–511) requires Federal agencies to display an OMB control number with their information collection request.

Many agencies have begun publishing numerous OMB control numbers as amendments to existing regulations in the CFR. These OMB numbers are placed as close as possible to the applicable recordkeeping or reporting requirements.

PAST PROVISIONS OF THE CODE

Provisions of the Code that are no longer in force and effect as of the revision date stated on the cover of each volume are not carried. Code users may find the text of provisions in effect on any given date in the past by using the appropriate List of CFR Sections Affected (LSA). For the convenience of the reader, a "List of CFR Sections Affected" is published at the end of each CFR volume. For changes to the Code prior to the LSA listings at the end of the volume, consult previous annual editions of the LSA. For changes to the Code prior to 2001, consult the List of CFR Sections Affected compilations, published for 1949-1963, 1964-1972, 1973-1985, and 1986-2000.

"[RESERVED]" TERMINOLOGY

The term "[Reserved]" is used as a place holder within the Code of Federal Regulations. An agency may add regulatory information at a "[Reserved]" location at any time. Occasionally "[Reserved]" is used editorially to indicate that a portion of the CFR was left vacant and not dropped in error.

INCORPORATION BY REFERENCE

What is incorporation by reference? Incorporation by reference was established by statute and allows Federal agencies to meet the requirement to publish regulations in the Federal Register by referring to materials already published elsewhere. For an incorporation to be valid, the Director of the Federal Register must approve it. The legal effect of incorporation by reference is that the material is treated as if it were published in full in the Federal Register (5 U.S.C. 552(a)). This material, like any other properly issued regulation, has the force of law.

What is a proper incorporation by reference? The Director of the Federal Register will approve an incorporation by reference only when the requirements of 1 CFR part 51 are met. Some of the elements on which approval is based are:

(a) The incorporation will substantially reduce the volume of material published in the Federal Register.

(b) The matter incorporated is in fact available to the extent necessary to afford fairness and uniformity in the administrative process.

(c) The incorporating document is drafted and submitted for publication in accordance with 1 CFR part 51.

What if the material incorporated by reference cannot be found? If you have any problem locating or obtaining a copy of material listed as an approved incorporation by reference, please contact the agency that issued the regulation containing that incorporation. If, after contacting the agency, you find the material is not available, please notify the Director of the Federal Register, National Archives and Records Administration, 8601 Adelphi Road, College Park, MD 20740-6001, or call 202-741-6010.

CFR INDEXES AND TABULAR GUIDES

A subject index to the Code of Federal Regulations is contained in a separate volume, revised annually as of January 1, entitled CFR INDEX AND FINDING AIDS. This volume contains the Parallel Table of Authorities and Rules. A list of CFR titles, chapters, subchapters, and parts and an alphabetical list of agencies publishing in the CFR are also included in this volume.

An index to the text of "Title 3—The President" is carried within that volume.

The Federal Register Index is issued monthly in cumulative form. This index is based on a consolidation of the "Contents" entries in the daily Federal Register.

A List of CFR Sections Affected (LSA) is published monthly, keyed to the revision dates of the 50 CFR titles.

REPUBLICATION OF MATERIAL

There are no restrictions on the republication of material appearing in the Code of Federal Regulations.

INQUIRIES

For a legal interpretation or explanation of any regulation in this volume, contact the issuing agency. The issuing agency's name appears at the top of odd-numbered pages.

For inquiries concerning CFR reference assistance, call 202-741-6000 or write to the Director, Office of the Federal Register, National Archives and Records Administration, 8601 Adelphi Road, College Park, MD 20740-6001 or e-mail *fedreg.info@nara.gov*.

THIS TITLE

Title 17—COMMODITY AND SECURITIES EXCHANGES is composed of five volumes. The first two volumes, containing parts 1–40 and 41–199, comprise Chapter I—Commodity Futures Trading Commission. The third volume contains Chapter II—Securities and Exchange Commission, parts 200–239. The fourth volume, comprising part 240, contains additional regulations of the Securities and Exchange Commission. The fifth volume, comprising part 241 to end, contains the remaining regulations of the Securities and Exchange Commission and Chapter IV—Department of the Treasury. The contents of these volumes represent all current regulations codified under this title by the Commodity Futures Trading Commission, the Securities and Exchange Commission, and the Department of the Treasury as of April 1, 2023.

The OMB control numbers for the Securities and Exchange Commission appear in §200.800 of chapter II. For the convenience of the user, §200.800 is reprinted in the Finding Aids sections of volume 4, containing part 240, and volume 5, containing part 241 to end.

For this volume, Robert J. Sheehan, III was Chief Editor. The Code of Federal Regulations publication program is under the direction of John Hyrum Martinez, assisted by Stephen J. Frattini.

Title 17—Commodity and Securities Exchanges

(This book contains part 241 to end)

	Part
CHAPTER II—Securities and Exchange Commission (Continued)	241
CHAPTER IV—Department of the Treasury	400

CHAPTER II—SECURITIES AND EXCHANGE COMMISSION (CONTINUED)

Part		Page
241	Interpretative releases relating to the Securities Exchange Act of 1934 and general rules and regulations thereunder	5
242	Regulations M, SHO, ATS, AC, NMS, and SBSR and customer margin requirements for security futures	11
243	Regulation FD	111
244	Regulation G	113
245	Regulation blackout trading restriction	115
246	Credit risk retention	121
247	Regulation R—Exemptions and definitions related to the exceptions for banks from the definition of broker	163
248	Regulations S-P, S-AM, and S-ID	177
249	Forms, Securities Exchange Act of 1934	228
249a	Forms, Securities Investor Protection Act of 1970 [Reserved]	
249b	Further forms, Securities Exchange Act of 1934	250
250	Cross-border antifraud law-enforcement authority	252
251–254	[Reserved]	
255	Proprietary trading and certain interests in and relationships with covered funds	252
256–259	[Reserved]	
260	General rules and regulations, Trust Indenture Act of 1939	299
261	Interpretative releases relating to the Trust Indenture Act of 1939 and general rules and regulations thereunder	316
269	Forms prescribed under the Trust Indenture Act of 1939	317
270	Rules and regulations, Investment Company Act of 1940	319
271	Interpretative releases relating to the Investment Company Act of 1940 and general rules and regulations thereunder	494

Part		Page
274	Forms prescribed under the Investment Company Act of 1940	497
275	Rules and regulations, Investment Advisers Act of 1940	505
276	Interpretative releases relating to the Investment Advisers Act of 1940 and general rules and regulations thereunder	554
279	Forms prescribed under the Investment Advisers Act of 1940	556
281	Interpretative releases relating to corporate reorganizations under Chapter X of the Bankruptcy Act	557
285	Rules and regulations pursuant to section 15(a) of the Bretton Woods Agreements Act	557
286	General rules and regulations pursuant to section 11(a) of the Inter-American Development Bank Act	559
287	General rules and regulations pursuant to section 11(a) of the Asian Development Bank Act	561
288	General rules and regulations pursuant to section 9(a) of the African Development Bank Act	563
289	General rules and regulations pursuant to section 13(a) of the International Finance Corporation Act	565
290	General rules and regulations pursuant to section 9(a) of the European Bank for Reconstruction and Development Act	567
300	Rules of the Securities Investor Protection Corporation	569
301	Forms, Securities Investor Protection Corporation	576
302	Orderly liquidation of covered brokers or dealers	577
303–399	[Reserved]	

PART 241—INTERPRETATIVE RELEASES RELATING TO THE SECURITIES EXCHANGE ACT OF 1934 AND GENERAL RULES AND REGULATIONS THEREUNDER

AUTHORITY: 15 U.S.C. 78a *et seq.*

Subject	Release No.	Date	Fed. Reg. Vol. and Page
Excerpt from letter relating to section 16(a)	21	Oct. 1, 1934	11 FR 10968.
Statement by Commission to correct the erroneous impression created by certain commercial institutions with respect to the necessity for filing reports with the Commission.	68	July 22, 1934	Do.
Letter of General Counsel relating to section 16(a)	116	Mar. 9, 1935	Do.
Opinion of General Counsel relating to section 16(a)	175	Apr. 16, 1935	Do.
Excerpt from a general letter relating to section 16(a)	227	May 14, 1935	Do.
Opinion of the Director of the Division of Forms and Regulations discussing the definition of "parent" as used in various forms under the Securities Act of 1933 and the Securities Exchange Act of 1934.	1131	Apr. 7, 1937	Do.
Statement by Commission with respect to the purpose of the disclosure requirements of section 14 and the rules adopted thereunder.	1350	Aug. 13, 1937	11 FR 10969.
Opinion of Director of the Trading and Exchange Division relating to Rules X-15C1-6 (17 CFR 240.15c1-6) and X-10B-2 (17 CFR 240.10b-2).	1411	Oct. 7, 1937	Do.
Opinion of Director of the Trading and Exchange Division relating to Rule X-15C1-1(a) (17 CFR, 240.15c1-1a).	1462	Nov. 15, 1937	Do.
Partial text of letter of February 2, 1938, from the Secretary of the New York Stock Exchange to its members, relating to Rules X-3B-3 (17 CFR 240.3b-3), X-10A-1 (17 CFR 240.10a-1), and X-10A-2 (17 CFR 240.10a-2), together with a letter from Director of Trading and Exchange Division, concurring in the opinions expressed by the Exchange.	1571	Feb. 5, 1938	Do.
Opinion of General Counsel relating to section 16(a)	1965	Dec. 21, 1938	11 FR 10970.
Letter of General Counsel concerning the services of former employees of the Commission in connection with matters with which such employees become familiar during their course of employment with the Commission.	2066	May 5, 1939	11 FR 10971.
Statement of Commission and separate statement by Commissioner Healy on the problem of regulating the "pegging, fixing and stabilizing" of security prices under sections 9(a)(2), 9(a)(6) and 15(c)(1) of the Securities Exchange Act.	2446	Mar. 18, 1940	Do.
Statement of Commission respecting distinctions between the reporting requirements of section 16(a) of the Securities Exchange Act of 1934 and section 30(f) of the Investment Company Act of 1940.	2687	Nov. 16, 1940	11 FR 10981.
Statement of Commission issued in connection with the adoption of Rules X-8C-1 (17 CFR, 240.8c-1) and X-15-C2-1 (17 CFR, 240.15c 2-1) under the Securities Exchange Act of 1934 relating to the hypothecation of customers' securities by members of national securities exchanges and other brokers and dealers.	2690	Nov. 15, 1940	11 FR 10982.
Opinion of General Counsel relating to paragraph (b)(2)(ii) of Rules X-8C-1 (17 CFR, 240.8c-1) and X-15C2-1 (17 CFR, 240.15C 2-1) under the Securities Exchange Act.	2822	Mar. 17, 1941	11 FR 10983.
Partial text of letter sent by Director of the Trading and Exchange Division to certain securities dealers who had failed to keep records of the times of their securities transactions, as required by Rules X-17A-3 (17 CFR, 240.17a-3) and X-17A-4 (17 CFR, 240.17a-4) under the Securities Exchange Act.	3040	Oct. 13, 1941	11 FR 10984.
Opinion of General Counsel relating to the anti-manipulation provisions of sections 9(a)(2), 10(b) and 15(c)(1) of the Securities Exchange Act of 1934, as well as section 17(a) of the Securities Act of 1933.	3056	Oct. 27, 1941	Do.
Opinion of Chief Counsel to the Corporation Finance Division relating to when-issued trading of securities the issuance of which has already been approved by a Federal district court under Chapter X of the Bankruptcy Act.	3069	Jan. 4, 1945	11 FR 10985.
Statement of Commission policy with respect to the acceleration of the effective date of a registration statement.	3085	Dec. 6, 1941	Do.
Letter of Director of the Corporation Finance Division relating to sections 14 and 18.	3380	Feb. 2, 1943	Do.
Excerpts from letters of Director of the Corporation Finance Division relating to section 14 and Schedule 14A under Regulation X-14 (17 CFR, 240.14a-9).	3385	Feb. 17, 1943	Do.
Opinion of Director of the Trading and Exchange Division relating to the anti-manipulation provisions of sections 9(a)(2), 10(b), and 15(c)(1) of the Securities Exchange Act of 1934, and 17(a) of the Securities Act of 1933.	3505	Nov. 16, 1943	11 FR 10986.

Pt. 241   17 CFR Ch. II (4-1-23 Edition)

Subject	Release No.	Date	Fed. Reg. Vol. and Page
Opinion of Director of the Trading and Exchange Division relating to the anti-manipulation provisions of sections 9(a)(2), 10(b), and 15(c)(1) of the Securities Exchange Act of 1934, and 17(a) of the Securities Act of 1933.	3506	Nov. 16, 1943	11 FR 10987.
Statement of the Commission relating to the anti-fraud provisions of section 17(a) of the Securities Act of 1933, and sections 10(b) and 15(c)(1) of the Securities Exchange Act of 1934.	3572	June 1, 1944	Do.
Letter of Director of the Corporation Finance Division relating to section 20 and to Rule X-14A-7 (17 CFR, 240.14a-7) under the Securities Exchange Act of 1934.	3638	Jan. 3, 1945	11 FR 10988.
Statement by Commission relating to section 3(a)(1)	3639	Jan. 4, 1945	Do.
Statement of the Commission in connection with the adoption of certain amendments to Form 3-M, one of the forms for registration of over-the-counter brokers or dealers under section 15(b) of the Securities Exchange Act of 1934, and to Rule X-15B-2 (17 CFR, 240.15b-2), the rule governing the filing of supplemental statements to such applications.	3674	Apr. 9, 1945	Do.
Statement by Commission relating to the adoption of Rule X-13A-6B (17 CFR, 240.13a-6b).	3803	Mar. 28, 1946	Do.
Statement of the Commission in connection with notice of opportunity to submit proposals for regulations or legislation regarding the stabilization of market prices by persons offering securities to the public.	4163	Sept. 16, 1948	13 FR 4163.
Statement of the Commission accompanying November 5, 1948, revision of § 240.14 of this chapter (Regulation X-14).	4185	Nov. 5, 1948	13 FR 6680.
Opinion of the General Counsel, relating to the use of "hedge clauses" by brokers, dealers, investment advisers, and others.	4593	Apr. 18, 1951	16 FR 3387.
Statement of the Commission regarding public offerings of investment contracts providing for the acquisition, sale or servicing of mortgages or deeds of trust.	5633	Jan. 31, 1958	23 FR 841.
Statement of the Commission as to the applicability of the Federal securities laws to real estate investment trusts.	6419	Nov. 18, 1960	25 FR 12178.
Statement of the Commission concerning standards of conduct for registered broker-dealers in the distribution of unregistered securities.	6721	Feb. 2, 1962	27 FR 1251.
Opinion of Philip A. Loomis, Jr., Director of Division of Trading and Exchanges of the Commission, on the application of section 11(d)(1), Securities Exchange Act of 1934, to broker-dealers engaged in "equity funding", "secured funding", and "life funding".	6726	Feb. 8, 1962	27 FR 1415.
Statement of the Commission cautioning broker-dealers about violating the anti-fraud provisions of the Federal securities laws when making short sales in which they delay effecting the covering transaction to acquire the security.	6778	Apr. 16, 1962	27 FR 3991.
Statement of Commission showing circumstances in 7 cases where profits in real estate transactions were not earned at time transactions were recorded but that the sales were designed to create the illusion of profits or value as a basis for the sale of securities.	6982	Dec. 28, 1962	28 FR 276.
Answer of the Commission to four questions relating to the solicitation of proxies.	7078	May 15, 1963	28 FR 5133.
Statement by the Commission on the maintenance of records of transactions by brokers-dealers as underwriters of investment company shares according to Rule 17a-3 under section 17(a) of the Securities Exchange Act of 1934 (17 CFR 240.17a-3).	7169	Nov. 13, 1963	28 FR 12617.
Opinion of the General Counsel relating to participation by broker-dealer firms in proxy solicitations.	7208	Jan. 7, 1964	29 FR 341.
Statement of the Commission re applicability of Securities Act of 1933 to offerings of securities outside the U.S. and re applicability of section 15(a) of the Securities Exchange Act of 1934 to foreign underwriters as part of program of Presidential Task Force to reduce U.S. balance of payments deficit and protect U.S. gold reserves.	7366	July 9, 1964	29 FR 9828.
Summary and interpretation by the Commission of amendments to the Securities Act of 1933 and Securities Exchange Act of 1934 as contained in the Securities Acts Amendments of 1964.	7425	Sept. 14, 1964	29 FR 13455.
Opinion and statement of the Commission in regard to proper reporting of deferred income taxes arising from installment sales.	7763	Dec. 7, 1965	30 FR 15420.
Statement of the Commission to clarify the meaning of "beneficial ownership of securities" as relates to beneficial ownership of securities held by family members.	7793	Jan. 19, 1966	31 FR 1005.
Program by the Commission which it requests that issuing companies follow in order to expedite the processing of proxy material.	7805	Jan. 26, 1966	31 FR 2475.
Statement of the Commission setting the date of May 1, 1966 after which filings must reflect beneficial ownership of securities held by family members.	7824	Feb. 14, 1966	31 FR 3175.
Policy statement by the Director of the Division of Trading and Markets re consummation of securities transactions by brokers-dealers when trading is suspended.	7920	July 19, 1966	31 FR 10076.

Securities and Exchange Commission

Pt. 241

Subject	Release No.	Date	Fed. Reg. Vol. and Page
Opinions of the Commission on the acceleration of the effective date of a registration statement under the Securities Act of 1933 and on the clearance of proxy material such as convertible preferred shares considered residual securities in determining earnings per share applicable to common stock.	8336	June 18, 1968	33 FR 10086.
Statement of the Commission to alert prospective borrowers obtaining loans for real estate development about recent fraudulent schemes.	8351	July 5, 1968	33 FR 10134.
Statement of the Commission warning broker-dealers to be prompt in the consummation of securities transactions and about the penalty for not so doing.	8363	July 29, 1968	33 FR 11150.
Statement of the Commission re broker-dealer registration of insurance companies acting as agents for distribution of "variable annuities" and application of regulations for such under the Securities Exchange Act of 1934.	8389	Aug. 29, 1968	33 FR 13005.
Statement of the Commission reminding broker-dealer managements to establish and maintain an effective supervisory system and failure to do so will result in disciplinary action against the firm and responsible individuals.	8404	Sept. 11, 1968	33 FR 14286.
Statement of the Commission clarifying that industrial revenue bonds sold according to Rule 131 (17 CFR 230.131) and Rule 3b–5 (17 CFR 240.3b–5) are not affected if acquired and paid for by the underwriters on or before December 31, 1968.	8409	Sept. 16, 1968	33 FR 14545.
Statement of the Commission cautioning brokers and dealers with respect to effecting transactions of "spin offs" and "shell corporations".	8638	July 2, 1969	34 FR 11581.
Commission's statement about publicity concerning the petroleum discoveries on the North Slope of Alaska.	8728	Oct. 20, 1969	34 FR 17433.
Commission's warning statement re sale and distribution of whisky warehouse receipts.	8733	Nov. 4, 1969	34 FR 18160.
Letter by Philip A. Loomis, Jr., General Counsel for the Commission, explaining obligations of mutual fund managements and brokers with respect to commissions on portfolio brokerage of mutual funds.	8746	Nov. 10, 1969	34 FR 18543.
Publication of the Commission's guidelines re applicability of Federal securities laws to offer and sale outside the U.S. of shares of registered open-end investment companies.	8907	June 23, 1970	35 FR 12103.
Statement of the Commission reminding reporting companies of obligation re Commission's rules to file reports on a timely basis.	8995	Oct. 15, 1970	35 FR 16733.
Commission's statement re exemption of certain industrial revenue bonds from registration, etc. requirements in view of amendment of Securities Act of 1933 and of Securities Exchange Act of 1934 by "section 401" (Pub. L. 91–1037).	9016	Nov. 6, 1970	35 FR 17990.
Commission's views relating to important questions re the accounting by registered investment companies for investment securities in their financial statements and in the periodic computations of net asset value for the purpose of pricing their shares.	9049	Dec. 23, 1970	35 FR 19986.
Publication of the Commission's procedure to be followed if requests are to be met for no action or interpretative letters and responses thereto to be made available for public use.	9065	Jan. 25, 1971	36 FR 2600.
Interpretations of the Commission in regard to requirements for registration statements and reports concerning information requested re description of business, summary of operations, and financial statements.	9083	Feb. 18, 1971	36 FR 4483.
Statement of the Commission warning the public about novel unsecured debt securities which appear to invite unwarranted comparisons with bank savings accounts, savings and loan association accounts, and bank time deposit certificates.	9148	Apr. 12, 1971	36 FR 8239.
Statement of the Commission prohibiting the reduction of fixed charges by amounts representing interest or investment income or gains on retirement of debt in registration statements or reports filed with the Commission.	9210	June 16, 1971	36 FR 11918.
Statement of the Commission calling attention to requirements in its forms and rules under the Securities Act of 1933 and the Securities and Exchange Act of 1934 for disclosure of legal proceedings and descriptions of registrant's business as these requirements relate to material matters involving the environment and civil rights.	9252	July 19, 1971	36 FR 13988.
Commission's policy requiring the inclusion in financial statements of the ratio of earnings to fixed charges for the total enterprise in equivalent prominence with the ratio for the registrant or registrant and consolidated subsidiaries.	9279	Aug. 10, 1971	36 FR 15527.
Policy of Commission's Division of Corporation Finance to defer processing registration statements and amendments filed under the Securities Act of 1933 by issuers whose reports are delinquent until such reports are brought up to date.	9345	Sept. 27, 1971	36 FR 19362.
Commission's statement concerning applicability of securities laws to multi-level distributorships and other business opportunities offered through pyramid sales plans.	9387	Nov. 30, 1971	36 FR 23289.
Statement by the Commission regarding payment of solicitation fees in tender offers.	9395	Nov. 24, 1971	36 FR 23359.

Pt. 241　　　　　　　　　　　　　　　　　　　　　　　　　　17 CFR Ch. II (4–1–23 Edition)

Subject	Release No.	Date	Fed. Reg. Vol. and Page
Commission's statement concerning offering and sale of securities in non-public offerings and applicability of antifraud provisions of securities acts.	9444	Jan. 14, 1972	37 FR 600.
Statement of the Commission's views on the present status of the securities markets and the direction in which the public interest requires that they evolve in the future.	....	Mar. 14, 1972	37 FR 5286
Commission endorses the establishment by all publicly held companies of audit committees composed of outside directors.	9548	Apr. 5, 1972	37 FR 6850.
Applicability of Commission's policy statement on the future structure of securities markets to selection of brokers and payment of commissions by institutional managers.	9598	May 18, 1972	37 FR 9988.
Commission's statement and policy on misleading pro rata stock distributions to shareholders.	9618	June 9, 1972	37 FR 11559.
Commission's guidelines on independence of certifying accountants; example cases and Commission's conclusions.	9662	June 19, 1972	37 FR 14294.
Commission's decisions on recommendations of advisory committee regarding commencement of enforcement proceedings and termination of staff investigations.	9796	Mar. 1, 1973	38 FR 5457.
Commission's interpretation of risk-sharing test in pooling-of-interest accounting.	9798	Oct. 5, 1972	37 FR 20937.
Commission's statement that short-selling securities prior to offering date is a possible violation of antifraud and antimanipulative laws.	9824	Oct. 25, 1972	37 FR 22796.
Commission reaffirms proper accounting treatment to be followed by a lessee when the lessor is created as a conduit for debt financing.	9867	Dec. 13, 1972	37 FR 26516.
Commission's interpretations of a rule (15c3–3) dealing with customer protection by securities brokers and dealers.	9922	Jan. 18, 1973	38 FR 1737.
Amendment of previous interpretation (AS–130) of risk-sharing test in pooling of interest accounting.	9927	Jan. 18, 1973	38 FR 1734.
Commission clarifies effective dates of Rule 15c3–3	9946	Feb. 5, 1973	38 FR 3313.
Commission's designation of control locations for foreign securities	9969	Feb. 5, 1973	Do.
Commission's findings on disclosure of projections of future economic performance by issuers of publicly traded securities.	9984	Mar. 19, 1973	38 FR 7220.
Commission's views on reporting cash flow and other related data	10041	Apr. 11, 1973	38 FR 9158.
Commission's statement on obligations of underwriters with respect to discretionary accounts.	10181	June 1, 1973	38 FR 17201.
Commission's opinion on net capital treatment of securities position, obligation and transactions in suspended securities.	10209	June 8, 1973	38 FR 16774.
Commission expresses concern with failure of issuers to timely and properly file periodic and current report.	10214	July 10, 1973	38 FR 18366.
Commission's statement and policy on application of minimum net capital requirement.	10304	Aug. 3, 1973	38 FR 20820.
Commission's conclusions as to certain problem relating to the effect of treasury stock transactions on accounting for business combinations.	10363	Sept. 10, 1973	38 FR 24635.
Commission's interpretation of market identification requirement of rule for reporting of market information on transactions in listed securities.	10388	Sept. 20, 1973	38 FR 26358.
Commission's response to the New York Stock Exchange's proposed interpretation of "affiliated person".	10391	Sept. 25, 1973	38 FR 26716.
Commission request for comments on Accounting Series Release No. 46	10422	Oct. 17, 1973	38 FR 28819.
Commission's guidelines for control locations for foreign securities	10429	Oct. 23, 1973	38 FR 29217.
Commission's views and comments relating to quarterly reporting on Form 10–Q and Form 10–QSB.	10547	Jan. 7, 1974	39 FR 1261.
Statement by the Commission on disclosure of the impact of possible fuel shortages on the operations of issuers.	10569	Jan. 10, 1974	39 FR 1511.
Commission's statement on disclosure of inventory profits reflected in income in periods of rising prices.	10580	Jan. 17, 1974	39 FR 2085.
Commission decision on trading in securities issued or guaranteed by the governments of Bulgaria, Hungary, and Romania.	10610	Jan. 31, 1974	39 FR 3932.
Commission views on disclosure of illegal campaign contributions	10673	Mar. 11, 1974	39 FR 10237.
Commission's statement of policy and interpretations	10363A	Apr. 12, 1974	39 FR 14588.
Commission's statement regarding maintenance of current books and records by brokers and dealers.	10756	May 9, 1974	39 FR 16440.
Commission's practices on reporting of natural gas reserve estimates	10857	June 14, 1974	39 FR 27556.
Commission's views on business combinations involving open-end investment companies.	10898	July 3, 1974	39 FR 26719.
Commission's guidelines for filings related to extractive reserves and natural gas supplies.	10899	July 3, 1974	39 FR 26720.
Commission's guidelines for registration and reporting	10961	Aug. 14, 1974	39 FR 31894.
Commission's requirements for financial statements; limited partnerships in annual reports.	11029	Sept. 27, 1974	39 FR 36578.
Commission's examples of unusual risks and uncertainties	11150	Dec. 23, 1994	40 FR 2678.
Letters of the Division of Corporation Finance with respect to certain proposed arrangements for the sale of gold bullion.	11156	Dec. 26, 1994	40 FR 1695.
Commission's statement on disclosure problems relating to LIFO accounting	11198	Jan. 23, 1975	40 FR 6483.
Commission's guidelines on Accounting Series Release No. 148	11470	June 13, 1975	40 FR 27441.

Securities and Exchange Commission

Pt. 241

Subject	Release No.	Date	Fed. Reg. Vol. and Page
Brokers and dealers effecting transactions in municipal securities	11854	Nov. 20, 1975	40 FR 57786.
Financial responsibility requirements of brokers and dealers	11969	Jan 2, 1976	41 FR 5277.
Brokers and dealers effecting transactions in municipal securities	12021	....	41 FR 3469.
Interpretation of certain terms in item 10 of Form BD	12078	Feb. 17, 1976	41 FR 7089.
Brokers and dealers effecting transactions in municipal securities	12288	Apr. 15, 1976	41 FR 15842.
Standards for disclosure; oil and gas reserve	12435	May 12, 1976	41 FR 21764.
Brokers and dealers effecting transactions in municipal securities	12496	June 11, 1976	41 FR 23668.
Statement of informal proposals for the rendering of staff advice with respect to shareholder proposals.	12599	July 20, 1976	41 FR 29989.
Guides for statistical disclosure by bank holding companies	12748	Aug. 31, 1976	41 FR 39007.
Uniform net capital rule	12766	Sept. 14, 1976	41 FR 39014.
Uniform net capital rule	12927	Oct. 27, 1976	41 FR 48335.
Brokers and dealers effecting transactions in municipal securities	12932	Oct. 27, 1976	41 FR 48336.
Brokers and dealers effecting transactions in municipal securities	13108	Jan. 4, 1977	42 FR 759.
Brokers and dealers effecting transactions in municipal securities	13362	Mar. 21, 1977	42 FR 15310.
Rescission of certain accounting series releases	13630	June 15, 1977	42 FR 33282.
Guideline regarding the preparation of integrated reports to shareholders	13639	June 17, 1977	42 FR 31780.
Industry segment determination	14523	Mar. 3, 1978	43 FR 9599.
Securities transactions by members of national securities exchanges	14563	Mar. 14, 1978	43 FR 11542.
Application of registration requirements to certain tender offers and the application of tender offer provisions to certain cash-option mergers.	14699	Apr. 24, 1978	43 FR 18163.
Reporting by certain institutional investors of beneficial ownership of certain equity securities which as of the end of any month exceeds ten percent of the class.	14830	June 13, 1978	43 FR 25420.
Division of investment management's interpretative positions relating to Rule 13f–1 and related Form 13F.	15292	Nov. 2, 1978	43 FR 52697.
Guides for disclosure of projections of future economic performance	15305	Nov. 7, 1978	43 FR 53246.
Commission's statement regarding disclosure of impact of Wage and Price Standards for 1979 on the operations of issuers.	15371	Nov. 29, 1978	43 FR 57596.
Statement of the views of the Commission's Division of Corporation Finance with respect to disclosure in proxy statements containing certain sale of assets transactions.	15572	Feb. 15, 1979	44 FR 11541.
Short sales; interpretation of rule	16150	Aug. 30, 1979	44 FR 53159.
Shareholder communications, shareholder participation in the corporate electoral process and corporate governance generally.	16163	Sept. 6, 1979	44 FR 53426.
Environmental disclosure requirements	16224	Sept. 27, 1979	44 FR 56924.
Pooled income funds	16478	Jan. 10, 1980	45 FR 3258.
Tender offer rules	16623	Mar. 5, 1980	45 FR 15521.
Proxy rules	16833	May 23, 1980	45 FR 36374.
Clearing agencies	16900	June 17, 1980	45 FR 41920.
Guides for statistical disclosure by bank holding companies	16961	July 8, 1980	45 FR 47142.
Transfer agents	17111	Sept. 2, 1980	45 FR 59840.
Amendments to guides	17114	Sept. 2, 1980	45 FR 63647.
Extension date of clearing agencies for form filing	17231	Oct. 20, 1980	45 FR 70857.
Beneficial ownership rules	17354	Dec. 4, 1980	45 FR 81559.
Distribution of proxy materials to beneficial shareowners	17424	Jan. 7, 1981	46 FR 3204.
Foreign Corrupt Practices Act of 1977	17500	Jan. 29, 1981	46 FR 11544.
Analysis of results of 1980 proxy statement disclosure monitoring program	17518	Feb. 5, 1981	46 FR 11954.
Option and option-related transactions during underwritten offerings	17609	Mar. 6, 1981	46 FR 16670.
Going private transactions under rule 13e–3	17719	Apr. 13, 1981	46 FR 22571.
Insider reporting and trading	18114	Sept. 23, 1981	46 FR 48147.
Retail repurchase agreements by banks and savings and loan associations	18122	Sept. 25, 1981	46 FR 48637.
Analysis of results of 1981 proxy statement disclosure monitoring program	18532	Mar. 3, 1982	47 FR 10794.
Rescission of guides and redesignation of industry guides (effective May 24, 1982).	18525	Mar. 3, 1982	47 FR 11481.
Amendments to guides	19337	Dec. 15, 1982	47 FR 57911.
Revision of financial statement requirements and industry guide disclosure for bank holding companies..	19570	Mar. 7, 1983	48 FR 11104.
Commission's views on *Colema Realty Corp.* v. *R. D. Bibow, et al*	19756	May 11, 1983	48 FR 23173.
Revision of industry guide disclosures for bank holding companies	20068	Aug. 11, 1983	48 FR 37609.
Public statements by corporate representatives	20560	Jan. 13, 1984	49 FR 2468.
Research reports	21332	Sept. 19, 1984	49 FR 37574.
Commission views on computer brokerage systems	21383	Oct. 9, 1984	49 FR 40159.
Guide for disclosures concerning reserves for unpaid claims and claim adjustment expenses of property-casualty underwriters.	21521	Nov. 27, 1984	49 FR 47601.
Brokerage and research services concerning scope of section 28(e) of Securities Exchange Act of 1934.	23170	Apr. 23, 1986	51 FR 16012.
Application of Rule 10b—6 under the Securities Exchange Act of 1934 to persons participating in shelf distributions.	23611	Sept. 11, 1986	51 FR 33248.
Industry guides for statistical disclosure by bank holding companies	23846	Nov. 25, 1986	51 FR 43599.
Tender offers rules	24296	Apr. 3, 1987	52 FR 11458.
Statement of the Commission Regarding Disclosure Obligations of Companies Affected by the Government's Defense Contract Procurement Inquiry and Related Issues.	25951	Aug. 1, 1988	53 FR 29228.

Subject	Release No.	Date	Fed. Reg. Vol. and Page
Statement of the Commission Regarding Disclosure by Issuers of interests in Publicly Offered Commodity Pools.	26508	Feb. 1, 1989	54 FR 5603.
Management's discussion and analysis of financial condition and results of operations; certain investment company disclosures.	26831	May 18, 1989	54 FR 22427.
Modifying and confirming the interpretation of municipal underwriter securities responsibilities.	26985	June 28, 1989	54 FR 28814.
Liquidation of Index Arbitrage Positions	27938	Apr. 30, 1990	55 FR 17949.
Ownership reports on trading by officers, directors and principal security holders.	29131	Apr. 26, 1991	56 FR 19928.
Limited partnership reorganizations and public offerings of limited partnership interests.	29314	June 17, 1991	56 FR 28986.
Registration of Successors to Broker-Dealers and Investment Advisors	31661	Jan. 4, 1993	58 FR 11.
Statement of the Commission regarding disclosure obligations of municipal securities issuers and others.	33741	Mar. 9, 1994	59 FR 12758.
Amendment of interpretation regarding substantive repossession of collateral	34061	May 12, 1994	59 FR 26109.
Use of electronic media for delivery purposes	36345	Oct. 6, 1995	60 FR 53467.
Use of electronic media for delivery purposes	37182	May 9, 1996	61 FR 24651.
Statement of the Commission Regarding Use of Internet Web Sites to Offer Securities, Solicit Securities Transactions or Advertise Investment Services Offshore.	39779	Mar. 23, 1998	63 FR 14813
Confirmation and Affirmation of Securities Trades; Matching	39829	Apr. 6, 1998	63 FR 17947
Statement of the Commission Regarding Disclosure of Year 2000 Issues and Consequences by Public Companies, Investment Advisers, Investment Companies, and Municipal Securities Issuers.	40277	July 29, 1998	63 FR 41404.
Use of electronic media	42728	Apr. 28, 2000	65 FR 25856.
Commission Guidance on Mini-Tender Offers and Limited Partnership Tender Offers.	43069	July 24, 2000	65 FR 46588.
Commission Guidance to Broker-Dealers on the Use of Electronic Storage Media Under the Electronic Signatures in Global and National Commerce Act of 2000 With Respect to Rule 17a–4(f).	44238	May 7, 2001	66 FR 22921.
Application of the Electronic Signatures in Global and National Commerce Act to Record Retention Requirements Pertaining to Issuers.	44424	June 21, 2001	66 FR 33176.
Calculation of Average Weekly Trading Volume	44820A	Sept. 27, 2001	66 FR 49274
Commission Guidance on the Scope of Section 28(e) of the Exchange Act	45194	Dec. 27, 2001	67 FR 8
Commission Guidance on Trading in Security Futures Products	46101	June 21, 2002	67 FR 43246
Electronic Storage of Broker-Dealer Records	47806	May 7, 2003	68 FR 25283
Books and Records Requirements for Brokers and Dealers Under the Securities Exchange Act of 1934.	47910	May 22, 2003	68 FR 32311
Commission Guidance on Rule 3b–3 and Married Put Transactions	48795	November 17, 2003	68 FR 65822
Commission Guidance Regarding Management's Discussion and Analysis of Financial Condition and Results of Operations.	48960	December 19, 2003	68 FR 75065
Commission Guidance Regarding the Public Company Accounting Oversight Board's Auditing and Related Profesional Practice Standard No. 1.	49708	May 14, 2004	69 FR 29066
Short Sales	50103	July 28, 2004	69 FR 48029
Prohibited Conduct in Connection with IPO Allocations	51500	April 7, 2005	70 FR 19677
Commission Guidance Regarding Accounting for Sales of Vaccines and Bioterror Countermeasures to the Federal Government for Placement Into the Pediatric Vaccine Stockpile or the Strategic National Stockpile.	52885	December 5, 2005	70 FR 73345
Commission Guidance Regarding Client Commission Practices Under Section 28(e) of the Securities and Exchange Act of 1934.	54165	July 18, 2006	71 FR 41996
Commission Guidance Regarding Management's Report on Internal Control Over Financial Reporting Under Section 13(a) or 15(d) of the Securities and Exchange Act of 1934.	55929	June 20, 2007	72 FR 35343
Commission Guidance Regarding and Amendment to the Rules Relating to Organization and Program Management Concerning Proposed Rule Changes Filed by Self-Regulatory Organizations.	58024	June 25, 2008	73 FR 40152
Commission Guidance on the Use of Company Web Sites	58288	Aug. 1, 2008	73 FR 45874
Commission Guidance and Revisions to the Cross-Border Tender Offer, Exchange Offer, Rights Offerings, and Business Combination Rules and Beneficial Ownership Reporting Rules for Certain Foreign Institutions.	58597	Sept. 19, 2008	73 FR 60094
Regulation SHO Amendments	58775	Oct. 14, 2008	73 FR 61706
Commission Guidance Regarding the Financial Accounting Standards Board's Accounting Standards Codification.	60519A	Aug. 25, 2009	74 FR 42773
Commission Guidance Regarding Disclosure Related to Climate Change	61469	Feb. 2, 2010	75 FR 62973
Amendment to Municipal Securities Disclosure	62184A	May 26, 2010	75 FR 33156
Commission Guidance on Presentation of Liquidity and Capital Resources Disclosures in Management's Discussion and Analysis.	62934	Sept. 17, 2010	75 FR 59897
Commission Guidance Regarding Auditing, Attestation, and Related Professional Practice Standards Related to Brokers and Dealers.	62991	Sept. 24, 2010	75 FR 60617
Commission Guidance Regarding Definitions of Mortgage Related Security and Small Business Related Security.	67448	July 17, 2012	77 FR 42988

Securities and Exchange Commission   Pt. 242

Subject	Release No.	Date	Fed. Reg. Vol. and Page
Further Definition of "Swap," "Security-Based Swap," and "Security-Based Swap Agreement"; Mixed Swaps; Security-Based Swap Agreement Recordkeeping.	67453	July 18, 2012	77 FR 48362
Application of "Security-Based Swap Dealer" and "Major Security-Based Swap Participant" Definitions to Cross-Border Security-Based Swap Activities.	34–72472	June 25, 2014	79 FR 47371
Commission Guidance Regarding the Definition of the Terms "Spouse" and "Marriage" Following the Supreme Court's Decision in *United States* v. *Windsor*.	34–75250	June 19, 2015	80 FR 37536
Interpretation of the SEC's Whistleblower Rules under Section 21F of the Securities Exchange Act of 1934.	34–75592	Aug. 4, 2015	80 FR 47831
Interpretation Regarding Automated Quotations Under Regulation NMS	34–78102	June 17, 2016	81 FR 40793
Commission Guidance Regarding Revenue Recognition for Bill-and-Hold Arrangements.	34–81428	Aug. 18, 2017	82 FR 41148
Updates to Commission Guidance Regarding Accounting for Sales of Vaccines and Bioterror Countermeasures to the Federal Government for Placement into the Pediatric Vaccine Stockpile or the Strategic National Stockpile.	34–81429	Aug. 18, 2017	82 FR 41150
Commission Interpretation and Guidance Regarding the Applicability of the Proxy Rules to Proxy Voting Advice.	34–86721	Aug. 21, 2019	84 FR 47419
Commission Guidance on Management's Discussion and Analysis of Financial Condition and Results of Operations.	34–88094	Jan. 30, 2020	85 FR 10571

PART 242—REGULATIONS M, SHO, ATS, AC, NMS, AND SBSR AND CUSTOMER MARGIN REQUIREMENTS FOR SECURITY FUTURES

REGULATION M

Sec.
242.100 Preliminary note; definitions.
242.101 Activities by distribution participants.
242.102 Activities by issuers and selling security holders during a distribution.
242.103 Nasdaq passive market making.
242.104 Stabilizing and other activities in connection with an offering.
242.105 Short selling in connection with a public offering.

REGULATION SHO—REGULATION OF SHORT SALES

242.200 Definition of "short sale" and marking requirements.
242.201 Circuit breaker.
242.203 Borrowing and delivery requirements.
242.204 Close-out requirement.

REGULATION ATS—ALTERNATIVE TRADING SYSTEMS

242.300 Definitions.
242.301 Requirements for alternative trading systems.
242.302 Recordkeeping requirements for alternative trading systems.
242.303 Record preservation requirements for alternative trading systems.
242.304 NMS Stock ATSs.

CUSTOMER MARGIN REQUIREMENTS FOR SECURITY FUTURES

242.400 Customer margin requirements for security futures—authority, purpose, interpretation, and scope.
242.401 Definitions.
242.402 General provisions.
242.403 Required margin.
242.404 Type, form and use of margin.
242.405 Withdrawal of margin.
242.406 Undermargined accounts.

REGULATION AC—ANALYST CERTIFICATION

242.500 Definitions
242.501 Certifications in connection with research reports.
242.502 Certifications in connection with public appearances.
242.503 Certain foreign research reports.
242.504 Notification to associated persons.
242.505 Exclusion for news media.

REGULATION NMS—REGULATION OF THE NATIONAL MARKET SYSTEM

242.600 NMS security designation and definitions.
242.601 Dissemination of transaction reports and last sale data with respect to transactions in NMS stocks.
242.602 Dissemination of quotations in NMS securities.
242.603 Distribution, consolidation, and display of information with respect to quotations for and transactions in NMS stocks.
242.604 Display of customer limit orders.
242.605 Disclosure of order execution information.
242.606 Disclosure of order routing information.

§ 242.100

242.607 Customer account statements.
242.608 Filing and amendment of national market system plans.
242.609 Registration of securities information processors: form of application and amendments.
242.610 Access to quotations.
242.610T Equity transaction fee pilot.
242.611 Order protection rule.
242.612 Minimum pricing increment.
242.613 Consolidated audit trail.
242.614 Registration and responsibilities of competing consolidators.

REGULATION SBSR—REGULATORY REPORTING AND PUBLIC DISSEMINATION OF SECURITY-BASED SWAP INFORMATION

242.900 Definitions
242.901 Reporting obligations.
242.902 Public dissemination of transaction reports.
242.903 Coded information.
242.904 Operating hours of registered security-based swap data repositories.
242.905 Correction of errors in security-based swap information.
242.906 Other duties of participants.
242.907 Policies and procedures of registered security-based swap data repositories.
242.908 Cross-border matters.
242.909 Registration of security-based swap data repository as a securities information processor.

Regulation SCI—Systems Compliance and Integrity

242.1000 Definitions.
242.1001 Obligations related to policies and procedures of SCI entities.
242.1002 Obligations related to SCI events.
242.1003 Obligations related to systems changes; SCI review.
242.1004 SCI entity business continuity and disaster recovery plans testing requirements for members or participants.
242.1005 Recordkeeping requirements related to compliance with Regulation SCI.
242.1006 Electronic filing and submission.
242.1007 Requirements for service bureaus.

AUTHORITY: 15 U.S.C. 77g, 77q(a), 77s(a), 78b, 78c, 78g(c)(2), 78i(a), 78j, 78k–1(c), 78*l*, 78m, 78n, 78o(b), 78o(c), 78o(g), 78q(a), 78q(b), 78q(h), 78w(a), 78dd–1, 78mm, 80a–23, 80a–29, and 80a–37.

SOURCE: 62 FR 544, Jan. 3, 1997, unless otherwise noted.

REGULATION M

§ 242.100 Preliminary note; definitions.

(a) *Preliminary note:* Any transaction or series of transactions, whether or not effected pursuant to the provisions of Regulation M (§§ 242.100–242.105 of this chapter), remain subject to the antifraud and antimanipulation provisions of the securities laws, including, without limitation, Section 17(a) of the Securities Act of 1933 [15 U.S.C. 77q(a)] and Sections 9, 10(b), and 15(c) of the Securities Exchange Act of 1934 [15 U.S.C. 78i, 78j(b), and 78o(c)].

(b) For purposes of regulation M (§§ 242.100 through 242.105 of this chapter) the following definitions shall apply:

ADTV means the worldwide average daily trading volume during the two full calendar months immediately preceding, or any 60 consecutive calendar days ending within the 10 calendar days preceding, the filing of the registration statement; or, if there is no registration statement or if the distribution involves the sale of securities on a delayed basis pursuant to § 230.415 of this chapter, two full calendar months immediately preceding, or any consecutive 60 calendar days ending within the 10 calendar days preceding, the determination of the offering price.

Affiliated purchaser means:

(1) A person acting, directly or indirectly, in concert with a distribution participant, issuer, or selling security holder in connection with the acquisition or distribution of any covered security; or

(2) An affiliate, which may be a separately identifiable department or division of a distribution participant, issuer, or selling security holder, that, directly or indirectly, controls the purchases of any covered security by a distribution participant, issuer, or selling security holder, whose purchases are controlled by any such person, or whose purchases are under common control with any such person; or

(3) An affiliate, which may be a separately identifiable department or division of a distribution participant, issuer, or selling security holder, that regularly purchases securities for its own account or for the account of others, or that recommends or exercises investment discretion with respect to the purchase or sale of securities; *Provided, however,* That this paragraph (3) shall not apply to such affiliate if the following conditions are satisfied:

(i) The distribution participant, issuer, or selling security holder:

Securities and Exchange Commission

(A) Maintains and enforces written policies and procedures reasonably designed to prevent the flow of information to or from the affiliate that might result in a violation of §§ 242.101, 242.102, and 242.104; and

(B) Obtains an annual, independent assessment of the operation of such policies and procedures; and

(ii) The affiliate has no officers (or persons performing similar functions) or employees (other than clerical, ministerial, or support personnel) in common with the distribution participant, issuer, or selling security holder that direct, effect, or recommend transactions in securities; and

(iii) The affiliate does not, during the applicable restricted period, act as a market maker (other than as a specialist in compliance with the rules of a national securities exchange), or engage, as a broker or a dealer, in solicited transactions or proprietary trading, in covered securities.

Agent independent of the issuer means a trustee or other person who is independent of the issuer. The agent shall be deemed to be independent of the issuer only if:

(1) The agent is not an affiliate of the issuer; and

(2) Neither the issuer nor any affiliate of the issuer exercises any direct or indirect control or influence over the prices or amounts of the securities to be purchased, the timing of, or the manner in which, the securities are to be purchased, or the selection of a broker or dealer (other than the independent agent itself) through which purchases may be executed; *Provided, however,* That the issuer or its affiliate will not be deemed to have such control or influence solely because it revises not more than once in any three-month period the source of the shares to fund the plan the basis for determining the amount of its contributions to a plan, or the basis for determining the frequency of its allocations to a plan, or any formula specified in a plan that determines the amount or timing of securities to be purchased by the agent.

Asset-backed security has the meaning contained in § 229.1101 of this chapter.

§ 242.100

At-the-market offering means an offering of securities at other than a fixed price.

Business day refers to a 24 hour period determined with reference to the principal market for the securities to be distributed, and that includes a complete trading session for that market.

Completion of participation in a distribution. Securities acquired in the distribution for investment by any person participating in a distribution, or any affiliated purchaser of such person, shall be deemed to be distributed. A person shall be deemed to have completed its participation in a distribution as follows:

(1) An issuer or selling security holder, when the distribution is completed;

(2) An underwriter, when such person's participation has been distributed, including all other securities of the same class that are acquired in connection with the distribution, and any stabilization arrangements and trading restrictions in connection with the distribution have been terminated; *Provided, however,* That an underwriter's participation will not be deemed to have been completed if a syndicate overallotment option is exercised in an amount that exceeds the net syndicate short position at the time of such exercise; and

(3) Any other person participating in the distribution, when such person's participation has been distributed.

Covered security means any security that is the subject of a distribution, or any reference security.

Current exchange rate means the current rate of exchange between two currencies, which is obtained from at least one independent entity that provides or disseminates foreign exchange quotations in the ordinary course of its business.

Distribution means an offering of securities, whether or not subject to registration under the Securities Act, that is distinguished from ordinary trading transactions by the magnitude of the offering and the presence of special selling efforts and selling methods.

Distribution participant means an underwriter, prospective underwriter, broker, dealer, or other person who has agreed to participate or is participating in a distribution.

§ 242.100

Electronic communications network has the meaning provided in § 242.600.

Employee has the meaning contained in Form S-8 (§ 239.16b of this chapter) relating to employee benefit plans.

Exchange Act means the Securities Exchange Act of 1934 (15 U.S.C. 78a *et seq.*).

Independent bid means a bid by a person who is not a distribution participant, issuer, selling security holder, or affiliated purchaser.

NASD means the National Association of Securities Dealers, Inc. or any of its subsidiaries.

Nasdaq means the electronic dealer quotation system owned and operated by The Nasdaq Stock Market, Inc.

Nasdaq security means a security that is authorized for quotation on Nasdaq, and such authorization is not suspended, terminated, or prohibited.

Net purchases means the amount by which a passive market maker's purchases exceed its sales.

Offering price means the price at which the security is to be or is being distributed.

Passive market maker means a market maker that effects bids or purchases in accordance with the provisions of § 242.103.

Penalty bid means an arrangement that permits the managing underwriter to reclaim a selling concession from a syndicate member in connection with an offering when the securities originally sold by the syndicate member are purchased in syndicate covering transactions.

Plan means any bonus, profit-sharing, pension, retirement, thrift, savings, incentive, stock purchase, stock option, stock ownership, stock appreciation, dividend reinvestment, or similar plan; or any dividend or interest reinvestment plan or employee benefit plan as defined in § 230.405 of this chapter.

Principal market means the single securities market with the largest aggregate reported trading volume for the class of securities during the 12 full calendar months immediately preceding the filing of the registration statement; or, if there is no registration statement or if the distribution involves the sale of securities on a delayed basis pursuant to § 230.415 of this chapter, during the 12 full calendar months immediately preceding the determination of the offering price. For the purpose of determining the aggregate trading volume in a security, the trading volume of depositary shares representing such security shall be included, and shall be multiplied by the multiple or fraction of the security represented by the depositary share. For purposes of this paragraph, depositary share means a security, evidenced by a depositary receipt, that represents another security, or a multiple or fraction thereof, deposited with a depositary.

Prospective underwriter means a person:

(1) Who has submitted a bid to the issuer or selling security holder, and who knows or is reasonably certain that such bid will be accepted, whether or not the terms and conditions of the underwriting have been agreed upon; or

(2) Who has reached, or is reasonably certain to reach, an understanding with the issuer or selling security holder, or managing underwriter that such person will become an underwriter, whether or not the terms and conditions of the underwriting have been agreed upon.

Public float value shall be determined in the manner set forth on the front page of Form 10-K (§ 249.310 of this chapter), even if the issuer of such securities is not required to file Form 10-K, relating to the aggregate market value of common equity securities held by non-affiliates of the issuer.

Reference period means the two full calendar months immediately preceding the filing of the registration statement or, if there is no registration statement or if the distribution involves the sale of securities on a delayed basis pursuant to § 230.415 of this chapter, the two full calendar months immediately preceding the determination of the offering price.

Reference security means a security into which a security that is the subject of a distribution ("subject security") may be converted, exchanged, or exercised or which, under the terms of the subject security, may in whole or in significant part determine the value of the subject security.

Restricted period means:

Securities and Exchange Commission

§ 242.101

(1) For any security with an ADTV value of $100,000 or more of an issuer whose common equity securities have a public float value of $25 million or more, the period beginning on the later of one business day prior to the determination of the offering price or such time that a person becomes a distribution participant, and ending upon such person's completion of participation in the distribution; and

(2) For all other securities, the period beginning on the later of five business days prior to the determination of the offering price or such time that a person becomes a distribution participant, and ending upon such person's completion of participation in the distribution.

(3) In the case of a distribution involving a merger, acquisition, or exchange offer, the period beginning on the day proxy solicitation or offering materials are first disseminated to security holders, and ending upon the completion of the distribution.

Securities Act means the Securities Act of 1933 (15 U.S.C. 77a *et seq.*).

Selling security holder means any person on whose behalf a distribution is made, other than an issuer.

Stabilize or stabilizing means the placing of any bid, or the effecting of any purchase, for the purpose of pegging, fixing, or maintaining the price of a security.

Syndicate covering transaction means the placing of any bid or the effecting of any purchase on behalf of the sole distributor or the underwriting syndicate or group to reduce a short position created in connection with the offering.

30% ADTV limitation means 30 percent of the market maker's ADTV in a covered security during the reference period, as obtained from the NASD.

Underwriter means a person who has agreed with an issuer or selling security holder:

(1) To purchase securities for distribution; or

(2) To distribute securities for or on behalf of such issuer or selling security holder; or

(3) To manage or supervise a distribution of securities. for or on behalf of such issuer or selling security holder.

[62 FR 544, Jan. 3, 1997, as amended at 62 FR 11323, Mar. 12, 1997; 70 FR 1623, Jan. 7, 2005; 70 FR 37619, June 29, 2005]

§ 242.101 Activities by distribution participants.

(a) *Unlawful Activity.* In connection with a distribution of securities, it shall be unlawful for a distribution participant or an affiliated purchaser of such person, directly or indirectly, to bid for, purchase, or attempt to induce any person to bid for or purchase, a covered security during the applicable restricted period; *Provided, however,* That if a distribution participant or affiliated purchaser is the issuer or selling security holder of the securities subject to the distribution, such person shall be subject to the provisions of § 242.102, rather than this section.

(b) *Excepted Activity.* The following activities shall not be prohibited by paragraph (a) of this section:

(1) *Research.* The publication or dissemination of any information, opinion, or recommendation, if the conditions of § 230.138, § 230.139, or § 230.139b of this chapter are met; or

(2) *Transactions complying with certain other sections.* Transactions complying with §§ 242.103 or 242.104; or

(3) *Odd-lot transactions.* Transactions in odd-lots; or transactions to offset odd-lots in connection with an odd-lot tender offer conducted pursuant to § 240.13e–4(h)(5) of this chapter; or

(4) *Exercises of securities.* The exercise of any option, warrant, right, or any conversion privilege set forth in the instrument governing a security; or

(5) *Unsolicited transactions.* Unsolicited brokerage transactions; or unsolicited purchases that are not effected from or through a broker or dealer, on a securities exchange, or through an inter-dealer quotation system or electronic communications network; or

(6) *Basket transactions.* (i) Bids or purchases, in the ordinary course of business, in connection with a basket of 20 or more securities in which a covered security does not comprise more than 5% of the value of the basket purchased; or

§ 242.102

(ii) Adjustments to such a basket in the ordinary course of business as a result of a change in the composition of a standardized index; or

(7) *De minimis transactions.* Purchases during the restricted period, other than by a passive market maker, that total less than 2% of the ADTV of the security being purchased, or unaccepted bids; *Provided, however,* That the person making such bid or purchase has maintained and enforces written policies and procedures reasonably designed to achieve compliance with the other provisions of this section; or

(8) *Transactions in connection with a distribution.* Transactions among distribution participants in connection with a distribution, and purchases of securities from an issuer or selling security holder in connection with a distribution, that are not effected on a securities exchange, or through an inter-dealer quotation system or electronic communications network; or

(9) *Offers to sell or the solicitation of offers to buy.* Offers to sell or the solicitation of offers to buy the securities being distributed (including securities acquired in stabilizing), or securities offered as principal by the person making such offer or solicitation; or

(10) *Transactions in Rule 144A securities.* Transactions in securities eligible for resale under § 230.144A(d)(3) of this chapter, or any reference security, if the Rule 144A securities are sold in the United States solely to:

(i) Qualified institutional buyers, as defined in § 230.144A(a)(1) of this chapter, or to purchasers that the seller and any person acting on behalf of the seller reasonably believes are qualified institutional buyers, in transactions exempt from registration under section 4(2) of the Securities Act (15 U.S.C. 77d(2)) or §§ 230.144A or § 230.500 *et seq* of this chapter; or

(ii) Persons not deemed to be "U.S. persons" for purposes of §§ 230.902(o)(2) or 230.902(o)(7) of this chapter, during a distribution qualifying under paragraph (b)(10)(i) of this section.

(c) *Excepted Securities.* The provisions of this section shall not apply to any of the following securities:

(1) *Actively-traded securities.* Securities that have an ADTV value of at least $1 million and are issued by an issuer whose common equity securities have a public float value of at least $150 million; *Provided, however,* That such securities are not issued by the distribution participant or an affiliate of the distribution participant; or

(2) *Investment grade nonconvertible and asset-backed securities.* Nonconvertible debt securities, nonconvertible preferred securities, and asset-backed securities, that are rated by at least one nationally recognized statistical rating organization, as that term is used in § 240.15c3–1 of this chapter, in one of its generic rating categories that signifies investment grade; or

(3) *Exempted securities.* "Exempted securities" as defined in section 3(a)(12) of the Exchange Act (15 U.S.C. 78c(a)(12)); or

(4) *Face-amount certificates or securities issued by an open-end management investment company or unit investment trust.* Face-amount certificates issued by a face-amount certificate company, or redeemable securities issued by an open-end management investment company or a unit investment trust. Any terms used in this paragraph (c)(4) that are defined in the Investment Company Act of 1940 (15 U.S.C. 80a–1 *et seq.*) shall have the meanings specified in such Act.

(d) *Exemptive authority.* Upon written application or upon its own motion, the Commission may grant an exemption from the provisions of this section, either unconditionally or on specified terms and conditions, to any transaction or class of transactions, or to any security or class of securities.

[62 FR 544, Jan. 3, 1997, as amended at 77 FR 18685, Mar. 28, 2012; 78 FR 44805, July 24, 2013; 83 FR 64222, Dec. 13, 2018]

§ 242.102 Activities by issuers and selling security holders during a distribution.

(a) *Unlawful Activity.* In connection with a distribution of securities effected by or on behalf of an issuer or selling security holder, it shall be unlawful for such person, or any affiliated purchaser of such person, directly or indirectly, to bid for, purchase, or attempt to induce any person to bid for or purchase, a covered security during the applicable restricted period; *Except*

Securities and Exchange Commission

§ 242.102

That if an affiliated purchaser is a distribution participant, such affiliated purchaser may comply with § 242.101, rather than this section.

(b) *Excepted Activity.* The following activities shall not be prohibited by paragraph (a) of this section:

(1) *Odd-lot transactions.* Transactions in odd-lots, or transactions to offset odd-lots in connection with an odd-lot tender offer conducted pursuant to § 240.13e–4(h)(5) of this chapter; or

(2) *Transactions by closed-end investment companies.* (i) Transactions complying with § 270.23c–3 of this chapter; or

(ii) Periodic tender offers of securities, at net asset value, conducted pursuant to § 240.13e–4 of this chapter by a closed-end investment company that engages in a continuous offering of its securities pursuant to § 230.415 of this chapter; *Provided, however,* That such securities are not traded on a securities exchange or through an inter-dealer quotation system or electronic communications network; or

(3) *Redemptions by commodity pools or limited partnerships.* Redemptions by commodity pools or limited partnerships, at a price based on net asset value, which are effected in accordance with the terms and conditions of the instruments governing the securities; *Provided, however,* That such securities are not traded on a securities exchange, or through an inter-dealer quotation system or electronic communications network; or

(4) *Exercises of securities.* The exercise of any option, warrant, right, or any conversion privilege set forth in the instrument governing a security; or

(5) *Offers to sell or the solicitation of offers to buy.* Offers to sell or the solicitation of offers to buy the securities being distributed; or

(6) *Unsolicited purchases.* Unsolicited purchases that are not effected from or through a broker or dealer, on a securities exchange, or through an inter-dealer quotation system or electronic communications network; or

(7) *Transactions in Rule 144A securities.* Transactions in securities eligible for resale under § 230.144A(d)(3) of this chapter, or any reference security, if the Rule 144A securities are sold in the United States solely to:

(i) Qualified institutional buyers, as defined in § 230.144A(a)(1) of this chapter, or to purchasers that the seller and any person acting on behalf of the seller reasonably believes are qualified institutional buyers, in transactions exempt from registration under section 4(2) of the Securities Act (15 U.S.C. 77d(2)) or §§ 230.144A or § 230.500 *et seq* of this chapter; or

(ii) Persons not deemed to be "U.S. persons" for purposes of §§ 230.902(o)(2) or 230.902(o)(7) of this chapter, during a distribution qualifying under paragraph (b)(7)(i) of this section.

(c) *Plans.* (1) Paragraph (a) of this section shall not apply to distributions of securities pursuant to a plan, which are made:

(i) Solely to employees or security holders of an issuer or its subsidiaries, or to a trustee or other person acquiring such securities for the accounts of such persons; or

(ii) To persons other than employees or security holders, if bids for or purchases of securities pursuant to the plan are effected solely by an agent independent of the issuer and the securities are from a source other than the issuer or an affiliated purchaser of the issuer.

(2) Bids for or purchases of any security made or effected by or for a plan shall be deemed to be a purchase by the issuer unless the bid is made, or the purchase is effected, by an agent independent of the issuer.

(d) *Excepted Securities.* The provisions of this section shall not apply to any of the following securities:

(1) *Actively-traded reference securities.* Reference securities with an ADTV value of at least $1 million that are issued by an issuer whose common equity securities have a public float value of at least $150 million; *Provided, however,* That such securities are not issued by the issuer, or any affiliate of the issuer, of the security in distribution.

(2) *Investment grade nonconvertible and asset-backed securities.* Nonconvertible debt securities, nonconvertible preferred securities, and asset-backed securities, that are rated by at least one nationally recognized statistical rating organization, as that term is used in § 240.15c3–1 of this chapter, in one of its

§ 242.103

generic rating categories that signifies investment grade; or

(3) *Exempted securities.* "Exempted securities" as defined in section 3(a)(12) of the Exchange Act (15 U.S.C. 78c(a)(12)); or

(4) *Face-amount certificates or securities issued by an open-end management investment company or unit investment trust.* Face-amount certificates issued by a face-amount certificate company, or redeemable securities issued by an open-end management investment company or a unit investment trust. Any terms used in this paragraph (d)(4) that are defined in the Investment Company Act of 1940 (15 U.S.C. 80a–1 *et seq.*) shall have the meanings specified in such Act.

(e) *Exemptive Authority.* Upon written application or upon its own motion, the Commission may grant an exemption from the provisions of this section, either unconditionally or on specified terms and conditions, to any transaction or class of transactions, or to any security or class of securities.

[62 FR 544, Jan. 3, 1997, as amended at 62 FR 11323, Mar. 12, 1997; 77 FR 18685, Mar. 28, 2012; 78 FR 44805, July 24, 2013]

§ 242.103 Nasdaq passive market making.

(a) *Scope of section.* This section permits broker-dealers to engage in market making transactions in covered securities that are Nasdaq securities without violating the provisions of § 242.101; *Except That* this section shall not apply to any security for which a stabilizing bid subject to § 242.104 is in effect, or during any at-the-market offering or best efforts offering.

(b) *Conditions to be met*—(1) *General limitations.* A passive market maker must effect all transactions in the capacity of a registered market maker on Nasdaq. A passive market maker shall not bid for or purchase a covered security at a price that exceeds the highest independent bid for the covered security at the time of the transaction, except as permitted by paragraph (b)(3) of this section or required by a rule promulgated by the Commission or the NASD governing the handling of customer orders.

(2) *Purchase limitation.* On each day of the restricted period, a passive market maker's net purchases shall not exceed the greater of its 30% ADTV limitation or 200 shares (together, "purchase limitation"); *Provided, however,* That a passive market maker may purchase all of the securities that are part of a single order that, when executed, results in its purchase limitation being equalled or exceeded. If a passive market maker's net purchases equal or exceed its purchase limitation, it shall withdraw promptly its quotations from Nasdaq. If a passive market maker withdraws its quotations pursuant to this paragraph, it may not effect any bid or purchase in the covered security for the remainder of that day, irrespective of any later sales during that day, unless otherwise permitted by § 242.101.

(3) *Requirement to lower the bid.* If all independent bids for a covered security are reduced to a price below the passive market maker's bid, the passive market maker must lower its bid promptly to a level not higher than the then highest independent bid; *Provided, however,* That a passive market maker may continue to bid and effect purchases at its bid at a price exceeding the then highest independent bid until the passive market maker purchases an aggregate amount of the covered security that equals or, through the purchase of all securities that are part of a single order, exceeds the lesser of two times the minimum quotation size for the security, as determined by NASD rules, or the passive market maker's remaining purchasing capacity under paragraph (b)(2) of this section.

(4) *Limitation on displayed size.* At all times, the passive market maker's displayed bid size may not exceed the lesser of the minimum quotation size for the covered security, or the passive market maker's remaining purchasing capacity under paragraph (b)(2) of this section; *Provided, however,* That a passive market maker whose purchasing capacity at any time is between one and 99 shares may display a bid size of 100 shares.

(5) *Identification of a passive market making bid.* The bid displayed by a passive market maker shall be designated as such.

(6) *Notification and reporting to the NASD.* A passive market maker shall

Securities and Exchange Commission § 242.104

notify the NASD in advance of its intention to engage in passive market making, and shall submit to the NASD information regarding passive market making purchases, in such form as the NASD shall prescribe.

(7) *Prospectus disclosure.* The prospectus for any registered offering in which any passive market maker intends to effect transactions in any covered security shall contain the information required in §§ 228.502, 228.508, 229.502, and 229.508 of this chapter.

(c) *Transactions at prices resulting from unlawful activity.* No transaction shall be made at a price that the passive market maker knows or has reason to know is the result of activity that is fraudulent, manipulative, or deceptive under the securities laws, or any rule or regulation thereunder.

§ 242.104 Stabilizing and other activities in connection with an offering.

(a) *Unlawful activity.* It shall be unlawful for any person, directly or indirectly, to stabilize, to effect any syndicate covering transaction, or to impose a penalty bid, in connection with an offering of any security, in contravention of the provisions of this section. No stabilizing shall be effected at a price that the person stabilizing knows or has reason to know is in contravention of this section, or is the result of activity that is fraudulent, manipulative, or deceptive under the securities laws, or any rule or regulation thereunder.

(b) *Purpose.* Stabilizing is prohibited except for the purpose of preventing or retarding a decline in the market price of a security.

(c) *Priority.* To the extent permitted or required by the market where stabilizing occurs, any person stabilizing shall grant priority to any independent bid at the same price irrespective of the size of such independent bid at the time that it is entered.

(d) *Control of stabilizing.* No sole distributor or syndicate or group stabilizing the price of a security or any member or members of such syndicate or group shall maintain more than one stabilizing bid in any one market at the same price at the same time.

(e) *At-the-market offerings.* Stabilizing is prohibited in an at-the-market offering.

(f) *Stabilizing levels*—(1) *Maximum stabilizing bid.* Notwithstanding the other provisions of this paragraph (f), no stabilizing shall be made at a price higher than the lower of the offering price or the stabilizing bid for the security in the principal market (or, if the principal market is closed, the stabilizing bid in the principal market at its previous close).

(2) *Initiating stabilizing*—(i) *Initiating stabilizing when the principal market is open.* After the opening of quotations for the security in the principal market, stabilizing may be initiated in any market at a price no higher than the last independent transaction price for the security in the principal market if the security has traded in the principal market on the day stabilizing is initiated or on the most recent prior day of trading in the principal market and the current asked price in the principal market is equal to or greater than the last independent transaction price. If both conditions of the preceding sentence are not satisfied, stabilizing may be initiated in any market after the opening of quotations in the principal market at a price no higher than the highest current independent bid for the security in the principal market.

(ii) *Initiating stabilizing when the principal market is closed.* (A) When the principal market for the security is closed, but immediately before the opening of quotations for the security in the market where stabilizing will be initiated, stabilizing may be initiated at a price no higher than the lower of:

(*1*) The price at which stabilizing could have been initiated in the principal market for the security at its previous close; or

(*2*) The most recent price at which an independent transaction in the security has been effected in any market since the close of the principal market, if the person stabilizing knows or has reason to know of such transaction.

(B) When the principal market for the security is closed, but after the opening of quotations in the market where stabilizing will be initiated, stabilizing may be initiated at a price no higher than the lower of:

§ 242.104

(*1*) The price at which stabilization could have been initiated in the principal market for the security at its previous close; or

(*2*) The last independent transaction price for the security in that market if the security has traded in that market on the day stabilizing is initiated or on the last preceding business day and the current asked price in that market is equal to or greater than the last independent transaction price. If both conditions of the preceding sentence are not satisfied, under this paragraph (f)(2)(ii)(B)(*2*), stabilizing may be initiated at a price no higher than the highest current independent bid for the security in that market.

(iii) *Initiating stabilizing when there is no market for the security or before the offering price is determined.* If no *bona fide* market for the security being distributed exists at the time stabilizing is initiated, no stabilizing shall be initiated at a price in excess of the offering price. If stabilizing is initiated before the offering price is determined, then stabilizing may be continued after determination of the offering price at the price at which stabilizing then could be initiated.

(3) *Maintaining or carrying over a stabilizing bid.* A stabilizing bid initiated pursuant to paragraph (f)(2) of this section, which has not been discontinued, may be maintained, or carried over into another market, irrespective of changes in the independent bids or transaction prices for the security.

(4) *Increasing or reducing a stabilizing bid.* A stabilizing bid may be increased to a price no higher than the highest current independent bid for the security in the principal market if the principal market is open, or, if the principal market is closed, to a price no higher than the highest independent bid in the principal market at the previous close thereof. A stabilizing bid may be reduced, or carried over into another market at a reduced price, irrespective of changes in the independent bids or transaction prices for the security. If stabilizing is discontinued, it shall not be resumed at a price higher than the price at which stabilizing then could be initiated.

(5) *Initiating, maintaining, or adjusting a stabilizing bid to reflect the current exchange rate.* If a stabilizing bid is expressed in a currency other than the currency of the principal market for the security, such bid may be initiated, maintained, or adjusted to reflect the current exchange rate, consistent with the provisions of this section. If, in initiating, maintaining, or adjusting a stabilizing bid pursuant to this paragraph (f)(5), the bid would be at or below the midpoint between two trading differentials, such stabilizing bid shall be adjusted downward to the lower differential.

(6) *Adjustments to stabilizing bid.* If a security goes ex-dividend, ex-rights, or ex-distribution, the stabilizing bid shall be reduced by an amount equal to the value of the dividend, right, or distribution. If, in reducing a stabilizing bid pursuant to this paragraph (f)(6), the bid would be at or below the midpoint between two trading differentials, such stabilizing bid shall be adjusted downward to the lower differential.

(7) *Stabilizing of components.* When two or more securities are being offered as a unit, the component securities shall not be stabilized at prices the sum of which exceeds the then permissible stabilizing price for the unit.

(8) *Special prices.* Any stabilizing price that otherwise meets the requirements of this section need not be adjusted to reflect special prices available to any group or class of persons (including employees or holders of warrants or rights).

(g) *Offerings with no U.S. stabilizing activities.* (1) Stabilizing to facilitate an offering of a security in the United States shall not be deemed to be in violation of this section if all of the following conditions are satisfied:

(i) No stabilizing is made in the United States;

(ii) Stabilizing outside the United States is made in a jurisdiction with statutory or regulatory provisions governing stabilizing that are comparable to the provisions of this section; and

(iii) No stabilizing is made at a price above the offering price in the United States, except as permitted by paragraph (f)(5) of this section.

(2) For purposes of this paragraph (g), the Commission by rule, regulation, or order may determine whether a foreign

Securities and Exchange Commission § 242.105

statute or regulation is comparable to this section considering, among other things, whether such foreign statute or regulation: specifies appropriate purposes for which stabilizing is permitted; provides for disclosure and control of stabilizing activities; places limitations on stabilizing levels; requires appropriate recordkeeping; provides other protections comparable to the provisions of this section; and whether procedures exist to enable the Commission to obtain information concerning any foreign stabilizing transactions.

(h) *Disclosure and notification.* (1) Any person displaying or transmitting a bid that such person knows is for the purpose of stabilizing shall provide prior notice to the market on which such stabilizing will be effected, and shall disclose its purpose to the person with whom the bid is entered.

(2) Any person effecting a syndicate covering transaction or imposing a penalty bid shall provide prior notice to the self-regulatory organization with direct authority over the principal market in the United States for the security for which the syndicate covering transaction is effected or the penalty bid is imposed.

(3) Any person subject to this section who sells to, or purchases for the account of, any person any security where the price of such security may be or has been stabilized, shall send to the purchaser at or before the completion of the transaction, a prospectus, offering circular, confirmation, or other document containing a statement similar to that comprising the statement provided for in Item 502(d) of Regulation S–B (§ 228.502(d) of this chapter) or Item 502(d) of Regulation S–K (§ 229.502(d) of this chapter).

(i) *Recordkeeping requirements.* A person subject to this section shall keep the information and make the notification required by § 240.17a–2 of this chapter.

(j) *Excepted securities.* The provisions of this section shall not apply to:

(1) *Exempted securities.* "Exempted securities," as defined in section 3(a)(12) of the Exchange Act (15 U.S.C. 78c(a)(12)); or

(2) *Transactions of Rule 144A securities.* Transactions in securities eligible for resale under § 230.144A(d)(3) of this chapter, if such securities are sold in the United States solely to:

(i) Qualified institutional buyers, as defined in § 230.144A(a)(1) of this chapter, or to purchasers that the seller and any person acting on behalf of the seller reasonably believes are qualified institutional buyers, in a transaction exempt from registration under section 4(2) of the Securities Act (15 U.S.C. 77d(2)) or §§ 230.144A or § 230.500 *et seq* of this chapter; or

(ii) Persons not deemed to be "U.S. persons" for purposes of §§ 230.902(o)(2) or 230.902(o)(7) of this chapter, during a distribution qualifying under paragraph (j)(2)(i) of this section.

(k) *Exemptive authority.* Upon written application or upon its own motion, the Commission may grant an exemption from the provisions of this section, either unconditionally or on specified terms and conditions, to any transaction or class of transactions, or to any security or class of securities.

[62 FR 544, Jan. 3, 1997, as amended at 62 FR 11323, Mar. 12, 1997; 62 FR 13213, Mar. 19, 1997; 77 FR 18685, Mar. 28, 2012; 78 FR 44805, July 24, 2013]

§ 242.105 Short selling in connection with a public offering.

(a) *Unlawful activity.* In connection with an offering of equity securities for cash pursuant to a registration statement or a notification on Form 1–A (§ 239.90 of this chapter) or Form 1–E (§ 239.200 of this chapter) filed under the Securities Act of 1933 ("offered securities"), it shall be unlawful for any person to sell short (as defined in § 242.200(a)) the security that is the subject of the offering and purchase the offered securities from an underwriter or broker or dealer participating in the offering if such short sale was effected during the period ("Rule 105 restricted period") that is the shorter of the period:

(1) Beginning five business days before the pricing of the offered securities and ending with such pricing; or

(2) Beginning with the initial filing of such registration statement or notification on Form 1–A or Form 1–E and ending with the pricing.

(b) *Excepted activity*—(1) *Bona fide purchase.* It shall not be prohibited for

§ 242.200

such person to purchase the offered securities as provided in paragraph (a) of this section if:

(i) Such person makes a bona fide purchase(s) of the security that is the subject of the offering that is:

(A) At least equivalent in quantity to the entire amount of the Rule 105 restricted period short sale(s);

(B) Effected during regular trading hours;

(C) Reported to an "effective transaction reporting plan" (as defined in § 242.600(b)(30); and

(D) Effected after the last Rule 105 restricted period short sale, and no later than the business day prior to the day of pricing; and

(ii) Such person did not effect a short sale, that is reported to an effective transaction reporting plan, within the 30 minutes prior to the close of regular trading hours (as defined in § 242.600(b)(77)) on the business day prior to the day of pricing.

(2) *Separate accounts.* Paragraph (a) of this section shall not prohibit the purchase of the offered security in an account of a person where such person sold short during the Rule 105 restricted period in a separate account, if decisions regarding securities transactions for each account are made separately and without coordination of trading or cooperation among or between the accounts.

(3) *Investment companies.* Paragraph (a) of this section shall not prohibit an investment company (as defined by Section 3 of the Investment Company Act) that is registered under Section 8 of the Investment Company Act, or a series of such company (investment company) from purchasing an offered security where any of the following sold the offered security short during the Rule 105 restricted period:

(i) An affiliated investment company, or any series of such a company; or

(ii) A separate series of the investment company.

(c) *Excepted offerings.* This section shall not apply to offerings that are not conducted on a firm commitment basis.

(d) *Exemptive authority.* Upon written application or upon its own motion, the Commission may grant an exemption from the provisions of this section, either unconditionally or on specified terms and conditions, to any transaction or class of transactions, or to any security or class of securities.

[62 FR 544, Jan. 3, 1997, as amended at 69 FR 48029, Aug. 6, 2004; 72 FR 45107, Aug. 10, 2007; 83 FR 58427, Nov. 19, 2018; 86 FR 18809, Apr. 9, 2021]

REGULATION SHO—REGULATION OF SHORT SALES

§ 242.200 Definition of "short sale" and marking requirements.

(a) The term *short sale* shall mean any sale of a security which the seller does not own or any sale which is consummated by the delivery of a security borrowed by, or for the account of, the seller.

(b) A person shall be deemed to own a security if:

(1) The person or his agent has title to it; or

(2) The person has purchased, or has entered into an unconditional contract, binding on both parties thereto, to purchase it, but has not yet received it; or

(3) The person owns a security convertible into or exchangeable for it and has tendered such security for conversion or exchange; or

(4) The person has an option to purchase or acquire it and has exercised such option; or

(5) The person has rights or warrants to subscribe to it and has exercised such rights or warrants; or

(6) The person holds a security futures contract to purchase it and has received notice that the position will be physically settled and is irrevocably bound to receive the underlying security.

(c) A person shall be deemed to own securities only to the extent that he has a net long position in such securities.

(d) A broker or dealer shall be deemed to own a security, even if it is not net long, if:

(1) The broker or dealer acquired that security while acting in the capacity of a block positioner; and

(2) If and to the extent that the broker or dealer's short position in the security is the subject of offsetting positions created in the course of bona

Securities and Exchange Commission § 242.201

fide arbitrage, risk arbitrage, or bona fide hedge activities.

(e) A broker-dealer shall be deemed to own a security even if it is not net long, if:

(1) The broker-dealer is unwinding index arbitrage position involving a long basket of stock and one or more short index futures traded on a board of trade or one or more standardized options contracts as defined in 17 CFR 240.9b–1(a)(4); and

(2) If and to the extent that the broker-dealer's short position in the security is the subject of offsetting positions created and maintained in the course of bona-fide arbitrage, risk arbitrage, or bona fide hedge activities; and

(3) The sale does not occur during a period commencing at the time that the NYSE Composite Index has declined by two percent or more from its closing value on the previous day and terminating upon the end of the trading day. The two percent shall be calculated at the beginning of each calendar quarter and shall be two percent, rounded down to the nearest 10 points, of the average closing value of the NYSE Composite Index for the last month of the previous quarter.

(f) In order to determine its net position, a broker or dealer shall aggregate all of its positions in a security unless it qualifies for independent trading unit aggregation, in which case each independent trading unit shall aggregate all of its positions in a security to determine its net position. Independent trading unit aggregation is available only if:

(1) The broker or dealer has a written plan of organization that identifies each aggregation unit, specifies its trading objective(s), and supports its independent identity;

(2) Each aggregation unit within the firm determines, at the time of each sale, its net position for every security that it trades;

(3) All traders in an aggregation unit pursue only the particular trading objective(s) or strategy(s) of that aggregation unit and do not coordinate that strategy with any other aggregation unit; and

(4) Individual traders are assigned to only one aggregation unit at any time.

(g) A broker or dealer must mark all sell orders of any equity security as "long," "short," or "short exempt."

(1) An order to sell shall be marked "long" only if the seller is deemed to own the security being sold pursuant to paragraphs (a) through (f) of this section and either:

(i) The security to be delivered is in the physical possession or control of the broker or dealer; or

(ii) It is reasonably expected that the security will be in the physical possession or control of the broker or dealer no later than the settlement of the transaction.

(2) A sale order shall be marked "short exempt" only if the provisions of § 242.201(c) or (d) are met.

(h) Upon written application or upon its own motion, the Commission may grant an exemption from the provisions of this section, either unconditionally or on specified terms and conditions, to any transaction or class of transactions, or to any security or class of securities, or to any person or class of persons.

[69 FR 48029, Aug. 6, 2004, as amended at 72 FR 36359, July 3, 2007; 72 FR 45557, Aug. 14, 2007; 75 FR 11323, Mar. 10, 2010]

§ 242.201 Circuit breaker.

(a) *Definitions.* For the purposes of this section:

(1) The term *covered security* shall mean any NMS stock as defined in § 242.600(b)(55).

(2) The term *effective transaction reporting plan for a covered security* shall have the same meaning as in § 242.600(b)(30).

(3) The term *listing market* shall have the same meaning as the term "primary listing exchange" as defined in § 242.600(b)(68).

(4) The term *national best bid* shall have the same meaning as in § 242.600(b)(50).

(5) The term *odd lot* shall have the same meaning as in § 242.600(b)(58).

(6) The term *plan processor* shall have the same meaning as in § 242.600(b)(67).

(7) The term *regular trading hours* shall have the same meaning as in § 242.600(b)(77).

(8) The term *riskless principal* shall mean a transaction in which a broker or dealer, after having received an

§ 242.201

order to buy a security, purchases the security as principal at the same price to satisfy the order to buy, exclusive of any explicitly disclosed markup or markdown, commission equivalent, or other fee, or, after having received an order to sell, sells the security as principal at the same price to satisfy the order to sell, exclusive of any explicitly disclosed markup or markdown, commission equivalent, or other fee.

(9) The term *trading center* shall have the same meaning as in § 242.600(b)(95).

(b)(1) A trading center shall establish, maintain, and enforce written policies and procedures reasonably designed to:

(i) Prevent the execution or display of a short sale order of a covered security at a price that is less than or equal to the current national best bid if the price of that covered security decreases by 10% or more from the covered security's closing price as determined by the listing market for the covered security as of the end of regular trading hours on the prior day; and

(ii) Impose the requirements of paragraph (b)(1)(i) of this section for the remainder of the day and the following day when a national best bid for the covered security is calculated and disseminated on a current and continuing basis pursuant to an effective national market system plan.

(iii) *Provided, however,* that the policies and procedures must be reasonably designed to permit:

(A) The execution of a displayed short sale order of a covered security by a trading center if, at the time of initial display of the short sale order, the order was at a price above the current national best bid; and

(B) The execution or display of a short sale order of a covered security marked "short exempt" without regard to whether the order is at a price that is less than or equal to the current national best bid.

(2) A trading center shall regularly surveil to ascertain the effectiveness of the policies and procedures required by paragraph (b)(1) of this section and shall take prompt action to remedy deficiencies in such policies and procedures.

(3) The determination regarding whether the price of a covered security has decreased by 10% or more from the covered security's closing price as determined by the listing market for the covered security as of the end of regular trading hours on the prior day shall be made by the listing market for the covered security and, if such decrease has occurred, the listing market shall immediately make such information available as provided in § 242.603(b).

(c) Following any determination and notification pursuant to paragraph (b)(3) of this section with respect to a covered security, a broker or dealer submitting a short sale order of the covered security in question to a trading center may mark the order "short exempt" if the broker or dealer identifies the order as being at a price above the current national best bid at the time of submission; *provided, however:*

(1) The broker or dealer that identifies a short sale order of a covered security as "short exempt" in accordance with this paragraph (c) must establish, maintain, and enforce written policies and procedures reasonably designed to prevent incorrect identification of orders for purposes of this paragraph; and

(2) The broker or dealer shall regularly surveil to ascertain the effectiveness of the policies and procedures required by paragraph (c)(1) of this section and shall take prompt action to remedy deficiencies in such policies and procedures.

(d) Following any determination and notification pursuant to paragraph (b)(3) of this section with respect to a covered security, a broker or dealer may mark a short sale order of a covered security "short exempt" if the broker or dealer has a reasonable basis to believe that:

(1) The short sale order of a covered security is by a person that is deemed to own the covered security pursuant to § 242.200, provided that the person intends to deliver the security as soon as all restrictions on delivery have been removed.

(2) The short sale order of a covered security is by a market maker to offset customer odd-lot orders or to liquidate an odd-lot position that changes such broker's or dealer's position by no more than a unit of trading.

Securities and Exchange Commission § 242.201

(3) The short sale order of a covered security is for a good faith account of a person who then owns another security by virtue of which he is, or presently will be, entitled to acquire an equivalent number of securities of the same class as the securities sold; provided such sale, or the purchase which such sale offsets, is effected for the bona fide purpose of profiting from a current difference between the price of the security sold and the security owned and that such right of acquisition was originally attached to or represented by another security or was issued to all the holders of any such securities of the issuer.

(4) The short sale order of a covered security is for a good faith account and submitted to profit from a current price difference between a security on a foreign securities market and a security on a securities market subject to the jurisdiction of the United States, provided that the short seller has an offer to buy on a foreign market that allows the seller to immediately cover the short sale at the time it was made. For the purposes of this paragraph (d)(4), a depository receipt of a security shall be deemed to be the same security as the security represented by such receipt.

(5)(i) The short sale order of a covered security is by an underwriter or member of a syndicate or group participating in the distribution of a security in connection with an over-allotment of securities; or

(ii) The short sale order of a covered security is for purposes of a lay-off sale by an underwriter or member of a syndicate or group in connection with a distribution of securities through a rights or standby underwriting commitment.

(6) The short sale order of a covered security is by a broker or dealer effecting the execution of a customer purchase or the execution of a customer "long" sale on a riskless principal basis. In addition, for purposes of this paragraph (d)(6), a broker or dealer must have written policies and procedures in place to assure that, at a minimum:

(i) The customer order was received prior to the offsetting transaction;

(ii) The offsetting transaction is allocated to a riskless principal or customer account within 60 seconds of execution; and

(iii) The broker or dealer has supervisory systems in place to produce records that enable the broker or dealer to accurately and readily reconstruct, in a time-sequenced manner, all orders on which a broker or dealer relies pursuant to this exception.

(7) The short sale order is for the sale of a covered security at the volume weighted average price (VWAP) that meets the following criteria:

(i) The VWAP for the covered security is calculated by:

(A) Calculating the values for every regular way trade reported in the consolidated system for the security during the regular trading session, by multiplying each such price by the total number of shares traded at that price;

(B) Compiling an aggregate sum of all values; and

(C) Dividing the aggregate sum by the total number of reported shares for that day in the security.

(ii) The transactions are reported using a special VWAP trade modifier.

(iii) The VWAP matched security:

(A) Qualifies as an "actively-traded security" pursuant to § 242.101 and § 242.102; or

(B) The proposed short sale transaction is being conducted as part of a basket transaction of twenty or more securities in which the subject security does not comprise more than 5% of the value of the basket traded.

(iv) The transaction is not effected for the purpose of creating actual, or apparent, active trading in or otherwise affecting the price of any security.

(v) A broker or dealer shall be permitted to act as principal on the contra-side to fill customer short sale orders only if the broker's or dealer's position in the covered security, as committed by the broker or dealer during the pre-opening period of a trading day and aggregated across all of its customers who propose to sell short the same security on a VWAP basis, does not exceed 10% of the covered security's relevant average daily trading volume.

25

§ 242.203

(e) No self-regulatory organization shall have any rule that is not in conformity with, or conflicts with, this section.

(f) Upon written application or upon its own motion, the Commission may grant an exemption from the provisions of this section, either unconditionally or on specified terms and conditions, to any person or class of persons, to any transaction or class of transactions, or to any security or class of securities to the extent that such exemption is necessary or appropriate, in the public interest, and is consistent with the protection of investors.

[75 FR 11323, Mar. 10, 2010, as amended at 83 FR 58427, Nov. 19, 2018; 86 FR 18809, Apr. 9, 2021]

§ 242.203 Borrowing and delivery requirements.

(a) *Long sales.* (1) If a broker or dealer knows or has reasonable grounds to believe that the sale of an equity security was or will be effected pursuant to an order marked "long," such broker or dealer shall not lend or arrange for the loan of any security for delivery to the purchaser's broker after the sale, or fail to deliver a security on the date delivery is due.

(2) The provisions of paragraph (a)(1) of this section shall not apply:

(i) To the loan of any security by a broker or dealer through the medium of a loan to another broker or dealer;

(ii) If the broker or dealer knows, or has been reasonably informed by the seller, that the seller owns the security, and that the seller would deliver the security to the broker or dealer prior to the scheduled settlement of the transaction, but the seller failed to do so; or

(iii) If, prior to any loan or arrangement to loan any security for delivery, or failure to deliver, a national securities exchange, in the case of a sale effected thereon, or a national securities association, in the case of a sale not effected on an exchange, finds:

(A) That such sale resulted from a mistake made in good faith;

(B) That due diligence was used to ascertain that the circumstances specified in § 242.200(g) existed; and

(C) Either that the condition of the market at the time the mistake was discovered was such that undue hardship would result from covering the transaction by a "purchase for cash" or that the mistake was made by the seller's broker and the sale was at a permissible price under any applicable short sale price test.

(b) *Short sales.* (1) A broker or dealer may not accept a short sale order in an equity security from another person, or effect a short sale in an equity security for its own account, unless the broker or dealer has:

(i) Borrowed the security, or entered into a bona-fide arrangement to borrow the security; or

(ii) Reasonable grounds to believe that the security can be borrowed so that it can be delivered on the date delivery is due; and

(iii) Documented compliance with this paragraph (b)(1).

(2) The provisions of paragraph (b)(1) of this section shall not apply to:

(i) A broker or dealer that has accepted a short sale order from another registered broker or dealer that is required to comply with paragraph (b)(1) of this section, unless the broker or dealer relying on this exception contractually undertook responsibility for compliance with paragraph (b)(1) of this section;

(ii) Any sale of a security that a person is deemed to own pursuant to § 242.200, provided that the broker or dealer has been reasonably informed that the person intends to deliver such security as soon as all restrictions on delivery have been removed. If the person has not delivered such security within 35 days after the trade date, the broker-dealer that effected the sale must borrow securities or close out the short position by purchasing securities of like kind and quantity;

(iii) Short sales effected by a market maker in connection with bona-fide market making activities in the security for which this exception is claimed; and

(iv) Transactions in security futures.

(3) If a participant of a registered clearing agency has a fail to deliver position at a registered clearing agency in a threshold security for thirteen

Securities and Exchange Commission § 242.203

consecutive settlement days, the participant shall immediately thereafter close out the fail to deliver position by purchasing securities of like kind and quantity:

(i) *Provided, however,* that a participant of a registered clearing agency that has a fail to deliver position at a registered clearing agency in a threshold security on the effective date of this amendment and which, prior to the effective date of this amendment, had been previously grandfathered from the close-out requirement in this paragraph (b)(3) (i.e., because the participant of a registered clearing agency had a fail to deliver position at a registered clearing agency on the settlement day preceding the day that the security became a threshold security), shall close out that fail to deliver position within thirty-five consecutive settlement days of the effective date of this amendment by purchasing securities of like kind and quantity;

(ii) *Provided, however,* that if a participant of a registered clearing agency has a fail to deliver position at a registered clearing agency in a threshold security that was sold pursuant to § 230.144 of this chapter for thirty-five consecutive settlement days, the participant shall immediately thereafter close out the fail to deliver position in the security by purchasing securities of like kind and quantity;

(iii) *Provided, however,* that a participant of a registered clearing agency that has a fail to deliver position at a registered clearing agency in a threshold security on the effective date of this amendment and which, prior to the effective date of this amendment, had been previously excepted from the close-out requirement in paragraph (b)(3) of this section (i.e., because the participant of a registered clearing agency had a fail to deliver position in the threshold security that is attributed to short sales effected by a registered options market maker to establish or maintain a hedge on options positions that were created before the security became a threshold security), shall immediately close out that fail to deliver position, including any adjustments to the fail to deliver position, within 35 consecutive settlement days of the effective date of this amendment by purchasing securities of like kind and quantity;

(iv) If a participant of a registered clearing agency has a fail to deliver position at a registered clearing agency in a threshold security for thirteen consecutive settlement days, the participant and any broker or dealer for which it clears transactions, including any market maker that would otherwise be entitled to rely on the exception provided in paragraph (b)(2)(iii) of this section, may not accept a short sale order in the threshold security from another person, or effect a short sale in the threshold security for its own account, without borrowing the security or entering into a bona-fide arrangement to borrow the security, until the participant closes out the fail to deliver position by purchasing securities of like kind and quantity;

(v) If a participant of a registered clearing agency entitled to rely on the 35 consecutive settlement day close-out requirement contained in paragraph (b)(3)(i), (b)(3)(ii), or (b)(3)(iii) of this section has a fail to deliver position at a registered clearing agency in the threshold security for 35 consecutive settlement days, the participant and any broker or dealer for which it clears transactions, including any market maker, that would otherwise be entitled to rely on the exception provided in paragraph (b)(2)(ii) of this section, may not accept a short sale order in the threshold security from another person, or effect a short sale in the threshold security for its own account, without borrowing the security or entering into a bona fide arrangement to borrow the security, until the participant closes out the fail to deliver position by purchasing securities of like kind and quantity;

(vi) If a participant of a registered clearing agency reasonably allocates a portion of a fail to deliver position to another registered broker or dealer for which it clears trades or for which it is responsible for settlement, based on such broker or dealer's short position, then the provisions of this paragraph (b)(3) relating to such fail to deliver position shall apply to the portion of such registered broker or dealer that was allocated the fail to deliver position, and not to the participant; and

§ 242.204

(vii) A participant of a registered clearing agency shall not be deemed to have fulfilled the requirements of this paragraph (b)(3) where the participant enters into an arrangement with another person to purchase securities as required by this paragraph (b)(3), and the participant knows or has reason to know that the other person will not deliver securities in settlement of the purchase.

(c) *Definitions.* (1) For purposes of this section, the term *market maker* has the same meaning as in section 3(a)(38) of the Securities Exchange Act of 1934 ("Exchange Act") (15 U.S.C. 78c(a)(38)).

(2) For purposes of this section, the term *participant* has the same meaning as in section 3(a)(24) of the Exchange Act (15 U.S.C. 78c(a)(24)).

(3) For purposes of this section, the term *registered clearing agency* means a clearing agency, as defined in section 3(a)(23)(A) of the Exchange Act (15 U.S.C. 78c(a)(23)(A)), that is registered with the Commission pursuant to section 17A of the Exchange Act (15 U.S.C. 78q-1).

(4) For purposes of this section, the term *security future* has the same meaning as in section 3(a)(55) of the Exchange Act (15 U.S.C. 78c(a)(55)).

(5) For purposes of this section, the term *settlement day* means any business day on which deliveries of securities and payments of money may be made through the facilities of a registered clearing agency.

(6) For purposes of this section, the term *threshold security* means any equity security of an issuer that is registered pursuant to section 12 of the Exchange Act (15 U.S.C. 78l) or for which the issuer is required to file reports pursuant to section 15(d) of the Exchange Act (15 U.S.C. 78o(d)):

(i) For which there is an aggregate fail to deliver position for five consecutive settlement days at a registered clearing agency of 10,000 shares or more, and that is equal to at least 0.5% of the issue's total shares outstanding;

(ii) Is included on a list disseminated to its members by a self-regulatory organization; and

(iii) *Provided, however,* that a security shall cease to be a threshold security if the aggregate fail to deliver position at a registered clearing agency does not exceed the level specified in paragraph (c)(6)(i) of this section for five consecutive settlement days.

(d) *Exemptive authority.* Upon written application or upon its own motion, the Commission may grant an exemption from the provisions of this section, either unconditionally or on specified terms and conditions, to any transaction or class of transactions, or to any security or class of securities, or to any person or class of persons.

[69 FR 48029, Aug. 6, 2004, as amended at 72 FR 45557, Aug. 14, 2007; 73 FR 61706, Oct. 17, 2008]

§ 242.204 Close-out requirement.

(a) A participant of a registered clearing agency must deliver securities to a registered clearing agency for clearance and settlement on a long or short sale in any equity security by settlement date, or if a participant of a registered clearing agency has a fail to deliver position at a registered clearing agency in any equity security for a long or short sale transaction in that equity security, the participant shall, by no later than the beginning of regular trading hours on the settlement day following the settlement date, immediately close out its fail to deliver position by borrowing or purchasing securities of like kind and quantity; *Provided, however:*

(1) If a participant of a registered clearing agency has a fail to deliver position at a registered clearing agency in any equity security and the participant can demonstrate on its books and records that such fail to deliver position resulted from a long sale, the participant shall by no later than the beginning of regular trading hours on the third consecutive settlement day following the settlement date, immediately close out the fail to deliver position by purchasing or borrowing securities of like kind and quantity;

(2) If a participant of a registered clearing agency has a fail to deliver position at a registered clearing agency in any equity security resulting from a sale of a security that a person is deemed to own pursuant to § 242.200 and that such person intends to deliver as soon as all restrictions on delivery have been removed, the participant shall, by no later than the begining of

Securities and Exchange Commission § 242.204

regular trading hours on the thirty-fifth consecutive calendar day following the trade date for the transaction, immediately close out the fail to deliver position by purchasing securities of like kind and quantity; or

(3) If a participant of a registered clearing agency has a fail to deliver position at a registered clearing agency in any equity security that is attributable to bona fide market making activities by a registered market maker, options market maker, or other market maker obligated to quote in the over-the-counter market, the participant shall by no later than the beginning of regular trading hours on the third consecutive settlement day following the settlement date, immediately close out the fail to deliver position by purchasing or borrowing securities of like kind and quantity.

(b) If a participant of a registered clearing agency has a fail to deliver position in any equity security at a registered clearing agency and does not close out such fail to deliver position in accordance with the requirements of paragraph (a) of this section, the participant and any broker or dealer from which it receives trades for clearance and settlement, including any market maker that would otherwise be entitled to rely on the exception provided in § 242.203(b)(2)(iii), may not accept a short sale order in the equity security from another person, or effect a short sale in the equity security for its own account, to the extent that the broker or dealer submits its short sales to that participant for clearance and settlement, without first borrowing the security, or entering into a bona fide arrangement to borrow the security, until the participant closes out the fail to deliver position by purchasing securities of like kind and quantity and that purchase has cleared and settled at a registered clearing agency; *Provided, however:* A broker or dealer shall not be subject to the requirements of this paragraph if the broker or dealer timely certifies to the participant of a registered clearing agency that it has not incurred a fail to deliver position on settlement date for a long or short sale in an equity security for which the participant has a fail to deliver position at a registered clearing agency or that the broker or dealer is in compliance with paragraph (e) of this section.

(c) The participant must notify any broker or dealer from which it receives trades for clearance and settlement, including any market maker that would otherwise be entitled to rely on the exception provided in § 242.203(b)(2)(iii):

(1) That the participant has a fail to deliver position in an equity security at a registered clearing agency that has not been closed out in accordance with the requirements of paragraph (a) of this section; and

(2) When the purchase that the participant has made to close out the fail to deliver position has cleared and settled at a registered clearing agency.

(d) If a participant of a registered clearing agency reasonably allocates a portion of a fail to deliver position to another registered broker or dealer for which it clears trades or from which it receives trades for settlement, based on such broker's or dealer's short position, the provisions of paragraphs (a) and (b) of this section relating to such fail to deliver position shall apply to such registered broker or dealer that was allocated the fail to deliver position, and not to the participant. A broker or dealer that has been allocated a portion of a fail to deliver position that does not comply with the provisions of paragraph (a) of this section must immediately notify the participant that it has become subject to the requirements of paragraph (b) of this section.

(e) Even if a participant of a registered clearing agency has not closed out a fail to deliver position at a registered clearing agency in accordance with paragraph (a) of this section, or has not allocated a fail to deliver position to a broker or dealer in accordance with paragraph (d) of this section, a broker or dealer shall not be subject to the requirements of paragraph (a) or (b) of this section if the broker or dealer purchases or borrows the securities, and if:

(1) The purchase or borrow is bona fide;

(2) The purchase or borrow is executed after trade date but by no later than the end of regular trading hours on settlement date for the transaction;

§ 242.300

(3) The purchase or borrow is of a quantity of securities sufficient to cover the entire amount of that broker's or dealer's fail to deliver position at a registered clearing agency in that security; and

(4) The broker or dealer can demonstrate that it has a net flat or net long position on its books and records on the day of the purchase or borrow.

(f) A participant of a registered clearing agency shall not be deemed to have fulfilled the requirements of this section where the participant enters into an arrangement with another person to purchase or borrow securities as required by this section, and the participant knows or has reason to know that the other person will not deliver securities in settlement of the purchase or borrow.

(g) *Definitions.* (1) For purposes of this section, the term *settlement date* shall mean the business day on which delivery of a security and payment of money is to be made through the facilities of a registered clearing agency in connection with the sale of a security.

(2) For purposes of this section, the term *regular trading hours* has the same meaning as in § 242.600(b)(77) (Rule 600(b)(77) of Regulation NMS).

[74 FR 38292, July 31, 2009, as amended at 83 FR 58427, Nov. 19, 2018; 86 FR 18809, Apr. 9, 2021]

REGULATION ATS—ALTERNATIVE TRADING SYSTEMS

SOURCE: Sections 242.300 through 242.303 appear at 63 FR 70921, Dec. 22, 1998, unless otherwise noted.

PRELIMINARY NOTES

1. An alternative trading system is required to comply with the requirements in this Regulation ATS, unless such alternative trading system:
(a) Is registered as a national securities exchange;
(b) Is exempt from registration as a national securities exchange based on the limited volume of transactions effected on the alternative trading system; or
(c) Trades only government securities and certain other related instruments.

All alternative trading systems must comply with the antifraud, antimanipulation, and other applicable provisions of the federal securities laws.

2. The requirements imposed upon an alternative trading system by Regulation ATS are in addition to any requirements applicable to broker-dealers registered under section 15 of the Act, (15 U.S.C. 78o).

3. An alternative trading system must comply with any applicable state law relating to the offer or sale of securities or the registration or regulation of persons or entities effecting transactions in securities.

4. The disclosures made pursuant to the provisions of this section are in addition to any other disclosure requirements under the federal securities laws.

§ 242.300 Definitions.

For purposes of this section, the following definitions shall apply:

(a) *Alternative trading system* means any organization, association, person, group of persons, or system:

(1) That constitutes, maintains, or provides a market place or facilities for bringing together purchasers and sellers of securities or for otherwise performing with respect to securities the functions commonly performed by a stock exchange within the meaning of § 240.3b–16 of this chapter; and

(2) That does not:

(i) Set rules governing the conduct of subscribers other than the conduct of such subscribers' trading on such organization, association, person, group of persons, or system; or

(ii) Discipline subscribers other than by exclusion from trading.

(b) *Subscriber* means any person that has entered into a contractual agreement with an alternative trading system to access such alternative trading system for the purpose of effecting transactions in securities or submitting, disseminating, or displaying orders on such alternative trading system, including a customer, member, user, or participant in an alternative trading system. A subscriber, however, shall not include a national securities exchange or national securities association.

(c) *Affiliate of a subscriber* means any person that, directly or indirectly, controls, is under common control with, or is controlled by, the subscriber, including any employee.

(d) *Debt security* shall mean any security other than an equity security, as defined in § 240.3a11–1 of this chapter, as well as non-participatory preferred stock.

Securities and Exchange Commission § 242.301

(e) *Order* means any firm indication of a willingness to buy or sell a security, as either principal or agent, including any bid or offer quotation, market order, limit order, or other priced order.

(f) *Control* means the power, directly or indirectly, to direct the management or policies of the broker-dealer of an alternative trading system, whether through ownership of securities, by contract, or otherwise. A person is presumed to *control* the broker-dealer of an alternative trading system, if that person:

(1) Is a director, general partner, or officer exercising executive responsibility (or having similar status or performing similar functions);

(2) Directly or indirectly has the right to vote 25 percent or more of a class of voting security or has the power to sell or direct the sale of 25 percent or more of a class of voting securities of the broker-dealer of the alternative trading system; or

(3) In the case of a partnership, has contributed, or has the right to receive upon dissolution, 25 percent or more of the capital of the broker-dealer of the alternative trading system.

(g) *NMS stock* shall have the meaning provided in § 242.600; *provided, however,* that a debt or convertible debt security shall not be deemed an NMS stock for purposes of this Regulation ATS.

(h) *Effective transaction reporting plan* shall have the meaning provided in § 242.600.

(i) *Corporate debt security* shall mean any security that:

(1) Evidences a liability of the issuer of such security;

(2) Has a fixed maturity date that is at least one year following the date of issuance; and

(3) Is not an exempted security, as defined in section 3(a)(12) of the Act (15 U.S.C. 78c(a)(12)).

(j) *Commercial paper* shall mean any note, draft, or bill of exchange which arises out of a current transaction or the proceeds of which have been or are to be used for current transactions, and which has a maturity at the time of issuance of not exceeding nine months, exclusive of days of grace, or any renewal thereof the maturity of which is likewise limited.

(k) *NMS Stock ATS* means an alternative trading system, as defined in paragraph (a) of this section, that trades NMS stocks, as defined in paragraph (g) of this section.

[62 FR 544, Jan. 3, 1997, as amended at 70 FR 37619, June 29, 2005; 74 FR 52372, Oct. 9, 2009; 83 FR 38911, Aug. 7, 2018]

§ 242.301 Requirements for alternative trading systems.

(a) *Scope of section.* An alternative trading system shall comply with the requirements in paragraph (b) of this section, unless such alternative trading system:

(1) Is registered as an exchange under section 6 of the Act, (15 U.S.C. 78f);

(2) Is exempted by the Commission from registration as an exchange based on the limited volume of transactions effected;

(3) Is operated by a national securities association;

(4)(i) Is registered as a broker-dealer under sections 15(b) or 15C of the Act (15 U.S.C. 78o(b), and 78o–5), or is a bank, and

(ii) Limits its securities activities to the following instruments:

(A) Government securities, as defined in section 3(a)(42) of the Act, (15 U.S.C. 78c(a)(42));

(B) Repurchase and reverse repurchase agreements solely involving securities included within paragraph (a)(4)(ii)(A) of this section;

(C) Any put, call, straddle, option, or privilege on a government security, other than a put, call, straddle, option, or privilege that:

(*1*) Is traded on one or more national securities exchanges; or

(*2*) For which quotations are disseminated through an automated quotation system operated by a registered securities association; and

(D) Commercial paper.

(5) Is exempted, conditionally or unconditionally, by Commission order, after application by such alternative trading system, from one or more of the requirements of paragraph (b) of this section or § 242.304. The Commission will grant such exemption only after determining that such an order is consistent with the public interest, the

§ 242.301

protection of investors, and the removal of impediments to, and perfection of the mechanisms of, a national market system.

(b) *Requirements.* Every alternative trading system subject to this Regulation ATS, pursuant to paragraph (a) of this section, shall comply with the requirements in this paragraph (b).

(1) *Broker-dealer registration.* The alternative trading system shall register as a broker-dealer under section 15 of the Act, (15 U.S.C. 78o).

(2) *Notice.* (i) The alternative trading system shall file an initial operation report on Form ATS, § 249.637 of this chapter, in accordance with the instructions therein, at least 20 days prior to commencing operation as an alternative trading system.

(ii) The alternative trading system shall file an amendment on Form ATS at least 20 calendar days prior to implementing a material change to the operation of the alternative trading system.

(iii) If any information contained in the initial operation report filed under paragraph (b)(2)(i) of this section becomes inaccurate for any reason and has not been previously reported to the Commission as an amendment on Form ATS, the alternative trading system shall file an amendment on Form ATS correcting such information within 30 calendar days after the end of each calendar quarter in which the alternative trading system has operated.

(iv) The alternative trading system shall promptly file an amendment on Form ATS correcting information previously reported on Form ATS after discovery that any information filed under paragraphs (b)(2)(i), (ii) or (iii) of this section was inaccurate when filed.

(v) The alternative trading system shall promptly file a cessation of operations report on Form ATS in accordance with the instructions therein upon ceasing to operate as an alternative trading system.

(vi) Every notice or amendment filed pursuant to this paragraph (b)(2) shall constitute a "report" within the meaning of sections 11A, 17(a), 18(a), and 32(a), (15 U.S.C. 78k–1, 78q(a), 78r(a), and 78ff(a)), and any other applicable provisions of the Act.

(vii) The reports provided for in paragraph (b)(2) of this section shall be considered filed upon receipt by the Division of Trading and Markets, at the Commission's principal office in Washington, DC. Duplicate originals of the reports provided for in paragraphs (b)(2)(i) through (v) of this section must be filed with surveillance personnel designated as such by any self-regulatory organization that is the designated examining authority for the alternative trading system pursuant to § 240.17d–1 of this chapter simultaneously with filing with the Commission. Duplicates of the reports required by paragraph (b)(9) of this section shall be provided to surveillance personnel of such self-regulatory authority upon request. All reports filed pursuant to this paragraph (b)(2) and paragraph (b)(9) of this section shall be deemed confidential when filed.

(viii) An NMS Stock ATS that is operating pursuant to an initial operation report on Form ATS on file with the Commission as of January 7, 2019 ("Legacy NMS Stock ATS") shall be subject to the requirements of paragraphs (b)(2)(i) through (vii) of this section until that ATS files an initial Form ATS–N with the Commission pursuant to § 242.304(a)(1)(iv)(A). Thereafter, the Legacy NMS Stock ATS shall file reports pursuant to § 242.304. An alternative trading system that trades NMS stocks and securities other than NMS stocks shall be subject to the requirements of § 242.304 of this chapter with respect to NMS stocks and paragraph (b)(2) of this section with respect to non-NMS stocks. As of January 7, 2019, an entity seeking to operate as an NMS Stock ATS shall not be subject to the requirements of paragraphs (b)(2)(i) through (vii) of this section and shall file reports pursuant to § 242.304.

(3) *Order display and execution access.* (i) An alternative trading system shall comply with the requirements set forth in paragraph (b)(3)(ii) of this section, with respect to any NMS stock in which the alternative trading system:

(A) Displays subscriber orders to any person (other than alternative trading system employees); and

(B) During at least 4 of the preceding 6 calendar months, had an average

Securities and Exchange Commission § 242.301

daily trading volume of 5 percent or more of the aggregate average daily share volume for such NMS stock as reported by an effective transaction reporting plan.

(ii) Such alternative trading system shall provide to a national securities exchange or national securities association the prices and sizes of the orders at the highest buy price and the lowest sell price for such NMS stock, displayed to more than one person in the alternative trading system, for inclusion in the quotation data made available by the national securities exchange or national securities association to vendors pursuant to § 242.602.

(iii) With respect to any order displayed pursuant to paragraph (b)(3)(ii) of this section, an alternative trading system shall provide to any broker-dealer that has access to the national securities exchange or national securities association to which the alternative trading system provides the prices and sizes of displayed orders pursuant to paragraph (b)(3)(ii) of this section, the ability to effect a transaction with such orders that is:

(A) Equivalent to the ability of such broker-dealer to effect a transaction with other orders displayed on the exchange or by the association; and

(B) At the price of the highest priced buy order or lowest priced sell order displayed for the lesser of the cumulative size of such priced orders entered therein at such price, or the size of the execution sought by such broker-dealer.

(4) *Fees.* The alternative trading system shall not charge any fee to broker-dealers that access the alternative trading system through a national securities exchange or national securities association, that is inconsistent with equivalent access to the alternative trading system required by paragraph (b)(3)(iii) of this section. In addition, if the national securities exchange or national securities association to which an alternative trading system provides the prices and sizes of orders under paragraphs (b)(3)(ii) and (b)(3)(iii) of this section establishes rules designed to assure consistency with standards for access to quotations displayed on such national securities exchange, or the market operated by such national securities association, the alternative trading system shall not charge any fee to members that is contrary to, that is not disclosed in the manner required by, or that is inconsistent with any standard of equivalent access established by such rules.

(5) *Fair access.* (i) An alternative trading system shall comply with the requirements in paragraph (b)(5)(ii) of this section, if during at least 4 of the preceding 6 calendar months, such alternative trading system had:

(A) With respect to any NMS stock, 5 percent or more of the average daily volume in that security reported by an effective transaction reporting plan;

(B) With respect to an equity security that is not an NMS stock and for which transactions are reported to a self-regulatory organization, 5 percent or more of the average daily trading volume in that security as calculated by the self-regulatory organization to which such transactions are reported;

(C) With respect to municipal securities, 5 percent or more of the average daily volume traded in the United States; or

(D) With respect to corporate debt securities, 5 percent or more of the average daily volume traded in the United States.

(ii) An alternative trading system shall:

(A) Establish written standards for granting access to trading on its system;

(B) Not unreasonably prohibit or limit any person in respect to access to services offered by such alternative trading system by applying the standards established under paragraph (b)(5)(ii)(A) of this section in an unfair or discriminatory manner;

(C) Make and keep records of:

(*1*) All grants of access including, for all subscribers, the reasons for granting such access; and

(*2*) All denials or limitations of access and reasons, for each applicant, for denying or limiting access; and

(D) Report the information required on Form ATS-R (§ 249.638 of this chapter) regarding grants, denials, and limitations of access.

(iii) Notwithstanding paragraph (b)(5)(i) of this section, an alternative trading system shall not be required to

§ 242.301

comply with the requirements in paragraph (b)(5)(ii) of this section, if such alternative trading system:

(A) Matches customer orders for a security with other customer orders;

(B) Such customers' orders are not displayed to any person, other than employees of the alternative trading system; and

(C) Such orders are executed at a price for such security disseminated by an effective transaction reporting plan, or derived from such prices.

(6) *Capacity, integrity, and security of automated systems.* (i) The alternative trading system shall comply with the requirements in paragraph (b)(6)(ii) of this section, if during at least 4 of the preceding 6 calendar months, such alternative trading system had:

(A) With respect to municipal securities, 20 percent or more of the average daily volume traded in the United States; or

(B) With respect to corporate debt securities, 20 percent or more of the average daily volume traded in the United States.

(ii) With respect to those systems that support order entry, order routing, order execution, transaction reporting, and trade comparison, the alternative trading system shall:

(A) Establish reasonable current and future capacity estimates;

(B) Conduct periodic capacity stress tests of critical systems to determine such system's ability to process transactions in an accurate, timely, and efficient manner;

(C) Develop and implement reasonable procedures to review and keep current its system development and testing methodology;

(D) Review the vulnerability of its systems and data center computer operations to internal and external threats, physical hazards, and natural disasters;

(E) Establish adequate contingency and disaster recovery plans;

(F) On an annual basis, perform an independent review, in accordance with established audit procedures and standards, of such alternative trading system's controls for ensuring that paragraphs (b)(6)(ii)(A) through (E) of this section are met, and conduct a review by senior management of a report containing the recommendations and conclusions of the independent review; and

(G) Promptly notify the Commission staff of material systems outages and significant systems changes.

(iii) Notwithstanding paragraph (b)(6)(i) of this section, an alternative trading system shall not be required to comply with the requirements in paragraph (b)(6)(ii) of this section, if such alternative trading system:

(A) Matches customer orders for a security with other customer orders;

(B) Such customers' orders are not displayed to any person, other than employees of the alternative trading system; and

(C) Such orders are executed at a price for such security disseminated by an effective transaction reporting plan, or derived from such prices.

(7) *Examinations, inspections, and investigations.* The alternative trading system shall permit the examination and inspection of its premises, systems, and records, and cooperate with the examination, inspection, or investigation of subscribers, whether such examination is being conducted by the Commission or by a self-regulatory organization of which such subscriber is a member.

(8) *Recordkeeping.* The alternative trading system shall:

(i) Make and keep current the records specified in § 242.302; and

(ii) Preserve the records specified in § 242.303.

(9) *Reporting.* The alternative trading system shall:

(i) Separately file the information required by Form ATS-R (§ 249.638 of this chapter) for transactions in NMS stocks, as defined in paragraph (g) of this section, and transactions in securities other than NMS stocks within 30 calendar days after the end of each calendar quarter in which the market has operated after the effective date of this section; and

(ii) Separately file the information required by Form ATS-R for transactions in NMS stocks and transactions in securities other than NMS stocks within 10 calendar days after an alternative trading system ceases to operate.

Securities and Exchange Commission § 242.303

(10) *Written procedures to ensure the confidential treatment of trading information.* (i) The alternative trading system shall establish adequate written safeguards and written procedures to protect subscribers' confidential trading information. Such written safeguards and written procedures shall include:

(A) Limiting access to the confidential trading information of subscribers to those employees of the alternative trading system who are operating the system or responsible for its compliance with these or any other applicable rules;

(B) Implementing standards controlling employees of the alternative trading system trading for their own accounts; and

(ii) The alternative trading system shall adopt and implement adequate written oversight procedures to ensure that the written safeguards and procedures established pursuant to paragraph (b)(10)(i) of this section are followed.

(11) *Name.* The alternative trading system shall not use in its name the word "exchange," or derivations of the word "exchange," such as the term "stock market."

[63 FR 70921, Dec. 22, 1998, as amended at 65 FR 13235, Mar. 13, 2000; 70 FR 37619, June 29, 2005; 74 FR 52372, Oct. 9, 2009; 79 FR 72436, Dec. 5, 2014; 83 FR 38911, Aug. 7, 2018]

§ 242.302 Recordkeeping requirements for alternative trading systems.

To comply with the condition set forth in paragraph (b)(8) of §242.301, an alternative trading system shall make and keep current the following records:

(a) A record of subscribers to such alternative trading system (identifying any affiliations between the alternative trading system and subscribers to the alternative trading system, including common directors, officers, or owners);

(b) Daily summaries of trading in the alternative trading system including:

(1) Securities for which transactions have been executed;

(2) Transaction volume, expressed with respect to equity securities in:
 (i) Number of trades;
 (ii) Number of shares traded; and
 (iii) Total settlement value in terms of U.S. dollars; and

(3) Transaction volume, expressed with respect to debt securities in:
 (i) Number of trades; and
 (ii) Total U.S. dollar value; and

(c) Time-sequenced records of order information in the alternative trading system, including:

(1) Date and time (expressed in terms of hours, minutes, and seconds) that the order was received;

(2) Identity of the security;

(3) The number of shares, or principal amount of bonds, to which the order applies;

(4) An identification of the order as related to a program trade or an index arbitrage trade as defined in New York Stock Exchange Rule 80A;

(5) The designation of the order as a buy or sell order;

(6) The designation of the order as a short sale order;

(7) The designation of the order as a market order, limit order, stop order, stop limit order, or other type or order;

(8) Any limit or stop price prescribed by the order;

(9) The date on which the order expires and, if the time in force is less than one day, the time when the order expires;

(10) The time limit during which the order is in force;

(11) Any instructions to modify or cancel the order;

(12) The type of account, i.e., retail, wholesale, employee, proprietary, or any other type of account designated by the alternative trading system, for which the order is submitted;

(13) Date and time (expressed in terms of hours, minutes, and seconds) that the order was executed;

(14) Price at which the order was executed;

(15) Size of the order executed (expressed in number of shares or units or principal amount); and

(16) Identity of the parties to the transaction.

§ 242.303 Record preservation requirements for alternative trading systems.

(a) To comply with the condition set forth in paragraph (b)(8) of §242.301, an alternative trading system shall preserve the following records:

(1) For a period of not less than three years, the first two years in an easily

§ 242.303

accessible place, an alternative trading system shall preserve:

(i) All records required to be made pursuant to § 242.302;

(ii) All notices provided by such alternative trading system to subscribers generally, whether written or communicated through automated means, including, but not limited to, notices addressing hours of system operations, system malfunctions, changes to system procedures, maintenance of hardware and software, instructions pertaining to access to the market and denials of, or limitations on, access to the alternative trading system;

(iii) If subject to paragraph (b)(5)(ii) of § 242.301, at least one copy of such alternative trading system's standards for access to trading, all documents relevant to the alternative trading systems decision to grant, deny, or limit access to any person, and all other documents made or received by the alternative trading system in the course of complying with paragraph (b)(5) of § 242.301; and

(iv) At least one copy of all documents made or received by the alternative trading system in the course of complying with paragraph (b)(6) of § 242.301, including all correspondence, memoranda, papers, books, notices, accounts, reports, test scripts, test results, and other similar records.

(v) At least one copy of the written safeguards and written procedures to protect subscribers' confidential trading information and the written oversight procedures created in the course of complying with paragraph (b)(10) of § 242.301.

(2) During the life of the enterprise and of any successor enterprise, an alternative trading system shall preserve:

(i) All partnership articles or, in the case of a corporation, all articles of incorporation or charter, minute books and stock certificate books; and

(ii) Copies of reports filed pursuant to paragraph (b)(2) of § 242.301 or § 242.304 of this chapter and records made pursuant to paragraph (b)(5) of § 242.301 of this chapter.

(b) The records required to be maintained and preserved pursuant to paragraph (a) of this section must be produced, reproduced, and maintained in paper form or in any of the forms permitted under § 240.17a–4(f) of this chapter.

(c) Alternative trading systems must comply with any other applicable recordkeeping or reporting requirement in the Act, and the rules and regulations thereunder. If the information in a record required to be made pursuant to this section is preserved in a record made pursuant to § 240.17a–3 or § 240.17a–4 of this chapter, or otherwise preserved by the alternative trading system (whether in summary or some other form), this section shall not require the sponsor to maintain such information in a separate file, provided that the sponsor can promptly sort and retrieve the information as if it had been kept in a separate file as a record made pursuant to this section, and preserves the information in accordance with the time periods specified in paragraph (a) of this section.

(d) The records required to be maintained and preserved pursuant to this section may be prepared or maintained by a service bureau, depository, or other recordkeeping service on behalf of the alternative trading system. An agreement with a service bureau, depository, or other recordkeeping service shall not relieve the alternative trading system from the responsibility to prepare and maintain records as specified in this section. The service bureau, depository, or other recordkeeping service shall file with the Commission a written undertaking in a form acceptable to the Commission, signed by a duly authorized person, to the effect that such records are the property of the alternative trading system required to be maintained and preserved and will be surrendered promptly on request of the alternative trading system, and shall include the following provision: With respect to any books and records maintained or preserved on behalf of (name of alternative trading system), the undersigned hereby undertakes to permit examination of such books and records at any time, or from time to time, during business hours by the staff of the Securities and Exchange Commission, any self-regulatory organization of which the alternative trading system is a member, or any State securities regulator having

Securities and Exchange Commission § 242.304

jurisdiction over the alternative trading system, and to promptly furnish to the Commission, self-regulatory organization of which the alternative trading system is a member, or any State securities regulator having jurisdiction over the alternative trading system a true, correct, complete and current hard copy of any, all, or any part of, such books and records.

(e) Every alternative trading system shall furnish to any representative of the Commission promptly upon request, legible, true, and complete copies of those records that are required to be preserved under this section.

[63 FR 70921, Dec. 22, 1998, as amended at 66 FR 55841, Nov. 2, 2001; 83 FR 38911, Aug. 7, 2018]

§ 242.304 NMS Stock ATSs.

(a) *Conditions to the exemption.* Unless not required to comply with Regulation ATS pursuant to § 242.301(a), an NMS Stock ATS must comply with §§ 242.300 through 242.304 (except § 242.301(b)(2)(i) through (vii)) to be exempt pursuant to § 240.3a1–1(a)(2).

(1) *Initial Form ATS–N.* (i) *Filing and effectiveness requirement.* No exemption is available to an NMS Stock ATS pursuant to § 240.3a1–1(a)(2) unless the NMS Stock ATS files with the Commission an initial Form ATS–N, in accordance with the conditions of this section, and the initial Form ATS–N is effective pursuant to paragraph (a)(1)(iii) or (a)(1)(iv)(A) of this section.

(ii) *Commission review period.* (A) The Commission may, by order, as provided in paragraph (a)(1)(iii) of this section, declare an initial Form ATS–N filed by an NMS Stock ATS ineffective no later than 120 calendar days from the date of filing with the Commission, or, if applicable, the end of the extended review period. The Commission may extend the initial Form ATS–N review period for:

(*1*) An additional 90 calendar days, if the Form ATS–N is unusually lengthy or raises novel or complex issues that require additional time for review, in which case the Commission will notify the NMS Stock ATS in writing within the initial 120-calendar day review period and will briefly describe the reason for the determination for which additional time for review is required; or

(*2*) Any extended review period to which a duly authorized representative of the NMS Stock ATS agrees in writing.

(B) During review by the Commission of the initial Form ATS–N, the NMS Stock ATS shall amend its initial Form ATS–N pursuant to the requirements of paragraphs (a)(2)(i)(B) and (C) of this section. To make material changes to its initial Form ATS–N during the Commission review period, the NMS Stock ATS shall withdraw its filed initial Form ATS–N and may refile an initial Form ATS–N pursuant to paragraph (a)(1) of this section.

(iii) *Effectiveness; Ineffectiveness determination.* (A) An initial Form ATS–N, as amended, filed by an NMS Stock ATS will become effective, unless declared ineffective, upon the earlier of:

(*1*) The completion of review by the Commission and publication pursuant to paragraph (b)(2)(i) of this section; or

(*2*) The expiration of the review period, or, if applicable, the end of the extended review period, pursuant to paragraph (a)(1)(ii) of this section.

(B) The Commission will, by order, declare an initial Form ATS–N ineffective if it finds, after notice and opportunity for hearing, that such action is necessary or appropriate in the public interest, and is consistent with the protection of investors. If the Commission declares an initial Form ATS–N ineffective, the NMS Stock ATS shall be prohibited from operating as an NMS Stock ATS pursuant to § 240.3a1–1(a)(2). An initial Form ATS–N declared ineffective does not prevent the NMS Stock ATS from subsequently filing a new Form ATS–N.

(iv) *Transition for Legacy NMS Stock ATSs.* (A) *Initial Form ATS–N filing requirements.* A Legacy NMS Stock ATS shall file with the Commission an initial Form ATS–N, in accordance with the conditions of this section, no earlier than January 7, 2019, and no later than February 8, 2019. An initial Form ATS–N filed by a Legacy NMS Stock ATS shall supersede and replace for purposes of the exemption the previously filed Form ATS of the Legacy NMS Stock ATS. The Legacy NMS

§ 242.304

Stock ATS may operate, on a provisional basis, pursuant to the filed initial Form ATS–N, and any amendments thereto, during the review of the initial Form ATS–N by the Commission. An initial Form ATS–N filed by a Legacy NMS Stock ATS, as amended, will become effective, unless declared ineffective, upon the earlier of:

(1) The completion of review by the Commission and publication pursuant to paragraph (b)(2)(i) of this section; or

(2) The expiration of the review period, or, if applicable, the end of the extended review period, pursuant to paragraph (a)(1)(iv)(B) of this section.

(B) *Commission review period; Ineffectiveness determination.* The Commission may, by order, as provided in paragraph (a)(1)(iii) of this section, declare an initial Form ATS–N filed by a Legacy NMS Stock ATS ineffective no later than 120 calendar days from the date of filing with the Commission, or, if applicable, the end of the extended review period. The Commission may extend the initial Form ATS–N review period for a Legacy NMS Stock ATS for:

(1) An additional 120 calendar days if the initial Form ATS–N is unusually lengthy or raises novel or complex issues that require additional time for review, in which case the Commission will notify the Legacy NMS Stock ATS in writing within the initial 120-calendar day review period and briefly describe the reason for the determination for which additional time for review is required; or

(2) Any extended review period to which a duly-authorized representative of the Legacy NMS Stock ATS agrees in writing.

(C) *Amendments to initial Form ATS–N.* During review by the Commission of the initial Form ATS–N filed by a Legacy NMS Stock ATS, the Legacy NMS Stock ATS shall amend its initial Form ATS–N pursuant to the requirements of paragraphs (a)(2)(i)(A) through (D) of this section.

(2) *Form ATS–N amendment.* (i) *Filing requirements.* An NMS Stock ATS shall amend a Form ATS–N, in accordance with the conditions of this section:

(A) At least 30 calendar days, except as provided by paragraph (a)(2)(i)(D) of this section, prior to the date of implementation of a material change to the operations of the NMS Stock ATS or to the activities of the broker-dealer operator or its affiliates that are subject to disclosure on Form ATS–N ("Material Amendment");

(B) No later than 30 calendar days after the end of each calendar quarter to correct information that has become inaccurate or incomplete for any reason and was not required to be reported to the Commission as a Form ATS–N amendment pursuant to paragraphs (a)(2)(i)(A), (C), or (D) of this section ("Updating Amendment");

(C) Promptly, to correct information in any previous disclosure on Form ATS–N, after discovery that any information previously filed on Form ATS–N was materially inaccurate or incomplete when filed ("Correcting Amendment"); or

(D) No later than seven calendar days after information required to be disclosed in Part III, Items 24 and 25 on Form ATS–N has become inaccurate or incomplete ("Order Display and Fair Access Amendment").

(ii) *Commission review period; Ineffectiveness determination.* The Commission will, by order, declare ineffective any Form ATS–N amendment filed pursuant to paragraphs (a)(2)(i)(A) through (D) of this section, no later than 30 calendar days from filing with the Commission, if the Commission finds that such action is necessary or appropriate in the public interest, and is consistent with the protection of investors. A Form ATS–N amendment declared ineffective shall prohibit the NMS Stock ATS from operating pursuant to the ineffective Form ATS–N amendment. A Form ATS–N amendment declared ineffective does not prevent the NMS Stock ATS from subsequently filing a new Form ATS–N amendment. During review by the Commission of a Material Amendment, the NMS Stock ATS shall amend the Material Amendment pursuant to the requirements of paragraphs (a)(2)(i)(B) through (C) of this section. To make material changes to a filed Material Amendment during the Commission review period, an NMS Stock ATS shall withdraw its filed Material Amendment and must file the new Material Amendment pursuant to (a)(2)(i)(A) of this section.

Securities and Exchange Commission § 242.304

(3) *Notice of cessation.* An NMS Stock ATS shall notice its cessation of operations on Form ATS–N at least 10 business days prior to the date the NMS Stock ATS will cease to operate as an NMS Stock ATS. The notice of cessation shall cause the Form ATS–N to become ineffective on the date designated by the NMS Stock ATS.

(4) *Suspension, limitation, and revocation of the exemption from the definition of exchange.* (i) The Commission will, by order, if it finds, after notice and opportunity for hearing, that such action is necessary or appropriate in the public interest, and is consistent with the protection of investors, suspend for a period not exceeding twelve months, limit, or revoke the exemption for an NMS Stock ATS pursuant to § 240.3a1-1(a)(2) of this chapter.

(ii) If the exemption for an NMS Stock ATS is suspended or revoked pursuant to paragraph (a)(4)(i) of this section, the NMS Stock ATS shall be prohibited from operating pursuant to the exemption pursuant to § 240.3a1-1(a)(2) of this chapter. If the exemption for an NMS Stock ATS is limited pursuant to paragraph (a)(4)(i) of this section, the NMS Stock ATS shall be prohibited from operating in a manner otherwise inconsistent with the terms and conditions of the Commission order.

(b) *Public disclosures.* (1) Every Form ATS–N filed pursuant to this section shall constitute a "report" within the meaning of sections 11A, 17(a), 18(a), and 32(a) (15 U.S.C. 78k-1, 78q(a), 78r(a), and 78ff(a)), and any other applicable provisions of the Act.

(2) The Commission will make public via posting on the Commission's website, each:

(i) Effective initial Form ATS–N, as amended;

(ii) Order of ineffective initial Form ATS–N;

(iii) Form ATS–N amendment to an effective Form ATS–N:

(A) *Material Amendments:* The cover page of the Material Amendment will be made public by the Commission upon filing and, unless the Commission declares the Material Amendment ineffective, the entirety of the Material Amendment, as amended, will be made public by the Commission following the expiration of the review period pursuant to paragraph (a)(2)(ii) of this section.

(B) *Updating, Correcting, and Order Display and Fair Access Amendments:* The entirety of Updating, Correcting, and Order Display and Fair Access Amendments will be made public by the Commission upon filing. Notwithstanding the foregoing, an Updating or Correcting Amendment filed to a Material Amendment will be made public by the Commission following the expiration of the review period for such Material Amendment pursuant to paragraph (a)(2)(ii) of this section.

(iv) Order of ineffective Form ATS–N amendment;

(v) Notice of cessation; and

(vi) Order suspending, limiting, or revoking the exemption for an NMS Stock ATS from the definition of an "exchange" pursuant to § 240.3a1-1(a)(2) of this chapter.

(3) Each NMS Stock ATS shall make public via posting on its website a direct URL hyperlink to the Commission's website that contains the documents enumerated in paragraph (b)(2) of this section.

(c) *Form ATS–N disclosure requirements.* (1) An NMS Stock ATS must file a Form ATS–N in accordance with the instructions therein.

(2) Any report required to be filed with the Commission under this section shall be filed on Form ATS–N, and include all information as prescribed in Form ATS–N and the instructions thereto. Such document shall be executed at, or prior to, the time Form ATS–N is filed and shall be retained by the NMS Stock ATS in accordance with §§ 242.303 and § 232.302 of this chapter, and the instructions in Form ATS–N.

[83 FR 38911, Aug. 7, 2018]

CUSTOMER MARGIN REQUIREMENTS FOR SECURITY FUTURES

SOURCE: 67 FR 53176, Aug. 14, 2002, unless otherwise noted.

§ 242.400 Customer margin requirements for security futures—authority, purpose, interpretation, and scope.

(a) *Authority and purpose.* Sections 242.400 through 242.406 and 17 CFR 41.42 through 41.49 ("this Regulation, §§ 242.400 through 242.406") are issued by the Securities and Exchange Commission ("Commission") jointly with the Commodity Futures Trading Commission ("CFTC"), pursuant to authority delegated by the Board of Governors of the Federal Reserve System under section 7(c)(2)(A) of the Securities Exchange Act of 1934 ("Act") (15 U.S.C. 78g(c)(2)(A)). The principal purpose of this Regulation (§§ 242.400 through 242.406) is to regulate customer margin collected by brokers, dealers, and members of national securities exchanges, including futures commission merchants required to register as brokers or dealers under section 15(b)(11) of the Act (15 U.S.C. 78o(b)(11)), relating to security futures.

(b) *Interpretation.* This Regulation (§§ 242.400 through 242.406) shall be jointly interpreted by the Commission and the CFTC, consistent with the criteria set forth in clauses (i) through (iv) of section 7(c)(2)(B) of the Act (15 U.S.C. 78g(c)(2)(B)) and the provisions of Regulation T (12 CFR part 220).

(c) *Scope.* (1) This Regulation (§§ 242.400 through 242.406) does not preclude a self-regulatory authority, under rules that are effective in accordance with section 19(b)(2) of the Act (15 U.S.C. 78s(b)(2)) or section 19(b)(7) of the Act (15 U.S.C. 78s(b)(7)) and, as applicable, section 5c(c) of the Commodity Exchange Act ("CEA") (7 U.S.C. 7a–2(c)), or a security futures intermediary from imposing additional margin requirements on security futures, including higher initial or maintenance margin levels, consistent with this Regulation (§§ 242.400 through 242.406), or from taking appropriate action to preserve its financial integrity.

(2) This Regulation (§§ 242.400 through 242.406) does not apply to:

(i) Financial relations between a customer and a security futures intermediary to the extent that they comply with a portfolio margining system under rules that meet the criteria set forth in section 7(c)(2)(B) of the Act (15 U.S.C. 78g(c)(2)(B)) and that are effective in accordance with section 19(b)(2) of the Act (15 U.S.C. 78s(b)(2)) and, as applicable, section 5c(c) of the CEA (7 U.S.C. 7a–2(c));

(ii) Financial relations between a security futures intermediary and a foreign person involving security futures traded on or subject to the rules of a foreign board of trade;

(iii) Margin requirements that clearing agencies registered under section 17A of the Exchange Act (15 U.S.C. 78q–1) or derivatives clearing organizations registered under section 5b of the CEA (7 U.S.C. 7a–1) impose on their members;

(iv) Financial relations between a security futures intermediary and a person based on a good faith determination by the security futures intermediary that such person is an exempted person; and

(v) Financial relations between a security futures intermediary and, or arranged by a security futures intermediary for, a person relating to trading in security futures by such person for its own account, if such person:

(A) Is a member of a national securities exchange or national securities association registered pursuant to section 15A(a) of the Act (15 U.S.C. 78o–3(a)); and

(B) Is registered with such exchange or such association as a security futures dealer pursuant to rules that are effective in accordance with section 19(b)(2) of the Act (15 U.S.C. 78s(b)(2)) and, as applicable, section 5c(c) of the CEA (7 U.S.C. 7a–2(c)), that:

(*1*) Require such member to be registered as a floor trader or a floor broker with the CFTC under Section 4f(a)(1) of the CEA (7 U.S.C. 6f(a)(1)), or as a dealer with the Commission under section 15(b) of the Act (15 U.S.C. 78o(b));

(*2*) Require such member to maintain records sufficient to prove compliance with this paragraph (c)(2)(v) and the rules of the exchange or association of which it is a member;

(*3*) Require such member to hold itself out as being willing to buy and sell security futures for its own account on a regular or continuous basis; and

Securities and Exchange Commission §242.401

(4) Provide for disciplinary action, including revocation of such member's registration as a security futures dealer, for such member's failure to comply with this Regulation (§§ 242.400 through 242.406) or the rules of the exchange or association.

(d) *Exemption.* The Commission may exempt, either unconditionally or on specified terms and conditions, financial relations involving any security futures intermediary, customer, position, or transaction, or any class of security futures intermediaries, customers, positions, or transactions, from one or more requirements of this Regulation (§§ 242.400 through 242.406), if the Commission determines that such exemption is necessary or appropriate in the public interest and consistent with the protection of investors. An exemption granted pursuant to this paragraph shall not operate as an exemption from any CFTC rules. Any exemption that may be required from such rules must be obtained separately from the CFTC.

§ 242.401 Definitions.

(a) For purposes of this Regulation (§§ 242.400 through 242.406) only, the following terms shall have the meanings set forth in this section.

(1) *Applicable margin rules* and *margin rules applicable to an account* mean the rules and regulations applicable to financial relations between a security futures intermediary and a customer with respect to security futures and related positions carried in a securities account or futures account as provided in § 242.402(a) of this Regulation (§§ 242.400 through 242.406).

(2) *Broker* shall have the meaning provided in section 3(a)(4) of the Act (15 U.S.C. 78c(a)(4)).

(3) *Contract multiplier* means the number of units of a narrow-based security index expressed as a dollar amount, in accordance with the terms of the security future contract.

(4) *Current market value* means, on any day:

(i) With respect to a security future:

(A) If the instrument underlying such security future is a stock, theproduct of the daily settlement price of such security future as shown by any regularly published reporting or quotation service, and the applicable number of shares per contract; or

(B) If the instrument underlying such security future is a narrow-based security index, as defined in section 3(a)(55)(B) of the Act (15 U.S.C. 78c(a)(55)(B)), the product of the daily settlement price of such security future as shown by any regularly published reporting or quotation service, and the applicable contract multiplier.

(ii) With respect to a security other than a security future, the most recent closing sale price of the security, as shown by any regularly published reporting or quotation service. If there is no recent closing sale price, the security futures intermediary may use any reasonable estimate of the market value of the security as of the most recent close of business.

(5) *Customer* excludes an exempted person and includes:

(i) Any person or persons acting jointly:

(A) On whose behalf a security futures intermediary effects a security futures transaction or carries a security futures position; or

(B) Who would be considered a customer of the security futures intermediary according to the ordinary usage of the trade;

(ii) Any partner in a security futures intermediary that is organized as a partnership who would be considered a customer of the security futures intermediary absent the partnership relationship; and

(iii) Any joint venture in which a security futures intermediary participates and which would be considered a customer of the security futures intermediary if the security futures intermediary were not a participant.

(6) *Daily settlement price* means, with respect to a security future, the settlement price of such security future determined at the close of trading each day, under the rules of the applicable exchange, clearing agency, or derivatives clearing organization.

(7) *Dealer* shall have the meaning provided in section 3(a)(5) of the Act (15 U.S.C. 78c(a)(5)).

(8) *Equity* means the equity or margin equity in a securities or futures account, as computed in accordance with

§ 242.401

the margin rules applicable to the account and subject to adjustment under § 242.404(c), (d) and (e) of this Regulation (§§ 242.400 through 242.406).

(9) *Exempted person* means:

(i) A member of a national securities exchange, a registered broker or dealer, or a registered futures commission merchant, a substantial portion of whose business consists of transactions in securities, commodity futures, or commodity options with persons other than brokers, dealers, futures commission merchants, floor brokers, or floor traders, and includes a person who:

(A) Maintains at least 1000 active accounts on an annual basis for persons other than brokers, dealers, persons associated with a broker or dealer, futures commission merchants, floor brokers, floor traders, and persons affiliated with a futures commission merchant, floor broker, or floor trader that are effecting transactions in securities, commodity futures, or commodity options;

(B) Earns at least $10 million in gross revenues on an annual basis from transactions in securities, commodity futures, or commodity options with persons other than brokers, dealers, persons associated with a broker or dealer, futures commission merchants, floor brokers, floor traders, and persons affiliated with a futures commission merchant, floor broker, or floor trader; or

(C) Earns at least 10 percent of its gross revenues on an annual basis from transactions in securities, commodity futures, or commodity options with persons other than brokers, dealers, persons associated with a broker or dealer, futures commission merchants, floor brokers, floor traders, and persons affiliated with a futures commission merchant, floor broker, or floor trader.

(ii) For purposes of paragraph (a)(9)(i) of this section only, persons affiliated with a futures commission merchant, floor broker, or floor trader means any partner, officer, director, or branch manager of such futures commission merchant, floor broker, or floor trader (or any person occupying a similar status or performing similar functions), any person directly or indirectly controlling, controlled by, or under common control with such futures commission merchant, floor broker, or floor trader, or any employee of such a futures commission merchant, floor broker, or floor trader.

(iii) A member of a national securities exchange, a registered broker or dealer, or a registered futures commission merchant that has been in existence for less than one year may meet the definition of exempted person based on a six-month period.

(10) *Exempted security* shall have the meaning provided in section 3(a)(12) of the Act (15 U.S.C. 78c(a)(12)).

(11) *Floor broker* shall have the meaning provided in Section 1a(16) of the CEA (7 U.S.C. 1a(16)).

(12) *Floor trader* shall have the meaning provided in Section 1a(17) of the CEA (7 U.S.C. 1a(17)).

(13) *Futures account* shall have the meaning provided in § 240.15c3–3(a) of this chapter.

(14) *Futures commission merchant* shall have the meaning provided in Section 1a of the CEA (7 U.S.C. 1a).

(15) *Good faith,* with respect to making a determination or accepting a statement concerning financial relations with a person, means that the security futures intermediary is alert to the circumstances surrounding such financial relations, and if in possession of information that would cause a prudent person not to make the determination or accept the notice or certification without inquiry, investigates and is satisfied that it is correct.

(16) *Listed option* means a put or call option that is:

(i) Issued by a clearing agency that is registered under section 17A of the Act (15 U.S.C. 17q–1) or cleared and guaranteed by a derivatives clearing organization that is registered under Section 5b of the CEA (7 U.S.C. 7a–1); and

(ii) Traded on or subject to the rules of a self-regulatory authority.

(17) *Margin call* means a demand by a security futures intermediary to a customer for a deposit of cash, securities or other assets to satisfy the required margin for security futures or related positions or a special margin requirement.

(18) *Margin deficiency* means the amount by which the required margin

Securities and Exchange Commission

§ 242.401

in an account is not satisfied by the equity in the account, as computed in accordance with § 242.404 of this Regulation (§§ 242.400 through 242.406).

(19) *Margin equity security* shall have the meaning provided in Regulation T.

(20) *Margin security* shall have the meaning provided in Regulation T.

(21) *Member* shall have the meaning provided in section 3(a)(3) of the Act (15 U.S.C. 78c(a)(3)), and shall include persons registered under section 15(b)(11) of the Act (15 U.S.C. 78o(b)(11)) that are permitted to effect transactions on a national securities exchange without the services of another person acting as executing broker.

(22) *Money market mutual fund* means any security issued by an investment company registered under section 8 of the Investment Company Act of 1940 (15 U.S.C. 80a–8) that is considered a money market fund under § 270.2a–7 of this chapter.

(23) *Persons associated with a broker or dealer* shall have the meaning provided in section 3(a)(18) of the Act (15 U.S.C. 78c(a)(18)).

(24) *Regulation T* means Regulation T promulgated by the Board of Governors of the Federal Reserve System, 12 CFR part 220, as amended from time to time.

(25) *Regulation T collateral value*, with respect to a security, means the current market value of the security reduced by the percentage of required margin for a position in the security held in a margin account under Regulation T.

(26) *Related position*, with respect to a security future, means any position in an account that is combined with the security future to create an offsetting position as provided in § 242.403(b)(2) of this Regulation (§§ 242.400 through 242.406).

(27) *Related transaction*, with respect to a position or transaction in a security future, means:

(i) Any transaction that creates, eliminates, increases or reduces an offsetting position involving a security future and a related position, as provided in § 242.403(b)(2) of this Regulation (§§ 242.400 through 242.406); or

(ii) Any deposit or withdrawal of margin for the security future or a related position, except as provided in § 242.405(b) of this Regulation (§§ 242.400 through 242.406).

(28) *Securities account* shall have the meaning provided in § 240.15c3–3(a) of this chapter.

(29) *Security futures intermediary* means any creditor as defined in Regulation T with respect to its financial relations with any person involving security futures.

(30) *Self-regulatory authority* means a national securities exchange registered under section 6 of the Act (15 U.S.C. 78f), a national securities association registered under section 15A of the Act (15 U.S.C. 78o–3), a contract market registered under Section 5 of the CEA (7 U.S.C. 7) or Section 5f of the CEA (7 U.S.C. 7b–1), or a derivatives transaction execution facility registered under Section 5a of the CEA (7 U.S.C. 7a).

(31) *Special margin requirement* shall have the meaning provided in § 242.404(e)(1)(ii) of this Regulation (§§ 242.400 through 242.406).

(32) *Variation settlement* means any credit or debit to a customer account, made on a daily or intraday basis, for the purpose of marking to market a security future or any other contract that is:

(i) Issued by a clearing agency that is registered under section 17A of the Act (15 U.S.C. 78q–1) or cleared and guaranteed by a derivatives clearing organization that is registered under Section 5b of the CEA (7 U.S.C. 7a–1); and

(ii) Traded on or subject to the rules of a self-regulatory authority.

(b) Terms used in this Regulation (§§ 242.400 through 242.406) and not otherwise defined in this section shall have the meaning set forth in the margin rules applicable to the account.

(c) Terms used in this Regulation (§§ 242.400 through 242.406) and not otherwise defined in this section or in the margin rules applicable to the account shall have the meaning set forth in the Act and the CEA; if the definitions of a term in the Act and the CEA are inconsistent as applied in particular circumstances, such term shall have the meaning set forth in rules, regulations, or interpretations jointly promulgated by the Commission and the CFTC.

§ 242.402 General provisions.

(a) *Applicable margin rules.* Except to the extent inconsistent with this Regulation (§§ 242.400 through 242.406):

(1) A security futures intermediary that carries a security future on behalf of a customer in a securities account shall record and conduct all financial relations with respect to such security future and related positions in accordance with Regulation T and the margin rules of the self-regulatory authorities of which the security futures intermediary is a member.

(2) A security futures intermediary that carries a security future on behalf of a customer in a futures account shall record and conduct all financial relations with respect to such security future and related positions in accordance with the margin rules of the self-regulatory authorities of which the security futures intermediary is a member.

(b) *Separation and consolidation of accounts.* (1) The requirements for security futures and related positions in one account may not be met by considering items in any other account, except as permitted or required under paragraph (b)(2) of this section or applicable margin rules. If withdrawals of cash, securities or other assets deposited as margin are permitted under this Regulation (§§ 242.400 through 242.406), bookkeeping entries shall be made when such cash, securities, or assets are used for purposes of meeting requirements in another account.

(2) Notwithstanding paragraph (b)(1) of this section, the security futures intermediary shall consider all futures accounts in which security futures and related positions are held that are within the same regulatory classification or account type and are owned by the same customer to be a single account for purposes of this Regulation (§§ 242.400 through 242.406). The security futures intermediary may combine such accounts with other futures accounts that are within the same regulatory classification or account type and are owned by the same customer for purposes of computing a customer's overall margin requirement, as permitted or required by applicable margin rules.

(c) *Accounts of partners.* If a partner of the security futures intermediary has an account with the security futures intermediary in which security futures or related positions are held, the security futures intermediary shall disregard the partner's financial relations with the firm (as shown in the partner's capital and ordinary drawing accounts) in calculating the margin or equity of any such account.

(d) *Contribution to joint venture.* If an account in which security futures or related positions are held is the account of a joint venture in which the security futures intermediary participates, any interest of the security futures intermediary in the joint account in excess of the interest which the security futures intermediary would have on the basis of its right to share in the profits shall be margined in accordance with this Regulation (§§ 242.400 through 242.406).

(e) *Extensions of credit.* (1) No security futures intermediary may extend or maintain credit to or for any customer for the purpose of evading or circumventing any requirement under this Regulation (§§ 242.400 through 242.406).

(2) A security futures intermediary may arrange for the extension or maintenance of credit to or for any customer by any person, provided that the security futures intermediary does not willfully arrange credit that would constitute a violation of Regulation T, U or X of the Board of Governors of the Federal Reserve System (12 CFR parts 220, 221, and 224) by such person.

(f) *Change in exempted person status.* Once a person ceases to qualify as an exempted person, it shall notify the security futures intermediary of this fact before entering into any new security futures transaction or related transaction that would require additional margin to be deposited under this Regulation (§§ 242.400 through 242.406). Financial relations with respect to any such transactions shall be subject to the provisions of this Regulation (§§ 242.400 through 242.406).

§ 242.403 Required margin.

(a) *Applicability.* Each security futures intermediary shall determine the

Securities and Exchange Commission § 242.404

required margin for the security futures and related positions held on behalf of a customer in a securities account or futures account as set forth in this section.

(b) *Required margin*—(1) *General rule.* The required margin for each long or short position in a security future shall be fifteen (15) percent of the current market value of such security future.

(2) *Offsetting positions.* Notwithstanding the margin levels specified in paragraph (b)(1) of this section, a self-regulatory authority may set the required initial or maintenance margin level for an offsetting position involving security futures and related positions at a level lower than the level that would be required under paragraph (b)(1) of this section if such positions were margined separately, pursuant to rules that meet the criteria set forth in section 7(c)(2)(B) of the Act (15 U.S.C. 78g(c)(2)(B)) and are effective in accordance with section 19(b)(2) of the Act (15 U.S.C. 78s(b)(2)) and, as applicable, Section 5c(c) of the CEA (7 U.S.C. 7a–2(c)).

(c) *Procedures for certain margin level adjustments.* An exchange registered under section 6(g) of the Act (15 U.S.C. 78f(g)), or a national securities association registered under section 15A(k) of the Act (15 U.S.C. 78o–3(k)), may raise or lower the required margin level for a security future to a level not lower than that specified in this section, in accordance with section 19(b)(7) of the Act (15 U.S.C. 78s(b)(7)).

[67 FR 53176, Aug. 14, 2002, as amended at 85 FR 75146, Nov. 24, 2020]

§ 242.404 Type, form and use of margin.

(a) *When margin is required.* Margin is required to be deposited whenever the required margin for security futures and related positions in an account is not satisfied by the equity in the account, subject to adjustment under paragraph (c) of this section.

(b) *Acceptable margin deposits.* (1) The required margin may be satisfied by a deposit of cash, margin securities (subject to paragraph (b)(2) of this section), exempted securities, any other asset permitted under Regulation T to satisfy a margin deficiency in a securities margin account, or any combination thereof, each as valued in accordance with paragraph (c) of this section.

(2) Shares of a money market mutual fund may be accepted as a margin deposit for purposes of this Regulation (§§ 242.400 through 242.406), *provided that:*

(i) The customer waives any right to redeem the shares without the consent of the security futures intermediary and instructs the fund or its transfer agent accordingly;

(ii) The security futures intermediary (or clearing agency or derivatives clearing organization with which the shares are deposited as margin) obtains the right to redeem the shares in cash, promptly upon request; and

(iii) The fund agrees to satisfy any conditions necessary or appropriate to ensure that the shares may be redeemed in cash, promptly upon request.

(c) *Adjustments*—(1) *Futures accounts.* For purposes of this section, the equity in a futures account shall be computed in accordance with the margin rules applicable to the account, subject to the following:

(i) A security future shall have no value;

(ii) Each net long or short position in a listed option on a contract for future delivery shall be valued in accordance with the margin rules applicable to the account;

(iii) Except as permitted in paragraph (e) of this section, each margin equity security shall be valued at an amount no greater than its Regulation T collateral value;

(iv) Each other security shall be valued at an amount no greater than its current market value reduced by the percentage specified for such security in § 240.15c3–1(c)(2)(vi) of this chapter;

(v) Freely convertible foreign currency may be valued at an amount no greater than its daily marked-to-market U.S. dollar equivalent;

(vi) Variation settlement receivable (or payable) by an account at the close of trading on any day shall be treated as a credit (or debit) to the account on that day; and

(vii) Each other acceptable margin deposit or component of equity shall be valued at an amount no greater than its value under Regulation T.

§ 242.404

(2) *Securities accounts.* For purposes of this section, the equity in a securities account shall be computed in accordance with the margin rules applicable to the account, subject to the following:

(i) A security future shall have no value;

(ii) Freely convertible foreign currency may be valued at an amount no greater than its daily mark-to-market U.S. dollar equivalent; and

(iii) Variation settlement receivable (or payable) to an account at the close of trading on any day shall be treated as a credit (or debit) by the account on that day.

(d) *Satisfaction restriction.* Any transaction, position or deposit that is used to satisfy the required margin for security futures or related positions under this Regulation (§§ 242.400 through 242.406), including a related position, shall be unavailable to satisfy the required margin for any other position or transaction or any other requirement.

(e) *Alternative collateral valuation for margin equity securities in a futures account.* (1) Notwithstanding paragraph (c)(1)(iii) of this section, a security futures intermediary need not value a margin equity security at its Regulation T collateral value when determining whether the required margin for the security futures and related positions in a futures account is satisfied, *provided that:*

(i) The margin equity security is valued at an amount no greater than the current market value of the security reduced by the lowest percentage level of margin required for a long position in the security held in a margin account under the rules of a national securities exchange registered pursuant to section 6(a) of the Act (15 U.S.C. 78f(a));

(ii) Additional margin is required to be deposited on any day when the day's security futures transactions and related transactions would create or increase a margin deficiency in the account if the margin equity securities were valued at their Regulation T collateral value, and shall be for the amount of the margin deficiency so created or increased (a "special margin requirement"); and

(iii) Cash, securities, or other assets deposited as margin for the positions in an account are not permitted to be withdrawn from the account at any time that:

(A) Additional cash, securities, or other assets are required to be deposited as margin under this section for a transaction in the account on the same or a previous day; or

(B) The withdrawal, together with other transactions, deposits, and withdrawals on the same day, would create or increase a margin deficiency if the margin equity securities were valued at their Regulation T collateral value.

(2) All security futures transactions and related transactions on any day shall be combined to determine the amount of a special margin requirement. Additional margin deposited to satisfy a special margin requirement shall be valued at an amount no greater than its Regulation T collateral value.

(3) If the alternative collateral valuation method set forth in paragraph (e) of this section is used with respect to an account in which security futures or related positions are carried:

(i) An account that is transferred from one security futures intermediary to another may be treated as if it had been maintained by the transferee from the date of its origin, if the transferee accepts, in good faith, a signed statement of the transferor (or, if that is not practicable, of the customer), that any margin call issued under this Regulation (§§ 242.400 through 242.406) has been satisfied; and

(ii) An account that is transferred from one customer to another as part of a transaction, not undertaken to avoid the requirements of this Regulation (§§ 242.400 through 242.406), may be treated as if it had been maintained for the transferee from the date of its origin, if the security futures intermediary accepts in good faith and keeps with the transferee account a signed statement of the transferor describing the circumstances for the transfer.

(f) *Guarantee of accounts.* No guarantee of a customer's account shall be given any effect for purposes of determining whether the required margin in

Securities and Exchange Commission

an account is satisfied, except as permitted under applicable margin rules.

§ 242.405 Withdrawal of margin.

(a) *By the customer.* Except as otherwise provided in § 242.404(e)(1)(ii) of this Regulation (§§ 242.400 through 242.406), cash, securities, or other assets deposited as margin for positions in an account may be withdrawn, provided that the equity in the account after such withdrawal is sufficient to satisfy the required margin for the security futures and related positions in the account under this Regulation (§§ 242.400 through 242.406).

(b) *By the security futures intermediary.* Notwithstanding paragraph (a) of this section, the security futures intermediary, in its usual practice, may deduct the following items from an account in which security futures or related positions are held if they are considered in computing the balance of such account:

(1) Variation settlement payable, directly or indirectly, to a clearing agency that is registered under section 17A of the Act (15 U.S.C. 78q–1) or a derivatives clearing organization that is registered under section 5b of the CEA (7 U.S.C. 7a–1);

(2) Interest charged on credit maintained in the account;

(3) Communication or shipping charges with respect to transactions in the account;

(4) Payment of commissions, brokerage, taxes, storage and other charges lawfully accruing in connection with the positions and transactions in the account;

(5) Any service charges that the security futures intermediary may impose; or

(6) Any other withdrawals that are permitted from a securities margin account under Regulation T, to the extent permitted under applicable margin rules.

§ 242.406 Undermargined accounts.

(a) *Failure to satisfy margin call.* If any margin call required by this Regulation (§§ 242.400 through 242.406) is not met in full, the security futures intermediary shall take the deduction required with respect to an undermargined account in computing its net capital under Commission or CFTC rules.

(b) *Accounts that liquidate to a deficit.* If at any time there is a liquidating deficit in an account in which security futures are held, the security futures intermediary shall take steps to liquidate positions in the account promptly and in an orderly manner.

(c) *Liquidation of undermargined accounts not required.* Notwithstanding Section 402(a) of this Regulation (§§ 242.400 through 242.406), section 220.4(d) of Regulation T (12 CFR 220.4(d)) respecting liquidation of positions in lieu of deposit shall not apply with respect to security futures carried in a securities account.

REGULATION AC—ANALYST CERTIFICATION

SOURCE: 68 FR 9492, February 27, 2003, unless otherwise noted.

§ 242.500 Definitions.

For purposes of Regulation AC (§§ 242.500 through 242.505 of this chapter) the term:

Covered person of a broker or dealer means an associated person of that broker or dealer but does not include:

(1) An associated person:

(i) If the associated person has no officers (or persons performing similar functions) or employees in common with the broker or dealer who can influence the activities of research analysts or the content of research reports; and

(ii) If the broker or dealer maintains and enforces written policies and procedures reasonably designed to prevent the broker or dealer, any controlling persons, officers (or persons performing similar functions), and employees of the broker or dealer from influencing the activities of research analysts and the content of research reports prepared by the associated person.

(2) An associated person who is an investment adviser:

(i) Not registered with the Commission as an investment adviser because of the prohibition of section 203A of the Investment Advisers Act of 1940 (15 U.S.C. 80b–3a); and

§ 242.501

(ii) Not registered or required to be registered with the Commission as a broker or dealer.

NOTE TO DEFINITION OF COVERED PERSON: An associated person of a broker or dealer who is not a covered person continues to be subject to the federal securities laws, including the anti-fraud provisions of the federal securities laws.

Foreign person means any person who is not a U.S. person.

Foreign security means a security issued by a foreign issuer for which a U.S. market is not the principal trading market.

Public appearance means any participation by a research analyst in a seminar, forum (including an interactive electronic forum), or radio or television or other interview, in which the research analyst makes a specific recommendation or provides information reasonably sufficient upon which to base an investment decision about a security or an issuer.

Registered broker or dealer means a broker or dealer registered or required to register pursuant to section 15 or section 15B of the Securities Exchange Act of 1934 (15 U.S.C. 78o or 78o–4) or a government securities broker or government securities dealer registered or required to register pursuant to section 15C(a)(1)(A) of the Securities Exchange Act of 1934 (15 U.S.C. 78o–5(a)(1)(A)).

Research analyst means any natural person who is primarily responsible for the preparation of the content of a research report.

Research report means a written communication (including an electronic communication) that includes an analysis of a security or an issuer and provides information reasonably sufficient upon which to base an investment decision.

Third party research analyst means:

(1) With respect to a broker or dealer, any research analyst not employed by that broker or dealer or any associated person of that broker or dealer; and

(2) With respect to a covered person of a broker or dealer, any research analyst not employed by that covered person, by the broker or dealer with whom that covered person is associated, or by any other associated person of the broker or dealer with whom that covered person is associated.

United States has the meaning contained in § 230.902(l) of this chapter.

U.S. person has the meaning contained in § 230.902(k) of this chapter.

§ 242.501 Certifications in connection with research reports.

(a) A broker or dealer or covered person that publishes, circulates, or provides a research report prepared by a research analyst to a U.S. person in the United States shall include in that research report a clear and prominent certification by the research analyst containing the following:

(1) A statement attesting that all of the views expressed in the research report accurately reflect the research analyst's personal views about any and all of the subject securities or issuers; and

(2)(i) A statement attesting that no part of the research analyst's compensation was, is, or will be, directly or indirectly, related to the specific recommendations or views expressed by the research analyst in the research report; or

(ii) A statement:

(A) Attesting that part or all of the research analyst's compensation was, is, or will be, directly or indirectly, related to the specific recommendations or views expressed by the research analyst in the research report;

(B) Identifying the source, amount, and purpose of such compensation; and

(C) Further disclosing that the compensation could influence the recommendations or views expressed in the research report.

(b) A broker or dealer or covered person that publishes, circulates, or provides a research report prepared by a third party research analyst to a U.S. person in the United States shall be exempt from the requirements of this section with respect to such research report if the following conditions are satisfied:

(1) The employer of the third party research analyst has no officers (or persons performing similar functions) or employees in common with the broker or dealer or covered person; and

(2) The broker or dealer (or, with respect to a covered person, the broker or dealer with whom the covered person is associated) maintains and enforces

written policies and procedures reasonably designed to prevent the broker or dealer, any controlling persons, officers (or persons performing similar functions), and employees of the broker or dealer from influencing the activities of the third party research analyst and the content of research reports prepared by the third party research analyst.

§ 242.502 Certifications in connection with public appearances.

(a) If a broker or dealer publishes, circulates, or provides a research report prepared by a research analyst employed by the broker or dealer or covered person to a U.S. person in the United States, the broker or dealer must make a record within 30 days after any calendar quarter in which the research analyst made a public appearance that contains the following:

(1) A statement by the research analyst attesting that the views expressed by the research analyst in all public appearances during the calendar quarter accurately reflected the research analyst's personal views at that time about any and all of the subject securities or issuers; and

(2) A statement by the research analyst attesting that no part of the research analyst's compensation was, is, or will be, directly or indirectly, related to the specific recommendations or views expressed by the research analyst in such public appearances.

(b) If the broker or dealer does not obtain a statement by the research analyst in accordance with paragraph (a) of this section:

(1) The broker or dealer shall promptly notify in writing its examining authority, designated pursuant to section 17(d) of the Securities Exchange Act of 1934 (15 U.S.C. 78q(d)) and §240.17d–2 of this chapter, that the research analyst did not provide the certifications specified in paragraph (a) of this section; and

(2) For 120 days following notification pursuant to paragraph (b)(1) of this section, the broker or dealer shall disclose in any research report prepared by the research analyst and published, circulated, or provided to a U.S. person in the United States that the research analyst did not provide the certifications specified in paragraph (a) of this section.

(c) In the case of a research analyst who is employed outside the United States by a foreign person located outside the United States, this section shall only apply to a public appearance while the research analyst is physically present in the United States.

(d) A broker or dealer shall preserve the records specified in paragraphs (a) and (b) of this section in accordance with §240.17a–4 of this chapter and for a period of not less than 3 years, the first 2 years in an accessible place.

§ 242.503 Certain foreign research reports.

A foreign person, located outside the United States and not associated with a registered broker or dealer, who prepares a research report concerning a foreign security and provides it to a U.S. person in the United States in accordance with the provisions of §240.15a–6(a)(2) of this chapter shall be exempt from the requirements of this regulation.

§ 242.504 Notification to associated persons.

A broker or dealer shall notify any person with whom that broker or dealer is associated who publishes, circulates, or provides research reports:

(a) Whether the broker or dealer maintains and enforces written policies and procedures reasonably designed to prevent the broker or dealer, any controlling persons, officers (or persons performing similar functions), or employees of the broker or dealer from influencing the activities of research analysts and the content of research reports prepared by the associated person; and

(b) Whether the associated person has any officers (or persons performing similar functions) or employees in common with the broker or dealer who can influence the activities of research analysts or the content of research reports and, if so, the identity of those persons.

§ 242.505 Exclusion for news media.

No provision of this Regulation AC shall apply to any person who:

49

§ 242.600

(a) Is the publisher of any bona fide newspaper, news magazine or business or financial publication of general and regular circulation; and

(b) Is not registered or required to be registered with the Commission as a broker or dealer or investment adviser.

REGULATION NMS—REGULATION OF THE NATIONAL MARKET SYSTEM

SOURCE: 70 FR 37620, June 29, 2005, unless otherwise noted.

§ 242.600 NMS security designation and definitions.

(a) The term *national market system security* as used in section 11A(a)(2) of the Act (15 U.S.C. 78k–1(a)(2)) shall mean any NMS security as defined in paragraph (b) of this section.

(b) For purposes of Regulation NMS (§§ 242.600 through 242.612), the following definitions shall apply:

(1) *Actionable indication of interest* means any indication of interest that explicitly or implicitly conveys all of the following information with respect to any order available at the venue sending the indication of interest:

(i) Symbol;

(ii) Side (buy or sell);

(iii) A price that is equal to or better than the national best bid for buy orders and the national best offer for sell orders; and

(iv) A size that is at least equal to one round lot.

(2) *Administrative data* means administrative, control, and other technical messages made available by national securities exchanges and national securities associations pursuant to the effective national market system plan or plans required under § 242.603(b) or the technical specifications thereto as of April 9, 2021.

(3) *Aggregate quotation size* means the sum of the quotation sizes of all responsible brokers or dealers who have communicated on any national securities exchange bids or offers for an NMS security at the same price.

(4) *Alternative trading system* has the meaning provided in § 242.300(a).

(5) *Auction information* means all information specified by national securities exchange rules or effective national market system plans that is generated by a national securities exchange leading up to and during auctions, including opening, reopening, and closing auctions, and publicly disseminated during the time periods and at the time intervals provided in such rules and plans.

(6) *Automated quotation* means a quotation displayed by a trading center that:

(i) Permits an incoming order to be marked as immediate-or-cancel;

(ii) Immediately and automatically executes an order marked as immediate-or-cancel against the displayed quotation up to its full size;

(iii) Immediately and automatically cancels any unexecuted portion of an order marked as immediate-or-cancel without routing the order elsewhere;

(iv) Immediately and automatically transmits a response to the sender of an order marked as immediate-or-cancel indicating the action taken with respect to such order; and

(v) Immediately and automatically displays information that updates the displayed quotation to reflect any change to its material terms.

(7) *Automated trading center* means a trading center that:

(i) Has implemented such systems, procedures, and rules as are necessary to render it capable of displaying quotations that meet the requirements for an automated quotation set forth in paragraph (b)(6) of this section;

(ii) Identifies all quotations other than automated quotations as manual quotations;

(iii) Immediately identifies its quotations as manual quotations whenever it has reason to believe that it is not capable of displaying automated quotations; and

(iv) Has adopted reasonable standards limiting when its quotations change from automated quotations to manual quotations, and vice versa, to specifically defined circumstances that promote fair and efficient access to its automated quotations and are consistent with the maintenance of fair and orderly markets.

(8) *Average effective spread* means the share-weighted average of effective spreads for order executions calculated, for buy orders, as double the amount of difference between the execution price and the midpoint of the

Securities and Exchange Commission

§ 242.600

national best bid and national best offer at the time of order receipt and, for sell orders, as double the amount of difference between the midpoint of the national best bid and national best offer at the time of order receipt and the execution price.

(9) *Average realized spread* means the share-weighted average of realized spreads for order executions calculated, for buy orders, as double the amount of difference between the execution price and the midpoint of the national best bid and national best offer five minutes after the time of order execution and, for sell orders, as double the amount of difference between the midpoint of the national best bid and national best offer five minutes after the time of order execution and the execution price; *provided, however*, that the midpoint of the final national best bid and national best offer disseminated for regular trading hours shall be used to calculate a realized spread if it is disseminated less than five minutes after the time of order execution.

(10) *Best bid and best offer* mean the highest priced bid and the lowest priced offer.

(11) *Bid* or *offer* means the bid price or the offer price communicated by a member of a national securities exchange or member of a national securities association to any broker or dealer, or to any customer, at which it is willing to buy or sell one or more round lots of an NMS security, as either principal or agent, but shall not include indications of interest.

(12) *Block size with respect to* an order means it is:

(i) Of at least 10,000 shares; or

(ii) For a quantity of stock having a market value of at least $200,000.

(13) *Categorized by order size* means dividing orders into separate categories for sizes from 100 to 499 shares, from 500 to 1999 shares, from 2000 to 4999 shares, and 5000 or greater shares.

(14) *Categorized by order type* means dividing orders into separate categories for market orders, marketable limit orders, inside-the-quote limit orders, at-the-quote limit orders, and near-the-quote limit orders.

(15) *Categorized by security* means dividing orders into separate categories for each NMS stock that is included in a report.

(16) *Competing consolidator* means a securities information processor required to be registered pursuant to § 242.614 (Rule 614) or a national securities exchange or national securities association that receives information with respect to quotations for and transactions in NMS stocks and generates a consolidated market data product for dissemination to any person.

(17) *Consolidated display* means:

(i) The prices, sizes, and market identifications of the national best bid and national best offer for a security; and

(ii) Consolidated last sale information for a security.

(18) *Consolidated last sale information* means the price, volume, and market identification of the most recent transaction report for a security that is disseminated pursuant to an effective national market system plan.

(19) *Consolidated market data* means the following data, consolidated across all national securities exchanges and national securities associations:

(i) Core data;

(ii) Regulatory data;

(iii) Administrative data;

(iv) Self-regulatory organization-specific program data; and

(v) Additional regulatory, administrative, or self-regulatory organization-specific program data elements defined as such pursuant to the effective national market system plan or plans required under § 242.603(b).

(20) *Consolidated market data product* means any data product developed by a competing consolidator that contains consolidated market data or data components of consolidated market data. For purposes of this paragraph (b)(20), data components of consolidated market data include the enumerated elements, and any subcomponent of the enumerated elements, of consolidated market data in paragraph (b)(19) of this section. All consolidated market data products must reflect data consolidated across all national securities exchanges and national securities associations.

(21) *Core data* means:

§ 242.600

(i) The following information with respect to quotations for, and transactions in, NMS stocks:
(A) Quotation sizes;
(B) Aggregate quotation sizes;
(C) Best bid and best offer;
(D) National best bid and national best offer;
(E) Protected bid and protected offer;
(F) Transaction reports;
(G) Last sale data;
(H) Odd-lot information;
(I) Depth of book data; and
(J) Auction information.

(ii) For purposes of the calculation and dissemination of core data by competing consolidators, as defined in paragraph (b)(16) of this section, and the calculation of core data by self-aggregators, as defined in paragraph (b)(84) of this section, the best bid and best offer, national best bid and national best offer, protected bid and protected offer, and depth of book data shall include odd-lots that when aggregated are equal to or greater than a round lot; such aggregation shall occur across multiple prices and shall be disseminated at the least aggressive price of all such aggregated odd-lots.

(iii) Competing consolidators shall represent the quotation sizes of the following data elements, if disseminated in a consolidated market data product as defined in paragraph (b)(20) of this section, as the number of shares rounded down to the nearest multiple of a round lot: The best bid and best offer, national best bid and national best offer, protected bid and protected offer, depth of book data, and auction information.

(iv) Competing consolidators shall attribute the following data elements, if disseminated in a consolidated market data product as defined in paragraph (b)(20) of this section, to the national securities exchange or national securities association that is the source of each such data element: Best bid and best offer, national best bid and national best offer, protected bid and protected offer, transaction reports, last sale data, odd-lot information, depth of book data, and auction information.

(22) *Covered order* means any market order or any limit order (including immediate-or-cancel orders) received by a market center during regular trading hours at a time when a national best bid and national best offer is being disseminated, and, if executed, is executed during regular trading hours, but shall exclude any order for which the customer requests special handling for execution, including, but not limited to, orders to be executed at a market opening price or a market closing price, orders submitted with stop prices, orders to be executed only at their full size, orders to be executed on a particular type of tick or bid, orders submitted on a "not held" basis, orders for other than regular settlement, and orders to be executed at prices unrelated to the market price of the security at the time of execution.

(23) *Customer* means any person that is not a broker or dealer.

(24) *Customer limit order* means an order to buy or sell an NMS stock at a specified price that is not for the account of either a broker or dealer; *provided, however,* that the term *customer limit* order shall include an order transmitted by a broker or dealer on behalf of a customer.

(25) *Customer order* means an order to buy or sell an NMS security that is not for the account of a broker or dealer, but shall not include any order for a quantity of a security having a market value of at least $50,000 for an NMS security that is an option contract and a market value of at least $200,000 for any other NMS security.

(26) *Depth of book data* means all quotation sizes at each national securities exchange and on a facility of a national securities association at each of the next five prices at which there is a bid that is lower than the national best bid and offer that is higher than the national best offer. For these five prices, the aggregate size available at each price, if any, at each national securities exchange and national securities association shall be attributed to such exchange or association.

(27) *Directed order* means an order from a customer that the customer specifically instructed the broker or dealer to route to a particular venue for execution.

(28) *Dynamic market monitoring device* means any service provided by a vendor

Securities and Exchange Commission

§ 242.600

on an interrogation device or other display that:

(i) Permits real-time monitoring, on a dynamic basis, of transaction reports, last sale data, or quotations with respect to a particular security; and

(ii) Displays the most recent transaction report, last sale data, or quotation with respect to that security until such report, data, or quotation has been superseded or supplemented by the display of a new transaction report, last sale data, or quotation reflecting the next reported transaction or quotation in that security.

(29) *Effective national market system plan* means any national market system plan approved by the Commission (either temporarily or on a permanent basis) pursuant to § 242.608.

(30) *Effective transaction reporting plan* means any transaction reporting plan approved by the Commission pursuant to § 242.601.

(31) *Electronic communications network* means, for the purposes of § 242.602(b)(5), any electronic system that widely disseminates to third parties orders entered therein by an exchange market maker or OTC market maker, and permits such orders to be executed against in whole or in part; except that the term *electronic communications network* shall not include:

(i) Any system that crosses multiple orders at one or more specified times at a single price set by the system (by algorithm or by any derivative pricing mechanism) and does not allow orders to be crossed or executed against directly by participants outside of such times; or

(ii) Any system operated by, or on behalf of, an OTC market maker or exchange market maker that executes customer orders primarily against the account of such market maker as principal, other than riskless principal.

(32) *Exchange market maker* means any member of a national securities exchange that is registered as a specialist or market maker pursuant to the rules of such exchange.

(33) *Exchange-traded security* means any NMS security or class of NMS securities listed and registered, or admitted to unlisted trading privileges, on a national securities exchange; *provided,* *however,* that securities not listed on any national securities exchange that are traded pursuant to unlisted trading privileges are excluded.

(34) *Executed at the quote* means, for buy orders, execution at a price equal to the national best offer at the time of order receipt and, for sell orders, execution at a price equal to the national best bid at the time of order receipt.

(35) *Executed outside the quote* means, for buy orders, execution at a price higher than the national best offer at the time of order receipt and, for sell orders, execution at a price lower than the national best bid at the time of order receipt.

(36) *Executed with price improvement* means, for buy orders, execution at a price lower than the national best offer at the time of order receipt and, for sell orders, execution at a price higher than the national best bid at the time of order receipt.

(37) *Inside-the-quote limit order, at-the-quote limit order,* and *near-the-quote limit order* mean non-marketable buy orders with limit prices that are, respectively, higher than, equal to, and lower by $0.10 or less than the national best bid at the time of order receipt, and non-marketable sell orders with limit prices that are, respectively, lower than, equal to, and higher by $0.10 or less than the national best offer at the time of order receipt.

(38) *Intermarket sweep order* means a limit order for an NMS stock that meets the following requirements:

(i) When routed to a trading center, the limit order is identified as an intermarket sweep order; and

(ii) Simultaneously with the routing of the limit order identified as an intermarket sweep order, one or more additional limit orders, as necessary, are routed to execute against the full displayed size of any protected bid, in the case of a limit order to sell, or the full displayed size of any protected offer, in the case of a limit order to buy, for the NMS stock with a price that is superior to the limit price of the limit order identified as an intermarket sweep order. These additional routed orders also must be marked as intermarket sweep orders.

(39) *Interrogation device* means any securities information retrieval system

§ 242.600

capable of displaying transaction reports, last sale data, or quotations upon inquiry, on a current basis on a terminal or other device.

(40) *Joint self-regulatory organization plan* means a plan as to which two or more self-regulatory organizations, acting jointly, are sponsors.

(41) *Last sale data* means any price or volume data associated with a transaction.

(42) *Listed equity security* means any equity security listed and registered, or admitted to unlisted trading privileges, on a national securities exchange.

(43) *Listed option* means any option traded on a registered national securities exchange or automated facility of a national securities association.

(44) *Make publicly available* means posting on an Internet Web site that is free and readily accessible to the public, furnishing a written copy to customers on request without charge, and notifying customers at least annually in writing that a written copy will be furnished on request.

(45) *Manual quotation* means any quotation other than an automated quotation.

(46) *Market center* means any exchange market maker, OTC market maker, alternative trading system, national securities exchange, or national securities association.

(47) *Marketable limit order* means any buy order with a limit price equal to or greater than the national best offer at the time of order receipt, or any sell order with a limit price equal to or less than the national best bid at the time of order receipt.

(48) *Moving ticker* means any continuous real-time moving display of transaction reports or last sale data (other than a dynamic market monitoring device) provided on an interrogation or other display device.

(49) *Nasdaq security* means any registered security listed on The Nasdaq Stock Market, Inc.

(50) *National best bid and national best offer* means, with respect to quotations for an NMS stock, the best bid and best offer for such stock that are calculated and disseminated on a current and continuing basis by a competing consolidator or calculated by a self-aggregator and, for NMS securities other than NMS stocks, the best bid and best offer for such security that are calculated and disseminated on a current and continuing basis by a plan processor pursuant to an effective national market system plan; provided, that in the event two or more market centers transmit to the plan processor, a competing consolidator or a self-aggregator identical bids or offers for an NMS security, the best bid or best offer (as the case may be) shall be determined by ranking all such identical bids or offers (as the case may be) first by size (giving the highest ranking to the bid or offer associated with the largest size), and then by time (giving the highest ranking to the bid or offer received first in time).

(51) *National market system plan* means any joint self-regulatory organization plan in connection with:

(i) The planning, development, operation or regulation of a national market system (or a subsystem thereof) or one or more facilities thereof; or

(ii) The development and implementation of procedures and/or facilities designed to achieve compliance by self-regulatory organizations and their members with any section of this Regulation NMS and part 240, subpart A of this chapter promulgated pursuant to section 11A of the Act (15 U.S.C. 78k–1).

(52) *National securities association* means any association of brokers and dealers registered pursuant to section 15A of the Act (15 U.S.C. 78o–3).

(53) *National securities exchange* means any exchange registered pursuant to section 6 of the Act (15 U.S.C. 78f).

(54) *NMS security* means any security or class of securities for which transaction reports are collected, processed, and made available pursuant to an effective transaction reporting plan, or an effective national market system plan for reporting transactions in listed options.

(55) *NMS stock* means any NMS security other than an option.

(56) *Non-directed order* means any order from a customer other than a directed order.

(57) *Non-marketable limit order* means any limit order other than a marketable limit order.

Securities and Exchange Commission § 242.600

(58) *Odd-lot* means an order for the purchase or sale of an NMS stock in an amount less than a round lot.

(59) *Odd-lot information* means:

(i) Odd-lot transaction data disseminated pursuant to the effective national market system plan or plans required under § 242.603(b) as of April 9, 2021; and

(ii) Odd-lots at a price greater than or equal to the national best bid and less than or equal to the national best offer, aggregated at each price level at each national securities exchange and national securities association.

(60) *Options class* means all of the put option or call option series overlying a security, as defined in section 3(a)(10) of the Act (15 U.S.C. 78c(a)(10)).

(61) *Options series* means the contracts in an options class that have the same unit of trade, expiration date, and exercise price, and other terms or conditions.

(62) *Orders providing liquidity* means orders that were executed against after resting at a trading center.

(63) *Orders removing liquidity* means orders that executed against resting trading interest at a trading center.

(64) *OTC market maker* means any dealer that holds itself out as being willing to buy from and sell to its customers, or others, in the United States, an NMS stock for its own account on a regular or continuous basis otherwise than on a national securities exchange in amounts of less than block size.

(65) *Participants*, when used in connection with a national market system plan, means any self-regulatory organization which has agreed to act in accordance with the terms of the plan but which is not a signatory of such plan.

(66) *Payment for order flow* has the meaning provided in § 240.10b–10 of this chapter.

(67) *Plan processor* means any self-regulatory organization or securities information processor acting as an exclusive processor in connection with the development, implementation and/or operation of any facility contemplated by an effective national market system plan.

(68) *Primary listing exchange* means, for each NMS stock, the national securities exchange identified as the primary listing exchange in the effective national market system plan or plans required under § 242.603(b).

(69) *Profit-sharing relationship* means any ownership or other type of affiliation under which the broker or dealer, directly or indirectly, may share in any profits that may be derived from the execution of non-directed orders.

(70) *Protected bid* or *protected offer* means a quotation in an NMS stock that:

(i) Is displayed by an automated trading center;

(ii) Is disseminated pursuant to an effective national market system plan; and

(iii) Is an automated quotation that is the best bid or best offer of a national securities exchange, or the best bid or best offer of a national securities association.

(71) *Protected quotation* means a protected bid or a protected offer.

(72) *Published aggregate quotation size* means the aggregate quotation size calculated by a national securities exchange and displayed by a vendor on a terminal or other display device at the time an order is presented for execution to a responsible broker or dealer.

(73) *Published bid and published offer* means the bid or offer of a responsible broker or dealer for an NMS security communicated by it to its national securities exchange or association pursuant to § 242.602 and displayed by a vendor on a terminal or other display device at the time an order is presented for execution to such responsible broker or dealer.

(74) *Published quotation size* means the quotation size of a responsible broker or dealer communicated by it to its national securities exchange or association pursuant to § 242.602 and displayed by a vendor on a terminal or other display device at the time an order is presented for execution to such responsible broker or dealer.

(75) *Quotation* means a bid or an offer.

(76) *Quotation size*, when used with respect to a responsible broker's or dealer's bid or offer for an NMS security, means:

(i) The number of shares (or units of trading) of that security which such responsible broker or dealer has specified, for purposes of dissemination to

§ 242.600

vendors, that it is willing to buy at the bid price or sell at the offer price comprising its bid or offer, as either principal or agent; or

(ii) In the event such responsible broker or dealer has not so specified, a normal unit of trading for that NMS security.

(77) *Regular trading hours* means the time between 9:30 a.m. and 4:00 p.m. Eastern Time, or such other time as is set forth in the procedures established pursuant to § 242.605(a)(2).

(78) *Regulatory data* means:

(i) Information required to be collected or calculated by the primary listing exchange for an NMS stock and provided to competing consolidators and self-aggregators pursuant to the effective national market system plan or plans required under § 242.603(b), including, at a minimum:

(A) Information regarding Short Sale Circuit Breakers pursuant to § 242.201;

(B) Information regarding Price Bands required pursuant to the Plan to Address Extraordinary Market Volatility (LULD Plan);

(C) Information relating to regulatory halts or trading pauses (news dissemination/pending, LULD, Market-Wide Circuit Breakers) and reopenings or resumptions;

(D) The official opening and closing prices of the primary listing exchange; and

(E) An indicator of the applicable round lot size.

(ii) Information required to be collected or calculated by the national securities exchange or national securities association on which an NMS stock is traded and provided to competing consolidators and self-aggregators pursuant to the effective national market system plan or plans required under § 242.603(b), including, at a minimum:

(A) Whenever such national securities exchange or national securities association receives a bid (offer) below (above) an NMS stock's lower (upper) LULD price band, an appropriate regulatory data flag identifying the bid (offer) as non-executable; and

(B) Other regulatory messages including subpenny execution and trade-though exempt indicators.

(iii) For purposes of paragraph (b)(78)(i)(C) of this section, the primary listing exchange that has the largest proportion of companies included in the S&P 500 Index shall monitor the S&P 500 Index throughout the trading day, determine whether a Level 1, Level 2, or Level 3 decline, as defined in self-regulatory organization rules related to Market-Wide Circuit Breakers, has occurred, and immediately inform the other primary listing exchanges of all such declines.

(79) *Responsible broker or dealer* means:

(i) When used with respect to bids or offers communicated on a national securities exchange, any member of such national securities exchange who communicates to another member on such national securities exchange, at the location (or locations) or through the facility or facilities designated by such national securities exchange for trading in an NMS security a bid or offer for such NMS security, as either principal or agent; *provided, however,* that, in the event two or more members of a national securities exchange have communicated on or through such national securities exchange bids or offers for an NMS security at the same price, each such member shall be considered a *responsible broker or dealer* for that bid or offer, subject to the rules of priority and precedence then in effect on that national securities exchange; and further provided, that for a bid or offer which is transmitted from one member of a national securities exchange to another member who undertakes to represent such bid or offer on such national securities exchange as agent, only the last member who undertakes to represent such bid or offer as agent shall be considered the *responsible broker or dealer* for that bid or offer; and

(ii) When used with respect to bids and offers communicated by a member of an association to a broker or dealer or a customer, the member communicating the bid or offer (regardless of whether such bid or offer is for its own account or on behalf of another person).

Securities and Exchange Commission

§ 242.600

(80) *Revised bid or offer* means a market maker's bid or offer which supersedes its published bid or published offer.

(81) *Revised quotation size* means a market maker's quotation size which supersedes its published quotation size.

(82) *Round lot* means:

(i) For any NMS stock for which the prior calendar month's average closing price on the primary listing exchange was $250.00 or less per share, an order for the purchase or sale of an NMS stock of 100 shares;

(ii) For any NMS stock for which the prior calendar month's average closing price on the primary listing exchange was $250.01 to $1,000.00 per share, an order for the purchase or sale of an NMS stock of 40 shares;

(iii) For any NMS stock for which the prior calendar month's average closing price on the primary listing exchange was $1,000.01 to $10,000.00 per share, an order for the purchase or sale of an NMS stock of 10 shares;

(iv) For any NMS stock for which the prior calendar month's average closing price on the primary listing exchange was $10,000.01 or more per share, an order for the purchase or sale of an NMS stock of 1 share; and

(v) For any NMS stock for which the prior calendar month's average closing price is not available, an order for the purchase or sale of an NMS stock of 100 shares.

(83) *Self-aggregator* means a broker, dealer, national securities exchange, national securities association, or investment adviser registered with the Commission that receives information with respect to quotations for and transactions in NMS stocks, including all data necessary to generate consolidated market data, and generates consolidated market data solely for internal use. A self-aggregator may make consolidated market data available to its affiliates that are registered with the Commission for their internal use. Except as provided in the preceding sentence, a self-aggregator may not disseminate or otherwise make available consolidated market data, or components of consolidated market data, as provided in paragraph (b)(20) of this section, to any person.

(84) *Self-regulatory organization* means any national securities exchange or national securities association.

(85) *Self-regulatory organization-specific program data* means:

(i) Information related to retail liquidity programs specified by the rules of national securities exchanges and disseminated pursuant to the effective national market system plan or plans required under § 242.603(b) as of April 9, 2021; and

(ii) Other self-regulatory organization-specific information with respect to quotations for or transactions in NMS stocks as specified by the effective national market system plan or plans required under § 242.603(b).

(86) *Specified persons*, when used in connection with any notification required to be provided pursuant to § 242.602(a)(3) and any election (or withdrawal thereof) permitted under § 242.602(a)(5), means:

(i) Each vendor;

(ii) Each plan processor; and

(iii) The processor for the Options Price Reporting Authority (in the case of a notification for a subject security which is a class of securities underlying options admitted to trading on any national securities exchange).

(87) *Sponsor*, when used in connection with a national market system plan, means any self-regulatory organization which is a signatory to such plan and has agreed to act in accordance with the terms of the plan.

(88) *SRO display-only facility* means a facility operated by or on behalf of a national securities exchange or national securities association that displays quotations in a security, but does not execute orders against such quotations or present orders to members for execution.

(89) *SRO trading facility* means a facility operated by or on behalf of a national securities exchange or a national securities association that executes orders in a security or presents orders to members for execution.

(90) *Subject security* means:

(i) With respect to a national securities exchange:

(A) Any exchange-traded security other than a security for which the executed volume of such exchange, during the most recent calendar quarter,

§ 242.601

comprised one percent or less of the aggregate trading volume for such security as reported pursuant to an effective transaction reporting plan or effective national market system plan; and

(B) Any other NMS security for which such exchange has in effect an election, pursuant to § 242.602(a)(5)(i), to collect, process, and make available to a vendor bids, offers, quotation sizes, and aggregate quotation sizes communicated on such exchange; and

(ii) With respect to a member of a national securities association:

(A) Any exchange-traded security for which such member acts in the capacity of an OTC market maker unless the executed volume of such member, during the most recent calendar quarter, comprised one percent or less of the aggregate trading volume for such security as reported pursuant to an effective transaction reporting plan or effective national market system plan; and

(B) Any other NMS security for which such member acts in the capacity of an OTC market maker and has in effect an election, pursuant to § 242.602(a)(5)(ii), to communicate to its association bids, offers, and quotation sizes for the purpose of making such bids, offers, and quotation sizes available to a vendor.

(91) *Time of order execution* means the time (to the second) that an order was executed at any venue.

(92) *Time of order receipt* means the time (to the second) that an order was received by a market center for execution.

(93) *Time of the transaction* has the meaning provided in § 240.10b–10 of this chapter.

(94) *Trade-through* means the purchase or sale of an NMS stock during regular trading hours, either as principal or agent, at a price that is lower than a protected bid or higher than a protected offer.

(95) *Trading center* means a national securities exchange or national securities association that operates an SRO trading facility, an alternative trading system, an exchange market maker, an OTC market maker, or any other broker or dealer that executes orders internally by trading as principal or crossing orders as agent.

(96) *Trading rotation* means, with respect to an options class, the time period on a national securities exchange during which:

(i) Opening, re-opening, or closing transactions in options series in such options class are not yet completed; and

(ii) Continuous trading has not yet commenced or has not yet ended for the day in options series in such options class.

(97) *Transaction report* means a report containing the price and volume associated with a transaction involving the purchase or sale of one or more round lots of a security.

(98) *Transaction reporting association* means any person authorized to implement or administer any transaction reporting plan on behalf of persons acting jointly under § 242.601(a).

(99) *Transaction reporting plan* means any plan for collecting, processing, making available or disseminating transaction reports with respect to transactions in securities filed with the Commission pursuant to, and meeting the requirements of, § 242.601.

(100) *Vendor* means any securities information processor engaged in the business of disseminating transaction reports, last sale data, or quotations with respect to NMS securities to brokers, dealers, or investors on a real-time or other current and continuing basis, whether through an electronic communications network, moving ticker, or interrogation device.

[70 FR 37620, June 29, 2005, as amended at 83 FR 58427, Nov. 19, 2018; 86 FR 18809, Apr. 9, 2021; 86 FR 29196, June 1, 2021]

§ 242.601 Dissemination of transaction reports and last sale data with respect to transactions in NMS stocks.

(a) *Filing and effectiveness of transaction reporting plans.* (1) Every national securities exchange shall file a transaction reporting plan regarding transactions in listed equity and Nasdaq securities executed through its facilities, and every national securities association shall file a transaction reporting plan regarding transactions in

Securities and Exchange Commission

§ 242.601

listed equity and Nasdaq securities executed by its members otherwise than on a national securities exchange.

(2) Any transaction reporting plan, or any amendment thereto, filed pursuant to this section shall be filed with the Commission, and considered for approval, in accordance with the procedures set forth in § 242.608(a) and (b). Any such plan, or amendment thereto, shall specify, at a minimum:

(i) The listed equity and Nasdaq securities or classes of such securities for which transaction reports shall be required by the plan;

(ii) Reporting requirements with respect to transactions in listed equity securities and Nasdaq securities, for any broker or dealer subject to the plan;

(iii) The manner of collecting, processing, sequencing, making available and disseminating transaction reports and last sale data reported pursuant to such plan;

(iv) The manner in which such transaction reports reported pursuant to such plan are to be consolidated with transaction reports from national securities exchanges and national securities associations reported pursuant to any other effective transaction reporting plan;

(v) The applicable standards and methods which will be utilized to ensure promptness of reporting, and accuracy and completeness of transaction reports;

(vi) Any rules or procedures which may be adopted to ensure that transaction reports or last sale data will not be disseminated in a fraudulent or manipulative manner;

(vii) Specific terms of access to transaction reports made available or disseminated pursuant to the plan; and

(viii) That transaction reports or last sale data made available to any vendor for display on an interrogation device identify the marketplace where each transaction was executed.

(3) No transaction reporting plan filed pursuant to this section, or any amendment to an effective transaction reporting plan, shall become effective unless approved by the Commission or otherwise permitted in accordance with the procedures set forth in § 242.608.

(b) *Prohibitions and reporting requirements.* (1) No broker or dealer may execute any transaction in, or induce or attempt to induce the purchase or sale of, any NMS stock:

(i) On or through the facilities of a national securities exchange unless there is an effective transaction reporting plan with respect to transactions in such security executed on or through such exchange facilities; or

(ii) Otherwise than on a national securities exchange unless there is an effective transaction reporting plan with respect to transactions in such security executed otherwise than on a national securities exchange by such broker or dealer.

(2) Every broker or dealer who is a member of a national securities exchange or national securities association shall promptly transmit to the exchange or association of which it is a member all information required by any effective transaction reporting plan filed by such exchange or association (either individually or jointly with other exchanges and/or associations).

(c) *Retransmission of transaction reports or last sale data.* Notwithstanding any provision of any effective transaction reporting plan, no national securities exchange or national securities association may, either individually or jointly, by rule, stated policy or practice, transaction reporting plan or otherwise, prohibit, condition or otherwise limit, directly or indirectly, the ability of any vendor to retransmit, for display in moving tickers, transaction reports or last sale data made available pursuant to any effective transaction reporting plan; *provided, however,* that a national securities exchange or national securities association may, by means of an effective transaction reporting plan, condition such retransmission upon appropriate undertakings to ensure that any charges for the distribution of transaction reports or last sale data in moving tickers permitted by paragraph (d) of this section are collected.

(d) *Charges.* Nothing in this section shall preclude any national securities exchange or national securities association, separately or jointly, pursuant to the terms of an effective transaction

§ 242.602

reporting plan, from imposing reasonable, uniform charges (irrespective of geographic location) for distribution of transaction reports or last sale data.

(e) *Appeals.* The Commission may, in its discretion, entertain appeals in connection with the implementation or operation of any effective transaction reporting plan in accordance with the provisions of § 242.608(d).

(f) *Exemptions.* The Commission may exempt from the provisions of this section, either unconditionally or on specified terms and conditions, any national securities exchange, national securities association, broker, dealer, or specified security if the Commission determines that such exemption is consistent with the public interest, the protection of investors and the removal of impediments to, and perfection of the mechanisms of, a national market system.

§ 242.602 Dissemination of quotations in NMS securities.

(a) *Dissemination requirements for national securities exchanges and national securities associations.* (1) Every national securities exchange and national securities association shall establish and maintain procedures and mechanisms for collecting bids, offers, quotation sizes, and aggregate quotation sizes from responsible brokers or dealers who are members of such exchange or association, processing such bids, offers, and sizes, and making such bids, offers, and sizes available to vendors, as follows:

(i) Each national securities exchange shall at all times such exchange is open for trading, collect, process, and make available to vendors the best bid, the best offer, and aggregate quotation sizes for each subject security listed or admitted to unlisted trading privileges which is communicated on any national securities exchange by any responsible broker or dealer, but shall not include:

(A) Any bid or offer executed immediately after communication and any bid or offer communicated by a responsible broker or dealer other than an exchange market maker which is cancelled or withdrawn if not executed immediately after communication; and

(B) Any bid or offer communicated during a period when trading in that security has been suspended or halted, or prior to the commencement of trading in that security on any trading day, on that exchange.

(ii) Each national securities association shall, at all times that last sale information with respect to NMS securities is reported pursuant to an effective transaction reporting plan, collect, process, and make available to vendors the best bid, best offer, and quotation sizes communicated otherwise than on an exchange by each member of such association acting in the capacity of an OTC market maker for each subject security and the identity of that member (excluding any bid or offer executed immediately after communication), except during any period when over-the-counter trading in that security has been suspended.

(2) Each national securities exchange shall, with respect to each published bid and published offer representing a bid or offer of a member for a subject security, establish and maintain procedures for ascertaining and disclosing to other members of that exchange, upon presentation of orders sought to be executed by them in reliance upon paragraph (b)(2) of this section, the identity of the responsible broker or dealer who made such bid or offer and the quotation size associated with it.

(3)(i) If, at any time a national securities exchange is open for trading, such exchange determines, pursuant to rules approved by the Commission pursuant to section 19(b)(2) of the Act (15 U.S.C. 78s(b)(2)), that the level of trading activities or the existence of unusual market conditions is such that the exchange is incapable of collecting, processing, and making available to vendors the data for a subject security required to be made available pursuant to paragraph (a)(1) of this section in a manner that accurately reflects the current state of the market on such exchange, such exchange shall immediately notify all specified persons of that determination. Upon such notification, responsible brokers or dealers that are members of that exchange shall be relieved of their obligation under paragraphs (b)(2) and (c)(3) of this section and such exchange shall be

Securities and Exchange Commission

§ 242.602

relieved of its obligations under paragraphs (a)(1) and (2) of this section for that security; *provided, however,* that such exchange will continue, to the maximum extent practicable under the circumstances, to collect, process, and make available to vendors data for that security in accordance with paragraph (a)(1) of this section.

(ii) During any period a national securities exchange, or any responsible broker or dealer that is a member of that exchange, is relieved of any obligation imposed by this section for any subject security by virtue of a notification made pursuant to paragraph (a)(3)(i) of this section, such exchange shall monitor the activity or conditions which formed the basis for such notification and shall immediately renotify all specified persons when that exchange is once again capable of collecting, processing, and making available to vendors the data for that security required to be made available pursuant to paragraph (a)(1) of this section in a manner that accurately reflects the current state of the market on such exchange. Upon such renotification, any exchange or responsible broker or dealer which had been relieved of any obligation imposed by this section as a consequence of the prior notification shall again be subject to such obligation.

(4) Nothing in this section shall preclude any national securities exchange or national securities association from making available to vendors indications of interest or bids and offers for a subject security at any time such exchange or association is not required to do so pursuant to paragraph (a)(1) of this section.

(5)(i) Any national securities exchange may make an election for purposes of the definition of *subject security* in § 242.600(b)(90) for any NMS security, by collecting, processing, and making available bids, offers, quotation sizes, and aggregate quotation sizes in that security; except that for any NMS security previously listed or admitted to unlisted trading privileges on only one exchange and not traded by any OTC market maker, such election shall be made by notifying all specified persons, and shall be effective at the opening of trading on the business day following notification.

(ii) Any member of a national securities association acting in the capacity of an OTC market maker may make an election for purposes of the definition of *subject security* in § 242.600(b)(90) for any NMS security, by communicating to its association bids, offers, and quotation sizes in that security; except that for any other NMS security listed or admitted to unlisted trading privileges on only one exchange and not traded by any other OTC market maker, such election shall be made by notifying its association and all specified persons, and shall be effective at the opening of trading on the business day following notification.

(iii) The election of a national securities exchange or member of a national securities association for any NMS security pursuant to this paragraph (a)(5) shall cease to be in effect if such exchange or member ceases to make available or communicate bids, offers, and quotation sizes in such security.

(b) *Obligations of responsible brokers and dealers.* (1) Each responsible broker or dealer shall promptly communicate to its national securities exchange or national securities association, pursuant to the procedures established by that exchange or association, its best bids, best offers, and quotation sizes for any subject security.

(2) Subject to the provisions of paragraph (b)(3) of this section, each responsible broker or dealer shall be obligated to execute any order to buy or sell a subject security, other than an odd-lot order, presented to it by another broker or dealer, or any other person belonging to a category of persons with whom such responsible broker or dealer customarily deals, at a price at least as favorable to such buyer or seller as the responsible broker's or dealer's published bid or published offer (exclusive of any commission, commission equivalent or differential customarily charged by such responsible broker or dealer in connection with execution of any such order) in any amount up to its published quotation size.

§ 242.602

(3)(i) No responsible broker or dealer shall be obligated to execute a transaction for any subject security as provided in paragraph (b)(2) of this section to purchase or sell that subject security in an amount greater than such revised quotation size if:

(A) Prior to the presentation of an order for the purchase or sale of a subject security, a responsible broker or dealer has communicated to its exchange or association, pursuant to paragraph (b)(1) of this section, a revised quotation size; or

(B) At the time an order for the purchase or sale of a subject security is presented, a responsible broker or dealer is in the process of effecting a transaction in such subject security, and immediately after the completion of such transaction, it communicates to its exchange or association a revised quotation size, such responsible broker or dealer shall not be obligated by paragraph (b)(2) of this section to purchase or sell that subject security in an amount greater than such revised quotation size.

(ii) No responsible broker or dealer shall be obligated to execute a transaction for any subject security as provided in paragraph (b)(2) of this section if:

(A) Before the order sought to be executed is presented, such responsible broker or dealer has communicated to its exchange or association pursuant to paragraph (b)(1) of this section, a revised bid or offer; or

(B) At the time the order sought to be executed is presented, such responsible broker or dealer is in the process of effecting a transaction in such subject security, and, immediately after the completion of such transaction, such responsible broker or dealer communicates to its exchange or association pursuant to paragraph (b)(1) of this section, a revised bid or offer; *provided, however,* that such responsible broker or dealer shall nonetheless be obligated to execute any such order in such subject security as provided in paragraph (b)(2) of this section at its revised bid or offer in any amount up to its published quotation size or revised quotation size.

(4) Subject to the provisions of paragraph (a)(4) of this section:

(i) No national securities exchange or OTC market maker may make available, disseminate or otherwise communicate to any vendor, directly or indirectly, for display on a terminal or other display device any bid, offer, quotation size, or aggregate quotation size for any NMS security which is not a subject security with respect to such exchange or OTC market maker; and

(ii) No vendor may disseminate or display on a terminal or other display device any bid, offer, quotation size, or aggregate quotation size from any national securities exchange or OTC market maker for any NMS security which is not a subject security with respect to such exchange or OTC market maker.

(5)(i) Entry of any priced order for an NMS security by an exchange market maker or OTC market maker in that security into an electronic communications network that widely disseminates such order shall be deemed to be:

(A) A bid or offer under this section, to be communicated to the market maker's exchange or association pursuant to this paragraph (b) for at least the minimum quotation size that is required by the rules of the market maker's exchange or association if the priced order is for the account of a market maker, or the actual size of the order up to the minimum quotation size required if the priced order is for the account of a customer; and

(B) A communication of a bid or offer to a vendor for display on a display device for purposes of paragraph (b)(4) of this section.

(ii) An exchange market maker or OTC market maker that has entered a priced order for an NMS security into an electronic communications network that widely disseminates such order shall be deemed to be in compliance with paragraph (b)(5)(i)(A) of this section if the electronic communications network:

(A)(*1*) Provides to a national securities exchange or national securities association (or an exclusive processor acting on behalf of one or more exchanges or associations) the prices and sizes of the orders at the highest buy price and the lowest sell price for such

Securities and Exchange Commission § 242.602

security entered in, and widely disseminated by, the electronic communications network by exchange market makers and OTC market makers for the NMS security, and such prices and sizes are included in the quotation data made available by such exchange, association, or exclusive processor to vendors pursuant to this section; and

(*2*) Provides, to any broker or dealer, the ability to effect a transaction with a priced order widely disseminated by the electronic communications network entered therein by an exchange market maker or OTC market maker that is:

(*i*) Equivalent to the ability of any broker or dealer to effect a transaction with an exchange market maker or OTC market maker pursuant to the rules of the national securities exchange or national securities association to which the electronic communications network supplies such bids and offers; and

(*ii*) At the price of the highest priced buy order or lowest priced sell order, or better, for the lesser of the cumulative size of such priced orders entered therein by exchange market makers or OTC market makers at such price, or the size of the execution sought by the broker or dealer, for such security; or

(B) Is an alternative trading system that:

(*1*) Displays orders and provides the ability to effect transactions with such orders under § 242.301(b)(3); and

(*2*) Otherwise is in compliance with Regulation ATS (§ 242.300 through § 242.303).

(c) *Transactions in listed options.* (1) A national securities exchange or national securities association:

(i) Shall not be required, under paragraph (a) of this section, to collect from responsible brokers or dealers who are members of such exchange or association, or to make available to vendors, the quotation sizes and aggregate quotation sizes for listed options, if such exchange or association establishes by rule and periodically publishes the quotation size for which such responsible brokers or dealers are obligated to execute an order to buy or sell an options series that is a subject security at its published bid or offer under paragraph (b)(2) of this section;

(ii) May establish by rule and periodically publish a quotation size, which shall not be for less than one contract, for which responsible brokers or dealers who are members of such exchange or association are obligated under paragraph (b)(2) of this section to execute an order to buy or sell a listed option for the account of a broker or dealer that is in an amount different from the quotation size for which it is obligated to execute an order for the account of a customer; and

(iii) May establish and maintain procedures and mechanisms for collecting from responsible brokers and dealers who are members of such exchange or association, and making available to vendors, the quotation sizes and aggregate quotation sizes in listed options for which such responsible broker or dealer will be obligated under paragraph (b)(2) of this section to execute an order from a customer to buy or sell a listed option and establish by rule and periodically publish the size, which shall not be less than one contract, for which such responsible brokers or dealers are obligated to execute an order for the account of a broker or dealer.

(2) If, pursuant to paragraph (c)(1) of this section, the rules of a national securities exchange or national securities association do not require its members to communicate to it their quotation sizes for listed options, a responsible broker or dealer that is a member of such exchange or association shall:

(i) Be relieved of its obligations under paragraph (b)(1) of this section to communicate to such exchange or association its quotation sizes for any listed option; and

(ii) Comply with its obligations under paragraph (b)(2) of this section by executing any order to buy or sell a listed option, in an amount up to the size established by such exchange's or association's rules under paragraph (c)(1) of this section.

(3) *Thirty second response.* Each responsible broker or dealer, within thirty seconds of receiving an order to buy or sell a listed option in an amount greater than the quotation size established by a national securities exchange's or national securities association's rules pursuant to paragraph

§ 242.603

(c)(1) of this section, or its published quotation size must:

(i) Execute the entire order; or

(ii)(A) Execute that portion of the order equal to at least:

(*1*) The quotation size established by a national securities exchange's or national securities association's rules, pursuant to paragraph (c)(1) of this section, to the extent that such exchange or association does not collect and make available to vendors quotation size and aggregate quotation size under paragraph (a) of this section; or

(*2*) Its published quotation size; and

(B) Revise its bid or offer.

(4) Notwithstanding paragraph (c)(3) of this section, no responsible broker or dealer shall be obligated to execute a transaction for any listed option as provided in paragraph (b)(2) of this section if:

(i) Any of the circumstances in paragraph (b)(3) of this section exist; or

(ii) The order for the purchase or sale of a listed option is presented during a trading rotation in that listed option.

(d) *Exemptions.* The Commission may exempt from the provisions of this section, either unconditionally or on specified terms and conditions, any responsible broker or dealer, electronic communications network, national securities exchange, or national securities association if the Commission determines that such exemption is consistent with the public interest, the protection of investors and the removal of impediments to and perfection of the mechanism of a national market system.

[70 FR 37620, June 29, 20051997, as amended at 83 FR 58427, Nov. 19, 2018; 86 FR 18811, Apr. 9, 2021]

§ 242.603 Distribution, consolidation, and display of information with respect to quotations for and transactions in NMS stocks.

(a) *Distribution of information.* (1) Any exclusive processor, or any broker or dealer with respect to information for which it is the exclusive source, that distributes information with respect to quotations for or transactions in an NMS stock to a securities information processor shall do so on terms that are fair and reasonable.

(2) Any national securities exchange, national securities association, broker, or dealer that distributes information with respect to quotations for or transactions in an NMS stock to a securities information processor, broker, dealer, or other persons shall do so on terms that are not unreasonably discriminatory.

(b) *Dissemination of information.* Every national securities exchange on which an NMS stock is traded and national securities association shall act jointly pursuant to one or more effective national market system plans for the dissemination of consolidated market data. Every national securities exchange on which an NMS stock is traded and national securities association shall make available to all competing consolidators and self-aggregators its information with respect to quotations for and transactions in NMS stocks, including all data necessary to generate consolidated market data, in the same manner and using the same methods, including all methods of access and the same format, as such national securities exchange or national securities association makes available any information with respect to quotations for and transactions in NMS stocks to any person.

(c) *Display of information.* (1) No securities information processor, broker, or dealer shall provide, in a context in which a trading or order-routing decision can be implemented, a display of any information with respect to quotations for or transactions in an NMS stock without also providing, in an equivalent manner, a consolidated display for such stock.

(2) The provisions of paragraph (c)(1) of this section shall not apply to a display of information on the trading floor or through the facilities of a national securities exchange or to a display in connection with the operation of a market linkage system implemented in accordance with an effective national market system plan.

(d) *Exemptions.* The Commission, by order, may exempt from the provisions of this section, either unconditionally or on specified terms and conditions,

Securities and Exchange Commission

any person, security, or item of information, or any class or classes of persons, securities, or items of information, if the Commission determines that such exemption is necessary or appropriate in the public interest, and is consistent with the protection of investors.

[70 FR 37620, June 29, 2005, as amended at 86 FR 18811, Apr. 9, 2021]

§ 242.604 Display of customer limit orders.

(a) *Specialists and OTC market makers.* For all NMS stocks:

(1) Each member of a national securities exchange that is registered by that exchange as a specialist, or is authorized by that exchange to perform functions substantially similar to that of a specialist, shall publish immediately a bid or offer that reflects:

(i) The price and the full size of each customer limit order held by the specialist that is at a price that would improve the bid or offer of such specialist in such security; and

(ii) The full size of each customer limit order held by the specialist that:

(A) Is priced equal to the bid or offer of such specialist for such security;

(B) Is priced equal to the national best bid or national best offer; and

(C) Represents more than a *de minimis* change in relation to the size associated with the specialist's bid or offer.

(2) Each registered broker or dealer that acts as an OTC market maker shall publish immediately a bid or offer that reflects:

(i) The price and the full size of each customer limit order held by the OTC market maker that is at a price that would improve the bid or offer of such OTC market maker in such security; and

(ii) The full size of each customer limit order held by the OTC market maker that:

(A) Is priced equal to the bid or offer of such OTC market maker for such security;

(B) Is priced equal to the national best bid or national best offer; and

(C) Represents more than a *de minimis* change in relation to the size associated with the OTC market maker's bid or offer.

§ 242.605

(b) *Exceptions.* The requirements in paragraph (a) of this section shall not apply to any customer limit order:

(1) That is executed upon receipt of the order.

(2) That is placed by a customer who expressly requests, either at the time that the order is placed or prior thereto pursuant to an individually negotiated agreement with respect to such customer's orders, that the order not be displayed.

(3) That is an odd-lot order.

(4) That is a block size order, unless a customer placing such order requests that the order be displayed.

(5) That is delivered immediately upon receipt to a national securities exchange or national securities association-sponsored system, or an electronic communications network that complies with the requirements of § 242.602(b)(5)(ii) with respect to that order.

(6) That is delivered immediately upon receipt to another exchange member or OTC market maker that complies with the requirements of this section with respect to that order.

(7) That is an "all or none" order.

(c) *Exemptions.* The Commission may exempt from the provisions of this section, either unconditionally or on specified terms and conditions, any responsible broker or dealer, electronic communications network, national securities exchange, or national securities association if the Commission determines that such exemption is consistent with the public interest, the protection of investors and the removal of impediments to and perfection of the mechanism of a national market system.

§ 242.605 Disclosure of order execution information.

This section requires market centers to make available standardized, monthly reports of statistical information concerning their order executions. This information is presented in accordance with uniform standards that are based on broad assumptions about order execution and routing practices. The information will provide a starting point to promote visibility and competition on the part of market centers and broker-dealers, particularly on the

§ 242.605

factors of execution price and speed. The disclosures required by this section do not encompass all of the factors that may be important to investors in evaluating the order routing services of a broker-dealer. In addition, any particular market center's statistics will encompass varying types of orders routed by different broker-dealers on behalf of customers with a wide range of objectives. Accordingly, the statistical information required by this section alone does not create a reliable basis to address whether any particular broker-dealer failed to obtain the most favorable terms reasonably available under the circumstances for customer orders.

(a) *Monthly electronic reports by market centers.* (1) Every market center shall make available for each calendar month, in accordance with the procedures established pursuant to paragraph (a)(2) of this section, a report on the covered orders in NMS stocks that it received for execution from any person. Such report shall be in electronic form; shall be categorized by security, order type, and order size; and shall include the following columns of information:

(i) For market orders, marketable limit orders, inside-the-quote limit orders, at-the-quote limit orders, and near-the-quote limit orders:

(A) The number of covered orders;

(B) The cumulative number of shares of covered orders;

(C) The cumulative number of shares of covered orders cancelled prior to execution;

(D) The cumulative number of shares of covered orders executed at the receiving market center;

(E) The cumulative number of shares of covered orders executed at any other venue;

(F) The cumulative number of shares of covered orders executed from 0 to 9 seconds after the time of order receipt;

(G) The cumulative number of shares of covered orders executed from 10 to 29 seconds after the time of order receipt;

(H) The cumulative number of shares of covered orders executed from 30 seconds to 59 seconds after the time of order receipt;

(I) The cumulative number of shares of covered orders executed from 60 seconds to 299 seconds after the time of order receipt;

(J) The cumulative number of shares of covered orders executed from 5 minutes to 30 minutes after the time of order receipt; and

(K) The average realized spread for executions of covered orders; and

(ii) For market orders and marketable limit orders:

(A) The average effective spread for executions of covered orders;

(B) The cumulative number of shares of covered orders executed with price improvement;

(C) For shares executed with price improvement, the share-weighted average amount per share that prices were improved;

(D) For shares executed with price improvement, the share-weighted average period from the time of order receipt to the time of order execution;

(E) The cumulative number of shares of covered orders executed at the quote;

(F) For shares executed at the quote, the share-weighted average period from the time of order receipt to the time of order execution;

(G) The cumulative number of shares of covered orders executed outside the quote;

(H) For shares executed outside the quote, the share-weighted average amount per share that prices were outside the quote; and

(I) For shares executed outside the quote, the share-weighted average period from the time of order receipt to the time of order execution.

(2) Every national securities exchange on which NMS stocks are traded and each national securities association shall act jointly in establishing procedures for market centers to follow in making available to the public the reports required by paragraph (a)(1) of this section in a uniform, readily accessible, and usable electronic form. In the event there is no effective national market system plan establishing such procedures, market centers shall prepare their reports in a consistent, usable, and machine-readable electronic format, and make such reports available for downloading from an Internet

Securities and Exchange Commission § 242.606

Web site that is free and readily accessible to the public. Every market center shall keep such reports posted on an internet website that is free and readily accessible to the public for a period of three years from the initial date of posting on the internet website.

(3) A market center shall make available the report required by paragraph (a)(1) of this section within one month after the end of the month addressed in the report.

(b) *Exemptions.* The Commission may, by order upon application, conditionally or unconditionally exempt any person, security, or transaction, or any class or classes of persons, securities, or transactions, from any provision or provisions of this section, if the Commission determines that such exemption is necessary or appropriate in the public interest, and is consistent with the protection of investors.

[70 FR 37620, June 29, 2005, as amended at 83 FR 58427, Nov. 19, 2018]

§ 242.606 Disclosure of order routing information.

(a) *Quarterly report on order routing.* (1) Every broker or dealer shall make publicly available for each calendar quarter a report on its routing of non-directed orders in NMS stocks that are submitted on a held basis and of non-directed orders that are customer orders in NMS securities that are option contracts during that quarter broken down by calendar month and keep such report posted on an internet website that is free and readily accessible to the public for a period of three years from the initial date of posting on the internet website. Such report shall include a section for NMS stocks—separated by securities that are included in the S&P 500 Index as of the first day of that quarter and other NMS stocks—and a separate section for NMS securities that are option contracts. Such report shall be made available using the most recent versions of the XML schema and the associated PDF renderer as published on the Commission's website for all reports required by this section. Each section in a report shall include the following information:

(i) The percentage of total orders for the section that were non-directed orders, and the percentages of total non-directed orders for the section that were market orders, marketable limit orders, non-marketable limit orders, and other orders;

(ii) The identity of the ten venues to which the largest number of total non-directed orders for the section were routed for execution and of any venue to which five percent or more of non-directed orders were routed for execution, the percentage of total non-directed orders for the section routed to the venue, and the percentages of total non-directed market orders, total non-directed marketable limit orders, total non-directed non-marketable limit orders, and total non-directed other orders for the section that were routed to the venue;

(iii) For each venue identified pursuant to paragraph (a)(1)(ii) of this section, the net aggregate amount of any payment for order flow received, payment from any profit-sharing relationship received, transaction fees paid, and transaction rebates received, both as a total dollar amount and per share, for each of the following non-directed order types:

(A) Market orders;
(B) Marketable limit orders;
(C) Non-marketable limit orders; and
(D) Other orders.

(iv) A discussion of the material aspects of the broker's or dealer's relationship with each venue identified pursuant to paragraph (a)(1)(ii) of this section, including a description of any arrangement for payment for order flow and any profit-sharing relationship and a description of any terms of such arrangements, written or oral, that may influence a broker's or dealer's order routing decision including, among other things:

(A) Incentives for equaling or exceeding an agreed upon order flow volume threshold, such as additional payments or a higher rate of payment;

(B) Disincentives for failing to meet an agreed upon minimum order flow threshold, such as lower payments or the requirement to pay a fee;

(C) Volume-based tiered payment schedules; and

(D) Agreements regarding the minimum amount of order flow that the broker-dealer would send to a venue.

§ 242.606

(2) A broker or dealer shall make the report required by paragraph (a)(1) of this section publicly available within one month after the end of the quarter addressed in the report.

(b) *Customer requests for information on order routing.* (1) Every broker or dealer shall, on request of a customer, disclose to its customer, for:

(i) Orders in NMS stocks that are submitted on a held basis;

(ii) Orders in NMS stocks that are submitted on a not held basis and the broker or dealer is not required to provide the customer a report under paragraph (b)(3) of this section; and

(iii) Orders in NMS securities that are option contracts, the identity of the venue to which the customer's orders were routed for execution in the six months prior to the request, whether the orders were directed orders or non-directed orders, and the time of the transactions, if any, that resulted from such orders. Such disclosure shall be made available using the most recent versions of the XML schema and the associated PDF renderer as published on the Commission's website for all reports required by this section.

(2) A broker or dealer shall notify customers in writing at least annually of the availability on request of the information specified in paragraph (b)(1) of this section.

(3) Except as provided for in paragraphs (b)(4) and (5) of this section, every broker or dealer shall, on request of a customer that places, directly or indirectly, one or more orders in NMS stocks that are submitted on a not held basis with the broker or dealer, disclose to such customer within seven business days of receiving the request, a report on its handling of such orders for that customer for the prior six months by calendar month. Such report shall be made available using the most recent versions of the XML schema and the associated PDF renderer as published on the Commission's website for all reports required by this section. For purposes of such report, the handling of a NMS stock order submitted by a customer to a broker-dealer on a not held basis includes the handling of all child orders derived from that order. Such report shall be divided into two sections: One for directed orders and one for non-directed orders. Each section of such report shall include, with respect to such order flow sent by the customer to the broker or dealer, the total number of shares sent to the broker or dealer by the customer during the relevant period; the total number of shares executed by the broker or dealer as principal for its own account; the total number of orders exposed by the broker or dealer through an actionable indication of interest; and the venue or venues to which orders were exposed by the broker or dealer through an actionable indication of interest, provided that, where applicable, a broker or dealer must disclose that it exposed a customer's order through an actionable indication of interest to other customers but need not disclose the identity of such customers. Each section of such report also shall include the following columns of information for each venue to which the broker or dealer routed such orders for the customer, in the aggregate:

(i) *Information on Order Routing.* (A) Total shares routed;

(B) Total shares routed marked immediate or cancel;

(C) Total shares routed that were further routable; and

(D) Average order size routed.

(ii) *Information on Order Execution.* (A) Total shares executed;

(B) Fill rate (shares executed divided by the shares routed);

(C) Average fill size;

(D) Average net execution fee or rebate (cents per 100 shares, specified to four decimal places);

(E) Total number of shares executed at the midpoint;

(F) Percentage of shares executed at the midpoint;

(G) Total number of shares executed that were priced on the side of the spread more favorable to the order;

(H) Percentage of total shares executed that were priced at the side of the spread more favorable to the order;

(I) Total number of shares executed that were priced on the side of the spread less favorable to the order; and

(J) Percentage of total shares executed that were priced on the side of the spread less favorable to the order.

(iii) *Information on Orders that Provided Liquidity.* (A) Total number of

Securities and Exchange Commission § 242.607

shares executed of orders providing liquidity;

(B) Percentage of shares executed of orders providing liquidity;

(C) Average time between order entry and execution or cancellation, for orders providing liquidity (in milliseconds); and

(D) Average net execution rebate or fee for shares of orders providing liquidity (cents per 100 shares, specified to four decimal places).

(iv) *Information on Orders that Removed Liquidity.* (A) Total number of shares executed of orders removing liquidity;

(B) Percentage of shares executed of orders removing liquidity; and

(C) Average net execution fee or rebate for shares of orders removing liquidity (cents per 100 shares, specified to four decimal places).

(4) Except as provided below, no broker or dealer shall be required to provide reports pursuant to paragraph (b)(3) of this section if the percentage of shares of not held orders in NMS stocks the broker or dealer received from its customers over the prior six calendar months was less than five percent of the total shares in NMS stocks the broker or dealer received from its customers during that time (the "five percent threshold" for purposes of this paragraph). A broker or dealer that equals or exceeds this five percent threshold shall be required (subject to paragraph (b)(5) of this section) to provide reports pursuant to paragraph (b)(3) of this section for at least six calendar months ("Compliance Period") regardless of the percentage of shares of not held orders in NMS stocks the broker or dealer receives from its customers during the Compliance Period. The Compliance Period shall begin the first calendar day of the next calendar month after the broker or dealer equaled or exceeded the five percent threshold, unless it is the first time the broker or dealer has equaled or exceeded the five percent threshold, in which case the Compliance Period shall begin the first calendar day four calendar months later. A broker or dealer shall not be required to provide reports pursuant to paragraph (b)(3) of this section for orders that the broker or dealer did not receive during a Compliance Period. If, at any time after the end of a Compliance Period, the percentage of shares of not held orders in NMS stocks the broker or dealer received from its customers was less than five percent of the total shares in NMS stocks the broker or dealer received from its customers over the prior six calendar months, the broker or dealer shall not be required to provide reports pursuant to paragraph (b)(3) of this section, except for orders that the broker or dealer received during the portion of a Compliance Period that remains covered by paragraph (b)(3) of this section.

(5) No broker or dealer shall be subject to the requirements of paragraph (b)(3) of this section with respect to a customer that traded on average each month for the prior six months less than $1,000,000 of notional value of not held orders in NMS stocks through the broker or dealer.

(c) *Exemptions.* The Commission may, by order upon application, conditionally or unconditionally exempt any person, security, or transaction, or any class or classes of persons, securities, or transactions, from any provision or provisions of this section, if the Commission determines that such exemption is necessary or appropriate in the public interest, and is consistent with the protection of investors.

[70 FR 37620, June 29, 2005, as amended at 83 FR 58427, Nov. 19, 2018]

§ 242.607 Customer account statements.

(a) No broker or dealer acting as agent for a customer may effect any transaction in, induce or attempt to induce the purchase or sale of, or direct orders for purchase or sale of, any NMS stock or a security authorized for quotation on an automated inter-dealer quotation system that has the characteristics set forth in section 17B of the Act (15 U.S.C. 78q–2), unless such broker or dealer informs such customer, in writing, upon opening a new account and on an annual basis thereafter, of the following:

(1) The broker's or dealer's policies regarding receipt of payment for order

§ 242.608

flow from any broker or dealer, national securities exchange, national securities association, or exchange member to which it routes customers' orders for execution, including a statement as to whether any payment for order flow is received for routing customer orders and a detailed description of the nature of the compensation received; and

(2) The broker's or dealer's policies for determining where to route customer orders that are the subject of payment for order flow absent specific instructions from customers, including a description of the extent to which orders can be executed at prices superior to the national best bid and national best offer.

(b) *Exemptions.* The Commission, upon request or upon its own motion, may exempt by rule or by order, any broker or dealer or any class of brokers or dealers, security or class of securities from the requirements of paragraph (a) of this section with respect to any transaction or class of transactions, either unconditionally or on specified terms and conditions, if the Commission determines that such exemption is consistent with the public interest and the protection of investors.

§ 242.608 **Filing and amendment of national market system plans.**

(a) *Filing of national market system plans and amendments thereto.* (1) Any two or more self-regulatory organizations, acting jointly, may file a national market system plan or may propose an amendment to an effective national market system plan ("proposed amendment") by submitting the text of the plan or amendment to the Commission by email, together with a statement of the purpose of such plan or amendment and, to the extent applicable, the documents and information required by paragraphs (a)(4) and (5) of this section.

(2) The Commission may propose amendments to any effective national market system plan by publishing the text thereof, together with a statement of the purpose of such amendment, in accordance with the provisions of paragraph (b) of this section.

(3) Self-regulatory organizations are authorized to act jointly in:

(i) Planning, developing, and operating any national market subsystem or facility contemplated by a national market system plan;

(ii) Preparing and filing a national market system plan or any amendment thereto; or

(iii) Implementing or administering an effective national market system plan.

(4) Every national market system plan filed pursuant to this section, or any amendment thereto, shall be accompanied by:

(i) Copies of all governing or constituent documents relating to any person (other than a self-regulatory organization) authorized to implement or administer such plan on behalf of its sponsors; and

(ii) To the extent applicable:

(A) A detailed description of the manner in which the plan or amendment, and any facility or procedure contemplated by the plan or amendment, will be implemented;

(B) A listing of all significant phases of development and implementation (including any pilot phase) contemplated by the plan or amendment, together with the projected date of completion of each phase;

(C) An analysis of the impact on competition of implementation of the plan or amendment or of any facility contemplated by the plan or amendment;

(D) A description of any written understandings or agreements between or among plan sponsors or participants relating to interpretations of the plan or conditions for becoming a sponsor or participant in the plan; and

(E) In the case of a proposed amendment, a statement that such amendment has been approved by the sponsors in accordance with the terms of the plan.

(5) Every national market system plan, or any amendment thereto, filed pursuant to this section shall include a description of the manner in which any facility contemplated by the plan or amendment will be operated. Such description shall include, to the extent applicable:

Securities and Exchange Commission § 242.608

(i) The terms and conditions under which brokers, dealers, and/or self-regulatory organizations will be granted or denied access (including specific procedures and standards governing the granting or denial of access);

(ii) The method by which any fees or charges collected on behalf of all of the sponsors and/or participants in connection with access to, or use of, any facility contemplated by the plan or amendment will be determined and imposed (including any provision for distribution of any net proceeds from such fees or charges to the sponsors and/or participants) and the amount of such fees or charges;

(iii) The method by which, and the frequency with which, the performance of any person acting as plan processor with respect to the implementation and/or operation of the plan will be evaluated; and

(iv) The method by which disputes arising in connection with the operation of the plan will be resolved.

(6) In connection with the selection of any person to act as plan processor with respect to any facility contemplated by a national market system plan (including renewal of any contract for any person to so act), the sponsors shall file with the Commission a statement identifying the person selected, describing the material terms under which such person is to serve as plan processor, and indicating the solicitation efforts, if any, for alternative plan processors, the alternatives considered and the reasons for selection of such person.

(7) Any national market system plan (or any amendment thereto) which is intended by the sponsors to satisfy a plan filing requirement contained in any other section of this Regulation NMS and part 240, subpart A of this chapter shall, in addition to compliance with this section, also comply with the requirements of such other section.

(8)(i) A participant in an effective national market system plan shall ensure that a current and complete version of the plan is posted on a plan website or on a website designated by plan participants within two business days after notification by the Commission of effectiveness of the plan. Each participant in an effective national market system plan shall ensure that such website is updated to reflect amendments to such plan within two business days after the plan participants have been notified by the Commission of its approval of a proposed amendment pursuant to paragraph (b) of this section. If the amendment is not effective for a certain period, the plan participants shall clearly indicate the effective date in the relevant text of the plan. Each plan participant also shall provide a link on its own website to the website with the current version of the plan.

(ii) The plan participants shall ensure that any proposed amendments filed pursuant to paragraph (a) of this section are posted on a plan website or a designated website no later than two business days after the filing of the proposed amendments with the Commission. If the plan participants do not post a proposed amendment on a plan website or a designated website on the same business day that they file such proposed amendment with the Commission, then the plan participants shall inform the Commission of the business day on which they posted such proposed amendment on a plan website or a designated website. The plan participants shall maintain any proposed amendment to the plan on a plan website or a designated website until the Commission approves the plan amendment and the plan participants update the website to reflect such amendment or the plan participants withdraw the proposed amendment or the plan participants are notified pursuant to paragraph (b)(1)(iii) of this section that the proposed amendment is not filed in compliance with requirements or the Commission disapproves the proposed amendment. If the plan participants withdraw a proposed amendment or are notified pursuant to paragraph (b)(1)(iii) of this section that a proposed amendment is not filed in compliance with requirements or the Commission disapproves a proposed amendment, the plan participants shall remove such amendment from the plan website or designated website within two business days of withdrawal, notification of non-compliant filing or disapproval. Each plan participant shall

§ 242.608

provide a link to the website with the current version of the plan.

(b) *Effectiveness of national market system plans.* (1) The Commission shall publish notice of the filing of any national market system plan, or any proposed amendment to any effective national market system plan (including any amendment initiated by the Commission), together with the terms of substance of the filing or a description of the subjects and issues involved, and shall provide interested persons an opportunity to submit written comments. No national market system plan, or any amendment thereto, shall become effective unless approved by the Commission or otherwise permitted in accordance with paragraph (b)(3) of this section.

(i) *Publication of national market system plans.* The Commission shall send the notice of the filing of a national market system plan to the FEDERAL REGISTER for publication thereof under this paragraph (b)(1) within 90 days of the business day on which such plan was filed with the Commission pursuant to paragraph (a) of this section. If the Commission fails to send the notice to the FEDERAL REGISTER for publication thereof within such 90-day period, then the date of publication shall be deemed to be the last day of such 90-day period.

(ii) *Publication of proposed amendments.* The Commission shall send the notice of the filing of a proposed amendment to the FEDERAL REGISTER for publication thereof under this paragraph (b)(1) within 15 days of the business day on which such proposed amendment was posted on a plan website or a website designated by plan participants pursuant to paragraph (a) of this section after being filed with the Commission pursuant to paragraph (a) of this section. If the Commission fails to send the notice to the FEDERAL REGISTER for publication thereof within such 15-day period, then the date of publication shall be deemed to be the business day on which such website posting was made.

(iii) A national market system plan or proposed amendment has not been filed with the Commission for purposes of this paragraph (b)(1) if, not later than 7 business days after the business day of receipt by the Commission, the Commission notifies the plan participants that the filing of the national market system plan or proposed amendment does not comply with paragraph (a) of this section or plan filing requirements in other sections of Regulation NMS and part 240, subpart A of this chapter, except that if the Commission determines that the plan or amendment is unusually lengthy and is complex or raises novel regulatory issues, the Commission shall inform the plan participants of such determination not later than 7 business days after the business day of receipt by the Commission and, for purposes of this paragraph (b)(1), the filing of such plan or amendment has not been made with the Commission if, not later than 21 days after the business day of receipt by the Commission, the Commission notifies the plan participants that the filing of such plan or amendment does not comply with paragraph (a) of this section or plan filing requirements in other sections of Regulation NMS and part 240, subpart A of this chapter.

(iv) For purposes of this section, a "business day" is any day other than a Saturday, Sunday, Federal holiday, a day that the Office of Personnel Management has announced that Federal agencies in the Washington, DC area are closed to the public, a day on which the Commission is subject to a Federal government shutdown or a day on which the Commission's Washington, DC office is otherwise not open for regular business; provided further, a filing received by the Commission or a website posting made at or before 5:30 p.m. Eastern Standard Time or Eastern Daylight Saving Time, whichever is currently in effect, on a business day, shall be deemed received or made on that business day, and a filing received by the Commission or a website posting made after 5:30 p.m. Eastern Standard Time or Eastern Daylight Saving Time, whichever is currently in effect, shall be deemed received or made on the next business day.

(2) The Commission shall approve a national market system plan or proposed amendment to an effective national market system plan, with such changes or subject to such conditions

Securities and Exchange Commission

§ 242.608

as the Commission may deem necessary or appropriate, if it finds that such plan or amendment is necessary or appropriate in the public interest, for the protection of investors and the maintenance of fair and orderly markets, to remove impediments to, and perfect the mechanisms of, a national market system, or otherwise in furtherance of the purposes of the Act. The Commission shall disapprove a national market system plan or proposed amendment if it does not make such a finding. Approval or disapproval of a national market system plan, or an amendment to an effective national market system plan (other than an amendment initiated by the Commission), shall be by order. Promulgation of an amendment to an effective national market system plan initiated by the Commission shall be by rule.

(i) Within 90 days of the date of publication of notice of the filing of a national market system plan or proposed amendment, or within such longer period as to which the plan participants consent, the Commission shall, by order, approve or disapprove the plan or amendment, or institute proceedings to determine whether the plan or amendment should be disapproved. Proceedings to determine whether the plan or amendment should be disapproved will be conducted pursuant to 17 CFR 201.700 and 201.701. Such proceedings shall include notice of the grounds for disapproval under consideration and opportunity for hearing and shall be concluded within 180 days of the date of publication of notice of the plan or amendment. At the conclusion of such proceedings the Commission shall, by order, approve or disapprove the plan or amendment. The time for conclusion of such proceedings may be extended for up to 60 days (up to 240 days from the date of notice publication) if the Commission determines that a longer period is appropriate and publishes the reasons for such determination or the plan participants consent to the longer period.

(ii) The time for conclusion of proceedings to determine whether a national market system plan or proposed amendment should be disapproved may be extended for an additional period up to 60 days beyond the period set forth in paragraph (b)(2)(i) of this section (up to 300 days from the date of notice publication) if the Commission determines that a longer period is appropriate and publishes the reasons for such determination or the plan participants consent to the longer period.

(3) A proposed amendment may be put into effect upon filing with the Commission if designated by the sponsors as:

(i) [Reserved]

(ii) Concerned solely with the administration of the plan, or involving the governing or constituent documents relating to any person (other than a self-regulatory organization) authorized to implement or administer such plan on behalf of its sponsors; or

(iii) Involving solely technical or ministerial matters. At any time within 60 days of the filing of any such amendment, the Commission may summarily abrogate the amendment and require that such amendment be refiled in accordance with paragraph (a)(1) of this section and reviewed in accordance with paragraph (b)(2) of this section, if it appears to the Commission that such action is necessary or appropriate in the public interest, for the protection of investors, or the maintenance of fair and orderly markets, to remove impediments to, and perfect the mechanisms of, a national market system or otherwise in furtherance of the purposes of the Act.

(4) Notwithstanding the provisions of paragraph (b)(1) of this section, a proposed amendment may be put into effect summarily upon publication of notice of such amendment, on a temporary basis not to exceed 120 days, if the Commission finds that such action is necessary or appropriate in the public interest, for the protection of investors or the maintenance of fair and orderly markets, to remove impediments to, and perfect the mechanisms of, a national market system or otherwise in furtherance of the purposes of the Act.

(5) Any plan (or amendment thereto) in connection with:

(i) The planning, development, operation, or regulation of a national market system (or a subsystem thereof) or one or more facilities thereof; or

§ 242.608

(ii) The development and implementation of procedures and/or facilities designed to achieve compliance by self-regulatory organizations and/or their members of any section of this Regulation NMS (§§ 242.600 through 242.612) and part 240, subpart A of this chapter promulgated pursuant to section 11A of the Act (15 U.S.C. 78k–1), approved by the Commission pursuant to section 11A of the Act (or pursuant to any rule or regulation thereunder) prior to the effective date of this section (either temporarily or permanently) shall be deemed to have been filed and approved pursuant to this section and no additional filing need be made by the sponsors with respect to such plan or amendment; *provided, however*, that all terms and conditions associated with any such approval (including time limitations) shall continue to be applicable; *provided, further*, that any amendment to such plan filed with or approved by the Commission on or after the effective date of this section shall be subject to the provisions of, and considered in accordance with the procedures specified in, this section.

(c) *Compliance with terms of national market system plans.* Each self-regulatory organization shall comply with the terms of any effective national market system plan of which it is a sponsor or a participant. Each self-regulatory organization also shall, absent reasonable justification or excuse, enforce compliance with any such plan by its members and persons associated with its members.

(d) *Appeals.* The Commission may, in its discretion, entertain appeals in connection with the implementation or operation of any effective national market system plan as follows:

(1) Any action taken or failure to act by any person in connection with an effective national market system plan (other than a prohibition or limitation of access reviewable by the Commission pursuant to section 11A(b)(5) or section 19(d) of the Act (15 U.S.C. 78k–1(b)(5) or 78s(d))) shall be subject to review by the Commission, on its own motion or upon application by any person aggrieved thereby (including, but not limited to, self-regulatory organizations, brokers, dealers, issuers, and vendors), filed not later than 30 days after notice of such action or failure to act or within such longer period as the Commission may determine.

(2) Application to the Commission for review, or the institution of review by the Commission on its own motion, shall not operate as a stay of any such action unless the Commission determines otherwise, after notice and opportunity for hearing on the question of a stay (which hearing may consist only of affidavits or oral arguments).

(3) In any proceedings for review, if the Commission, after appropriate notice and opportunity for hearing (which hearing may consist solely of consideration of the record of any proceedings conducted in connection with such action or failure to act and an opportunity for the presentation of reasons supporting or opposing such action or failure to act) and upon consideration of such other data, views, and arguments as it deems relevant, finds that the action or failure to act is in accordance with the applicable provisions of such plan and that the applicable provisions are, and were, applied in a manner consistent with the public interest, the protection of investors, the maintenance of fair and orderly markets, and the removal of impediments to, and the perfection of the mechanisms of a national market system, the Commission, by order, shall dismiss the proceeding. If the Commission does not make any such finding, or if it finds that such action or failure to act imposes any burden on competition not necessary or appropriate in furtherance of the purposes of the Act, the Commission, by order, shall set aside such action and/or require such action with respect to the matter reviewed as the Commission deems necessary or appropriate in the public interest, for the protection of investors, and the maintenance of fair and orderly markets, or to remove impediments to, and perfect the mechanisms of, a national market system.

(e) *Exemptions.* The Commission may exempt from the provisions of this section, either unconditionally or on specified terms and conditions, any self-regulatory organization, member thereof, or specified security, if the Commission determines that such exemption is consistent with the public interest, the protection of investors,

Securities and Exchange Commission § 242.610

the maintenance of fair and orderly markets and the removal of impediments to, and perfection of the mechanisms of, a national market system.

[70 FR 37620, June 29, 2005; 71 FR 232, Jan. 4, 2006, as amended at 85 FR 65497, Oct. 15, 2020]

§ 242.609 Registration of securities information processors: form of application and amendments.

(a) An application for the registration of a securities information processor shall be filed on Form SIP (§ 249.1001 of this chapter) in accordance with the instructions contained therein.

(b) If any information reported in items 1–13 or item 21 of Form SIP or in any amendment thereto is or becomes inaccurate for any reason, whether before or after the registration has been granted, the securities information processor shall promptly file an amendment on Form SIP correcting such information.

(c) The Commission, upon its own motion or upon application by any securities information processor, may conditionally or unconditionally exempt any securities information processor from any provision of the rules or regulations adopted under section 11A(b) of the Act (15 U.S.C. 78k–1(b)).

(d) Every amendment filed pursuant to this section shall constitute a "report" within the meaning of sections 17(a), 18(a) and 32(a) of the Act (15 U.S.C. 78q(a), 78r(a), and 78ff(a)).

§ 242.610 Access to quotations.

(a) *Quotations of SRO trading facility.* A national securities exchange or national securities association shall not impose unfairly discriminatory terms that prevent or inhibit any person from obtaining efficient access through a member of the national securities exchange or national securities association to the quotations in an NMS stock displayed through its SRO trading facility.

(b) *Quotations of SRO display-only facility.* (1) Any trading center that displays quotations in an NMS stock through an SRO display-only facility shall provide a level and cost of access to such quotations that is substantially equivalent to the level and cost of access to quotations displayed by SRO trading facilities in that stock.

(2) Any trading center that displays quotations in an NMS stock through an SRO display-only facility shall not impose unfairly discriminatory terms that prevent or inhibit any person from obtaining efficient access to such quotations through a member, subscriber, or customer of the trading center.

(c) *Fees for access to quotations.* A trading center shall not impose, nor permit to be imposed, any fee or fees for the execution of an order against a protected quotation of the trading center or against any other quotation of the trading center that is the best bid or best offer of a national securities exchange, the best bid or best offer of The Nasdaq Stock Market, Inc., or the best bid or best offer of a national securities association other than the best bid or best offer of The Nasdaq Stock Market, Inc. in an NMS stock that exceed or accumulate to more than the following limits:

(1) If the price of a protected quotation or other quotation is $1.00 or more, the fee or fees cannot exceed or accumulate to more than $0.003 per share; or

(2) If the price of a protected quotation or other quotation is less than $1.00, the fee or fees cannot exceed or accumulate to more than 0.3% of the quotation price per share.

(d) *Locking or crossing quotations.* Each national securities exchange and national securities association shall establish, maintain, and enforce written rules that:

(1) Require its members reasonably to avoid:

(i) Displaying quotations that lock or cross any protected quotation in an NMS stock; and

(ii) Displaying manual quotations that lock or cross any quotation in an NMS stock disseminated pursuant to an effective national market system plan;

(2) Are reasonably designed to assure the reconciliation of locked or crossed quotations in an NMS stock; and

(3) Prohibit its members from engaging in a pattern or practice of displaying quotations that lock or cross any protected quotation in an NMS

§ 242.610T

stock, or of displaying manual quotations that lock or cross any quotation in an NMS stock disseminated pursuant to an effective national market system plan, other than displaying quotations that lock or cross any protected or other quotation as permitted by an exception contained in its rules established pursuant to paragraph (d)(1) of this section.

(e) *Exemptions.* The Commission, by order, may exempt from the provisions of this section, either unconditionally or on specified terms and conditions, any person, security, quotations, orders, or fees, or any class or classes of persons, securities, quotations, orders, or fees, if the Commission determines that such exemption is necessary or appropriate in the public interest, and is consistent with the protection of investors.

§ 242.610T Equity transaction fee pilot.

(a) *Pilot pricing restrictions.* Notwithstanding § 242.610(c), on a pilot basis for the period specified in paragraph (c) of this section, in connection with a transaction in an NMS stock, a national securities exchange shall not:

(1) For *Test Group 1*, impose, or permit to be imposed, any fee or fees for the display of, or execution against, the displayed best bid or best offer of such market that exceed or accumulate to more than *$0.0010* per share;

(2) For *Test Group 2*, provide to any person, or permit to be provided to any person, a rebate or other remuneration in connection with an execution, or offer, or permit to be offered, any linked pricing that provides a discount or incentive on transaction fees applicable to removing (providing) liquidity that is linked to providing (removing) liquidity, except to the extent the exchange has a rule to provide non-rebate linked pricing to its registered market makers in consideration for meeting market quality metrics; and

(3) For the *Control Group*, impose, or permit to be imposed, any fee or fees in contravention of the limits specified in § 242.610(c).

(b) *Pilot securities*—(1) *Initial List of Pilot Securities.* (i) The Commission shall designate by notice the initial List of Pilot Securities, and shall assign each Pilot Security to one Test Group or the Control Group. Further, the Commission may designate by notice the assignment of NMS stocks that are interlisted on a Canadian securities exchange to Test Group 2 or the Control Group.

(ii) For purposes of this section, "Pilot Securities" means the NMS stocks designated by the Commission on the initial List of Pilot Securities pursuant to paragraph (b)(1)(i) of this section and any successors to such NMS stocks. At the time of selection by the Commission, an NMS stock must have a minimum share price of $2 to be included in the Pilot and must have an unlimited duration or a duration beyond the end of the post-Pilot Period. In addition, an NMS stock must have an average daily volume of 30,000 shares or more to be included in the Pilot. If the share price of a Pilot Security in one of the Test Groups or the Control Group closes below $1 at the end of a trading day, it shall be removed from the Pilot.

(iii) For purposes of this section, "primary listing exchange" means the national securities exchange on which the NMS stock is listed. If an NMS stock is listed on more than one national securities exchange, the national securities exchange upon which the NMS stock has been listed the longest shall be the primary listing exchange.

(2) *Pilot Securities Exchange Lists.* (i) After the Commission selects the initial List of Pilot Securities and prior to the beginning of trading on the first day of the Pilot Period each primary listing exchange shall publicly post on its website downloadable files containing a list, in pipe-delimited ASCII format, of the Pilot Securities for which the exchange serves as the primary listing exchange. Each primary listing exchange shall maintain and update this list as necessary prior to the beginning of trading on each business day that the U.S. equities markets are open for trading through the end of the post-Pilot Period.

(ii) The Pilot Securities Exchange Lists shall contain the following fields:

(A) Ticker Symbol;
(B) Security Name;
(C) Primary Listing Exchange;
(D) Security Type;

Securities and Exchange Commission

§ 242.610T

(*1*) Common Stock;
(*2*) ETP;
(*3*) Preferred Stock;
(*4*) Warrant;
(*5*) Closed-End Fund;
(*6*) Structured Product;
(*7*) ADR; and
(*8*) Other;
(E) Pilot Group:
(*1*) Control Group;
(*2*) Test Group 1; and
(*3*) Test Group 2;
(F) Stratum Code; and
(G) Date the Entry Was Last Updated.

(3) *Pilot Securities Change Lists.* (i) Prior to the beginning of trading on each trading day the U.S. equities markets are open for trading throughout the end of the post-Pilot Period, each primary listing exchange shall publicly post on its website downloadable files containing a Pilot Securities Change List, in pipe-delimited ASCII format, that lists each separate change applicable to any Pilot Securities for which it serves or has served as the primary listing exchange. The Pilot Securities Change List will provide a cumulative list of all changes to the Pilot Securities that the primary listing exchange has made to the Pilot Securities Exchange List published pursuant to paragraph (b)(2) of this section.

(ii) In addition to the fields required for the Pilot Securities Exchange List, the Pilot Securities Change Lists shall contain the following fields:

(A) New Ticker Symbol (if applicable);
(B) New Security Name (if applicable);
(C) Deleted Date (if applicable);
(D) Date Security Closed Below $1 (if applicable);
(E) Effective Date of Change; and
(F) Reason for the Change.

(4) *Posting requirement.* All information publicly posted in downloadable files pursuant to paragraphs (b)(2) and (3) of this section shall be and remain freely and persistently available and easily accessible by the general public on the primary listing exchange's website for a period of not less than five years from the conclusion of the post-Pilot Period. In addition, the information shall be presented in a manner that facilitates access by machines without encumbrance, and shall not be subject to any restrictions, including restrictions on access, retrieval, distribution and reuse.

(c) *Pilot duration.* (1) The Pilot shall include:

(i) A six-month "pre-Pilot Period;"

(ii) A two-year "Pilot Period" with an automatic sunset at the end of the first year unless, no later than thirty days prior to that time, the Commission publishes a notice that the Pilot shall continue for up to one additional year; and

(iii) A six-month "post-Pilot Period."

(2) The Commission shall designate by notice the commencement and termination dates of the pre-Pilot Period, Pilot Period, and post-Pilot Period, including any suspension of the one-year sunset of the Pilot Period.

(d) *Order routing datasets.* Throughout the duration of the Pilot, including the pre-Pilot Period and post-Pilot Period, each national securities exchange that facilitates trading in NMS stocks shall prepare and transmit to the Commission a file, in pipe-delimited ASCII format, no later than the last day of each month, containing sets of order routing data, for the prior month, in accordance with the specifications in paragraphs (d)(1) and (2) of this section. For the pre-Pilot Period, order routing datasets shall include each NMS stock. For the Pilot Period and post-Pilot Period, order routing datasets shall include each Pilot Security. Each national securities exchange shall treat the order routing datasets as regulatory information and shall not access or use that information for any commercial or non-regulatory purpose.

(1) Dataset of daily volume statistics, with field names as the first record and a consistent naming convention that indicates the exchange and date of the file, that include the following specifications of liquidity-providing orders by security and separating orders by order designation (exchanges may exclude auction orders) and order capacity:

(i) Code identifying the submitting exchange.

(ii) Eight-digit code identifying the date of the calendar day of trading in the format "yyyymmdd."

77

§ 242.610T

(iii) Symbol assigned to an NMS stock (including ETPs) under the national market system plan to which the consolidated best bid and offer for such a security are disseminated.
(iv) The broker-dealer's CRD number and MPID.
(v) Order type code:
(A) Inside-the-quote orders;
(B) At-the-quote limit orders; and
(C) Near-the-quote limit orders.
(vi) Order size codes:
(A) <100 share bucket;
(B) 100–499 share bucket;
(C) 500–1,999 share bucket;
(D) 2,000–4,999 share bucket;
(E) 5,000–9,999 share bucket; and
(F) ≥10,000 share bucket.
(vii) Number of orders received.
(viii) Cumulative number of shares of orders received.
(ix) Cumulative number of shares of orders cancelled prior to execution.
(x) Cumulative number of shares of orders executed at receiving market center.
(xi) Cumulative number of shares of orders routed to another execution venue.
(xii) Cumulative number of shares of orders executed within:
(A) 0 to < 100 microseconds of order receipt;
(B) 100 microseconds to < 100 milliseconds of order receipt;
(C) 100 milliseconds to < 1 second of order receipt;
(D) 1 second to < 30 seconds of order receipt;
(E) 30 seconds to < 60 seconds of order receipt;
(F) 60 seconds to < 5 minutes of order receipt;
(G) 5 minutes to < 30 minutes of order receipt; and
(H) ≥ 30 minutes of order receipt.
(2) Dataset of daily volume statistics, with field names as the first record and a consistent naming convention that indicates the exchange and date of the file, that include the following specifications of liquidity-taking orders by security and separating orders by order designation (exchanges may exclude auction orders) and order capacity:
(i) Code identifying the submitting exchange.

(ii) Eight-digit code identifying the date of the calendar day of trading in the format "yyyymmdd."
(iii) Symbol assigned to an NMS stock (including ETPs) under the national market system plan to which the consolidated best bid and offer for such a security are disseminated.
(iv) The broker-dealer's CRD number and MPID.
(v) Order type code:
(A) Market orders; and
(B) Marketable limit orders.
(vi) Order size codes:
(A) <100 share bucket;
(B) 100–499 share bucket;
(C) 500–1,999 share bucket;
(D) 2,000–4,999 share bucket;
(E) 5,000–9,999 share bucket; and
(F) ≥10,000 share bucket.
(vii) Number of orders received.
(viii) Cumulative number of shares of orders received.
(ix) Cumulative number of shares of orders cancelled prior to execution.
(x) Cumulative number of shares of orders executed at receiving market center.
(xi) Cumulative number of shares of orders routed to another execution venue.
(e) *Exchange Transaction Fee Summary.* Throughout the duration of the Pilot, including the pre-Pilot Period and post-Pilot Period, each national securities exchange that facilitates trading in NMS stocks shall publicly post on its website downloadable files containing information relating to transaction fees and rebates and changes thereto (applicable to securities having a price equal to or greater than $1). Each national securities exchange shall post its initial Exchange Transaction Fee Summary prior to the start of trading on the first day of the pre-Pilot Period and update its Exchange Transaction Fee Summary on a monthly basis within 10 business days of the first day of each calendar month, to reflect data collected for the prior month. The information prescribed by this section shall be made available using the most recent version of the XML schema published on the Commission's website. All information publicly posted pursuant to this paragraph (e) shall be and remain freely and persistently available and easily accessible on

Securities and Exchange Commission §242.611

the national securities exchange's website for a period of not less than five years from the conclusion of the post-Pilot Period. In addition, the information shall be presented in a manner that facilitates access by machines without encumbrance, and shall not be subject to any restrictions, including restrictions on access, retrieval, distribution, and reuse. The Exchange Transaction Fee Summary shall contain the following fields:

(1) Exchange Name;
(2) Record Type Indicator:
  (i) Reported Fee is the Monthly Average;
  (ii) Reported Fee is the Median; and
  (iii) Reported Fee is the Spot Monthly;
(3) Participant Type:
  (i) Registered Market Maker; and
  (ii) All Others;
(4) Pilot Group:
  (i) Control Group;
  (ii) Test Group 1; and
  (iii) Test Group 2;
(5) Applicability to Displayed and Non-Displayed Interest:
  (i) Displayed only;
  (ii) Non-displayed only; and
  (iii) Both displayed and non-displayed;
(6) Applicability to Top and Depth of Book Interest:
  (i) Top of book only;
  (ii) Depth of book only; and
  (iii) Both top and depth of book;
(7) Effective Date of Fee or Rebate;
(8) End Date of Currently Reported Fee or Rebate (if applicable);
(9) Month and Year of the monthly realized reported average and median per share fees and rebates;
(10) Pre/Post Fee Changes Indicator (if applicable) denoting implementation of a new fee or rebate on a day other than the first day of the month;
(11) Base and Top Tier Fee or Rebate:
  (i) Take (to remove):
    (A) Base Fee/Rebate reflecting the standard amount assessed or rebated before any applicable discounts, tiers, caps, or other incentives are applied; and
    (B) Top Tier Fee/Rebate reflecting the amount assessed or rebated after any applicable discounts, tiers, caps, or other incentives are applied; and
  (ii) Make (to provide):
    (A) Base Fee/Rebate reflecting the standard amount assessed or rebated before any applicable discounts, tiers, caps, or other incentives are applied; and
    (B) Top Tier Fee/Rebate reflecting the amount assessed or rebated after any applicable discounts, tiers, caps, or other incentives are applied;
(12) Average Take Fee (Rebate)/Average Make Rebate (Fee), by Participant Type, Test Group, Displayed/Non-Displayed, and Top/Depth of Book; and
(13) Median Take Fee (Rebate)/Median Make Fee (Rebate), by Participant Type, Test Group, Displayed/Non-Displayed, and Top/Depth of Book.

[84 FR 5298, Feb. 20, 2019]

EFFECTIVE DATE NOTE: At 84 FR 5298, Feb. 20, 2019, §242.610T was added, effective Apr. 22, 2019, through Dec. 29, 2023.

§242.611 Order protection rule.

(a) *Reasonable policies and procedures.* (1) A trading center shall establish, maintain, and enforce written policies and procedures that are reasonably designed to prevent trade-throughs on that trading center of protected quotations in NMS stocks that do not fall within an exception set forth in paragraph (b) of this section and, if relying on such an exception, that are reasonably designed to assure compliance with the terms of the exception.

(2) A trading center shall regularly surveil to ascertain the effectiveness of the policies and procedures required by paragraph (a)(1) of this section and shall take prompt action to remedy deficiencies in such policies and procedures.

(b) *Exceptions.* (1) The transaction that constituted the trade-through was effected when the trading center displaying the protected quotation that was traded through was experiencing a failure, material delay, or malfunction of its systems or equipment.

(2) The transaction that constituted the trade-through was not a "regular way" contract.

(3) The transaction that constituted the trade-through was a single-priced opening, reopening, or closing transaction by the trading center.

(4) The transaction that constituted the trade-through was executed at a time when a protected bid was priced

higher than a protected offer in the NMS stock.

(5) The transaction that constituted the trade-through was the execution of an order identified as an intermarket sweep order.

(6) The transaction that constituted the trade-through was effected by a trading center that simultaneously routed an intermarket sweep order to execute against the full displayed size of any protected quotation in the NMS stock that was traded through.

(7) The transaction that constituted the trade-through was the execution of an order at a price that was not based, directly or indirectly, on the quoted price of the NMS stock at the time of execution and for which the material terms were not reasonably determinable at the time the commitment to execute the order was made.

(8) The trading center displaying the protected quotation that was traded through had displayed, within one second prior to execution of the transaction that constituted the trade-through, a best bid or best offer, as applicable, for the NMS stock with a price that was equal or inferior to the price of the trade-through transaction.

(9) The transaction that constituted the trade-through was the execution by a trading center of an order for which, at the time of receipt of the order, the trading center had guaranteed an execution at no worse than a specified price (a "stopped order"), where:

(i) The stopped order was for the account of a customer;

(ii) The customer agreed to the specified price on an order-by-order basis; and

(iii) The price of the trade-through transaction was, for a stopped buy order, lower than the national best bid in the NMS stock at the time of execution or, for a stopped sell order, higher than the national best offer in the NMS stock at the time of execution.

(c) *Intermarket sweep orders.* The trading center, broker, or dealer responsible for the routing of an intermarket sweep order shall take reasonable steps to establish that such order meets the requirements set forth in § 242.600(b)(38).

(d) *Exemptions.* The Commission, by order, may exempt from the provisions of this section, either unconditionally or on specified terms and conditions, any person, security, transaction, quotation, or order, or any class or classes of persons, securities, quotations, or orders, if the Commission determines that such exemption is necessary or appropriate in the public interest, and is consistent with the protection of investors.

[70 FR 37620, June 29, 2005, as amended at 83 FR 58429, Nov. 19, 2018; 86 FR 18811, Apr. 9, 2021]

§ 242.612 Minimum pricing increment.

(a) No national securities exchange, national securities association, alternative trading system, vendor, or broker or dealer shall display, rank, or accept from any person a bid or offer, an order, or an indication of interest in any NMS stock priced in an increment smaller than $0.01 if that bid or offer, order, or indication of interest is priced equal to or greater than $1.00 per share.

(b) No national securities exchange, national securities association, alternative trading system, vendor, or broker or dealer shall display, rank, or accept from any person a bid or offer, an order, or an indication of interest in any NMS stock priced in an increment smaller than $0.0001 if that bid or offer, order, or indication of interest is priced less than $1.00 per share.

(c) The Commission, by order, may exempt from the provisions of this section, either unconditionally or on specified terms and conditions, any person, security, quotation, or order, or any class or classes of persons, securities, quotations, or orders, if the Commission determines that such exemption is necessary or appropriate in the public interest, and is consistent with the protection of investors.

§ 242.613 Consolidated audit trail.

(a) *Creation of a national market system plan governing a consolidated audit trail.* (1) Each national securities exchange and national securities association shall jointly file on or before 270 days from the date of publication of the Adopting Release in the FEDERAL REGISTER a national market system plan to govern the creation, implementation, and maintenance of a consolidated audit trail and central repository

Securities and Exchange Commission § 242.613

as required by this section. The national market system plan shall discuss the following considerations:

(i) The method(s) by which data will be reported to the central repository including, but not limited to, the sources of such data and the manner in which the central repository will receive, extract, transform, load, and retain such data; and the basis for selecting such method(s);

(ii) The time and method by which the data in the central repository will be made available to regulators, in accordance with paragraph (e)(1) of this section, to perform surveillance or analyses, or for other purposes as part of their regulatory and oversight responsibilities;

(iii) The reliability and accuracy of the data reported to and maintained by the central repository throughout its lifecycle, including transmission and receipt from market participants; data extraction, transformation and loading at the central repository; data maintenance and management at the central repository; and data access by regulators;

(iv) The security and confidentiality of the information reported to the central repository;

(v) The flexibility and scalability of the systems used by the central repository to collect, consolidate and store consolidated audit trail data, including the capacity of the consolidated audit trail to efficiently incorporate, in a cost-effective manner, improvements in technology, additional capacity, additional order data, information about additional securities or transactions, changes in regulatory requirements, and other developments;

(vi) The feasibility, benefits, and costs of broker-dealers reporting to the consolidated audit trail in a timely manner:

(A) The identity of all market participants (including broker-dealers and customers) that are allocated NMS securities, directly or indirectly, in a primary market transaction;

(B) The number of such securities each such market participant is allocated; and

(C) The identity of the broker-dealer making each such allocation;

(vii) The detailed estimated costs for creating, implementing, and maintaining the consolidated audit trail as contemplated by the national market system plan, which estimated costs should specify:

(A) An estimate of the costs to the plan sponsors for establishing and maintaining the central repository;

(B) An estimate of the costs to members of the plan sponsors, initially and on an ongoing basis, for reporting the data required by the national market system plan;

(C) An estimate of the costs to the plan sponsors, initially and on an ongoing basis, for reporting the data required by the national market system plan; and

(D) How the plan sponsors propose to fund the creation, implementation, and maintenance of the consolidated audit trail, including the proposed allocation of such estimated costs among the plan sponsors, and between the plan sponsors and members of the plan sponsors;

(viii) An analysis of the impact on competition, efficiency and capital formation of creating, implementing, and maintaining of the national market system plan;

(ix) A plan to eliminate existing rules and systems (or components thereof) that will be rendered duplicative by the consolidated audit trail, including identification of such rules and systems (or components thereof); to the extent that any existing rules or systems related to monitoring quotes, orders, and executions provide information that is not rendered duplicative by the consolidated audit trail, an analysis of:

(A) Whether the collection of such information remains appropriate;

(B) If still appropriate, whether such information should continue to be separately collected or should instead be incorporated into the consolidated audit trail; and

(C) If no longer appropriate, how the collection of such information could be efficiently terminated; the steps the plan sponsors propose to take to seek Commission approval for the elimination of such rules and systems (or components thereof); and a timetable

§ 242.613

for such elimination, including a description of how the plan sponsors propose to phase in the consolidated audit trail and phase out such existing rules and systems (or components thereof);

(x) Objective milestones to assess progress toward the implementation of the national market system plan;

(xi) The process by which the plan sponsors solicited views of their members and other appropriate parties regarding the creation, implementation, and maintenance of the consolidated audit trail, a summary of the views of such members and other parties, and how the plan sponsors took such views into account in preparing the national market system plan; and

(xii) Any reasonable alternative approaches to creating, implementing, and maintaining a consolidated audit trail that the plan sponsors considered in developing the national market system plan including, but not limited to, a description of any such alternative approach; the relative advantages and disadvantages of each such alternative, including an assessment of the alternative's costs and benefits; and the basis upon which the plan sponsors selected the approach reflected in the national market system plan.

(2) The national market system plan, or any amendment thereto, filed pursuant to this section shall comply with the requirements in § 242.608(a), if applicable, and be filed with the Commission pursuant to § 242.608.

(3) The national market system plan submitted pursuant to this section shall require each national securities exchange and national securities association to:

(i) Within two months after effectiveness of the national market system plan jointly (or under the governance structure described in the plan) select a person to be the plan processor;

(ii) Within four months after effectiveness of the national market system plan synchronize their business clocks and require members of each such exchange and association to synchronize their business clocks in accordance with paragraph (d) of this section;

(iii) Within one year after effectiveness of the national market system plan provide to the central repository the data specified in paragraph (c) of this section;

(iv) Within fourteen months after effectiveness of the national market system plan implement a new or enhanced surveillance system(s) as required by paragraph (f) of this section;

(v) Within two years after effectiveness of the national market system plan require members of each such exchange and association, except those members that qualify as small broker-dealers as defined in § 240.0–10(c) of this chapter, to provide to the central repository the data specified in paragraph (c) of this section; and

(vi) Within three years after effectiveness of the national market system plan require members of each such exchange and association that qualify as small broker-dealers as defined in § 240.0–10(c) of this chapter to provide to the central repository the data specified in paragraph (c) of this section.

(4) Each national securities exchange and national securities association shall be a sponsor of the national market system plan submitted pursuant to this section and approved by the Commission.

(5) No national market system plan filed pursuant to this section, or any amendment thereto, shall become effective unless approved by the Commission or otherwise permitted in accordance with the procedures set forth in § 242.608. In determining whether to approve the national market system plan, or any amendment thereto, and whether the national market system plan or any amendment thereto is in the public interest under § 242.608(b)(2), the Commission shall consider the impact of the national market system plan or amendment, as applicable, on efficiency, competition, and capital formation.

(b) *Operation and administration of the national market system plan.* (1) The national market system plan submitted pursuant to this section shall include a governance structure to ensure fair representation of the plan sponsors, and administration of the central repository, including the selection of the plan processor.

(2) The national market system plan submitted pursuant to this section shall include a provision addressing the

Securities and Exchange Commission

§ 242.613

requirements for the admission of new sponsors of the plan and the withdrawal of existing sponsors from the plan.

(3) The national market system plan submitted pursuant to this section shall include a provision addressing the percentage of votes required by the plan sponsors to effectuate amendments to the plan.

(4) The national market system plan submitted pursuant to this section shall include a provision addressing the manner in which the costs of operating the central repository will be allocated among the national securities exchanges and national securities associations that are sponsors of the plan, including a provision addressing the manner in which costs will be allocated to new sponsors to the plan.

(5) The national market system plan submitted pursuant to this section shall require the appointment of a Chief Compliance Officer to regularly review the operation of the central repository to assure its continued effectiveness in light of market and technological developments, and make any appropriate recommendations for enhancements to the nature of the information collected and the manner in which it is processed.

(6) The national market system plan submitted pursuant to this section shall include a provision requiring the plan sponsors to provide to the Commission, at least every two years after effectiveness of the national market system plan, a written assessment of the operation of the consolidated audit trail. Such document shall include, at a minimum:

(i) An evaluation of the performance of the consolidated audit trail including, at a minimum, with respect to data accuracy (consistent with paragraph (e)(6) of this section), timeliness of reporting, comprehensiveness of data elements, efficiency of regulatory access, system speed, system downtime, system security (consistent with paragraph (e)(4) of this section), and other performance metrics to be determined by the Chief Compliance Officer, along with a description of such metrics;

(ii) A detailed plan, based on such evaluation, for any potential improvements to the performance of the consolidated audit trail with respect to any of the following: improving data accuracy; shortening reporting timeframes; expanding data elements; adding granularity and details regarding the scope and nature of Customer-IDs; expanding the scope of the national market system plan to include new instruments and new types of trading and order activities; improving the efficiency of regulatory access; increasing system speed; reducing system downtime; and improving performance under other metrics to be determined by the Chief Compliance Officer;

(iii) An estimate of the costs associated with any such potential improvements to the performance of the consolidated audit trail, including an assessment of the potential impact on competition, efficiency, and capital formation; and

(iv) An estimated implementation timeline for any such potential improvements, if applicable.

(7) The national market system plan submitted pursuant to this section shall include an Advisory Committee which shall function in accordance with the provisions set forth in this paragraph (b)(7). The purpose of the Advisory Committee shall be to advise the plan sponsors on the implementation, operation, and administration of the central repository.

(i) The national market system plan submitted pursuant to this section shall set forth the term and composition of the Advisory Committee, which composition shall include representatives of the member firms of the plan sponsors.

(ii) Members of the Advisory Committee shall have the right to attend any meetings of the plan sponsors, to receive information concerning the operation of the central repository, and to provide their views to the plan sponsors; provided, however, that the plan sponsors may meet without the Advisory Committee members in executive session if, by affirmative vote of a majority of the plan sponsors, the plan sponsors determine that such an executive session is required.

(c) *Data recording and reporting.* (1) The national market system plan submitted pursuant to this section shall

§ 242.613

provide for an accurate, time-sequenced record of orders beginning with the receipt or origination of an order by a member of a national securities exchange or national securities association, and further documenting the life of the order through the process of routing, modification, cancellation, and execution (in whole or in part) of the order.

(2) The national market system plan submitted pursuant to this section shall require each national securities exchange, national securities association, and member to report to the central repository the information required by paragraph (c)(7) of this section in a uniform electronic format, or in a manner that would allow the central repository to convert the data to a uniform electronic format, for consolidation and storage.

(3) The national market system plan submitted pursuant to this section shall require each national securities exchange, national securities association, and member to record the information required by paragraphs (c)(7)(i) through (v) of this section contemporaneously with the reportable event. The national market system plan shall require that information recorded pursuant to paragraphs (c)(7)(i) through (v) of this section must be reported to the central repository by 8:00 a.m. Eastern Time on the trading day following the day such information has been recorded by the national securities exchange, national securities association, or member. The national market system plan may accommodate voluntary reporting prior to 8:00 a.m. Eastern Time, but shall not impose an earlier reporting deadline on the reporting parties.

(4) The national market system plan submitted pursuant to this section shall require each member of a national securities exchange or national securities association to record and report to the central repository the information required by paragraphs (c)(7)(vi) through (viii) of this section by 8:00 a.m. Eastern Time on the trading day following the day the member receives such information. The national market system plan may accommodate voluntary reporting prior to 8:00 a.m. Eastern Time, but shall not impose an earlier reporting deadline on the reporting parties.

(5) The national market system plan submitted pursuant to this section shall require each national securities exchange and its members to record and report to the central repository the information required by paragraph (c)(7) of this section for each NMS security registered or listed for trading on such exchange or admitted to unlisted trading privileges on such exchange.

(6) The national market system plan submitted pursuant to this section shall require each national securities association and its members to record and report to the central repository the information required by paragraph (c)(7) of this section for each NMS security for which transaction reports are required to be submitted to the association.

(7) The national market system plan submitted pursuant to this section shall require each national securities exchange, national securities association, and any member of such exchange or association to record and electronically report to the central repository details for each order and each reportable event, including, but not limited to, the following information:

(i) For original receipt or origination of an order:

(A) Customer-ID(s) for each customer;

(B) The CAT–Order-ID;

(C) The CAT–Reporter-ID of the broker-dealer receiving or originating the order;

(D) Date of order receipt or origination;

(E) Time of order receipt or origination (using time stamps pursuant to paragraph (d)(3) of this section); and

(F) Material terms of the order.

(ii) For the routing of an order, the following information:

(A) The CAT-Order-ID;

(B) Date on which the order is routed;

(C) Time at which the order is routed (using time stamps pursuant to paragraph (d)(3) of this section);

(D) The CAT-Reporter-ID of the broker-dealer or national securities exchange routing the order;

Securities and Exchange Commission § 242.613

(E) The CAT-Reporter-ID of the broker-dealer, national securities exchange, or national securities association to which the order is being routed;

(F) If routed internally at the broker-dealer, the identity and nature of the department or desk to which an order is routed; and

(G) Material terms of the order.

(iii) For the receipt of an order that has been routed, the following information:

(A) The CAT-Order-ID;

(B) Date on which the order is received;

(C) Time at which the order is received (using time stamps pursuant to paragraph (d)(3) of this section);

(D) The CAT-Reporter-ID of the broker-dealer, national securities exchange, or national securities association receiving the order;

(E) The CAT-Reporter-ID of the broker-dealer or national securities exchange routing the order; and

(F) Material terms of the order.

(iv) If the order is modified or cancelled, the following information:

(A) The CAT-Order-ID;

(B) Date the modification or cancellation is received or originated;

(C) Time the modification or cancellation is received or originated (using time stamps pursuant to paragraph (d)(3) of this section);

(D) Price and remaining size of the order, if modified;

(E) Other changes in material terms of the order, if modified; and

(F) The CAT-Reporter-ID of the broker-dealer or Customer-ID of the person giving the modification or cancellation instruction.

(v) If the order is executed, in whole or part, the following information:

(A) The CAT-Order-ID;

(B) Date of execution;

(C) Time of execution (using time stamps pursuant to paragraph (d)(3) of this section);

(D) Execution capacity (principal, agency, riskless principal);

(E) Execution price and size;

(F) The CAT-Reporter-ID of the national securities exchange or broker-dealer executing the order; and

(G) Whether the execution was reported pursuant to an effective transaction reporting plan or the Plan for Reporting of Consolidated Options Last Sale Reports and Quotation Information.

(vi) If the order is executed, in whole or part, the following information:

(A) The account number for any sub-accounts to which the execution is allocated (in whole or part);

(B) The CAT-Reporter-ID of the clearing broker or prime broker, if applicable; and

(C) The CAT-Order-ID of any contra-side order(s).

(vii) If the trade is cancelled, a cancelled trade indicator.

(viii) For original receipt or origination of an order, the following information:

(A) Information of sufficient detail to identify the customer; and

(B) Customer account information.

(8) All plan sponsors and their members shall use the same Customer-ID and CAT-Reporter-ID for each customer and broker-dealer.

(d) *Clock synchronization and time stamps.* The national market system plan submitted pursuant to this section shall require:

(1) Each national securities exchange, national securities association, and member of such exchange or association to synchronize its business clocks that are used for the purposes of recording the date and time of any reportable event that must be reported pursuant to this section to the time maintained by the National Institute of Standards and Technology, consistent with industry standards;

(2) Each national securities exchange and national securities association to evaluate annually the clock synchronization standard to determine whether it should be shortened, consistent with changes in industry standards; and

(3) Each national securities exchange, national securities association, and member of such exchange or association to utilize the time stamps required by paragraph (c)(7) of this section, with at minimum the granularity set forth in the national market system plan submitted pursuant to this section, which shall reflect current industry standards and be at least to the millisecond. To the extent that the relevant order handling and execution

§ 242.613

systems of any national securities exchange, national securities association, or member of such exchange or association utilize time stamps in increments finer than the minimum required by the national market system plan, the plan shall require such national securities exchange, national securities association, or member to utilize time stamps in such finer increments when providing data to the central repository, so that all reportable events reported to the central repository by any national securities exchange, national securities association, or member can be accurately sequenced. The national market system plan shall require the sponsors of the national market system plan to annually evaluate whether industry standards have evolved such that the required time stamp standard should be in finer increments.

(e) *Central repository.* (1) The national market system plan submitted pursuant to this section shall provide for the creation and maintenance of a central repository. Such central repository shall be responsible for the receipt, consolidation, and retention of all information reported pursuant to paragraph (c)(7) of this section. The central repository shall store and make available to regulators data in a uniform electronic format, and in a form in which all events pertaining to the same originating order are linked together in a manner that ensures timely and accurate retrieval of the information required by paragraph (c)(7) of this section for all reportable events for that order.

(2) Each national securities exchange, national securities association, and the Commission shall have access to the central repository, including all systems operated by the central repository, and access to and use of the data reported to and consolidated by the central repository under paragraph (c) of this section, for the purpose of performing its respective regulatory and oversight responsibilities pursuant to the federal securities laws, rules, and regulations. The national market system plan submitted pursuant to this section shall provide that such access to and use of such data by each national securities exchange, national securities association, and the Commission for the purpose of performing its regulatory and oversight responsibilities pursuant to the federal securities laws, rules, and regulations shall not be limited.

(3) The national market system plan submitted pursuant to this section shall include a provision requiring the creation and maintenance by the plan processor of a method of access to the consolidated data stored in the central repository that includes the ability to run searches and generate reports.

(4) The national market system plan submitted pursuant to this section shall include policies and procedures, including standards, to be used by the plan processor to:

(i) Ensure the security and confidentiality of all information reported to the central repository by requiring that:

(A) All plan sponsors and their employees, as well as all employees of the central repository, agree to use appropriate safeguards to ensure the confidentiality of such data and agree not to use such data for any purpose other than surveillance and regulatory purposes, provided that nothing in this paragraph (e)(4)(i)(A) shall be construed to prevent a plan sponsor from using the data that it reports to the central repository for regulatory, surveillance, commercial, or other purposes as otherwise permitted by applicable law, rule, or regulation;

(B) Each plan sponsor adopt and enforce rules that:

(*1*) Require information barriers between regulatory staff and non-regulatory staff with regard to access and use of data in the central repository; and

(*2*) Permit only persons designated by plan sponsors to have access to the data in the central repository;

(C) The plan processor:

(*1*) Develop and maintain a comprehensive information security program for the central repository, with dedicated staff, that is subject to regular reviews by the Chief Compliance Officer;

(*2*) Have a mechanism to confirm the identity of all persons permitted to access the data; and

Securities and Exchange Commission

§ 242.613

(3) Maintain a record of all instances where such persons access the data; and

(D) The plan sponsors adopt penalties for non-compliance with any policies and procedures of the plan sponsors or central repository with respect to information security.

(ii) Ensure the timeliness, accuracy, integrity, and completeness of the data provided to the central repository pursuant to paragraph (c) of this section; and

(iii) Ensure the accuracy of the consolidation by the plan processor of the data provided to the central repository pursuant to paragraph (c) of this section.

(5) The national market system plan submitted pursuant to this section shall address whether there will be an annual independent evaluation of the security of the central repository and:

(i) If so, provide a description of the scope of such planned evaluation; and

(ii) If not, provide a detailed explanation of the alternative measures for evaluating the security of the central repository that are planned instead.

(6) The national market system plan submitted pursuant to this section shall:

(i) Specify a maximum error rate to be tolerated by the central repository for any data reported pursuant to paragraphs (c)(3) and (c)(4) of this section; describe the basis for selecting such maximum error rate; explain how the plan sponsors will seek to reduce such maximum error rate over time; describe how the plan will seek to ensure compliance with such maximum error rate and, in the event of noncompliance, will promptly remedy the causes thereof;

(ii) Require the central repository to measure the error rate each business day and promptly take appropriate remedial action, at a minimum, if the error rate exceeds the maximum error rate specified in the plan;

(iii) Specify a process for identifying and correcting errors in the data reported to the central repository pursuant to paragraphs (c)(3) and (c)(4) of this section, including the process for notifying the national securities exchanges, national securities association, and members who reported erroneous data to the central repository of such errors, to help ensure that such errors are promptly corrected by the reporting entity, and for disciplining those who repeatedly report erroneous data; and

(iv) Specify the time by which data that has been corrected will be made available to regulators.

(7) The national market system plan submitted pursuant to this section shall require the central repository to collect and retain on a current and continuing basis and in a format compatible with the information consolidated and stored pursuant to paragraph (c)(7) of this section:

(i) Information, including the size and quote condition, on the national best bid and national best offer for each NMS security;

(ii) Transaction reports reported pursuant to an effective transaction reporting plan filed with the Commission pursuant to, and meeting the requirements of, § 242.601; and

(iii) Last sale reports reported pursuant to the Plan for Reporting of Consolidated Options Last Sale Reports and Quotation Information filed with the Commission pursuant to, and meeting the requirements of, § 242.608.

(8) The national market system plan submitted pursuant to this section shall require the central repository to retain the information collected pursuant to paragraphs (c)(7) and (e)(7) of this section in a convenient and usable standard electronic data format that is directly available and searchable electronically without any manual intervention for a period of not less than five years.

(f) *Surveillance.* Every national securities exchange and national securities association subject to this section shall develop and implement a surveillance system, or enhance existing surveillance systems, reasonably designed to make use of the consolidated information contained in the consolidated audit trail.

(g) *Compliance by members.* (1) Each national securities exchange and national securities association shall file with the Commission pursuant to section 19(b)(2) of the Act (15 U.S.C. 78s(b)(2)) and § 240.19b–4 of this chapter on or before 60 days from approval of

§ 242.613

the national market system plan a proposed rule change to require its members to comply with the requirements of this section and the national market system plan approved by the Commission.

(2) Each member of a national securities exchange or national securities association shall comply with all the provisions of any approved national market system plan applicable to members.

(3) The national market system plan submitted pursuant to this section shall include a provision requiring each national securities exchange and national securities association to agree to enforce compliance by its members with the provisions of any approved plan.

(4) The national market system plan submitted pursuant to this section shall include a mechanism to ensure compliance with the requirements of any approved plan by the members of a national securities exchange or national securities association.

(h) *Compliance by national securities exchanges and national securities associations.* (1) Each national securities exchange and national securities association shall comply with the provisions of the national market system plan approved by the Commission.

(2) Any failure by a national securities exchange or national securities association to comply with the provisions of the national market system plan approved by the Commission shall be considered a violation of this section.

(3) The national market system plan submitted pursuant to this section shall include a mechanism to ensure compliance by the sponsors of the plan with the requirements of any approved plan. Such enforcement mechanism may include penalties where appropriate.

(i) *Other securities and other types of transactions.* The national market system plan submitted pursuant to this section shall include a provision requiring each national securities exchange and national securities association to jointly provide to the Commission within six months after effectiveness of the national market system plan a document outlining how such exchanges and associations could incorporate into the consolidated audit trail information with respect to equity securities that are not NMS securities, debt securities, primary market transactions in equity securities that are not NMS securities, and primary market transactions in debt securities, including details for each order and reportable event that may be required to be provided, which market participants may be required to provide the data, an implementation timeline, and a cost estimate.

(j) *Definitions.* As used in this section:

(1) The term *CAT–Order-ID* shall mean a unique order identifier or series of unique order identifiers that allows the central repository to efficiently and accurately link all reportable events for an order, and all orders that result from the aggregation or disaggregation of such order.

(2) The term *CAT–Reporter-ID* shall mean, with respect to each national securities exchange, national securities association, and member of a national securities exchange or national securities association, a code that uniquely and consistently identifies such person for purposes of providing data to the central repository.

(3) The term *customer* shall mean:

(i) The account holder(s) of the account at a registered broker-dealer originating the order; and

(ii) Any person from whom the broker-dealer is authorized to accept trading instructions for such account, if different from the account holder(s).

(4) The term *customer account information* shall include, but not be limited to, account number, account type, customer type, date account opened, and large trader identifier (if applicable).

(5) The term *Customer-ID* shall mean, with respect to a customer, a code that uniquely and consistently identifies such customer for purposes of providing data to the central repository.

(6) The term *error rate* shall mean the percentage of reportable events collected by the central repository in which the data reported does not fully and accurately reflect the order event that occurred in the market.

(7) The term *material terms of the order* shall include, but not be limited to, the NMS security symbol; security type;

Securities and Exchange Commission § 242.614

price (if applicable); size (displayed and non-displayed); side (buy/sell); order type; if a sell order, whether the order is long, short, short exempt; open/close indicator; time in force (if applicable); if the order is for a listed option, option type (put/call), option symbol or root symbol, underlying symbol, strike price, expiration date, and open/close; and any special handling instructions.

(8) The term *order* shall include:

(i) Any order received by a member of a national securities exchange or national securities association from any person;

(ii) Any order originated by a member of a national securities exchange or national securities association; or

(iii) Any bid or offer.

(9) The term *reportable event* shall include, but not be limited to, the original receipt or origination, modification, cancellation, routing, and execution (in whole or in part) of an order, and receipt of a routed order.

[77 FR 45808, Aug. 1, 2012]

§ 242.614 Registration and responsibilities of competing consolidators.

(a) *Competing consolidator registration*—(1) *Initial Form CC*—(i) *Filing and effectiveness requirement.* No person, other than a national securities exchange or a national securities association:

(A) May receive directly, pursuant to an effective national market system plan, from a national securities exchange or national securities association information with respect to quotations for and transactions in NMS stocks; and

(B) Generate a consolidated market data product for dissemination to any person unless the person files with the Commission an initial Form CC and the initial Form CC has become effective pursuant to paragraph (a)(1)(v) of this section.

(ii) *Electronic filing and submission.* Any reports to the Commission required under this section shall be filed electronically on Form CC (17 CFR 249.1002), include all information as prescribed in Form CC and the instructions thereto, and contain an electronic signature as defined in § 240.19b–4(j) of this chapter.

(iii) *Commission review period.* The Commission may, by order, as provided in paragraph (a)(1)(v)(B) of this section, declare an initial Form CC filed by a competing consolidator ineffective no later than 90 calendar days from the date of filing with the Commission.

(iv) *Withdrawal of initial Form CC due to inaccurate or incomplete disclosures.* During the review by the Commission of the initial Form CC, if any information disclosed in the initial Form CC is or becomes inaccurate or incomplete, the competing consolidator shall promptly withdraw the initial Form CC and may refile an initial Form CC pursuant to paragraph (a)(1) of this section.

(v) *Effectiveness; ineffectiveness determination.* (A) An initial Form CC filed by a competing consolidator will become effective, unless declared ineffective, no later than the expiration of the review period provided in paragraph (a)(1)(iii) of this section and publication pursuant to paragraph (b)(2)(i) of this section.

(B) The Commission shall, by order, declare an initial Form CC ineffective if it finds, after notice and opportunity for hearing, that such action is necessary or appropriate in the public interest, and is consistent with the protection of investors. If the Commission declares an initial Form CC ineffective, the competing consolidator shall be prohibited from operating as a competing consolidator. An initial Form CC declared ineffective does not prevent the competing consolidator from subsequently filing a new Form CC.

(2) *Form CC amendments.* A competing consolidator shall amend a Form CC:

(i) Prior to the implementation of a material change to the pricing, connectivity, or products offered ("material amendment"); and

(ii) No later than 30 calendar days after the end of each calendar year to correct information that has become inaccurate or incomplete for any reason and to provide an Annual Report as required under Form CC (each a "Form CC amendment").

(3) *Notice of cessation.* A competing consolidator shall notice its cessation of operations on Form CC at least 90 calendar days prior to the date the competing consolidator will cease to

§ 242.614

operate as a competing consolidator. The notice of cessation shall cause the Form CC to become ineffective on the date designated by the competing consolidator.

(4) *Date of filing.* For purposes of filings made pursuant to this section:

(i) The term *business day* shall have the same meaning as defined in § 240.19b–4(b)(2) of this chapter.

(ii) If the conditions of this section and Form CC are otherwise satisfied, all filings submitted electronically on or before 5:30 p.m. Eastern Standard Time or Eastern Daylight Saving Time, whichever is currently in effect, on a business day, shall be deemed filed on that business day, and all filings submitted after 5:30 p.m. Eastern Standard Time or Eastern Daylight Saving Time, whichever is currently in effect, shall be deemed filed on the next business day.

(b) *Public disclosures.* (1) Every Form CC filed pursuant to this section shall constitute a "report" within the meaning of sections 11A, 17(a), 18(a), and 32(a) of the Act (15 U.S.C. 78k–1, 78q(a), 78r(a), and 78ff(a)), and any other applicable provisions of the Act.

(2) The Commission will make public via posting on the Commission's website:

(i) Identification of each competing consolidator that has filed an initial Form CC with the Commission and the date of filing;

(ii) Each effective initial Form CC, as amended;

(iii) Each order of ineffective initial Form CC;

(iv) Each Form CC amendment. The Commission will make public the entirety of any Form CC amendment no later than 30 calendar days from the date of filing thereof with the Commission; and

(v) Each notice of cessation.

(c) *Posting of hyperlink to the Commission's website.* Each competing consolidator shall make public via posting on its website a direct URL hyperlink to the Commission's website that contains the documents enumerated in paragraphs (b)(2)(ii) through (v) of this section.

(d) *Responsibilities of competing consolidators.* Each competing consolidator shall:

(1) Collect from each national securities exchange and national securities association, either directly or indirectly, any information with respect to quotations for and transactions in NMS stocks as provided in § 242.603(b) that is necessary to create a consolidated market data product, as defined in § 242.600(b)(20).

(2) Calculate and generate a consolidated market data product, as defined in § 242.600(b)(20), from the information collected pursuant to paragraph (d)(1) of this section.

(3) Make a consolidated market data product, as defined in § 242.600(b)(20), as timestamped as required by paragraph (d)(4) of this section and including the national securities exchange and national securities association data generation timestamp required to be provided by the national securities exchange and national securities association participants by paragraph (e)(2) of this section, available to subscribers on a consolidated basis on terms that are not unreasonably discriminatory.

(4) Timestamp the information collected pursuant to paragraph (d)(1) of this section upon:

(i) Receipt from each national securities exchange and national securities association;

(ii) Receipt of such information at its aggregation mechanism; and

(iii) Dissemination of a consolidated market data product to subscribers.

(5) Within 15 calendar days after the end of each month, publish prominently on its website monthly performance metrics, as defined by the effective national market system plan(s) for NMS stocks, that shall include at least the information in paragraphs (d)(5)(i) through (v) of this section. All information must be publicly posted in downloadable files and must remain free and accessible (without any encumbrances or restrictions) by the general public on the website for a period of not less than three years from the initial date of posting.

(i) Capacity statistics;

(ii) Message rate and total statistics;

(iii) System availability;

(iv) Network delay statistics; and

(v) Latency statistics for the following, with distribution statistics up to the 99.99th percentile:

Securities and Exchange Commission § 242.614

(A) When a national securities exchange or national securities association sends an inbound message to a competing consolidator network and when the competing consolidator network receives the inbound message;

(B) When the competing consolidator network receives the inbound message and when the competing consolidator network sends the corresponding consolidated message to a subscriber; and

(C) When a national securities exchange or national securities association sends an inbound message to a competing consolidator network and when the competing consolidator network sends the corresponding consolidated message to a subscriber.

(6) Within 15 calendar days after the end of each month, publish prominently on its website the information in paragraphs (d)(6)(i) through (v) of this section. All information must be publicly posted and must remain free and accessible (without any encumbrances or restrictions) by the general public on the website for a period of not less than three years from the initial date of posting.

(i) Data quality issues;
(ii) System issues;
(iii) Any clock synchronization protocol utilized;
(iv) For the clocks used to generate the timestamps described in paragraph (d)(4) of this section, the clock drift averages and peaks, and the number of instances of clock drift greater than 100 microseconds; and
(v) Vendor alerts.

(7) Keep and preserve at least one copy of all documents, including all correspondence, memoranda, papers, books, notices, accounts, and such other records as shall be made or received by it in the course of its business as such and in the conduct of its business. Competing consolidators shall keep all such documents for a period of no less than five years, the first two years in an easily accessible place.

(8) Upon request of any representative of the Commission, promptly furnish to the possession of such representative copies of any documents required to be kept and preserved by it.

(9) Each competing consolidator that is not required to comply with the requirements of §§ 242.1000 through 242.1007 regarding systems compliance and integrity (Regulation SCI) shall comply with the following:

(i) *Definitions.* For purposes of this paragraph (d)(9), the following definitions shall apply:

Systems disruption means an event in a competing consolidator's systems involved in the collection and consolidation of consolidated market data, and dissemination of consolidated market data products, that disrupts, or significantly degrades, the normal operation of such systems.

Systems intrusion means any unauthorized entry into a competing consolidator's systems involved in the collection and consolidation of consolidated market data, and dissemination of consolidated market data products.

(ii) *Obligations relating to policies and procedures.* (A)(*1*) Establish, maintain, and enforce written policies and procedures reasonably designed to ensure: That its systems involved in the collection and consolidation of consolidated market data, and dissemination of consolidated market data products have levels of capacity, integrity, resiliency, availability, and security adequate to maintain the competing consolidator's operational capability and promote the maintenance of fair and orderly markets; and the prompt, accurate, and reliable dissemination of consolidated market data products.

(*2*) Such policies and procedures shall be deemed to be reasonably designed if they are consistent with current industry standards, which shall be comprised of information technology practices that are widely available to information technology professionals in the financial sector and issued by an authoritative body that is a U.S. governmental entity or agency, association of U.S. governmental entities or agencies, or widely recognized organization. Compliance with such current industry standards, however, shall not be the exclusive means to comply with the requirements of this paragraph (d)(9)(ii)(A);

(B) Periodically review the effectiveness of the policies and procedures required by paragraph (d)(9)(ii)(A) of this section, and take prompt action to remedy deficiencies in such policies and procedures; and

§ 242.614

(C) Establish, maintain, and enforce reasonably designed written policies and procedures that include the criteria for identifying responsible personnel, the designation and documentation of responsible personnel, and escalation procedures to quickly inform responsible personnel of potential systems disruptions and systems intrusions; and periodically review the effectiveness of the policies and procedures, and take prompt action to remedy deficiencies.

(iii) *Systems disruptions or systems intrusions.* (A) Upon responsible personnel having a reasonable basis to conclude that a systems disruption or systems intrusion has occurred, begin to take appropriate corrective action which shall include, at a minimum, mitigating potential harm to investors and market integrity resulting from the event and devoting adequate resources to remedy the event as soon as reasonably practicable.

(B) Promptly upon responsible personnel having a reasonable basis to conclude that a systems disruption (other than a system disruption that has had, or the competing consolidator reasonably estimates would have, no or a de minimis impact on the competing consolidator's operations or on market participants) has occurred, publicly disseminate information relating to the event (including the system(s) affected and a summary description); when known, promptly publicly disseminate additional information relating to the event (including a detailed description, an assessment of those potentially affected, a description of the progress of corrective action and when the event has been or is expected to be resolved); and until resolved, provide regular updates with respect to such information.

(C) Concurrent with public dissemination of information relating to a systems disruption pursuant to paragraph (d)(9)(iii)(B) of this section, or promptly upon responsible personnel having a reasonable basis to conclude that a systems intrusion (other than a system intrusion that has had, or the competing consolidator reasonably estimates would have, no or a de minimis impact on the competing consolidator's operations or on market participants) has occurred, provide the Commission notification and, until resolved, updates of such event. Notifications required pursuant to this paragraph (d)(9)(iii)(C) shall include information relating to the event (including the system(s) affected and a summary description); when known, additional information relating to the event (including a detailed description, an assessment of those potentially affected, a description of the progress of corrective action and when the event has been or is expected to be resolved); and until resolved, regular updates with respect to such information. Notifications relating to systems disruptions and systems intrusions pursuant to this paragraph (d)(9)(iii)(C) shall be submitted to the Commission on Form CC.

(iv) *Coordinated testing.* Participate in the industry- or sector-wide coordinated testing of business recovery and disaster recovery plans required of SCI entities pursuant to § 242.1004(c).

(e) *Amendment of the effective national market system plan(s) for NMS stocks.* The participants to the effective national market system plan(s) for NMS stocks shall file with the Commission, pursuant to § 242.608, an amendment that includes the following provisions within 150 calendar days from June 8, 2021:

(1) Conforming the effective national market system plan(s) for NMS stocks to reflect provision of information with respect to quotations for and transactions in NMS stocks that is necessary to generate consolidated market data by the national securities exchange and national securities association participants to competing consolidators and self-aggregators;

(2) The application of timestamps by the national securities exchange and national securities association participants on all information with respect to quotations for and transactions in NMS stocks that is necessary to generate consolidated market data, including the time that such information was generated as applicable by the national securities exchange or national securities association and the time the national securities exchange or national securities association made such information available to competing consolidators and self-aggregators;

Securities and Exchange Commission

§ 242.900

(3) Assessments of competing consolidator performance, including speed, reliability, and cost of data provision and the provision of an annual report of such assessment to the Commission, and the Commission will make the annual report publicly available on the Commission's website;

(4) The development, maintenance, and publication of a list that identifies the primary listing exchange for each NMS stock; and

(5) The calculation and publication on a monthly basis of consolidated market data gross revenues for NMS stocks as specified by:

(i) Listed on the New York Stock Exchange (NYSE);
(ii) Listed on Nasdaq; and
(iii) Listed on exchanges other than NYSE or Nasdaq.

[86 FR 18811, Apr. 9, 2021]

REGULATION SBSR—REGULATORY REPORTING AND PUBLIC DISSEMINATION OF SECURITY-BASED SWAP INFORMATION

SOURCE: 80 FR 14728, Mar. 19, 2015, unless otherwise noted.

§ 242.900 Definitions.

Terms used in §§ 242.900 through 242.909 that appear in Section 3 of the Exchange Act (15 U.S.C. 78c) have the same meaning as in Section 3 of the Exchange Act and the rules or regulations thereunder. In addition, for purposes of Regulation SBSR (§§ 242.900 through 242.909), the following definitions shall apply:

(a) *Affiliate* means any person that, directly or indirectly, controls, is controlled by, or is under common control with, a person.

(b) *Asset class* means those security-based swaps in a particular broad category, including, but not limited to, credit derivatives and equity derivatives.

(c) [Reserved].

(d) *Branch ID* means the UIC assigned to a branch or other unincorporated office of a participant.

(e) *Broker ID* means the UIC assigned to a person acting as a broker for a participant.

(f) *Business day* means a day, based on U.S. Eastern Time, other than a Saturday, Sunday, or a U.S. federal holiday.

(g) *Clearing transaction* means a security-based swap that has a registered clearing agency as a direct counterparty.

(h) *Control* means, for purposes of §§ 242.900 through 242.909, the possession, direct or indirect, of the power to direct or cause the direction of the management and policies of a person, whether through the ownership of voting securities, by contract, or otherwise. A person is presumed to control another person if the person:

(1) Is a director, general partner or officer exercising executive responsibility (or having similar status or functions);

(2) Directly or indirectly has the right to vote 25 percent or more of a class of voting securities or has the power to sell or direct the sale of 25 percent or more of a class of voting securities; or

(3) In the case of a partnership, has the right to receive, upon dissolution, or has contributed, 25 percent or more of the capital.

(i) *Counterparty* means a person that is a direct counterparty or indirect counterparty of a security-based swap.

(j) *Counterparty ID* means the UIC assigned to a counterparty to a security-based swap.

(k) *Direct counterparty* means a person that is a primary obligor on a security-based swap.

(l) *Direct electronic access* has the same meaning as in § 240.13n–4(a)(5) of this chapter.

(m) *Exchange Act* means the Securities Exchange Act of 1934 (15 U.S.C. 78a et seq.), as amended.

(n) *Execution agent ID* means the UIC assigned to any person other than a broker or trader that facilitates the execution of a security-based swap on behalf of a direct counterparty.

(o) *Foreign branch* has the same meaning as in § 240.3a71–3(a)(1) of this chapter.

(p) *Indirect counterparty* means a guarantor of a direct counterparty's performance of any obligation under a security-based swap such that the direct counterparty on the other side can exercise rights of recourse against the indirect counterparty in connection

§ 242.900

with the security-based swap; for these purposes a direct counterparty has rights of recourse against a guarantor on the other side if the direct counterparty has a conditional or unconditional legally enforceable right, in whole or in part, to receive payments from, or otherwise collect from, the guarantor in connection with the security-based swap.

(q) *Life cycle event* means, with respect to a security-based swap, any event that would result in a change in the information reported to a registered security-based swap data repository under § 242.901(c), (d), or (i), including: An assignment or novation of the security-based swap; a partial or full termination of the security-based swap; a change in the cash flows originally reported; for a security-based swap that is not a clearing transaction, any change to the title or date of any master agreement, collateral agreement, margin agreement, or any other agreement incorporated by reference into the security-based swap contract; or a corporate action affecting a security or securities on which the security-based swap is based (e.g., a merger, dividend, stock split, or bankruptcy). Notwithstanding the above, a life cycle event shall not include the scheduled expiration of the security-based swap, a previously described and anticipated interest rate adjustment (such as a quarterly interest rate adjustment), or other event that does not result in any change to the contractual terms of the security-based swap.

(r) *Non-mandatory report* means any information provided to a registered security-based swap data repository by or on behalf of a counterparty other than as required by §§ 242.900 through 242.909.

(s) *Non-U.S. person* means a person that is not a U.S. person.

(t) *Parent* means a legal person that controls a participant.

(u) *Participant,* with respect to a registered security-based swap data repository, means:

(1) A counterparty, that meets the criteria of § 242.908(b), of a security-based swap that is reported to that registered security-based swap data repository to satisfy an obligation under § 242.901(a);

17 CFR Ch. II (4–1–23 Edition)

(2) A platform that reports a security-based swap to that registered security-based swap data repository to satisfy an obligation under § 242.901(a);

(3) A registered clearing agency that is required to report to that registered security-based swap data repository whether or not it has accepted a security-based swap for clearing pursuant to § 242.901(e)(1)(ii); or

(4) A registered broker-dealer (including a registered security-based swap execution facility) that is required to report a security-based swap to that registered security-based swap data repository by § 242.901(a).

(v) *Platform* means a national securities exchange or security-based swap execution facility that is registered or exempt from registration.

(w) *Platform ID* means the UIC assigned to a platform on which a security-based swap is executed.

(x) *Post-trade processor* means any person that provides affirmation, confirmation, matching, reporting, or clearing services for a security-based swap transaction.

(y) *Pre-enactment security-based swap* means any security-based swap executed before July 21, 2010 (the date of enactment of the Dodd-Frank Act (Pub. L. 111–203, H.R. 4173)), the terms of which had not expired as of that date.

(z) *Price* means the price of a security-based swap transaction, expressed in terms of the commercial conventions used in that asset class.

(aa) *Product* means a group of security-based swap contracts each having the same material economic terms except those relating to price and size.

(bb) *Product ID* means the UIC assigned to a product.

(cc) *Publicly disseminate* means to make available through the Internet or other electronic data feed that is widely accessible and in machine-readable electronic format.

(dd) [Reserved].

(ee) *Registered clearing agency* means a person that is registered with the Commission as a clearing agency pursuant to section 17A of the Exchange Act (15 U.S.C. 78q–1) and any rules or regulations thereunder.

Securities and Exchange Commission § 242.901

(ff) *Registered security-based swap data repository* means a person that is registered with the Commission as a security-based swap data repository pursuant to section 13(n) of the Exchange Act (15 U.S.C. 78m(n)) and any rules or regulations thereunder.

(gg) *Reporting side* means the side of a security-based swap identified by § 242.901(a)(2).

(hh) *Side* means a direct counterparty and any guarantor of that direct counterparty's performance who meets the definition of indirect counterparty in connection with the security-based swap.

(ii) *Time of execution* means the point at which the counterparties to a security-based swap become irrevocably bound under applicable law.

(jj) *Trader ID* means the UIC assigned to a natural person who executes one or more security-based swaps on behalf of a direct counterparty.

(kk) *Trading desk* means, with respect to a counterparty, the smallest discrete unit of organization of the participant that purchases or sells security-based swaps for the account of the participant or an affiliate thereof.

(ll) *Trading desk ID* means the UIC assigned to the trading desk of a participant.

(mm) *Transaction ID* means the UIC assigned to a specific security-based swap transaction.

(nn) *Transitional security-based swap* means a security-based swap executed on or after July 21, 2010, and before the first date on which trade-by-trade reporting of security-based swaps in that asset class to a registered security-based swap data repository is required pursuant to §§ 242.900 through 242.909.

(oo) *Ultimate parent* means a legal person that controls a participant and that itself has no parent.

(pp) *Ultimate parent ID* means the UIC assigned to an ultimate parent of a participant.

(qq) *Unique Identification Code* or *UIC* means a unique identification code assigned to a person, unit of a person, product, or transaction.

(rr) *United States* has the same meaning as in § 240.3a71–3(a)(5) of this chapter.

(ss) *U.S. person* has the same meaning as in § 240.3a71–3(a)(4) of this chapter.

(tt) *Widely accessible,* as used in paragraph (cc) of this section, means widely available to users of the information on a non-fee basis.

[80 FR 14728, Mar. 19, 2015, as amended at 81 FR 53653, Aug. 12, 2016]

§ 242.901 Reporting obligations.

(a) *Assigning reporting duties.* A security-based swap, including a security-based swap that results from the allocation, termination, novation, or assignment of another security-based swap, shall be reported as follows:

(1) *Platform-executed security-based swaps that will be submitted to clearing.* If a security-based swap is executed on a platform and will be submitted to clearing, the platform on which the transaction was executed shall report to a registered security-based swap data repository the counterparty ID or the execution agent ID of each direct counterparty, as applicable, and the information set forth in paragraph (c) of this section (except that, with respect to paragraph (c)(5) of this section, the platform need indicate only if both direct counterparties are registered security-based swap dealers) and paragraphs (d)(9) and (10) of this section.

(2) *All other security-based swaps.* For all security-based swaps other than platform-executed security-based swaps that will be submitted to clearing, the reporting side shall provide the information required by §§ 242.900 through 242.909 to a registered security-based swap data repository. The reporting side shall be determined as follows:

(i) *Clearing transactions.* For a clearing transaction, the reporting side is the registered clearing agency that is a counterparty to the transaction.

(ii) *Security-based swaps other than clearing transactions.* (A) If both sides of the security-based swap include a registered security-based swap dealer, the sides shall select the reporting side.

(B) If only one side of the security-based swap includes a registered security-based swap dealer, that side shall be the reporting side.

(C) If both sides of the security-based swap include a registered major security-based swap participant, the sides shall select the reporting side.

§ 242.901

(D) If one side of the security-based swap includes a registered major security-based swap participant and the other side includes neither a registered security-based swap dealer nor a registered major security-based swap participant, the side including the registered major security-based swap participant shall be the reporting side.

(E) If neither side of the security-based swap includes a registered security-based swap dealer or registered major security-based swap participant:

(*1*) If both sides include a U.S. person, the sides shall select the reporting side.

(*2*) If one side includes a non-U.S. person that falls within § 242.908(b)(5) or a U.S. person and the other side includes a non-U.S. person that falls within § 242.908(b)(5), the sides shall select the reporting side.

(*3*) If one side includes only non-U.S. persons that do not fall within § 242.908(b)(5) and the other side includes a non-U.S. person that falls within § 242.908(b)(5) or a U.S. person, the side including a non-U.S. person that falls within § 242.908(b)(5) or a U.S. person shall be the reporting side.

(*4*) If neither side includes a U.S. person and neither side includes a non-U.S. person that falls within § 242.908(b)(5) but the security-based swap is effected by or through a registered broker-dealer (including a registered security-based swap execution facility), the registered broker-dealer (including a registered security-based swap execution facility) shall report the counterparty ID or the execution agent ID of each direct counterparty, as applicable, and the information set forth in paragraph (c) of this section (except that, with respect to paragraph (c)(5) of this section, the registered broker-dealer (including a registered security-based swap execution facility) need indicate only if both direct counterparties are registered security-based swap dealers) and paragraphs (d)(9) and (10) of this section.

(3) *Notification to registered clearing agency.* A person who, under paragraph (a)(1) or (a)(2)(ii) of this section, has a duty to report a security-based swap that has been submitted to clearing at a registered clearing agency shall promptly provide that registered clearing agency with the transaction ID of the submitted security-based swap and the identity of the registered security-based swap data repository to which the transaction will be reported or has been reported.

(b) *Alternate recipient of security-based swap information.* If there is no registered security-based swap data repository that will accept the report required by § 242.901(a), the person required to make such report shall instead provide the required information to the Commission.

(c) *Primary trade information.* The reporting side shall report the following information within the timeframe specified in paragraph (j) of this section:

(1) The product ID, if available. If the security-based swap has no product ID, or if the product ID does not include the following information, the reporting side shall report:

(i) Information that identifies the security-based swap, including the asset class of the security-based swap and the specific underlying reference asset(s), reference issuer(s), or reference index;

(ii) The effective date;

(iii) The scheduled termination date;

(iv) The terms of any standardized fixed or floating rate payments, and the frequency of any such payments; and

(v) If the security-based swap is customized to the extent that the information provided in paragraphs (c)(1)(i) through (iv) of this section does not provide all of the material information necessary to identify such customized security-based swap or does not contain the data elements necessary to calculate the price, a flag to that effect;

(2) The date and time, to the second, of execution, expressed using Coordinated Universal Time (UTC);

(3) The price, including the currency in which the price is expressed and the amount(s) and currenc(ies) of any upfront payments;

(4) The notional amount(s) and the currenc(ies) in which the notional amount(s) is expressed;

(5) If both sides of the security-based swap include a registered security-

Securities and Exchange Commission § 242.901

based swap dealer, an indication to that effect;

(6) Whether the direct counterparties intend that the security-based swap will be submitted to clearing; and

(7) If applicable, any flags pertaining to the transaction that are specified in the policies and procedures of the registered security-based swap data repository to which the transaction will be reported.

(d) *Secondary trade information.* In addition to the information required under paragraph (c) of this section, for each security-based swap for which it is the reporting side, the reporting side shall report the following information within the timeframe specified in paragraph (j) of this section:

(1) The counterparty ID or the execution agent ID of each counterparty, as applicable;

(2) As applicable, the branch ID, broker ID, execution agent ID, trader ID, and trading desk ID of the direct counterparty on the reporting side;

(3) To the extent not provided pursuant to paragraph (c)(1) of this section, the terms of any fixed or floating rate payments, or otherwise customized or non-standard payment streams, including the frequency and contingencies of any such payments;

(4) For a security-based swap that is not a clearing transaction and that will not be allocated after execution, the title and date of any master agreement, collateral agreement, margin agreement, or any other agreement incorporated by reference into the security-based swap contract;

(5) To the extent not provided pursuant to paragraph (c) of this section or other provisions of this paragraph (d), any additional data elements included in the agreement between the counterparties that are necessary for a person to determine the market value of the transaction;

(6) If applicable, and to the extent not provided pursuant to paragraph (c) of this section, the name of the clearing agency to which the security-based swap will be submitted for clearing;

(7) If the direct counterparties do not intend to submit the security-based swap to clearing, whether they have invoked the exception in Section 3C(g) of the Exchange Act (15 U.S.C. 78c–3(g));

(8) To the extent not provided pursuant to the other provisions of this paragraph (d), if the direct counterparties do not submit the security-based swap to clearing, a description of the settlement terms, including whether the security-based swap is cash-settled or physically settled, and the method for determining the settlement value;

(9) The platform ID, if applicable, or if a registered broker-dealer (including a registered security-based swap execution facility) is required to report the security-based swap by § 242.901(a)(2)(ii)(E)(*4*), the broker ID of that registered broker-dealer (including a registered security-based swap execution facility); and

(10) If the security-based swap arises from the allocation, termination, novation, or assignment of one or more existing security-based swaps, the transaction ID of the allocated, terminated, assigned, or novated security-based swap(s), except in the case of a clearing transaction that results from the netting or compression of other clearing transactions.

(e) *Reporting of life cycle events.* (1)(i) *Generally.* A life cycle event, and any adjustment due to a life cycle event, that results in a change to information previously reported pursuant to paragraph (c), (d), or (i) of this section shall be reported by the reporting side, except that the reporting side shall not report whether or not a security-based swap has been accepted for clearing.

(ii) *Acceptance for clearing.* A registered clearing agency shall report whether or not it has accepted a security-based swap for clearing.

(2) All reports of life cycle events and adjustments due to life cycle events shall, within the timeframe specified in paragraph (j) of this section, be reported to the entity to which the original security-based swap transaction will be reported or has been reported and shall include the transaction ID of the original transaction.

(f) *Time stamping incoming information.* A registered security-based swap data repository shall time stamp, to the second, its receipt of any information submitted to it pursuant to paragraph (c), (d), (e), or (i) of this section.

§ 242.901

(g) *Assigning transaction ID.* A registered security-based swap data repository shall assign a transaction ID to each security-based swap, or establish or endorse a methodology for transaction IDs to be assigned by third parties.

(h) *Format of reported information.* A person having a duty to report shall electronically transmit the information required under this section in a format required by the registered security-based swap data repository to which it reports.

(i) *Reporting of pre-enactment and transitional security-based swaps.* With respect to any pre-enactment security-based swap or transitional security-based swap in a particular asset class, and to the extent that information about such transaction is available, the reporting side shall report all of the information required by paragraphs (c) and (d) of this section to a registered security-based swap data repository that accepts security-based swaps in that asset class and indicate whether the security-based swap was open as of the date of such report.

(j) *Interim timeframe for reporting.* The reporting timeframe for paragraphs (c) and (d) of this section shall be 24 hours after the time of execution (or acceptance for clearing in the case of a security-based swap that is subject to regulatory reporting and public dissemination solely by operation of § 242.908(a)(1)(ii)), or, if 24 hours after the time of execution or acceptance, as applicable, would fall on a day that is not a business day, by the same time on the next day that is a business day. The reporting timeframe for paragraph (e) of this section shall be 24 hours after the occurrence of the life cycle event or the adjustment due to the life cycle event.

APPENDIX TO 17 CFR 242.901 REPORTS REGARDING THE ESTABLISHMENT OF BLOCK THRESHOLDS AND REPORTING DELAYS FOR REGULATORY REPORTING OF SECURITY-BASED SWAP TRANSACTION DATA

This appendix sets forth guidelines applicable to reports that the Commission has directed its staff to make in connection with the determination of block thresholds and reporting delays for security-based swap transaction data. The Commission intends to use these reports to inform its specification of the criteria for determining what constitutes a large notional security-based swap transaction (block trade) for particular markets and contracts; and the appropriate time delay for reporting large notional security-based swap transactions (block trades) to the public in order to implement regulatory requirements under Section 13 of the Act (15 U.S.C. 78m). In producing these reports, the staff shall consider security-based swap data collected by the Commission pursuant to other Title VII rules, as well as any other applicable information as the staff may determine to be appropriate for its analysis.

(a) *Report topics.* As appropriate, based on the availability of data and information, the reports should address the following topics for each asset class:

(1) *Price impact.* In connection with the Commission's obligation to specify criteria for determining what constitutes a block trade and the appropriate reporting delay for block trades, the report generally should assess the effect of notional amount and observed reporting delay on price impact of trades in the security-based swap market.

(2) *Hedging.* In connection with the Commission's obligation to specify criteria for determining what constitutes a block trade and the appropriate reporting delay for block trades, the report generally should consider potential relationships between observed reporting delays and the incidence and cost of hedging large trades in the security-based swap market, and whether these relationships differ for interdealer trades and dealer to customer trades.

(3) *Price efficiency.* In connection with the Commission's obligation to specify criteria for determining what constitutes a block trade and the appropriate reporting delay for block trades, the report generally should assess the relationship between reporting delays and the speed with which transaction information is impounded into market prices, estimating this relationship for trades of different notional amounts.

(4) *Other topics.* Any other analysis of security-based swap data and information, such as security-based swap market liquidity and price volatility, that the Commission or the staff deem relevant to the specification of:

(i) The criteria for determining what constitutes a large notional security-based swap transaction (block trade) for particular markets and contracts; and

(ii) The appropriate time delay for reporting large notional security-based swap transactions (block trades).

(b) *Timing of reports.* Each report shall be complete no later than two years following the initiation of public dissemination of security-based swap transaction data by the first registered SDR in that asset class.

(c) *Public comment on the report.* Following completion of the report, the report shall be

Securities and Exchange Commission § 242.903

published in the FEDERAL REGISTER for public comment.

[80 FR 14728, Mar. 19, 2015, as amended at 81 FR 53653, Aug. 12, 2016]

§ 242.902 **Public dissemination of transaction reports.**

(a) *General.* Except as provided in paragraph (c) of this section, a registered security-based swap data repository shall publicly disseminate a transaction report of a security-based swap, or a life cycle event or adjustment due to a life cycle event, immediately upon receipt of information about the security-based swap, or upon re-opening following a period when the registered security-based swap data repository was closed. The transaction report shall consist of all the information reported pursuant to § 242.901(c), plus any condition flags contemplated by the registered security-based swap data repository's policies and procedures that are required by § 242.907.

(b) [Reserved].

(c) *Non-disseminated information.* A registered security-based swap data repository shall not disseminate:

(1) The identity of any counterparty to a security-based swap;

(2) With respect to a security-based swap that is not cleared at a registered clearing agency and that is reported to the registered security-based swap data repository, any information disclosing the business transactions and market positions of any person;

(3) Any information regarding a security-based swap reported pursuant to § 242.901(i);

(4) Any non-mandatory report;

(5) Any information regarding a security-based swap that is required to be reported pursuant to §§ 242.901 and 242.908(a)(1) but is not required to be publicly disseminated pursuant to § 242.908(a)(2);

(6) Any information regarding a clearing transaction that arises from the acceptance of a security-based swap for clearing by a registered clearing agency or that results from netting other clearing transactions;

(7) Any information regarding the allocation of a security-based swap; or

(8) Any information regarding a security-based swap that has been rejected from clearing or rejected by a prime broker if the original transaction report has not yet been publicly disseminated.

(d) *Temporary restriction on other market data sources.* No person shall make available to one or more persons (other than a counterparty or a post-trade processor) transaction information relating to a security-based swap before the primary trade information about the security-based swap is sent to a registered security-based swap data repository.

[80 FR 14728, Mar. 19, 2015, as amended at 81 FR 53654, Aug. 12, 2016]

§ 242.903 **Coded information.**

(a) If an internationally recognized standards-setting system that imposes fees and usage restrictions on persons that obtain UICs for their own usage that are fair and reasonable and not unreasonably discriminatory and that meets the criteria of paragraph (b) of this section is recognized by the Commission and has assigned a UIC to a person, unit of a person, or product (or has endorsed a methodology for assigning transaction IDs), the registered security-based swap data repository shall employ that UIC (or methodology for assigning transaction IDs). If no such system has been recognized by the Commission, or a recognized system has not assigned a UIC to a particular person, unit of a person, or product (or has not endorsed a methodology for assigning transaction IDs), the registered security-based swap data repository shall assign a UIC to that person, unit of person, or product using its own methodology (or endorse a methodology for assigning transaction IDs). If the Commission has recognized such a system that assigns UICs to persons, each participant of a registered security-based swap data repository shall obtain a UIC from or through that system for identifying itself, and each participant that acts as a guarantor of a direct counterparty's performance of any obligation under a security-based swap that is subject to § 242.908(a) shall, if the direct counterparty has not already done so, obtain a UIC for identifying the direct counterparty from or through that system, if that system

§ 242.904

permits third-party registration without a requirement to obtain prior permission of the direct counterparty.

(b) A registered security-based swap data repository may permit information to be reported pursuant to § 242.901, and may publicly disseminate that information pursuant to § 242.902, using codes in place of certain data elements, provided that the information necessary to interpret such codes is widely available to users of the information on a non-fee basis.

§ 242.904 Operating hours of registered security-based swap data repositories.

A registered security-based swap data repository shall have systems in place to continuously receive and disseminate information regarding security-based swaps pursuant to §§ 242.900 through 242.909, subject to the following exceptions:

(a) A registered security-based swap data repository may establish normal closing hours during periods when, in its estimation, the U.S. market and major foreign markets are inactive. A registered security-based swap data repository shall provide reasonable advance notice to participants and to the public of its normal closing hours.

(b) A registered security-based swap data repository may declare, on an *ad hoc* basis, special closing hours to perform system maintenance that cannot wait until normal closing hours. A registered security-based swap data repository shall, to the extent reasonably possible under the circumstances, avoid scheduling special closing hours during periods when, in its estimation, the U.S. market and major foreign markets are most active; and provide reasonable advance notice of its special closing hours to participants and to the public.

(c) During normal closing hours, and to the extent reasonably practicable during special closing hours, a registered security-based swap data repository shall have the capability to receive and hold in queue information regarding security-based swaps that has been reported pursuant to §§ 242.900 through 242.909.

(d) When a registered security-based swap data repository re-opens following normal closing hours or special closing hours, it shall disseminate transaction reports of security-based swaps held in queue, in accordance with the requirements of § 242.902.

(e) If a registered security-based swap data repository could not receive and hold in queue transaction information that was required to be reported pursuant to §§ 242.900 through 242.909, it must immediately upon re-opening send a message to all participants that it has resumed normal operations. Thereafter, any participant that had an obligation to report information to the registered security-based swap data repository pursuant to §§ 242.900 through 242.909, but could not do so because of the registered security-based swap data repository's inability to receive and hold in queue data, must promptly report the information to the registered security-based swap data repository.

§ 242.905 Correction of errors in security-based swap information.

(a) *Duty to correct.* Any counterparty or other person having a duty to report a security-based swap that discovers an error in information previously reported pursuant to §§ 242.900 through 242.909 shall correct such error in accordance with the following procedures:

(1) If a person that was not the reporting side for a security-based swap transaction discovers an error in the information reported with respect to such security-based swap, that person shall promptly notify the person having the duty to report the security-based swap of the error; and

(2) If the person having the duty to report a security-based swap transaction discovers an error in the information reported with respect to a security-based swap, or receives notification from a counterparty of an error, such person shall promptly submit to the entity to which the security-based swap was originally reported an amended report pertaining to the original transaction report. If the person having the duty to report reported the initial transaction to a registered security-based swap data repository, such person shall submit an amended report to the registered security-based swap data repository in a manner consistent

Securities and Exchange Commission

with the policies and procedures contemplated by § 242.907(a)(3).

(b) *Duty of security-based swap data repository to correct.* A registered security-based swap data repository shall:

(1) Upon discovery of an error or receipt of a notice of an error, verify the accuracy of the terms of the security-based swap and, following such verification, promptly correct the erroneous information regarding such security-based swap contained in its system; and

(2) If such erroneous information relates to a security-based swap that the registered security-based swap data repository previously disseminated and falls into any of the categories of information enumerated in § 242.901(c), publicly disseminate a corrected transaction report of the security-based swap promptly following verification of the trade by the counterparties to the security-based swap, with an indication that the report relates to a previously disseminated transaction.

[80 FR 14728, Mar. 19, 2015, as amended at 81 FR 53654, Aug. 12, 2016]

§ 242.906 Other duties of participants.

(a) *Identifying missing UIC information.* A registered security-based swap data repository shall identify any security-based swap reported to it for which the registered security-based swap data repository does not have the counterparty ID and (if applicable) the broker ID, branch ID, execution agent ID, trading desk ID, and trader ID of each direct counterparty. Once a day, the registered security-based swap data repository shall send a report to each participant of the registered security-based swap data repository or, if applicable, an execution agent, identifying, for each security-based swap to which that participant is a counterparty, the security-based swap(s) for which the registered security-based swap data repository lacks counterparty ID and (if applicable) broker ID, branch ID, execution agent ID, trading desk ID, and trader ID. A participant of a registered security-based swap data repository that receives such a report shall provide the missing information with respect to its side of each security-based swap referenced in the report to the registered security-based swap data repository within 24 hours.

(b) *Duty to provide ultimate parent and affiliate information.* Each participant of a registered security-based swap data repository that is not a platform, a registered clearing agency, an externally managed investment vehicle, or a registered broker-dealer (including a registered security-based swap execution facility) that becomes a participant solely as a result of making a report to satisfy an obligation under § 242.901(a)(2)(ii)(E)(*4*) shall provide to the registered security-based swap data repository information sufficient to identify its ultimate parent(s) and any affiliate(s) of the participant that also are participants of the registered security-based swap data repository, using ultimate parent IDs and counterparty IDs. Any such participant shall promptly notify the registered security-based swap data repository of any changes to that information.

(c) *Policies and procedures to support reporting compliance.* Each participant of a registered security-based swap data repository that is a registered security-based swap dealer, registered major security-based swap participant, registered clearing agency, platform, or registered broker-dealer (including a registered security-based swap execution facility) that becomes a participant solely as a result of making a report to satisfy an obligation under § 242.901(a)(2)(ii)(E)(*4*) shall establish, maintain, and enforce written policies and procedures that are reasonably designed to ensure that it complies with any obligations to report information to a registered security-based swap data repository in a manner consistent with §§ 242.900 through 242.909. Each such participant shall review and update its policies and procedures at least annually.

[81 FR 53654, Aug. 12, 2016]

§ 242.907 Policies and procedures of registered security-based swap data repositories.

(a) *General policies and procedures.* With respect to the receipt, reporting, and dissemination of data pursuant to §§ 242.900 through 242.909, a registered security-based swap data repository

§ 242.908

shall establish and maintain written policies and procedures:

(1) That enumerate the specific data elements of a security-based swap that must be reported, which shall include, at a minimum, the data elements specified in § 242.901(c) and (d);

(2) That specify one or more acceptable data formats (each of which must be an open-source structured data format that is widely used by participants), connectivity requirements, and other protocols for submitting information;

(3) For specifying procedures for reporting life cycle events and corrections to previously submitted information, making corresponding updates or corrections to transaction records, and applying an appropriate flag to the transaction report to indicate that the report is an error correction required to be disseminated by § 242.905(b)(2), or is a life cycle event, or any adjustment due to a life cycle event, required to be disseminated by § 242.902(a);

(4) For:

(i) Identifying characteristic(s) of a security-based swap, or circumstances associated with the execution or reporting of the security-based swap, that could, in the fair and reasonable estimation of the registered security-based swap data repository, cause a person without knowledge of these characteristic(s) or circumstance(s), to receive a distorted view of the market;

(ii) Establishing flags to denote such characteristic(s) or circumstance(s);

(iii) Directing participants that report security-based swaps to apply such flags, as appropriate, in their reports to the registered security-based swap data repository; and

(iv) Applying such flags:

(A) To disseminated reports to help to prevent a distorted view of the market; or

(B) In the case of a transaction referenced in § 242.902(c), to suppress the report from public dissemination entirely, as appropriate;

(5) For assigning UICs in a manner consistent with § 242.903; and

(6) For periodically obtaining from each participant other than a platform, registered clearing agency, externally managed investment vehicle, or registered broker-dealer (including a registered security-based swap execution facility) that becomes a participant solely as a result of making a report to satisfy an obligation under § 242.901(a)(2)(ii)(E)(4) information that identifies the participant's ultimate parent(s) and any participant(s) with which the participant is affiliated, using ultimate parent IDs and counterparty IDs.

(b) [Reserved].

(c) *Public availability of policies and procedures.* A registered security-based swap data repository shall make the policies and procedures required by §§ 242.900 through 242.909 publicly available on its Web site.

(d) *Updating of policies and procedures.* A registered security-based swap data repository shall review, and update as necessary, the policies and procedures required by §§ 242.900 through 242.909 at least annually. Such policies and procedures shall indicate the date on which they were last reviewed.

(e) A registered security-based swap data repository shall provide to the Commission, upon request, information or reports related to the timeliness, accuracy, and completeness of data reported to it pursuant to §§ 242.900 through 242.909 and the registered security-based swap data repository's policies and procedures thereunder.

[80 FR 14728, Mar. 19, 2015, as amended at 81 FR 53655, Aug. 12, 2016]

§ 242.908 Cross-border matters.

(a) *Application of Regulation SBSR to cross-border transactions.* (1) A security-based swap shall be subject to regulatory reporting and public dissemination if:

(i) There is a direct or indirect counterparty that is a U.S. person on either or both sides of the transaction;

(ii) The security-based swap is accepted for clearing by a clearing agency having its principal place of business in the United States;

(iii) The security-based swap is executed on a platform having its principal place of business in the United States;

(iv) The security-based swap is effected by or through a registered broker-dealer (including a registered security-based swap execution facility); or

Securities and Exchange Commission § 242.908

(v) The transaction is connected with a non-U.S. person's security-based swap dealing activity and is arranged, negotiated, or executed by personnel of such non-U.S. person located in a U.S. branch or office, or by personnel of an agent of such non-U.S. person located in a U.S. branch or office.

(2) A security-based swap that is not included within paragraph (a)(1) of this section shall be subject to regulatory reporting but not public dissemination if there is a direct or indirect counterparty on either or both sides of the transaction that is a registered security-based swap dealer or a registered major security-based swap participant.

(b) *Limitation on obligations.* Notwithstanding any other provision of §§ 242.900 through 242.909, a person shall not incur any obligation under §§ 242.900 through 242.909 unless it is:

(1) A U.S. person;

(2) A registered security-based swap dealer or registered major security-based swap participant;

(3) A platform;

(4) A registered clearing agency; or

(5) A non-U.S. person that, in connection with such person's security-based swap dealing activity, arranged, negotiated, or executed the security-based swap using its personnel located in a U.S. branch or office, or using personnel of an agent located in a U.S. branch or office.

(c) *Substituted compliance*—(1) *General.* Compliance with the regulatory reporting and public dissemination requirements in sections 13(m) and 13A of the Act (15 U.S.C. 78m(m) and 78m–1), and the rules and regulations thereunder, may be satisfied by compliance with the rules of a foreign jurisdiction that is the subject of a Commission order described in paragraph (c)(2) of this section, provided that at least one of the direct counterparties to the security-based swap is either a non-U.S. person or a foreign branch.

(2) *Procedure.* (i) The Commission may, conditionally or unconditionally, by order, make a substituted compliance determination regarding regulatory reporting and public dissemination of security-based swaps with respect to a foreign jurisdiction if that jurisdiction's requirements for the regulatory reporting and public dissemination of security-based swaps are comparable to otherwise applicable requirements. The Commission may, conditionally or unconditionally, by order, make a substituted compliance determination regarding regulatory reporting of security-based swaps that are subject to § 242.908(a)(2) with respect to a foreign jurisdiction if that jurisdiction's requirements for the regulatory reporting of security-based swaps are comparable to otherwise applicable requirements.

(ii) A party that potentially would comply with requirements under §§ 242.900 through 242.909 pursuant to a substituted compliance order or any foreign financial regulatory authority or authorities supervising such a person's security-based swap activities may file an application, pursuant to the procedures set forth in § 240.0–13 of this chapter, requesting that the Commission make a substituted compliance determination regarding regulatory reporting and public dissemination with respect to a foreign jurisdiction the rules of which also would require reporting and public dissemination of those security-based swaps.

(iii) In making such a substituted compliance determination, the Commission shall take into account such factors as the Commission determines are appropriate, such as the scope and objectives of the relevant foreign regulatory requirements, as well as the effectiveness of the supervisory compliance program administered, and the enforcement authority exercised, by the foreign financial regulatory authority to support oversight of its regulatory reporting and public dissemination system for security-based swaps. The Commission shall not make such a substituted compliance determination unless it finds that:

(A) The data elements that are required to be reported pursuant to the rules of the foreign jurisdiction are comparable to those required to be reported pursuant to § 242.901;

(B) The rules of the foreign jurisdiction require the security-based swap to be reported and publicly disseminated in a manner and a timeframe comparable to those required by §§ 242.900

§ 242.909

through 242.909 (or, in the case of transactions that are subject to § 242.908(a)(2) but not to § 242.908(a)(1), the rules of the foreign jurisdiction require the security-based swap to be reported in a manner and a timeframe comparable to those required by §§ 242.900 through 242.909);

(C) The Commission has direct electronic access to the security-based swap data held by a trade repository or foreign regulatory authority to which security-based swaps are reported pursuant to the rules of that foreign jurisdiction; and

(D) Any trade repository or foreign regulatory authority in the foreign jurisdiction that receives and maintains required transaction reports of security-based swaps pursuant to the laws of that foreign jurisdiction is subject to requirements regarding data collection and maintenance; systems capacity, integrity, resiliency, availability, and security; and recordkeeping that are comparable to the requirements imposed on security-based swap data repositories by the Commission's rules and regulations.

(iv) Before issuing a substituted compliance order pursuant to this section, the Commission shall have entered into memoranda of understanding and/or other arrangements with the relevant foreign financial regulatory authority or authorities under such foreign financial regulatory system addressing supervisory and enforcement cooperation and other matters arising under the substituted compliance determination.

(v) The Commission may, on its own initiative, modify or withdraw such order at any time, after appropriate notice and opportunity for comment.

[80 FR 14728, Mar. 19, 2015, as amended at 81 FR 53655, Aug. 12, 2016]

§ 242.909 Registration of security-based swap data repository as a securities information processor.

A registered security-based swap data repository shall also register with the Commission as a securities information processor on Form SDR (§ 249.1500 of this chapter).

Regulation SCI—Systems Compliance and Integrity

SOURCE: 79 FR 72436, Dec. 5, 2014, unless otherwise noted.

§ 242.1000 Definitions.

For purposes of Regulation SCI (§§ 242.1000 through 242.1007), the following definitions shall apply:

Critical SCI systems means any SCI systems of, or operated by or on behalf of, an SCI entity that:

(1) Directly support functionality relating to:

(i) Clearance and settlement systems of clearing agencies;

(ii) Openings, reopenings, and closings on the primary listing market;

(iii) Trading halts;

(iv) Initial public offerings;

(v) The provision of market data by a plan processor; or

(vi) Exclusively-listed securities; or

(2) Provide functionality to the securities markets for which the availability of alternatives is significantly limited or nonexistent and without which there would be a material impact on fair and orderly markets.

Electronic signature has the meaning set forth in § 240.19b-4(j) of this chapter.

Exempt clearing agency subject to ARP means an entity that has received from the Commission an exemption from registration as a clearing agency under Section 17A of the Act, and whose exemption contains conditions that relate to the Commission's Automation Review Policies (ARP), or any Commission regulation that supersedes or replaces such policies.

Indirect SCI systems means any systems of, or operated by or on behalf of, an SCI entity that, if breached, would be reasonably likely to pose a security threat to SCI systems.

Major SCI event means an SCI event that has had, or the SCI entity reasonably estimates would have:

(1) Any impact on a critical SCI system; or

(2) A significant impact on the SCI entity's operations or on market participants.

Plan processor has the meaning set forth in § 242.600(b)(67).

Responsible SCI personnel means, for a particular SCI system or indirect SCI

Securities and Exchange Commission

§ 242.1000

system impacted by an SCI event, such senior manager(s) of the SCI entity having responsibility for such system, and their designee(s).

SCI alternative trading system or *SCI ATS* means an alternative trading system, as defined in § 242.300(a), which during at least four of the preceding six calendar months:

(1) Had with respect to NMS stocks:

(i) Five percent (5%) or more in any single NMS stock, and one-quarter percent (0.25%) or more in all NMS stocks, of the average daily dollar volume reported by applicable transaction reporting plans; or

(ii) One percent (1%) or more in all NMS stocks of the average daily dollar volume reported by applicable transaction reporting plans; or

(2) Had with respect to equity securities that are not NMS stocks and for which transactions are reported to a self-regulatory organization, five percent (5%) or more of the average daily dollar volume as calculated by the self-regulatory organization to which such transactions are reported;

(3) Provided, however, that such SCI ATS shall not be required to comply with the requirements of Regulation SCI until six months after satisfying any of paragraphs (1) or (2) of this definition, as applicable, for the first time.

SCI competing consolidator means:

(1) Any competing consolidator, as defined in § 242.600, which, during at least four of the preceding six calendar months, accounted for five percent (5%) or more of consolidated market data gross revenue paid to the effective national market system plan or plans required under § 242.603(b), for NMS stocks:

(i) Listed on the New York Stock Exchange LLC;

(ii) Listed on The Nasdaq Stock Market LLC; or

(iii) Listed on exchanges other than the New York Stock Exchange LLC or The Nasdaq Stock Market LLC, as reported by such plan or plans pursuant to the terms thereof.

(2) Provided, however, that such SCI competing consolidator shall not be required to comply with the requirements of this section and §§ 242.1001 through 242.1007 (Regulation SCI) until six months after satisfying any of paragraph (1) of this definition, as applicable, for the first time; and

(3) Provided, however, that such SCI competing consolidator shall not be required to comply with the requirements of Regulation SCI prior to one year after the compliance date for § 242.614(d)(3).

SCI entity means an SCI self-regulatory organization, SCI alternative trading system, plan processor, exempt clearing agency subject to ARP, or SCI competing consolidator.

SCI event means an event at an SCI entity that constitutes:

(1) A systems disruption;

(2) A systems compliance issue; or

(3) A systems intrusion.

SCI review means a review, following established procedures and standards, that is performed by objective personnel having appropriate experience to conduct reviews of SCI systems and indirect SCI systems, and which review contains:

(1) A risk assessment with respect to such systems of an SCI entity; and

(2) An assessment of internal control design and effectiveness of its SCI systems and indirect SCI systems to include logical and physical security controls, development processes, and information technology governance, consistent with industry standards.

SCI self-regulatory organization or *SCI SRO* means any national securities exchange, registered securities association, or registered clearing agency, or the Municipal Securities Rulemaking Board; *provided however,* that for purposes of this section, the term SCI self-regulatory organization shall not include an exchange that is notice registered with the Commission pursuant to 15 U.S.C. 78f(g) or a limited purpose national securities association registered with the Commission pursuant to 15 U.S.C. 78o-3(k).

SCI systems means all computer, network, electronic, technical, automated, or similar systems of, or operated by or on behalf of, an SCI entity that, with respect to securities, directly support trading, clearance and settlement, order routing, market data, market regulation, or market surveillance.

Senior management means, for purposes of Rule 1003(b), an SCI entity's

§ 242.1001

Chief Executive Officer, Chief Technology Officer, Chief Information Officer, General Counsel, and Chief Compliance Officer, or the equivalent of such employees or officers of an SCI entity.

Systems compliance issue means an event at an SCI entity that has caused any SCI system of such entity to operate in a manner that does not comply with the Act and the rules and regulations thereunder or the entity's rules or governing documents, as applicable.

Systems disruption means an event in an SCI entity's SCI systems that disrupts, or significantly degrades, the normal operation of an SCI system.

Systems intrusion means any unauthorized entry into the SCI systems or indirect SCI systems of an SCI entity.

[79 FR 72436, Dec. 5, 2014, as amended at 80 FR 81454, Dec. 30, 2015; 83 FR 58429, Nov. 19, 2018; 86 FR 18814, Apr. 9, 2021]

§ 242.1001 Obligations related to policies and procedures of SCI entities.

(a) *Capacity, integrity, resiliency, availability, and security.* (1) Each SCI entity shall establish, maintain, and enforce written policies and procedures reasonably designed to ensure that its SCI systems and, for purposes of security standards, indirect SCI systems, have levels of capacity, integrity, resiliency, availability, and security, adequate to maintain the SCI entity's operational capability and promote the maintenance of fair and orderly markets.

(2) Policies and procedures required by paragraph (a)(1) of this section shall include, at a minimum:

(i) The establishment of reasonable current and future technological infrastructure capacity planning estimates;

(ii) Periodic capacity stress tests of such systems to determine their ability to process transactions in an accurate, timely, and efficient manner;

(iii) A program to review and keep current systems development and testing methodology for such systems;

(iv) Regular reviews and testing, as applicable, of such systems, including backup systems, to identify vulnerabilities pertaining to internal and external threats, physical hazards, and natural or manmade disasters;

(v) Business continuity and disaster recovery plans that include maintaining backup and recovery capabilities sufficiently resilient and geographically diverse and that are reasonably designed to achieve next business day resumption of trading and two-hour resumption of critical SCI systems following a wide-scale disruption;

(vi) Standards that result in such systems being designed, developed, tested, maintained, operated, and surveilled in a manner that facilitates the successful collection, processing, and dissemination of market data; and

(vii) Monitoring of such systems to identify potential SCI events.

(3) Each SCI entity shall periodically review the effectiveness of the policies and procedures required by this paragraph (a), and take prompt action to remedy deficiencies in such policies and procedures.

(4) For purposes of this paragraph (a), such policies and procedures shall be deemed to be reasonably designed if they are consistent with current SCI industry standards, which shall be comprised of information technology practices that are widely available to information technology professionals in the financial sector and issued by an authoritative body that is a U.S. governmental entity or agency, association of U.S. governmental entities or agencies, or widely recognized organization. Compliance with such current SCI industry standards, however, shall not be the exclusive means to comply with the requirements of this paragraph (a).

(b) *Systems compliance.* (1) Each SCI entity shall establish, maintain, and enforce written policies and procedures reasonably designed to ensure that its SCI systems operate in a manner that complies with the Act and the rules and regulations thereunder and the entity's rules and governing documents, as applicable.

(2) Policies and procedures required by paragraph (b)(1) of this section shall include, at a minimum:

(i) Testing of all SCI systems and any changes to SCI systems prior to implementation;

(ii) A system of internal controls over changes to SCI systems;

(iii) A plan for assessments of the functionality of SCI systems designed to detect systems compliance issues,

Securities and Exchange Commission §242.1002

including by responsible SCI personnel and by personnel familiar with applicable provisions of the Act and the rules and regulations thereunder and the SCI entity's rules and governing documents; and

(iv) A plan of coordination and communication between regulatory and other personnel of the SCI entity, including by responsible SCI personnel, regarding SCI systems design, changes, testing, and controls designed to detect and prevent systems compliance issues.

(3) Each SCI entity shall periodically review the effectiveness of the policies and procedures required by this paragraph (b), and take prompt action to remedy deficiencies in such policies and procedures.

(4) *Safe harbor from liability for individuals.* Personnel of an SCI entity shall be deemed not to have aided, abetted, counseled, commanded, caused, induced, or procured the violation by an SCI entity of this paragraph (b) if the person:

(i) Has reasonably discharged the duties and obligations incumbent upon such person by the SCI entity's policies and procedures; and

(ii) Was without reasonable cause to believe that the policies and procedures relating to an SCI system for which such person was responsible, or had supervisory responsibility, were not established, maintained, or enforced in accordance with this paragraph (b) in any material respect.

(c) *Responsible SCI personnel.* (1) Each SCI entity shall establish, maintain, and enforce reasonably designed written policies and procedures that include the criteria for identifying responsible SCI personnel, the designation and documentation of responsible SCI personnel, and escalation procedures to quickly inform responsible SCI personnel of potential SCI events.

(2) Each SCI entity shall periodically review the effectiveness of the policies and procedures required by paragraph (c)(1) of this section, and take prompt action to remedy deficiencies in such policies and procedures.

§242.1002 Obligations related to SCI events.

(a) *Corrective action.* Upon any responsible SCI personnel having a reasonable basis to conclude that an SCI event has occurred, each SCI entity shall begin to take appropriate corrective action which shall include, at a minimum, mitigating potential harm to investors and market integrity resulting from the SCI event and devoting adequate resources to remedy the SCI event as soon as reasonably practicable.

(b) *Commission notification and recordkeeping of SCI events.* Each SCI entity shall:

(1) Upon any responsible SCI personnel having a reasonable basis to conclude that an SCI event has occurred, notify the Commission of such SCI event immediately;

(2) Within 24 hours of any responsible SCI personnel having a reasonable basis to conclude that the SCI event has occurred, submit a written notification pertaining to such SCI event to the Commission, which shall be made on a good faith, best efforts basis and include:

(i) A description of the SCI event, including the system(s) affected; and

(ii) To the extent available as of the time of the notification: The SCI entity's current assessment of the types and number of market participants potentially affected by the SCI event; the potential impact of the SCI event on the market; a description of the steps the SCI entity has taken, is taking, or plans to take, with respect to the SCI event; the time the SCI event was resolved or timeframe within which the SCI event is expected to be resolved; and any other pertinent information known by the SCI entity about the SCI event;

(3) Until such time as the SCI event is resolved and the SCI entity's investigation of the SCI event is closed, provide updates pertaining to such SCI event to the Commission on a regular basis, or at such frequency as reasonably requested by a representative of the Commission, to correct any materially incorrect information previously provided, or when new material information is discovered, including but not limited to, any of the information listed in paragraph (b)(2)(ii) of this section;

(4)(i)(A) If an SCI event is resolved and the SCI entity's investigation of

§ 242.1002

the SCI event is closed within 30 calendar days of the occurrence of the SCI event, then within five business days after the resolution of the SCI event and closure of the investigation regarding the SCI event, submit a final written notification pertaining to such SCI event to the Commission containing the information required in paragraph (b)(4)(ii) of this section.

(B)(*1*) If an SCI event is not resolved or the SCI entity's investigation of the SCI event is not closed within 30 calendar days of the occurrence of the SCI event, then submit an interim written notification pertaining to such SCI event to the Commission within 30 calendar days after the occurrence of the SCI event containing the information required in paragraph (b)(4)(ii) of this section, to the extent known at the time.

(*2*) Within five business days after the resolution of such SCI event and closure of the investigation regarding such SCI event, submit a final written notification pertaining to such SCI event to the Commission containing the information required in paragraph (b)(4)(ii) of this section.

(ii) Written notifications required by paragraph (b)(4)(i) of this section shall include:

(A) A detailed description of: The SCI entity's assessment of the types and number of market participants affected by the SCI event; the SCI entity's assessment of the impact of the SCI event on the market; the steps the SCI entity has taken, is taking, or plans to take, with respect to the SCI event; the time the SCI event was resolved; the SCI entity's rule(s) and/or governing document(s), as applicable, that relate to the SCI event; and any other pertinent information known by the SCI entity about the SCI event;

(B) A copy of any information disseminated pursuant to paragraph (c) of this section by the SCI entity to date regarding the SCI event to any of its members or participants; and

(C) An analysis of parties that may have experienced a loss, whether monetary or otherwise, due to the SCI event, the number of such parties, and an estimate of the aggregate amount of such loss.

(5) The requirements of paragraphs (b)(1) through (4) of this section shall not apply to any SCI event that has had, or the SCI entity reasonably estimates would have, no or a de minimis impact on the SCI entity's operations or on market participants. For such events, each SCI entity shall:

(i) Make, keep, and preserve records relating to all such SCI events; and

(ii) Submit to the Commission a report, within 30 calendar days after the end of each calendar quarter, containing a summary description of such systems disruptions and systems intrusions, including the SCI systems and, for systems intrusions, indirect SCI systems, affected by such systems disruptions and systems intrusions during the applicable calendar quarter.

(c) *Dissemination of SCI events.* (1) Each SCI entity shall:

(i) Promptly after any responsible SCI personnel has a reasonable basis to conclude that an SCI event that is a systems disruption or systems compliance issue has occurred, disseminate the following information about such SCI event:

(A) The system(s) affected by the SCI event; and

(B) A summary description of the SCI event; and

(ii) When known, promptly further disseminate the following information about such SCI event:

(A) A detailed description of the SCI event;

(B) The SCI entity's current assessment of the types and number of market participants potentially affected by the SCI event; and

(C) A description of the progress of its corrective action for the SCI event and when the SCI event has been or is expected to be resolved; and

(iii) Until resolved, provide regular updates of any information required to be disseminated under paragraphs (c)(1)(i) and (ii) of this section.

(2) Each SCI entity shall, promptly after any responsible SCI personnel has a reasonable basis to conclude that a SCI event that is a systems intrusion has occurred, disseminate a summary description of the systems intrusion, including a description of the corrective action taken by the SCI entity and when the systems intrusion has been or

Securities and Exchange Commission

§ 242.1004

is expected to be resolved, unless the SCI entity determines that dissemination of such information would likely compromise the security of the SCI entity's SCI systems or indirect SCI systems, or an investigation of the systems intrusion, and documents the reasons for such determination.

(3) The information required to be disseminated under paragraphs (c)(1) and (2) of this section promptly after any responsible SCI personnel has a reasonable basis to conclude that an SCI event has occurred, shall be promptly disseminated by the SCI entity to those members or participants of the SCI entity that any responsible SCI personnel has reasonably estimated may have been affected by the SCI event, and promptly disseminated to any additional members or participants that any responsible SCI personnel subsequently reasonably estimates may have been affected by the SCI event; *provided, however,* that for major SCI events, the information required to be disseminated under paragraphs (c)(1) and (2) of this section shall be promptly disseminated by the SCI entity to all of its members or participants.

(4) The requirements of paragraphs (c)(1) through (3) of this section shall not apply to:

(i) SCI events to the extent they relate to market regulation or market surveillance systems; or

(ii) Any SCI event that has had, or the SCI entity reasonably estimates would have, no or a de minimis impact on the SCI entity's operations or on market participants.

§ 242.1003 Obligations related to systems changes; SCI review.

(a) *Systems changes.* Each SCI entity shall:

(1) Within 30 calendar days after the end of each calendar quarter, submit to the Commission a report describing completed, ongoing, and planned material changes to its SCI systems and the security of indirect SCI systems, during the prior, current, and subsequent calendar quarters, including the dates or expected dates of commencement and completion. An SCI entity shall establish reasonable written criteria for identifying a change to its SCI systems and the security of indirect SCI systems as material and report such changes in accordance with such criteria.

(2) Promptly submit a supplemental report notifying the Commission of a material error in or material omission from a report previously submitted under this paragraph (a).

(b) *SCI review.* Each SCI entity shall:

(1) Conduct an SCI review of the SCI entity's compliance with Regulation SCI not less than once each calendar year; *provided, however,* that:

(i) Penetration test reviews of the network, firewalls, and production systems shall be conducted at a frequency of not less than once every three years; and

(ii) Assessments of SCI systems directly supporting market regulation or market surveillance shall be conducted at a frequency based upon the risk assessment conducted as part of the SCI review, but in no case less than once every three years; and

(2) Submit a report of the SCI review required by paragraph (b)(1) of this section to senior management of the SCI entity for review no more than 30 calendar days after completion of such SCI review; and

(3) Submit to the Commission, and to the board of directors of the SCI entity or the equivalent of such board, a report of the SCI review required by paragraph (b)(1) of this section, together with any response by senior management, within 60 calendar days after its submission to senior management of the SCI entity.

§ 242.1004 SCI entity business continuity and disaster recovery plans testing requirements for members or participants.

With respect to an SCI entity's business continuity and disaster recovery plans, including its backup systems, each SCI entity shall:

(a) Establish standards for the designation of those members or participants that the SCI entity reasonably determines are, taken as a whole, the minimum necessary for the maintenance of fair and orderly markets in the event of the activation of such plans;

§ 242.1005

(b) Designate members or participants pursuant to the standards established in paragraph (a) of this section and require participation by such designated members or participants in scheduled functional and performance testing of the operation of such plans, in the manner and frequency specified by the SCI entity, provided that such frequency shall not be less than once every 12 months; and

(c) Coordinate the testing of such plans on an industry- or sector-wide basis with other SCI entities.

§ 242.1005 Recordkeeping requirements related to compliance with Regulation SCI.

(a) An SCI SRO shall make, keep, and preserve all documents relating to its compliance with Regulation SCI as prescribed in § 240.17a-1 of this chapter.

(b) An SCI entity that is not an SCI SRO shall:

(1) Make, keep, and preserve at least one copy of all documents, including correspondence, memoranda, papers, books, notices, accounts, and other such records, relating to its compliance with Regulation SCI, including, but not limited to, records relating to any changes to its SCI systems and indirect SCI systems;

(2) Keep all such documents for a period of not less than five years, the first two years in a place that is readily accessible to the Commission or its representatives for inspection and examination; and

(3) Upon request of any representative of the Commission, promptly furnish to the possession of such representative copies of any documents required to be kept and preserved by it pursuant to paragraphs (b)(1) and (2) of this section.

(c) Upon or immediately prior to ceasing to do business or ceasing to be registered under the Securities Exchange Act of 1934, an SCI entity shall take all necessary action to ensure that the records required to be made, kept, and preserved by this section shall be accessible to the Commission and its representatives in the manner required by this section and for the remainder of the period required by this section.

§ 242.1006 Electronic filing and submission.

(a) Except with respect to notifications to the Commission made pursuant to § 242.1002(b)(1) or updates to the Commission made pursuant to paragraph § 242.1002(b)(3), any notification, review, description, analysis, or report to the Commission required to be submitted under Regulation SCI shall be filed electronically on Form SCI (§ 249.1900 of this chapter), include all information as prescribed in Form SCI and the instructions thereto, and contain an electronic signature; and

(b) The signatory to an electronically filed Form SCI shall manually sign a signature page or document, in the manner prescribed by Form SCI, authenticating, acknowledging, or otherwise adopting his or her signature that appears in typed form within the electronic filing. Such document shall be executed before or at the time Form SCI is electronically filed and shall be retained by the SCI entity in accordance with § 242.1005.

§ 242.1007 Requirements for service bureaus.

If records required to be filed or kept by an SCI entity under Regulation SCI are prepared or maintained by a service bureau or other recordkeeping service on behalf of the SCI entity, the SCI entity shall ensure that the records are available for review by the Commission and its representatives by submitting a written undertaking, in a form acceptable to the Commission, by such service bureau or other recordkeeping service, signed by a duly authorized person at such service bureau or other recordkeeping service. Such a written undertaking shall include an agreement by the service bureau to permit the Commission and its representatives to examine such records at any time or from time to time during business hours, and to promptly furnish to the Commission and its representatives true, correct, and current electronic files in a form acceptable to the Commission or its representatives or hard copies of any or all or any part of such records, upon request, periodically, or continuously and, in any case, within the same time periods as would apply to the SCI entity for such records. The preparation or maintenance of records by a service bureau or other recordkeeping service shall not relieve an SCI entity from its obligation to prepare, maintain, and provide the Commission and its representatives access to such records.

PART 243—REGULATION FD

Sec.
243.100 General rule regarding selective disclosure.
243.101 Definitions.
243.102 No effect on antifraud liability.
243.103 No effect on Exchange Act reporting status.

AUTHORITY: 15 U.S.C. 78c, 78i, 78j, 78m, 78o, 78w, 78mm, and 80a-29, unless otherwise noted.

SOURCE: 65 FR 51738, Aug. 24, 2000, unless otherwise noted.

§ 243.100 General rule regarding selective disclosure.

(a) Whenever an issuer, or any person acting on its behalf, discloses any material nonpublic information regarding that issuer or its securities to any person described in paragraph (b)(1) of this section, the issuer shall make public disclosure of that information as provided in § 243.101(e):

(1) Simultaneously, in the case of an intentional disclosure; and

(2) Promptly, in the case of a non-intentional disclosure.

(b)(1) Except as provided in paragraph (b)(2) of this section, paragraph (a) of this section shall apply to a disclosure made to any person outside the issuer:

(i) Who is a broker or dealer, or a person associated with a broker or dealer, as those terms are defined in Section 3(a) of the Securities Exchange Act of 1934 (15 U.S.C. 78c(a));

(ii) Who is an investment adviser, as that term is defined in Section 202(a)(11) of the Investment Advisers Act of 1940 (15 U.S.C. 80b–2(a)(11)); an institutional investment manager, as that term is defined in Section 13(f)(6) of the Securities Exchange Act of 1934 (15 U.S.C. 78m(f)(6)), that filed a report on Form 13F (17 CFR 249.325) with the Commission for the most recent quarter ended prior to the date of the disclosure; or a person associated with either of the foregoing. For purposes of this paragraph, a "person associated with an investment adviser or institutional investment manager" has the meaning set forth in Section 202(a)(17) of the Investment Advisers Act of 1940 (15 U.S.C. 80b–2(a)(17)), assuming for these purposes that an institutional investment manager is an investment adviser;

(iii) Who is an investment company, as defined in Section 3 of the Investment Company Act of 1940 (15 U.S.C. 80a–3), or who would be an investment company but for Section 3(c)(1) (15 U.S.C. 80a–3(c)(1)) or Section 3(c)(7) (15 U.S.C. 80a–3(c)(7)) thereof, or an affiliated person of either of the foregoing. For purposes of this paragraph, "affiliated person" means only those persons described in Section 2(a)(3)(C), (D), (E), and (F) of the Investment Company Act of 1940 (15 U.S.C. 80a–2(a)(3)(C), (D), (E), and (F)), assuming for these purposes that a person who would be an investment company but for Section 3(c)(1) (15 U.S.C. 80a–3(c)(1)) or Section 3(c)(7) (15 U.S.C. 80a–3(c)(7)) of the Investment Company Act of 1940 is an investment company; or

(iv) Who is a holder of the issuer's securities, under circumstances in which it is reasonably foreseeable that the person will purchase or sell the issuer's securities on the basis of the information.

(2) Paragraph (a) of this section shall not apply to a disclosure made:

(i) To a person who owes a duty of trust or confidence to the issuer (such as an attorney, investment banker, or accountant);

(ii) To a person who expressly agrees to maintain the disclosed information in confidence;

(iii) In connection with a securities offering registered under the Securities Act, other than an offering of the type described in any of Rule 415(a)(1)(i) through (vi) under the Securities Act (§ 230.415(a)(1)(i) through (vi) of this chapter) (except an offering of the type described in Rule 415(a)(1)(i) under the Securities Act (§ 230.415(a)(1)(i) of this chapter) also involving a registered offering, whether or not underwritten, for capital formation purposes for the account of the issuer (unless the issuer's offering is being registered for the purpose of evading the requirements of this section)), if the disclosure is by any of the following means:

(A) A registration statement filed under the Securities Act, including a prospectus contained therein;

(B) A free writing prospectus used after filing of the registration statement for the offering or a communication falling within the exception to the definition of prospectus contained in clause (a) of section 2(a)(10) of the Securities Act;

(C) Any other Section 10(b) prospectus;

(D) A notice permitted by Rule 135 under the Securities Act (§ 230.135 of this chapter);

(E) A communication permitted by Rule 134 under the Securities Act (§ 230.134 of this chapter); or

(F) An oral communication made in connection with the registered securities offering after filing of the registration statement for the offering under the Securities Act.

[65 FR 51738, Aug. 24, 2000, as amended at 70 FR 44829, Aug. 3, 2005; 74 FR 63865, Dec. 4, 2009; 75 FR 61051, Oct. 4, 2010; 76 FR 71877, Nov. 21, 2011]

§ 243.101 Definitions.

This section defines certain terms as used in Regulation FD (§§ 243.100–243.103).

(a) *Intentional.* A selective disclosure of material nonpublic information is "intentional" when the person making the disclosure either knows, or is reckless in not knowing, that the information he or she is communicating is both material and nonpublic.

(b) *Issuer.* An "issuer" subject to this regulation is one that has a class of securities registered under Section 12 of the Securities Exchange Act of 1934 (15 U.S.C. 78*l*), or is required to file reports under Section 15(d) of the Securities Exchange Act of 1934 (15 U.S.C. 78o(d)), including any closed-end investment company (as defined in Section 5(a)(2) of the Investment Company Act of 1940) (15 U.S.C. 80a–5(a)(2)), but not including any other investment company or any foreign government or foreign private issuer, as those terms are defined in Rule 405 under the Securities Act (§ 230.405 of this chapter).

(c) *Person acting on behalf of an issuer.* "Person acting on behalf of an issuer" means any senior official of the issuer (or, in the case of a closed-end investment company, a senior official of the issuer's investment adviser), or any other officer, employee, or agent of an issuer who regularly communicates with any person described in § 243.100(b)(1)(i), (ii), or (iii), or with holders of the issuer's securities. An officer, director, employee, or agent of an issuer who discloses material nonpublic information in breach of a duty of trust or confidence to the issuer shall not be considered to be acting on behalf of the issuer.

(d) *Promptly.* "Promptly" means as soon as reasonably practicable (but in no event after the later of 24 hours or the commencement of the next day's trading on the New York Stock Exchange) after a senior official of the issuer (or, in the case of a closed-end investment company, a senior official of the issuer's investment adviser) learns that there has been a non-intentional disclosure by the issuer or person acting on behalf of the issuer of information that the senior official knows, or is reckless in not knowing, is both material and nonpublic.

(e) *Public disclosure.* (1) Except as provided in paragraph (e)(2) of this section, an issuer shall make the "public disclosure" of information required by § 243.100(a) by furnishing to or filing with the Commission a Form 8–K (17 CFR 249.308) disclosing that information.

(2) An issuer shall be exempt from the requirement to furnish or file a Form 8–K if it instead disseminates the information through another method (or combination of methods) of disclosure that is reasonably designed to provide broad, non-exclusionary distribution of the information to the public.

(f) *Senior official.* "Senior official" means any director, executive officer (as defined in § 240.3b–7 of this chapter), investor relations or public relations officer, or other person with similar functions.

(g) *Securities offering.* For purposes of § 243.100(b)(2)(iv):

Securities and Exchange Commission

§ 244.100

(1) *Underwritten offerings.* A securities offering that is underwritten commences when the issuer reaches an understanding with the broker-dealer that is to act as managing underwriter and continues until the later of the end of the period during which a dealer must deliver a prospectus or the sale of the securities (unless the offering is sooner terminated);

(2) *Non-underwritten offerings.* A securities offering that is not underwritten:

(i) If covered by Rule 415(a)(1)(x) (§ 230.415(a)(1)(x) of this chapter), commences when the issuer makes its first bona fide offer in a takedown of securities and continues until the later of the end of the period during which each dealer must deliver a prospectus or the sale of the securities in that takedown (unless the takedown is sooner terminated);

(ii) If a business combination as defined in Rule 165(f)(1) (§ 230.165(f)(1) of this chapter), commences when the first public announcement of the transaction is made and continues until the completion of the vote or the expiration of the tender offer, as applicable (unless the transaction is sooner terminated);

(iii) If an offering other than those specified in paragraphs (a) and (b) of this section, commences when the issuer files a registration statement and continues until the later of the end of the period during which each dealer must deliver a prospectus or the sale of the securities (unless the offering is sooner terminated).

§ 243.102 No effect on antifraud liability.

No failure to make a public disclosure required solely by § 243.100 shall be deemed to be a violation of Rule 10b-5 (17 CFR 240.10b-5) under the Securities Exchange Act.

§ 243.103 No effect on Exchange Act reporting status.

A failure to make a public disclosure required solely by § 243.100 shall not affect whether:

(a) For purposes of Forms S-3 (17 CFR 239.13), S-8 (17 CFR 239.16b) and SF-3 (17 CFR 239.45) under the Securities Act of 1933 (15 U.S.C. 77a *et seq.*), or Form N-2 (17 CFR 239.14 and 274.11a-1) under the Securities Act of 1933 (15 U.S.C. 77a *et seq.*) and the Investment Company Act of 1940 (15 U.S.C. 80a-1 *et seq.*), an issuer is deemed to have filed all the material required to be filed pursuant to Section 13 or 15(d) of the Securities Exchange Act of 1934 (15 U.S.C. 78m or 78o(d)) or where applicable, has made those filings in a timely manner; or

(b) There is adequate current public information about the issuer for purposes of § 230.144(c) of this chapter (Rule 144(c)).

[65 FR 51738, Aug. 24, 2000, as amended at 79 FR 57344, Sept. 24, 2014; 85 FR 33360, June 1, 2020]

PART 244—REGULATION G

Sec.
244.100 General rules regarding disclosure of non-GAAP financial measures.
244.101 Definitions.
244.102 No effect on antifraud liability.

AUTHORITY: 15 U.S.C. 7261, 78c, 78i, 78j, 78m, 78o, 78w, 78mm, and 80a-29

SOURCE: 68 FR 4832, Jan. 30, 2003, unless otherwise noted.

§ 244.100 General rules regarding disclosure of non-GAAP financial measures.

(a) Whenever a registrant, or person acting on its behalf, publicly discloses material information that includes a non-GAAP financial measure, the registrant must accompany that non-GAAP financial measure with:

(1) A presentation of the most directly comparable financial measure calculated and presented in accordance with Generally Accepted Accounting Principles (GAAP); and

(2) A reconciliation (by schedule or other clearly understandable method), which shall be quantitative for historical non-GAAP measures presented, and quantitative, to the extent available without unreasonable efforts, for forward-looking information, of the differences between the non-GAAP financial measure disclosed or released with the most comparable financial measure or measures calculated and presented in accordance with GAAP identified in paragraph (a)(1) of this section.

§ 244.101

(b) A registrant, or a person acting on its behalf, shall not make public a non-GAAP financial measure that, taken together with the information accompanying that measure and any other accompanying discussion of that measure, contains an untrue statement of a material fact or omits to state a material fact necessary in order to make the presentation of the non-GAAP financial measure, in light of the circumstances under which it is presented, not misleading.

(c) This section shall not apply to a disclosure of a non-GAAP financial measure that is made by or on behalf of a registrant that is a foreign private issuer if the following conditions are satisfied:

(1) The securities of the registrant are listed or quoted on a securities exchange or inter-dealer quotation system outside the United States;

(2) The non-GAAP financial measure is not derived from or based on a measure calculated and presented in accordance with generally accepted accounting principles in the United States; and

(3) The disclosure is made by or on behalf of the registrant outside the United States, or is included in a written communication that is released by or on behalf of the registrant outside the United States.

(d) This section shall not apply to a non-GAAP financial measure included in disclosure relating to a proposed business combination, the entity resulting therefrom or an entity that is a party thereto, if the disclosure is contained in a communication that is subject to § 230.425 of this chapter, § 240.14a–12 or § 240.14d–2(b)(2) of this chapter or § 229.1015 of this chapter.

NOTES TO § 244.100: 1. If a non-GAAP financial measure is made public orally, telephonically, by Web cast, by broadcast, or by similar means, the requirements of paragraphs (a)(1)(i) and (a)(1)(ii) of this section will be satisfied if:

(i) The required information in those paragraphs is provided on the registrant's Web site at the time the non-GAAP financial measure is made public; and

(ii) The location of the web site is made public in the same presentation in which the non-GAAP financial measure is made public.

2. The provisions of paragraph (c) of this section shall apply notwithstanding the existence of one or more of the following circumstances:

(i) A written communication is released in the United States as well as outside the United States, so long as the communication is released in the United States contemporaneously with or after the release outside the United States and is not otherwise targeted at persons located in the United States;

(ii) Foreign journalists, U.S. journalists or other third parties have access to the information;

(iii) The information appears on one or more web sites maintained by the registrant, so long as the web sites, taken together, are not available exclusively to, or targeted at, persons located in the United States; or

(iv) Following the disclosure or release of the information outside the United States, the information is included in a submission by the registrant to the Commission made under cover of a Form 6–K.

§ 244.101 Definitions.

This section defines certain terms as used in Regulation G (§§ 244.100 through 244.102).

(a)(1) *Non-GAAP financial measure.* A non-GAAP financial measure is a numerical measure of a registrant's historical or future financial performance, financial position or cash flows that:

(i) Excludes amounts, or is subject to adjustments that have the effect of excluding amounts, that are included in the most directly comparable measure calculated and presented in accordance with GAAP in the statement of income, balance sheet or statement of cash flows (or equivalent statements) of the issuer; or

(ii) Includes amounts, or is subject to adjustments that have the effect of including amounts, that are excluded from the most directly comparable measure so calculated and presented.

(2) A non-GAAP financial measure does not include operating and other financial measures and ratios or statistical measures calculated using exclusively one or both of:

(i) Financial measures calculated in accordance with GAAP; and

(ii) Operating measures or other measures that are not non-GAAP financial measures.

(3) A non-GAAP financial measure does not include financial measures required to be disclosed by GAAP, Commission rules, or a system of regulation of a government or governmental

Securities and Exchange Commission

§ 245.100

authority or self-regulatory organization that is applicable to the registrant.

(b) *GAAP.* GAAP refers to generally accepted accounting principles in the United States, except that:

(1) In the case of foreign private issuers whose primary financial statements are prepared in accordance with non-U.S. generally accepted accounting principles, GAAP refers to the principles under which those primary financial statements are prepared; and

(2) In the case of foreign private issuers that include a non-GAAP financial measure derived from a measure calculated in accordance with U.S. generally accepted accounting principles, GAAP refers to U.S. generally accepted accounting principles for purposes of the application of the requirements of Regulation G to the disclosure of that measure.

(c) *Registrant.* A registrant subject to this regulation is one that has a class of securities registered under Section 12 of the Securities Exchange Act of 1934 (15 U.S.C. 78*l*), or is required to file reports under Section 15(d) of the Securities Exchange Act of 1934 (15 U.S.C. 78o(d)), excluding any investment company registered under Section 8 of the Investment Company Act of 1940 (15 U.S.C. 80a-8).

(d) *United States.* United States means the United States of America, its territories and possessions, any State of the United States, and the District of Columbia.

§ 244.102 No effect on antifraud liability.

Neither the requirements of this Regulation G (17 CFR 244.100 through 244.102) nor a person's compliance or non-compliance with the requirements of this Regulation shall in itself affect any person's liability under Section 10(b) (15 U.S.C. 78j(b)) of the Securities Exchange Act of 1934 or § 240.10b-5 of this chapter.

PART 245—REGULATION BLACKOUT TRADING RESTRICTION

[Regulation BTR—Blackout Trading Restriction]

Sec.
245.100 Definitions.
245.101 Prohibition of insider trading during pension fund blackout periods.
245.102 Exceptions to definition of blackout period.
245.103 Issuer right of recovery; right of action by equity security owner.
245.104 Notice.

AUTHORITY: 15 U.S.C. 78w(a), unless otherwise noted.

Sections 245.100–245.104 are also issued under secs. 3(a) and 306(a), Pub. L. 107–204, 116 Stat. 745.

SOURCE: 68 FR 4355, Jan. 28, 2003, unless otherwise noted.

§ 245.100 Definitions.

As used in Regulation BTR (§§ 245.100 through 245.104), unless the context otherwise requires:

(a) The term *acquired in connection with service or employment as a director or executive officer,* when applied to a director or executive officer, means that he or she acquired, directly or indirectly, an equity security:

(1) At a time when he or she was a director or executive officer, under a compensatory plan, contract, authorization or arrangement, including, but not limited to, an option, warrants or rights plan, a pension, retirement or deferred compensation plan or a bonus, incentive or profit-sharing plan (whether or not set forth in any formal plan document), including a compensatory plan, contract, authorization or arrangement with a parent, subsidiary or affiliate;

(2) At a time when he or she was a director or executive officer, as a result of any transaction or business relationship described in paragraph (a) of Item 404 of Regulation S-K (§ 229.404 of this chapter) or, in the case of a foreign private issuer, Item 7.B of Form 20-F (§ 249.220f of this chapter) (but without application of the disclosure thresholds of such provisions), to the extent that he or she has a pecuniary interest (as defined in paragraph (*l*) of this section) in the equity securities;

(3) At a time when he or she was a director or executive officer, as directors' qualifying shares or other securities that he or she must hold to satisfy minimum ownership requirements or guidelines for directors or executive officers;

(4) Prior to becoming, or while, a director or executive officer where the

§ 245.100

equity security was acquired as a direct or indirect inducement to service or employment as a director or executive officer; or

(5) Prior to becoming, or while, a director or executive officer where the equity security was received as a result of a business combination in respect of an equity security of an entity involved in the business combination that he or she had acquired in connection with service or employment as a director or executive officer of such entity.

(b) Except as provided in § 245.102, the term *blackout period*:

(1) With respect to the equity securities of any issuer (other than a foreign private issuer), means any period of more than three consecutive business days during which the ability to purchase, sell or otherwise acquire or transfer an interest in any equity security of such issuer held in an individual account plan is temporarily suspended by the issuer or by a fiduciary of the plan with respect to not fewer than 50% of the participants or beneficiaries located in the United States and its territories and possessions under all individual account plans (as defined in paragraph (j) of this section) maintained by the issuer that permit participants or beneficiaries to acquire or hold equity securities of the issuer;

(2) With respect to the equity securities of any foreign private issuer (as defined in § 240.3b–4(c) of this chapter), means any period of more than three consecutive business days during which both:

(i) The conditions of paragraph (b)(1) of this section are met; and

(ii)(A) The number of participants and beneficiaries located in the United States and its territories and possessions subject to the temporary suspension exceeds 15% of the total number of employees of the issuer and its consolidated subsidiaries; or

(B) More than 50,000 participants and beneficiaries located in the United States and its territories and possessions are subject to the temporary suspension.

(3) In determining the individual account plans (as defined in paragraph (j) of this section) maintained by an issuer for purposes of this paragraph (b):

(i) The rules under section 414(b), (c), (m) and (o) of the Internal Revenue Code (26 U.S.C. 414(b), (c), (m) and (o)) are to be applied; and

(ii) An individual account plan that is maintained outside of the United States primarily for the benefit of persons substantially all of whom are nonresident aliens (within the meaning of section 104(b)(4) of the Employee Retirement Income Security Act of 1974 (29 U.S.C. 1003(b)(4))) is not to be considered.

(4) In determining the number of participants and beneficiaries in an individual account plan (as defined in paragraph (j) of this section) maintained by an issuer:

(i) The determination may be made as of any date within the 12-month period preceding the beginning date of the temporary suspension in question; provided that if there has been a significant change in the number of participants or beneficiaries in an individual account plan since the date selected, the determination for such plan must be made as of the most recent practicable date that reflects such change; and

(ii) The determination may be made without regard to overlapping plan participation.

(c)(1) The term *director* has, except as provided in paragraph (c)(2) of this section, the meaning set forth in section 3(a)(7) of the Exchange Act (15 U.S.C. 78c(a)(7)).

(2) In the case of a foreign private issuer (as defined in § 240.3b–4(c) of this chapter), the term *director* means an individual within the definition set forth in section 3(a)(7) of the Exchange Act who is a management employee of the issuer.

(d) The term *derivative security* has the meaning set forth in § 240.16a–1(c) of this chapter.

(e) The term *equity security* has the meaning set forth in section 3(a)(11) of the Exchange Act (15 U.S.C. 78c(a)(11)) and § 240.3a11–1 of this chapter.

(f) The term *equity security of the issuer* means any equity security or derivative security relating to an issuer, whether or not issued by that issuer.

(g) The term *Exchange Act* means the Securities Exchange Act of 1934 (15 U.S.C. 78a *et seq.*).

Securities and Exchange Commission

§ 245.101

(h)(1) The term *executive officer* has, except as provided in paragraph (h)(2) of this section, the meaning set forth in § 240.16a–1(f) of this chapter.

(2) In the case of a foreign private issuer (as defined in § 240.3b–4(c) of this chapter), the term *executive officer* means the principal executive officer or officers, the principal financial officer or officers and the principal accounting officer or officers of the issuer.

(i) The term *exempt security* has the meaning set forth in section 3(a)(12) of the Exchange Act (15 U.S.C. 78c(a)(12)).

(j) The term *individual account plan* means a pension plan which provides for an individual account for each participant and for benefits based solely upon the amount contributed to the participant's account, and any income, expenses, gains and losses, and any forfeitures of accounts of other participants which may be allocated to such participant's account, except that such term does not include a one-participant retirement plan (within the meaning of section 101(i)(8)(B) of the Employee Retirement Income Security Act of 1974 (29 U.S.C. 1021(i)(8)(B))), nor does it include a pension plan in which participation is limited to directors of the issuer.

(k) The term *issuer* means an issuer (as defined in section 3(a)(8) of the Exchange Act (15 U.S.C. 78c(a)(8))), the securities of which are registered under section 12 of the Exchange Act (15 U.S.C. 78*l*) or that is required to file reports under section 15(d) of the Exchange Act (15 U.S.C. 78o(d)) or that files or has filed a registration statement that has not yet become effective under the Securities Act of 1933 (15 U.S.C. 77a *et seq.*) and that it has not withdrawn.

(l) The term *pecuniary interest* has the meaning set forth in § 240.16a–1(a)(2)(i) of this chapter and the term *indirect pecuniary interest* has the meaning set forth in § 240.16a–1(a)(2)(ii) of this chapter. Section 240.16a–1(a)(2)(iii) of this chapter also shall apply to determine pecuniary interest for purposes of this regulation.

[68 FR 4355, Jan. 28, 2003, as amended at 71 FR 53263, Sept. 8, 2006]

§ 245.101 Prohibition of insider trading during pension fund blackout periods.

(a) Except to the extent otherwise provided in paragraph (c) of this section, it is unlawful under section 306(a)(1) of the Sarbanes-Oxley Act of 2002 (15 U.S.C. 7244(a)(1)) for any director or executive officer of an issuer of any equity security (other than an exempt security), directly or indirectly, to purchase, sell or otherwise acquire or transfer any equity security of the issuer (other than an exempt security) during any blackout period with respect to such equity security, if such director or executive officer acquires or previously acquired such equity security in connection with his or her service or employment as a director or executive officer.

(b) For purposes of section 306(a)(1) of the Sarbanes-Oxley Act of 2002, any sale or other transfer of an equity security of the issuer during a blackout period will be treated as a transaction involving an equity security "acquired in connection with service or employment as a director or executive officer" (as defined in § 245.100(a)) to the extent that the director or executive officer has a pecuniary interest (as defined in § 245.100(l)) in such equity security, unless the director or executive officer establishes by specific identification of securities that the transaction did not involve an equity security "acquired in connection with service or employment as a director or executive officer." To establish that the equity security was not so acquired, a director or executive officer must identify the source of the equity securities and demonstrate that he or she has utilized the same specific identification for any purpose related to the transaction (such as tax reporting and any applicable disclosure and reporting requirements).

(c) The following transactions are exempt from section 306(a)(1) of the Sarbanes-Oxley Act of 2002:

(1) Any acquisition of equity securities resulting from the reinvestment of dividends in, or interest on, equity securities of the same issuer if the acquisition is made pursuant to a plan providing for the regular reinvestment of dividends or interest and the plan provides for broad-based participation,

117

§ 245.101

does not discriminate in favor of employees of the issuer and operates on substantially the same terms for all plan participants;

(2) Any purchase or sale of equity securities of the issuer pursuant to a contract, instruction or written plan entered into by the director or executive officer that satisfies the affirmative defense conditions of § 240.10b5–1(c) of this chapter; provided that the director or executive officer did not enter into or modify the contract, instruction or written plan during the blackout period (as defined in § 245.100(b)) in question, or while aware of the actual or approximate beginning or ending dates of that blackout period (whether or not the director or executive officer received notice of the blackout period as required by Section 306(a)(6) of the Sarbanes-Oxley Act of 2002 (15 U.S.C. 7244(a)(6)));

(3) Any purchase or sale of equity securities, other than a Discretionary Transaction (as defined in § 240.16b–3(b)(1) of this chapter), pursuant to a Qualified Plan (as defined in § 240.16b–3(b)(4) of this chapter), an Excess Benefit Plan (as defined in § 240.16b–3(b)(2) of this chapter) or a Stock Purchase Plan (as defined in § 240.16b–3(b)(5) of this chapter) (or, in the case of a foreign private issuer, pursuant to an employee benefit plan that either (i) has been approved by the taxing authority of a foreign jurisdiction, or (ii) is eligible for preferential treatment under the tax laws of a foreign jurisdiction because the plan provides for broad-based employee participation); provided that a Discretionary Transaction that meets the conditions of paragraph (c)(2) of this section also shall be exempt;

(4) Any grant or award of an option, stock appreciation right or other equity compensation pursuant to a plan that, by its terms:

(i) Permits directors or executive officers to receive grants or awards; and

(ii) Either:

(A) States the amount and price of securities to be awarded to designated directors and executive officers or categories of directors and executive officers (though not necessarily to others who may participate in the plan) and specifies the timing of awards to directors and executive officers; or

(B) Sets forth a formula that determines the amount, price and timing, using objective criteria (such as earnings of the issuer, value of the securities, years of service, job classification, and compensation levels);

(5) Any exercise, conversion or termination of a derivative security that the director or executive officer did not write or acquire during the blackout period (as defined in § 245.100(b)) in question, or while aware of the actual or approximate beginning or ending dates of that blackout period (whether or not the director or executive officer received notice of the blackout period as required by Section 306(a)(6) of the Sarbanes-Oxley Act of 2002; and either:

(i) The derivative security, by its terms, may be exercised, converted or terminated only on a fixed date, with no discretionary provision for earlier exercise, conversion or termination; or

(ii) The derivative security is exercised, converted or terminated by a counterparty and the director or executive officer does not exercise any influence on the counterparty with respect to whether or when to exercise, convert or terminate the derivative security;

(6) Any acquisition or disposition of equity securities involving a bona fide gift or a transfer by will or the laws of descent and distribution;

(7) Any acquisition or disposition of equity securities pursuant to a domestic relations order, as defined in the Internal Revenue Code or Title I of the Employment Retirement Income Security Act of 1974, or the rules thereunder;

(8) Any sale or other disposition of equity securities compelled by the laws or other requirements of an applicable jurisdiction;

(9) Any acquisition or disposition of equity securities in connection with a merger, acquisition, divestiture or similar transaction occurring by operation of law;

(10) The increase or decrease in the number of equity securities held as a result of a stock split or stock dividend applying equally to all securities of that class, including a stock dividend in which equity securities of a different

Securities and Exchange Commission § 245.103

issuer are distributed; and the acquisition of rights, such as shareholder or pre-emptive rights, pursuant to a pro rata grant to all holders of the same class of equity securities; and

(11) Any acquisition or disposition of an asset-backed security, as defined in § 229.1101 of this chapter.

[70 FR 1623, Jan. 7, 2005]

§ 245.102 Exceptions to definition of blackout period.

The term "blackout period," as defined in § 245.100(b), does not include:

(a) A regularly scheduled period in which participants and beneficiaries may not purchase, sell or otherwise acquire or transfer an interest in any equity security of an issuer, if a description of such period, including its frequency and duration and the plan transactions to be suspended or otherwise affected, is:

(1) Incorporated into the individual account plan or included in the documents or instruments under which the plan operates; and

(2) Disclosed to an employee before he or she formally enrolls, or within 30 days following formal enrollment, as a participant under the individual account plan or within 30 days after the adoption of an amendment to the plan. For purposes of this paragraph (a)(2), the disclosure may be provided in any graphic form that is reasonably accessible to the employee; or

(b) Any trading suspension described in § 245.100(b) that is imposed in connection with a corporate merger, acquisition, divestiture or similar transaction involving the plan or plan sponsor, the principal purpose of which is to permit persons affiliated with the acquired or divested entity to become participants or beneficiaries, or to cease to be participants or beneficiaries, in an individual account plan; provided that the persons who become participants or beneficiaries in an individual account plan are not able to participate in the same class of equity securities after the merger, acquisition, divestiture or similar transaction as before the transaction.

§ 245.103 Issuer right of recovery; right of action by equity security owner.

(a) *Recovery of profits.* Section 306(a)(2) of the Sarbanes-Oxley Act of 2002 (15 U.S.C. 7244(a)(2)) provides that any profit realized by a director or executive officer from any purchase, sale or other acquisition or transfer of any equity security of an issuer in violation of section 306(a)(1) of that Act (15 U.S.C. 7244(a)(1)) will inure to and be recoverable by the issuer, regardless of any intention on the part of the director or executive officer in entering into the transaction.

(b) *Actions to recover profit.* Section 306(a)(2) of the Sarbanes-Oxley Act of 2002 provides that an action to recover profit may be instituted at law or in equity in any court of competent jurisdiction by the issuer, or by the owner of any equity security of the issuer in the name and on behalf of the issuer if the issuer fails or refuses to bring such action within 60 days after the date of request, or fails diligently to prosecute the action thereafter, except that no such suit may be brought more than two years after the date on which such profit was realized.

(c) *Measurement of profit.* (1) In determining the profit recoverable in an action undertaken pursuant to section 306(a)(2) of the Sarbanes-Oxley Act of 2002 from a transaction that involves a purchase, sale or other acquisition or transfer (other than a grant, exercise, conversion or termination of a derivative security) in violation of section 306(a)(1) of that Act of an equity security of an issuer that is registered pursuant to section 12(b) or 12(g) of the Exchange Act (15 U.S.C. 78*l*(b) or (g)) and listed on a national securities exchange or listed in an automated inter-dealer quotation system of a national securities association, profit (including any loss avoided) may be measured by comparing the difference between the amount paid or received for the equity security on the date of the transaction during the blackout period and the average market price of the equity security calculated over the first three trading days after the ending date of the blackout period.

(2) In determining the profit recoverable in an action undertaken pursuant

§ 245.104

to section 306(a)(2) of the Sarbanes-Oxley Act of 2002 from a transaction that is not described in paragraph (c)(1) of this section, profit (including any loss avoided) may be measured in a manner that is consistent with the objective of identifying the amount of any gain realized or loss avoided by a director or executive officer as a result of a transaction taking place in violation of section 306(a)(1) of that Act during the blackout period as opposed to taking place outside of such blackout period.

(3) The terms of this section do not limit in any respect the authority of the Commission to seek or determine remedies as the result of a transaction taking place in violation of section 306(a)(1) of the Sarbanes-Oxley Act.

§ 245.104 Notice.

(a) In any case in which a director or executive officer is subject to section 306(a)(1) of the Sarbanes-Oxley Act of 2002 (15 U.S.C. 7244(a)(1)) in connection with a blackout period (as defined in § 245.100(b)) with respect to any equity security, the issuer of the equity security must timely notify each director or officer and the Commission of the blackout period.

(b) For purposes of this section:

(1) The notice must include:

(i) The reason or reasons for the blackout period;

(ii) A description of the plan transactions to be suspended during, or otherwise affected by, the blackout period;

(iii) A description of the class of equity securities subject to the blackout period;

(iv) The length of the blackout period by reference to:

(A) The actual or expected beginning date and ending date of the blackout period; or

(B) The calendar week during which the blackout period is expected to begin and the calendar week during which the blackout period is expected to end, provided that the notice to directors and executive officers describes how, during such week or weeks, a director or executive officer may obtain, without charge, information as to whether the blackout period has begun or ended; and provided further that the notice to the Commission describes how, during the blackout period and for a period of two years after the ending date of the blackout period, a security holder or other interested person may obtain, without charge, the actual beginning and ending dates of the blackout period.

(C) For purposes of this paragraph (b)(1)(iv), a *calendar week* means a seven-day period beginning on Sunday and ending on Saturday; and

(v) The name, address and telephone number of the person designated by the issuer to respond to inquiries about the blackout period, or, in the absence of such a designation, the issuer's human resources director or person performing equivalent functions.

(2) (i) Notice to an affected director or executive officer will be considered timely if the notice described in paragraph (b)(1) of this section is provided (in graphic form that is reasonably accessible to the recipient):

(A) No later than five business days after the issuer receives the notice required by section 101(i)(2)(E) of the Employment Retirement Income Security Act of 1974 (29 U.S.C. 1021(i)(2)(E)); or

(B) If no such notice is received by the issuer, a date that is at least 15 calendar days before the actual or expected beginning date of the blackout period.

(ii) Notwithstanding paragraph (b)(2)(i) of this section, the requirement to give advance notice will not apply in any case in which the inability to provide advance notice of the blackout period is due to events that were unforeseeable to, or circumstances that were beyond the reasonable control of, the issuer, and the issuer reasonably so determines in writing. Determinations described in the preceding sentence must be dated and signed by an authorized representative of the issuer. In any case in which this exception to the advance notice requirement applies, the issuer must provide the notice described in paragraph (b)(1) of this section, as well as a copy of the written determination, to all affected directors and executive officers as soon as reasonably practicable.

(iii) If there is a subsequent change in the beginning or ending dates of the

Securities and Exchange Commission

blackout period as provided in the notice to directors and executive officers under paragraph (b)(2)(i) of this section, an issuer must provide directors and executive officers with an updated notice explaining the reasons for the change in the date or dates and identifying all material changes in the information contained in the prior notice. The updated notice is required to be provided as soon as reasonably practicable, unless such notice in advance of the termination of a blackout period is impracticable.

(3) Notice to the Commission will be considered timely if:

(i) The issuer, except as provided in paragraph (b)(3)(ii) of this section, files a current report on Form 8–K (§ 249.308 of this chapter) within the time prescribed for filing the report under the instructions for the form; or

(ii) In the case of a foreign private issuer (as defined in § 240.3b–4(c) of this chapter), the issuer includes the information set forth in paragraph (b)(1) of this section in the first annual report on Form 20–F (§ 249.220f of this chapter) or 40–F (§ 249.240f of this chapter) required to be filed after the receipt of the notice of a blackout period required by 29 CFR 2520.101–3(c) within the time prescribed for filing the report under the instructions for the form or in an earlier filed report on Form 6–K (§ 249.306).

(iii) If there is a subsequent change in the beginning or ending dates of the blackout period as provided in the notice to the Commission under paragraph (b)(3)(i) of this section, an issuer must file a current report on Form 8–K containing the updated beginning or ending dates of the blackout period, explaining the reasons for the change in the date or dates and identifying all material changes in the information contained in the prior report. The updated notice is required to be provided as soon as reasonably practicable.

PART 246—CREDIT RISK RETENTION

Subpart A—Authority, Purpose, Scope and Definitions

Sec.
246.1 [Reserved]
246.2 Definitions.

Subpart B—Credit Risk Retention

246.3 Base risk retention requirement.
246.4 Standard risk retention.
246.5 Revolving pool securitizations.
246.6 Eligible ABCP conduits.
246.7 Commercial mortgage-backed securities.
246.8 Federal National Mortgage Association and Federal Home Loan Mortgage Corporation ABS.
246.9 Open market CLOs.
246.10 Qualified tender option bonds.

Subpart C—Transfer of Risk Retention

246.11 Allocation of risk retention to an originator.
246.12 Hedging, transfer and financing prohibitions.

Subpart D—Exceptions and Exemptions

246.13 Exemption for qualified residential mortgages.
246.14 Definitions applicable to qualifying commercial loans, commercial real estate loans, and automobile loans.
246.15 Qualifying commercial loans, commercial real estate loans, and automobile loans.
246.16 Underwriting standards for qualifying commercial loans.
246.17 Underwriting standards for qualifying CRE loans.
246.18 Underwriting standards for qualifying automobile loans.
246.19 General exemptions.
246.20 Safe harbor for certain foreign-related transactions.
246.21 Additional exemptions.
246.22 Periodic review of the QRM definition, exempted three-to-four unit residential mortgage loans, and community-focused residential mortgage exemption.

AUTHORITY: 15 U.S.C. 77g, 77j, 77s, 77z–3, 78c, 78m, 78o, 78o–11, 78w, 78mm.

SOURCE: 79 FR 77740, Dec. 24, 2014, unless otherwise noted.

Subpart A—Authority, Purpose, Scope and Definitions

§ 246.1 Purpose, scope, and authority.

(a) *Authority and purpose.* This part (Regulation RR) is issued by the Securities and Exchange Commission ("Commission") jointly with the Board of Governors of the Federal Reserve System, the Federal Deposit Insurance Corporation, the Office of the Comptroller of the Currency, and, in the case of the securitization of any residential

§ 246.2

mortgage asset, together with the Secretary of Housing and Urban Development and the Federal Housing Finance Agency, pursuant to Section 15G of the Securities Exchange Act of 1934 (15 U.S.C. 78o-11). The Commission also is issuing this part pursuant to its authority under Sections 7, 10, 19(a), and 28 of the Securities Act and Sections 3, 13, 15, 23, and 36 of the Exchange Act. This part requires securitizers to retain an economic interest in a portion of the credit risk for any asset that the securitizer, through the issuance of an asset-backed security, transfers, sells, or conveys to a third party. This part specifies the permissible types, forms, and amounts of credit risk retention, and establishes certain exemptions for securitizations collateralized by assets that meet specified underwriting standards or otherwise qualify for an exemption.

(b) The authority of the Commission under this part shall be in addition to the authority of the Commission to otherwise enforce the federal securities laws, including, without limitation, the antifraud provisions of the securities laws.

[79 FR 77766, Dec. 24, 2014]

§ 246.2 Definitions.

For purposes of this part, the following definitions apply:

ABS interest means:

(1) Any type of interest or obligation issued by an issuing entity, whether or not in certificated form, including a security, obligation, beneficial interest or residual interest (other than an uncertificated regular interest in a REMIC that is held by another REMIC, where both REMICs are part of the same structure and a single REMIC in that structure issues ABS interests to investors, or a non-economic residual interest issued by a REMIC), payments on which are primarily dependent on the cash flows of the collateral owned or held by the issuing entity; and

(2) Does not include common or preferred stock, limited liability interests, partnership interests, trust certificates, or similar interests that:

(i) Are issued primarily to evidence ownership of the issuing entity; and

(ii) The payments, if any, on which are not primarily dependent on the cash flows of the collateral held by the issuing entity; and

(3) Does not include the right to receive payments for services provided by the holder of such right, including servicing, trustee services and custodial services.

Affiliate of, or a person *affiliated* with, a specified person means a person that directly, or indirectly through one or more intermediaries, controls, or is controlled by, or is under common control with, the person specified.

Appropriate Federal banking agency has the same meaning as in section 3 of the Federal Deposit Insurance Act (12 U.S.C. 1813).

Asset means a self-liquidating financial asset (including but not limited to a loan, lease, mortgage, or receivable).

Asset-backed security has the same meaning as in section 3(a)(79) of the Securities Exchange Act of 1934 (15 U.S.C. 78c(a)(79)).

Collateral means, with respect to any issuance of ABS interests, the assets that provide the cash flow and the servicing assets that support such cash flow for the ABS interests irrespective of the legal structure of issuance, including security interests in assets or other property of the issuing entity, fractional undivided property interests in the assets or other property of the issuing entity, or any other property interest in or rights to cash flow from such assets and related servicing assets. Assets or other property *collateralize* an issuance of ABS interests if the assets or property serve as collateral for such issuance.

Commercial real estate loan has the same meaning as in § 246.14.

Commission means the Securities and Exchange Commission.

Control including the terms "controlling," "controlled by" and "under common control with":

(1) Means the possession, direct or indirect, of the power to direct or cause the direction of the management and policies of a person, whether through the ownership of voting securities, by contract, or otherwise.

(2) Without limiting the foregoing, a person shall be considered to control another person if the first person:

(i) Owns, controls or holds with power to vote 25 percent or more of any

Securities and Exchange Commission §246.2

class of voting securities of the other person; or

(ii) Controls in any manner the election of a majority of the directors, trustees or persons performing similar functions of the other person.

Credit risk means:

(1) The risk of loss that could result from the failure of the borrower in the case of a securitized asset, or the issuing entity in the case of an ABS interest in the issuing entity, to make required payments of principal or interest on the asset or ABS interest on a timely basis;

(2) The risk of loss that could result from bankruptcy, insolvency, or a similar proceeding with respect to the borrower or issuing entity, as appropriate; or

(3) The effect that significant changes in the underlying credit quality of the asset or ABS interest may have on the market value of the asset or ABS interest.

Creditor has the same meaning as in 15 U.S.C. 1602(g).

Depositor means:

(1) The person that receives or purchases and transfers or sells the securitized assets to the issuing entity;

(2) The sponsor, in the case of a securitization transaction where there is not an intermediate transfer of the assets from the sponsor to the issuing entity; or

(3) The person that receives or purchases and transfers or sells the securitized assets to the issuing entity in the case of a securitization transaction where the person transferring or selling the securitized assets directly to the issuing entity is itself a trust.

Eligible horizontal residual interest means, with respect to any securitization transaction, an ABS interest in the issuing entity:

(1) That is an interest in a single class or multiple classes in the issuing entity, provided that each interest meets, individually or in the aggregate, all of the requirements of this definition;

(2) With respect to which, on any payment date or allocation date on which the issuing entity has insufficient funds to satisfy its obligation to pay all contractual interest or principal due, any resulting shortfall will reduce amounts payable to the eligible horizontal residual interest prior to any reduction in the amounts payable to any other ABS interest, whether through loss allocation, operation of the priority of payments, or any other governing contractual provision (until the amount of such ABS interest is reduced to zero); and

(3) That, with the exception of any non-economic REMIC residual interest, has the most subordinated claim to payments of both principal and interest by the issuing entity.

Eligible horizontal cash reserve account means an account meeting the requirements of §246.4(b).

Eligible vertical interest means, with respect to any securitization transaction, a single vertical security or an interest in each class of ABS interests in the issuing entity issued as part of the securitization transaction that constitutes the same proportion of each such class.

Federal banking agencies means the Office of the Comptroller of the Currency, the Board of Governors of the Federal Reserve System, and the Federal Deposit Insurance Corporation.

GAAP means generally accepted accounting principles as used in the United States.

Issuing entity means, with respect to a securitization transaction, the trust or other entity:

(1) That owns or holds the pool of assets to be securitized; and

(2) In whose name the asset-backed securities are issued.

Majority-owned affiliate of a person means an entity (other than the issuing entity) that, directly or indirectly, majority controls, is majority controlled by or is under common majority control with, such person. For purposes of this definition, majority control means ownership of more than 50 percent of the equity of an entity, or ownership of any other controlling financial interest in the entity, as determined under GAAP.

Originator means a person who:

(1) Through an extension of credit or otherwise, creates an asset that collateralizes an asset-backed security; and

§ 246.3

(2) Sells the asset directly or indirectly to a securitizer or issuing entity.

REMIC has the same meaning as in 26 U.S.C. 860D.

Residential mortgage means:

(1) A transaction that is a covered transaction as defined in § 1026.43(b) of Regulation Z (12 CFR 1026.43(b)(1));

(2) Any transaction that is exempt from the definition of "covered transaction" under § 1026.43(a) of Regulation Z (12 CFR 1026.43(a)); and

(3) Any other loan secured by a residential structure that contains one to four units, whether or not that structure is attached to real property, including an individual condominium or cooperative unit and, if used as a residence, a mobile home or trailer.

Retaining sponsor means, with respect to a securitization transaction, the sponsor that has retained or caused to be retained an economic interest in the credit risk of the securitized assets pursuant to subpart B of this part.

Securitization transaction means a transaction involving the offer and sale of asset-backed securities by an issuing entity.

Securitized asset means an asset that:

(1) Is transferred, sold, or conveyed to an issuing entity; and

(2) Collateralizes the ABS interests issued by the issuing entity.

Securitizer means, with respect to a securitization transaction, either:

(1) The depositor of the asset-backed securities (if the depositor is not the sponsor); or

(2) The sponsor of the asset-backed securities.

Servicer means any person responsible for the management or collection of the securitized assets or making allocations or distributions to holders of the ABS interests, but does not include a trustee for the issuing entity or the asset-backed securities that makes allocations or distributions to holders of the ABS interests if the trustee receives such allocations or distributions from a servicer and the trustee does not otherwise perform the functions of a servicer.

Servicing assets means rights or other assets designed to assure the servicing or timely distribution of proceeds to ABS interest holders and rights or other assets that are related or incidental to purchasing or otherwise acquiring and holding the issuing entity's securitized assets. Servicing assets include amounts received by the issuing entity as proceeds of securitized assets, including proceeds of rights or other assets, whether as remittances by obligors or as other recoveries.

Single vertical security means, with respect to any securitization transaction, an ABS interest entitling the sponsor to a specified percentage of the amounts paid on each class of ABS interests in the issuing entity (other than such single vertical security).

Sponsor means a person who organizes and initiates a securitization transaction by selling or transferring assets, either directly or indirectly, including through an affiliate, to the issuing entity.

State has the same meaning as in Section 3(a)(16) of the Securities Exchange Act of 1934 (15 U.S.C. 78c(a)(16)).

United States or U.S. means the United States of America, including its territories and possessions, any State of the United States, and the District of Columbia.

Wholly-owned affiliate means a person (other than an issuing entity) that, directly or indirectly, wholly controls, is wholly controlled by, or is wholly under common control with, another person. For purposes of this definition, "wholly controls" means ownership of 100 percent of the equity of an entity.

Subpart B—Credit Risk Retention

§ 246.3 Base risk retention requirement.

(a) *Base risk retention requirement.* Except as otherwise provided in this part, the sponsor of a securitization transaction (or majority-owned affiliate of the sponsor) shall retain an economic interest in the credit risk of the securitized assets in accordance with any one of §§ 246.4 through 246.10. Credit risk in securitized assets required to be retained and held by any person for purposes of compliance with this part, whether a sponsor, an originator, an originator-seller, or a third-party purchaser, except as otherwise provided in this part, may be acquired and held by any of such person's majority-owned

Securities and Exchange Commission

§ 246.4

affiliates (other than an issuing entity).

(b) *Multiple sponsors.* If there is more than one sponsor of a securitization transaction, it shall be the responsibility of each sponsor to ensure that at least one of the sponsors of the securitization transaction (or at least one of their majority-owned or wholly-owned affiliates, as applicable) retains an economic interest in the credit risk of the securitized assets in accordance with any one of §§ 246.4, 246.5, 246.8, 246.9, or 246.10.

§ 246.4 Standard risk retention.

(a) *General requirement.* Except as provided in §§ 246.5 through 246.10, the sponsor of a securitization transaction must retain an eligible vertical interest or eligible horizontal residual interest, or any combination thereof, in accordance with the requirements of this section.

(1) If the sponsor retains only an eligible vertical interest as its required risk retention, the sponsor must retain an eligible vertical interest in a percentage of not less than 5 percent.

(2) If the sponsor retains only an eligible horizontal residual interest as its required risk retention, the amount of the interest must equal at least 5 percent of the fair value of all ABS interests in the issuing entity issued as a part of the securitization transaction, determined using a fair value measurement framework under GAAP.

(3) If the sponsor retains both an eligible vertical interest and an eligible horizontal residual interest as its required risk retention, the percentage of the fair value of the eligible horizontal residual interest and the percentage of the eligible vertical interest must equal at least five.

(4) The percentage of the eligible vertical interest, eligible horizontal residual interest, or combination thereof retained by the sponsor must be determined as of the closing date of the securitization transaction.

(b) *Option to hold base amount in eligible horizontal cash reserve account.* In lieu of retaining all or any part of an eligible horizontal residual interest under paragraph (a) of this section, the sponsor may, at closing of the securitization transaction, cause to be established and funded, in cash, an eligible horizontal cash reserve account in the amount equal to the fair value of such eligible horizontal residual interest or part thereof, provided that the account meets all of the following conditions:

(1) The account is held by the trustee (or person performing similar functions) in the name and for the benefit of the issuing entity;

(2) Amounts in the account are invested only in cash and cash equivalents; and

(3) Until all ABS interests in the issuing entity are paid in full, or the issuing entity is dissolved:

(i) Amounts in the account shall be released only to:

(A) Satisfy payments on ABS interests in the issuing entity on any payment date on which the issuing entity has insufficient funds from any source to satisfy an amount due on any ABS interest; or

(B) Pay critical expenses of the trust unrelated to credit risk on any payment date on which the issuing entity has insufficient funds from any source to pay such expenses and:

(*1*) Such expenses, in the absence of available funds in the eligible horizontal cash reserve account, would be paid prior to any payments to holders of ABS interests; and

(*2*) Such payments are made to parties that are not affiliated with the sponsor; and

(ii) Interest (or other earnings) on investments made in accordance with paragraph (b)(2) of this section may be released once received by the account.

(c) *Disclosures.* A sponsor relying on this section shall provide, or cause to be provided, to potential investors, under the caption "Credit Risk Retention", a reasonable period of time prior to the sale of the asset-backed securities in the securitization transaction the following disclosures in written form and within the time frames set forth in this paragraph (c):

(1) *Horizontal interest.* With respect to any eligible horizontal residual interest held under paragraph (a) of this section, a sponsor must disclose:

(i) A reasonable period of time prior to the sale of an asset-backed security

§ 246.4

issued in the same offering of ABS interests,

(A) The fair value (expressed as a percentage of the fair value of all of the ABS interests issued in the securitization transaction and dollar amount (or corresponding amount in the foreign currency in which the ABS interests are issued, as applicable)) of the eligible horizontal residual interest that the sponsor expects to retain at the closing of the securitization transaction. If the specific prices, sizes, or rates of interest of each tranche of the securitization are not available, the sponsor must disclose a range of fair values (expressed as a percentage of the fair value of all of the ABS interests issued in the securitization transaction and dollar amount (or corresponding amount in the foreign currency in which the ABS interests are issued, as applicable)) of the eligible horizontal residual interest that the sponsor expects to retain at the close of the securitization transaction based on a range of bona fide estimates or specified prices, sizes, or rates of interest of each tranche of the securitization. A sponsor disclosing a range of fair values based on a range of bona fide estimates or specified prices, sizes or rates of interest of each tranche of the securitization must also disclose the method by which it determined any range of prices, tranche sizes, or rates of interest.

(B) A description of the material terms of the eligible horizontal residual interest to be retained by the sponsor;

(C) A description of the valuation methodology used to calculate the fair values or range of fair values of all classes of ABS interests, including any portion of the eligible horizontal residual interest retained by the sponsor;

(D) All key inputs and assumptions or a comprehensive description of such key inputs and assumptions that were used in measuring the estimated total fair value or range of fair values of all classes of ABS interests, including the eligible horizontal residual interest to be retained by the sponsor.

(E) To the extent applicable to the valuation methodology used, the disclosure required in paragraph (c)(1)(i)(D) of this section shall include,

17 CFR Ch. II (4–1–23 Edition)

but should not be limited to, quantitative information about each of the following:

(*1*) Discount rates;

(*2*) Loss given default (recovery);

(*3*) Prepayment rates;

(*4*) Default rates;

(*5*) Lag time between default and recovery; and

(*6*) The basis of forward interest rates used.

(F) The disclosure required in paragraphs (c)(1)(i)(C) and (D) of this section shall include, at a minimum, descriptions of all inputs and assumptions that either could have a material impact on the fair value calculation or would be material to a prospective investor's ability to evaluate the sponsor's fair value calculations. To the extent the disclosure required in this paragraph (c)(1) includes a description of a curve or curves, the description shall include a description of the methodology that was used to derive each curve and a description of any aspects or features of each curve that could materially impact the fair value calculation or the ability of a prospective investor to evaluate the sponsor's fair value calculation. To the extent a sponsor uses information about the securitized assets in its calculation of fair value, such information shall not be as of a date more than 60 days prior to the date of first use with investors; provided that for a subsequent issuance of ABS interests by the same issuing entity with the same sponsor for which the securitization transaction distributes amounts to investors on a quarterly or less frequent basis, such information shall not be as of a date more than 135 days prior to the date of first use with investors; provided further, that the balance or value (in accordance with the transaction documents) of the securitized assets may be increased or decreased to reflect anticipated additions or removals of assets the sponsor makes or expects to make between the cut-off date or similar date for establishing the composition of the asset pool collateralizing such asset-backed security and the closing date of the securitization.

Securities and Exchange Commission § 246.5

(G) A summary description of the reference data set or other historical information used to develop the key inputs and assumptions referenced in paragraph (c)(1)(i)(D) of this section, including loss given default and default rates;

(ii) A reasonable time after the closing of the securitization transaction:

(A) The fair value (expressed as a percentage of the fair value of all of the ABS interests issued in the securitization transaction and dollar amount (or corresponding amount in the foreign currency in which the ABS are issued, as applicable)) of the eligible horizontal residual interest the sponsor retained at the closing of the securitization transaction, based on actual sale prices and finalized tranche sizes;

(B) The fair value (expressed as a percentage of the fair value of all of the ABS interests issued in the securitization transaction and dollar amount (or corresponding amount in the foreign currency in which the ABS are issued, as applicable)) of the eligible horizontal residual interest that the sponsor is required to retain under this section; and

(C) To the extent the valuation methodology or any of the key inputs and assumptions that were used in calculating the fair value or range of fair values disclosed prior to sale and required under paragraph (c)(1)(i) of this section materially differs from the methodology or key inputs and assumptions used to calculate the fair value at the time of closing, descriptions of those material differences.

(iii) If the sponsor retains risk through the funding of an eligible horizontal cash reserve account:

(A) The amount to be placed (or that is placed) by the sponsor in the eligible horizontal cash reserve account at closing, and the fair value (expressed as a percentage of the fair value of all of the ABS interests issued in the securitization transaction and dollar amount (or corresponding amount in the foreign currency in which the ABS interests are issued, as applicable)) of the eligible horizontal residual interest that the sponsor is required to fund through the eligible horizontal cash reserve account in order for such account, together with other retained interests, to satisfy the sponsor's risk retention requirement;

(B) A description of the material terms of the eligible horizontal cash reserve account; and

(C) The disclosures required in paragraphs (c)(1)(i) and (ii) of this section.

(2) *Vertical interest.* With respect to any eligible vertical interest retained under paragraph (a) of this section, the sponsor must disclose:

(i) A reasonable period of time prior to the sale of an asset-backed security issued in the same offering of ABS interests,

(A) The form of the eligible vertical interest;

(B) The percentage that the sponsor is required to retain as a vertical interest under this section; and

(C) A description of the material terms of the vertical interest and the amount that the sponsor expects to retain at the closing of the securitization transaction.

(ii) A reasonable time after the closing of the securitization transaction, the amount of the vertical interest the sponsor retained at closing, if that amount is materially different from the amount disclosed under paragraph (c)(2)(i) of this section.

(d) *Record maintenance.* A sponsor must retain the certifications and disclosures required in paragraphs (a) and (c) of this section in its records and must provide the disclosure upon request to the Commission and its appropriate Federal banking agency, if any, until three years after all ABS interests are no longer outstanding.

§ 246.5 Revolving pool securitizations.

(a) *Definitions.* For purposes of this section, the following definitions apply:

Revolving pool securitization means an issuing entity that is established to issue on multiple issuance dates more than one series, class, subclass, or tranche of asset-backed securities that are collateralized by a common pool of securitized assets that will change in composition over time, and that does not monetize excess interest and fees from its securitized assets.

Seller's interest means an ABS interest or ABS interests:

§ 246.5

(1) Collateralized by the securitized assets and servicing assets owned or held by the issuing entity, other than the following that are not considered a component of seller's interest:

(i) Servicing assets that have been allocated as collateral only for a specific series in connection with administering the revolving pool securitization, such as a principal accumulation or interest reserve account; and

(ii) Assets that are not eligible under the terms of the securitization transaction to be included when determining whether the revolving pool securitization holds aggregate securitized assets in specified proportions to aggregate outstanding investor ABS interests issued; and

(2) That is *pari passu* with each series of investor ABS interests issued, or partially or fully subordinated to one or more series in identical or varying amounts, with respect to the allocation of all distributions and losses with respect to the securitized assets prior to early amortization of the revolving securitization (as specified in the securitization transaction documents); and

(3) That adjusts for fluctuations in the outstanding principal balance of the securitized assets in the pool.

(b) *General requirement.* A sponsor satisfies the risk retention requirements of § 246.3 with respect to a securitization transaction for which the issuing entity is a revolving pool securitization if the sponsor maintains a seller's interest of not less than 5 percent of the aggregate unpaid principal balance of all outstanding investor ABS interests in the issuing entity.

(c) *Measuring the seller's interest.* In measuring the seller's interest for purposes of meeting the requirements of paragraph (b) of this section:

(1) The unpaid principal balance of the securitized assets for the numerator of the 5 percent ratio shall not include assets of the types excluded from the definition of seller's interest in paragraph (a) of this section;

(2) The aggregate unpaid principal balance of outstanding investor ABS interests in the denominator of the 5 percent ratio may be reduced by the amount of funds held in a segregated principal accumulation account for the repayment of outstanding investor ABS interests, if:

(i) The terms of the securitization transaction documents prevent funds in the principal accumulation account from being applied for any purpose other than the repayment of the unpaid principal of outstanding investor ABS interests; and

(ii) Funds in that account are invested only in the types of assets in which funds held in an eligible horizontal cash reserve account pursuant to § 246.4 are permitted to be invested;

(3) If the terms of the securitization transaction documents set minimum required seller's interest as a proportion of the unpaid principal balance of outstanding investor ABS interests for one or more series issued, rather than as a proportion of the aggregate outstanding investor ABS interests in all outstanding series combined, the percentage of the seller's interest for each such series must, when combined with the percentage of any minimum seller's interest set by reference to the aggregate outstanding investor ABS interests, equal at least 5 percent;

(4) The 5 percent test must be determined and satisfied at the closing of each issuance of ABS interests to investors by the issuing entity, and

(i) At least monthly at a seller's interest measurement date specified under the securitization transaction documents, until no ABS interest in the issuing entity is held by any person not a wholly-owned affiliate of the sponsor; or

(ii) If the revolving pool securitization fails to meet the 5 percent test as of any date described in paragraph (c)(4)(i) of this section, and the securitization transaction documents specify a cure period, the 5 percent test must be determined and satisfied within the earlier of the cure period, or one month after the date described in paragraph (c)(4)(i).

(d) *Measuring outstanding investor ABS interests.* In measuring the amount of outstanding investor ABS interests for purposes of this section, ABS interests held for the life of such ABS interests by the sponsor or its wholly-owned affiliates may be excluded.

Securities and Exchange Commission § 246.5

(e) *Holding and retention of the seller's interest; legacy trusts.* (1) Notwithstanding § 246.12(a), the seller's interest, and any offsetting horizontal retention interest retained pursuant to paragraph (g) of this section, must be retained by the sponsor or by one or more wholly-owned affiliates of the sponsor, including one or more depositors of the revolving pool securitization.

(2) If one revolving pool securitization issues collateral certificates representing a beneficial interest in all or a portion of the securitized assets held by that securitization to another revolving pool securitization, which in turn issues ABS interests for which the collateral certificates are all or a portion of the securitized assets, a sponsor may satisfy the requirements of paragraphs (b) and (c) of this section by retaining the seller's interest for the assets represented by the collateral certificates through either of the revolving pool securitizations, so long as both revolving pool securitizations are retained at the direction of the same sponsor or its wholly-owned affiliates.

(3) If the sponsor retains the seller's interest associated with the collateral certificates at the level of the revolving pool securitization that issues those collateral certificates, the proportion of the seller's interest required by paragraph (b) of this section retained at that level must equal the proportion that the principal balance of the securitized assets represented by the collateral certificates bears to the principal balance of the securitized assets in the revolving pool securitization that issues the ABS interests, as of each measurement date required by paragraph (c) of this section.

(f) *Offset for pool-level excess funding account.* The 5 percent seller's interest required on each measurement date by paragraph (c) of this section may be reduced on a dollar-for-dollar basis by the balance, as of such date, of an excess funding account in the form of a segregated account that:

(1) Is funded in the event of a failure to meet the minimum seller's interest requirements or other requirement to maintain a minimum balance of securitized assets under the securitization transaction documents by distributions otherwise payable to the holder of the seller's interest;

(2) Is invested only in the types of assets in which funds held in a horizontal cash reserve account pursuant to § 246.4 are permitted to be invested; and

(3) In the event of an early amortization, makes payments of amounts held in the account to holders of investor ABS interests in the same manner as payments to holders of investor ABS interests of amounts received on securitized assets.

(g) *Combined seller's interests and horizontal interest retention.* The 5 percent seller's interest required on each measurement date by paragraph (c) of this section may be reduced to a percentage lower than 5 percent to the extent that, for all series of investor ABS interests issued after the applicable effective date of this § 246.5, the sponsor, or notwithstanding § 246.12(a) a wholly-owned affiliate of the sponsor, retains, at a minimum, a corresponding percentage of the fair value of ABS interests issued in each series, in the form of one or more of the horizontal residual interests meeting the requirements of paragraphs (h) or (i).

(h) *Residual ABS interests in excess interest and fees.* The sponsor may take the offset described in paragraph (g) of this section for a residual ABS interest in excess interest and fees, whether certificated or uncertificated, in a single or multiple classes, subclasses, or tranches, that meets, individually or in the aggregate, the requirements of this paragraph (h);

(1) Each series of the revolving pool securitization distinguishes between the series' share of the interest and fee cash flows and the series' share of the principal repayment cash flows from the securitized assets collateralizing the revolving pool securitization, which may according to the terms of the securitization transaction documents, include not only the series' ratable share of such cash flows but also excess cash flows available from other series;

(2) The residual ABS interest's claim to any part of the series' share of the interest and fee cash flows for any interest payment period is subordinated to all accrued and payable interest due

§ 246.5

on the payment date to more senior ABS interests in the series for that period, and further reduced by the series' share of losses, including defaults on principal of the securitized assets collateralizing the revolving pool securitization (whether incurred in that period or carried over from prior periods) to the extent that such payments would have been included in amounts payable to more senior interests in the series;

(3) The revolving pool securitization continues to revolve, with one or more series, classes, subclasses, or tranches of asset-backed securities that are collateralized by a common pool of assets that change in composition over time; and

(4) For purposes of taking the offset described in paragraph (g) of this section, the sponsor determines the fair value of the residual ABS interest in excess interest and fees, and the fair value of the series of outstanding investor ABS interests to which it is subordinated and supports using the fair value measurement framework under GAAP, as of:

(i) The closing of the securitization transaction issuing the supported ABS interests; and

(ii) The seller's interest measurement dates described in paragraph (c)(4) of this section, except that for these periodic determinations the sponsor must update the fair value of the residual ABS interest in excess interest and fees for the numerator of the percentage ratio, but may at the sponsor's option continue to use the fair values determined in (h)(4)(i) for the outstanding investor ABS interests in the denominator.

(i) *Offsetting eligible horizontal residual interest.* The sponsor may take the offset described in paragraph (g) of this section for ABS interests that would meet the definition of eligible horizontal residual interests in § 246.2 but for the sponsor's simultaneous holding of subordinated seller's interests, residual ABS interests in excess interests and fees, or a combination of the two, if:

(1) The sponsor complies with all requirements of paragraphs (b) through (e) of this section for its holdings of subordinated seller's interest, and paragraph (h) for its holdings of residual ABS interests in excess interests and fees, as applicable;

(2) For purposes of taking the offset described in paragraph (g) of this section, the sponsor determines the fair value of the eligible horizontal residual interest as a percentage of the fair value of the outstanding investor ABS interests in the series supported by the eligible horizontal residual interest, determined using the fair value measurement framework under GAAP:

(i) As of the closing of the securitization transaction issuing the supported ABS interests; and

(ii) Without including in the numerator of the percentage ratio any fair value based on:

(A) The subordinated seller's interest or residual ABS interest in excess interest and fees;

(B) the interest payable to the sponsor on the eligible horizontal residual interest, if the sponsor is including the value of residual ABS interest in excess interest and fees pursuant to paragraph (h) of this section in taking the offset in paragraph (g) of this section; and,

(C) the principal payable to the sponsor on the eligible horizontal residual interest, if the sponsor is including the value of the seller's interest pursuant to paragraphs (b) through (f) of this section and distributions on that seller's interest are available to reduce charge-offs that would otherwise be allocated to reduce principal payable to the offset eligible horizontal residual interest.

(j) *Specified dates.* A sponsor using data about the revolving pool securitization's collateral, or ABS interests previously issued, to determine the closing-date percentage of a seller's interest, residual ABS interest in excess interest and fees, or eligible horizontal residual interest pursuant to this § 246.5 may use such data prepared as of specified dates if:

(1) The sponsor describes the specified dates in the disclosures required by paragraph (k) of this section; and

(2) The dates are no more than 60 days prior to the date of first use with investors of disclosures required for the interest by paragraph (k) of this section, or for revolving pool securitizations that make distributions

Securities and Exchange Commission § 246.5

to investors on a quarterly or less frequent basis, no more than 135 days prior to the date of first use with investors of such disclosures.

(k) *Disclosure and record maintenance.* (1) *Disclosure.* A sponsor relying on this section shall provide, or cause to be provided, to potential investors, under the caption "Credit Risk Retention" the following disclosure in written form and within the time frames set forth in this paragraph (k):

(i) A reasonable period of time prior to the sale of an asset-backed security, a description of the material terms of the seller's interest, and the percentage of the seller's interest that the sponsor expects to retain at the closing of the securitization transaction, measured in accordance with the requirements of this § 246.5, as a percentage of the aggregate unpaid principal balance of all outstanding investor ABS interests issued, or as a percentage of the aggregate unpaid principal balance of outstanding investor ABS interests for one or more series issued, as required by the terms of the securitization transaction;

(ii) A reasonable time after the closing of the securitization transaction, the amount of seller's interest the sponsor retained at closing, if that amount is materially different from the amount disclosed under paragraph (k)(1)(i) of this section; and

(iii) A description of the material terms of any horizontal residual interests offsetting the seller's interest in accordance with paragraphs (g), (h), and (i) of this section; and

(iv) Disclosure of the fair value of those horizontal residual interests retained by the sponsor for the series being offered to investors and described in the disclosures, as a percentage of the fair value of the outstanding investor ABS interests issued, described in the same manner and within the same timeframes required for disclosure of the fair values of eligible horizontal residual interests specified in § 246.4(c).

(2) *Adjusted data.* Disclosures required by this paragraph (k) to be made a reasonable period of time prior to the sale of an asset-backed security of the amount of seller's interest, residual ABS interest in excess interest and fees, or eligible horizontal residual interest may include adjustments to the amount of securitized assets for additions or removals the sponsor expects to make before the closing date and adjustments to the amount of outstanding investor ABS interests for expected increases and decreases of those interests under the control of the sponsor.

(3) *Record maintenance.* A sponsor must retain the disclosures required in paragraph (k)(1) of this section in its records and must provide the disclosure upon request to the Commission and its appropriate Federal banking agency, if any, until three years after all ABS interests are no longer outstanding.

(l) *Early amortization of all outstanding series.* A sponsor that organizes a revolving pool securitization that relies on this § 246.5 to satisfy the risk retention requirements of § 246.3, does not violate the requirements of this part if its seller's interest falls below the level required by § 246. 5 after the revolving pool securitization commences early amortization, pursuant to the terms of the securitization transaction documents, of all series of outstanding investor ABS interests, if:

(1) The sponsor was in full compliance with the requirements of this section on all measurement dates specified in paragraph (c) of this section prior to the commencement of early amortization;

(2) The terms of the seller's interest continue to make it *pari passu* with or subordinate in identical or varying amounts to each series of outstanding investor ABS interests issued with respect to the allocation of all distributions and losses with respect to the securitized assets;

(3) The terms of any horizontal interest relied upon by the sponsor pursuant to paragraph (g) to offset the minimum seller's interest amount continue to require the interests to absorb losses in accordance with the terms of paragraph (h) or (i) of this section, as applicable; and

(4) The revolving pool securitization issues no additional ABS interests after early amortization is initiated to any person not a wholly-owned affiliate of the sponsor, either at the time of

§ 246.6

issuance or during the amortization period.

§ 246.6 Eligible ABCP conduits.

(a) *Definitions.* For purposes of this section, the following additional definitions apply:

100 percent liquidity coverage means an amount equal to the outstanding balance of all ABCP issued by the conduit plus any accrued and unpaid interest without regard to the performance of the ABS interests held by the ABCP conduit and without regard to any credit enhancement.

ABCP means asset-backed commercial paper that has a maturity at the time of issuance not exceeding 397 days, exclusive of days of grace, or any renewal thereof the maturity of which is likewise limited.

ABCP conduit means an issuing entity with respect to ABCP.

Eligible ABCP conduit means an ABCP conduit, *provided that:*

(1) The ABCP conduit is bankruptcy remote or otherwise isolated for insolvency purposes from the sponsor of the ABCP conduit and from any intermediate SPV;

(2) The ABS interests acquired by the ABCP conduit are:

(i) ABS interests collateralized solely by assets originated by an originator-seller and by servicing assets;

(ii) Special units of beneficial interest (or similar ABS interests) in a trust or special purpose vehicle that retains legal title to leased property underlying leases originated by an originator-seller that were transferred to an intermediate SPV in connection with a securitization collateralized solely by such leases and by servicing assets;

(iii) ABS interests in a revolving pool securitization collateralized solely by assets originated by an originator-seller and by servicing assets; or

(iv) ABS interests described in paragraph (2)(i), (ii), or (iii) of this definition that are collateralized, in whole or in part, by assets acquired by an originator-seller in a business combination that qualifies for business combination accounting under GAAP, and, if collateralized in part, the remainder of such assets are assets described in paragraph (2)(i), (ii), or (iii) of this definition; and

(v) Acquired by the ABCP conduit in an initial issuance by or on behalf of an intermediate SPV:

(A) Directly from the intermediate SPV,

(B) From an underwriter of the ABS interests issued by the intermediate SPV, or

(C) From another person who acquired the ABS interests directly from the intermediate SPV;

(3) The ABCP conduit is collateralized solely by ABS interests acquired from intermediate SPVs as described in paragraph (2) of this definition and servicing assets; and

(4) A regulated liquidity provider has entered into a legally binding commitment to provide 100 percent liquidity coverage (in the form of a lending facility, an asset purchase agreement, a repurchase agreement, or other similar arrangement) to all the ABCP issued by the ABCP conduit by lending to, purchasing ABCP issued by, or purchasing assets from, the ABCP conduit in the event that funds are required to repay maturing ABCP issued by the ABCP conduit. With respect to the 100 percent liquidity coverage, in the event that the ABCP conduit is unable for any reason to repay maturing ABCP issued by the issuing entity, the liquidity provider shall be obligated to pay an amount equal to any shortfall, and the total amount that may be due pursuant to the 100 percent liquidity coverage shall be equal to 100 percent of the amount of the ABCP outstanding at any time plus accrued and unpaid interest (amounts due pursuant to the required liquidity coverage may not be subject to credit performance of the ABS interests held by the ABCP conduit or reduced by the amount of credit support provided to the ABCP conduit and liquidity support that only funds performing loans or receivables or performing ABS interests does not meet the requirements of this section).

Intermediate SPV means a special purpose vehicle that:

(1) (i) Is a direct or indirect wholly-owned affiliate of the originator-seller; or

(ii) Has nominal equity owned by a trust or corporate service provider that specializes in providing independent ownership of special purpose vehicles,

Securities and Exchange Commission § 246.6

and such trust or corporate service provider is not affiliated with any other transaction parties;

(2) Is bankruptcy remote or otherwise isolated for insolvency purposes from the eligible ABCP conduit and from each originator-seller and each majority-owned affiliate in each case that, directly or indirectly, sells or transfers assets to such intermediate SPV;

(3) Acquires assets from the originator-seller that are originated by the originator-seller or acquired by the originator-seller in the acquisition of a business that qualifies for business combination accounting under GAAP or acquires ABS interests issued by another intermediate SPV of the originator-seller that are collateralized solely by such assets; and

(4) Issues ABS interests collateralized solely by such assets, as applicable.

Originator-seller means an entity that originates assets and sells or transfers those assets, directly or through a majority-owned affiliate, to an intermediate SPV, and includes (except for the purposes of identifying the sponsorship and affiliation of an intermediate SPV pursuant to this §246.6) any affiliate of the originator-seller that, directly or indirectly, majority controls, is majority controlled by or is under common majority control with, the originator-seller. For purposes of this definition, majority control means ownership of more than 50 percent of the equity of an entity, or ownership of any other controlling financial interest in the entity, as determined under GAAP.

Regulated liquidity provider means:

(1) A depository institution (as defined in section 3 of the Federal Deposit Insurance Act (12 U.S.C. 1813));

(2) A bank holding company (as defined in 12 U.S.C. 1841), or a subsidiary thereof;

(3) A savings and loan holding company (as defined in 12 U.S.C. 1467a), provided all or substantially all of the holding company's activities are permissible for a financial holding company under 12 U.S.C. 1843(k), or a subsidiary thereof; or

(4) A foreign bank whose home country supervisor (as defined in §211.21 of the Federal Reserve Board's Regulation K (12 CFR 211.21)) has adopted capital standards consistent with the Capital Accord of the Basel Committee on Banking Supervision, as amended, and that is subject to such standards, or a subsidiary thereof.

(b) *In general.* An ABCP conduit sponsor satisfies the risk retention requirement of §246.3 with respect to the issuance of ABCP by an eligible ABCP conduit in a securitization transaction if, for each ABS interest the ABCP conduit acquires from an intermediate SPV:

(1) An originator-seller of the intermediate SPV retains an economic interest in the credit risk of the assets collateralizing the ABS interest acquired by the eligible ABCP conduit in the amount and manner required under §246.4 or §246.5; and

(2) The ABCP conduit sponsor:

(i) Approves each originator-seller permitted to sell or transfer assets, directly or indirectly, to an intermediate SPV from which an eligible ABCP conduit acquires ABS interests;

(ii) Approves each intermediate SPV from which an eligible ABCP conduit is permitted to acquire ABS interests;

(iii) Establishes criteria governing the ABS interests, and the securitized assets underlying the ABS interests, acquired by the ABCP conduit;

(iv) Administers the ABCP conduit by monitoring the ABS interests acquired by the ABCP conduit and the assets supporting those ABS interests, arranging for debt placement, compiling monthly reports, and ensuring compliance with the ABCP conduit documents and with the ABCP conduit's credit and investment policy; and

(v) Maintains and adheres to policies and procedures for ensuring that the requirements in this paragraph (b) of this section have been met.

(c) *Originator-seller compliance with risk retention.* The use of the risk retention option provided in this section by an ABCP conduit sponsor does not relieve the originator-seller that sponsors ABS interests acquired by an eligible ABCP conduit from such originator-seller's obligation to comply with its own risk retention obligations under this part.

§ 246.6

(d) *Disclosures*—(1) *Periodic disclosures to investors.* An ABCP conduit sponsor relying upon this section shall provide, or cause to be provided, to each purchaser of ABCP, before or contemporaneously with the first sale of ABCP to such purchaser and at least monthly thereafter, to each holder of commercial paper issued by the ABCP conduit, in writing, each of the following items of information, which shall be as of a date not more than 60 days prior to date of first use with investors:

(i) The name and form of organization of the regulated liquidity provider that provides liquidity coverage to the eligible ABCP conduit, including a description of the material terms of such liquidity coverage, and notice of any failure to fund.

(ii) With respect to each ABS interest held by the ABCP conduit:

(A) The asset class or brief description of the underlying securitized assets;

(B) The standard industrial category code (SIC Code) for the originator-seller that will retain (or has retained) pursuant to this section an interest in the securitization transaction; and

(C) A description of the percentage amount of risk retention pursuant to the rule by the originator-seller, and whether it is in the form of an eligible horizontal residual interest, vertical interest, or revolving pool securitization seller's interest, as applicable.

(2) *Disclosures to regulators regarding originator-sellers.* An ABCP conduit sponsor relying upon this section shall provide, or cause to be provided, upon request, to the Commission and its appropriate Federal banking agency, if any, in writing, all of the information required to be provided to investors in paragraph (d)(1) of this section, and the name and form of organization of each originator-seller that will retain (or has retained) pursuant to this section an interest in the securitization transaction.

(e) *Sale or transfer of ABS interests between eligible ABCP conduits.* At any time, an eligible ABCP conduit that acquired an ABS interest in accordance with the requirements set forth in this section may transfer, and another eligible ABCP conduit may acquire, such ABS interest, if the following conditions are satisfied:

(1) The sponsors of both eligible ABCP conduits are in compliance with this section; and

(2) The same regulated liquidity provider has entered into one or more legally binding commitments to provide 100 percent liquidity coverage to all the ABCP issued by both eligible ABCP conduits.

(f) *Duty to comply.* (1) The ABCP conduit sponsor shall be responsible for compliance with this section.

(2) An ABCP conduit sponsor relying on this section:

(i) Shall maintain and adhere to policies and procedures that are reasonably designed to monitor compliance by each originator-seller which is satisfying a risk retention obligation in respect of ABS interests acquired by an eligible ABCP conduit with the requirements of paragraph (b)(1) of this section; and

(ii) In the event that the ABCP conduit sponsor determines that an originator-seller no longer complies with the requirements of paragraph (b)(1) of this section, shall:

(A) Promptly notify the holders of the ABCP, and upon request, the Commission and its appropriate Federal banking agency, if any, in writing of:

(*1*) The name and form of organization of any originator-seller that fails to retain risk in accordance with paragraph (b)(1) of this section and the amount of ABS interests issued by an intermediate SPV of such originator-seller and held by the ABCP conduit;

(*2*) The name and form of organization of any originator-seller that hedges, directly or indirectly through an intermediate SPV, its risk retention in violation of paragraph (b)(1) of this section and the amount of ABS interests issued by an intermediate SPV of such originator-seller and held by the ABCP conduit; and

(*3*) Any remedial actions taken by the ABCP conduit sponsor or other party with respect to such ABS interests; and

(B) Take other appropriate steps pursuant to the requirements of paragraphs (b)(2)(iv) and (v) of this section which may include, as appropriate, curing any breach of the requirements in

Securities and Exchange Commission § 246.7

this section, or removing from the eligible ABCP conduit any ABS interest that does not comply with the requirements in this section.

§ 246.7 Commercial mortgage-backed securities.

(a) *Definitions*. For purposes of this section, the following definition shall apply:

Special servicer means, with respect to any securitization of commercial real estate loans, any servicer that, upon the occurrence of one or more specified conditions in the servicing agreement, has the right to service one or more assets in the transaction.

(b) *Third-party purchaser*. A sponsor may satisfy some or all of its risk retention requirements under § 246.3 with respect to a securitization transaction if a third party (or any majority-owned affiliate thereof) purchases and holds for its own account an eligible horizontal residual interest in the issuing entity in the same form, amount, and manner as would be held by the sponsor under § 246.4 and all of the following conditions are met:

(1) *Number of third-party purchasers*. At any time, there are no more than two third-party purchasers of an eligible horizontal residual interest. If there are two third-party purchasers, each third-party purchaser's interest must be *pari passu* with the other third-party purchaser's interest.

(2) *Composition of collateral*. The securitization transaction is collateralized solely by commercial real estate loans and servicing assets.

(3) *Source of funds*. (i) Each third-party purchaser pays for the eligible horizontal residual interest in cash at the closing of the securitization transaction.

(ii) No third-party purchaser obtains financing, directly or indirectly, for the purchase of such interest from any other person that is a party to, or an affiliate of a party to, the securitization transaction (including, but not limited to, the sponsor, depositor, or servicer other than a special servicer affiliated with the third-party purchaser), other than a person that is a party to the transaction solely by reason of being an investor.

(4) *Third-party review*. Each third-party purchaser conducts an independent review of the credit risk of each securitized asset prior to the sale of the asset-backed securities in the securitization transaction that includes, at a minimum, a review of the underwriting standards, collateral, and expected cash flows of each commercial real estate loan that is collateral for the asset-backed securities.

(5) *Affiliation and control rights*. (i) Except as provided in paragraph (b)(5)(ii) of this section, no third-party purchaser is affiliated with any party to the securitization transaction (including, but not limited to, the sponsor, depositor, or servicer) other than investors in the securitization transaction.

(ii) Notwithstanding paragraph (b)(5)(i) of this section, a third-party purchaser may be affiliated with:

(A) The special servicer for the securitization transaction; or

(B) One or more originators of the securitized assets, as long as the assets originated by the affiliated originator or originators collectively comprise less than 10 percent of the unpaid principal balance of the securitized assets included in the securitization transaction at the cut-off date or similar date for establishing the composition of the securitized assets collateralizing the asset-backed securities issued pursuant to the securitization transaction.

(6) *Operating Advisor*. The underlying securitization transaction documents shall provide for the following:

(i) The appointment of an operating advisor (the Operating Advisor) that:

(A) Is not affiliated with other parties to the securitization transaction;

(B) Does not directly or indirectly have any financial interest in the securitization transaction other than in fees from its role as Operating Advisor; and

(C) Is required to act in the best interest of, and for the benefit of, investors as a collective whole;

(ii) Standards with respect to the Operating Advisor's experience, expertise and financial strength to fulfill its duties and responsibilities under the applicable transaction documents over the life of the securitization transaction;

§ 246.7

(iii) The terms of the Operating Advisor's compensation with respect to the securitization transaction;

(iv) When the eligible horizontal residual interest has been reduced by principal payments, realized losses, and appraisal reduction amounts (which reduction amounts are determined in accordance with the applicable transaction documents) to a principal balance of 25 percent or less of its initial principal balance, the special servicer for the securitized assets must consult with the Operating Advisor in connection with, and prior to, any material decision in connection with its servicing of the securitized assets, including, without limitation:

(A) Any material modification of, or waiver with respect to, any provision of a loan agreement (including a mortgage, deed of trust, or other security agreement);

(B) Foreclosure upon or comparable conversion of the ownership of a property; or

(C) Any acquisition of a property.

(v) The Operating Advisor shall have adequate and timely access to information and reports necessary to fulfill its duties under the transaction documents, including all reports made available to holders of ABS interests and third-party purchasers, and shall be responsible for:

(A) Reviewing the actions of the special servicer;

(B) Reviewing all reports provided by the special servicer to the issuing entity or any holder of ABS interests;

(C) Reviewing for accuracy and consistency with the transaction documents calculations made by the special servicer; and

(D) Issuing a report to investors (including any third-party purchasers) and the issuing entity on a periodic basis concerning:

(1) Whether the Operating Advisor believes, in its sole discretion exercised in good faith, that the special servicer is operating in compliance with any standard required of the special servicer in the applicable transaction documents; and

(2) Which, if any, standards the Operating Advisor believes, in its sole discretion exercised in good faith, the special servicer has failed to comply.

(vi)(A) The Operating Advisor shall have the authority to recommend that the special servicer be replaced by a successor special servicer if the Operating Advisor determines, in its sole discretion exercised in good faith, that:

(1) The special servicer has failed to comply with a standard required of the special servicer in the applicable transaction documents; and

(2) Such replacement would be in the best interest of the investors as a collective whole; and

(B) If a recommendation described in paragraph (b)(6)(vi)(A) of this section is made, the special servicer shall be replaced upon the affirmative vote of a majority of the outstanding principal balance of all ABS interests voting on the matter, with a minimum of a quorum of ABS interests voting on the matter. For purposes of such vote, the applicable transaction documents shall specify the quorum and may not specify a quorum of more than the holders of 20 percent of the outstanding principal balance of all ABS interests in the issuing entity, with such quorum including at least three ABS interest holders that are not affiliated with each other.

(7) *Disclosures.* The sponsor provides, or causes to be provided, to potential investors a reasonable period of time prior to the sale of the asset-backed securities as part of the securitization transaction and, upon request, to the Commission and its appropriate Federal banking agency, if any, the following disclosure in written form under the caption "Credit Risk Retention":

(i) The name and form of organization of each initial third-party purchaser that acquired an eligible horizontal residual interest at the closing of a securitization transaction;

(ii) A description of each initial third-party purchaser's experience in investing in commercial mortgage-backed securities;

(iii) Any other information regarding each initial third-party purchaser or each initial third-party purchaser's retention of the eligible horizontal residual interest that is material to investors in light of the circumstances of the particular securitization transaction;

Securities and Exchange Commission § 246.7

(iv) The fair value (expressed as a percentage of the fair value of all of the ABS interests issued in the securitization transaction and dollar amount (or corresponding amount in the foreign currency in which the ABS interests are issued, as applicable)) of the eligible horizontal residual interest that will be retained (or was retained) by each initial third-party purchaser, as well as the amount of the purchase price paid by each initial third-party purchaser for such interest;

(v) The fair value (expressed as a percentage of the fair value of all of the ABS interests issued in the securitization transaction and dollar amount (or corresponding amount in the foreign currency in which the ABS interests are issued, as applicable)) of the eligible horizontal residual interest in the securitization transaction that the sponsor would have retained pursuant to § 246.4 if the sponsor had relied on retaining an eligible horizontal residual interest in that section to meet the requirements of § 246.3 with respect to the transaction;

(vi) A description of the material terms of the eligible horizontal residual interest retained by each initial third-party purchaser, including the same information as is required to be disclosed by sponsors retaining horizontal interests pursuant to § 246.4;

(vii) The material terms of the applicable transaction documents with respect to the Operating Advisor, including without limitation:

(A) The name and form of organization of the Operating Advisor;

(B) A description of any material conflict of interest or material potential conflict of interest between the Operating Advisor and any other party to the transaction;

(C) The standards required by paragraph (b)(6)(ii) of this section and a description of how the Operating Advisor satisfies each of the standards; and

(D) The terms of the Operating Advisor's compensation under paragraph (b)(6)(iii) of this section; and

(viii) The representations and warranties concerning the securitized assets, a schedule of any securitized assets that are determined not to comply with such representations and warranties, and what factors were used to make the determination that such securitized assets should be included in the pool notwithstanding that the securitized assets did not comply with such representations and warranties, such as compensating factors or a determination that the exceptions were not material.

(8) *Hedging, transfer and pledging*—(i) *General rule.* Except as set forth in paragraph (b)(8)(ii) of this section, each third-party purchaser and its affiliates must comply with the hedging and other restrictions in § 246.12 as if it were the retaining sponsor with respect to the securitization transaction and had acquired the eligible horizontal residual interest pursuant to § 246.4; provided that, the hedging and other restrictions in § 246.12 shall not apply on or after the date that each CRE loan (as defined in § 246.14) that serves as collateral for outstanding ABS interests has been defeased. For purposes of this section, a loan is deemed to be defeased if:

(A) cash or cash equivalents of the types permitted for an eligible horizontal cash reserve account pursuant to § 246.4 whose maturity corresponds to the remaining debt service obligations, have been pledged to the issuing entity as collateral for the loan and are in such amounts and payable at such times as necessary to timely generate cash sufficient to make all remaining debt service payments due on such loan; and

(B) the issuing entity has an obligation to release its lien on the loan.

(ii) *Exceptions*—(A) *Transfer by initial third-party purchaser or sponsor.* An initial third-party purchaser that acquired an eligible horizontal residual interest at the closing of a securitization transaction in accordance with this section, or a sponsor that acquired an eligible horizontal residual interest at the closing of a securitization transaction in accordance with this section, may, on or after the date that is five years after the date of the closing of the securitization transaction, transfer that interest to a subsequent third-party purchaser that complies with paragraph (b)(8)(ii)(C) of this section. The initial third-party purchaser shall provide the sponsor with complete identifying information

137

§ 246.8

for the subsequent third-party purchaser.

(B) *Transfer by subsequent third-party purchaser.* At any time, a subsequent third-party purchaser that acquired an eligible horizontal residual interest pursuant to this section may transfer its interest to a different third-party purchaser that complies with paragraph (b)(8)(ii)(C) of this section. The transferring third-party purchaser shall provide the sponsor with complete identifying information for the acquiring third-party purchaser.

(C) *Requirements applicable to subsequent third-party purchasers.* A subsequent third-party purchaser is subject to all of the requirements of paragraphs (b)(1), (b)(3) through (5), and (b)(8) of this section applicable to third-party purchasers, provided that obligations under paragraphs (b)(1), (b)(3) through (5), and (b)(8) of this section that apply to initial third-party purchasers at or before the time of closing of the securitization transaction shall apply to successor third-party purchasers at or before the time of the transfer of the eligible horizontal residual interest to the successor third-party purchaser.

(c) *Duty to comply.* (1) The retaining sponsor shall be responsible for compliance with this section by itself and for compliance by each initial or subsequent third-party purchaser that acquired an eligible horizontal residual interest in the securitization transaction.

(2) A sponsor relying on this section:

(i) Shall maintain and adhere to policies and procedures to monitor each third-party purchaser's compliance with the requirements of paragraphs (b)(1), (b)(3) through (5), and (b)(8) of this section; and

(ii) In the event that the sponsor determines that a third-party purchaser no longer complies with one or more of the requirements of paragraphs (b)(1), (b)(3) through (5), or (b)(8) of this section, shall promptly notify, or cause to be notified, the holders of the ABS interests issued in the securitization transaction of such noncompliance by such third-party purchaser.

17 CFR Ch. II (4–1–23 Edition)

§ 246.8 **Federal National Mortgage Association and Federal Home Loan Mortgage Corporation ABS.**

(a) *In general.* A sponsor satisfies its risk retention requirement under this part if the sponsor fully guarantees the timely payment of principal and interest on all ABS interests issued by the issuing entity in the securitization transaction and is:

(1) The Federal National Mortgage Association or the Federal Home Loan Mortgage Corporation operating under the conservatorship or receivership of the Federal Housing Finance Agency pursuant to section 1367 of the Federal Housing Enterprises Financial Safety and Soundness Act of 1992 (12 U.S.C. 4617) with capital support from the United States; or

(2) Any limited-life regulated entity succeeding to the charter of either the Federal National Mortgage Association or the Federal Home Loan Mortgage Corporation pursuant to section 1367(i) of the Federal Housing Enterprises Financial Safety and Soundness Act of 1992 (12 U.S.C. 4617(i)), provided that the entity is operating with capital support from the United States.

(b) *Certain provisions not applicable.* The provisions of § 246.12(b), (c), and (d) shall not apply to a sponsor described in paragraph (a)(1) or (2) of this section, its affiliates, or the issuing entity with respect to a securitization transaction for which the sponsor has retained credit risk in accordance with the requirements of this section.

(c) *Disclosure.* A sponsor relying on this section shall provide to investors, in written form under the caption "Credit Risk Retention" and, upon request, to the Federal Housing Finance Agency and the Commission, a description of the manner in which it has met the credit risk retention requirements of this part.

§ 246.9 **Open market CLOs.**

(a) *Definitions.* For purposes of this section, the following definitions shall apply:

CLO means a special purpose entity that:

(i) Issues debt and equity interests, and

(ii) Whose assets consist primarily of loans that are securitized assets and servicing assets.

CLO-eligible loan tranche means a term loan of a syndicated facility that meets the criteria set forth in paragraph (c) of this section.

CLO manager means an entity that manages a CLO, which entity is registered as an investment adviser under the Investment Advisers Act of 1940, as amended (15 U.S.C. 80b-1 *et seq.*), or is an affiliate of such a registered investment adviser and itself is managed by such registered investment adviser.

Commercial borrower means an obligor under a corporate credit obligation (including a loan).

Initial loan syndication transaction means a transaction in which a loan is syndicated to a group of lenders.

Lead arranger means, with respect to a CLO-eligible loan tranche, an institution that:

(i) Is active in the origination, structuring and syndication of commercial loan transactions (as defined in § 246.14) and has played a primary role in the structuring, underwriting and distribution on the primary market of the CLO-eligible loan tranche.

(ii) Has taken an allocation of the funded portion of the syndicated credit facility under the terms of the transaction that includes the CLO-eligible loan tranche of at least 20 percent of the aggregate principal balance at origination, and no other member (or members affiliated with each other) of the syndication group that funded at origination has taken a greater allocation; and

(iii) Is identified in the applicable agreement governing the CLO-eligible loan tranche; represents therein to the holders of the CLO-eligible loan tranche and to any holders of participation interests in such CLO-eligible loan tranche that such lead arranger satisfies the requirements of paragraph (i) of this definition and, at the time of initial funding of the CLO-eligible tranche, will satisfy the requirements of paragraph (ii) of this definition; further represents therein (solely for the purpose of assisting such holders to determine the eligibility of such CLO-eligible loan tranche to be held by an open market CLO) that in the reasonable judgment of such lead arranger, the terms of such CLO-eligible loan tranche are consistent with the requirements of paragraphs (c)(2) and (3) of this section; and covenants therein to such holders that such lead arranger will fulfill the requirements of paragraph (c)(1) of this section.

Open market CLO means a CLO:

(i) Whose assets consist of senior, secured syndicated loans acquired by such CLO directly from the sellers thereof in open market transactions and of servicing assets,

(ii) That is managed by a CLO manager, and

(iii) That holds less than 50 percent of its assets, by aggregate outstanding principal amount, in loans syndicated by lead arrangers that are affiliates of the CLO or the CLO manager or originated by originators that are affiliates of the CLO or the CLO manager.

Open market transaction means:

(i) Either an initial loan syndication transaction or a secondary market transaction in which a seller offers senior, secured syndicated loans to prospective purchasers in the loan market on market terms on an arm's length basis, which prospective purchasers include, but are not limited to, entities that are not affiliated with the seller, or

(ii) A reverse inquiry from a prospective purchaser of a senior, secured syndicated loan through a dealer in the loan market to purchase a senior, secured syndicated loan to be sourced by the dealer in the loan market.

Secondary market transaction means a purchase of a senior, secured syndicated loan not in connection with an initial loan syndication transaction but in the secondary market.

Senior, secured syndicated loan means a loan made to a commercial borrower that:

(i) Is not subordinate in right of payment to any other obligation for borrowed money of the commercial borrower,

(ii) Is secured by a valid first priority security interest or lien in or on specified collateral securing the commercial borrower's obligations under the loan, and

§ 246.9

(iii) The value of the collateral subject to such first priority security interest or lien, together with other attributes of the obligor (including, without limitation, its general financial condition, ability to generate cash flow available for debt service and other demands for that cash flow), is adequate (in the commercially reasonable judgment of the CLO manager exercised at the time of investment) to repay the loan and to repay all other indebtedness of equal seniority secured by such first priority security interest or lien in or on the same collateral, and the CLO manager certifies, on or prior to each date that it acquires a loan constituting part of a new CLO-eligible tranche, that it has policies and procedures to evaluate the likelihood of repayment of loans acquired by the CLO and it has followed such policies and procedures in evaluating each CLO-eligible loan tranche.

(b) *In general.* A sponsor satisfies the risk retention requirements of § 246.3 with respect to an open market CLO transaction if:

(1) The open market CLO does not acquire or hold any assets other than CLO-eligible loan tranches that meet the requirements of paragraph (c) of this section and servicing assets;

(2) The governing documents of such open market CLO require that, at all times, the assets of the open market CLO consist of senior, secured syndicated loans that are CLO-eligible loan tranches and servicing assets;

(3) The open market CLO does not invest in ABS interests or in credit derivatives other than hedging transactions that are servicing assets to hedge risks of the open market CLO;

(4) All purchases of CLO-eligible loan tranches and other assets by the open market CLO issuing entity or through a warehouse facility used to accumulate the loans prior to the issuance of the CLO's ABS interests are made in open market transactions on an armslength basis;

(5) The CLO manager of the open market CLO is not entitled to receive any management fee or gain on sale at the time the open market CLO issues its ABS interests.

(c) *CLO-eligible loan tranche.* To qualify as a CLO-eligible loan tranche, a term loan of a syndicated credit facility to a commercial borrower must have the following features:

(1) A minimum of 5 percent of the face amount of the CLO-eligible loan tranche is retained by the lead arranger thereof until the earliest of the repayment, maturity, involuntary and unscheduled acceleration, payment default, or bankruptcy default of such CLO-eligible loan tranche, provided that such lead arranger complies with limitations on hedging, transferring and pledging in § 246.12 with respect to the interest retained by the lead arranger.

(2) Lender voting rights within the credit agreement and any intercreditor or other applicable agreements governing such CLO-eligible loan tranche are defined so as to give holders of the CLO-eligible loan tranche consent rights with respect to, at minimum, any material waivers and amendments of such applicable documents, including but not limited to, adverse changes to the calculation or payments of amounts due to the holders of the CLO-eligible tranche, alterations to *pro rata* provisions, changes to voting provisions, and waivers of conditions precedent; and

(3) The pro rata provisions, voting provisions, and similar provisions applicable to the security associated with such CLO-eligible loan tranches under the CLO credit agreement and any intercreditor or other applicable agreements governing such CLO-eligible loan tranches are not materially less advantageous to the holder(s) of such CLO-eligible tranche than the terms of other tranches of comparable seniority in the broader syndicated credit facility.

(d) *Disclosures.* A sponsor relying on this section shall provide, or cause to be provided, to potential investors a reasonable period of time prior to the sale of the asset-backed securities in the securitization transaction and at least annually with respect to the information required by paragraph (d)(1) of this section and, upon request, to the Commission and its appropriate Federal banking agency, if any, the following disclosure in written form under the caption "Credit Risk Retention":

Securities and Exchange Commission § 246.10

(1) *Open market CLOs.* A complete list of every asset held by an open market CLO (or before the CLO's closing, in a warehouse facility in anticipation of transfer into the CLO at closing), including the following information:

(i) The full legal name, Standard Industrial Classification (SIC) category code, and legal entity identifier (LEI) issued by a utility endorsed or otherwise governed by the Global LEI Regulatory Oversight Committee or the Global LEI Foundation (if an LEI has been obtained by the obligor) of the obligor of the loan or asset;

(ii) The full name of the specific loan tranche held by the CLO;

(iii) The face amount of the entire loan tranche held by the CLO, and the face amount of the portion thereof held by the CLO;

(iv) The price at which the loan tranche was acquired by the CLO; and

(v) For each loan tranche, the full legal name of the lead arranger subject to the sales and hedging restrictions of § 246.12; and

(2) *CLO manager.* The full legal name and form of organization of the CLO manager.

§ 246.10 Qualified tender option bonds.

(a) *Definitions.* For purposes of this section, the following definitions shall apply:

Municipal security or *municipal securities* shall have the same meaning as the term "municipal securities" in Section 3(a)(29) of the Securities Exchange Act of 1934 (15 U.S.C. 78c(a)(29)) and any rules promulgated pursuant to such section.

Qualified tender option bond entity means an issuing entity with respect to tender option bonds for which each of the following applies:

(i) Such entity is collateralized solely by servicing assets and by municipal securities that have the same municipal issuer and the same underlying obligor or source of payment (determined without regard to any third-party credit enhancement), and such municipal securities are not subject to substitution.

(ii) Such entity issues no securities other than:

(A) A single class of tender option bonds with a preferred variable return payable out of capital that meets the requirements of paragraph (b) of this section, and

(B) One or more residual equity interests that, in the aggregate, are entitled to all remaining income of the issuing entity.

(C) The types of securities referred to in paragraphs (ii)(A) and (B) of this definition must constitute asset-backed securities.

(iii) The municipal securities held as assets by such entity are issued in compliance with Section 103 of the Internal Revenue Code of 1986, as amended (the "IRS Code", 26 U.S.C. 103), such that the interest payments made on those securities are excludable from the gross income of the owners under Section 103 of the IRS Code.

(iv) The terms of all of the securities issued by the entity are structured so that all holders of such securities who are eligible to exclude interest received on such securities will be able to exclude that interest from gross income pursuant to Section 103 of the IRS Code or as "exempt-interest dividends" pursuant to Section 852(b)(5) of the IRS Code (26 U.S.C. 852(b)(5)) in the case of regulated investment companies under the Investment Company Act of 1940, as amended.

(v) Such entity has a legally binding commitment from a regulated liquidity provider as defined in § 246.6(a), to provide a 100 percent guarantee or liquidity coverage with respect to all of the issuing entity's outstanding tender option bonds.

(vi) Such entity qualifies for monthly closing elections pursuant to IRS Revenue Procedure 2003–84, as amended or supplemented from time to time.

Tender option bond means a security which has features which entitle the holders to tender such bonds to the issuing entity for purchase at any time upon no more than 397 days' notice, for a purchase price equal to the approximate amortized cost of the security, plus accrued interest, if any, at the time of tender.

(b) *Risk retention options.* Notwithstanding anything in this section, the sponsor with respect to an issuance of tender option bonds may retain an eligible vertical interest or eligible horizontal residual interest, or any combination thereof, in accordance with the requirements of §246.4. In order to satisfy its risk retention requirements under this section, the sponsor with respect to an issuance of tender option bonds by a qualified tender option bond entity may retain:

(1) An eligible vertical interest or an eligible horizontal residual interest, or any combination thereof, in accordance with the requirements of §246.4; or

(2) An interest that meets the requirements set forth in paragraph (c) of this section; or

(3) A municipal security that meets the requirements set forth in paragraph (d) of this section; or

(4) Any combination of interests and securities described in paragraphs (b)(1) through (b)(3) of this section such that the sum of the percentages held in each form equals at least five.

(c) *Tender option termination event.* The sponsor with respect to an issuance of tender option bonds by a qualified tender option bond entity may retain an interest that upon issuance meets the requirements of an eligible horizontal residual interest but that upon the occurrence of a "tender option termination event" as defined in Section 4.01(5) of IRS Revenue Procedure 2003–84, as amended or supplemented from time to time will meet the requirements of an eligible vertical interest.

(d) *Retention of a municipal security outside of the qualified tender option bond entity.* The sponsor with respect to an issuance of tender option bonds by a qualified tender option bond entity may satisfy its risk retention requirements under this Section by holding municipal securities from the same issuance of municipal securities deposited in the qualified tender option bond entity, the face value of which retained municipal securities is equal to 5 percent of the face value of the municipal securities deposited in the qualified tender option bond entity.

(e) *Disclosures.* The sponsor shall provide, or cause to be provided, to potential investors a reasonable period of time prior to the sale of the asset-backed securities as part of the securitization transaction and, upon request, to the Commission and its appropriate Federal banking agency, if any, the following disclosure in written form under the caption "Credit Risk Retention":

(1) The name and form of organization of the qualified tender option bond entity;

(2) A description of the form and subordination features of such retained interest in accordance with the disclosure obligations in §246.4(c);

(3) To the extent any portion of the retained interest is claimed by the sponsor as an eligible horizontal residual interest (including any interest held in compliance with §246.10(c)), the fair value of that interest (expressed as a percentage of the fair value of all of the ABS interests issued in the securitization transaction and as a dollar amount);

(4) To the extent any portion of the retained interest is claimed by the sponsor as an eligible vertical interest (including any interest held in compliance with §246.10(c)), the percentage of ABS interests issued represented by the eligible vertical interest; and

(5) To the extent any portion of the retained interest claimed by the sponsor is a municipal security held outside of the qualified tender option bond entity, the name and form of organization of the qualified tender option bond entity, the identity of the issuer of the municipal securities, the face value of the municipal securities deposited into the qualified tender option bond entity, and the face value of the municipal securities retained by the sponsor or its majority-owned affiliates and subject to the transfer and hedging prohibition.

(f) *Prohibitions on Hedging and Transfer.* The prohibitions on transfer and hedging set forth in §246.12, apply to any interests or municipal securities retained by the sponsor with respect to an issuance of tender option bonds by a qualified tender option bond entity pursuant to of this section.

Subpart C—Transfer of Risk Retention

§ 246.11 Allocation of risk retention to an originator.

(a) *In general.* A sponsor choosing to retain an eligible vertical interest or an eligible horizontal residual interest (including an eligible horizontal cash reserve account), or combination thereof under § 246.4, with respect to a securitization transaction may offset the amount of its risk retention requirements under § 246.4 by the amount of the eligible interests, respectively, acquired by an originator of one or more of the securitized assets if:

(1) At the closing of the securitization transaction:

(i) The originator acquires the eligible interest from the sponsor and retains such interest in the same manner and proportion (as between horizontal and vertical interests) as the sponsor under § 246.4, as such interest was held prior to the acquisition by the originator;

(ii) The ratio of the percentage of eligible interests acquired and retained by the originator to the percentage of eligible interests otherwise required to be retained by the sponsor pursuant to § 246.4, does not exceed the ratio of:

(A) The unpaid principal balance of all the securitized assets originated by the originator; to

(B) The unpaid principal balance of all the securitized assets in the securitization transaction;

(iii) The originator acquires and retains at least 20 percent of the aggregate risk retention amount otherwise required to be retained by the sponsor pursuant to § 246.4; and

(iv) The originator purchases the eligible interests from the sponsor at a price that is equal, on a dollar-for-dollar basis, to the amount by which the sponsor's required risk retention is reduced in accordance with this section, by payment to the sponsor in the form of:

(A) Cash; or

(B) A reduction in the price received by the originator from the sponsor or depositor for the assets sold by the originator to the sponsor or depositor for inclusion in the pool of securitized assets.

(2) *Disclosures.* In addition to the disclosures required pursuant to § 246.4(c), the sponsor provides, or causes to be provided, to potential investors a reasonable period of time prior to the sale of the asset-backed securities as part of the securitization transaction and, upon request, to the Commission and its appropriate Federal banking agency, if any, in written form under the caption "Credit Risk Retention", the name and form of organization of any originator that will acquire and retain (or has acquired and retained) an interest in the transaction pursuant to this section, including a description of the form and amount (expressed as a percentage and dollar amount (or corresponding amount in the foreign currency in which the ABS interests are issued, as applicable)) and nature (*e.g.*, senior or subordinated) of the interest, as well as the method of payment for such interest under paragraph (a)(1)(iv) of this section.

(3) *Hedging, transferring and pledging.* The originator and each of its affiliates complies with the hedging and other restrictions in § 246.12 with respect to the interests retained by the originator pursuant to this section as if it were the retaining sponsor and was required to retain the interest under subpart B of this part.

(b) *Duty to comply.* (1) The retaining sponsor shall be responsible for compliance with this section.

(2) A retaining sponsor relying on this section:

(i) Shall maintain and adhere to policies and procedures that are reasonably designed to monitor the compliance by each originator that is allocated a portion of the sponsor's risk retention obligations with the requirements in paragraphs (a)(1) and (3) of this section; and

(ii) In the event the sponsor determines that any such originator no longer complies with any of the requirements in paragraphs (a)(1) and (3) of this section, shall promptly notify, or cause to be notified, the holders of the ABS interests issued in the securitization transaction of such noncompliance by such originator.

§ 246.12 Hedging, transfer and financing prohibitions.

(a) *Transfer.* Except as permitted by § 246.7(b)(8), and subject to § 246.5, a retaining sponsor may not sell or otherwise transfer any interest or assets that the sponsor is required to retain pursuant to subpart B of this part to any person other than an entity that is and remains a majority-owned affiliate of the sponsor and each such majority-owned affiliate shall be subject to the same restrictions.

(b) *Prohibited hedging by sponsor and affiliates.* A retaining sponsor and its affiliates may not purchase or sell a security, or other financial instrument, or enter into an agreement, derivative or other position, with any other person if:

(1) Payments on the security or other financial instrument or under the agreement, derivative, or position are materially related to the credit risk of one or more particular ABS interests that the retaining sponsor (or any of its majority-owned affiliates) is required to retain with respect to a securitization transaction pursuant to subpart B of this part or one or more of the particular securitized assets that collateralize the asset-backed securities issued in the securitization transaction; and

(2) The security, instrument, agreement, derivative, or position in any way reduces or limits the financial exposure of the sponsor (or any of its majority-owned affiliates) to the credit risk of one or more of the particular ABS interests that the retaining sponsor (or any of its majority-owned affiliates) is required to retain with respect to a securitization transaction pursuant to subpart B of this part or one or more of the particular securitized assets that collateralize the asset-backed securities issued in the securitization transaction.

(c) *Prohibited hedging by issuing entity.* The issuing entity in a securitization transaction may not purchase or sell a security or other financial instrument, or enter into an agreement, derivative or position, with any other person if:

(1) Payments on the security or other financial instrument or under the agreement, derivative or position are materially related to the credit risk of one or more particular ABS interests that the retaining sponsor for the transaction (or any of its majority-owned affiliates) is required to retain with respect to the securitization transaction pursuant to subpart B of this part; and

(2) The security, instrument, agreement, derivative, or position in any way reduces or limits the financial exposure of the retaining sponsor (or any of its majority-owned affiliates) to the credit risk of one or more of the particular ABS interests that the sponsor (or any of its majority-owned affiliates) is required to retain pursuant to subpart B of this part.

(d) *Permitted hedging activities.* The following activities shall not be considered prohibited hedging activities under paragraph (b) or (c) of this section:

(1) Hedging the interest rate risk (which does not include the specific interest rate risk, known as spread risk, associated with the ABS interest that is otherwise considered part of the credit risk) or foreign exchange risk arising from one or more of the particular ABS interests required to be retained by the sponsor (or any of its majority-owned affiliates) under subpart B of this part or one or more of the particular securitized assets that underlie the asset-backed securities issued in the securitization transaction; or

(2) Purchasing or selling a security or other financial instrument or entering into an agreement, derivative, or other position with any third party where payments on the security or other financial instrument or under the agreement, derivative, or position are based, directly or indirectly, on an index of instruments that includes asset-backed securities if:

(i) Any class of ABS interests in the issuing entity that were issued in connection with the securitization transaction and that are included in the index represents no more than 10 percent of the dollar-weighted average (or corresponding weighted average in the currency in which the ABS interests are issued, as applicable) of all instruments included in the index; and

(ii) All classes of ABS interests in all issuing entities that were issued in

Securities and Exchange Commission § 246.12

connection with any securitization transaction in which the sponsor (or any of its majority-owned affiliates) is required to retain an interest pursuant to subpart B of this part and that are included in the index represent, in the aggregate, no more than 20 percent of the dollar-weighted average (or corresponding weighted average in the currency in which the ABS interests are issued, as applicable) of all instruments included in the index.

(e) *Prohibited non-recourse financing.* Neither a retaining sponsor nor any of its affiliates may pledge as collateral for any obligation (including a loan, repurchase agreement, or other financing transaction) any ABS interest that the sponsor is required to retain with respect to a securitization transaction pursuant to subpart B of this part unless such obligation is with full recourse to the sponsor or affiliate, respectively.

(f) *Duration of the hedging and transfer restrictions*—(1) *General rule.* Except as provided in paragraph (f)(2) of this section, the prohibitions on sale and hedging pursuant to paragraphs (a) and (b) of this section shall expire on or after the date that is the latest of:

(i) The date on which the total unpaid principal balance (if applicable) of the securitized assets that collateralize the securitization transaction has been reduced to 33 percent of the total unpaid principal balance of the securitized assets as of the cut-off date or similar date for establishing the composition of the securitized assets collateralizing the asset-backed securities issued pursuant to the securitization transaction;

(ii) The date on which the total unpaid principal obligations under the ABS interests issued in the securitization transaction has been reduced to 33 percent of the total unpaid principal obligations of the ABS interests at closing of the securitization transaction; or

(iii) Two years after the date of the closing of the securitization transaction.

(2) *Securitizations of residential mortgages.* (i) If all of the assets that collateralize a securitization transaction subject to risk retention under this part are residential mortgages, the prohibitions on sale and hedging pursuant to paragraphs (a) and (b) of this section shall expire on or after the date that is the later of:

(A) Five years after the date of the closing of the securitization transaction; or

(B) The date on which the total unpaid principal balance of the residential mortgages that collateralize the securitization transaction has been reduced to 25 percent of the total unpaid principal balance of such residential mortgages at the cut-off date or similar date for establishing the composition of the securitized assets collateralizing the asset-backed securities issued pursuant to the securitization transaction.

(ii) Notwithstanding paragraph (f)(2)(i) of this section, the prohibitions on sale and hedging pursuant to paragraphs (a) and (b) of this section shall expire with respect to the sponsor of a securitization transaction described in paragraph (f)(2)(i) of this section on or after the date that is seven years after the date of the closing of the securitization transaction.

(3) *Conservatorship or receivership of sponsor.* A conservator or receiver of the sponsor (or any other person holding risk retention pursuant to this part) of a securitization transaction is permitted to sell or hedge any economic interest in the securitization transaction if the conservator or receiver has been appointed pursuant to any provision of federal or State law (or regulation promulgated thereunder) that provides for the appointment of the Federal Deposit Insurance Corporation, or an agency or instrumentality of the United States or of a State as conservator or receiver, including without limitation any of the following authorities:

(i) 12 U.S.C. 1811;
(ii) 12 U.S.C. 1787;
(iii) 12 U.S.C. 4617; or
(iv) 12 U.S.C. 5382.

(4) *Revolving pool securitizations.* The provisions of paragraphs (f)(1) and (2) are not available to sponsors of revolving pool securitizations with respect to the forms of risk retention specified in § 246.5.

§ 246.13

Subpart D—Exceptions and Exemptions

§ 246.13 Exemption for qualified residential mortgages.

(a) *Definitions.* For purposes of this section, the following definitions shall apply:

Currently performing means the borrower in the mortgage transaction is not currently thirty (30) days or more past due, in whole or in part, on the mortgage transaction.

Qualified residential mortgage means a "qualified mortgage" as defined in section 129C of the Truth in Lending Act (15 U.S.C.1639c) and regulations issued thereunder, as amended from time to time.

(b) *Exemption.* A sponsor shall be exempt from the risk retention requirements in subpart B of this part with respect to any securitization transaction, if:

(1) All of the assets that collateralize the asset-backed securities are qualified residential mortgages or servicing assets;

(2) None of the assets that collateralize the asset-backed securities are asset-backed securities;

(3) As of the cut-off date or similar date for establishing the composition of the securitized assets collateralizing the asset-backed securities issued pursuant to the securitization transaction, each qualified residential mortgage collateralizing the asset-backed securities is currently performing; and

(4)(i) The depositor with respect to the securitization transaction certifies that it has evaluated the effectiveness of its internal supervisory controls with respect to the process for ensuring that all assets that collateralize the asset-backed security are qualified residential mortgages or servicing assets and has concluded that its internal supervisory controls are effective; and

(ii) The evaluation of the effectiveness of the depositor's internal supervisory controls must be performed, for each issuance of an asset-backed security in reliance on this section, as of a date within 60 days of the cut-off date or similar date for establishing the composition of the asset pool collateralizing such asset-backed security; and

(iii) The sponsor provides, or causes to be provided, a copy of the certification described in paragraph (b)(4)(i) of this section to potential investors a reasonable period of time prior to the sale of asset-backed securities in the issuing entity, and, upon request, to the Commission and its appropriate Federal banking agency, if any.

(c) *Repurchase of loans subsequently determined to be non-qualified after closing.* A sponsor that has relied on the exemption provided in paragraph (b) of this section with respect to a securitization transaction shall not lose such exemption with respect to such transaction if, after closing of the securitization transaction, it is determined that one or more of the residential mortgage loans collateralizing the asset-backed securities does not meet all of the criteria to be a qualified residential mortgage *provided that:*

(1) The depositor complied with the certification requirement set forth in paragraph (b)(4) of this section;

(2) The sponsor repurchases the loan(s) from the issuing entity at a price at least equal to the remaining aggregate unpaid principal balance and accrued interest on the loan(s) no later than 90 days after the determination that the loans do not satisfy the requirements to be a qualified residential mortgage; and

(3) The sponsor promptly notifies, or causes to be notified, the holders of the asset-backed securities issued in the securitization transaction of any loan(s) included in such securitization transaction that is (or are) required to be repurchased by the sponsor pursuant to paragraph (c)(2) of this section, including the amount of such repurchased loan(s) and the cause for such repurchase.

§ 246.14 Definitions applicable to qualifying commercial loans, qualifying commercial real estate loans, and qualifying automobile loans.

The following definitions apply for purposes of §§ 246.15 through 246.18:

Appraisal Standards Board means the board of the Appraisal Foundation that develops, interprets, and amends the Uniform Standards of Professional Appraisal Practice (USPAP), establishing

Securities and Exchange Commission §246.14

generally accepted standards for the appraisal profession.

Automobile loan:

(1) Means any loan to an individual to finance the purchase of, and that is secured by a first lien on, a passenger car or other passenger vehicle, such as a minivan, van, sport-utility vehicle, pickup truck, or similar light truck for personal, family, or household use; and

(2) Does not include any:

(i) Loan to finance fleet sales;

(ii) Personal cash loan secured by a previously purchased automobile;

(iii) Loan to finance the purchase of a commercial vehicle or farm equipment that is not used for personal, family, or household purposes;

(iv) Lease financing;

(v) Loan to finance the purchase of a vehicle with a salvage title; or

(vi) Loan to finance the purchase of a vehicle intended to be used for scrap or parts.

Combined loan-to-value (CLTV) ratio means, at the time of origination, the sum of the principal balance of a first-lien mortgage loan on the property, plus the principal balance of any junior-lien mortgage loan that, to the creditor's knowledge, would exist at the closing of the transaction and that is secured by the same property, divided by:

(1) For acquisition funding, the lesser of the purchase price or the estimated market value of the real property based on an appraisal that meets the requirements set forth in §246.17(a)(2)(ii); or

(2) For refinancing, the estimated market value of the real property based on an appraisal that meets the requirements set forth in §246.17(a)(2)(ii).

Commercial loan means a secured or unsecured loan to a company or an individual for business purposes, other than any:

(1) Loan to purchase or refinance a one-to-four family residential property;

(2) Commercial real estate loan.

Commercial real estate (CRE) loan means:

(1) A loan secured by a property with five or more single family units, or by nonfarm nonresidential real property, the primary source (50 percent or more) of repayment for which is expected to be:

(i) The proceeds of the sale, refinancing, or permanent financing of the property; or

(ii) Rental income associated with the property;

(2) Loans secured by improved land if the obligor owns the fee interest in the land and the land is leased to a third party who owns all improvements on the land, and the improvements are nonresidential or residential with five or more single family units; and

(3) Does not include:

(i) A land development and construction loan (including 1- to 4-family residential or commercial construction loans);

(ii) Any other land loan; or

(iii) An unsecured loan to a developer.

Debt service coverage (DSC) ratio means:

(1) For qualifying leased CRE loans, qualifying multi-family loans, and other CRE loans:

(i) The annual NOI less the annual replacement reserve of the CRE property at the time of origination of the CRE loan(s) divided by

(ii) The sum of the borrower's annual payments for principal and interest (calculated at the fully-indexed rate) on any debt obligation.

(2) For commercial loans:

(i) The borrower's EBITDA as of the most recently completed fiscal year divided by

(ii) The sum of the borrower's annual payments for principal and interest on all debt obligations.

Debt to income (DTI) ratio means the borrower's total debt, including the monthly amount due on the automobile loan, divided by the borrower's monthly income.

Earnings before interest, taxes, depreciation, and amortization (EBITDA) means the annual income of a business before expenses for interest, taxes, depreciation and amortization are deducted, as determined in accordance with GAAP.

Environmental risk assessment means a process for determining whether a property is contaminated or exposed to any condition or substance that could

§ 246.14

result in contamination that has an adverse effect on the market value of the property or the realization of the collateral value.

First lien means a lien or encumbrance on property that has priority over all other liens or encumbrances on the property.

Junior lien means a lien or encumbrance on property that is lower in priority relative to other liens or encumbrances on the property.

Leverage ratio means the borrower's total debt divided by the borrower's EBITDA.

Loan-to-value (LTV) ratio means, at the time of origination, the principal balance of a first-lien mortgage loan on the property divided by:

(1) For acquisition funding, the lesser of the purchase price or the estimated market value of the real property based on an appraisal that meets the requirements set forth in § 246.17(a)(2)(ii); or

(2) For refinancing, the estimated market value of the real property based on an appraisal that meets the requirements set forth in § 246.17(a)(2)(ii).

Model year means the year determined by the manufacturer and reflected on the vehicle's Motor Vehicle Title as part of the vehicle description.

Net operating income (NOI) refers to the income a CRE property generates for the owner after all expenses have been deducted for federal income tax purposes, except for depreciation, debt service expenses, and federal and state income taxes, and excluding any unusual and nonrecurring items of income.

Operating affiliate means an affiliate of a borrower that is a lessor or similar party with respect to the commercial real estate securing the loan.

Payments-in-kind means payments of accrued interest that are not paid in cash when due, and instead are paid by increasing the principal balance of the loan or by providing equity in the borrowing company.

Purchase money security interest means a security interest in property that secures the obligation of the obligor incurred as all or part of the price of the property.

Purchase price means the amount paid by the borrower for the vehicle net of any incentive payments or manufacturer cash rebates.

Qualified tenant means:

(1) A tenant with a lease who has satisfied all obligations with respect to the property in a timely manner; or

(2) A tenant who originally had a lease that subsequently expired and currently is leasing the property on a month-to-month basis, has occupied the property for at least three years prior to the date of origination, and has satisfied all obligations with respect to the property in a timely manner.

Qualifying leased CRE loan means a CRE loan secured by commercial non-farm real property, other than a multi-family property or a hotel, inn, or similar property:

(1) That is occupied by one or more qualified tenants pursuant to a lease agreement with a term of no less than one (1) month; and

(2) Where no more than 20 percent of the aggregate gross revenue of the property is payable from one or more tenants who:

(i) Are subject to a lease that will terminate within six months following the date of origination; or

(ii) Are not qualified tenants.

Qualifying multi-family loan means a CRE loan secured by any residential property (excluding a hotel, motel, inn, hospital, nursing home, or other similar facility where dwellings are not leased to residents):

(1) That consists of five or more dwelling units (including apartment buildings, condominiums, cooperatives and other similar structures) primarily for residential use; and

(2) Where at least 75 percent of the NOI is derived from residential rents and tenant amenities (including income from parking garages, health or swim clubs, and dry cleaning), and not from other commercial uses.

Rental income means:

(1) Income derived from a lease or other occupancy agreement between the borrower or an operating affiliate of the borrower and a party which is not an affiliate of the borrower for the use of real property or improvements

Securities and Exchange Commission § 246.15

serving as collateral for the applicable loan; and

(2) Other income derived from hotel, motel, dormitory, nursing home, assisted living, mini-storage warehouse or similar properties that are used primarily by parties that are not affiliates or employees of the borrower or its affiliates.

Replacement reserve means the monthly capital replacement or maintenance amount based on the property type, age, construction and condition of the property that is adequate to maintain the physical condition and NOI of the property.

Salvage title means a form of vehicle title branding, which notes that the vehicle has been severely damaged and/or deemed a total loss and uneconomical to repair by an insurance company that paid a claim on the vehicle.

Total debt, with respect to a borrower, means:

(1) In the case of an automobile loan, the sum of:

(i) All monthly housing payments (rent- or mortgage-related, including property taxes, insurance and home owners association fees); and

(ii) Any of the following that is dependent upon the borrower's income for payment:

(A) Monthly payments on other debt and lease obligations, such as credit card loans or installment loans, including the monthly amount due on the automobile loan;

(B) Estimated monthly amortizing payments for any term debt, debts with other than monthly payments and debts not in repayment (such as deferred student loans, interest-only loans); and

(C) Any required monthly alimony, child support or court-ordered payments; and

(2) In the case of a commercial loan, the outstanding balance of all long-term debt (obligations that have a remaining maturity of more than one year) and the current portion of all debt that matures in one year or less.

Total liabilities ratio means the borrower's total liabilities divided by the sum of the borrower's total liabilities and equity, less the borrower's intangible assets, with each component determined in accordance with GAAP.

Trade-in allowance means the amount a vehicle purchaser is given as a credit at the purchase of a vehicle for the fair exchange of the borrower's existing vehicle to compensate the dealer for some portion of the vehicle purchase price, not to exceed the highest trade-in value of the existing vehicle, as determined by a nationally recognized automobile pricing agency and based on the manufacturer, year, model, features, mileage, and condition of the vehicle, less the payoff balance of any outstanding debt collateralized by the existing vehicle.

Uniform Standards of Professional Appraisal Practice (USPAP) means generally accepted standards for professional appraisal practice issued by the Appraisal Standards Board of the Appraisal Foundation.

§ 246.15 Qualifying commercial loans, commercial real estate loans, and automobile loans.

(a) *General exception for qualifying assets.* Commercial loans, commercial real estate loans, and automobile loans that are securitized through a securitization transaction shall be subject to a 0 percent risk retention requirement under subpart B, provided that the following conditions are met:

(1) The assets meet the underwriting standards set forth in §§ 246.16 (qualifying commercial loans), 246.17 (qualifying CRE loans), or 246.18 (qualifying automobile loans) of this part, as applicable;

(2) The securitization transaction is collateralized solely by loans of the same asset class and by servicing assets;

(3) The securitization transaction does not permit reinvestment periods; and

(4) The sponsor provides, or causes to be provided, to potential investors a reasonable period of time prior to the sale of asset-backed securities of the issuing entity, and, upon request, to the Commission, and to its appropriate Federal banking agency, if any, in written form under the caption "Credit Risk Retention", a description of the

§ 246.16

manner in which the sponsor determined the aggregate risk retention requirement for the securitization transaction after including qualifying commercial loans, qualifying CRE loans, or qualifying automobile loans with 0 percent risk retention.

(b) *Risk retention requirement.* For any securitization transaction described in paragraph (a) of this section, the percentage of risk retention required under § 246.3(a) is reduced by the percentage evidenced by the ratio of the unpaid principal balance of the qualifying commercial loans, qualifying CRE loans, or qualifying automobile loans (as applicable) to the total unpaid principal balance of commercial loans, CRE loans, or automobile loans (as applicable) that are included in the pool of assets collateralizing the asset-backed securities issued pursuant to the securitization transaction (the qualifying asset ratio); provided that:

(1) The qualifying asset ratio is measured as of the cut-off date or similar date for establishing the composition of the securitized assets collateralizing the asset-backed securities issued pursuant to the securitization transaction;

(2) If the qualifying asset ratio would exceed 50 percent, the qualifying asset ratio shall be deemed to be 50 percent; and

(3) The disclosure required by paragraph (a)(4) of this section also includes descriptions of the qualifying commercial loans, qualifying CRE loans, and qualifying automobile loans (qualifying assets) and descriptions of the assets that are not qualifying assets, and the material differences between the group of qualifying assets and the group of assets that are not qualifying assets with respect to the composition of each group's loan balances, loan terms, interest rates, borrower credit information, and characteristics of any loan collateral.

(c) *Exception for securitizations of qualifying assets only.* Notwithstanding other provisions of this section, the risk retention requirements of subpart B of this part shall not apply to securitization transactions where the transaction is collateralized solely by servicing assets and either qualifying commercial loans, qualifying CRE loans, or qualifying automobile loans.

(d) *Record maintenance.* A sponsor must retain the disclosures required in paragraphs (a) and (b) of this section and the certifications required in §§ 246.16(a)(8), 246.17(a)(10), and 246.18(a)(8), as applicable, in its records until three years after all ABS interests issued in the securitization are no longer outstanding. The sponsor must provide the disclosures and certifications upon request to the Commission and the sponsor's appropriate Federal banking agency, if any.

§ 246.16 **Underwriting standards for qualifying commercial loans.**

(a) *Underwriting, product and other standards.* (1) Prior to origination of the commercial loan, the originator:

(i) Verified and documented the financial condition of the borrower:

(A) As of the end of the borrower's two most recently completed fiscal years; and

(B) During the period, if any, since the end of its most recently completed fiscal year;

(ii) Conducted an analysis of the borrower's ability to service its overall debt obligations during the next two years, based on reasonable projections;

(iii) Determined that, based on the previous two years' actual performance, the borrower had:

(A) A total liabilities ratio of 50 percent or less;

(B) A leverage ratio of 3.0 or less; and

(C) A DSC ratio of 1.5 or greater;

(iv) Determined that, based on the two years of projections, which include the new debt obligation, following the closing date of the loan, the borrower will have:

(A) A total liabilities ratio of 50 percent or less;

(B) A leverage ratio of 3.0 or less; and

(C) A DSC ratio of 1.5 or greater.

(2) Prior to, upon or promptly following the inception of the loan, the originator:

(i) If the loan is originated on a secured basis, obtains a perfected security interest (by filing, title notation or otherwise) or, in the case of real property, a recorded lien, on all of the property pledged to collateralize the loan; and

(ii) If the loan documents indicate the purpose of the loan is to finance

Securities and Exchange Commission §246.16

the purchase of tangible or intangible property, or to refinance such a loan, obtains a first lien on the property.

(3) The loan documentation for the commercial loan includes covenants that:

(i) Require the borrower to provide to the servicer of the commercial loan the borrower's financial statements and supporting schedules on an ongoing basis, but not less frequently than quarterly;

(ii) Prohibit the borrower from retaining or entering into a debt arrangement that permits payments-in-kind;

(iii) Impose limits on:

(A) The creation or existence of any other security interest or lien with respect to any of the borrower's property that serves as collateral for the loan;

(B) The transfer of any of the borrower's assets that serve as collateral for the loan; and

(C) Any change to the name, location or organizational structure of the borrower, or any other party that pledges collateral for the loan;

(iv) Require the borrower and any other party that pledges collateral for the loan to:

(A) Maintain insurance that protects against loss on the collateral for the commercial loan at least up to the amount of the loan, and that names the originator or any subsequent holder of the loan as an additional insured or loss payee;

(B) Pay taxes, charges, fees, and claims, where non-payment might give rise to a lien on any collateral;

(C) Take any action required to perfect or protect the security interest and first lien (as applicable) of the originator or any subsequent holder of the loan in any collateral for the commercial loan or the priority thereof, and to defend any collateral against claims adverse to the lender's interest;

(D) Permit the originator or any subsequent holder of the loan, and the servicer of the loan, to inspect any collateral for the commercial loan and the books and records of the borrower; and

(E) Maintain the physical condition of any collateral for the commercial loan.

(4) Loan payments required under the loan agreement are:

(i) Based on level monthly payments of principal and interest (at the fully indexed rate) that fully amortize the debt over a term that does not exceed five years from the date of origination; and

(ii) To be made no less frequently than quarterly over a term that does not exceed five years.

(5) The primary source of repayment for the loan is revenue from the business operations of the borrower.

(6) The loan was funded within the six (6) months prior to the cut-off date or similar date for establishing the composition of the securitized assets collateralizing the asset-backed securities issued pursuant to the securitization transaction.

(7) At the cut-off date or similar date for establishing the composition of the securitized assets collateralizing the asset-backed securities issued pursuant to the securitization transaction, all payments due on the loan are contractually current.

(8)(i) The depositor of the asset-backed security certifies that it has evaluated the effectiveness of its internal supervisory controls with respect to the process for ensuring that all qualifying commercial loans that collateralize the asset-backed security and that reduce the sponsor's risk retention requirement under §246.15 meet all of the requirements set forth in paragraphs (a)(1) through (7) of this section and has concluded that its internal supervisory controls are effective;

(ii) The evaluation of the effectiveness of the depositor's internal supervisory controls referenced in paragraph (a)(8)(i) of this section shall be performed, for each issuance of an asset-backed security, as of a date within 60 days of the cut-off date or similar date for establishing the composition of the asset pool collateralizing such asset-backed security; and

(iii) The sponsor provides, or causes to be provided, a copy of the certification described in paragraph (a)(8)(i) of this section to potential investors a reasonable period of time prior to the sale of asset-backed securities in the issuing entity, and, upon request, to its appropriate Federal banking agency, if any.

§ 246.17

(b) *Cure or buy-back requirement.* If a sponsor has relied on the exception provided in § 246.15 with respect to a qualifying commercial loan and it is subsequently determined that the loan did not meet all of the requirements set forth in paragraphs (a)(1) through (7) of this section, the sponsor shall not lose the benefit of the exception with respect to the commercial loan if the depositor complied with the certification requirement set forth in paragraph (a)(8) of this section and:

(1) The failure of the loan to meet any of the requirements set forth in paragraphs (a)(1) through (7) of this section is not material; or

(2) No later than 90 days after the determination that the loan does not meet one or more of the requirements of paragraphs (a)(1) through (7) of this section, the sponsor:

(i) Effectuates cure, establishing conformity of the loan to the unmet requirements as of the date of cure; or

(ii) Repurchases the loan(s) from the issuing entity at a price at least equal to the remaining principal balance and accrued interest on the loan(s) as of the date of repurchase.

(3) If the sponsor cures or repurchases pursuant to paragraph (b)(2) of this section, the sponsor must promptly notify, or cause to be notified, the holders of the asset-backed securities issued in the securitization transaction of any loan(s) included in such securitization transaction that is required to be cured or repurchased by the sponsor pursuant to paragraph (b)(2) of this section, including the principal amount of such loan(s) and the cause for such cure or repurchase.

§ 246.17 Underwriting standards for qualifying CRE loans.

(a) *Underwriting, product and other standards.* (1) The CRE loan must be secured by the following:

(i) An enforceable first lien, documented and recorded appropriately pursuant to applicable law, on the commercial real estate and improvements;

(ii)(A) An assignment of:

(*1*) Leases and rents and other occupancy agreements related to the commercial real estate or improvements or the operation thereof for which the borrower or an operating affiliate is a lessor or similar party and all payments under such leases and occupancy agreements; and

(*2*) All franchise, license and concession agreements related to the commercial real estate or improvements or the operation thereof for which the borrower or an operating affiliate is a lessor, licensor, concession granter or similar party and all payments under such other agreements, whether the assignments described in this paragraph (a)(1)(ii)(A)(*2*) are absolute or are stated to be made to the extent permitted by the agreements governing the applicable franchise, license or concession agreements;

(B) An assignment of all other payments due to the borrower or due to any operating affiliate in connection with the operation of the property described in paragraph (a)(1)(i) of this section; and

(C) The right to enforce the agreements described in paragraph (a)(1)(ii)(A) of this section and the agreements under which payments under paragraph (a)(1)(ii)(B) of this section are due against, and collect amounts due from, each lessee, occupant or other obligor whose payments were assigned pursuant to paragraphs (a)(1)(ii)(A) or (B) of this section upon a breach by the borrower of any of the terms of, or the occurrence of any other event of default (however denominated) under, the loan documents relating to such CRE loan; and

(iii) A security interest:

(A) In all interests of the borrower and any applicable operating affiliate in all tangible and intangible personal property of any kind, in or used in the operation of or in connection with, pertaining to, arising from, or constituting, any of the collateral described in paragraphs (a)(1)(i) or (ii) of this section; and

(B) In the form of a perfected security interest if the security interest in such property can be perfected by the filing of a financing statement, fixture filing, or similar document pursuant to the law governing the perfection of such security interest;

(2) Prior to origination of the CRE loan, the originator:

Securities and Exchange Commission § 246.17

(i) Verified and documented the current financial condition of the borrower and each operating affiliate;

(ii) Obtained a written appraisal of the real property securing the loan that:

(A) Had an effective date not more than six months prior to the origination date of the loan by a competent and appropriately State-certified or State-licensed appraiser;

(B) Conforms to generally accepted appraisal standards as evidenced by the USPAP and the appraisal requirements [1] of the Federal banking agencies; and

(C) Provides an "as is" opinion of the market value of the real property, which includes an income approach;[2]

(iii) Qualified the borrower for the CRE loan based on a monthly payment amount derived from level monthly payments consisting of both principal and interest (at the fully-indexed rate) over the term of the loan, not exceeding 25 years, or 30 years for a qualifying multi-family property;

(iv) Conducted an environmental risk assessment to gain environmental information about the property securing the loan and took appropriate steps to mitigate any environmental liability determined to exist based on this assessment;

(v) Conducted an analysis of the borrower's ability to service its overall debt obligations during the next two years, based on reasonable projections (including operating income projections for the property);

(vi)(A) Determined that based on the two years' actual performance immediately preceding the origination of the loan, the borrower would have had:

(1) A DSC ratio of 1.5 or greater, if the loan is a qualifying leased CRE loan, net of any income derived from a tenant(s) who is not a qualified tenant(s);

(2) A DSC ratio of 1.25 or greater, if the loan is a qualifying multi-family property loan; or

(3) A DSC ratio of 1.7 or greater, if the loan is any other type of CRE loan;

(B) If the borrower did not own the property for any part of the last two years prior to origination, the calculation of the DSC ratio, for purposes of paragraph (a)(2)(vi)(A) of this section, shall include the property's operating income for any portion of the two-year period during which the borrower did not own the property;

(vii) Determined that, based on two years of projections, which include the new debt obligation, following the origination date of the loan, the borrower will have:

(A) A DSC ratio of 1.5 or greater, if the loan is a qualifying leased CRE loan, net of any income derived from a tenant(s) who is not a qualified tenant(s);

(B) A DSC ratio of 1.25 or greater, if the loan is a qualifying multi-family property loan; or

(C) A DSC ratio of 1.7 or greater, if the loan is any other type of CRE loan.

(3) The loan documentation for the CRE loan includes covenants that:

(i) Require the borrower to provide the borrower's financial statements and supporting schedules to the servicer on an ongoing basis, but not less frequently than quarterly, including information on existing, maturing and new leasing or rent-roll activity for the property securing the loan, as appropriate; and

(ii) Impose prohibitions on:

(A) The creation or existence of any other security interest with respect to the collateral for the CRE loan described in paragraphs (a)(1)(i) and (a)(1)(ii)(A) of this section, except as provided in paragraph (a)(4) of this section;

(B) The transfer of any collateral for the CRE loan described in paragraph (a)(1)(i) or (a)(1)(ii)(A) of this section or of any other collateral consisting of fixtures, furniture, furnishings, machinery or equipment other than any such fixture, furniture, furnishings, machinery or equipment that is obsolete or surplus; and

(C) Any change to the name, location or organizational structure of any borrower, operating affiliate or other pledgor unless such borrower, operating affiliate or other pledgor shall have given the holder of the loan at

---

[1] 12 CFR part 34, subpart C (OCC); 12 CFR part 208, subpart E, and 12 CFR part 225, subpart G (Board); and 12 CFR part 323 (FDIC).

[2] See USPAP, Standard 1.

§ 246.17

least 30 days advance notice and, pursuant to applicable law governing perfection and priority, the holder of the loan is able to take all steps necessary to continue its perfection and priority during such 30-day period.

(iii) Require each borrower and each operating affiliate to:

(A) Maintain insurance that protects against loss on collateral for the CRE loan described in paragraph (a)(1)(i) of this section for an amount no less than the replacement cost of the property improvements, and names the originator or any subsequent holder of the loan as an additional insured or lender loss payee;

(B) Pay taxes, charges, fees, and claims, where non-payment might give rise to a lien on collateral for the CRE loan described in paragraphs (a)(1)(i) and (ii) of this section;

(C) Take any action required to:

(*1*) Protect the security interest and the enforceability and priority thereof in the collateral described in paragraphs (a)(1)(i) and (a)(1)(ii)(A) of this section and defend such collateral against claims adverse to the originator's or any subsequent holder's interest; and

(*2*) Perfect the security interest of the originator or any subsequent holder of the loan in any other collateral for the CRE loan to the extent that such security interest is required by this section to be perfected;

(D) Permit the originator or any subsequent holder of the loan, and the servicer, to inspect any collateral for the CRE loan and the books and records of the borrower or other party relating to any collateral for the CRE loan;

(E) Maintain the physical condition of collateral for the CRE loan described in paragraph (a)(1)(i) of this section;

(F) Comply with all environmental, zoning, building code, licensing and other laws, regulations, agreements, covenants, use restrictions, and proffers applicable to collateral for the CRE loan described in paragraph (a)(1)(i) of this section;

(G) Comply with leases, franchise agreements, condominium declarations, and other documents and agreements relating to the operation of collateral for the CRE loan described in paragraph (a)(1)(i) of this section, and to not modify any material terms and conditions of such agreements over the term of the loan without the consent of the originator or any subsequent holder of the loan, or the servicer; and

(H) Not materially alter collateral for the CRE loan described in paragraph (a)(1)(i) of this section without the consent of the originator or any subsequent holder of the loan, or the servicer.

(4) The loan documentation for the CRE loan prohibits the borrower and each operating affiliate from obtaining a loan secured by a junior lien on collateral for the CRE loan described in paragraph (a)(1)(i) or (a)(1)(ii)(A) of this section, unless:

(i) The sum of the principal amount of such junior lien loan, plus the principal amount of all other loans secured by collateral described in paragraph (a)(1)(i) or (a)(1)(ii)(A) of this section, does not exceed the applicable CLTV ratio in paragraph (a)(5) of this section, based on the appraisal at origination of such junior lien loan; or

(ii) Such loan is a purchase money obligation that financed the acquisition of machinery or equipment and the borrower or operating affiliate (as applicable) pledges such machinery and equipment as additional collateral for the CRE loan.

(5) At origination, the applicable loan-to-value ratios for the loan are:

(i) LTV less than or equal to 65 percent and CLTV less than or equal to 70 percent; or

(ii) LTV less than or equal to 60 percent and CLTV less than or equal to 65 percent, if an appraisal used to meet the requirements set forth in paragraph (a)(2)(ii) of this section used a direct capitalization rate, and that rate is less than or equal to the sum of:

(A) The 10-year swap rate, as reported in the Federal Reserve's H.15 Report (or any successor report) as of the date concurrent with the effective date of such appraisal; and

(B) 300 basis points.

(iii) If the appraisal required under paragraph (a)(2)(ii) of this section included a direct capitalization method using an overall capitalization rate, that rate must be disclosed to potential investors in the securitization.

Securities and Exchange Commission § 246.17

(6) All loan payments required to be made under the loan agreement are:

(i) Based on level monthly payments of principal and interest (at the fully indexed rate) to fully amortize the debt over a term that does not exceed 25 years, or 30 years for a qualifying multifamily loan; and

(ii) To be made no less frequently than monthly over a term of at least ten years.

(7) Under the terms of the loan agreement:

(i) Any maturity of the note occurs no earlier than ten years following the date of origination;

(ii) The borrower is not permitted to defer repayment of principal or payment of interest; and

(iii) The interest rate on the loan is:

(A) A fixed interest rate;

(B) An adjustable interest rate and the borrower, prior to or concurrently with origination of the CRE loan, obtained a derivative that effectively results in a fixed interest rate; or

(C) An adjustable interest rate and the borrower, prior to or concurrently with origination of the CRE loan, obtained a derivative that established a cap on the interest rate for the term of the loan, and the loan meets the underwriting criteria in paragraphs (a)(2)(vi) and (vii) of this section using the maximum interest rate allowable under the interest rate cap.

(8) The originator does not establish an interest reserve at origination to fund all or part of a payment on the loan.

(9) At the cut-off date or similar date for establishing the composition of the securitized assets collateralizing the asset-backed securities issued pursuant to the securitization transaction, all payments due on the loan are contractually current.

(10)(i) The depositor of the asset-backed security certifies that it has evaluated the effectiveness of its internal supervisory controls with respect to the process for ensuring that all qualifying CRE loans that collateralize the asset-backed security and that reduce the sponsor's risk retention requirement under § 246.15 meet all of the requirements set forth in paragraphs (a)(1) through (9) of this section and has concluded that its internal supervisory controls are effective;

(ii) The evaluation of the effectiveness of the depositor's internal supervisory controls referenced in paragraph (a)(10)(i) of this section shall be performed, for each issuance of an asset-backed security, as of a date within 60 days of the cut-off date or similar date for establishing the composition of the asset pool collateralizing such asset-backed security;

(iii) The sponsor provides, or causes to be provided, a copy of the certification described in paragraph (a)(10)(i) of this section to potential investors a reasonable period of time prior to the sale of asset-backed securities in the issuing entity, and, upon request, to its appropriate Federal banking agency, if any; and

(11) Within two weeks of the closing of the CRE loan by its originator or, if sooner, prior to the transfer of such CRE loan to the issuing entity, the originator shall have obtained a UCC lien search from the jurisdiction of organization of the borrower and each operating affiliate, that does not report, as of the time that the security interest of the originator in the property described in paragraph (a)(1)(iii) of this section was perfected, other higher priority liens of record on any property described in paragraph (a)(1)(iii) of this section, other than purchase money security interests.

(b) *Cure or buy-back requirement.* If a sponsor has relied on the exception provided in § 246.15 with respect to a qualifying CRE loan and it is subsequently determined that the CRE loan did not meet all of the requirements set forth in paragraphs (a)(1) through (9) and (a)(11) of this section, the sponsor shall not lose the benefit of the exception with respect to the CRE loan if the depositor complied with the certification requirement set forth in paragraph (a)(10) of this section, and:

(1) The failure of the loan to meet any of the requirements set forth in paragraphs (a)(1) through (9) and (a)(11) of this section is not material; or;

(2) No later than 90 days after the determination that the loan does not meet one or more of the requirements of paragraphs (a)(1) through (9) or (a)(11) of this section, the sponsor:

§ 246.18

(i) Effectuates cure, restoring conformity of the loan to the unmet requirements as of the date of cure; or

(ii) Repurchases the loan(s) from the issuing entity at a price at least equal to the remaining principal balance and accrued interest on the loan(s) as of the date of repurchase.

(3) If the sponsor cures or repurchases pursuant to paragraph (b)(2) of this section, the sponsor must promptly notify, or cause to be notified, the holders of the asset-backed securities issued in the securitization transaction of any loan(s) included in such securitization transaction that is required to be cured or repurchased by the sponsor pursuant to paragraph (b)(2) of this section, including the principal amount of such repurchased loan(s) and the cause for such cure or repurchase.

§ 246.18 Underwriting standards for qualifying automobile loans.

(a) *Underwriting, product and other standards.* (1) Prior to origination of the automobile loan, the originator:

(i) Verified and documented that within 30 days of the date of origination:

(A) The borrower was not currently 30 days or more past due, in whole or in part, on any debt obligation;

(B) Within the previous 24 months, the borrower has not been 60 days or more past due, in whole or in part, on any debt obligation;

(C) Within the previous 36 months, the borrower has not:

(*1*) Been a debtor in a proceeding commenced under Chapter 7 (Liquidation), Chapter 11 (Reorganization), Chapter 12 (Family Farmer or Family Fisherman plan), or Chapter 13 (Individual Debt Adjustment) of the U.S. Bankruptcy Code; or

(*2*) Been the subject of any federal or State judicial judgment for the collection of any unpaid debt;

(D) Within the previous 36 months, no one-to-four family property owned by the borrower has been the subject of any foreclosure, deed in lieu of foreclosure, or short sale; or

(E) Within the previous 36 months, the borrower has not had any personal property repossessed;

(ii) Determined and documented that the borrower has at least 24 months of credit history; and

(iii) Determined and documented that, upon the origination of the loan, the borrower's DTI ratio is less than or equal to 36 percent.

(A) For the purpose of making the determination under paragraph (a)(1)(iii) of this section, the originator must:

(*1*) Verify and document all income of the borrower that the originator includes in the borrower's effective monthly income (using payroll stubs, tax returns, profit and loss statements, or other similar documentation); and

(*2*) On or after the date of the borrower's written application and prior to origination, obtain a credit report regarding the borrower from a consumer reporting agency that compiles and maintain files on consumers on a nationwide basis (within the meaning of 15 U.S.C. 1681a(p)) and verify that all outstanding debts reported in the borrower's credit report are incorporated into the calculation of the borrower's DTI ratio under paragraph (a)(1)(iii) of this section;

(2) An originator will be deemed to have met the requirements of paragraph (a)(1)(i) of this section if:

(i) The originator, no more than 30 days before the closing of the loan, obtains a credit report regarding the borrower from a consumer reporting agency that compiles and maintains files on consumers on a nationwide basis (within the meaning of 15 U.S.C. 1681a(p));

(ii) Based on the information in such credit report, the borrower meets all of the requirements of paragraph (a)(1)(i) of this section, and no information in a credit report subsequently obtained by the originator before the closing of the loan contains contrary information; and

(iii) The originator obtains electronic or hard copies of the credit report.

(3) At closing of the automobile loan, the borrower makes a down payment from the borrower's personal funds and trade-in allowance, if any, that is at least equal to the sum of:

(i) The full cost of the vehicle title, tax, and registration fees;

(ii) Any dealer-imposed fees;

Securities and Exchange Commission § 246.19

(iii) The full cost of any additional warranties, insurance or other products purchased in connection with the purchase of the vehicle; and

(iv) 10 percent of the vehicle purchase price.

(4) The originator records a first lien securing the loan on the purchased vehicle in accordance with State law.

(5) The terms of the loan agreement provide a maturity date for the loan that does not exceed the lesser of:

(i) Six years from the date of origination; or

(ii) 10 years minus the difference between the current model year and the vehicle's model year.

(6) The terms of the loan agreement:

(i) Specify a fixed rate of interest for the life of the loan;

(ii) Provide for a level monthly payment amount that fully amortizes the amount financed over the loan term;

(iii) Do not permit the borrower to defer repayment of principal or payment of interest; and

(iv) Require the borrower to make the first payment on the automobile loan within 45 days of the loan's contract date.

(7) At the cut-off date or similar date for establishing the composition of the securitized assets collateralizing the asset-backed securities issued pursuant to the securitization transaction, all payments due on the loan are contractually current; and

(8)(i) The depositor of the asset-backed security certifies that it has evaluated the effectiveness of its internal supervisory controls with respect to the process for ensuring that all qualifying automobile loans that collateralize the asset-backed security and that reduce the sponsor's risk retention requirement under § 246.15 meet all of the requirements set forth in paragraphs (a)(1) through (7) of this section and has concluded that its internal supervisory controls are effective;

(ii) The evaluation of the effectiveness of the depositor's internal supervisory controls referenced in paragraph (a)(8)(i) of this section shall be performed, for each issuance of an asset-backed security, as of a date within 60 days of the cut-off date or similar date for establishing the composition of the asset pool collateralizing such asset-backed security; and

(iii) The sponsor provides, or causes to be provided, a copy of the certification described in paragraph (a)(8)(i) of this section to potential investors a reasonable period of time prior to the sale of asset-backed securities in the issuing entity, and, upon request, to its appropriate Federal banking agency, if any.

(b) *Cure or buy-back requirement.* If a sponsor has relied on the exception provided in § 246.15 with respect to a qualifying automobile loan and it is subsequently determined that the loan did not meet all of the requirements set forth in paragraphs (a)(1) through (7) of this section, the sponsor shall not lose the benefit of the exception with respect to the automobile loan if the depositor complied with the certification requirement set forth in paragraph (a)(8) of this section, and:

(1) The failure of the loan to meet any of the requirements set forth in paragraphs (a)(1) through (7) of this section is not material; or

(2) No later than ninety (90) days after the determination that the loan does not meet one or more of the requirements of paragraphs (a)(1) through (7) of this section, the sponsor:

(i) Effectuates cure, establishing conformity of the loan to the unmet requirements as of the date of cure; or

(ii) Repurchases the loan(s) from the issuing entity at a price at least equal to the remaining principal balance and accrued interest on the loan(s) as of the date of repurchase.

(3) If the sponsor cures or repurchases pursuant to paragraph (b)(2) of this section, the sponsor must promptly notify, or cause to be notified, the holders of the asset-backed securities issued in the securitization transaction of any loan(s) included in such securitization transaction that is required to be cured or repurchased by the sponsor pursuant to paragraph (b)(2) of this section, including the principal amount of such loan(s) and the cause for such cure or repurchase.

§ 246.19 General exemptions.

(a) *Definitions.* For purposes of this section, the following definitions shall apply:

§ 246.19

Community-focused residential mortgage means a residential mortgage exempt from the definition of "covered transaction" under § 1026.43(a)(3)(iv) and (v) of the CFPB's Regulation Z (12 CFR 1026.43(a)).

First pay class means a class of ABS interests for which all interests in the class are entitled to the same priority of payment and that, at the time of closing of the transaction, is entitled to repayments of principal and payments of interest prior to or pro-rata with all other classes of securities collateralized by the same pool of first-lien residential mortgages, until such class has no principal or notional balance remaining.

Inverse floater means an ABS interest issued as part of a securitization transaction for which interest or other income is payable to the holder based on a rate or formula that varies inversely to a reference rate of interest.

Qualifying three-to-four unit residential mortgage loan means a mortgage loan that is:

(i) Secured by a dwelling (as defined in 12 CFR 1026.2(a)(19)) that is owner occupied and contains three-to-four housing units;

(ii) Is deemed to be for business purposes for purposes of Regulation Z under 12 CFR part 1026, Supplement I, paragraph 3(a)(5)(i); and

(iii) Otherwise meets all of the requirements to qualify as a qualified mortgage under § 1026.43(e) and (f) of Regulation Z (12 CFR 1026.43(e) and (f)) as if the loan were a covered transaction under that section.

(b) This part shall not apply to:

(1) *U.S. Government-backed securitizations.* Any securitization transaction that:

(i) Is collateralized solely by residential, multifamily, or health care facility mortgage loan assets that are insured or guaranteed (in whole or in part) as to the payment of principal and interest by the United States or an agency of the United States, and servicing assets; or

(ii) Involves the issuance of asset-backed securities that:

(A) Are insured or guaranteed as to the payment of principal and interest by the United States or an agency of the United States; and

(B) Are collateralized solely by residential, multifamily, or health care facility mortgage loan assets or interests in such assets, and servicing assets.

(2) *Certain agricultural loan securitizations.* Any securitization transaction that is collateralized solely by loans or other assets made, insured, guaranteed, or purchased by any institution that is subject to the supervision of the Farm Credit Administration, including the Federal Agricultural Mortgage Corporation, and servicing assets;

(3) *State and municipal securitizations.* Any asset-backed security that is a security issued or guaranteed by any State, or by any political subdivision of a State, or by any public instrumentality of a State that is exempt from the registration requirements of the Securities Act of 1933 by reason of section 3(a)(2) of that Act (15 U.S.C. 77c(a)(2)); and

(4) *Qualified scholarship funding bonds.* Any asset-backed security that meets the definition of a qualified scholarship funding bond, as set forth in section 150(d)(2) of the Internal Revenue Code of 1986 (26 U.S.C. 150(d)(2)).

(5) *Pass-through resecuritizations.* Any securitization transaction that:

(i) Is collateralized solely by servicing assets, and by asset-backed securities:

(A) For which credit risk was retained as required under subpart B of this part; or

(B) That were exempted from the credit risk retention requirements of this part pursuant to subpart D of this part;

(ii) Is structured so that it involves the issuance of only a single class of ABS interests; and

(iii) Provides for the pass-through of all principal and interest payments received on the underlying asset-backed securities (net of expenses of the issuing entity) to the holders of such class.

(6) *First-pay-class securitizations.* Any securitization transaction that:

(i) Is collateralized solely by servicing assets, and by first-pay classes of asset-backed securities collateralized by first-lien residential mortgages on properties located in any state:

Securities and Exchange Commission § 246.19

(A) For which credit risk was retained as required under subpart B of this part; or

(B) That were exempted from the credit risk retention requirements of this part pursuant to subpart D of this part;

(ii) Does not provide for any ABS interest issued in the securitization transaction to share in realized principal losses other than pro rata with all other ABS interests issued in the securitization transaction based on the current unpaid principal balance of such ABS interests at the time the loss is realized;

(iii) Is structured to reallocate prepayment risk;

(iv) Does not reallocate credit risk (other than as a consequence of reallocation of prepayment risk); and

(v) Does not include any inverse floater or similarly structured ABS interest.

(7) *Seasoned loans.* (i) Any securitization transaction that is collateralized solely by servicing assets, and by seasoned loans that meet the following requirements:

(A) The loans have not been modified since origination; and

(B) None of the loans have been delinquent for 30 days or more.

(ii) For purposes of this paragraph, a *seasoned loan* means:

(A) With respect to asset-backed securities collateralized by residential mortgages, a loan that has been outstanding and performing for the longer of:

(*1*) A period of five years; or

(*2*) Until the outstanding principal balance of the loan has been reduced to 25 percent of the original principal balance.

(3) Notwithstanding paragraphs (b)(7)(ii)(A)(*1*) and (*2*) of this section, any residential mortgage loan that has been outstanding and performing for a period of at least seven years shall be deemed a seasoned loan.

(B) With respect to all other classes of asset-backed securities, a loan that has been outstanding and performing for the longer of:

(*1*) A period of at least two years; or

(*2*) Until the outstanding principal balance of the loan has been reduced to 33 percent of the original principal balance.

(8) *Certain public utility securitizations.* (i) Any securitization transaction where the asset-back securities issued in the transaction are secured by the intangible property right to collect charges for the recovery of specified costs and such other assets, if any, of an issuing entity that is wholly owned, directly or indirectly, by an investor owned utility company that is subject to the regulatory authority of a State public utility commission or other appropriate State agency.

(ii) For purposes of this paragraph:

(A) *Specified cost* means any cost identified by a State legislature as appropriate for recovery through securitization pursuant to specified cost recovery legislation; and

(B) *Specified cost recovery legislation* means legislation enacted by a State that:

(*1*) Authorizes the investor owned utility company to apply for, and authorizes the public utility commission or other appropriate State agency to issue, a financing order determining the amount of specified costs the utility will be allowed to recover;

(*2*) Provides that pursuant to a financing order, the utility acquires an intangible property right to charge, collect, and receive amounts necessary to provide for the full recovery of the specified costs determined to be recoverable, and assures that the charges are non-bypassable and will be paid by customers within the utility's historic service territory who receive utility goods or services through the utility's transmission and distribution system, even if those customers elect to purchase these goods or services from a third party; and

(*3*) Guarantees that neither the State nor any of its agencies has the authority to rescind or amend the financing order, to revise the amount of specified costs, or in any way to reduce or impair the value of the intangible property right, except as may be contemplated by periodic adjustments authorized by the specified cost recovery legislation.

(c) *Exemption for securitizations of assets issued, insured or guaranteed by the United States.* This part shall not apply

159

§ 246.19

to any securitization transaction if the asset-backed securities issued in the transaction are:

(1) Collateralized solely by obligations issued by the United States or an agency of the United States and servicing assets;

(2) Collateralized solely by assets that are fully insured or guaranteed as to the payment of principal and interest by the United States or an agency of the United States (other than those referred to in paragraph (b)(1)(i) of this section) and servicing assets; or

(3) Fully guaranteed as to the timely payment of principal and interest by the United States or any agency of the United States;

(d) *Federal Deposit Insurance Corporation securitizations.* This part shall not apply to any securitization transaction that is sponsored by the Federal Deposit Insurance Corporation acting as conservator or receiver under any provision of the Federal Deposit Insurance Act or of Title II of the Dodd-Frank Wall Street Reform and Consumer Protection Act.

(e) *Reduced requirement for certain student loan securitizations.* The 5 percent risk retention requirement set forth in § 246.4 shall be modified as follows:

(1) With respect to a securitization transaction that is collateralized solely by student loans made under the Federal Family Education Loan Program ("FFELP loans") that are guaranteed as to 100 percent of defaulted principal and accrued interest, and servicing assets, the risk retention requirement shall be 0 percent;

(2) With respect to a securitization transaction that is collateralized solely by FFELP loans that are guaranteed as to at least 98 percent but less than 100 percent of defaulted principal and accrued interest, and servicing assets, the risk retention requirement shall be 2 percent; and

(3) With respect to any other securitization transaction that is collateralized solely by FFELP loans, and servicing assets, the risk retention requirement shall be 3 percent.

(f) *Community-focused lending securitizations.* (1) This part shall not apply to any securitization transaction if the asset-backed securities issued in the transaction are collateralized solely by community-focused residential mortgages and servicing assets.

(2) For any securitization transaction that includes both community-focused residential mortgages and residential mortgages that are not exempt from risk retention under this part, the percent of risk retention required under § 246.4(a) is reduced by the ratio of the unpaid principal balance of the community-focused residential mortgages to the total unpaid principal balance of residential mortgages that are included in the pool of assets collateralizing the asset-backed securities issued pursuant to the securitization transaction (the community-focused residential mortgage asset ratio); provided that:

(i) The community-focused residential mortgage asset ratio is measured as of the cut-off date or similar date for establishing the composition of the pool assets collateralizing the asset-backed securities issued pursuant to the securitization transaction; and

(ii) If the community-focused residential mortgage asset ratio would exceed 50 percent, the community-focused residential mortgage asset ratio shall be deemed to be 50 percent.

(g) *Exemptions for securitizations of certain three-to-four unit mortgage loans.* A sponsor shall be exempt from the risk retention requirements in subpart B of this part with respect to any securitization transaction if:

(1)(i) The asset-backed securities issued in the transaction are collateralized solely by qualifying three-to-four unit residential mortgage loans and servicing assets; or

(ii) The asset-backed securities issued in the transaction are collateralized solely by qualifying three-to-four unit residential mortgage loans, qualified residential mortgages as defined in § 246.13, and servicing assets.

(2) The depositor with respect to the securitization provides the certifications set forth in § 246.13(b)(4) with respect to the process for ensuring that all assets that collateralize the asset-backed securities issued in the transaction are qualifying three-to-four unit residential mortgage loans, qualified residential mortgages, or servicing assets; and

Securities and Exchange Commission

§ 246.20

(3) The sponsor of the securitization complies with the repurchase requirements in § 246.13(c) with respect to a loan if, after closing, it is determined that the loan does not meet all of the criteria to be either a qualified residential mortgage or a qualifying three-to-four unit residential mortgage loan, as appropriate.

(h) *Rule of construction.* Securitization transactions involving the issuance of asset-backed securities that are either issued, insured, or guaranteed by, or are collateralized by obligations issued by, or loans that are issued, insured, or guaranteed by, the Federal National Mortgage Association, the Federal Home Loan Mortgage Corporation, or a Federal home loan bank shall not on that basis qualify for exemption under this part.

§ 246.20 Safe harbor for certain foreign-related transactions.

(a) *Definitions.* For purposes of this section, the following definition shall apply:

U.S. person means:

(i) Any of the following:

(A) Any natural person resident in the United States;

(B) Any partnership, corporation, limited liability company, or other organization or entity organized or incorporated under the laws of any State or of the United States;

(C) Any estate of which any executor or administrator is a U.S. person (as defined under any other clause of this definition);

(D) Any trust of which any trustee is a U.S. person (as defined under any other clause of this definition);

(E) Any agency or branch of a foreign entity located in the United States;

(F) Any non-discretionary account or similar account (other than an estate or trust) held by a dealer or other fiduciary for the benefit or account of a U.S. person (as defined under any other clause of this definition);

(G) Any discretionary account or similar account (other than an estate or trust) held by a dealer or other fiduciary organized, incorporated, or (if an individual) resident in the United States; and

(H) Any partnership, corporation, limited liability company, or other organization or entity if:

(*1*) Organized or incorporated under the laws of any foreign jurisdiction; and

(*2*) Formed by a U.S. person (as defined under any other clause of this definition) principally for the purpose of investing in securities not registered under the Act; and

(ii) "U.S. person(s)" does not include:

(A) Any discretionary account or similar account (other than an estate or trust) held for the benefit or account of a person not constituting a U.S. person (as defined in paragraph (i) of this section) by a dealer or other professional fiduciary organized, incorporated, or (if an individual) resident in the United States;

(B) Any estate of which any professional fiduciary acting as executor or administrator is a U.S. person (as defined in paragraph (i) of this section) if:

(*1*) An executor or administrator of the estate who is not a U.S. person (as defined in paragraph (i) of this section) has sole or shared investment discretion with respect to the assets of the estate; and

(*2*) The estate is governed by foreign law;

(C) Any trust of which any professional fiduciary acting as trustee is a U.S. person (as defined in paragraph (i) of this section), if a trustee who is not a U.S. person (as defined in paragraph (i) of this section) has sole or shared investment discretion with respect to the trust assets, and no beneficiary of the trust (and no settlor if the trust is revocable) is a U.S. person (as defined in paragraph (i) of this section);

(D) An employee benefit plan established and administered in accordance with the law of a country other than the United States and customary practices and documentation of such country;

(E) Any agency or branch of a U.S. person (as defined in paragraph (i) of this section) located outside the United States if:

(*1*) The agency or branch operates for valid business reasons; and

(*2*) The agency or branch is engaged in the business of insurance or banking and is subject to substantive insurance

§ 246.21

or banking regulation, respectively, in the jurisdiction where located;

(F) The International Monetary Fund, the International Bank for Reconstruction and Development, the Inter-American Development Bank, the Asian Development Bank, the African Development Bank, the United Nations, and their agencies, affiliates and pension plans, and any other similar international organizations, their agencies, affiliates and pension plans.

(b) *In general.* This part shall not apply to a securitization transaction if all the following conditions are met:

(1) The securitization transaction is not required to be and is not registered under the Securities Act of 1933 (15 U.S.C. 77a *et seq.*);

(2) No more than 10 percent of the dollar value (or equivalent amount in the currency in which the ABS interests are issued, as applicable) of all classes of ABS interests in the securitization transaction are sold or transferred to U.S. persons or for the account or benefit of U.S. persons;

(3) Neither the sponsor of the securitization transaction nor the issuing entity is:

(i) Chartered, incorporated, or organized under the laws of the United States or any State;

(ii) An unincorporated branch or office (wherever located) of an entity chartered, incorporated, or organized under the laws of the United States or any State; or

(iii) An unincorporated branch or office located in the United States or any State of an entity that is chartered, incorporated, or organized under the laws of a jurisdiction other than the United States or any State; and

(4) If the sponsor or issuing entity is chartered, incorporated, or organized under the laws of a jurisdiction other than the United States or any State, no more than 25 percent (as determined based on unpaid principal balance) of the assets that collateralize the ABS interests sold in the securitization transaction were acquired by the sponsor or issuing entity, directly or indirectly, from:

(i) A majority-owned affiliate of the sponsor or issuing entity that is chartered, incorporated, or organized under the laws of the United States or any State; or

(ii) An unincorporated branch or office of the sponsor or issuing entity that is located in the United States or any State.

(c) *Evasions prohibited.* In view of the objective of these rules and the policies underlying Section 15G of the Exchange Act, the safe harbor described in paragraph (b) of this section is not available with respect to any transaction or series of transactions that, although in technical compliance with paragraphs (a) and (b) of this section, is part of a plan or scheme to evade the requirements of section 15G and this part. In such cases, compliance with section 15G and this part is required.

§ 246.21 Additional exemptions.

(a) *Securitization transactions.* The federal agencies with rulewriting authority under section 15G(b) of the Exchange Act (15 U.S.C. 78o-11(b)) with respect to the type of assets involved may jointly provide a total or partial exemption of any securitization transaction as such agencies determine may be appropriate in the public interest and for the protection of investors.

(b) *Exceptions, exemptions, and adjustments.* The Federal banking agencies and the Commission, in consultation with the Federal Housing Finance Agency and the Department of Housing and Urban Development, may jointly adopt or issue exemptions, exceptions or adjustments to the requirements of this part, including exemptions, exceptions or adjustments for classes of institutions or assets in accordance with section 15G(e) of the Exchange Act (15 U.S.C. 78o-11(e)).

§ 246.22 Periodic review of the QRM definition, exempted three-to-four unit residential mortgage loans, and community-focused residential mortgage exemption

(a) The Federal banking agencies and the Commission, in consultation with the Federal Housing Finance Agency and the Department of Housing and Urban Development, shall commence a review of the definition of qualified residential mortgage in § 246.13, a review of the community-focused residential mortgage exemption in

Securities and Exchange Commission

§ 246.19(f), and a review of the exemption for qualifying three-to-four unit residential mortgage loans in § 246.19(g):

(1) No later than four years after the effective date of the rule (as it relates to securitizers and originators of asset-backed securities collateralized by residential mortgages), five years following the completion of such initial review, and every five years thereafter; and

(2) At any time, upon the request of any Federal banking agency, the Commission, the Federal Housing Finance Agency or the Department of Housing and Urban Development, specifying the reason for such request, including as a result of any amendment to the definition of qualified mortgage or changes in the residential housing market.

(b) The Federal banking agencies, the Commission, the Federal Housing Finance Agency and the Department of Housing and Urban Development shall publish in the FEDERAL REGISTER notice of the commencement of a review and, in the case of a review commenced under paragraph (a)(2) of this section, the reason an agency is requesting such review. After completion of any review, but no later than six months after the publication of the notice announcing the review, unless extended by the agencies, the agencies shall jointly publish a notice disclosing the determination of their review. If the agencies determine to amend the definition of qualified residential mortgage, the agencies shall complete any required rulemaking within 12 months of publication in the FEDERAL REGISTER of such notice disclosing the determination of their review, unless extended by the agencies.

PART 247—REGULATION R—EXEMPTIONS AND DEFINITIONS RELATED TO THE EXCEPTIONS FOR BANKS FROM THE DEFINITION OF BROKER

Sec.
247.100 Definition.
247.700 Defined terms relating to the networking exception from the definition of "broker."
247.701 Exemption from the definition of "broker" for certain institutional referrals.
247.721 Defined terms relating to the trust and fiduciary activities exception from the definition of "broker."
247.722 Exemption allowing banks to calculate trust and fiduciary compensation on a bank-wide basis.
247.723 Exemptions for special accounts, transferred accounts, foreign branches, and a *de minimis* number of accounts.
247.740 Defined terms relating to the sweep accounts exception from the definition of "broker."
247.741 Exemption for banks effecting transactions in money market funds.
247.760 Exemption from definition of "broker" for banks accepting orders to effect transactions in securities from or on behalf of custody accounts.
247.771 Exemption from the definition of "broker" for banks effecting transactions in securities issued pursuant to Regulation S.
247.772 Exemption from the definition of "broker" for banks engaging in securities lending transactions.
247.775 Exemption from the definition of "broker" for banks effecting certain excepted or exempted transactions in investment company securities.
247.776 Exemption from the definition of "broker" for banks effecting certain excepted or exempted transactions in a company's securities for its employee benefit plans.
247.780 Exemption for banks from liability under section 29 of the Securities Exchange Act of 1934.
247.781 Exemption from the definition of "broker" for banks for a limited period of time.

AUTHORITY: 15 U.S.C. 78c, 78o, 78q, 78w, and 78mm.

SOURCE: 72 FR 56554, Oct. 3, 2007, unless otherwise noted.

§ 247.100 Definition.

For purposes of this part the following definition shall apply: *Act* means the Securities Exchange Act of 1934 (15 U.S.C. 78a *et seq.*).

§ 247.700 Defined terms relating to the networking exception from the definition of "broker."

When used with respect to the Third Party Brokerage Arrangements ("Networking") Exception from the definition of the term "broker" in section 3(a)(4)(B)(i) of the Act (15 U.S.C.

§ 247.700

78c(a)(4)(B)(i)) in the context of transactions with a customer, the following terms shall have the meaning provided:

(a) *Contingent on whether the referral results in a transaction* means dependent on whether the referral results in a purchase or sale of a security; whether an account is opened with a broker or dealer; whether the referral results in a transaction involving a particular type of security; or whether it results in multiple securities transactions; provided, however, that a referral fee may be contingent on whether a customer:

(1) Contacts or keeps an appointment with a broker or dealer as a result of the referral; or

(2) Meets any objective, base-line qualification criteria established by the bank or broker or dealer for customer referrals, including such criteria as minimum assets, net worth, income, or marginal federal or state income tax rate, or any requirement for citizenship or residency that the broker or dealer, or the bank, may have established generally for referrals for securities brokerage accounts.

(b)(1) *Incentive compensation* means compensation that is intended to encourage a bank employee to refer customers to a broker or dealer or give a bank employee an interest in the success of a securities transaction at a broker or dealer. The term does not include compensation paid by a bank under a bonus or similar plan that is:

(i) Paid on a discretionary basis; and

(ii) Based on multiple factors or variables and:

(A) Those factors or variables include multiple significant factors or variables that are not related to securities transactions at the broker or dealer;

(B) A referral made by the employee is not a factor or variable in determining the employee's compensation under the plan; and

(C) The employee's compensation under the plan is not determined by reference to referrals made by any other person.

(2) Nothing in this paragraph (b) shall be construed to prevent a bank from compensating an officer, director or employee under a bonus or similar plan on the basis of any measure of the overall profitability or revenue of:

(i) The bank, either on a stand-alone or consolidated basis;

(ii) Any affiliate of the bank (other than a broker or dealer), or any operating unit of the bank or an affiliate (other than a broker or dealer), if the affiliate or operating unit does not over time predominately engage in the business of making referrals to a broker or dealer; or

(iii) A broker or dealer if:

(A) Such measure of overall profitability or revenue is only one of multiple factors or variables used to determine the compensation of the officer, director or employee;

(B) The factors or variables used to determine the compensation of the officer, director or employee include multiple significant factors or variables that are not related to the profitability or revenue of the broker or dealer;

(C) A referral made by the employee is not a factor or variable in determining the employee's compensation under the plan; and

(D) The employee's compensation under the plan is not determined by reference to referrals made by any other person.

(c) *Nominal one-time cash fee of a fixed dollar amount* means a cash payment for a referral, to a bank employee who was personally involved in referring the customer to the broker or dealer, in an amount that meets any of the following standards:

(1) The payment does not exceed:

(i) Twice the average of the minimum and maximum hourly wage established by the bank for the current or prior year for the job family that includes the employee; or

(ii) 1/1000th of the average of the minimum and maximum annual base salary established by the bank for the current or prior year for the job family that includes the employee;

(2) The payment does not exceed twice the employee's actual base hourly wage or 1/1000th of the employee's actual annual base salary; or

(3) The payment does not exceed twenty-five dollars ($25), as adjusted in accordance with paragraph (f) of this section.

Securities and Exchange Commission §247.701

(d) *Job family* means a group of jobs or positions involving similar responsibilities, or requiring similar skills, education or training, that a bank, or a separate unit, branch or department of a bank, has established and uses in the ordinary course of its business to distinguish among its employees for purposes of hiring, promotion, and compensation.

(e) *Referral* means the action taken by one or more bank employees to direct a customer of the bank to a broker or dealer for the purchase or sale of securities for the customer's account.

(f) *Inflation adjustment*—(1) *In general.* On April 1, 2012, and on the 1st day of each subsequent 5-year period, the dollar amount referred to in paragraph (c)(3) of this section shall be adjusted by:

(i) Dividing the annual value of the Employment Cost Index For Wages and Salaries, Private Industry Workers (or any successor index thereto), as published by the Bureau of Labor Statistics, for the calendar year preceding the calendar year in which the adjustment is being made by the annual value of such index (or successor) for the calendar year ending December 31, 2006; and

(ii) Multiplying the dollar amount by the quotient obtained in paragraph (f)(1)(i) of this section.

(2) *Rounding.* If the adjusted dollar amount determined under paragraph (f)(1) of this section for any period is not a multiple of $1, the amount so determined shall be rounded to the nearest multiple of $1.

§247.701 Exemption from the definition of "broker" for certain institutional referrals.

(a) *General.* A bank that meets the requirements for the exception from the definition of "broker" under section 3(a)(4)(B)(i) of the Act (15 U.S.C. 78c(a)(4)(B)(i)), other than section 3(a)(4)(B)(i)(VI) of the Act (15 U.S.C. 78c(a)(4)(B)(i)(VI)), is exempt from the conditions of section 3(a)(4)(B)(i)(VI) of the Act solely to the extent that a bank employee receives a referral fee for referring a high net worth customer or institutional customer to a broker or dealer with which the bank has a contractual or other written arrangement of the type specified in section 3(a)(4)(B)(i) of the Act, if:

(1) *Bank employee.* (i) The bank employee is:

(A) Not registered or approved, or otherwise required to be registered or approved, in accordance with the qualification standards established by the rules of any self-regulatory organization;

(B) Predominantly engaged in banking activities other than making referrals to a broker or dealer; and

(C) Not subject to statutory disqualification, as that term is defined in section 3(a)(39) of the Act (15 U.S.C. 78c(a)(39)), except subparagraph (E) of that section; and

(ii) The high net worth customer or institutional customer is encountered by the bank employee in the ordinary course of the employee's assigned duties for the bank.

(2) *Bank determinations and obligations*—(i) *Disclosures.* The bank provides the high net worth customer or institutional customer the information set forth in paragraph (b) of this section

(A) In writing prior to or at the time of the referral; or

(B) Orally prior to or at the time of the referral and

(*1*) The bank provides such information to the customer in writing within 3 business days of the date on which the bank employee refers the customer to the broker or dealer; or

(*2*) The written agreement between the bank and the broker or dealer provides for the broker or dealer to provide such information to the customer in writing in accordance with paragraph (a)(3)(i) of this section.

(ii) *Customer qualification.* (A) In the case of a customer that is a not a natural person, the bank has a reasonable basis to believe that the customer is an institutional customer before the referral fee is paid to the bank employee.

(B) In the case of a customer that is a natural person, the bank has a reasonable basis to believe that the customer is a high net worth customer prior to or at the time of the referral.

(iii) *Employee qualification information.* Before a referral fee is paid to a bank employee under this section, the bank provides the broker or dealer the name of the employee and such other

§ 247.701

identifying information that may be necessary for the broker or dealer to determine whether the bank employee is registered or approved, or otherwise required to be registered or approved, in accordance with the qualification standards established by the rules of any self-regulatory organization or is subject to statutory disqualification, as that term is defined in section 3(a)(39) of the Act (15 U.S.C. 78c(a)(39)), except subparagraph (E) of that section.

(iv) *Good faith compliance and corrections.* A bank that acts in good faith and that has reasonable policies and procedures in place to comply with the requirements of this section shall not be considered a "broker" under section 3(a)(4) of the Act (15 U.S.C. 78c(a)(4)) solely because the bank fails to comply with the provisions of this paragraph (a)(2) with respect to a particular customer if the bank:

(A) Takes reasonable and prompt steps to remedy the error (such as, for example, by promptly making the required determination or promptly providing the broker or dealer the required information); and

(B) Makes reasonable efforts to reclaim the portion of the referral fee paid to the bank employee for the referral that does not, following any required remedial action, meet the requirements of this section and that exceeds the amount otherwise permitted under section 3(a)(4)(B)(i)(VI) of the Act (15 U.S.C. 78c(a)(4)(B)(i)(VI)) and § 247.700.

(3) *Provisions of written agreement.* The written agreement between the bank and the broker or dealer shall require that:

(i) *Broker-dealer written disclosures.* If, pursuant to paragraph (a)(2)(i)(B)(*2*) of this section, the broker or dealer is to provide the customer in writing the disclosures set forth in paragraph (b) of this section, the broker or dealer provides such information to the customer in writing:

(A) Prior to or at the time the customer begins the process of opening an account at the broker or dealer, if the customer does not have an account with the broker or dealer; or

(B) Prior to the time the customer places an order for a securities transaction with the broker or dealer as a result of the referral, if the customer already has an account at the broker or dealer.

(ii) *Customer and employee qualifications.* Before the referral fee is paid to the bank employee:

(A) The broker or dealer determine that the bank employee is not subject to statutory disqualification, as that term is defined in section 3(a)(39) of the Act (15 U.S.C. 78c(a)(39)), except subparagraph (E) of that section; and

(B) The broker or dealer has a reasonable basis to believe that the customer is a high net worth customer or an institutional customer.

(iii) *Suitability or sophistication determination by broker or dealer*—(A) *Contingent referral fees.* In any case in which payment of the referral fee is contingent on completion of a securities transaction at the broker or dealer, the broker or dealer, before such securities transaction is conducted, perform a suitability analysis of the securities transaction in accordance with the rules of the broker or dealer's applicable self-regulatory organization as if the broker or dealer had recommended the securities transaction.

(B) *Non-contingent referral fees.* In any case in which payment of the referral fee is not contingent on the completion of a securities transaction at the broker or dealer, the broker or dealer, before the referral fee is paid, either:

(*1*) Determine that the customer:

(*i*) Has the capability to evaluate investment risk and make independent decisions; and

(*ii*) Is exercising independent judgment based on the customer's own independent assessment of the opportunities and risks presented by a potential investment, market factors and other investment considerations; or

(*2*) Perform a suitability analysis of all securities transactions requested by the customer contemporaneously with the referral in accordance with the rules of the broker or dealer's applicable self-regulatory organization as if the broker or dealer had recommended the securities transaction.

(iv) *Notice to the customer.* The broker or dealer inform the customer if the broker or dealer determines that the

Securities and Exchange Commission § 247.701

customer or the securities transaction(s) to be conducted by the customer does not meet the applicable standard set forth in paragraph (a)(3)(iii) of this section.

(v) *Notice to the bank.* The broker or dealer promptly inform the bank if the broker or dealer determines that:

(A) The customer is not a high net worth customer or institutional customer, as applicable; or

(B) The bank employee is subject to statutory disqualification, as that term is defined in section 3(a)(39) of the Act (15 U.S.C. 78c(a)(39)), except subparagraph (E) of that section.

(b) *Required disclosures.* The disclosures provided to the high net worth customer or institutional customer pursuant to paragraphs (a)(2)(i) or (a)(3)(i) of this section shall clearly and conspicuously disclose:

(1) The name of the broker or dealer; and

(2) That the bank employee participates in an incentive compensation program under which the bank employee may receive a fee of more than a nominal amount for referring the customer to the broker or dealer and payment of this fee may be contingent on whether the referral results in a transaction with the broker or dealer.

(c) *Receipt of other compensation.* Nothing in this section prevents or prohibits a bank from paying or a bank employee from receiving any type of compensation that would not be considered incentive compensation under § 247.700(b)(1) or that is described in § 247.700(b)(2).

(d) *Definitions.* When used in this section:

(1) *High net worth customer*—(i) *General. High net worth customer* means:

(A) Any natural person who, either individually or jointly with his or her spouse, has at least $5 million in net worth excluding the primary residence and associated liabilities of the person and, if applicable, his or her spouse; and

(B) Any revocable, inter vivos or living trust the settlor of which is a natural person who, either individually or jointly with his or her spouse, meets the net worth standard set forth in paragraph (d)(1)(i)(A) of this section.

(ii) *Individual and spousal assets.* In determining whether any person is a high net worth customer, there may be included in the assets of such person

(A) Any assets held individually;

(B) If the person is acting jointly with his or her spouse, any assets of the person's spouse (whether or not such assets are held jointly); and

(C) If the person is not acting jointly with his or her spouse, fifty percent of any assets held jointly with such person's spouse and any assets in which such person shares with such person's spouse a community property or similar shared ownership interest.

(2) *Institutional customer* means any corporation, partnership, limited liability company, trust or other nonnatural person that has, or is controlled by a non-natural person that has, at least:

(i) $10 million in investments; or

(ii) $20 million in revenues; or

(iii) $15 million in revenues if the bank employee refers the customer to the broker or dealer for investment banking services.

(3) *Investment banking services* includes, without limitation, acting as an underwriter in an offering for an issuer; acting as a financial adviser in a merger, acquisition, tender offer or similar transaction; providing venture capital, equity lines of credit, private investment-private equity transactions or similar investments; serving as placement agent for an issuer; and engaging in similar activities.

(4) *Referral fee* means a fee (paid in one or more installments) for the referral of a customer to a broker or dealer that is:

(i) A predetermined dollar amount, or a dollar amount determined in accordance with a predetermined formula (such as a fixed percentage of the dollar amount of total assets placed in an account with the broker or dealer), that does not vary based on:

(A) The revenue generated by or the profitability of securities transactions conducted by the customer with the broker or dealer; or

(B) The quantity, price, or identity of securities transactions conducted over time by the customer with the broker or dealer; or

§ 247.721

(C) The number of customer referrals made; or

(ii) A dollar amount based on a fixed percentage of the revenues received by the broker or dealer for investment banking services provided to the customer.

(e) *Inflation adjustments*—(1) *In general.* On April 1, 2012, and on the 1st day of each subsequent 5-year period, each dollar amount in paragraphs (d)(1) and (d)(2) of this section shall be adjusted by:

(i) Dividing the annual value of the Personal Consumption Expenditures Chain-Type Price Index (or any successor index thereto), as published by the Department of Commerce, for the calendar year preceding the calendar year in which the adjustment is being made by the annual value of such index (or successor) for the calendar year ending December 31, 2006; and

(ii) Multiplying the dollar amount by the quotient obtained in paragraph (e)(1)(i) of this section.

(2) *Rounding.* If the adjusted dollar amount determined under paragraph (e)(1) of this section for any period is not a multiple of $100,000, the amount so determined shall be rounded to the nearest multiple of $100,000.

[72 FR 56554, Oct. 3, 2007, as amended at 73 FR 20780, Apr. 17, 2008]

§ 247.721 Defined terms relating to the trust and fiduciary activities exception from the definition of "broker."

(a) *Defined terms for chiefly compensated test.* For purposes of this part and section 3(a)(4)(B)(ii) of the Act (15 U.S.C. 78c(a)(4)(B)(ii)), the following terms shall have the meaning provided:

(1) *Chiefly compensated—account-by-account test.* Chiefly compensated shall mean the *relationship-total compensation percentage* for each *trust or fiduciary account* of the bank is greater than 50 percent.

(2) The *relationship-total compensation percentage* for a *trust or fiduciary account* shall be the mean of the *yearly compensation percentage* for the account for the immediately preceding year and the *yearly compensation percentage* for the account for the year immediately preceding that year.

(3) The *yearly compensation percentage* for a *trust or fiduciary account* shall be

(i) Equal to the relationship compensation attributable to the *trust or fiduciary account* during the year divided by the total compensation attributable to the *trust or fiduciary account* during that year, with the quotient expressed as a percentage; and

(ii) Calculated within 60 days of the end of the year.

(4) *Relationship compensation* means any compensation a bank receives attributable to a trust or fiduciary account that consists of:

(i) An administration fee, including, without limitation, a fee paid—

(A) For personal services, tax preparation, or real estate settlement services;

(B) For disbursing funds from, or for recording receipt of payments to, a trust or fiduciary account;

(C) In connection with securities lending or borrowing transactions;

(D) For custody services; or

(E) In connection with an investment in shares of an investment company for personal service, the maintenance of shareholder accounts or any service described in paragraph (a)(4)(iii)(C) of this section;

(ii) An annual fee (payable on a monthly, quarterly or other basis), including, without limitation, a fee paid for assessing investment performance or for reviewing compliance with applicable investment guidelines or restrictions;

(iii) A fee based on a percentage of assets under management, including, without limitation, a fee paid

(A) Pursuant to a plan under § 270.12b–1;

(B) In connection with an investment in shares of an investment company for personal service or the maintenance of shareholder accounts;

(C) Based on a percentage of assets under management for any of the following services—

(*1*) Providing transfer agent or sub-transfer agent services for beneficial owners of investment company shares;

(*2*) Aggregating and processing purchase and redemption orders for investment company shares;

(*3*) Providing beneficial owners with account statements showing their purchases, sales, and positions in the investment company;

168

Securities and Exchange Commission § 247.722

(4) Processing dividend payments for the investment company;

(5) Providing sub-accounting services to the investment company for shares held beneficially;

(6) Forwarding communications from the investment company to the beneficial owners, including proxies, shareholder reports, dividend and tax notices, and updated prospectuses; or

(7) Receiving, tabulating, and transmitting proxies executed by beneficial owners of investment company shares;

(D) Based on the financial performance of the assets in an account; or

(E) For the types of services described in paragraph (a)(4)(i)(C) or (D) of this section if paid based on a percentage of assets under management;

(iv) A flat or capped per order processing fee, paid by or on behalf of a customer or beneficiary, that is equal to not more than the cost incurred by the bank in connection with executing securities transactions for trust or fiduciary accounts; or

(v) Any combination of such fees.

(5) *Trust or fiduciary account* means an account for which the bank acts in a trustee or fiduciary capacity as defined in section 3(a)(4)(D) of the Act (15 U.S.C. 78c(a)(4)(D)).

(6) *Year* means a calendar year, or fiscal year consistently used by the bank for recordkeeping and reporting purposes.

(b) *Revenues derived from transactions conducted under other exceptions or exemptions.* For purposes of calculating the *yearly compensation percentage* for a *trust or fiduciary account*, a bank may at its election exclude the compensation associated with any securities transaction conducted in accordance with the exceptions in section 3(a)(4)(B)(i) or sections 3(a)(4)(B)(iii)–(xi) of the Act (15 U.S.C. 78c(a)(4)(B)(i) or 78c(a)(4)(B)(iii)–(xi)) and the rules issued thereunder, including any exemption related to such exceptions jointly adopted by the Commission and the Board, *provided that* if the bank elects to exclude such compensation, the bank must exclude the compensation from both the relationship compensation (if applicable) and total compensation for the account.

(c) *Advertising restrictions*—(1) *In general.* A bank complies with the advertising restriction in section 3(a)(4)(B)(ii)(II) of the Act (15 U.S.C. 78c(a)(4)(B)(ii)(II)) if advertisements by or on behalf of the bank do not advertise—

(i) That the bank provides securities brokerage services for trust or fiduciary accounts except as part of advertising the bank's broader trust or fiduciary services; and

(ii) The securities brokerage services provided by the bank to trust or fiduciary accounts more prominently than the other aspects of the trust or fiduciary services provided to such accounts.

(2) *Advertisement.* For purposes of this section, the term *advertisement* has the same meaning as in § 247.760(h)(2).

[72 FR 56554, Oct. 3, 2007, as amended at 73 FR 20780, Apr. 17, 2008]

§ 247.722 Exemption allowing banks to calculate trust and fiduciary compensation on a bank-wide basis.

(a) *General.* A bank is exempt from meeting the "chiefly compensated" condition in section 3(a)(4)(B)(ii)(I) of the Act (15 U.S.C. 78c(a)(4)(B)(ii)(I)) to the extent that it effects transactions in securities for any account in a trustee or fiduciary capacity within the scope of section 3(a)(4)(D) of the Act (15 U.S.C. 78c(a)(4)(D)) if:

(1) The bank meets the other conditions for the exception from the definition of the term "broker" under sections 3(a)(4)(B)(ii) and 3(a)(4)(C) of the Act (15 U.S.C. 78c(a)(4)(B)(ii) and 15 U.S.C. 78c(a)(4)(C)), including the advertising restrictions in section 3(a)(4)(B)(ii)(II) of the Act (15 U.S.C. 78c(a)(4)(B)(ii)(II) as implemented by § 247.721(c); and

(2) The aggregate relationship-total compensation percentage for the bank's trust and fiduciary business is at least 70 percent.

(b) *Aggregate relationship-total compensation percentage.* For purposes of this section, the *aggregate relationship-total compensation percentage* for a bank's trust and fiduciary business shall be the mean of the bank's *yearly bank-wide compensation percentage* for the immediately preceding year and the bank's *yearly bank-wide compensation percentage* for the year immediately preceding that year.

§ 247.723

(c) *Yearly bank-wide compensation percentage.* For purposes of this section, a bank's *yearly bank-wide compensation percentage* for a year shall be

(1) Equal to the *relationship compensation* attributable to the bank's trust and fiduciary business as a whole during the year divided by the total compensation attributable to the bank's trust and fiduciary business as a whole during that year, with the quotient expressed as a percentage; and

(2) Calculated within 60 days of the end of the year.

(d) *Revenues derived from transactions conducted under other exceptions or exemptions.* For purposes of calculating the *yearly compensation percentage* for a *trust or fiduciary account,* a bank may at its election exclude the compensation associated with any securities transaction conducted in accordance with the exceptions in section 3(a)(4)(B)(i) or sections 3(a)(4)(B)(iii)–(xi) of the Act (15 U.S.C. 78c(a)(4)(B)(i) or 78c(a)(4)(B)(iii)–(xi)) and the rules issued thereunder, including any exemption related to such sections jointly adopted by the Commission and the Board, *provided that* if the bank elects to exclude such compensation, the bank must exclude the compensation from both the relationship compensation (if applicable) and total compensation of the bank.

§ 247.723 Exemptions for special accounts, transferred accounts, foreign branches and a de minimis number of accounts.

(a) *Short-term accounts.* A bank may, in determining its compliance with the chiefly compensated test in § 247.721(a)(1) or § 247.722(a)(2), exclude any trust or fiduciary account that had been open for a period of less than 3 months during the relevant year.

(b) *Accounts acquired as part of a business combination or asset acquisition.* For purposes of determining compliance with the chiefly compensated test in § 247.721(a)(1) or § 247.722(a)(2), any *trust or fiduciary account* that a bank acquired from another person as part of a merger, consolidation, acquisition, purchase of assets or similar transaction may be excluded by the bank for 12 months after the date the bank acquired the account from the other person.

(c) *Non-shell foreign branches*—(1) *Exemption.* For purposes of determining compliance with the chiefly compensated test in § 247.722(a)(2), a bank may exclude the trust or fiduciary accounts held at a non-shell foreign branch of the bank if the bank has reasonable cause to believe that trust or fiduciary accounts of the foreign branch held by or for the benefit of a U.S. person as defined in 17 CFR 230.902(k) constitute less than 10 percent of the total number of trust or fiduciary accounts of the foreign branch.

(2) *Rules of construction.* Solely for purposes of this paragraph (c), a bank will be deemed to have reasonable cause to believe that a trust or fiduciary account of a foreign branch of the bank is not held by or for the benefit of a U.S. person if

(i) The principal mailing address maintained and used by the foreign branch for the accountholder(s) and beneficiary(ies) of the account is not in the United States; or

(ii) The records of the foreign branch indicate that the accountholder(s) and beneficiary(ies) of the account is not a U.S. person as defined in 17 CFR 230.902(k).

(3) *Non-shell foreign branch.* Solely for purposes of this paragraph (c), a non-shell foreign branch of a bank means a branch of the bank

(i) That is located outside the United States and provides banking services to residents of the foreign jurisdiction in which the branch is located; and

(ii) For which the decisions relating to day-to-day operations and business of the branch are made at that branch and are not made by an office of the bank located in the United States.

(d) *Accounts transferred to a broker or dealer or other unaffiliated entity.* Notwithstanding section 3(a)(4)(B)(ii)(I) of the Act (15 U.S.C. 78c(a)(4)(B)(ii)(I)) and § 247.721(a)(1) of this part, a bank operating under § 247.721(a)(1) shall not be considered a broker for purposes of section 3(a)(4) of the Act (15 U.S.C. 78c(a)(4)) solely because a *trust or fiduciary account* does not meet the chiefly compensated standard in § 247.721(a)(1) if, within 3 months of the end of the year in which the account fails to meet

Securities and Exchange Commission § 247.741

such standard, the bank transfers the account or the securities held by or on behalf of the account to a broker or dealer registered under section 15 of the Act (15 U.S.C. 78o) or another entity that is not an affiliate of the bank and is not required to be registered as a broker or dealer.

(e) *De minimis exclusion.* A bank may, in determining its compliance with the chiefly compensated test in § 247.721(a)(1), exclude a *trust or fiduciary account* if:

(1) The bank maintains records demonstrating that the securities transactions conducted by or on behalf of the account were undertaken by the bank in the exercise of its trust or fiduciary responsibilities with respect to the account;

(2) The total number of accounts excluded by the bank under this paragraph (d) does not exceed the lesser of—

(i) 1 percent of the total number of trust or fiduciary accounts held by the bank, *provided that* if the number so obtained is less than 1 the amount shall be rounded up to 1; or

(ii) 500; and

(3) The bank did not rely on this paragraph (e) with respect to such account during the immediately preceding year.

[72 FR 56554, Oct. 3, 2007, as amended at 73 FR 20780, Apr. 17, 2008]

§ 247.740 Defined terms relating to the sweep accounts exception from the definition of "broker."

For purposes of section 3(a)(4)(B)(v) of the Act (15 U.S.C. 78c(a)(4)(B)(v)), the following terms shall have the meaning provided:

(a) *Deferred sales load* has the same meaning as in 17 CFR 270.6c–10.

(b) *Money market fund* means an open-end company registered under the Investment Company Act of 1940 (15 U.S.C. 80a–1 et seq.) that is regulated as a money market fund pursuant to 17 CFR 270.2a–7.

(c)(1) *No-load*, in the context of an investment company or the securities issued by an investment company, means, for securities of the class or series in which a bank effects transactions, that:

(i) That class or series is not subject to a sales load or a deferred sales load; and

(ii) Total charges against net assets of that class or series of the investment company's securities for sales or sales promotion expenses, for personal service, or for the maintenance of shareholder accounts do not exceed 0.25 of 1% of average net assets annually.

(2) For purposes of this definition, charges for the following will not be considered charges against net assets of a class or series of an investment company's securities for sales or sales promotion expenses, for personal service, or for the maintenance of shareholder accounts:

(i) Providing transfer agent or sub-transfer agent services for beneficial owners of investment company shares;

(ii) Aggregating and processing purchase and redemption orders for investment company shares;

(iii) Providing beneficial owners with account statements showing their purchases, sales, and positions in the investment company;

(iv) Processing dividend payments for the investment company;

(v) Providing sub-accounting services to the investment company for shares held beneficially;

(vi) Forwarding communications from the investment company to the beneficial owners, including proxies, shareholder reports, dividend and tax notices, and updated prospectuses; or

(vii) Receiving, tabulating, and transmitting proxies executed by beneficial owners of investment company shares.

(d) *Open-end company* has the same meaning as in section 5(a)(1) of the Investment Company Act of 1940 (15 U.S.C. 80a–5(a)(1)).

(e) *Sales load* has the same meaning as in section 2(a)(35) of the Investment Company Act of 1940 (15 U.S.C. 80a–2(a)(35)).

§ 247.741 Exemption for banks effecting transactions in money market funds.

(a) A bank is exempt from the definition of the term "broker" under section 3(a)(4) of the Act (15 U.S.C. 78c(a)(4)) to the extent that it effects transactions on behalf of a customer in

§ 247.760

securities issued by a money market fund, provided that:

(1) The bank either

(i) Provides the customer, directly or indirectly, any other product or service, the provision of which would not, in and of itself, require the bank to register as a broker or dealer under section 15(a) of the Act (15 U.S.C. 78o(a)); or

(ii) Effects the transactions on behalf of another bank as part of a program for the investment or reinvestment of deposit funds of, or collected by, the other bank; and

(2)(i) The class or series of securities is no-load; or

(ii) If the class or series of securities is not no-load

(A) The bank or, if applicable, the other bank described in paragraph (a)(1)(B) of this section provides the customer, not later than at the time the customer authorizes the securities transactions, a prospectus for the securities; and

(B) The bank and, if applicable, the other bank described in paragraph (a)(1)(B) of this section do not characterize or refer to the class or series of securities as no-load.

(b) *Definitions.* For purposes of this section:

(1) *Money market fund* has the same meaning as in § 247.740(b).

(2) *No-load* has the same meaning as in § 247.740(c).

[72 FR 56554, Oct. 3, 2007, as amended at 73 FR 20780, Apr. 17, 2008]

§ 247.760 Exemption from definition of "broker" for banks accepting orders to effect transactions in securities from or on behalf of custody accounts.

(a) *Employee benefit plan accounts and individual retirement accounts or similar accounts.* A bank is exempt from the definition of the term "broker" under section 3(a)(4) of the Act (15 U.S.C. 78c(a)(4)) to the extent that, as part of its customary banking activities, the bank accepts orders to effect transactions in securities for an employee benefit plan account or an individual retirement account or similar account for which the bank acts as a custodian if:

(1) *Employee compensation restriction and additional conditions.* The bank complies with the employee compensation restrictions in paragraph (c) of this section *and* the other conditions in paragraph (d) of this section;

(2) *Advertisements.* Advertisements by or on behalf of the bank do not:

(i) Advertise that the bank accepts orders for securities transactions for employee benefit plan accounts or individual retirement accounts or similar accounts, except as part of advertising the other custodial or safekeeping services the bank provides to these accounts; or

(ii) Advertise that such accounts are securities brokerage accounts or that the bank's safekeeping and custody services substitute for a securities brokerage account; and

(3) *Advertisements and sales literature for individual retirement or similar accounts.* Advertisements and sales literature issued by or on behalf of the bank do not describe the securities order-taking services provided by the bank to individual retirement accounts or similar accounts more prominently than the other aspects of the custody or safekeeping services provided by the bank to these accounts.

(b) *Accommodation trades for other custodial accounts.* A bank is exempt from the definition of the term "broker" under section 3(a)(4) of the Act (15 U.S.C. 78c(a)(4)) to the extent that, as part of its customary banking activities, the bank accepts orders to effect transactions in securities for an account for which the bank acts as custodian other than an employee benefit plan account or an individual retirement account or similar account if:

(1) *Accommodation.* The bank accepts orders to effect transactions in securities for the account only as an accommodation to the customer;

(2) *Employee compensation restriction and additional conditions.* The bank complies with the employee compensation restrictions in paragraph (c) of this section and the other conditions in paragraph (d) of this section;

(3) *Bank fees.* Any fee charged or received by the bank for effecting a securities transaction for the account does not vary based on:

Securities and Exchange Commission § 247.760

(i) Whether the bank accepted the order for the transaction; or

(ii) The quantity or price of the securities to be bought or sold;

(4) *Advertisements.* Advertisements by or on behalf of the bank do not state that the bank accepts orders for securities transactions for the account;

(5) *Sales literature.* Sales literature issued by or on behalf of the bank:

(i) Does not state that the bank accepts orders for securities transactions for the account except as part of describing the other custodial or safekeeping services the bank provides to the account; and

(ii) Does not describe the securities order-taking services provided to the account more prominently than the other aspects of the custody or safekeeping services provided by the bank to the account; and

(6) *Investment advice and recommendations.* The bank does not provide investment advice or research concerning securities to the account, make recommendations to the account concerning securities or otherwise solicit securities transactions from the account; provided, however, that nothing in this paragraph (b)(6) shall prevent a bank from:

(i) Publishing, using or disseminating advertisements and sales literature in accordance with paragraphs (b)(4) and (b)(5) of this section; and

(ii) Responding to customer inquiries regarding the bank's safekeeping and custody services by providing:

(A) Advertisements or sales literature consistent with the provisions of paragraphs (b)(4) and (b)(5) of this section describing the safekeeping, custody and related services that the bank offers;

(B) A prospectus prepared by a registered investment company, or sales literature prepared by a registered investment company or by the broker or dealer that is the principal underwriter of the registered investment company pertaining to the registered investment company's products;

(C) Information based on the materials described in paragraphs (b)(6)(ii)(A) and (B) of this section; or

(iii) Responding to inquiries regarding the bank's safekeeping, custody or other services, such as inquiries concerning the customer's account or the availability of sweep or other services, so long as the bank does not provide investment advice or research concerning securities to the account or make a recommendation to the account concerning securities.

(c) *Employee compensation restriction.* A bank may accept orders pursuant to this section for a securities transaction for an account described in paragraph (a) or (b) of this section only if no bank employee receives compensation, including a fee paid pursuant to a plan under 17 CFR 270.12b–1, from the bank, the executing broker or dealer, or any other person that is based on whether a securities transaction is executed for the account or that is based on the quantity, price, or identity of securities purchased or sold by such account, provided that nothing in this paragraph shall prohibit a bank employee from receiving compensation that would not be considered incentive compensation under § 247.700(b)(1) as if a referral had been made by the bank employee, or any compensation described in § 247.700(b)(2).

(d) *Other conditions.* A bank may accept orders for a securities transaction for an account for which the bank acts as a custodian under this section only if the bank:

(1) Does not act in a trustee or fiduciary capacity (as defined in section 3(a)(4)(D) of the Act (15 U.S.C. 78c(a)(4)(D)) with respect to the account, other than as a directed trustee;

(2) Complies with section 3(a)(4)(C) of the Act (15 U.S.C. 78c(a)(4)(C)) in handling any order for a securities transaction for the account; and

(3) Complies with section 3(a)(4)(B)(viii)(II) of the Act (15 U.S.C. 78c(a)(4)(B)(viii)(II)) regarding carrying broker activities.

(e) *Non-fiduciary administrators and recordkeepers.* A bank that acts as a non-fiduciary and non-custodial administrator or recordkeeper for an employee benefit plan account for which another bank acts as custodian may rely on the exemption provided in this section if:

(1) Both the custodian bank and the administrator or recordkeeper bank comply with paragraphs (a), (c) and (d) of this section; and

§ 247.760

(2) The administrator or recordkeeper bank does not execute a cross-trade with or for the employee benefit plan account or net orders for securities for the employee benefit plan account, other than:

(i) Crossing or netting orders for shares of open-end investment companies not traded on an exchange, or

(ii) Crossing orders between or netting orders for accounts of the custodian bank that contracted with the administrator or recordkeeper bank for services.

(f) *Subcustodians.* A bank that acts as a subcustodian for an account for which another bank acts as custodian may rely on the exemptions provided in this section if:

(1) For employee benefit plan accounts and individual retirement accounts or similar accounts, both the custodian bank and the subcustodian bank meet the requirements of paragraphs (a), (c) and (d) of this section;

(2) For other custodial accounts, both the custodian bank and the subcustodian bank meet the requirements of paragraphs (b), (c) and (d) of this section; and

(3) The subcustodian bank does not execute a cross-trade with or for the account or net orders for securities for the account, other than:

(i) Crossing or netting orders for shares of open-end investment companies not traded on an exchange, or

(ii) Crossing orders between or netting orders for accounts of the custodian bank.

(g) *Evasions.* In considering whether a bank meets the terms of this section, both the form and substance of the relevant account(s), transaction(s) and activities (including advertising activities) of the bank will be considered in order to prevent evasions of the requirements of this section.

(h) *Definitions.* When used in this section:

(1) *Account for which the bank acts as a custodian* means an account that is:

(i) An employee benefit plan account for which the bank acts as a custodian;

(ii) An individual retirement account or similar account for which the bank acts as a custodian;

(iii) An account established by a written agreement between the bank and the customer that sets forth the terms that will govern the fees payable to, and rights and obligations of, the bank regarding the safekeeping or custody of securities; or

(iv) An account for which the bank acts as a directed trustee.

(2) *Advertisement* means any material that is published or used in any electronic or other public media, including any Web site, newspaper, magazine or other periodical, radio, television, telephone or tape recording, videotape display, signs or billboards, motion pictures, or telephone directories (other than routine listings).

(3) *Directed trustee* means a trustee that does not exercise investment discretion with respect to the account.

(4) *Employee benefit plan account* means a pension plan, retirement plan, profit sharing plan, bonus plan, thrift savings plan, incentive plan, or other similar plan, including, without limitation, an employer-sponsored plan qualified under section 401(a) of the Internal Revenue Code (26 U.S.C. 401(a)), a governmental or other plan described in section 457 of the Internal Revenue Code (26 U.S.C. 457), a tax-deferred plan described in section 403(b) of the Internal Revenue Code (26 U.S.C. 403(b)), a church plan, governmental, multiemployer or other plan described in section 414(d), (e) or (f) of the Internal Revenue Code (26 U.S.C. 414(d), (e) or (f)), an incentive stock option plan described in section 422 of the Internal Revenue Code (26 U.S.C. 422); a Voluntary Employee Beneficiary Association Plan described in section 501(c)(9) of the Internal Revenue Code (26 U.S.C. 501(c)(9)), a non-qualified deferred compensation plan (including a rabbi or secular trust), a supplemental or mirror plan, and a supplemental unemployment benefit plan.

(5) *Individual retirement account or similar account* means an individual retirement account as defined in section 408 of the Internal Revenue Code (26 U.S.C. 408), Roth IRA as defined in section 408A of the Internal Revenue Code (26 U.S.C. 408A), health savings account as defined in section 223(d) of the Internal Revenue Code (26 U.S.C. 223(d)), Archer medical savings account as defined in section 220(d) of the Internal

Securities and Exchange Commission § 247.772

Revenue Code (26 U.S.C. 220(d)), Coverdell education savings account as defined in section 530 of the Internal Revenue Code (26 U.S.C. 530), or other similar account.

(6) *Sales literature* means any written or electronic communication, other than an advertisement, that is generally distributed or made generally available to customers of the bank or the public, including circulars, form letters, brochures, telemarketing scripts, seminar texts, published articles, and press releases concerning the bank's products or services.

(7) *Principal underwriter* has the same meaning as in section 2(a)(29) of the Investment Company Act of 1940 (15 U.S.C. 80a–2(a)(29)).

§ 247.771 Exemption from the definition of "broker" for banks effecting transactions in securities issued pursuant to Regulation S.

(a) A bank is exempt from the definition of the term "broker" under section 3(a)(4) of the Act (15 U.S.C. 78c(a)(4)), to the extent that, as agent, the bank:

(1) Effects a sale in compliance with the requirements of 17 CFR 230.903 of an eligible security to a purchaser who is not in the United States;

(2) Effects, by or on behalf of a person who is not a U.S. person under 17 CFR 230.902(k), a resale of an eligible security after its initial sale with a reasonable belief that the eligible security was initially sold outside of the United States within the meaning of and in compliance with 17 CFR 230.903 to a purchaser who is not in the United States or a registered broker or dealer, provided that if the resale is made prior to the expiration of any applicable distribution compliance period specified in 17 CFR 230.903(b)(2) or (b)(3), the resale is made in compliance with the requirements of 17 CFR 230.904; or

(3) Effects, by or on behalf of a registered broker or dealer, a resale of an eligible security after its initial sale with a reasonable belief that the eligible security was initially sold outside of the United States within the meaning of and in compliance with the requirements of 17 CFR 230.903 to a purchaser who is not in the United States, provided that if the resale is made prior to the expiration of any applicable distribution compliance period specified in 17 CFR 230.903(b)(2) or (b)(3), the resale is made in compliance with the requirements of 17 CFR 230.904.

(b) *Definitions.* For purposes of this section:

(1) *Distributor* has the same meaning as in 17 CFR 230.902(d).

(2) *Eligible security* means a security that:

(i) Is not being sold from the inventory of the bank or an affiliate of the bank; and

(ii) Is not being underwritten by the bank or an affiliate of the bank on a firm-commitment basis, unless the bank acquired the security from an unaffiliated distributor that did not purchase the security from the bank or an affiliate of the bank.

(3) *Purchaser* means a person who purchases an eligible security and who is not a U.S. person under 17 CFR 230.902(k).

§ 247.772 Exemption from the definition of "broker" for banks engaging in securities lending transactions.

(a) A bank is exempt from the definition of the term "broker" under section 3(a)(4) of the Act (15 U.S.C. 78c(a)(4)), to the extent that, as an agent, it engages in or effects securities lending transactions, and any securities lending services in connection with such transactions, with or on behalf of a person the bank reasonably believes to be:

(1) A qualified investor as defined in section 3(a)(54)(A) of the Act (15 U.S.C. 78c(a)(54)(A)); or

(2) Any employee benefit plan that owns and invests on a discretionary basis, not less than $ 25,000,000 in investments.

(b) *Securities lending transaction* means a transaction in which the owner of a security lends the security temporarily to another party pursuant to a written securities lending agreement under which the lender retains the economic interests of an owner of such securities, and has the right to terminate the transaction and to recall the loaned securities on terms agreed by the parties.

§ 247.775

(c) *Securities lending services* means:

(1) Selecting and negotiating with a borrower and executing, or directing the execution of the loan with the borrower;

(2) Receiving, delivering, or directing the receipt or delivery of loaned securities;

(3) Receiving, delivering, or directing the receipt or delivery of collateral;

(4) Providing mark-to-market, corporate action, recordkeeping or other services incidental to the administration of the securities lending transaction;

(5) Investing, or directing the investment of, cash collateral; or

(6) Indemnifying the lender of securities with respect to various matters.

§ 247.775 Exemption from the definition of "broker" for banks effecting certain excepted or exempted transactions in investment company securities.

(a) A bank that meets the conditions for an exception or exemption from the definition of the term "broker" except for the condition in section 3(a)(4)(C)(i) of the Act (15 U.S.C. 78c(a)(4)(C)(i)), is exempt from such condition to the extent that it effects a transaction in a *covered security*, if:

(1) Any such security is neither traded on a national securities exchange nor through the facilities of a national securities association or an interdealer quotation system;

(2) The security is distributed by a registered broker or dealer, or the sales charge is no more than the amount permissible for a security sold by a registered broker or dealer pursuant to any applicable rules adopted pursuant to section 22(b)(1) of the Investment Company Act of 1940 (15 U.S.C. 80a–22(b)(1)) by a securities association registered under section 15A of the Act (15 U.S.C. 78o–3); and

(3) Any such transaction is effected:

(i) Through the National Securities Clearing Corporation; or

(ii) Directly with a transfer agent or with an insurance company or separate account that is excluded from the definition of transfer agent in Section 3(a)(25) of the Act.

(b) *Definitions.* For purposes of this section:

(1) *Covered security* means:

(i) Any security issued by an open-end company, as defined by section 5(a)(1) of the Investment Company Act (15 U.S.C. 80a–5(a)(1)), that is registered under that Act; and

(ii) Any variable insurance contract funded by a separate account, as defined by section 2(a)(37) of the Investment Company Act (15 U.S.C. 80a–2(a)(37)), that is registered under that Act.

(2) *Interdealer quotation system* has the same meaning as in 17 CFR 240.15c2–11.

(3) *Insurance company* has the same meaning as in 15 U.S.C. 77b(a)(13).

[72 FR 56554, Oct. 3, 2007, as amended at 73 FR 20780, Apr. 17, 2008]

§ 247.776 Exemption from the definition of "broker" for banks effecting certain excepted or exempted transactions in a company's securities for its employee benefit plans.

(a) A bank that meets the conditions for an exception or exemption from the definition of the term "broker" except for the condition in section 3(a)(4)(C)(i) of the Act (15 U.S.C. 78c(a)(4)(C)(i)), is exempt from such condition to the extent that it effects a transaction in the securities of a company directly with a transfer agent acting for the company that issued the security, if:

(1) No commission is charged with respect to the transaction;

(2) The transaction is conducted by the bank solely for the benefit of an employee benefit plan account;

(3) Any such security is obtained directly from:

(i) The company; or

(ii) An employee benefit plan of the company; and

(4) Any such security is transferred only to:

(i) The company; or

(ii) An employee benefit plan of the company.

(b) For purposes of this section, the term *employee benefit plan account* has the same meaning as in § 247.760(h)(4).

§ 247.780 Exemption for banks from liability under section 29 of the Securities Exchange Act of 1934.

(a) No contract entered into before March 31, 2009, shall be void or considered voidable by reason of section 29(b) of the Act (15 U.S.C. 78cc(b)) because

Securities and Exchange Commission

any bank that is a party to the contract violated the registration requirements of section 15(a) of the Act (15 U.S.C. 78o(a)), any other applicable provision of the Act, or the rules and regulations thereunder based solely on the bank's status as a broker when the contract was created.

(b) No contract shall be void or considered voidable by reason of section 29(b) of the Act (15 U.S.C. 78cc(b)) because any bank that is a party to the contract violated the registration requirements of section 15(a) of the Act (15 U.S.C. 78o(a)) or the rules and regulations thereunder based solely on the bank's status as a broker when the contract was created, if:

(1) At the time the contract was created, the bank acted in good faith and had reasonable policies and procedures in place to comply with section 3(a)(4)(B) of the Act (15 U.S.C. 78c(a)(4)(B)) and the rules and regulations thereunder; and

(2) At the time the contract was created, any violation of the registration requirements of section 15(a) of the Act by the bank did not result in any significant harm or financial loss or cost to the person seeking to void the contract.

§ 247.781 Exemption from the definition of "broker" for banks for a limited period of time.

A bank is exempt from the definition of the term "broker" under section 3(a)(4) of the Act (15 U.S.C. 78c(a)(4)) until the first day of its first fiscal year commencing after September 30, 2008.

PART 248—REGULATIONS S–P, S–AM, AND S–ID

Subpart A—Regulation S-P: Privacy of Consumer Financial Information and Safeguarding Personal Information

Sec.
248.1 Purpose and scope.
248.2 Model privacy form: rule of construction.
248.3 Definitions.

PRIVACY AND OPT OUT NOTICES

248.4 Initial privacy notice to consumers required.
248.5 Annual privacy notice to customers required.
248.6 Information to be included in privacy notices.
248.7 Form of opt out notice to consumers; opt out methods.
248.8 Revised privacy notices.
248.9 Delivering privacy and opt out notices.

LIMITS ON DISCLOSURES

248.10 Limits on disclosure of nonpublic personal information to nonaffiliated third parties.
248.11 Limits on redisclosure and reuse of information.
248.12 Limits on sharing account number information for marketing purposes.

EXCEPTIONS

248.13 Exception to opt out requirements for service providers and joint marketing.
248.14 Exceptions to notice and opt out requirements for processing and servicing transactions.
248.15 Other exceptions to notice and opt out requirements.

RELATION TO OTHER LAWS; EFFECTIVE DATE

248.16 Protection of Fair Credit Reporting Act.
248.17 Relation to State laws.
248.18 Effective date; transition rule.
248.19–248.29 [Reserved]
248.30 Procedures to safeguard customer records and information.
248.31–248.100 [Reserved]

APPENDIX A TO SUBPART A OF PART 248—FORMS

Subpart B—Regulation S-AM: Limitations on Affiliate Marketing

248.101 Purpose and scope.
248.102 Examples.
248.103–248.119 [Reserved]
248.120 Definitions.
248.121 Affiliate marketing opt out and exceptions.
248.122 Scope and duration of opt out.
248.123 Contents of opt out notice; consolidated and equivalent notices.
248.124 Reasonable opportunity to opt out.
248.125 Reasonable and simple methods of opting out.
248.126 Delivery of opt out notices.
248.127 Renewal of opt out elections.
248.128 Effective date, compliance date, and prospective application.

APPENDIX TO SUBPART B OF PART 248—MODEL FORMS

§ 248.1

Subpart C—Regulation S–ID: Identity Theft Red Flags

248.201 Duties regarding the detection, prevention, and mitigation of identity theft.
248.202 Duties of card issuers regarding changes of address.

APPENDIX A TO SUBPART C OF PART 248—INTERAGENCY GUIDELINES ON IDENTITY THEFT DETECTION, PREVENTION, AND MITIGATION

AUTHORITY: 15 U.S.C. 78q, 78q-1, 78*o*-4, 78*o*-5, 78w, 78mm, 80a-30, 80a-37, 80b-4, 80b-11, 1681m(e), 1681s(b), 1681s-3 and note, 1681w(a)(1), 6801–6809, and 6825; Pub. L. 111–203, secs. 1088(a)(8), (a)(10), and sec. 1088(b), 124 Stat. 1376 (2010).

SOURCE: 65 FR 40362, June 29, 2000, unless otherwise noted.

EDITORIAL NOTE: Nomenclature changes to part 248 appear at 74 FR 40431, Aug. 11, 2009.

Subpart A—Regulation S-P: Privacy of Consumer Financial Information and Safeguarding Personal Information

§ 248.1 Purpose and scope.

(a) *Purpose.* This subpart governs the treatment of nonpublic personal information about consumers by the financial institutions listed in paragraph (b) of this section. This subpart:

(1) Requires a financial institution to provide notice to customers about its privacy policies and practices;

(2) Describes the conditions under which a financial institution may disclose nonpublic personal information about consumers to nonaffiliated third parties; and

(3) Provides a method for consumers to prevent a financial institution from disclosing that information to most nonaffiliated third parties by "opting out" of that disclosure, subject to the exceptions in §§ 248.13, 248.14, and 248.15.

(b) *Scope.* Except with respect to § 248.30(b), this subpart applies only to nonpublic personal information about individuals who obtain financial products or services primarily for personal, family, or household purposes from the institutions listed below. This subpart does not apply to information about companies or about individuals who obtain financial products or services primarily for business, commercial, or agricultural purposes. This part applies to brokers, dealers, and investment companies, as well as to investment advisers that are registered with the Commission. It also applies to foreign (non-resident) brokers, dealers, investment companies and investment advisers that are registered with the Commission. These entities are referred to in this subpart as "you." This subpart does not apply to foreign (non-resident) brokers, dealers, investment companies and investment advisers that are not registered with the Commission. Nothing in this subpart modifies, limits, or supersedes the standards governing individually identifiable health information promulgated by the Secretary of Health and Human Services under the authority of sections 262 and 264 of the Health Insurance Portability and Accountability Act of 1996 (42 U.S.C. 1320d–1320d-8).

[65 FR 40362, June 29, 2000, as amended at 69 FR 71329, Dec. 8, 2004]

§ 248.2 Model privacy form: rule of construction.

(a) *Model privacy form.* Use of the model privacy form in appendix A to subpart A of this part, consistent with the instructions in appendix A to subpart A, constitutes compliance with the notice content requirements of §§ 248.6 and 248.7 of this part, although use of the model privacy form is not required.

(b) *Examples.* The examples in this part provide guidance concerning the rule's application in ordinary circumstances. The facts and circumstances of each individual situation, however, will determine whether compliance with an example, to the extent practicable, constitutes compliance with this part.

(c) *Substituted compliance with CFTC financial privacy rules by futures commission merchants and introducing brokers.* Except with respect to § 248.30(b), any futures commission merchant or introducing broker (as those terms are defined in the Commodity Exchange Act (7 U.S.C. 1, *et seq.*)) registered by notice with the Commission for the purpose of conducting business in security futures products pursuant to section 15(b)(11)(A) of the Securities Exchange Act of 1934 (15 U.S.C. 78*o*(b)(11)(A)) that is subject to and in compliance with

Securities and Exchange Commission § 248.3

the financial privacy rules of the Commodity Futures Trading Commission (17 CFR part 160) will be deemed to be in compliance with this part.

[74 FR 62984, Dec. 1, 2009]

§ 248.3 Definitions.

As used in this subpart, unless the context requires otherwise:

(a) *Affiliate* of a broker, dealer, or investment company, or an investment adviser registered with the Commission means any company that controls, is controlled by, or is under common control with the broker, dealer, or investment company, or investment adviser registered with the Commission. In addition, a broker, dealer, or investment company, or an investment adviser registered with the Commission will be deemed an affiliate of a company for purposes of this subpart if:

(1) That company is regulated under Title V of the GLBA by the Federal Trade Commission or by a Federal functional regulator other than the Commission; and

(2) Rules adopted by the Federal Trade Commission or another federal functional regulator under Title V of the GLBA treat the broker, dealer, or investment company, or investment adviser registered with the Commission as an affiliate of that company.

(b) *Broker* has the same meaning as in section 3(a)(4) of the Securities Exchange Act of 1934 (15 U.S.C. 78c(a)(4)).

(c)(1) *Clear and conspicuous* means that a notice is reasonably understandable and designed to call attention to the nature and significance of the information in the notice.

(2) *Examples*—(i) *Reasonably understandable.* You make your notice reasonably understandable if you:

(A) Present the information in the notice in clear, concise sentences, paragraphs, and sections;

(B) Use short explanatory sentences or bullet lists whenever possible;

(C) Use definite, concrete, everyday words and active voice whenever possible;

(D) Avoid multiple negatives;

(E) Avoid legal and highly technical business terminology whenever possible; and

(F) Avoid explanations that are imprecise and readily subject to different interpretations.

(ii) *Designed to call attention.* You design your notice to call attention to the nature and significance of the information in it if you:

(A) Use a plain-language heading to call attention to the notice;

(B) Use a typeface and type size that are easy to read;

(C) Provide wide margins and ample line spacing;

(D) Use boldface or italics for key words; and

(E) Use distinctive type size, style, and graphic devices, such as shading or sidebars when you combine your notice with other information.

(iii) *Notices on web sites.* If you provide a notice on a web page, you design your notice to call attention to the nature and significance of the information in it if you use text or visual cues to encourage scrolling down the page if necessary to view the entire notice and ensure that other elements on the web site (such as text, graphics, hyperlinks, or sound) do not distract attention from the notice, and you either:

(A) Place the notice on a screen that consumers frequently access, such as a page on which transactions are conducted; or

(B) Place a link on a screen that consumers frequently access, such as a page on which transactions are conducted, that connects directly to the notice and is labeled appropriately to convey the importance, nature, and relevance of the notice.

(d) *Collect* means to obtain information that you organize or can retrieve by the name of an individual or by identifying number, symbol, or other identifying particular assigned to the individual, irrespective of the source of the underlying information.

(e) *Commission* means the Securities and Exchange Commission.

(f) *Company* means any corporation, limited liability company, business trust, general or limited partnership, association, or similar organization.

(g)(1) *Consumer* means an individual who obtains or has obtained a financial product or service from you that is to be used primarily for personal, family,

§ 248.3

or household purposes, or that individual's legal representative.

(2) *Examples.* (i) An individual is your consumer if he or she provides nonpublic personal information to you in connection with obtaining or seeking to obtain brokerage services or investment advisory services, whether or not you provide brokerage services to the individual or establish a continuing relationship with the individual.

(ii) An individual is not your consumer if he or she provides you only with his or her name, address, and general areas of investment interest in connection with a request for a prospectus, an investment adviser brochure, or other information about financial products or services.

(iii) An individual is not your consumer if he or she has an account with another broker or dealer (the introducing broker-dealer) that carries securities for the individual in a special omnibus account with you (the clearing broker-dealer) in the name of the introducing broker-dealer, and when you receive only the account numbers and transaction information of the introducing broker-dealer's consumers in order to clear transactions.

(iv) If you are an investment company, an individual is not your consumer when the individual purchases an interest in shares you have issued only through a broker or dealer or investment adviser who is the record owner of those shares.

(v) An individual who is a consumer of another financial institution is not your consumer solely because you act as agent for, or provide processing or other services to, that financial institution.

(vi) An individual is not your consumer solely because he or she has designated you as trustee for a trust.

(vii) An individual is not your consumer solely because he or she is a beneficiary of a trust for which you are a trustee.

(viii) An individual is not your consumer solely because he or she is a participant or a beneficiary of an employee benefit plan that you sponsor or for which you act as a trustee or fiduciary.

(h) *Consumer reporting agency* has the same meaning as in section 603(f) of the Fair Credit Reporting Act (15 U.S.C. 1681a(f)).

(i) *Control* of a company means the power to exercise a controlling influence over the management or policies of a company whether through ownership of securities, by contract, or otherwise. Any person who owns beneficially, either directly or through one or more controlled companies, more than 25 percent of the voting securities of any company is presumed to control the company. Any person who does not own more than 25 percent of the voting securities of any company will be presumed not to control the company. Any presumption regarding control may be rebutted by evidence, but, in the case of an investment company, will continue until the Commission makes a decision to the contrary according to the procedures described in section 2(a)(9) of the Investment Company Act of 1940 (15 U.S.C. 80a–2(a)(9)).

(j) *Customer* means a consumer who has a customer relationship with you.

(k)(1) *Customer relationship* means a continuing relationship between a consumer and you under which you provide one or more financial products or services to the consumer that are to be used primarily for personal, family, or household purposes.

(2) *Examples*—(i) *Continuing relationship.* A consumer has a continuing relationship with you if:

(A) The consumer has a brokerage account with you, or if a consumer's account is transferred to you from another broker-dealer;

(B) The consumer has an investment advisory contract with you (whether written or oral);

(C) The consumer is the record owner of securities you have issued if you are an investment company;

(D) The consumer holds an investment product through you, such as when you act as a custodian for securities or for assets in an Individual Retirement Arrangement;

(E) The consumer purchases a variable annuity from you;

(F) The consumer has an account with an introducing broker or dealer that clears transactions with and for its customers through you on a fully disclosed basis;

Securities and Exchange Commission

§ 248.3

(G) You hold securities or other assets as collateral for a loan made to the consumer, even if you did not make the loan or do not effect any transactions on behalf of the consumer; or

(H) You regularly effect or engage in securities transactions with or for a consumer even if you do not hold any assets of the consumer.

(ii) *No continuing relationship.* A consumer does not, however, have a continuing relationship with you if you open an account for the consumer solely for the purpose of liquidating or purchasing securities as an accommodation, i.e., on a one time basis, without the expectation of engaging in other transactions.

(l) *Dealer* has the same meaning as in section 3(a)(5) of the Securities Exchange Act of 1934 (15 U.S.C. 78c(a)(5)).

(m) *Federal functional regulator* means:

(1) The Board of Governors of the Federal Reserve System;

(2) The Office of the Comptroller of the Currency;

(3) The Board of Directors of the Federal Deposit Insurance Corporation;

(4) The Director of the Office of Thrift Supervision;

(5) The National Credit Union Administration Board

(6) The Securities and Exchange Commission; and

(7) The Commodity Futures Trading Commission.

(n)(1) *Financial institution* means any institution the business of which is engaging in activities that are financial in nature or incidental to such financial activities as described in section 4(k) of the Bank Holding Company Act of 1956 (12 U.S.C. 1843(k)).

(2) *Financial institution* does not include:

(i) The Federal Agricultural Mortgage Corporation or any entity chartered and operating under the Farm Credit Act of 1971 (12 U.S.C. 2001 *et seq.*); or

(ii) Institutions chartered by Congress specifically to engage in securitizations, secondary market sales (including sales of servicing rights), or similar transactions related to a transaction of a consumer, as long as such institutions do not sell or transfer nonpublic personal information to a nonaffiliated third party.

(o)(1) *Financial product or service* means any product or service that a financial holding company could offer by engaging in an activity that is financial in nature or incidental to such a financial activity under section 4(k) of the Bank Holding Company Act of 1956 (12 U.S.C. 1843(k)).

(2) *Financial service* includes your evaluation or brokerage of information that you collect in connection with a request or an application from a consumer for a financial product or service.

(p) *GLBA* means the Gramm-Leach-Bliley Act (Pub. L. No. 106–102, 113 Stat. 1338 (1999)).

(q) *Investment adviser* has the same meaning as in section 202(a)(11) of the Investment Advisers Act of 1940 (15 U.S.C. 80b–2(a)(11)).

(r) *Investment company* has the same meaning as in section 3 of the Investment Company Act of 1940 (15 U.S.C. 80a–3), and includes a separate series of the investment company.

(s)(1) *Nonaffiliated third party* means any person except:

(i) Your affiliate; or

(ii) A person employed jointly by you and any company that is not your affiliate (but *nonaffiliated third party* includes the other company that jointly employs the person).

(2) *Nonaffiliated third party* includes any company that is an affiliate solely by virtue of your or your affiliate's direct or indirect ownership or control of the company in conducting merchant banking or investment banking activities of the type described in section 4(k)(4)(H) or insurance company investment activities of the type described in section 4(k)(4)(I) of the Bank Holding Company Act (12 U.S.C. 1843(k)(4)(H) and (I)).

(t)(1) *Nonpublic personal information* means:

(i) Personally identifiable financial information; and

(ii) Any list, description, or other grouping of consumers (and publicly available information pertaining to them) that is derived using any personally identifiable financial information that is not publicly available information.

§ 248.3

(2) *Nonpublic personal information* does not include:

(i) Publicly available information, except as included on a list described in paragraph (t)(1)(ii) of this section or when the publicly available information is disclosed in a manner that indicates the individual is or has been your consumer; or

(ii) Any list, description, or other grouping of consumers (and publicly available information pertaining to them) that is derived without using any personally identifiable financial information that is not publicly available information.

(3) *Examples of lists.* (i) Nonpublic personal information includes any list of individuals' names and street addresses that is derived in whole or in part using personally identifiable financial information that is not publicly available information, such as account numbers.

(ii) Nonpublic personal information does not include any list of individuals' names and addresses that contains only publicly available information, is not derived in whole or in part using personally identifiable financial information that is not publicly available information, and is not disclosed in a manner that indicates that any of the individuals on the list is a consumer of a financial institution.

(u)(1) *Personally identifiable financial information* means any information:

(i) A consumer provides to you to obtain a financial product or service from you;

(ii) About a consumer resulting from any transaction involving a financial product or service between you and a consumer; or

(iii) You otherwise obtain about a consumer in connection with providing a financial product or service to that consumer.

(2) *Examples*—(i) *Information included.* Personally identifiable financial information includes:

(A) Information a consumer provides to you on an application to obtain a loan, credit card, or other financial product or service;

(B) Account balance information, payment history, overdraft history, and credit or debit card purchase information;

(C) The fact that an individual is or has been one of your customers or has obtained a financial product or service from you;

(D) Any information about your consumer if it is disclosed in a manner that indicates that the individual is or has been your consumer;

(E) Any information that a consumer provides to you or that you or your agent otherwise obtain in connection with collecting on a loan or servicing a loan;

(F) Any information you collect through an Internet "cookie" (an information collecting device from a web server); and

(G) Information from a consumer report.

(ii) *Information not included.* Personally identifiable financial information does not include:

(A) A list of names and addresses of customers of an entity that is not a financial institution; or

(B) Information that does not identify a consumer, such as aggregate information or blind data that does not contain personal identifiers such as account numbers, names, or addresses.

(v)(1) *Publicly available information* means any information that you reasonably believe is lawfully made available to the general public from:

(i) Federal, State, or local government records;

(ii) Widely distributed media; or

(iii) Disclosures to the general public that are required to be made by federal, State, or local law.

(2) *Examples*—(i) *Reasonable belief.* (A) You have a reasonable belief that information about your consumer is made available to the general public if you have confirmed, or your consumer has represented to you, that the information is publicly available from a source described in paragraphs (v)(1)(i)–(iii) of this section;

(B) You have a reasonable belief that information about your consumer is made available to the general public if you have taken steps to submit the information, in accordance with your internal procedures and policies and with applicable law, to a keeper of federal, State, or local government records that is required by law to make the information publicly available.

Securities and Exchange Commission § 248.4

(C) You have a reasonable belief that an individual's telephone number is lawfully made available to the general public if you have located the telephone number in the telephone book or the consumer has informed you that the telephone number is not unlisted.

(D) You do not have a reasonable belief that information about a consumer is publicly available solely because that information would normally be recorded with a keeper of federal, State, or local government records that is required by law to make the information publicly available, if the consumer has the ability in accordance with applicable law to keep that information nonpublic, such as where a consumer may record a deed in the name of a blind trust.

(ii) *Government records.* Publicly available information in government records includes information in government real estate records and security interest filings.

(iii) *Widely distributed media.* Publicly available information from widely distributed media includes information from a telephone book, a television or radio program, a newspaper, or a web site that is available to the general public on an unrestricted basis. A web site is not restricted merely because an Internet service provider or a site operator requires a fee or a password, so long as access is available to the general public.

(w) *You* means:

(1) Any broker or dealer;

(2) Any investment company; and

(3) Any investment adviser registered with the Commission under the Investment Advisers Act of 1940.

[65 FR 40362, June 29, 2000, as amended at 66 FR 45147, Aug. 27, 2001; 74 FR 40431, Aug. 11, 2009]

PRIVACY AND OPT OUT NOTICES

§ 248.4 Initial privacy notice to consumers required.

(a) *Initial notice requirement.* You must provide a clear and conspicuous notice that accurately reflects your privacy policies and practices to:

(1) *Customer.* An individual who becomes your customer, not later than when you establish a customer relationship, except as provided in paragraph (e) of this section; and

(2) *Consumer.* A consumer, before you disclose any nonpublic personal information about the consumer to any nonaffiliated third party, if you make such a disclosure other than as authorized by §§ 248.14 and 248.15.

(b) *When initial notice to a consumer is not required.* You are not required to provide an initial notice to a consumer under paragraph (a) of this section if:

(1) You do not disclose any nonpublic personal information about the consumer to any nonaffiliated third party, other than as authorized by §§ 248.14 and 248.15; and

(2) You do not have a customer relationship with the consumer.

(c) *When you establish a customer relationship*—(1) *General rule.* You establish a customer relationship when you and the consumer enter into a continuing relationship.

(2) *Special rule for loans.* You do not have a customer relationship with a consumer if you buy a loan made to the consumer but do not have the servicing rights for that loan.

(3) *Examples of establishing customer relationship.* You establish a customer relationship when the consumer:

(i) Effects a securities transaction with you or opens a brokerage account with you under your procedures;

(ii) Opens a brokerage account with an introducing broker or dealer that clears transactions with and for its customers through you on a fully disclosed basis;

(iii) Enters into an advisory contract with you (whether in writing or orally); or

(iv) Purchases shares you have issued (and the consumer is the record owner of the shares), if you are an investment company.

(d) *Existing customers.* When an existing customer obtains a new financial product or service from you that is to be used primarily for personal, family, or household purposes, you satisfy the initial notice requirements of paragraph (a) of this section as follows:

(1) You may provide a revised privacy notice, under § 248.8, that covers the customer's new financial product or service; or

§ 248.5

(2) If the initial, revised, or annual notice that you most recently provided to that customer was accurate with respect to the new financial product or service, you do not need to provide a new privacy notice under paragraph (a) of this section.

(e) *Exceptions to allow subsequent delivery of notice.* (1) You may provide the initial notice required by paragraph (a)(1) of this section within a reasonable time after you establish a customer relationship if:

(i) Establishing the customer relationship is not at the customer's election;

(ii) Providing notice not later than when you establish a customer relationship would substantially delay the customer's transaction and the customer agrees to receive the notice at a later time; or

(iii) A nonaffiliated broker or dealer or investment adviser establishes a customer relationship between you and a consumer without your prior knowledge.

(2) *Examples of exceptions*—(i) *Not at customer's election.* Establishing a customer relationship is not at the customer's election if the customer's account is transferred to you by a trustee selected by the Securities Investor Protection Corporation ("SIPC") and appointed by a United States Court.

(ii) *Substantial delay of customer's transaction.* Providing notice not later than when you establish a customer relationship would substantially delay the customer's transaction when you and the individual agree over the telephone to enter into a customer relationship involving prompt delivery of the financial product or service.

(iii) *No substantial delay of customer's transaction.* Providing notice not later than when you establish a customer relationship would not substantially delay the customer's transaction when the relationship is initiated in person at your office or through other means by which the customer may view the notice, such as on a web site.

(f) *Delivery.* When you are required to deliver an initial privacy notice by this section, you must deliver it according to § 248.9. If you use a short-form initial notice for non-customers according to

17 CFR Ch. II (4–1–23 Edition)

§ 248.6(d), you may deliver your privacy notice according to § 248.6(d)(3).

§ 248.5 Annual privacy notice to customers required.

(a)(1) *General rule.* You must provide a clear and conspicuous notice to customers that accurately reflects your privacy policies and practices not less than annually during the continuation of the customer relationship. *Annually* means at least once in any period of 12 consecutive months during which that relationship exists. You may define the 12-consecutive-month period, but you must apply it to the customer on a consistent basis.

(2) *Example.* You provide a notice annually if you define the 12-consecutive-month period as a calendar year and provide the annual notice to the customer once in each calendar year following the calendar year in which you provided the initial notice. For example, if a customer opens an account on any day of year 1, you must provide an annual notice to that customer by December 31 of year 2.

(b)(1) *Termination of customer relationship.* You are not required to provide an annual notice to a former customer.

(2) *Examples.* Your customer becomes a former customer when:

(i) The individual's brokerage account is closed;

(ii) The individual's investment advisory contract is terminated;

(iii) You are an investment company and the individual is no longer the record owner of securities you have issued; or

(iv) You are an investment company and your customer has been determined to be a lost securityholder as defined in 17 CFR 240.17a–24(b).

(c) *Special rule for loans.* If you do not have a customer relationship with a consumer under the special provision for loans in § 248.4(c)(2), then you need not provide an annual notice to that consumer under this section.

(d) *Delivery.* When you are required to deliver an annual privacy notice by this section, you must deliver it according to § 248.9.

§ 248.6 Information to be included in privacy notices.

(a) *General rule.* The initial, annual, and revised privacy notices that you provide under §§ 248.4, 248.5, and 248.8 must include each of the following items of information that applies to you or to the consumers to whom you send your privacy notice, in addition to any other information you wish to provide:

(1) The categories of nonpublic personal information that you collect;

(2) The categories of nonpublic personal information that you disclose;

(3) The categories of affiliates and nonaffiliated third parties to whom you disclose nonpublic personal information, other than those parties to whom you disclose information under §§ 248.14 and 248.15;

(4) The categories of nonpublic personal information about your former customers that you disclose and the categories of affiliates and nonaffiliated third parties to whom you disclose nonpublic personal information about your former customers, other than those parties to whom you disclose information under §§ 248.14 and 248.15;

(5) If you disclose nonpublic personal information to a nonaffiliated third party under § 248.13 (and no other exception applies to that disclosure), a separate statement of the categories of information you disclose and the categories of third parties with whom you have contracted;

(6) An explanation of the consumer's right under § 248.10(a) to opt out of the disclosure of nonpublic personal information to nonaffiliated third parties, including the method(s) by which the consumer may exercise that right at that time;

(7) Any disclosures that you make under section 603(d)(2)(A)(iii) of the Fair Credit Reporting Act (15 U.S.C. 1681a(d)(2)(A)(iii)) (that is, notices regarding the ability to opt out of disclosures of information among affiliates);

(8) Your policies and practices with respect to protecting the confidentiality and security of nonpublic personal information; and

(9) Any disclosure that you make under paragraph (b) of this section.

(b) *Description of nonaffiliated third parties subject to exceptions.* If you disclose nonpublic personal information to third parties as authorized under §§ 248.14 and 248.15, you are not required to list those exceptions in the initial or annual privacy notices required by §§ 248.4 and 248.5. When describing the categories with respect to those parties, it is sufficient to state that you make disclosures to other nonaffiliated companies:

(1) For your everyday business purposes such as [*include all that apply*] to process transactions, maintain account(s), respond to court orders and legal investigations, or report to credit bureaus; or

(2) As permitted by law.

(c) *Examples*—(1) *Categories of nonpublic personal information that you collect.* You satisfy the requirement to categorize the nonpublic personal information that you collect if you list the following categories, as applicable:

(i) Information from the consumer;

(ii) Information about the consumer's transactions with you or your affiliates;

(iii) Information about the consumer's transactions with nonaffiliated third parties; and

(iv) Information from a consumer-reporting agency.

(2) *Categories of nonpublic personal information you disclose.* (i) You satisfy the requirement to categorize the nonpublic personal information that you disclose if you list the categories described in paragraph (e)(1) of this section, as applicable, and a few examples to illustrate the types of information in each category.

(ii) If you reserve the right to disclose all of the nonpublic personal information about consumers that you collect, you may simply state that fact without describing the categories or examples of the nonpublic personal information you disclose.

(3) *Categories of affiliates and nonaffiliated third parties to whom you disclose.* You satisfy the requirement to categorize the affiliates and nonaffiliated third parties to whom you

§ 248.6

disclose nonpublic personal information if you list the following categories, as applicable, and a few examples to illustrate the types of third parties in each category:

(i) Financial service providers;
(ii) Non-financial companies; and
(iii) Others.

(4) *Disclosures under exception for service providers and joint marketers.* If you disclose nonpublic personal information under the exception in § 248.13 to a nonaffiliated third party to market products or services that you offer alone or jointly with another financial institution, you satisfy the disclosure requirement of paragraph (a)(5) of this section if you:

(i) List the categories of nonpublic personal information you disclose, using the same categories and examples you used to meet the requirements of paragraph (a)(2) of this section, as applicable; and

(ii) State whether the third party is:

(A) A service provider that performs marketing services on your behalf or on behalf of you and another financial institution; or

(B) A financial institution with which you have a joint marketing agreement.

(5) *Simplified notices.* If you do not disclose, and do not wish to reserve the right to disclose, nonpublic personal information to affiliates or nonaffiliated third parties except as authorized under §§ 248.14 and 248.15, you may simply state that fact, in addition to the information you must provide under paragraphs (a)(1), (a)(8), (a)(9), and (b) of this section.

(6) *Confidentiality and security.* You describe your policies and practices with respect to protecting the confidentiality and security of nonpublic personal information if you do both of the following:

(i) Describe in general terms who is authorized to have access to the information; and

(ii) State whether you have security practices and procedures in place to ensure the confidentiality of the information in accordance with your policy. You are not required to describe technical information about the safeguards you use.

(d) *Short-form initial notice with opt out notice for non-customers.* (1) You may satisfy the initial notice requirements in §§ 248.4(a)(2), 248.7(b), and 248.7(c) for a consumer who is not a customer by providing a short-form initial notice at the same time as you deliver an opt out notice as required in § 248.7.

(2) A short-form initial notice must:

(i) Be clear and conspicuous;

(ii) State that your privacy notice is available upon request; and

(iii) Explain a reasonable means by which the consumer may obtain the privacy notice.

(3) You must deliver your short-form initial notice according to § 248.9. You are not required to deliver your privacy notice with your short-form initial notice. You instead may simply provide the consumer a reasonable means to obtain your privacy notice. If a consumer who receives your short-form notice requests your privacy notice, you must deliver your privacy notice according to § 248.9.

(4) *Examples of obtaining privacy notice.* You provide a reasonable means by which a consumer may obtain a copy of your privacy notice if you:

(i) Provide a toll-free telephone number that the consumer may call to request the notice; or

(ii) For a consumer who conducts business in person at your office, maintain copies of the notice on hand that you provide to the consumer immediately upon request.

(e) *Future disclosures.* Your notice may include:

(1) Categories of nonpublic personal information that you reserve the right to disclose in the future, but do not currently disclose; and

(2) Categories of affiliates or nonaffiliated third parties to whom you reserve the right in the future to disclose, but to whom you do not currently disclose, nonpublic personal information.

(f) *Model privacy form.* Pursuant to § 248.2(a) and appendix A to subpart A of this part, Form S-P meets the notice content requirements of this section.

[65 FR 40362, June 29, 2000, as amended at 74 FR 62985, Dec. 1, 2009]

Securities and Exchange Commission § 248.7

§ 248.7 Form of opt out notice to consumers; opt out methods.

(a)(1) *Form of opt out notice.* If you are required to provide an opt out notice under § 248.10(a), you must provide a clear and conspicuous notice to each of your consumers that accurately explains the right to opt out under that section. The notice must state:

(i) That you disclose or reserve the right to disclose nonpublic personal information about your consumer to a nonaffiliated third party;

(ii) That the consumer has the right to opt out of that disclosure; and

(iii) A reasonable means by which the consumer may exercise the opt out right.

(2) *Examples*—(i) *Adequate opt out notice.* You provide adequate notice that the consumer can opt out of the disclosure of nonpublic personal information to a nonaffiliated third party if you:

(A) Identify all of the categories of nonpublic personal information that you disclose or reserve the right to disclose, and all of the categories of nonaffiliated third parties to which you disclose the information, as described in § 248.6(a)(2) and (3) and state that the consumer can opt out of the disclosure of that information; and

(B) Identify the financial products or services that the consumer obtains from you, either singly or jointly, to which the opt out direction would apply.

(ii) *Reasonable opt out means.* You provide a reasonable means to exercise an opt out right if you:

(A) Designate check-off boxes in a prominent position on the relevant forms with the opt out notice;

(B) Include a reply form together with the opt out notice;

(C) Provide an electronic means to opt out, such as a form that can be sent via electronic mail or a process at your web site, if the consumer agrees to the electronic delivery of information; or

(D) Provide a toll-free telephone number that consumers may call to opt out.

(iii) *Unreasonable opt out means.* You do not provide a reasonable means of opting out if:

(A) The only means of opting out is for the consumer to write his or her own letter to exercise that opt out right; or

(B) The only means of opting out as described in any notice subsequent to the initial notice is to use a check-off box that you provided with the initial notice but did not include with the subsequent notice.

(iv) *Specific opt out means.* You may require each consumer to opt out through a specific means, as long as that means is reasonable for that consumer.

(b) *Same form as initial notice permitted.* You may provide the opt out notice together with or on the same written or electronic form as the initial notice you provide in accordance with § 248.4.

(c) *Initial notice required when opt out notice delivered subsequent to initial notice.* If you provide the opt out notice after the initial notice in accordance with § 248.4, you must also include a copy of the initial notice with the opt out notice in writing or, if the consumer agrees, electronically.

(d) *Joint relationships.* (1) If two or more consumers jointly obtain a financial product or service from you, you may provide a single opt out notice. Your opt out notice must explain how you will treat an opt out direction by a joint consumer.

(2) Any of the joint consumers may exercise the right to opt out. You may either:

(i) Treat an opt out direction by a joint consumer as applying to all of the associated joint consumers; or

(ii) Permit each joint consumer to opt out separately.

(3) If you permit each joint consumer to opt out separately, you must permit one of the joint consumers to opt out on behalf of all of the joint consumers.

(4) You may not require *all* joint consumers to opt out before you implement *any* opt out direction.

(5) *Example.* If John and Mary have a joint brokerage account with you and arrange for you to send statements to John's address, you may do any of the following, but you must explain in your opt out notice which opt out policy you will follow:

(i) Send a single opt out notice to John's address, but you must accept an

§ 248.8

opt out direction from either John or Mary;

(ii) Treat an opt out direction by either John or Mary as applying to the entire account. If you do so, and John opts out, you may not require Mary to opt out as well before implementing John's opt out direction; or

(iii) Permit John and Mary to make different opt out directions. If you do so,

(A) You must permit John and Mary to opt out for each other.

(B) If both opt out, you must permit both to notify you in a single response (such as on a form or through a telephone call).

(C) If John opts out and Mary does not, you may only disclose nonpublic personal information about Mary, but not about John and not about John and Mary jointly.

(e) *Time to comply with opt out.* You must comply with a consumer's opt out direction as soon as reasonably practicable after you receive it.

(f) *Continuing right to opt out.* A consumer may exercise the right to opt out at any time.

(g) *Duration of consumer's opt out direction.* (1) A consumer's direction to opt out under this section is effective until the consumer revokes it in writing or, if the consumer agrees, electronically.

(2) When a customer relationship terminates, the customer's opt out direction continues to apply to the nonpublic personal information that you collected during or related to that relationship. If the individual subsequently establishes a new customer relationship with you, the opt out direction that applied to the former relationship does not apply to the new relationship.

(h) *Delivery.* When you are required to deliver an opt out notice by this section, you must deliver it according to § 248.9.

(i) *Model privacy form.* Pursuant to § 248.2(a) and appendix A to subpart A of this part, Form S-P meets the notice content requirements of this section.

[65 FR 40362, June 29, 2000, as amended at 74 FR 62985, Dec. 1, 2009]

§ 248.8 Revised privacy notices.

(a) *General rule.* Except as otherwise authorized in this subpart, you must not, directly or through any affiliate, disclose any nonpublic personal information about a consumer to a nonaffiliated third party other than as described in the initial notice that you provided to that consumer under § 248.4, unless:

(1) You have provided to the consumer a clear and conspicuous revised notice that accurately describes your policies and practices;

(2) You have provided to the consumer a new opt out notice;

(3) You have given the consumer a reasonable opportunity, before you disclose the information to the nonaffiliated third party, to opt out of the disclosure; and

(4) The consumer does not opt out.

(b) *Examples.* (1) Except as otherwise permitted by §§ 248.13, 248.14, and 248.15, you must provide a revised notice before you:

(i) Disclose a new category of nonpublic personal information to any nonaffiliated third party;

(ii) Disclose nonpublic personal information to a new category of nonaffiliated third party; or

(iii) Disclose nonpublic personal information about a former customer to a nonaffiliated third party, if that former customer has not had the opportunity to exercise an opt out right regarding that disclosure.

(2) A revised notice is not required if you disclose nonpublic personal information to a new nonaffiliated third party that you adequately described in your prior notice.

(c) *Delivery.* When you are required to deliver a revised privacy notice by this section, you must deliver it according to § 248.9.

§ 248.9 Delivering privacy and opt out notices.

(a) *How to provide notices.* You must provide any privacy notices and opt out notices, including short-form initial notices that this subpart requires so that each consumer can reasonably be expected to receive actual notice in writing or, if the consumer agrees, electronically.

Securities and Exchange Commission

§ 248.10

(b)(1) *Examples of reasonable expectation of actual notice.* You may reasonably expect that a consumer will receive actual notice if you:

(i) Hand-deliver a printed copy of the notice to the consumer;

(ii) Mail a printed copy of the notice to the last known address of the consumer;

(iii) For the consumer who conducts transactions electronically, post the notice on the electronic site and require the consumer to acknowledge receipt of the notice as a necessary step to obtaining a particular financial product or service; or

(iv) For an isolated transaction with the consumer, such as an ATM transaction, post the notice on the ATM screen and require the consumer to acknowledge receipt of the notice as a necessary step to obtaining the particular financial product or service.

(2) *Examples of unreasonable expectation of actual notice.* You may not, however, reasonably expect that a consumer will receive actual notice of your privacy policies and practices if you:

(i) Only post a sign in your branch or office or generally publish advertisements of your privacy policies and practices; or

(ii) Send the notice via electronic mail to a consumer who does not obtain a financial product or service from you electronically.

(c) *Annual notices only.* (1) You may reasonably expect that a customer will receive actual notice of your annual privacy notice if:

(i) The customer uses your web site to access financial products and services electronically and agrees to receive notices at the web site and you post your current privacy notice continuously in a clear and conspicuous manner on the web site; or

(ii) The customer has requested that you refrain from sending any information regarding the customer relationship, and your current privacy notice remains available to the customer upon request.

(2) *Example of reasonable expectation of receipt of annual privacy notice.* You may reasonably expect that consumers who share an address will receive actual notice of your annual privacy notice if you deliver the notice with or in a stockholder or shareholder report under the conditions in 17 CFR 270.30d–1(f) or 17 CFR 270.30d–2(b), or with or in a prospectus under the conditions in 17 CFR 230.154.

(d) *Oral description of notice insufficient.* You may not provide any notice required by this subpart solely by orally explaining the notice, either in person or over the telephone.

(e) *Retention or accessibility of notices for customers.* (1) For customers only, you must provide the initial notice required by § 248.4(a)(1), the annual notice required by § 248.5(a), and the revised notice required by § 248.8, so that the customer can retain them or obtain them later in writing or, if the customer agrees, electronically.

(2) *Examples of retention or accessibility.* You provide a privacy notice to the customer so that the customer can retain it or obtain it later if you:

(i) Hand-deliver a printed copy of the notice to the customer;

(ii) Mail a printed copy of the notice to the last known address of the customer; or

(iii) Make your current privacy notice available on a web site (or a link to another web site) for the customer who obtains a financial product or service electronically and agrees to receive the notice at the web site.

(f) *Joint notice with other financial institutions.* You may provide a joint notice from you and one or more of your affiliates or other financial institutions, as identified in the notice, as long as the notice is accurate with respect to you and the other institutions.

(g) *Joint relationships.* If two or more consumers jointly obtain a financial product or service from you, you may satisfy the initial, annual, and revised notice requirements of paragraph (a) of this section by providing one notice to those consumers jointly.

LIMITS ON DISCLOSURES

§ 248.10 Limits on disclosure of nonpublic personal information to nonaffiliated third parties.

(a)(1) *Conditions for disclosure.* Except as otherwise authorized in this subpart, you may not, directly or through any affiliate, disclose any nonpublic

§ 248.11

personal information about a consumer to a nonaffiliated third party unless:

(i) You have provided to the consumer an initial notice as required under § 248.4;

(ii) You have provided to the consumer an opt out notice as required in § 248.7;

(iii) You have given the consumer a reasonable opportunity, before you disclose the information to the nonaffiliated third party, to opt out of the disclosure; and

(iv) The consumer does not opt out.

(2) *Opt out definition.* Opt out means a direction by the consumer that you not disclose nonpublic personal information about that consumer to a nonaffiliated third party, other than as permitted by §§ 248.13, 248.14, and 248.15.

(3) *Examples of reasonable opportunity to opt out.* You provide a consumer with a reasonable opportunity to opt out if:

(i) *By mail.* You mail the notices required in paragraph (a)(1) of this section to the consumer and allow the consumer to opt out by mailing a form, calling a toll-free telephone number, or any other reasonable means within 30 days after the date you mailed the notices.

(ii) *By electronic means.* A customer opens an on-line account with you and agrees to receive the notices required in paragraph (a)(1) of this section electronically, and you allow the customer to opt out by any reasonable means within 30 days after the date that the customer acknowledges receipt of the notices in conjunction with opening the account.

(iii) *Isolated transaction with consumer.* For an isolated transaction, such as the provision of brokerage services to a consumer as an accommodation, you provide the consumer with a reasonable opportunity to opt out if you provide the notices required in paragraph (a)(1) of this section at the time of the transaction and request that the consumer decide, as a necessary part of the transaction, whether to opt out before completing the transaction.

(b) *Application of opt out to all consumers and all nonpublic personal information.* (1) You must comply with this section, regardless of whether you and the consumer have established a customer relationship.

(2) Unless you comply with this section, you may not, directly or through any affiliate, disclose any nonpublic personal information about a consumer that you have collected, regardless of whether you collected it before or after receiving the direction to opt out from the consumer.

(c) *Partial opt out.* You may allow a consumer to select certain nonpublic personal information or certain nonaffiliated third parties with respect to which the consumer wishes to opt out.

§ 248.11 Limits on redisclosure and reuse of information.

(a)(1) *Information you receive under an exception.* If you receive nonpublic personal information from a nonaffiliated financial institution under an exception in § 248.14 or § 248.15, your disclosure and use of that information is limited as follows:

(i) You may disclose the information to the affiliates of the financial institution from which you received the information;

(ii) You may disclose the information to your affiliates, but your affiliates may, in turn, disclose and use the information only to the extent that you may disclose and use the information; and

(iii) You may disclose and use the information pursuant to an exception in § 248.14 or § 248.15 in the ordinary course of business to carry out the activity covered by the exception under which you received the information.

(2) *Example.* If you receive a customer list from a nonaffiliated financial institution in order to provide account-processing services under the exception in § 248.14(a), you may disclose that information under any exception in § 248.14 or § 248.15 in the ordinary course of business in order to provide those services. You could also disclose that information in response to a properly authorized subpoena or in the ordinary course of business to your attorneys, accountants, and auditors. You could not disclose that information to a third party for marketing purposes or use that information for your own marketing purposes.

Securities and Exchange Commission

§ 248.12

(b)(1) *Information you receive outside of an exception.* If you receive nonpublic personal information from a nonaffiliated financial institution other than under an exception in § 248.14 or § 248.15, you may disclose the information only:

(i) To the affiliates of the financial institution from which you received the information;

(ii) To your affiliates, but your affiliates may, in turn, disclose the information only to the extent that you can disclose the information; and

(iii) To any other person, if the disclosure would be lawful if made directly to that person by the financial institution from which you received the information.

(2) *Example.* If you obtain a customer list from a nonaffiliated financial institution outside of the exceptions in §§ 248.14 and 248.15:

(i) You may use that list for your own purposes;

(ii) You may disclose that list to another nonaffiliated third party only if the financial institution from which you purchased the list could have lawfully disclosed the list to that third party. That is, you may disclose the list in accordance with the privacy policy of the financial institution from which you received the list, as limited by the opt out direction of each consumer whose nonpublic personal information you intend to disclose, and you may disclose the list in accordance with an exception in § 248.14 or § 248.15, such as in the ordinary course of business to your attorneys, accountants, or auditors.

(c) *Information you disclose under an exception.* If you disclose nonpublic personal information to a nonaffiliated third party under an exception in § 248.14 or § 248.15, the third party may disclose and use that information only as follows:

(1) The third party may disclose the information to your affiliates;

(2) The third party may disclose the information to its affiliates, but its affiliates may, in turn, disclose and use the information only to the extent that the third party may disclose and use the information; and

(3) The third party may disclose and use the information pursuant to an exception in § 248.14 or § 248.15 in the ordinary course of business to carry out the activity covered by the exception under which it received the information.

(d) *Information you disclose outside of an exception.* If you disclose nonpublic personal information to a nonaffiliated third party other than under an exception in § 248.14 or § 248.15, the third party may disclose the information only:

(1) To your affiliates;

(2) To its affiliates, but its affiliates, in turn, may disclose the information only to the extent the third party can disclose the information; and

(3) To any other person, if the disclosure would be lawful if you made it directly to that person.

§ 248.12 Limits on sharing account number information for marketing purposes.

(a) *General prohibition on disclosure of account numbers.* You must not, directly or through an affiliate, disclose, other than to a consumer reporting agency, an account number or similar form of access number or access code for a consumer's credit card account, deposit account, or transaction account to any nonaffiliated third party for use in telemarketing, direct mail marketing, or other marketing through electronic mail to the consumer.

(b) *Exceptions.* Paragraph (a) of this section does not apply if you disclose an account number or similar form of access number or access code:

(1) To your agent or service provider solely in order to perform marketing for your own products or services, as long as the agent or service provider is not authorized to directly initiate charges to the account; or

(2) To a participant in a private label credit card program or an affinity or similar program where the participants in the program are identified to the customer when the customer enters into the program.

(c) *Example—Account number.* An account number, or similar form of access number or access code, does not include a number or code in an encrypted form, as long as you do not

§ 248.13

provide the recipient with a means to decode the number or code.

EXCEPTIONS

§ 248.13 Exception to opt out requirements for service providers and joint marketing.

(a) *General rule.* (1) The opt out requirements in §§ 248.7 and 248.10 do not apply when you provide nonpublic personal information to a nonaffiliated third party to perform services for you or functions on your behalf, if you:

(i) Provide the initial notice in accordance with § 248.4; and

(ii) Enter into a contractual agreement with the third party that prohibits the third party from disclosing or using the information other than to carry out the purposes for which you disclosed the information, including use under an exception in § 248.14 or § 248.15 in the ordinary course of business to carry out those purposes.

(2) *Example.* If you disclose nonpublic personal information under this section to a financial institution with which you perform joint marketing, your contractual agreement with that institution meets the requirements of paragraph (a)(1)(ii) of this section if it prohibits the institution from disclosing or using the nonpublic personal information except as necessary to carry out the joint marketing or under an exception in § 248.14 or § 248.15 in the ordinary course of business to carry out that joint marketing.

(b) *Service may include joint marketing.* The services a nonaffiliated third party performs for you under paragraph (a) of this section may include marketing of your own products or services or marketing of financial products or services offered pursuant to joint agreements between you and one or more financial institutions.

(c) *Definition of joint agreement.* For purposes of this section, *joint agreement* means a written contract pursuant to which you and one or more financial institutions jointly offer, endorse, or sponsor a financial product or service.

§ 248.14 Exceptions to notice and opt out requirements for processing and servicing transactions.

(a) *Exceptions for processing and servicing transactions at consumer's request.* The requirements for initial notice in § 248.4(a)(2), for the opt out in §§ 248.7 and 248.10, and for initial notice in § 248.13 in connection with service providers and joint marketing, do not apply if you disclose nonpublic personal information as necessary to effect, administer, or enforce a transaction that a consumer requests or authorizes, or in connection with:

(1) Processing or servicing a financial product or service that a consumer requests or authorizes;

(2) Maintaining or servicing the consumer's account with you, or with another entity as part of a private label credit card program or other extension of credit on behalf of such entity; or

(3) A proposed or actual securitization, secondary market sale (including sales of servicing rights), or similar transaction related to a transaction of the consumer.

(b) *Necessary to effect, administer, or enforce a transaction* means that the disclosure is:

(1) Required, or is one of the lawful or appropriate methods, to enforce your rights or the rights of other persons engaged in carrying out the financial transaction or providing the product or service; or

(2) Required, or is a usual, appropriate, or acceptable method:

(i) To carry out the transaction or the product or service business of which the transaction is a part, and record, service, or maintain the consumer's account in the ordinary course of providing the financial service or financial product;

(ii) To administer or service benefits or claims relating to the transaction or the product or service business of which it is a part;

(iii) To provide a confirmation, statement, or other record of the transaction, or information on the status or value of the financial service or financial product to the consumer or the consumer's agent or broker;

(iv) To accrue or recognize incentives or bonuses associated with the transaction that are provided by you or any other party;

(v) To underwrite insurance at the consumer's request or for reinsurance purposes, or for any of the following purposes as they relate to a consumer's

Securities and Exchange Commission § 248.15

insurance: Account administration, reporting, investigating, or preventing fraud or material misrepresentation, processing premium payments, processing insurance claims, administering insurance benefits (including utilization review activities), participating in research projects, or as otherwise required or specifically permitted by federal or State law; or

(vi) In connection with:

(A) The authorization, settlement, billing, processing, clearing, transferring, reconciling or collection of amounts charged, debited, or otherwise paid using a debit, credit, or other payment card, check, or account number, or by other payment means;

(B) The transfer of receivables, accounts, or interests therein; or

(C) The audit of debit, credit, or other payment information.

§ 248.15 Other exceptions to notice and opt out requirements.

(a) *Exceptions to notice and opt out requirements.* The requirements for initial notice in § 248.4(a)(2), for the opt out in §§ 248.7 and 248.10, and for initial notice in § 248.13 in connection with service providers and joint marketing do not apply when you disclose nonpublic personal information:

(1) With the consent or at the direction of the consumer, provided that the consumer has not revoked the consent or direction;

(2)(i) To protect the confidentiality or security of your records pertaining to the consumer, service, product, or transaction;

(ii) To protect against or prevent actual or potential fraud, unauthorized transactions, claims, or other liability;

(iii) For required institutional risk control or for resolving consumer disputes or inquiries;

(iv) To persons holding a legal or beneficial interest relating to the consumer; or

(v) To persons acting in a fiduciary or representative capacity on behalf of the consumer;

(3) To provide information to insurance rate advisory organizations, guaranty funds or agencies, agencies that are rating you, persons that are assessing your compliance with industry standards, and your attorneys, accountants, and auditors;

(4) To the extent specifically permitted or required under other provisions of law and in accordance with the Right to Financial Privacy Act of 1978 (12 U.S.C. 3401 *et seq.*), to law enforcement agencies (including a federal functional regulator, the Secretary of the Treasury, with respect to 31 U.S.C. Chapter 53, Subchapter II (Records and Reports on Monetary Instruments and Transactions) and 12 U.S.C. Chapter 21 (Financial Recordkeeping), a State insurance authority, with respect to any person domiciled in that insurance authority's State that is engaged in providing insurance, and the Federal Trade Commission), self-regulatory organizations, or for an investigation on a matter related to public safety;

(5)(i) To a consumer reporting agency in accordance with the Fair Credit Reporting Act (15 U.S.C. 1681 *et seq.*), or

(ii) From a consumer report reported by a consumer reporting agency;

(6) In connection with a proposed or actual sale, merger, transfer, or exchange of all or a portion of a business or operating unit if the disclosure of nonpublic personal information concerns solely consumers of such business or unit; or

(7)(i) To comply with federal, State, or local laws, rules and other applicable legal requirements;

(ii) To comply with a properly authorized civil, criminal, or regulatory investigation, or subpoena or summons by federal, State, or local authorities; or

(iii) To respond to judicial process or government regulatory authorities having jurisdiction over you for examination, compliance, or other purposes as authorized by law.

(b) *Examples of consent and revocation of consent.* (1) A consumer may specifically consent to your disclosure to a nonaffiliated mortgage lender of the value of the assets in the consumer's brokerage or investment advisory account so that the lender can evaluate the consumer's application for a mortgage loan.

(2) A consumer may revoke consent by subsequently exercising the right to

opt out of future disclosures of nonpublic personal information as permitted under § 248.7(f).

RELATION TO OTHER LAWS; EFFECTIVE DATE

§ 248.16 Protection of Fair Credit Reporting Act.

Nothing in this subpart shall be construed to modify, limit, or supersede the operation of the Fair Credit Reporting Act (15 U.S.C. 1681 *et seq.*), and no inference shall be drawn on the basis of the provisions of this subpart regarding whether information is transaction or experience information under section 603 of that Act.

§ 248.17 Relation to State laws.

(a) *In general.* This subpart shall not be construed as superseding, altering, or affecting any statute, regulation, order, or interpretation in effect in any State, except to the extent that such State statute, regulation, order, or interpretation is inconsistent with the provisions of this subpart, and then only to the extent of the inconsistency.

(b) *Greater protection under State law.* For purposes of this section, a State statute, regulation, order, or interpretation is not inconsistent with the provisions of this subpart if the protection such statute, regulation, order, or interpretation affords any consumer is greater than the protection provided under this subpart, as determined by the Federal Trade Commission, after consultation with the Commission, on the Federal Trade Commission's own motion, or upon the petition of any interested party.

§ 248.18 Effective date; transition rule.

(a) *Effective date.* This subpart is effective November 13, 2000. In order to provide sufficient time for you to establish policies and systems to comply with the requirements of this subpart, the compliance date for this subpart is July 1, 2001.

(b)(1) *Notice requirement for consumers who are your customers on the compliance date.* By July 1, 2001, you must have provided an initial notice, as required by § 248.4, to consumers who are your customers on July 1, 2001.

(2) *Example.* You provide an initial notice to consumers who are your customers on July 1, 2001, if, by that date, you have established a system for providing an initial notice to all new customers and have mailed the initial notice to all your existing customers.

(c) *Two-year grandfathering of service agreements.* Until July 1, 2002, a contract that you have entered into with a nonaffiliated third party to perform services for you or functions on your behalf satisfies the provisions of § 248.13(a)(2), even if the contract does not include a requirement that the third party maintain the confidentiality of nonpublic personal information, as long as you entered into the agreement on or before July 1, 2000.

§§ 248.19–248.29 [Reserved]

§ 248.30 Procedures to safeguard customer records and information; disposal of consumer report information.

(a) Every broker, dealer, and investment company, and every investment adviser registered with the Commission must adopt written policies and procedures that address administrative, technical, and physical safeguards for the protection of customer records and information. These written policies and procedures must be reasonably designed to:

(1) Insure the security and confidentiality of customer records and information;

(2) Protect against any anticipated threats or hazards to the security or integrity of customer records and information; and

(3) Protect against unauthorized access to or use of customer records or information that could result in substantial harm or inconvenience to any customer.

(b) *Disposal of consumer report information and records*—(1) *Definitions* (i) *Consumer report* has the same meaning as in section 603(d) of the Fair Credit Reporting Act (15 U.S.C. 1681a(d)).

(ii) *Consumer report information* means any record about an individual, whether in paper, electronic or other form, that is a consumer report or is derived from a consumer report. Consumer report information also means a compilation of such records. Consumer report

Securities and Exchange Commission

information does not include information that does not identify individuals, such as aggregate information or blind data.

(iii) *Disposal* means:

(A) The discarding or abandonment of consumer report information; or

(B) The sale, donation, or transfer of any medium, including computer equipment, on which consumer report information is stored.

(iv) *Notice-registered broker-dealers* means a broker or dealer registered by notice with the Commission under section 15(b)(11) of the Securities Exchange Act of 1934 (15 U.S.C. 78o(b)(11)).

(v) *Transfer agent* has the same meaning as in section 3(a)(25) of the Securities Exchange Act of 1934 (15 U.S.C. 78c(a)(25)).

(2) *Proper disposal requirements*—(i) *Standard.* Every broker and dealer other than notice-registered broker-dealers, every investment company, and every investment adviser and transfer agent registered with the Commission, that maintains or otherwise possesses consumer report information for a business purpose must properly dispose of the information by taking reasonable measures to protect against unauthorized access to or use of the information in connection with its disposal.

Pt. 248, Subpt. A, App. A

(ii) *Relation to other laws.* Nothing in this section shall be construed:

(A) To require any broker, dealer, or investment company, or any investment adviser or transfer agent registered with the Commission to maintain or destroy any record pertaining to an individual that is not imposed under other law; or

(B) To alter or affect any requirement imposed under any other provision of law to maintain or destroy any of those records.

[65 FR 40362, June 29, 2000, as amended at 69 FR 71329, Dec. 8, 2004]

§§ 248.31–248.100 [Reserved]

APPENDIX A TO SUBPART A OF PART 248—FORMS

A. Any person may view and print this form at: *http://www.sec.gov/about/forms/secforms.htm.*

B. Use of Form S–P by brokers, dealers, and investment companies, and investment advisers registered with the Commission constitutes compliance with the notice content requirements of §§ 248.6 and 248.7 of this part.

FORM S–P—MODEL PRIVACY FORM

A. The Model Privacy Form

Pt. 248, Subpt. A, App. A

Version 1: Model Form With No Opt-Out.

Rev. [insert date]

FACTS	WHAT DOES [NAME OF FINANCIAL INSTITUTION] DO WITH YOUR PERSONAL INFORMATION?
Why?	Financial companies choose how they share your personal information. Federal law gives consumers the right to limit some but not all sharing. Federal law also requires us to tell you how we collect, share, and protect your personal information. Please read this notice carefully to understand what we do.
What?	The types of personal information we collect and share depend on the product or service you have with us. This information can include: ■ Social Security number and [income] ■ [account balances] and [payment history] ■ [credit history] and [credit scores] When you are *no longer* our customer, we continue to share your information as described in this notice.
How?	All financial companies need to share customers' personal information to run their everyday business. In the section below, we list the reasons financial companies can share their customers' personal information; the reasons [name of financial institution] chooses to share; and whether you can limit this sharing.

Reasons we can share your personal information	Does [name of financial institution] share?	Can you limit this sharing?
For our everyday business purposes— such as to process your transactions, maintain your account(s), respond to court orders and legal investigations, or report to credit bureaus		
For our marketing purposes— to offer our products and services to you		
For joint marketing with other financial companies		
For our affiliates' everyday business purposes— information about your transactions and experiences		
For our affiliates' everyday business purposes— information about your creditworthiness		
For our affiliates to market to you		
For nonaffiliates to market to you		

Questions?	Call [phone number] or go to [website]

Securities and Exchange Commission   **Pt. 248, Subpt. A, App. A**

Page 2

Who we are

Who is providing this notice?	[insert]

What we do

How does [name of financial institution] protect my personal information?	To protect your personal information from unauthorized access and use, we use security measures that comply with federal law. These measures include computer safeguards and secured files and buildings. [insert]
How does [name of financial institution] collect my personal information?	We collect your personal information, for example, when you ■ [open an account] or [deposit money] ■ [pay your bills] or [apply for a loan] ■ [use your credit or debit card] [We also collect your personal information from other companies.] OR [We also collect your personal information from others, such as credit bureaus, affiliates, or other companies.]
Why can't I limit all sharing?	Federal law gives you the right to limit only ■ sharing for affiliates' everyday business purposes—information about your creditworthiness ■ affiliates from using your information to market to you ■ sharing for nonaffiliates to market to you State laws and individual companies may give you additional rights to limit sharing. [See below for more on your rights under state law.]

Definitions

Affiliates	Companies related by common ownership or control. They can be financial and nonfinancial companies. ■ [affiliate information]
Nonaffiliates	Companies not related by common ownership or control. They can be financial and nonfinancial companies. ■ [nonaffiliate information]
Joint marketing	A formal agreement between nonaffiliated financial companies that together market financial products or services to you. ■ [joint marketing information]

Other important information

[insert other important information]

Pt. 248, Subpt. A, App. A   17 CFR Ch. II (4-1-23 Edition)

Version 2: Model Form with Opt-Out by Telephone and/or Online.

Rev. [Insert date]

FACTS	WHAT DOES [NAME OF FINANCIAL INSTITUTION] DO WITH YOUR PERSONAL INFORMATION?
Why?	Financial companies choose how they share your personal information. Federal law gives consumers the right to limit some but not all sharing. Federal law also requires us to tell you how we collect, share, and protect your personal information. Please read this notice carefully to understand what we do.
What?	The types of personal information we collect and share depend on the product or service you have with us. This information can include: ■ Social Security number and [income] ■ [account balances] and [payment history] ■ [credit history] and [credit scores]
How?	All financial companies need to share customers' personal information to run their everyday business. In the section below, we list the reasons financial companies can share their customers' personal information; the reasons [name of financial institution] chooses to share; and whether you can limit this sharing.

Reasons we can share your personal information	Does [name of financial institution] share?	Can you limit this sharing?
For our everyday business purposes— such as to process your transactions, maintain your account(s), respond to court orders and legal investigations, or report to credit bureaus		
For our marketing purposes— to offer our products and services to you		
For joint marketing with other financial companies		
For our affiliates' everyday business purposes— information about your transactions and experiences		
For our affiliates' everyday business purposes— information about your creditworthiness		
For our affiliates to market to you		
For nonaffiliates to market to you		

To limit our sharing	■ Call [phone number]—our menu will prompt you through your choice(s) or ■ Visit us online: [website] Please note: If you are a *new* customer, we can begin sharing your information [30] days from the date we sent this notice. When you are *no longer* our customer, we continue to share your information as described in this notice. However, you can contact us at any time to limit our sharing.
Questions?	Call [phone number] or go to [website]

198

Securities and Exchange Commission Pt. 248, Subpt. A, App. A

Page 2

Who we are	
Who is providing this notice?	[insert]

What we do	
How does [name of financial institution] protect my personal information?	To protect your personal information from unauthorized access and use, we use security measures that comply with federal law. These measures include computer safeguards and secured files and buildings. [insert]
How does [name of financial institution] collect my personal information?	We collect your personal information, for example, when you ■ [open an account] or [deposit money] ■ [pay your bills] or [apply for a loan] ■ [use your credit or debit card] [We also collect your personal information from other companies.] OR [We also collect your personal information from others, such as credit bureaus, affiliates, or other companies.]
Why can't I limit all sharing?	Federal law gives you the right to limit only ■ sharing for affiliates' everyday business purposes—information about your creditworthiness ■ affiliates from using your information to market to you ■ sharing for nonaffiliates to market to you State laws and individual companies may give you additional rights to limit sharing. [See below for more on your rights under state law.]
What happens when I limit sharing for an account I hold jointly with someone else?	[Your choices will apply to everyone on your account.] OR [Your choices will apply to everyone on your account—unless you tell us otherwise.]

Definitions	
Affiliates	Companies related by common ownership or control. They can be financial and nonfinancial companies. ■ [affiliate information]
Nonaffiliates	Companies not related by common ownership or control. They can be financial and nonfinancial companies. ■ [nonaffiliate information]
Joint marketing	A formal agreement between nonaffiliated financial companies that together market financial products or services to you. ■ [joint marketing information]

Other important information	
[insert other important information]	

Pt. 248, Subpt. A, App. A   17 CFR Ch. II (4–1–23 Edition)

Version 3: Model Form with Mail-In Opt-Out Form.

Rev. [insert date]

FACTS	WHAT DOES [NAME OF FINANCIAL INSTITUTION] DO WITH YOUR PERSONAL INFORMATION?
Why?	Financial companies choose how they share your personal information. Federal law gives consumers the right to limit some but not all sharing. Federal law also requires us to tell you how we collect, share, and protect your personal information. Please read this notice carefully to understand what we do.
What?	The types of personal information we collect and share depend on the product or service you have with us. This information can include: ■ Social Security number and [income] ■ [account balances] and [payment history] ■ [credit history] and [credit scores]
How?	All financial companies need to share customers' personal information to run their everyday business. In the section below, we list the reasons financial companies can share their customers' personal information; the reasons [name of financial institution] chooses to share; and whether you can limit this sharing.

Reasons we can share your personal information	Does [name of financial institution] share?	Can you limit this sharing?
For our everyday business purposes— such as to process your transactions, maintain your account(s), respond to court orders and legal investigations, or report to credit bureaus		
For our marketing purposes— to offer our products and services to you		
For joint marketing with other financial companies		
For our affiliates' everyday business purposes— information about your transactions and experiences		
For our affiliates' everyday business purposes— information about your creditworthiness		
For our affiliates to market to you		
For nonaffiliates to market to you		

To limit our sharing	■ Call [phone number]—our menu will prompt you through your choice(s) ■ Visit us online: [website] or ■ Mail the form below **Please note:** If you are a *new* customer, we can begin sharing your information [30] days from the date we sent this notice. When you are *no longer* our customer, we continue to share your information as described in this notice. However, you can contact us at any time to limit our sharing.
Questions?	Call [phone number] or go to [website]

✂--

Mail-in Form		
Leave Blank OR [If you have a joint account, your choice(s) will apply to everyone on your account unless you mark below. ❏ Apply my choices only to me]	Mark any/all you want to limit: ❏ Do not share information about my creditworthiness with your affiliates for their everyday business purposes. ❏ Do not allow your affiliates to use my personal information to market to me. ❏ Do not share my personal information with nonaffiliates to market their products and services to me. Name Address City, State, Zip [Account #]	Mail to: [Name of Financial Institution] [Address1] [Address2] [City], [ST] [ZIP]

200

Securities and Exchange Commission Pt. 248, Subpt. A, App. A

Page 2

Who we are

Who is providing this notice?	[insert]

What we do

How does [name of financial institution] protect my personal information?	To protect your personal information from unauthorized access and use, we use security measures that comply with federal law. These measures include computer safeguards and secured files and buildings. [insert]
How does [name of financial institution] collect my personal information?	We collect your personal information, for example, when you - [open an account] or [deposit money] - [pay your bills] or [apply for a loan] - [use your credit or debit card] [We also collect your personal information from other companies.] OR [We also collect your personal information from others, such as credit bureaus, affiliates, or other companies.]
Why can't I limit all sharing?	Federal law gives you the right to limit only - sharing for affiliates' everyday business purposes—information about your creditworthiness - affiliates from using your information to market to you - sharing for nonaffiliates to market to you State laws and individual companies may give you additional rights to limit sharing. [See below for more on your rights under state law.]
What happens when I limit sharing for an account I hold jointly with someone else?	[Your choices will apply to everyone on your account.] OR [Your choices will apply to everyone on your account—unless you tell us otherwise.]

Definitions

Affiliates	Companies related by common ownership or control. They can be financial and nonfinancial companies. - [affiliate information]
Nonaffiliates	Companies not related by common ownership or control. They can be financial and nonfinancial companies. - [nonaffiliate information]
Joint marketing	A formal agreement between nonaffiliated financial companies that together market financial products or services to you. - [joint marketing information]

Other important information

[insert other important information]

Pt. 248, Subpt. A, App. A   17 CFR Ch. II (4–1–23 Edition)

Version 4. Optional Mail-in Form.

Mail-in Form

Leave Blank OR [If you have a joint account, your choice(s) will apply to everyone on your account unless you mark below. ☐ Apply my choices only to me]	Mark any/all you want to limit: ☐ Do not share information about my creditworthiness with your affiliates for their everyday business purposes. ☐ Do not allow your affiliates to use my personal information to market to me. ☐ Do not share my personal information with nonaffiliates to market their products and services to me.
	Name
	Address
	City, State, Zip
	[Account #]

Mail To: [Name of Financial Institution], [Address1]
[Address2], [City], [ST] [ZIP]

B. General Instructions

1. How the Model Privacy Form is Used

(a) The model form may be used, at the option of a financial institution, including a group of financial institutions that use a common privacy notice, to meet the content requirements of the privacy notice and opt-out notice set forth in §§ 248.6 and 248.7 of this part.

(b) The model form is a standardized form, including page layout, content, format, style, pagination, and shading. Institutions seeking to obtain the safe harbor through use of the model form may modify it only as described in these instructions.

(c) Note that disclosure of certain information, such as assets, income, and information from a consumer reporting agency, may give rise to obligations under the Fair Credit Reporting Act [15 U.S.C. 1681–1681x] (FCRA), such as a requirement to permit a consumer to opt out of disclosures to affiliates or designation as a consumer reporting agency if disclosures are made to nonaffiliated third parties.

(d) The word "customer" may be replaced by the word "member" whenever it appears in the model form, as appropriate.

2. The Contents of the Model Privacy Form

The model form consists of two pages, which may be printed on both sides of a single sheet of paper, or may appear on two separate pages. Where an institution provides a long list of institutions at the end of the model form in accordance with Instruction C.3(a)(1), or provides additional information in accordance with Instruction C.3(c), and such list or additional information exceeds the space available on page two of the model form, such list or additional information may extend to a third page.

(a) *Page One.* The first page consists of the following components:

(1) Date last revised (upper right-hand corner).

(2) Title.

(3) Key frame (Why?, What?, How?).

(4) Disclosure table ("Reasons we can share your personal information").

(5) "To limit our sharing" box, as needed, for the financial institution's opt-out information.

(6) "Questions" box, for customer service contact information.

(7) Mail-in opt-out form, as needed.

(b) *Page Two.* The second page consists of the following components:

(1) Heading (Page 2).

(2) Frequently Asked Questions ("Who we are" and "What we do").

(3) Definitions.

(4) "Other important information" box, as needed.

3. The Format of the Model Privacy Form

The format of the model form may be modified only as described below.

(a) *Easily readable type font.* Financial institutions that use the model form must use an easily readable type font. While a number of factors together produce easily readable type font, institutions are required to use a minimum of 10-point font (unless otherwise expressly permitted in these Instructions) and sufficient spacing between the lines of type.

(b) *Logo.* A financial institution may include a corporate logo on any page of the notice, so long as it does not interfere with the

Securities and Exchange Commission

readability of the model form or the space constraints of each page.

(c) *Page size and orientation.* Each page of the model form must be printed on paper in portrait orientation, the size of which must be sufficient to meet the layout and minimum font size requirements, with sufficient white space on the top, bottom, and sides of the content.

(d) *Color.* The model form must be printed on white or light color paper (such as cream) with black or other contrasting ink color. Spot color may be used to achieve visual interest, so long as the color contrast is distinctive and the color does not detract from the readability of the model form. Logos may also be printed in color.

(e) *Languages.* The model form may be translated into languages other than English.

C. *Information Required in the Model Privacy Form*

The information in the model form may be modified only as described below:

1. Name of the Institution or Group of Affiliated Institutions Providing the Notice

Insert the name of the financial institution providing the notice or a common identity of affiliated institutions jointly providing the notice on the form wherever [name of financial institution] appears.

2. Page One

(a) *Last revised date.* The financial institution must insert in the upper right-hand corner the date on which the notice was last revised. The information shall appear in minimum 8-point font as "rev. [month/year]" using either the name or number of the month, such as "rev. July 2009" or "rev. 7/09".

(b) *General instructions for the "What?" box.* (1) The bulleted list identifies the types of personal information that the institution collects and shares. All institutions must use the term "Social Security number" in the first bullet.

(2) Institutions must use five (5) of the following terms to complete the bulleted list: income; account balances; payment history; transaction history; transaction or loss history; credit history; credit scores; assets; investment experience; credit-based insurance scores; insurance claim history; medical information; overdraft history; purchase history; account transactions; risk tolerance; medical-related debts; credit card or other debt; mortgage rates and payments; retirement assets; checking account information; employment information; wire transfer instructions.

(c) *General instructions for the disclosure table.* The left column lists reasons for sharing or using personal information. Each rea-

Pt. 248, Subpt. A, App. A

son correlates to a specific legal provision described in paragraph C.2(d) of this Instruction. In the middle column, each institution must provide a "Yes" or "No" response that accurately reflects its information sharing policies and practices with respect to the reason listed on the left. In the right column, each institution must provide in each box one of the following three (3) responses, as applicable, that reflects whether a consumer can limit such sharing: "Yes" if it is required to or voluntarily provides an opt-out; "No" if it does not provide an opt-out; or "We don't share" if it answers "No" in the middle column. Only the sixth row ("For our affiliates to market to you") may be omitted at the option of the institution. *See* paragraph C.2(d)(6) of this Instruction.

(d) *Specific disclosures and corresponding legal provisions.* (1) *For our everyday business purposes.* This reason incorporates sharing information under §§ 248.14 and 248.15 and with service providers pursuant to § 248.13 of this part other than the purposes specified in paragraphs C.2(d)(2) or C.2(d)(3) of these Instructions.

(2) *For our marketing purposes.* This reason incorporates sharing information with service providers by an institution for its own marketing pursuant to § 248.13 of this part. An institution that shares for this reason may choose to provide an opt-out.

(3) *For joint marketing with other financial companies.* This reason incorporates sharing information under joint marketing agreements between two or more financial institutions and with any service provider used in connection with such agreements pursuant to § 248.13 of this part. An institution that shares for this reason may choose to provide an opt-out.

(4) *For our affiliates' everyday business purposes—information about transactions and experiences.* This reason incorporates sharing information specified in sections 603(d)(2)(A)(i) and (ii) of the FCRA. An institution that shares for this reason may choose to provide an opt-out.

(5) *For our affiliates' everyday business purposes—information about creditworthiness.* This reason incorporates sharing information pursuant to section 603(d)(2)(A)(iii) of the FCRA. An institution that shares for this reason must provide an opt-out.

(6) *For our affiliates to market to you.* This reason incorporates sharing information specified in section 624 of the FCRA. This reason may be omitted from the disclosure table when: the institution does not have affiliates (or does not disclose personal information to its affiliates); the institution's affiliates do not use personal information in a manner that requires an opt-out; or the institution provides the affiliate marketing notice separately. Institutions that include

this reason must provide an opt-out of indefinite duration. An institution that is required to provide an affiliate marketing opt-out, but does not include that opt-out in the model form under this part, must comply with section 624 of the FCRA and 17 CFR part 248, subpart B, with respect to the initial notice and opt-out and any subsequent renewal notice and opt-out. An institution not required to provide an opt-out under this subparagraph may elect to include this reason in the model form.

(7) *For nonaffiliates to market to you.* This reason incorporates sharing described in §§ 248.7 and 248.10(a) of this part. An institution that shares personal information for this reason must provide an opt-out.

(e) *To limit our sharing:* A financial institution must include this section of the model form *only* if it provides an opt-out. The word "choice" may be written in either the singular or plural, as appropriate. Institutions must select one or more of the applicable opt-out methods described: telephone, such as by a toll-free number; a Web site; or use of a mail-in opt-out form. Institutions may include the words "toll-free" before telephone, as appropriate. An institution that allows consumers to opt online must provide either a specific Web address that takes consumers directly to the opt-out page or a general Web address that provides a clear and conspicuous direct link to the opt-out page. The opt-out choices made available to the consumer who contacts the institution through these methods must correspond accurately to the "Yes" responses in the third column of the disclosure table. In the part titled "Please note" institutions may insert a number that is 30 or greater in the space marked "[30]." Instructions on voluntary or state privacy law opt-out information are in paragraph C.2(g)(5) of these Instructions.

(f) *Questions box.* Customer service contact information must be inserted as appropriate, where [phone number] or [Web site] appear. Institutions may elect to provide either a phone number, such as a toll-free number, or a Web address, or both. Institutions may include the words "toll-free" before the telephone number, as appropriate.

(g) *Mail-in opt-out form.* Financial institutions must include this mail-in form *only* if they state in the "To limit our sharing" box that consumers can opt out by mail. The mail-in form must provide opt-out options that correspond accurately to the "Yes" responses in the third column in the disclosure table. Institutions that require customers to provide only name and address may omit the section identified as "[account #]." Institutions that require additional or different information, such as a random opt-out number or a truncated account number, to implement an opt-out election should modify the "[account #]" reference accordingly. This includes institutions that require customers with multiple accounts to identify each account to which the opt-out should apply. An institution must enter its opt-out mailing address: in the far right of this form (*see* version 3); or below the form (*see* version 4). The reverse side of the mail-in opt-out form must not include any content of the model form.

(1) *Joint accountholder.* Only institutions that provide their joint accountholders the choice to opt out for only one accountholder, in accordance with paragraph C.3(a)(5) of these Instructions, must include in the far left column of the mail-in form the following statement: "If you have a joint account, your choice(s) will apply to everyone on your account unless you mark below. ☐ Apply my choice(s) only to me." The word "choice" may be written in either the singular or plural, as appropriate. Financial institutions that provide insurance products or services, provide this option, and elect to use the model form may substitute the word "policy" for "account" in this statement. Institutions that do not provide this option may eliminate this left column from the mail-in form.

(2) *FCRA Section 603(d)(2)(A)(iii) opt-out.* If the institution shares personal information pursuant to section 603(d)(2)(A)(iii) of the FCRA, it must include in the mail-in opt-out form the following statement: "☐ Do not share information about my creditworthiness with your affiliates for their everyday business purposes."

(3) *FCRA Section 624 opt-out.* If the institution incorporates section 624 of the FCRA in accord with paragraph C.2(d)(6) of these Instructions, it must include in the mail-in opt-out form the following statement: "☐ Do not allow your affiliates to use my personal information to market to me."

(4) *Nonaffiliate opt-out.* If the financial institution shares personal information pursuant to § 248.10(a) of this part, it must include in the mail-in opt-out form the following statement: "☐ Do not share my personal information with nonaffiliates to market their products and services to me."

(5) *Additional opt-outs.* Financial institutions that use the disclosure table to provide opt-out options beyond those required by Federal law must provide those opt-outs in this section of the model form. A financial institution that chooses to offer an opt-out for its own marketing in the mail-in opt-out form must include one of the two following statements: "☐ Do not share my personal information to market to me." *or* "☐ Do not use my personal information to market to me." A financial institution that chooses to offer an opt-out for joint marketing must include the following statement: "☐ Do not share my personal information with other financial institutions to jointly market to me."

Securities and Exchange Commission

Pt. 248, Subpt. A, App. A

(h) *Barcodes.* A financial institution may elect to include a barcode and/or "tagline" (an internal identifier) in 6-point font at the bottom of page one, as needed for information internal to the institution, so long as these do not interfere with the clarity or text of the form.

3. Page Two

(a) *General Instructions for the Questions.* Certain of the Questions may be customized as follows:

(1) *"Who is providing this notice?"* This question may be omitted where only one financial institution provides the model form and that institution is clearly identified in the title on page one. Two or more financial institutions that jointly provide the model form must use this question to identify themselves as required by § 248.9(f) of this part. Where the list of institutions exceeds four (4) lines, the institution must describe in the response to this question the general types of institutions jointly providing the notice and must separately identify those institutions, in minimum 8-point font, directly following the "Other important information" box, or, if that box is not included in the institution's form, directly following the "Definitions." The list may appear in a multi-column format.

(2) *"How does [name of financial institution] protect my personal information?"* The financial institution may only provide additional information pertaining to its safeguards practices following the designated response to this question. Such information may include information about the institution's use of cookies or other measures it uses to safeguard personal information. Institutions are limited to a maximum of 30 additional words.

(3) *"How does [name of financial institution] collect my personal information?"* Institutions must use five (5) of the following terms to complete the bulleted list for this question: open an account; deposit money; pay your bills; apply for a loan; use your credit or debit card; seek financial or tax advice; apply for insurance; pay insurance premiums; file an insurance claim; seek advice about your investments; buy securities from us; sell securities to us; direct us to buy securities; direct us to sell your securities; make deposits or withdrawals from your account; enter into an investment advisory contract; give us your income information; provide employment information; give us your employment history; tell us about your investment or retirement portfolio; tell us about your investment or retirement earnings; apply for financing; apply for a lease; provide account information; give us your contact information; pay us by check; give us your wage statements; provide your mortgage information; make a wire transfer; tell us who receives the money; tell us where to send the money; show your government-issued ID; show your driver's license; order a commodity futures or option trade. Institutions that collect personal information from their affiliates and/or credit bureaus must include after the bulleted list the following statement: "We also collect your personal information from others, such as credit bureaus, affiliates, or other companies." Institutions that do not collect personal information from their affiliates or credit bureaus but do collect information from other companies must include the following statement instead: "We also collect your personal information from other companies." Only institutions that do not collect any personal information from affiliates, credit bureaus, or other companies can omit both statements.

(4) *"Why can't I limit all sharing?"* Institutions that describe state privacy law provisions in the *"Other important information"* box must use the bracketed sentence: "See below for more on your rights under state law." Other institutions must omit this sentence.

(5) *"What happens when I limit sharing for an account I hold jointly with someone else?"* Only financial institutions that provide opt-out options must use this question. Other institutions must omit this question. Institutions must choose one of the following two statements to respond to this question: "Your choices will apply to everyone on your account." or "Your choices will apply to everyone on your account—unless you tell us otherwise." Financial institutions that provide insurance products or services and elect to use the model form may substitute the word "policy" for "account" in these statements.

(b) *General Instructions for the Definitions.* The financial institution must customize the space below the responses to the three definitions in this section. This specific information must be in italicized lettering to set off the information from the standardized definitions.

(1) *Affiliates.* As required by § 248.6(a)(3) of this part, where [*affiliate information*] appears, the financial institution must:

(i) If it has no affiliates, state: "[*name of financial institution*] has no affiliates;"

(ii) If it has affiliates but does not share personal information, state: "[*name of financial institution*] does not share with our affiliates;" or

(iii) If it shares with its affiliates, state, as applicable: "Our affiliates include companies with a [*common corporate identity of financial institution*] name; financial companies such as [*insert illustrative list of companies*]; non-financial companies, such as [*insert illustrative list of companies*] and others, such as [*insert illustrative list*]."

(2) *Nonaffiliates.* As required by § 248.6(c)(3) of this part, where [*nonaffiliate information*] appears, the financial institution must:

205

§ 248.101

(i) If it does not share with nonaffiliated third parties, state: "[*name of financial institution*] does not share with nonaffiliates so they can market to you;" or

(ii) If it shares with nonaffiliated third parties, state, as applicable: "Nonaffiliates we share with can include [*list categories of companies such as mortgage companies, insurance companies, direct marketing companies, and nonprofit organizations*]."

(3) *Joint Marketing.* As required by § 248.13 of this part, where [*joint marketing*] appears, the financial institution must:

(i) If it does not engage in joint marketing, state: "[*name of financial institution*] doesn't jointly market;" or

(ii) If it shares personal information for joint marketing, state, as applicable: "Our joint marketing partners include [*list categories of companies such as credit card companies*]."

(c) *General instructions for the "Other important information" box.* This box is optional. The space provided for information in this box is not limited. Only the following types of information can appear in this box.

(1) State and/or international privacy law information; and/or

(2) Acknowledgment of receipt form.

[74 FR 62985, Dec. 1, 2009]

Subpart B—Regulation S-AM: Limitations on Affiliate Marketing

Source: 74 FR 40431, Aug. 11, 2009, unless otherwise noted.

§ 248.101 Purpose and scope.

(a) *Purpose.* The purpose of this subpart is to implement section 624 of the Fair Credit Reporting Act, 15 U.S.C. 1681, *et seq.* ("FCRA"). Section 624, which was added to the FCRA by section 214 of the Fair and Accurate Credit Transactions Act of 2003, Public Law 108–159, 117 Stat. 1952 (2003) ("FACT Act" or "Act"), regulates the use of consumer information received from an affiliate to make marketing solicitations.

(b) *Scope.* This subpart applies to any broker or dealer other than a notice-registered broker or dealer, to any investment company, and to any investment adviser or transfer agent registered with the Commission. These entities are referred to in this subpart as "you."

§ 248.102 Examples.

The examples in this subpart are not exclusive. The examples in this subpart provide guidance concerning the rules' application in ordinary circumstances. The facts and circumstances of each individual situation, however, will determine whether compliance with an example, to the extent applicable, constitutes compliance with this subpart. Examples in a paragraph illustrate only the issue described in the paragraph and do not illustrate any other issue that may arise under this subpart. Similarly, the examples do not illustrate any issues that may arise under other laws or regulations.

§§ 248.103–248.119 [Reserved]

§ 248.120 Definitions.

As used in this subpart, unless the context requires otherwise:

(a) *Affiliate* of a broker, dealer, or investment company, or an investment adviser or transfer agent registered with the Commission means any person that is related by common ownership or common control with the broker, dealer, or investment company, or the investment adviser or transfer agent registered with the Commission. In addition, a broker, dealer, or investment company, or an investment adviser or transfer agent registered with the Commission will be deemed an affiliate of a company for purposes of this subpart if:

(1) That company is regulated under section 214 of the FACT Act, Public Law 108–159, 117 Stat. 1952 (2003), by a government regulator other than the Commission; and

(2) Rules adopted by the other government regulator under section 214 of the FACT Act treat the broker, dealer, or investment company, or investment adviser or transfer agent registered with the Commission as an affiliate of that company.

(b) *Broker* has the same meaning as in section 3(a)(4) of the Securities Exchange Act of 1934 (15 U.S.C. 78c(a)(4)). A "broker" does not include a broker registered by notice with the Commission under section 15(b)(11) of the Securities Exchange Act of 1934 (15 U.S.C. 78o(b)(11)).

(c) *Clear and conspicuous* means reasonably understandable and designed to call attention to the nature and significance of the information presented.

Securities and Exchange Commission § 248.120

(d) *Commission* means the Securities and Exchange Commission.

(e) *Company* means any corporation, limited liability company, business trust, general or limited partnership, association, or similar organization.

(f) *Concise*—(1) *In general.* The term "concise" means a reasonably brief expression or statement.

(2) *Combination with other required disclosures.* A notice required by this subpart may be concise even if it is combined with other disclosures required or authorized by Federal or State law.

(g) *Consumer* means an individual.

(h) *Control* of a company means the power to exercise a controlling influence over the management or policies of a company whether through ownership of securities, by contract, or otherwise. Any person who owns beneficially, either directly or through one or more controlled companies, more than 25 percent of the voting securities of any company is presumed to control the company. Any person who does not own more than 25 percent of the voting securities of any company will be presumed not to control the company. Any presumption regarding control may be rebutted by evidence, but, in the case of an investment company, will continue until the Commission makes a decision to the contrary according to the procedures described in section 2(a)(9) of the Investment Company Act of 1940 (15 U.S.C. 80a–2(a)(9)).

(i) *Dealer* has the same meaning as in section 3(a)(5) of the Securities Exchange Act of 1934 (15 U.S.C. 78c(a)(5)). A "dealer" does not include a dealer registered by notice with the Commission under section 15(b)(11) of the Securities Exchange Act of 1934 (15 U.S.C. 78o(b)(11)).

(j) *Eligibility information* means any information the communication of which would be a consumer report if the exclusions from the definition of "consumer report" in section 603(d)(2)(A) of the FCRA did not apply. Eligibility information does not include aggregate or blind data that does not contain personal identifiers such as account numbers, names, or addresses.

(k) *FCRA* means the Fair Credit Reporting Act (15 U.S.C. 1681, *et seq.*).

(l) *GLBA* means the Gramm-Leach-Bliley Act (15 U.S.C. 6801, *et seq.*).

(m) *Investment adviser* has the same meaning as in section 202(a)(11) of the Investment Advisers Act of 1940 (15 U.S.C. 80b–2(a)(11)).

(n) *Investment company* has the same meaning as in section 3 of the Investment Company Act of 1940 (15 U.S.C. 80a–3) and includes a separate series of the investment company.

(o) *Marketing solicitation*—(1) *In general.* The term "marketing solicitation" means the marketing of a product or service initiated by a person to a particular consumer that is:

(i) Based on eligibility information communicated to that person by its affiliate as described in this subpart; and

(ii) Intended to encourage the consumer to purchase or obtain such product or service.

(2) *Exclusion of marketing directed at the general public.* A marketing solicitation does not include marketing communications that are directed at the general public. For example, television, general circulation magazine, billboard advertisements and publicly available Web sites that are not directed to particular consumers would not constitute marketing solicitations, even if those communications are intended to encourage consumers to purchase products and services from the person initiating the communications.

(3) *Examples of marketing solicitations.* A marketing solicitation would include, for example, a telemarketing call, direct mail, e-mail, or other form of marketing communication directed to a particular consumer that is based on eligibility information received from an affiliate.

(p) *Person* means any individual, partnership, corporation, trust, estate, cooperative, association, government or governmental subdivision or agency, or other entity.

(q) *Pre-existing business relationship*—(1) *In general.* The term "pre-existing business relationship" means a relationship between a person, or a person's licensed agent, and a consumer based on:

(i) A financial contract between the person and the consumer which is in force on the date on which the consumer is sent a solicitation covered by this subpart;

§ 248.120

(ii) The purchase, rental, or lease by the consumer of the person's goods or services, or a financial transaction (including holding an active account or a policy in force or having another continuing relationship) between the consumer and the person, during the 18-month period immediately preceding the date on which the consumer is sent a solicitation covered by this subpart; or

(iii) An inquiry or application by the consumer regarding a product or service offered by that person during the three-month period immediately preceding the date on which the consumer is sent a solicitation covered by this subpart.

(2) *Examples of pre-existing business relationships.* (i) If a consumer has a brokerage account with a broker-dealer that is currently in force, the broker-dealer has a pre-existing business relationship with the consumer and can use eligibility information it receives from its affiliates to make solicitations to the consumer about its products or services.

(ii) If a consumer has an investment advisory contract with a registered investment adviser, the investment adviser has a pre-existing business relationship with the consumer and can use eligibility information it receives from its affiliates to make solicitations to the consumer about its products or services.

(iii) If a consumer was the record owner of securities issued by an investment company, but the consumer redeems these securities, the investment company has a pre-existing business relationship with the consumer and can use eligibility information it receives from its affiliates to make solicitations to the consumer about its products or services for 18 months after the date the consumer redeemed the investment company's securities.

(iv) If a consumer applies for a margin account offered by a broker-dealer, but does not obtain a product or service from or enter into a financial contract or transaction with the broker-dealer, the broker-dealer has a pre-existing business relationship with the consumer and can therefore use eligibility information it receives from its affiliates to make solicitations to the consumer about its products or services for three months after the date of the application.

(v) If a consumer makes a telephone inquiry to a broker-dealer about its products or services and provides contact information to the broker-dealer, but does not obtain a product or service from or enter into a financial contract or transaction with the institution, the broker-dealer has a pre-existing business relationship with the consumer and can therefore use eligibility information it receives from its affiliates to make solicitations to the consumer about its products or services for three months after the date of the inquiry.

(vi) If a consumer makes an inquiry by e-mail to a broker-dealer about one of its affiliated investment company's products or services but does not obtain a product or service from, or enter into a financial contract or transaction with the broker-dealer or the investment company, the broker-dealer and the investment company both have a pre-existing business relationship with the consumer and can therefore use eligibility information they receive from their affiliates to make solicitations to the consumer about their products or services for three months after the date of the inquiry.

(vii) If a consumer who has a pre-existing business relationship with an investment company that is part of a group of affiliated companies makes a telephone call to the centralized call center for the affiliated companies to inquire about products or services offered by a broker-dealer affiliated with the investment company, and provides contact information to the call center, the call constitutes an inquiry to the broker-dealer. In these circumstances, the broker-dealer has a pre-existing business relationship with the consumer and can therefore use eligibility information it receives from the investment company to make solicitations to the consumer about its products or services for three months after the date of the inquiry.

(3) *Examples where no pre-existing business relationship is created.* (i) If a consumer makes a telephone call to a centralized call center for a group of affiliated companies to inquire about the

consumer's existing account at a broker-dealer, the call does not constitute an inquiry to any affiliate other than the broker-dealer that holds the consumer's account and does not establish a pre-existing business relationship between the consumer and any affiliate of the account-holding broker-dealer.

(ii) If a consumer who has an advisory contract with a registered investment adviser makes a telephone call to an affiliate of the investment adviser to ask about the affiliate's retail locations and hours, but does not make an inquiry about the affiliate's products or services, the call does not constitute an inquiry and does not establish a pre-existing business relationship between the consumer and the affiliate. Also, the affiliate's capture of the consumer's telephone number does not constitute an inquiry and does not establish a pre-existing business relationship between the consumer and the affiliate.

(iii) If a consumer makes a telephone call to a broker-dealer in response to an advertisement offering a free promotional item to consumers who call a toll-free number, but the advertisement does not indicate that the broker-dealer's products or services will be marketed to consumers who call in response, the call does not create a pre-existing business relationship between the consumer and the broker-dealer because the consumer has not made an inquiry about a product or service offered by the institution, but has merely responded to an offer for a free promotional item.

(r) *Transfer agent* has the same meaning as in section 3(a)(25) of the Securities Exchange Act of 1934 (15 U.S.C. 78c(a)(25)).

(s) *You* means:

(1) Any broker or dealer other than a broker or dealer registered by notice with the Commission under section 15(b)(11) of the Securities Exchange Act of 1934 (15 U.S.C. 78o(b)(11));

(2) Any investment company;

(3) Any investment adviser registered with the Commission under the Investment Advisers Act of 1940 (15 U.S.C. 80b-1, *et seq.*); and

(4) Any transfer agent registered with the Commission under section 17A of the Securities Exchange Act of 1934 (15 U.S.C. 78q-1).

§ 248.121 **Affiliate marketing opt out and exceptions.**

(a) *Initial notice and opt out requirement*—(1) *In general.* You may not use eligibility information about a consumer that you receive from an affiliate to make a marketing solicitation to the consumer, unless:

(i) It is clearly and conspicuously disclosed to the consumer in writing or, if the consumer agrees, electronically, in a concise notice that you may use eligibility information about that consumer received from an affiliate to make marketing solicitations to the consumer;

(ii) The consumer is provided a reasonable opportunity and a reasonable and simple method to "opt out," or the consumer prohibits you from using eligibility information to make marketing solicitations to the consumer; and

(iii) The consumer has not opted out.

(2) *Example.* A consumer has a brokerage account with a broker-dealer. The broker-dealer furnishes eligibility information about the consumer to its affiliated investment adviser. Based on that eligibility information, the investment adviser wants to make a marketing solicitation to the consumer about its discretionary advisory accounts. The investment adviser does not have a pre-existing business relationship with the consumer and none of the other exceptions apply. The investment adviser is prohibited from using eligibility information received from its broker-dealer affiliate to make marketing solicitations to the consumer about its discretionary advisory accounts unless the consumer is given a notice and opportunity to opt out and the consumer does not opt out.

(3) *Affiliates who may provide the notice.* The notice required by this paragraph must be provided:

(i) By an affiliate that has or has previously had a pre-existing business relationship with the consumer; or

(ii) As part of a joint notice from two or more members of an affiliated group of companies, provided that at least one of the affiliates on the joint notice

§ 248.121

has or has previously had a pre-existing business relationship with the consumer.

(b) *Making marketing solicitations*—(1) *In general.* For purposes of this subpart, you make a marketing solicitation if:

(i) You receive eligibility information from an affiliate;

(ii) You use that eligibility information to do one or more of the following:

(A) Identify the consumer or type of consumer to receive a marketing solicitation;

(B) Establish criteria used to select the consumer to receive a marketing solicitation; or

(C) Decide which of your products or services to market to the consumer or tailor your marketing solicitation to that consumer; and

(iii) As a result of your use of the eligibility information, the consumer is provided a marketing solicitation.

(2) *Receiving eligibility information from an affiliate, including through a common database.* You may receive eligibility information from an affiliate in various ways, including when the affiliate places that information into a common database that you may access.

(3) *Receipt or use of eligibility information by your service provider.* Except as provided in paragraph (b)(5) of this section, you receive or use an affiliate's eligibility information if a service provider acting on your behalf (whether an affiliate or a nonaffiliated third party) receives or uses that information in the manner described in paragraph (b)(1)(i) or (b)(1)(ii) of this section. All relevant facts and circumstances will determine whether a person is acting as your service provider when it receives or uses an affiliate's eligibility information in connection with marketing your products and services.

(4) *Use by an affiliate of its own eligibility information.* Unless you have used eligibility information that you receive from an affiliate in the manner described in paragraph (b)(1)(ii) of this section, you do not make a marketing solicitation subject to this subpart if your affiliate:

(i) Uses its own eligibility information that it obtained in connection with a pre-existing business relationship it has or had with the consumer to market your products or services to the affiliate's consumer; or

(ii) Directs its service provider to use the affiliate's own eligibility information that it obtained in connection with a pre-existing business relationship it has or had with the consumer to market your products or services to the consumer, and you do not communicate directly with the service provider regarding that use.

(5) *Use of eligibility information by a service provider*—(i) *In general.* You do not make a marketing solicitation subject to this subpart if a service provider (including an affiliated or third-party service provider that maintains or accesses a common database that you may access) receives eligibility information from your affiliate that your affiliate obtained in connection with a pre-existing business relationship it has or had with the consumer and uses that eligibility information to market your products or services to that affiliate's consumer, so long as:

(A) Your affiliate controls access to and use of its eligibility information by the service provider (including the right to establish the specific terms and conditions under which the service provider may use such information to market your products or services);

(B) Your affiliate establishes specific terms and conditions under which the service provider may access and use your affiliate's eligibility information to market your products and services (or those of affiliates generally) to your affiliate's consumers, such as the identity of the affiliated companies whose products or services may be marketed to the affiliate's consumers by the service provider, the types of products or services of affiliated companies that may be marketed, and the number of times your affiliate's consumers may receive marketing materials, and periodically evaluates the service provider's compliance with those terms and conditions;

(C) Your affiliate requires the service provider to implement reasonable policies and procedures designed to ensure that the service provider uses your affiliate's eligibility information in accordance with the terms and conditions established by your affiliate relating to

Securities and Exchange Commission § 248.121

the marketing of your products or services;

(D) Your affiliate is identified on or with the marketing materials provided to the consumer; and

(E) You do not directly use your affiliate's eligibility information in the manner described in paragraph (b)(1)(ii) of this section.

(ii) *Writing requirements.* (A) The requirements of paragraphs (b)(5)(i)(A) and (C) of this section must be set forth in a written agreement between your affiliate and the service provider; and

(B) The specific terms and conditions established by your affiliate as provided in paragraph (b)(5)(i)(B) of this section must be set forth in writing.

(6) *Examples of making marketing solicitations.* (i) A consumer has an investment advisory contract with a registered investment adviser that is affiliated with a broker-dealer. The broker-dealer receives eligibility information about the consumer from the investment adviser. The broker-dealer uses that eligibility information to identify the consumer to receive a marketing solicitation about brokerage products and services, and, as a result, the broker-dealer provides a marketing solicitation to the consumer about its brokerage services. Pursuant to paragraph (b)(1) of this section, the broker-dealer has made a marketing solicitation to the consumer.

(ii) The same facts as in the example in paragraph (b)(6)(i) of this section, except that after using the eligibility information to identify the consumer to receive a marketing solicitation about brokerage products and services, the broker-dealer asks the registered investment adviser to send the marketing solicitation to the consumer and the investment adviser does so. Pursuant to paragraph (b)(1) of this section, the broker-dealer has made a marketing solicitation to the consumer because it used eligibility information about the consumer that it received from an affiliate to identify the consumer to receive a marketing solicitation about its products or services, and, as a result, a marketing solicitation was provided to the consumer about the broker-dealer's products and services.

(iii) The same facts as in the example in paragraph (b)(6)(i) of this section, except that eligibility information about consumers who have an investment advisory contract with a registered investment adviser is placed into a common database that all members of the affiliated group of companies may independently access and use. Without using the investment adviser's eligibility information, the broker-dealer develops selection criteria and provides those criteria, marketing materials, and related instructions to the investment adviser. The investment adviser reviews eligibility information about its own consumers using the selection criteria provided by the broker-dealer to determine which consumers should receive the broker-dealer's marketing materials and sends the broker-dealer's marketing materials to those consumers. Even though the broker-dealer has received eligibility information through the common database as provided in paragraph (b)(2) of this section, it did not use that information to identify consumers or establish selection criteria; instead, the investment adviser used its own eligibility information. Therefore, pursuant to paragraph (b)(4)(i) of this section, the broker-dealer has not made a marketing solicitation to the consumer.

(iv) The same facts as in the example in paragraph (b)(6)(iii) of this section, except that the registered investment adviser provides the broker-dealer's criteria to the investment adviser's service provider and directs the service provider to use the investment adviser's eligibility information to identify investment adviser consumers who meet the criteria and to send the broker-dealer's marketing materials to those consumers. The broker-dealer does not communicate directly with the service provider regarding the use of the investment adviser's information to market its products or services to the investment adviser's consumers. Pursuant to paragraph (b)(4)(ii) of this section, the broker-dealer has not made a marketing solicitation to the consumer.

(v) An affiliated group of companies includes an investment company, a principal underwriter for the investment company, a retail broker-dealer,

§ 248.121

and a transfer agent that also acts as a service provider. Each affiliate in the group places information about its consumers into a common database. The service provider has access to all information in the common database. The investment company controls access to and use of its eligibility information by the service provider. This control is set forth in a written agreement between the investment company and the service provider. The written agreement also requires the service provider to establish reasonable policies and procedures designed to ensure that the service provider uses the investment company's eligibility information in accordance with specific terms and conditions established by the investment company relating to the marketing of the products and services of all affiliates, including the principal underwriter and the retail broker-dealer. In a separate written communication, the investment company specifies the terms and conditions under which the service provider may use the investment company's eligibility information to market the retail broker-dealer's products and services to the investment company's consumers. The specific terms and conditions are: a list of affiliated companies (including the retail broker-dealer) whose products or services may be marketed to the investment company's consumers by the service provider; the specific products or services or types of products or services that may be marketed to the investment company's consumers by the service provider; the categories of eligibility information that may be used by the service provider in marketing products or services to the investment company's consumers; the types or categories of the investment company's consumers to whom the service provider may market products or services of investment company affiliates; the number and types of marketing communications that the service provider may send to the investment company's consumers; and the length of time during which the service provider may market the products or services of the investment company's affiliates to its consumers. The investment company periodically evaluates the service provider's compliance with these terms and conditions. The retail broker-dealer asks the service provider to market brokerage services to certain of the investment company's consumers. Without using the investment company's eligibility information, the retail broker-dealer develops selection criteria and provides those criteria, its marketing materials, and related instructions to the service provider. The service provider uses the investment company's eligibility information from the common database to identify the investment company's consumers to whom brokerage services will be marketed. When the retail broker-dealer's marketing materials are provided to the identified consumers, the name of the investment company is displayed on the retail broker-dealer's marketing materials, an introductory letter that accompanies the marketing materials, an account statement that accompanies the marketing materials, or the envelope containing the marketing materials. The requirements of paragraph (b)(5) of this section have been satisfied, and the retail broker-dealer has not made a marketing solicitation to the consumer.

(vi) The same facts as in the example in paragraph (b)(6)(v) of this section, except that the terms and conditions permit the service provider to use the investment company's eligibility information to market the products and services of other affiliates to the investment company's consumers whenever the service provider deems it appropriate to do so. The service provider uses the investment company's eligibility information in accordance with the discretion afforded to it by the terms and conditions. Because the terms and conditions are not specific, the requirements of paragraph (b)(5) of this section have not been satisfied.

(c) *Exceptions.* The provisions of this subpart do not apply to you if you use eligibility information that you receive from an affiliate:

(1) To make a marketing solicitation to a consumer with whom you have a pre-existing business relationship;

(2) To facilitate communications to an individual for whose benefit you provide employee benefit or other services pursuant to a contract with an employer related to and arising out of the

Securities and Exchange Commission § 248.121

current employment relationship or status of the individual as a participant or beneficiary of an employee benefit plan;

(3) To perform services on behalf of an affiliate, except that this paragraph shall not be construed as permitting you to send marketing solicitations on behalf of an affiliate if the affiliate would not be permitted to send the marketing solicitation as a result of the election of the consumer to opt out under this subpart;

(4) In response to a communication about your products or services initiated by the consumer;

(5) In response to an authorization or request by the consumer to receive solicitations; or

(6) If your compliance with this subpart would prevent you from complying with any provision of State insurance laws pertaining to unfair discrimination in any State in which you are lawfully doing business.

(d) *Examples of exceptions*—(1) *Example of the pre-existing business relationship exception.* A consumer has a brokerage account with a broker-dealer. The consumer also has a deposit account with the broker-dealer's affiliated depository institution. The broker-dealer receives eligibility information about the consumer from its depository institution affiliate and uses that information to make a marketing solicitation to the consumer about the broker-dealer's college savings accounts. The broker-dealer may make this marketing solicitation even if the consumer has not been given a notice and opportunity to opt out because the broker-dealer has a pre-existing business relationship with the consumer.

(2) *Examples of service provider exception.* (i) A consumer has a brokerage account with a broker-dealer. The broker-dealer furnishes eligibility information about the consumer to its affiliate, a registered investment adviser. Based on that eligibility information, the investment adviser wants to make a marketing solicitation to the consumer about its advisory services. The investment adviser does not have a pre-existing business relationship with the consumer and none of the other exceptions in paragraph (c) of this section apply. The consumer has been given an opt out notice and has elected to opt out of receiving such marketing solicitations. The investment adviser asks a service provider to send the marketing solicitation to the consumer on its behalf. The service provider may not send the marketing solicitation on behalf of the investment adviser because, as a result of the consumer's opt out election, the investment adviser is not permitted to make the marketing solicitation.

(ii) The same facts as in paragraph (d)(2)(i) of this section, except the consumer has been given an opt out notice, but has not elected to opt out. The investment adviser asks a service provider to send the solicitation to the consumer on its behalf. The service provider may send the marketing solicitation on behalf of the investment adviser because, as a result of the consumer's not opting out, the investment adviser is permitted to make the marketing solicitation.

(3) *Examples of consumer-initiated communications.* (i) A consumer who is the record owner of shares in an investment company initiates a communication with an affiliated registered investment adviser about advisory services. The affiliated investment adviser may use eligibility information about the consumer it obtains from the investment company or any other affiliate to make marketing solicitations regarding the affiliated investment adviser's services in response to the consumer-initiated communication.

(ii) A consumer who has a brokerage account with a broker-dealer contacts the broker-dealer to request information about how to save and invest for a child's college education without specifying the type of savings or investment vehicle in which the consumer may be interested. Information about a range of different products or services offered by the broker-dealer and one or more of its affiliates may be responsive to that communication. Such products, services, and investments may include the following: investments in affiliated investment companies; investments in section 529 plans offered by the broker-dealer; or trust services offered by a different financial institution in the affiliated group. Any affiliate offering

§ 248.121

products or services that would be responsive to the consumer's request for information about saving and investing for a child's college education may use eligibility information to make marketing solicitations to the consumer in response to this communication.

(iii) A registered investment adviser makes a marketing call to the consumer without using eligibility information received from an affiliate. The investment adviser leaves a voice-mail message that invites the consumer to call a toll-free number to receive information about services offered by the investment adviser. If the consumer calls the toll-free number to inquire about the investment advisory services, the call is a consumer-initiated communication about a product or service, and the investment adviser may now use eligibility information it receives from its affiliates to make marketing solicitations to the consumer.

(iv) A consumer calls a broker-dealer to ask about retail locations and hours, but does not request information about its products or services. The broker-dealer may not use eligibility information it receives from an affiliate to make marketing solicitations to the consumer because the consumer-initiated communication does not relate to the broker-dealer's products or services. Thus, the use of eligibility information received from an affiliate would not be responsive to the communication and the exception does not apply.

(v) A consumer calls a broker-dealer to ask about retail locations and hours. The customer service representative asks the consumer if there is a particular product or service about which the consumer is seeking information. The consumer responds that the consumer wants to stop in and find out about mutual funds (i.e., registered open-end investment companies). The customer service representative offers to provide that information by telephone and mail additional information to the consumer. The consumer agrees and provides or confirms contact information for receipt of the materials to be mailed. The broker-dealer may use eligibility information it receives from an affiliate to make marketing solicitations to the consumer about mutual funds because such marketing solicitations would respond to the consumer-initiated communication about mutual funds.

(4) *Examples of consumer authorization or request for marketing solicitations.* (i) A consumer who has a brokerage account with a broker-dealer authorizes or requests information about life insurance offered by the broker-dealer's insurance affiliate. The authorization or request, whether given to the broker-dealer or the insurance affiliate, would permit the insurance affiliate to use eligibility information about the consumer it obtains from the broker-dealer or any other affiliate to make marketing solicitations to the consumer about life insurance.

(ii) A consumer completes an online application to open an online brokerage account with a broker-dealer. The broker-dealer's online application contains a blank check box that the consumer may check to authorize or request information from the broker-dealer's affiliates. The consumer checks the box. The consumer has authorized or requested marketing solicitations from the broker-dealer's affiliates.

(iii) A consumer completes an online application to open an online brokerage account with a broker-dealer. The broker-dealer's online application contains a check box indicating that the consumer authorizes or requests information from the broker-dealer's affiliates. The consumer does not deselect the check box. The consumer has not authorized or requested marketing solicitations from the broker-dealer's affiliates.

(iv) The terms and conditions of a brokerage account agreement contain preprinted boilerplate language stating that by applying to open an account the consumer authorizes or requests to receive solicitations from the broker-dealer's affiliates. The consumer has not authorized or requested marketing solicitations from the broker-dealer's affiliates.

(e) *Relation to affiliate-sharing notice and opt out.* Nothing in this subpart limits the responsibility of a person to comply with the notice and opt out provisions of Section 603(d)(2)(A)(iii) of

Securities and Exchange Commission § 248.122

the FCRA (15 U.S.C. 1681a(d)(2)(A)(iii)) where applicable.

§ 248.122 Scope and duration of opt out.

(a) *Scope of opt out*—(1) *In general.* Except as otherwise provided in this section, the consumer's election to opt out prohibits any affiliate covered by the opt out notice from using eligibility information received from another affiliate as described in the notice to make marketing solicitations to the consumer.

(2) *Continuing relationship*—(i) *In general.* If the consumer establishes a continuing relationship with you or your affiliate, an opt out notice may apply to eligibility information obtained in connection with:

(A) A single continuing relationship or multiple continuing relationships that the consumer establishes with you or your affiliates, including continuing relationships established subsequent to delivery of the opt out notice, so long as the notice adequately describes the continuing relationships covered by the opt out; or

(B) Any other transaction between the consumer and you or your affiliates as described in the notice.

(ii) *Examples of continuing relationships.* A consumer has a continuing relationship with you or your affiliate if the consumer:

(A) Opens a brokerage account or enters into an advisory contract with you or your affiliate;

(B) Obtains a loan for which you or your affiliate owns the servicing rights;

(C) Purchases investment company shares in his or her own name;

(D) Holds an investment through you or your affiliate; such as when you act or your affiliate acts as a custodian for securities or for assets in an individual retirement arrangement;

(E) Enters into an agreement or understanding with you or your affiliate whereby you or your affiliate undertakes to arrange or broker a home mortgage loan for the consumer;

(F) Enters into a lease of personal property with you or your affiliate; or

(G) Obtains financial, investment, or economic advisory services from you or your affiliate for a fee.

(3) *No continuing relationship*—(i) *In general.* If there is no continuing relationship between a consumer and you or your affiliate, and you or your affiliate obtain eligibility information about a consumer in connection with a transaction with the consumer, such as an isolated transaction or an application that is denied, an opt out notice provided to the consumer only applies to eligibility information obtained in connection with that transaction.

(ii) *Examples of isolated transactions.* An isolated transaction occurs if:

(A) The consumer uses your or your affiliate's ATM to withdraw cash from an account at another financial institution; or

(B) A broker-dealer opens a brokerage account for the consumer solely for the purpose of liquidating or purchasing securities as an accommodation, i.e., on a one-time basis, without the expectation of engaging in other transactions.

(4) *Menu of alternatives.* A consumer may be given the opportunity to choose from a menu of alternatives when electing to prohibit solicitations, such as by electing to prohibit solicitations from certain types of affiliates covered by the opt out notice but not other types of affiliates covered by the notice, electing to prohibit marketing solicitations based on certain types of eligibility information but not other types of eligibility information, or electing to prohibit marketing solicitations by certain methods of delivery but not other methods of delivery. However, one of the alternatives must allow the consumer to prohibit all marketing solicitations from all of the affiliates that are covered by the notice.

(5) *Special rule for a notice following termination of all continuing relationships*—(i) *In general.* A consumer must be given a new opt out notice if, after all continuing relationships with you or your affiliate(s) are terminated, the consumer subsequently establishes another continuing relationship with you or your affiliate(s) and the consumer's eligibility information is to be used to make a marketing solicitation. The new opt out notice must apply, at a minimum, to eligibility information obtained in connection with the new continuing relationship. Consistent

§ 248.123

with paragraph (b) of this section, the consumer's decision not to opt out after receiving the new opt out notice would not override a prior opt out election by the consumer that applies to eligibility information obtained in connection with a terminated relationship, regardless of whether the new opt out notice applies to eligibility information obtained in connection with the terminated relationship.

(ii) *Example.* A consumer has an advisory contract with a company that is registered with the Commission as both a broker-dealer and an investment adviser, and that is part of an affiliated group. The consumer terminates the advisory contract. One year after terminating the advisory contract, the consumer opens a brokerage account with the same company. The consumer must be given a new notice and opportunity to opt out before the company's affiliates may make marketing solicitations to the consumer using eligibility information obtained by the company in connection with the new brokerage account relationship, regardless of whether the consumer opted out in connection with the advisory contract.

(b) *Duration of opt out.* The election of a consumer to opt out must be effective for a period of at least five years (the "opt out period") beginning when the consumer's opt out election is received and implemented, unless the consumer subsequently revokes the opt out in writing or, if the consumer agrees, electronically. An opt out period of more than five years may be established, including an opt out period that does not expire unless revoked by the consumer.

(c) *Time of opt out.* A consumer may opt out at any time.

§ 248.123 Contents of opt out notice; consolidated and equivalent notices.

(a) *Contents of opt out notice*—(1) *In general.* A notice must be clear, conspicuous, and concise, and must accurately disclose:

(i) *The name of the affiliate(s) providing the notice.* If the notice is provided jointly by multiple affiliates and each affiliate shares a common name, such as "ABC," then the notice may indicate that it is being provided by multiple companies with the ABC name or multiple companies in the ABC group or family of companies, for example, by stating that the notice is provided by "all of the ABC companies," "the ABC banking, credit card, insurance, and securities companies," or by listing the name of each affiliate providing the notice. But if the affiliates providing the joint notice do not all share a common name, then the notice must either separately identify each affiliate by name or identify each of the common names used by those affiliates, for example, by stating that the notice is provided by "all of the ABC and XYZ companies" or by "the ABC bank and securities companies and the XYZ insurance companies";

(ii) A list of the affiliates or types of affiliates whose use of eligibility information is covered by the notice, which may include companies that become affiliates after the notice is provided to the consumer. If each affiliate covered by the notice shares a common name, such as "ABC," then the notice may indicate that it applies to multiple companies with the ABC name or multiple companies in the ABC group or family of companies, for example, by stating that the notice is provided by "all of the ABC companies," "the ABC banking, credit card, insurance, and securities companies," or by listing the name of each affiliate providing the notice. But if the affiliates covered by the notice do not all share a common name, then the notice must either separately identify each covered affiliate by name or identify each of the common names used by those affiliates, for example, by stating that the notice applies to "all of the ABC and XYZ companies" or to "the ABC banking and securities companies and the XYZ insurance companies";

(iii) A general description of the types of eligibility information that may be used to make marketing solicitations to the consumer;

(iv) That the consumer may elect to limit the use of eligibility information to make marketing solicitations to the consumer;

(v) That the consumer's election will apply for the specified period of time stated in the notice and, if applicable,

Securities and Exchange Commission § 248.124

that the consumer will be allowed to renew the election once that period expires;

(vi) If the notice is provided to consumers who may have previously opted out, such as if a notice is provided to consumers annually, that the consumer who has chosen to limit marketing solicitations does not need to act again until the consumer receives a renewal notice; and

(vii) A reasonable and simple method for the consumer to opt out.

(2) *Joint relationships.* (i) If two or more consumers jointly obtain a product or service, a single opt out notice may be provided to the joint consumers. Any of the joint consumers may exercise the right to opt out.

(ii) The opt out notice must explain how an opt out direction by a joint consumer will be treated. An opt out direction by a joint consumer may be treated as applying to all of the associated joint consumers, or each joint consumer may be permitted to opt out separately. If each joint consumer is permitted to opt out separately, one of the joint consumers must be permitted to opt out on behalf of all of the joint consumers and the joint consumers must be permitted to exercise their separate rights to opt out in a single response.

(iii) It is impermissible to require all joint consumers to opt out before implementing any opt out direction.

(3) *Alternative contents.* If the consumer is afforded a broader right to opt out of receiving marketing than is required by this subpart, the requirements of this section may be satisfied by providing the consumer with a clear, conspicuous, and concise notice that accurately discloses the consumer's opt out rights.

(4) *Model notices.* Model notices are provided in the Appendix to this subpart.

(b) *Coordinated and consolidated notices.* A notice required by this subpart may be coordinated and consolidated with any other notice or disclosure required to be issued under any other provision of law by the entity providing the notice, including but not limited to the notice described in section 603(d)(2)(A)(iii) of the FCRA (15 U.S.C. 1681a(d)(2)(A)(iii)) and the GLBA privacy notice.

(c) *Equivalent notices.* A notice or other disclosure that is equivalent to the notice required by this subpart, and that is provided to a consumer together with disclosures required by any other provision of law, satisfies the requirements of this section.

§ 248.124 **Reasonable opportunity to opt out.**

(a) *In general.* You must not use eligibility information that you receive from an affiliate to make marketing solicitations to a consumer about your products or services unless the consumer is provided a reasonable opportunity to opt out, as required by § 248.121(a)(1)(ii).

(b) *Examples of a reasonable opportunity to opt out.* The consumer is given a reasonable opportunity to opt out if:

(1) *By mail.* The opt out notice is mailed to the consumer. The consumer is given 30 days from the date the notice is mailed to elect to opt out by any reasonable means.

(2) *By electronic means.* (i) The opt out notice is provided electronically to the consumer, such as by posting the notice at an Internet Web site at which the consumer has obtained a product or service. The consumer acknowledges receipt of the electronic notice. The consumer is given 30 days after the date the consumer acknowledges receipt to elect to opt out by any reasonable means.

(ii) The opt out notice is provided to the consumer by e-mail where the consumer has agreed to receive disclosures by e-mail from the person sending the notice. The consumer is given 30 days after the e-mail is sent to elect to opt out by any reasonable means.

(3) *At the time of an electronic transaction.* The opt out notice is provided to the consumer at the time of an electronic transaction, such as a transaction conducted on an Internet Web site. The consumer is required to decide, as a necessary part of proceeding with the transaction, whether to opt out before completing the transaction. There is a simple process that the consumer may use to opt out at that time using the same mechanism through which the transaction is conducted.

217

(4) *At the time of an in-person transaction.* The opt out notice is provided to the consumer in writing at the time of an in-person transaction. The consumer is required to decide, as a necessary part of proceeding with the transaction, whether to opt out before completing the transaction, and is not permitted to complete the transaction without making a choice. There is a simple process that the consumer may use during the course of the in-person transaction to opt out, such as completing a form that requires consumers to write a "yes" or "no" to indicate their opt out preference or that requires the consumer to check one of two blank check boxes—one that allows consumers to indicate that they want to opt out and one that allows consumers to indicate that they do not want to opt out.

(5) *By including in a privacy notice.* The opt out notice is included in a GLBA privacy notice. The consumer is allowed to exercise the opt out within a reasonable period of time and in the same manner as the opt out under that privacy notice.

§ 248.125 Reasonable and simple methods of opting out.

(a) *In general.* You must not use eligibility information about a consumer that you receive from an affiliate to make a marketing solicitation to the consumer about your products or services, unless the consumer is provided a reasonable and simple method to opt out, as required by § 248.121(a)(1)(ii).

(b) *Examples*—(1) *Reasonable and simple opt out methods.* Reasonable and simple methods for exercising the opt out right include:

(i) Designating a check-off box in a prominent position on the opt out form;

(ii) Including a reply form and a self-addressed envelope together with the opt out notice;

(iii) Providing an electronic means to opt out, such as a form that can be electronically mailed or processed at an Internet Web site, if the consumer agrees to the electronic delivery of information;

(iv) Providing a toll-free telephone number that consumers may call to opt out; or

(v) Allowing consumers to exercise all of their opt out rights described in a consolidated opt out notice that includes the GLBA privacy, FCRA affiliate sharing, and FCRA affiliate marketing opt outs, by a single method, such as by calling a single toll-free telephone number.

(2) *Opt out methods that are not reasonable and simple.* Reasonable and simple methods for exercising an opt out right *do not* include:

(i) Requiring the consumer to write his or her own letter;

(ii) Requiring the consumer to call or write to obtain a form for opting out, rather than including the form with the opt out notice; or

(iii) Requiring the consumer who receives the opt out notice in electronic form only, such as through posting at an Internet Web site, to opt out solely by paper mail or by visiting a different Web site without providing a link to that site.

(c) *Specific opt out means.* Each consumer may be required to opt out through a specific means, as long as that means is reasonable and simple for that consumer.

§ 248.126 Delivery of opt out notices.

(a) *In general.* The opt out notice must be provided so that each consumer can reasonably be expected to receive actual notice. For opt out notices provided electronically, the notice may be provided in compliance with either the electronic disclosure provisions in this subpart or the provisions in section 101 of the Electronic Signatures in Global and National Commerce Act, 15 U.S.C. 7001, *et seq.*

(b) *Examples of reasonable expectation of actual notice.* A consumer may reasonably be expected to receive actual notice if the affiliate providing the notice:

(1) Hand-delivers a printed copy of the notice to the consumer;

(2) Mails a printed copy of the notice to the last known mailing address of the consumer;

(3) Provides a notice by e-mail to a consumer who has agreed to receive electronic disclosures by e-mail from the affiliate providing the notice; or

Securities and Exchange Commission § 248.127

(4) Posts the notice on the Internet Web site at which the consumer obtained a product or service electronically and requires the consumer to acknowledge receipt of the notice.

(c) *Examples of no reasonable expectation of actual notice.* A consumer may not reasonably be expected to receive actual notice if the affiliate providing the notice:

(1) Only posts the notice on a sign in a branch or office or generally publishes the notice in a newspaper;

(2) Sends the notice by e-mail to a consumer who has not agreed to receive electronic disclosures by e-mail from the affiliate providing the notice; or

(3) Posts the notice on an Internet Web site without requiring the consumer to acknowledge receipt of the notice.

§ 248.127 Renewal of opt out elections.

(a) *Renewal notice and opt out requirement*—(1) *In general.* After the opt out period expires, you may not make marketing solicitations to a consumer who previously opted out, unless:

(i) The consumer has been given a renewal notice that complies with the requirements of this section and §§ 248.124 through 248.126, and a reasonable opportunity and a reasonable and simple method to renew the opt out, and the consumer does not renew the opt out; or

(ii) An exception in § 248.121(c) applies.

(2) *Renewal period.* Each opt out renewal must be effective for a period of at least five years as provided in § 248.122(b).

(3) *Affiliates who may provide the notice.* The notice required by this paragraph must be provided:

(i) By the affiliate that provided the previous opt out notice, or its successor; or

(ii) As part of a joint renewal notice from two or more members of an affiliated group of companies, or their successors, that jointly provided the previous opt out notice.

(b) *Contents of renewal notice.* The renewal notice must be clear, conspicuous, and concise, and must accurately disclose:

(1) The name of the affiliate(s) providing the notice. If the notice is provided jointly by multiple affiliates and each affiliate shares a common name, such as "ABC," then the notice may indicate it is being provided by multiple companies with the ABC name or multiple companies in the ABC group or family of companies, for example, by stating that the notice is provided by "all of the ABC companies," "the ABC banking, credit card, insurance, and securities companies," or by listing the name of each affiliate providing the notice. But if the affiliates providing the joint notice do not all share a common name, then the notice must either separately identify each affiliate by name or identify each of the common names used by those affiliates, for example, by stating that the notice is provided by "all of the ABC and XYZ companies" or by "the ABC banking and securities companies and the XYZ insurance companies";

(2) A list of the affiliates or types of affiliates whose use of eligibility information is covered by the notice, which may include companies that become affiliates after the notice is provided to the consumer. If each affiliate covered by the notice shares a common name, such as "ABC," then the notice may indicate that it applies to multiple companies with the ABC name or multiple companies in the ABC group or family of companies, for example, by stating that the notice is provided by "all of the ABC companies," "the ABC banking, credit card, insurance, and securities companies," or by listing the name of each affiliate providing the notice. But if the affiliates covered by the notice do not all share a common name, then the notice must either separately identify each covered affiliate by name or identify each of the common names used by those affiliates, for example, by stating that the notice applies to "all of the ABC and XYZ companies" or to "the ABC banking and securities companies and the XYZ insurance companies";

(3) A general description of the types of eligibility information that may be used to make marketing solicitations to the consumer;

§ 248.128

(4) That the consumer previously elected to limit the use of certain information to make marketing solicitations to the consumer;

(5) That the consumer's election has expired or is about to expire;

(6) That the consumer may elect to renew the consumer's previous election;

(7) If applicable, that the consumer's election to renew will apply for the specified period of time stated in the notice and that the consumer will be allowed to renew the election once that period expires; and

(8) A reasonable and simple method for the consumer to opt out.

(c) *Timing of the renewal notice*—(1) *In general.* A renewal notice may be provided to the consumer either:

(i) A reasonable period of time before the expiration of the opt out period; or

(ii) Any time after the expiration of the opt out period but before marketing solicitations that would have been prohibited by the expired opt out are made to the consumer.

(2) *Combination with annual privacy notice.* If you provide an annual privacy notice under the GLBA, providing a renewal notice with the last annual privacy notice provided to the consumer before expiration of the opt out period is a reasonable period of time before expiration of the opt out in all cases.

(d) *No effect on opt out period.* An opt out period may not be shortened by sending a renewal notice to the consumer before expiration of the opt out period, even if the consumer does not renew the opt out.

§ 248.128 Effective date, compliance date, and prospective application.

(a) *Effective date.* This subpart is effective September 10, 2009.

(b) *Mandatory compliance date.* Compliance with this subpart is required not later than January 1, 2010.

(c) *Prospective application.* The provisions of this subpart do not prohibit you from using eligibility information that you receive from an affiliate to make a marketing solicitation to a consumer if you receive such information prior to January 1, 2010. For purposes of this section, you are deemed to receive eligibility information when such information is placed into a common database and is accessible by you.

APPENDIX TO SUBPART B OF PART 248—MODEL FORMS

a. Although you and your affiliates are not required to use the model forms in this Appendix, use of a model form (if applicable to each person that uses it) complies with the requirement in section 624 of the FCRA for clear, conspicuous, and concise notices.

b. Although you may need to change the language or format of a model form to reflect your actual policies and procedures, any such changes may not be so extensive as to affect the substance, clarity, or meaningful sequence of the language in the model forms. Acceptable changes include, for example:

1. Rearranging the order of the references to "your income," "your account history," and "your credit score."

2. Substituting other types of information for "income," "account history," or "credit score" for accuracy, such as "payment history," "credit history," "payoff status," or "claims history."

3. Substituting a clearer and more accurate description of the affiliates providing or covered by the notice for phrases such as "the [ABC] group of companies."

4. Substituting other types of affiliates covered by the notice for "credit card," "insurance," or "securities" affiliates.

5. Omitting items that are not accurate or applicable. For example, if a person does not limit the duration of the opt out period, the notice may omit information about the renewal notice.

6. Adding a statement informing the consumer how much time they have to opt out before shared eligibility information may be used to make solicitations to them.

7. Adding a statement that the consumer may exercise the right to opt out at any time.

8. Adding the following statement, if accurate: "If you previously opted out, you do not need to do so again."

9. Providing a place on the form for the consumer to fill in identifying information, such as his or her name and address.

10. Adding disclosures regarding the treatment of opt-outs by joint consumers to comply with § 248.123(a)(2), if applicable.

Securities and Exchange Commission

A-1—Model Form for Initial Opt Out Notice (Single-Affiliate Notice)

A-2—Model Form for Initial Opt Out Notice (Joint Notice)

A-3—Model Form for Renewal Notice (Single-Affiliate Notice)

A-4—Model Form for Renewal Notice (Joint Notice)

A-5—Model Form for Voluntary "No Marketing" Notice

A-1—MODEL FORM FOR INITIAL OPT OUT NOTICE (SINGLE-AFFILIATE NOTICE)—[YOUR CHOICE TO LIMIT MARKETING]/[MARKETING OPT OUT]

• [Name of Affiliate] is providing this notice.

• [Optional: Federal law gives you the right to limit some but not all marketing from our affiliates. Federal law also requires us to give you this notice to tell you about your choice to limit marketing from our affiliates.]

• You may limit our affiliates in the [ABC] group of companies, such as our [investment adviser, broker, transfer agent, and investment company] affiliates, from marketing their products or services to you based on your personal information that we collect and share with them. This information includes your [income], your [account history with us], and your [credit score].

• Your choice to limit marketing offers from our affiliates will apply [until you tell us to change your choice]/[for x years from when you tell us your choice]/[for at least 5 years from when you tell us your choice]. [Include if the opt out period expires.] Once that period expires, you will receive a renewal notice that will allow you to continue to limit marketing offers from our affiliates for [another x years]/[at least another 5 years].

• [Include, if applicable, in a subsequent notice, including an annual notice, for consumers who may have previously opted out.] If you have already made a choice to limit marketing offers from our affiliates, you do not need to act again until you receive the renewal notice.

To limit marketing offers, contact us [include all that apply]:

• By telephone: 1-877-###-####
• On the Web: www.—.com
• By mail: check the box and complete the form below, and send the form to:

[Company name]

[Company address]

☐ Do not allow your affiliates to use my personal information to market to me.

A-2—MODEL FORM FOR INITIAL OPT OUT NOTICE (JOINT NOTICE)—[YOUR CHOICE TO LIMIT MARKETING]/[MARKETING OPT OUT]

• The [ABC group of companies] is providing this notice.

• [Optional: Federal law gives you the right to limit some but not all marketing from the [ABC] companies. Federal law also requires us to give you this notice to tell you about your choice to limit marketing from the [ABC] companies.]

• You may limit the [ABC] companies, such as the [ABC investment companies, investment advisers, transfer agents, and broker-dealers] affiliates, from marketing their products or services to you based on your personal information that they receive from other [ABC] companies. This information includes your [income], your [account history], and your [credit score].

• Your choice to limit marketing offers from the [ABC] companies will apply [until you tell us to change your choice]/[for x years from when you tell us your choice]/[for at least 5 years from when you tell us your choice]. [Include if the opt out period expires.] Once that period expires, you will receive a renewal notice that will allow you to continue to limit marketing offers from the [ABC] companies for [another x years]/[at least another 5 years].

• [Include, if applicable, in a subsequent notice, including an annual notice, for consumers who may have previously opted out.] If you have already made a choice to limit marketing offers from the [ABC] companies, you do not need to act again until you receive the renewal notice.

To limit marketing offers, contact us [include all that apply]:

• By telephone: 1-877-###-####
• On the Web: www.—.com
• By mail: check the box and complete the form below, and send the form to:

[Company name]

[Company address]

☐ Do not allow any company [in the ABC group of companies] to use my personal information to market to me.

A-3—MODEL FORM FOR RENEWAL NOTICE (SINGLE-AFFILIATE NOTICE)—[RENEWING YOUR CHOICE TO LIMIT MARKETING]/[RENEWING YOUR MARKETING OPT OUT]

• [Name of Affiliate] is providing this notice.

• [Optional: Federal law gives you the right to limit some but not all marketing from our affiliates. Federal law also requires us to give you this notice to tell you about your choice to limit marketing from our affiliates.]

• You previously chose to limit our affiliates in the [ABC] group of companies, such

§ 248.201

as our [investment adviser, investment company, transfer agent, and broker-dealer] affiliates, from marketing their products or services to you based on your personal information that we share with them. This information includes your [income], your [account history with us], and your [credit score].

• Your choice has expired or is about to expire.

To renew your choice to limit marketing for [x] more years, contact us [include all that apply]:

• By telephone: 1-877-###-####
• On the Web: *www.—.com*
• By mail: check the box and complete the form below, and send the form to:

[Company name]

[Company address]

Renew my choice to limit marketing for [x] more years.

A-4—MODEL FORM FOR RENEWAL NOTICE (JOINT NOTICE)—[RENEWING YOUR CHOICE TO LIMIT MARKETING]/[RENEWING YOUR MARKETING OPT OUT]

• The [ABC group of companies] is providing this notice.

• [Optional: Federal law gives you the right to limit some but not all marketing from the [ABC] companies. Federal law also requires us to give you this notice to tell you about your choice to limit marketing from the [ABC] companies.]

• You previously chose to limit the [ABC] companies, such as the [ABC investment adviser, investment company, transfer agent, and broker-dealer] affiliates, from marketing their products or services to you based on your personal information that they receive from other ABC companies. This information includes your [income], your [account history], and your [credit score].

• Your choice has expired or is about to expire.

To renew your choice to limit marketing for [x] more years, contact us [include all that apply]:

• By telephone: 1-877-###-####
• On the Web: *www.—.com*
• By mail: check the box and complete the form below, and send the form to:

[Company name]

[Company address]

Renew my choice to limit marketing for [x] more years.

A-5—MODEL FORM FOR VOLUNTARY "NO MARKETING" NOTICE—YOUR CHOICE TO STOP MARKETING

• [Name of Affiliate] is providing this notice.

• You may choose to stop all marketing from us and our affiliates.

• [Your choice to stop marketing from us and our affiliates will apply until you tell us to change your choice.]

To stop all marketing, contact us [include all that apply]:

• By telephone: 1-877-###-####
• On the Web: *www.—.com*
• By mail: check the box and complete the form below, and send the form to:

[Company name]

[Company address]

Do not market to me.

Subpart C—Regulation S–ID: Identity Theft Red Flags

SOURCE: 78 FR 23663, Apr. 17, 2013, unless otherwise noted.

§ 248.201 Duties regarding the detection, prevention, and mitigation of identity theft.

(a) *Scope.* This section applies to a *financial institution* or *creditor*, as defined in the Fair Credit Reporting Act (15 U.S.C. 1681), that is:

(1) A broker, dealer or any other person that is registered or required to be registered under the Securities Exchange Act of 1934;

(2) An investment company that is registered or required to be registered under the Investment Company Act of 1940, that has elected to be regulated as a business development company under that Act, or that operates as an employees' securities company under that Act; or

(3) An investment adviser that is registered or required to be registered under the Investment Advisers Act of 1940.

(b) *Definitions.* For purposes of this subpart, and Appendix A of this subpart, the following definitions apply:

(1) *Account* means a continuing relationship established by a person with a financial institution or creditor to obtain a product or service for personal, family, household or business purposes. Account includes a brokerage account, a *mutual fund* account (*i.e.*, an account with an open-end investment company), and an investment advisory account.

(2) The term *board of directors* includes:

(i) In the case of a branch or agency of a foreign financial institution or

Securities and Exchange Commission

§ 248.201

creditor, the managing official of that branch or agency; and

(ii) In the case of a financial institution or creditor that does not have a board of directors, a designated employee at the level of senior management.

(3) *Covered account* means:

(i) An account that a financial institution or creditor offers or maintains, primarily for personal, family, or household purposes, that involves or is designed to permit multiple payments or transactions, such as a brokerage account with a broker-dealer or an account maintained by a mutual fund (or its agent) that permits wire transfers or other payments to third parties; and

(ii) Any other account that the financial institution or creditor offers or maintains for which there is a reasonably foreseeable risk to customers or to the safety and soundness of the financial institution or creditor from identity theft, including financial, operational, compliance, reputation, or litigation risks.

(4) *Credit* has the same meaning as in 15 U.S.C. 1681a(r)(5).

(5) *Creditor* has the same meaning as in 15 U.S.C. 1681m(e)(4).

(6) *Customer* means a person that has a covered account with a financial institution or creditor.

(7) *Financial institution* has the same meaning as in 15 U.S.C. 1681a(t).

(8) *Identifying information* means any name or number that may be used, alone or in conjunction with any other information, to identify a specific person, including any—

(i) Name, Social Security number, date of birth, official State or government issued driver's license or identification number, alien registration number, government passport number, employer or taxpayer identification number;

(ii) Unique biometric data, such as fingerprint, voice print, retina or iris image, or other unique physical representation;

(iii) Unique electronic identification number, address, or routing code; or

(iv) Telecommunication identifying information or access device (as defined in 18 U.S.C. 1029(e)).

(9) *Identity theft* means a fraud committed or attempted using the identifying information of another person without authority.

(10) *Red Flag* means a pattern, practice, or specific activity that indicates the possible existence of identity theft.

(11) *Service provider* means a person that provides a service directly to the financial institution or creditor.

(12) *Other definitions.*

(i) *Broker* has the same meaning as in section 3(a)(4) of the Securities Exchange Act of 1934 (15 U.S.C. 78c(a)(4)).

(ii) *Commission* means the Securities and Exchange Commission.

(iii) *Dealer* has the same meaning as in section 3(a)(5) of the Securities Exchange Act of 1934 (15 U.S.C. 78c(a)(5)).

(iv) *Investment adviser* has the same meaning as in section 202(a)(11) of the Investment Advisers Act of 1940 (15 U.S.C. 80b-2(a)(11)).

(v) *Investment company* has the same meaning as in section 3 of the Investment Company Act of 1940 (15 U.S.C. 80a-3), and includes a separate series of the investment company.

(vi) Other terms not defined in this subpart have the same meaning as in the Fair Credit Reporting Act (15 U.S.C. 1681 *et seq.*).

(c) *Periodic identification of covered accounts.* Each financial institution or creditor must periodically determine whether it offers or maintains covered accounts. As a part of this determination, a financial institution or creditor must conduct a risk assessment to determine whether it offers or maintains covered accounts described in paragraph (b)(3)(ii) of this section, taking into consideration:

(1) The methods it provides to open its accounts;

(2) The methods it provides to access its accounts; and

(3) Its previous experiences with identity theft.

(d) *Establishment of an Identity Theft Prevention Program—*

(1) *Program requirement.* Each financial institution or creditor that offers or maintains one or more covered accounts must develop and implement a written Identity Theft Prevention Program (Program) that is designed to detect, prevent, and mitigate identity theft in connection with the opening of

§ 248.202

a covered account or any existing covered account. The Program must be appropriate to the size and complexity of the financial institution or creditor and the nature and scope of its activities.

(2) *Elements of the Program.* The Program must include reasonable policies and procedures to:

(i) Identify relevant Red Flags for the covered accounts that the financial institution or creditor offers or maintains, and incorporate those Red Flags into its Program;

(ii) Detect Red Flags that have been incorporated into the Program of the financial institution or creditor;

(iii) Respond appropriately to any Red Flags that are detected pursuant to paragraph (d)(2)(ii) of this section to prevent and mitigate identity theft; and

(iv) Ensure the Program (including the Red Flags determined to be relevant) is updated periodically, to reflect changes in risks to customers and to the safety and soundness of the financial institution or creditor from identity theft.

(e) *Administration of the Program.* Each financial institution or creditor that is required to implement a Program must provide for the continued administration of the Program and must:

(1) Obtain approval of the initial written Program from either its board of directors or an appropriate committee of the board of directors;

(2) Involve the board of directors, an appropriate committee thereof, or a designated employee at the level of senior management in the oversight, development, implementation and administration of the Program;

(3) Train staff, as necessary, to effectively implement the Program; and

(4) Exercise appropriate and effective oversight of service provider arrangements.

(f) *Guidelines.* Each financial institution or creditor that is required to implement a Program must consider the guidelines in Appendix A to this subpart and include in its Program those guidelines that are appropriate.

§ 248.202 Duties of card issuers regarding changes of address.

(a) *Scope.* This section applies to a person described in § 248.201(a) that issues a credit or debit card (card issuer).

(b) *Definitions.* For purposes of this section:

(1) *Cardholder* means a consumer who has been issued a *credit card* or *debit card* as defined in 15 U.S.C. 1681a(r).

(2) *Clear and conspicuous* means reasonably understandable and designed to call attention to the nature and significance of the information presented.

(3) Other terms not defined in this subpart have the same meaning as in the Fair Credit Reporting Act (15 U.S.C. 1681 *et seq.*).

(c) *Address validation requirements.* A card issuer must establish and implement reasonable written policies and procedures to assess the validity of a change of address if it receives notification of a change of address for a consumer's debit or credit card account and, within a short period of time afterwards (during at least the first 30 days after it receives such notification), the card issuer receives a request for an additional or replacement card for the same account. Under these circumstances, the card issuer may not issue an additional or replacement card, until, in accordance with its reasonable policies and procedures and for the purpose of assessing the validity of the change of address, the card issuer:

(1)(i) Notifies the cardholder of the request:

(A) At the cardholder's former address; or

(B) By any other means of communication that the card issuer and the cardholder have previously agreed to use; and

(ii) Provides to the cardholder a reasonable means of promptly reporting incorrect address changes; or

(2) Otherwise assesses the validity of the change of address in accordance with the policies and procedures the card issuer has established pursuant to § 248.201.

(d) *Alternative timing of address validation.* A card issuer may satisfy the requirements of paragraph (c) of this section if it validates an address pursuant to the methods in paragraph (c)(1) or

Securities and Exchange Commission

(c)(2) of this section when it receives an address change notification, before it receives a request for an additional or replacement card.

(e) *Form of notice.* Any written or electronic notice that the card issuer provides under this paragraph must be clear and conspicuous and be provided separately from its regular correspondence with the cardholder.

APPENDIX A TO SUBPART C OF PART 248—INTERAGENCY GUIDELINES ON IDENTITY THEFT DETECTION, PREVENTION, AND MITIGATION

Section 248.201 requires each financial institution and creditor that offers or maintains one or more covered accounts, as defined in § 248.201(b)(3), to develop and provide for the continued administration of a written Program to detect, prevent, and mitigate identity theft in connection with the opening of a covered account or any existing covered account. These guidelines are intended to assist financial institutions and creditors in the formulation and maintenance of a Program that satisfies the requirements of § 248.201.

I. THE PROGRAM

In designing its Program, a financial institution or creditor may incorporate, as appropriate, its existing policies, procedures, and other arrangements that control reasonably foreseeable risks to customers or to the safety and soundness of the financial institution or creditor from identity theft.

II. IDENTIFYING RELEVANT RED FLAGS

(a) *Risk Factors.* A financial institution or creditor should consider the following factors in identifying relevant Red Flags for covered accounts, as appropriate:

(1) The types of covered accounts it offers or maintains;

(2) The methods it provides to open its covered accounts;

(3) The methods it provides to access its covered accounts; and

(4) Its previous experiences with identity theft.

(b) *Sources of Red Flags.* Financial institutions and creditors should incorporate relevant Red Flags from sources such as:

(1) Incidents of identity theft that the financial institution or creditor has experienced;

(2) Methods of identity theft that the financial institution or creditor has identified that reflect changes in identity theft risks; and

(3) Applicable regulatory guidance.

(c) *Categories of Red Flags.* The Program should include relevant Red Flags from the following categories, as appropriate. Examples of Red Flags from each of these categories are appended as Supplement A to this Appendix A.

(1) Alerts, notifications, or other warnings received from consumer reporting agencies or service providers, such as fraud detection services;

(2) The presentation of suspicious documents;

(3) The presentation of suspicious personal identifying information, such as a suspicious address change;

(4) The unusual use of, or other suspicious activity related to, a covered account; and

(5) Notice from customers, victims of identity theft, law enforcement authorities, or other persons regarding possible identity theft in connection with covered accounts held by the financial institution or creditor.

III. DETECTING RED FLAGS

The Program's policies and procedures should address the detection of Red Flags in connection with the opening of covered accounts and existing covered accounts, such as by:

(a) Obtaining identifying information about, and verifying the identity of, a person opening a covered account, for example, using the policies and procedures regarding identification and verification set forth in the Customer Identification Program rules implementing 31 U.S.C. 5318(*l*) (31 CFR 1023.220 (broker-dealers) and 1024.220 (mutual funds)); and

(b) Authenticating customers, monitoring transactions, and verifying the validity of change of address requests, in the case of existing covered accounts.

IV. PREVENTING AND MITIGATING IDENTITY THEFT

The Program's policies and procedures should provide for appropriate responses to the Red Flags the financial institution or creditor has detected that are commensurate with the degree of risk posed. In determining an appropriate response, a financial institution or creditor should consider aggravating factors that may heighten the risk of identity theft, such as a data security incident that results in unauthorized access to a customer's account records held by the financial institution, creditor, or third party, or notice that a customer has provided information related to a covered account held by the financial institution or creditor to someone fraudulently claiming to represent the financial institution or creditor or to a fraudulent Web site. Appropriate responses may include the following:

(a) Monitoring a covered account for evidence of identity theft;

(b) Contacting the customer;

Pt. 248, Subpt. C, App. A

(c) Changing any passwords, security codes, or other security devices that permit access to a covered account;
(d) Reopening a covered account with a new account number;
(e) Not opening a new covered account;
(f) Closing an existing covered account;
(g) Not attempting to collect on a covered account or not selling a covered account to a debt collector;
(h) Notifying law enforcement; or
(i) Determining that no response is warranted under the particular circumstances.

V. UPDATING THE PROGRAM

Financial institutions and creditors should update the Program (including the Red Flags determined to be relevant) periodically, to reflect changes in risks to customers or to the safety and soundness of the financial institution or creditor from identity theft, based on factors such as:
(a) The experiences of the financial institution or creditor with identity theft;
(b) Changes in methods of identity theft;
(c) Changes in methods to detect, prevent, and mitigate identity theft;
(d) Changes in the types of accounts that the financial institution or creditor offers or maintains; and
(e) Changes in the business arrangements of the financial institution or creditor, including mergers, acquisitions, alliances, joint ventures, and service provider arrangements.

VI. METHODS FOR ADMINISTERING THE PROGRAM

(a) *Oversight of Program.* Oversight by the board of directors, an appropriate committee of the board, or a designated employee at the level of senior management should include:
(1) Assigning specific responsibility for the Program's implementation;
(2) Reviewing reports prepared by staff regarding compliance by the financial institution or creditor with §248.201; and
(3) Approving material changes to the Program as necessary to address changing identity theft risks.
(b) *Reports.* (1) *In general.* Staff of the financial institution or creditor responsible for development, implementation, and administration of its Program should report to the board of directors, an appropriate committee of the board, or a designated employee at the level of senior management, at least annually, on compliance by the financial institution or creditor with §248.201.
(2) *Contents of report.* The report should address material matters related to the Program and evaluate issues such as: The effectiveness of the policies and procedures of the financial institution or creditor in addressing the risk of identity theft in connection with the opening of covered accounts and with respect to existing covered accounts; service provider arrangements; significant incidents involving identity theft and management's response; and recommendations for material changes to the Program.

(c) *Oversight of service provider arrangements.* Whenever a financial institution or creditor engages a service provider to perform an activity in connection with one or more covered accounts the financial institution or creditor should take steps to ensure that the activity of the service provider is conducted in accordance with reasonable policies and procedures designed to detect, prevent, and mitigate the risk of identity theft. For example, a financial institution or creditor could require the service provider by contract to have policies and procedures to detect relevant Red Flags that may arise in the performance of the service provider's activities, and either report the Red Flags to the financial institution or creditor, or to take appropriate steps to prevent or mitigate identity theft.

VII. OTHER APPLICABLE LEGAL REQUIREMENTS

Financial institutions and creditors should be mindful of other related legal requirements that may be applicable, such as:
(a) For financial institutions and creditors that are subject to 31 U.S.C. 5318(g), filing a Suspicious Activity Report in accordance with applicable law and regulation;
(b) Implementing any requirements under 15 U.S.C. 1681c-1(h) regarding the circumstances under which credit may be extended when the financial institution or creditor detects a fraud or active duty alert;
(c) Implementing any requirements for furnishers of information to consumer reporting agencies under 15 U.S.C. 1681s-2, for example, to correct or update inaccurate or incomplete information, and to not report information that the furnisher has reasonable cause to believe is inaccurate; and
(d) Complying with the prohibitions in 15 U.S.C. 1681m on the sale, transfer, and placement for collection of certain debts resulting from identity theft.

Supplement A to Appendix A

In addition to incorporating Red Flags from the sources recommended in section II.b. of the Guidelines in Appendix A to this subpart, each financial institution or creditor may consider incorporating into its Program, whether singly or in combination, Red Flags from the following illustrative examples in connection with covered accounts:

Alerts, Notifications or Warnings From a Consumer Reporting Agency

1. A fraud or active duty alert is included with a consumer report.

Securities and Exchange Commission

2. A consumer reporting agency provides a notice of credit freeze in response to a request for a consumer report.
3. A consumer reporting agency provides a notice of address discrepancy, as referenced in Sec. 605(h) of the Fair Credit Reporting Act (15 U.S.C. 1681c(h)).
4. A consumer report indicates a pattern of activity that is inconsistent with the history and usual pattern of activity of an applicant or customer, such as:
  a. A recent and significant increase in the volume of inquiries;
  b. An unusual number of recently established credit relationships;
  c. A material change in the use of credit, especially with respect to recently established credit relationships; or
  d. An account that was closed for cause or identified for abuse of account privileges by a financial institution or creditor.

Suspicious Documents

5. Documents provided for identification appear to have been altered or forged.
6. The photograph or physical description on the identification is not consistent with the appearance of the applicant or customer presenting the identification.
7. Other information on the identification is not consistent with information provided by the person opening a new covered account or customer presenting the identification.
8. Other information on the identification is not consistent with readily accessible information that is on file with the financial institution or creditor, such as a signature card or a recent check.
9. An application appears to have been altered or forged, or gives the appearance of having been destroyed and reassembled.

Suspicious Personal Identifying Information

10. Personal identifying information provided is inconsistent when compared against external information sources used by the financial institution or creditor. For example:
  a. The address does not match any address in the consumer report; or
  b. The Social Security Number (SSN) has not been issued, or is listed on the Social Security Administration's Death Master File.
11. Personal identifying information provided by the customer is not consistent with other personal identifying information provided by the customer. For example, there is a lack of correlation between the SSN range and date of birth.
12. Personal identifying information provided is associated with known fraudulent activity as indicated by internal or third-party sources used by the financial institution or creditor. For example:
  a. The address on an application is the same as the address provided on a fraudulent application; or

b. The phone number on an application is the same as the number provided on a fraudulent application.
13. Personal identifying information provided is of a type commonly associated with fraudulent activity as indicated by internal or third-party sources used by the financial institution or creditor. For example:
  a. The address on an application is fictitious, a mail drop, or a prison; or
  b. The phone number is invalid, or is associated with a pager or answering service.
14. The SSN provided is the same as that submitted by other persons opening an account or other customers.
15. The address or telephone number provided is the same as or similar to the address or telephone number submitted by an unusually large number of other persons opening accounts or by other customers.
16. The person opening the covered account or the customer fails to provide all required personal identifying information on an application or in response to notification that the application is incomplete.
17. Personal identifying information provided is not consistent with personal identifying information that is on file with the financial institution or creditor.
18. For financial institutions and creditors that use challenge questions, the person opening the covered account or the customer cannot provide authenticating information beyond that which generally would be available from a wallet or consumer report.

Unusual Use of, or Suspicious Activity Related to, the Covered Account

19. Shortly following the notice of a change of address for a covered account, the institution or creditor receives a request for a new, additional, or replacement means of accessing the account or for the addition of an authorized user on the account.
20. A covered account is used in a manner that is not consistent with established patterns of activity on the account. There is, for example:
  a. Nonpayment when there is no history of late or missed payments;
  b. A material increase in the use of available credit;
  c. A material change in purchasing or spending patterns; or
  d. A material change in electronic fund transfer patterns in connection with a deposit account.
21. A covered account that has been inactive for a reasonably lengthy period of time is used (taking into consideration the type of account, the expected pattern of usage and other relevant factors).
22. Mail sent to the customer is returned repeatedly as undeliverable although transactions continue to be conducted in connection with the customer's covered account.

23. The financial institution or creditor is notified that the customer is not receiving paper account statements.
24. The financial institution or creditor is notified of unauthorized charges or transactions in connection with a customer's covered account.

Notice From Customers, Victims of Identity Theft, Law Enforcement Authorities, or Other Persons Regarding Possible Identity Theft in Connection With Covered Accounts Held by the Financial Institution or Creditor

25. The financial institution or creditor is notified by a customer, a victim of identity theft, a law enforcement authority, or any other person that it has opened a fraudulent account for a person engaged in identity theft.

PART 249—FORMS, SECURITIES EXCHANGE ACT OF 1934

Sec.
249.0–1 Availability of forms.

Subpart A—Forms for Registration or Exemption of, and Notification of Action Taken by, National Securities Exchanges

249.1 Form 1, for application for, and amendments to applications for, registration as a national securities exchange or exemption from registration pursuant to Section 5 of the Exchange Act.
249.10 Form 1–N for notice registration as a national securities exchange.
249.11 Form R31 for reporting covered sales and covered round turn transactions under section 31 of the Act.
249.25 Form 25, for notification of removal from listing and/or registration.
249.26 Form 26, for notification of the admission to trading of a substituted or additional class of security under Rule 12a–5 (§ 240.12a–5 of this chapter).

Subpart B—Forms for Reports To Be Filed by Officers, Directors, and Security Holders

249.103 Form 3, initial statement of beneficial ownership of securities.
249.104 Form 4, statement of changes in beneficial ownership of securities.
249.105 Form 5, annual statement of beneficial ownership of securities.

Subpart C—Forms for Applications for Registration of Securities on National Securities Exchanges and Similar Matters

249.208 [Reserved]
249.208a Form 8–A, for registration of certain classes of securities pursuant to section 12(b) or (g) of the Securities Exchange Act of 1934.
249.208b–249.208c [Reserved]
249.210 Form 10, general form for registration of securities pursuant to section 12(b) or (g) of the Securities Exchange Act of 1934.
249.210b [Reserved]
249.218 Form 18, for foreign governments and political subdivisions thereof.
249.220f Form 20–F, registration of securities of foreign private issuers pursuant to section 12(b) or (g), annual and transition reports pursuant to sections 13 and 15(d), and shell company reports required under Rule 13a–19 or 15d–19 (§ 240.13a–19 or § 240.15d–19 of this chapter).
249.240f Form 40–F, for registration of securities of certain Canadian issuers pursuant to section 12(b) or (g) and for reports pursuant to section 15(d) and Rule 15d–4 (§ 240.15d–4 of this chapter).
249.250 Form F–X, for appointment of agent for service of process by issuers registering securities on Form F–8, F–9, F–10 or F–80 (§ 239.38, 239.39, 239.40 or 239.41 of this chapter), or registering securities or filing periodic reports on Form 40–F (§ 249.240f of this chapter), or by any issuer or other non-U.S. person filing tender offer documents on Schedule 13E–4F, 14D–1F or 14D–9F (§ 240.13e–102, 240.14d–102 or 240.14d–103 of this chapter), or by any non-U.S. person acting as trustee with respect to securities registered on Form F–7 (§ 249.37 of this chapter), F–8, F–9, F–10 or F–80.

Subpart D—Forms for Annual and Other Reports of Issuers Required Under Sections 13 and 15(d) of the Securities Exchange Act of 1934

249.306 Form 6–K report of foreign issuer pursuant to Rules 13a–16 (§ 240.13a–16 of this chapter) and 15d–16 (§ 240.15d–16 of this chapter) under the Securities Exchange Act of 1934.
249.308 Form 8–K, for current reports.
249.308a Form 10–Q, for quarterly and transition reports under sections 13 or 15(d) of the Securities Exchange Act of 1934.
249.310 Form 10–K, for annual and transition reports pursuant to sections 13 or 15(d) of the Securities Exchange Act of 1934.
249.310b–249.310c [Reserved]
249.311 Form 11–K, for annual reports of employee stock purchase, savings and similar plans pursuant to section 15(d) of the Securities Exchange Act of 1934.
249.312 Form 10–D, periodic distribution reports by asset-backed issuers.
249.318 Form 18–K, annual report for foreign governments and political subdivisions thereof.
249.322 Form 12b–25—Notification of late filing.

Securities and Exchange Commission Pt. 249

249.323 Form 15, certification of termination of registration of a class of security under section 12(g) or notice of suspension of duty to file reports pursuant to sections 13 and 15(d) of the Act.
249.324 Form 15F, certification by a foreign private issuer regarding the termination of registration of a class of securities under section 12(g) or the duty to file reports under section 13(a) or section 15(d).
249.325 Form 13F, report of institutional investment manager pursuant to section 13(f) of the Securities Exchange Act of 1934.
249.326 Form N-PX, annual report of proxy voting record.
249.327 Form 13H, Information required on large traders pursuant to Section 13(h) of the Securities Exchange Act of 1934 and rules thereunder.
249.328T Form 17-H, Risk assessment report for brokers and dealers pursuant to section 17(h) of the Securities Exchange Act of 1934 and rules thereunder.
249.330 Form N-CEN, annual report of registered investment companies.
249.331 Form N-CSR, certified shareholder report.
249.332 [Reserved]
249.444 Form SE, form for submission of paper format exhibits by electronic filers.
249.445 [Reserved]
249.446 Form ID, uniform application for access codes to file on EDGAR.
249.447 Form TH—Notification of reliance on temporary hardship exemption.

Subpart E—Forms for Statements Made in Connection With Exempt Tender Offers

249.480 Form CB, tender offer statement in connection with a tender offer for a foreign private issuer.

Subpart F—Forms for Registration of Brokers and Dealers Transacting Business on Over-the-Counter Markets

249.501 Form BD, for application for registration as a broker and dealer or to amend or supplement such an application.
249.501a Form BDW, notice of withdrawal from registration as broker-dealer pursuant to §240.15b6-1, §240.15Bc3-1, or §240.15Cc1-1 of this chapter.
249.501b Form BD-N for notice registration as a broker-dealer.
249.507 Form 7-M, consent to service of process by an individual nonresident broker-dealer.
249.508 Form 8-M, consent to service of process by a corporation which is a nonresident broker-dealer.
249.509 Form 9-M, consent to service of process by a partnership nonresident broker-dealer.
249.510 Form 10-M, consent to service of process by a nonresident general partner of a broker-dealer firm.

Subpart G—Forms for Reports To Be Made by Certain Exchange Members, Brokers, Dealers, Security-Based Swap Dealers, and Major Security-Based Swap Participants

249.617 Form X-17A-5, information required of certain brokers, dealers, security-based swap dealers, and major security-based swap participants pursuant to sections 15F and 17 of the Securities Exchange Act of 1934 and §§240.17a-5, 240.17a-10, 240.17a-11, 240.17a-12, and 240.18a-79 of this chapter, as applicable.
249.618 Form BD-Y2K, information required of broker-dealers pursuant to section 17 of the Securities Exchange Act of 1934 and §240.17a-5 of this chapter.
249.619 Form TA-Y2K, information required of transfer agents pursuant to section 17 of the Securities Exchange Act of 1934 and §240.17Ad-18 of this chapter.
249.620–249.634 [Reserved]
249.635 Form X-17A-19, report by national securities exchanges and registered national securities associations of changes in the membership status of any of their members.
249.636 [Reserved]
249.637 Form ATS, information required of alternative trading systems pursuant to §242.301(b)(2) of this chapter.
249.638 Form ATS-R, information required of alternative trading systems pursuant to §242.301(b)(8) of this chapter.
249.639 Form custody.
249.640 Form ATS-N, information required of NMS Stock ATSs pursuant to §242.304(a) of this chapter.
249.641 Form CRS, Relationship Summary for Brokers and Dealers Providing Services to Retail Investors, pursuant to §240.17a-14 of this chapter.

Subpart H—Forms for Reports as to Stabilization

249.709 [Reserved]

Subpart I—Forms for Self-Regulatory Organization Rule Changes and Forms for Registration of and Reporting by National Securities Associations and Affiliated Securities Associations

249.801 Form X-15AA-1, for application for registration as a national securities association or affiliated securities association.

249.802 Form X–15AJ–1, for amendatory and/or supplementary statements to registration statement of a national securities association or an affiliated securities association.
249.803 Form X–15AJ–2, for annual consolidated supplement of a national securities association or an affiliated securities association.
249.819 Form 19b–4, for electronic filings with respect to proposed rule changes, advance notices and security-based swap submissions by all self-regulatory organizations.
249.820 Form 19b–4(e) for the listing and trading of new derivative securities products by self-regulatory organizations that are not deemed proposed rule changes pursuant to Rule 19b–4(e)(§ 240.19b–4(e)).
249.821 Form PILOT, information required of self-regulatory organizations operating pilot trading systems pursuant to § 240.19b–5 of this chapter.
249.822 Form 19b–7, for electronic filing with respect to proposed rule changes by self-regulatory organizations under Section 19(b)(7)(A) of the Securities Exchange Act of 1934.

Subpart J [Reserved]

Subpart K—Forms for Registration of, and Reporting by Securities Information Processors

249.1001 Form SIP, for application for registration as a securities information processor or to amend such an application or registration.
249.1002 Form CC, for application for registration as a competing consolidator or to amend such an application or registration.

Subpart L—Forms for Registration of Municipal Securities Dealers

249.1100 Form MSD, application for registration as a municipal securities dealer pursuant to rule 15Ba2–1 under the Securities Exchange Act of 1934 or amendment to such application.
249.1110 Form MSDW, notice of withdrawal from registration as a municipal securities dealer pursuant to Rule 15Bc3–1 (17 CFR 240.15Bc3–1).

Subpart M—Forms for Reporting and Inquiry With Respect to Missing, Lost, Stolen, or Counterfeit Securities

249.1200 Form X–17F–1A—Report for missing, lost, stolen or counterfeit securities.

Subpart N—Forms for Registration of Municipal Advisors and for Providing Information Regarding Certain Natural Persons

249.1300 Form MA, for registration as a municipal advisor, and for amendments to registration.
249.1300T Form MA–T, for temporary registration as a municipal advisor, and for amendments to, and withdrawals from, temporary registration.
249.1310 Form MA–I, for providing information regarding natural person municipal advisors, and for amendments to such information.
249.1320 Form MA–W, for withdrawal from registration as a municipal advisor.
249.1330 Form MA–NR, for appointment of agent for service of process by non-resident municipal advisor, non-resident general partner or managing agent of a municipal advisor, and non-resident natural person associated with a municipal advisor.

Subpart O—Forms for Asset-Backed Securities

249.1400 Form ABS–15G, Asset-backed securitizer report pursuant to Section 15G of the Securities Exchange Act of 1934.
249.1401 Form ABS–EE, for submission of the asset-data file exhibits and related documents.

Subpart P—Forms for Registration of Security-Based Swap Data Repositories

249.1500 Form SDR, for application for registration as a security-based swap data repository, amendments thereto, or withdrawal from registration.

Subpart Q—Registration of Security-Based Swap Dealers and Major Security-Based Swap Participants

249.1600 Form SBSE, for application for registration as a security-based swap dealer or major security-based swap participant or to amend such an application for registration.
249.1600a Form SBSE–A, for application for registration as a security-based swap

Securities and Exchange Commission

§ 249.1

dealer or major security-based swap participant or to amend such an application for registration by firms registered or registering with the Commodity Futures Trading Commission as a swap dealer or major swap participant that are not also registered or registering with the Commission as a broker or dealer.

249.1600b Form SBSE–BD, for application for registration as a security-based swap dealer or major security-based swap participant or to amend such an application for registration by firms registered or registering with the Commission as a broker or dealer.

249.1600c Form SBSE–C, for certification by security-based swap dealers and major security-based swap participants.

249.1601 Form SBSE–W, for withdrawal from registration as a security-based swap dealer or major security-based swap participant or to amend such an application for registration.

Subparts R—S [Reserved]

Subpart T—Form SCI, for filing notices and reports as required by Regulation SCI.

249.1900 Form SCI, for filing notices and reports as required by Regulation SCI.

Subpart U—Forms for Registration of Funding Portals

249.2000 Form Funding Portal.

AUTHORITY: 15 U.S.C. 78a *et seq.* and 7201 *et seq.*; 12 U.S.C. 5461 *et seq.*; 18 U.S.C. 1350; Sec. 953(b) Pub. L. 111–203, 124 Stat. 1904; Sec. 102(a)(3) Pub. L. 112–106, 126 Stat. 309 (2012), Sec. 107 Pub. L. 112–106, 126 Stat. 313 (2012), Sec. 72001 Pub. L. 114–94, 129 Stat. 1312 (2015), and secs. 2 and 3 Pub. L. 116–222, 134 Stat. 1063 (2020), unless otherwise noted.

Section 249.220f is also issued under secs. 3(a), 202, 208, 302, 306(a), 401(a), 401(b), 406 and 407, Pub. L. 107–204, 116 Stat. 745, and secs. 2 and 3, Pub. L. 116–222, 134 Stat. 1063.

Section 249.240f is also issued under secs. 3(a), 202, 208, 302, 306(a), 401(a), 406 and 407, Pub. L. 107–204, 116 Stat. 745.

Section 249.308 is also issued under 15 U.S.C. 80a–29 and 80a–37.

Section 249.308a is also issued under secs. 3(a) and 302, Pub. L. 107–204, 116 Stat. 745.

Section 249.308b is also issued under secs. 3(a) and 302, Pub. L. 107–204, 116 Stat. 745.

Section 249.310 is also issued under secs. 3(a), 202, 208, 302, 406 and 407, Pub. L. 107–204, 116 Stat. 745.

Section 249.326(T) also issued under section 13(f)(1) (15 U.S.C. 78m(f)(1)).

Section 249.330 is also issued under 15 U.S.C. 80a–29(a).

Section 249.331 is also issued under 15 U.S.C. 78j–1, 7202, 7233, 7241, 7264, 7265; and 18 U.S.C. 1350.

Section 249.617 is also issued under Pub. L. 111–203, § 939, 939A, 124. Stat. 1376 (2010) (15 U.S.C. 78c, 15 U.S.C. 78*o*–7 note)..

Section 249.640 is also issued under Public Law 111–203, sec. 913, 124 Stat. 1376 (2010).

Section 249.819 is also issued under 12 U.S.C. 5465(e).

Section 249.1400 is also issued under sec. 943, Pub. L. 111–203, 124 Stat. 1376.

EDITORIAL NOTE: Nomenclature changes to part 249 appear at 57 FR 36501, Aug. 13, 1992, and 57 FR 47409, Oct. 16, 1992.

§ 249.0–1 Availability of forms.

(a) This part identifies and describes the forms prescribed for use under the Securities Exchange Act of 1934.

(b) Any person may obtain a copy of any form prescribed for use in this part by written request to the Securities and Exchange Commission, 100 F Street, NE, Washington, DC 20549. Any person may inspect the forms at this address and at the Commission's regional offices. (*See* § 200.11 of this chapter for the addresses of SEC regional offices.)

[46 FR 17757, Mar. 20, 1981, as amended at 47 FR 26820, June 22, 1982; 59 FR 5946, Feb. 9, 1994; 73 FR 979, Jan. 4, 2008]

Subpart A—Forms for Registration or Exemption of, and Notification of Action Taken by, National Securities Exchanges

§ 249.1 Form 1, for application for, and amendments to applications for, registration as a national securities exchange or exemption from registration pursuant to Section 5 of the Exchange Act.

The form shall be used for application for, and amendments to applications for, registration as a national securities exchange or exemption from registration pursuant to Section 5 of the Act, (15 U.S.C. 78e).

[63 FR 70925, Dec. 22, 1998]

EDITORIAL NOTE: For FEDERAL REGISTER citations affecting Form 1, see the List of CFR Sections Affected, which appears in the Finding Aids section of the printed volume and at *www.govinfo.gov.*

§ 249.10 Form 1-N for notice registration as a national securities exchange.

This form shall be used for notice, and amendments to the notice, to permit an exchange to register as a national securities exchange solely for the purposes of trading security futures products pursuant to Section 6(g) of the Act (15 U.S.C. 78f(g)).

[66 FR 43743, Aug. 20, 2001]

EDITORIAL NOTE: For FEDERAL REGISTER citations affecting Form 1–10, see the List of CFR Sections Affected, which appears in the Finding Aids section of the printed volume and at *www.govinfo.gov*.

§ 249.11 Form R31 for reporting covered sales and covered round turn transactions under section 31 of the Act.

This form shall be used by each national securities exchange to report to the Commission within ten business days after the end of every month the aggregate dollar amount of sales of securities that occurred on the exchange, had a charge date in the month of the report, and are subject to fees pursuant to section 31(b) of the Act (15 U.S.C. 78ee) and § 240.31 of this chapter; and the total number of round turn transactions in security futures that occurred on the exchange, had a charge date in the month of the report, and are subject to assessments pursuant to section 31(d) of the Act and § 240.31 of this chapter. This form also shall be used by a national securities association to report to the Commission within ten business days after the end of every month the aggregate dollar amount of sales of securities that occurred by or through a member of the association otherwise than on a national securities exchange, had a charge date in the month of the report, and are subject to fees pursuant to section 31(c) of the Act and § 240.31 of this chapter; and the total number of round turn transactions in security futures that occurred by or through any member of the association otherwise than on a national securities exchange, had a charge date in the month of the report, and are subject to assessments pursuant to section 31(d) of the Act and § 240.31 of this chapter.

[69 FR 41080, July 7, 2004]

EDITORIAL NOTE: For FEDERAL REGISTER citations affecting Form R31, see the List of CFR Sections Affected, which appears in the Finding Aids section of the printed volume and at *www.govinfo.gov*.

§ 249.25 Form 25, for notification of removal from listing and/or registration.

This form shall be used by registered national securities exchanges and issuers for notification of removal of a class of securities from listing on a national securities exchange and/or withdrawal of registration under section 12(b) of the Act (15 U.S.C. 78l(b)).

[70 FR 42469, July 22, 2005]

EDITORIAL NOTE: For FEDERAL REGISTER citations affecting Form 25, see the List of CFR Sections Affected, which appears in the Finding Aids section of the printed volume and at *www.govinfo.gov*.

§ 249.26 Form 26, for notification of the admission to trading of a substituted or additional class of security under Rule 12a–5 (§ 240.12a–5 of this chapter).

This form shall be used by a registered national securities exchange for notification of the admission to trading of a substituted or additional class of security under Rule 12a–5.

[33 FR 18995, Dec. 20, 1968]

EDITORIAL NOTE: For FEDERAL REGISTER citations affecting Form 26, see the List of CFR Sections Affected, which appears in the Finding Aids section of the printed volume and at *www.govinfo.gov*.

Subpart B—Forms for Reports To Be Filed by Officers, Directors, and Security Holders

§ 249.103 Form 3, initial statement of beneficial ownership of securities.

This Form shall be filed pursuant to Rule 16a–3 (§ 240.16a–3 of this chapter) for initial statements of beneficial ownership of securities. The Commission is authorized to solicit the information required by this Form pursuant to sections 16(a) and 23(a) of the Securities Exchange Act of 1934 (15 U.S.C. 78p(a) and 78w(a)); and sections 30(h)

Securities and Exchange Commission § 249.105

and 38 of the Investment Company Act of 1940 (15 U.S.C. 80a-29(h) and 80a-37), and the rules and regulations thereunder. Disclosure of information specified on this Form is mandatory. The information will be used for the primary purpose of disclosing the holdings of directors, officers and beneficial owners of registered companies. Information disclosed will be a matter of public record and available for inspection by members of the public. The Commission can use the information in investigations or litigation involving the federal securities laws or other civil, criminal, or regulatory statutes or provisions, as well as for referral to other governmental authorities and self-regulatory organizations. Failure to disclose required information may result in civil or criminal action against persons involved for violations of the federal securities laws and rules.

[56 FR 7274, Feb. 21, 1991, as amended at 72 FR 45112, Aug. 10, 2007]

EDITORIAL NOTE: For FEDERAL REGISTER citations affecting Form 3, see the List of CFR Sections Affected, which appears in the Finding Aids section of the printed volume and at *www.govinfo.gov*.

§ 249.104 Form 4, statement of changes in beneficial ownership of securities.

This Form shall be filed pursuant to Rule 16a-3 (§ 240.16a-3 of this chapter) for statements of changes in beneficial ownership of securities. The Commission is authorized to solicit the information required by this Form pursuant to sections 16(a) and 23(a) of the Securities Exchange Act of 1934 (15 U.S.C. 78p(a) and 78w(a)); and sections 30(h) and 38 of the Investment Company Act of 1940 (15 U.S.C. 80a-29(h) and 80a-37), and the rules and regulations thereunder. Disclosure of information specified on this Form is mandatory. The information will be used for the primary purpose of disclosing the holdings of directors, officers and beneficial owners of registered companies. Information disclosed will be a matter of public record and available for inspection by members of the public. The Commission can use the information in investigations or litigation involving the federal securities laws or other civil, criminal, or regulatory statutes or provisions, as well as for referral to other governmental authorities and self-regulatory organizations. Failure to disclose required information may result in civil or criminal action against persons involved for violations of the federal securities laws and rules.

[56 FR 7274, Feb. 21, 1991, as amended at 72 FR 45112, Aug. 10, 2007]

EDITORIAL NOTE: For FEDERAL REGISTER citations affecting Form 4, see the List of CFR Sections Affected, which appears in the Finding Aids section of the printed volume and at *www.govinfo.gov*.

§ 249.105 Form 5, annual statement of beneficial ownership of securities.

This Form shall be filed pursuant to Rule 16a-3 (§ 240.16a-3 of this chapter) for annual statements of beneficial ownership of securities. The Commission is authorized to solicit the information required by this Form pursuant to sections 16(a) and 23(a) of the Securities Exchange Act of 1934 (15 U.S.C. 78p(a) and 78w(a)); and sections 30(h) and 38 of the Investment Company Act of 1940 (15 U.S.C. 80a-29(h) and 80a-37), and the rules and regulations thereunder. Disclosure of information specified on this Form is mandatory. The information will be used for the primary purpose of disclosing the holdings of directors, officers and beneficial owners of registered companies. Information disclosed will be a matter of public record and available for inspection by members of the public. The Commission can use the information in investigations or litigation involving the federal securities laws or other civil, criminal, or regulatory statutes or provisions, as well as for referral to other governmental authorities and self-regulatory organizations. Failure to disclose required information may result in civil or criminal action against persons involved for violations of the federal securities laws and rules.

[56 FR 7274, Feb. 21, 1991, as amended at 72 FR 45112, Aug. 10, 2007]

EDITORIAL NOTE: For FEDERAL REGISTER citations affecting Form 5, see the List of CFR Sections Affected, which appears in the Finding Aids section of the printed volume and at *www.govinfo.gov*.

Subpart C—Forms for Applications for Registration of Securities on National Securities Exchanges and Similar Matters

§ 249.208 [Reserved]

§ 249.208a Form 8–A, for registration of certain classes of securities pursuant to section 12 (b) or (g) of the Securities Exchange Act of 1934.

(a) Subject to paragraph (b) of this section, this form may be used for registration pursuant to section 12(b) or (g) of the Securities Exchange Act of 1934 of any class of securities of any issuer which:

(1) Is required to file reports pursuant to sections 13 and 15(d) of that Act;

(2) Is concurrently qualifying a Tier 2 offering statement relating to that class of securities using the Form S–1 or Form S–11 disclosure models; or

(3) Pursuant to an order exempting the exchange on which the issuer has securities listed from registration as a national securities exchange.

(b) If the registrant would be required to file an annual report pursuant to section 15(d) of the Act for its last fiscal year, except for the fact that the registration statement on this form will become effective before such report is required to be filed, an annual report for such fiscal year shall nevertheless be filed within the period specified in the appropriate annual report form.

(c) If this form is used for the registration of a class of securities under Section 12(b) of the Act (15 U.S.C. 78l(b)), it shall become effective;

(1) If a class of securities is not concurrently being registered under the Securities Act of 1933 (15 U.S.C. 77a *et seq.*)("Securities Act"), upon the later of receipt by the Commission of certification from the national securities exchange listed on the form or the filing of the Form 8–A with the Commission; or

(2) If a class of securities is concurrently being registered under the Securities Act, upon the later of the Filing of the Form 8–A with the Commission, receipt by the Commission of certification from the national securities exchange listed on the form, or the effectiveness of the Securities Act registration statement relating to the class of securities.

(d) If this form is used for the registration of a class of securities under Section 12(g) of the Act (15 U.S.C. 78l(g)), it shall become effective:

(1) If a class of securities is not concurrently being registered under the Securities Act, upon the filing of the Form 8–A with the Commission; or

(2) If a class of securities is concurrently being registered under the Securities Act, upon the later of the filing of the Form 8–A with the Commission or the effectiveness of the Securities registration statement relating to the class of securities.

(e) Notwithstanding the foregoing in paragraphs (c) and (d) of this section, if the form is used for registration of a class of securities being offered under Regulation A, it shall become effective:

(1) For the registration of a class of securities under Section 12(b), upon the latest of the filing of the form with the Commission, the qualification of the Regulation A offering statement or the receipt by the Commission of certification from the national securities exchange listed on the form; or

(2) For the registration of a class of securities under Section 12(g), upon the later of the filing of the form and qualification of that Regulation A offering statement.

[43 FR 21663, May 19, 1978]

EDITORIAL NOTE: For FEDERAL REGISTER citations affecting Form 8–A, see the List of CFR Sections Affected, which appears in the Finding Aids section of the printed volume and at *www.govinfo.gov.*

§§ 249.208b–249.208c [Reserved]

EDITORIAL NOTE: Amended Form 8–A replaces former Form 8–C; see § 249.208a of this chapter.

§ 249.210 Form 10, general form for registration of securities pursuant to section 12(b) or (g) of the Securities Exchange Act of 1934.

This form shall be used for registration pursuant to section 12 (b) or (g) of the Securities Exchange Act of 1934 of

Securities and Exchange Commission § 249.240f

classes of securities of issuers for which no other form is prescribed.

(Secs. 7, 10, 19(a), 48 Stat. 78, 81, 85; secs. 205, 209, 48 Stat. 906, 908; sec. 8, 68 Stat. 685; 15 U.S.C. 77g, 77j, 77s(a); secs. 12, 13, 14, 15(d), 23, 48 Stat. 892, 894, 895, 901; sec. 203(a), 49 Stat. 704; secs. 1, 3, 8, 49 Stat. 1375, 1377, 1379; sec. 202, 68 Stat. 686; secs. 3, 4, 5, 6, 10, 78 Stat. 565–568, 569, 570–574, 88a; secs. 1, 2, 3, 82 Stat. 454, 455; secs.1, 2, 3–5, 28(c), 84 Stat. 1435, 1479; sec. 105(b), 88 Stat. 1503; secs. 8, 9, 10, 18, 89 Stat. 117, 118, 119, 155 (15 U.S.C. 78*l*, 78m, 78n, 78o(d), 78w))

[33 FR 18995, Dec. 20, 1968]

EDITORIAL NOTE: For FEDERAL REGISTER citations affecting Form 10 see the List of CFR Sections Affected, which appears in the Finding Aids section of the printed volume and at *www.govinfo.gov*.

§ 249.210b [Reserved]

§ 249.218 Form 18, for foreign governments and political subdivisions thereof.

This form shall be used for the registration of securities of any foreign government or political subdivision thereof.

[47 FR 54781, Dec. 6, 1982]

EDITORIAL NOTE: For FEDERAL REGISTER citations affecting Form 18, see the List of CFR Sections Affected, which appears in the Finding Aids section of the printed volume and at *www.govinfo.gov*.

§ 249.220f Form 20-F, registration of securities of foreign private issuers pursuant to section 12(b) or (g), annual and transition reports pursuant to sections 13 and 15(d), and shell company reports required under Rule 13a-19 or 15d-19 (§ 240.13a-19 or § 240.15d-19 of this chapter).

(a) Any foreign private issuer, other than an asset-backed issuer (as defined in § 229.1101 of this chapter), may use this form as a registration statement under section 12 (15 U.S.C. 78l) of the Securities Exchange Act of 1934 (the "Exchange Act") (15 U.S.C. 78a *et seq.*), as an annual or transition report filed under section 13(a) or 15(d) of the Exchange Act (15 U.S.C. 78m(a) or 78o(d)), or as a shell company report required under Rule 13a-19 or Rule 15d-19 under the Exchange Act (§ 240.13a-19 or 240.15d-19 of this chapter).

(b) An annual report on this form shall be filed within six months after the end of the fiscal year covered by such report.

(c) A transition report on this form shall be filed in accordance with the requirements set forth in § 240.13a-10 or § 240.15d-10 applicable when the issuer changes its fiscal year end.

[47 FR 54781, Dec. 6, 1982, as amended at 70 FR 1625, Jan. 7, 2005; 70 FR 42248, July 21, 2005]

EDITORIAL NOTE: For FEDERAL REGISTER citations affecting Form 20-F, see the List of CFR Sections Affected, which appears in the Finding Aids section of the printed volume and at *www.govinfo.gov*.

§ 249.240f Form 40-F, for registration of securities of certain Canadian issuers pursuant to section 12(b) or (g) and for reports pursuant to section 15(d) and Rule 15d-4 (§ 240.15d-4 of this chapter).

(a) Form 40-F may be used to file reports with the Commission pursuant to section 15(d) of the Securities Exchange Act of 1934 (the "Exchange Act") and Rule 15d-4 (17 CFR 240.15d-4) thereunder by registrants that are subject to the reporting requirements of that section solely by reason of their having filed a registration statement on Form F-7, F-8, F-10 or F-80 under the Securities Act of 1933 (the "Securities Act").

NOTE TO PARAGRAPH (a): No reporting obligation arises under section 15(d) of the Securities Act from the registration of securities on Form F-7, F-8 or F-80 if the issuer, at the time of filing such Form, is exempt from the requirements of section 12(g) of the Exchange Act pursuant to Rule 12g3-2(b). See Rule 12h-4 under the Exchange Act.

(b) Form 40-F may be used to register securities with the Commission pursuant to section 12(b) or 12(g) of the Exchange Act, to file reports with the Commission pursuant to section 13(a) of the Exchange Act and Rule 13a-3 (17 CFR 240.13a-3) thereunder, and to file reports with the Commission pursuant to section 15(d) of the Exchange Act if:

(1) The registrant is incorporated or organized under the laws of Canada or any Canadian province or territory;

(2) The registrant is a foreign private issuer or a crown corporation;

§ 249.240f

(3) The registrant has been subject to the periodic reporting requirements of any securities commission or equivalent regulatory authority in Canada for a period of at least 12 calendar months immediately preceding the filing of this Form and is currently in compliance with such obligations; and

(4) The aggregate market value of the public float of the registrant's outstanding equity shares is $75 million or more.

Instructions

1. For purposes of this Form, "foreign private issuer" shall be construed in accordance with Rule 405 under the Securities Act.

2. For purposes of this Form, the term "crown corporation" shall mean a corporation all of whose common shares or comparable equity is owned directly or indirectly by the Government of Canada or a Province or Territory of Canada.

3. For purposes of this Form, the "public float" of specified securities shall mean only such securities held by persons other than affiliates of the issuer.

4. For the purposes of this Form, an "affiliate" of a person is anyone who beneficially owns directly or indirectly, or exercises control or direction over, more than 10 percent of the outstanding equity shares of such person. The determination of a person's affiliates shall be made as of the end of such person's most recently completed fiscal year.

5. For purposes of this Form, "equity shares" shall mean common shares, non-voting equity shares and subordinate or restricted voting equity shares, but shall not include preferred shares.

6. For purposes of this Form, the market value of outstanding equity shares (whether or not held by affiliates) shall be computed by use of the price at which the shares were last sold, or the average of the bid and asked prices of such shares, in the principal market for such shares as of a date within 60 days prior to the date of filing. If there is no market for any of such securities, the book value of such securities computed as of the latest practicable date prior to the filing of this Form shall be used for purposes of calculating the market value, unless the issuer of such securities is in bankruptcy or receivership or has an accumulated capital deficit, in which case one-third of the principal amount, par value or stated value of such securities shall be used.

(c) If the registrant is a successor registrant subsisting after a business combination, it shall be deemed to meet the 12-month reporting requirement of paragraph (b)(3) of this section if:

(1) The time the successor registrant has been subject to the continuous disclosure requirements of any securities commission or equivalent regulatory authority in Canada, when added separately to the time each predecessor had been subject to such requirements at the time of the business combination, in each case equals at least 12 calendar months, *provided, however,* that any predecessor need not be considered for purposes of the reporting history calculation if the reporting histories of predecessors whose assets and gross revenues, respectively, would contribute at least 80 percent of the total assets and gross revenues from continuing operations of the successor registrant, as measured based on pro forma combination of such participating companies' most recently completed fiscal years immediately prior to the business combination, when combined with the reporting history of the successor registrant in each case satisfy such 12-month reporting requirement; and

(2) The successor registrant has been subject to such continuous disclosure requirements since the business combination, and is currently in compliance with its obligations thereunder.

(d) This Form shall not be used if the registrant is an investment company registered or required to be registered under the Investment Company Act of 1940.

(e) Registrants registering securities on this Form, and registrants filing annual reports on this Form who have not previously filed a Form F-X (§ 249.250 of this chapter) in connection with the class of securities in relation to which the obligation to file this report arises, shall file a Form F-X with the Commission together with this Form.

[56 FR 30075, July 1, 1991]

EDITORIAL NOTE: For FEDERAL REGISTER citations affecting Form 40-F, see the List of CFR Sections Affected, which appears in the Finding Aids section of the printed volume and at *www.govinfo.gov*.

Securities and Exchange Commission § 249.308a

§ 249.250 Form F-X, for appointment of agent for service of process by issuers registering securities on Form F-8, F-9, F-10 or F-80 (§ 239.38, 239.39, 239.40 or 239.41 of this chapter), or registering securities or filing periodic reports on Form 40-F (§ 249.240f of this chapter), or by any issuer or other non-U.S. person filing tender offer documents on Schedule 13E-4F, 14D-1F or 14D-9F (§ 240.13e-102, 240.14d-102 or 240.14d-103 of this chapter), or by any non-U.S. person acting as trustee with respect to securities registered on Form F-7 (§ 249.37 of this chapter), F-8, F-9, F-10 or F-80.

Form F-X shall be filed with the Commission:

(a) By any issuer registering securities on Form F-8, F-9, F-10 or F-80 under the Securities Act of 1933;

(b) By any issuer registering securities on Form 40-F under the Securities Exchange Act of 1934;

(c) By any issuer filing a periodic report on Form 40-F, if it has not previously filed a Form F-X in connection with the class of securities in relation to which the obligation to file a report on Form 40-F arises;

(d) By any issuer or other non-U.S. person filing tender offer documents on Schedule 13E-4F, 14D-1F or 14D-9F; and

(e) By any non-U.S. person acting as trustee with respect to securities registered on Form F-7, F-8, F-9, F-10 or F-80.

[56 FR 30076, July 1, 1991]

EDITORIAL NOTE: For FEDERAL REGISTER citations affecting Form F-X, see the List of CFR Sections Affected, which appears in the Finding Aids section of the printed volume and at www.govinfo.gov.

Subpart D—Forms for Annual and Other Reports of Issuers Required Under Sections 13 and 15(d) of the Securities Exchange Act of 1934

EFFECTIVE DATE NOTE: At 87 FR 78808, Dec. 22, 2022, the heading to Subpart D of part 249 was revised, effective July 1, 2024. For the convenience of the user, the revised text is set forth as follows:

Subpart D—Forms for Annual and Other Reports of Issuers and Other Persons Required Under Sections 13, 14A, and 15(d) of the Securities Exchange Act of 1934

§ 249.306 Form 6-K, report of foreign issuer pursuant to Rules 13a-16 (§ 240.13a-16 of this chapter) and 15d-16 (§ 240.15d-16 of this chapter) under the Securities Exchange Act of 1934.

This form shall be used by foreign issuers which are required to furnish reports pursuant to Rule 13a-16 (§ 240.13a-16 of this chapter) or 15d-16 (§ 240.15d-16 of this chapter) under the Securities Exchange Act of 1934.

[33 FR 18995, Dec. 20, 1968]

EDITORIAL NOTE: For FEDERAL REGISTER citations affecting Form 6-K, see the List of CFR Sections Affected, which appears in the Finding Aids section of the printed volume and at www.govinfo.gov.

§ 249.308 Form 8-K, for current reports.

This form shall be used for the current reports required by Rule 13a-11 or Rule 15d-11 (§ 240.13a-11 or § 240.15d-11 of this chapter) and for reports of nonpublic information required to be disclosed by Regulation FD (§§ 243.100 and 243.101 of this chapter).

[33 FR 18995, Dec. 20, 1968]

EDITORIAL NOTE: For FEDERAL REGISTER citations affecting Form 8-K, see the List of CFR Sections Affected, which appears in the Finding Aids section of the printed volume and at www.govinfo.gov.

§ 249.308a Form 10-Q, for quarterly and transition reports under sections 13 or 15(d) of the Securities Exchange Act of 1934.

(a) Form 10-Q shall be used for quarterly reports under section 13 or 15(d) of the Securities Exchange Act of 1934 (15 U.S.C. 78m or 78o(d)), required to be filed pursuant to § 240.13a-13 or § 240.15d-13 of this chapter. A quarterly report on this form pursuant to § 240.13a-13 or § 240.15d-13 of this chapter shall be filed within the following period after the end of the first three fiscal quarters of each fiscal year, but no quarterly report need be filed for the fourth quarter of any fiscal year:

§ 249.310

(1) 40 days after the end of the fiscal quarter for large accelerated filers and accelerated filers (as defined in § 240.12b–2 of this chapter); and

(2) 45 days after the end of the fiscal quarter for all other registrants.

(b) Form 10–Q also shall be used for transition and quarterly reports filed pursuant to § 240.13a–10 or § 240.15d–10 of this chapter. Such transition or quarterly reports shall be filed in accordance with the requirements set forth in § 240.13a–10 or § 240.15d–10 of this chapter applicable when the registrant changes its fiscal year end.

[67 FR 58506, Sept. 16, 2002, as amended at 69 FR 68236, Nov. 23, 2004; 70 FR 76642, Dec. 27, 2005]

EDITORIAL NOTE: For FEDERAL REGISTER citations affecting Form 10–Q, see the List of CFR Sections Affected, which appears in the Finding Aids section of the printed volume and at www.govinfo.gov.

§ 249.310 Form 10–K, for annual and transition reports pursuant to sections 13 or 15(d) of the Securities Exchange Act of 1934.

(a) This form shall be used for annual reports pursuant to sections 13 or 15(d) of the Securities Exchange Act of 1934 (15 U.S.C. 78m or 78o(d)) for which no other form is prescribed. This form also shall be used for transition reports filed pursuant to section 13 or 15(d) of the Securities Exchange Act of 1934.

(b) Annual reports on this form shall be filed within the following period:

(1) 60 days after the end of the fiscal year covered by the report (75 days for fiscal years ending before December 15, 2006) for large accelerated filers (as defined in § 240.12b–2 of this chapter);

(2) 75 days after the end of the fiscal year covered by the report for accelerated filers (as defined in § 240.12b–2 of this chapter); and

(3) 90 days after the end of the fiscal year covered by the report for all other registrants.

(c) Transition reports on this form shall be filed in accordance with the requirements set forth in § 240.13a–10 or § 240.15d–10 of this chapter applicable when the registrant changes its fiscal year end.

(d) Notwithstanding paragraphs (b) and (c) of this section, all schedules required by Article 12 of Regulation S–X (§§ 210.12–01–210.12–29 of this chapter) may, at the option of the registrant, be filed as an amendment to the report not later than 30 days after the applicable due date of the report.

[70 FR 76642, Dec. 27, 2005]

EDITORIAL NOTE: For FEDERAL REGISTER citations affecting Form 10–K, see the List of CFR Sections Affected, which appears in the Finding Aids section of the printed volume and at www.govinfo.gov.

§§ 249.310b–249.310c [Reserved]

§ 249.311 Form 11–K, for annual reports of employee stock purchase, savings and similar plans pursuant to section 15(d) of the Securities Exchange Act of 1934.

This form shall be used for annual reports pursuant to section 15(d) of the Securities Exchange Act of 1934 with respect to employee stock purchase, savings and similar plans, interests in which constitute securities which have been registered under the Securities Act of 1933. Such a report is required to be filed even though the issuer of the securities offered to employees pursuant to the plan also files annual reports pursuant to section 13 or 15(d) of the Securities Exchange Act of 1934. However, attention is directed to Rule 15d–21 (§ 240.15d–21 of this chapter) which provides that in certain cases the information required by this form may be furnished with respect to the plan as a part of the annual report of such issuer. Reports on this form shall be filed within 90 days after the end of the fiscal year of the plan, or, in the case of a plan subject to the Employee Retirement Income Security Act of 1974, within 180 days after the plan's fiscal year end.

[43 FR 21663, May 19, 1978]

EDITORIAL NOTE: For FEDERAL REGISTER citations affecting Form 11–K, see the List of CFR Sections Affected, which appears in the Finding Aids section of the printed volume and at www.govinfo.gov.

§ 249.312 Form 10–D, periodic distribution reports by asset-backed issuers.

This form shall be used by asset-backed issuers to file periodic distribution reports pursuant to § 240.13a–17 or

Securities and Exchange Commission § 249.323

§ 240.15d–17 of this chapter. A distribution report on this form pursuant to § 240.13a–17 or § 240.15d–17 of this chapter shall be filed within 15 days after each required distribution date on the asset-backed securities, as specified in the governing documents for such securities.

[70 FR 1626, Jan. 7, 2005]

EDITORIAL NOTE: For FEDERAL REGISTER citations affecting Form 10–D, see the List of CFR Sections Affected, which appears in the Finding Aids section of the printed volume and at www.govinfo.gov.

§ 249.318 Form 18–K, annual report for foreign governments and political subdivisions thereof.

This form shall be used for the annual reports of foreign governments or political subdivisions thereof.

[47 FR 54790, Dec. 6, 1982]

EDITORIAL NOTE: For FEDERAL REGISTER citations affecting Form 18–K, see the List of CFR Sections Affected, which appears in the Finding Aids section of the printed volume and at www.govinfo.gov.

§ 249.322 Form 12b–25—Notification of late filing.

(a) This form shall be filed pursuant to § 240.12b–25 of this chapter by issuers who are unable to file timely all or any required portion of an annual or transition report on Form 10–K and Form 10–KSB, 20–F, or 11–K (§ 249.310, 249.310b, 249.220f or 249.311), a quarterly or transition report on Form 10–Q and Form 10–QSB (§§ 249.308a and 249.308b), or a distribution report on Form 10–D (§ 249.312) pursuant to section 13 or 15(d) of the Act (15 U.S.C. 78m or 78o(d)) or an annual report on Form N–CEN (§§ 249.330; 274.101) or a semi-annual or annual report on Form N–CSR (§§ 249.331; 274.128) pursuant to section 13 or 15(d) of the Act or section 30 of the Investment Company Act of 1940 (15 U.S.C. 80a–29). The filing shall consist of a signed original and three conformed copies, and shall be filed with the Commission at Washington, DC 20549, no later than one business day after the due date for the periodic report in question. Copies of this form may be obtained from "Publications," Securities and Exchange Commission, 100 F Street, NE., Washington, DC 20549 and at our Web site at http://www.sec.gov.

(b) This form shall not be used by electronic filers unable to timely file a report solely due to electronic difficulties. Filers unable to submit a report within the time period prescribed due to electronic difficulties should comply with either Rule 201 or Rule 202 of Regulation S–T (§ 232.201 or § 232.202 of this chapter), or apply for an adjustment in filing date pursuant to Rule 13(b) of Regulation S–T (§ 232.13(b) of this chapter).

(c) *Interactive data submissions.* This form shall not be used by electronic filers with respect to the submission or posting of an Interactive Data File (§ 232.11 of this chapter). Electronic filers unable to submit or post an Interactive Data File within the time period prescribed should comply with either Rule 201 or 202 of Regulation S–T (§§ 232.201 and 232.202 of this chapter).

[50 FR 1449, Jan. 11, 1985, as amended at 70 FR 1630, Jan. 7, 2005; 73 FR 32228, June 5, 2008; 74 FR 6821, Feb. 10, 2009; 81 FR 82020, June 1, 2018]

EDITORIAL NOTE: For FEDERAL REGISTER citations affecting Form 12b–25, see the List of CFR Sections Affected, which appears in the Finding Aids section of the printed volume and at www.govinfo.gov.

§ 249.323 Form 15, certification of termination of registration of a class of security under section 12(g) or notice of suspension of duty to file reports pursuant to sections 13 and 15(d) of the Act.

(a) This form shall be filed by each issuer to certify that the number of holders of record of a class of security registered under section 12(g) of the Act is reduced to less than 300 persons, or that the number of holders of record of a class of security registered under section 12(g) of the Act is reduced to less than 500 persons and the total assets of the issuer have not exceeded $10 million on the last day of each of the issuer's most recent three fiscal years. Registration terminates 90 days after the filing of the certificate or within such shorter time as the Commission may direct.

(b) This form shall also be filed by each issuer required to file reports pursuant to section 15(d) of the Act, as a notification that the duty to file such

§ 249.324

reports is suspended pursuant to section 15(d) of the Act because all securities of each class of such issuer registered under the Securities Act of 1933 are held of record by less than 300 persons at the beginning of its fiscal year, or otherwise pursuant to the provisions of Rule 12h–3 (17 CFR 240.12h–3).

(Secs. 12(g)(4), 12(h), 13(a), 15(d), 23(a), 48 Stat. 892, 894, 895, 901; sec. 203(a), 49 Stat. 704; secs. 3, 8, 49 Stat. 1377, 1379; secs. 3, 4, 6, 78 Stat. 565–568, 569, 570–574; sec. 18, 89 Stat. 155; sec. 204, 91 Stat. 1500; 15 U.S.C. 78*l*(g)(4), 78*l*(h), 78m(a), 78o(d), 78w(a))

[49 FR 12690, Mar. 30, 1984, as amended at 51 FR 25362, July 14, 1986; 61 FR 21356, May 9, 1996]

EDITORIAL NOTE: For FEDERAL REGISTER citations affecting Form 15, see the List of CFR Sections Affected, which appears in the Finding Aids section of the printed volume and at *www.govinfo.gov*.

§ 249.324 Form 15F, certification by a foreign private issuer regarding the termination of registration of a class of securities under section 12(g) or the duty to file reports under section 13(a) or section 15(d).

This form shall be filed by a foreign private issuer to disclose and certify the information on the basis of which it meets the requirements specified in Rule 12h–6 (§ 240.12h–6 of this chapter) to terminate the registration of a class of securities under section 12(g) of the Act (15 U.S.C. 78*l*(g)) or the duty to file reports under section 13(a) of the Act (15 U.S.C. 78m(a)) or section 15(d) of the Act (15 U.S.C. 78o(d)). In each instance, unless the Commission objects, termination occurs 90 days, or such shorter time as the Commission may direct, after the filing of Form 15F.

[72 FR 16958, Apr. 5, 2007]

EDITORIAL NOTE: For FEDERAL REGISTER citations affecting Form 15F, see the List of CFR Sections Affected, which appears in the Finding Aids section of the printed volume and at *www.govinfo.gov*.

§ 249.325 Form 13F, report of institutional investment manager pursuant to section 13(f) of the Securities Exchange Act of 1934.

This form shall be used by institutional investment managers which are required to furnish reports pursuant to section 13(f) of the Securities Exchange Act of 1934. (15 U.S.C. 78m(f)) and Rule 13f–1 thereunder (§ 240.13f–1 of this chapter).

[43 FR 26705, June 22, 1978]

EDITORIAL NOTE: For FEDERAL REGISTER citations affecting Form 13F, see the List of CFR Sections Affected, which appears in the Finding Aids section of the printed volume and at *www.govinfo.gov*.

§ 249.326 Form N–PX, annual report of proxy voting record.

This form shall be used by institutional investment managers to file an annual report pursuant to § 240.14Ad–1 of this chapter containing the manager's proxy voting record.

[87 FR 78808, Dec. 22, 2022]

EFFECTIVE DATE NOTE: At 87 FR 78808, Dec. 22, 2022, § 249.326 was added, effective July 1, 2024.

§ 249.327 Form 13H, Information required on large traders pursuant to Section 13(h) of the Securities Exchange Act of 1934 and rules thereunder.

This form shall be used by persons that are large traders required to furnish identifying information to the Commission pursuant to Section 13(h)(1) of the Securities Exchange Act of 1934 [15 U.S.C. 78m(h)(1)] and § 240.13h–1(b) of this chapter.

[76 FR 47004, Aug. 3, 2011]

EDITORIAL NOTE: For FEDERAL REGISTER citations affecting Form 13H, see the List of CFR Sections Affected, which appears in the Finding Aids section of the printed volume and at *www.govinfo.gov*.

§ 249.328T Form 17–H, Risk assessment report for brokers and dealers pursuant to section 17(h) of the Securities Exchange Act of 1934 and rules thereunder.

This form shall be used by brokers and dealers in reporting information to the Commission concerning certain of their associated persons pursuant to section 17(h) of the Securities Exchange Act of 1934 [15 U.S.C. 78q(h)] and Rules 17h–1T and 17h–2T thereunder [§§ 240.17h–1T and 240.17h–2T of this chapter].

[57 FR 32171, July 21, 1992]

EDITORIAL NOTE: For FEDERAL REGISTER citations affecting Form 17–H, see the List of CFR Sections Affected, which appears in the

Securities and Exchange Commission § 249.447

Finding Aids section of the printed volume and at *www.govinfo.gov*.

§ 249.330 Form N–CEN, annual report of registered investment companies.

This form shall be used by registered unit investment trusts and small business investment companies for annual reports to be filed pursuant to § 270.30a–1 of this chapter in satisfaction of the requirement of section 30(a) of the Investment Company Act of 1940 (15 U.S.C. 80a–29(a)) that every registered investment company must file annually with the Commission such information, documents, and reports as investment companies having securities registered on a national securities exchange are required to file annually pursuant to section 13(a) of the Securities Exchange Act of 1934 (15 U.S.C. 78m(a)) and the rules and regulations thereunder.

NOTE: The text of Form N–CEN will not appear in the *Code of Federal Regulations*.

[81 FR 82020, Nov. 18, 2016]

EDITORIAL NOTE: For FEDERAL REGISTER citations affecting Form N–CEN, see the List of CFR Sections Affected, which appears in the Finding Aids section of the printed volume and at *www.govinfo.gov*.

§ 249.331 Form N–CSR, certified shareholder report.

This form shall be used by registered management investment companies to file reports pursuant to § 270.30b2–1(a) of this chapter not later than 10 days after the transmission to stockholders of any report that is required to be transmitted to stockholders under § 270.30e–1 of this chapter.

[68 FR 5365, Feb. 3, 2003]

EDITORIAL NOTE: For FEDERAL REGISTER citations affecting Form N–CSR, see the List of CFR Sections Affected, which appears in the Finding Aids section of the printed volume and at *www.govinfo.gov*.

§ 249.332 [Reserved]

§ 249.444 Form SE, form for submission of paper format exhibits by electronic filers.

This form shall be used by an electronic filer for the submission of any paper format document relating to an otherwise electronic filing, as provided in Rule 311 of Regulation S–T (§ 232.311 of this chapter).

[58 FR 14686, Mar. 18, 1993]

EDITORIAL NOTE: For FEDERAL REGISTER citations affecting Form SE, see the List of CFR Sections Affected, which appears in the Finding Aids section of the printed volume and at *www.govinfo.gov*.

§ 249.445 [Reserved]

§ 249.446 Form ID, uniform application for access codes to file on EDGAR.

Form ID must be filed by registrants, third party filers, or their agents, , to request the following access codes to permit filing on EDGAR:

(a) Central Index Key (CIK)—uniquely identifies each filer, filing agent, and training agent.

(b) CIK Confirmation Code (CCC)—used in the header of a filing in conjunction with the CIK of the filer to ensure that the filing has been authorized by the filer.

(c) Password (PW)—allows a filer, filing agent or training agent to log on to the EDGAR system, submit filings, and change its CCC.

(d) Password Modification Authorization Code (PMAC)—allows a filer, filing agent or training agent to change its Password.

[69 FR 22710, Apr. 26, 2004, as amended at 86 FR 25805, May 11, 2021]

EDITORIAL NOTE: For FEDERAL REGISTER citations affecting Form ID, see the List of CFR Sections Affected, which appears in the Finding Aids section of the printed volume and at *www.govinfo.gov*.

§ 249.447 Form TH—Notification of reliance on temporary hardship exemption.

Form TH shall be filed by any electronic filer who submits to the Commission, pursuant to a temporary hardship exemption, a document in paper format that otherwise would be required to be submitted electronically, as prescribed by Rule 201(a) of Regulation S–T (§ 232.201(a) of this chapter).

[58 FR 14686, Mar. 18, 1993]

EDITORIAL NOTE: For FEDERAL REGISTER citations affecting Form TH, see the List of CFR Sections Affected, which appears in the Finding Aids section of the printed volume and at *www.govinfo.gov*.

§ 249.480

Subpart E—Forms for Statements Made in Connection With Exempt Tender Offers

SOURCE: 64 FR 61406, Nov. 10, 1999, unless otherwise noted.

§ 249.480 Form CB, tender offer statement in connection with a tender offer for a foreign private issuer.

This form is used to report an issuer tender offer conducted in compliance with § 240.13e-4(h)(8) of this chapter and a third-party tender offer conducted in compliance with § 240.14d-1(c) of this chapter. This report also is used by a subject company pursuant to § 240.14e-2(d) of this chapter.

[64 FR 61406, Nov. 10, 1999]

EDITORIAL NOTE: For FEDERAL REGISTER citations affecting Form CB, see the List of CFR Sections Affected, which appears in the Finding Aids section of the printed volume and at *www.govinfo.gov.*

Subpart F—Forms for Registration of Brokers and Dealers Transacting Business on Over-the-Counter Markets

§ 249.501 Form BD, for application for registration as a broker and dealer or to amend or supplement such an application.

(a) This form shall be used for application for registration as a broker-dealer under the Securities Exchange Act of 1934, or to amend such application.

(b) Interim Form BD shall be used for application for registration as broker-dealer under the Securities Exchange Act of 1934, or to amend such application, only by order of the Commission. In the event broker-dealers are required to comply with their filing obligations on Interim Form BD, the form will be made available at the Commission's Publication Office at (202) 942-4040.

[33 FR 18995, Dec. 20, 1968]

EDITORIAL NOTE: For FEDERAL REGISTER citations affecting Form BD, see the List of CFR Sections Affected, which appears in the Finding Aids section of the printed volume and at *www.govinfo.gov.*

§ 249.501a Form BDW, notice of withdrawal from registration as broker-dealer pursuant to § 240.15b6-1, § 240.15Bc3-1, or § 240.15Cc1-1 of this chapter.

(a) This form shall be used for filing a notice of withdrawal as broker-dealer pursuant to Rule 15b6-1 (§ 240.15b6-1 of this chapter), Rule 15Bc3-1 § 240.15B3-1 of this chapter), or Rule 15Cc1-1 (§ 240.15Cc1-1 of this chapter). Under sections 15(b), 15B, 15C, 17(a), and 23(a) of the Securities Exchange Act of 1934 (17 CFR part 240), and the rules and regulations thereunder, the Commission is authorized to solicit the information required to be supplied by this form from registrants desiring to withdraw their registration as a broker-dealer. Disclosure of the information specified in this form is mandatory prior to processing of applications for withdrawal, except for social security account numbers, disclosure of which is voluntary. The information will be used for the primary purpose of determining whether it is in the public interest to permit a broker-dealer to withdraw his registration. This notice will be made a matter of public record. Therefore, any information, given will be available for inspection by any member of the public. Because of the public nature of the information the Commission can utilize it for a variety of purposes, including referral to other governmental authorities or securities self-regulatory organizations for investigatory purposes or in connection with litigation involving the Federal securities laws and other civil, criminal or regulatory statutes or provisions. Social security account numbers, if furnished, will assist the Commission in identifying registrants and, therefore, in promptly processing applications for withdrawal. Failure to disclose the information requested by Form BDW, except for social security account numbers, may result in the registrant not being permitted to withdraw his registration.

(b) Interim Form BDW shall be used for application for registration as broker-dealer under the Securities Exchange Act of 1934, or to amend such application, only by order of the Commission. In the event broker-dealers are required to comply with their filing

Securities and Exchange Commission § 249.617

obligations on Interim Form BD, the form will be made available at the Commission's Publication Office at (202) 942–4040.

[52 FR 16844, May 6, 1987]

EDITORIAL NOTE: For FEDERAL REGISTER citations affecting Form BDW, see the List of CFR Sections Affected, which appears in the Finding Aids section of the printed volume and at *www.govinfo.gov*.

§ 249.501b Form BD-N for notice registration as a broker-dealer.

This form shall be used for notice of registration as a broker-dealer pursuant to Section 15(b)(11)(A) of the Act (15 U.S.C. 78o(b)(11)(A)) for the limited purpose of trading security futures products, or to amend such notice.

[66 FR 45147, Aug. 27, 2001]

EDITORIAL NOTE: For FEDERAL REGISTER citations affecting Form BD–N, see the List of CFR Sections Affected, which appears in the Finding Aids section of the printed volume and at *www.govinfo.gov*.

§ 249.507 Form 7–M, consent to service of process by an individual nonresident broker-dealer.

This form shall be filed pursuant to Rule 15b1–5 (§ 240.15b1–5 of this chapter) by each individual nonresident broker-dealer registered or applying for registration pursuant to section 15 of the Act.

[33 FR 18995, Dec. 20, 1968]

EDITORIAL NOTE: For FEDERAL REGISTER citations affecting Form 7–M, see the List of CFR Sections Affected, which appears in the Finding Aids section of the printed volume and at *www.govinfo.gov*.

§ 249.508 Form 8–M, consent to service of process by a corporation which is a nonresident broker-dealer.

This form shall be filed pursuant to Rule 15b1–5 (§ 240.15b1–5 of this chapter) by each corporate nonresident broker-dealer registered or applying for registration pursuant to section 15 of the Act.

[33 FR 18995, Dec. 20, 1968]

EDITORIAL NOTE: For FEDERAL REGISTER citations affecting Form 8–M, see the List of CFR Sections Affected, which appears in the Finding Aids section of the printed volume and at *www.govinfo.gov*.

§ 249.509 Form 9–M, consent to service of process by a partnership nonresident broker-dealer.

This form shall be filed pursuant to Rule 15b1–5 (§ 240.15b1–5 of this chapter) by each partnership nonresident broker-dealer registered or applying for registration pursuant to section 15 of the Act.

[33 FR 18995, Dec. 20, 1968]

EDITORIAL NOTE: For FEDERAL REGISTER citations affecting Form 9–M, see the List of CFR Sections Affected, which appears in the Finding Aids section of the printed volume and at *www.govinfo.gov*.

§ 249.510 Form 10–M, consent to service of process by a nonresident general partner of a broker-dealer firm.

This form shall be filed pursuant to Rule 15b1–5 (§ 240.15b1–5 of this chapter) by each nonresident general partner of a broker-dealer firm registered or applying for registration pursuant to section 15 of the Act.

[33 FR 18995, Dec. 20, 1968]

EDITORIAL NOTE: For FEDERAL REGISTER citations affecting Form 10–M, see the List of CFR Sections Affected, which appears in the Finding Aids section of the printed volume and at *www.govinfo.gov*.

Subpart G—Forms for Reports To Be Made by Certain Exchange Members, Brokers, Dealers, Security-Based Swap Dealers, and Major Security-Based Swap Participants

§ 249.617 Form X–17A–5, information required of certain brokers, dealers, security-based swap dealers, and major security-based swap participants pursuant to sections 15F and 17 of the Securities Exchange Act of 1934 and §§ 240.17a–5, 240.17a–10, 240.17a–11, 240.17a–12, and 240.18a–79 of this chapter, as applicable.

Appropriate parts of Form X–17A–5, as applicable, shall be used by brokers, dealers, security-based swap dealers, and major security-based swap participants required to file reports under §§ 240.17a–5, 240.17a–10, 240.17a–11, 240.17a–12, and 240.18a–7 of this chapter, as applicable.

[84 FR 68669, Dec. 16, 2019]

§ 249.618

EDITORIAL NOTE: For FEDERAL REGISTER citations affecting Form X–17A–5, see the List of CFR Sections Affected, which appears in the Finding Aids section of the printed volume and at *www.govinfo.gov*.

§ 249.618 Form BD-Y2K, information required of broker-dealers pursuant to section 17 of the Securities Exchange Act of 1934 and § 240.17a–5 of this chapter.

This form shall be used by every broker-dealer required to file reports under § 240.17a–5(e) of this chapter.

[63 FR 37674, July 13, 1998]

EDITORIAL NOTE: For FEDERAL REGISTER citations affecting Form BD-Y2K, see the List of CFR Sections Affected, which appears in the Finding Aids section of the printed volume and at *www.govinfo.gov*.

§ 249.619 Form TA-Y2K, information required of transfer agents pursuant to section 17 of the Securities Exchange Act of 1934 and § 240.17Ad–18 of this chapter.

This form shall be used by every registered transfer agent required to file reports under § 240.17Ad–18 of this chapter.

[63 FR 37694, July 13, 1998]

EDITORIAL NOTE: For FEDERAL REGISTER citations affecting Form TA-Y2K, see the List of CFR Sections Affected, which appears in the Finding Aids section of the printed volume and at *www.govinfo.gov*.

§§ 249.620–249.634 [Reserved]

§ 249.635 Form X–17A–19, report by national securities exchanges and registered national securities associations of changes in the membership status of any of their members.

This form shall be completed and filed by each national securities exchange or registered national securities association as required by § 240.17a–19 of this chapter within 5 business days of the occurrence of the initiation of the membership of any person or the suspension or termination of the membership of any of its members.

[45 FR 39841, June 12, 1980]

EDITORIAL NOTE: For FEDERAL REGISTER citations affecting Form X–17A–19, see the List of CFR Sections Affected, which appears in the Finding Aids section of the printed volume and at *www.govinfo.gov*.

§ 249.636 [Reserved]

§ 249.637 Form ATS, information required of alternative trading systems pursuant to § 242.301(b)(2) of this chapter.

This form shall be used by every alternative trading system to file required notices, reports and amendments under § 242.301(b)(2) of this chapter.

[63 FR 70933, Dec. 22, 1998]

EDITORIAL NOTE: For FEDERAL REGISTER citations affecting Form ATS, see the List of CFR Sections Affected, which appears in the Finding Aids section of the printed volume and at *www.govinfo.gov*.

§ 249.638 Form ATS-R, information required of alternative trading systems pursuant to § 242.301(b)(8) of this chapter.

This form shall be used by every alternative trading system to file required reports under § 242.301(b)(8) of this chapter.

[63 FR 70943, Dec. 22, 1998]

EDITORIAL NOTE: For FEDERAL REGISTER citations affecting Form ATS-R, see the List of CFR Sections Affected, which appears in the Finding Aids section of the printed volume and at *www.govinfo.gov*.

§ 249.639 Form custody.

This form shall be used for reports of information required by § 240.17a–5 of this chapter.

EDITORIAL NOTE: For FEDERAL REGISTER citations affecting Form Custody, see the List of CFR Sections Affected, which appears in the Finding Aids section of the printed volume and at *www.govinfo.gov*.

[78 FR 51994, Aug. 21, 2013]

§ 249.640 Form ATS–N, information required of NMS Stock ATSs pursuant to § 242.304(a) of this chapter.

This form shall be used by every NMS Stock ATS to file required reports under § 242.304(a) of this chapter.

[83 FR 38913, Aug. 7, 2018]

EDITORIAL NOTE: For FEDERAL REGISTER citations affecting Form ATS–N, see the List of CFR Sections Affected, which appears in the Finding Aids section of the printed volume and at *www.govinfo.gov*.

Securities and Exchange Commission

§ 249.819

§ 249.641 Form CRS, Relationship Summary for Brokers and Dealers Providing Services to Retail Investors, pursuant to § 240.17a–14 of this chapter.

This form shall be prepared and filed by brokers and dealers registered with the Securities and Exchange Commission pursuant to Section 15 of the Act that offer services to a retail investor pursuant to § 240.17a–14 of this chapter.

[84 FR 33630, July 12, 2019]

EDITORIAL NOTE: For FEDERAL REGISTER citations affecting Form CRS, see the List of CFR Sections Affected, which appears in the Finding Aids section of the printed volume and at www.govinfo.gov.

Subpart H—Forms For Reports as to Stabilization

§ 249.709 [Reserved]

Subpart I—Forms for Self-Regulatory Organization Rule Changes and Forms for Registration of and Reporting by National Securities Associations and Affiliated Securities Associations

§ 249.801 Form X–15AA–1, for application for registration as a national securities association or affiliated securities association.

This form shall be filed as an application for registration as a national securities association or as an affiliated securities association pursuant to Rule 15Aa–1 (§ 240.15Aa–1 of this chapter).

[33 FR 18995, Dec. 20, 1968]

EDITORIAL NOTE: For FEDERAL REGISTER citations affecting Form X–15AA–1, see the List of CFR Sections Affected, which appears in the Finding Aids section of the printed volume and at www.govinfo.gov.

§ 249.802 Form X–15AJ–1, for amendatory and/or supplementary statements to registration statement of a national securities association or an affiliated securities association.

This form shall be filed pursuant to Rule 15Aj–1 (§ 240.15Aj–1 of this chapter) as amendatory and/or supplementary statements to registration statement of a national securities association or an affiliated securities association.

[33 FR 18995, Dec. 20, 1968]

EDITORIAL NOTE: For FEDERAL REGISTER citations affecting Form X–15AJ–1, see the List of CFR Sections Affected, which appears in the Finding Aids section of the printed volume and at www.govinfo.gov.

§ 249.803 Form X–15AJ–2, for annual consolidated supplement of a national securities association or an affiliated securities association.

This form shall be filed pursuant to Rule 15Aj–1 (§ 240.15Aj–1 of this chapter) for the annual consolidated supplement to registration statement of a national securities association or an affiliated securities association.

[33 FR 18995, Dec. 20, 1968]

EDITORIAL NOTE: For FEDERAL REGISTER citations affecting Form X–15AJ–2, see the List of CFR Sections Affected, which appears in the Finding Aids section of the printed volume and at www.govinfo.gov.

§ 249.819 Form 19b–4, for electronic filings with respect to proposed rule changes, advance notices and security-based swap submissions by all self-regulatory organizations.

This form shall be used by all self-regulatory organizations, as defined in Section 3(a)(26) of the Securities Exchange Act of 1934 (15 U.S.C. 78c(a)(26)), to file electronically proposed rule changes with the Commission pursuant to Section 19(b) of the Act (15 U.S.C. 78s(b)) and § 240.19b–4 of this chapter, advance notices with the Commission pursuant to Section 806(e) of the Payment, Clearing and Settlement Supervision Act (12 U.S.C. 5465(e)) and § 240.19b–4 of this chapter and security-based swap submissions with the Commission pursuant to Section 3C(b)(2) of the Act (15 U.S.C. 78c–3(b)(2)) and § 240.19b–4 of this chapter.

[77 FR 41650, July 13, 2012]

EDITORIAL NOTE: Copies of Form 19b–4 have been filed with the Office of the Federal Register and will be forwarded to the self-regulatory organizations. Copies may be requested from the Commission.

§ 249.820

§ 249.820 Form 19b–4(e) for the listing and trading of new derivative securities products by self-regulatory organizations that are not deemed proposed rule changes pursuant to Rule 19b–4(e)(§ 240.19b–4(e)).

This form shall be used by all self-regulatory organizations, as defined in section 3(a)(26) of the Act, to notify the Commission of a self-regulatory organization's listing and trading of a new derivative securities product that is not deemed a proposed rule change, pursuant to Rule 19b–4(e) under the Act (17 CFR 240.19b–4(e)).

[63 FR 70967, Dec. 22, 1998]

EDITORIAL NOTE: For FEDERAL REGISTER citations affecting Form 19b–4(e), see the List of CFR Sections Affected, which appears in the Finding Aids section of the printed volume and at *www.govinfo.gov*.

§ 249.821 Form PILOT, information required of self-regulatory organizations operating pilot trading systems pursuant to § 240.19b–5 of this chapter.

This form shall be used by all self-regulatory organizations, as defined in section 3(a)(26) of the Act, (15 U.S.C 78c(a)(26)), to file required information and reports with regard to pilot trading systems pursuant to § 240.19b–5 of this chapter.

[63 FR 70946, Dec. 22, 1998]

EDITORIAL NOTE: For FEDERAL REGISTER citations affecting Form PILOT, see the List of CFR Sections Affected, which appears in the Finding Aids section of the printed volume and at *www.govinfo.gov*.

§ 249.822 Form 19b–7, for electronic filing with respect to proposed rule changes by self-regulatory organizations under Section 19(b)(7)(A) of the Securities Exchange Act of 1934.

This form shall be used by self-regulatory organizations, as defined in section 3(a)(25) of the Securities Exchange Act of 1934 (15 U.S.C. 78c(a)(25)), to file electronically proposed rule changes with the Commission pursuant to section 19(b)(7) of the Act (15 U.S.C. 78s(b)(7)) and § 240.19b–7 of this chapter.

[73 FR 16190, Mar. 27, 2008]

Subpart J [Reserved]

Subpart K—Form for Registration of, and Reporting by Securities Information Processors

§ 249.1001 Form SIP, for application for registration as a securities information processor or to amend such an application or registration.

This form shall be used for application for registration as a securities information processor, pursuant to section 11A(b) of the Securities Exchange Act of 1934 (15 U.S.C. 78k–1(b)) and § 242.609 of this chapter, or to amend such an application or registration.

[70 FR 37632, June 29, 2005]

EDITORIAL NOTE: For FEDERAL REGISTER citations affecting Form SIP, see the List of CFR Sections Affected, which appears in the Finding Aids section of the printed volume and at *www.govinfo.gov*.

§ 249.1002 Form CC, for application for registration as a competing consolidator or to amend such an application or registration.

This form shall be used for application for registration as a competing consolidator, pursuant to section 11A of the Securities Exchange Act of 1934 (15 U.S.C. 78k–1) and § 242.614 of this chapter, or to amend such an application or registration.

[86 FR 18814, Apr. 9, 2021]

Subpart L—Forms for Registration of Municipal Securities Dealers

§ 249.1100 Form MSD, application for registration as a municipal securities dealer pursuant to rule 15Ba2–1 under the Securities Exchange Act of 1934 or amendment to such application.

This Form is to be used by a bank or a separately identifiable department or division of a bank (as defined by the Municipal Securities Rulemaking Board) to apply for registration as a municipal securities dealer with the Securities and Exchange Commission pursuant to section 15B(a) of the Securities Exchange Act of 1934 (the "Act"), or to amend such application.

NOTE: Copies of Form MSD have been filed with the Office of the Federal Register as part of this document. Copies of Forms BD and MSD may be obtained from the Office of Reports and Information Services; Securities

Securities and Exchange Commission § 249.1310

and Exchange Commission, 500 North Capitol Street, Washington, DC, 20549. Only printed copies of Form MSD should be used to apply for registration with the Commission.

[40 FR 49777, Oct. 24, 1975; 40 FR 54425, Nov. 24, 1975]

EDITORIAL NOTE: For FEDERAL REGISTER citations affecting Form MSD, see the List of CFR Sections Affected, which appears in the Finding Aids section of the printed volume and at *www.govinfo.gov*.

§ 249.1110 Form MSDW, notice of withdrawal from registration as a municipal securities dealer pursuant to Rule 15Bc3-1 (17 CFR 240.15Bc3-1).

This form is to be used by a bank or a separately identifiable department or division of a bank (as defined by the Municipal Securities Rulemaking Board) to withdraw from registration with the Securities and Exchange Commission as a municipal securities dealer pursuant to section 15B(c) of the Securities Exchange Act of 1934.

NOTE: Copies of Form MSDW have been filed with the Office of the Federal Register as part of this document. Copies of Form MSDW may be obtained from the Publications Section, Securities and Exchange Commission, 500 North Capitol Street, Washington, DC 20549.

[41 FR 28949, July 14, 1976]

EDITORIAL NOTE: For FEDERAL REGISTER citations affecting Form MSDW, see the List of CFR Sections Affected, which appears in the Finding Aids section of the printed volume and at *www.govinfo.gov*.

Subpart M—Forms for Reporting and Inquiry With Respect to Missing, Lost, Stolen, or Counterfeit Securities

§ 249.1200 Form X-17F-1A—Report for missing, lost, stolen or counterfeit securities.

This form is to be filed with the Commission or its designee pursuant to paragraph (c) of § 240.17f-1 of this chapter by all reporting institutions subject to section 17(f)(1) of the Securities Exchange Act of 1934.

[44 FR 31504, May 31, 1979]

EDITORIAL NOTE: For FEDERAL REGISTER citations affecting Form X-17F-1A, see the List of CFR Sections Affected, which appears in the Finding Aids section of the printed volume and at *www.govinfo.gov*.

Subpart N—Forms for Registration of Municipal Advisors and for Providing Information Regarding Certain Natural Persons

SOURCE: 78 FR 67639, Nov. 12, 2013, unless otherwise noted.

§ 249.1300 Form MA, for registration as a municipal advisor, and for amendments to registration.

The form shall be used for registration as a municipal advisor pursuant to section 15B of the Securities Exchange Act of 1934 (15 U.S.C. 78o-4) and for amendments to registrations.

EDITORIAL NOTE: For FEDERAL REGISTER citations affecting Form MA-T, see the List of CFR Sections Affected, which appears in the Finding Aids section of the printed volume and at *www.govinfo.gov*.

§ 249.1300T Form MA-T, for temporary registration as a municipal advisor, and for amendments to, and withdrawals from, temporary registration.

The form shall be used for temporary registration as a municipal advisor, and for amendments to, and withdrawals from, temporary registration pursuant to Section 15B of the Exchange Act, (15 U.S.C. 78o-4).

EDITORIAL NOTE: For FEDERAL REGISTER citations affecting Form MA-T, see the List of CFR Sections Affected, which appears in the Finding Aids section of the printed volume and at *www.govinfo.gov*.

§ 249.1310 Form MA-I, for providing information regarding natural person municipal advisors, and for amendments to such information.

The form shall be used for providing information regarding natural person municipal advisors, and for amendments to such information.

EDITORIAL NOTE: For FEDERAL REGISTER citations affecting Form MA-I, see the List of CFR Sections Affected, which appears in the Finding Aids section of the printed volume and at *www.govinfo.gov*.

§ 249.1320

§ 249.1320 Form MA–W, for withdrawal from registration as a municipal advisor.

The form shall be used for filing a notice of withdrawal from registration as a municipal advisor pursuant to section 15B of the Securities Exchange Act of 1934 (15 U.S.C. 78o-4).

EDITORIAL NOTE: For FEDERAL REGISTER citations affecting Form MA–W, see the List of CFR Sections Affected, which appears in the Finding Aids section of the printed volume and at *www.govinfo.gov*.

§ 249.1330 Form MA–NR, for appointment of agent for service of process by non-resident municipal advisor, non-resident general partner or managing agent of a municipal advisor, and non-resident natural person associated with a municipal advisor.

The form shall be used to furnish information pertaining to the appointment of agent for service of process by a non-resident municipal advisor and by registered municipal advisors to furnish the same for each of its non-resident general partner or managing agent, or non-resident natural person associated with a municipal advisor pursuant to section 15B of the Securities Exchange Act of 1934 (15 U.S.C. 78o-4).

EDITORIAL NOTE: For FEDERAL REGISTER citations affecting Form MA–NR, see the List of CFR Sections Affected, which appears in the Finding Aids section of the printed volume and at *www.govinfo.gov*.

Subpart O—Forms for Asset-Backed Securities

§ 249.1400 Form ABS–15G, Asset-backed securitizer report pursuant to Section 15G of the Securities Exchange Act of 1934.

This form shall be used for reports of information required by Rule 15Ga–1 (§ 240.15Ga–1 of this chapter).

[76 FR 4515, Jan. 26, 2011]

EDITORIAL NOTE: For FEDERAL REGISTER citations affecting Form ABS–15G, see the List of CFR Sections Affected, which appears in the Finding Aids section of the printed volume and at *www.govinfo.gov*.

§ 249.1401 Form ABS–EE, for submission of the asset-data file exhibits and related documents.

This Form shall be used by an electronic filer for the submission of information required by Item 1111(h) (§ 229.1111(h) of this chapter).

[79 FR 57346, Sept. 24, 2014]

EDITORIAL NOTE: For FEDERAL REGISTER citations affecting Form ABS–EE, see the List of CFR Sections Affected, which appears in the Finding Aids section of the printed volume and at *www.govinfo.gov*.

Subpart P—Forms for Registration of Security-Based Swap Data Repositories

§ 249.1500 Form SDR, for application for registration as a security-based swap data repository, amendments thereto, or withdrawal from registration.

The form shall be used for registration as a security-based swap data repository, and for the amendments to and withdrawal from such registration pursuant to section 13(n) of the Exchange Act (15 U.S.C. 78m(n)).

[80 FR 14557, Mar. 19, 2015]

EDITORIAL NOTE: For FEDERAL REGISTER citations affecting Form SDR, see the List of CFR Sections Affected, which appears in the Finding Aids section of the printed volume and at *www.govinfo.gov*.

Subpart Q—Registration of Security-Based Swap Dealers and Major Security-Based Swap Participants

SOURCE: 80 FR 49017 Aug. 14, 2015, unless otherwise noted.

§ 249.1600 Form SBSE, for application for registration as a security-based swap dealer or major security-based swap participant or to amend such an application for registration.

This form shall be used for application for registration as a security-based swap dealer or major security-based swap participant by firms that are not registered with the Commission as a broker or dealer and that are not registered or registering with the Commodity Futures Trading Commission

Securities and Exchange Commission § 249.1601

as a swap dealer or major swap participant, pursuant to Section 15F(b) of the Securities Exchange Act of 1934 (15 U.S.C. 78o–10(b)) and to amend such an application for registration.

EDITORIAL NOTE: For FEDERAL REGISTER citations affecting Form SBSE, see the List of CFR Sections Affected, which appears in the Finding Aids section of the printed volume and at *www.govinfo.gov*.

§ 249.1600a Form SBSE–A, for application for registration as a security-based swap dealer or major security-based swap participant or to amend such an application for registration by firms registered or registering with the Commodity Futures Trading Commission as a swap dealer or major swap participant that are not also registered or registering with the Commission as a broker or dealer.

This form shall be used instead of Form SBSE (§ 249.1600) to apply for registration as a security-based swap dealer or major security-based swap participant by firms that are not registered or registering with the Commission as a broker or dealer but that are registered or registering with the Commodity Futures Trading Commission as a swap dealer or major swap participant, pursuant to Section 15F(b) of the Securities Exchange Act of 1934 (15 U.S.C. 78o–10(b)) and to amend such an application for registration. An entity that is registered or registering with the Commission as a broker or dealer and is also registered or registering with the Commodity Futures Trading Commission as a swap dealer or major swap participant shall apply for registration as a security-based swap dealer or major security-based swap participant on Form SBSE–BD (§ 249.1600b) and not on this Form SBSE–A.

EDITORIAL NOTE: For FEDERAL REGISTER citations affecting Form SBSE–A, see the List of CFR Sections Affected, which appears in the Finding Aids section of the printed volume and at *www.govinfo.gov*.

§ 249.1600b Form SBSE–BD, for application for registration as a security-based swap dealer or major security-based swap participant or to amend such an application for registration by firms registered or registering with the Commission as a broker or dealer.

This form shall be used instead of either Form SBSE (§ 249.1600) or SBSE–A (§ 249.1600a) to apply for registration as a security-based swap dealer or major security-based swap participant solely by firms registered or registering with the Commission as a broker or dealer, pursuant to Section 15F(b) of the Securities Exchange Act of 1934 (15 U.S.C. 78o–10(b)) and to amend such an application for registration. An entity that is registered or registering with the Commission as a broker or dealer and is also registered or registering with the Commodity Futures Trading Commission as a swap dealer or major swap participant, shall apply for registration as a security-based swap dealer or major security-based swap participant on this Form SBSE–BD and not on Form SBSE–A.

EDITORIAL NOTE: For FEDERAL REGISTER citations affecting Form SBSE–BD, see the List of CFR Sections Affected, which appears in the Finding Aids section of the printed volume and at *www.govinfo.gov*.

§ 249.1600c Form SBSE–C, for certification by security-based swap dealers and major security-based swap participants.

This form shall be used to file required certifications on Form SBSE–C pursuant to § 240.15Fb2–1(a) of this chapter.

EDITORIAL NOTE: For FEDERAL REGISTER citations affecting Form SBSE–C, see the List of CFR Sections Affected, which appears in the Finding Aids section of the printed volume and at *www.govinfo.gov*.

§ 249.1601 Form SBSE–W, for withdrawal from registration as a security-based swap dealer or major security-based swap participant or to amend such an application for registration.

This form shall be used to withdraw from registration as a security-based swap dealer or major security-based swap participant, pursuant to Section

§ 249.1900.

15F(b) of the Securities Exchange Act of 1934 (15 U.S.C. 78o-10(b)).

EDITORIAL NOTE: For FEDERAL REGISTER citations affecting Form SBSE-W, see the List of CFR Sections Affected, which appears in the Finding Aids section of the printed volume and at *www.govinfo.gov*.

Subparts R–S [Reserved]

Subpart T—Form SCI, for filing notices and reports as required by Regulation SCI.

§ 249.1900 **Form SCI, for filing notices and reports as required by Regulation SCI.**

Form SCI shall be used to file notices and reports as required by Regulation SCI (§§ 242.1000 through 242.1007).

[79 FR 72440, Dec. 5, 2014]

EDITORIAL NOTE: For FEDERAL REGISTER citations affecting Form SCI, see the List of CFR Sections Affected, which appears in the Finding Aids section of the printed volume and at *www.govinfo.gov*.

Subpart U—Forms for Registration of Funding Portals

§ 249.2000 **Form Funding Portal.**

This form shall be used for filings by funding portals under Regulation Crowdfunding (part 227 of this chapter).

[80 FR 71570, Nov. 16, 2015]

EDITORIAL NOTE: For FEDERAL REGISTER citations affecting Form Funding Portal, see the List of CFR Sections Affected, which appears in the Finding Aids section of the printed volume and at *www.govinfo.gov*.

PART 249a—FORMS, SECURITIES INVESTOR PROTECTION ACT OF 1970 [RESERVED]

PART 249b—FURTHER FORMS, SECURITIES EXCHANGE ACT OF 1934

Sec.
249b.1–249b.99 [Reserved]
249b.100 Form TA-1, uniform form for registration as a transfer agent pursuant to section 17A of the Securities Exchange Act of 1934.
249b.101 Form TA-W, notice of withdrawal from registration as transfer agent.
249b.102 Form TA-2, form to be used by transfer agents registered pursuant to section 17A of the Securities Exchange Act of 1934 for the annual report of transfer agent activities.
249b.200 Form CA-1, form for registration or for exemption from registration as a clearing agency and for amendment to registration as a clearing agency pursuant to section 17A of the Securities Exchange Act of 1934.
249b.300 FORM NRSRO, application for registration as a nationally recognized statistical rating organization pursuant to section 15E of the Securities Exchange Act of 1934 and § 240.17g-1 of this chapter.
249b.400 Form SD, specialized disclosure report.

AUTHORITY: 15 U.S.C. 78a *et seq.*, unless otherwise noted;

Sections 249b.100 and 249b.102 also issued under secs. 17, 17A and 23(a); 48 Stat. 897, as amended, 89 Stat. 137, 141 and 48 Stat. 901 (15 U.S.C. 78q, 78q-1, 78w(a)).

Section 249b.400 is also issued under secs. 1502 and 1504, Pub. L. 111-203, 124 Stat. 2213 and 2220.

§§ 249b.1–249b.99 [Reserved]

§ 249b.100 **Form TA-1,[1] uniform form for registration as a transfer agent pursuant to section 17A of the Securities Exchange Act of 1934.**

This form shall be used for application for registration as a transfer agent and for amendment to registration as a transfer agent pursuant to section 17A of the Securities Exchange Act of 1934.

[40 FR 51184, Nov. 4, 1975, as amended at 51 FR 12127, Apr. 9, 1986; 73 FR 32228, June 5, 2008]

EDITORIAL NOTE: For FEDERAL REGISTER citations affecting Form TA-1, see the List of CFR Sections Affected, which appears in the Finding Aids section of the printed volume and at *www.govinfo.gov*.

§ 249b.101 **Form TA-W, notice of withdrawal from registration as transfer agent.**

This form shall be used for withdrawing, pursuant to section 17A of the Securities Exchange Act of 1934, the

---

[1] Copies of the form may be obtained from the Publications Section, Securities and Exchange Commission, 100 F Street, NE., Washington, DC 20549 and from each of the Commission's regional offices.

Securities and Exchange Commission

registration of transfer agents registered with the Commission.

(Secs. 2, 17, 17A and 23(a); (15 U.S.C. 78b, 78a, 78a-1 and 78w(a)))

[42 FR 44984, Sept. 8, 1977]

EDITORIAL NOTE: For FEDERAL REGISTER citations affecting Form TA-W, see the List of CFR Sections Affected, which appears in the Finding Aids section of the printed volume and at *www.govinfo.gov*.

§ 249b.102 Form TA-2,[1] form to be used by transfer agents registered pursuant to section 17A of the Securities Exchange Act of 1934 for the annual report of transfer agent activities.

This form shall be used on an annual basis for registered transfer agents for reporting their business activities.

[51 FR 12134, Apr. 9, 1986, as amended at 73 FR 32228, June 5, 2008]

EDITORIAL NOTE: For FEDERAL REGISTER citations affecting Form TA-2, see the List of CFR Sections Affected, which appears in the Finding Aids section of the printed volume and at *www.govinfo.gov*.

§ 249b.200 Form CA-1,[1] form for registration or for exemption from registration as a clearing agency and for amendment to registration as a clearing agency pursuant to section 17A of the Securities Exchange Act of 1934.

This form shall be used for application for registration or for exemption from registration as a clearing agency and for amendment to registration as a clearing agency pursuant to section 17A of the Securities Exchange Act of 1934.

[40 FR 52359, Nov. 10, 1975, as amended at 51 FR 12134, Apr. 9, 1986; 73 FR 32228, June 5, 2008]

EDITORIAL NOTE: For FEDERAL REGISTER citations affecting Form CA-1, see the List of CFR Sections Affected, which appears in the Finding Aids section of the printed volume and at *www.govinfo.gov*.

§ 249b.300 FORM NRSRO, application for registration as a nationally recognized statistical rating organization pursuant to section 15E of the Securities Exchange Act of 1934 and § 240.17g-1 of this chapter.

This Form shall be used for an initial application for and an application to add a class of credit ratings to, a supplement to an initial application for and an application to add a class of credit ratings to, an update and amendment to an application for, and a withdrawal from a registration as a nationally recognized statistical rating organization pursuant to section 15E of the Securities Exchange Act of 1934 (15 U.S.C. 78o-7) and § 240.17g-1 of this chapter.

[72 FR 33624, June 18, 2007]

EDITORIAL NOTE: For FEDERAL REGISTER citations affecting Form NRSRO, see the List of CFR Sections Affected, which appears in the Finding Aids section of the printed volume and at *www.govinfo.gov*.

§ 249b.400 Form SD, specialized disclosure report.

(a) This Form shall be filed pursuant to § 240.13p-1 of this chapter by registrants that file reports with the Commission pursuant to Sections 13(a) or 15(d) of the Securities Exchange Act of 1934 and are required to disclose the information required by Section 13(p) under the Securities Exchange Act of 1934 and Rule 13p-1 (§ 240.13p-1) of this chapter.

(b) This Form shall be filed pursuant to Rule 13q-1 (§ 240.13q-1) of this chapter by resource extraction issuers that are required to disclose the information required by Section 13(q) of the Securities Exchange Act of 1934 (15 U.S.C. 78m(q)) and Rule 13q-1 of this chapter.

[77 FR 56362, Sept. 12, 2012, as amended at 77 FR 56418, Sept. 12, 2012]

EDITORIAL NOTE: For FEDERAL REGISTER citations affecting Form SD, see the List of CFR Sections Affected, which appears in the Finding Aids section of the printed volume and at *www.govinfo.gov*.

---

[1] Copies of the form may be obtained from the Publication Section, Securities and Exchange Commission, 100 F Street, NE., Washington, DC 20549 and from each of the Commission's regional offices.

[1] Copies of the form may be obtained from the Publication Section, Securities and Exchange Commission, 100 F Street, NE., Washington, DC 20549 and from each of the Commission's regional offices.

PART 250—CROSS-BORDER ANTI-FRAUD LAW-ENFORCEMENT AUTHORITY

AUTHORITY: 15 U.S.C. 77s, 77v(c), 78w, 78aa(b), 80b–11, and 80b–14(b).

SOURCE: 79 FR 47372, Aug. 12, 2014, unless otherwise noted.

§ 250.1 Cross-border antifraud law-enforcement authority.

(a) Notwithstanding any other Commission rule or regulation, the antifraud provisions of the securities laws apply to:

(1) Conduct within the United States that constitutes significant steps in furtherance of the violation; or

(2) Conduct occurring outside the United States that has a foreseeable substantial effect within the United States.

(b) The antifraud provisions of the securities laws apply to conduct described in paragraph (a)(1) of this section even if:

(1) The violation relates to a securities transaction or securities transactions occurring outside the United States that involves only foreign investors; or

(2) The violation is committed by a foreign adviser and involves only foreign investors.

(c) Violations of the antifraud provisions of the securities laws described in this section may be pursued in judicial proceedings brought by the Commission or the United States.

PARTS 251–254 [RESERVED]

PART 255—PROPRIETARY TRADING AND CERTAIN INTERESTS IN AND RELATIONSHIPS WITH COVERED FUNDS

Subpart A—Authority and Definitions

Sec.
255.1 Authority, purpose, scope, and relationship to other authorities
255.2 Definitions.

Subpart B—Proprietary Trading

255.3 Prohibition on proprietary trading.
255.4 Permitted underwriting and market making-related activities.
255.5 Permitted risk-mitigating hedging activities.
255.6 Other permitted proprietary trading activities.
255.7 Limitations on permitted proprietary trading activities.
255.8–255.9 [Reserved]

Subpart C—Covered Fund Activities and Investments

255.10 Prohibition on acquiring or retaining an ownership interest in and having certain relationships with a covered fund.
255.11 Permitted organizing and offering, underwriting, and market making with respect to a covered fund.
255.12 Permitted investment in a covered fund.
255.13 Other permitted covered fund activities and investments.
255.14 Limitations on relationships with a covered fund.
255.15 Other limitations on permitted covered fund activities and investments.
255.16 Ownership of interests in and sponsorship of issuers of certain collateralized debt obligations backed by trust-preferred securities.
255.17–255.19 [Reserved]

Subpart D—Compliance Program Requirement; Violations

255.20 Program for compliance; reporting.
255.21 Termination of activities or investments; penalties for violations.

APPENDIX A TO PART 255—REPORTING AND RECORDKEEPING REQUIREMENTS FOR COVERED TRADING ACTIVITIES

AUTHORITY: 12 U.S.C. 1851.

SOURCE: 79 FR 5779, 5805, Jan. 31, 2014, unless otherwise noted.

Subpart A—Authority and Definitions

§ 255.1 Authority, purpose, scope, and relationship to other authorities.

(a) *Authority.* This part is issued by the SEC under section 13 of the Bank Holding Company Act of 1956, as amended (12 U.S.C. 1851).

(b) *Purpose.* Section 13 of the Bank Holding Company Act establishes prohibitions and restrictions on proprietary trading and investments in or relationships with covered funds by certain banking entities, including registered broker-dealers, registered investment advisers, and registered security-based swap dealers, among others identified in section 2(12)(B) of the

Securities and Exchange Commission § 255.2

Dodd-Frank Wall Street Reform and Consumer Protection Act of 2010 (12 U.S.C. 5301(12)(B)). This part implements section 13 of the Bank Holding Company Act by defining terms used in the statute and related terms, establishing prohibitions and restrictions on proprietary trading and investments in or relationships with covered funds, and explaining the statute's requirements.

(c) *Scope*. This part implements section 13 of the Bank Holding Company Act with respect to banking entities for which the SEC is the primary financial regulatory agency, as defined in this part, but does not include such entities to the extent they are not within the definition of banking entity in § 255.2(c).

(d) *Relationship to other authorities*. Except as otherwise provided under section 13 of the Bank Holding Company Act, and notwithstanding any other provision of law, the prohibitions and restrictions under section 13 of Bank Holding Company Act shall apply to the activities and investments of a banking entity identified in paragraph (c) of this section, even if such activities and investments are authorized for the banking entity under other applicable provisions of law.

(e) *Preservation of authority*. Nothing in this part limits in any way the authority of the SEC to impose on a banking entity identified in paragraph (c) of this section additional requirements or restrictions with respect to any activity, investment, or relationship covered under section 13 of the Bank Holding Company Act or this part, or additional penalties for violation of this part provided under any other applicable provision of law.

[79 FR 5805, Jan. 31, 2014, as amended at 84 FR 35022, July 22, 2019]

§ 255.2 Definitions.

Unless otherwise specified, for purposes of this part:

(a) *Affiliate* has the same meaning as in section 2(k) of the Bank Holding Company Act of 1956 (12 U.S.C. 1841(k)).

(b) *Bank holding company* has the same meaning as in section 2 of the Bank Holding Company Act of 1956 (12 U.S.C. 1841).

(c) *Banking entity*. (1) Except as provided in paragraph (c)(2) of this section, *banking entity* means:

(i) Any insured depository institution;

(ii) Any company that controls an insured depository institution;

(iii) Any company that is treated as a bank holding company for purposes of section 8 of the International Banking Act of 1978 (12 U.S.C. 3106); and

(iv) Any affiliate or subsidiary of any entity described in paragraph (c)(1)(i), (ii), or (iii) of this section.

(2) Banking entity does not include:

(i) A covered fund that is not itself a banking entity under paragraph (c)(1)(i), (ii), or (iii) of this section;

(ii) A portfolio company held under the authority contained in section 4(k)(4)(H) or (I) of the BHC Act (12 U.S.C. 1843(k)(4)(H), (I)), or any portfolio concern, as defined under 13 CFR 107.50, that is controlled by a small business investment company, as defined in section 103(3) of the Small Business Investment Act of 1958 (15 U.S.C. 662), so long as the portfolio company or portfolio concern is not itself a banking entity under paragraph (c)(1)(i), (ii), or (iii) of this section; or

(iii) The FDIC acting in its corporate capacity or as conservator or receiver under the Federal Deposit Insurance Act or Title II of the Dodd-Frank Wall Street Reform and Consumer Protection Act.

(d) *Board* means the Board of Governors of the Federal Reserve System.

(e) *CFTC* means the Commodity Futures Trading Commission.

(f) *Dealer* has the same meaning as in section 3(a)(5) of the Exchange Act (15 U.S.C. 78c(a)(5)).

(g) *Depository institution* has the same meaning as in section 3(c) of the Federal Deposit Insurance Act (12 U.S.C. 1813(c)).

(h) *Derivative*. (1) Except as provided in paragraph (h)(2) of this section, *derivative* means:

(i) Any swap, as that term is defined in section 1a(47) of the Commodity Exchange Act (7 U.S.C. 1a(47)), or security-based swap, as that term is defined in section 3(a)(68) of the Exchange Act (15 U.S.C. 78c(a)(68));

§ 255.2

(ii) Any purchase or sale of a commodity, that is not an excluded commodity, for deferred shipment or delivery that is intended to be physically settled;

(iii) Any foreign exchange forward (as that term is defined in section 1a(24) of the Commodity Exchange Act (7 U.S.C. 1a(24)) or foreign exchange swap (as that term is defined in section 1a(25) of the Commodity Exchange Act (7 U.S.C. 1a(25));

(iv) Any agreement, contract, or transaction in foreign currency described in section 2(c)(2)(C)(i) of the Commodity Exchange Act (7 U.S.C. 2(c)(2)(C)(i));

(v) Any agreement, contract, or transaction in a commodity other than foreign currency described in section 2(c)(2)(D)(i) of the Commodity Exchange Act (7 U.S.C. 2(c)(2)(D)(i)); and

(vi) Any transaction authorized under section 19 of the Commodity Exchange Act (7 U.S.C. 23(a) or (b));

(2) A derivative does not include:

(i) Any consumer, commercial, or other agreement, contract, or transaction that the CFTC and SEC have further defined by joint regulation, interpretation, or other action as not within the definition of swap, as that term is defined in section 1a(47) of the Commodity Exchange Act (7 U.S.C. 1a(47)), or security-based swap, as that term is defined in section 3(a)(68) of the Exchange Act (15 U.S.C. 78c(a)(68)); or

(ii) Any identified banking product, as defined in section 402(b) of the Legal Certainty for Bank Products Act of 2000 (7 U.S.C. 27(b)), that is subject to section 403(a) of that Act (7 U.S.C. 27a(a)).

(i) *Employee* includes a member of the immediate family of the employee.

(j) *Exchange Act* means the Securities Exchange Act of 1934 (15 U.S.C. 78a *et seq.*).

(k) *Excluded commodity* has the same meaning as in section 1a(19) of the Commodity Exchange Act (7 U.S.C. 1a(19)).

(l) *FDIC* means the Federal Deposit Insurance Corporation.

(m) *Federal banking agencies* means the Board, the Office of the Comptroller of the Currency, and the FDIC.

(n) *Foreign banking organization* has the same meaning as in § 211.21(o) of the Board's Regulation K (12 CFR 211.21(o)), but does not include a foreign bank, as defined in section 1(b)(7) of the International Banking Act of 1978 (12 U.S.C. 3101(7)), that is organized under the laws of the Commonwealth of Puerto Rico, Guam, American Samoa, the United States Virgin Islands, or the Commonwealth of the Northern Mariana Islands.

(o) *Foreign insurance regulator* means the insurance commissioner, or a similar official or agency, of any country other than the United States that is engaged in the supervision of insurance companies under foreign insurance law.

(p) *General account* means all of the assets of an insurance company except those allocated to one or more separate accounts.

(q) *Insurance company* means a company that is organized as an insurance company, primarily and predominantly engaged in writing insurance or reinsuring risks underwritten by insurance companies, subject to supervision as such by a state insurance regulator or a foreign insurance regulator, and not operated for the purpose of evading the provisions of section 13 of the BHC Act (12 U.S.C. 1851).

(r) *Insured depository institution* has the same meaning as in section 3(c) of the Federal Deposit Insurance Act (12 U.S.C. 1813(c)), but does not include:

(1) An insured depository institution that is described in section 2(c)(2)(D) of the BHC Act (12 U.S.C. 1841(c)(2)(D)); or

(2) An insured depository institution if it has, and if every company that controls it has, total consolidated assets of $10 billion or less and total trading assets and trading liabilities, on a consolidated basis, that are 5 percent or less of total consolidated assets.

(s) *Limited trading assets and liabilities* means with respect to a banking entity that:

(1)(i) The banking entity has, together with its affiliates and subsidiaries, trading assets and liabilities (excluding trading assets and liabilities attributable to trading activities permitted pursuant to § 255.6(a)(1) and (2) of subpart B) the average gross sum of which over the previous consecutive four quarters, as measured as of the last day of each of the four previous

Securities and Exchange Commission

§ 255.2

calendar quarters, is less than $1 billion; and

(ii) The SEC has not determined pursuant to § 255.20(g) or (h) of this part that the banking entity should not be treated as having limited trading assets and liabilities.

(2) With respect to a banking entity other than a banking entity described in paragraph (s)(3) of this section, trading assets and liabilities for purposes of this paragraph (s) means trading assets and liabilities (excluding trading assets and liabilities attributable to trading activities permitted pursuant to § 255.6(a)(1) and (2) of subpart B) on a worldwide consolidated basis.

(3)(i) With respect to a banking entity that is a foreign banking organization or a subsidiary of a foreign banking organization, trading assets and liabilities for purposes of this paragraph (s) means the trading assets and liabilities (excluding trading assets and liabilities attributable to trading activities permitted pursuant to § 255.6(a)(1) and (2) of subpart B) of the combined U.S. operations of the top-tier foreign banking organization (including all subsidiaries, affiliates, branches, and agencies of the foreign banking organization operating, located, or organized in the United States).

(ii) For purposes of paragraph (s)(3)(i) of this section, a U.S. branch, agency, or subsidiary of a banking entity is located in the United States; however, the foreign bank that operates or controls that branch, agency, or subsidiary is not considered to be located in the United States solely by virtue of operating or controlling the U.S. branch, agency, or subsidiary. For purposes of paragraph (s)(3)(i) of this section, all foreign operations of a U.S. agency, branch, or subsidiary of a foreign banking organization are considered to be located in the United States, including branches outside the United States that are managed or controlled by a U.S. branch or agency of the foreign banking organization, for purposes of calculating the banking entity's U.S. trading assets and liabilities.

(t) *Loan* means any loan, lease, extension of credit, or secured or unsecured receivable that is not a security or derivative.

(u) *Moderate trading assets and liabilities* means, with respect to a banking entity, that the banking entity does not have significant trading assets and liabilities or limited trading assets and liabilities.

(v) *Primary financial regulatory agency* has the same meaning as in section 2(12) of the Dodd-Frank Wall Street Reform and Consumer Protection Act (12 U.S.C. 5301(12)).

(w) *Purchase* includes any contract to buy, purchase, or otherwise acquire. For security futures products, purchase includes any contract, agreement, or transaction for future delivery. With respect to a commodity future, purchase includes any contract, agreement, or transaction for future delivery. With respect to a derivative, purchase includes the execution, termination (prior to its scheduled maturity date), assignment, exchange, or similar transfer or conveyance of, or extinguishing of rights or obligations under, a derivative, as the context may require.

(x) *Qualifying foreign banking organization* means a foreign banking organization that qualifies as such under § 211.23(a), (c) or (e) of the Board's Regulation K (12 CFR 211.23(a), (c), or (e)).

(y) *SEC* means the Securities and Exchange Commission.

(z) *Sale* and *sell* each include any contract to sell or otherwise dispose of. For security futures products, such terms include any contract, agreement, or transaction for future delivery. With respect to a commodity future, such terms include any contract, agreement, or transaction for future delivery. With respect to a derivative, such terms include the execution, termination (prior to its scheduled maturity date), assignment, exchange, or similar transfer or conveyance of, or extinguishing of rights or obligations under, a derivative, as the context may require.

(aa) *Security* has the meaning specified in section 3(a)(10) of the Exchange Act (15 U.S.C. 78c(a)(10)).

(bb) *Security-based swap dealer* has the same meaning as in section 3(a)(71) of the Exchange Act (15 U.S.C. 78c(a)(71)).

(cc) *Security future* has the meaning specified in section 3(a)(55) of the Exchange Act (15 U.S.C. 78c(a)(55)).

(dd) *Separate account* means an account established and maintained by an insurance company in connection with one or more insurance contracts to hold assets that are legally segregated from the insurance company's other assets, under which income, gains, and losses, whether or not realized, from assets allocated to such account, are, in accordance with the applicable contract, credited to or charged against such account without regard to other income, gains, or losses of the insurance company.

(ee) *Significant trading assets and liabilities* means with respect to a banking entity that: (1)(i) The banking entity has, together with its affiliates and subsidiaries, trading assets and liabilities the average gross sum of which over the previous consecutive four quarters, as measured as of the last day of each of the four previous calendar quarters, equals or exceeds $20 billion; or

(ii) The SEC has determined pursuant to §255.20(h) of this part that the banking entity should be treated as having significant trading assets and liabilities.

(2) With respect to a banking entity, other than a banking entity described in paragraph (ee)(3) of this section, trading assets and liabilities for purposes of this paragraph (ee) means trading assets and liabilities (excluding trading assets and liabilities attributable to trading activities permitted pursuant to §255.6(a)(1) and (2) of subpart B) on a worldwide consolidated basis.

(3)(i) With respect to a banking entity that is a foreign banking organization or a subsidiary of a foreign banking organization, trading assets and liabilities for purposes of this paragraph (ee) means the trading assets and liabilities (excluding trading assets and liabilities attributable to trading activities permitted pursuant to §255.6(a)(1) and (2) of subpart B) of the combined U.S. operations of the top-tier foreign banking organization (including all subsidiaries, affiliates, branches, and agencies of the foreign banking organization operating, located, or organized in the United States as well as branches outside the United States that are managed or controlled by a branch or agency of the foreign banking entity operating, located or organized in the United States).

(ii) For purposes of paragraph (ee)(3)(i) of this section, a U.S. branch, agency, or subsidiary of a banking entity is located in the United States; however, the foreign bank that operates or controls that branch, agency, or subsidiary is not considered to be located in the United States solely by virtue of operating or controlling the U.S. branch, agency, or subsidiary. For purposes of paragraph (ee)(3)(i) of this section, all foreign operations of a U.S. agency, branch, or subsidiary of a foreign banking organization are considered to be located in the United States for purposes of calculating the banking entity's U.S. trading assets and liabilities.

(ff) *State* means any State, the District of Columbia, the Commonwealth of Puerto Rico, Guam, American Samoa, the United States Virgin Islands, and the Commonwealth of the Northern Mariana Islands.

(gg) *Subsidiary* has the same meaning as in section 2(d) of the Bank Holding Company Act of 1956 (12 U.S.C. 1841(d)).

(hh) *State insurance regulator* means the insurance commissioner, or a similar official or agency, of a State that is engaged in the supervision of insurance companies under State insurance law.

(ii) *Swap dealer* has the same meaning as in section 1(a)(49) of the Commodity Exchange Act (7 U.S.C. 1a(49)).

[84 FR 62237, Nov. 14, 2019]

Subpart B—Proprietary Trading

§255.3 Prohibition on proprietary trading.

(a) *Prohibition.* Except as otherwise provided in this subpart, a banking entity may not engage in proprietary trading. *Proprietary trading* means engaging as principal for the trading account of the banking entity in any purchase or sale of one or more financial instruments.

(b) *Definition of trading account.* (1) *Trading account.* Trading account means:

(i) Any account that is used by a banking entity to purchase or sell one

Securities and Exchange Commission § 255.3

or more financial instruments principally for the purpose of short-term resale, benefitting from actual or expected short-term price movements, realizing short-term arbitrage profits, or hedging one or more of the positions resulting from the purchases or sales of financial instruments described in this paragraph;

(ii) Any account that is used by a banking entity to purchase or sell one or more financial instruments that are both market risk capital rule covered positions and trading positions (or hedges of other market risk capital rule covered positions), if the banking entity, or any affiliate with which the banking entity is consolidated for regulatory reporting purposes, calculates risk-based capital ratios under the market risk capital rule; or

(iii) Any account that is used by a banking entity to purchase or sell one or more financial instruments, if the banking entity:

(A) Is licensed or registered, or is required to be licensed or registered, to engage in the business of a dealer, swap dealer, or security-based swap dealer, to the extent the instrument is purchased or sold in connection with the activities that require the banking entity to be licensed or registered as such; or

(B) Is engaged in the business of a dealer, swap dealer, or security-based swap dealer outside of the United States, to the extent the instrument is purchased or sold in connection with the activities of such business.

(2) *Trading account application for certain banking entities.* (i) A banking entity that is subject to paragraph (b)(1)(ii) of this section in determining the scope of its trading account is not subject to paragraph (b)(1)(i) of this section.

(ii) A banking entity that does not calculate risk-based capital ratios under the market risk capital rule and is not a consolidated affiliate for regulatory reporting purposes of a banking entity that calculates risk based capital ratios under the market risk capital rule may elect to apply paragraph (b)(1)(ii) of this section in determining the scope of its trading account as if it were subject to that paragraph. A banking entity that elects under this section to apply paragraph (b)(1)(ii) of this section in determining the scope of its trading account as if it were subject to that paragraph is not required to apply paragraph (b)(1)(i) of this section.

(3) *Consistency of account election for certain banking entities.* (i) Any election or change to an election under paragraph (b)(2)(ii) of this section must apply to the electing banking entity and all of its wholly owned subsidiaries. The primary financial regulatory agency of a banking entity that is affiliated with but is not a wholly owned subsidiary of such electing banking entity may require that the banking entity be subject to this uniform application requirement if the primary financial regulatory agency determines that it is necessary to prevent evasion of the requirements of this part after notice and opportunity for response as provided in subpart D.

(ii) A banking entity that does not elect under paragraph (b)(2)(ii) of this section to be subject to the trading account definition in (b)(1)(ii) may continue to apply the trading account definition in paragraph (b)(1)(i) of this section for one year from the date on which it becomes, or becomes a consolidated affiliate for regulatory reporting purposes with, a banking entity that calculates risk-based capital ratios under the market risk capital rule.

(4) *Rebuttable presumption for certain purchases and sales.* The purchase (or sale) of a financial instrument by a banking entity shall be presumed not to be for the trading account of the banking entity under paragraph (b)(1)(i) of this section if the banking entity holds the financial instrument for sixty days or longer and does not transfer substantially all of the risk of the financial instrument within sixty days of the purchase (or sale).

(c) *Financial instrument.* (1) *Financial instrument* means:

(i) A security, including an option on a security;

(ii) A derivative, including an option on a derivative; or

(iii) A contract of sale of a commodity for future delivery, or option on a contract of sale of a commodity for future delivery.

§ 255.3

(2) A financial instrument does not include:
(i) A loan;
(ii) A commodity that is not:
(A) An excluded commodity (other than foreign exchange or currency);
(B) A derivative;
(C) A contract of sale of a commodity for future delivery; or
(D) An option on a contract of sale of a commodity for future delivery; or
(iii) Foreign exchange or currency.

(d) *Proprietary trading.* Proprietary trading does not include:
(1) Any purchase or sale of one or more financial instruments by a banking entity that arises under a repurchase or reverse repurchase agreement pursuant to which the banking entity has simultaneously agreed, in writing, to both purchase and sell a stated asset, at stated prices, and on stated dates or on demand with the same counterparty;
(2) Any purchase or sale of one or more financial instruments by a banking entity that arises under a transaction in which the banking entity lends or borrows a security temporarily to or from another party pursuant to a written securities lending agreement under which the lender retains the economic interests of an owner of such security, and has the right to terminate the transaction and to recall the loaned security on terms agreed by the parties;
(3) Any purchase or sale of a security, foreign exchange forward (as that term is defined in section 1a(24) of the Commodity Exchange Act (7 U.S.C. 1a(24)), foreign exchange swap (as that term is defined in section 1a(25) of the Commodity Exchange Act (7 U.S.C. 1a(25)), or cross-currency swap by a banking entity for the purpose of liquidity management in accordance with a documented liquidity management plan of the banking entity that:
(i) Specifically contemplates and authorizes the particular financial instruments to be used for liquidity management purposes, the amount, types, and risks of these financial instruments that are consistent with liquidity management, and the liquidity circumstances in which the particular financial instruments may or must be used;

(ii) Requires that any purchase or sale of financial instruments contemplated and authorized by the plan be principally for the purpose of managing the liquidity of the banking entity, and not for the purpose of short-term resale, benefitting from actual or expected short-term price movements, realizing short-term arbitrage profits, or hedging a position taken for such short-term purposes;
(iii) Requires that any financial instruments purchased or sold for liquidity management purposes be highly liquid and limited to financial instruments the market, credit, and other risks of which the banking entity does not reasonably expect to give rise to appreciable profits or losses as a result of short-term price movements;
(iv) Limits any financial instruments purchased or sold for liquidity management purposes, together with any other financial instruments purchased or sold for such purposes, to an amount that is consistent with the banking entity's near-term funding needs, including deviations from normal operations of the banking entity or any affiliate thereof, as estimated and documented pursuant to methods specified in the plan;
(v) Includes written policies and procedures, internal controls, analysis, and independent testing to ensure that the purchase and sale of financial instruments that are not permitted under § 255.6(a) or (b) of this subpart are for the purpose of liquidity management and in accordance with the liquidity management plan described in this paragraph (d)(3); and
(vi) Is consistent with the SEC's regulatory requirements regarding liquidity management;
(4) Any purchase or sale of one or more financial instruments by a banking entity that is a derivatives clearing organization or a clearing agency in connection with clearing financial instruments;
(5) Any excluded clearing activities by a banking entity that is a member of a clearing agency, a member of a derivatives clearing organization, or a member of a designated financial market utility;

Securities and Exchange Commission

§ 255.3

(6) Any purchase or sale of one or more financial instruments by a banking entity, so long as:

(i) The purchase (or sale) satisfies an existing delivery obligation of the banking entity or its customers, including to prevent or close out a failure to deliver, in connection with delivery, clearing, or settlement activity; or

(ii) The purchase (or sale) satisfies an obligation of the banking entity in connection with a judicial, administrative, self-regulatory organization, or arbitration proceeding;

(7) Any purchase or sale of one or more financial instruments by a banking entity that is acting solely as agent, broker, or custodian;

(8) Any purchase or sale of one or more financial instruments by a banking entity through a deferred compensation, stock-bonus, profit-sharing, or pension plan of the banking entity that is established and administered in accordance with the law of the United States or a foreign sovereign, if the purchase or sale is made directly or indirectly by the banking entity as trustee for the benefit of persons who are or were employees of the banking entity;

(9) Any purchase or sale of one or more financial instruments by a banking entity in the ordinary course of collecting a debt previously contracted in good faith, provided that the banking entity divests the financial instrument as soon as practicable, and in no event may the banking entity retain such instrument for longer than such period permitted by the SEC;

(10) Any purchase or sale of one or more financial instruments that was made in error by a banking entity in the course of conducting a permitted or excluded activity or is a subsequent transaction to correct such an error;

(11) Contemporaneously entering into a customer-driven swap or customer-driven security-based swap and a matched swap or security-based swap if:

(i) The banking entity retains no more than minimal price risk; and

(ii) The banking entity is not a registered dealer, swap dealer, or security-based swap dealer;

(12) Any purchase or sale of one or more financial instruments that the banking entity uses to hedge mortgage servicing rights or mortgage servicing assets in accordance with a documented hedging strategy; or

(13) Any purchase or sale of a financial instrument that does not meet the definition of trading asset or trading liability under the applicable reporting form for a banking entity as of January 1, 2020.

(e) *Definition of other terms related to proprietary trading.* For purposes of this subpart:

(1) *Anonymous* means that each party to a purchase or sale is unaware of the identity of the other party(ies) to the purchase or sale.

(2) *Clearing agency* has the same meaning as in section 3(a)(23) of the Exchange Act (15 U.S.C. 78c(a)(23)).

(3) *Commodity* has the same meaning as in section 1a(9) of the Commodity Exchange Act (7 U.S.C. 1a(9)), except that a commodity does not include any security;

(4) *Contract of sale of a commodity for future delivery* means a contract of sale (as that term is defined in section 1a(13) of the Commodity Exchange Act (7 U.S.C. 1a(13)) for future delivery (as that term is defined in section 1a(27) of the Commodity Exchange Act (7 U.S.C. 1a(27))).

(5) *Cross-currency swap* means a swap in which one party exchanges with another party principal and interest rate payments in one currency for principal and interest rate payments in another currency, and the exchange of principal occurs on the date the swap is entered into, with a reversal of the exchange of principal at a later date that is agreed upon when the swap is entered into.

(6) *Derivatives clearing organization* means:

(i) A derivatives clearing organization registered under section 5b of the Commodity Exchange Act (7 U.S.C. 7a–1);

(ii) A derivatives clearing organization that, pursuant to CFTC regulation, is exempt from the registration requirements under section 5b of the Commodity Exchange Act (7 U.S.C. 7a–1); or

§ 255.3

(iii) A foreign derivatives clearing organization that, pursuant to CFTC regulation, is permitted to clear for a foreign board of trade that is registered with the CFTC.

(7) *Exchange,* unless the context otherwise requires, means any designated contract market, swap execution facility, or foreign board of trade registered with the CFTC, or, for purposes of securities or security-based swaps, an exchange, as defined under section 3(a)(1) of the Exchange Act (15 U.S.C. 78c(a)(1)), or security-based swap execution facility, as defined under section 3(a)(77) of the Exchange Act (15 U.S.C. 78c(a)(77)).

(8) *Excluded clearing activities* means:

(i) With respect to customer transactions cleared on a derivatives clearing organization, a clearing agency, or a designated financial market utility, any purchase or sale necessary to correct trading errors made by or on behalf of a customer provided that such purchase or sale is conducted in accordance with, for transactions cleared on a derivatives clearing organization, the Commodity Exchange Act, CFTC regulations, and the rules or procedures of the derivatives clearing organization, or, for transactions cleared on a clearing agency, the rules or procedures of the clearing agency, or, for transactions cleared on a designated financial market utility that is neither a derivatives clearing organization nor a clearing agency, the rules or procedures of the designated financial market utility;

(ii) Any purchase or sale in connection with and related to the management of a default or threatened imminent default of a customer provided that such purchase or sale is conducted in accordance with, for transactions cleared on a derivatives clearing organization, the Commodity Exchange Act, CFTC regulations, and the rules or procedures of the derivatives clearing organization, or, for transactions cleared on a clearing agency, the rules or procedures of the clearing agency, or, for transactions cleared on a designated financial market utility that is neither a derivatives clearing organization nor a clearing agency, the rules or procedures of the designated financial market utility;

(iii) Any purchase or sale in connection with and related to the management of a default or threatened imminent default of a member of a clearing agency, a member of a derivatives clearing organization, or a member of a designated financial market utility;

(iv) Any purchase or sale in connection with and related to the management of the default or threatened default of a clearing agency, a derivatives clearing organization, or a designated financial market utility; and

(v) Any purchase or sale that is required by the rules or procedures of a clearing agency, a derivatives clearing organization, or a designated financial market utility to mitigate the risk to the clearing agency, derivatives clearing organization, or designated financial market utility that would result from the clearing by a member of security-based swaps that reference the member or an affiliate of the member.

(9) *Designated financial market utility* has the same meaning as in section 803(4) of the Dodd-Frank Act (12 U.S.C. 5462(4)).

(10) *Issuer* has the same meaning as in section 2(a)(4) of the Securities Act of 1933 (15 U.S.C. 77b(a)(4)).

(11) *Market risk capital rule covered position and trading position* means a financial instrument that meets the criteria to be a covered position and a trading position, as those terms are respectively defined, without regard to whether the financial instrument is reported as a covered position or trading position on any applicable regulatory reporting forms:

(i) In the case of a banking entity that is a bank holding company, savings and loan holding company, or insured depository institution, under the market risk capital rule that is applicable to the banking entity; and

(ii) In the case of a banking entity that is affiliated with a bank holding company or savings and loan holding company, other than a banking entity to which a market risk capital rule is applicable, under the market risk capital rule that is applicable to the affiliated bank holding company or savings and loan holding company.

(12) *Market risk capital rule* means the market risk capital rule that is contained in 12 CFR part 3, subpart F, with

Securities and Exchange Commission § 255.4

respect to a banking entity for which the OCC is the primary financial regulatory agency, 12 CFR part 217 with respect to a banking entity for which the Board is the primary financial regulatory agency, or 12 CFR part 324 with respect to a banking entity for which the FDIC is the primary financial regulatory agency.

(13) *Municipal security* means a security that is a direct obligation of or issued by, or an obligation guaranteed as to principal or interest by, a State or any political subdivision thereof, or any agency or instrumentality of a State or any political subdivision thereof, or any municipal corporate instrumentality of one or more States or political subdivisions thereof.

(14) *Trading desk* means a unit of organization of a banking entity that purchases or sells financial instruments for the trading account of the banking entity or an affiliate thereof that is:

(i)(A) Structured by the banking entity to implement a well-defined business strategy;

(B) Organized to ensure appropriate setting, monitoring, and management review of the desk's trading and hedging limits, current and potential future loss exposures, and strategies; and

(C) Characterized by a clearly defined unit that:

(*1*) Engages in coordinated trading activity with a unified approach to its key elements;

(*2*) Operates subject to a common and calibrated set of risk metrics, risk levels, and joint trading limits;

(*3*) Submits compliance reports and other information as a unit for monitoring by management; and

(*4*) Books its trades together; or

(ii) For a banking entity that calculates risk-based capital ratios under the market risk capital rule, or a consolidated affiliate for regulatory reporting purposes of a banking entity that calculates risk-based capital ratios under the market risk capital rule, established by the banking entity or its affiliate for purposes of market risk capital calculations under the market risk capital rule.

[79 FR 5779, 5805, Jan. 31, 2014, as amended at 84 FR 62239, Nov. 14, 2019]

§ 255.4 Permitted underwriting and market making-related activities.

(a) *Underwriting activities*—(1) *Permitted underwriting activities.* The prohibition contained in § 255.3(a) does not apply to a banking entity's underwriting activities conducted in accordance with this paragraph (a).

(2) *Requirements.* The underwriting activities of a banking entity are permitted under paragraph (a)(1) of this section only if:

(i) The banking entity is acting as an underwriter for a distribution of securities and the trading desk's underwriting position is related to such distribution;

(ii)(A) The amount and type of the securities in the trading desk's underwriting position are designed not to exceed the reasonably expected near term demands of clients, customers, or counterparties, taking into account the liquidity, maturity, and depth of the market for the relevant types of securities; and

(B) Reasonable efforts are made to sell or otherwise reduce the underwriting position within a reasonable period, taking into account the liquidity, maturity, and depth of the market for the relevant types of securities;

(iii) In the case of a banking entity with significant trading assets and liabilities, the banking entity has established and implements, maintains, and enforces an internal compliance program required by subpart D of this part that is reasonably designed to ensure the banking entity's compliance with the requirements of paragraph (a) of this section, including reasonably designed written policies and procedures, internal controls, analysis and independent testing identifying and addressing:

(A) The products, instruments or exposures each trading desk may purchase, sell, or manage as part of its underwriting activities;

(B) Limits for each trading desk, in accordance with paragraph (a)(2)(ii)(A) of this section;

(C) Written authorization procedures, including escalation procedures that require review and approval of any trade that would exceed a trading desk's limit(s), demonstrable analysis

§ 255.4

of the basis for any temporary or permanent increase to a trading desk's limit(s), and independent review of such demonstrable analysis and approval; and

(D) Internal controls and ongoing monitoring and analysis of each trading desk's compliance with its limits.

(iv) A banking entity with significant trading assets and liabilities may satisfy the requirements in paragraphs (a)(2)(iii)(B) and (C) of this section by complying with the requirements set forth below in paragraph (c) of this section;

(v) The compensation arrangements of persons performing the activities described in this paragraph (a) are designed not to reward or incentivize prohibited proprietary trading; and

(vi) The banking entity is licensed or registered to engage in the activity described in this paragraph (a) in accordance with applicable law.

(3) *Definition of distribution.* For purposes of this paragraph (a), a distribution of securities means:

(i) An offering of securities, whether or not subject to registration under the Securities Act of 1933, that is distinguished from ordinary trading transactions by the presence of special selling efforts and selling methods; or

(ii) An offering of securities made pursuant to an effective registration statement under the Securities Act of 1933.

(4) *Definition of underwriter.* For purposes of this paragraph (a), *underwriter* means:

(i) A person who has agreed with an issuer or selling security holder to:

(A) Purchase securities from the issuer or selling security holder for distribution;

(B) Engage in a distribution of securities for or on behalf of the issuer or selling security holder; or

(C) Manage a distribution of securities for or on behalf of the issuer or selling security holder; or

(ii) A person who has agreed to participate or is participating in a distribution of such securities for or on behalf of the issuer or selling security holder.

(5) *Definition of selling security holder.* For purposes of this paragraph (a), *selling security holder* means any person, other than an issuer, on whose behalf a distribution is made.

(6) *Definition of underwriting position.* For purposes of this section, *underwriting position* means the long or short positions in one or more securities held by a banking entity or its affiliate, and managed by a particular trading desk, in connection with a particular distribution of securities for which such banking entity or affiliate is acting as an underwriter.

(7) *Definition of client, customer, and counterparty.* For purposes of this paragraph (a), the terms *client, customer, and counterparty,* on a collective or individual basis, refer to market participants that may transact with the banking entity in connection with a particular distribution for which the banking entity is acting as underwriter.

(b) *Market making-related activities—* (1) *Permitted market making-related activities.* The prohibition contained in § 255.3(a) does not apply to a banking entity's market making-related activities conducted in accordance with this paragraph (b).

(2) *Requirements.* The market making-related activities of a banking entity are permitted under paragraph (b)(1) of this section only if:

(i) The trading desk that establishes and manages the financial exposure, routinely stands ready to purchase and sell one or more types of financial instruments related to its financial exposure, and is willing and available to quote, purchase and sell, or otherwise enter into long and short positions in those types of financial instruments for its own account, in commercially reasonable amounts and throughout market cycles on a basis appropriate for the liquidity, maturity, and depth of the market for the relevant types of financial instruments;

(ii) The trading desk's market-making related activities are designed not to exceed, on an ongoing basis, the reasonably expected near term demands of clients, customers, or counterparties, taking into account the liquidity, maturity, and depth of the market for the relevant types of financial instruments;

Securities and Exchange Commission § 255.4

(iii) In the case of a banking entity with significant trading assets and liabilities, the banking entity has established and implements, maintains, and enforces an internal compliance program required by subpart D of this part that is reasonably designed to ensure the banking entity's compliance with the requirements of paragraph (b) of this section, including reasonably designed written policies and procedures, internal controls, analysis and independent testing identifying and addressing:

(A) The financial instruments each trading desk stands ready to purchase and sell in accordance with paragraph (b)(2)(i) of this section;

(B) The actions the trading desk will take to demonstrably reduce or otherwise significantly mitigate promptly the risks of its financial exposure consistent with the limits required under paragraph (b)(2)(iii)(C) of this section; the products, instruments, and exposures each trading desk may use for risk management purposes; the techniques and strategies each trading desk may use to manage the risks of its market making-related activities and positions; and the process, strategies, and personnel responsible for ensuring that the actions taken by the trading desk to mitigate these risks are and continue to be effective;

(C) Limits for each trading desk, in accordance with paragraph (b)(2)(ii) of this section;

(D) Written authorization procedures, including escalation procedures that require review and approval of any trade that would exceed a trading desk's limit(s), demonstrable analysis of the basis for any temporary or permanent increase to a trading desk's limit(s), and independent review of such demonstrable analysis and approval; and

(E) Internal controls and ongoing monitoring and analysis of each trading desk's compliance with its limits.

(iv) A banking entity with significant trading assets and liabilities may satisfy the requirements in paragraphs (b)(2)(iii)(C) and (D) of this section by complying with the requirements set forth below in paragraph (c) of this section;

(v) The compensation arrangements of persons performing the activities described in this paragraph (b) are designed not to reward or incentivize prohibited proprietary trading; and

(vi) The banking entity is licensed or registered to engage in activity described in this paragraph (b) in accordance with applicable law.

(3) *Definition of client, customer, and counterparty.* For purposes of paragraph (b) of this section, the terms *client, customer, and counterparty,* on a collective or individual basis refer to market participants that make use of the banking entity's market making-related services by obtaining such services, responding to quotations, or entering into a continuing relationship with respect to such services, provided that:

(i) A trading desk or other organizational unit of another banking entity is not a client, customer, or counterparty of the trading desk if that other entity has trading assets and liabilities of $50 billion or more as measured in accordance with the methodology described in §255.2(ee) of this part, unless:

(A) The trading desk documents how and why a particular trading desk or other organizational unit of the entity should be treated as a client, customer, or counterparty of the trading desk for purposes of paragraph (b)(2) of this section; or

(B) The purchase or sale by the trading desk is conducted anonymously on an exchange or similar trading facility that permits trading on behalf of a broad range of market participants.

(ii) [Reserved]

(4) *Definition of financial exposure.* For purposes of this section, *financial exposure* means the aggregate risks of one or more financial instruments and any associated loans, commodities, or foreign exchange or currency, held by a banking entity or its affiliate and managed by a particular trading desk as part of the trading desk's market making-related activities.

(5) *Definition of market-maker positions.* For the purposes of this section, *market-maker positions* means all of the positions in the financial instruments for which the trading desk stands ready to make a market in accordance with paragraph (b)(2)(i) of this section,

§ 255.4

that are managed by the trading desk, including the trading desk's open positions or exposures arising from open transactions.

(c) *Rebuttable presumption of compliance*—(1) *Internal limits.* (i) A banking entity shall be presumed to meet the requirement in paragraph (a)(2)(ii)(A) or (b)(2)(ii) of this section with respect to the purchase or sale of a financial instrument if the banking entity has established and implements, maintains, and enforces the internal limits for the relevant trading desk as described in paragraph (c)(1)(ii) of this section.

(ii)(A) With respect to underwriting activities conducted pursuant to paragraph (a) of this section, the presumption described in paragraph (c)(1)(i) of this section shall be available to each trading desk that establishes, implements, maintains, and enforces internal limits that should take into account the liquidity, maturity, and depth of the market for the relevant types of securities and are designed not to exceed the reasonably expected near term demands of clients, customers, or counterparties, based on the nature and amount of the trading desk's underwriting activities, on the:

(*1*) Amount, types, and risk of its underwriting position;

(*2*) Level of exposures to relevant risk factors arising from its underwriting position; and

(*3*) Period of time a security may be held.

(B) With respect to market making-related activities conducted pursuant to paragraph (b) of this section, the presumption described in paragraph (c)(1)(i) of this section shall be available to each trading desk that establishes, implements, maintains, and enforces internal limits that should take into account the liquidity, maturity, and depth of the market for the relevant types of financial instruments and are designed not to exceed the reasonably expected near term demands of clients, customers, or counterparties, based on the nature and amount of the trading desk's market-making related activities, that address the:

(*1*) Amount, types, and risks of its market-maker positions;

(*2*) Amount, types, and risks of the products, instruments, and exposures the trading desk may use for risk management purposes;

(*3*) Level of exposures to relevant risk factors arising from its financial exposure; and

(*4*) Period of time a financial instrument may be held.

(2) *Supervisory review and oversight.* The limits described in paragraph (c)(1) of this section shall be subject to supervisory review and oversight by the SEC on an ongoing basis.

(3) *Limit breaches and increases.* (i) With respect to any limit set pursuant to paragraphs (c)(1)(ii)(A) or (c)(1)(ii)(B) of this section, a banking entity shall maintain and make available to the SEC upon request records regarding any limit that is exceeded and any temporary or permanent increase to any limit(s), in each case in the form and manner as directed by the SEC.

(ii) In the event of a breach or increase of any limit set pursuant to paragraph (c)(1)(ii)(A) or (B) of this section, the presumption described in paragraph (c)(1)(i) of this section shall continue to be available only if the banking entity:

(A) Takes action as promptly as possible after a breach to bring the trading desk into compliance; and

(B) Follows established written authorization procedures, including escalation procedures that require review and approval of any trade that exceeds a trading desk's limit(s), demonstrable analysis of the basis for any temporary or permanent increase to a trading desk's limit(s), and independent review of such demonstrable analysis and approval.

(4) *Rebutting the presumption.* The presumption in paragraph (c)(1)(i) of this section may be rebutted by the SEC if the SEC determines, taking into account the liquidity, maturity, and depth of the market for the relevant types of financial instruments and based on all relevant facts and circumstances, that a trading desk is engaging in activity that is not based on the reasonably expected near term demands of clients, customers, or counterparties. The SEC's rebuttal of the presumption in paragraph (c)(1)(i)

Securities and Exchange Commission § 255.5

must be made in accordance with the notice and response procedures in subpart D of this part.

[84 FR 62241, Nov. 14, 2019]

§ 255.5 Permitted risk-mitigating hedging activities.

(a) *Permitted risk-mitigating hedging activities.* The prohibition contained in § 255.3(a) does not apply to the risk-mitigating hedging activities of a banking entity in connection with and related to individual or aggregated positions, contracts, or other holdings of the banking entity and designed to reduce the specific risks to the banking entity in connection with and related to such positions, contracts, or other holdings.

(b) *Requirements.* (1) The risk-mitigating hedging activities of a banking entity that has significant trading assets and liabilities are permitted under paragraph (a) of this section only if:

(i) The banking entity has established and implements, maintains and enforces an internal compliance program required by subpart D of this part that is reasonably designed to ensure the banking entity's compliance with the requirements of this section, including:

(A) Reasonably designed written policies and procedures regarding the positions, techniques and strategies that may be used for hedging, including documentation indicating what positions, contracts or other holdings a particular trading desk may use in its risk-mitigating hedging activities, as well as position and aging limits with respect to such positions, contracts or other holdings;

(B) Internal controls and ongoing monitoring, management, and authorization procedures, including relevant escalation procedures; and

(C) The conduct of analysis and independent testing designed to ensure that the positions, techniques and strategies that may be used for hedging may reasonably be expected to reduce or otherwise significantly mitigate the specific, identifiable risk(s) being hedged;

(ii) The risk-mitigating hedging activity:

(A) Is conducted in accordance with the written policies, procedures, and internal controls required under this section;

(B) At the inception of the hedging activity, including, without limitation, any adjustments to the hedging activity, is designed to reduce or otherwise significantly mitigate one or more specific, identifiable risks, including market risk, counterparty or other credit risk, currency or foreign exchange risk, interest rate risk, commodity price risk, basis risk, or similar risks, arising in connection with and related to identified positions, contracts, or other holdings of the banking entity, based upon the facts and circumstances of the identified underlying and hedging positions, contracts or other holdings and the risks and liquidity thereof;

(C) Does not give rise, at the inception of the hedge, to any significant new or additional risk that is not itself hedged contemporaneously in accordance with this section;

(D) Is subject to continuing review, monitoring and management by the banking entity that:

(*1*) Is consistent with the written hedging policies and procedures required under paragraph (b)(1)(i) of this section;

(*2*) Is designed to reduce or otherwise significantly mitigate the specific, identifiable risks that develop over time from the risk-mitigating hedging activities undertaken under this section and the underlying positions, contracts, and other holdings of the banking entity, based upon the facts and circumstances of the underlying and hedging positions, contracts and other holdings of the banking entity and the risks and liquidity thereof; and

(*3*) Requires ongoing recalibration of the hedging activity by the banking entity to ensure that the hedging activity satisfies the requirements set out in paragraph (b)(1)(ii) of this section and is not prohibited proprietary trading; and

(iii) The compensation arrangements of persons performing risk-mitigating hedging activities are designed not to reward or incentivize prohibited proprietary trading.

(2) The risk-mitigating hedging activities of a banking entity that does not have significant trading assets and

§ 255.5

liabilities are permitted under paragraph (a) of this section only if the risk-mitigating hedging activity:

(i) At the inception of the hedging activity, including, without limitation, any adjustments to the hedging activity, is designed to reduce or otherwise significantly mitigate one or more specific, identifiable risks, including market risk, counterparty or other credit risk, currency or foreign exchange risk, interest rate risk, commodity price risk, basis risk, or similar risks, arising in connection with and related to identified positions, contracts, or other holdings of the banking entity, based upon the facts and circumstances of the identified underlying and hedging positions, contracts or other holdings and the risks and liquidity thereof; and

(ii) Is subject, as appropriate, to ongoing recalibration by the banking entity to ensure that the hedging activity satisfies the requirements set out in paragraph (b)(2) of this section and is not prohibited proprietary trading.

(c) *Documentation requirement.* (1) A banking entity that has significant trading assets and liabilities must comply with the requirements of paragraphs (c)(2) and (3) of this section, unless the requirements of paragraph (c)(4) of this section are met, with respect to any purchase or sale of financial instruments made in reliance on this section for risk-mitigating hedging purposes that is:

(i) Not established by the specific trading desk establishing or responsible for the underlying positions, contracts, or other holdings the risks of which the hedging activity is designed to reduce;

(ii) Established by the specific trading desk establishing or responsible for the underlying positions, contracts, or other holdings the risks of which the purchases or sales are designed to reduce, but that is effected through a financial instrument, exposure, technique, or strategy that is not specifically identified in the trading desk's written policies and procedures established under paragraph (b)(1) of this section or under § 255.4(b)(2)(iii)(B) of this subpart as a product, instrument, exposure, technique, or strategy such trading desk may use for hedging; or

(iii) Established to hedge aggregated positions across two or more trading desks.

(2) In connection with any purchase or sale identified in paragraph (c)(1) of this section, a banking entity must, at a minimum, and contemporaneously with the purchase or sale, document:

(i) The specific, identifiable risk(s) of the identified positions, contracts, or other holdings of the banking entity that the purchase or sale is designed to reduce;

(ii) The specific risk-mitigating strategy that the purchase or sale is designed to fulfill; and

(iii) The trading desk or other business unit that is establishing and responsible for the hedge.

(3) A banking entity must create and retain records sufficient to demonstrate compliance with the requirements of this paragraph (c) for a period that is no less than five years in a form that allows the banking entity to promptly produce such records to the SEC on request, or such longer period as required under other law or this part.

(4) The requirements of paragraphs (c)(2) and (3) of this section do not apply to the purchase or sale of a financial instrument described in paragraph (c)(1) of this section if:

(i) The financial instrument purchased or sold is identified on a written list of pre-approved financial instruments that are commonly used by the trading desk for the specific type of hedging activity for which the financial instrument is being purchased or sold; and

(ii) At the time the financial instrument is purchased or sold, the hedging activity (including the purchase or sale of the financial instrument) complies with written, pre-approved limits for the trading desk purchasing or selling the financial instrument for hedging activities undertaken for one or more other trading desks. The limits shall be appropriate for the:

(A) Size, types, and risks of the hedging activities commonly undertaken by the trading desk;

(B) Financial instruments purchased and sold for hedging activities by the trading desk; and

Securities and Exchange Commission § 255.6

(C) Levels and duration of the risk exposures being hedged.

[79 FR 5779, 5805, Jan. 31, 2014, as amended at 84 FR 62243, Nov. 14, 2019]

§ 255.6 Other permitted proprietary trading activities.

(a) *Permitted trading in domestic government obligations.* The prohibition contained in § 255.3(a) does not apply to the purchase or sale by a banking entity of a financial instrument that is:

(1) An obligation of, or issued or guaranteed by, the United States;

(2) An obligation, participation, or other instrument of, or issued or guaranteed by, an agency of the United States, the Government National Mortgage Association, the Federal National Mortgage Association, the Federal Home Loan Mortgage Corporation, a Federal Home Loan Bank, the Federal Agricultural Mortgage Corporation or a Farm Credit System institution chartered under and subject to the provisions of the Farm Credit Act of 1971 (12 U.S.C. 2001 *et seq.*);

(3) An obligation of any State or any political subdivision thereof, including any municipal security; or

(4) An obligation of the FDIC, or any entity formed by or on behalf of the FDIC for purpose of facilitating the disposal of assets acquired or held by the FDIC in its corporate capacity or as conservator or receiver under the Federal Deposit Insurance Act or Title II of the Dodd-Frank Wall Street Reform and Consumer Protection Act.

(b) *Permitted trading in foreign government obligations*—(1) *Affiliates of foreign banking entities in the United States.* The prohibition contained in § 255.3(a) does not apply to the purchase or sale of a financial instrument that is an obligation of, or issued or guaranteed by, a foreign sovereign (including any multinational central bank of which the foreign sovereign is a member), or any agency or political subdivision of such foreign sovereign, by a banking entity, so long as:

(i) The banking entity is organized under or is directly or indirectly controlled by a banking entity that is organized under the laws of a foreign sovereign and is not directly or indirectly controlled by a top-tier banking entity that is organized under the laws of the United States;

(ii) The financial instrument is an obligation of, or issued or guaranteed by, the foreign sovereign under the laws of which the foreign banking entity referred to in paragraph (b)(1)(i) of this section is organized (including any multinational central bank of which the foreign sovereign is a member), or any agency or political subdivision of that foreign sovereign; and

(iii) The purchase or sale as principal is not made by an insured depository institution.

(2) *Foreign affiliates of a U.S. banking entity.* The prohibition contained in § 255.3(a) does not apply to the purchase or sale of a financial instrument that is an obligation of, or issued or guaranteed by, a foreign sovereign (including any multinational central bank of which the foreign sovereign is a member), or any agency or political subdivision of that foreign sovereign, by a foreign entity that is owned or controlled by a banking entity organized or established under the laws of the United States or any State, so long as:

(i) The foreign entity is a foreign bank, as defined in section 211.2(j) of the Board's Regulation K (12 CFR 211.2(j)), or is regulated by the foreign sovereign as a securities dealer;

(ii) The financial instrument is an obligation of, or issued or guaranteed by, the foreign sovereign under the laws of which the foreign entity is organized (including any multinational central bank of which the foreign sovereign is a member), or any agency or political subdivision of that foreign sovereign; and

(iii) The financial instrument is owned by the foreign entity and is not financed by an affiliate that is located in the United States or organized under the laws of the United States or of any State.

(c) *Permitted trading on behalf of customers*—(1) *Fiduciary transactions.* The prohibition contained in § 255.3(a) does not apply to the purchase or sale of financial instruments by a banking entity acting as trustee or in a similar fiduciary capacity, so long as:

(i) The transaction is conducted for the account of, or on behalf of, a customer; and

§ 255.6

(ii) The banking entity does not have or retain beneficial ownership of the financial instruments.

(2) *Riskless principal transactions.* The prohibition contained in § 255.3(a) does not apply to the purchase or sale of financial instruments by a banking entity acting as riskless principal in a transaction in which the banking entity, after receiving an order to purchase (or sell) a financial instrument from a customer, purchases (or sells) the financial instrument for its own account to offset a contemporaneous sale to (or purchase from) the customer.

(d) *Permitted trading by a regulated insurance company.* The prohibition contained in § 255.3(a) does not apply to the purchase or sale of financial instruments by a banking entity that is an insurance company or an affiliate of an insurance company if:

(1) The insurance company or its affiliate purchases or sells the financial instruments solely for:

(i) The general account of the insurance company; or

(ii) A separate account established by the insurance company;

(2) The purchase or sale is conducted in compliance with, and subject to, the insurance company investment laws, regulations, and written guidance of the State or jurisdiction in which such insurance company is domiciled; and

(3) The appropriate Federal banking agencies, after consultation with the Financial Stability Oversight Council and the relevant insurance commissioners of the States and foreign jurisdictions, as appropriate, have not jointly determined, after notice and comment, that a particular law, regulation, or written guidance described in paragraph (d)(2) of this section is insufficient to protect the safety and soundness of the covered banking entity, or the financial stability of the United States.

(e) *Permitted trading activities of foreign banking entities.* (1) The prohibition contained in § 255.3(a) does not apply to the purchase or sale of financial instruments by a banking entity if:

(i) The banking entity is not organized or directly or indirectly controlled by a banking entity that is organized under the laws of the United States or of any State;

(ii) The purchase or sale by the banking entity is made pursuant to paragraph (9) or (13) of section 4(c) of the BHC Act; and

(iii) The purchase or sale meets the requirements of paragraph (e)(3) of this section.

(2) A purchase or sale of financial instruments by a banking entity is made pursuant to paragraph (9) or (13) of section 4(c) of the BHC Act for purposes of paragraph (e)(1)(ii) of this section only if:

(i) The purchase or sale is conducted in accordance with the requirements of paragraph (e) of this section; and

(ii)(A) With respect to a banking entity that is a foreign banking organization, the banking entity meets the qualifying foreign banking organization requirements of section 211.23(a), (c) or (e) of the Board's Regulation K (12 CFR 211.23(a), (c) or (e)), as applicable; or

(B) With respect to a banking entity that is not a foreign banking organization, the banking entity is not organized under the laws of the United States or of any State and the banking entity, on a fully-consolidated basis, meets at least two of the following requirements:

(*1*) Total assets of the banking entity held outside of the United States exceed total assets of the banking entity held in the United States;

(*2*) Total revenues derived from the business of the banking entity outside of the United States exceed total revenues derived from the business of the banking entity in the United States; or

(*3*) Total net income derived from the business of the banking entity outside of the United States exceeds total net income derived from the business of the banking entity in the United States.

(3) A purchase or sale by a banking entity is permitted for purposes of this paragraph (e) if:

(i) The banking entity engaging as principal in the purchase or sale (including relevant personnel) is not located in the United States or organized under the laws of the United States or of any State;

(ii) The banking entity (including relevant personnel) that makes the decision to purchase or sell as principal is

Securities and Exchange Commission § 255.7

not located in the United States or organized under the laws of the United States or of any State; and

(iii) The purchase or sale, including any transaction arising from risk-mitigating hedging related to the instruments purchased or sold, is not accounted for as principal directly or on a consolidated basis by any branch or affiliate that is located in the United States or organized under the laws of the United States or of any State.

(4) For purposes of this paragraph (e), a U.S. branch, agency, or subsidiary of a foreign banking entity is considered to be located in the United States; however, the foreign bank that operates or controls that branch, agency, or subsidiary is not considered to be located in the United States solely by virtue of operating or controlling the U.S. branch, agency, or subsidiary.

(f) *Permitted trading activities of qualifying foreign excluded funds.* The prohibition contained in § 255.3(a) does not apply to the purchase or sale of a financial instrument by a qualifying foreign excluded fund. For purposes of this paragraph (f), a qualifying foreign excluded fund means a banking entity that:

(1) Is organized or established outside the United States, and the ownership interests of which are offered and sold solely outside the United States;

(2)(i) Would be a covered fund if the entity were organized or established in the United States, or

(ii) Is, or holds itself out as being, an entity or arrangement that raises money from investors primarily for the purpose of investing in financial instruments for resale or other disposition or otherwise trading in financial instruments;

(3) Would not otherwise be a banking entity except by virtue of the acquisition or retention of an ownership interest in, sponsorship of, or relationship with the entity, by another banking entity that meets the following:

(i) The banking entity is not organized, or directly or indirectly controlled by a banking entity that is organized, under the laws of the United States or of any State; and

(ii) The banking entity's acquisition or retention of an ownership interest in or sponsorship of the fund meets the requirements for permitted covered fund activities and investments solely outside the United States, as provided in § 255.13(b);

(4) Is established and operated as part of a bona fide asset management business; and

(5) Is not operated in a manner that enables the banking entity that sponsors or controls the qualifying foreign excluded fund, or any of its affiliates, to evade the requirements of section 13 of the BHC Act or this part.

[79 FR 5779, 5805, Jan. 31, 2014, as amended at 84 FR 62244, Nov. 14, 2019; 85 FR 46522, July 31, 2020]

§ 255.7 **Limitations on permitted proprietary trading activities.**

(a) No transaction, class of transactions, or activity may be deemed permissible under §§ 255.4 through 255.6 if the transaction, class of transactions, or activity would:

(1) Involve or result in a material conflict of interest between the banking entity and its clients, customers, or counterparties;

(2) Result, directly or indirectly, in a material exposure by the banking entity to a high-risk asset or a high-risk trading strategy; or

(3) Pose a threat to the safety and soundness of the banking entity or to the financial stability of the United States.

(b) *Definition of material conflict of interest.* (1) For purposes of this section, a material conflict of interest between a banking entity and its clients, customers, or counterparties exists if the banking entity engages in any transaction, class of transactions, or activity that would involve or result in the banking entity's interests being materially adverse to the interests of its client, customer, or counterparty with respect to such transaction, class of transactions, or activity, and the banking entity has not taken at least one of the actions in paragraph (b)(2) of this section.

(2) Prior to effecting the specific transaction or class or type of transactions, or engaging in the specific activity, the banking entity:

(i) *Timely and effective disclosure.* (A) Has made clear, timely, and effective disclosure of the conflict of interest, together with other necessary information, in reasonable detail and in a manner sufficient to permit a reasonable client, customer, or counterparty to meaningfully understand the conflict of interest; and

(B) Such disclosure is made in a manner that provides the client, customer, or counterparty the opportunity to negate, or substantially mitigate, any materially adverse effect on the client, customer, or counterparty created by the conflict of interest; or

(ii) *Information barriers.* Has established, maintained, and enforced information barriers that are memorialized in written policies and procedures, such as physical separation of personnel, or functions, or limitations on types of activity, that are reasonably designed, taking into consideration the nature of the banking entity's business, to prevent the conflict of interest from involving or resulting in a materially adverse effect on a client, customer, or counterparty. A banking entity may not rely on such information barriers if, in the case of any specific transaction, class or type of transactions or activity, the banking entity knows or should reasonably know that, notwithstanding the banking entity's establishment of information barriers, the conflict of interest may involve or result in a materially adverse effect on a client, customer, or counterparty.

(c) *Definition of high-risk asset and high-risk trading strategy.* For purposes of this section:

(1) *High-risk asset* means an asset or group of related assets that would, if held by a banking entity, significantly increase the likelihood that the banking entity would incur a substantial financial loss or would pose a threat to the financial stability of the United States.

(2) *High-risk trading strategy* means a trading strategy that would, if engaged in by a banking entity, significantly increase the likelihood that the banking entity would incur a substantial financial loss or would pose a threat to the financial stability of the United States.

§§ 255.8–255.9 [Reserved]

Subpart C—Covered Funds Activities and Investments

§ 255.10 Prohibition on acquiring or retaining an ownership interest in and having certain relationships with a covered fund.

(a) *Prohibition.* (1) Except as otherwise provided in this subpart, a banking entity may not, as principal, directly or indirectly, acquire or retain any ownership interest in or sponsor a covered fund.

(2) Paragraph (a)(1) of this section does not include acquiring or retaining an ownership interest in a covered fund by a banking entity:

(i) Acting solely as agent, broker, or custodian, so long as;

(A) The activity is conducted for the account of, or on behalf of, a customer; and

(B) The banking entity and its affiliates do not have or retain beneficial ownership of such ownership interest;

(ii) Through a deferred compensation, stock-bonus, profit-sharing, or pension plan of the banking entity (or an affiliate thereof) that is established and administered in accordance with the law of the United States or a foreign sovereign, if the ownership interest is held or controlled directly or indirectly by the banking entity as trustee for the benefit of persons who are or were employees of the banking entity (or an affiliate thereof);

(iii) In the ordinary course of collecting a debt previously contracted in good faith, provided that the banking entity divests the ownership interest as soon as practicable, and in no event may the banking entity retain such ownership interest for longer than such period permitted by the SEC; or

(iv) On behalf of customers as trustee or in a similar fiduciary capacity for a customer that is not a covered fund, so long as:

(A) The activity is conducted for the account of, or on behalf of, the customer; and

(B) The banking entity and its affiliates do not have or retain beneficial ownership of such ownership interest.

Securities and Exchange Commission § 255.10

(b) *Definition of covered fund.* (1) Except as provided in paragraph (c) of this section, covered fund means:

(i) An issuer that would be an investment company, as defined in the Investment Company Act of 1940 (15 U.S.C. 80a-1 *et seq.*), *but for* section 3(c)(1) or 3(c)(7) of that Act (15 U.S.C. 80a-3(c)(1) or (7));

(ii) Any commodity pool under section 1a(10) of the Commodity Exchange Act (7 U.S.C. 1a(10)) for which:

(A) The commodity pool operator has claimed an exemption under 17 CFR 4.7; or

(B)(*1*) A commodity pool operator is registered with the CFTC as a commodity pool operator in connection with the operation of the commodity pool;

(*2*) Substantially all participation units of the commodity pool are owned by qualified eligible persons under 17 CFR 4.7(a)(2) and (3); and

(*3*) Participation units of the commodity pool have not been publicly offered to persons who are not qualified eligible persons under 17 CFR 4.7(a)(2) and (3); or

(iii) For any banking entity that is, or is controlled directly or indirectly by a banking entity that is, located in or organized under the laws of the United States or of any State, an entity that:

(A) Is organized or established outside the United States and the ownership interests of which are offered and sold solely outside the United States;

(B) Is, or holds itself out as being, an entity or arrangement that raises money from investors primarily for the purpose of investing in securities for resale or other disposition or otherwise trading in securities; and

(C)(*1*) Has as its sponsor that banking entity (or an affiliate thereof); or

(*2*) Has issued an ownership interest that is owned directly or indirectly by that banking entity (or an affiliate thereof).

(2) An issuer shall not be deemed to be a covered fund under paragraph (b)(1)(iii) of this section if, were the issuer subject to U.S. securities laws, the issuer could rely on an exclusion or exemption from the definition of "investment company" under the Investment Company Act of 1940 (15 U.S.C. 80a-1 *et seq.*) other than the exclusions contained in section 3(c)(1) and 3(c)(7) of that Act.

(3) For purposes of paragraph (b)(1)(iii) of this section, a U.S. branch, agency, or subsidiary of a foreign banking entity is located in the United States; however, the foreign bank that operates or controls that branch, agency, or subsidiary is not considered to be located in the United States solely by virtue of operating or controlling the U.S. branch, agency, or subsidiary.

(c) Notwithstanding paragraph (b) of this section, unless the appropriate Federal banking agencies, the SEC, and the CFTC jointly determine otherwise, a covered fund does not include:

(1) *Foreign public funds.* (i) Subject to paragraphs (c)(1)(ii) and (iii) of this section, an issuer that:

(A) Is organized or established outside of the United States; and

(B) Is authorized to offer and sell ownership interests, and such interests are offered and sold, through one or more public offerings.

(ii) With respect to a banking entity that is, or is controlled directly or indirectly by a banking entity that is, located in or organized under the laws of the United States or of any State and any issuer for which such banking entity acts as sponsor, the sponsoring banking entity may not rely on the exemption in paragraph (c)(1)(i) of this section for such issuer unless more than 75 percent of the ownership interests in the issuer are sold to persons other than:

(A) Such sponsoring banking entity;

(B) Such issuer;

(C) Affiliates of such sponsoring banking entity or such issuer; and

(D) Directors and senior executive officers as defined in § 225.71(c) of the Board's Regulation Y (12 CFR 225.71(c)) of such entities.

(iii) For purposes of paragraph (c)(1)(i)(B) of this section, the term "public offering" means a distribution (as defined in § 255.4(a)(3)) of securities in any jurisdiction outside the United States to investors, including retail investors, provided that:

(A) The distribution is subject to substantive disclosure and retail investor protection laws or regulations;

(B) With respect to an issuer for which the banking entity serves as the investment manager, investment adviser, commodity trading advisor, commodity pool operator, or sponsor, the distribution complies with all applicable requirements in the jurisdiction in which such distribution is being made;

(C) The distribution does not restrict availability to investors having a minimum level of net worth or net investment assets; and

(D) The issuer has filed or submitted, with the appropriate regulatory authority in such jurisdiction, offering disclosure documents that are publicly available.

(2) *Wholly-owned subsidiaries.* An entity, all of the outstanding ownership interests of which are owned directly or indirectly by the banking entity (or an affiliate thereof), except that:

(i) Up to five percent of the entity's outstanding ownership interests, less any amounts outstanding under paragraph (c)(2)(ii) of this section, may be held by employees or directors of the banking entity or such affiliate (including former employees or directors if their ownership interest was acquired while employed by or in the service of the banking entity); and

(ii) Up to 0.5 percent of the entity's outstanding ownership interests may be held by a third party if the ownership interest is acquired or retained by the third party for the purpose of establishing corporate separateness or addressing bankruptcy, insolvency, or similar concerns.

(3) *Joint ventures.* A joint venture between a banking entity or any of its affiliates and one or more unaffiliated persons, provided that the joint venture:

(i) Is composed of no more than 10 unaffiliated co-venturers;

(ii) Is in the business of engaging in activities that are permissible for the banking entity or affiliate, other than investing in securities for resale or other disposition; and

(iii) Is not, and does not hold itself out as being, an entity or arrangement that raises money from investors primarily for the purpose of investing in securities for resale or other disposition or otherwise trading in securities.

(4) *Acquisition vehicles.* An issuer:

(i) Formed solely for the purpose of engaging in a *bona fide* merger or acquisition transaction; and

(ii) That exists only for such period as necessary to effectuate the transaction.

(5) *Foreign pension or retirement funds.* A plan, fund, or program providing pension, retirement, or similar benefits that is:

(i) Organized and administered outside the United States;

(ii) A broad-based plan for employees or citizens that is subject to regulation as a pension, retirement, or similar plan under the laws of the jurisdiction in which the plan, fund, or program is organized and administered; and

(iii) Established for the benefit of citizens or residents of one or more foreign sovereigns or any political subdivision thereof.

(6) *Insurance company separate accounts.* A separate account, provided that no banking entity other than the insurance company participates in the account's profits and losses.

(7) *Bank owned life insurance.* A separate account that is used solely for the purpose of allowing one or more banking entities to purchase a life insurance policy for which the banking entity or entities is beneficiary, provided that no banking entity that purchases the policy:

(i) Controls the investment decisions regarding the underlying assets or holdings of the separate account; or

(ii) Participates in the profits and losses of the separate account other than in compliance with applicable requirements regarding bank owned life insurance.

(8) *Loan securitizations.* (i) *Scope.* An issuing entity for asset-backed securities that satisfies all the conditions of this paragraph (c)(8) and the assets or holdings of which are composed solely of:

(A) Loans as defined in § 255.2(t);

(B) Rights or other assets designed to assure the servicing or timely distribution of proceeds to holders of such securities and rights or other assets that are related or incidental to purchasing or otherwise acquiring and holding the loans, provided that each asset that is a security (other than special units of

Securities and Exchange Commission

§ 255.10

beneficial interest and collateral certificates meeting the requirements of paragraph (c)(8)(v) of this section) meets the requirements of paragraph (c)(8)(iii) of this section;

(C) Interest rate or foreign exchange derivatives that meet the requirements of paragraph (c)(8)(iv) of this section;

(D) Special units of beneficial interest and collateral certificates that meet the requirements of paragraph (c)(8)(v) of this section; and

(E) Debt securities, other than asset-backed securities and convertible securities, provided that:

(1) The aggregate value of such debt securities does not exceed five percent of the aggregate value of loans held under paragraph (c)(8)(i)(A) of this section, cash and cash equivalents held under paragraph (c)(8)(iii)(A) of this section, and debt securities held under this paragraph (c)(8)(i)(E); and

(2) The aggregate value of the loans, cash and cash equivalents, and debt securities for purposes of this paragraph is calculated at par value at the most recent time any such debt security is acquired, except that the issuing entity may instead determine the value of any such loan, cash equivalent, or debt security based on its fair market value if:

(i) The issuing entity is required to use the fair market value of such assets for purposes of calculating compliance with concentration limitations or other similar calculations under its transaction agreements, and

(ii) The issuing entity's valuation methodology values similarly situated assets consistently.

(ii) *Impermissible assets.* For purposes of this paragraph (c)(8), except as permitted under paragraph (c)(8)(i)(E) of this section, the assets or holdings of the issuing entity shall not include any of the following:

(A) A security, including an asset-backed security, or an interest in an equity or debt security other than as permitted in paragraphs (c)(8)(iii), (iv), or (v) of this section;

(B) A derivative, other than a derivative that meets the requirements of paragraph (c)(8)(iv) of this section; or

(C) A commodity forward contract.

(iii) *Permitted securities.* Notwithstanding paragraph (c)(8)(ii)(A) of this section, the issuing entity may hold securities, other than debt securities permitted under paragraph (c)(8)(i)(E) of this section, if those securities are:

(A) Cash equivalents—which, for the purposes of this paragraph, means high quality, highly liquid investments whose maturity corresponds to the securitization's expected or potential need for funds and whose currency corresponds to either the underlying loans or the asset-backed securities—for purposes of the rights and assets in paragraph (c)(8)(i)(B) of this section; or

(B) Securities received in lieu of debts previously contracted with respect to the loans supporting the asset-backed securities.

(iv) *Derivatives.* The holdings of derivatives by the issuing entity shall be limited to interest rate or foreign exchange derivatives that satisfy all of the following conditions:

(A) The written terms of the derivatives directly relate to the loans, the asset-backed securities, the contractual rights or other assets described in paragraph (c)(8)(i)(B) of this section, or the debt securities described in paragraph (c)(8)(i)(E) of this section; and

(B) The derivatives reduce the interest rate and/or foreign exchange risks related to the loans, the asset-backed securities, the contractual rights or other assets described in paragraph (c)(8)(i)(B) of this section, or the debt securities described in paragraph (c)(8)(i)(E) of this section.

(v) *Special units of beneficial interest and collateral certificates.* The assets or holdings of the issuing entity may include collateral certificates and special units of beneficial interest issued by a special purpose vehicle, provided that:

(A) The special purpose vehicle that issues the special unit of beneficial interest or collateral certificate meets the requirements in this paragraph (c)(8);

(B) The special unit of beneficial interest or collateral certificate is used for the sole purpose of transferring to the issuing entity for the loan securitization the economic risks and benefits of the assets that are permissible for loan securitizations under this paragraph (c)(8) and does not directly or indirectly transfer any interest in

273

§ 255.10

any other economic or financial exposure;

(C) The special unit of beneficial interest or collateral certificate is created solely to satisfy legal requirements or otherwise facilitate the structuring of the loan securitization; and

(D) The special purpose vehicle that issues the special unit of beneficial interest or collateral certificate and the issuing entity are established under the direction of the same entity that initiated the loan securitization.

(9) *Qualifying asset-backed commercial paper conduits.* (i) An issuing entity for asset-backed commercial paper that satisfies all of the following requirements:

(A) The asset-backed commercial paper conduit holds only:

(*1*) Loans and other assets permissible for a loan securitization under paragraph (c)(8)(i) of this section; and

(*2*) Asset-backed securities supported solely by assets that are permissible for loan securitizations under paragraph (c)(8)(i) of this section and acquired by the asset-backed commercial paper conduit as part of an initial issuance either directly from the issuing entity of the asset-backed securities or directly from an underwriter in the distribution of the asset-backed securities;

(B) The asset-backed commercial paper conduit issues only asset-backed securities, comprised of a residual interest and securities with a legal maturity of 397 days or less; and

(C) A regulated liquidity provider has entered into a legally binding commitment to provide full and unconditional liquidity coverage with respect to all of the outstanding asset-backed securities issued by the asset-backed commercial paper conduit (other than any residual interest) in the event that funds are required to redeem maturing asset-backed securities.

(ii) For purposes of this paragraph (c)(9), a regulated liquidity provider means:

(A) A depository institution, as defined in section 3(c) of the Federal Deposit Insurance Act (12 U.S.C. 1813(c));

(B) A bank holding company, as defined in section 2(a) of the Bank Holding Company Act of 1956 (12 U.S.C. 1841(a)), or a subsidiary thereof;

(C) A savings and loan holding company, as defined in section 10a of the Home Owners' Loan Act (12 U.S.C. 1467a), provided all or substantially all of the holding company's activities are permissible for a financial holding company under section 4(k) of the Bank Holding Company Act of 1956 (12 U.S.C. 1843(k)), or a subsidiary thereof;

(D) A foreign bank whose home country supervisor, as defined in § 211.21(q) of the Board's Regulation K (12 CFR 211.21(q)), has adopted capital standards consistent with the Capital Accord for the Basel Committee on banking Supervision, as amended, and that is subject to such standards, or a subsidiary thereof; or

(E) The United States or a foreign sovereign.

(10). *Qualifying covered bonds*—(i) *Scope.* An entity owning or holding a dynamic or fixed pool of loans or other assets as provided in paragraph (c)(8) of this section for the benefit of the holders of covered bonds, provided that the assets in the pool are composed solely of assets that meet the conditions in paragraph (c)(8)(i) of this section.

(ii) *Covered bond.* For purposes of this paragraph (c)(10), a covered bond means:

(A) A debt obligation issued by an entity that meets the definition of foreign banking organization, the payment obligations of which are fully and unconditionally guaranteed by an entity that meets the conditions set forth in paragraph (c)(10)(i) of this section; or

(B) A debt obligation of an entity that meets the conditions set forth in paragraph (c)(10)(i) of this section, provided that the payment obligations are fully and unconditionally guaranteed by an entity that meets the definition of foreign banking organization and the entity is a wholly-owned subsidiary, as defined in paragraph (c)(2) of this section, of such foreign banking organization.

(11) *SBICs and public welfare investment funds.* An issuer:

(i) That is a small business investment company, as defined in section 103(3) of the Small Business Investment Act of 1958 (15 U.S.C. 662), or that has

Securities and Exchange Commission § 255.10

received from the Small Business Administration notice to proceed to qualify for a license as a small business investment company, which notice or license has not been revoked, or that has voluntarily surrendered its license to operate as a small business investment company in accordance with 13 CFR 107.1900 and does not make any new investments (other than investments in cash equivalents, which, for the purposes of this paragraph, means high quality, highly liquid investments whose maturity corresponds to the issuer's expected or potential need for funds and whose currency corresponds to the issuer's assets) after such voluntary surrender;

(ii) The business of which is to make investments that are:

(A) Designed primarily to promote the public welfare, of the type permitted under paragraph (11) of section 5136 of the Revised Statutes of the United States (12 U.S.C. 24), including the welfare of low- and moderate-income communities or families (such as providing housing, services, or jobs) and including investments that qualify for consideration under the regulations implementing the Community Reinvestment Act (12 U.S.C. 2901 et seq.); or

(B) Qualified rehabilitation expenditures with respect to a qualified rehabilitated building or certified historic structure, as such terms are defined in section 47 of the Internal Revenue Code of 1986 or a similar State historic tax credit program;

(iii) That has elected to be regulated or is regulated as a rural business investment company, as described in 15 U.S.C. 80b–3(b)(8)(A) or (B), or that has terminated its participation as a rural business investment company in accordance with 7 CFR 4290.1900 and does not make any new investments (other than investments in cash equivalents, which, for the purposes of this paragraph, means high quality, highly liquid investments whose maturity corresponds to the issuer's expected or potential need for funds and whose currency corresponds to the issuer's assets) after such termination; or

(iv) That is a qualified opportunity fund, as defined in 26 U.S.C. 1400Z–2(d).

(12) *Registered investment companies and excluded entities.* An issuer:

(i) That is registered as an investment company under section 8 of the Investment Company Act of 1940 (15 U.S.C. 80a–8), or that is formed and operated pursuant to a written plan to become a registered investment company as described in §255.20(e)(3) of subpart D and that complies with the requirements of section 18 of the Investment Company Act of 1940 (15 U.S.C. 80a–18);

(ii) That may rely on an exclusion or exemption from the definition of "investment company" under the Investment Company Act of 1940 (15 U.S.C. 80a–1 et seq.) other than the exclusions contained in section 3(c)(1) and 3(c)(7) of that Act; or

(iii) That has elected to be regulated as a business development company pursuant to section 54(a) of that Act (15 U.S.C. 80a–53) and has not withdrawn its election, or that is formed and operated pursuant to a written plan to become a business development company as described in §255.20(e)(3) of subpart D and that complies with the requirements of section 61 of the Investment Company Act of 1940 (15 U.S.C. 80a–60).

(13) *Issuers in conjunction with the FDIC's receivership or conservatorship operations.* An issuer that is an entity formed by or on behalf of the FDIC for the purpose of facilitating the disposal of assets acquired in the FDIC's capacity as conservator or receiver under the Federal Deposit Insurance Act or Title II of the Dodd-Frank Wall Street Reform and Consumer Protection Act.

(14) *Other excluded issuers.* (i) Any issuer that the appropriate Federal banking agencies, the SEC, and the CFTC jointly determine the exclusion of which is consistent with the purposes of section 13 of the BHC Act.

(ii) A determination made under paragraph (c)(14)(i) of this section will be promptly made public.

(15) *Credit funds.* Subject to paragraphs (c)(15)(iii), (iv), and (v) of this section, an issuer that satisfies the asset and activity requirements of paragraphs (c)(15)(i) and (ii) of this section.

(i) *Asset requirements.* The issuer's assets must be composed solely of:

(A) Loans as defined in §255.2(t);

(B) Debt instruments, subject to paragraph (c)(15)(iv) of this section;

275

§ 255.10

(C) Rights and other assets that are related or incidental to acquiring, holding, servicing, or selling such loans or debt instruments, provided that:

(*1*) Each right or asset held under this paragraph (c)(15)(i)(C) that is a security is either:

(*i*) A cash equivalent (which, for the purposes of this paragraph, means high quality, highly liquid investments whose maturity corresponds to the issuer's expected or potential need for funds and whose currency corresponds to either the underlying loans or the debt instruments);

(*ii*) A security received in lieu of debts previously contracted with respect to such loans or debt instruments; or

(*iii*) An equity security (or right to acquire an equity security) received on customary terms in connection with such loans or debt instruments; and

(*2*) Rights or other assets held under this paragraph (c)(15)(i)(C) of this section may not include commodity forward contracts or any derivative; and

(D) Interest rate or foreign exchange derivatives, if:

(*1*) The written terms of the derivative directly relate to the loans, debt instruments, or other rights or assets described in paragraph (c)(15)(i)(C) of this section; and

(*2*) The derivative reduces the interest rate and/or foreign exchange risks related to the loans, debt instruments, or other rights or assets described in paragraph (c)(15)(i)(C) of this section.

(ii) *Activity requirements.* To be eligible for the exclusion of paragraph (c)(15) of this section, an issuer must:

(A) Not engage in any activity that would constitute proprietary trading under § 255.3(b)(l)(i), as if the issuer were a banking entity; and

(B) Not issue asset-backed securities.

(iii) *Requirements for a sponsor, investment adviser, or commodity trading advisor.* A banking entity that acts as a sponsor, investment adviser, or commodity trading advisor to an issuer that meets the conditions in paragraphs (c)(15)(i) and (ii) of this section may not rely on this exclusion unless the banking entity:

(A) Provides in writing to any prospective and actual investor in the issuer the disclosures required under

17 CFR Ch. II (4-1-23 Edition)

§ 255.11(a)(8) of this subpart, as if the issuer were a covered fund;

(B) Ensures that the activities of the issuer are consistent with safety and soundness standards that are substantially similar to those that would apply if the banking entity engaged in the activities directly; and

(C) Complies with the limitations imposed in § 255.14, as if the issuer were a covered fund, except the banking entity may acquire and retain any ownership interest in the issuer.

(iv) *Additional Banking Entity Requirements.* A banking entity may not rely on this exclusion with respect to an issuer that meets the conditions in paragraphs (c)(15)(i) and (ii) of this section unless:

(A) The banking entity does not, directly or indirectly, guarantee, assume, or otherwise insure the obligations or performance of the issuer or of any entity to which such issuer extends credit or in which such issuer invests; and

(B) Any assets the issuer holds pursuant to paragraphs (c)(15)(i)(B) or (i)(C)(*1*)(*iii*) of this section would be permissible for the banking entity to acquire and hold directly under applicable federal banking laws and regulations.

(v) *Investment and Relationship Limits.* A banking entity's investment in, and relationship with, the issuer must:

(A) Comply with the limitations imposed in § 255.15, as if the issuer were a covered fund; and

(B) Be conducted in compliance with, and subject to, applicable banking laws and regulations, including applicable safety and soundness standards.

(16) *Qualifying venture capital funds.* (i) Subject to paragraphs (c)(16)(ii) through (iv) of this section, an issuer that:

(A) Is a venture capital fund as defined in 17 CFR 275.203(l)–1; and

(B) Does not engage in any activity that would constitute proprietary trading under § 255.3(b)(1)(i), as if the issuer were a banking entity.

(ii) A banking entity that acts as a sponsor, investment adviser, or commodity trading advisor to an issuer that meets the conditions in paragraph (c)(16)(i) of this section may not rely on

276

Securities and Exchange Commission § 255.10

this exclusion unless the banking entity:

(A) Provides in writing to any prospective and actual investor in the issuer the disclosures required under § 255.11(a)(8), as if the issuer were a covered fund;

(B) Ensures that the activities of the issuer are consistent with safety and soundness standards that are substantially similar to those that would apply if the banking entity engaged in the activities directly; and

(C) Complies with the restrictions in § 255.14 as if the issuer were a covered fund (except the banking entity may acquire and retain any ownership interest in the issuer).

(iii) The banking entity must not, directly or indirectly, guarantee, assume, or otherwise insure the obligations or performance of the issuer.

(iv) A banking entity's ownership interest in or relationship with the issuer must:

(A) Comply with the limitations imposed in § 255.15, as if the issuer were a covered fund; and

(B) Be conducted in compliance with, and subject to, applicable banking laws and regulations, including applicable safety and soundness standards.

(17) *Family wealth management vehicles.* (i) Subject to paragraph (c)(17)(ii) of this section, any entity that is not, and does not hold itself out as being, an entity or arrangement that raises money from investors primarily for the purpose of investing in securities for resale or other disposition or otherwise trading in securities, and:

(A) If the entity is a trust, the grantor(s) of the entity are all family customers; and

(B) If the entity is not a trust:

(*1*) A majority of the voting interests in the entity are owned (directly or indirectly) by family customers;

(*2*) A majority of the interests in the entity are owned (directly or indirectly) by family customers;

(*3*) The entity is owned only by family customers and up to 5 closely related persons of the family customers; and

(C) Notwithstanding paragraph (c)(17)(i)(A) and (B) of this section, up to an aggregate 0.5 percent of the entity's outstanding ownership interests may be acquired or retained by one or more entities that are not family customers or closely related persons if the ownership interest is acquired or retained by such parties for the purpose of and to the extent necessary for establishing corporate separateness or addressing bankruptcy, insolvency, or similar concerns.

(ii) A banking entity may rely on the exclusion in paragraph (c)(17)(i) of this section with respect to an entity provided that the banking entity (or an affiliate):

(A) Provides bona fide trust, fiduciary, investment advisory, or commodity trading advisory services to the entity;

(B) Does not, directly or indirectly, guarantee, assume, or otherwise insure the obligations or performance of such entity;

(C) Complies with the disclosure obligations under § 255.11(a)(8), as if such entity were a covered fund, provided that the content may be modified to prevent the disclosure from being misleading and the manner of disclosure may be modified to accommodate the specific circumstances of the entity;

(D) Does not acquire or retain, as principal, an ownership interest in the entity, other than as described in paragraph (c)(17)(i)(C) of this section;

(E) Complies with the requirements of §§ 255.14(b) and 255.15, as if such entity were a covered fund; and

(F) Except for riskless principal transactions as defined in paragraph (d)(11) of this section, complies with the requirements of 12 CFR 223.15(a), as if such banking entity and its affiliates were a member bank and the entity were an affiliate thereof.

(iii) For purposes of paragraph (c)(17) of this section, the following definitions apply:

(A) *Closely related person* means a natural person (including the estate and estate planning vehicles of such person) who has longstanding business or personal relationships with any family customer.

(B) *Family customer* means:

(*1*) A family client, as defined in Rule 202(a)(11)(G)–1(d)(4) of the Investment Advisers Act of 1940 (17 CFR 275.202(a)(11)(G)–1(d)(4)); or

277

§ 255.10

(2) Any natural person who is a father-in-law, mother-in-law, brother-in-law, sister-in-law, son-in-law or daughter-in-law of a family client, or a spouse or a spousal equivalent of any of the foregoing.

(18) *Customer facilitation vehicles.* (i) Subject to paragraph (c)(18)(ii) of this section, an issuer that is formed by or at the request of a customer of the banking entity for the purpose of providing such customer (which may include one or more affiliates of such customer) with exposure to a transaction, investment strategy, or other service provided by the banking entity.

(ii) A banking entity may rely on the exclusion in paragraph (c)(18)(i) of this section with respect to an issuer provided that:

(A) All of the ownership interests of the issuer are owned by the customer (which may include one or more of its affiliates) for whom the issuer was created;

(B) Notwithstanding paragraph (c)(18)(ii)(A) of this section, up to an aggregate 0.5 percent of the issuer's outstanding ownership interests may be acquired or retained by one or more entities that are not customers if the ownership interest is acquired or retained by such parties for the purpose of and to the extent necessary for establishing corporate separateness or addressing bankruptcy, insolvency, or similar concerns; and

(C) The banking entity and its affiliates:

(*1*) Maintain documentation outlining how the banking entity intends to facilitate the customer's exposure to such transaction, investment strategy, or service;

(*2*) Do not, directly or indirectly, guarantee, assume, or otherwise insure the obligations or performance of such issuer;

(*3*) Comply with the disclosure obligations under § 255.11(a)(8), as if such issuer were a covered fund, provided that the content may be modified to prevent the disclosure from being misleading and the manner of disclosure may be modified to accommodate the specific circumstances of the issuer;

(*4*) Do not acquire or retain, as principal, an ownership interest in the issuer, other than as described in paragraph (c)(18)(ii)(B) of this section;

(*5*) Comply with the requirements of §§ 255.14(b) and 255.15, as if such issuer were a covered fund; and

(*6*) Except for riskless principal transactions as defined in paragraph (d)(11) of this section, comply with the requirements of 12 CFR 223.15(a), as if such banking entity and its affiliates were a member bank and the issuer were an affiliate thereof.

(d) *Definition of other terms related to covered funds.* For purposes of this subpart:

(1) *Applicable accounting standards* means U.S. generally accepted accounting principles, or such other accounting standards applicable to a banking entity that the SEC determines are appropriate and that the banking entity uses in the ordinary course of its business in preparing its consolidated financial statements.

(2) *Asset-backed security* has the meaning specified in Section 3(a)(79) of the Exchange Act (15 U.S.C. 78c(a)(79).

(3) *Director* has the same meaning as provided in section 215.2(d)(1) of the Board's Regulation O (12 CFR 215.2(d)(1)).

(4) *Issuer* has the same meaning as in section 2(a)(22) of the Investment Company Act of 1940 (15 U.S.C. 80a-2(a)(22)).

(5) *Issuing entity* means with respect to asset-backed securities the special purpose vehicle that owns or holds the pool assets underlying asset-backed securities and in whose name the asset-backed securities supported or serviced by the pool assets are issued.

(6) *Ownership interest.* (i) *Ownership interest* means any equity, partnership, or other similar interest. An "other similar interest" means an interest that:

(A) Has the right to participate in the selection or removal of a general partner, managing member, member of the board of directors or trustees, investment manager, investment adviser, or commodity trading advisor of the covered fund, excluding:

(*1*) The rights of a creditor to exercise remedies upon the occurrence of an event of default or an acceleration event; and

(*2*) The right to participate in the removal of an investment manager for "cause" or participate in the selection of a replacement manager upon an investment manager's resignation or removal. For purposes of this paragraph (d)(6)(i)(A)(*2*), "cause" for removal of an investment manager means one or more of the following events:

(*i*) The bankruptcy, insolvency, conservatorship or receivership of the investment manager;

(*ii*) The breach by the investment manager of any material provision of the covered fund's transaction agreements applicable to the investment manager;

(*iii*) The breach by the investment manager of material representations or warranties;

(*iv*) The occurrence of an act that constitutes fraud or criminal activity in the performance of the investment manager's obligations under the covered fund's transaction agreements;

(*v*) The indictment of the investment manager for a criminal offense, or the indictment of any officer, member, partner or other principal of the investment manager for a criminal offense materially related to his or her investment management activities;

(*vi*) A change in control with respect to the investment manager;

(*vii*) The loss, separation or incapacitation of an individual critical to the operation of the investment manager or primarily responsible for the management of the covered fund's assets; or

(*viii*) Other similar events that constitute "cause" for removal of an investment manager, provided that such events are not solely related to the performance of the covered fund or the investment manager's exercise of investment discretion under the covered fund's transaction agreements;

(B) Has the right under the terms of the interest to receive a share of the income, gains or profits of the covered fund;

(C) Has the right to receive the underlying assets of the covered fund after all other interests have been redeemed and/or paid in full (excluding the rights of a creditor to exercise remedies upon the occurrence of an event of default or an acceleration event);

(D) Has the right to receive all or a portion of excess spread (the positive difference, if any, between the aggregate interest payments received from the underlying assets of the covered fund and the aggregate interest paid to the holders of other outstanding interests);

(E) Provides under the terms of the interest that the amounts payable by the covered fund with respect to the interest could be reduced based on losses arising from the underlying assets of the covered fund, such as allocation of losses, write-downs or charge-offs of the outstanding principal balance, or reductions in the amount of interest due and payable on the interest;

(F) Receives income on a pass-through basis from the covered fund, or has a rate of return that is determined by reference to the performance of the underlying assets of the covered fund; or

(G) Any synthetic right to have, receive, or be allocated any of the rights in paragraphs (d)(6)(i)(A) through (F) of this section.

(ii) Ownership interest does not include:

(A) Restricted profit interest, which is an interest held by an entity (or an employee or former employee thereof) in a covered fund for which the entity (or employee thereof) serves as investment manager, investment adviser, commodity trading advisor, or other service provider, so long as:

(*1*) The sole purpose and effect of the interest is to allow the entity (or employee or former employee thereof) to share in the profits of the covered fund as performance compensation for the investment management, investment advisory, commodity trading advisory, or other services provided to the covered fund by the entity (or employee or former employee thereof), provided that the entity (or employee or former employee thereof) may be obligated under the terms of such interest to return profits previously received;

(*2*) All such profit, once allocated, is distributed to the entity (or employee or former employee thereof) promptly after being earned or, if not so distributed, is retained by the covered fund for the sole purpose of establishing a reserve amount to satisfy contractual obligations with respect to subsequent

§ 255.10

losses of the covered fund and such undistributed profit of the entity (or employee or former employee thereof) does not share in the subsequent investment gains of the covered fund;

(3) Any amounts invested in the covered fund, including any amounts paid by the entity in connection with obtaining the restricted profit interest, are within the limits of § 255.12 of this subpart; and

(4) The interest is not transferable by the entity (or employee or former employee thereof) except to an affiliate thereof (or an employee of the banking entity or affiliate), to immediate family members, or through the intestacy, of the employee or former employee, or in connection with a sale of the business that gave rise to the restricted profit interest by the entity (or employee or former employee thereof) to an unaffiliated party that provides investment management, investment advisory, commodity trading advisory, or other services to the fund.

(B) Any senior loan or senior debt interest that has the following characteristics:

(*1*) Under the terms of the interest the holders of such interest do not have the right to receive a share of the income, gains, or profits of the covered fund, but are entitled to receive only:

(*i*) Interest at a stated interest rate, as well as commitment fees or other fees, which are not determined by reference to the performance of the underlying assets of the covered fund; and

(*ii*) Repayment of a fixed principal amount, on or before a maturity date, in a contractually-determined manner (which may include prepayment premiums intended solely to reflect, and compensate holders of the interest for, forgone income resulting from an early prepayment);

(*2*) The entitlement to payments under the terms of the interest are absolute and could not be reduced based on losses arising from the underlying assets of the covered fund, such as allocation of losses, write-downs or charge-offs of the outstanding principal balance, or reductions in the amount of interest due and payable on the interest; and

(*3*) The holders of the interest are not entitled to receive the underlying assets of the covered fund after all other interests have been redeemed or paid in full (excluding the rights of a creditor to exercise remedies upon the occurrence of an event of default or an acceleration event).

(7) *Prime brokerage transaction* means any transaction that would be a covered transaction, as defined in section 23A(b)(7) of the Federal Reserve Act (12 U.S.C. 371c(b)(7)), that is provided in connection with custody, clearance and settlement, securities borrowing or lending services, trade execution, financing, or data, operational, and administrative support.

(8) *Resident of the United States* means a person that is a "U.S. person" as defined in rule 902(k) of the SEC's Regulation S (17 CFR 230.902(k)).

(9) *Sponsor* means, with respect to a covered fund:

(i) To serve as a general partner, managing member, or trustee of a covered fund, or to serve as a commodity pool operator with respect to a covered fund as defined in (b)(1)(ii) of this section;

(ii) In any manner to select or to control (or to have employees, officers, or directors, or agents who constitute) a majority of the directors, trustees, or management of a covered fund; or

(iii) To share with a covered fund, for corporate, marketing, promotional, or other purposes, the same name or a variation of the same name, except as permitted under § 255.11(a)(6).

(10) *Trustee.* (i) For purposes of paragraph (d)(9) of this section and § 255.11 of subpart C, a trustee does not include:

(A) A trustee that does not exercise investment discretion with respect to a covered fund, including a trustee that is subject to the direction of an unaffiliated named fiduciary who is not a trustee pursuant to section 403(a)(1) of the Employee's Retirement Income Security Act (29 U.S.C. 1103(a)(1)); or

(B) A trustee that is subject to fiduciary standards imposed under foreign law that are substantially equivalent to those described in paragraph (d)(10)(i)(A) of this section;

(ii) Any entity that directs a person described in paragraph (d)(10)(i) of this section, or that possesses authority and discretion to manage and control the investment decisions of a covered fund for which such person serves as trustee, shall be considered to be a trustee of such covered fund.

(11) *Riskless principal transaction.* Riskless principal transaction means a transaction in which a banking entity, after receiving an order from a customer to buy (or sell) a security, purchases (or sells) the security in the secondary market for its own account to offset a contemporaneous sale to (or purchase from) the customer.

[79 FR 5779, 5805, Jan. 31, 2014, as amended at 84 FR 35022, July 22, 2019; 84 FR 62244, Nov. 14, 2019; 85 FR 46523, July 31, 2020]

§ 255.11 Permitted organizing and offering, underwriting, and market making with respect to a covered fund.

(a) *Organizing and offering a covered fund in general.* Notwithstanding § 255.10(a) of this subpart, a banking entity is not prohibited from acquiring or retaining an ownership interest in, or acting as sponsor to, a covered fund in connection with, directly or indirectly, organizing and offering a covered fund, including serving as a general partner, managing member, trustee, or commodity pool operator of the covered fund and in any manner selecting or controlling (or having employees, officers, directors, or agents who constitute) a majority of the directors, trustees, or management of the covered fund, including any necessary expenses for the foregoing, only if:

(1) The banking entity (or an affiliate thereof) provides *bona fide* trust, fiduciary, investment advisory, or commodity trading advisory services;

(2) The covered fund is organized and offered only in connection with the provision of *bona fide* trust, fiduciary, investment advisory, or commodity trading advisory services and only to persons that are customers of such services of the banking entity (or an affiliate thereof), pursuant to a written plan or similar documentation outlining how the banking entity or such affiliate intends to provide advisory or similar services to its customers through organizing and offering such fund;

(3) The banking entity and its affiliates do not acquire or retain an ownership interest in the covered fund except as permitted under § 255.12 of this subpart;

(4) The banking entity and its affiliates comply with the requirements of § 255.14 of this subpart;

(5) The banking entity and its affiliates do not, directly or indirectly, guarantee, assume, or otherwise insure the obligations or performance of the covered fund or of any covered fund in which such covered fund invests;

(6) The covered fund, for corporate, marketing, promotional, or other purposes:

(i) Does not share the same name or a variation of the same name with the banking entity (or an affiliate thereof) except that a covered fund may share the same name or a variation of the same name with a banking entity that is an investment adviser to the covered fund if:

(A) The investment adviser is not an insured depository institution, a company that controls an insured depository institution, or a company that is treated as a bank holding company for purposes of section 8 of the International Banking Act of 1978 (12 U.S.C. 3106); and

(B) The investment adviser does not share the same name or a variation of the same name as an insured depository institution, a company that controls an insured depository institution, or a company that is treated as a bank holding company for purposes of section 8 of the International Banking Act of 1978 (12 U.S.C. 3106); and

(ii) Does not use the word "bank" in its name;

(7) No director or employee of the banking entity (or an affiliate thereof) takes or retains an ownership interest in the covered fund, except for any director or employee of the banking entity or such affiliate who is directly engaged in providing investment advisory, commodity trading advisory, or other services to the covered fund at the time the director or employee takes the ownership interest; and

(8) The banking entity:

(i) Clearly and conspicuously discloses, in writing, to any prospective and actual investor in the covered fund (such as through disclosure in the covered fund's offering documents):

§ 255.12

(A) That "any losses in [such covered fund] will be borne solely by investors in [the covered fund] and not by [the banking entity] or its affiliates; therefore, [the banking entity's] losses in [such covered fund] will be limited to losses attributable to the ownership interests in the covered fund held by [the banking entity] and any affiliate in its capacity as investor in the [covered fund] or as beneficiary of a restricted profit interest held by [the banking entity] or any affiliate";

(B) That such investor should read the fund offering documents before investing in the covered fund;

(C) That the "ownership interests in the covered fund are not insured by the FDIC, and are not deposits, obligations of, or endorsed or guaranteed in any way, by any banking entity" (unless that happens to be the case); and

(D) The role of the banking entity and its affiliates and employees in sponsoring or providing any services to the covered fund; and

(ii) Complies with any additional rules of the appropriate Federal banking agencies, the SEC, or the CFTC, as provided in section 13(b)(2) of the BHC Act, designed to ensure that losses in such covered fund are borne solely by investors in the covered fund and not by the covered banking entity and its affiliates.

(b) *Organizing and offering an issuing entity of asset-backed securities.* (1) Notwithstanding § 255.10(a) of this subpart, a banking entity is not prohibited from acquiring or retaining an ownership interest in, or acting as sponsor to, a covered fund that is an issuing entity of asset-backed securities in connection with, directly or indirectly, organizing and offering that issuing entity, so long as the banking entity and its affiliates comply with all of the requirements of paragraph (a)(3) through (8) of this section.

(2) For purposes of this paragraph (b), organizing and offering a covered fund that is an issuing entity of asset-backed securities means acting as the securitizer, as that term is used in section 15G(a)(3) of the Exchange Act (15 U.S.C. 78*o*–11(a)(3)) of the issuing entity, or acquiring or retaining an ownership interest in the issuing entity as required by section 15G of that Act (15 U.S.C.78*o*–11) and the implementing regulations issued thereunder.

(c) *Underwriting and market making in ownership interests of a covered fund.* The prohibition contained in § 255.10(a) of this subpart does not apply to a banking entity's underwriting activities or market making-related activities involving a covered fund so long as:

(1) Those activities are conducted in accordance with the requirements of § 255.4(a) or § 255.4(b) of subpart B, respectively; and

(2) With respect to any banking entity (or any affiliate thereof) that: Acts as a sponsor, investment adviser or commodity trading advisor to a particular covered fund or otherwise acquires and retains an ownership interest in such covered fund in reliance on paragraph (a) of this section; or acquires and retains an ownership interest in such covered fund and is either a securitizer, as that term is used in section 15G(a)(3) of the Exchange Act (15 U.S.C. 78*o*–11(a)(3)), or is acquiring and retaining an ownership interest in such covered fund in compliance with section 15G of that Act (15 U.S.C.78*o*–11) and the implementing regulations issued thereunder each as permitted by paragraph (b) of this section, then in each such case any ownership interests acquired or retained by the banking entity and its affiliates in connection with underwriting and market making related activities for that particular covered fund are included in the calculation of ownership interests permitted to be held by the banking entity and its affiliates under the limitations of § 255.12(a)(2)(ii); § 255.12(a)(2)(iii), and § 255.12(d) of this subpart.

[79 FR 5779, 5805, Jan. 31, 2014, as amended at 84 FR 35022, July 22, 2019; 84 FR 62244, Nov. 14, 2019]

§ 255.12 Permitted investment in a covered fund.

(a) *Authority and limitations on permitted investments in covered funds.* (1) Notwithstanding the prohibition contained in § 255.10(a) of this subpart, a banking entity may acquire and retain an ownership interest in a covered fund that the banking entity or an affiliate thereof organizes and offers pursuant to §255.11, for the purposes of:

(i) *Establishment.* Establishing the fund and providing the fund with sufficient initial equity for investment to permit the fund to attract unaffiliated investors, subject to the limits contained in paragraphs (a)(2)(i) and (iii) of this section; or

(ii) *De minimis investment.* Making and retaining an investment in the covered fund subject to the limits contained in paragraphs (a)(2)(ii) and (iii) of this section.

(2) *Investment limits*—(i) *Seeding period.* With respect to an investment in any covered fund made or held pursuant to paragraph (a)(1)(i) of this section, the banking entity and its affiliates:

(A) Must actively seek unaffiliated investors to reduce, through redemption, sale, dilution, or other methods, the aggregate amount of all ownership interests of the banking entity in the covered fund to the amount permitted in paragraph (a)(2)(i)(B) of this section; and

(B) Must, no later than 1 year after the date of establishment of the fund (or such longer period as may be provided by the Board pursuant to paragraph (e) of this section), conform its ownership interest in the covered fund to the limits in paragraph (a)(2)(ii) of this section;

(ii) *Per-fund limits.* (A) Except as provided in paragraph (a)(2)(ii)(B) of this section, an investment by a banking entity and its affiliates in any covered fund made or held pursuant to paragraph (a)(1)(ii) of this section may not exceed 3 percent of the total number or value of the outstanding ownership interests of the fund.

(B) An investment by a banking entity and its affiliates in a covered fund that is an issuing entity of asset-backed securities may not exceed 3 percent of the total fair market value of the ownership interests of the fund measured in accordance with paragraph (b)(3) of this section, unless a greater percentage is retained by the banking entity and its affiliates in compliance with the requirements of section 15G of the Exchange Act (15 U.S.C. 78*o*–11) and the implementing regulations issued thereunder, in which case the investment by the banking entity and its affiliates in the covered fund may not exceed the amount, number, or value of ownership interests of the fund required under section 15G of the Exchange Act and the implementing regulations issued thereunder.

(iii) *Aggregate limit.* The aggregate value of all ownership interests of the banking entity and its affiliates in all covered funds acquired or retained under this section may not exceed 3 percent of the tier 1 capital of the banking entity, as provided under paragraph (c) of this section, and shall be calculated as of the last day of each calendar quarter.

(iv) *Date of establishment.* For purposes of this section, the date of establishment of a covered fund shall be:

(A) *In general.* The date on which the investment adviser or similar entity to the covered fund begins making investments pursuant to the written investment strategy for the fund;

(B) *Issuing entities of asset-backed securities.* In the case of an issuing entity of asset-backed securities, the date on which the assets are initially transferred into the issuing entity of asset-backed securities.

(b) *Rules of construction*—(1) *Attribution of ownership interests to a covered banking entity.* (i) For purposes of paragraph (a)(2) of this section, the amount and value of a banking entity's permitted investment in any single covered fund shall include any ownership interest held under §255.12 directly by the banking entity, including any affiliate of the banking entity.

(ii) *Treatment of registered investment companies, SEC-regulated business development companies, and foreign public funds.* For purposes of paragraph (b)(1)(i) of this section, a registered investment company, SEC-regulated business development companies, or foreign public fund as described in §255.10(c)(1) will not be considered to be an affiliate of the banking entity so long as:

(A) The banking entity, together with its affiliates, does not own, control, or hold with the power to vote 25 percent or more of the voting shares of the company or fund; and

§ 255.12

(B) The banking entity, or an affiliate of the banking entity, provides investment advisory, commodity trading advisory, administrative, and other services to the company or fund in compliance with the limitations under applicable regulation, order, or other authority.

(iii) *Covered funds.* For purposes of paragraph (b)(1)(i) of this section, a covered fund will not be considered to be an affiliate of a banking entity so long as the covered fund is held in compliance with the requirements of this subpart.

(iv) *Treatment of employee and director investments financed by the banking entity.* For purposes of paragraph (b)(1)(i) of this section, an investment by a director or employee of a banking entity who acquires an ownership interest in his or her personal capacity in a covered fund sponsored by the banking entity will be attributed to the banking entity if the banking entity, directly or indirectly, extends financing for the purpose of enabling the director or employee to acquire the ownership interest in the fund and the financing is used to acquire such ownership interest in the covered fund.

(2) *Calculation of permitted ownership interests in a single covered fund.* Except as provided in paragraph (b)(3) or (4), for purposes of determining whether an investment in a single covered fund complies with the restrictions on ownership interests under paragraphs (a)(2)(i)(B) and (a)(2)(ii)(A) of this section:

(i) The aggregate number of the outstanding ownership interests held by the banking entity shall be the total number of ownership interests held under this section by the banking entity in a covered fund divided by the total number of ownership interests held by all entities in that covered fund, as of the last day of each calendar quarter (both measured without regard to committed funds not yet called for investment);

(ii) The aggregate value of the outstanding ownership interests held by the banking entity shall be the aggregate fair market value of all investments in and capital contributions made to the covered fund by the banking entity, divided by the value of all investments in and capital contributions made to that covered fund by all entities, as of the last day of each calendar quarter (all measured without regard to committed funds not yet called for investment). If fair market value cannot be determined, then the value shall be the historical cost basis of all investments in and contributions made by the banking entity to the covered fund;

(iii) For purposes of the calculation under paragraph (b)(2)(ii) of this section, once a valuation methodology is chosen, the banking entity must calculate the value of its investment and the investments of all others in the covered fund in the same manner and according to the same standards.

(3) *Issuing entities of asset-backed securities.* In the case of an ownership interest in an issuing entity of asset-backed securities, for purposes of determining whether an investment in a single covered fund complies with the restrictions on ownership interests under paragraphs (a)(2)(i)(B) and (a)(2)(ii)(B) of this section:

(i) For securitizations subject to the requirements of section 15G of the Exchange Act (15 U.S.C. 78o–11), the calculations shall be made as of the date and according to the valuation methodology applicable pursuant to the requirements of section 15G of the Exchange Act (15 U.S.C. 78o–11) and the implementing regulations issued thereunder; or

(ii) For securitization transactions completed prior to the compliance date of such implementing regulations (or as to which such implementing regulations do not apply), the calculations shall be made as of the date of establishment as defined in paragraph (a)(2)(iv)(B) of this section or such earlier date on which the transferred assets have been valued for purposes of transfer to the covered fund, and thereafter only upon the date on which additional securities of the issuing entity of asset-backed securities are priced for purposes of the sales of ownership interests to unaffiliated investors.

(iii) For securitization transactions completed prior to the compliance date of such implementing regulations (or as to which such implementing regulations do not apply), the aggregate

Securities and Exchange Commission § 255.12

value of the outstanding ownership interests in the covered fund shall be the fair market value of the assets transferred to the issuing entity of the securitization and any other assets otherwise held by the issuing entity at such time, determined in a manner that is consistent with its determination of the fair market value of those assets for financial statement purposes.

(iv) For purposes of the calculation under paragraph (b)(3)(iii) of this section, the valuation methodology used to calculate the fair market value of the ownership interests must be the same for both the ownership interests held by a banking entity and the ownership interests held by all others in the covered fund in the same manner and according to the same standards.

(4) *Multi-tier fund investments*—(i) *Master-feeder fund investments.* If the principal investment strategy of a covered fund (the "feeder fund") is to invest substantially all of its assets in another single covered fund (the "master fund"), then for purposes of the investment limitations in paragraphs (a)(2)(i)(B) and (a)(2)(ii) of this section, the banking entity's permitted investment in such funds shall be measured only by reference to the value of the master fund. The banking entity's permitted investment in the master fund shall include any investment by the banking entity in the master fund, as well as the banking entity's pro-rata share of any ownership interest in the master fund that is held through the feeder fund; and

(ii) *Fund-of-funds investments.* If a banking entity organizes and offers a covered fund pursuant to § 255.11 for the purpose of investing in other covered funds (a "fund of funds") and that fund of funds itself invests in another covered fund that the banking entity is permitted to own, then the banking entity's permitted investment in that other fund shall include any investment by the banking entity in that other fund, as well as the banking entity's pro-rata share of any ownership interest in the fund that is held through the fund of funds. The investment of the banking entity may not represent more than 3 percent of the amount or value of any single covered fund.

(5) *Parallel Investments and Co-Investments.* (i) A banking entity shall not be required to include in the calculation of the investment limits under paragraph (a)(2) of this section any investment the banking entity makes alongside a covered fund as long as the investment is made in compliance with applicable laws and regulations, including applicable safety and soundness standards.

(ii) A banking entity shall not be restricted under this section in the amount of any investment the banking entity makes alongside a covered fund as long as the investment is made in compliance with applicable laws and regulations, including applicable safety and soundness standards.

(c) *Aggregate permitted investments in all covered funds.* (1)(i) For purposes of paragraph (a)(2)(iii) of this section, the aggregate value of all ownership interests held by a banking entity shall be the sum of all amounts paid or contributed by the banking entity in connection with acquiring or retaining an ownership interest in covered funds (together with any amounts paid by the entity in connection with obtaining a restricted profit interest under § 255.10(d)(6)(ii)), on a historical cost basis;

(ii) Treatment of employee and director restricted profit interests financed by the banking entity. For purposes of paragraph (c)(1)(i) of this section, an investment by a director or employee of a banking entity who acquires a restricted profit interest in his or her personal capacity in a covered fund sponsored by the banking entity will be attributed to the banking entity if the banking entity, directly or indirectly, extends financing for the purpose of enabling the director or employee to acquire the restricted profit interest in the fund and the financing is used to acquire such ownership interest in the covered fund.

(2) *Calculation of tier 1 capital.* For purposes of paragraph (a)(2)(iii) of this section:

(i) *Entities that are required to hold and report tier 1 capital.* If a banking entity is required to calculate and report tier 1 capital, the banking entity's tier 1 capital shall be equal to the amount of tier 1 capital of the banking entity

§ 255.12

as of the last day of the most recent calendar quarter, as reported to its primary financial regulatory agency; and

(ii) If a banking entity is not required to calculate and report tier 1 capital, the banking entity's tier 1 capital shall be determined to be equal to:

(A) In the case of a banking entity that is controlled, directly or indirectly, by a depository institution that calculates and reports tier 1 capital, be equal to the amount of tier 1 capital reported by such controlling depository institution in the manner described in paragraph (c)(2)(i) of this section;

(B) In the case of a banking entity that is not controlled, directly or indirectly, by a depository institution that calculates and reports tier 1 capital:

(*1*) *Bank holding company subsidiaries.* If the banking entity is a subsidiary of a bank holding company or company that is treated as a bank holding company, be equal to the amount of tier 1 capital reported by the top-tier affiliate of such covered banking entity that calculates and reports tier 1 capital in the manner described in paragraph (c)(2)(i) of this section; and

(*2*) *Other holding companies and any subsidiary or affiliate thereof.* If the banking entity is not a subsidiary of a bank holding company or a company that is treated as a bank holding company, be equal to the total amount of shareholders' equity of the top-tier affiliate within such organization as of the last day of the most recent calendar quarter that has ended, as determined under applicable accounting standards.

(iii) *Treatment of foreign banking entities*—(A) *Foreign banking entities.* Except as provided in paragraph (c)(2)(iii)(B) of this section, with respect to a banking entity that is not itself, and is not controlled directly or indirectly by, a banking entity that is located or organized under the laws of the United States or of any State, the tier 1 capital of the banking entity shall be the consolidated tier 1 capital of the entity as calculated under applicable home country standards.

(B) *U.S. affiliates of foreign banking entities.* With respect to a banking entity that is located or organized under the laws of the United States or any State and is controlled by a foreign banking entity identified under paragraph (c)(2)(iii)(A) of this section, the banking entity's tier 1 capital shall be as calculated under paragraphs (c)(2)(i) or (ii) of this section.

(d) *Capital treatment for a permitted investment in a covered fund.* For purposes of calculating compliance with the applicable regulatory capital requirements, a banking entity shall deduct from the banking entity's tier 1 capital (as determined under paragraph (c)(2) of this section) the greater of:

(1)(i) The sum of all amounts paid or contributed by the banking entity in connection with acquiring or retaining an ownership interest (together with any amounts paid by the entity in connection with obtaining a restricted profit interest under § 255.10(d)(6)(ii) of subpart C of this part), on a historical cost basis, plus any earnings received; and

(ii) The fair market value of the banking entity's ownership interests in the covered fund as determined under paragraph (b)(2)(ii) or (b)(3) of this section (together with any amounts paid by the entity in connection with obtaining a restricted profit interest under § 255.10(d)(6)(ii) of subpart C of this part), if the banking entity accounts for the profits (or losses) of the fund investment in its financial statements.

(2) Treatment of employee and director restricted profit interests financed by the banking entity. For purposes of paragraph (d)(1) of this section, an investment by a director or employee of a banking entity who acquires a restricted profit interest in his or her personal capacity in a covered fund sponsored by the banking entity will be attributed to the banking entity if the banking entity, directly or indirectly, extends financing for the purpose of enabling the director or employee to acquire the restricted profit interest in the fund and the financing is used to acquire such ownership interest in the covered fund.

(e) *Extension of time to divest an ownership interest.* (1) *Extension period.* Upon application by a banking entity, the Board may extend the period under paragraph (a)(2)(i) of this section for up to 2 additional years if the Board finds that an extension would be consistent

Securities and Exchange Commission § 255.13

with safety and soundness and not detrimental to the public interest.

(2) *Application requirements.* An application for extension must:

(i) Be submitted to the Board at least 90 days prior to the expiration of the applicable time period;

(ii) Provide the reasons for application, including information that addresses the factors in paragraph (e)(3) of this section; and

(iii) Explain the banking entity's plan for reducing the permitted investment in a covered fund through redemption, sale, dilution or other methods as required in paragraph (a)(2) of this section.

(3) *Factors governing the Board determinations.* In reviewing any application under paragraph (e)(1) of this section, the Board may consider all the facts and circumstances related to the permitted investment in a covered fund, including:

(i) Whether the investment would result, directly or indirectly, in a material exposure by the banking entity to high-risk assets or high-risk trading strategies;

(ii) The contractual terms governing the banking entity's interest in the covered fund;

(iii) The date on which the covered fund is expected to have attracted sufficient investments from investors unaffiliated with the banking entity to enable the banking entity to comply with the limitations in paragraph (a)(2)(i) of this section;

(iv) The total exposure of the covered banking entity to the investment and the risks that disposing of, or maintaining, the investment in the covered fund may pose to the banking entity and the financial stability of the United States;

(v) The cost to the banking entity of divesting or disposing of the investment within the applicable period;

(vi) Whether the investment or the divestiture or conformance of the investment would involve or result in a material conflict of interest between the banking entity and unaffiliated parties, including clients, customers, or counterparties to which it owes a duty;

(vii) The banking entity's prior efforts to reduce through redemption, sale, dilution, or other methods its ownership interests in the covered fund, including activities related to the marketing of interests in such covered fund;

(viii) Market conditions; and

(ix) Any other factor that the Board believes appropriate.

(4) *Authority to impose restrictions on activities or investment during any extension period.* The Board may impose such conditions on any extension approved under paragraph (e)(1) of this section as the Board determines are necessary or appropriate to protect the safety and soundness of the banking entity or the financial stability of the United States, address material conflicts of interest or other unsound banking practices, or otherwise further the purposes of section 13 of the BHC Act and this part.

(5) *Consultation.* In the case of a banking entity that is primarily regulated by another Federal banking agency, the SEC, or the CFTC, the Board will consult with such agency prior to acting on an application by the banking entity for an extension under paragraph (e)(1) of this section.

[79 FR 5779, 5805, Jan. 31, 2014, as amended at 84 FR 62244, Nov. 14, 2019; 85 FR 46527, July 31, 2020]

§ 255.13 Other permitted covered fund activities and investments.

(a) *Permitted risk-mitigating hedging activities.* (1) The prohibition contained in § 255.10(a) of this subpart does not apply with respect to an ownership interest in a covered fund acquired or retained by a banking entity that is designed to reduce or otherwise significantly mitigate the specific, identifiable risks to the banking entity in connection with:

(i) A compensation arrangement with an employee of the banking entity or an affiliate thereof that directly provides investment advisory, commodity trading advisory or other services to the covered fund; or

(ii) A position taken by the banking entity when acting as intermediary on behalf of a customer that is not itself a banking entity to facilitate the exposure by the customer to the profits and losses of the covered fund.

§ 255.13

(2) The risk-mitigating hedging activities of a banking entity are permitted under this paragraph (a) only if:

(i) The banking entity has established and implements, maintains and enforces an internal compliance program in accordance with subpart D of this part that is reasonably designed to ensure the banking entity's compliance with the requirements of this section, including:

(A) Reasonably designed written policies and procedures; and

(B) Internal controls and ongoing monitoring, management, and authorization procedures, including relevant escalation procedures; and

(ii) The acquisition or retention of the ownership interest:

(A) Is made in accordance with the written policies, procedures, and internal controls required under this section;

(B) At the inception of the hedge, is designed to reduce or otherwise significantly mitigate one or more specific, identifiable risks arising:

(*1*) Out of a transaction conducted solely to accommodate a specific customer request with respect to the covered fund; or

(*2*) In connection with the compensation arrangement with the employee that directly provides investment advisory, commodity trading advisory, or other services to the covered fund;

(C) Does not give rise, at the inception of the hedge, to any significant new or additional risk that is not itself hedged contemporaneously in accordance with this section; and

(D) Is subject to continuing review, monitoring and management by the banking entity.

(iii) With respect to risk-mitigating hedging activity conducted pursuant to paragraph (a)(1)(i) of this section, the compensation arrangement relates solely to the covered fund in which the banking entity or any affiliate has acquired an ownership interest pursuant to paragraph (a)(1)(i) and such compensation arrangement provides that any losses incurred by the banking entity on such ownership interest will be offset by corresponding decreases in amounts payable under such compensation arrangement.

(b) *Certain permitted covered fund activities and investments outside of the United States.* (1) The prohibition contained in § 255.10(a) of this subpart does not apply to the acquisition or retention of any ownership interest in, or the sponsorship of, a covered fund by a banking entity only if:

(i) The banking entity is not organized or directly or indirectly controlled by a banking entity that is organized under the laws of the United States or of one or more States;

(ii) The activity or investment by the banking entity is pursuant to paragraph (9) or (13) of section 4(c) of the BHC Act;

(iii) No ownership interest in the covered fund is offered for sale or sold to a resident of the United States; and

(iv) The activity or investment occurs solely outside of the United States.

(2) An activity or investment by the banking entity is pursuant to paragraph (9) or (13) of section 4(c) of the BHC Act for purposes of paragraph (b)(1)(ii) of this section only if:

(i) The activity or investment is conducted in accordance with the requirements of this section; and

(ii)(A) With respect to a banking entity that is a foreign banking organization, the banking entity meets the qualifying foreign banking organization requirements of section 211.23(a), (c) or (e) of the Board's Regulation K (12 CFR 211.23(a), (c) or (e)), as applicable; or

(B) With respect to a banking entity that is not a foreign banking organization, the banking entity is not organized under the laws of the United States or of one or more States and the banking entity, on a fully-consolidated basis, meets at least two of the following requirements:

(*1*) Total assets of the banking entity held outside of the United States exceed total assets of the banking entity held in the United States;

(*2*) Total revenues derived from the business of the banking entity outside of the United States exceed total revenues derived from the business of the banking entity in the United States; or

(*3*) Total net income derived from the business of the banking entity outside of the United States exceeds total net

Securities and Exchange Commission § 255.13

income derived from the business of the banking entity in the United States.

(3) An ownership interest in a covered fund is not offered for sale or sold to a resident of the United States for purposes of paragraph (b)(1)(iii) of this section only if it is not sold and has not been sold pursuant to an offering that targets residents of the United States in which the banking entity or any affiliate of the banking entity participates. If the banking entity or an affiliate sponsors or serves, directly or indirectly, as the investment manager, investment adviser, commodity pool operator or commodity trading advisor to a covered fund, then the banking entity or affiliate will be deemed for purposes of this paragraph (b)(3) to participate in any offer or sale by the covered fund of ownership interests in the covered fund.

(4) An activity or investment occurs solely outside of the United States for purposes of paragraph (b)(1)(iv) of this section only if:

(i) The banking entity acting as sponsor, or engaging as principal in the acquisition or retention of an ownership interest in the covered fund, is not itself, and is not controlled directly or indirectly by, a banking entity that is located in the United States or organized under the laws of the United States or of any State;

(ii) The banking entity (including relevant personnel) that makes the decision to acquire or retain the ownership interest or act as sponsor to the covered fund is not located in the United States or organized under the laws of the United States or of any State; and

(iii) The investment or sponsorship, including any transaction arising from risk-mitigating hedging related to an ownership interest, is not accounted for as principal directly or indirectly on a consolidated basis by any branch or affiliate that is located in the United States or organized under the laws of the United States or of any State.

(5) For purposes of this section, a U.S. branch, agency, or subsidiary of a foreign bank, or any subsidiary thereof, is located in the United States; however, a foreign bank of which that branch, agency, or subsidiary is a part is not considered to be located in the United States solely by virtue of operation of the U.S. branch, agency, or subsidiary.

(c) Permitted covered fund interests and activities by a regulated insurance company. The prohibition contained in § 255.10(a) of this subpart does not apply to the acquisition or retention by an insurance company, or an affiliate thereof, of any ownership interest in, or the sponsorship of, a covered fund only if:

(1) The insurance company or its affiliate acquires and retains the ownership interest solely for the general account of the insurance company or for one or more separate accounts established by the insurance company;

(2) The acquisition and retention of the ownership interest is conducted in compliance with, and subject to, the insurance company investment laws and regulations of the State or jurisdiction in which such insurance company is domiciled; and

(3) The appropriate Federal banking agencies, after consultation with the Financial Stability Oversight Council and the relevant insurance commissioners of the States and foreign jurisdictions, as appropriate, have not jointly determined, after notice and comment, that a particular law or regulation described in paragraph (c)(2) of this section is insufficient to protect the safety and soundness of the banking entity, or the financial stability of the United States.

(d) *Permitted covered fund activities and investments of qualifying foreign excluded funds.* (1) The prohibition contained in § 255.10(a) does not apply to a qualifying foreign excluded fund.

(2) For purposes of this paragraph (d), a qualifying foreign excluded fund means a banking entity that:

(i) Is organized or established outside the United States, and the ownership interests of which are offered and sold solely outside the United States;

(ii)(A) Would be a covered fund if the entity were organized or established in the United States, or

(B) Is, or holds itself out as being, an entity or arrangement that raises money from investors primarily for the

§ 255.14

purpose of investing in financial instruments for resale or other disposition or otherwise trading in financial instruments;

(iii) Would not otherwise be a banking entity except by virtue of the acquisition or retention of an ownership interest in, sponsorship of, or relationship with the entity, by another banking entity that meets the following:

(A) The banking entity is not organized, or directly or indirectly controlled by a banking entity that is organized, under the laws of the United States or of any State; and

(B) The banking entity's acquisition of an ownership interest in or sponsorship of the fund by the foreign banking entity meets the requirements for permitted covered fund activities and investments solely outside the United States, as provided in § 255.13(b);

(iv) Is established and operated as part of a bona fide asset management business; and

(v) Is not operated in a manner that enables the banking entity that sponsors or controls the qualifying foreign excluded fund, or any of its affiliates, to evade the requirements of section 13 of the BHC Act or this part.

[79 FR 5779, 5805, Jan. 31, 2014, as amended at 84 FR 62244, Nov. 14, 2019; 85 FR 46528, July 31, 2020]

§ 255.14 Limitations on relationships with a covered fund.

(a) *Relationships with a covered fund.* (1) Except as provided for in paragraph (a)(2) of this section, no banking entity that serves, directly or indirectly, as the investment manager, investment adviser, commodity trading advisor, or sponsor to a covered fund, that organizes and offers a covered fund pursuant to § 255.11 of this subpart, or that continues to hold an ownership interest in accordance with § 255.11(b) of this subpart, and no affiliate of such entity, may enter into a transaction with the covered fund, or with any other covered fund that is controlled by such covered fund, that would be a covered transaction as defined in section 23A of the Federal Reserve Act (12 U.S.C. 371c(b)(7)), as if such banking entity and the affiliate thereof were a member bank and the covered fund were an affiliate thereof.

(2) Notwithstanding paragraph (a)(1) of this section, a banking entity may:

(i) Acquire and retain any ownership interest in a covered fund in accordance with the requirements of §§ 255.11, 255.12, or 255.13;

(ii) Enter into any prime brokerage transaction with any covered fund in which a covered fund managed, sponsored, or advised by such banking entity (or an affiliate thereof) has taken an ownership interest, if:

(A) The banking entity is in compliance with each of the limitations set forth in § 255.11 of this subpart with respect to a covered fund organized and offered by such banking entity (or an affiliate thereof);

(B) The chief executive officer (or equivalent officer) of the banking entity certifies in writing annually no later than March 31 to the SEC (with a duty to update the certification if the information in the certification materially changes) that the banking entity does not, directly or indirectly, guarantee, assume, or otherwise insure the obligations or performance of the covered fund or of any covered fund in which such covered fund invests; and

(C) The Board has not determined that such transaction is inconsistent with the safe and sound operation and condition of the banking entity; and

(iii) Enter into a transaction with a covered fund that would be an exempt covered transaction under 12 U.S.C. 371c(d) or § 223.42 of the Board's Regulation W (12 CFR 223.42) subject to the limitations specified under 12 U.S.C. 371c(d) or § 223.42 of the Board's Regulation W (12 CFR 223.42), as applicable,

(iv) Enter into a riskless principal transaction with a covered fund; and

(v) Extend credit to or purchase assets from a covered fund, provided:

(A) Each extension of credit or purchase of assets is in the ordinary course of business in connection with payment transactions; settlement services; or futures, derivatives, and securities clearing;

(B) Each extension of credit is repaid, sold, or terminated by the end of five business days; and

(C) The banking entity making each extension of credit meets the requirements of § 223.42(l)(1)(i) and (ii) of the Board's Regulation W (12 CFR

Securities and Exchange Commission § 255.15

223.42(1)(1)(i) and(ii)), as if the extension of credit was an intraday extension of credit, regardless of the duration of the extension of credit.

(3) Any transaction or activity permitted under paragraphs (a)(2)(iii), (iv) or (v) must comply with the limitations in § 255.15.

(b) *Restrictions on transactions with covered funds.* A banking entity that serves, directly or indirectly, as the investment manager, investment adviser, commodity trading advisor, or sponsor to a covered fund, or that organizes and offers a covered fund pursuant to § 255.11 of this subpart, or that continues to hold an ownership interest in accordance with § 255.11(b) of this subpart, shall be subject to section 23B of the Federal Reserve Act (12 U.S.C. 371c–1), as if such banking entity were a member bank and such covered fund were an affiliate thereof.

(c) *Restrictions on other permitted transactions.* Any transaction permitted under paragraphs (a)(2)(ii), (iii), or (iv) of this section shall be subject to section 23B of the Federal Reserve Act (12 U.S.C. 371c–1) as if the counterparty were an affiliate of the banking entity under section 23B.

[79 FR 5779, 5805, Jan. 31, 2014, as amended at 84 FR 62245, Nov. 14, 2019; 85 FR 46528, Oct. 1, 2020]

§ 255.15 Other limitations on permitted covered fund activities.

(a) No transaction, class of transactions, or activity may be deemed permissible under §§ 255.11 through 255.13 of this subpart if the transaction, class of transactions, or activity would:

(1) Involve or result in a material conflict of interest between the banking entity and its clients, customers, or counterparties;

(2) Result, directly or indirectly, in a material exposure by the banking entity to a high-risk asset or a high-risk trading strategy; or

(3) Pose a threat to the safety and soundness of the banking entity or to the financial stability of the United States.

(b) *Definition of material conflict of interest.* (1) For purposes of this section, a material conflict of interest between a banking entity and its clients, customers, or counterparties exists if the banking entity engages in any transaction, class of transactions, or activity that would involve or result in the banking entity's interests being materially adverse to the interests of its client, customer, or counterparty with respect to such transaction, class of transactions, or activity, and the banking entity has not taken at least one of the actions in paragraph (b)(2) of this section.

(2) Prior to effecting the specific transaction or class or type of transactions, or engaging in the specific activity, the banking entity:

(i) *Timely and effective disclosure.* (A) Has made clear, timely, and effective disclosure of the conflict of interest, together with other necessary information, in reasonable detail and in a manner sufficient to permit a reasonable client, customer, or counterparty to meaningfully understand the conflict of interest; and

(B) Such disclosure is made in a manner that provides the client, customer, or counterparty the opportunity to negate, or substantially mitigate, any materially adverse effect on the client, customer, or counterparty created by the conflict of interest; or

(ii) *Information barriers.* Has established, maintained, and enforced information barriers that are memorialized in written policies and procedures, such as physical separation of personnel, or functions, or limitations on types of activity, that are reasonably designed, taking into consideration the nature of the banking entity's business, to prevent the conflict of interest from involving or resulting in a materially adverse effect on a client, customer, or counterparty. A banking entity may not rely on such information barriers if, in the case of any specific transaction, class or type of transactions or activity, the banking entity knows or should reasonably know that, notwithstanding the banking entity's establishment of information barriers, the conflict of interest may involve or result in a materially adverse effect on a client, customer, or counterparty.

(c) *Definition of high-risk asset and high-risk trading strategy.* For purposes of this section:

(1) *High-risk asset* means an asset or group of related assets that would, if

§ 255.16

held by a banking entity, significantly increase the likelihood that the banking entity would incur a substantial financial loss or would pose a threat to the financial stability of the United States.

(2) *High-risk trading strategy* means a trading strategy that would, if engaged in by a banking entity, significantly increase the likelihood that the banking entity would incur a substantial financial loss or would pose a threat to the financial stability of the United States.

§ 255.16 Ownership of interests in and sponsorship of issuers of certain collateralized debt obligations backed by trust-preferred securities.

(a) The prohibition contained in § 255.10(a)(1) does not apply to the ownership by a banking entity of an interest in, or sponsorship of, any issuer if:

(1) The issuer was established, and the interest was issued, before May 19, 2010;

(2) The banking entity reasonably believes that the offering proceeds received by the issuer were invested primarily in Qualifying TruPS Collateral; and

(3) The banking entity acquired such interest on or before December 10, 2013 (or acquired such interest in connection with a merger with or acquisition of a banking entity that acquired the interest on or before December 10, 2013).

(b) For purposes of this § 255.16, *Qualifying TruPS Collateral* shall mean any trust preferred security or subordinated debt instrument issued prior to May 19, 2010 by a depository institution holding company that, as of the end of any reporting period within 12 months immediately preceding the issuance of such trust preferred security or subordinated debt instrument, had total consolidated assets of less than $15,000,000,000 or issued prior to May 19, 2010 by a mutual holding company.

(c) Notwithstanding paragraph (a)(3) of this section, a banking entity may act as a market maker with respect to the interests of an issuer described in paragraph (a) of this section in accordance with the applicable provisions of §§ 255.4 and 255.11.

(d) Without limiting the applicability of paragraph (a) of this section, the Board, the FDIC and the OCC will make public a non-exclusive list of issuers that meet the requirements of paragraph (a). A banking entity may rely on the list published by the Board, the FDIC and the OCC.

[79 FR 5228, Jan. 31, 2014]

§§ 255.17–255.19 [Reserved]

Subpart D—Compliance Program Requirement; Violations

§ 255.20 Program for compliance; reporting.

(a) *Program requirement.* Each banking entity (other than a banking entity with limited trading assets and liabilities or a qualifying foreign excluded fund under section 255.6(f) or 255.13(d)) shall develop and provide for the continued administration of a compliance program reasonably designed to ensure and monitor compliance with the prohibitions and restrictions on proprietary trading and covered fund activities and investments set forth in section 13 of the BHC Act and this part. The terms, scope, and detail of the compliance program shall be appropriate for the types, size, scope, and complexity of activities and business structure of the banking entity.

(b) *Banking entities with significant trading assets and liabilities.* With respect to a banking entity with significant trading assets and liabilities, the compliance program required by paragraph (a) of this section, at a minimum, shall include:

(1) Written policies and procedures reasonably designed to document, describe, monitor and limit trading activities subject to subpart B (including those permitted under §§ 255.3 to 255.6 of subpart B), including setting, monitoring and managing required limits set out in § 2554 and § 2555, and activities and investments with respect to a covered fund subject to subpart C (including those permitted under §§ 255.11 through 255.14 of subpart C) conducted by the banking entity to ensure that all activities and investments conducted by the banking entity that are subject to section 13 of the BHC Act

Securities and Exchange Commission § 255.20

and this part comply with section 13 of the BHC Act and this part;

(2) A system of internal controls reasonably designed to monitor compliance with section 13 of the BHC Act and this part and to prevent the occurrence of activities or investments that are prohibited by section 13 of the BHC Act and this part;

(3) A management framework that clearly delineates responsibility and accountability for compliance with section 13 of the BHC Act and this part and includes appropriate management review of trading limits, strategies, hedging activities, investments, incentive compensation and other matters identified in this part or by management as requiring attention;

(4) Independent testing and audit of the effectiveness of the compliance program conducted periodically by qualified personnel of the banking entity or by a qualified outside party;

(5) Training for trading personnel and managers, as well as other appropriate personnel, to effectively implement and enforce the compliance program; and

(6) Records sufficient to demonstrate compliance with section 13 of the BHC Act and this part, which a banking entity must promptly provide to the SEC upon request and retain for a period of no less than 5 years or such longer period as required by the SEC.

(c) *CEO attestation.* The CEO of a banking entity that has significant trading assets and liabilities must, based on a review by the CEO of the banking entity, attest in writing to the SEC, each year no later than March 31, that the banking entity has in place processes to establish, maintain, enforce, review, test and modify the compliance program required by paragraph (b) of this section in a manner reasonably designed to achieve compliance with section 13 of the BHC Act and this part. In the case of a U.S. branch or agency of a foreign banking entity, the attestation may be provided for the entire U.S. operations of the foreign banking entity by the senior management officer of the U.S. operations of the foreign banking entity who is located in the United States.

(d) *Reporting requirements under appendix A to this part.* (1) A banking entity (other than a qualifying foreign excluded fund under section 255.6(f) or 255.13(d)) engaged in proprietary trading activity permitted under subpart B shall comply with the reporting requirements described in appendix A to this part, if:

(i) The banking entity has significant trading assets and liabilities; or

(ii) The SEC notifies the banking entity in writing that it must satisfy the reporting requirements contained in appendix A to this part.

(2) Frequency of reporting: Unless the SEC notifies the banking entity in writing that it must report on a different basis, a banking entity subject to appendix A to this part shall report the information required by appendix A for each quarter within 30 days of the end of the quarter.

(e) *Additional documentation for covered funds.* A banking entity with significant trading assets and liabilities (other than a qualifying foreign excluded fund under section 255.6(f) or 255.13(d)) shall maintain records that include:

(1) Documentation of the exclusions or exemptions other than sections 3(c)(1) and 3(c)(7) of the Investment Company Act of 1940 relied on by each fund sponsored by the banking entity (including all subsidiaries and affiliates) in determining that such fund is not a covered fund;

(2) For each fund sponsored by the banking entity (including all subsidiaries and affiliates) for which the banking entity relies on one or more of the exclusions from the definition of covered fund provided by §§ 255.10(c)(1), 255.10(c)(5), 255.10(c)(8), 255.10(c)(9), or 255.10(c)(10) of subpart C, documentation supporting the banking entity's determination that the fund is not a covered fund pursuant to one or more of those exclusions;

(3) For each seeding vehicle described in § 255.10(c)(12)(i) or (iii) of subpart C that will become a registered investment company or SEC-regulated business development company, a written plan documenting the banking entity's determination that the seeding vehicle will become a registered investment company or SEC-regulated business development company; the period of time during which the vehicle will operate

§ 255.20

as a seeding vehicle; and the banking entity's plan to market the vehicle to third-party investors and convert it into a registered investment company or SEC-regulated business development company within the time period specified in § 255.12(a)(2)(i)(B) of subpart C;

(4) For any banking entity that is, or is controlled directly or indirectly by a banking entity that is, located in or organized under the laws of the United States or of any State, if the aggregate amount of ownership interests in foreign public funds that are described in § 255.10(c)(1) of subpart C owned by such banking entity (including ownership interests owned by any affiliate that is controlled directly or indirectly by a banking entity that is located in or organized under the laws of the United States or of any State) exceeds $50 million at the end of two or more consecutive calendar quarters, beginning with the next succeeding calendar quarter, documentation of the value of the ownership interests owned by the banking entity (and such affiliates) in each foreign public fund and each jurisdiction in which any such foreign public fund is organized, calculated as of the end of each calendar quarter, which documentation must continue until the banking entity's aggregate amount of ownership interests in foreign public funds is below $50 million for two consecutive calendar quarters; and

(5) For purposes of paragraph (e)(4) of this section, a U.S. branch, agency, or subsidiary of a foreign banking entity is located in the United States; however, the foreign bank that operates or controls that branch, agency, or subsidiary is not considered to be located in the United States solely by virtue of operating or controlling the U.S. branch, agency, or subsidiary.

(f) *Simplified programs for less active banking entities*—(1) *Banking entities with no covered activities.* A banking entity that does not engage in activities or investments pursuant to subpart B or subpart C (other than trading activities permitted pursuant to § 255.6(a) of subpart B) may satisfy the requirements of this section by establishing the required compliance program prior to becoming engaged in such activities or making such investments (other than trading activities permitted pursuant to § 255.6(a) of subpart B).

(2) *Banking entities with moderate trading assets and liabilities.* A banking entity with moderate trading assets and liabilities may satisfy the requirements of this section by including in its existing compliance policies and procedures appropriate references to the requirements of section 13 of the BHC Act and this part and adjustments as appropriate given the activities, size, scope, and complexity of the banking entity.

(g) *Rebuttable presumption of compliance for banking entities with limited trading assets and liabilities*—(1) *Rebuttable presumption.* Except as otherwise provided in this paragraph, a banking entity with limited trading assets and liabilities shall be presumed to be compliant with subpart B and subpart C of this part and shall have no obligation to demonstrate compliance with this part on an ongoing basis.

(2) *Rebuttal of presumption.* If upon examination or audit, the SEC determines that the banking entity has engaged in proprietary trading or covered fund activities that are otherwise prohibited under subpart B or subpart C of this part, the SEC may require the banking entity to be treated under this part as if it did not have limited trading assets and liabilities. The SEC's rebuttal of the presumption in this paragraph must be made in accordance with the notice and response procedures in paragraph (i) of this section.

(h) *Reservation of authority.* Notwithstanding any other provision of this part, the SEC retains its authority to require a banking entity without significant trading assets and liabilities to apply any requirements of this part that would otherwise apply if the banking entity had significant or moderate trading assets and liabilities if the SEC determines that the size or complexity of the banking entity's trading or investment activities, or the risk of evasion of subpart B or subpart C of this part, does not warrant a presumption of compliance under paragraph (g) of this section or treatment as a banking entity with moderate trading assets and liabilities, as applicable. The SEC's exercise of this reservation of authority must be made in accordance with the notice and response procedures in paragraph (i) of this section.

(i) *Notice and response procedures*—(1) *Notice.* The SEC will notify the banking entity in writing of any determination requiring notice under this part and will provide an explanation of the determination.

(2) *Response.* The banking entity may respond to any or all items in the notice described in paragraph (i)(1) of this section. The response should include any matters that the banking entity would have the SEC consider in deciding whether to make the determination. The response must be in writing and delivered to the designated SEC official within 30 days after the date on which the banking entity received the notice. The SEC may shorten the time period when, in the opinion of the SEC, the activities or condition of the banking entity so requires, provided that the banking entity is informed of the time period at the time of notice, or with the consent of the banking entity. In its discretion, the SEC may extend the time period for good cause.

(3) *Waiver.* Failure to respond within 30 days or such other time period as may be specified by the SEC shall constitute a waiver of any objections to the SEC's determination.

(4) *Decision.* The SEC will notify the banking entity of the decision in writing. The notice will include an explanation of the decision.

[79 FR 5779, 5805, Jan. 31, 2014, as amended at 84 FR 62245, Nov. 14, 2019; 85 FR 46529, July 31, 2020]

§ 255.21 Termination of activities or investments; penalties for violations.

(a) Any banking entity that engages in an activity or makes an investment in violation of section 13 of the BHC Act or this part, or acts in a manner that functions as an evasion of the requirements of section 13 of the BHC Act or this part, including through an abuse of any activity or investment permitted under subparts B or C, or otherwise violates the restrictions and requirements of section 13 of the BHC Act or this part, shall, upon discovery, promptly terminate the activity and, as relevant, dispose of the investment.

(b) Whenever the SEC finds reasonable cause to believe any banking entity has engaged in an activity or made an investment in violation of section 13 of the BHC Act or this part, or engaged in any activity or made any investment that functions as an evasion of the requirements of section 13 of the BHC Act or this part, the SEC may take any action permitted by law to enforce compliance with section 13 of the BHC Act and this part, including directing the banking entity to restrict, limit, or terminate any or all activities under this part and dispose of any investment.

APPENDIX A TO PART 255—REPORTING AND RECORDKEEPING REQUIREMENTS FOR COVERED TRADING ACTIVITIES

I. PURPOSE

a. This appendix sets forth reporting and recordkeeping requirements that certain banking entities must satisfy in connection with the restrictions on proprietary trading set forth in subpart B ("proprietary trading restrictions"). Pursuant to § 255.20(d), this appendix applies to a banking entity that, together with its affiliates and subsidiaries, has significant trading assets and liabilities. These entities are required to (i) furnish periodic reports to the SEC regarding a variety of quantitative measurements of their covered trading activities, which vary depending on the scope and size of covered trading activities, and (ii) create and maintain records documenting the preparation and content of these reports. The requirements of this appendix must be incorporated into the banking entity's internal compliance program under § 255.20.

b. The purpose of this appendix is to assist banking entities and the SEC in:

(1) Better understanding and evaluating the scope, type, and profile of the banking entity's covered trading activities;

(2) Monitoring the banking entity's covered trading activities;

(3) Identifying covered trading activities that warrant further review or examination by the banking entity to verify compliance with the proprietary trading restrictions;

(4) Evaluating whether the covered trading activities of trading desks engaged in market making-related activities subject to § 255.4(b) are consistent with the requirements governing permitted market making-related activities;

(5) Evaluating whether the covered trading activities of trading desks that are engaged in permitted trading activity subject to § 255.4, § 255.5, or § 255.6(a) and (b) (*i.e.*, underwriting and market making-related activity,

Pt. 255, App. A

risk-mitigating hedging, or trading in certain government obligations) are consistent with the requirement that such activity not result, directly or indirectly, in a material exposure to high-risk assets or high-risk trading strategies;

(6) Identifying the profile of particular covered trading activities of the banking entity, and the individual trading desks of the banking entity, to help establish the appropriate frequency and scope of examination by SEC of such activities; and

(7) Assessing and addressing the risks associated with the banking entity's covered trading activities.

c. Information that must be furnished pursuant to this appendix is not intended to serve as a dispositive tool for the identification of permissible or impermissible activities.

d. In addition to the quantitative measurements required in this appendix, a banking entity may need to develop and implement other quantitative measurements in order to effectively monitor its covered trading activities for compliance with section 13 of the BHC Act and this part and to have an effective compliance program, as required by § 255.20. The effectiveness of particular quantitative measurements may differ based on the profile of the banking entity's businesses in general and, more specifically, of the particular trading desk, including types of instruments traded, trading activities and strategies, and history and experience (e.g., whether the trading desk is an established, successful market maker or a new entrant to a competitive market). In all cases, banking entities must ensure that they have robust measures in place to identify and monitor the risks taken in their trading activities, to ensure that the activities are within risk tolerances established by the banking entity, and to monitor and examine for compliance with the proprietary trading restrictions in this part.

e. On an ongoing basis, banking entities must carefully monitor, review, and evaluate all furnished quantitative measurements, as well as any others that they choose to utilize in order to maintain compliance with section 13 of the BHC Act and this part. All measurement results that indicate a heightened risk of impermissible proprietary trading, including with respect to otherwise-permitted activities under §§ 255.4 through 255.6(a) and (b), or that result in a material exposure to high-risk assets or high-risk trading strategies, must be escalated within the banking entity for review, further analysis, explanation to SEC, and remediation, where appropriate. The quantitative measurements discussed in this appendix should be helpful to banking entities in identifying and managing the risks related to their covered trading activities.

17 CFR Ch. II (4–1–23 Edition)

II. DEFINITIONS

The terms used in this appendix have the same meanings as set forth in §§ 255.2 and 255.3. In addition, for purposes of this appendix, the following definitions apply:

Applicability identifies the trading desks for which a banking entity is required to calculate and report a particular quantitative measurement based on the type of covered trading activity conducted by the trading desk.

Calculation period means the period of time for which a particular quantitative measurement must be calculated.

Comprehensive profit and loss means the net profit or loss of a trading desk's material sources of trading revenue over a specific period of time, including, for example, any increase or decrease in the market value of a trading desk's holdings, dividend income, and interest income and expense.

Covered trading activity means trading conducted by a trading desk under § 255.4, § 255.5, § 255.6(a), or § 255.6(b). A banking entity may include in its covered trading activity trading conducted under § 255.3(d), § 255.6(c), § 255.6(d), or § 255.6(e).

Measurement frequency means the frequency with which a particular quantitative metric must be calculated and recorded.

Trading day means a calendar day on which a trading desk is open for trading.

III. REPORTING AND RECORDKEEPING

a. Scope of Required Reporting

1. Quantitative measurements. Each banking entity made subject to this appendix by § 255.20 must furnish the following quantitative measurements, as applicable, for each trading desk of the banking entity engaged in covered trading activities and calculate these quantitative measurements in accordance with this appendix:

i. Internal Limits and Usage;
ii. Value-at-Risk;
iii. Comprehensive Profit and Loss Attribution;
iv. Positions; and
v. Transaction Volumes.

2. Trading desk information. Each banking entity made subject to this appendix by § 255.20 must provide certain descriptive information, as further described in this appendix, regarding each trading desk engaged in covered trading activities.

3. Quantitative measurements identifying information. Each banking entity made subject to this appendix by § 255.20 must provide certain identifying and descriptive information, as further described in this appendix, regarding its quantitative measurements.

4. Narrative statement. Each banking entity made subject to this appendix by § 255.20 may provide an optional narrative statement, as further described in this appendix.

Securities and Exchange Commission Pt. 255, App. A

5. File identifying information. Each banking entity made subject to this appendix by §255.20 must provide file identifying information in each submission to the SEC pursuant to this appendix, including the name of the banking entity, the RSSD ID assigned to the top-tier banking entity by the Board, and identification of the reporting period and creation date and time.

b. Trading Desk Information

1. Each banking entity must provide descriptive information regarding each trading desk engaged in covered trading activities, including:

i. Name of the trading desk used internally by the banking entity and a unique identification label for the trading desk;

ii. Identification of each type of covered trading activity in which the trading desk is engaged;

iii. Brief description of the general strategy of the trading desk;

v. A list identifying each Agency receiving the submission of the trading desk;

2. Indication of whether each calendar date is a trading day or not a trading day for the trading desk; and

3. Currency reported and daily currency conversion rate.

c. Quantitative Measurements Identifying Information

Each banking entity must provide the following information regarding the quantitative measurements:

1. An Internal Limits Information Schedule that provides identifying and descriptive information for each limit reported pursuant to the Internal Limits and Usage quantitative measurement, including the name of the limit, a unique identification label for the limit, a description of the limit, the unit of measurement for the limit, the type of limit, and identification of the corresponding risk factor attribution in the particular case that the limit type is a limit on a risk factor sensitivity and profit and loss attribution to the same risk factor is reported; and

2. A Risk Factor Attribution Information Schedule that provides identifying and descriptive information for each risk factor attribution reported pursuant to the Comprehensive Profit and Loss Attribution quantitative measurement, including the name of the risk factor or other factor, a unique identification label for the risk factor or other factor, a description of the risk factor or other factor, and the risk factor or other factor's change unit.

d. Narrative Statement

Each banking entity made subject to this appendix by §255.20 may submit in a separate electronic document a Narrative Statement to the SEC with any information the banking entity views as relevant for assessing the information reported. The Narrative Statement may include further description of or changes to calculation methods, identification of material events, description of and reasons for changes in the banking entity's trading desk structure or trading desk strategies, and when any such changes occurred.

e. Frequency and Method of Required Calculation and Reporting

A banking entity must calculate any applicable quantitative measurement for each trading day. A banking entity must report the Trading Desk Information, the Quantitative Measurements Identifying Information, and each applicable quantitative measurement electronically to the SEC on the reporting schedule established in §255.20 unless otherwise requested by the SEC. A banking entity must report the Trading Desk Information, the Quantitative Measurements Identifying Information, and each applicable quantitative measurement to the SEC in accordance with the XML Schema specified and published on the SEC's website.

f. Recordkeeping

A banking entity must, for any quantitative measurement furnished to the SEC pursuant to this appendix and §255.20(d), create and maintain records documenting the preparation and content of these reports, as well as such information as is necessary to permit the SEC to verify the accuracy of such reports, for a period of five years from the end of the calendar year for which the measurement was taken. A banking entity must retain the Narrative Statement, the Trading Desk Information, and the Quantitative Measurements Identifying Information for a period of five years from the end of the calendar year for which the information was reported to the SEC.

IV. QUANTITATIVE MEASUREMENTS

a. Risk-Management Measurements

1. Internal Limits and Usage

i. *Description:* For purposes of this appendix, Internal Limits are the constraints that define the amount of risk and the positions that a trading desk is permitted to take at a point in time, as defined by the banking entity for a specific trading desk. Usage represents the value of the trading desk's risk or positions that are accounted for by the current activity of the desk. Internal limits and their usage are key compliance and risk management tools used to control and monitor risk taking and include, but are not limited to, the limits set out in §§255.4 and 255.5.

Pt. 255, App. A

A trading desk's risk limits, commonly including a limit on "Value-at-Risk," are useful in the broader context of the trading desk's overall activities, particularly for the market making activities under § 255.4(b) and hedging activity under § 255.5. Accordingly, the limits required under §§ 255.4(b)(2)(iii)(C) and 255.5(b)(1)(i)(A) must meet the applicable requirements under §§ 255.4(b)(2)(iii)(C) and 255.5(b)(1)(i)(A) and also must include appropriate metrics for the trading desk limits including, at a minimum, "Value-at-Risk" except to the extent the "Value-at-Risk" metric is demonstrably ineffective for measuring and monitoring the risks of a trading desk based on the types of positions traded by, and risk exposures of, that desk.

A. A banking entity must provide the following information for each limit reported pursuant to this quantitative measurement: The unique identification label for the limit reported in the Internal Limits Information Schedule, the limit size (distinguishing between an upper and a lower limit), and the value of usage of the limit.

ii. *Calculation Period:* One trading day.

iii. *Measurement Frequency:* Daily.

iv. *Applicability:* All trading desks engaged in covered trading activities.

2. Value-at-Risk

i. *Description:* For purposes of this appendix, Value-at-Risk ("VaR") is the measurement of the risk of future financial loss in the value of a trading desk's aggregated positions at the ninety-nine percent confidence level over a one-day period, based on current market conditions.

ii. *Calculation Period:* One trading day.

iii. *Measurement Frequency:* Daily.

iv. *Applicability:* All trading desks engaged in covered trading activities.

b. *Source-of-Revenue Measurements*

1. Comprehensive Profit and Loss Attribution

i. *Description:* For purposes of this appendix, Comprehensive Profit and Loss Attribution is an analysis that attributes the daily fluctuation in the value of a trading desk's positions to various sources. First, the daily profit and loss of the aggregated positions is divided into two categories: (i) Profit and loss attributable to a trading desk's existing positions that were also positions held by the trading desk as of the end of the prior day ("existing positions"); and (ii) profit and loss attributable to new positions resulting from the current day's trading activity ("new positions").

A. The comprehensive profit and loss associated with existing positions must reflect changes in the value of these positions on the applicable day. The comprehensive profit and loss from existing positions must be further attributed, as applicable, to (i) changes in the specific risk factors and other factors that are monitored and managed as part of the trading desk's overall risk management policies and procedures; and (ii) any other applicable elements, such as cash flows, carry, changes in reserves, and the correction, cancellation, or exercise of a trade.

B. For the attribution of comprehensive profit and loss from existing positions to specific risk factors and other factors, a banking entity must provide the following information for the factors that explain the preponderance of the profit or loss changes due to risk factor changes: The unique identification label for the risk factor or other factor listed in the Risk Factor Attribution Information Schedule, and the profit or loss due to the risk factor or other factor change.

C. The comprehensive profit and loss attributed to new positions must reflect commissions and fee income or expense and market gains or losses associated with transactions executed on the applicable day. New positions include purchases and sales of financial instruments and other assets/liabilities and negotiated amendments to existing positions. The comprehensive profit and loss from new positions may be reported in the aggregate and does not need to be further attributed to specific sources.

D. The portion of comprehensive profit and loss from existing positions that is not attributed to changes in specific risk factors and other factors must be allocated to a residual category. Significant unexplained profit and loss must be escalated for further investigation and analysis.

ii. *Calculation Period:* One trading day.

iii. *Measurement Frequency:* Daily.

iv. *Applicability:* All trading desks engaged in covered trading activities.

c. *Positions and Transaction Volumes Measurements*

1. Positions

i. *Description:* For purposes of this appendix, Positions is the value of securities and derivatives positions managed by the trading desk. For purposes of the Positions quantitative measurement, do not include in the Positions calculation for "securities" those securities that are also "derivatives," as those terms are defined under subpart A; instead, report those securities that are also derivatives as "derivatives."[1] A banking entity must separately report the trading

---

[1] *See* § 255.2(h), (aa). For example, under this part, a security-based swap is both a "security" and a "derivative." For purposes of the Positions quantitative measurement, security-based swaps are reported as derivatives rather than securities.

Securities and Exchange Commission

desk's market value of long securities positions, short securities positions, derivatives receivables, and derivatives payables.

ii. *Calculation Period:* One trading day.
iii. *Measurement Frequency:* Daily.
iv. *Applicability:* All trading desks that rely on §255.4(a) or (b) to conduct underwriting activity or market-making-related activity, respectively.

2. Transaction Volumes

i. *Description:* For purposes of this appendix, Transaction Volumes measures three exclusive categories of covered trading activity conducted by a trading desk. A banking entity is required to report the value and number of security and derivative transactions conducted by the trading desk with: (i) Customers, excluding internal transactions; (ii) non-customers, excluding internal transactions; and (iii) trading desks and other organizational units where the transaction is booked into either the same banking entity or an affiliated banking entity. For securities, value means gross market value. For derivatives, value means gross notional value. For purposes of calculating the Transaction Volumes quantitative measurement, do not include in the Transaction Volumes calculation for "securities" those securities that are also "derivatives," as those terms are defined under subpart A; instead, report those securities that are also derivatives as "derivatives."[2] Further, for purposes of the Transaction Volumes quantitative measurement, a customer of a trading desk that relies on §255.4(a) to conduct underwriting activity is a market participant identified in §255.4(a)(7), and a customer of a trading desk that relies on §255.4(b) to conduct market making-related activity is a market participant identified in §255.4(b)(3).

ii. *Calculation Period:* One trading day.
iii. *Measurement Frequency:* Daily.
iv. *Applicability:* All trading desks that rely on §255.4(a) or (b) to conduct underwriting activity or market-making-related activity, respectively.

[84 FR 62246, Nov. 14, 2019]

PARTS 256–259 [RESERVED]

PART 260—GENERAL RULES AND REGULATIONS, TRUST INDENTURE ACT OF 1939

TERMS USED IN THE RULES AND REGULATIONS

Sec.
260.0–1 Application of definitions contained in the act.

[2] *See* §255.2(h), (aa).

260.0–2 Definitions of terms used in the rules and regulations.
260.0–3 Definition of "rules and regulations" as used in certain sections of the Act.
260.0–4 Sequential numbering of documents filed with the Commission.

OFFICE OF THE COMMISSION

260.0–5 Business hours of the Commission.
260.0–6 Nondisclosure of information obtained in the course of examinations and investigations.
260.0–7 Small entities for purposes of the Regulatory Flexibility Act.
260.0–11 Liability for certain statements by issuers.

RULES UNDER SECTION 303

260.3(4)–1 Definition of "commission from an underwriter or dealer not in excess of the usual and customary distributors' or sellers' commissions" in section 303(4), for certain transactions.
260.3(4)–2 Definition of "distribution" in section 303(4) for certain transactions.
260.3(4)–3 Definitions of "participates" and "participation" as used in section 303(4), in relation to certain transactions.

RULES UNDER SECTION 304

260.4a–1 Exempted securities under section 304(a)(8).
260.4a–2 Exempted securities under section 304(d).
260.4a–3 Exempted securities under section 304(a)(9).
260.4c–1 Form for applications under section 304(c).
260.4c–2 General requirements as to form and content of applications.
260.4c–3 Number of copies; filing; signatures; binding.
260.4c–4 Applications under section 304(c)(1).
260.4c–5 Applications under section 304(c)(2).
260.4d–7 Application for exemption from one or more provisions of the Act.
260.4d–8 Content.
260.4d–9 Exemption for Canadian Trust Indentures from Specified Provisions of the Act.
260.4d–10 Exemption for securities issued pursuant to §230.802 of this chapter.
260.4d–11 Exemption for security-based swaps offered and sold in reliance on Rule 239 under the Securities Act of 1933 (17 CFR 230.239).
260.4d–12 Exemption for security-based swaps offered and sold in reliance on Securities Act of 1933 Rule 240 (§230.240).

RULES UNDER SECTION 305

260.5a–1 Forms for statements of eligibility and qualification.
260.5a–2 General requirements as to form and content of statements of eligibility and qualification.

Pt. 260

260.5a-3 Number of copies; filing; signatures; binding.
260.5b-1 Application pursuant to section 305(b)(2) of the Trust Indenture Act for determining eligibility of a person designated as trustee for offerings on a delayed basis.
260.5b-2 General requirements as to form and content of applications.
260.5b-3 Number of copies—Filing—Signatures.

Rules Under Section 307

Applications for Qualification of Indentures

260.7a-1 Form for application.
260.7a-2 Powers of agent for service named in application.
260.7a-3 Number of copies; filing; signatures; binding.
260.7a-4 Calculation of time.
260.7a-5 Filing of amendments; number of copies.
260.7a-6 Telegraphic delaying amendments.
260.7a-7 Effective date of amendment filed under section 8(a) of the Securities Act with the consent of the Commission.
260.7a-8 Effective date of amendment filed under section 8(a) of the Securities Act pursuant to order of Commission.
260.7a-9 Delaying amendments.

General Requirements as to Form and Content of Applications, Statements and Reports

General

260.7a-15 Scope of §§ 260.7a-15 to 260.7a-37.

Formal Requirements

260.7a-16 Inclusion of items, differentiation between items and answers, omission of instructions.
260.7a-17 Quality, color and size of paper.
260.7a-18 Legibility.
260.7a-19 Margin for binding.
260.7a-20 Riders; inserts.

General Requirements as to Contents

260.7a-21 Clarity.
260.7a-22 Information unknown or not reasonably available.
260.7a-23 Statements required where item is inapplicable or where answer is "none".
260.7a-24 Words relating to periods of time in the past.
260.7a-25 Words relating to the future.
260.7a-26 Disclaimer of control.
260.7a-27 Title of securities.

Incorporation by Reference

260.7a-28 Incorporation of matter in application, statement or report, other than exhibits, as answer to item.
260.7a-29 Incorporation of exhibits as such.
260.7a-30 Identification of material incorporated; form of incorporation.
260.7a-31 Incorporation by reference of contested material.
260.7a-32 Incorporation by reference rendering document incomplete, unclear, or confusing.

Exhibits

260.7a-33 Additional exhibits.
260.7a-34 Omission of substantially identical documents.

Amendments

260.7a-35 Formal requirements as to amendments.
260.7a-36 Signatures to amendments.

Inspection and Publication of Applications, Statements and Reports

260.7a-37 Inspection of applications, statements and reports.

Rules Under Section 310

260.10a-1 Application for determining eligibility of a foreign person to act as sole trustee pursuant to section 310(a)(1) of the Act.
260.10a-2 General requirements as to form and content of applications.
260.10a-3 Number of copies—Filing—Signatures.
260.10a-4 Consent of trustee to service of process.
260.10a-5 Eligibility of Canadian Trustees.
260.10b-1 Calculation of percentages.
260.10b-2 Applications under section 310(b)(1)(ii).
260.10b-3 Applications relative to affiliations between trustees and underwriters.
260.10b-4 Application for stay of trustee's duty to resign pursuant to section 310(b) of the Act.
260.10b-5 Content.
260.10b-6 Notices—Exemptive Application Procedure.

Rules Under Section 311

260.11b-4 Definition of "cash transaction" in section 311(b)(4).
260.11b-6 Definition of "self-liquidating paper" in section 311(b)(6).

Rules Under Section 314

Periodic Reports

260.14a-1 Application of §§ 260.7a-15 to 260.7a-38.
260.19a-1 Compliance with Section 314(a)(1) of the Trust Indenture Act for certain eligible indenture obligors.

AUTHORITY: 15 U.S.C. 77c, 77ddd, 77eee, 77ggg, 77nnn, 77sss, 78ll (d), 80b-3, 80b-4, and 80b-11, unless otherwise noted.

Securities and Exchange Commission § 260.0-3

Source: 5 FR 293, Jan. 25, 1940, unless otherwise noted.

Editorial Note: Nomenclature changes to part 260 appear at 57 FR 36501, Aug. 13, 1992, and 57 FR 47409, Oct. 16, 1992.

Note: In §§ 260.0-1 to 260.14a-1 the numbers to the right of the decimal point correspond with the respective rule number of the general rules and regulations under the Trust Indenture Act of 1939.

ATTENTION ELECTRONIC FILERS

THIS REGULATION SHOULD BE READ IN CONJUNCTION WITH REGULATION S-T (PART 232 OF THIS CHAPTER), WHICH GOVERNS THE PREPARATION AND SUBMISSION OF DOCUMENTS IN ELECTRONIC FORMAT. MANY PROVISIONS RELATING TO THE PREPARATION AND SUBMISSION OF DOCUMENTS IN PAPER FORMAT CONTAINED IN THIS REGULATION ARE SUPERSEDED BY THE PROVISIONS OF REGULATION S-T FOR DOCUMENTS REQUIRED TO BE FILED IN ELECTRONIC FORMAT.

Terms Used in the Rules and Regulations

§ 260.0-1 Application of definitions contained in the act.

Unless the context otherwise requires, the terms defined in the act shall, when used in the rules and regulations, have the respective meanings given in the act.

§ 260.0-2 Definitions of terms used in the rules and regulations.

Unless the context otherwise requires, the following terms, when used in this part, shall have the respective meanings indicated in this section:

(a) *Act.* The term "act" means the Trust Indenture Act of 1939. (53 Stat. 1149; 15 U.S.C. 77aaa)

(b) *Affiliate.* The term "affiliate" means a person controlling, controlled by, or under common control with, another person. The terms "affiliated" and "affiliation" have meanings correlative to the foregoing.

(c) *Agent for service.* The term "agent for service" means the person authorized to receive notices and communications from the Commission.

(d) *Amount.* The term "amount" when used in regard to securities, shall have the meaning given in § 260.10b-1(c).

(e) *Class.* The term "class", when used in regard to securities, shall have the meaning given in § 260.10b-1(e).

(f) *Control.* The term "control" means the power to direct the management and policies of a person, directly or through one or more intermediaries, whether through the ownership of voting securities, by contract, or otherwise. The terms "controlling" and "controlled" have meanings correlative to the foregoing. (See § 260.a-26.)

(g) *Electronic filer.* The term *electronic filer* means a person or an entity that submits filings electronically pursuant to Rules 100 and 101 of Regulation S-T (§§ 232.100 and 232.101 of this chapter, respectively).

(h) *Electronic filing.* The term *electronic filing* means a document under the federal securities laws that is transmitted or delivered to the Commission in electronic format.

(i) *Outstanding.* The term "outstanding", when used in regard to securities, shall have the meaning given in § 260.10b-1(d).

(j) *Parent.* The term "parent" means a person controlling one or more other persons.

(k) *Rules and regulations.* The term "rules and regulations" means all rules and regulations adopted by the Commission pursuant to the act, including the forms and instructions thereto.

(l) *Section.* The term "section" means a section of the act.[1]

(m) *Subsidiary.* The term "subsidiary" means a person controlled by another person.

[5 FR 293, Jan. 25, 1940, as amended at 58 FR 14686, Mar. 18, 1993; 62 FR 36459, July 8, 1997]

§ 260.0-3 Definition of "rules and regulations" as used in certain sections of the Act.

(a) The term *rules and regulations* as used in section 305 of the Act shall include the forms for registration of securities under the Securities Act of 1933 and the related instructions thereto, and the forms for information, documents and statements under section 305 of the Act.

---

[1] References to "this section" or to section number preceded by a section symbol are to sections in the Code of Federal Regulations.

§ 260.0-4

(b) The term *rules and regulations* as used in section 307 of the Act shall include the forms for applications under section 307 of the Act and the related instructions thereto.

[21 FR 1046, Feb. 15, 1956]

§ 260.0-4 Sequential numbering of documents filed with the Commission.

The manually signed original (or in the case of duplicate originals, one duplicate original) of all registrations, applications, statements, reports, or other documents filed under the Trust Indenture Act of 1939 shall be numbered sequentially (in addition to any internal numbering which otherwise may be present) by handwritten, typed, printed, or other legible form of notation from the facing page of the document through the last page of that document and any exhibits or attachments thereto. Further, the total number of pages contained in a numbered original shall be set forth on the first page of the document.

[44 FR 4666, Jan. 23, 1979, as amended at 76 FR 71877, Nov. 21, 2011]

OFFICE OF THE COMMISSION

§ 260.0-5 Business hours of the Commission.

(a) *General.* The principal office of the Commission, at 100 F Street, NE., Washington, DC 20549, is open each day, except Saturdays, Sundays and federal holidays, from 9 a.m. to 5:30 p.m., Eastern Standard Time or Eastern Daylight Saving Time, whichever is currently in effect, *provided that* the hours for the filing of documents with the Commission are as set forth in paragraphs (b) and (c) of this section.

(b) *Submissions made in paper.* Paper documents filed with or otherwise furnished to the Commission may be submitted to the Commission each day, except Saturdays, Sundays and federal holidays, from 8 a.m. to 5:30 p.m., Eastern Standard Time or Eastern Daylight Saving Time, whichever is currently in effect.

(c) *Electronic filings.* Filings made by direct transmission may be submitted to the Commission each day, except Saturdays, Sundays, and Federal holidays, from 6 a.m. to 10 p.m., Eastern Standard Time or Eastern Daylight Saving Time, whichever is currently in effect.

[58 FR 14687, Mar. 18, 1993, as amended at 65 FR 24802, Apr. 27, 2000; 68 FR 25800, May 13, 2003; 73 FR 32228, June 5, 2008; 88 FR 12209, Feb. 27, 2023]

§ 260.0-6 Nondisclosure of information obtained in the course of examinations and investigations.

Information or documents obtained by officers or employees of the Commission in the course of any examination or investigation under section 8(e) of the Securities Act of 1933 (48 Stat. 79; 15 U.S.C. 77h), pursuant to section 307(c) of the Trust Indenture Act of 1939 (53 Stat. 1156; 15 U.S.C. 77ggg), or any examination or investigation under section 20(a) of the Securities Act of 1933 (48 Stat. 86; 15 U.S.C. 77t), pursuant to section 321(a) of the Trust Indenture Act of 1939 (53 Stat. 1174; 15 U.S.C. 77uuu), shall, unless made a matter of public record, be deemed confidential. Except as provided by 17 CFR 203.2, officers and employees are hereby prohibited from making such confidential information or documents or any other non-public records of the Commission available to anyone other than a member, officer or employee of the Commission, unless the Commission or the General Counsel, pursuant to delegated authority, authorizes the disclosure of such information or the production of such documents as not being contrary to the public interest. Any officer or employee who is served with a subpoena requiring the disclosure of such information or the production of such documents shall appear in court and, unless the authorization described in the preceding sentence shall have been given, shall respectfully decline to disclose the information or produce the documents called for, basing his or her refusal upon this section. Any officer or employee who is served with such a subpoena shall promptly advise the General Counsel of the service of such subpoena, the nature of the information or documents sought, and any circumstances which may bear upon the desirability of making available such information or documents.

[44 FR 50836, Aug. 30, 1979, as amended at 53 FR 17459, May 17, 1988; 54 FR 33501, Aug. 15, 1989; 76 FR 71877, Nov. 21, 2011]

Securities and Exchange Commission § 260.0–11

§ 260.0–7 Small entities for purposes of the Regulatory Flexibility Act.

For purposes of Commission rulemaking in accordance with the provisions of Chapter Six of the Administrative Procedure Act (5 U.S.C. 601 *et seq.*), and unless otherwise defined for purposes of a particular rulemaking proceeding, the term "small business" or "small organization," for purposes of the Trust Indenture Act of 1939 shall mean an issuer whose total assets on the last day of its most recent fiscal year were $5 million or less that is engaged or proposing to engage in small business financing. An issuer is considered to be engaged or proposing to be engaged in small business financing under this section if it is conducting or proposing to conduct an offering of securities which does not exceed the dollar limitation prescribed by § 260.4a–2.

[47 FR 5223, Feb. 4, 1982, as amended at 51 FR 25362, July 14, 1986]

§ 260.0–11 Liability for certain statements by issuers.

(a) A statement within the coverage of paragraph (b) below which is made by or on behalf of an issuer or by an outside reviewer retained by the issuer shall be deemed not to be a fraudulent statement (as defined in paragraph (d) of this section), unless it is shown that such statement was made or reaffirmed without a reasonable basis or was disclosed other than in good faith.

(b) This rule applies to the following statements:

(1) A forward-looking statement (as defined in paragraph (c) of this section) made in a document filed with the Commission, in Part I of a quarterly report on Form 10–Q, § 249.308a of this chapter, or in an annual report to security holders meeting the requirements of Rules 14a–3(b) and (c) or 14c–3(a) and (b) under the Securities Exchange Act of 1934 (§ 240.14a–3(b) and (c) or § 240.14c–3(a) and (b) of this chapter), a statement reaffirming such forward-looking statement after the date the document was filed or the annual report was made publicly available, or a forward-looking statement made before the date the document was filed or the date the annual report was made publicly available if such statement is reaffirmed in a filed document, in Part I of a quarterly report on Form 10–Q, or in an annual report made publicly available within a reasonable time after the making of such forward-looking statement; *Provided, that:*

(i) At the time such statements are made or reaffirmed, either the issuer is subject to the reporting requirements of section 13(a) or 15(d) of the Securities Exchange Act of 1934 and has complied with the requirements of Rule 13a–1 or 15d–1 (§ 240.13a–1 or § 240.15d–1 of this chapter) thereunder, if applicable, to file its most recent annual report on Form 10–K, Form 20–F, or Form 40–F; or if the issuer is not subject to the reporting requirements of section 13(a) or 15(d) of the Securities Exchange Act of 1934, the statements are made in a registration statement filed under the Securities Act of 1933 or pursuant to section 12(b) or (g) of the Securities Exchange Act of 1934; and

(ii) The statements are not made by or on behalf of an issuer that is an investment company registered under the Investment Company Act of 1940; and

(2) Information relating to the effects of changing prices on the business enterprise presented voluntarily or pursuant to Item 303 of Regulation S–K (§ 229.303 of this chapter), Item 5 of Form 20–F (§ 249.220f of this chapter), "Operating and Financial Review and Prospects," Item 302 of Regulation S–K (§ 229.302 of this chapter), "Supplementary Financial Information," or Rule 3–20(c) of Regulation S–X (§ 210.3–20(c) of this chapter), and disclosed in a document filed with the Commission, in Part I of a quarterly report on Form 10–Q, or in an annual report to shareholders meeting the requirements of Rules 14a–3(b) and (c) or 14c–3(a) and (b) (§ 240.14a–3(b) and (c) or § 240.14c–3(a) and (b)) under the Securities Exchange Act of 1934.

(c) For the purpose of this rule, the term *forward-looking statement* shall mean and shall be limited to:

(1) A statement containing a projection of revenues, income (loss), earnings (loss) per share, capital expenditures, dividends, capital structure or other financial items;

(2) A statement of management's plans and objectives for future operations;

§ 260.3(4)-1

(3) A statement of future economic performance contained in management's discussion and analysis of financial condition and results of operations included pursuant to Item 303 of Regulation S–K (§ 229.303 of this chapter) or Item 5 of Form 20–F; or

(4) Disclosed statements of the assumptions underlying or relating to any of the statements described in paragraphs (c) (1), (2), or (3) of this section.

(d) For the purpose of this rule the term *fraudulent statement* shall mean a statement which is an untrue statement of a material fact, a statement false or misleading with respect to any material fact, an omission to state a material fact necessary to make a statement not misleading, or which constitutes the employment of a manipulative, deceptive, or fraudulent device, contrivance, scheme, transaction, act, practice, course of business, or an artifice to defraud, as those terms are used in the Trust Indenture Act of 1939 and other acts referred to in section 323(b) thereof or the rules or regulations promulgated thereunder.

[46 FR 19458, Mar. 31, 1981, as amended at 47 FR 54790, Dec. 26, 1982; 56 FR 30077, July 1, 1991; 64 FR 53925, Oct. 5, 1999; 73 FR 982, Jan. 4, 2008]

RULES UNDER SECTION 303

§ 260.3(4)–1 Definition of "commission from an underwriter or dealer not in excess of the usual and customary distributors' or sellers' commissions" in section 303(4), for certain transactions.

(a) The term *commission* in section 303(4) shall include such remuneration, commonly known as a spread, as may be received by a distributor or dealer as a consequence of reselling securities bought from an underwriter or dealer at a price below the offering price of such securities, where such resales afford the distributor or dealer a margin of profit not in excess of what is usual and customary in such transactions.

(b) The term *commission from an underwriter or dealer* in section 303(4) shall include commissions paid by an underwriter or dealer affiliated with the issuer.

(c) The term *usual and customary distributors' or sellers' commission* in section 303(4) shall mean a commission or remuneration, commonly known as a spread, paid to or received by any person selling securities either for his own account or for the account of others, which is not in excess of the amount usual and customary in the distribution and sale of issues of similar type and size, and not in excess of the amount allowed to other persons, if any, for comparable service in the distribution of the particular issue; but such term shall not include amounts paid to any person whose function is the management of the distribution of all of a substantial part of the particular issue, or who performs the functions normally performed by an underwriter or underwriting syndicate.

§ 260.3(4)–2 Definition of "distribution" in section 303(4) for certain transactions.

A person, the chief part of the business of which consists in the purchase of the securities of any one issuer and/or its affiliate and in the sale of its own securities to furnish the proceeds with which to acquire the securities of such issuer and/or affiliate, is to be regarded as engaged in the distribution of the securities of such issuer and/or affiliate within the meaning of section 303(4).

§ 260.3(4)–3 Definitions of "participates" and "participation" as used in section 303(4), in relation to certain transactions.

(a) The terms *participates* and *participation* in section 303(4) shall not include the interest of a person (1) who is neither in privity of contract with the issuer nor affiliated with the issuer, and (2) who has no association with any principal underwriter of the securities being distributed, and (3) whose function in the distribution is confined to an undertaking to purchase all or some specified proportion of the securities remaining unsold after the lapse of some specified period of time, and (4) who purchases such securities for investment and not with a view to distribution.

(b) As used in this section:

(1) The term *association* shall include a relationship between two persons under which one (i) is affiliated with the other, or (ii) has, in common with

Securities and Exchange Commission § 260.4c-4

the other, one or more partners, directors, officers, trustees, branch managers, or other persons occupying a similar status or performing similar functions or (iii) has a participation, direct or indirect, in the profits of the other, or has a financial stake, by debtor-creditor relationship, stock ownership, contract or otherwise, in the income or business of the other.

(2) The term *principal underwriter* means an underwriter in privity of contract with the issuer of the securities as to which he is underwriter.

RULES UNDER SECTION 304

§ 260.4a-1 Exempted securities under section 304(a)(8).

The provisions of the Trust Indenture Act of 1939 shall not apply to any security that has been or will be issued otherwise than under an indenture. The same issuer may not claim this exemption within a period of twelve consecutive months for more than $50,000,000 aggregate principal amount of any securities.

[80 FR 21925, Apr. 20, 2015]

§ 260.4a-2 Exempted securities under section 304(d).

The provisions of the Trust Indenture Act of 1939 shall not apply to any security that has been issued or will be issued in accordance with the provisions of Regulation A (17 CFR 230.251 *et seq.*) under the Securities Act of 1933.

[57 FR 36501, Aug. 13, 1992]

§ 260.4a-3 Exempted securities under section 304(a)(9).

The provisions of the Trust Indenture Act of 1939 shall not apply to any security which has been or is to be issued under an indenture which limits the aggregate principal amount of securities at any time outstanding thereunder to $10,000,000 or less, but this exemption shall not be applied within a period of thirty-six consecutive months to more than $10,000,000 aggregate principal amount of securities of the same issuer.

(Secs. 304(a)(8) and 304(a)(9) of the Trust Indenture Act of 1939, (sec. 302, Pub. L. 96-477; secs. 304(a)(8), 304(a)(9), 53 Stat. 1153; 15 U.S.C. 77ddd(a)(8), 77ddd(a)(9)))

[46 FR 63256, Dec. 31, 1981. Redesignated and amended at 57 FR 36501, Aug. 13, 1992]

§ 260.4c-1 Form for applications under section 304(c).

Form T-4 shall be used for applications for exemption filed pursuant to section 304(c) of the act.

[6 FR 981, Feb. 15, 1941]

§ 260.4c-2 General requirements as to form and content of applications.

Sections 260.7a-15 to 260.7a-38 shall be applicable to applications on Form T-4.

[6 FR 981, Feb. 15, 1941]

§ 260.4c-3 Number of copies; filing; signatures; binding.

(a) Three copies of every application and of every amendment thereto shall be filed with the Commission at its principal office.

(b) At least the original of each application or amendment filed with the Commission shall be signed in the manner prescribed by Form T-4 (§ 269.4 of this chapter).

(c) The application proper and the exhibits thereto shall be bound on the left side in one or more parts, but without stiff covers.

[16 FR 8737, Aug. 29, 1951]

§ 260.4c-4 Applications under section 304(c)(1).

(a) An applicant under section 304(c)(1) may, if it so desires, waive a hearing and request the Commission to decide the application without a formal hearing on the basis of the application and such other information and documents as the Commission shall designate as a part of the record. However, a hearing may be called upon order of the Commission notwithstanding that the applicant shall have filed such a waiver and request whenever, in the judgment of the Commission, such a hearing is necessary or appropriate in the public interest.

(b) If the applicant waives a hearing and requests the Commission to decide

§ 260.4c-5

the application without a hearing and if no hearing has been ordered by the Commission:

(1) The applicant shall, at the request of the Commission, furnish such additional information or documents as the Commission may deem necessary to decide the application.

(2) The Commission may, with the consent of the applicant, make a part of the record any pertinent information or documents filed with the Commission by the applicant or by any other person.

(3) The Commission shall, in its order deciding the application, designate and describe the information and documents comprising the record on which the decision is based.

[6 FR 981, Feb. 15, 1941]

§ 260.4c-5 Applications under section 304(c)(2).

A hearing shall be held upon every application filed pursuant to section 304(c)(2).

[6 FR 981, Feb. 15, 1941]

§ 260.4d-7 Application for exemption from one or more provisions of the Act.

(a) Three copies of every application for an order under section 304(d) of the Act (15 U.S.C. 77ddd(d)) and of every amendment thereto shall be filed with the Commission at its principal office.

(b) One copy shall be manually signed by a duly authorized officer of the applicant (or individual customarily performing similar functions with respect to an organization, whether incorporated or unincorporated), or by a natural person seeking exemption under section 304(d) of the Act.

(c) Such applications shall be on paper no larger 8½ × 11 inches in size. If reduction of large documents would render them illegible, such documents may be filed on paper larger than 8½ × 11 inches in size. The left margin shall be at least 1½ inches wide and if the application is bound, it shall be bound on the left side.

(d) The application shall be typed, printed, copied, or prepared by a process which produces copies suitable for repeated photocopying and microfilming. All typewritten or printed matter shall be set forth in black ink to permit photocopying. If printed, the application shall be in type not smaller than 10-point, roman type, at least two points leaded.

(e) Rules 7a-28 through 7a-32 (§§ 260.7a-28 through 260.7a-32 of this chapter) relating to incorporation by reference shall be applicable to applications for exemption pursuant to section 304(d) of the Act.

[56 FR 22319, May 15, 1991]

§ 260.4d-8 Content.

(a) Each application for an order under section 304(d) of the Act (15 U.S.C. 77ddd(d)) shall contain the name, address, and telephone number of each applicant and the name, address, and telephone number of any person to which such applicant wishes any questions regarding the application to be directed.

(b) Each application shall contain a statement of the relevant facts on which the request for relief is based, including a justification for the exemption(s) requested and a discussion of any benefit expected for security holders, trustees and/or obligors.

[56 FR 22319, May 15, 1991]

§ 260.4d-9 Exemption for Canadian Trust Indentures from Specified Provisions of the Act.

Any trust indenture filed in connection with offerings on a registration statement on Form S-1, (§ 239.1 of this chapter) F-7, F-8, F-9, F-10 or F-80 (§§ 239.37 through 239.41 of this chapter) shall be exempt from the operation of sections 310(a)(3) and 310(a)(4), sections 310(b) through 316(a), and sections 316(c) through 318(a) of the Act; provided that the trust indenture is subject to:

(a) The Canada Business Corporations Act, R. S. C. 1985;

(b) The Bank Act, R. S. C. 1985;

(c) The Business Corporations Act, 1982 (Ontario), S. O. 1982; or

(d) The Company Act, R.S.B.C. 1979, C. 59.

[56 FR 30077, July 1, 1991, as amended at 57 FR 36501, Aug. 13, 1992; 58 FR 33190, June 16, 1993; 73 FR 983, Jan. 4, 2008]

§ 260.4d-10 Exemption for securities issued pursuant to § 230.802 of this chapter.

Any debt security, whether or not issued under an indenture, is exempt from the Act if made in compliance with § 230.802 of this chapter.

[64 FR 61406, Nov. 10, 1999]

§ 260.4d-11 Exemption for security-based swaps offered and sold in reliance on Rule 239 under the Securities Act of 1933 (17 CFR 230.239).

Any security-based swap offered and sold in reliance on Rule 239 under the Securities Act of 1933 (17 CFR 230.239), whether or not issued under an indenture, is exempt from the Act.

[77 FR 20549, Apr. 5, 2012]

§ 260.4d-12 Exemption for security-based swaps offered and sold in reliance on Securities Act of 1933 Rule 240 (§ 230.240).

Any security-based swap offered and sold in reliance on § 230.240 of this chapter, whether or not issued under an indenture, is exempt from the Act. This section will expire on February 11, 2018.

[82 FR 10707, Feb. 15, 2017]

RULES UNDER SECTION 305

§ 260.5a-1 Forms for statements of eligibility and qualification.

(a) Form T-1 shall be used for statements of eligibility and qualification of corporations designated to act as trustees under trust indentures to be qualified pursuant to section 305 or 307 of the Act.

(b) Form T-2 shall be used for statements of eligibility and qualification of individuals designated to act as trustees under trust indentures to be qualified pursuant to section 305 or 307 of the Act.

§ 260.5a-2 General requirements as to form and content of statements of eligibility and qualification.

Rules 7a-15 through 7a-37 (§§ 260.7a-15 through 260.7a-37 of this chapter) under section 307 under the Trust Indenture Act shall be applicable to statements filed on Forms T-1, T-2, and T-6.

[56 FR 22320, May 15, 1991]

§ 260.5a-3 Number of copies; filing; signatures; binding.

(a) Three copies of each statement of eligibility and qualification shall be filed with the registration statement or application for qualification.

(b) At least the original of each statement of eligibility and qualification filed with the Commission shall be signed in the manner prescribed by the particular form.

(c) Each statement of eligibility and qualification and the exhibits thereto shall be bound on the left-hand side in one or more parts, without stiff covers. The binding shall be made in such manner as to leave the reading matter legible.

(d) The statement or statements shall be filed by the obligor upon the indenture securities as a separate part of the registration statement or application for qualification, as the case may be.

[6 FR 667, Jan. 30, 1941, as amended at 16 FR 8737, Aug. 29, 1951]

§ 260.5b-1 Application pursuant to section 305(b)(2) of the Trust Indenture Act for determining eligibility of a person designated as trustee for offerings on a delayed basis.

Forms T-1 and T-2 (17 CFR 269.1 and 269.2) shall be used for applications filed for the purpose of determining the eligibility under section 310(a) of the Act of a person designated as trustee for debt securities registered under the Securities Act of 1933 which are eligible to be issued, offered, or sold on a delayed basis by or on behalf of the registrant.

[56 FR 22320, May 15, 1991]

§ 260.5b-2 General requirements as to form and content of applications.

Rule 5a-2 (§ 260.5a-2 of this chapter) and rules 7a-15 through 7a-37 [§§ 260.7a-15 through 260.7a-37 of this chapter] shall be applicable to applications pursuant to rule 5b-1 (§ 260.56b-1 of this chapter).

[56 FR 22320, May 15, 1991]

§ 260.5b-3 Number of copies—Filing—Signatures.

(a) Three copies of every application pursuant to rule 5b-1 (§ 260.5b-1 of this

§ 260.7a-1

chapter) and of every amendment thereto shall be filed with the Commission at its principal office by the issuer upon the indenture securities. Such application shall be filed no later than the second business day following the initial date of public offering or sales after effectiveness of the registration statement with respect to such securities, or transmitted by a means reasonably calculated to result in filing with the Commission by that date.

(b) One copy shall be manually signed by the applicant's duly authorized officer (or individual customarily performing similar functions with respect to any organization, whether incorporated or unincorporated), or by the individual trustee, as applicable.

[56 FR 22320, May 15, 1991]

RULES UNDER SECTION 307

APPLICATIONS FOR QUALIFICATION OF INDENTURES

§ 260.7a-1 Form for application.

Form T-3 shall be used for applications for qualification of indentures pursuant to section 307(a).

§ 260.7a-2 Powers of agent for service named in application.

Every applicant shall be deemed, in the absence of a statement to the contrary, to confer upon the agent for service the following powers:

(a) A power to amend the application for qualification by altering the date of the proposed offering of the indenture securities.

(b) A power to make application pursuant to § 260.7 for the Commission's consent to the filing of an amendment.

(c) A power to withdraw the application for qualification or any amendment thereto.

(d) A power to consent to the entry of an order under section 8(b) of the Securities Act of 1933 (48 Stat. 79; 15 U.S.C. 77l), waiving notice and hearing, such order being entered without prejudice to the right of the applicant thereafter to have the order vacated upon a showing to the Commission that the application for qualification, as amended, is no longer incomplete or inaccurate on its face in any material respect.

§ 260.7a-3 Number of copies; filing; signatures; binding.

(a) Three copies of the complete application shall be filed with the Commission at its principal office.

(b) At least the original of each application filed with the Commission shall be signed in the manner prescribed by Form T-3 (§ 269.3 of this chapter).

(c) The application proper and the exhibits thereto shall be bound on the left side in one or more parts, but without stiff covers. The binding shall be made in such manner as to leave the reading matter legible.

[16 FR 8737, Aug. 29, 1951]

§ 260.7a-4 Calculation of time.

Saturdays, Sundays and holidays shall be counted in computing the effective date of applications for qualification filed under section 307(a) of the Act. The twentieth day shall be deemed to begin at the expiration of nineteen periods of twenty-four hours each from 5:30 p.m., eastern standard time or eastern daylight-saving time, whichever is in effect at the principal office of the Commission on the date of filing.

[12 FR 2941, May 2, 1947]

§ 260.7a-5 Filing of amendments; number of copies.

Except as provided in § 260.7a-6, three copies of every amendment to an application shall be filed with the Commission.

[16 FR 8737, Aug. 29, 1951]

§ 260.7a-6 Telegraphic delaying amendments.

An amendment altering the proposed date of the public offering may be made by the agent for service by telegram. In each case, such telegraphic amendment shall be confirmed within a reasonable time by the filing of three copies, one of which shall be signed by the agent for service. Such confirmation shall not be deemed an amendment.

§ 260.7a-7 Effective date of amendment filed under section 8(a) of the Securities Act with the consent of the Commission.

An applicant desiring the Commission's consent to the filing of an amendment with the effect provided in section 8(a) of the Securities Act of 1933 may apply for such consent at or before the time of filing the amendment. The application shall be signed by the applicant or the agent for service and shall state fully the grounds upon which made. The Commission's consent shall be deemed to be given and the amendment shall be treated as a part of the application for qualification upon the sending of written or telegraphic notice to that effect.

§ 260.7a-8 Effective date of amendment filed under section 8(a) of the Securities Act pursuant to order of Commission.

An amendment made prior to the effective date of the application of qualification shall be deemed to be made pursuant to an order of the Commission within the meaning of section 8(a) of the Securities Act of 1933 so as to be treated as part of the application for qualification only when the Commission shall, after the filing of such amendment, find that it has been filed pursuant to its order.

§ 260.7a-9 Delaying amendments.

(a) An amendment in the following form filed with an application for qualification, or as an amendment to such an application which has not become effective, shall be deemed to be filed on such date or dates as may be necessary to delay the effective date of such application for the period specified in such amendment:

The obligor hereby amends this application for qualification on such date or dates as may be necessary to delay its effectiveness until (i) the 20th day after the filing of a further amendment which specifically states that it shall supersede this amendment, or (ii) such date as the Commission, acting pursuant to section 307(c) of the Act, may determine upon the written request of the obligor.

(b) An amendment pursuant to paragraph (a) of this section which is filed with an application for qualification shall be set forth on the facing page thereof. Any such amendment filed after the filing of the application may be made by letter or telegram and may be signed by the agent for service. Any amendment filed to supersede an amendment filed pursuant to paragraph (a) of this section may also be made by letter or telegram. Every such telegraphic amendment shall be confirmed in writing within a reasonable time by filing a signed copy of the amendment. Such confirmation shall not be deemed an amendment.

[30 FR 12387, Sept. 29, 1965]

GENERAL REQUIREMENTS AS TO FORM AND CONTENT OF APPLICATIONS, STATEMENTS AND REPORTS

GENERAL

§ 260.7a-15 Scope of §§ 260.7a-15 to 260.7a-37.

The rules contained in §§ 260.7a-15 to 260.7a-37 shall govern applications for exemption filed pursuant to section 304(c) or 304(d) of the Act, applications for qualification of indentures filed pursuant to section 307, statements of eligibility and qualifications of trustees filed pursuant to section 305, 307, or 310(a) of the Act, applications for the stay of the trustee's duty to resign filed pursuant to section 310(b) of the Act, and reports filed pursuant to section 314(a) of the Act.

[56 FR 22320, May 15, 1991]

FORMAL REQUIREMENTS

§ 260.7a-16 Inclusion of items, differentiation between items and answers, omission of instructions.

Except as expressly provided otherwise in the particular form, the application, statement, or report shall contain all of the items of the form as well as the answers thereto. The items shall be made to stand out from the answers by variation in margin or type or by other means. All instructions shall be omitted.

[6 FR 981, Feb. 15, 1941]

§ 260.7a-17 Quality, color and size of paper.

The application, statement or report, including all amendments and, where practicable, all papers and documents filed as a part thereof, shall be on good quality, unglazed, white paper, no larger than 8½ × 11 inches in size. To the extent that the reduction of larger documents would render them illegible,

§ 260.7a-18

such documents may be filed on paper larger than 8½ × 11 inches in size.

[47 FR 58239, Dec. 30, 1982]

§ 260.7a-18 Legibility.

(a) The application, statement or report, including all amendments and, where practicable, all papers and documents filed as a part thereof, shall be clear, easily readable and shall be typewritten, mimeographed, printed or prepared by any similar process which, in the opinion of the Commission, produces copies suitable for repeated photocopying and microfilming.

(b) If printed, the application, statement or report shall be in type not smaller than 10-point, roman type, at least two points leaded.

(c) All printing, mimeographing, typing or other markings shall be in black ink, except that debits in credit categories and credits in debit categories may be set forth in red or black ink, but shall in all cases be designated in such manner as to be clearly distinguishable as such on photocopies.

[5 FR 293, Jan. 25, 1940, as amended at 47 FR 58239, Dec. 30, 1982]

§ 260.7a-19 Margin for binding.

The application, statement or report, including all amendments and, where practicable, all papers and documents filed as a part thereof, shall have a back or stitching margin of at least 1½ inches for binding.

§ 260.7a-20 Riders; inserts.

Riders shall not be used. If the application, statement or report is typed on a printed form, and the space provided for the answer to any given item is insufficient, reference shall be made in such space to a full insert page or pages on which the item number and item shall be restated and a complete answer given.

GENERAL REQUIREMENTS AS TO CONTENTS

§ 260.7a-21 Clarity.

The answer to each item of the particular form shall be so worded as to be intelligible without the necessity of referring to the instructions or to this part.

§ 260.7a-22 Information unknown or not reasonably available.

Information required shall be given insofar as it is known or can be obtained by reasonable investigation. Responsibility for the accuracy or completeness of information obtained from persons other than affiliates may be disclaimed. As to information which is unknown and is unavailable after reasonable investigation, there shall be included a statement as to the nature of the investigation.

§ 260.7a-23 Statements required where item is inapplicable or where answer is "none".

If any item is inapplicable or the answer is "none", a statement to such effect shall be made.

§ 260.7a-24 Words relating to periods of time in the past.

Unless the context clearly shows otherwise, wherever any fixed period of time in the past is indicated, such period shall be computed from the date of filing with the Commission.

§ 260.7a-25 Words relating to the future.

Unless the context clearly shows otherwise, whenever words relate to the future, they have reference solely to present intention.

§ 260.7a-26 Disclaimer of control.

If the existence of control is open to reasonable doubt in any instance, the applicant or the trustee, as the case may be, may disclaim the existence of control and any admission thereof; in such case, however, a statement shall be made of the material facts pertinent to the possible existence of control.

§ 260.7a-27 Title of securities.

Where the title of securities is required to be furnished in an application, statement or report, the following requirements shall be met:

(a) In the case of shares, there shall be given the full designation of the class of shares and, if not included therein, the par or stated value, if any, and the rate of dividends, if fixed, and whether cumulative or non-cumulative.

Securities and Exchange Commission

§ 260.7a–33

(b) In the case of funded debt, there shall be given the full designation of the issue and, if not included therein, the rate of interest and the date of maturity. If the issue matures serially, a brief indication shall be given of the serial maturities: For example, "maturing serially from 1950 to 1960". If the payment of interest or principal is contingent, such contingency shall be appropriately indicated. The rate of interest, however, may be omitted from the title of indenture securities on the facing page of Form T–1 and Form T–2, if the rate of interest is not determined at the time these forms are filed.

(c) In the case of other securities, a similar designation shall be given.

[5 FR 293, Jan. 25, 1940, as amended at 9 FR 750, Jan. 20, 1944]

INCORPORATION BY REFERENCE

§ 260.7a–28 Incorporation of matter in application, statement or report, other than exhibits, as answer to item.

Matter contained in any part of the application, statement or report, other than exhibits, may be incorporated by reference as answer, or partial answer, to any item in the same application, statement or report.

§ 260.7a–29 Incorporation of exhibits as such.

(a) Any exhibit or part thereof previously or concurrently filed with the Commission pursuant to any Act administered by the Commission, may, subject to the limitations of § 228.10(f) and § 229.10(d) of this chapter, be incorporated by reference as an exhibit to any application, statement or report filed with the Commission by the same or any other person. Any exhibit or part thereof so filed with a trustee pursuant to the Trust Indenture Act of 1939 may be incorporated by reference as an exhibit to any report filed with such trustee pursuant to section 314(a) of that Act by the same or any other person.

(b) If any modification has occurred in the text of any exhibit incorporated by reference since the filing thereof, there shall be filed with the reference a statement containing the text of any such modification and the date thereof.

(c) If the number of copies of any exhibit previously or concurrently filed is less than the number required to be filed with the application, statement or report which incorporates such exhibit, there shall be filed with the application, statement or report as many additional copies of the exhibit as may be necessary to meet the requirements of such application, statement or report.

[6 FR 667, Jan. 30, 1941, as amended at 29 FR 2421, Feb. 13, 1964; 60 FR 32825, June 23, 1995; 76 FR 71877, Nov. 21, 2011]

§ 260.7a–30 Identification of material incorporated; form of incorporation.

In each case of incorporation by reference, the matter incorporated shall be clearly identified in the reference. An express statement shall be made to the effect that the specified matter is incorporated in the application, statement or report at the particular place where the information is required.

§ 260.7a–31 Incorporation by reference of contested material.

Notwithstanding any particular provision permitting incorporation by reference, no application, statement or report shall incorporate by reference any matter which is subject, at the time of filing the application, statement or report, to pending proceedings under section 8(b) or 8(d) of the Securities Act of 1933 (whether pursuant to the provisions of the Trust Indenture Act of 1939, or otherwise) or to an order entered under either of those sections.

§ 260.7a–32 Incorporation by reference rendering document incomplete, unclear, or confusing.

Notwithstanding any particular provision permitting incorporation by reference, the Commission may refuse to permit such incorporation in any case in which in its judgment such incorporation would render the application, statement or report incomplete, unclear or confusing.

EXHIBITS

§ 260.7a–33 Additional exhibits.

Any application, statement or report may include exhibits in addition to those required by the particular form.

§ 260.7a-34

Such additional exhibits shall be so marked as to indicate clearly the items to which they refer.

§ 260.7a-34 Omission of substantially identical documents.

In any case where two or more documents required to be filed as exhibits are substantially identical in all material respects except as to the parties thereto, dates of execution or other details, a copy of only one of such documents need be filed, with a schedule identifying the documents omitted and setting forth the material details in which such documents differ from the document, a copy of which is filed: *Provided, however,* That the Commission may at any time in its discretion require the filing of copies of any documents so omitted.

AMENDMENTS

§ 260.7a-35 Formal requirements as to amendments.

(a) Amendments to an application, statement or report shall comply with §§ 260.7a-17 to 260.7a-19.

(b) All amendments relating to a particular application, statements or report shall be numbered consecutively in the order in which they are filed with the Commission. Amendments shall be numbered separately for each separate application, statement or report.

(c) Every amendment to an item of an application, statement or report shall contain the item number, the caption and the text of the item being amended and the complete amended answer thereto.

(d) If at any time the application, statement or report becomes unclear or confusing because of the number of amendments filed or the length or complexity thereof, there may be filed, and at the written request of the Commission there shall be filed, a complete new application, statement or report, as amended, but no additional copies of exhibits need be filed.

§ 260.7a-36 Signatures to amendments.

Subject to § 260.7a-2, at least the original of every amendment to an application, statement or report shall be signed in the manner prescribed by the particular form on which the application, statement or report was filed.

[16 FR 8737, Aug. 29, 1951]

INSPECTION AND PUBLICATION OF APPLICATIONS, STATEMENTS AND REPORTS

§ 260.7a-37 Inspection of applications, statements and reports.

All applications, statements and reports are available for public inspection during business hours at the principal office of the Commission.

[16 FR 8737, Aug. 29, 1951]

RULE UNDER SECTION 310

§ 260.10a-1 Application for determining eligibility of a foreign person to act as sole trustee pursuant to section 310(a)(1) of the Act.

Form T-6 (17 CFR 269.9 of this chapter) shall be used for an application filed to obtain authorization for a corporation or other person organized and doing business under the laws of a foreign government to act as sole trustee under an indenture qualified or to be qualified under the Act.

[56 FR 22320, May 15, 1991]

§ 260.10a-2 General requirements as to form and content of applications.

Rule 5a-2 (§ 260.5a-2 of this chapter) and rules 7a-15 through 7a-37 [§§ 260.7a-15 through 260.7a-37 of this chapter] under section 307 of the Act shall be applicable to applications on Form T-6 pursuant to section 310(a)(1) of the Act and Rule 10a-1 (§ 260.10a-1 of this chapter).

[56 FR 22320, May 15, 1991]

§ 260.10a-3 Number of copies—Filing—Signatures.

(a) Three copies of every application pursuant to rule 10a-1 (§ 260.10a-1 of this chapter) and of every amendment thereto shall be filed with the Commission at its principal office.

(b) One copy shall be manually signed by the applicant's duly authorized officer (or individual customarily performing similar functions with respect to any organization, whether incorporated or unincorporated).

[56 FR 22320, May 15, 1991]

Securities and Exchange Commission § 260.10b-1

§ 260.10a-4 Consent of trustee to service of process.

At the time of filing an application pursuant to Rule 10a-1 (§ 260.10a-1 of this chapter) and at such time as it files a statement of eligibility to act as trustee under an indenture qualified under the Act, an indenture trustee organized and doing business under the laws of a foreign government shall furnish to the Commission on Form F-X (§ 249.250 of this chapter) a written consent of the trustee and power of attorney designating a U. S. person with an address in the United States as agent upon whom may be served any process, pleadings, subpoenas or other papers in any Commission investigation or administrative proceeding and any civil suit or action brought against the trustee or to which the trustee has been joined as defendant or respondent, in any appropriate court in any place subject to the jurisdiction of any state or of the United States, or of the District of Columbia or Puerto Rico, where the investigation, proceeding or cause of action arises out of or relates to or concerns the securities in relation to which the indenture trustee proposes to act as trustee pursuant to any rule or order under section 310(a) of the Act and stipulates and agrees that any such suit, action or proceeding may be commenced by the service of process upon said agent for service of process, and that such service shall be taken and held in all courts to be as valid and binding as if due personal service thereof had been made.

[56 FR 30077, July 1, 1991]

§ 260.10a-5 Eligibility of Canadian Trustees.

(a) Subject to paragraph (b) of this section, any trust company, acting as trustee under an indenture qualified or to be qualified under the Act and filed in connection with offerings on a registration statement on Form S-1 (§ 239.11 of this chapter) F-7, F-8, F-9, F-10 or F-80 (§§ 239.37 through 239.41 of this chapter) that is incorporated and regulated as a trust company under the laws of Canada or any of its political subdivisions and that is subject to supervision or examination pursuant to the Trust Companies Act (Canada), R.S.C. 1985, or the Canada Deposit Insurance Corporation Act, R.S.C. 1985 shall not be subject to the requirement of domicile in the United States under section 310(a) of the Act (15 U.S.C. 77jjj(a)).

(b) Each trustee eligible for appointment under this section (17 CFR 260.10a-5) shall file as part of the registration statement for the securities to which the trusteeship relates a consent to service of process and power of attorney on Form F-X (§ 269.5 of this chapter).

[56 FR 30077, July 1, 1991, as amended at 57 FR 36501, Aug. 13, 1992; 58 FR 33191, June 16, 1993; 73 FR 983, Jan. 4, 2008]

§ 260.10b-1 Calculation of percentages.

The percentages of voting securities and other securities specified in section 310(b) of the Act shall be calculated in accordance with the following provisions:

(a) A specified percentage of the voting securities of a person means such amount of the outstanding voting securities of such person as entitles the holder or holders thereof to cast such specified percentage of the aggregate votes which the holders of all the outstanding voting securities of such person are entitled to cast in the direction or management of the affairs of such person.

(b) A specified percentage of a class of securities of a person means such percentage of the aggregate amount of securities of the class outstanding.

(c) The term *amount*, when used in regard to securities, means the principal amount if relating to evidences of indebtedness, the number of shares if relating to capital shares, and the number of units if relating to any other kind of security.

(d) The term *outstanding* means issued and not held by or for the account of the issuer. The following securities shall not be deemed outstanding within the meaning of this definition:

(1) Securities of an issuer held in a sinking fund relating to securities of the issuer of the same class;

(2) Securities of an issuer held in a sinking fund relating to another class of securities of the issuer, if the obligation evidenced by such other class of

§ 260.10b-2

securities is not in default as to principal or interest or otherwise;

(3) Securities pledged by the issuer thereof as security for an obligation of the issuer not in default as to principal or interest or otherwise;

(4) Securities held in escrow is placed in escrow by the issuer otherwise;

Provided, however, That any voting securities of an issuer shall be deemed outstanding if any person other than the issuer is entitled to exercise the voting rights thereof.

(e) A security shall be deemed to be of the same class as another security if both securities confer upon the holder or holders thereof substantially the same rights and privileges: *Provided, however,* That, in the case of secured evidences of indebtedness, all of which are issued under a single indenture, differences in the interest rates or maturity dates of various series thereof shall not be deemed sufficient to constitute such series different classes: *And, provided further,* That, in the case of unsecured evidences of indebtedness, differences in the interest rates or maturity dates thereof shall not be deemed sufficient to constitute them securities of different classes, whether or not they are issued under a single indenture.

§ 260.10b-2 Applications under section 310(b)(1)(ii).

If an application filed with the Commission pursuant to clause (ii) of section 310(b)(1) (53 Stat. 1157; 15 U.S.C. 77jjj) of the Act is based upon the claim that no material conflict of interest will be involved because prior to or concurrently with the delivery of the securities to be issued under the indenture to be qualified all securities outstanding under the other indenture or indentures, under which the person designated to act as indenture trustee is also a trustee, will be discharged or:

(a) Funds sufficient to discharge the securities will be deposited in trust for that purpose.

(b) The securities, if not presently maturing, will be called for redemption or irrevocable power to make the call will be given to some third person.

(c) All liens securing the securities will be released or all steps necessary to effect the release at the maturity or redemption date will be taken.

The application shall be deemed to have been granted unless, within 7 days after it is filed, the Commission orders a hearing thereon.

[6 FR 808, Feb. 7, 1941]

§ 260.10b-3 Applications relative to affiliations between trustees and underwriters.

(a) Any person proposing to act as trustee under indentures to be qualified under the act may make application for a finding by the Commission as to whether such person is or is not an affiliate of any specified person who may be named as an underwriter for an obligor in any registration statement or application for qualification subsequently filed with the Commission.

(b) Every application pursuant to this section shall be filed in triplicate and shall contain a statement of the material facts necessary to enable the Commission to make the finding request. The applicant may incorporate by reference in the application any information or documents contained in a statement of eligibility and qualification of the applicant filed with the Commission. The Commission may with the consent of the applicant or at the applicant's request, make a part of the record the record in any prior proceeding in which the same issues were involved.

(c) A hearing will be held, after confirmed telegraphic notice to the applicant, upon every application filed pursuant to this section.

(d) Every finding by the Commission pursuant to this section shall be limited to the facts disclosed in the application and in the hearing thereon, and shall be made solely for the purposes of sections 305(b) and 307(c) of the Act.

[6 FR 2376, May 13, 1941]

§ 260.10b-4 Application for stay of trustee's duty to resign pursuant to section 310(b) of the Act.

(a) Three copies of every application for a stay of a trustee's duty to resign under section 310(b) of the Act and of every amendment thereto shall be filed with the Commission at its principal office.

Securities and Exchange Commission § 260.11b-4

(b) One copy shall be manually signed by a duly authorized officer of the applicant (or individual customarily performing similar functions with respect to an organization, whether incorporated or unincorporated) or by a natural person seeking a stay under section 310(b) of the Act.

(c) Such applications shall be on paper no larger than 8½ × 11 inches in size. If reduction of large documents would render them illegible, such documents may be filed on paper larger than 8½ × 11 inches in size. The left margin shall be at least 1½ inches wide and if the application is bound, it shall be bound on the left side.

(d) The application shall be typed, printed, copied, or prepared by a process which produces copies suitable for repeated photocopying and microfilming. All typewritten or printed matter shall be set forth in black ink to permit photocopying. If printed, the application shall be in type not smaller than 10-point, roman type, at least two points leaded.

(e) Rules 7a-28 through 7a-32 [§§ 260.7a-28 through 260.7a-32 of this chapter] relating to incorporation by reference shall be applicable to applications for stay pursuant to section 310(b) of the Act.

[56 FR 22320, May 15, 1991]

§ 260.10b-5 Content.

(a) Each application for a stay of a trustee's duty to resign under section 310(b) of the Act shall contain the name, address, and telephone number of each applicant and the name, address, and telephone number of any person to which such applicant wishes any questions regarding the application to be directed.

(b) Each application shall contain a statement of the reasons why the applicant is deemed to be entitled to a stay of resignation with reference to the provisions of section 310(b) of the Act. The statement shall address the nature of the default, the reasonableness of the period before the default will be cured or waived, the procedures to be used to cure or obtain a waiver of the default, and the reasons why a stay will not be inconsistent with the interests of the holders of the indenture securities.

[56 FR 22321, May 15, 1991]

§ 260.10b-6 Notices—Exemptive Application Procedure.

(a) A proposed notice of the proceeding indicated by the filing of the application shall accompany each application for a stay of a trustee's duty to resign under section 310(b) as an exhibit thereto and if necessary shall be modified to reflect any amendments to such application.

(b) Notice of the initiation of the proceeding will be published in the FEDERAL REGISTER and will indicate the earliest date upon which an order disposing of the matter may be entered. The notice will also provide that any interested person may, within the period specified therein, submit to the Commission in writing any facts bearing upon the desirability of a hearing on the matter, and may request that a hearing be held stating the person's reasons therefore and the nature of his or her interest in the matter.

(c) An order disposing of the matter will be issued following the expiration of the period of time referred to in paragraph (b) of this section, unless the Commission thereafter orders a hearing on the matter.

(d) The Commission will order a hearing on the matter, if it appears that a hearing is necessary or appropriate in the public interest or for the protection of investors:

(1) Upon the request of any interested person, or

(2) Upon its own motion.

[56 FR 22321, May 15, 1991]

RULES UNDER SECTION 311

§ 260.11b-4 Definition of "cash transaction" in section 311(b)(4).

The term "cash transaction", as used in section 311(b)(4), means any transaction in which full payment for goods or securities sold is made within 7 days after delivery of the goods or securities in currency or in checks or other orders drawn upon banks or bankers and payable upon demand.

315

§ 260.11b-6 Definition of "self-liquidating paper" in section 311(b)(6).

The term *self-liquidating paper*, as used in section 311(b)(6) of the Act, means any draft, bill of exchange, acceptance or obligation which is made, drawn, negotiated or incurred by the obligor for the purpose of financing the purchase, processing, manufacture, shipment, storage or sale of goods, wares or merchandise and which is secured by documents evidencing title to, possession of or a lien upon the goods, wares or merchandise or the receivables or proceeds arising from the sale of the goods, wares or merchandise previously constituting the security: *Provided*, The security is received by the trustee simultaneously with the creation of the creditor relationship with the obligor arising from the making, drawing, negotiating or incurring of the draft, bill of exchange, acceptance or obligation.

RULES UNDER SECTION 314

PERIODIC REPORTS

§ 260.14a-1 Application of §§ 260.7a-15 to 260.7a-38.

Sections 260.7a-15 to 260.7a-38 shall be applicable to annual reports under section 314(a).

§ 260.19a-1 Compliance with Section 314(a)(1) of the Trust Indenture Act for certain eligible indenture obligors.

(a) This section is applicable only to an "eligible indenture obligor" as defined in paragraph (b) of this section.

(b) For purposes of paragraph (c) of this section, an "eligible indenture obligor" is any obligor that:

(1) Is required to file reports with the Commission pursuant to Section 13 or Section 15(d) of the Securities Exchange Act of 1934 (15 U.S.C. §§ 78m or 78o(d)) (the "Exchange Act"); and

(2) May rely on any of the provisions of Release No. 34–45589 (March 18, 2002) (which may be viewed on the Commission's website at *www.sec.gov*) with regard to the filing of reports with the Commission pursuant to Section 13 or Section 15(d) of the Exchange Act (14 U.S.C. 78m or 78o(d)).

(c) An "eligible indenture obligor" that files with the indenture trustee those Exchange Act reports filed with the Commission in accordance with the Release referred to in paragraph (b)(2) of this section has met its duty under Section 314(a)(1) of the Act (15 U.S.C. 77nnn(a)(1)) to file with the indenture trustee all reports required to be filed with the Commission pursuant to Section 13 or Section 15(d) of the Securities Exchange Act of 1934.

[67 FR 13538, Mar. 22, 2002, as amended at 76 FR 71877, Nov. 21, 2011]

PART 261—INTERPRETATIVE RELEASES RELATING TO THE TRUST INDENTURE ACT OF 1939 AND GENERAL RULES AND REGULATIONS THEREUNDER

Subject	Release No.	Date	Fed. Reg. Vol. and Page
Opinion of the General Counsel relating to application of section 310(b) where trustee under one indenture is trustee under another indenture for securities of an affiliate of the obligor.	16	Nov. 14, 1941	11 FR 10989.
Opinion of the Chief Counsel to the Corporation Finance Division relating to when-issued trading of securities the issuance of which is subject to approval by a Federal district court under Chapter X of the Bankruptcy Act.	30	Aug. 28, 1944	Do.
Opinion of the Chief Counsel to the Corporation Finance Division relating to when-issued trading of securities the issuance of which has already been approved by a Federal district court under Chapter X of the Bankruptcy Act.	31	Jan. 4, 1945	11 FR 10990.
Interpretation with reference to the securities of the International Bank for Reconstruction and Development.	37	June 25, 1947	12 FR 4450.
Statement of the Commission to clarify the meaning of "beneficial ownership of securities" as relates to beneficial ownership of securities held by family members.	227	Jan. 25, 1966	31 FR 1005.
Statement of the Commission setting the date of May 1, 1966 after which filings must reflect beneficial ownership of securities held by family members.	229	Feb. 14, 1966	31 FR 3175.

Securities and Exchange Commission § 269.1

Subject	Release No.	Date	Fed. Reg. Vol. and Page
Commissions statement re exemption of certain industrial revenue bonds from registration, etc. requirements in view of amendment of Securities Act of 1933 and of Securities Exchange Act of 1934 by "section 401" (Pub. L. 91–1037).	284	Nov. 6, 1970	35 FR 17990.
Publication of the Commission's procedure to be followed if requests are to be met for no action or interpretative letters and responses thereto to be made available for public use.	289	Jan. 25, 1971	36 FR 2600.
Offerings of debt securities pursuant to trust indentures	524	Apr. 25, 1979	44 FR 26739.
No-action position respecting public offerings of debt securities registered on Form SB–2 without qualification of an indenture under the Trust Indenture Act.	542	Oct. 16, 1979	44 FR 61941.
Simplified form of trust indenture	605	Jan. 8, 1981	46 FR 3500.
Retail repurchase agreements by banks and Savings and Loan Associations	658	Sept. 25, 1981	46 FR 48637.
Application of the registration provisions of the Securities Act of 1933 to the offer and sale of securities by United States branches and agencies of foreign banks.	2038	Sept. 23, 1986	51 FR 34462.

PART 269—FORMS PRESCRIBED UNDER THE TRUST INDENTURE ACT OF 1939

Sec.
269.0–1 Availability of forms.
269.1 Form T–1, for statement of eligibility and qualification for corporate trustees.
269.2 Form T–2, for statement of eligibility and qualification for individual trustees.
269.3 Form T–3, for application for qualification of trust indentures.
269.4 Form T–4, for application for exemption pursuant to section 304(c) of the Act.
269.5 Form F–X, for appointment of agent for service of process by issuers registering securities on Form F–8, F–9, F–10 or F–80 (§§ 239.38, 239.39, 239.40 or 239.41 of this chapter), or registering securities or filing periodic reports on Form 40–F (§ 249.240f of this chapter), or by any issuer or other non-U.S. person filing tender offer documents on Schedule 13E–4F, 14D–1F or 14D–9F (§§ 240.13e–102, 240.14d–102 or 240.14d–103 of this chapter), or by any non-U.S. person acting as trustee with respect to securities registered on Form F–7 (§ 239.37 of this chapter), F–8, F–9, F–10 or F–80.
269.6 [Reserved]
269.7 Form ID, uniform application for access codes to file on EDGAR.
269.8 Form SE, form for submission of paper format exhibits by electronic filers.
269.9 Form T–6 for application under section 310(a)(1) of the Trust Indenture Act for determination of the eligibility of a foreign person to act as institutional trustee.
269.10 Form TH—Notification of reliance on temporary hardship exemption.

AUTHORITY: 15 U.S.C. 77ddd(c), 77eee, 77ggg, 77hhh, 77iii, 77jjj, 77sss, and 78␢l(d), unless otherwise noted.

SOURCE: 33 FR 19002, Dec. 20, 1968, unless otherwise noted.

§ 269.0–1 Availability of forms.

(a) This part identifies and describes the forms prescribed for use under the Trust Indenture Act of 1939.

(b) Any person may obtain a copy of any form prescribed for use in this part by written request to the Securities and Exchange Commission, 100 F Street, NE., Washington, DC 20549. Any person may inspect the forms at this address and at the Commission's regional offices. (See § 200.11 of this chapter for the addresses of SEC regional offices.)

[46 FR 17757, Mar. 20, 1981, as amended at 47 FR 26820, June 22, 1982; 59 FR 5946, Feb. 9, 1994; 73 FR 983, Jan. 4, 2008]

§ 269.1 Form T–1, for statement of eligibility and qualification for corporate trustees.

This form shall be filed pursuant to Rule 5a–1(a) (§ 260.5a–1(a) of this chapter) for statements of eligibility and qualification of corporations designated to act as trustees under thrust indentures to be qualified pursuant to section 305 or 307 of the Trust Indenture Act of 1939.

EDITORIAL NOTE: For FEDERAL REGISTER citations affecting Form T–1, see the List of CFR Sections Affected, which appears in the Finding Aids section of the printed volume and at *www.govinfo.gov*.

§ 269.2 Form T-2, for statement of eligibility and qualification for individual trustees.

This form shall be filed pursuant to Rule 5a–1(b) (§ 260.5a–1(b) of this chapter) for statements of eligibility and qualification of individuals designated to act as trustees under trust indentures to be qualified pursuant to section 305 or 307 of the Trust Indenture Act of 1939. Under sections 307, 308, 309, 310 and 319 of the Trust Indenture Act of 1939 (17 CFR part 260), the Commission is authorized to solicit the information required to be supplied by this form for statements of eligibility and qualification of individuals designated to act as trustees. Disclosure of the information specified in this form is mandatory before processing statements of eligibility and qualification. The information will be used for the primary purpose of determining relationships of trustees and whether there are any conflicting interests. This statement will be made a matter of public record. Therefore, any information given will be available for inspection by any member of the public. Because of the public nature of the information, the Commission can utilize it for a variety of purposes, including referral to other governmental authorities or securities self-regulatory organizations for investigatory purposes or in connection with litigation involving the Federal securities laws or other civil, criminal or regulatory statutes or provisions. Failure to disclose the information requested by this form may result in enforcement action by the Commission to compel compliance with the Federal securities laws.

[40 FR 55320, Nov. 28, 1975, as amended at 62 FR 35342, July 1, 1997]

EDITORIAL NOTE: For FEDERAL REGISTER citations affecting Form T-2, see the List of CFR Sections Affected, which appears in the Finding Aids section of the printed volume and at *www.govinfo.gov.*

§ 269.3 Form T-3, for application for qualification of trust indentures.

This form shall be filed pursuant to Rule 7a–1 (§ 260.7a–1 of this chapter) for applications for qualification of indentures pursuant to section 307(a) of the Trust Indenture Act of 1939, but only when securities to be issued thereunder are not required to be registered under the Securities Act of 1933 (15 U.S.C. 77a et seq.).

EDITORIAL NOTE: For FEDERAL REGISTER citations affecting Form T-3, see the List of CFR Sections Affected, which appears in the Finding Aids section of the printed volume and at *www.govinfo.gov.*

§ 269.4 Form T-4, for application for exemption pursuant to section 304(c) of the Act.

This form shall be filed pursuant to Rule 4c–1 (§ 260.4c–1 of this chapter) for applications for exemption filed pursuant to section 304(c) of the Trust Indenture Act of 1939.

EDITORIAL NOTE: For FEDERAL REGISTER citations affecting Form T-4, see the List of CFR Sections Affected, which appears in the Finding Aids section of the printed volume and at *www.govinfo.gov.*

§ 269.5 Form F-X, for appointment of agent for service of process by issuers registering securities on Form F-8, F-9, F-10 or F-80 (§§ 239.38, 239.39, 239.40 or 239.41 of this chapter), or registering securities or filing periodic reports on Form 40-F (§ 249.240f of this chapter), or by any issuer or other non-U.S. person filing tender offer documents on Schedule 13E-4F, 14D-1F or 14D-9F (§§ 240.13e-102, 240.14d-102 or 240.14d-103 of this chapter), or by any non-U.S. person acting as trustee with respect to securities registered on Form F-7 (§ 239.37 of this chapter), F-8, F-9, F-10 or F-80.

Form F-X shall be filed with the Commission:

(a) By any issuer registering securities on Form F-8, F-9, F-10 or F-80 under the Securities Act of 1933;

(b) By any issuer registering securities on Form 40-F under the Securities Exchange Act of 1934;

(c) By any issuer filing a periodic report on Form 40-F, if it has not previously filed a Form F-X in connection with the class of securities in relation to which the obligation to file a report on Form 40-F arises;

(d) By any issuer or other non-U.S. person filing tender offer documents on Schedule 13E-4F, 14D-1F or 14D-9F; and

Securities and Exchange Commission

Pt. 270

(e) By non-U.S. person acting as trustee with respect to securities registered on Form F-7, F-8, F-9, F-10 or F-80.

[56 FR 30078, July 1, 1991]

EDITORIAL NOTE: For FEDERAL REGISTER citations affecting Form F-X, see the List of CFR Sections Affected, which appears in the Finding Aids section of the printed volume and at *www.govinfo.gov*.

§ 269.6 [Reserved]

§ 269.7 Form ID, uniform application for access codes to file on EDGAR.

Form ID must be filed by registrants, third party filers, or their agents, to request the following access codes to permit filing on EDGAR:

(a) Central Index Key (CIK)—uniquely identifies each filer, filing agent, and training agent.

(b) CIK Confirmation Code (CCC)—used in the header of a filing in conjunction with the CIK of the filer to ensure that the filing has been authorized by the filer.

(c) Password (PW)—allows a filer, filing agent or training agent to log on to the EDGAR system, submit filings, and change its CCC.

(d) Password Modification Authorization Code (PMAC)—allows a filer, filing agent or training agent to change its Password.

[69 FR 22710, Apr. 26, 2004, as amended at 86 FR 25805, May 11, 2021]

EDITORIAL NOTE: For FEDERAL REGISTER citations affecting Form ID, see the List of CFR Sections Affected, which appears in the Finding Aids section of the printed volume and at *www.govinfo.gov*.

§ 269.8 Form SE, form for submission of paper format exhibits by electronic filers.

This form shall be used by an electronic filer for the submission of any paper format document relating to an otherwise electronic filing, as provided in Rule 311 of Regulation S-T (§ 232.311 of this chapter).

[58 FR 14687, Mar. 18, 1993]

EDITORIAL NOTE: For FEDERAL REGISTER citations affecting Form SE, see the List of CFR Sections Affected, which appears in the Finding Aids section of the printed volume and at *www.govinfo.gov*.

§ 269.9 Form T-6 for application under section 310(a)(1) of the Trust Indenture Act for determination of the eligibility of a foreign person to act as institutional trustee.

This form shall be used for the filing of an application pursuant to rule 10a-1 [§ 260.10a-1 of this chapter] to obtain authorization for a corporation or other person organized and doing business under the laws of a foreign government to act as sole trustee under an indenture qualified or to be qualified under the Act.

[56 FR 22321, May 15, 1991]

EDITORIAL NOTE: For FEDERAL REGISTER citations affecting Form T-6, see the List of CFR Sections Affected, which appears in the Finding Aids section of the printed volume and at *www.govinfo.gov*.

§ 269.10 Form TH—Notification of reliance on temporary hardship exemption.

Form TH shall be filed by any electronic filer who submits to the Commission, pursuant to a temporary hardship exemption, a document in paper format that otherwise would be required to be submitted electronically, as prescribed by Rule 201(a) of Regulation S-T (§ 232.201(a) of this chapter).

[58 FR 14687, Mar. 18, 1993]

EDITORIAL NOTE: For FEDERAL REGISTER citations affecting Form TH, see the List of CFR Sections Affected, which appears in the Finding Aids section of the printed volume and at *www.govinfo.gov*.

PART 270—RULES AND REGULATIONS, INVESTMENT COMPANY ACT OF 1940

Sec.
270.0-1 Definition of terms used in this part.
270.0-2 General requirements of papers and applications.
270.0-3 Amendments to registration statements and reports.
270.0-4 Incorporation by reference.
270.0-5 Procedure with respect to applications and other matters.
270.0-8 Payment of filing fees.
270.0-9 [Reserved]
270.0-10 Small entities under the Investment Company Act for purposes of the Regulatory Flexibility Act.
270.0-11 Customer identification programs.
270.2a-1 Valuation of portfolio securities in special cases.

270.2a-2 Effect of eliminations upon valuation of portfolio securities.
270.2a3-1 Investment company limited partners not deemed affiliated persons.
270.2a-4 Definition of "current net asset value" for use in computing periodically the current price of redeemable security.
270.2a-5 Fair value determination and readily available market quotations.
270.2a-6 Certain transactions not deemed assignments.
270.2a-7 Money market funds.
270.2a19-2 Investment company general partners not deemed interested persons.
270.2a19-3 Certain investment company directors not considered interested persons because of ownership of index fund securities.
270.2a41-1 Valuation of standby commitments by registered investment companies.
270.2a-46 Certain issuers as eligible portfolio companies.
270.2a51-1 Definition of investments for purposes of section 2(a)(51) (definition of "qualified purchaser"); certain calculations.
270.2a51-2 Definitions of beneficial owner for certain purposes under sections 2(a)(51) and 3(c)(7) and determining indirect ownership interests.
270.2a51-3 Certain companies as qualified purchasers.
270.3a-1 Certain prima facie investment companies.
270.3a-2 Transient investment companies.
270.3a-3 Certain investment companies owned by companies which are not investment companies.
270.3a-4 Status of investment advisory programs.
270.3a-5 Exemption for subsidiaries organized to finance the operations of domestic or foreign companies.
270.3a-6 Foreign banks and foreign insurance companies.
270.3a-7 Issuers of asset-backed securities.
270.3a-8 Certain research and development companies.
270.3a-9 Crowdfunding vehicle.
270.3c-1 Definition of beneficial ownership for certain section 3(c)(1) funds.
270.3c-2 Definition of beneficial ownership in small business investment companies.
270.3c-3 Definition of certain terms used in section 3(c)(1) of the Act with respect to certain debt securities offered by small business investment companies.
270.3c-4 Definition of "common trust fund" as used in section 3(c)(3) of the Act.
270.3c-5 Beneficial ownership by knowledgeable employees and certain other persons.
270.3c-6 Certain transfers of interests in section 3(c)(1) and section 3(c)(7) funds.
270.5b-1 Definition of "total assets."
270.5b-2 Exclusion of certain guarantees as securities of the guarantor.
270.5b-3 Acquisition of repurchase agreement or refunded security treated as acquisition of underlying securities.
270.6a-5 Purchase of certain debt securities by companies relying on section 6(a)(5) of the Act.
270.6b-1 Exemption of employees' securities company pending determination of application.
270.6c-3 Exemptions for certain registered variable life insurance separate accounts.
270.6c-6 Exemption for certain registered separate accounts and other persons.
270.6c-7 Exemptions from certain provisions of sections 22(e) and 27 for registered separate accounts offering variable annuity contracts to participants in the Texas Optional Retirement Program.
270.6c-8 Exemptions for registered separate accounts to impose a deferred sales load and to deduct certain administrative charges.
270.6c-10 Exemption for certain open-end management investment companies to impose deferred sales loads.
270.6c-11 Exchange-traded funds.
270.6d-1 Exemption for certain closed-end investment companies.
270.6e-2 Exemptions for certain variable life insurance separate accounts.
270.6e-3 Exemptions for flexible premium variable life insurance separate accounts.
270.7d-1 Specification of conditions and arrangements for Canadian management investment companies requesting order permitting registration.
270.7d-2 Definition of "public offering" as used in section 7(d) of the Act with respect to certain Canadian tax-deferred retirement savings accounts.
270.8b-1 Scope of §§ 270.8b-1 to 270.8b-31.
270.8b-2 Definitions.
270.8b-3 Title of securities.
270.8b-4 Interpretation of requirements.
270.8b-5 Time of filing original registration statement.
270.8b-6 [Reserved]
270.8b-10 Requirements as to proper form.
270.8b-11 Number of copies; signatures; binding.
270.8b-12 Requirements as to paper, printing and language.
270.8b-13 Preparation of registration statement or report.
270.8b-14 Riders; inserts.
270.8b-15 Amendments.
270.8b-16 Amendments to registration statement.
270.8b-20 Additional information.
270.8b-21 Information unknown or not available.
270.8b-22 Disclaimer of control.
270.8b-23—270.8b-24 [Reserved]

Securities and Exchange Commission

270.8b-25 Extension of time for furnishing information.
270.8b-30 Additional exhibits.
270.8b-31 Omission of substantially identical documents.
270.8b-32 [Reserved]
270.8f-1 Deregistration of certain registered investment companies.
270.10b-1 Definition of regular broker or dealer.
270.10e-1 Death, disqualification, or bona fide resignation of directors.
270.10f-1 Conditional exemption of certain underwriting transactions.
270.10f-2 Exercise of warrants or rights received on portfolio securities.
270.10f-3 Exemption for the acquisition of securities during the existence of an underwriting or selling syndicate.
270.11a-1 Definition of "exchange" for purposes of section 11 of the Act.
270.11a-2 Offers of exchange by certain registered separate accounts or others the terms of which do not require prior Commission approval.
270.11a-3 Offers of exchange by open-end investment companies other than separate accounts.
270.12b-1 Distribution of shares by registered open-end management investment company.
270.12d1-1 Exemptions for investments in money market funds.
270.12d1-2 [Reserved]
270.12d1-3 Exemptions for investment companies relying on section 12(d)(1)(F) of the Act.
270.12d1-4 Exemptions for investments in certain investment companies.
270.12d2-1 Definition of insurance company for purposes of sections 12(d)(2) and 12(g) of the Act.
270.12d3-1 Exemption of acquisitions of securities issued by persons engaged in securities related businesses.
270.13a-1 Exemption for change of status by temporarily diversified company.
270.14a-1 Use of notification pursuant to regulation E under the Securities Act of 1933.
270.14a-2 Exemption from section 14(a) of the Act for certain registered separate accounts and their principal underwriters.
270.14a-3 Exemption from section 14(a) of the Act for certain registered unit investment trusts and their principal underwriters.
270.15a-1 Exemption from stockholders' approval of certain small investment advisory contracts.
270.15a-2 Annual continuance of contracts.
270.15a-3 Exemption for initial period of investment adviser of certain registered separate accounts from requirement of security holder approval of investment advisory contract.
270.15a-4 Temporary exemption for certain investment advisers.
270.16a-1 Exemption for initial period of directors of certain registered accounts from requirements of election by security holders.
270.17a-1 Exemption of certain underwriting transactions exempted by § 270.10f-1.
270.17a-2 Exemption of certain purchase, sale, or borrowing transactions.
270.17a-3 Exemption of transactions with fully owned subsidiaries.
270.17a-4 Exemption of transactions pursuant to certain contracts.
270.17a-5 Pro rata distribution neither "sale" nor "purchase."
270.17a-6 Exemption for transactions with portfolio affiliates.
270.17a-7 Exemption of certain purchase or sale transactions between an investment company and certain affiliated persons thereof.
270.17a-8 Mergers of affiliated companies.
270.17a-9 Purchase of certain securities from a money market fund by an affiliate, or an affiliate of an affiliate.
270.17a-10 Exemption for transactions with certain subadvisory affiliates.
270.17d-1 Applications regarding joint enterprises or arrangements and certain profit-sharing plans.
270.17d-2 Form for report by small business investment company and affiliated bank.
270.17d-3 Exemption relating to certain joint enterprises or arrangements concerning payment for distribution of shares of a registered open-end management investment company.
270.17e-1 Brokerage transactions on a securities exchange.
270.17f-1 Custody of securities with members of national securities exchanges.
270.17f-2 Custody of investments by registered management investment company.
270.17f-3 Free cash accounts for investment companies with bank custodians.
270.17f-4 Custody of investment company assets with a securities depository.
270.17f-5 Custody of investment company assets outside the United States.
270.17f-6 Custody of investment company assets with Futures Commission Merchants and Commodity Clearing Organizations.
270.17f-7 Custody of investment company assets with a foreign securities depository.
270.17g-1 Bonding of officers and employees of registered management investment companies.
270.17j-1 Personal investment activities of investment company personnel.
270.18c-1 Exemption of privately held indebtedness.

270.18c-2 Exemptions of certain debentures issued by small business investment companies.
270.18f-1 Exemption from certain requirements of section 18(f)(1) (of the Act) for registered open-end investment companies which have the right to redeem in kind.
270.18f-2 Fair and equitable treatment for holders of each class or series of stock of series investment companies.
270.18f-3 Multiple class companies.
270.18f-4 Exemption from the requirements of section 18 and section 61 for certain senior securities transactions.
270.19a-1 Written statement to accompany dividend payments by management companies.
270.19b-1 Frequency of distribution of capital gains.
270.20a-1 Solicitation of proxies, consents and authorizations.
270.20a-2—270.20a-4 [Reserved]
270.22c-1 Pricing of redeemable securities for distribution, redemption and repurchase.
270.22c-2 Redemption fees for redeemable securities.
270.22d-1 Exemption from section 22(d) to permit sales of redeemable securities at prices which reflect sales loads set pursuant to a schedule.
270.22d-2 Exemption from section 22(d) for certain registered separate accounts.
270.22e-1 Exemption from section 22(e) of the Act during annuity payment period of variable annuity contracts participating in certain registered separate accounts.
270.22e-2 Pricing of redemption requests in accordance with Rule 22c-1.
270.22e-3 Exemption for liquidation of money market funds.
270.22e-4 Liquidity risk management programs.
270.23c-1 Repurchase of securities by closed-end companies.
270.23c-2 Call and redemption of securities issued by registered closed-end companies.
270.23c-3 Repurchase offers by closed-end companies.
270.24b-1 Definitions.
270.24b-2 Filing copies of sales literature.
270.24b-3 Sales literature deemed filed.
270.24b-4 Filing copies of covered investment fund research reports.
270.24e-1 Filing of certain prospectuses as post-effective amendments to registration statements under the Securities Act of 1933.
270.24f-2 Registration under the Securities Act of 1933 of certain investment company securities.
270.26a-1 Payment of administrative fees to the depositor or principal underwriter of a unit investment trust; exemptive relief for separate accounts.
270.26a-2 Exemptions from certain provisions of sections 26 and 27 for registered separate accounts and others regarding custodianship of and deduction of certain fees and charges from the assets of such accounts.
270.27c-1 [Reserved]
270.27d-1 Reserve requirements for principal underwriters and depositors to carry out the obligations to refund charges required by section 27(d) and section 27(f) of the Act.
270.27d-2 [Reserved]
270.27e-1 [Reserved]
270.27f-1 [Reserved]
270.27g-1 [Reserved]
270.27h-1 [Reserved]
270.27i-1 Exemption from Section 27(i)(2)(A) of the Act during annuity payment period of variable annuity contracts participating in certain registered separate accounts.
270.28b-1 Investment in loans partially or wholly guaranteed under the Servicemen's Readjustment Act of 1944, as amended.
270.30a-1 Annual report for registered investment companies.
270.30a-2 Certification of Form N-CSR.
270.30a-3 Controls and procedures.
270.30a-4 Annual report for wholly-owned registered management investment company subsidiary of registered management investment company.
270.30b1-1—270.30b1-3 [Reserved]
270.30b1-4 Report of proxy voting record.
270.30b1-5 [Reserved]
270.30b1-7 Monthly report for money market funds.
270.30b1-8 Current report for money market funds.
270.30b1-9 Monthly report.
270.30b1-9(T) Temporary rule regarding monthly report.
270.30b1-10 Current report for open-end and closed-end management investment companies.
270.30b2-1 Filing of reports to stockholders.
270.30d-1 Filing of copies of reports to shareholders.
270.30e-1 Reports to stockholders of management companies.
270.30e-2 Reports to shareholders of unit investment trusts.
270.30e-3 Internet availability of reports to shareholders.
270.30h-1 Applicability of section 16 of the Exchange Act to section 30(h).
270.31a-1 Records to be maintained by registered investment companies, certain majority-owned subsidiaries thereof, and other persons having transactions with registered investment companies.
270.31a-2 Records to be preserved by registered investment companies, certain

Securities and Exchange Commission Pt. 270

majority-owned subsidiaries thereof, and other persons having transactions with registered investment companies.

270.31a–3 Records prepared or maintained by other than person required to maintain and preserve them.

270.31a–4 Records to be maintained and preserved by registered investment companies relating to fair value determinations.

270.32a–1 Exemption of certain companies from affiliation provisions of section 32(a).

270.32a–2 Exemption for initial period from vote of security holders on independent public accountant for certain registered separate accounts.

270.32a–3 Exemption from provision of section 32(a)(1) regarding the time period during which a registered management investment company must select an independent public accountant.

270.32a–4 Independent audit committees.

270.34b–1 Sales literature deemed to be misleading.

270.35d–1 Investment company names.

270.38a–1 Compliance procedures and practices of certain investment companies.

270.45a–1 Confidential treatment of names and addresses of dealers of registered investment company securities.

270.55a–1 Investment activities of business development companies.

270.57b–1 Exemption for downstream affiliates of business development companies.

270.60a–1 Exemption for certain business development companies.

AUTHORITY: 15 U.S.C. 80a–1 *et seq.*, 80a–34(d), 80a–37, 80a–39, and Pub. L. 111–203, sec. 939A, 124 Stat. 1376 (2010), unless otherwise noted.

Section 270.0–1 also issued under sec. 38(a) (15 U.S.C. 80a–37(a));

Section 270.0–1(a)(7) is also issued under 15 U.S.C. 80a–10(e);

Section 270.0–11 also issued under secs. 8, 24, 30 and 38, Investment Company Act (15 U.S.C. 80a–8, 80a–24, 80a–29 and 80a–37), secs. 6, 7, 8, 10 and 19(a), Securities Act (15 U.S.C. 77f, 77g, 77h, 77j, 77s(a)) and secs. 3(b), 12, 13, 14, 15(d) and 23(a), Exchange Act (15 U.S.C. 78c(b), 78l, 78m, 78n, 78o(d) and 78w(a));

Section 270.6a–5 is also issued under 15 U.S.C. 80a–6(a)(5)(A)(iv)(I).

Section 270.6c–9 is also issued under secs. 6(c) (15 U.S.C. 80a–6(c)) and 38(a) (15 U.S.C. 80a–37(a));

Section 270.6c–10 is also issued under sec. 6(c) (15 U.S.C. 80a–6(c));

Section 270.6c–11 is also issued under 15 U.S.C. 80a–6(c) and 80a–37(a).

Section 270.6e–3 is also issued under 15 U.S.C. 80a–5(e);

Section 270.8b–11 is also issued under 15 U.S.C. 77s, 80a–8, and 80a–37;

Section 270.10e–1 is also issued under 15 U.S.C. 80a–10(e);

Sections 270.12d1–1, 270.12d1–2, and 270.12d1–3 are also issued under 15 U.S.C. 80a–6(c), 80a–12(d)(1)(J), and 80a–37(a).

Section 270.12d3–1 is also issued under 15 U.S.C. 80a–6(c);

Section 270.17a–8 is also issued under 15 U.S.C. 80a–6(c) and 80a–37(a);

Section 270.17d–1 is also issued under 15 U.S.C. 80a–6(c), 80a–17(d), and 80a–37(a);

Section 270.17e–1 is also issued under 15 U.S.C. 80a–6(c), 80a–30(a), and 80a–37(a);

Section 270.17f–5 also issued under sec. 6(c) (15 U.S.C. 80a–6(c);

Section 270.17g–1 is also issued under 15 U.S.C. 80a–6(c), 80a–17(d), 80a–17(g), and 80a–37(a);

Section 270.17j–1 is also issued under secs. 206(4) and 211(a), Investment Advisers Act (15 U.S.C. 80b–6(4) and 80b–11(a));

Section 270.19b–1 is also issued under secs. 6(c) (15 U.S.C. 80a–6(c)), 19 (a) and (b) (15 U.S.C 80a–19 (a) and (b)), and 38(a) (15 U.S.C. 80a–37(a));

Section 270.22c–1 also issued under secs. 6(c), 22(c), and 38(a) (15 U.S.C. 80a–6(c), 80a–22(c), and 80a–37(a));

Section 270.23c–3 also issued under 15 U.S.C. 80a–23(c).

Section 270.24f–2 also issued under 15 U.S.C. 80a–24(f)(4).

Section 270.30a–1 is also issued under 15 U.S.C. 78m, 78o(d), 80a–8, and 80a–29.

Section 270.30a–2 is also issued under 15 U.S.C. 78m, 78o(d), 80a–8, 80a–29, 7202, and 7241; and 18 U.S.C. 1350, unless otherwise noted.

Section 270.30a–3 is also issued under 15 U.S.C. 78m, 78o(d), 80a–8, and 80a–29, and secs. 3(a) and 302, Pub. L. 107–204, 116 Stat. 745.

Section 270.30b1–1 is also issued under 15 U.S.C. 78m, 78o(d), 80a–8, and 80a–29.

Section 270.30b2–1 is also issued under 15 U.S.C. 78m, 78o(d), 80a–8, 80a–29, and secs. 3(a) and 302, Pub. L. 107–204, 116 Stat. 745.

Section 270.30d–1 is also issued under 15 U.S.C. 78m, 78o(d), 80a–8, and 80a–29, and secs. 3(a) and 302, Pub. L. 107–204, 116 Stat. 745.

Section 270.30e–1 is also issued under 15 U.S.C. 77f, 77g, 77h, 77j, 77s, 78l, 78m, 78n, 78o(d), 78w(a), 80a–8, 80a–29, and 80a–37;

Section 270.31a–2 is also issued under 15 U.S.C. 80a–30.

ATTENTION ELECTRONIC FILERS

THIS REGULATION SHOULD BE READ IN CONJUNCTION WITH REGULATION S-T (PART 232 OF THIS CHAPTER), WHICH GOVERNS THE PREPARATION AND SUBMISSION OF DOCUMENTS IN ELECTRONIC FORMAT. MANY PROVISIONS RELATING TO THE PREPARATION AND SUBMISSION OF DOCUMENTS IN PAPER FORMAT CONTAINED IN THIS REGULATION ARE SUPERSEDED BY THE PROVISIONS OF REGULATION S-T FOR DOCUMENTS REQUIRED TO BE FILED IN ELECTRONIC FORMAT.

§ 270.0–1 Definition of terms used in this part.

(a) As used in the rules and regulations prescribed by the Commission pursuant to the Investment Company Act of 1940, unless the context otherwise requires:

(1) The term *Commission* means the Securities and Exchange Commission.

(2) The term *act* means the Investment Company Act of 1940.

(3) The term *section* refers to a section of the act.

(4) The terms *rule* and *regulations* refer to the rules and regulations adopted by the Commission pursuant to the Act, including the forms for registration and reports and the accompanying instructions thereto.

(5) The term *administrator* means any person who provides significant administrative or business affairs management services to an investment company.

(6)(i) A person is an *independent legal counsel* with respect to the directors who are not interested persons of an investment company ("disinterested directors") if:

(A) A majority of the disinterested directors reasonably determine in the exercise of their judgment (and record the basis for that determination in the minutes of their meeting) that any representation by the person of the company's investment adviser, principal underwriter, administrator ("management organizations"), or any of their control persons, since the beginning of the fund's last two completed fiscal years, is or was sufficiently limited that it is unlikely to adversely affect the professional judgment of the person in providing legal representation to the disinterested directors; and

(B) The disinterested directors have obtained an undertaking from such person to provide them with information necessary to make their determination and to update promptly that information when the person begins to represent, or materially increases his representation of, a management organization or control person.

(ii) The disinterested directors are entitled to rely on the information obtained from the person, unless they know or have reason to believe that the information is materially false or incomplete. The disinterested directors must re-evaluate their determination no less frequently than annually (and record the basis accordingly), except as provided in paragraph (iii) of this section.

(iii) After the disinterested directors obtain information that the person has begun to represent, or has materially increased his representation of, a management organization (or any of its control persons), the person may continue to be an independent legal counsel, for purposes of paragraph (a)(6)(i) of this section, for no longer than three months unless during that period the disinterested directors make a new determination under that paragraph.

(iv) For purposes of paragraphs (a)(6)(i)–(iii) of this section:

(A) The term *person* has the same meaning as in section 2(a)(28) of the Act (15 U.S.C. 80a–2(a)(28)) and, in addition, includes a partner, co-member, or employee of any person; and

(B) The term *control person* means any person (other than an investment company) directly or indirectly controlling, controlled by, or under common control with any of the investment company's management organizations.

(7) *Fund governance standards.* The board of directors of an investment company ("fund") satisfies the *fund governance standards* if:

(i) At least seventy-five percent of the directors of the fund are not interested persons of the fund ("disinterested directors") or, if the fund has three directors, all but one are disinterested directors;

(ii) The disinterested directors of the fund select and nominate any other disinterested director of the fund;

(iii) Any person who acts as legal counsel for the disinterested directors of the fund is an independent legal counsel as defined in paragraph (a)(6) of this section;

(iv) A disinterested director serves as chairman of the board of directors of the fund, presides over meetings of the board of directors and has substantially the same responsibilities as would a chairman of a board of directors;

(v) The board of directors evaluates at least once annually the performance

Securities and Exchange Commission § 270.0-2

of the board of directors and the committees of the board of directors, which evaluation must include a consideration of the effectiveness of the committee structure of the fund board and the number of funds on whose boards each director serves;

(vi) The disinterested directors meet at least once quarterly in a session at which no directors who are interested persons of the fund are present; and

(vii) The disinterested directors have been authorized to hire employees and to retain advisers and experts necessary to carry out their duties.

(b) Unless otherwise specifically provided, the terms used in the rules and regulations in this part shall have the meaning defined in the Act. The terms "EDGAR," "EDGAR Filer Manual," "electronic filer," "electronic filing," "electronic format," "electronic submission," "paper format," and "signature" shall have the meanings assigned to such terms in Regulation S-T—General Rules for Electronic Filings (Part 232 of this chapter).

(c) A rule or regulation which defines a term without express reference to the act or to the rules and regulations, or to a portion thereof, defines such terms for all purposes as used both in the act and in the rules and regulations in this part, unless the context otherwise requires.

(d) Unless otherwise specified or the context otherwise requires, the term "prospectus" means a prospectus meeting the requirements of section 10(a) of the Securities Act of 1933 as amended.

(e) Definition of separate account and conditions for availability of exemption under §§ 270.6c-6, 270.6c-7, 270.6c-8, 270.11a-2, 270.14a-2, 270.15a-3, 270.16a-1, 270.22c-1, 270.22d-2, 270.22e-1, 270.26a-1, 270.27i-1, and 270.32a-2 (Rules 6c-6, 6c-7, 6c-8, 11a-2, 14a-2, 15a-3, 16a-1, 22c-1, 22d-2, 22e-1, 26a-1, 27i-1, and 32a-2).

(1) As used in the rules and regulations prescribed by the Commission pursuant to the Investment Company Act of 1940, unless otherwise specified or the context otherwise requires, the term "separate account" shall mean an account established and maintained by an insurance company pursuant to the laws of any state or territory of the United States, or of Canada or any province thereof, under which income, gains and losses, whether or not realized, from assets allocated to such account, are, in accordance with the applicable contract, credited to or charged against such account without regard to other income, gains or losses of the insurance company and the term "variable annuity contract" shall mean any accumulation or annuity contract, any portion thereof, or any unit of interest or participation therein pursuant to which the value of the contract, either prior or subsequent to annuitization, or both, varies according to the investment experience of the separate account in which the contract participates.

(2) As conditions to the availability of exemptive Rules 6c-6, 6c-7, 6c-8, 11a-2, 14a-2, 15a-2, 16a-1, 22c-1, 22d-2, 22e-1, 26a-1, 27i-1, and 32a-2, the separate account shall be legally segregated, the assets of the separate account shall, at the time during the year that adjustments in the reserves are made, have a value at least equal to the reserves and other contract liabilities with respect to such account, and at all other times, shall have a value approximately equal to or in excess of such reserves and liabilities; and that portion of such assets having a value equal to, or approximately equal to, such reserves and contract liabilities shall not be chargeable with liabilities arising out of any other business which the insurance company may conduct.

[Rule N-1, 5 FR 4316, Oct. 31, 1940, as amended at 19 FR 6730, Oct. 20, 1954; 30 FR 829, Jan. 27, 1965; 48 FR 36098, Aug. 9, 1983; 50 FR 42682, Oct. 22, 1985; 58 FR 14859, Mar. 18, 1993; 66 FR 3757, Jan. 16, 2001; 69 FR 46389, Aug. 2, 2004; 85 FR 26101, May 1, 2020]

§ 270.0-2 General requirements of papers and applications.

(a) *Filing of papers.* All papers required to be filed with the Commission pursuant to the Act or the rules and regulations thereunder shall, unless otherwise provided by the rules and regulations in this part, be delivered through the mails or otherwise to the Secretary of the Securities and Exchange Commission, Washington, DC 20549. Except as otherwise provided by the rules and regulations, the date on which papers are actually received by

§ 270.0-2

the Commission shall be the date of filing thereof. If the last day for the timely filing of such papers falls on a Saturday, Sunday, or holiday, such papers may be filed on the first business day following.

(b) *Formal specifications respecting applications.* Every application for an order under any provision of the Act, for which a form with instructions is not specifically prescribed, and every amendment to such application shall be filed in quintuplicate. One copy shall be signed by the applicant but the other four copies may have facsimile or typed signatures. Such applications should be on paper no larger than 8½ × 11 inches in size. To the extent that the reduction of larger documents would render them illegible, such documents may be filed on paper larger than 8½ × 11 inches in size. The left margin should be at least 1½ inches wide and, if the application is bound, it should be bound on the left side. All typewritten or printed matter (including deficits in financial statements) should be set forth in black so as to permit photocopying.

(c) *Authorizations respecting applications.* (1) Every application for an order under any provision of the act, for which a form with instructions is not specifically prescribed and which is executed by a corporation, partnership, or other company and filed with the Commission, shall contain a concise statement of the applicable provisions of the articles of incorporation, bylaws, or similar documents, relating to the right of the person signing and filing such application to take such action on behalf of the applicant, and a statement that all such requirements have been complied with and that the person signing and filing the same is fully authorized to do so. If such authorization is dependent on resolutions of stockholders, directors, or other bodies, such resolutions shall be attached as an exhibit to, or the pertinent provisions thereof shall be quoted in, the application.

(2) If an amendment to any such application shall be filed, such amendment shall contain a similar statement or, in lieu thereof, shall state that the authorization described in the original application is applicable to the individual who signs such amendment and that such authorization still remains in effect.

(3) When any such application or amendment is signed by an agent or attorney, the power of attorney evidencing his authority to sign shall contain similar statements and shall be filed with the Commission.

(d) *Verification of applications and statements of fact.* Every application for an order under any provision of the Act, for which a form with instructions is not specifically prescribed and every amendment to such application, and every statement of fact formally filed in support of, or in opposition to, any application or declaration shall be verified by the person executing the same. An instrument executed on behalf of a corporation shall be verified in substantially the following form, but suitable changes may be made in such form for other kinds of companies and for individuals:

The undersigned states that he or she has duly executed the attached _____ dated _____, 20 ____ for and on behalf of (*name of company*); that he or she is (*title of officer*) of such company; and that all action by stockholders, directors, and other bodies necessary to authorize the undersigned to execute and file such instrument has been taken. The undersigned further states that he or she is familiar with such instrument, and the contents thereof, and that the facts therein set forth are true to the best of his or her knowledge, information and belief.

(Signature)

(e) *Statement of grounds for application.* Each application should contain a brief statement of the reasons why the applicant is deemed to be entitled to the action requested with a reference to the provisions of the act and of the rules and regulations under which application is made.

(f) *Name and address.* Every application shall contain the name and address of each applicant and the name and address of any person to whom any applicant wishes any question regarding the application to be directed.

(g) The manually signed original (or in the case of duplicate originals, one duplicate original) of all registrations, applications, statements, reports, or other documents filed under the Investment Company Act of 1940, as amended,

Securities and Exchange Commission § 270.0–4

shall be numbered sequentially (in addition to any internal numbering which otherwise may be present) by handwritten, typed, printed, or other legible form of notation from the facing page of the document through the last page of that document and any exhibits or attachments thereto. Further, the total number of pages contained in a numbered original shall be set forth on the first page of the document.

[Rule N–2, 5 FR 4316, Oct. 31, 1940, as amended at 33 FR 9391, June 27, 1968; 33 FR 23325, Aug. 29, 1973; 44 FR 4666, Jan. 23, 1979; 47 FR 58239, Dec. 30, 1982; 48 FR 17065, Apr. 21, 1983; 58 FR 14859, Mar. 18, 1993; 73 FR 65525, Nov. 4, 2008; 87 FR 38976, June 30, 2022; 87 FR 41060, July 11, 2022]

§ 270.0–3 Amendments to registration statements and reports.

Registration statements filed with the Commission pursuant to section 8 (54 Stat. 803; 15 U.S.C. 80a–8) and reports filed with the Commission pursuant to section 30 (54 Stat. 836; 15 U.S.C. 80a–35) may be amended in the following manner:

(a) Each amendment shall conform to the requirements for the registration statement or report it amends with regard to filing, number of copies filed, size, paper, ink, margins, binding, and similar formal matters.

(b) Each amendment to a particular statement or report shall have a facing sheet as follows:

SECURITIES AND EXCHANGE COMMISSION

Washington, DC 20549

Amendment No._____

to

Form_____
File No._____
(Describe the nature of the statement or report)
Dated_____, 19___,
Pursuant to Section _____ of the Investment Company Act of 1940

Name of Registrant

Address of Principal Office of Registrant

The facing sheet shall contain in addition any other information required on the facing sheet of the form for the statement or report which is being amended. Amendments to a particular statement or report which is being consecutively in the order in which filed with the Commission.

(c) Each amendment shall contain in the manner required in the original statement or report the text of every item to which it relates and shall set out a complete amended answer to each such item. However, amendments to financial statements may contain only the particular statements or schedules in fact amended.

(d) Each amendment shall have a signature sheet containing the form of signature required in the statement or report it amends.

(Secs. 8, 30, 54 Stat. 803, 74 Stat. 201; 15 U.S.C. 80a–8, 80a–29)

[Rule N–3, 6 FR 3966, Aug. 8, 1941, as amended at 33 FR 3217, Feb. 21, 1968]

§ 270.0–4 Incorporation by reference.

(a) *Registration statements and reports.* Except as provided by this section or in the appropriate form, information may be incorporated by reference in answer, or partial answer, to any item of a registration statement or report. Where an item requires a summary or outline of the provisions of any document, the summary or outline may incorporate by reference particular items, sections, or paragraphs of any exhibit and may be qualified in its entirety by such reference.

(b) *Financial information.* Except as provided in the Commission's rules, financial information required to be given in comparative form for two or more fiscal years or periods must not be incorporated by reference unless the information incorporated by reference includes the entire period for which the comparative data is given. In the financial statements, incorporating by reference, or cross-referencing to, information outside of the financial statements is not permitted unless otherwise specifically permitted or required by the Commission's rules or by U.S. Generally Accepted Accounting Principles or International Financial Reporting Standards as issued by the International Accounting Standards Board, whichever is applicable.

(c) *Exhibits.* Any document or part thereof, including any financial statement or part thereof, filed with the Commission pursuant to any Act administered by the Commission may be incorporated by reference as an exhibit to any registration statement, application, or report filed with the Commission by the same or any other person. If any modification has occurred in the text of any document incorporated by reference since the filing thereof, the registrant must file with the reference a statement containing the text of any such modification and the date thereof.

(d) *Hyperlinks.* Include an active hyperlink to information incorporated into a registration statement, application, or report by reference if such information is publicly available on the Commission's Electronic Data Gathering, Analysis and Retrieval System ("EDGAR") at the time the registration statement, application, or report is filed. For hyperlinking to exhibits, please refer to the appropriate form.

(e) *General.* Include an express statement clearly describing the specific location of the information you are incorporating by reference. The statement must identify the document where the information was originally filed or submitted and the location of the information within that document. The statement must be made at the particular place where the information is required, if applicable. Information must not be incorporated by reference in any case where such incorporation would render the disclosure incomplete, unclear, or confusing. For example, unless expressly permitted or required, disclosure must not be incorporated by reference from a second document if that second document incorporates information pertinent to such disclosure by reference to a third document.

[84 FR 12732, Apr. 2, 2019]

§ 270.0-5 **Procedure with respect to applications and other matters.**

The procedure herein below set forth will be followed with respect to any proceeding initiated by the filing of an application, or upon the Commission's own motion, pursuant to any section of the Act or any rule or regulation thereunder, unless in the particular case a different procedure is provided:

(a) Notice of the initiation of the proceeding will be published in the FEDERAL REGISTER and will indicate the earliest date upon which an order disposing of the matter may be entered. The notice will also provide that any interested person may, within the period of time specified therein, submit to the Commission in writing any facts bearing upon the desirability of a hearing on the matter and may request that a hearing be held, stating his reasons therefor and the nature of his interest in the matter.

(b) An order disposing of the matter will be issued as of course, following the expiration of the period of time referred to in paragraph (a) of this section, unless the Commission thereafter orders a hearing on the matter.

(c) The Commission will order a hearing on the matter, if it appears that a hearing is necessary or appropriate in the public interest or for the protection of investors, (1) upon the request of an interested person or (2) upon its own motion.

(d)(1) An applicant may request expedited review of an application if such application is substantially identical to two other applications for which an order granting the requested relief has been issued within three years of the date of the application's initial filing.

(2) For purposes of this section, "substantially identical" applications are applications requesting relief from the same sections of the Act and this part, containing identical terms and conditions, and differing only with respect to factual differences that are not material to the relief requested.

(e) An application submitted for expedited review must include:

(1) A notation on the cover page of the application that states prominently, "EXPEDITED REVIEW REQUESTED UNDER 17 CFR 270.0-5(d)";

(2) Exhibits with marked copies of the application showing changes from the final versions of the two applications identified as substantially identical under paragraph (e)(3) of this section; and

(3) An accompanying cover letter, signed, on behalf of the applicant, by the person executing the application:

(i) Identifying two substantially identical applications and explaining why the applicant chose those particular applications, and if more recent applications of the same type have been approved, why the applications

Securities and Exchange Commission § 270.0–10

chosen, rather than the more recent applications, are appropriate; and

(ii) Certifying that the applicant believes the application meets the requirements of paragraph (d) of this section and that the marked copies required by paragraph (e)(2) of this section are complete and accurate.

(f)(1) No later than 45 days from the date of filing of an application for which expedited review is requested:

(i) Notice of an application will be issued in accordance with paragraph (a) of this section; or

(ii) The applicant will be notified that the application is not eligible for expedited review because it does not meet the criteria set forth in paragraph (d) or (e) of this section or because additional time is necessary for appropriate consideration of the application.

(2) For purposes of paragraph (f)(1) of this section:

(i) The 45-day period will stop running upon:

(A) Any request for modification of an application and will resume running on the 14th day after the applicant has filed an amended application responsive to such request, including a marked copy showing any changes made and a certification signed by the person executing the application that such marked copy is complete and accurate;

(B) Any unsolicited amendment of the application and will resume running on the 30th day after such an amendment, provided that the amendment includes a marked copy showing changes made and a certification signed by the person executing the application that such marked copy is complete and accurate; and

(C) Any irregular closure of the Commission's Washington, DC office to the public for normal business, including, but not limited to, closure due to a lapse in Federal appropriations, national emergency, inclement weather, or ad hoc Federal holiday, and will resume upon the reopening of the Commission's Washington, DC office to the public for normal business.

(ii) If the applicant does not file an amendment responsive to any request for modification within 30 days of receiving such request, including a marked copy showing any changes made and a certification signed by the person executing the application that such marked copy is complete and accurate, the application will be deemed withdrawn.

(g) If an applicant has not responded in writing to any request for clarification or modification of an application filed under this section, other than an application that is under expedited review under paragraphs (d) and (e) of this section, within 120 days after the request, the application will be deemed withdrawn.

[38 FR 23325, Aug. 29, 1973, as amended at 61 FR 49961, Sept. 24, 1996; 86 FR 57107, Sept. 15, 2020]

§ 270.0–8 Payment of filing fees.

All payment of filing fees shall be made by wire transfer, debit card, credit card, or via the Automated Clearing House Network. Payment of filing fees required by this section shall be made in accordance with the directions set forth in § 202.3a of this chapter.

[86 FR 70262, Dec. 9, 2021]

§ 270.0–9 [Reserved]

§ 270.0–10 Small entities under the Investment Company Act for purposes of the Regulatory Flexibility Act.

(a) *General.* For purposes of Commission rulemaking in accordance with the provisions of Chapter Six of the Administrative Procedure Act (5 U.S.C. 601 *et seq.*) and unless otherwise defined for purposes of a particular rulemaking, the term *small business* or *small organization* for purposes of the Investment Company Act of 1940 shall mean an investment company that, together with other investment companies in the same group of related investment companies, has net assets of $50 million or less as of the end of its most recent fiscal year. For purposes of this section:

(1) In the case of a management company, the term *group of related investment companies* shall mean two or more management companies (including series thereof) that:

(i) Hold themselves out to investors as related companies for purposes of investment and investor services; and

(ii) Either:

§ 270.0-11

(A) Have a common investment adviser or have investment advisers that are affiliated persons of each other; or

(B) Have a common administrator; and

(2) In the case of a unit investment trust, the term *group of related investment companies* shall mean two or more unit investment trusts (including series thereof) that have a common sponsor.

(b) *Special rule for insurance company separate accounts.* In determining whether an insurance company separate account is a *small business* or *small entity* pursuant to paragraph (a) of this section, the assets of the separate account shall be cumulated with the assets of the general account and all other separate accounts of the insurance company.

(c) *Determination of net assets.* The Commission may calculate its determination of the net assets of a group of related investment companies based on the net assets of each investment company in the group as of the end of such company's fiscal year.

[63 FR 35514, June 30, 1998]

§ 270.0-11 Customer identification programs.

Each registered open-end company is subject to the requirements of 31 U.S.C. 5318(l) and the implementing regulation at 31 CFR 103.131, which requires a customer identification program to be implemented as part of the anti-money laundering program required under subchapter II of chapter 53 of title 31, United States Code and the implementing regulations issued by the Department of the Treasury at 31 CFR part 103. Where 31 CFR 103.131 and this chapter use different definitions for the same term, the definition in 31 CFR 103.131 shall be used for the purpose of compliance with 31 CFR 103.131. Where 31 CFR 103.131 and this chapter require the same records to be preserved for different periods of time, such records shall be preserved for the longer period of time.

[68 FR 25146, May 9, 2003]

§ 270.2a-1 Valuation of portfolio securities in special cases.

(a) Any investment company whose securities are qualified for sale, or for whose securities application for such qualification has been made, in any State in which the securities owned by such company are required by applicable State law or regulations to be valued at cost or on some other basis different from that prescribed by clause (A) of section 2(a)(41) of the Act for the purpose of determining the percentage of its assets invested in any particular type or classification of securities or in the securities of any one issuer, may, in valuing its securities for the purposes of sections 5 and 12 of the Act, use the same basis of valuation as that used in complying with such State law or regulations in lieu of the method of valuation prescribed by clause (A) of section 2(a)(41) of the Act.

(b) Any open-end company which has heretofore valued its securities at cost for the purpose of qualifying as a "mutual investment company" under the Internal Revenue Code, prior to its amendment by the Revenue Act of 1942, shall henceforth, for the purposes of sections 5 and 12 of the Act, value its securities in accordance with the method prescribed in clause (A) of section 2(a)(41) of the Act unless such company is permitted under paragraph (a) of this section to use a different method of valuation.

(c) A registered investment company which has adopted for the purposes of sections 5 and 12 of the Act a method of valuation permitted by paragraph (a) of this section, shall state in its registration statement filed pursuant to section 8 (54 Stat. 803; 15 U.S.C. 80a–8) of the Act, or in a report filed pursuant to section 30 (54 Stat. 836; 15 U.S.C. 80a–30) of the Act, the method of valuation adopted and the facts which justify the adoption of such method. A registered investment company which has adopted for the purposes of sections 5 and 12 of the Act a method of valuation permitted by paragraph (a) of this section, unless it shall have adopted such method for the purpose or partly for the purpose of qualifying as a "mutual investment company" under the Internal Revenue Code, shall continue to use that method until it has notified the

Commission of its desire to use a different method, and has received from the Commission permission for such change. Such permission may be made effective on a fixed date or within such reasonable time thereafter as may be deemed advisable under the circumstances.

(d) If at any time it appears that the method of valuation adopted by any company pursuant to paragraph (a) of this section is no longer justified by the facts, the Commission may require a change in the method of valuation within a reasonable period of time either to the method prescribed in clause (A) of section 2(a)(41) of the Act or to some other method permitted by paragraph (a) of this section which is justified by the existing facts.

[Rule N-2A-1, 8 FR 3567, Mar. 24, 1943, as amended at 38 FR 8593, Apr. 4, 1973]

§ 270.2a-2 Effect of eliminations upon valuation of portfolio securities.

During any fiscal quarter in which elimination of securities from the portfolio of an investment company occur, the securities remaining in the portfolio shall, for the purpose of sections 5 and 12 of the Act (54 Stat. 800, 808; 15 U.S.C. 80a-5, 80a-12), be so valued as to give effect to the eliminations in accordance with one of the following methods:

(a) Specific certificate,
(b) First in—first out,
(c) Last in—first out, or
(d) Average value.

For these purposes, a single method of elimination shall be used consistently with respect to all portfolio securities. In giving effect to eliminations pursuant to this section values shall be computed in accordance with section 2(a)(41)(A) of the Act (54 Stat. 790; 15 U.S.C. 80a-2(a)(41)(A)).

[38 FR 8593, Apr. 4, 1973]

§ 270.2a3-1 Investment company limited partners not deemed affiliated persons.

PRELIMINARY NOTE TO § 270.2a3-1: This § 270.2a3-1 excepts from the definition of affiliated person in section 2(a)(3)) (15 U.S.C. 80a-2(a)(3)) those limited partners of investment companies organized in limited partnership form that are affiliated persons solely because they are partners under section 2(a)(3)(D) (15 U.S.C. 80a-2(a)(3)(D)). Reliance on this § 270.2a3-1 does not except a limited partner that is an affiliated person by virtue of any other provision.

No limited partner of a registered management company or a business development company, organized as a limited partnership and relying on § 270.2a19-2, shall be deemed to be an affiliated person of such company, or any other partner of such company, solely by reason of being a limited partner of such company.

[58 FR 45838, Aug. 31, 1993]

§ 270.2a-4 Definition of "current net asset value" for use in computing periodically the current price of redeemable security.

(a) The current net asset value of any redeemable security issued by a registered investment company used in computing periodically the current price for the purpose of distribution, redemption, and repurchase means an amount which reflects calculations, whether or not recorded in the books of account, made substantially in accordance with the following, with estimates used where necessary or appropriate.

(1) Portfolio securities with respect to which market quotations are readily available shall be valued at current market value, and other securities and assets shall be valued at fair value as determined in good faith by the board of directors of the registered company.

(2) Changes in holdings of portfolio securities shall be reflected no later than in the first calculation on the first business day following the trade date.

(3) Changes in the number of outstanding shares of the registered company resulting from distributions, redemptions, and repurchases shall be reflected no later than in the first calculation on the first business day following such change.

(4) Expenses, including any investment advisory fees, shall be included to date of calculation. Appropriate provision shall be made for Federal income taxes if required. Investment companies which retain realized capital gains designated as a distribution to shareholders shall comply with paragraph (h) of § 210.6-03 of Regulation S-X.

(5) Dividends receivable shall be included to date of calculation either at

§ 270.2a-5

ex-dividend dates or record dates, as appropriate.

(6) Interest income and other income shall be included to date of calculation.

(b) The items which would otherwise be required to be reflected by paragraphs (a) (4) and (6) of this section need not be so reflected if cumulatively, when netted, they do not amount to as much as one cent per outstanding share.

(c) Notwithstanding the requirements of paragraph (a) of this section, any interim determination of current net asset value between calculations made as of the close of the New York Stock Exchange on the preceding business day and the current business day may be estimated so as to reflect any change in current net asset value since the closing calculation on the preceding business day.

(Secs. 7, 19(a), 48 Stat. 78, 85, 908, 15 U.S.C. 77g, 77s(a); secs. 12, 13, 15(d), 23(a), 48 Stat. 892, 894, 895, 901; secs. 3, 8, 49 Stat. 1377, 1379, secs. 3, 4, 78 Stat. 569, 570, secs. 1, 2, 82 Stat. 454, 15 U.S.C. 78l, 78m, 78o(d), 78w(a); secs. 8, 22, 30, 31(c), 38(a), 54 Stat. 803, 823, 836, 838, 841, 15 U.S.C. 80a-8, 80a-22, 80a-29, 80a-30(c))

[29 FR 19101, Dec. 30, 1964, as amended at 35 FR 314, Jan. 8, 1970; 47 FR 56844, Dec. 21, 1982]

§ 270.2a-5 Fair value determination and readily available market quotations.

(a) *Fair value determination.* For purposes of section 2(a)(41) of the Act (15 U.S.C. 80a-2(a)(41)) and § 270.2a-4, determining fair value in good faith with respect to a fund requires:

(1) *Assess and manage risks.* Periodically assessing any material risks associated with the determination of the fair value of fund investments ("valuation risks"), including material conflicts of interest, and managing those identified valuation risks;

(2) *Establish and apply fair value methodologies.* Performing each of the following, taking into account the fund's valuation risks:

(i) Selecting and applying in a consistent manner an appropriate methodology or methodologies for determining (and calculating) the fair value of fund investments, provided that a selected methodology may be changed if a different methodology is equally or more representative of the fair value of fund investments, including specifying the key inputs and assumptions specific to each asset class or portfolio holding;

(ii) Periodically reviewing the appropriateness and accuracy of the methodologies selected and making any necessary changes or adjustments thereto; and

(iii) Monitoring for circumstances that may necessitate the use of fair value;

(3) *Test fair value methodologies.* Testing the appropriateness and accuracy of the fair value methodologies that have been selected, including identifying the testing methods to be used and the minimum frequency with which such testing methods are to be used; and

(4) *Evaluate pricing services.* Overseeing pricing service providers, if used, including establishing the process for approving, monitoring, and evaluating each pricing service provider and initiating price challenges as appropriate.

(b) *Performance of fair value determinations.* The board of the fund must determine fair value in good faith for any or all fund investments by carrying out the functions required in paragraph (a) of this section. The board may choose to designate the valuation designee to perform the fair value determination relating to any or all fund investments, which shall carry out all of the functions required in paragraph (a) of this section, subject to the requirements of this paragraph (b).

(1) *Oversight and reporting.* The board oversees the valuation designee, and the valuation designee reports to the fund's board, in writing, including such information as may be reasonably necessary for the board to evaluate the matters covered in the report, as follows:

(i) *Periodic reporting.* (A) At least quarterly:

(*1*) Any reports or materials requested by the board related to the fair value of designated investments or the valuation designee's process for fair valuing fund investments; and

(*2*) A summary or description of material fair value matters that occurred in the prior quarter, including:

Securities and Exchange Commission § 270.2a–5

(*i*) Any material changes in the assessment and management of valuation risks required under paragraph (a)(1) of this section, including any material changes in conflicts of interest of the valuation designee (and any other service provider);

(*ii*) Any material changes to, or material deviations from, the fair value methodologies established under paragraph (a)(2) of this section; and

(*iii*) Any material changes to the valuation designee's process for selecting and overseeing pricing services, as well as any material events related to the valuation designee's oversight of pricing services; and

(B) At least annually, an assessment of the adequacy and effectiveness of the valuation designee's process for determining the fair value of the designated portfolio of investments, including, at a minimum:

(*1*) A summary of the results of the testing of fair value methodologies required under paragraph (a)(3) of this section; and

(*2*) An assessment of the adequacy of resources allocated to the process for determining the fair value of designated investments, including any material changes to the roles or functions of the persons responsible for determining fair value under paragraph (b)(2) of this section; and

(ii) *Prompt board notification and reporting.* The valuation designee notifies the board of the occurrence of matters that materially affect the fair value of the designated portfolio of investments, including a significant deficiency or material weakness in the design or effectiveness of the valuation designee's fair value determination process, or material errors in the calculation of net asset value, (any such matter or error, a "material matter") within a time period determined by the board (but in no event later than five business days after the valuation designee becomes aware of the material matter), with such timely follow-on reporting as the board may determine appropriate; and

(2) *Specify responsibilities.* The valuation designee specifies the titles of the persons responsible for determining the fair value of the designated investments, including by specifying the particular functions for which they are responsible, and reasonably segregates fair value determinations from the portfolio management of the fund such that the portfolio manager(s) may not determine, or effectively determine by exerting substantial influence on, the fair values ascribed to portfolio investments.

(c) *Readily available market quotations.* For purposes of section 2(a)(41) of the Act (15 U.S.C. 80a–2(a)(41)), a market quotation is readily available only when that quotation is a quoted price (unadjusted) in active markets for identical investments that the fund can access at the measurement date, provided that a quotation will not be readily available if it is not reliable.

(d) *Unit investment trusts.* If the fund is a unit investment trust, and the initial deposit of portfolio securities into the unit investment trust occurs *after* March 8, 2021, the fund's trustee or depositor must carry out the requirements of paragraph (a) of this section. If the initial deposit of portfolio securities into the unit investment trust occurred *before* March 8, 2021, and an entity other than the fund's trustee or depositor has been designated to carry out the fair value determination, that entity must carry out the requirements of paragraph (a) of this section.

(e) *Definitions.* For purposes of this section:

(1) *Fund* means a registered investment company or business development company.

(2) *Fair value* means the value of a portfolio investment for which market quotations are not readily available under paragraph (c) of this section.

(3) *Board* means either the fund's entire board of directors or a designated committee of such board composed of a majority of directors who are not interested persons of the fund.

(4) *Valuation designee* means the investment adviser, other than a sub-adviser, of a fund or, if the fund does not have an investment adviser, an officer or officers of the fund.

[86 FR 807, Jan. 6, 2021]

§ 270.2a-6 Certain transactions not deemed assignments.

A transaction which does not result in a change of actual control or management of the investment adviser to, or principal underwriter of, an investment company is not an assignment for purposes of section 15(a)(4) or section 15(b)(2) of the act, respectively.

(Secs. 6(c) and 38(a) (15 U.S.C. 80a-6(c) and 80a-37(a)))

[45 FR 1861, Jan. 9, 1980]

§ 270.2a-7 Money market funds.

(a) *Definitions*—(1) *Acquisition (or acquire)* means any purchase or subsequent rollover (but does not include the failure to exercise a demand feature).

(2) *Amortized cost method of valuation* means the method of calculating an investment company's net asset value whereby portfolio securities are valued at the fund's acquisition cost as adjusted for amortization of premium or accretion of discount rather than at their value based on current market factors.

(3) *Asset-backed security* means a fixed income security (other than a government security) issued by a special purpose entity (as defined in this paragraph (a)(3)), substantially all of the assets of which consist of qualifying assets (as defined in this paragraph (a)(3)). *Special purpose entity* means a trust, corporation, partnership or other entity organized for the sole purpose of issuing securities that entitle their holders to receive payments that depend primarily on the cash flow from qualifying assets, but does not include a registered investment company. *Qualifying assets* means financial assets, either fixed or revolving, that by their terms convert into cash within a finite time period, plus any rights or other assets designed to assure the servicing or timely distribution of proceeds to security holders.

(4) *Business day* means any day, other than Saturday, Sunday, or any customary business holiday.

(5) *Collateralized fully* has the same meaning as defined in § 270.5b-3(c)(1) except that § 270.5b-3(c)(1)(iv)(C) shall not apply.

(6) *Conditional demand feature* means a demand feature that is not an unconditional demand feature. A conditional demand feature is not a guarantee.

(7) *Conduit security* means a security issued by a municipal issuer (as defined in this paragraph (a)(7)) involving an arrangement or agreement entered into, directly or indirectly, with a person other than a municipal issuer, which arrangement or agreement provides for or secures repayment of the security. *Municipal issuer* means a state or territory of the United States (including the District of Columbia), or any political subdivision or public instrumentality of a state or territory of the United States. A conduit security does not include a security that is:

(i) Fully and unconditionally guaranteed by a municipal issuer;

(ii) Payable from the general revenues of the municipal issuer or other municipal issuers (other than those revenues derived from an agreement or arrangement with a person who is not a municipal issuer that provides for or secures repayment of the security issued by the municipal issuer);

(iii) Related to a project owned and operated by a municipal issuer; or

(iv) Related to a facility leased to and under the control of an industrial or commercial enterprise that is part of a public project which, as a whole, is owned and under the control of a municipal issuer.

(8) *Daily liquid assets* means:

(i) Cash;

(ii) Direct obligations of the U.S. Government;

(iii) Securities that will mature, as determined without reference to the exceptions in paragraph (i) of this section regarding interest rate readjustments, or are subject to a demand feature that is exercisable and payable, within one business day; or

(iv) Amounts receivable and due unconditionally within one business day on pending sales of portfolio securities.

(9) *Demand feature* means a feature permitting the holder of a security to sell the security at an exercise price equal to the approximate amortized cost of the security plus accrued interest, if any, at the later of the time of

Securities and Exchange Commission § 270.2a–7

exercise or the settlement of the transaction, paid within 397 calendar days of exercise.

(10) *Demand feature issued by a noncontrolled person* means a demand feature issued by:

(i) A person that, directly or indirectly, does not control, and is not controlled by or under common control with the issuer of the security subject to the demand feature (*control* means "control" as defined in section 2(a)(9) of the Act) (15 U.S.C. 80a–2(a)(9)); or

(ii) A sponsor of a special purpose entity with respect to an asset-backed security.

(11) *Eligible security* means a security:

(i) With a remaining maturity of 397 calendar days or less that the fund's board of directors determines presents minimal credit risks to the fund, which determination must include an analysis of the capacity of the security's issuer or guarantor (including for this paragraph (a)(11)(i) the provider of a conditional demand feature, when applicable) to meet its financial obligations, and such analysis must include, to the extent appropriate, consideration of the following factors with respect to the security's issuer or guarantor:

(A) Financial condition;

(B) Sources of liquidity;

(C) Ability to react to future market-wide and issuer- or guarantor-specific events, including ability to repay debt in a highly adverse situation; and

(D) Strength of the issuer or guarantor's industry within the economy and relative to economic trends, and issuer or guarantor's competitive position within its industry.

(ii) That is issued by a registered investment company that is a money market fund; or

(iii) That is a government security.

NOTE TO PARAGRAPH (a)(11): For a discussion of additional factors that may be relevant in evaluating certain specific asset types see Investment Company Act Release No. IC–31828 (9/16/15).

(12) *Event of insolvency* has the same meaning as defined in § 270.5b–3(c)(2).

(13) *Floating rate security* means a security the terms of which provide for the adjustment of its interest rate whenever a specified interest rate changes and that, at any time until the final maturity of the instrument or the period remaining until the principal amount can be recovered through demand, can reasonably be expected to have a market value that approximates its amortized cost.

(14) *Government money market fund* means a money market fund that invests 99.5 percent or more of its total assets in cash, government securities, and/or repurchase agreements that are collateralized fully.

(15) *Government security* has the same meaning as defined in section 2(a)(16) of the Act (15 U.S.C. 80a–2(a)(16)).

(16) *Guarantee:*

(i) Means an unconditional obligation of a person other than the issuer of the security to undertake to pay, upon presentment by the holder of the guarantee (if required), the principal amount of the underlying security plus accrued interest when due or upon default, or, in the case of an unconditional demand feature, an obligation that entitles the holder to receive upon the later of exercise or the settlement of the transaction the approximate amortized cost of the underlying security or securities, plus accrued interest, if any. A guarantee includes a letter of credit, financial guaranty (bond) insurance, and an unconditional demand feature (other than an unconditional demand feature provided by the issuer of the security).

(ii) The sponsor of a special purpose entity with respect to an asset-backed security shall be deemed to have provided a guarantee with respect to the entire principal amount of the asset-backed security for purposes of this section, except paragraphs (a)(11) (definition of eligible security), (d)(2)(ii) (credit substitution), (d)(3)(iv)(A) (fractional guarantees) and (e) (guarantees not relied on) of this section, unless the money market fund's board of directors has determined that the fund is not relying on the sponsor's financial strength or its ability or willingness to provide liquidity, credit or other support to determine the quality (pursuant to paragraph (d)(2) of this section) or liquidity (pursuant to paragraph (d)(4) of this section) of the asset-backed security, and maintains a record of this determination (pursuant to paragraphs (g)(7) and (h)(6) of this section).

§ 270.2a–7

(17) *Guarantee issued by a non-controlled person* means a guarantee issued by:

(i) A person that, directly or indirectly, does not control, and is not controlled by or under common control with the issuer of the security subject to the guarantee (*control* means "control" as defined in section 2(a)(9) of the Act) (15 U.S.C. 80a–2(a)(9))); or

(ii) A sponsor of a special purpose entity with respect to an asset-backed security.

(18) *Illiquid security* means a security that cannot be sold or disposed of in the ordinary course of business within seven calendar days at approximately the value ascribed to it by the fund.

(19) *Penny-rounding method* of pricing means the method of computing an investment company's price per share for purposes of distribution, redemption and repurchase whereby the current net asset value per share is rounded to the nearest one percent.

(20) *Refunded security* has the same meaning as defined in § 270.5b–3(c)(4).

(21) *Retail money market fund* means a money market fund that has policies and procedures reasonably designed to limit all beneficial owners of the fund to natural persons.

(22) *Single state fund* means a tax exempt fund that holds itself out as seeking to maximize the amount of its distributed income that is exempt from the income taxes or other taxes on investments of a particular state and, where applicable, subdivisions thereof.

(23) *Tax exempt fund* means any money market fund that holds itself out as distributing income exempt from regular federal income tax.

(24) *Total assets* means, with respect to a money market fund using the Amortized Cost Method, the total amortized cost of its assets and, with respect to any other money market fund, means the total value of the money market fund's assets, as defined in section 2(a)(41) of the Act (15 U.S.C. 80a–2(a)(41)) and the rules thereunder.

(25) *Unconditional demand feature* means a demand feature that by its terms would be readily exercisable in the event of a default in payment of principal or interest on the underlying security or securities.

(26) *United States dollar-denominated* means, with reference to a security, that all principal and interest payments on such security are payable to security holders in United States dollars under all circumstances and that the interest rate of, the principal amount to be repaid, and the timing of payments related to such security do not vary or float with the value of a foreign currency, the rate of interest payable on foreign currency borrowings, or with any other interest rate or index expressed in a currency other than United States dollars.

(27) *Variable rate security* means a security the terms of which provide for the adjustment of its interest rate on set dates (such as the last day of a month or calendar quarter) and that, upon each adjustment until the final maturity of the instrument or the period remaining until the principal amount can be recovered through demand, can reasonably be expected to have a market value that approximates its amortized cost.

(28) *Weekly liquid assets* means:

(i) Cash;

(ii) Direct obligations of the U.S. Government;

(iii) Government securities that are issued by a person controlled or supervised by and acting as an instrumentality of the government of the United States pursuant to authority granted by the Congress of the United States that:

(A) Are issued at a discount to the principal amount to be repaid at maturity without provision for the payment of interest; and

(B) Have a remaining maturity date of 60 days or less.

(iv) Securities that will mature, as determined without reference to the exceptions in paragraph (i) of this section regarding interest rate readjustments, or are subject to a demand feature that is exercisable and payable, within five business days; or

(v) Amounts receivable and due unconditionally within five business days on pending sales of portfolio securities.

(b) *Holding out and use of names and titles*—(1) *Holding out.* It shall be an untrue statement of material fact within the meaning of section 34(b) of the Act

Securities and Exchange Commission

§ 270.2a–7

(15 U.S.C. 80a–33(b)) for a registered investment company, in any registration statement, application, report, account, record, or other document filed or transmitted pursuant to the Act, including any advertisement, pamphlet, circular, form letter, or other sales literature addressed to or intended for distribution to prospective investors that is required to be filed with the Commission by section 24(b) of the Act (15 U.S.C. 80a–24(b)), to hold itself out to investors as a money market fund or the equivalent of a money market fund, unless such registered investment company complies with this section.

(2) *Names.* It shall constitute the use of a materially deceptive or misleading name or title within the meaning of section 35(d) of the Act (15 U.S.C. 80a–34(d)) for a registered investment company to adopt the term "money market" as part of its name or title or the name or title of any redeemable securities of which it is the issuer, or to adopt a name that suggests that it is a money market fund or the equivalent of a money market fund, unless such registered investment company complies with this section.

(3) *Titles.* For purposes of paragraph (b)(2) of this section, a name that suggests that a registered investment company is a money market fund or the equivalent thereof includes one that uses such terms as "cash," "liquid," "money," "ready assets" or similar terms.

(c) *Pricing and Redeeming Shares*—(1) *Share price calculation.*

(i) The current price per share, for purposes of distribution, redemption and repurchase, of any redeemable security issued by a government money market fund or retail money market fund, notwithstanding the requirements of section 2(a)(41) of the Act (15 U.S.C. 80a–2(a)(41)) and of §§ 270.2a–4 and 270.22c–1 thereunder, may be computed by use of the amortized cost method and/or the penny-rounding method. To use these methods, the board of directors of the government or retail money market fund must determine, in good faith, that it is in the best interests of the fund and its shareholders to maintain a stable net asset value per share or stable price per share, by virtue of either the amortized cost method and/ or the penny-rounding method. The government or retail money market fund may continue to use such methods only so long as the board of directors believes that they fairly reflect the market-based net asset value per share and the fund complies with the other requirements of this section.

(ii) Any money market fund that is not a government money market fund or a retail money market fund must compute its price per share for purposes of distribution, redemption and repurchase by rounding the fund's current net asset value per share to a minimum of the fourth decimal place in the case of a fund with a $1.0000 share price or an equivalent or more precise level of accuracy for money market funds with a different share price (e.g. $10.000 per share, or $100.00 per share).

(2) *Liquidity fees and temporary suspensions of redemptions.* Except as provided in paragraphs (c)(2)(iii) and (v) of this section, and notwithstanding sections 22(e) and 27(i) of the Act (15 U.S.C. 80a–22(e) and 80a–27(i)) and § 270.22c–1:

(i) *Discretionary liquidity fees and temporary suspensions of redemptions.* If, at any time, the money market fund has invested less than thirty percent of its total assets in weekly liquid assets, the fund may institute a liquidity fee (not to exceed two percent of the value of the shares redeemed) or suspend the right of redemption temporarily, subject to paragraphs (c)(2)(i)(A) and (B) of this section, if the fund's board of directors, including a majority of the directors who are not interested persons of the fund, determines that the fee or suspension of redemptions is in the best interests of the fund.

(A) *Duration and application of discretionary liquidity fee.* Once imposed, a discretionary liquidity fee must be applied to all shares redeemed and must remain in effect until the money market fund's board of directors, including a majority of the directors who are not interested persons of the fund, determines that imposing such liquidity fee is no longer in the best interests of the fund. Provided however, that if, at the end of a business day, the money market fund has invested thirty percent or

§ 270.2a–7

more of its total assets in weekly liquid assets, the fund must cease charging the liquidity fee, effective as of the beginning of the next business day.

(B) *Duration of temporary suspension of redemptions.* The temporary suspension of redemptions must apply to all shares and must remain in effect until the fund's board of directors, including a majority of the directors who are not interested persons of the fund, determines that the temporary suspension of redemptions is no longer in the best interests of the fund. Provided, however, that the fund must restore the right of redemption on the earlier of:

(*1*) The beginning of the next business day following a business day that ended with the money market fund having invested thirty percent or more of its total assets in weekly liquid assets; or

(*2*) The beginning of the next business day following ten business days after suspending redemptions. The money market fund may not suspend the right of redemption pursuant to this section for more than ten business days in any rolling ninety calendar day period.

(ii) *Default liquidity fees.* If, at the end of a business day, the money market fund has invested less than ten percent of its total assets in weekly liquid assets, the fund must institute a liquidity fee, effective as of the beginning of the next business day, as described in paragraphs (c)(2)(ii)(A) and (B) of this section, unless the fund's board of directors, including a majority of the directors who are not interested persons of the fund, determines that imposing the fee is not in the best interests of the fund.

(A) *Amount of default liquidity fee.* The default liquidity fee shall be one percent of the value of shares redeemed unless the money market fund's board of directors, including a majority of the directors who are not interested persons of the fund, determines, at the time of initial imposition or later, that a higher or lower fee level is in the best interests of the fund. A liquidity fee may not exceed two percent of the value of the shares redeemed.

(B) *Duration and application of default liquidity fee.* Once imposed, the default liquidity fee must be applied to all shares redeemed and shall remain in effect until the money market fund's board of directors, including a majority of the directors who are not interested persons of the fund, determines that imposing such liquidity fee is not in the best interests of the fund. Provided however, that if, at the end of a business day, the money market fund has invested thirty percent or more of its total assets in weekly liquid assets, the fund must cease charging the liquidity fee, effective as of the beginning of the next business day.

(iii) *Government money market funds.* The requirements of paragraphs (c)(2)(i) and (ii) of this section shall not apply to a government money market fund. A government money market fund may, however, choose to rely on the ability to impose liquidity fees and suspend redemptions consistent with the requirements of paragraph (c)(2)(i) and/or (ii) of this section and any other requirements that apply to liquidity fees and temporary suspensions of redemptions (e.g., Item 4(b)(1)(ii) of Form N–1A (§ 274.11A of this chapter)).

(iv) *Variable contracts.* Notwithstanding section 27(i) of the Act (15 U.S.C. 80a–27(i)), a variable insurance contract issued by a registered separate account funding variable insurance contracts or the sponsoring insurance company of such separate account may apply a liquidity fee or temporary suspension of redemptions pursuant to paragraph (c)(2) of this section to contract owners who allocate all or a portion of their contract value to a subaccount of the separate account that is either a money market fund or that invests all of its assets in shares of a money market fund.

(v) *Master feeder funds.* Any money market fund (a "feeder fund") that owns, pursuant to section 12(d)(1)(E) of the Act (15 U.S.C. 80a–12(d)(1)(E)), shares of another money market fund (a "master fund") may not impose liquidity fees or temporary suspensions of redemptions under paragraphs (c)(2)(i) and (ii) of this section, provided however, that if a master fund, in which the feeder fund invests, imposes a liquidity fee or temporary suspension of redemptions pursuant to paragraphs (c)(2)(i) and (ii) of this section, then the

Securities and Exchange Commission

§ 270.2a–7

feeder fund shall pass through to its investors the fee or redemption suspension on the same terms and conditions as imposed by the master fund.

(d) *Risk-limiting conditions*—(1) *Portfolio maturity.* The money market fund must maintain a dollar-weighted average portfolio maturity appropriate to its investment objective; provided, however, that the money market fund must not:

(i) Acquire any instrument with a remaining maturity of greater than 397 calendar days;

(ii) Maintain a dollar-weighted average portfolio maturity ("WAM") that exceeds 60 calendar days; or

(iii) Maintain a dollar-weighted average portfolio maturity that exceeds 120 calendar days, determined without reference to the exceptions in paragraph (i) of this section regarding interest rate readjustments ("WAL").

(2) *Portfolio quality*—(i) *General.* The money market fund must limit its portfolio investments to those United States dollar-denominated securities that at the time of acquisition are eligible securities.

(ii) *Securities subject to guarantees.* A security that is subject to a guarantee may be determined to be an eligible security based solely on whether the guarantee is an eligible security, provided however, that the issuer of the guarantee, or another institution, has undertaken to promptly notify the holder of the security in the event the guarantee is substituted with another guarantee (if such substitution is permissible under the terms of the guarantee).

(iii) *Securities subject to conditional demand features.* A security that is subject to a conditional demand feature ("underlying security") may be determined to be an eligible security only if:

(A) The conditional demand feature is an eligible security;

(B) The underlying security or any guarantee of such security is an eligible security, except that the underlying security or guarantee may have a remaining maturity of more than 397 calendar days.

(C) At the time of the acquisition of the underlying security, the money market fund's board of directors has determined that there is minimal risk that the circumstances that would result in the conditional demand feature not being exercisable will occur; and

(*1*) The conditions limiting exercise either can be monitored readily by the fund or relate to the taxability, under federal, state or local law, of the interest payments on the security; or

(*2*) The terms of the conditional demand feature require that the fund will receive notice of the occurrence of the condition and the opportunity to exercise the demand feature in accordance with its terms; and

(D) The issuer of the conditional demand feature, or another institution, has undertaken to promptly notify the holder of the security in the event the conditional demand feature is substituted with another conditional demand feature (if such substitution is permissible under the terms of the conditional demand feature).

(3) *Portfolio diversification*—(i) *Issuer diversification.* The money market fund must be diversified with respect to issuers of securities acquired by the fund as provided in paragraphs (d)(3)(i) and (ii) of this section, other than with respect to government securities.

(A) *Taxable and national funds.* Immediately after the acquisition of any security, a money market fund other than a single state fund must not have invested more than:

(*1*) Five percent of its total assets in securities issued by the issuer of the security, provided, however, that with respect to paragraph (d)(3)(i)(A) of this section, such a fund may invest up to twenty-five percent of its total assets in the securities of a single issuer for a period of up to three business days after the acquisition thereof; provided, further, that the fund may not invest in the securities of more than one issuer in accordance with the foregoing proviso in this paragraph (d)(3)(i)(A)(*1*) at any time; and

(*2*) Ten percent of its total assets in securities issued by or subject to demand features or guarantees from the institution that issued the demand feature or guarantee, provided, however, that a tax exempt fund need only comply with this paragraph (d)(3)(i)(A)(*2*) with respect to eighty-five percent of its total assets, subject to paragraph (d)(3)(iii) of this section.

339

§ 270.2a-7

(B) *Single state funds.* Immediately after the acquisition of any security, a single state fund must not have invested:

(*1*) With respect to seventy-five percent of its total assets, more than five percent of its total assets in securities issued by the issuer of the security; and

(*2*) With respect to seventy-five percent of its total assets, more than ten percent of its total assets in securities issued by or subject to demand features or guarantees from the institution that issued the demand feature or guarantee, subject to paragraph (d)(3)(iii) of this section.

(ii) *Issuer diversification calculations.* For purposes of making calculations under paragraph (d)(3)(i) of this section:

(A) *Repurchase agreements.* The acquisition of a repurchase agreement may be deemed to be an acquisition of the underlying securities, provided the obligation of the seller to repurchase the securities from the money market fund is collateralized fully and the fund's board of directors has evaluated the seller's creditworthiness.

(B) *Refunded securities.* The acquisition of a refunded security shall be deemed to be an acquisition of the escrowed government securities.

(C) *Conduit securities.* A conduit security shall be deemed to be issued by the person (other than the municipal issuer) ultimately responsible for payments of interest and principal on the security.

(D) *Asset-backed securities—*(*1*) *General.* An asset-backed security acquired by a fund ("primary ABS") shall be deemed to be issued by the special purpose entity that issued the asset-backed security, provided:

(*i*) *Holdings of primary ABS.* Any person whose obligations constitute ten percent or more of the principal amount of the qualifying assets of the primary ABS ("ten percent obligor") shall be deemed to be an issuer of the portion of the primary ABS such obligations represent; and

(*ii*) *Holdings of secondary ABS.* If a ten percent obligor of a primary ABS is itself a special purpose entity issuing asset-backed securities ("secondary ABS"), any ten percent obligor of such secondary ABS also shall be deemed to be an issuer of the portion of the primary ABS that such ten percent obligor represents.

(*2*) *Restricted special purpose entities.* A ten percent obligor with respect to a primary or secondary ABS shall not be deemed to have issued any portion of the assets of a primary ABS as provided in paragraph (d)(3)(ii)(D)(*1*) of this section if that ten percent obligor is itself a special purpose entity issuing asset-backed securities ("restricted special purpose entity"), and the securities that it issues (other than securities issued to a company that controls, or is controlled by or under common control with, the restricted special purpose entity and which is not itself a special purpose entity issuing asset-backed securities) are held by only one other special purpose entity.

((*3*) *Demand features and guarantees.* In the case of a ten percent obligor deemed to be an issuer, the fund must satisfy the diversification requirements of paragraph (d)(3)(iii) of this section with respect to any demand feature or guarantee to which the ten percent obligor's obligations are subject.

(E) *Shares of other money market funds.* A money market fund that acquires shares issued by another money market fund in an amount that would otherwise be prohibited by paragraph (d)(3)(i) of this section shall nonetheless be deemed in compliance with this section if the board of directors of the acquiring money market fund reasonably believes that the fund in which it has invested is in compliance with this section.

(F) *Treatment of certain affiliated entities—*(*1*) *General.* The money market fund, when calculating the amount of its total assets invested in securities issued by any particular issuer for purposes of paragraph (d)(3)(i) of this section, must treat as a single issuer two or more issuers of securities owned by the money market fund if one issuer controls the other, is controlled by the other issuer, or is under common control with the other issuer, provided that "control" for this purpose means ownership of more than 50 percent of the issuer's voting securities.

340

Securities and Exchange Commission § 270.2a-7

(2) *Equity owners of asset-backed commercial paper special purpose entities.* The money market fund is not required to aggregate an asset-backed commercial paper special purpose entity and its equity owners under paragraph (d)(3)(ii)(F)*(1)* of this section provided that a primary line of business of its equity owners is owning equity interests in special purpose entities and providing services to special purpose entities, the independent equity owners' activities with respect to the SPEs are limited to providing management or administrative services, and no qualifying assets of the special purpose entity were originated by the equity owners.

(3) *Ten percent obligors.* For purposes of determining ten percent obligors pursuant to paragraph (d)(3)(ii)(D)*(1)(i)* of this section, the money market fund must treat as a single person two or more persons whose obligations in the aggregate constitute ten percent or more of the principal amount of the qualifying assets of the primary ABS if one person controls the other, is controlled by the other person, or is under common control with the person, provided that "control" for this purpose means ownership of more than 50 percent of the person's voting securities.

(iii) *Diversification rules for demand features and guarantees.* The money market fund must be diversified with respect to demand features and guarantees acquired by the fund as provided in paragraphs (d)(3)(i), (iii), and (iv) of this section, other than with respect to a demand feature issued by the same institution that issued the underlying security, or with respect to a guarantee or demand feature that is itself a government security.

(A) *General.* Immediately after the acquisition of any demand feature or guarantee, any security subject to a demand feature or guarantee, or a security directly issued by the issuer of a demand feature or guarantee, a money market fund must not have invested more than ten percent of its total assets in securities issued by or subject to demand features or guarantees from the institution that issued the demand feature or guarantee, subject to paragraphs (d)(3)(i) and (d)(3)(iii)(B) of this section.

(B) *Tax exempt funds.* Immediately after the acquisition of any demand feature or guarantee, any security subject to a demand feature or guarantee, or a security directly issued by the issuer of a demand feature or guarantee (any such acquisition, a "demand feature or guarantee acquisition"), a tax exempt fund, with respect to eighty-five percent of its total assets, must not have invested more than ten percent of its total assets in securities issued by or subject to demand features or guarantees from the institution that issued the demand feature or guarantee; provided that any demand feature or guarantee acquisition in excess of ten percent of the fund's total assets in accordance with this paragraph must be a demand feature or guarantee issued by a non-controlled person.

(iv) *Demand feature and guarantee diversification calculations*—(A) *Fractional demand features or guarantees.* In the case of a security subject to a demand feature or guarantee from an institution by which the institution guarantees a specified portion of the value of the security, the institution shall be deemed to guarantee the specified portion thereof.

(B) *Layered demand features or guarantees.* In the case of a security subject to demand features or guarantees from multiple institutions that have not limited the extent of their obligations as described in paragraph (d)(3)(iv)(A) of this section, each institution shall be deemed to have provided the demand feature or guarantee with respect to the entire principal amount of the security.

(v) *Diversification safe harbor.* A money market fund that satisfies the applicable diversification requirements of paragraphs (d)(3) and (e) of this section shall be deemed to have satisfied the diversification requirements of section 5(b)(1) of the Act (15 U.S.C. 80a-5(b)(1)) and the rules adopted thereunder.

(4) *Portfolio liquidity.* The money market fund must hold securities that are sufficiently liquid to meet reasonably foreseeable shareholder redemptions in light of the fund's obligations under section 22(e) of the Act (15 U.S.C. 80a-22(e)) and any commitments the fund

§ 270.2a–7

has made to shareholders; provided, however, that:

(i) *Illiquid securities.* The money market fund may not acquire any illiquid security if, immediately after the acquisition, the money market fund would have invested more than five percent of its total assets in illiquid securities.

(ii) *Minimum daily liquidity requirement.* The money market fund may not acquire any security other than a daily liquid asset if, immediately after the acquisition, the fund would have invested less than ten percent of its total assets in daily liquid assets. This provision does not apply to tax exempt funds.

(iii) *Minimum weekly liquidity requirement.* The money market fund may not acquire any security other than a weekly liquid asset if, immediately after the acquisition, the fund would have invested less than thirty percent of its total assets in weekly liquid assets.

(e) *Demand features and guarantees not relied upon.* If the fund's board of directors has determined that the fund is not relying on a demand feature or guarantee to determine the quality (pursuant to paragraph (d)(2) of this section), or maturity (pursuant to paragraph (i) of this section), or liquidity of a portfolio security (pursuant to paragraph (d)(4) of this section), and maintains a record of this determination (pursuant to paragraphs (g)(3) and (h)(7) of this section), then the fund may disregard such demand feature or guarantee for all purposes of this section.

(f) *Defaults and other events*—(1) *Adverse events.* Upon the occurrence of any of the events specified in paragraphs (f)(1)(i) through (iii) of this section with respect to a portfolio security, the money market fund shall dispose of such security as soon as practicable consistent with achieving an orderly disposition of the security, by sale, exercise of any demand feature or otherwise, absent a finding by the board of directors that disposal of the portfolio security would not be in the best interests of the money market fund (which determination may take into account, among other factors, market conditions that could affect the orderly disposition of the portfolio security):

(i) The default with respect to a portfolio security (other than an immaterial default unrelated to the financial condition of the issuer);

(ii) A portfolio security ceases to be an eligible security (e.g., no longer presents minimal credit risks); or

(iii) An event of insolvency occurs with respect to the issuer of a portfolio security or the provider of any demand feature or guarantee.

(2) *Notice to the Commission.* The money market fund must notify the Commission of the occurrence of certain material events, as specified in Form N–CR (§ 274.222 of this chapter).

(3) *Defaults for purposes of paragraphs (f)(1) and (2) of this section.* For purposes of paragraphs (f)(1) and (2) of this section, an instrument subject to a demand feature or guarantee shall not be deemed to be in default (and an event of insolvency with respect to the security shall not be deemed to have occurred) if:

(i) In the case of an instrument subject to a demand feature, the demand feature has been exercised and the fund has recovered either the principal amount or the amortized cost of the instrument, plus accrued interest;

(ii) The provider of the guarantee is continuing, without protest, to make payments as due on the instrument; or

(iii) The provider of a guarantee with respect to an asset-backed security pursuant to paragraph (a)(16)(ii) of this section is continuing, without protest, to provide credit, liquidity or other support as necessary to permit the asset-backed security to make payments as due.

(g) *Required procedures.* The money market fund's board of directors must adopt written procedures including the following:

(1) *Funds using amortized cost.* In the case of a government or retail money market fund that uses the amortized cost method of valuation, in supervising the money market fund's operations and delegating special responsibilities involving portfolio management to the money market fund's investment adviser, the money market

Securities and Exchange Commission § 270.2a-7

fund's board of directors, as a particular responsibility within the overall duty of care owed to its shareholders, shall establish written procedures reasonably designed, taking into account current market conditions and the money market fund's investment objectives, to stabilize the money market fund's net asset value per share, as computed for the purpose of distribution, redemption and repurchase, at a single value.

(i) *Specific procedures.* Included within the procedures adopted by the board of directors shall be the following:

(A) *Shadow pricing.* Written procedures shall provide:

(*1*) That the extent of deviation, if any, of the current net asset value per share calculated using available market quotations (or an appropriate substitute that reflects current market conditions) from the money market fund's amortized cost price per share, shall be calculated at least daily, and at such other intervals that the board of directors determines appropriate and reasonable in light of current market conditions;

(*2*) For the periodic review by the board of directors of the amount of the deviation as well as the methods used to calculate the deviation; and

(*3*) For the maintenance of records of the determination of deviation and the board's review thereof.

(B) *Prompt consideration of deviation.* In the event such deviation from the money market fund's amortized cost price per share exceeds ½ of 1 percent, the board of directors shall promptly consider what action, if any, should be initiated by the board of directors.

(C) *Material dilution or unfair results.* Where the board of directors believes the extent of any deviation from the money market fund's amortized cost price per share may result in material dilution or other unfair results to investors or existing shareholders, it shall cause the fund to take such action as it deems appropriate to eliminate or reduce to the extent reasonably practicable such dilution or unfair results.

(ii) [Reserved]

(2) *Funds using penny rounding.* In the case of a government or retail money market fund that uses the penny rounding method of pricing, in supervising the money market fund's operations and delegating special responsibilities involving portfolio management to the money market fund's investment adviser, the money market fund's board of directors, as a particular responsibility within the overall duty of care owed to its shareholders, must establish written procedures reasonably designed, taking into account current market conditions and the money market fund's investment objectives, to assure to the extent reasonably practicable that the money market fund's price per share as computed for the purpose of distribution, redemption and repurchase, rounded to the nearest one percent, will not deviate from the single price established by the board of directors.

(3) *Ongoing Review of Credit Risks.* The written procedures must require the adviser to provide ongoing review of whether each security (other than a government security) continues to present minimal credit risks. The review must:

(i) Include an assessment of each security's credit quality, including the capacity of the issuer or guarantor (including conditional demand feature provider, when applicable) to meet its financial obligations; and

(ii) Be based on, among other things, financial data of the issuer of the portfolio security or provider of the guarantee or demand feature, as the case may be, and in the case of a security subject to a conditional demand feature, the issuer of the security whose financial condition must be monitored under paragraph (d)(2)(iii) of this section, whether such data is publicly available or provided under the terms of the security's governing documents.

(4) *Securities subject to demand features or guarantees.* In the case of a security subject to one or more demand features or guarantees that the fund's board of directors has determined that the fund is not relying on to determine the quality (pursuant to paragraph (d)(2) of this section), maturity (pursuant to paragraph (i) of this section) or liquidity (pursuant to paragraph (d)(4) of this section) of the security subject to the demand feature or guarantee, written

§ 270.2a–7

procedures must require periodic evaluation of such determination.

(5) *Adjustable rate securities without demand features.* In the case of a variable rate or floating rate security that is not subject to a demand feature and for which maturity is determined pursuant to paragraph (i)(1), (i)(2) or (i)(4) of this section, written procedures shall require periodic review of whether the interest rate formula, upon readjustment of its interest rate, can reasonably be expected to cause the security to have a market value that approximates its amortized cost value.

(6) *Ten percent obligors of asset-backed securities.* In the case of an asset-backed security, written procedures must require the fund to periodically determine the number of ten percent obligors (as that term is used in paragraph (d)(3)(ii)(D) of this section) deemed to be the issuers of all or a portion of the asset-backed security for purposes of paragraph (d)(3)(ii)(D) of this section; provided, however, written procedures need not require periodic determinations with respect to any asset-backed security that a fund's board of directors has determined, at the time of acquisition, will not have, or is unlikely to have, ten percent obligors that are deemed to be issuers of all or a portion of that asset-backed security for purposes of paragraph (d)(3)(ii)(D) of this section, and maintains a record of this determination.

(7) *Asset-backed securities not subject to guarantees.* In the case of an asset-backed security for which the fund's board of directors has determined that the fund is not relying on the sponsor's financial strength or its ability or willingness to provide liquidity, credit or other support in connection with the asset-backed security to determine the quality (pursuant to paragraph (d)(2) of this section) or liquidity (pursuant to paragraph (d)(4) of this section) of the asset-backed security, written procedures must require periodic evaluation of such determination.

(8) *Stress Testing.* Written procedures must provide for:

(i) *General.* The periodic stress testing, at such intervals as the board of directors determines appropriate and reasonable in light of current market conditions, of the money market fund's ability to have invested at least ten percent of its total assets in weekly liquid assets, and the fund's ability to minimize principal volatility (and, in the case of a money market fund using the amortized cost method of valuation or penny rounding method of pricing as provided in paragraph (c)(1) of this section, the fund's ability to maintain the stable price per share established by the board of directors for the purpose of distribution, redemption and repurchase), based upon specified hypothetical events that include, but are not limited to:

(A) Increases in the general level of short-term interest rates, in combination with various levels of an increase in shareholder redemptions;

(B) An event indicating or evidencing credit deterioration, such as a downgrade or default of particular portfolio security positions, each representing various portions of the fund's portfolio (with varying assumptions about the resulting loss in the value of the security), in combination with various levels of an increase in shareholder redemptions;

(C) A widening of spreads compared to the indexes to which portfolio securities are tied in various sectors in the fund's portfolio (in which a sector is a logically related subset of portfolio securities, such as securities of issuers in similar or related industries or geographic region or securities of a similar security type), in combination with various levels of an increase in shareholder redemptions; and

(D) Any additional combinations of events that the adviser deems relevant.

(ii) A report on the results of such testing to be provided to the board of directors at its next regularly scheduled meeting (or sooner, if appropriate in light of the results), which report must include:

(A) The date(s) on which the testing was performed and an assessment of the money market fund's ability to have invested at least ten percent of its total assets in weekly liquid assets and to minimize principal volatility (and, in the case of a money market fund using the amortized cost method of valuation or penny rounding method of pricing as provided in paragraph (c)(1) of this section to maintain the stable

Securities and Exchange Commission §270.2a-7

price per share established by the board of directors); and

(B) An assessment by the fund's adviser of the fund's ability to withstand the events (and concurrent occurrences of those events) that are reasonably likely to occur within the following year, including such information as may reasonably be necessary for the board of directors to evaluate the stress testing conducted by the adviser and the results of the testing. The fund adviser must include a summary of the significant assumptions made when performing the stress tests.

(h) *Recordkeeping and reporting*—(1) *Written procedures.* For a period of not less than six years following the replacement of existing procedures with new procedures (the first two years in an easily accessible place), a written copy of the procedures (and any modifications thereto) described in this section must be maintained and preserved.

(2) *Board considerations and actions.* For a period of not less than six years (the first two years in an easily accessible place) a written record must be maintained and preserved of the board of directors' considerations and actions taken in connection with the discharge of its responsibilities, as set forth in this section, to be included in the minutes of the board of directors' meetings.

(3) *Credit risk analysis.* For a period of not less than three years from the date that the credit risks of a portfolio security were most recently reviewed, a written record must be maintained and preserved in an easily accessible place of the determination that a portfolio security is an eligible security, including the determination that it presents minimal credit risks at the time the fund acquires the security, or at such later times (or upon such events) that the board of directors determines that the investment adviser must reassess whether the security presents minimal credit risks.

(4) *Determinations with respect to adjustable rate securities.* For a period of not less than three years from the date when the assessment was most recently made, a written record must be preserved and maintained, in an easily accessible place, of the determination required by paragraph (g)(5) of this section (that a variable rate or floating rate security that is not subject to a demand feature and for which maturity is determined pursuant to paragraph (i)(1), (i)(2) or (i)(4) of this section can reasonably be expected, upon readjustment of its interest rate at all times during the life of the instrument, to have a market value that approximates its amortized cost).

(5) *Determinations with respect to asset-backed securities.* For a period of not less than three years from the date when the determination was most recently made, a written record must be preserved and maintained, in an easily accessible place, of the determinations required by paragraph (g)(6) of this section (the number of ten percent obligors (as that term is used in paragraph (d)(3)(ii)(D) of this section) deemed to be the issuers of all or a portion of the asset-backed security for purposes of paragraph (d)(3)(ii)(D) of this section). The written record must include:

(i) The identities of the ten percent obligors (as that term is used in paragraph (d)(3)(ii)(D) of this section), the percentage of the qualifying assets constituted by the securities of each ten percent obligor and the percentage of the fund's total assets that are invested in securities of each ten percent obligor; and

(ii) Any determination that an asset-backed security will not have, or is unlikely to have, ten percent obligors deemed to be issuers of all or a portion of that asset-backed security for purposes of paragraph (d)(3)(ii)(D) of this section.

(6) *Evaluations with respect to asset-backed securities not subject to guarantees.* For a period of not less than three years from the date when the evaluation was most recently made, a written record must be preserved and maintained, in an easily accessible place, of the evaluation required by paragraph (g)(7) of this section (regarding asset-backed securities not subject to guarantees).

(7) *Evaluations with respect to securities subject to demand features or guarantees.* For a period of not less than three years from the date when the evaluation was most recently made, a written record must be preserved and maintained, in an easily accessible place, of

the evaluation required by paragraph (g)(4) of this section (regarding securities subject to one or more demand features or guarantees).

(8) *Reports with respect to stress testing.* For a period of not less than six years (the first two years in an easily accessible place), a written copy of the report required under paragraph (g)(8)(ii) of this section must be maintained and preserved.

(9) *Inspection of records.* The documents preserved pursuant to paragraph (h) of this section are subject to inspection by the Commission in accordance with section 31(b) of the Act (15 U.S.C. 80a–30(b)) as if such documents were records required to be maintained pursuant to rules adopted under section 31(a) of the Act (15 U.S.C. 80a–30(a)).

(10) *Web site disclosure of portfolio holdings and other fund information.* The money market fund must post prominently on its Web site the following information:

(i) For a period of not less than six months, beginning no later than the fifth business day of the month, a schedule of its investments, as of the last business day or subsequent calendar day of the preceding month, that includes the following information:

(A) With respect to the money market fund and each class of redeemable shares thereof:

(*1*) The WAM; and

(*2*) The WAL.

(B) With respect to each security held by the money market fund:

(*1*) Name of the issuer;

(*2*) Category of investment (indicate the category that identifies the instrument from among the following: U.S. Treasury Debt; U.S. Government Agency Debt; Non-U.S. Sovereign, Sub-Sovereign and Supra-National debt; Certificate of Deposit; Non-Negotiable Time Deposit; Variable Rate Demand Note; Other Municipal Security; Asset Backed Commercial Paper; Other Asset Backed Securities; U.S. Treasury Repurchase Agreement, if collateralized only by U.S. Treasuries (including Strips) and cash; U.S. Government Agency Repurchase Agreement, collateralized only by U.S. Government Agency securities, U.S. Treasuries, and cash; Other Repurchase Agreement, if any collateral falls outside Treasury, Government Agency and cash; Insurance Company Funding Agreement; Investment Company; Financial Company Commercial Paper; and Non-Financial Company Commercial Paper. If Other Instrument, include a brief description);

(*3*) CUSIP number (if any);

(*4*) Principal amount;

(*5*) The maturity date determined by taking into account the maturity shortening provisions in paragraph (i) of this section (*i.e.*, the maturity date used to calculate WAM under paragraph (d)(1)(ii) of this section);

(*6*) The maturity date determined without reference to the exceptions in paragraph (i) of this section regarding interest rate readjustments (*i.e.*, the maturity used to calculate WAL under paragraph (d)(1)(iii) of this section);

(*7*) Coupon or yield; and

(*8*) Value.

(ii) A schedule, chart, graph, or other depiction, which must be updated each business day as of the end of the preceding business day, showing, as of the end of each business day during the preceding six months:

(A) The percentage of the money market fund's total assets invested in daily liquid assets;

(B) The percentage of the money market fund's total assets invested in weekly liquid assets; and

(C) The money market fund's net inflows or outflows.

(iii) A schedule, chart, graph, or other depiction showing the money market fund's net asset value per share (which the fund must calculate based on current market factors before applying the amortized cost or penny-rounding method, if used), rounded to the fourth decimal place in the case of funds with a $1.000 share price or an equivalent level of accuracy for funds with a different share price (e.g., $10.00 per share), as of the end of each business day during the preceding six months, which must be updated each business day as of the end of the preceding business day.

(iv) A link to a Web site of the Securities and Exchange Commission where a user may obtain the most recent 12 months of publicly available information filed by the money market fund pursuant to §270.30b1–7.

Securities and Exchange Commission § 270.2a-7

(v) For a period of not less than one year, beginning no later than the same business day on which the money market fund files an initial report on Form N–CR (§ 274.222 of this chapter) in response to the occurrence of any event specified in Parts C, E, F, or G of Form N–CR, the same information that the money market fund is required to report to the Commission on Part C (Items C.1, C.2, C.3, C.4, C.5, C.6, and C.7), Part E (Items E.1, E.2, E.3, and E.4), Part F (Items F.1 and F.2), or Part G of Form N–CR concerning such event, along with the following statement: "The Fund was required to disclose additional information about this event [or "these events," as appropriate] on Form N–CR and to file this form with the Securities and Exchange Commission. Any Form N–CR filing submitted by the Fund is available on the EDGAR Database on the Securities and Exchange Commission's Internet site at *http://www.sec.gov.*"

(11) *Processing of transactions.* A government money market fund and a retail money market fund (or its transfer agent) must have the capacity to redeem and sell securities issued by the fund at a price based on the current net asset value per share pursuant to § 270.22c–1. Such capacity must include the ability to redeem and sell securities at prices that do not correspond to a stable price per share.

(i) *Maturity of portfolio securities.* For purposes of this section, the maturity of a portfolio security shall be deemed to be the period remaining (calculated from the trade date or such other date on which the fund's interest in the security is subject to market action) until the date on which, in accordance with the terms of the security, the principal amount must unconditionally be paid, or in the case of a security called for redemption, the date on which the redemption payment must be made, except as provided in paragraphs (i)(1) through (i)(8) of this section:

(1) *Adjustable rate government securities.* A government security that is a variable rate security where the variable rate of interest is readjusted no less frequently than every 397 calendar days shall be deemed to have a maturity equal to the period remaining until the next readjustment of the interest rate. A government security that is a floating rate security shall be deemed to have a remaining maturity of one day.

(2) *Short-term variable rate securities.* A variable rate security, the principal amount of which, in accordance with the terms of the security, must unconditionally be paid in 397 calendar days or less shall be deemed to have a maturity equal to the earlier of the period remaining until the next readjustment of the interest rate or the period remaining until the principal amount can be recovered through demand.

(3) *Long-term variable rate securities.* A variable rate security, the principal amount of which is scheduled to be paid in more than 397 calendar days, that is subject to a demand feature, shall be deemed to have a maturity equal to the longer of the period remaining until the next readjustment of the interest rate or the period remaining until the principal amount can be recovered through demand.

(4) *Short-term floating rate securities.* A floating rate security, the principal amount of which, in accordance with the terms of the security, must unconditionally be paid in 397 calendar days or less shall be deemed to have a maturity of one day, except for purposes of determining WAL under paragraph (d)(1)(iii) of this section, in which case it shall be deemed to have a maturity equal to the period remaining until the principal amount can be recovered through demand.

(5) *Long-term floating rate securities.* A floating rate security, the principal amount of which is scheduled to be paid in more than 397 calendar days, that is subject to a demand feature, shall be deemed to have a maturity equal to the period remaining until the principal amount can be recovered through demand.

(6) *Repurchase agreements.* A repurchase agreement shall be deemed to have a maturity equal to the period remaining until the date on which the repurchase of the underlying securities is scheduled to occur, or, where the agreement is subject to demand, the notice period applicable to a demand for the repurchase of the securities.

§ 270.2a19–2

(7) *Portfolio lending agreements.* A portfolio lending agreement shall be treated as having a maturity equal to the period remaining until the date on which the loaned securities are scheduled to be returned, or where the agreement is subject to demand, the notice period applicable to a demand for the return of the loaned securities.

(8) *Money market fund securities.* An investment in a money market fund shall be treated as having a maturity equal to the period of time within which the acquired money market fund is required to make payment upon redemption, unless the acquired money market fund has agreed in writing to provide redemption proceeds to the investing money market fund within a shorter time period, in which case the maturity of such investment shall be deemed to be the shorter period.

(j) *Delegation.* The money market fund's board of directors may delegate to the fund's investment adviser or officers the responsibility to make any determination required to be made by the board of directors under this section other than the determinations required by paragraphs (c)(1) (board findings), (c)(2)(i) and (ii) (determinations related to liquidity fees and temporary suspensions of redemptions), (f)(1) (adverse events), (g)(1) and (2) (amortized cost and penny rounding procedures), and (g)(8) (stress testing procedures) of this section.

(1) *Written guidelines.* The board of directors must establish and periodically review written guidelines (including guidelines for determining whether securities present minimal credit risks as required in paragraphs (d)(2) and (g)(3) of this section) and procedures under which the delegate makes such determinations.

(2) *Oversight.* The board of directors must take any measures reasonably necessary (through periodic reviews of fund investments and the delegate's procedures in connection with investment decisions and prompt review of the adviser's actions in the event of the default of a security or event of insolvency with respect to the issuer of the security or any guarantee or demand feature to which it is subject that requires notification of the Commission under paragraph (f)(2) of this section by reference to Form N–CR (§ 274.222 of this chapter)) to assure that the guidelines and procedures are being followed.

[79 FR 47958, Aug. 14, 2014, as amended at 80 FR 58153, Sept. 25, 2015]

§ 270.2a19–2 Investment company general partners not deemed interested persons.

PRELIMINARY NOTE TO § 270.2a19–2: This § 270.2a19–2 conditionally excepts from the definition of interested person in section 2(a)(19) (15 U.S.C. 80a–2(a)(19)) general partners of investment companies organized in limited partnership form. Compliance with the conditions of this § 270.2a19–2 does not relieve an investment company of any other requirement of this Act, or except a general partner that is an interested person by virtue of any other provision.

(a) *Director General Partners Not Deemed Interested Persons.* A general partner serving as a director of a limited partnership investment company shall not be deemed to be an interested person of such company, or of any investment adviser of, or principal underwriter for, such company, solely by reason of being a partner of the limited partnership investment company, or a copartner in the limited partnership investment company with any investment adviser of, or principal underwriter for, the company, *provided* that the Limited Partnership Agreement contains in substance the following:

(1) Only general partners who are natural persons shall serve as, and perform the functions of, directors of the limited partnership investment company, except that any general partner may act as provided in paragraph (a)(2)(iii) of this section.

(2) A general partner shall not have the authority to act individually on behalf of, or to bind, the Limited Partnership Investment Company, except:

(i) In such person's capacity as investment adviser, principal underwriter, or administrator;

(ii) Within the scope of such person's authority as delegated by the board of directors; or

(iii) In the event that no director of the company remains, to the extent necessary to continue the Limited Partnership Investment Company, for such limited periods as are permitted under the Act to fill director vacancies.

Securities and Exchange Commission

§ 270.2a-46

(3) Limited partners shall have all of the rights afforded shareholders under the Act. If a limited partnership interest is transferred in a manner that is effective under the Partnership Agreement, the transferee shall have all of the rights afforded shareholders under the Act.

(4) A general partner shall not withdraw from the Limited Partnership Investment Company or reduce its Federal Tax Status Contribution without giving at least one year's prior written notice to the Limited Partnership Investment Company, if such withdrawal or reduction is likely to cause the company to lose its partnership tax classification. This paragraph (a)(4) shall not apply to an investment adviser general partner if the company terminates its advisory agreement with such general partner.

(b) *Definitions.* (1) "Federal Tax Status Contribution" shall mean the interest (including limited partnership interest) in each material item of partnership income, gain, loss, deduction, or credit, and other contributions, required to be held or made by general partners, pursuant to section 4 of Internal Revenue Service Revenue Procedure 89-12, or any successor provisions thereto.

(2) "Limited Partnership Investment Company" shall mean a registered management company or a business development company that is organized as a limited partnership under state law.

(3) "Partnership Agreement" shall mean the agreement of the partners of the Limited Partnership Investment Company as to the affairs of the limited partnership and the conduct of its business.

[58 FR 45838, Aug. 31, 1993; 58 FR 64353, Dec. 6, 1993; 59 FR 15501, Apr. 1, 1994]

§ 270.2a19-3 Certain investment company directors not considered interested persons because of ownership of index fund securities.

If a director of a registered investment company ("Fund") owns shares of a registered investment company (including the Fund) with an investment objective to replicate the performance of one or more broad-based securities indices ("Index Fund"), ownership of the Index Fund shares will not cause the director to be considered an "interested person" of the Fund or of the Fund's investment adviser or principal underwriter (as defined by section 2(a)(19)(A)(iii) and (B)(iii) of the Act (15 U.S.C. 80a–2(a)(19)(A)(iii) and (B)(iii)).

[66 FR 3758, Jan. 16, 2001]

§ 270.2a41-1 Valuation of standby commitments by registered investment companies.

(a) A standby commitment means a right to sell a specified underlying security or securities within a specified period of time and at an exercise price equal to the amortized cost of the underlying security or securities plus accrued interest, if any, at the time of exercise, that may be sold, transferred or assigned only with the underlying security or securities. A standby commitment entitles the holder to receive same day settlement, and will be considered to be from the party to whom the investment company will look for payment of the exercise price. A standby commitment may be assigned a fair value of zero, Provided, That:

(1) The standby commitment is not used to affect the company's valuation of the security or securities underlying the standby commitment; and

(2) Any consideration paid by the company for the standby commitment, whether paid in cash or by paying a premium for the underlying security or securities, is accounted for by the company as unrealized depreciation until the standby commitment is exercised or expires.

(b) [Reserved]

[51 FR 9779, Mar. 21, 1986, as amended at 56 FR 8128, Feb. 27, 1991; 61 FR 13982, Mar. 28, 1996; 62 FR 64986, Dec. 9, 1997]

§ 270.2a-46 Certain issuers as eligible portfolio companies.

The term *eligible portfolio company* shall include any issuer that meets the requirements set forth in paragraphs (A) and (B) of section 2(a)(46) of the Act (15 U.S.C. 80a–2(a)(46)(A) and (B)) and that:

(a) Does not have any class of securities listed on a national securities exchange; or

(b) Has a class of securities listed on a national securities exchange, but has

§ 270.2a51–1

an aggregate market value of outstanding voting and non-voting common equity of less than $250 million. For purposes of this paragraph:

(1) The *aggregate market value* of an issuer's outstanding voting and non-voting common equity shall be computed by use of the price at which the common equity was last sold, or the average of the bid and asked prices of such common equity, in the principal market for such common equity as of a date within 60 days prior to the date of acquisition of its securities by a business development company; and

(2) *Common equity* has the same meaning as in 17 CFR 230.405.

[73 FR 29051, May 20, 2008]

§ 270.2a51–1 Definition of investments for purposes of section 2(a)(51) (definition of "qualified purchaser"); certain calculations.

(a) *Definitions.* As used in this section:

(1) The term *Commodity Interests* means commodity futures contracts, options on commodity futures contracts, and options on physical commodities traded on or subject to the rules of:

(i) Any contract market designated for trading such transactions under the Commodity Exchange Act and the rules thereunder; or

(ii) Any board of trade or exchange outside the United States, as contemplated in Part 30 of the rules under the Commodity Exchange Act [17 CFR 30.1 through 30.11].

(2) The term *Family Company* means a company described in paragraph (A)(ii) of section 2(a)(51) of the Act [15 U.S.C. 80a–2(a)(51)].

(3) The term *Investment Vehicle* means an investment company, a company that would be an investment company but for the exclusions provided by sections 3(c)(1) through 3(c)(9) of the Act [15 U.S.C. 80a–3(c)(1) through 3(c)(9)] or the exemptions provided by §§ 270.3a–6 or 270.3a–7, or a commodity pool.

(4) The term *Investments* has the meaning set forth in paragraph (b) of this section.

(5) The term *Physical Commodity* means any physical commodity with respect to which a Commodity Interest is traded on a market specified in paragraph (a)(1) of this section.

(6) The term *Prospective Qualified Purchaser* means a person seeking to purchase a security of a Section 3(c)(7) Company.

(7) The term *Public Company* means a company that:

(i) Files reports pursuant to section 13 or 15(d) of the Securities Exchange Act of 1934 [15 U.S.C. 78m or 78o(d)]; or

(ii) Has a class of securities that are listed on a "designated offshore securities market" as such term is defined by Regulation S under the Securities Act of 1933 [17 CFR 230.901 through 230.904].

(8) The term *Related Person* means a person who is related to a Prospective Qualified Purchaser as a sibling, spouse or former spouse, or is a direct lineal descendant or ancestor by birth or adoption of the Prospective Qualified Purchaser, or is a spouse of such descendant or ancestor, *provided that*, in the case of a Family Company, a Related Person includes any owner of the Family Company and any person who is a Related Person of such owner.

(9) The term *Relying Person* means a Section 3(c)(7) Company or a person acting on its behalf.

(10) The term *Section 3(c)(7) Company* means a company that would be an investment company but for the exclusion provided by section 3(c)(7) of the Act [15 U.S.C. 80a–3(c)(7)].

(b) *Types of Investments.* For purposes of section 2(a)(51) of the Act [15 U.S.C. 80a–2(a)(51)], the term *Investments* means:

(1) Securities (as defined by section 2(a)(1) of the Securities Act of 1933 [15 U.S.C. 77b(a)(1)]), other than securities of an issuer that controls, is controlled by, or is under common control with, the Prospective Qualified Purchaser that owns such securities, unless the issuer of such securities is:

(i) An Investment Vehicle;

(ii) A Public Company; or

(iii) A company with shareholders' equity of not less than $50 million (determined in accordance with generally accepted accounting principles) as reflected on the company's most recent financial statements, *provided that* such financial statements present the information as of a date within 16 months

Securities and Exchange Commission § 270.2a51–1

preceding the date on which the Prospective Qualified Purchaser acquires the securities of a Section 3(c)(7) Company;

(2) Real estate held for investment purposes;

(3) Commodity Interests held for investment purposes;

(4) Physical Commodities held for investment purposes;

(5) To the extent not securities, financial contracts (as such term is defined in section 3(c)(2)(B)(ii) of the Act [15 U.S.C. 80a–3(c)(2)(B)(ii)] entered into for investment purposes;

(6) In the case of a Prospective Qualified Purchaser that is a Section 3(c)(7) Company, a company that would be an investment company but for the exclusion provided by section 3(c)(1) of the Act [15 U.S.C. 80a–3(c)(1)], or a commodity pool, any amounts payable to such Prospective Qualified Purchaser pursuant to a firm agreement or similar binding commitment pursuant to which a person has agreed to acquire an interest in, or make capital contributions to, the Prospective Qualified Purchaser upon the demand of the Prospective Qualified Purchaser; and

(7) Cash and cash equivalents (including foreign currencies) held for investment purposes. For purposes of this section, cash and cash equivalents include:

(i) Bank deposits, certificates of deposit, bankers acceptances and similar bank instruments held for investment purposes; and

(ii) The net cash surrender value of an insurance policy.

(c) *Investment Purposes.* For purposes of this section:

(1) Real estate shall not be considered to be held for investment purposes by a Prospective Qualified Purchaser if it is used by the Prospective Qualified Purchaser or a Related Person for personal purposes or as a place of business, or in connection with the conduct of the trade or business of the Prospective Qualified Purchaser or a Related Person, *provided that* real estate owned by a Prospective Qualified Purchaser who is engaged primarily in the business of investing, trading or developing real estate in connection with such business may de deemed to be held for investment purposes. Residential real estate shall not be deemed to be used for personal purposes if deductions with respect to such real estate are not disallowed by section 280A of the Internal Revenue Code [26 U.S.C. 280A].

(2) A Commodity Interest or Physical Commodity owned, or a financial contract entered into, by the Prospective Qualified Purchaser who is engaged primarily in the business of investing, reinvesting, or trading in Commodity Interests, Physical Commodities or financial contracts in connection with such business may be deemed to be held for investment purposes.

(d) *Valuation.* For purposes of determining whether a Prospective Qualified Purchaser is a qualified purchaser, the aggregate amount of Investments owned and invested on a discretionary basis by the Prospective Qualified Purchaser shall be the Investments' fair market value on the most recent practicable date or their cost, *provided that:*

(1) In the case of Commodity Interests, the amount of Investments shall be the value of the initial margin or option premium deposited in connection with such Commodity Interests; and

(2) In each case, there shall be deducted from the amount of Investments owned by the Prospective Qualified Purchaser the amounts specified in paragraphs (e) and (f) of this section, as applicable.

(e) *Deductions.* In determining whether any person is a qualified purchaser there shall be deducted from the amount of such person's Investments the amount of any outstanding indebtedness incurred to acquire or for the purpose of acquiring the Investments owned by such person.

(f) *Deductions: Family Companies.* In determining whether a Family Company is a qualified purchaser, in addition to the amounts specified in paragraph (e) of this section, there shall be deducted from the value of such Family Company's Investments any outstanding indebtedness incurred by an owner of the Family Company to acquire such Investments.

(g) *Special rules for certain Prospective Qualified Purchasers*—1) *Qualified institutional buyers.* Any Prospective Qualified Purchaser who is, or who a Relying

§ 270.2a51–2

Person reasonably believes is, a qualified institutional buyer as defined in paragraph (a) of § 230.144A of this chapter, acting for its own account, the account of another qualified institutional buyer, or the account of a qualified purchaser, shall be deemed to be a qualified purchaser *provided:*

(i) That a dealer described in paragraph (a)(1)(ii) of § 230.144A of this chapter shall own and invest on a discretionary basis at least $25 million in securities of issuers that are not affiliated persons of the dealer; and

(ii) That a plan referred to in paragraph (a)(1)(i)(D) or (a)(1)(i)(E) of § 230.144A of this chapter, or a trust fund referred to in paragraph (a)(1)(i)(F) of § 230.144A of this chapter that holds the assets of such a plan, will not be deemed to be acting for its own account if investment decisions with respect to the plan are made by the beneficiaries of the plan, except with respect to investment decisions made solely by the fiduciary, trustee or sponsor of such plan.

(2) *Joint Investments.* In determining whether a natural person is a qualified purchaser, there may be included in the amount of such person's Investments any Investments held jointly with such person's spouse, or Investments in which such person shares with such person's spouse a community property or similar shared ownership interest. In determining whether spouses who are making a joint investment in a Section 3(c)(7) Company are qualified purchasers, there may be included in the amount of each spouse's Investments any Investments owned by the other spouse (whether or not such Investments are held jointly). In each case, there shall be deducted from the amount of any such Investments the amounts specified in paragraph (e) of this section incurred by each spouse.

(3) *Investments by Subsidiaries.* For purposes of determining the amount of Investments owned by a company under section 2(a)(51)(A)(iv) of the Act [15 U.S.C. 80a–2(a)(51)(A)(iv)], there may be included Investments owned by majority-owned subsidiaries of the company and Investments owned by a company ("Parent Company") of which the company is a majority-owned subsidiary, or by a majority-owned subsidiary of the company and other majority-owned subsidiaries of the Parent Company.

(4) *Certain Retirement Plans and Trusts.* In determining whether a natural person is a qualified purchaser, there may be included in the amount of such person's Investments any Investments held in an individual retirement account or similar account the Investments of which are directed by and held for the benefit of such person.

(h) *Reasonable Belief.* The term "qualified purchaser" as used in section 3(c)(7) of the Act [15 U.S.C. 80a–3(c)(7)] means any person that meets the definition of qualified purchaser in section 2(a)(51)(A) of the Act [15 U.S.C. 80a–2(a)(51)(A)]) and the rules thereunder, or that a Relying Person reasonably believes meets such definition.

[62 FR 17526, Apr. 9, 1997]

§ 270.2a51–2 **Definitions of beneficial owner for certain purposes under sections 2(a)(51) and 3(c)(7) and determining indirect ownership interests.**

(a) *Beneficial ownership: General.* Except as set forth in this section, for purposes of sections 2(a)(51)(C) and 3(c)(7)(B)(ii) of the Act [15 U.S.C. 80a–2(a)(51)(C) and –3(c)(7)(B)(ii)], the beneficial owners of securities of an excepted investment company (as defined in section 2(a)(51)(C) of the Act [15 U.S.C. 80a–2(a)(51)(C)]) shall be determined in accordance with section 3(c)(1) of the Act [15 U.S.C. 80a–3(c)(1)].

(b) *Beneficial ownership: Grandfather provision.* For purposes of section 3(c)(7)(B)(ii) of the Act [15 U.S.C. 80a–3(c)(7)(B)(ii)], securities of an issuer beneficially owned by a company (without giving effect to section 3(c)(1)(A) of the Act [15 U.S.C. 80a–3(c)(1)(A)]) ("owning company") shall be deemed to be beneficially owned by one person unless:

(1) The owning company is an investment company or an excepted investment company;

(2) The owning company, directly or indirectly, controls, is controlled by, or is under common control with, the issuer; and

(3) On October 11, 1996, under section 3(c)(1)(A) of the Act as then in effect, the voting securities of the issuer were

Securities and Exchange Commission

§ 270.2a51-3

deemed to be beneficially owned by the holders of the owning company's outstanding securities (other than short-term paper), in which case, such holders shall be deemed to be beneficial owners of the issuer's outstanding voting securities.

(c) *Beneficial ownership: Consent provision.* For purposes of section 2(a)(51)(C) of the Act [15 U.S.C. 80a-2(a)(51)(C)], securities of an excepted investment company beneficially owned by a company (without giving effect to section 3(c)(1)(A) of the Act [15 U.S.C. 80a-3(c)(1)(A)]) ("owning company") shall be deemed to be beneficially owned by one person unless:

(1) The owning company is an excepted investment company;

(2) The owning company directly or indirectly controls, is controlled by, or is under common control with, the excepted investment company or the company with respect to which the excepted investment company is, or will be, a qualified purchaser; and

(3) On April 30, 1996, under section 3(c)(1)(A) of the Act as then in effect, the voting securities of the excepted investment company were deemed to be beneficially owned by the holders of the owning company's outstanding securities (other than short-term paper), in which case the holders of such excepted company's securities shall be deemed to be beneficial owners of the excepted investment company's outstanding voting securities.

(d) *Indirect ownership: Consent provision.* For purposes of section 2(a)(51)(C) of the Act [15 U.S.C. 80a-2(a)(51)(C)], an excepted investment company shall not be deemed to indirectly own the securities of an excepted investment company seeking a consent to be treated as a qualified purchaser ("qualified purchaser company") unless such excepted investment company, directly or indirectly, controls, is controlled by, or is under common control with, the qualified purchaser company or a company with respect to which the qualified purchaser company is or will be a qualified purchaser.

(e) *Required consent: Consent provision.* For purposes of section 2(a)(51)(C) of the Act [15 U.S.C. 80a-2(a)(51)(C)], the consent of the beneficial owners of an excepted investment company ("owning company") that beneficially owns securities of an excepted investment company that is seeking the consents required by section 2(a)(51)(C) ("consent company") shall not be required unless the owning company directly or indirectly controls, is controlled by, or is under common control with, the consent company or the company with respect to which the consent company is, or will be, a qualified purchaser.

NOTES TO § 270.2a51-2: 1. On both April 30, 1996 and October 11, 1996, section 3(c)(1)(A) of the Act as then in effect provided that: (A) Beneficial ownership by a company shall be deemed to be beneficial ownership by one person, except that, if the company owns 10 per centum or more of the outstanding voting securities of the issuer, the beneficial ownership shall be deemed to be that of the holders of such company's outstanding securities (other than short-term paper) unless, as of the date of the most recent acquisition by such company of securities of that issuer, the value of all securities owned by such company of all issuers which are or would, but for the exception set forth in this subparagraph, be excluded from the definition of investment company solely by this paragraph, does not exceed 10 per centum of the value of the company's total assets. Such issuer nonetheless is deemed to be an investment company for purposes of section 12(d)(1).

2. Issuers seeking the consent required by section 2(a)(51)(C) of the Act should note that section 2(a)(51)(C) requires an issuer to obtain the consent of the beneficial owners of its securities and the beneficial owners of securities of any "excepted investment company" that directly or indirectly owns the securities of the issuer. Except as set forth in paragraphs (d) (with respect to indirect owners) and (e) (with respect to direct owners) of this section, nothing in this section is designed to limit this consent requirement.

[62 FR 17528, Apr. 9, 1997]

§ 270.2a51-3 Certain companies as qualified purchasers.

(a) For purposes of section 2(a)(51)(A) (ii) and (iv) of the Act [15 U.S.C. 80a-2(a)(51)(A) (ii) and (iv)], a company shall not be deemed to be a qualified purchaser if it was formed for the specific purpose of acquiring the securities offered by a company excluded from the definition of investment company by section 3(c)(7) of the Act [15 U.S.C. 80a-3(c)(7)] unless each beneficial owner of the company's securities is a qualified purchaser.

§ 270.3a–1

(b) For purposes of section 2(a)(51) of the Act [15 U.S.C. 80a–2(a)(51)], a company may be deemed to be a qualified purchaser if each beneficial owner of the company's securities is a qualified purchaser.

[62 FR 17528, Apr. 9, 1997]

§ 270.3a–1 Certain prima facie investment companies.

Notwithstanding section 3(a)(1)(C) of the Act (15 U.S.C. 80a–3(a)(1)(c)), an issuer will be deemed not to be an investment company under the Act; *Provided,* That:

(a) No more than 45 percent of the value (as defined in section 2(a)(41) of the Act) of such issuer's total assets (exclusive of Government securities and cash items) consists of, and no more than 45 percent of such issuer's net income after taxes (for the last four fiscal quarters combined) is derived from, securites other than:

(1) Government securities;

(2) Securities issued by employees' securities companies;

(3) Securities issued by majority-owned subsidiaries of the issuer (other than subsidiaries relying on the exclusion from the definition of investment company in section 3(b)(3) or (c)(1) of the Act) which are not investment companies; and

(4) Securities issued by companies:

(i) Which are controlled primarily by such issuer;

(ii) Through which such issuer engages in a business other than that of investing, reinvesting, owning, holding or trading in securities; and

(iii) Which are not investment companies;

(b) The issuer is not an investment company as defined in section 3(a)(1)(A) or 3(a)(1)(B) of the Act (15 U.S.C. 80a–3(a)(1)(A) or 80a–3(a)(1)(B)) and is not a special situation investment company; and

(c) The percentages described in paragraph (a) of this section are determined on an unconsolidated basis, except that the issuer shall consolidate its financial statements with the financial statements of any wholly-owned subsidiaries.

[46 FR 6881, Jan. 22, 1981, as amended at 67 FR 43536, June 28, 2002]

§ 270.3a–2 Transient investment companies.

(a) For purposes of sections 3(a)(1)(A) and 3(a)(1)(C) of the Act (15 U.S.C. 80a–3(a)(1)(A) and 80a–3(a)(1)(C)), an issuer is deemed not to be engaged in the business of investing, reinvesting, owning, holding or trading in securities during a period of time not to exceed one year; *Provided,* That the issuer has a *bona fide* intent to be engaged primarily, as soon as is reasonably possible (in any event by the termination of such period of time), in a business other than that of investing, reinvesting, owning, holding or trading in securities, such intent to be evidenced by:

(1) The issuer's business activities; and

(2) An appropriate resolution of the issuer's board of directors, or by an appropriate action of the person or persons performing similar functions for any issuer not having a board of directors, which resolution or action has been recorded contemporaneously in its minute books or comparable documents.

(b) For purposes of this rule, the period of time described in paragraph (a) shall commence on the earlier of:

(1) The date on which an issuer owns securities and/or cash having a value exceeding 50 percent of the value of such issuer's total assets on either a consolidated or unconsolidated basis; or

(2) The date on which an issuer owns or proposes to acquire investment securities (as defined in section 3(a) of the Act) having a value exceeding 40 per centum of the value of such issuer's total assets (exclusive of Government securities and cash items) on an unconsolidated basis.

(c) No issuer may rely on this section more frequently than once during any three-year period.

[46 FR 6883, Jan. 22, 1981, as amended at 67 FR 43536, June 28, 2002]

§ 270.3a–3 Certain investment companies owned by companies which are not investment companies.

Notwithstanding section 3(a)(1)(A) or section 3(a)(1)(C) of the Act (15 U.S.C. 80a–3(a)(1)(A) or 80a–3(a)(1)(C)), an issuer will be deemed not to be an investment company for purposes of the Act; *Provided,* That all of the outstanding securities of the issuer (other than short-term paper, directors' qualifying shares, and debt securities owned by the Small Business Administration) are directly or indirectly owned by a company which satisfies the conditions of § 270.3a–1(a) and which is:

(a) A company that is not an investment company as defined in section 3(a) of the Act;

(b) A company that is an investment company as defined in section 3(a)(1)(C) of the Act (15 U.S.C. 80a–3(a)(1)(C)), but which is excluded from the definition of the term "investment company" by section 3(b)(1) or 3(b)(2) of the Act (15 U.S.C. 80a–3(b)(1) or 80a–3(b)(2)); or

(c) A company that is deemed not to be an investment company for purposes of the Act by rule 3a–1.

[46 FR 6884, Jan. 22, 1981, as amended at 67 FR 43536, June 28, 2002]

§ 270.3a–4 Status of investment advisory programs.

NOTE: This section is a nonexclusive safe harbor from the definition of investment company for programs that provide discretionary investment advisory services to clients. There is no registration requirement under section 5 of the Securities Act of 1933 [15 U.S.C. 77e] with respect to programs that are organized and operated in the manner described in § 270.3a–4. The section is not intended, however, to create any presumption about a program that is not organized and operated in the manner contemplated by the section.

(a) Any program under which discretionary investment advisory services are provided to clients that has the following characteristics will not be deemed to be an investment company within the meaning of the Act [15 U.S.C. 80a, *et seq.*]:

(1) Each client's account in the program is managed on the basis of the client's financial situation and investment objectives and in accordance with any reasonable restrictions imposed by the client on the management of the account.

(2)(i) At the opening of the account, the sponsor or another person designated by the sponsor obtains information from the client regarding the client's financial situation and investment objectives, and gives the client the opportunity to impose reasonable restrictions on the management of the account;

(ii) At least annually, the sponsor or another person designated by the sponsor contacts the client to determine whether there have been any changes in the client's financial situation or investment objectives, and whether the client wishes to impose any reasonable restrictions on the management of the account or reasonably modify existing restrictions;

(iii) At least quarterly, the sponsor or another person designated by the sponsor notifies the client in writing to contact the sponsor or such other person if there have been any changes in the client's financial situation or investment objectives, or if the client wishes to impose any reasonable restrictions on the management of the client's account or reasonably modify existing restrictions, and provides the client with a means through which such contact may be made; and

(iv) The sponsor and personnel of the manager of the client's account who are knowledgeable about the account and its management are reasonably available to the client for consultation.

(3) Each client has the ability to impose reasonable restrictions on the management of the client's account, including the designation of particular securities or types of securities that should not be purchased for the account, or that should be sold if held in the account; *Provided, however,* that nothing in this section requires that a client have the ability to require that particular securities or types of securities be purchased for the account.

(4) The sponsor or person designated by the sponsor provides each client with a statement, at least quarterly, containing a description of all activity in the client's account during the preceding period, including all transactions made on behalf of the account, all contributions and withdrawals made by the client, all fees and expenses charged to the account, and the value of the account at the beginning and end of the period.

§ 270.3a–5

(5) Each client retains, with respect to all securities and funds in the account, to the same extent as if the client held the securities and funds outside the program, the right to:

(i) Withdraw securities or cash;

(ii) Vote securities, or delegate the authority to vote securities to another person;

(iii) Be provided in a timely manner with a written confirmation or other notification of each securities transaction, and all other documents required by law to be provided to security holders; and

(iv) Proceed directly as a security holder against the issuer of any security in the client's account and not be obligated to join any person involved in the operation of the program, or any other client of the program, as a condition precedent to initiating such proceeding.

(b) As used in this section, the term sponsor refers to any person who receives compensation for sponsoring, organizing or administering the program, or for selecting, or providing advice to clients regarding the selection of, persons responsible for managing the client's account in the program. If a program has more than one sponsor, one person shall be designated the principal sponsor, and such person shall be considered the sponsor of the program under this section.

[62 FR 15109, Mar. 31, 1997]

§ 270.3a–5 Exemption for subsidiaries organized to finance the operations of domestic or foreign companies.

(a) A finance subsidiary will not be considered an investment company under section 3(a) of the Act (15 U.S.C. 80a–3(a)) and securities of a finance subsidiary held by the parent company or a company controlled by the parent company will not be considered "investment securities" under section 3(a)(1)(C) of the Act (15 U.S.C. 80a–3(a)(1)(C)); *Provided,* That:

(1) Any debt securities of the finance subsidiary issued to or held by the public are unconditionally guaranteed by the parent company as to the payment of principal, interest, and premium, if any (except that the guarantee may be subordinated in right of payment to other debt of the parent company);

(2) Any non-voting preferred stock of the finance subsidiary issued to or held by the public is unconditionally guaranteed by the parent company as to payment of dividends, payment of the liquidation preference in the event of liquidation, and payments to be made under a sinking fund, if a sinking fund is to be provided (except that the guarantee may be subordinated in right of payment to other debt of the parent company);

(3) The parent company's guarantee provides that in the event of a default in payment of principal, interest, premium, dividends, liquidation preference or payments made under a sinking fund on any debt securities or non-voting preferred stock issued by the finance subsidiary, the holders of those securities may institute legal proceedings directly against the parent company (or, in the case of a partnership or joint venture, against the partners or participants in the joint venture) to enforce the guarantee without first proceeding against the finance subsidiary;

(4) Any securities issued by the finance subsidiary which are convertible or exchangeable are convertible or exchangeable only for securities issued by the parent company (and, in the case of a partnership or joint venture, for securities issued by the partners or participants in the joint venture) or for debt securities or non-voting preferred stock issued by the finance subsidiary meeting the applicable requirements of paragraphs (a)(1) through (a)(3);

(5) The finance subsidiary invests in or loans to its parent company or a company controlled by its parent company at least 85% of any cash or cash equivalents raised by the finance subsidiary through an offering of its debt securities or non-voting preferred stock or through other borrowings as soon as practicable, but in no event later than six months after the finance subsidiary's receipt of such cash or cash equivalents;

(6) The finance subsidiary does not invest in, reinvest in, own, hold or trade in securities other than Government securities, securities of its parent company or a company controlled by its parent company (or in the case of a

partnership or joint venture, the securities of the partners or participants in the joint venture) or debt securities (including repurchase agreements) which are exempted from the provisions of the Securities Act of 1933 by section 3(a)(3) of that Act; and

(7) Where the parent company is a foreign bank as the term is used in rule 3a–6 (17 CFR 270.3a–6 of this chapter), the parent company may, in lieu of the guaranty required by paragraph (a)(1) or (a)(2) of this section, issue, in favor of the holders of the finance subsidiary's debt securities or non-voting preferred stock, as the case may be, an irrevocable letter of credit in an amount sufficient to fund all of the amounts required to be guaranteed by paragraphs (a)(1) and (a)(2) of this section, *provided*, that:

(i) Payment on such letter of credit shall be conditional only upon the presentation of customary documentation, and

(ii) The beneficiary of such letter of credit is not required by either the letter of credit or applicable law to institute proceedings against the finance subsidiary before enforcing its remedies under the letter of credit.

(b) For purposes of this rule,

(1) A *finance subsidiary* shall mean any corporation—

(i) All of whose securities other than debt securities or non-voting preferred stock meeting the applicable requirements of paragraphs (a)(1) through (3) or directors' qualifying shares are owned by its parent company or a company controlled by its parent company; and

(ii) The primary purpose of which is to finance the business operations of its parent company or companies controlled by its parent company;

(2) A *parent company* shall mean any corporation, partnership or joint venture:

(i) That is not considered an investment company under section 3(a) or that is excepted or exempted by order from the definition of investment company by section 3(b) or by the rules or regulations under section 3(a);

(ii) That is organized or formed under the laws of the United States or of a state or that is a foreign private issuer, or that is a foreign bank or foreign insurance company as those terms are used in rule 3a–6 (17 CFR 270.3a–6 of this chapter); and

(iii) In the case of a partnership or joint venture, each partner or participant in the joint venture meets the requirements of paragraphs (b)(2)(i) and (ii).

(3) A *company controlled by the parent company* shall mean any corporation, partnership or joint venture:

(i) That is not considered an investment company under section 3(a) or that is excepted or exempted by order from the definition of investment company by section 3(b) or by the rules or regulations under section 3(a);

(ii) That is either organized or formed under the laws of the United States or of a state or that is a foreign private issuer, or that is a foreign bank or foreign insurance company as those terms are used in rule 3a–6; and

(iii) In the case of a corporation, more than 25 percent of whose outstanding voting securities are beneficially owned directly or indirectly by the parent company; or

(iv) In the case of a partnership or joint venture, each partner or participant in the joint venture meets the requirements of paragraphs (b)(3) (i) and (ii), and the parent company has the power to exercise a controlling influence over the management or policies of the partnership or joint venture.

(4) A *foreign private issuer* shall mean any issuer which is incorporated or organized under the laws of a foreign country, but not a foreign government or political subdivision of a foreign government.

[49 FR 49446, Dec. 20, 1984, as amended at 56 FR 56299, Nov. 4, 1991; 67 FR 43536, June 28, 2002]

§ 270.3a–6 Foreign banks and foreign insurance companies.

(a) Notwithstanding section 3(a)(1)(A) or section 3(a)(1)(C) of the Act (15 U.S.C. 80a–3(a)(1)(A) or 80a–3(a)(1)(C)), a foreign bank or foreign insurance company shall not be considered an investment company for purposes of the Act.

(b) For purposes of this section:

(1)(i) *Foreign bank* means a banking institution incorporated or organized under the laws of a country other than

§ 270.3a-7

the United States, or a political subdivision of a country other than the United States, that is:

(A) Regulated as such by that country's or subdivision's government or any agency thereof;

(B) Engaged substantially in commercial banking activity; and

(C) Not operated for the purpose of evading the provisions of the Act;

(ii) The term *foreign bank* shall also include:

(A) A trust company or loan company that is:

(*1*) Organized or incorporated under the laws of Canada or a political subdivision thereof;

(*2*) Regulated as a trust company or a loan company by that country's or subdivision's government or any agency thereof; and

(*3*) Not operated for the purpose of evading the provisions of the Act; and

(B) A building society that is:

(*1*) Organized under the laws of the United Kingdom or a political subdivision thereof;

(*2*) Regulated as a building society by the country's or subdivision's government or any agency thereof; and

(*3*) Not operated for the purpose of evading the provisions of the Act.

(iii) Nothing in this section shall be construed to include within the definition of *foreign bank* a common or collective trust or other separate pool of assets organized in the form of a trust or otherwise in which interests are separately offered.

(2) *Engaged substantially in commercial banking activity* means engaged regularly in, and deriving a substantial portion of its business from, extending commercial and other types of credit, and accepting demand and other types of deposits, that are customary for commercial banks in the country in which the head office of the banking institution is located.

(3) *Foreign insurance company* means an insurance company incorporated or organized under the laws of a country other than the United States, or a political subdivision of a country other than the United States, that is:

(i) Regulated as such by that country's or subdivision's government or any agency thereof;

(ii) Engaged primarily and predominantly in:

(A) The writing of insurance agreements of the type specified in section 3(a)(8) of the Securities Act of 1933 (15 U.S.C. 77c(a)(8)), except for the substitution of supervision by foreign government insurance regulators for the regulators referred to in that section; or

(B) The reinsurance of risks on such agreements underwritten by insurance companies; and

(iii) Not operated for the purpose of evading the provisions of the Act. Nothing in this section shall be construed to include within the definition of "foreign insurance company" a separate account or other pool of assets organized in the form of a trust or otherwise in which interests are separately offered.

NOTE: Foreign banks and foreign insurance companies (and certain of their finance subsidiaries and holding companies) relying on rule 3a-6 for exemption from the Act may be required by rule 489 (17 CFR 230.489) under the Securities Act of 1933 (15 U.S.C. 77a *et seq.*) to file Form F-N with the Commission in connection with the filing of a registration statement under the Securities Act of 1933.

[56 FR 56299, Nov. 4, 1991, as amended at 67 FR 43536, June 28, 2002]

§ 270.3a-7 Issuers of asset-backed securities.

(a) Notwithstanding section 3(a) of the Act, any issuer who is engaged in the business of purchasing, or otherwise acquiring, and holding eligible assets (and in activities related or incidental thereto), and who does not issue redeemable securities will not be deemed to be an investment company; *Provided That:*

(1) The issuer issues fixed-income securities or other securities which entitle their holders to receive payments that depend primarily on the cash flow from eligible assets;

(2) Securities sold by the issuer or any underwriter thereof are fixed-income securities rated, at the time of initial sale, in one of the four highest categories assigned long-term debt or in an equivalent short-term category (within either of which there may be sub-categories or gradations indicating

Securities and Exchange Commission

§ 270.3a–7

relative standing) by at least one nationally recognized statistical rating organization that is not an affiliated person of the issuer or of any person involved in the organization or operation of the issuer, except that:

(i) Any fixed-income securities may be sold to accredited investors as defined in paragraphs (1), (2), (3), and (7) of rule 501(a) under the Securities Act of 1933 (17 CFR 230.501(a)) and any entity in which all of the equity owners come within such paragraphs; and

(ii) Any securities may be sold to qualified institutional buyers as defined in rule 144A under the Securities Act (17 CFR 230.144A) and to persons (other than any rating organization rating the issuer's securities) involved in the organization or operation of the issuer or an affiliate, as defined in rule 405 under the Securities Act (17 CFR 230.405), of such a person;

Provided, That the issuer or any underwriter thereof effecting such sale exercises reasonable care to ensure that such securities are sold and will be resold to persons specified in paragraphs (a)(2) (i) and (ii) of this section;

(3) The issuer acquires additional eligible assets, or disposes of eligible assets, only if:

(i) The assets are acquired or disposed of in accordance with the terms and conditions set forth in the agreements, indentures, or other instruments pursuant to which the issuer's securities are issued;

(ii) The acquisition or disposition of the assets does not result in a downgrading in the rating of the issuer's outstanding fixed-income securities; and

(iii) The assets are not acquired or disposed of for the primary purpose of recognizing gains or decreasing losses resulting from market value changes; and

(4) If the issuer issues any securities other than securities exempted from the Securities Act by section 3(a)(3) thereof (15 U.S.C. 77c(a)(3)), the issuer:

(i) Appoints a trustee that meets the requirements of section 26(a)(1) of the Act and that is not affiliated, as that term is defined in rule 405 under the Securities Act (17 CFR 230.405), with the issuer or with any person involved in the organization or operation of the issuer, which does not offer or provide credit or credit enhancement to the issuer, and that executes an agreement or instrument concerning the issuer's securities containing provisions to the effect set forth in section 26(a)(3) of the Act;

(ii) Takes reasonable steps to cause the trustee to have a perfected security interest or ownership interest valid against third parties in those eligible assets that principally generate the cash flow needed to pay the fixed-income security holders, provided that such assets otherwise required to be held by the trustee may be released to the extent needed at the time for the operation of the issuer; and

(iii) Takes actions necessary for the cash flows derived from eligible assets for the benefit of the holders of fixed-income securities to be deposited periodically in a segregated account that is maintained or controlled by the trustee consistent with the rating of the outstanding fixed-income securities.

(b) For purposes of this section:

(1) *Eligible assets* means financial assets, either fixed or revolving, that by their terms convert into cash within a finite time period plus any rights or other assets designed to assure the servicing or timely distribution of proceeds to security holders.

(2) *Fixed-income securities* means any securities that entitle the holder to receive:

(i) A stated principal amount; or

(ii) Interest on a principal amount (which may be a notional principal amount) calculated by reference to a fixed rate or to a standard or formula which does not reference any change in the market value or fair value of eligible assets; or

(iii) Interest on a principal amount (which may be a notional principal amount) calculated by reference to auctions among holders and prospective holders, or through remarketing of the security; or

(iv) An amount equal to specified fixed or variable portions of the interest received on the assets held by the issuer; or

(v) Any combination of amounts described in paragraphs (b)(2) (i), (ii), (iii), and (iv) of this section;

359

§ 270.3a-8

Provided, That substantially all of the payments to which the holders of such securities are entitled consist of the foregoing amounts.

[57 FR 56256, Nov. 27, 1992]

§ 270.3a-8 Certain research and development companies.

(a) Notwithstanding sections 3(a)(1)(A) and 3(a)(1)(C) of the Act (15 U.S.C. 80a-3(a)(1)(A) and 80a-3(a)(1)(C)), an issuer will be deemed not to be an investment company if:

(1) Its research and development expenses, for the last four fiscal quarters combined, are a substantial percentage of its total expense for the same period;

(2) Its net income derived from investments in securities, for the last four fiscal quarters combined, does not exceed twice the amount of its research and development expenses for the same period;

(3) Its expenses for investment advisory and management activities, investment research and custody, for the last four fiscal quarters, combined, do not exceed five percent of its total expenses for the same period;

(4) Its investments in securities are capital preservation investments, except that:

(i) No more than 10 percent of the issuer's total assets may consist of other investments, or

(ii) No more than 25 percent of the issuer's total assets may consist of other investments, provided that at least 75 percent of such other investments are investments made pursuant to a collaborative research and development arrangement;

(5) It does not hold itself out as being engaged in the business of investing, reinvesting or trading in securities, and it is not a special situation investment company;

(6) It is primarily engaged, directly, through majority-owned subsidiaries, or through companies which it controls primarily, in a business or businesses other than that of investing, reinvesting, owning, holding, or trading in securities, as evidenced by:

(i) The activities of its officers, directors and employees;

(ii) Its public representations of policies;

(iii) Its historical development; and

(iv) An appropriate resolution of its board of directors, which resolution or action has been recorded contemporaneously in its minute books or comparable documents; and

(7) Its board of directors has adopted a written investment policy with respect to the issuer's capital preservation investments.

(b) For purposes of this section:

(1) All assets shall be valued in accordance with section 2(a)(41)(A) of the Act (15 U.S.C. 80a-2(a)(41)(A));

(2) The percentages described in this section are determined on an unconsolidated basis, except that the issuer shall consolidate its financial statements with the financial statements of any wholly-owned subsidiaries;

(3) *Board of directors* means the issuer's board of directors or an appropriate person or persons performing similar functions for any issuer not having a board of directors;

(4) *Capital preservation investment* means an investment that is made to conserve capital and liquidity until the funds are used in the issuer's primary business or businesses;

(5) *Controlled primarily* means controlled within the meaning of section 2(a)(9) of the Act (15 U.S.C. 80a-2(a)(9)) with a degree of control that is greater than that of any other person;

(6) *Investment made pursuant to a collaborative research and development arrangement* means an investment in an investee made pursuant to a business relationship which:

(i) Is designed to achieve narrowly focused goals that are directly related to, and an integral part of, the issue's research and development activities;

(ii) Calls for the issuer to conduct joint research and development activities with the investee or a company controlled primarily by, or which controls primarily, the investee; and

(iii) Is not entered into for the purpose of avoiding regulation under the Act;

(7) *Investments in securities* means all securities other than securities issued by majority-owned subsidiaries and companies controlled primarily by the issuer that conduct similar types of businesses, through which the issuer is engaged primarily in a business other than that of investing, reinvesting,

Securities and Exchange Commission § 270.3c–1

owning, holding, or trading in securities;

(8) *Other investment* means an investment in securities that is not a capital preservation investment; and

(9) *Research and development expenses* means research and development costs as defined in FASB ASC Topic 730, *Research and Development*, as currently in effect or as it may be subsequently revised.

[68 FR 37052, June 20, 2003, as amended at 76 FR 50123, Aug. 12, 2011]

§ 270.3a–9 Crowdfunding vehicle.

(a) Notwithstanding section 3(a) of the Act, a crowdfunding vehicle will be deemed not to be an investment company if the vehicle:

(1) Is organized and operated for the sole purpose of directly acquiring, holding, and disposing of securities issued by a single crowdfunding issuer and raising capital in one or more offerings made in compliance with §§ 227.100 through 227.504 (Regulation Crowdfunding);

(2) Does not borrow money and uses the proceeds from the sale of its securities solely to purchase a single class of securities of a single crowdfunding issuer;

(3) Issues only one class of securities in one or more offerings under Regulation Crowdfunding in which the crowdfunding vehicle and the crowdfunding issuer are deemed to be co-issuers under the Securities Act (15 U.S.C. 77a *et seq.*);

(4) Receives a written undertaking from the crowdfunding issuer to fund or reimburse the expenses associated with its formation, operation, or winding up, receives no other compensation, and any compensation paid to any person operating the vehicle is paid solely by the crowdfunding issuer;

(5) Maintains the same fiscal year-end as the crowdfunding issuer;

(6) Maintains a one-to-one relationship between the number, denomination, type and rights of crowdfunding issuer securities it owns and the number, denomination, type and rights of its securities outstanding;

(7) Seeks instructions from the holders of its securities with regard to:

(i) The voting of the crowdfunding issuer securities it holds and votes the crowdfunding issuer securities only in accordance with such instructions; and

(ii) Participating in tender or exchange offers or similar transactions conducted by the crowdfunding issuer and participates in such transactions only in accordance with such instructions;

(8) Receives, from the crowdfunding issuer, all disclosures and other information required under Regulation Crowdfunding and the crowdfunding vehicle promptly provides such disclosures and other information to the investors and potential investors in the crowdfunding vehicle's securities and to the relevant intermediary; and

(9) Provides to each investor the right to direct the crowdfunding vehicle to assert the rights under State and Federal law that the investor would have if he or she had invested directly in the crowdfunding issuer and provides to each investor any information that it receives from the crowdfunding issuer as a shareholder of record of the crowdfunding issuer.

(b) For purposes of this section:

(1) *Crowdfunding issuer* means a company that seeks to raise capital as a co-issuer with a crowdfunding vehicle in an offering that complies with all of the requirements under section 4(a)(6) of the Securities Act (15 U.S.C. 77d(a)(6)) and Regulation Crowdfunding.

(2) *Crowdfunding vehicle* means an issuer formed by or on behalf of a crowdfunding issuer for the purpose of conducting an offering under section 4(a)(6) of the Securities Act (15 U.S.C. 77d(a)(6)) as a co-issuer with the crowdfunding issuer, which offering is controlled by the crowdfunding issuer.

(3) *Regulation Crowdfunding* means the regulations set forth in §§ 227.100 through 227.504 of this chapter.

[86 FR 3602, Jan. 14, 2021]

§ 270.3c–1 Definition of beneficial ownership for certain 3(c)(1) funds.

(a) As used in this section:

(1) The term *Covered Company* means a company that is an investment company, a Section 3(c)(1) Company or a Section 3(c)(7) Company.

§ 270.3c-2

(2) The term *Section 3(c)(1) Company* means a company that would be an investment company but for the exclusion provided by section 3(c)(1) of the Act [15 U.S.C. 80a-3(c)(1)].

(3) The term *Section 3(c)(7) Company* means a company that would be an investment company but for the exclusion provided by section 3(c)(7) of the Act [15 U.S.C. 80a-3(c)(7)].

(b) For purposes of section 3(c)(1)(A) of the Act [15 U.S.C. 80a-3(c)(1)(A)], beneficial ownership by a Covered Company owning 10 percent or more of the outstanding voting securities of a Section 3(c)(1) Company shall be deemed to be beneficial ownership by one person, *provided that:*

(1) On April 1, 1997, the Covered Company owned 10 percent or more of the outstanding voting securities of the Section 3(c)(1) Company or non-voting securities that, on such date and in accordance with the terms of such securities, were convertible into or exchangeable for voting securities that, if converted or exchanged on or after such date, would have constituted 10 percent or more of the outstanding voting securities of the Section 3(c)(1) Company; and

(2) On the date of any acquisition of securities of the Section 3(c)(1) Company by the Covered Company, the value of all securities owned by the Covered Company of all issuers that are Section 3(c)(1) or Section 3(c)(7) Companies does not exceed 10 percent of the Covered Company's total assets.

[62 FR 17529, Apr. 9, 1997]

§ 270.3c-2 Definition of beneficial ownership in small business investment companies.

For the purpose of section 3(c)(1) of the Act, beneficial ownership by a company owning 10 per centum or more of the outstanding voting securities of any issuer which is a small business investment company licensed to operate under the Small Business Investment Act of 1958, or which has received from the Small Business Administration notice to proceed to qualify for a license, which notice or license has not been revoked, shall be deemed to be beneficial ownership by one person (a) if and so long as the value of all securities of small business investments companies owned by such company does not exceed 5 per centum of the value of its total assets; or (b) if and so long as such stock of the small business investment company shall be owned by a state development corporation which has been created by or pursuant to an act of the State legislature to promote and assist the growth and development of the economy within such State on a state-wide basis: *Provided,* That such State development corporation is not, or as a result of its investment in the small business investment company (considering such investment as an investment security) would not be, an investment company as defined in section 3 of the Act.

(Sec. 6, 74 Stat. 412; 15 U.S.C. 80a-6)

[33 FR 11451, Aug. 13, 1968]

§ 270.3c-3 Definition of certain terms used in section 3(c)(1) of the Act with respect to certain debt securities offered by small business investment companies.

The term *public offering* as used in section 3(c)(1) of the Act shall not be deemed to include the offer and sale by a small business investment company, licensed under the Small Business Investment Act of 1958, of any debt security issued by it which is (a) not convertible into, exchangeable for, or accompanied by any equity security, and (b) guaranteed as to timely payment of principal and interest by the Small Business Administration and backed by the full faith and credit of the United States. The holders of any securities offered and sold as described in this section shall be counted, in the aggregate, as one person for purposes of section 3(c)(1) of the Act.

[37 FR 7590, Apr. 18, 1972]

§ 270.3c-4 Definition of "common trust fund" as used in section 3(c)(3) of the Act.

The term *common trust fund* as used in section 3(c)(3) of the Act (15 U.S.C. 80a-3(c)(3)) shall include a common trust fund which is maintained by a bank which is a member of an affiliated group, as defined in section 1504(a) of the Internal Revenue Code of 1954 (26

Securities and Exchange Commission § 270.3c-5

U.S.C. 1504(a)), and which is maintained exclusively for the collective investment and reinvestment of monies contributed thereto by one or more bank members of such affiliated group in the capacity of trustee, executor, administrator, or guardian; *Provided, That*:

(a) The common trust fund is operated in compliance with the same State and Federal regulatory requirements as would apply if the bank maintaining such fund and any other contributing banks were the same entity; and

(b) The rights of persons for whose benefit a contributing bank acts as trustee, executor, administrator, or guardian would not be diminished by reason of the maintenance of such common trust fund by another bank member of the affiliated group.

(15 U.S.C. 80a-6(c), 80a-37(a))

[43 FR 2393, Jan. 17, 1978]

§ 270.3c-5 **Beneficial ownership by knowledgeable employees and certain other persons.**

(a) As used in this section:

(1) The term *Affiliated Management Person* means an affiliated person, as such term is defined in section 2(a)(3) of the Act [15 U.S.C. 80a-2(a)(3)], that manages the investment activities of a Covered Company. For purposes of this definition, the term "investment company" as used in section 2(a)(3) of the Act includes a Covered Company.

(2) The term *Covered Company* means a Section 3(c)(1) Company or a Section 3(c)(7) Company.

(3) The term *Executive Officer* means the president, any vice president in charge of a principal business unit, division or function (such as sales, administration or finance), any other officer who performs a policy-making function, or any other person who performs similar policy-making functions, for a Covered Company or for an Affiliated Management Person of the Covered Company.

(4) The term *Knowledgeable Employee* with respect to any Covered Company means any natural person who is:

(i) An Executive Officer, director, trustee, general partner, advisory board member, or person serving in a similar capacity, of the Covered Company or an Affiliated Management Person of the Covered Company; or

(ii) An employee of the Covered Company or an Affiliated Management Person of the Covered Company (other than an employee performing solely clerical, secretarial or administrative functions with regard to such company or its investments) who, in connection with his or her regular functions or duties, participates in the investment activities of such Covered Company, other Covered Companies, or investment companies the investment activities of which are managed by such Affiliated Management Person of the Covered Company, *provided that* such employee has been performing such functions and duties for or on behalf of the Covered Company or the Affiliated Management Person of the Covered Company, or substantially similar functions or duties for or on behalf of another company for at least 12 months.

(5) The term *Section 3(c)(1) Company* means a company that would be an investment company but for the exclusion provided by section 3(c)(1) of the Act [15 U.S.C. 80a-3(c)(1)].

(6) The term *Section 3(c)(7) Company* means a company that would be an investment company but for the exclusion provided by section 3(c)(7) of the Act [15 U.S.C. 80a-3(c)(7)].

(b) For purposes of determining the number of beneficial owners of a Section 3(c)(1) Company, and whether the outstanding securities of a Section 3(c)(7) Company are owned exclusively by qualified purchasers, there shall be excluded securities beneficially owned by:

(1) A person who at the time such securities were acquired was a Knowledgeable Employee of such Company;

(2) A company owned exclusively by Knowledgeable Employees;

(3) Any person who acquires securities originally acquired by a Knowledgeable Employee in accordance with this section, provided that such securities were acquired by such person in accordance with § 270.3c-6

[62 FR 17529, Apr. 9, 1997]

§ 270.3c–6 Certain transfers of interests in section 3(c)(1) and section 3(c)(7) funds.

(a) As used in this section:

(1) The term *Donee* means a person who acquires a security of a Covered Company (or a security or other interest in a company referred to in paragraph (b)(3) of this section) as a gift or bequest or pursuant to an agreement relating to a legal separation or divorce.

(2) The term *Section 3(c)(1) Company* means a company that would be an investment company but for the exclusion provided by section 3(c)(1) of the Act [15 U.S.C. 80a–3(c)(1)].

(3) The term *Section 3(c)(7) Company* means a company that would be an investment company but for the exclusion provided by section 3(c)(7) of the Act [15 U.S.C. 80a–3(c)(7)].

(4) The term *Transferee* means a Section 3(c)(1) Transferee or a Qualified Purchaser Transferee, in each case as defined in paragraph (b) of this section.

(5) The term *Transferor* means a Section 3(c)(1) Transferor or a Qualified Purchaser Transferor, in each case as defined in paragraph (b) of this section.

(b) Beneficial ownership by any person ("Section 3(c)(1) Transferee") who acquires securities or interests in securities of a Section 3(c)(1) Company from a person other than the Section 3(c)(1) Company shall be deemed to be beneficial ownership by the person from whom such transfer was made ("Section 3(c)(1) Transferor"), and securities of a Section 3(c)(7) Company that are owned by persons who received the securities from a qualified purchaser other than the Section 3(c)(7) Company ("Qualified Purchaser Transferor") or a person deemed to be a qualified purchaser by this section shall be deemed to be acquired by a qualified purchaser ("Qualified Purchaser Transferee"), provided that the Transferee is:

(1) The estate of the Transferor;

(2) A Donee; or

(3) A company established by the Transferor exclusively for the benefit of (or owned exclusively by) the Transferor and the persons specified in paragraphs (b)(1) and (b)(2) of this section.

[62 FR 17529, Apr. 9, 1997]

§ 270.5b–1 Definition of "total assets."

The term *total assets*, when used in computing values for the purposes of sections 5 and 12 of the Act, shall mean the gross assets of the company with respect to which the computation is made, taken as of the end of the fiscal quarter of the company last preceding the date of computation. This section shall not apply to any company which has adopted either of the alternative methods of valuation permitted by § 270.2a–1.

[Rule N–5B–1, 6 FR 5920, Nov. 22, 1941]

§ 270.5b–2 Exclusion of certain guarantees as securities of the guarantor.

(a) For the purposes of section 5 of the act, a guarantee of a security shall not be deemed to be a security issued by the guarantor: *Provided*, That the value of all securities issued or guaranteed by the guarantor, and owned by the management company, does not exceed 10 percent of the value of the total assets of such management company.

(b) Notwithstanding paragraph (a) of this section, for the purposes of section 5 of the Act, a guarantee by a railroad company of a security issued by a terminal company, warehouse company, switching company, or bridge company, shall not be deemed to be a security issued by such railroad company: *Provided:*

(1) The security is guaranteed jointly or severally by more than one railroad company; and

(2) No one of such guaranteeing railroad companies directly or indirectly controls all of its co-guarantors.

(c) For the purposes of section 5 of the Act, a lease or other arrangement whereby a railroad company is or becomes obligated to pay a stipulated annual sum of rental either to another railroad company or to the security holders of such other railroad company shall not be deemed in itself a guarantee.

[Rule N–5B–2, 10 FR 581, Jan. 16, 1945]

§ 270.5b–3 Acquisition of repurchase agreement or refunded security treated as acquisition of underlying securities.

(a) *Repurchase Agreements.* For purposes of sections 5 and 12(d)(3) of the

Securities and Exchange Commission § 270.5b-3

Act (15 U.S.C. 80a-5 and 80a-12(d)(3)), the acquisition of a repurchase agreement may be deemed to be an acquisition of the underlying securities, provided the obligation of the seller to repurchase the securities from the investment company is Collateralized Fully.

(b) *Refunded Securities.* For purposes of section 5 of the Act (15 U.S.C. 80a-5), the acquisition of a Refunded Security is deemed to be an acquisition of the escrowed Government Securities.

(c) *Definitions.* As used in this section:

(1) *Collateralized Fully* in the case of a repurchase agreement means that:

(i) The value of the securities collateralizing the repurchase agreement (reduced by the transaction costs (including loss of interest) that the investment company reasonably could expect to incur if the seller defaults) is, and during the entire term of the repurchase agreement remains, at least equal to the Resale Price provided in the agreement;

(ii) The investment company has perfected its security interest in the collateral;

(iii) The collateral is maintained in an account of the investment company with its custodian or a third party that qualifies as a custodian under the Act;

(iv) The collateral consists entirely of:

(A) Cash items;

(B) Government Securities; or

(C) Securities that the investment company's board of directors, or its delegate, determines at the time the repurchase agreement is entered into:

(*1*) Each issuer of which has an exceptionally strong capacity to meet its financial obligations; and

NOTE TO PARAGRAPH (c)(1)(iv)(C)(*1*): For a discussion of the phrase "exceptionally strong capacity to meet its financial obligations" see Investment Company Act Release No. 30847, (December 27, 2013).

(*2*) Are sufficiently liquid that they can be sold at approximately their carrying value in the ordinary course of business within seven calendar days; and

(v) Upon an Event of Insolvency with respect to the seller, the repurchase agreement would qualify under a provision of applicable insolvency law providing an exclusion from any automatic stay of creditors' rights against the seller.

(2) *Event of Insolvency* means, with respect to a person:

(i) An admission of insolvency, the application by the person for the appointment of a trustee, receiver, rehabilitator, or similar officer for all or substantially all of its assets, a general assignment for the benefit of creditors, the filing by the person of a voluntary petition in bankruptcy or application for reorganization or an arrangement with creditors; or

(ii) The institution of similar proceedings by another person which proceedings are not contested by the person; or

(iii) The institution of similar proceedings by a government agency responsible for regulating the activities of the person, whether or not contested by the person.

(3) *Government Security* means any "Government Security" as defined in section 2(a)(16) of the Act (15 U.S.C. 80a-2(a)(16)).

(4) *Issuer,* as used in paragraph (c)(1)(iv)(C)(*1*) of this section, means the issuer of a collateral security or the issuer of an unconditional obligation of a person other than the issuer of the collateral security to undertake to pay, upon presentment by the holder of the obligation (if required), the principal amount of the underlying collateral security plus accrued interest when due or upon default.

(5) *Refunded Security* means a debt security the principal and interest payments of which are to be paid by Government Securities ("deposited securities") that have been irrevocably placed in an escrow account pursuant to an agreement between the issuer of the debt security and an escrow agent that is not an "affiliated person," as defined in section 2(a)(3)(C) of the Act (15 U.S.C. 80a-2(a)(3)(C)), of the issuer of the debt security, and, in accordance with such escrow agreement, are pledged only to the payment of the debt security and, to the extent that excess proceeds are available after all payments of principal, interest, and applicable premiums on the Refunded Securities, the expenses of the escrow

§ 270.6a–5

agent and, thereafter, to the issuer or another party; *provided* that:

(i) The deposited securities are not redeemable prior to their final maturity;

(ii) The escrow agreement prohibits the substitution of the deposited securities unless the substituted securities are Government Securities; and

(iii) At the time the deposited securities are placed in the escrow account, or at the time a substitution of the deposited securities is made, an independent certified public accountant has certified to the escrow agent that the deposited securities will satisfy all scheduled payments of principal, interest and applicable premiums on the Refunded Securities.

(6) *Resale Price* means the acquisition price paid to the seller of the securities plus the accrued resale premium on such acquisition price. The accrued resale premium is the amount specified in the repurchase agreement or the daily amortization of the difference between the acquisition price and the resale price specified in the repurchase agreement.

[66 FR 36161, July 11, 2001, as amended at 74 FR 52373, Oct. 9, 2009; 79 FR 1329, Jan. 8, 2014]

§ 270.6a–5 Purchase of certain debt securities by companies relying on section 6(a)(5) of the Act.

For purposes of reliance on the exemption for certain companies under section 6(a)(5)(A) of the Act (15 U.S.C. 80a–6(a)(5)(A)), a company shall be deemed to have met the requirement for credit-worthiness of certain debt securities under section 6(a)(5)(A)(iv)(I) of the Investment Company Act (15 U.S.C. 80a–6(a)(5)(A)(iv)(I)) if, at the time of purchase, the board of directors (or its delegate) determines or members of the company (or their delegate) determine that the debt security is:

(a) Subject to no greater than moderate credit risk; and

(b) Sufficiently liquid that it can be sold at or near its carrying value within a reasonably short period of time.

[77 FR 70120, Nov. 23, 2012]

§ 270.6b–1 Exemption of employees' securities company pending determination of application.

Any employees' securities company which files an application for an order of exemption under section 6(b) of the Act (54 Stat. 801; 15 U.S.C. 80a–6) shall be exempt, pending final determination of such application by the Commission, from all provisions of the Act applicable to investment companies as such.

[Rule N–6B–1, 6 FR 6126, Dec. 2, 1941]

§ 270.6c–3 Exemptions for certain registered variable life insurance separate accounts.

A separate account which meets the requirements of paragraph (a) of Rule 6e–2 (17 CFR 270.6e–2) or paragraph (a) of Rule 6e–3(T) (17 CFR 270.6e–3(T)) and registers as an investment company under section 8(a) of the Act (15 U.S.C. 80a–8(a)), and the investment adviser, principal underwriter and depositor of such separate account, shall be exempt from the provisions of the Act specified in paragraph (b) of Rule 6e–2 or paragraph (b) of Rule 6e–3(T), except for sections 7 (15 U.S.C. 80a–7) and 8(a) of the Act, under the same terms and conditions as a separate account claiming exemption under Rule 6e–2 or Rule 6e–3(T).

(Secs. 6(c); 15 U.S.C. 80a–6(C) and 38(a))

[49 FR 49228, Dec. 3, 1984]

§ 270.6c–6 Exemption for certain registered separate accounts and other persons.

(a) As used in this section,

(1) *Revenue Ruling* shall mean Revenue Ruling 81–225, 1981–41 I.R.B. (October 13, 1981), issued by the Internal Revenue Service on September 25, 1981.

(2) *Existing separate account* shall mean a separate account which is, or is a part of, a unit investment trust registered under the Act, engaged in a continuous offering of its securities on September 25, 1981.

(3) *Existing portfolio company* shall mean a registered open-end management investment company, engaged in a continuous offering of its securities on September 25, 1981, all or part of whose securities were owned by an existing separate account on September 25, 1981.

Securities and Exchange Commission § 270.6c-6

(4) *New portfolio company* shall mean any registered open-end management investment company the shares of which will be sold to one or more registered separate accounts for the purpose of minimizing the impact of the Revenue Ruling on the contractowners of an existing separate account, which new portfolio company has the same:

(i) Investment objectives,

(ii) Fundamental policies, and

(iii) Voting rights as the existing portfolio company and has an advisory fee schedule, including expenses assumed by the adviser, that is at least as advantageous to the new portfolio company as was the fee schedule of the existing portfolio company.

(5) *New separate account* shall mean a separate account which

(i) Is, or is a part of, a unit investment trust registered under the Act;

(ii) Is intended to minimize the impact of the Revenue Ruling on the contractowners of an existing separate account;

(iii) Invests solely in one or more new portfolio companies;

(iv) Has the same

(A) Sales loads,

(B) Depositor, and

(C) Custodial arrangements

As the existing separate account; and

(v) Has

(A) Asset charges,

(B) Administrative fees, and

(C) Any other fees and charges (not including taxes) that correspond only to fees of the existing separate account and are no greater than those corresponding fees.

(b) Any order of the Commission under the Act, granted to an existing separate account on or before September 25, 1981, shall remain in full force and effect notwithstanding that the existing separate account invests in one or more new portfolio companies in lieu of, or in addition to, investing in one or more existing portfolio companies; *Provided*, That:

(1) No material changes in the facts upon which the order was based have occurred;

(2) All representations, undertakings, and conditions made or agreed to by the existing separate account, and any other person or persons, other than any existing portfolio company, in connection with the issuance of the order are, and continue to be, applicable to the existing separate account and any such other person or persons, unless modified in accordance with this section;

(3) All representations, undertakings, and conditions made or agreed to by the existing portfolio company in connection with the issuance of the order are made or agreed to by the new portfolio company, unless modified in accordance with this section; and

(4) Part II of the Registration Statement under the Securities Act of 1933 of the existing separate account

(i) Indicates that the existing separate account is relying upon paragraph (b) of this section,

(ii) Lists the Investment Company Act release numbers of any orders upon which the existing separate account intends to rely, and

(iii) Contains a representation that the provisions of this paragraph (b) have been complied with.

(c) Any order of the Commission under the Act, granted to an existing separate account on or before September 25, 1981, shall apply with full force and effect to a new separate account and the depositor of and principal underwriter for the new separate account notwithstanding that the new separate account invests in one or more new portfolio companies; *Provided*, That:

(1) No material changes in the facts upon which the order was based have occurred;

(2) All representations, undertakings, and conditions made or agreed to by the depositor, principal underwriter, and any other person or persons other than the existing separate account or any existing portfolio companies, in connection with the issuance of the order are, and continue to be, applicable to such depositor, principal underwriter, and other person or persons, unless modified in accordance with this section;

(3) All representations, undertakings, and conditions made or agreed to by the existing separate account in connection with the issuance of the order are made or agreed to by the new separate account, unless modified in accordance with this section;

§ 270.6c–6

(4) All representations, undertakings, and conditions made or agreed to by an existing portfolio company in connection with the issuance of the order are made or agreed to by the new portfolio company, unless modified in accordance with this section; and

(5) Part II of the Registration Statement under the Securities Act of 1933 of the new separate account

(i) Indicates that the new separate account is relying upon paragraph (c) of this section,

(ii) Lists the Investment Company Act release numbers of any orders upon which the new separate account intends to rely, and

(iii) Contains a representation that the provisions of this paragraph (c) have been complied with.

(d) Any affiliated person or depositor of or principal underwriter for a new or existing separate account or any affiliated person of or principal underwriter for a new or existing portfolio company, and any affiliated person of such persons, principal underwriters, or depositor shall be exempt from section 17(d) of the Act (15 U.S.C 80a–17(d)) and rule 17d–1 thereunder (17 CFR 270.17d–1) to the extent necessary to permit the organization of one or more new portfolio companies; *Provided*, That, any expenses borne by the existing portfolio company or the new portfolio company in connection with such organization are necessary and appropriate and are allocated in a manner that is fair and reasonable to all of the shareholders of these companies.

(e) Any affiliated person or depositor of or principal underwriter for a new or existing separate account and any affiliated persons of such a person, principal underwriter, or depositor shall be exempt from section 17(d) of the Act and Rule 17d–1 thereunder to the extent necessary to permit such person to bear any reasonable expenses arising out of the organization of one or more new portfolio companies or the new separate account.

(f) Any affiliated persons or depositor of or principal underwriter for a new or existing separate account or any affiliated person of or principal underwriter for a new or existing portfolio company, and any affiliated person of such persons, principal underwriters, or depositor shall be exempt from section 17(a) (15 U.S.C. 80a–17(a)), and any existing portfolio company which has made an election pursuant to Rule 18f–1 (17 CFR 270.18f–1) shall be permitted to revoke that election to the extent necessary to permit transactions involving the transfer of assets from the existing portfolio company to a new portfolio company; *Provided*, That:

(1) Such assets are transferred without the imposition of any fees or charges;

(2) The board of directors of the existing portfolio company, including a majority of the directors of the company who are not interested persons of such company, determines that the transfer of assets is fair and reasonable to all shareholders of the company and such determination, and the basis upon which it was made, is recorded in the minute book of the existing portfolio company;

(3) Any securities involved are valued by the existing portfolio company for purposes of the transfer in accordance with its valuation practices for determining net asset value per share; and

(4) With respect to Rule 18f–1, the existing separate account requests that the existing portfolio company redeem in kind the shares of the portfolio company held by the separate account.

(g) The new portfolio company shall be exempt from section 2(a)(41) (15 U.S.C. 80a–2(a)(41)) of the Act and rules 2a–4 (17 CFR 270.2a–4) and 22c–1 (17 CFR 270.22c–1) under the Act to the extent necessary to permit it to use the same method of valuation for the purpose of pricing its shares for sale, redemption, and repurchase, as the existing portfolio company; *Provided*, That:

(1) The existing portfolio company had on September 25, 1981, an order of the Commission exempting it, for the purposes of pricing its shares for sale, redemption, and repurchase, from:

(i) Section 2(a)(41) of the Act and rules 2a–4 and 22c–1 under the Act to the extent necessary to permit it to use the amortized cost valuation method or

(ii) Rules 2a–4 and 22c–1 under the Act to the extent necessary to permit it to calculate its net asset value per share to the nearest one cent on share values of $1.00;

Securities and Exchange Commission

§ 270.6c–6

(2) All representations, undertakings, and conditions made or agreed to by the existing portfolio company in connection with the order are made or agreed to by the new portfolio company unless modified in accordance with this section; and

(3) Part II of the Registration Statement under the Securities Act of 1933 of the new portfolio company

(i) Indicates that the new portfolio company is relying upon paragraph (g) of this section,

(ii) Lists the Investment Company Act release numbers of any orders upon which the new portfolio company intends to rely, and

(iii) Contains a representation that the provisions of paragraph (g) have been complied with.

(h) The depositor or trustee of an existing separate account shall be exempt from section 26(c) of the Act (15 U.S.C. 80a–26(c)) to the extent necessary to permit the substitution of securities of the new portfolio company for securities of the existing portfolio company; *Provided;* That, within thirty days of such substitution:

(1) The existing separate account notifies all contractowners of the substitution of securities and any determinations of the board of directors of the new portfolio company required by paragraph (d) of this section;

(2) The existing separate account delivers a copy of the prospectus of the new portfolio company to all contractowners; and

(3) The existing separate account, concurrently with the notification referred to in paragraph (h)(1) of this section or the delivery of the prospectus of the new portfolio company referred to in paragraph (h)(2) of this section, whichever is later, offers to those contractowners who would otherwise have surrender rights under their contracts the right, for a period of at least thirty days from the receipt of this offer, to surrender their contracts without the imposition of any withdrawal charge or contingent deferred sales load, and any surrendering contractowner receives the price next determined after the request for surrender is received by the insurance company.

(i) The existing separate account shall be exempt from section 22(d) of the Act (15 U.S.C. 80a–22(d)) to the extent necessary to permit it to comply with paragraph (h) of this section and the principal underwriter for or depositor of the existing separate account shall be exempt from section 26(a)(4)(B) of the Act (15 U.S.C. 80a–26(a)(4)(B)) to the extent necessary to permit them to rely on paragraph (h) of this section.

(j) Notwithstanding section 11 of the Act (15 U.S.C. 80a–11), the existing separate account or any principal underwriter for the existing separate account may make or cause to be made to the contractowners of the existing separate account an offer to exchange a security funded by an existing portfolio company for a security funded by a new portfolio company without the terms of that offer having first been submitted to and approved by the Commission; *Provided,* That the exchange is to be made on the basis of the relative net asset values of the securities to be exchanged without the imposition of any fees or charges.

(k) Notwithstanding section 11 of the Act, the new separate account or any principal underwriter for the new separate account may make or cause to be made an offer to the contractowners of the existing separate account to exchange their securities for securities of the new separate account without the terms of that offer having first been submitted to and approved by the Commission;

Provided, That:

(1) The exchange is to be made on the basis of the relative net asset values of the securities to be exchanged without the imposition of any fees or charges; and

(2) If the new separate account imposes a contingent deferred sales load ("sales load") on the securities to be acquired in the exchange

(i) At the time this sales load is imposed, it is calculated as if

(A) The contractowner had been a contractowner of the new separate account from the date on which he became a contractowner of the existing separate account, in the case of a sales load based on the amount of time the contractowner has been invested in the new separate account, and

§ 270.6c-7

(B) Amounts attributable to purchase payments made to the existing separate account had been made to the new separate account on the date on which they were made to the existing separate account, in the case of a sales load based on the amount of time purchase payments have been invested in the new separate account, and

(ii) The total sales load imposed does not exceed 9 percent of the sum of the purchase payments made to the new separate account and that portion of purchase payments made to the existing separate account attributable to the securities exchanged.

(1) Notwithstanding the foregoing, the provisions of this section will be available to a new separate account or new portfolio company, or to any affiliated person or depositor of or principal underwriter for such a new separate account, to any affiliated person of or principal underwriter for such a new portfolio company, to any affiliated person of such persons, depositor, or principal underwriters, or to any substitution of securities effected in reliance on this section, only if such new separate account or new portfolio company is registered under the Act or such substitution is effected prior to September 21, 1983.

[47 FR 42559, Sept. 28, 1982, as amended at 67 FR 43536, June 28, 2002]

§ 270.6c-7 Exemptions from certain provisions of sections 22(e) and 27 for registered separate accounts offering variable annuity contracts to participants in the Texas Optional Retirement Program.

A registered separate account, and any depositor of or underwriter for such account, shall be exempt from the provisions of sections 22(e), 27(i)(2)(A), and 27(d) of the Act (15 U.S.C. 80a-22(e), 80a-27(i)(2)(A), and 80a-27(d), respectively) with respect to any variable annuity contract participating in such account to the extent necessary to permit compliance with the Texas Optional Retirement Program ("Program"), Provided, That the separate, account, depositor, or underwriter for such account:

(a) Includes appropriate disclosure regarding the restrictions on redemption imposed by the Program in each registration statement, including the prospectus, used in connection with the Program;

(b) Includes appropriate disclosure regarding the restrictions on redemption imposed by the Program in any sales literature used in connection with the offer of annuity contracts to potential Program participants;

(c) Instructs salespeople who solicit Program participants to purchase annuity contracts specifically to bring the restrictions on redemption imposed by the Program to the attention of potential Program participants;

(d) Obtains from each Program participant who purchases an annuity contract in connection with the Program, prior to or at the time of such purchase, a signed statement acknowledging the restrictions on redemption imposed by the Program; and

(e) Includes in Part II of the separate account's registration statement under the Securities Act of 1933 a representation that this section is being relied upon and that the provisions of paragraphs (a) through (d) of this section have been complied with.

[49 FR 1479, Jan. 12, 1984, as amended at 85 FR 26102, May 1, 2020]

§ 270.6c-8 Exemptions for registered separate accounts to impose a deferred sales load and to deduct certain administrative charges.

(a) As used in this section *Deferred sales load* shall mean any sales load, including a contingent deferred sales load, that is deducted upon redemption or annuitization of amounts representing all or a portion of a securityholder's interest in a registered separate account.

(b) A registered separate account, and any depositor of or principal underwriter for such account, shall be exempt from the provisions of sections 22(c) and 27(i)(2)(A) of the Act (15 U.S.C. 80a-22(c) and 80a-27(i)(2)(A), respectively) and § 270.22c-1 (Rule 22c-1) to the extent necessary to permit them to impose a deferred sales load on any variable annuity contract participating in such account; provided that the terms of any offer to exchange another

Securities and Exchange Commission

contract for the contract are in compliance with the requirements of paragraph (d) or (e) of §270.11a–2 (Rule 11a–2).

(c) A registered separate account, and any depositor of or principal underwriter for such account, shall be exempt from sections 22(c) and 27(i)(2)(A) of the Act (15 U.S.C. 80a–22(c) and 80a–27(i)(2)(A), respectively) and §270.22c–1 (Rule 22c–1) to the extent necessary to permit them to deduct from the value of any variable annuity contract participating in such account, upon total redemption of the contract prior to the last day of the year, the full annual fee for administrative services that otherwise would have been deducted on that date.

[48 FR 36098, Aug. 9, 1983, as amended at 85 FR 26102, May 1, 2020]

§ 270.6c–10 Exemption for certain open-end management investment companies to impose deferred sales loads.

(a) A company and any exempted person shall be exempt from the provisions of sections 2(a)(32), 2(a)(35), and 22(d) of the Act [15 U.S.C. 80a–2(a)(32), 80a–2(a)(35), and 80a–22(d), respectively] and §270.22c–1 to the extent necessary to permit a deferred sales load to be imposed on shares issued by the company, *Provided*, that:

(1) The amount of the deferred sales load does not exceed a specified percentage of the net asset value or the offering price at the time of purchase;

(2) The terms of the deferred sales load are covered by the provisions of Rule 2830 of the Conduct Rules of the National Association of Securities Dealers, Inc.; and

(3) The same deferred sales load is imposed on all shareholders, except that scheduled variations in or elimination of a deferred sales load may be offered to a particular class of shareholders or transactions, *Provided*, that the conditions in §270.22d–1 are satisfied. Nothing in this paragraph (a) shall prevent a company from offering to existing shareholders a new scheduled variation that would waive or reduce the amount of a deferred sales load not yet paid.

(b) For purposes of this section:

§ 270.6c–11

(1) *Company* means a registered open-end management investment company, other than a registered separate account, and includes a separate series of the company;

(2) *Exempted person* means any principal underwriter of, dealer in, and any other person authorized to consummate transactions in, securities issued by a company; and

(3) *Deferred sales load* means any amount properly chargeable to sales or promotional expenses that is paid by a shareholder after purchase but before or upon redemption.

[61 FR 49016, Sept. 17, 1996]

§ 270.6c–11 Exchange-traded funds.

(a) *Definitions.* (1) For purposes of this section:

Authorized participant means a member or participant of a clearing agency registered with the Commission, which has a written agreement with the exchange-traded fund or one of its service providers that allows the authorized participant to place orders for the purchase and redemption of creation units.

Basket means the securities, assets or other positions in exchange for which an exchange-traded fund issues (or in return for which it redeems) creation units.

Business day means any day the exchange-traded fund is open for business, including any day when it satisfies redemption requests as required by section 22(e) of the Act (15 U.S.C. 80a–22(e)).

Cash balancing amount means an amount of cash to account for any difference between the value of the basket and the net asset value of a creation unit.

Creation unit means a specified number of exchange-traded fund shares that the exchange-traded fund will issue to (or redeem from) an authorized participant in exchange for the deposit (or delivery) of a basket and a cash balancing amount if any.

Custom basket means:

(A) A basket that is composed of a non-representative selection of the exchange-traded fund's portfolio holdings; or

(B) A representative basket that is different from the initial basket used

§ 270.6c–11

in transactions on the same business day.

Exchange-traded fund means a registered open-end management company:

(A) That issues (and redeems) creation units to (and from) authorized participants in exchange for a basket and a cash balancing amount if any; and

(B) Whose shares are listed on a national securities exchange and traded at market-determined prices.

Exchange-traded fund share means a share of stock issued by an exchange-traded fund.

Foreign investment means any security, asset or other position of the ETF issued by a foreign issuer as that term is defined in § 240.3b–4 of this title, and that is traded on a trading market outside of the United States.

Market price means:

(A) The official closing price of an exchange-traded fund share; or

(B) If it more accurately reflects the market value of an exchange-traded fund share at the time as of which the exchange-traded fund calculates current net asset value per share, the price that is the midpoint between the national best bid and national best offer as of that time.

National securities exchange means an exchange that is registered with the Commission under section 6 of the Securities Exchange Act of 1934 (15 U.S.C. 78f).

Portfolio holdings means the securities, assets or other positions held by the exchange-traded fund.

Premium or discount means the positive or negative difference between the market price of an exchange-traded fund share at the time as of which the current net asset value is calculated and the exchange-traded fund's current net asset value per share, expressed as a percentage of the exchange-traded fund share's current net asset value per share.

(2) Notwithstanding the definition of exchange-traded fund in paragraph (a)(1) of this section, an exchange-traded fund is not prohibited from selling (or redeeming) individual shares on the day of consummation of a reorganization, merger, conversion or liquidation, and is not limited to transactions with authorized participants under these circumstances.

(b) *Application of the Act to exchange-traded funds.* If the conditions of paragraph (c) of this section are satisfied:

(1) *Redeemable security.* An exchange-traded fund share is considered a "redeemable security" within the meaning of section 2(a)(32) of the Act (15 U.S.C. 80a-2(a)(32)).

(2) *Pricing.* A dealer in exchange-traded fund shares is exempt from section 22(d) of the Act (15 U.S.C. 80a-22(d)) and § 270.22c–1(a) with regard to purchases, sales and repurchases of exchange-traded fund shares at market-determined prices.

(3) *Affiliated transactions.* A person who is an affiliated person of an exchange-traded fund (or who is an affiliated person of such a person) solely by reason of the circumstances described in paragraphs (b)(3)(i) and (ii) of this section is exempt from sections 17(a)(1) and 17(a)(2) of the Act (15 U.S.C. 80a–17(a)(1) and (a)(2)) with regard to the deposit and receipt of baskets:

(i) Holding with the power to vote 5% or more of the exchange-traded fund's shares; or

(ii) Holding with the power to vote 5% or more of any investment company that is an affiliated person of the exchange-traded fund.

(4) *Postponement of redemptions.* If an exchange-traded fund includes a foreign investment in its basket, and if a local market holiday, or series of consecutive holidays, or the extended delivery cycles for transferring foreign investments to redeeming authorized participants prevents timely delivery of the foreign investment in response to a redemption request, the exchange-traded fund is exempt, with respect to the delivery of the foreign investment, from the prohibition in section 22(e) of the Act (15 U.S.C. 80a-22(e)) against postponing the date of satisfaction upon redemption for more than seven days after the tender of a redeemable security if the exchange-traded fund delivers the foreign investment as soon as practicable, but in no event later than 15 days after the tender of the exchange-traded fund shares.

(c) *Conditions.* (1) Each business day, an exchange-traded fund must disclose

Securities and Exchange Commission § 270.6c–11

prominently on its website, which is publicly available and free of charge:

(i) Before the opening of regular trading on the primary listing exchange of the exchange-traded fund shares, the following information (as applicable) for each portfolio holding that will form the basis of the next calculation of current net asset value per share:

(A) Ticker symbol;
(B) CUSIP or other identifier;
(C) Description of holding;
(D) Quantity of each security or other asset held; and
(E) Percentage weight of the holding in the portfolio;

(ii) The exchange-traded fund's current net asset value per share, market price, and premium or discount, each as of the end of the prior business day;

(iii) A table showing the number of days the exchange-traded fund's shares traded at a premium or discount during the most recently completed calendar year and the most recently completed calendar quarters since that year (or the life of the exchange-traded fund, if shorter);

(iv) A line graph showing exchange-traded fund share premiums or discounts for the most recently completed calendar year and the most recently completed calendar quarters since that year (or the life of the exchange-traded fund, if shorter);

(v) The exchange-traded fund's median bid-ask spread, expressed as a percentage rounded to the nearest hundredth, computed by:

(A) Identifying the exchange-traded fund's national best bid and national best offer as of the end of each 10 second interval during each trading day of the last 30 calendar days;

(B) Dividing the difference between each such bid and offer by the midpoint of the national best bid and national best offer; and

(C) Identifying the median of those values; and

(vi) If the exchange-traded fund's premium or discount is greater than 2% for more than seven consecutive trading days, a statement that the exchange-traded fund's premium or discount, as applicable, was greater than 2% and a discussion of the factors that are reasonably believed to have materially contributed to the premium or discount, which must be maintained on the website for at least one year thereafter.

(2) The portfolio holdings that form the basis for the exchange-traded fund's next calculation of current net asset value per share must be the ETF's portfolio holdings as of the close of business on the prior business day.

(3) An exchange-traded fund must adopt and implement written policies and procedures that govern the construction of baskets and the process that will be used for the acceptance of baskets; *provided, however*, if the exchange-traded fund utilizes a custom basket, these written policies and procedures also must:

(i) Set forth detailed parameters for the construction and acceptance of custom baskets that are in the best interests of the exchange-traded fund and its shareholders, including the process for any revisions to, or deviations from, those parameters; and

(ii) Specify the titles or roles of the employees of the exchange-traded fund's investment adviser who are required to review each custom basket for compliance with those parameters.

(4) An exchange-traded fund that seeks, directly or indirectly, to provide investment returns that correspond to the performance of a market index by a specified multiple, or to provide investment returns that have an inverse relationship to the performance of a market index, over a predetermined period of time, must comply with all applicable provisions of §270.18f–4.

(d) *Recordkeeping*. The exchange-traded fund must maintain and preserve for a period of not less than five years, the first two years in an easily accessible place:

(1) All written agreements (or copies thereof) between an authorized participant and the exchange-traded fund or one of its service providers that allows the authorized participant to place orders for the purchase or redemption of creation units;

(2) For each basket exchanged with an authorized participant, records setting forth:

(i) The ticker symbol, CUSIP or other identifier, description of holding, quantity of each holding, and percentage weight of each holding composing

§ 270.6d–1

the basket exchanged for creation units;

(ii) If applicable, identification of the basket as a custom basket and a record stating that the custom basket complies with policies and procedures that the exchange-traded fund adopted pursuant to paragraph (c)(3) of this section;

(iii) Cash balancing amount (if any); and

(iv) Identity of authorized participant transacting with the exchange-traded fund.

[84 FR 57234, Oct. 24, 2019, as amended at 85 FR 83291, Dec. 21, 2020]

§ 270.6d–1 Exemption for certain closed-end investment companies.

(a) An application under section 6(d) of the Act shall contain the following information:

(1) A brief description of the character of the business and investment policy of the applicant.

(2) The information relied upon by the applicant to satisfy the conditions of paragraphs (1) and (2) of section 6(d) of the Act.

(3) The number of holders of each class of the applicant's outstanding securities.

(4) An unconsolidated balance sheet as of a date not earlier than the end of the applicant's first fiscal year, together with a schedule specifying the title, the amount, the book value and, if determinable, the market value of each security in the applicant's portfolio.

(5) An unconsolidated profit and loss statement for the applicant's last fiscal year.

(6) A statement of each provision of the act from which the applicant seeks exemption, together with a statement of the facts by reason of which, in the applicant's opinion, such exemption is not contrary to the public interest or inconsistent with the protection of investors.

(b) There shall be attached to each copy of the application a copy of Form N–8A. The form need not be executed, but it shall be clearly marked on its facing page as an exhibit to the application. The filing of Form N–8A in this manner shall not be construed as the filing of a notification of registration under section 8(a) of the Act.

(c) The application may contain any additional information which the applicant desires to submit.

[Rule N–6D–1, 5 FR 4346, Nov. 2, 1940]

§ 270.6e–2 Exemptions for certain variable life insurance separate accounts.

(a) A separate account, and the investment adviser, principal underwriter and depositor of such separate account, shall, except for the exemptions provided in paragraph (b) of this section, be subject to all provisions of the Act and this part as though such separate account were a registered investment company issuing periodic payment plan certificates if:

(1) Such separate account is established and maintained by a life insurance company pursuant to the insurance laws or code of:

(i) Any state or territory of the United States or the District of Columbia; or

(ii) Canada or any province thereof, if it complies to the extent necessary with § 270.7d–1 (Rule 7d–1) under the Act;

(2) The assets of the separate account are derived solely from the sale of variable life insurance contracts as defined in paragraph (c) of this section, and advances made by the life insurance company which established and maintains the separate account ("life insurer") in connection with the operation of such separate account;

(3) The separate account is not used for variable annuity contracts or for funds corresponding to dividend accumulations or other contract liabilities not involving life contingencies;

(4) The income, gains and losses, whether or not realized, from assets allocated to such separate account, are, in accordance with the applicable variable life insurance contract, credited to or charged against such account without regard to other income, gains or losses of the life insurer;

(5) The separate account is legally segregated, and that portion of its assets having a value equal to, or approximately equal to, the reserves and other contract liabilities with respect to such separate account are not

Securities and Exchange Commission

§ 270.6e–2

chargeable with liabilities arising out of any other business that the life insurer may conduct;

(6) The assets of the separate account have, at each time during the year that adjustments in the reserves are made, a value at least equal to the reserves and other contract liabilities with respect to such separate account, and at all other times, except pursuant to an order of the Commission, have a value approximately equal to or in excess of such reserves and liabilities; and

(7) The investment adviser of the separate account is registered under the Investment Advisers Act of 1940.

(b) If a separate account meets the requirements of paragraph (a) of this section, then such separate account and the other persons described in paragraph (a) of this section shall be exempt from the provisions of the Act as follows:

(1) Section 7 (15 U.S.C. 80a–7).

(2) Section 8 (15 U.S.C. 80a–8) to the extent that:

(i) For purposes of paragraph (a) of section 8, the separate account shall file with the Commission a notification on § 274.301 of this chapter (Form N–6EI–1) which identifies such separate account; and

(ii) For purposes of paragraph (b) of section 8, the separate account shall file with the Commission a form to be designated by the Commission within 90 days after filing the notification on Form N–6EI–1; provided, however, that if the fiscal year of the separate account ends within this 90 day period the form may be filed within ninety days after the end of such fiscal year.

(3) Section 9 (15 U.S.C. 80a–9) to the extent that:

(i) The eligibility restrictions of section 9(a) shall not be applicable to those persons who are officers, directors and employees of the life insurer or its affiliates who do not participate directly in the management or administration of the separate account or in the sale of variable life insurance contracts funded by such separate account; and

(ii) A life insurer shall be ineligible pursuant to paragraph (3) of section 9(a) to serve as investment adviser, depositor of or principal underwriter for a variable life insurance separate account only if an affiliated person of such life insurer, ineligible by reason of paragraph (1) or (2) of section 9(a), participates directly in the management or administration of the separate account or in the sale of variable life insurance contracts funded by such separate account.

(4) Section 13(a) (15 U.S.C. 80a–13(a)) to the extent that:

(i) An insurance regulatory authority may require pursuant to insurance law or regulation that the separate account make (or refrain from making) certain investments which would result in changes in the subclassification or investment policies of the separate account;

(ii) Changes in the investment policy of the separate account initiated by contractholders or the board of directors of the separate account may be disapproved by the life insurer, provided that such disapproval is reasonable and is based upon a determination by the life insurer in good faith that:

(A) Such change would be contrary to state law; or

(B) Such change would be inconsistent with the investment objectives of the separate account or would result in the purchase of securities for the separate account which vary from the general quality and nature of investments and investment techniques utilized by other separate accounts of the life insurer or of an affiliated life insurance company, which separate accounts have investment objectives similar to the separate account; and

(iii) Any action taken in accordance with paragraph (b)(4)(i) or (ii) of this section and the reasons therefor shall be disclosed in the proxy statement for the next meeting of variable life insurance contractholders of the separate account.

(5) Section 14(a) (15 U.S.C. 80a–14(a)).

(6)(i) Section 15(a) (15 U.S.C. 80a–15(a)) to the extent this section requires that the initial written contract pursuant to which the investment adviser serves or acts shall have been approved by the vote of a majority of the outstanding voting securities of the registered company; provided that:

(A) Such investment adviser is selected and a written contract is entered into before the effective date of

§ 270.6e-2

the registration statement under the Securities Act of 1933, as amended, for variable life insurance contracts which are funded by the separate account, and that the terms of the contract are fully disclosed in such registration statement; and

(B) A written contract is submitted to a vote of variable life insurance contractholders at their first meeting after the effective date of the registration statement under the Securities Act of 1933, as amended, on condition that such meeting shall take place within one year after such effective date, unless the time for the holding of such meeting shall be extended by the Commission upon written request for good cause shown; and

(ii) Sections 15(a), (b) and (c) (15 U.S.C. 80a-15(a), (b), and (c)) to the extent that:

(A) An insurance regulatory authority may disapprove pursuant to insurance law or regulation any contract between the separate account and an investment adviser or principal underwriter;

(B) Changes in the principal underwriter for the separate account initiated by contractholders or the board of directors of the separate account may be disapproved by the life insurer; provided that such disapproval is reasonable;

(C) Changes in the investment adviser of the separate account initiated by contractholders or the board of directors of the separate account may be disapproved by the life insurer; provided that such disapproval is reasonable and is based upon a determination by the life insurer in good faith that:

(1) The rate of the proposed investment advisory fee will exceed the maximum rate that is permitted to be charged against the assets of the separate account for such services as specified by any variable life insurance contract funded by such separate account; or

(2) The proposed investment adviser may be expected to employ investment techniques which vary from the general techniques utilized by the current investment adviser to the separate account, or advise the purchase or sale of securities which would be inconsistent with the investment objectives of the separate account, or which would vary from the quality and nature of investments made by other separate accounts of the life insurer or of an affiliated life insurance company, which separate accounts have investment objectives similar to the separate account; and

(D) Any action taken in accordance with paragraph (b)(6)(ii)(A), (B), or (C) of this section and the reasons therefor shall be disclosed in the proxy statement for the next meeting of variable life insurance contractholders of the separate account.

(7) Section 16(a) (15 U.S.C. 80a-16(a)) to the extent that:

(i) Persons serving as directors of the separate account prior to the first meeting of such account's variable life insurance contractholders are exempt from the requirement of section 16(a) that such persons be elected by the holders of outstanding voting securities of such account at an annual or special meeting called for that purpose; provided that:

(A) Such persons have been appointed directors of such account by the life insurer before the effective date of the registration statement under the Securities Act of 1933, as amended, for variable life insurance contracts which are funded by the separate account and are identified in such registration statement (or are replacements appointed by the life insurer for any such persons who have become unable to serve as directors); and

(B) An election of directors for such account shall be held at the first meeting of variable life insurance contractholders after the effective date of the registration statement under the Securities Act of 1933, as amended, relating to contracts funded by such account, which meeting shall take place within one year after such effective date, unless the time for holding such meeting shall be extended by the Commission upon written request for good cause shown; and

(ii) A member of the board of directors of such separate account may be disapproved or removed by the appropriate insurance regulatory authority if such person is ineligible to serve as a director of the separate account pursuant to insurance law or regulation of

Securities and Exchange Commission § 270.6e-2

the jurisdiction in which the life insurer is domiciled.

(8) Section 17(f) (15 U.S.C. 80a–17(f)) to the extent that the securities and similar investments of the separate account may be maintained in the custody of the life insurer or an insurance company which is an affiliated person of such life insurer; provided that:

(i) The securities and similar investments allocated to such separate account are clearly identified as to ownership by such account, and such securities and similar investments are maintained in the vault of an insurance company which meets the qualifications set forth in paragraph (b)(8)(ii) of this section, and whose procedures and activities with respect to such safekeeping function are supervised by the insurance regulatory authorities of the jurisdiction in which the securities and similar investments will be held;

(ii) The insurance company maintaining such investments must file with an insurance regulatory authority of a State or territory of the United States or the District of Columbia an annual statement of its financial condition in the form prescribed by the National Association of Insurance Commissioners, must be subject to supervision and inspection by such authority and must be examined periodically as to its financial condition and other affairs by such authority, must hold the securities and similar investments of the separate account in its vault, which vault must be equivalent to that of a bank which is a member of the Federal Reserve System, and must have a combined capital and surplus, if a stock company, or an unassigned surplus, if a mutual company, of not less than $1,000,000 as set forth in its most recent annual statement filed with such authority;

(iii) Access to such securities and similar investments shall be limited to employees of or agents authorized by the Commission, representatives of insurance regulatory authorities, independent public accountants for the separate account, accountants for the life insurer and to no more than 20 persons authorized pursuant to a resolution of the board of directors of the separate account, which persons shall be directors of the separate account, officers and responsible employees of the life insurer or officers and responsible employees of the affiliated insurance company in whose vault such investments are maintained (if applicable), and access to such securities and similar investments shall be had only by two or more such persons jointly, at least one of whom shall be a director of the separate account or officer of the life insurer;

(iv) The requirement in paragraph (b)(8)(i) of this section that the securities and similar investments of the separate account be maintained in the vault of a qualified insurance company shall not apply to securities deposited with insurance regulatory authorities or deposited in a system for the central handling of securities established by a national securities exchange or national securities association registered with the Commission under the Securities Exchange Act of 1934, as amended, or such person as may be permitted by the Commission, or to securities on loan which are collateralized to the extent of their full market value, or to securities hypothecated, pledged, or placed in escrow for the account of such separate account in connection with a loan or other transaction authorized by specific resolution of the board of directors of the separate account, or to securities in transit in connection with the sale, exchange, redemption, maturity or conversion, the exercise of warrants or rights, assents to changes in terms of the securities, or to other transactions necessary or appropriate in the ordinary course of business relating to the management of securities;

(v) Each person when depositing such securities or similar investments in or withdrawing them from the depository or when ordering their withdrawal and delivery from the custody of the life insurer or affiliated insurance company, shall sign a notation in respect of such deposit, withdrawal or order which shall show:

(A) The date and time of the deposit, withdrawal, or order;

(B) The title and amount of the securities or other investments deposited, withdrawn or ordered to be withdrawn, and an identification thereof by certificate numbers or otherwise;

(C) The manner of acquisition of the securities or similar investments deposited or the purpose for which they have been withdrawn, or ordered to be withdrawn; and

(D) If withdrawn and delivered to another person the name of such person. Such notation shall be transmitted promptly to an officer or director of the separate account or the life insurer designated by the board of directors of the separate account who shall not be a person designated for the purpose of paragraph (b)(8)(iii) of this section. Such notation shall be on serially numbered forms and shall be preserved for at least one year;

(vi) Such securities and similar investments shall be verified by complete examination by an independent public accountant retained by the separate account at least three times during each fiscal year, at least two of which shall be chosen by such accountant without prior notice to such separate account. A certificate of such accountant stating that he has made an examination of such securities and investments and describing the nature and extent of the examination shall be transmitted to the Commission by the accountant promptly after each examination; and

(vii) Securities and similar investments of a separate account maintained with a bank or other company whose functions and physical facilities are supervised by Federal or state authorities pursuant to any arrangement whereby the directors, officers, employees or agents of the separate account or the life insurer are authorized or permitted to withdraw such investments upon their mere receipt are deemed to be in the custody of the life insurer and shall be exempt from the requirements of section 17(f) so long as the arrangement complies with all provisions of paragraph (b)(8) of this section, except that such securities will be maintained in the vault of a bank or other company rather than the vault of an insurance company.

(9) Section 18(i) (15 U.S.C. 80a–18(i)) to the extent that:

(i) For the purposes of any section of the Act which provides for the vote of securityholders on matters relating to the investment company:

(A) Variable life insurance contractholders shall have one vote for each $100 of cash value funded by the separate account, with fractional votes allocated for amounts less than $100;

(B) The life insurer shall have one vote for each $100 of assets of the separate account not otherwise attributable to contractholders pursuant to paragraph (b)(9)(i)(A) of this section, with fractional votes allocated for amounts less than $100; provided that after the commencement of sales of variable life insurance contracts funded by the separate account, the life insurer shall cast its votes for and against each matter which may be voted upon by contractholders in the same proportion as the votes cast by contractholders; and

(C) The number of votes to be allocated shall be determined as of a record date not more than 90 days prior to any meeting at which such vote is held; provided that if a quorum is not present at the meeting, the meeting may be adjourned for up to 60 days without fixing a new record date; and

(ii) The requirement of this section that every share of stock issued by a registered management investment company (except a common-law trust of the character described in section 16(c)) shall be a voting stock and have equal voting rights with every other outstanding voting stock shall not be deemed to be violated by actions specifically permitted by any provision of this section.

(10) Section 19 (15 U.S.C. 80a–19) to the extent that the provisions of this section shall not be applicable to any dividend or similar distribution paid or payable pursuant to provisions of participating variable life insurance contracts.

(11) Sections 22(d), 22(e), and 27(i)(2)(A) (15 U.S.C. 80a–22(d), 80a–22(e), and 80a–27(i)(2)(A), respectively) and §270.22c–1 (Rule 22c–1) promulgated under section 22(c) to the extent:

(i) That the amount payable on death and the cash surrender value of each variable life insurance contract shall be determined on each day during which the New York Stock Exchange is open for trading, not less frequently

Securities and Exchange Commission § 270.6e–2

than once daily as of the time of the close of trading on such exchange; provided that the amount payable on death need not be determined more than once each contract month if such determination does not reduce the participation of the contract in the investment experience of the separate account; provided further, however, that if the net valuation premium for such contract is transferred at least annually, then the amount payable on death need be determined only when such net premium is transferred; and

(ii) Necessary for compliance with this section or with insurance laws and regulations and established administrative procedures of the life insurer with respect to issuance, transfer and redemption procedures for variable life insurance contracts funded by the separate account including, but not limited to, premium rate structure and premium processing, insurance underwriting standards, and the particular benefit afforded by the contract; provided, however, that any procedure or action shall be reasonable, fair and not discriminatory to the interests of the affected contractholder and to all other holders of contracts of the same class or series funded by the separate account; and, further provided that any such action shall be disclosed in the form required to be filed by the separate account with the Commission pursuant to paragraph (b)(2)(ii) of this section.

(12) Section 27(i)(2)(A) (15 U.S.C. 80a–27(i)(A)), to the extent that such sections require that the variable life insurance contract be redeemable or provide for a refund in cash; provided that such contract provides for election by the contractholder of a cash surrender value or certain non-forfeiture and settlement options which are required or permitted by the insurance law or regulation of the jurisdiction in which the contract is offered; and further provided that unless required by the insurance law or regulation of the jurisdiction in which the contract is offered or unless elected by the contractholder, such contract shall not provide for the automatic imposition of any option, including, but not limited to, an automatic premium loan, which would involve the accrual or payment of an interest or similar charge;

(13) Section 32(a)(2) (15 U.S.C. 80a–31(a)(2)); provided that:

(i) The independent public accountant is selected before the effective date of the registration statement under the Securities Act of 1933, as amended, for variable life insurance contracts which are funded by the separate account, and the identity of such accountant is disclosed in such registration statement; and

(ii) The selection of such accountant is submitted for ratification or rejection to variable life insurance contractholders at their first meeting after the effective date of the registration statement under the Securities Act of 1933, as amended, on condition that such meeting shall take place within one year after such effective date, unless the time for the holding of such meeting shall be extended by the Commission upon written request for good cause shown.

(14) If the separate account is organized as a unit investment trust, all the assets of which consist of the shares of one or more registered management investment companies which offer their shares exclusively to variable life insurance separate accounts of the life insurer or of any affiliated life insurance company:

(i) The eligibility restrictions of section 9(a) (15 U.S.C. 80a–9(a)) shall not be applicable to those persons who are officers, directors, and employees of the life insurer or its affiliates who do not participate directly in the management or administration of any registered management investment company described in paragraph (b)(14) introductory text;

(ii) The life insurer shall be ineligible pursuant to paragraph (3) of section 9(a) to serve as investment adviser of or principal underwriter for any registered management investment company described in paragraph (b)(14) of this section only if an affiliated person of such life insurer, ineligible by reason of paragraph (1) or (2) of section 9(a), participates in the management or administration of such company;

(iii) The life insurer may vote shares of the registered management investment companies held by the separate

§ 270.6e-3

account without regard to instructions from contractholders of the separate account if such instructions would require such shares to be voted:

(A) To cause such companies to make (or refrain from making) certain investments which would result in changes in the sub-classification or investment objectives of such companies or to approve or disapprove any contract between such companies and an investment adviser when required to do so by an insurance regulatory authority subject to the provisions of paragraphs (b)(4)(i) and (b)(6)(ii)(A) of this section; or

(B) In favor of changes in investment objectives, investment adviser of or principal underwriter for such companies subject to the provisions of paragraphs (b)(4)(ii) and (b)(6)(ii)(B) and (C) of this section;

(iv) Any action taken in accordance with paragraph (b)(14)(iii)(A) or (B) of this section and the reasons therefor shall be disclosed in the next report to contractholders made pursuant to section 30(e) (15 U.S.C. 80a-29(e)) and § 270.30e-2 (Rule 30e-2);

(v) Any registered management investment company established by the insurer and described in paragraph (b)(14) of this section shall be exempt from section 14(a); and

(vi) Any registered management investment company established by the insurer and described in paragraph (b)(14) of this section shall be exempt from sections 15(a), 16(a), and 32(a)(2) (15 U.S.C. 80a-15(a), 80-16(a), and 80-31(a)(2), respectively), to the extent prescribed by paragraphs (b)(6)(i), (b)(7)(i), and (b)(13) of this section, provided that such company complies with the conditions set forth in those paragraphs as if it were a separate account.

(c) When used in this section, *variable life insurance contract* means a contract of life insurance, subject to regulation under the insurance laws or code of every jurisdiction in which it is offered, funded by a separate account of a life insurer, which contract, so long as premium payments are duly paid in accordance with its terms, provides for:

(1) A death benefit and cash surrender value which vary to reflect the investment experience of the separate account;

17 CFR Ch. II (4-1-23 Edition)

(2) An initial stated dollar amount of death benefit, and payment of a death benefit guaranteed by the life insurer to be at least equal to such stated amount; and

(3) Assumption of the mortality and expense risks thereunder by the life insurer for which a charge against the assets of the separate account may be assessed. Such charge shall be disclosed in the prospectus and shall not be less than fifty per centum of the maximum charge for risk assumption as disclosed in the prospectus and as provided for in the contract.

[85 FR 26102, May 1, 2020]

§ 270.6e-3 Exemptions for flexible premium variable life insurance separate accounts.

(a) A separate account, and its investment adviser, principal underwriter and depositor, shall, except as provided in paragraph (b) of this section, comply with all provisions of the Investment Company Act of 1940 (15 U.S.C. 80a-1 *et seq.*) and this part that apply to a registered investment company issuing periodic payment plan certificates if:

(1) It is a separate account within the meaning of section 2(a)(37) of the Act (15 U.S.C. 80a-2(a)(37)) and is established and maintained by a life insurance company pursuant to the insurance laws or code of:

(i) Any state or territory of the United States or the District of Columbia; or

(ii) Canada or any province thereof, if it complies with § 270.7d-1 (Rule 7d-1) under the Act (the "life insurer");

(2) The assets of the separate account are derived solely from:

(i) The sale of flexible premium variable life insurance contracts ("flexible contracts") as defined in paragraph (c)(1) of this section;

(ii) The sale of scheduled premium variable life insurance contracts ("scheduled contracts") as defined in paragraph (c) of § 270.6e-2 (Rule 6e-2) under the Act;

(iii) Funds corresponding to dividend accumulations with respect to such contracts; and

(iv) Advances made by the life insurer in connection with the operation of such separate account;

Securities and Exchange Commission § 270.6e-3

(3) The separate account is not used for variable annuity contracts or other contract liabilities not involving life contingencies;

(4) The separate account is legally segregated, and that part of its assets with a value approximately equal to the reserves and other contract liabilities for such separate account are not chargeable with liabilities arising from any other business of the life insurer;

(5) The value of the assets of the separate account, each time adjustments in the reserves are made, is at least equal to the reserves and other contract liabilities of the separate account, and at all other times approximately equals or exceeds the reserves and liabilities; and

(6) The investment adviser of the separate account is registered under the Investment Advisers Act of 1940 (15 U.S.C. 80b–1 *et seq.*).

(b) A separate account that meets the requirements of paragraph (a) of this section, and its investment adviser, principal underwriter and depositor shall be exempt with respect to flexible contracts funded by the separate account from the following provisions of the Act:

(1) Subject to section 26(f) of the Act, in connection with any sales charge deducted under the flexible contract, the separate account and other persons shall be exempt from sections 12(b), 22(c), and 27(i)(2)(A) (15 U.S.C. 80a–12(b), 80–22(c), and 80a–27(i)(2)(A), respectively) of the Act, and §§ 270.12b–1 (Rule 12b–1) and 270.22c–1 (Rule 22c–1) under the Act.

(2) Section 7 (15 U.S.C. 80a–7).

(3) Section 8 (15 U.S.C. 80a–8), to the extent that:

(i) For purposes of paragraph (a) of section 8, the separate account filed with the Commission a notification on § 274.301 of this chapter (Form N–6EI–1) which identifies the separate account; and

(ii) For purposes of paragraph (b) of section 8, the separate account shall file with the Commission the form designated by the Commission within ninety days after filing the notification on Form N–6EI–1; provided, however, that if the fiscal year of the separate account end within this ninety day period, the form may be filed within ninety days after the end of such fiscal year.

(4) Section 9 (15 U.S.C. 80a–9), to the extent that:

(i) The eligibility restrictions of section 9(a) shall not apply to persons who are officers, directors or employees of the life insurer or its affiliates and who do not participate directly in the management or administration of the separate account or in the sale of flexible contracts; and

(ii) A life insurer shall be ineligible under paragraph (3) of section 9(a) to serve as investment adviser, depositor of or principal underwriter for the separate account only if an affiliated person of such life insurer, ineligible by reason of paragraphs (1) or (2) of section 9(a), participates directly in the management or administration of the separate account or in the sale of flexible contracts.

(5) Section 13(a) (15 U.S.C. 80a–13(a)), to the extent that:

(i) An insurance regulatory authority may require pursuant to insurance law or regulation that the separate account make (or refrain from making) certain investments which would result in changes in the subclassification or investment policies of the separate account;

(ii) Changes in the investment policy of the separate account initiated by its contractholders or board of directors may be disapproved by the life insurer, if the disapproval is reasonable and is based on a good faith determination by the life insurer that:

(A) The change would violate state law; or

(B) The change would not be consistent with the investment objectives of the separate account or would result in the purchase of securities for the separate account which vary from the general quality and nature of investments and investment techniques used by other separate accounts of the life insurer or of an affiliated life insurance company with similar investment objectives; and

(iii) Any action described in paragraph (b)(5)(i) or (ii) of this section and the reasons for it shall be disclosed in the next communication to contractholders, but in no case, later than twelve months from the date of such action.

(6) Section 14(a) (15 U.S.C. 80a–14(a)).

(7)(i) Section 15(a) (15 U.S.C. 80a–15(a)), to the extent it requires that the initial written contract with the investment adviser shall have been approved by the vote of a majority of the outstanding voting securities of the registered investment company; provided that:

(A) The investment adviser is selected and a written contract is entered into before the effective date of the 1933 Act registration statement for flexible contracts, and that the terms of the contract are fully disclosed in the registration statement; and

(B) A written contract is submitted to a vote of contractholders at their first meeting and within one year after the effective date of the 1933 Act registration statement, unless the Commission upon written request and for good cause shown extends the time for the holding of such meeting; and

(ii) Sections 15(a), (b), and (c), to the extent that:

(A) An insurance regulatory authority may disapprove pursuant to insurance law or regulation any contract between the separate account and an investment adviser or principal underwriter;

(B) Changes in the principal underwriter for the separate account initiated by contractholders or the board of directors of the separate account may be disapproved by the life insurer; provided that such disapproval is reasonable;

(C) Changes in the investment adviser of the separate account initiated by contractholders or the board of directors of the separate account may be disapproved by the life insurer; provided that such disapproval is reasonable and is based on a good faith determination by the life insurer that:

(1) The proposed investment advisory fee will exceed the maximum rate specified in any flexible contract that may be charged against the assets of the separate account for such services; or

(2) The proposed investment adviser may be expected to employ investment techniques which vary from the general techniques used by the current investment adviser to the separate account, or advise the purchase or sale of securities which would not be consistent with the investment objectives of the separate account, or which would vary from the quality and nature of investments made by other separate accounts with similar investment objectives of the life insurer or an affiliated life insurance company; and

(D) Any action described in paragraph (b)(7)(ii)(A), (B), or (C) of this section and the reasons for it shall be disclosed in the next communication to contractholders, but in no case, later than twelve months from the date of such action.

(8) Section 16(a) (15 U.S.C. 80a–16(a)), to the extent that:

(i) Directors of the separate account serving before the first meeting of the account's contractholders are exempt from the requirement of section 16(a) that they be elected by the holders of outstanding voting securities of the account at an annual or special meeting called for that purpose; provided that:

(A) Such persons were appointed directors of the account by the life insurer before the effective date of the 1933 Act registration statement for flexible contracts and are identified in the registration statement (or are replacements appointed by the life insurer for any such persons who have become unable to serve as directors); and

(B) An election of directors for the account is held at the first meeting of contractholders and within one year after the effective date of the 1933 Act registration statement for flexible contracts, unless the time for holding the meeting is extended by the Commission upon written request and for good cause shown; and

(ii) A member of the board of directors of the separate account may be disapproved or removed by an insurance regulatory authority if the person is not eligible to be a director of the separate account under the law of the life insurer's domicile.

(9) Section 17(f) (15 U.S.C. 80a–17(f)), to the extent that the securities and similar investments of a separate account organized as a management investment company may be maintained in the custody of the life insurer or of an affiliated life insurance company; provided that:

Securities and Exchange Commission

§ 270.6e-3

(i) The securities and similar investments allocated to the separate account are clearly identified as owned by the account, and the securities and similar investments are kept in the vault of an insurance company which meets the qualifications in paragraph (b)(9)(ii) of this section, and whose safekeeping function is supervised by the insurance regulatory authorities of the jurisdiction in which the securities and similar investments will be held;

(ii) The insurance company maintaining such investments must file with an insurance regulatory authority of a state or territory of the United States or the District of Columbia an annual statement of its financial condition in the form prescribed by the National Association of Insurance Commissioners, must be subject to supervision and inspection by such authority and must be examined periodically as to its financial condition and other affairs by such authority, must hold the securities and similar investments of the separate account in its vault, which vault must be equivalent to that of a bank which is a member of the Federal Reserve System, and must have a combined capital and surplus, if a stock company, or an unassigned surplus, if a mutual company, of not less than $1,000,000 as set forth in its most recent annual statement filed with such authority;

(iii) Access to such securities and similar investments shall be limited to employees of the Commission, representatives of insurance regulatory authorities, independent public accountants retained by the separate account (or on its behalf by the life insurer), accountants for the life insurer, and to no more than 20 persons authorized by a resolution of the board of directors of the separate account, which persons shall be directors of the separate account, officers and responsible employees of the life insurer or officers and responsible employees of the affiliated life insurance company in whose vault the investments are kept (if applicable), and access to such securities and similar investments shall be had only by two or more such persons jointly, at least one of whom shall be a director of the separate account or officer of the life insurer;

(iv) The requirement in paragraph (b)(9)(i) of this section that the securities and similar investments of the separate account be maintained in the vault of a qualified insurance company shall not apply to securities deposited with insurance regulatory authorities or deposited in accordance with any rule under section 17(f), or to securities on loan which are collateralized to the extent of their full market value, or to securities hypothecated, pledged, or placed in escrow for the account of such separate account in connection with a loan or other transaction authorized by specific resolution of the board of directors of the separate account, or to securities in transit in connection with the sale, exchange, redemption, maturity or conversion, the exercise of warrants or rights, assents to changes in terms of the securities, or to other transactions necessary or appropriate in the ordinary course of business relating to the management of securities;

(v) Each person when depositing such securities or similar investments in or withdrawing them from the depository or when ordering their withdrawal and delivery from the custody of the life insurer or affiliated life insurance company, shall sign a notation showing:

(A) The date and time of the deposit, withdrawal or order;

(B) The title and amount of the securities or other investments deposited, withdrawn or ordered to be withdrawn, and an identification thereof by certificate numbers or otherwise;

(C) The manner of acquisition of the securities or similar investments deposited or the purpose for which they have been withdrawn, or ordered to be withdrawn; and

(D) If withdrawn and delivered to another person, the name of such person. The notation shall be sent promptly to an officer or director of the separate account or the life insurer designated by the board of directors of the separate account who is not himself permitted to have access to the securities or investments under paragraph (b)(9)(iii) of this section. The notation shall be on serially numbered forms and shall be kept for at least one year;

(vi) The securities and similar investments shall be verified by complete examination by an independent public accountant retained by the separate account (or on its behalf by the life insurer) at least three times each fiscal year, at least two of which shall be chosen by the accountant without prior notice to the separate account. A certificate of the accountant stating that he has made an examination of such securities and investments and describing the nature and extent of the examination shall be sent to the Commission by the accountant promptly after each examination; and

(vii) Securities and similar investments of a separate account maintained with a bank or other company whose functions and physical facilities are supervised by Federal or state authorities under any arrangement whereby the directors, officers, employees or agents of the separate account or the life insurer are authorized or permitted to withdraw such investments upon their mere receipt are deemed to be in the custody of the life insurer and shall be exempt from the requirements of section 17(f) so long as the arrangement complies with all provisions of paragraph (b)(9) of this section, except that such securities will be maintained in the vault of a bank or other company rather than the vault of an insurance company.

(10) Section 18(i) (15 U.S.C. 80a–18(i)), to the extent that:

(i) For the purposes of any section of the Act which provides for the vote of securityholders on matters relating to the investment company:

(A) Flexible contractholders shall have one vote for each $100 of cash value funded by the separate account, with fractional votes allocated for amounts less than $100;

(B) The life insurer shall have one vote for each $100 of assets of the separate account not otherwise attributable to contractholders under paragraph (b)(10)(i)(A) of this section, with fractional votes allocated for amounts less than $100; provided that after the commencement of sales of flexible contracts, the life insurer shall cast its votes for and against each matter which may be voted upon by contractholders in the same proportion as the votes cast by contractholders; and

(C) The number of votes to be allocated shall be determined as of a record date not more than 90 days before any meeting at which such vote is held; provided that if a quorum is not present at the meeting, the meeting may be adjourned for up to 60 days without fixing a new record date; and

(ii) The requirement of section 18(i) that every share of stock issued by a registered management investment company (except a common-law trust of the character described in section 16(c) (15 U.S.C. 80a–16(c))) shall be a voting stock and have equal voting rights with every other outstanding voting stock shall not be deemed to be violated by actions specifically permitted by any provisions of this section.

(11) Section 19 (15 U.S.C. 80a–19), to the extent that the provisions of this section shall not apply to any dividend or similar distribution paid or payable under provisions of participating flexible contracts.

(12) Sections 22(c), 22(d), 22(e) and 27(i)(2)(A) (15 U.S.C. 80a–22(c)), 80a–22(d), 80a–22(e), and 80a–27(i)(2)(A), respectively) and §270.22c–1 (Rule 22c–1) to the extent:

(i) The cash value of each flexible contract shall be computed in accordance with Rule 22c–1(b); provided, however, that where actual computation is not necessary for the operation of a particular contract, then the cash value of that contract must only be capable of computation; and provided further that to the extent the calculation of the cash value reflects deductions for the cost of insurance and other insurance benefits or administrative expenses and fees or sales charges, such deductions need only be made at such times as specified in the contract or as necessary for compliance with insurance laws and regulations;

(ii) The death benefit, unless required by insurance laws and regulations, shall be computed on any day that the investment experience of the separate account would affect the death benefit under the terms of the contract provided that such terms are reasonable, fair, and nondiscriminatory; and

Securities and Exchange Commission

§ 270.6e-3

(iii) Necessary to comply with this section or with insurance laws and regulations and established administrative procedures of the life insurer for issuance, increases in or additions of insurance benefits, transfer and redemption of flexible contracts, including, but not limited to, premium rate structure and premium processing, insurance underwriting standards, and the particular benefit afforded by the contract; provided, however, that any procedure or action shall be reasonable, fair, and not discriminatory to the interests of the affected contractholders and to all other holders of contracts of the same class or series funded by the separate account; and provided further that any such action shall be disclosed in the form filed by the separate account with the Commission under paragraph (b)(3)(ii) of this section.

(13) Sections 27(i)(2)(A) and 22(c) (15 U.S.C. 80a–27(i)(2)(A) and 80a–22(c)) and § 270.22c–1 (Rule 22c–1), to the extent that:

(i) Such sections require that the flexible contract be redeemable or provide for a refund in cash; provided that the contract provides for election by the contractholder of a cash surrender value or certain non-forfeiture and settlement options which are required or permitted by the insurance law or regulation of the jurisdiction in which the contract is offered; and provided further that unless required by the insurance law or regulation of the jurisdiction in which the contract is offered or unless elected by the contractholder, the contract shall not provide for the automatic imposition of any option, including, but not limited to, an automatic premium loan, which would involve the accrual or payment of an interest or similar charge.

(ii) Notwithstanding the provisions of paragraph (b)(13)(i) of this section, if the amounts available under the contract to pay the charges due under the contract on any contract processing day are less than such charges due, the contract may provide that the cash surrender value shall be applied to purchase a non-forfeiture option specified by the life insurer in such contract; provided that the contract also provides that Contract processing days occur not less frequently than monthly.

(iii) Subject to section 26(f) (15 U.S.C. 80a–26(f)), sales charges and administrative expenses or fees may be deducted upon redemption.

(14) Section 32(a)(2) (15 U.S.C. 80a–31(a)(2)); provided that:

(i) The independent public accountant is selected before the effective date of the 1933 Act registration statement for flexible contracts, and the identity of the accountant is disclosed in the registration statement; and

(ii) The selection of the accountant is submitted for ratification or rejection to flexible contractholders at their first meeting and within one year after the effective date of the 1933 Act registration statement for flexible contracts, unless the time for holding the meeting is extended by order of the Commission.

(15) If the separate account is organized as a unit investment trust, all the assets of which consist of the shares of one or more registered management investment companies which offer their shares exclusively to separate accounts of the life insurer, or of any affiliated life insurance company, offering either scheduled contracts or flexible contracts, or both; or which also offer their shares to variable annuity separate accounts of the life insurer or of an affiliated life insurance company, or which offer their shares to any such life insurance company in consideration solely for advances made by the life insurer in connection with the operation of the separate account; provided that the board of directors of each investment company, constituted with a majority of disinterested directors, will monitor such company for the existence of any material irreconcilable conflict between the interests of variable annuity contractholders and scheduled or flexible contractholders investing in such company; the life insurer agrees that it will be responsible for reporting any potential or existing conflicts to the directors; and if a conflict arises, the life insurer will, at its own cost, remedy such conflict up to and including establishing a new registered management investment company and segregating the assets

§ 270.6e-3

underlying the variable annuity contracts and the scheduled or flexible contracts; then:

(i) The eligibility restrictions of section 9(a) shall not apply to those persons who are officers, directors or employees of the life insurer or its affiliates who do not participate directly in the management or administration of any registered management investment company described in paragraph (b)(15) of this section;

(ii) The life insurer shall be ineligible under paragraph (3) of section 9(a) to serve as investment adviser of or principal underwriter for any registered management investment company described in paragraph (b)(15) of this section only if an affiliated person of such life insurer, ineligible by reason of paragraphs (1) or (2) of section 9(a), participates in the management or administration of such company;

(iii) For purposes of any section of the Act which provides for the vote of securityholders on matters relating to the separate account or the underlying registered investment company, the voting provisions of paragraphs (b)(10)(i) and (ii) of this section apply; provided that:

(A) The life insurer may vote shares of the registered management investment companies held by the separate account without regard to instructions from contractholders of the separate account if such instructions would require such shares to be voted:

(1) To cause such companies to make (or refrain from making) certain investments which would result in changes in the sub-classification or investment objectives of such companies or to approve or disapprove any contract between such companies and an investment adviser when required to do so by an insurance regulatory authority subject to the provisions of paragraphs (b)(5)(i) and (b)(7)(ii)(A) of this section; or

(2) In favor of changes in investment objectives, investment adviser of or principal underwriter for such companies subject to the provisions of paragraphs (b)(5)(ii) and (b)(7)(ii)(B) and (C) of this section;

(B) Any action taken in accordance with paragraph (b)(15)(iii)(A)(1) or (2) of this section and the reasons therefor shall be disclosed in the next report contractholders made under section 30(e) (15 U.S.C. 80a-29(e)) and § 270.30e-2 (Rule 30e-2);

(iv) Any registered management investment company established by the life insurer and described in paragraph (b)(15) of this section shall be exempt from section 14(a); and

(v) Any registered management investment company established by the life insurer and described in paragraph (b)(14) of this section shall be exempt from sections 15(a), 16(a), and 32(a)(2) (15 U.S.C. 80a-15(a), 80-16(a), and 80-31(a)(2), respectively), to the extent prescribed by paragraphs (b)(7)(i), (b)(8)(i), and (b)(14) of this section; provided that the company complies with the conditions set forth in paragraphs (b)(7)(i), (b)(8)(i), and (b)(14) of this section as if it were a separate account.

(c) When used in this section:

(1) *Flexible premium variable life insurance contract* means a contract of life insurance, subject to regulation under the insurance laws or code of every jurisdiction in which it is offered, funded by a separate account of a life insurer, which contract provides for:

(i) Premium payments which are not fixed by the life insurer as to both timing and amount; provided, however, that the life insurer may fix the timing and minimum amount of premium payments for the first two contract periods following issuance of the contract or of an increase in or addition of insurance benefits, and may prescribe a reasonable minimum amount for any additional premium payment;

(ii) A death benefit the amount or duration of which may vary to reflect the investment experience of the separate account;

(iii) A cash value which varies to reflect the investment experience of the separate account; and

(iv) There is a reasonable expectation that subsequent premium payments will be made.

(2) *Contract period* means the period from a contract issue or anniversary date to the earlier of the next following anniversary date (or, if later, the last day of any grace period commencing before such next following anniversary date) or the termination date of the contract.

Securities and Exchange Commission § 270.7d-1

(3) *Cash value* means the amount that would be available in cash upon voluntary termination of a contract by its owner before it becomes payable by death or maturity, without regard to any charges that may be assessed upon such termination and before deduction of any outstanding contract loan.

(4) *Cash surrender value* means the amount available in cash upon voluntary termination of a contract by its owner before it becomes payable by death or maturity, after any charges assessed in connection with the termination have been deducted and before deduction of any outstanding contract loan.

(5) *Contract processing day* means any day on which charges under the contract are deducted from the separate account.

[85 FR 26105, May 1, 2020]

§ 270.7d-1 **Specification of conditions and arrangements for Canadian management investment companies requesting order permitting registration.**

(a) A management investment company organized under the laws of Canada or any province thereof may obtain an order pursuant to section 7(d) permitting its registration under the act and the public offering of its securities, if otherwise appropriate, upon the filing of an application complying with paragraph (b) of this section. All such applications will be considered by the Commission pursuant to the procedure set forth in § 270.0-5 and other applicable rules. Conditions and arrangements proposed by investment companies organized under the laws of other countries will be considered by the Commission in the light of the special circumstances and local laws involved in each case.

(b) An application filed pursuant to this section shall contain, inter alia, the following undertakings and agreements of the applicant:

(1) Applicant will cause each present and future officer, director, investment adviser, principal underwriter and custodian of the applicant to enter into an agreement, to be filed by applicant with the Commission upon the filing of its registration statement or upon the assumption of such office by such person which will provide, among other things, that each such person agrees (i) to comply with the applicant's Letters Patent (Charter) and By Laws, the act and the rules thereunder, and the undertakings and agreements contained in said application insofar as applicable to such person; (ii) to do nothing inconsistent with the applicant's undertakings and agreements required by this section; (iii) that the undertakings enumerated as paragraphs (b)(1)(i) and (ii) of this section constitute representations and inducements to the Commission to issue its order in the premises and continue the same in effect, as the case may be; (iv) that each such agreement constitutes a contract between such person and the applicant and its shareholders with the intent that applicant's shareholders shall be beneficiaries of and shall have the status of parties to such agreement so as to enable them to maintain actions at law or in equity within the United States and Canada for any violation thereof. In addition the agreement of each officer and director will contain provisions similar to those contained in paragraph (b)(6) of this section.

(2) That every agreement and undertaking of the applicant, its officers, directors, investment adviser, principal underwriter and custodian required by this section (i) constitute inducements to the Commission for the issuance and continuance in effect of, and conditions to, the Commission's order to be entered under this section; (ii) constitute a contract among applicant and applicant's shareholders with the same intent as set forth in paragraph (b)(1)(iv) of this section; and (iii) failure by the applicant or any of the above enumerated persons to comply with any such agreement and undertaking, unless permitted by the Commission, shall constitute a violation of the order entered under this section.

(3) That the Commission, in its discretion, may revoke its order permitting registration of the applicant and the public offering of its securities if it shall find after notice and opportunity for hearing that there shall have been a violation of such order or the act and may determine whether distribution of

§ 270.7d-1

applicant's assets is necessary or appropriate in the interests of investors and may so direct.

(4) That applicant will perform every action and thing necessary to cause and assist the custodian of its assets to distribute the same, or the proceeds thereof, if the Commission or a court of competent jurisdiction, shall have so directed by a final order.

(5) That any shareholder of the applicant or the Commission on its own motion or on request of shareholders shall have the right to initiate a proceeding (i) before the Commission for the revocation of the order permitting registration of the applicant or (ii) before a court of competent jurisdiction for the liquidation of applicant and a distribution of its assets to its shareholders and creditors. Such court may enter such order in the event that it shall find, after notice and opportunity for hearing that applicant, its officers, directors, investment adviser, principal underwriter or custodian shall have violated any provision of the act or the Commission's order of registration of the applicant.

A court of competent jurisdiction for the purpose of paragraphs (b)(4) and (5) of this paragraph means the District Court of the United States of the district in which the assets of the applicant are maintained.

(6) That any shareholder of the applicant shall have the right to bring suit at law or in equity, in any court of the United States or Canada having jurisdiction over applicant, its assets or any of its officers or directors to enforce compliance by applicant, its officers and directors with any provision of applicant's Charter or By Laws, the act and the rules thereunder, or undertakings and agreements required by this section, insofar as applicable to such persons. That such court may appoint a trustee or receiver of the applicant with all powers necessary to implement the purposes of such suit, including the administration of the estate, the collection of corporate property including choses-in-action, and distribution of applicant's assets to its creditors and shareholders. That applicant and its officers and directors waive any objection they may be entitled to raise and any right they may have to object to the power and right of any shareholder of the applicant to bring such suit, reserving, however, their right to maintain that they have complied with the aforesaid provisions, undertakings and agreements, and otherwise to dispute such suit on its merits. Applicant, its officers and directors also agree that any final judgment or decree of any United States court as aforesaid, may be granted full faith and credit by a court of competent jurisdiction of Canada and consent that such Canadian court may enter judgment or decree thereon at the instance of any shareholder, receiver or trustee of the applicant.

(7) Applicant will file, and will cause each of its present or future directors, officers, or investment advisers who is not a resident of the United States to file with the Commission irrevocable designation of the applicant's custodian as an agent in the United States to accept service of process in any suit, action or proceeding before the Commission or any appropriate court to enforce the provisions of the acts administered by the Commission, or to enforce any right or liability based upon applicant's Charter, By Laws, contracts, or the respective undertakings and agreements of any such person required by this section, or which alleges a liability on the part of any such persons arising out of their service, acts of transactions relating to the applicant.

(8) Applicant's Charter and By Laws, taken together, will contain, so long as applicant is registered under the act in substance the following:

(i) The provisions of the Act as follows: Section 2(a): *Provided,* That the term "government securities" defined in section 2(a)(16) may include securities issued or guaranteed by Canada or any instrumentality of the government of Canada; the term "value" defined in section 2(a)(41) may be defined solely for the purposes of sections 5 and 12 in accordance with the provisions of § 270.2a-1 (Rule 2a-1) if the same shall be necessary or desirable to comply with Canadian regulatory or revenue laws or rules or regulations thereunder; the term "bank" defined in section 2(a)(5) shall be defined solely for the purposes of section 9 and 10, as any banking institution; section 4; section

Securities and Exchange Commission § 270.7d-1

5; section 6(c); section 9; section 10 (a), (b), (c), (e), (f) and (g): *Provided,* That the provisions of section 10(d) may be substituted for the provisions of section 10(a) and 10(b)(2) if applicable; section 11; section 12 (a), (b), (c), and (d); section 13(a); section 15 (a), (b), and (c); section 16(a); sections 17, 18, 19, 20 and 21; section 22(d); section 22(e): *Provided,* That the Toronto Stock Exchange or the Montreal Stock Exchange or both may be included in addition to the New York Stock Exchange; section 22(f); section 22(g); section 23; section 25 (a) and (b); section 30 (a), (b), (d), (e), and (f); section 31; section 32(a): *Provided,* That provision may be made for the selection and termination of employment of the accountant in compliance with The Companies Act of Canada; section 32(b). Where a provision of the act prohibits or directs action by an investment company, or its directors, officers or employees, the Charter or By Laws shall state that the applicant of its directors, officers or employees shall or shall not act, as the case may be, in conformity with the intent of the statute; where the provision applies to others, such as principal underwriters, investment advisers, controlled companies and affiliated persons, the Charter or By Laws shall also state that the applicant will not permit the prohibited conduct or will obtain the required action. Any of the provisions of sections 11, 12, 15, 18, 22, 23, 30, and 31 may be omitted if not applicable to a company of applicant's classification or subclassification as defined in section 4 or 5 of the act or if not applicable because the subject matter of such provisions is prohibited by the Charter or By Laws. Other provisions of the act not specified above may be incorporated in the applicant's Charter or By Laws at its option.

(ii) Any question of interpretation of any term or provision of the Charter or By Laws having a counterpart in or otherwise derived from a term or provision of the act shall be resolved by reference to interpretations, if any, of the corresponding term or provision of the act by the courts of the United States of America or, in the absence of any controlling decision of any such court, by rules, regulations, orders or interpretations of the Commission.

(iii) Applicant will maintain the original or duplicate copies of its books and records at the office of its custodian or other office located within the United States.

(iv) At least a majority of the directors and of the officers of the applicant will be United States citizens of whom a majority will be resident in the United States.

(v) Except as provided in § 270.17f–5 and § 270.17f–7, applicant will appoint, by contract, a bank, as defined in section 2(a)(5) of the Act (15 U.S.C. 80a–2(a)(5)) and having the qualification described in section 26(a)(1) of the Act (15 U.S.C. 80a–26(a)(1)), to act as trustee of, and maintain in its sole custody in the United States, all of applicant's securities and cash, other than cash necessary to meet applicant's current administrative expenses. The contract will provide, *inter alia,* that the custodian will:

(A) Consummate all purchases and sales of securities by applicant, other than purchases and sales on an established securities exchange, through the delivery of securities and receipt of cash, or *vice versa* as the case may be, within the United States, and (B) redeem in the United States such of applicant's shares as shall be surrendered therefor, and (C) distribute applicant's assets, or the proceeds thereof, to applicant's creditors and shareholders, upon service upon the custodian of an order of the Commission or court directing such distribution as provided in paragraphs (b) (3) and (5) of this section.

(vi) Applicant's principal underwriter for the sale of its shares will be a citizen and resident of the United States or a corporation organized under the laws of a state of the United States, and having its principal place of business therein, and if redeemable shares are offered, also a member in good standing of a securities association registered under section 15A of the Securities Exchange Act of 1934.

(vii) Applicant will appoint an accountant, qualified to act as an independent public accountant for the applicant under the act and the rules thereunder, who maintains a permanent office and place of business in the United States.

(viii) Any contract entered into between the applicant and its investment adviser and principal underwriter will contain provisions in compliance with the requirements of sections 15, 17(i) and 31 and the rules thereunder, and require that the investment adviser maintain in the United States its books and records or duplicate copies thereof relating to applicant.

(ix) Applicant's Charter and By Laws will not be changed in any manner inconsistent with this paragraph or the Act and the rules thereunder unless authorized by the Commission.

(9) Contracts of the applicant, other than those executed on an established securities exchange which do not involve affiliated persons, will provide that:

(i) Such contracts, irrespective of the place of their execution or performance, will be performed in accordance with the requirements of the Act, the Securities Act of 1933, and the Securities Exchange Act of 1934, if the subject matter of such contracts is within the purview of such acts; and

(ii) In effecting the purchase or sale of assets the parties thereto will utilize the United States mails or means of interstate commerce.

(10) Applicant will furnish to the Commission with its registration statement filed under the Act a list of persons affiliated with it and with its investment adviser and principal underwriter and will furnish revisions of such list, if any, concurrently with the filing of periodic reports required to be filed under the Act.

(Sec. 7, 54 Stat. 802; 15 U.S.C. 80a–7; secs. 6(c); 15 U.S.C. 80a–6(c); and 38(a); 15 U.S.C. 80a–37(a) of the Act)

[19 FR 2585, May 5, 1954, as amended at 38 FR 8593, Apr. 4, 1973; 49 FR 36084, Sept. 14, 1984; 65 FR 25637, May 3, 2000]

§ 270.7d–2 Definition of "public offering" as used in section 7(d) of the Act with respect to certain Canadian tax-deferred retirement savings accounts.

(a) *Definitions.* As used in this section:

(1) *Canadian law* means the federal laws of Canada, the laws of any province or territory of Canada, and the rules or regulations of any federal, provincial, or territorial regulatory authority, or any self-regulatory authority, of Canada.

(2) *Canadian Retirement Account* means a trust or other arrangement, including, but not limited to, a "Registered Retirement Savings Plan" or "Registered Retirement Income Fund" administered under Canadian law, that is managed by the Participant and:

(i) Operated to provide retirement benefits to a Participant; and

(ii) Established in Canada, administered under Canadian law, and qualified for tax-deferred treatment under Canadian law.

(3) *Eligible Security* means a security issued by a Qualified Company that:

(i) Is offered to a Participant, or sold to his or her Canadian Retirement Account, in reliance on this section; and

(ii) May also be purchased by Canadians other than Participants.

(4) *Foreign Government* means the government of any foreign country or of any political subdivision of a foreign country.

(5) *Foreign Issuer* means any issuer that is a Foreign Government, a national of any foreign country or a corporation or other organization incorporated or organized under the laws of any foreign country, except an issuer meeting the following conditions:

(i) More than 50 percent of the outstanding voting securities of the issuer are held of record either directly or through voting trust certificates or depositary receipts by residents of the United States; and

(ii) Any of the following:

(A) The majority of the executive officers or directors are United States citizens or residents;

(B) More than 50 percent of the assets of the issuer are located in the United States; or

(C) The business of the issuer is administered principally in the United States.

(iii) For purposes of this definition, the term *resident,* as applied to security holders, means any person whose address appears on the records of the issuer, the voting trustee, or the depositary as being located in the United States.

(6) *Participant* means a natural person who is a resident of the United States,

Securities and Exchange Commission § 270.8b–2

or is temporarily present in the United States, and who contributes to, or is or will be entitled to receive the income and assets from, a Canadian Retirement Account.

(7) *Qualified Company* means a Foreign Issuer whose securities are qualified for investment on a tax-deferred basis by a Canadian Retirement Account under Canadian law.

(8) *United States* means the United States of America, its territories and possessions, any State of the United States, and the District of Columbia.

(b) *Public Offering.* For purposes of section 7(d) of the Act (15 U.S.C. 80a–7(d)), the term "public offering" does not include the offer to a Participant, or the sale to his or her Canadian Retirement Account, of Eligible Securities issued by a Qualified Company, if the Qualified Company:

(1) Includes in any written offering materials delivered to a Participant, or to his or her Canadian Retirement Account, a prominent statement that the Eligible Security, and the Qualified Company that issued the Eligible Security, are not registered with the U.S. Securities and Exchange Commission, and that the Eligible Security and the Qualified Company are relying on exemptions from registration.

(2) Has not asserted that Canadian law, or the jurisdiction of the courts of Canada, does not apply in a proceeding involving an Eligible Security.

[65 FR 37677, June 15, 2000]

§ 270.8b–1 Scope of §§ 270.8b–1 through 270.8b–31.

The rules contained in §§ 270.8b–1 through 270.8b–31 shall govern all registration statements pursuant to section 8 of the Act (15 U.S.C. 80a–8), including notifications of registration pursuant to section 8(a), and all reports pursuant to section 30(a) or (b) of the Act (15 U.S.C. 80a–29(a) or (b)), including all amendments to such statements and reports, except that any provision in a form covering the same subject matter as any such rule shall be controlling.

[83 FR 40880, Aug. 16, 2018, as amended at 85 FR 26109, May 1, 2020]

§ 270.8b–2 Definitions.

Unless the context otherwise requires, the terms in paragraphs (a) through (m) of this section, when used in the rules contained in §§ 270.8b–1 through 270.8b–32, in the rules under section 30(a) or (b) of the Act or in the forms for registration statements and reports pursuant to section 8 or 30(a) or (b) of the Act, shall have the respective meanings indicated in this section. The terms "EDGAR," "EDGAR Filer Manual," "electronic filer," "electronic filing," "electronic format," "electronic submission," "paper format," and "signature" shall have the meanings assigned to such terms in part 232 of this chapter (Regulation S–T—General Rules for Electronic Filings).

(a) *Amount.* The term "amount", when used in regard to securities, means the principal amount if relating to evidences of indebtedness, the number of shares if relating to shares, and the number of units if relating to any other kind of security.

(b) *Certified.* The term "certified", when used in regard to financial statements, means certified by an independent public or independent certified public accountant or accountants.

(c) *Charter.* The term "charter" includes articles of incorporation, declaration of trust, articles of association or partnership, or any similar instrument, as amended, effecting (either with or without filing with any governmental agency) the organization or creation of an incorporated or unincorporated person.

(d) *Employee.* The term "employee" does not include a director, trustee, officer or member of the advisory board.

(e) *Fiscal year.* The term "fiscal year" means the annual accounting period or, if no closing date has been adopted, the calendar year ending on December 31.

(f) *Investment income.* The term "investment income" means the aggregate of net operating income or loss from real estate and gross income from interest, dividends and all other sources, exclusive of profit or loss on sales of securities or other properties.

(g) *Material.* The term "material", when used to qualify a requirement for the furnishing of information as to any subject, limits the information required to those matters as to which an average prudent investor ought reasonably to be informed before buying or selling any security of the particular company.

(h) *Parent.* A "parent" of a specified person is an affiliated person who controls the specified person directly or indirectly through one or more intermediaries.

(i) *Previously filed or reported.* The terms "previously filed" and "previously reported" means previously filed with, or reported in, a registration statement filed under section 8 of the Act or under the Securities Act of 1933, a report filed under section 30 of the Act or section 13 or 15(d) of the Securities Exchange Act of 1934, a definitive proxy statement filed under section 20 of the Act or section 14 of the Securities Exchange Act of 1934, or a prospectus filed under the Securities Act of 1933: *Provided,* That information contained in any such document shall be deemed to have been previously filed with, or reported to, an exchange only if such document is filed with such exchange.

(j) *Share.* The term "share" means a share of stock in a corporation or unit of interest in an unincorporated person.

(k) *Significant subsidiary.* The term "significant subsidiary" means a subsidiary, including its subsidiaries, which meets any of the following conditions, using amounts determined under U.S. Generally Accepted Accounting Principles and, if applicable, section 2(a)(41) of the Act:

(1) *Investment test.* The value of the registrant's and its other subsidiaries' investments in and advances to the tested subsidiary exceed 10 percent of the value of the total investments of the registrant and its subsidiaries consolidated as of the end of the most recently completed fiscal year; or

(2) *Income test.* The absolute value of the sum of combined investment income from dividends, interest, and other income, the net realized gains and losses on investments, and the net change in unrealized gains and losses on investments from the tested subsidiary, for the most recently completed fiscal year exceeds:

(i) 80 percent of the absolute value of the change in net assets resulting from operations of the registrant and its subsidiaries consolidated for the most recently completed fiscal year; or

(ii) 10 percent of the absolute value of the change in net assets resulting from operations of the registrant and its subsidiaries consolidated for the most recently completed fiscal year and the investment test (paragraph (k)(1) of this section) condition exceeds 5 percent. However, if the absolute value of the change in net assets resulting from operations of the registrant and its subsidiaries consolidated is at least 10 percent lower than the average of the absolute value of such amounts for each of its last five fiscal years, then the registrant may compute both conditions of the income test using the average of the absolute value of such amounts for the registrant and its subsidiaries consolidated for each of its last five fiscal years.

(l) *Subsidiary.* A "subsidiary" of a specified person is an affiliated person who is controlled by the specified person, directly or indirectly, through one or more intermediaries.

(m) *Totally-held subsidiary.* The term "totally-held subsidiary" means a subsidiary (1) substantially all of whose outstanding securities are owned by its parent and/or the parent's other totally-held subsidiaries, and (2) which is not indebted to any person other than its parent and/or the parent's other totally-held subsidiaries in an amount which is material in relation to the particular subsidiary, excepting indebtedness incurred in the ordinary course of business which is not overdue and which matures within one year from the date of its creation, whether evidenced by securities or not.

[18 FR 8575, Dec. 19, 1953, as amended at 19 FR 2779, May 14, 1954; 58 FR 14860, Mar. 18, 1993; 65 FR 24802, Apr. 27, 2000; 70 FR 6572, Feb. 8, 2005; 83 FR 40878, Aug. 16, 2018; 85 FR 54073, Aug. 31, 2020]

§ 270.8b-3 Title of securities.

Wherever the title of securities is required to be stated, there shall be given such information as will indicate the type and general character of the securities, including the following:

(a) In the case of shares, the par or stated value, if any; the rate of dividends, if fixed, and whether cumulative

Securities and Exchange Commission

or noncumulative; a brief indication of the preference, if any; and if convertible, a statement to that effect.

(b) In the case of funded debt, the rate of interest; the date of maturity, or if the issue matures serially, a brief indication of the serial maturities, such as "maturing serially from 1950 to 1960"; if the payment of principal or interest is contingent, an appropriate indication of such contingency; a brief indication of the priority of the issue; and if convertible, a statement to that effect.

(c) In the case of any other kind of security, appropriate information of comparable character.

[18 FR 8575, Dec. 19, 1953]

§ 270.8b-4 Interpretation of requirements.

Unless the context clearly shows otherwise:

(a) The forms require information only as to the company filing the registration statement or report.

(b) Whenever any fixed period of time in the past is indicated, such period shall be computed from the date of filing.

(c) Whenever words relate to the future, they have reference solely to present intention.

(d) Any words indicating the holder of a position or office include persons, by whatever titles designated, whose duties are those ordinarily performed by holders of such positions or officers.

[18 FR 8575, Dec. 18, 1953]

§ 270.8b-5 Time of filing original registration statement.

An investment company shall file a registration statement with the Commission on the appropriate form within three months after the filing of notification of registration under section 8(a) of the Act, provided that if the fiscal year of the company ends within the three months period, its registration statement may be filed within three months after the end of such fiscal year.

[19 FR 2779, May 14, 1954]

§ 270.8b-6 [Reserved]

§ 270.8b-10 Requirements as to proper form.

Every registration statement or report shall be prepared in accordance with the form prescribed therefor by the Commission, as in effect on the date of filing. Any such statement or report shall be deemed to be filed on the proper form unless objection to the form is made by the Commission within thirty days after the date of filing.

[18 FR 8576, Dec. 19, 1953]

§ 270.8b-11 Number of copies; signatures; binding.

(a) Three complete copies of each registration statement or report, including exhibits and all other papers and documents filed as a part thereof, shall be filed with the Commission.

(b) In the case of a registration statement filed on Form N-1A (§ 239.15A and § 274.11A of this chapter), Form N-2 (§ 239.14 and § 274.11a-1 of this chapter), Form N-3 (§ 239.17a and § 274.11b of this chapter), Form N-4 (§ 239.17b and § 274.11c of this chapter), or Form N-6 (§ 239.17c and § 274.11d of this chapter), three complete copies of each part of the registration statement (including, if applicable, exhibits and all other papers and documents filed as part of Part C of the registration statement) shall be filed with the Commission.

(c) At least one copy of the registration statement or report shall be signed in the manner prescribed by the appropriate form. Unsigned copies shall be conformed. If the signature of any person is affixed pursuant to a power of attorney or other similar authority, a copy of such power of attorney or other authority shall also be filed with the registration statement or report.

(d) Each copy of a registration statement or report filed with the Commission shall be bound in one or more parts without stiff covers. The binding shall be made on the left-hand side and in such manner as to leave the reading matter legible.

(e) *Signatures.* Where the Act or the rules thereunder, including paragraph (c) of this section, require a document filed with or furnished to the Commission to be signed, the document should

§ 270.8b–12

be manually signed, or signed using either typed signatures or duplicated or facsimile versions of manual signatures. When typed, duplicated, or facsimile signatures are used, each signatory to the filing shall manually or electronically sign a signature page or other document authenticating, acknowledging, or otherwise adopting his or her signature that appears in the filing ("authentication document"). Execute each such authentication document before or at the time the filing is made and retain for a period of five years. The requirements set forth in § 232.302(b) must be met with regards to the use of an electronically signed authentication document pursuant to this paragraph (e). Upon request, the registrant shall furnish to the Commission or its staff a copy of any or all documents retained pursuant to this section.

[49 FR 32059, Aug. 10, 1984, as amended at 50 FR 26160, June 25, 1985; 57 FR 56835, Dec. 1, 1992; 60 FR 26622, May 17, 1995; 63 FR 13944, Mar. 23, 1998; 67 FR 19870, Apr. 23, 2002; 85 FR 78320, Dec. 4, 2020]

§ 270.8b–12 Requirements as to paper, printing and language.

(a) Registration statements and reports shall be filed on good quality, unglazed, white paper, no larger than 8½ × 11 inches in size, insofar as practicable. To the extent that the reduction of larger documents would render them illegible, such documents may be filed on paper larger than 8½ × 11 inches in size.

(b) In the case of a registration statement filed on Form N–1A (§§ 239.15A and 274.11A of this chapter), Form N–2 (§§ 239.14 and 274.11a–1 of this chapter), Form N–3 (§§ 239.17a and 274.11b of this chapter), Form N–4 (§§ 239.17b and 274.11c of this chapter), or Form N–6 (§ 239.17c and § 274.11d of this chapter), Part C of the registration statement shall be filed on good quality, unglazed, white paper, no larger than 8½ × 11 inches in size, insofar as practicable. The prospectus and, if applicable, the Statement of Additional Information, however, may be filed on smaller-sized paper provided that the size of paper used in each document is uniform.

(c) The registration statement or report and, insofar as practicable all papers and documents filed as a part thereof, shall be printed, lithographed, mimeographed or typewritten. However, the registration statement or report or any portion thereof may be prepared by any similar process which, in the opinion of the Commission, produces copies suitable for permanent record. Irrespective of the process used, all copies of any such material shall be clear, easily readable and suitable for repeated photocopying. Debits in credit categories and credits in debit categories shall be designated so as to be clearly distinguishable as such on photocopies.

(d) The body of all printed registration statements and reports and all notes to financial statements and other tabular data included therein shall be in roman type at least as large as 10-point modern type. However, to the extent necessary for convenient presentation, financial statements and other statistical or tabular data, including tabular data in notes, may be set in type at least as large and as legible as 8-point modern type. All type shall be leaded at least 2-points.

(e) Registration statements and reports shall be in the English language. If any exhibit or other paper or document filed with a registration statement or report is in a foreign language, it shall be accompanied by a translation into the English language.

(f) Where a registration statement or report is distributed through an electronic medium, issuers may satisfy legibility requirements applicable to printed documents, such as paper size, type size and font, bold-face type, italics and red ink, by presenting all required information in a format readily communicated to investors, and where indicated, in a manner reasonably calculated to draw investor attention to specific information.

[49 FR 32060, Aug. 10, 1984, as amended at 50 FR 26160, June 25, 1985; 57 FR 56836, Dec. 1, 1992; 61 FR 24657, May 15, 1996; 67 FR 19870, Apr. 23, 2002]

§ 270.8b–13 Preparation of registration statement or report.

The registration statement or report shall contain the numbers and captions of all items of the appropriate form,

Securities and Exchange Commission

§ 270.8b–16

but the text of the items may be omitted provided the answers thereto are so prepared as to indicate to the reader the coverage of the items without the necessity of his referring to the text of the items or instructions thereto. However, where any item requires information to be given in tabular form, it shall be given in substantially the tabular form specified in the item. All instructions, whether appearing under the items of the form or elsewhere therein, are to be omitted from the registration statement or report. Unless expressly provided otherwise, if any item is inapplicable or the answer thereto is in the negative, an appropriate statement to that effect shall be made.

[18 FR 8576, Dec. 19, 1953]

§ 270.8b–14 Riders; inserts.

Riders shall not be used. If the registration statement or report is typed on a printed form, and the space provided for the answer to any given item is insufficient, reference shall be made in such space to a full insert page or pages on which the item number and caption and the complete answer are given.

[18 FR 8576, Dec. 19, 1953]

§ 270.8b–15 Amendments.

All amendments shall be filed under cover of the facing sheet of the appropriate form, shall be clearly identified as amendments, and shall comply with all pertinent requirements applicable to registration statements and reports. Amendments shall be filed separately for each separate registration or report amended. Except as permitted under rule 102(b) of Regulation S-T (§ 232.102(b) of this chapter), any amendment filed under this section shall state the complete text of each item amended. An amendment to any report required to include the certifications as specified in § 270.30a-2(a) must include new certifications by each principal executive and principal financial officer of the registrant, and an amendment to any report required to be accompanied by the certifications as specified in § 240.13a-14(b) or § 240.15d-14(b) and § 270.30a-2(b) must be accompanied by new certifications by each principal executive and principal financial officer of the registrant.

[18 FR 8576, Dec. 19, 1953, as amended at 58 FR 14860, Mar. 18, 1993; 68 FR 5365, Feb. 3, 2003; 68 FR 36671, June 18, 2003]

§ 270.8b–16 Amendments to registration statement.

(a) Every registered management investment company which is required to file an annual report on Form N-CEN, as prescribed by § 270.30a–1 of this chaptershall amend the registration statement required pursuant to Section 8(b) by filing, not more than 120 days after the close of each fiscal year ending on or after the date upon which such registration statement was filed, the appropriate form prescribed for such amendments.

(b) Paragraph (a) of this section shall not apply to a registered closed-end management investment company whose registration statement was filed on Form N–2; provided that the following information is transmitted to shareholders in its annual report to shareholders:

(1) If the company offers a dividend reinvestment plan to shareholders, information about the plan required to be disclosed in the company's prospectus by Item 10.1.e of Form N–2 (17 CFR 274.11a–1);

(2) The company's investment objectives and policies (described in Item 8.2 of Form N–2), and any material changes to same that have not been approved by shareholders;

(3) Any changes in the company's charter or by-laws that would delay or prevent a change of control of the company (described in Item 10.1.f of Form N–2) that have not been approved by shareholders;

(4) The principal risk factors associated with investment in the company (described in Item 8.3 of Form N–2), and any material changes to same; and

(5) Any changes in the persons who are primarily responsible for the day-to-day management of the company's portfolio (described in Item 9.1.c of Form N–2), including any new person's business experience during the past five years and the length of time he or she has been responsible for the management of the portfolio.

§ 270.8b-20

(c) In lieu of including a description of the dividend reinvestment plan in its annual report, a company may comply with the disclosure requirement of paragraph (b)(1) of this section concerning a company's dividend reinvestment plan by delivering to each shareholder annually a separate document containing the information about the plan required to be disclosed in the company's prospectus by Item 10.1.e of Form N-2. Any such document shall be deemed to be a record or document subject to the record-keeping requirements of section 31 (15 U.S.C. 80a-30) and the rules adopted thereunder (17 CFR 270.31a-1 et seq.).

(d) The changes required to be disclosed by paragraphs (b)(2) through (b)(5) of this section are those that occurred since the later of either the effective date of the company's registration statement relating to its initial offering of securities under the Securities Act of 1933 (15 U.S.C. 77a et seq.) (or the most recent post-effective amendment thereto) or the close of the period covered by the previously transmitted annual shareholder report.

(e) The changes required to be disclosed by paragraphs (b)(2) through (5) of this section must be described in enough detail to allow investors to understand each change and how it may affect the fund. Such disclosures must be prefaced with the following legend: "The following information [in this annual report] is a summary of certain changes since [date]. This information may not reflect all of the changes that have occurred since you purchased [this fund]."

[54 FR 10321, Mar. 13, 1989, as amended at 57 FR 56836, Dec. 1, 1992; 81 FR 82020, Nov. 18, 2016; 85 FR 33360, June 1, 2020]

§ 270.8b-20 Additional information.

In addition to the information expressly required to be included in a registration statement or report, there shall be added such further material information, if any, as may be necessary to make the required statements, in the light of the circumstances under which they are made, not misleading.

[18 FR 8576, Dec. 19, 1953]

§ 270.8b-21 Information unknown or not available.

Information required need be given only insofar as it is known or reasonably available to the registrant. If any required information is unknown and not reasonably available to the registrant, either because the obtaining thereof would involve unreasonable effort or expense, or because it rests peculiarly within the knowledge of another person not affiliated with the registrant, the information may be omitted subject to the following conditions:

(a) The registrant shall give such information on the subject as it possesses or can acquire without unreasonable effort or expense, together with the sources thereof.

(b) The registrant shall include a statement either showing that unreasonable effort or expense would be involved or indicating the absence of any affiliation with the person within whose knowledge the information rests and stating the result of a request made to such person for the information.

[18 FR 8576, Dec. 19, 1953]

§ 270.8b-22 Disclaimer of control.

If the existence of control is open to reasonable doubt in any instance, the registrant may disclaim the existence of control and any admission thereof; in such case, however, the registrant shall state the material facts pertinent to the possible existence of control.

[18 FR 8576, Dec. 19, 1953]

§§ 270.8b-23—270.8b-24 [Reserved]

§ 270.8b-25 Extension of time for furnishing information.

(a) Subject to paragraph (b) of this section, if it is impractical to furnish any required information, document or report at the time it is required to be filed, there may be filed with the Commission as a separate document an application (a) identifying the information, document or report in question, (b) stating why the filing thereof at the time required is impracticable, and (c) requesting an extension of time for filing the information, document or report to a specified date not more than

Securities and Exchange Commission § 270.10b–1

60 days after the date it would otherwise have to be filed. The application shall be deemed granted unless the Commission, within 10 days after receipt thereof, shall enter an order denying the application. Section 270.0–5 (Rule N–5) shall not apply to such applications.

(b) If it is impracticable to furnish any document or report required to be filed in electronic format at the time it is required to be filed, the electronic filer may file under the temporary hardship provision of rule 201 of Regulation S-T (§ 232.201 of this chapter) or may submit a written application for a continuing hardship exemption, in accordance with rule 202 of Regulation S-T (§ 232.202 of this chapter). Applications for such exemptions shall be considered in accordance with the provisions of those sections and paragraphs (h) and (i) of § 200.30–5 of this chapter.

[18 FR 8576, Dec. 19, 1953, as amended at 58 FR 14860, Mar. 18, 1993; 60 FR 14630, Mar. 20, 1995]

§ 270.8b–30 Additional exhibits.

A company may file such exhibits as it may desire, in addition to those required by the appropriate form. Such exhibits shall be so marked as to indicate clearly the subject matters to which they refer.

[18 FR 8576, Dec. 19, 1953]

§ 270.8b–31 Omission of substantially identical documents.

In any case where two or more indentures, contracts, franchises, or other documents required to be filed as exhibits are substantially identical in all material respects except as to the parties thereto, the dates of execution, or other details, copies of only one of such documents need be filed, with a schedule identifying the other documents omitted and setting forth the material details in which such documents differ from the documents filed. The Commission may at any time in its discretion require the filing of copies of any documents so omitted.

[18 FR 8576, Dec. 19, 1953]

§ 270.8b–32 [Reserved]

§ 270.8f–1 Deregistration of certain registered investment companies.

A registered investment company that seeks a Commission order declaring that it is no longer an investment company may file an application with the Commission on Form N–8F (17 CFR 274.218) if the investment company:

(a) Has sold substantially all of its assets to another registered investment company or merged into or consolidated with another registered investment company;

(b) Has distributed substantially all of its assets to its shareholders and has completed, or is in the process of, winding up its affairs;

(c) Qualifies for an exclusion from the definition of "investment company" under section 3(c)(1) (15 U.S.C. 80a–3(c)(1)) or section 3(c)(7) (15 U.S.C. 80a–3(c)(7)) of the Act; or

(d) Has become a business development company.

NOTE TO § 270.8f–1: Applicants who are not eligible to use Form N–8F to file an application to deregister may follow the general guidance for filing applications under rule 0–2 (17 CFR 270.0–2) of this chapter.

[64 FR 19471, Apr. 21, 1999]

§ 270.10b–1 Definition of regular broker or dealer.

The term *regular broker or dealer* of an investment company shall mean:

(a) One of the ten brokers or dealers that received the greatest dollar amount of brokerage commissions by virtue of direct or indirect participation in the company's portfolio transactions during the company's most recent fiscal year;

(b) One of the ten brokers or dealers that engaged as principal in the largest dollar amount of portfolio transactions of the investment company during the company's most recent fiscal year; or

(c) One of the ten brokers or dealers that sold the largest dollar amount of securities of the investment company during the company's most recent fiscal year.

[49 FR 40572, Oct. 17, 1984]

§ 270.10e-1 Death, disqualification, or bona fide resignation of directors.

If a registered investment company, by reason of the death, disqualification, or bona fide resignation of any director, does not meet any requirement of the Act or any rule or regulation thereunder regarding the composition of the company's board of directors, the operation of the relevant subsection of the Act, rule, or regulation will be suspended as to the company:

(a) For 90 days if the vacancy may be filled by action of the board of directors; or

(b) For 150 days if a vote of stockholders is required to fill the vacancy.

[66 FR 3758, Jan. 16, 2001]

§ 270.10f-1 Conditional exemption of certain underwriting transactions.

Any purchase or other acquisition by a registered management company acting, pursuant to a written agreement, as an underwriter of securities of an issuer which is not an investment company shall be exempt from the provisions of section 10(f) (54 Stat. 806; 15 U.S.C. 80a–10) upon the following conditions:

(a) The party to such agreement other than such registered company is a principal underwriter of such securities, which principal underwriter (1) is a person primarily engaged in the business of underwriting and distributing securities issued by other persons, selling securities to customers, or related activities, whose gross income normally is derived principally from such business or related activities, and (2) does not control or is not under common control with such registered company.

(b) No public offering of the securities underwritten by such agreement has been made prior to the execution thereof.

(c) Such securities have been effectively registered pursuant to the Securities Act of 1933 (48 Stat. 74; 15 U.S.C. 77a-aa) prior to the execution of such agreement.

(d) In regard to any securities underwritten, whether or not purchased, by the registered company pursuant to such agreement, such company shall be allowed a rate of gross commission, spread, concession or other profit not less than the amount allowed to such principal underwriter, exclusive of any amounts received by such principal underwriter as a management fee from other principal underwriters.

(e) Such agreement is authorized by resolution adopted by a vote of not less than a majority of the board of directors of such registered company, none of which majority is an affiliated person of such principal underwriter, of the issuer of the securities underwritten pursuant to such agreement or of any person engaged in a business described in paragraph (a)(1) of this section.

(f) The resolution required in paragraph (e) of this section shall state that it has been adopted pursuant to this section, and shall incorporate the terms of the proposed agreement by attaching a copy thereof as an exhibit or otherwise.

(g) A copy of the resolution required in paragraph (e) of this section, signed by each member of the board of directors of the registered company who voted in favor of its adoption, shall be transmitted to the Commission not later than the fifth day succeeding the date on which such agreement is executed.

[Rule N-10F-1, 6 FR 1191, Feb. 28, 1941]

§ 270.10f-2 Exercise of warrants or rights received on portfolio securities.

Any purchase or other acquisition of securities by a registered investment company pursuant to the exercise of warrants or rights to subscribe to or to purchase securities shall be exempt from the provisions of section 10(f) (section 10(f), 54 Stat. 807; 15 U.S.C. 80a–10) of the Act, *Provided,* That the warrants or rights so exercised (a) were offered or issued to such company as a security holder on the same basis as all other holders of the class or classes of securities to whom such warrants or rights were offered or issued, and (b) do not exceed 5 percent of the total amount of such warrants or rights so issued.

[Rule N-10F-2, 9 FR 339, Jan. 8, 1944]

Securities and Exchange Commission

§ 270.10f-3

§ 270.10f-3 Exemption for the acquisition of securities during the existence of an underwriting or selling syndicate.

(a) *Definitions*—(1) *Domestic Issuer* means any issuer other than a foreign government, a national of any foreign country, or a corporation or other organization incorporated or organized under the laws of any foreign country.

(2) *Eligible Foreign Offering* means a public offering of securities, conducted under the laws of a country other than the United States, that meets the following conditions:

(i) The offering is subject to regulation by a "foreign financial regulatory authority," as defined in section 2(a)(50) of the Act [15 U.S.C. 80a-2(a)(50)], in such country;

(ii) The securities are offered at a fixed price to all purchasers in the offering (except for any rights to purchase securities that are required by law to be granted to existing security holders of the issuer);

(iii) Financial statements, prepared and audited in accordance with standards required or permitted by the appropriate foreign financial regulatory authority in such country, for the two years prior to the offering, are made available to the public and prospective purchasers in connection with the offering; and

(iv) If the issuer is a Domestic Issuer, it meets the following conditions:

(A) It has a class of securities registered pursuant to section 12(b) or 12(g) of the Securities Exchange Act of 1934 [15 U.S.C. 78*l*(b) or 78*l*(g)] or is required to file reports pursuant to section 15(d) of the Securities Exchange Act of 1934 [15 U.S.C. 78o(d)]; and

(B) It has filed all the material required to be filed pursuant to section 13(a) or 15(d) of the Securities Exchange Act of 1934 [15 U.S.C. 78m(a) or 78o(d)] for a period of at least twelve months immediately preceding the sale of securities made in reliance upon this (or for such shorter period that the issuer was required to file such material).

(3) *Eligible Municipal Securities* means "municipal securities," as defined in section 3(a)(29) of the Securities Exchange Act of 1934 (15 U.S.C. 78c(a)(29)), that are sufficiently liquid that they can be sold at or near their carrying value within a reasonably short period of time and either:

(i) Are subject to no greater than moderate credit risk; or

(ii) If the issuer of the municipal securities, or the entity supplying the revenues or other payments from which the issue is to be paid, has been in continuous operation for less than three years, including the operation of any predecessors, the securities are subject to a minimal or low amount of credit risk.

(4) *Eligible Rule 144A Offering* means an offering of securities that meets the following conditions:

(i) The securities are offered or sold in transactions exempt from registration under section 4(2) of the Securities Act of 1933 [15 U.S.C. 77d(2)], rule 144A thereunder [§ 230.144A of this chapter], or rules 501–508 thereunder [§§ 230.501–230.508 of this chapter];

(ii) The securities are sold to persons that the seller and any person acting on behalf of the seller reasonably believe to include qualified institutional buyers, as defined in § 230.144A(a)(1) of this chapter; and

(iii) The seller and any person acting on behalf of the seller reasonably believe that the securities are eligible for resale to other qualified institutional buyers pursuant to § 230.144A of this chapter.

(5) *Managed portion* of a portfolio of a registered investment company means a discrete portion of a portfolio of a registered investment company for which a subadviser is responsible for providing investment advice, provided that:

(i) The subadviser is not an affiliated person of any investment adviser, promoter, underwriter, officer, director, member of an advisory board, or employee of the registered investment company; and

(ii) The subadviser's advisory contract:

(A) Prohibits it from consulting with any subadviser of the investment company that is a principal underwriter or an affiliated person of a principal underwriter concerning transactions of the investment company in securities or other assets; and

399

§ 270.10f-3

(B) Limits its responsibility in providing advice to providing advice with respect to such portion.

(6) *Series of a series company* means any class or series of a registered investment company that issues two or more classes or series of preferred or special stock, each of which is preferred over all other classes or series with respect to assets specifically allocated to that class or series.

(7) *Subadviser* means an investment adviser as defined in section 2(a)(20)(B) of the Act (15 U.S.C. 80a–2(a)(20)(B)).

(b) *Exemption for purchases by series companies and investment companies with managed portions.* For purposes of this section and section 10(f) of the Act (15 U.S.C. 80a–10(f)), each Series of a Series Company, and each Managed Portion of a registered investment company, is deemed to be a separate investment company. Therefore, a purchase or acquisition of a security by a registered investment company is exempt from the prohibitions of section 10(f) of the Act if section 10(f) of the Act would not prohibit such purchase if each Series and each Managed Portion of the company were a separately registered investment company.

(c) *Exemption for other purchases.* Any purchase of securities by a registered investment company prohibited by section 10(f) of the Act [15 U.S.C. 80a–10(f)] shall be exempt from the provisions of such section if the following conditions are met:

(1) *Type of Security.* The securities to be purchased are:

(i) Part of an issue registered under the Securities Act of 1933 (15 U.S.C. 77a—aa) that is being offered to the public;

(ii) Part of an issue of government securities, as defined in section 2(a)(16) of the Act (15 U.S.C. 80a–2(a)(16));

(iii) Eligible Municipal Securities;

(iv) Securities sold in an Eligible Foreign Offering; or

(v) Securities sold in an Eligible Rule 144A Offering.

(2) *Timing and Price.* (i) The securities are purchased prior to the end of the first day on which any sales are made, at a price that is not more than the price paid by each other purchaser of securities in that offering or in any concurrent offering of the securities (except, in the case of an Eligible Foreign Offering, for any rights to purchase that are required by law to be granted to existing security holders of the issuer); and

(ii) If the securities are offered for subscription upon exercise of rights, the securities shall be purchased on or before the fourth day preceding the day on which the rights offering terminates.

(3) *Reasonable reliance.* For purposes of determining compliance with paragraphs (c)(1)(v) and (c)(2)(i) of this section, an investment company may reasonably rely upon written statements made by the issuer or a syndicate manager, or by an underwriter or seller of the securities through which such investment company purchases the securities.

(4) *Continuous operation.* If the securities to be purchased are part of an issue registered under the Securities Act of 1933 (15 U.S.C. 77a-aa) that is being offered to the public, are government securities (as defined in section 2(a)(16) of the Act (15 U.S.C. 80a–2(a)(16))), or are purchased pursuant to an Eligible Foreign Offering or an Eligible Rule 144A Offering, the issuer of the securities must have been in continuous operation for not less than three years, including the operations of any predecessors.

(5) *Firm Commitment Underwriting.* The securities are offered pursuant to an underwriting or similar agreement under which the underwriters are committed to purchase all of the securities being offered, except those purchased by others pursuant to a rights offering, if the underwriters purchase any of the securities.

(6) *Reasonable commission.* The commission, spread or profit received or to be received by the principal underwriters is reasonable and fair compared to the commission, spread or profit received by other such persons in connection with the underwriting of similar securities being sold during a comparable period of time.

(7) *Percentage limit*—(i) *Generally.* The amount of securities of any class of such issue to be purchased by the investment company, aggregated with purchases by any other investment company advised by the investment

Securities and Exchange Commission § 270.11a–1

company's investment adviser, and any purchases by another account with respect to which the investment adviser has investment discretion if the investment adviser exercised such investment discretion with respect to the purchase, does not exceed the following limits:

(A) If purchased in an offering other than an Eligible Rule 144A Offering, 25 percent of the principal amount of the offering of such class; or

(B) If purchased in an Eligible Rule 144A Offering, 25 percent of the total of:

(*1*) The principal amount of the offering of such class sold by underwriters or members of the selling syndicate to qualified institutional buyers, as defined in § 230.144A(a)(1) of this chapter; plus

(*2*) The principal amount of the offering of such class in any concurrent public offering.

(ii) *Exemption from percentage limit.* The requirement in paragraph (c)(7)(i) of this section applies only if the investment adviser of the investment company is, or is an affiliated person of, a principal underwriter of the security; and

(iii) *Separate aggregation.* The requirement in paragraph (c)(7)(i) of this section applies independently with respect to each investment adviser of the investment company that is, or is an affiliated person of, a principal underwriter of the security.

(8) *Prohibition of Certain Affiliate Transactions.* Such investment company does not purchase the securities being offered directly or indirectly from an officer, director, member of an advisory board, investment adviser or employee of such investment company or from a person of which any such officer, director, member of an advisory board, investment adviser or employee is an affiliated person; *provided,* that a purchase from a syndicate manager shall not be deemed to be a purchase from a specific underwriter if:

(i) Such underwriter does not benefit directly or indirectly from the transaction; or

(ii) In respect to the purchase of Eligible Municipal Securities, such purchase is not designated as a group sale or otherwise allocated to the account of any person from whom this paragraph prohibits the purchase.

(9) [Reserved]

(10) *Board review.* The board of directors of the investment company, including a majority of the directors who are not interested persons of the investment company:

(i) Has approved procedures, pursuant to which such purchases may be effected for the company, that are reasonably designed to provide that the purchases comply with all the conditions of this section;

(ii) Approves such changes to the procedures as the board deems necessary; and

(iii) Determines no less frequently than quarterly that all purchases made during the preceding quarter were effected in compliance with such procedures.

(11) *Board composition.* The board of directors of the investment company satisfies the fund governance standards defined in § 270.0–1(a)(7).

(12) *Maintenance of records.* The investment company:

(i) Shall maintain and preserve permanently in an easily accessible place a written copy of the procedures, and any modification thereto, described in paragraphs (c)(10)(i) and (c)(10)(ii) of this section; and

(ii) Shall maintain and preserve for a period not less than six years from the end of the fiscal year in which any transactions occurred, the first two years in an easily accessible place, a written record of each such transaction, setting forth from whom the securities were acquired, the identity of the underwriting syndicate's members, the terms of the transaction, and the information or materials upon which the determination described in paragraph (c)(10)(iii) of this section was made.

[62 FR 42408, Aug. 7, 1997, as amended at 66 FR 3758, Jan. 16, 2001; 67 FR 31079, May 8, 2002; 68 FR 3152, Jan. 22, 2003; 69 FR 46389, Aug. 7, 2004; 74 FR 52373, Oct. 9, 2009; 81 FR 82020, Nov. 18, 2016]

§ 270.11a–1 Definition of "exchange" for purposes of section 11 of the Act.

(a) For the purposes of section 11 of the Act, the term *exchange* as used

§ 270.11a–2

therein shall include the issuance of any security by a registered investment company in an amount equal to the proceeds, or any portion of the proceeds, paid or payable—

(1) Upon the repurchase, by or at the instance of such issuer, of an outstanding security the terms of which provide for its termination, retirement or cancellation, or

(2) Upon the termination, retirement or cancellation of an outstanding security of such issuer in accordance with the terms thereof.

(b) A security shall not be deemed to have been repurchased by or at the instance of the issuer, or terminated, retired or canceled in accordance with the terms of the security if—

(1) The security was redeemed or repurchased at the instance of the holder; or

(2) A security holder's account was closed for failure to make payments as prescribed in the security or instruments pursuant to which the security was issued, and notice of intention to close the account was mailed to the security holder, and he had a reasonable time in which to meet the deficiency; or

(3) Sale of the security was restricted to a specified, limited group of persons and, in accordance with the terms of the security or the instruments pursuant to which the security was issued, upon its being transferred by the holder to a person not a member of the group eligible to purchase the security, the issuer required the surrender of the security and paid the redemption price thereof.

(c) The provisions of paragraph (a) of this section shall not apply if, following the repurchase of an outstanding security by or at the instance of the issuer or the termination, retirement or cancellation of an outstanding security in accordance with the terms thereof—

(1) The proceeds are actually paid to the security holder by or on behalf of the issuer within 7 days, and

(2) No sale and no offer (other than by way of exchange) of any security of the issuer is made by or on behalf of the issuer to the person to whom such proceeds were paid, within 60 days after such payment.

(d) The provisions of paragraph (a) of this section shall not apply to the repurchase, termination, retirement, or cancellation of a security outstanding on the effective date of this section or issued pursuant to a subscription agreement or other plan of acquisition in effect on such date.

(Sec. 11, 54 Stat. 808; 15 U.S.C. 80a–11)

[32 FR 10728, July 21, 1967]

§ 270.11a–2 Offers of exchange by certain registered separate accounts or others the terms of which do not require prior Commission approval.

(a) As used in this section:

(1) *Deferred sales load* shall mean any sales load, including a contingent deferred sales load, that is deducted upon redemption or annuitization of amounts representing all or a portion of a securityholder's interest in a separate account;

(2) *Exchanged security* shall include not only the security or securities (or portion[s] thereof) of a securityholder actually exchanged pursuant to an exchange offer but also any security or securities (or portion[s] thereof) of the securityholder previously exchanged for the exchanged security or its predecessors;

(3) *Front-end sales load* shall mean any sales load that is deducted from one or more purchase payments made by a securityholder before they are invested in a separate account; and

(4) *Purchase payments made for the acquired security*, as used in paragraphs (c)(2) and (d)(2) of this section, shall not include any purchase payments made for the exchanged security or any appreciation attributable to those purchase payments that are transferred to the offering account in connection with an exchange.

(b) Notwithstanding section 11 of the Act [15 U.S.C. 80a–11], any registered separate account or any principal underwriter for such an account (collectively, the "offering account") may make or cause to be made an offer to the holder of a security of the offering account, or of any other registered separate account having the same insurance company depositor or sponsor as the offering account or having an insurance company depositor or sponsor

Securities and Exchange Commission § 270.11a–3

that is an affiliate of the offering account's depositor or sponsor, to exchange his security (or portion thereof) (the "exchanged security") for a security (or portion thereof) of the offering account (the "acquired security") without the terms of such exchange offer first having been submitted to and approved by the Commission, as provided below:

(1) If the securities (or portions thereof) involved are variable annuity contracts, then

(i) The exchange must be made on the basis of the relative net asset values of the securities to be exchanged, except that the offering account may deduct at the time of the exchange

(A) An administrative fee which is disclosed in the part of the offering account's registration statement under the Securities Act of 1933 relating to the prospectus, and

(B) Any front-end sales load permitted by paragraph (c) of this section, and

(ii) Any deferred sales load imposed on the acquired security by the offering account shall be calculated in the manner prescribed by paragraph (d) or (e) of this section; or

(2) If the securities (or portions thereof) involved are variable life insurance contracts offered by a separate account registered under the Act as a unit investment trust, then the exchange must be made on the basis of the relative net asset values of the securities to be exchanged, except that the offering account may deduct at the time of the exchange an administrative fee which is disclosed in the part of the offering account's registration statement under the Securities Act of 1933 relating to the prospectus.

(c) If the offering account imposes a front-end sales load on the acquired security, then such sales load shall be a percentage that is no greater than the excess of the rate of the front-end sales load otherwise applicable to that security over the rate of any front-end sales load previously paid on the exchanged security.

(d) If the offering account imposes a deferred sales load on the acquired security and the exchanged security was also subject to a deferred sales load, then any deferred sales load imposed on the acquired security shall be calculated as if:

(1) The holder of the acquired security had been the holder of that security from the date on which he became the holder of the exchanged security; and

(2) Purchase payments made for the exchanged security had been made for the acquired security on the date on which they were made for the exchanged security.

(e) If the offering account imposes a deferred sales load on the acquired security and a front-end sales load was paid on the exchanged security, then any deferred sales load imposed on the acquired security may not be imposed on purchase payments made for the exchanged security or any appreciation attributable to purchase payments made for the exchanged security that are transferred in connection with the exchange.

(f) Notwithstanding the foregoing, no offer of exchange shall be made in reliance on this section if both a front-end sales load and a deferred sales load are to be imposed on the acquired security or if both such sales loads are imposed on the exchanged security.

[48 FR 36245, Aug. 10, 1983, as amended at 85 FR 26109, May 1, 2020]

§ 270.11a–3 Offers of exchange by open-end investment companies other than separate accounts.

(a) For purposes of this rule:

(1) *Acquired security* means the security held by a securityholder after completing an exchange pursuant to an exchange offer;

(2) *Administrative fee* means any fee, other than a sales load, deferred sales load or redemption fee, that is

(i) Reasonably intended to cover the costs incurred in processing exchanges of the type for which the fee is charged, *Provided that:* the offering company will maintain and preserve records of any determination of the costs incurred in connection with exchanges for a period of not less than six years, the first two years in an easily accessible place. The records preserved under this provision shall be subject to inspection by the Commission in accordance with section 31(b) of the Act (15 U.S.C. 80a–30(b)) as if such records

§ 270.11a-3

were records required to be maintained under rules adopted under section 31(a) of the Act (15 U.S.C. 80a-30a)); or

(ii) A nominal fee as defined in paragraph (a)(8) of this section;

(3) *Deferred sales load* means any amount properly chargeable to sales or promotional expenses that is paid by a shareholder after purchase but before or upon redemption;

(4) *Exchanged security* means

(i) The security actually exchanged pursuant to an exchange offer, and

(ii) Any security previously exchanged for such security or for any of its predecessors;

(5) *Group of investment companies* means any two or more registered open-end investment companies that hold themselves out to investors as related companies for purposes of investment and investor services, and

(i) That have a common investment adviser or principal underwriter, or

(ii) The investment adviser or principal underwriter of one of the companies is an affiliated person as defined in section 2(a)(3) of the Act (15 U.S.C. 80a-2(a)(3)) of the investment adviser or principal underwriter of each of the other companies;

(6) *Offering company* means a registered open-end investment company (other than a registered separate account) or any principal underwriter thereof that makes an offer (an "exchange offer") to the holder of a security of that company, or of another open-end investment company within the same group of investment companies as the offering company, to exchange that security for a security of the offering company;

(7) *Redemption fee* means a fee that is imposed by the fund pursuant to section 270.22c-2; and

(8) *Nominal fee* means a slight or *de minimis* fee.

(b) Notwithstanding section 11(a) of the Act (15 U.S.C. 80a-11(a)), and except as provided in paragraphs (d) and (e) of this section, in connection with an exchange offer an offering company may cause a securityholder to be charged a sales load on the acquired security, a redemption fee, an administrative fee, or any combination of the foregoing, *Provided that:*

(1) Any administrative fee or scheduled variation thereof is applied uniformly to all securityholders of the class specified;

(2) Any redemption fee charged with respect to the exchanged security or any scheduled variation thereof

(i) Is applied uniformly to all securityholders of the class specified, and

(ii) Does not exceed the redemption fee applicable to a redemption of the exchanged security in the absence of an exchange.

(3) No deferred sales load is imposed on the exchanged security at the time of an exchange;

(4) Any sales load charged with respect to the acquired security is a percentage that is no greater than the excess, if any, of the rate of the sales load applicable to that security in the absence of an exchange over the sum of the rates of all sales loads previously paid on the exchanged security, *Provided that:*

(i) The percentage rate of any sales load charged when the acquired security is redeemed, that is solely the result of a deferred sales load imposed on the exchanged security, may be no greater than the excess, if any, of the applicable rate of such sales load, calculated in accordance with paragraph (b)(5) of this section, over the sum of the rates of all sales loads previously paid on the acquired security, and

(ii) In no event may the sum of the rates of all sales loads imposed prior to and at the time the acquired security is redeemed, including any sales load paid or to be paid with respect to the exchanged security, exceed the maximum sales load rate, calculated in accordance with paragraph (b)(5) of this section, that would be applicable in the absence of an exchange to the security (exchanged or acquired) with the highest such rate;

(5) Any deferred sales load charged at the time the acquired security is redeemed is calculated as if the holder of the acquired security had held that security from the date on which he became the holder of the exchanged security, *Provided that:*

(i) The time period during which the acquired security is held need not be

Securities and Exchange Commission

§ 270.11a-3

included when the amount of the deferred sales load is calculated, if the deferred sales load is

(A) reduced by the amount of any fees collected on the acquired security under the terms of any plan of distribution adopted in accordance with rule 12b-1 under the Act (17 CFR 270.12b-1) (a "12b-1 plan"), and

(B) Solely the result of a sales load imposed on the exchanged security, and no other sales loads, including deferred sales loads, are imposed with respect to the acquired security,

(ii) The time period during which the exchanged security is held need not be included when the amount of the deferred sales load on the acquired security is calculated, if

(A) The deferred sales load is reduced by the amount of any fees previously collected on the exchanged security under the terms of any 12b-1 plan, and

(B) The exchanged security was not subject to any sales load, and

(iii) The holding periods in this subsection may be computed as of the end of the calendar month in which a security was purchased or redeemed;

(6) The prospectus of the offering company discloses

(i) The amount of any administrative or redemption fee imposed on an exchange transaction for its securities, as well as the amount of any administrative or redemption fee imposed on its securityholders to acquire the securities of other investment companies in an exchange transaction, and

(ii) If the offering company reserves the right to change the terms of or terminate an exchange offer, that the exchange offer is subject to termination and its terms are subject to change;

(7) Any sales literature or advertising that mentions the existence of the exchange offer also discloses

(i) The existence of any administrative fee or redemption fee that would be imposed at the time of an exchange; and

(ii) If the offering company reserves the right to change the terms of or terminate the exchange offer, that the exchange offer is subject to termination and its terms are subject to change;

(8) Whenever an exchange offer is to be terminated or its terms are to be amended materially, any holder of a security subject to that offer shall be given prominent notice of the impending termination or amendment at least 60 days prior to the date of termination or the effective date of the amendment, *Provided that:*

(i) No such notice need be given if the only material effect of an amendment is to reduce or eliminate an administrative fee, sales load or redemption fee payable at the time of an exchange, and

(ii) No notice need be given if, under extraordinary circumstances, either

(A) There is a suspension of the redemption of the exchanged security under section 22(e) of the Act [15 U.S.C. 80a-22(e)] and the rules and regulations thereunder, or

(B) The offering company temporarily delays or ceases the sale of the acquired security because it is unable to invest amounts effectively in accordance with applicable investment objectives, policies and restrictions; and

(9) In calculating any sales load charged with respect to the acquired security:

(i) If a securityholder exchanges less than all of his securities, the security upon which the highest sales load rate was previously paid is deemed exchanged first; and

(ii) If the exchanged security was acquired through reinvestment of dividends or capital gains distributions, that security is deemed to have been sold with a sales load rate equal to the sales load rate previously paid on the security on which the dividend was paid or distribution made.

(c) If either no sales load is imposed on the acquired security or the sales load imposed is less than the maximum allowed by paragraph (b)(4) of this section, the offering company may require the exchanging securityholder to have held the exchanged security for a minimum period of time previously established by the offering company and applied uniformly to all securityholders of the class specified.

(d) Any offering company that has previously made an offer of exchange may continue to impose fees or sales loads permitted by an order under section 11(a) of the Act upon shares purchased before the earlier of (1) One year after the effective date of this section, or (2) When the offer has been brought into compliance with the terms of this section, and upon shares acquired through reinvestment of dividends or capital gains distributions based on such shares, until such shares are redeemed.

(e) Any offering company that has previously made an offer of exchange cannot rely on this section to amend such prior offer unless

(1) The offering company's prospectus disclosed, during at least the two year period prior to the amendment of the offer (or, if the fund is less than two years old, at all times the offer has been outstanding) that the terms of the offer were subject to change, or

(2) The only effect of such change is to reduce or eliminate an administrative fee, sales load or redemption fee payable at the time of an exchange.

[54 FR 35185, Aug. 24, 1989, as amended at 61 FR 49016; Sept. 17, 1996; 70 FR 13341, Mar. 18, 2005]

§ 270.12b-1 Distribution of shares by registered open-end management investment company.

(a)(1) Except as provided in this section, it shall be unlawful for any registered open-end management investment company (other than a company complying with the provisions of section 10(d) of the Act (15 U.S.C. 80a-10(d))) to act as a distributor of securities of which it is the issuer, except through an underwriter;

(2) For purposes of this section, such a company will be deemed to be acting as a distributor of securities of which it is the issuer, other than through an underwriter, if it engages directly or indirectly in financing any activity which is primarily intended to result in the sale of shares issued by such company, including, but not necessarily limited to, advertising, compensation of underwriters, dealers, and sales personnel, the printing and mailing of prospectuses to other than current shareholders, and the printing and mailing of sales literature.

(b) A registered, open-end management investment company ("Company") may act as a distributor of securities of which it is the issuer: *Provided,* That any payments made by such company in connection with such distribution are made pursuant to a written plan describing all material aspects of the proposed financing of distribution and that all agreements with any person relating to implementation of the plan are in writing: *And further provided,* That:

(1) Such plan has been approved by a vote of at least a majority of the outstanding voting securities of such company, if adopted after any public offering of the company's voting securities or the sale of such securities to persons who are not affiliated persons of the company, affiliated persons of such persons, promoters of the company, or affiliated persons of such promoters;

(2) Such plan, together with any related agreements, has been approved by a vote of the board of directors of such company, and of the directors who are not interested persons of the company and have no direct or indirect financial interest in the operation of the plan or in any agreements related to the plan, cast in person at a meeting called for the purpose of voting on such plan or agreements;

(3) Such plan or agreement provides, in substance:

(i) That it shall continue in effect for a period of more than one year from the date of its execution or adoption only so long as such continuance is specifically approved at least annually in the manner described in paragraph (b)(2) of this section;

(ii) That any person authorized to direct the disposition of monies paid or payable by such company pursuant to the plan or any related agreement shall provide to the company's board of directors, and the directors shall review, at least quarterly, a written report of the amounts so expended and the purposes for which such expenditures were made; and

(iii) In the case of a plan, that it may be terminated at any time by vote of a majority of the members of the board of directors of the company who are not interested persons of the company and have no direct or indirect financial interest in the operation of the plan or in any agreements related to the plan or by vote of a majority of the outstanding voting securities of such company;

Securities and Exchange Commission § 270.12b-1

(iv) In the case of an agreement related to a plan:
(A) That it may be terminated at any time, without the payment of any penalty, by vote of a majority of the members of the board of directors of such company who are not interested persons of the company and have no direct or indirect financial interest in the operation of the plan or in any agreements related to the plan or by vote of a majority of the outstanding voting securities of such company on not more than sixty days' written notice to any other party to the agreement, and
(B) For its automatic termination in the event of its assignment;
(4) Such plan provides that it may not be amended to increase materially the amount to be spent for distribution without shareholder approval and that all material amendments of the plan must be approved in the manner described in paragraph (b)(2) of this section; and
(5) Such plan is implemented and continued in a manner consistent with the provisions of paragraphs (c), (d), and (e) of this section;
(c) A registered open-end management investment company may rely on the provisions of paragraph (b) of this section only if its board of directors satisfies the fund governance standards as defined in § 270.0–1(a)(7);
(d) In considering whether a registered open-end management investment company should implement or continue a plan in reliance on paragraph (b) of this section, the directors of such company shall have a duty to request and evaluate, and any person who is a party to any agreement with such company relating to such plan shall have a duty to furnish, such information as may reasonably be necessary to an informed determination of whether such plan should be implemented or continued; in fulfilling their duties under this paragraph the directors should consider and give appropriate weight to all pertinent factors, and minutes describing the factors considered and the basis for the decision to use company assets for distribution must be made and preserved in accordance with paragraph (f) of this section;

NOTE: For a discussion of factors which may be relevant to a decision to use company assets for distribution, see Investment Company Act Releases Nos. 10862, September 7, 1979, and 11414, October 28, 1980.

(e) A registered open-end management investment company may implement or continue a plan pursuant to paragraph (b) of this section only if the directors who vote to approve such implementation or continuation conclude, in the exercise of reasonable business judgment and in light of their fiduciary duties under state law and under sections 36(a) and (b) (15 U.S.C. 80a–35 (a) and (b)) of the Act, that there is a reasonable likelihood that the plan will benefit the company and its shareholders;

(f) A registered open-end management investment company must preserve copies of any plan, agreement or report made pursuant to this section for a period of not less than six years from the date of such plan, agreement or report, the first two years in an easily accessible place;

(g) If a plan covers more than one series or class of shares, the provisions of the plan must be severable for each series or class, and whenever this rule provides for any action to be taken with respect to a plan, that action must be taken separately for each series or class affected by the matter. Nothing in this paragraph (g) shall affect the rights of any purchase class under § 270.18f–3(f)(2)(iii).

(h) Notwithstanding any other provision of this section, a company may not:
(1) Compensate a broker or dealer for any promotion or sale of shares issued by that company by directing to the broker or dealer:
(i) The company's portfolio securities transactions; or
(ii) Any remuneration, including but not limited to any commission, mark-up, mark-down, or other fee (or portion thereof) received or to be received from the company's portfolio transactions effected through any other broker (including a government securities broker) or dealer (including a municipal securities dealer or a government securities dealer); and
(2) Direct its portfolio securities transactions to a broker or dealer that promotes or sells shares issued by the

§ 270.12d1-1

company, unless the company (or its investment adviser):

(i) Is in compliance with the provisions of paragraph (h)(1) of this section with respect to that broker or dealer; and

(ii) Has implemented, and the company's board of directors (including a majority of directors who are not interested persons of the company) has approved, policies and procedures reasonably designed to prevent:

(A) The persons responsible for selecting brokers and dealers to effect the company's portfolio securities transactions from taking into account the brokers' and dealers' promotion or sale of shares issued by the company or any other registered investment company; and

(B) The company, and any investment adviser and principal underwriter of the company, from entering into any agreement (whether oral or written) or other understanding under which the company directs, or is expected to direct, portfolio securities transactions, or any remuneration described in paragraph (h)(1)(ii) of this section, to a broker (including a government securities broker) or dealer (including a municipal securities dealer or a government securities dealer) in consideration for the promotion or sale of shares issued by the company or any other registered investment company.

[45 FR 73905, Nov. 7, 1980, as amended at 60 FR 11885, Mar. 2, 1995; 61 FR 49011, Sept. 17, 1996; 62 FR 51765, Oct. 3, 1997; 66 FR 3758, Jan. 16, 2001; 69 FR 46389, Aug. 2, 2004; 69 FR 54733, Sept. 9, 2004; 78 FR 79299, Dec. 30, 2013]

§ 270.12d1-1 Exemptions for investments in money market funds.

(a) *Exemptions for acquisition of money market fund shares.* If the conditions of paragraph (b) of this section are satisfied, notwithstanding sections 12(d)(1)(A), 12(d)(1)(B), 12(d)(1)(G), 17(a), and 57 of the Act (15 U.S.C. 80a-12(d)(1)(A), 80a-12(d)(1)(B), 80a-12(d)(1)(G), 80a-17(a), and 80a-56)) and § 270.17d-1:

(1) An investment company (*acquiring fund*) may purchase and redeem shares issued by a money market fund; and

(2) A money market fund, any principal underwriter thereof, and a broker or a dealer may sell or otherwise dispose of shares issued by the money market fund to any acquiring fund.

(b) Conditions—(1) *Fees.* The acquiring fund pays no sales charge, as defined in rule 2830(b)(8) of the Conduct Rules of the NASD ("sales charge"), or service fee, as defined in rule 2830(b)(9) of the Conduct Rules of the NASD, charged in connection with the purchase, sale, or redemption of securities issued by a money market fund ("service fee"); or the acquiring fund's investment adviser waives its advisory fee in an amount necessary to offset any sales charge or service fee.

(2) *Unregistered money market funds.* If the money market fund is not an investment company registered under the Act:

(i) The acquiring fund reasonably believes that the money market fund satisfies the following conditions as if it were a registered open-end investment company:

(A) Operates in compliance with § 270.2a-7;

(B) Complies with sections 17(a), (d), (e), 18, and 22(e) of the Act (15 U.S.C. 80a-17(a), (d), (e), 80a-18, and 80a-22(e));

(C) Has adopted procedures designed to ensure that it complies with sections 17(a), (d), (e), 18, and 22(e) of the Act (15 U.S.C. 80a-17(a), (d), (e), 80a-18, and 80a-22(e)), periodically reviews and updates those procedures, and maintains books and records describing those procedures;

(D) Maintains the records required by §§ 270.31a-1(b)(1), 270.31a-1(b)(2)(ii), 270.31a-1(b)(2)(iv), and 270.31a-1(b)(9); and

(E) Preserves permanently, the first two years in an easily accessible place, all books and records required to be made under paragraphs (b)(2)(i)(C) and (D) of this section, and makes those records available for examination on request by the Commission or its staff; and

(ii) The adviser to the money market fund is registered with the Commission as an investment adviser under section 203 of the Investment Advisers Act of 1940 (15 U.S.C. 80b-3).

(c) *Exemption from certain monitoring and recordkeeping requirements under § 270.17e-1.* Notwithstanding the requirements of §§ 270.17e-1(b)(3) and

Securities and Exchange Commission § 270.12d1–4

270.17e–1(d)(2), the payment of a commission, fee, or other remuneration to a broker shall be deemed as not exceeding the usual and customary broker's commission for purposes of section 17(e)(2)(A) of the Act if:

(1) The commission, fee, or other remuneration is paid in connection with the sale of securities to or by an acquiring fund;

(2) The broker and the acquiring fund are affiliated persons because each is an affiliated person of the same money market fund; and

(3) The acquiring fund is an affiliated person of the money market fund solely because the acquiring fund owns, controls, or holds with power to vote five percent or more of the outstanding securities of the money market fund.

(d) *Definitions.* (1) *Investment company* includes a company that would be an investment company under section 3(a) of the Act (15 U.S.C. 80a–3(a)) but for the exceptions to that definition provided for in sections 3(c)(1) and 3(c)(7) of the Act (15 U.S.C. 80a–3(c)(1) and 80a–3(c)(7)).

(2) *Money market fund* means:

(i) An open-end management investment company registered under the Act that is regulated as a money market fund under § 270.2a–7; or

(ii) A company that would be an investment company under section 3(a) of the Act (15 U.S.C. 80a–3(a)) but for the exceptions to that definition provided for in sections 3(c)(1) and 3(c)(7) of the Act (15 U.S.C. 80a–3(c)(1) and 80a–3(c)(7)) and that:

(A) Is limited to investing in the types of securities and other investments in which a money market fund may invest under § 270.2a–7; and

(B) Undertakes to comply with all the other requirements of § 270.2a–7, except that, if the company has no board of directors, the company's investment adviser performs the duties of the board of directors.

[71 FR 36655, June 27, 2006, as amended at 85 FR 74005, Nov. 19, 2020]

§ 270.12d1–2 [Reserved]

§ 270.12d1–3 Exemptions for investment companies relying on section 12(d)(1)(F) of the Act.

(a) *Exemption from sales charge limits.* A registered investment company ("acquiring fund") that relies on section 12(d)(1)(F) of the Act (15 U.S.C. 80a–12(d)(1)(F)) to acquire securities issued by an investment company ("acquired fund") may offer or sell any security it issues through a principal underwriter or otherwise at a public offering price that includes a sales load of more than 1½ percent if any sales charges and service fees charged with respect to the acquiring fund's securities do not exceed the limits set forth in rule 2830 of the Conduct Rules of the NASD applicable to a fund of funds.

(b) *Definitions.* For purposes of this section, the terms *fund of funds,* sales charge, and *service fee* have the same meanings as in rule 2830(b) of the Conduct Rules of the NASD.

[71 FR 36655, June 27, 2006]

§ 270.12d1–4 Exemptions for investments in certain investment companies.

(a) *Exemptions for acquisition and sale of acquired fund shares.* If the conditions of paragraph (b) of this section are satisfied, notwithstanding sections 12(d)(1)(A), 12(d)(1)(B), 12(d)(1)(C), 17(a), 57(a)(1)–(2), and 57(d)(1)–(2) of the Act (15 U.S.C. 80a–12(d)(1)(A), 80a–12(d)(1)(C), 80a–17(a), 80a–56(a)(1)–(2), and 80a–56(d)(1)–(2)):

(1) A registered investment company (other than a face-amount certificate company) or business development company (an *acquiring fund*) may purchase or otherwise acquire the securities issued by another registered investment company (other than a face-amount certificate company) or business development company (an *acquired fund*);

(2) An acquired fund, any principal underwriter thereof, and any broker or dealer registered under the Securities Exchange Act of 1934 may sell or otherwise dispose of the securities issued by the acquired fund to any acquiring fund and any acquired fund may redeem or repurchase any securities

§ 270.12d1–4

issued by the acquired fund from any acquiring fund; and

(3) An acquiring fund that is an affiliated person of an exchange-traded fund (or who is an affiliated person of such a fund) solely by reason of the circumstances described in § 270.6c–11(b)(3)(i) and (ii), may deposit and receive the exchange-traded fund's baskets, provided that the acquired exchange-traded fund is not otherwise an affiliated person (or affiliated person of an affiliated person) of the acquiring fund.

(b) *Conditions*—(1) *Control.* (i) The acquiring fund and its advisory group will not control (individually or in the aggregate) an acquired fund;

(ii) If the acquiring fund and its advisory group, in the aggregate,

(A) Hold more than 25% of the outstanding voting securities of an acquired fund that is a registered open-end management investment company or registered unit investment trust as a result of a decrease in the outstanding voting securities of the acquired fund, or

(B) Hold more than 10% of the outstanding voting securities of an acquired fund that is a registered closed-end management investment company or business development company, each of those holders will vote its securities in the same proportion as the vote of all other holders of such securities; provided, however, that in circumstances where all holders of the outstanding voting securities of the acquired fund are required by this section or otherwise under section 12(d)(1) to vote securities of the acquired fund in the same proportion as the vote of all other holders of such securities, the acquiring fund will seek instructions from its security holders with regard to the voting of all proxies with respect to such acquired fund securities and vote such proxies only in accordance with such instructions; and

(iii) The conditions in paragraphs (b)(1)(i) through (ii) of this section do not apply if:

(A) The acquiring fund is in the same group of investment companies as an acquired fund; or

(B) The acquiring fund's investment sub-adviser or any person controlling, controlled by, or under common control with such investment sub-adviser acts as an acquired fund's investment adviser or depositor.

(2) *Findings and agreements.* (i) Management companies.

(A) If the acquiring fund is a management company, prior to the initial acquisition of an acquired fund in excess of the limits in section 12(d)(1)(A)(i) of the Act (15 U.S.C. 80a–12(d)(1)(A)(i)), the acquiring fund's investment adviser must evaluate the complexity of the structure and fees and expenses associated with the acquiring fund's investment in the acquired fund, and find that the acquiring fund's fees and expenses do not duplicate the fees and expenses of the acquired fund;

(B) If the acquired fund is a management company, prior to the initial acquisition of an acquired fund in excess of the limits in section 12(d)(1)(A)(i) of the Act (15 U.S.C. 80a–12(d)(1)(A)(i)), the acquired fund's investment adviser must find that any undue influence concerns associated with the acquiring fund's investment in the acquired fund are reasonably addressed and, as part of this finding, the investment adviser must consider at a minimum the following items:

(*1*) The scale of contemplated investments by the acquiring fund and any maximum investment limits;

(*2*) The anticipated timing of redemption requests by the acquiring fund;

(*3*) Whether and under what circumstances the acquiring fund will provide advance notification of investments and redemptions; and

(*4*) The circumstances under which the acquired fund may elect to satisfy redemption requests in kind rather than in cash and the terms of any such redemptions in kind; and

(C) The investment adviser to each acquiring or acquired management company must report its evaluation, finding, and the basis for its evaluations or findings required by paragraphs (b)(2)(i)(A) or (B) of this section, as applicable, to the fund's board of directors, no later than the next regularly scheduled board of directors meeting.

(ii) Unit investment trusts. If the acquiring fund is a unit investment trust (*UIT*) and the date of initial deposit of portfolio securities into the UIT occurs

Securities and Exchange Commission §270.12d1–4

after the effective date of this section, the UIT's principal underwriter or depositor must evaluate the complexity of the structure associated with the UIT's investment in acquired funds and, on or before such date of initial deposit, find that the UIT's fees and expenses do not duplicate the fees and expenses of the acquired funds that the UIT holds or will hold at the date of deposit.

(iii) *Separate accounts funding variable insurance contracts.* With respect to a separate account funding variable insurance contracts that invests in an acquiring fund, the acquiring fund must obtain a certification from the insurance company offering the separate account that the insurance company has determined that the fees and expenses borne by the separate account, acquiring fund, and acquired fund, in the aggregate, are consistent with the standard set forth in section 26(f)(2)(A) of the Act (15 U.S.C. 80a–26(f)(2)(A)).

(iv) *Fund of funds investment agreement.* Unless the acquiring fund's investment adviser acts as the acquired fund's investment adviser and such adviser is not acting as the sub-adviser to either fund, the acquiring fund must enter into an agreement with the acquired fund effective for the duration of the funds' reliance on this section, which must include the following:

(A) Any material terms regarding the acquiring fund's investment in the acquired fund necessary to make the finding required under paragraph (b)(2)(i) through (ii) of this section;

(B) A termination provision whereby either the acquiring fund or acquired fund may terminate the agreement subject to advance written notice no longer than 60 days; and

(C) A requirement that the acquired fund provide the acquiring fund with information on the fees and expenses of the acquired fund reasonably requested by the acquiring fund.

(3) *Complex fund structures.* (i) No investment company may rely on section 12(d)(1)(G) of the Act (15 U.S.C. 80a–12(d)(1)(G)) or this section to purchase or otherwise acquire, in excess of the limits in section 12(d)(1)(A) of the Act (15 U.S.C. 80a–12(d)(1)(A)), the outstanding voting securities of an investment company (a *second-tier fund*) that relies on this section to acquire the securities of an acquired fund, unless the second-tier fund makes investments permitted by paragraph (b)(3)(ii) of this section; and

(ii) No acquired fund may purchase or otherwise acquire the securities of an investment company or private fund if immediately after such purchase or acquisition, the securities of investment companies and private funds owned by the acquired fund have an aggregate value in excess of 10 percent of the value of the total assets of the acquired fund; provided, however, that the 10 percent limitation of this paragraph shall not apply to investments by the acquired fund in:

(A) Reliance on section 12(d)(1)(E) of the Act (15 U.S.C. 80a–12(d)(1)(E));

(B) Reliance on §270.12d1–1;

(C) A subsidiary that is wholly-owned and controlled by the acquired fund;

(D) Securities received as a dividend or as a result of a plan of reorganization of a company; or

(E) Securities of another investment company received pursuant to exemptive relief from the Commission to engage in interfund borrowing and lending transactions.

(c) *Recordkeeping.* The acquiring and acquired funds relying upon this section must maintain and preserve for a period of not less than five years, the first two years in an easily accessible place, as applicable:

(1) A copy of each fund of funds investment agreement that is in effect, or at any time within the past five years was in effect, and any amendments thereto;

(2) A written record of the evaluations and findings required by paragraph (b)(2)(i) of this section, and the basis therefor within the past five years;

(3) A written record of the finding required by paragraph (b)(2)(ii) of this section and the basis for such finding; and

(4) The certification from each insurance company required by paragraph (b)(2)(iii) of this section.

(d) *Definitions.* For purposes of this section:

Advisory group means either:

§ 270.12d2-1

(1) An acquiring fund's investment adviser or depositor, and any person controlling, controlled by, or under common control with such investment adviser or depositor; or

(2) An acquiring fund's investment sub-adviser and any person controlling, controlled by, or under common control with such investment sub-adviser.

Baskets has the same meaning as in 17 CFR 270.6c–11(a)(1).

Exchange-traded fund means a fund or class, the shares of which are listed and traded on a national securities exchange, and that has formed and operates in reliance on § 6c–11 or under an exemptive order granted by the Commission.

Group of investment companies means any two or more registered investment companies or business development companies that hold themselves out to investors as related companies for purposes of investment and investor services.

Private fund means an issuer that would be an investment company under section 3(a) of the Act but for the exclusions from that definition provided for in section 3(c)(1) or section 3(c)(7) of the Act (15 U.S.C. 80a–3(c)(1) or 80a–3(c)(7)).

[85 FR 74005, Nov. 19, 2020]

§ 270.12d2–1 Definition of insurance company for purposes of sections 12(d)(2) and 12(g) of the Act.

For purposes of sections 12(d)(2) and 12(g) of the Act [15 U.S.C. 80a–12(d)(2) and 80a–12(g)], *insurance company* shall include a foreign insurance company as that term is used in rule 3a–6 under the Act (17 CFR 270.3a–6).

[56 FR 56300, Nov. 4, 1991]

§ 270.12d3–1 Exemption of acquisitions of securities issued by persons engaged in securities related businesses.

(a) Notwithstanding section 12(d)(3) of the Act, a registered investment company, or any company or companies controlled by such registered investment company ("acquiring company") may acquire any security issued by any person that, in its most recent fiscal year, derived 15 percent or less of its gross revenues from securities related activities unless the acquiring company would control such person after the acquisition.

(b) Notwithstanding section 12(d)(3) of the Act, an acquiring company may acquire any security issued by a person that, in its most recent fiscal year, derived more than 15 percent of its gross revenues from securities related activities, *provided that:*

(1) Immediately after the acquisition of any equity security, the acquiring company owns not more than five percent of the outstanding securities of that class of the issuer's equity securities;

(2) Immediately after the acquisition of any debt security, the acquiring company owns not more than ten percent of the outstanding principal amount of the issuer's debt securities; and

(3) Immediately after any such acquisition, the acquiring company has invested not more than five percent of the value of its total assets in the securities of the issuer.

(c) Notwithstanding paragraphs (a) and (b) of this section, this section does not exempt the acquisition of:

(1) A general partnership interest; or

(2) A security issued by the acquiring company's promoter, principal underwriter, or any affiliated person of such promoter, or principal underwriter; or

(3) A security issued by the acquiring company's investment adviser, or an affiliated person of the acquiring company's investment adviser, other than a security issued by a subadviser or an affiliated person of a subadviser of the acquiring company provided that:

(i) *Prohibited relationships.* The subadviser that is (or whose affiliated person is) the issuer is not, and is not an affiliated person of, an investment adviser responsible for providing advice with respect to the portion of the acquiring company that is acquiring the securities, or of any promoter, underwriter, officer, director, member of an advisory board, or employee of the acquiring company;

(ii) *Advisory contract.* The advisory contracts of the Subadviser that is (or whose affiliated person is) the issuer, and any Subadviser that is advising the portion of the acquiring company that is purchasing the securities:

Securities and Exchange Commission § 270.13a–1

(A) Prohibit them from consulting with each other concerning transactions of the acquiring company in securities or other assets, other than for purposes of complying with the conditions of paragraphs (a) and (b) of this section; and

(B) Limit their responsibility in providing advice to providing advice with respect to a discrete portion of the acquiring company's portfolio.

(d) For purposes of this section:

(1) *Securities related activities* are a person's activities as a broker, a dealer, an underwriter, an investment adviser registered under the Investment Advisers Act of 1940, as amended, or as an investment adviser to a registered investment company.

(2) An issuer's gross revenues from its own securities related activities and from its ratable share of the securities related activities of enterprises of which it owns 20 percent or more of the voting or equity interest should be considered in determining the degree to which an issuer is engaged in securities related activities. Such information may be obtained from the issuer's annual report to shareholders, the issuer's annual reports or registration statement filed with the Commission, or the issuer's chief financial officer.

(3) *Equity security* is as defined in § 240.3a–11 of this chapter.

(4) *Debt security* includes all securities other than equity securities.

(5) Determination of the percentage of an acquiring company's ownership of any class of outstanding equity securities of an issuer shall be made in accordance with the procedures described in the rules under § 240.16 of this chapter.

(6) Where an acquiring company is considering acquiring or has acquired options, warrants, rights, or convertible securities of a securities related business, the determination required by paragraph (b) of this section shall be made as though such options, warrants, rights, or conversion privileges had been exercised.

(7) The following transactions will not be deemed to be an acquisition of securities of a securities related business:

(i) Receipt of stock dividends on securities acquired in compliance with this section;

(ii) Receipt of securities arising from a stock-for-stock split on securities acquired in compliance with this section;

(iii) Exercise of options, warrants, or rights acquired in compliance with this section;

(iv) Conversion of convertible securities acquired in compliance with this section; and

(v) Acquisition of Demand Features or Guarantees, as these terms are defined in §§ 270.2a–7(a)(9) and 270.2a–7(a)(16) respectively, provided that, immediately after the acquisition of any Demand Feature or Guarantee, the company will not, with respect to 75 percent of the total value of its assets, have invested more than ten percent of the total value of its assets in securities underlying Demand Features or Guarantees from the same institution. For the purposes of this section, a Demand Feature or Guarantee will be considered to be from the party to whom the company will look for a payment of the exercise price.

(8) Any class or series of an investment company that issues two or more classes or series of preferred or special stock, each of which is preferred over all other classes or series with respect to assets specifically allocated to that class or series, shall be treated as if it is a registered investment company.

(9) *Subadviser* means an investment adviser as defined in section 2(a)(20)(B) of the Act (15 U.S.C. 80a-2(a)(20)(B)).

[58 FR 49427, Sept. 23, 1993, as amended at 61 FR 13982, Mar. 28, 1996; 62 FR 64986, Dec. 9, 1997; 66 FR 36162, July 11, 2001; 68 FR 3152, Jan. 22, 2003; 79 FR 47967, Aug. 14, 2014; 80 FR 58155, Sept. 25, 2015]

§ 270.13a–1 Exemption for change of status by temporarily diversified company.

A change of its subclassification by a registered management company from that of a diversified company to that of a nondiversified company shall be exempt from the provisions of section 13(a)(1) of the Act (54 Stat. 811; 15 U.S.C. 80a-13), if such change occurs under the following circumstances:

(a) Such company was a nondiversified company at the time of its

§ 270.14a-1

registration pursuant to section 8(a) (54 Stat. 803; 15 U.S.C. 80a–8), or thereafter legally became a nondiversified company.

(b) After its registration and within 3 years prior to such change, such company became a diversified company.

(c) At the time such company became a diversified company, its registration statement filed pursuant to section 8(b) (54 Stat. 803; 15 U.S.C. 80a–8), as supplemented and modified by any amendments and reports theretofore filed, did not stated that the registrant proposed to become a diversified company.

[Rule N–13A–1, 6 FR 3967, Aug. 8, 1941]

§ 270.14a-1 Use of notification pursuant to regulation E under the Securities Act of 1933.

For the purposes of section 14(a)(3) of the Act, registration of securities under the Securities Act of 1933 by a small business investment company operating under the Small Business Investment Act of 1958 shall be deemed to include the filing of a notification under Rule 604 of Regulation E promulgated under said Act if provision is made in connection with such notification which in the opinion of the Commission adequately insures (a) that after the effective date of such notification such company will not issue any security or receive any proceeds of any subscription for any security until firm agreements have been made with such company by not more than twenty-five responsible persons to purchase from it securities to be issued by it for an aggregate net amount which plus the then net worth of the company, if any, will equal at least $100,000; (b) that said aggregate net amount will be paid into such company before any subscriptions for such securities will be accepted from any persons in excess of twenty-five; (c) that arrangements will be made whereby any proceeds so paid in, as well as any sales load, will be refunded to any subscriber on demand without any deduction, in the event that the net proceeds so received by the company do not result in the company having a net worth of at least $100,000 within ninety days after such notification becomes effective.

[25 FR 3512, Apr. 22, 1960]

§ 270.14a-2 Exemption from section 14(a) of the Act for certain registered separate accounts and their principal underwriters.

(a) A registered separate account, and any principal underwriter for such account, shall be exempt from section 14(a) of the Act (15 U.S.C. 80a–14(a)) with respect to a public offering of variable annuity contracts participating in such account.

(b) Any registered management investment company which has as a promoter an insurance company and which offers its securities to separate accounts of such insurance company that offer variable annuity contracts and are registered under the Act as unit investment trusts ("trust accounts"), and any principal underwriter for such investment company, shall be exempt from section 14(a) with respect to such offering and to the offering of such securities to trust accounts of other insurance companies.

(c) Any registered management investment company exempt from section 14(a) of the Act pursuant to paragraph (b) of this section shall be exempt from sections 15(a), 16(a), and 32(a)(2) of the Act (15 U.S.C. 80a–15(a), 80a–16(a), and 80a–31(a)(2)), to the extent prescribed in §§ 270.15a–3, 270.16a–1, and 270.32a–2 (Rules 15a–3, 16a–1, and 32a–2 under the Act), provided that such investment company complies with the conditions set forth in Rules 15a–3, 16a–1, and 32a–2 as if it were a separate account.

[85 FR 26109, May 1, 2020]

§ 270.14a-3 Exemption from section 14(a) of the Act for certain registered unit investment trusts and their principal underwriters.

(a) A registered unit investment trust (hereinafter referred to as the "Trust") engaged exclusively in the business of investing in eligible trust securities, and any principal underwriter for the Trust, shall be exempt from section 14(a) of the Act with respect to a public offering of Trust units: *Provided,* That:

(1) At the commencement of such offering the Trust holds at least $100,000 principal amount of eligible trust securities (or delivery statements relating to contracts for the purchase of any

Securities and Exchange Commission § 270.15a-1

such securities which, together with cash or an irrevocable letter of credit issued by a bank in the amount required for their purchase, are held by the Trust for purchase of the securities);

(2) If, within ninety days from the time that the Trust's registration statement has become effective under the Securities Act of 1933 (15 U.S.C. 77a *et seq.*) the net worth of the Trust declines to less than $100,000 or the Trust is terminated, the sponsor for the Trust shall—

(i) Refund, on demand and without deduction, all sales charges to any unitholders who purchased Trust units from the sponsor (or from any underwriter or dealer participating in the distribution), and

(ii) Liquidate the eligible trust securities held by the Trust and distribute the proceeds thereof to the unitholders of the Trust;

(3) The sponsor instructs the trustee when the eligible trust securities are deposited in the Trust that, in the event that redemptions by the sponsor or any underwriter of units constituting a part of the unsold units results in the Trust having a net worth of less than 40 percent of the principal amount of the eligible trust securities (or delivery statements relating to contracts for the purchase of any such securities which, together with cash or an irrevocable letter of credit issued by a bank in the amount required for their purchase, are held by the Trust for purchase of the securities) initially deposited in the Trust—

(i) The trustee shall terminate the Trust and distribute the assets thereof to the unitholders of the Trust, and

(ii) The sponsor for the Trust shall refund, on demand and without deduction, all sales charges to any unitholder who purchased Trust units from the sponsor or from any underwriter or dealer participating in the distribution.

(b) For the purposes of determining the availability of the exemption provided by the foregoing subsection, the term "eligible trust securities" shall mean:

(1) Securities (other than convertible securities) which are issued by a corporation and which have their interest or dividend rate fixed at the time they are issued;

(2) Interest bearing obligations issued by a state, or by any agency, instrumentality, authority or political subdivision thereof;

(3) Government securities; and

(4) Units of a previously issued series of the Trust: *Provided,* That:

(i) The aggregate principal amount of units of existing series so deposited shall not exceed 10% of the aggregate principal amount of the portfolio of the new series;

(ii) The aggregate principal amount of units of any particular existing series so deposited shall not exceed 5% of the aggregate principal amount of the portfolio of the new series;

(iii) No units shall be so deposited which do not substantially meet investment quality criteria at least as high as those applicable to the new series in which such units are deposited;

(iv) The value of the eligible trust securities underlying units of an existing series deposited in a new series shall not, by reason of maturity of such securities according to their terms within ten years following the date of deposit, be reduced sufficiently for such existing series to be voluntarily terminated;

(v) Units of existing series so deposited shall constitute units purchased by the sponsor as market maker and not remaining unsold units from the original distribution of such units; and

(vi) The sponsor shall deposit units of existing series in the new series without a sales charge.

(Secs. 6(c) and 38(a) (15 U.S.C. 80a-6(c) and 15 U.S.C. 80a-37(a)))

[44 FR 29646, May 22, 1979; 44 FR 40064, July 9, 1979]

§ 270.15a-1 Exemption from stockholders' approval of certain small investment advisory contracts.

An investment adviser of a registered investment company shall be exempt from the requirement of sections 15(a) and 15(e) of the Act (54 Stat. 812; 15 U.S.C. 80a-15) that the written contract pursuant to which he acts shall have been approved by the vote of a majority of the outstanding votingsecurities of such company, if the following conditions are met:

§ 270.15a-2

(a) Such investment adviser is not an affiliated person of such company (except as investment adviser) nor of any principal underwriter for such company.

(b) His compensation as investment adviser of such company in any fiscal year of the company during which any such contract is in effect either (1) is not more than $100 or (2) is not more than $2,500 and not more than 1/40 of 1 percent of the value of the company's net assets averaged over the year or taken as of a definite date or dates within the year.

(c) The aggregate compensation of all investment advisers of such company exempted pursuant to this section in any fiscal year of the company either (1) is not more than $200 or (2) is not more than 1/20 of 1 percent of the value of the company's net assets averaged over the year or taken as of a definite date or dates within the year.

[Rule N-15A-1, 6 FR 2275, Jan. 8, 1944]

§ 270.15a-2 Annual continuance of contracts.

(a) For purposes of sections 15(a) and 15(b) of the Act, the continuance of a contract for a period more than two years after the date of its execution shall be deemed to have been specifically approved at least annually by the board of directors or by a vote of a majority of the outstanding voting securities of a registered investment company if such approval occurs:

(1) With respect to the first continuance of a contract, during the 90 days prior to and including the earlier of (i) the date specified in such contract for its termination in the absence of such approval, or (ii) the second anniversary of the date upon which such contract was executed; or

(2) With respect to any subsequent continuance of a contract, during the 90 days prior to and including the first anniversary of the date upon which the most recent previous annual continuance of such contract became effective.

(b) The provisions of paragraph (a) of this section shall not apply to any continuance of a contract which shall have been approved not later than 90 days after the date of adoption of this section, provided that such contract shall expire, by its terms, not later than 17 months from the date of adoption of this section.

NOTE: This section does not establish the exclusive method of complying with the Act. It provides one procedure by which a registered investment company may comply with the applicable provisions of sections 15(a) and 15(b) of the Act; it does not preclude any other appropriate procedure. Any annual continuance of a contract approved in accordance with the provisions of paragraph (a)(1) or (a)(2) of § 270.15a-2 will constitute a renewal of such contract for the purposes of section 15(c) of the Act, and therefore such renewal must be approved by the disinterested directors within the times specified in the section for a continuance.

[41 FR 41911, Sept. 24, 1976]

§ 270.15a-3 Exemption for initial period of investment adviser of certain registered separate accounts from requirement of security holder approval of investment advisory contract.

(a) An investment adviser of a registered separate account shall be exempt from the requirement under section 15(a) of the Act that the initial written contract pursuant to which the investment adviser serves or acts shall have been approved by the vote of a majority of the outstanding voting securities of such registered separate account, subject to the following conditions:

(1) Such registered separate account qualifies for exemption from section 14(a) of the Act pursuant to § 270.14a-2, or is exempt therefrom by order of the Commission upon application; and

(2) Such written contract shall be submitted to a vote of variable annuity contract owners at their first meeting after the effective date of the registration statement under the Securities Act of 1933, as amended (15 U.S.C. 77a *et seq.*) relating to variable annuity contracts participating in such account: *Provided,* That such meeting shall take place within 1 year after such effective date, unless the time for the holding of such meeting shall be extended by the Commission upon written request showing good cause therefor.

(Sec. 6, 54 Stat. 800; 15 U.S.C. 80a-6)

[34 FR 12695, Aug. 5, 1969]

Securities and Exchange Commission

§ 270.15a-4

§ 270.15a-4 Temporary exemption for certain investment advisers.

(a) For purposes of this section:

(1) *Fund* means an investment company, and includes a separate series of the company.

(2) *Interim contract* means a written investment advisory contract:

(i) That has not been approved by a majority of the fund's outstanding voting securities; and

(ii) That has a duration no greater than 150 days following the date on which the previous contract terminates.

(3) *Previous contract* means an investment advisory contract that has been approved by a majority of the fund's outstanding voting securities and has been terminated.

(b) Notwithstanding section 15(a) of the Act (15 U.S.C. 80a-15(a)), a person may act as investment adviser for a fund under an interim contract after the termination of a previous contract as provided in paragraphs (b)(1) or (b)(2) of this section:

(1) In the case of a previous contract terminated by an event described in section 15(a)(3) of the Act (15 U.S.C. 80a-15(a)(3)), by the failure to renew the previous contract, or by an assignment (other than an assignment by an investment adviser or a controlling person of the investment adviser in connection with which assignment the investment adviser or a controlling person directly or indirectly receives money or other benefit):

(i) The compensation to be received under the interim contract is no greater than the compensation the adviser would have received under the previous contract; and

(ii) The fund's board of directors, including a majority of the directors who are not interested persons of the fund, has approved the interim contract within 10 business days after the termination, at a meeting in which directors may participate by any means of communication that allows all directors participating to hear each other simultaneously during the meeting.

(2) In the case of a previous contract terminated by an assignment by an investment adviser or a controlling person of the investment adviser in connection with which assignment the investment adviser or a controlling person directly or indirectly receives money or other benefit:

(i) The compensation to be received under the interim contract is no greater than the compensation the adviser would have received under the previous contract;

(ii) The board of directors, including a majority of the directors who are not interested persons of the fund, has voted in person to approve the interim contract before the previous contract is terminated;

(iii) The board of directors, including a majority of the directors who are not interested persons of the fund, determines that the scope and quality of services to be provided to the fund under the interim contract will be at least equivalent to the scope and quality of services provided under the previous contract;

(iv) The interim contract provides that the fund's board of directors or a majority of the fund's outstanding voting securities may terminate the contract at any time, without the payment of any penalty, on not more than 10 calendar days' written notice to the investment adviser;

(v) The interim contract contains the same terms and conditions as the previous contract, with the exception of its effective and termination dates, provisions governed by paragraphs (b)(2)(i), (b)(2)(iv), and (b)(2)(vi) of this section, and any other differences in terms and conditions that the board of directors, including a majority of the directors who are not interested persons of the fund, finds to be immaterial;

(vi) The interim contract contains the following provisions:

(A) The compensation earned under the contract will be held in an interest-bearing escrow account with the fund's custodian or a bank;

(B) If a majority of the fund's outstanding voting securities approve a contract with the investment adviser by the end of the 150-day period, the amount in the escrow account (including interest earned) will be paid to the investment adviser; and

(C) If a majority of the fund's outstanding voting securities do not approve a contract with the investment adviser, the investment adviser will be paid, out of the escrow account, the lesser of:

(1) Any costs incurred in performing the interim contract (plus interest earned on that amount while in escrow); or

(2) The total amount in the escrow account (plus interest earned); and

(vii) The board of directors of the investment company satisfies the fund governance standards defined in § 270.0–1(a)(7).

[64 FR 68023, Dec. 6, 1999, as amended 66 FR 3758, Jan. 16, 2001; 69 FR 46389, Aug. 2, 2004]

§ 270.16a–1 Exemption for initial period of directors of certain registered accounts from requirements of election by security holders.

(a) Persons serving as the directors of a registered separate account shall, prior to the first meeting of such account's variable annuity contract owners, be exempt from the requirement of section 16(a) of the Act that such persons be elected by the holders of outstanding voting securities of such account at an annual or special meeting called for that purpose, subject to the following conditions:

(1) Such registered separate account qualifies for exemption from section 14(a) of the Act pursuant to § 270.14a–1 or is exempt therefrom by order of the Commission upon application; and

(2) Such persons have been appointed directors of such account by the establishing insurance company; and

(3) An election of directors for such account shall be held at the first meeting of variable annuity contract owners after the effective date of the registration statement under the Securities Act of 1933, as amended (15 U.S.C. 77a *et seq.*), relating to contracts participating in such account: *Provided*, That such meeting shall take place within 1 year after such effective date, unless the time for the holding of such meeting shall be extended by the Commission upon written request showing good cause therefor.

(Sec. 6, 54 Stat. 800; 15 U.S.C. 80a–6)

[34 FR 12695, Aug. 5, 1969]

§ 270.17a–1 Exemption of certain underwriting transactions exempted by § 270.10f–1.

Any transaction exempted pursuant to § 270.10f–1 shall be exempt from the provisions of section 17(a)(1) of the Act (54 Stat. 815; 15 U.S.C. 80a–17).

[Rule N–17A–1, 6 FR 1191, Feb. 28, 1941]

§ 270.17a–2 Exemption of certain purchase, sale, or borrowing transactions.

Purchase, sale or borrowing transactions occurring in the usual course of business between affiliated persons of registered investment companies shall be exempt from section 17(a) of the Act provided (a) the transactions involve notes, drafts, time payment contracts, bills of exchange, acceptance or other property of a commercial character rather than of an investment character; (b) the buyer or lender is a bank; and (c) the seller or borrower is a bank or is engaged principally in the business of installment financing.

[Rule N–17A–2, 12 FR 5008, July 29, 1947]

§ 270.17a–3 Exemption of transactions with fully owned subsidiaries.

(a) The following transactions shall be exempt from section 17(a) of the Act:

(1) Transactions solely between a registered investment company and one or more of its fully owned subsidiaries or solely between two or more fully owned subsidiaries of such company.

(2) Transactions solely between any subsidiary of a registered investment company and one or more fully owned subsidiaries of such subsidiary or solely between two or more fully owned subsidiaries of such subsidiary.

(b) The term *fully owned subsidiary* as used in this section, means a subsidiary (1) all of whose outstanding securities, other than directors' qualifying shares, are owned by its parent and/or the parent's other fully owned subsidiaries, and (2) which is not indebted to any person other than its parent and/or the parent's other fully owned subsidiaries in an amount which is material in relation to the particular subsidiary, excepting (i) indebtedness incurred in the ordinary course of business which is not overdue and which

Securities and Exchange Commission

§ 270.17a-6

matures within one year from the date of its creation, whether evidenced by securities or not, and (ii) any other indebtedness to one or more banks or insurance companies.

[Rule N-17A-3, 12 FR 3442, May 28, 1947]

§ 270.17a-4 Exemption of transactions pursuant to certain contracts.

Transactions pursuant to a contract shall be exempt from section 17(a) of the Act if at the time of the making of the contract and for a period of at least six months prior thereto no affiliation or other relationship existed which would operate to make such contract or the subsequent performance thereof subject to the provisions of said section 17(a).

[Rule N-17A-4, 12 FR 5008, July 29, 1947]

§ 270.17a-5 Pro rata distribution neither "sale" nor "purchase."

When a company makes a pro rata distribution in cash or in kind among its common stockholders without giving any election to any stockholder as to the specific assets which such stockholders shall receive, such distribution shall not be deemed to involve a sale to or a purchase from such distributing company as those terms are used in section 17(a) of the Act.

[20 FR 7447, Oct. 6, 1955]

§ 270.17a-6 Exemption for transactions with portfolio affiliates.

(a) *Exemption for transactions with portfolio affiliates.* A transaction to which a fund, or a company controlled by a fund, and a portfolio affiliate of the fund are parties is exempt from the provisions of section 17(a) of the Act (15 U.S.C. 80a–17(a)), provided that none of the following persons is a party to the transaction, or has a direct or indirect financial interest in a party to the transaction other than the fund:

(1) An officer, director, employee, investment adviser, member of an advisory board, depositor, promoter of or principal underwriter for the fund;

(2) A person directly or indirectly controlling the fund;

(3) A person directly or indirectly owning, controlling or holding with power to vote five percent or more of the outstanding voting securities of the fund;

(4) A person directly or indirectly under common control with the fund, other than:

(i) A portfolio affiliate of the fund; or

(ii) A fund whose sole interest in the transaction or a party to the transaction is an interest in the portfolio affiliate; or

(5) An affiliated person of any of the persons mentioned in paragraphs (a)(1)–(4) of this section, other than the fund or a portfolio affiliate of the fund.

(b) *Definitions*—(1) *Financial interest.* (i) The term *financial interest* as used in this section does not include:

(A) Any interest through ownership of securities issued by the fund;

(B) Any interest of a wholly-owned subsidiary of a fund;

(C) Usual and ordinary fees for services as a director;

(D) An interest of a non-executive employee;

(E) An interest of an insurance company arising from a loan or policy made or issued by it in the ordinary course of business to a natural person;

(F) An interest of a bank arising from a loan or account made or maintained by it in the ordinary course of business to or with a natural person, unless it arises from a loan to a person who is an officer, director or executive of a company which is a party to the transaction, or from a loan to a person who directly or indirectly owns, controls, or holds with power to vote, five percent or more of the outstanding voting securities of a company which is a party to the transaction;

(G) An interest acquired in a transaction described in paragraph (d)(3) of § 270.17d–1; or

(H) Any other interest that the board of directors of the fund, including a majority of the directors who are not interested persons of the fund, finds to be not material, provided that the directors record the basis for that finding in the minutes of their meeting.

(ii) A person has a financial interest in any party in which it has a financial interest, in which it had a financial interest within six months prior to the transaction, or in which it will acquire

419

§ 270.17a-7

a financial interest pursuant to an arrangement in existence at the time of the transaction.

(2) *Fund* means a registered investment company or separate series of a registered investment company.

(3) *Portfolio affiliate of a fund* means a person that is an affiliated person (or an affiliated person of an affiliated person) of a fund solely because the fund, a fund under common control with the fund, or both:

(i) Controls such person (or an affiliated person of such person); or

(ii) Owns, controls, or holds with power to vote five percent or more of the outstanding voting securities of such person (or an affiliated person of such person).

[68 FR 3153, Jan. 22, 2003]

§ 270.17a-7 Exemption of certain purchase or sale transactions between an investment company and certain affiliated persons thereof.

A purchase or sale transaction between registered investment companies or separate series of registered investment companies, which are affiliated persons, or affiliated persons of affiliated persons, of each other, between separate series of a registered investment company, or between a registered investment company or a separate series of a registered investment company and a person which is an affiliated person of such registered investment company (or affiliated person of such person) solely by reason of having a common investment adviser or investment advisers which are affiliated persons of each other, common directors, and/or common officers, is exempt from section 17(a) of the Act; *Provided,* That:

(a) The transaction is a purchase or sale, for no consideration other than cash payment against prompt delivery of a security for which market quotations are readily available;

(b) The transaction is effected at the independent current market price of the security. For purposes of this paragraph the "current market price" shall be:

(1) If the security is an "NMS stock" as that term is defined in 17 CFR 242.600, the last sale price with respect to such security reported in the consolidated transaction reporting system ("consolidated system") or the average of the highest current independent bid and lowest current independent offer for such security (reported pursuant to 17 CFR 242.602) if there are no reported transactions in the consolidated system that day; or

(2) If the security is not a reported security, and the principal market for such security is an exchange, then the last sale on such exchange or the average of the highest current independent bid and lowest current independent offer on such exchange if there are no reported transactions on such exchange that day; or

(3) If the security is not a reported security and is quoted in the NASDAQ System, then the average of the highest current independent bid and lowest current independent offer reported on Level 1 of NASDAQ; or

(4) For all other securities, the average of the highest current independent bid and lowest current independent offer determined on the basis of reasonable inquiry;

(c) The transaction is consistent with the policy of each registered investment company and separate series of a registered investment company participating in the transaction, as recited in its registration statement and reports filed under the Act;

(d) No brokerage commission, fee (except for customary transfer fees), or other remuneration is paid in connection with the transaction;

(e) The board of directors of the investment company, including a majority of the directors who are not interested persons of such investment company,

(1) Adopts procedures pursuant to which such purchase or sale transactions may be effected for the company, which are reasonably designed to provide that all of the conditions of this section in paragraphs (a) through (d) have been complied with,

(2) Makes and approves such changes as the board deems necessary, and

(3) Determines no less frequently than quarterly that all such purchases or sales made during the preceding quarter were effected in compliance with such procedures;

Securities and Exchange Commission § 270.17a-8

(f) The board of directors of the investment company satisfies the fund governance standards defined in § 270.0-1(a)(7); and

(g) The investment company (1) maintains and preserves permanently in an easily accessible place a written copy of the procedures (and any modifications thereto) described in paragraph (e) of this section, and (2) maintains and preserves for a period not less than six years from the end of the fiscal year in which any transactions occurred, the first two years in an easily accessible place, a written record of each such transaction setting forth a description of the security purchased or sold, the identity of the person on the other side of the transaction, the terms of the purchase or sale transaction, and the information or materials upon which the determinations described in paragraph (e)(3) of this section were made.

[46 FR 17013, Mar. 17, 1981, as amended at 58 FR 49921, Sept. 24, 1993; 66 FR 3758, Jan. 16, 2001; 69 FR 46389, Aug. 2, 2004; 70 FR 37632, June 29, 2005]

§ 270.17a-8 Mergers of affiliated companies.

(a) *Exemption of affiliated mergers.* A Merger of a registered investment company (or a series thereof) and one or more other registered investment companies (or series thereof) or Eligible Unregistered Funds is exempt from sections 17(a)(1) and (2) of the Act (15 U.S.C. 80a–17(a)(1)–(2)) if:

(1) *Surviving company.* The Surviving Company is a registered investment company (or a series thereof).

(2) *Board determinations.* As to any registered investment company (or series thereof) participating in the Merger ("Merging Company"):

(i) The board of directors, including a majority of the directors who are not interested persons of the Merging Company or of any other company or series participating in the Merger, determines that:

(A) Participation in the Merger is in the best interests of the Merging Company; and

(B) The interests of the Merging Company's existing shareholders will not be diluted as a result of the Merger.

NOTE TO PARAGRAPH (a)(2)(i): For a discussion of factors that may be relevant to the determinations in paragraph (a)(2)(i) of this section, see Investment Company Act Release No. 25666, July 18, 2002.

(ii) The directors have requested and evaluated such information as may reasonably be necessary to their determinations in paragraph (a)(2)(i) of this section, and have considered and given appropriate weight to all pertinent factors.

(iii) The directors, in making the determination in paragraph (a)(2)(i)(B) of this section, have approved procedures for the valuation of assets to be conveyed by each Eligible Unregistered Fund participating in the Merger. The approved procedures provide for the preparation of a report by an Independent Evaluator, to be considered in assessing the value of any securities (or other assets) for which market quotations are not readily available, that sets forth the fair value of each such asset as of the date of the Merger.

(iv) The determinations required in paragraph (a)(2)(i) of this section and the bases thereof, including the factors considered by the directors pursuant to paragraph (a)(2)(ii) of this section, are recorded fully in the minute books of the Merging Company.

(3) *Shareholder approval.* Participation in the Merger is approved by the vote of a majority of the outstanding voting securities (as provided in section 2(a)(42) of the Act (15 U.S.C. 80a–2(a)(42))) of any Merging Company that is not a Surviving Company, unless—

(i) No policy of the Merging Company that under section 13 of the Act (15 U.S.C. 80a–13) could not be changed without a vote of a majority of its outstanding voting securities, is materially different from a policy of the Surviving Company;

(ii) No advisory contract between the Merging Company and any investment adviser thereof is materially different from an advisory contract between the Surviving Company and any investment adviser thereof, except for the identity of the investment companies as a party to the contract;

(iii) Directors of the Merging Company who are not interested persons of the Merging Company and who were

§ 270.17a–9

elected by its shareholders, will comprise a majority of the directors of the Surviving Company who are not interested persons of the Surviving Company; and

(iv) Any distribution fees (as a percentage of the fund's average net assets) authorized to be paid by the Surviving Company pursuant to a plan adopted in accordance with § 270.12b–1 are no greater than the distribution fees (as a percentage of the fund's average net assets) authorized to be paid by the Merging Company pursuant to such a plan.

(4) *Board composition.* The board of directors of the Merging Company satisfies the fund governance standards defined in § 270.0–1(a)(7).

(5) *Merger records.* Any Surviving Company preserves written records that describe the Merger and its terms for six years after the Merger (and for the first two years in an easily accessible place).

(b) *Definitions.* For purposes of this section:

(1) *Merger* means the merger, consolidation, or purchase or sale of substantially all of the assets between a registered investment company (or a series thereof) and another company;

(2) *Eligible Unregistered Fund* means:

(i) A collective trust fund, as described in section 3(c)(11) of the Act (15 U.S.C. 80a–3(c)(11));

(ii) A common trust fund or similar fund, as described in section 3(c)(3) of the Act (15 U.S.C. 80a–3(c)(3)); or

(iii) A separate account, as described in section 2(a)(37) of the Act (15 U.S.C. 80a–2(a)(37)), that is neither registered under section 8 of the Act, nor required to be so registered;

(3) *Independent Evaluator* means a person who has expertise in the valuation of securities and other financial assets and who is not an interested person, as defined in section 2(a)(19) of the Act (15 U.S.C. 80a–2(a)(19)), of the Eligible Unregistered Fund or any affiliate thereof except the Merging Company; and

(4) *Surviving Company* means a company in which shareholders of a Merging Company will obtain an interest as a result of a Merger.

[67 FR 48518, July 24, 2002, as amended at 69 FR 46389, Aug. 2, 2004]

§ 270.17a–9 Purchase of certain securities from a money market fund by an affiliate, or an affiliate of an affiliate.

The purchase of a security from the portfolio of an open-end investment company holding itself out as a money market fund by any affiliated person or promoter of or principal underwriter for the money market fund or any affiliated person of such person shall be exempt from section 17(a) of the Act (15 U.S.C. 80a–17(a)); provided that:

(a) In the case of a portfolio security that has ceased to be an Eligible Security (as defined in § 270.2a–7(a)(12)), or has defaulted (other than an immaterial default unrelated to the financial condition of the issuer):

(1) The purchase price is paid in cash; and

(2) The purchase price is equal to the greater of the amortized cost of the security or its market price (in each case, including accrued interest).

(b) In the case of any other portfolio security:

(1) The purchase price meets the requirements of paragraph (a)(1) and (2) of this section; and

(2) In the event that the purchaser thereafter sells the security for a higher price than the purchase price paid to the money market fund, the purchaser shall promptly pay to the fund the amount by which the subsequent sale price exceeds the purchase price paid to the fund.

[75 FR 10117, Mar. 4, 2010]

§ 270.17a–10 Exemption for transactions with certain subadvisory affiliates.

(a) *Exemption.* A person that is prohibited by section 17(a) of the Act (15 U.S.C. 80a–17(a)) from entering into a transaction with a fund solely because such person is, or is an affiliated person of, a subadviser of the fund, or a subadviser of a fund that is under common control with the fund, may nonetheless enter into such transaction, if:

(1) *Prohibited relationship.* The person is not, and is not an affiliated person of, an investment adviser responsible for providing advice with respect to the portion of the fund for which the transaction is entered into, or of any promoter, underwriter, officer, director,

Securities and Exchange Commission

§ 270.17d-1

member of an advisory board, or employee of the fund.

(2) *Prohibited conduct.* The advisory contracts of the subadviser that is (or whose affiliated person is) entering into the transaction, and any subadviser that is advising the fund (or portion of the fund) entering into the transaction:

(i) Prohibit them from consulting with each other concerning transactions for the fund in securities or other assets; and

(ii) If both such subadvisers are responsible for providing investment advice to the fund, limit the subadvisers' responsibility in providing advice with respect to a discrete portion of the fund's portfolio.

(b) *Definitions.* (1) *Fund* means a registered investment company and includes a separate series of a registered investment company.

(2) *Subadviser* means an investment adviser as defined in section 2(a)(20)(B) of the Act (15 U.S.C. 80a–2(a)(20)(B)).

[68 FR 3153, Jan. 22, 2003]

§ 270.17d-1 Applications regarding joint enterprises or arrangements and certain profit-sharing plans.

(a) No affiliated person of or principal underwriter for any registered investment company (other than a company of the character described in section 12(d)(3) (A) and (B) of the Act) and no affiliated person of such a person or principal underwriter, acting as principal, shall participate in, or effect any transaction in connection with, any joint enterprise or other joint arrangement or profit-sharing plan in which any such registered company, or a company controlled by such registered company, is a participant, and which is entered into, adopted or modified subsequent to the effective date of this rule, unless an application regarding such joint enterprise, arrangement or profit-sharing plan has been filed with the Commission and has been granted by an order entered prior to the submission of such plan or modification to security holders for approval, or prior to such adoption or modification if not so submitted, except that the provisions of this rule shall not preclude any affiliated person from acting as manager of any underwriting syndicate or other group in which such registered or controlled company is a participant and receiving compensation therefor.

(b) In passing upon such applications, the Commission will consider whether the participation of such registered or controlled company in such joint enterprise, joint arrangement or profit-sharing plan on the basis proposed is consistent with the provisions, policies and purposes of the Act and the extent to which such participation is on a basis different from or less advantageous than that of other participants.

(c) "Joint enterprise or other joint arrangement or profit-sharing plan" as used in this section shall mean any written or oral plan, contract, authorization or arrangement, or any practice or understanding concerning an enterprise or undertaking whereby a registered investment company or a controlled company thereof and any affiliated person of or a principal underwriter for such registered investment company, or any affiliated person of such a person or principal underwriter, have a joint or a joint and several participation, or share in the profits of such enterprise or undertaking, including, but not limited to, any stock option or stock purchase plan, but shall not include an investment advisory contract subject to section 15 of the Act.

(d) Notwithstanding the requirements of paragraph (a) of this section, no application need be filed pursuant to this section with respect to any of the following:

(1) Any profit-sharing, stock option or stock purchase plan provided by any controlled company which is not an investment company for its officers, directors or employees, or the purchase of stock or the granting, modification or exercise of options pursuant to such a plan, provided:

(i) No individual participates therein who is either:

(*a*) An affiliated person of any investment company which is an affiliated person of such controlled company; or

(*b*) An affiliated person of the investment adviser or principal underwriter of such investment company; and

§ 270.17d-1

(ii) No participant has been an affiliated person of such investment company, its investment adviser or principal underwriter during the life of the plan and for six months prior to, as the case may be:

(a) Institution of the profit-sharing plan;

(b) The purchase of stock pursuant to a stock purchase plan; or

(c) The granting of any options pursuant to a stock option plan.

(2) Any plan provided by any registered investment company or any controlled company for its officers or employees if such plan has been qualified under section 401 of the Internal Revenue Code of 1954 and all contributions paid under said plan by the employer qualify as deductible under section 404 of said Code.

(3) Any loan or advance of credit to, or acquisition of securities or other property of, a small business concern, or any agreement to do any of the foregoing ("Investments"), made by a bank and a small business investment company (SBIC) licensed under the Small Business Investment Act of 1958, whether such transactions are contemporaneous or separated in time, where the bank is an affiliated person of either (i) the SBIC or (ii) an affiliated person of the SBIC; but reports containing pertinent details as to Investments and transactions relating thereto shall be made at such time, on such forms and by such persons as the Commission may from time to time prescribe.

(4) The issuance by a registered investment company which is licensed by the Small Business Administration pursuant to the Small Business Investment Act of 1958 of stock options which qualify under section 422 of the Internal Revenue Code, as amended, and which conform to § 107.805(b) of Chapter I of Title 13 of the Code of Federal Regulations.

(5) Any joint enterprise or other joint arrangement or profit-sharing plan ("joint enterprise") in which a registered investment company or a company controlled by such a company, is a participant, and in which a portfolio affiliate (as defined in § 270.17a–6(b)(3)) of such registered investment company is also a participant, provided that:

(i) None of the persons identified in § 270.17a–6(a) is a participant in the joint enterprise, or has a direct or indirect financial interest in a participant in the joint enterprise (other than the registered investment company);

(ii) *Financial interest.* (A) The term *financial interest* as used in this section does not include:

(1) Any interest through ownership of securities issued by the registered investment company;

(2) Any interest of a wholly owned subsidiary of the registered investment company;

(3) Usual and ordinary fees for services as a director;

(4) An interest of a non-executive employee;

(5) An interest of an insurance company arising from a loan or policy made or issued by it in the ordinary course of business to a natural person;

(6) An interest of a bank arising from a loan to a person who is an officer, director, or executive of a company which is a participant in the joint transaction or from a loan to a person who directly or indirectly owns, controls, or holds with power to vote, five percent or more of the outstanding voting securities of a company which is a participant in the joint transaction;

(7) An interest acquired in a transaction described in paragraph (d)(3) of this section; or

(8) Any other interest that the board of directors of the investment company, including a majority of the directors who are not interested persons of the investment company, finds to be not material, provided that the directors record the basis for that finding in the minutes of their meeting.

(B) A person has a financial interest in any party in which it has a financial interest, in which it had a financial interest within six months prior to the investment company's participation in the enterprise, or in which it will acquire a financial interest pursuant to an arrangement in existence at the time of the investment company's participation in the enterprise.

(6) The receipt of securities and/or cash by an investment company or a controlled company thereof and an affiliated person of such investment company or an affiliated person of such

person pursuant to a plan of reorganization: *Provided*, That no person identified in § 270.17a–6(a)(1) or any company in which such a person has a direct or indirect financial interest (as defined in paragraph (d)(5)(ii) of this section):

(i) Has a direct or indirect financial interest in the corporation under reorganization, except owning securities of each class or classes owned by such investment company or controlled company;

(ii) Receives pursuant to such plan any securities or other property, except securities of the same class and subject to the same terms as the securities received by such investment company or controlled company, and/or cash in the same proportion as is received by the investment company or controlled company based on securities of the company under reorganization owned by such persons; and

(iii) Is, or has a direct or indirect financial interest in any person (other than such investment company or controlled company) who is:

(A) Purchasing assets from the company under reorganization; or

(B) Exchanging shares with such person in a transaction not in compliance with the standards described in this paragraph (d)(6).

(7) Any arrangement regarding liability insurance policies (other than a bond required pursuant to rule 17g–1 (§ 270.17g–1) under the Act); *Provided,* That

(i) The investment company's participation in the joint liability insurance policy is in the best interests of the investment company;

(ii) The proposed premium for the joint liability insurance policy to be allocated to the investment company, based upon its proportionate share of the sum of the premiums that would have been paid if such insurance coverage were purchased separately by the insured parties, is fair and reasonable to the investment company;

(iii) The joint liability insurance policy does not exclude coverage for bona fide claims made against any director who is not an interested person of the investment company, or against the investment company if it is a co-defendant in the claim with the disinterested director, by another person insured under the joint liability insurance policy;

(iv) The board of directors of the investment company, including a majority of the directors who are not interested persons with respect thereto, determine no less frequently than annually that the standards described in paragraphs (d)(7)(i) and (ii) of this section have been satisfied; and

(v) The board of directors of the investment company satisfies the fund governance standards defined in § 270.0–1(a)(7).

(8) An investment adviser's bearing expenses in connection with a merger, consolidation or purchase or sale of substantially all of the assets of a company which involves a registered investment company of which it is an affiliated person.

[22 FR 426, Jan. 23, 1957, as amended at 26 FR 11240, Nov. 29, 1961; 35 FR 13123, Aug. 18, 1970; 39 FR 37973, Oct. 25, 1974; 44 FR 58503, Oct. 10, 1979; 44 FR 58908, Oct. 12, 1979; 45 FR 12409, Feb. 26, 1980; 66 FR 3758, Jan. 16, 2001; 68 FR 3153, Jan. 22, 2003; 69 FR 46389, Aug. 2, 2004; 78 FR 79299, Dec. 30, 2013]

§ 270.17d–2 **Form for report by small business investment company and affiliated bank.**

Form N–17D–1 is hereby prescribed as the form for reports required by paragraph (d)(3) of § 270.17d–1.

[26 FR 11240, Nov. 29, 1961]

§ 270.17d–3 **Exemption relating to certain joint enterprises or arrangements concerning payment for distribution of shares of a registered open-end management investment company.**

An affiliated person of, or principal underwriter for, a registered open-end management investment company and an affiliated person of such a person or principal underwriter shall be exempt from section 17(d) of the Act (15 U.S.C. 80a–17(d)) and rule 17d–1 thereunder (17 CFR 270.17d–1), to the extent necessary to permit any such person or principal underwriter to enter into a written agreement with such company whereby the company will make payments in connection with the distribution of its shares, *Provided,* That:

(a) Such agreement is made in compliance with the provisions of §270.12b–1; and

(b) No other registered management investment company which is either an affiliated person of such company or an affiliated person of such a person is a party to such agreement.

[45 FR 73905, Nov. 7, 1980]

§270.17e–1 Brokerage transactions on a securities exchange.

For purposes of section 17(e)(2)(A) of the Act [15 U.S.C. 80a–17(e)(2)(A)], a commission, fee or other remuneration shall be deemed as not exceeding the usual and customary broker's commission, if:

(a) The commission, fee, or other remuneration received or to be received is reasonable and fair compared to the commission, fee or other remuneration received by other brokers in connection with comparable transactions involving similar securities being purchased or sold on a securities exchange during a comparable period of time;

(b) The board of directors, including a majority of the directors of the investment company who are not interested persons thereof:

(1) Has adopted procedures which are reasonably designed to provide that such commission, fee, or other remuneration is consistent with the standard described in paragraph (a) of this section;

(2) Makes and approves such changes as the board deems necessary; and

(3) Determines no less frequently than quarterly that all transactions effected pursuant to this section during the preceding quarter (other than transactions in which the person acting as broker is a person permitted to enter into a transaction with the investment company by §270.17a–10) were effected in compliance with such procedures;

(c) The board of directors of the investment company satisfies the fund governance standards defined in §270.0–1(a)(7); and

(d) The investment company:

(1) Shall maintain and preserve permanently in an easily accessible place a copy of the procedures (and any modification thereto) described in paragraph (b)(1) of this section; and

(2) Shall maintain and preserve for a period not less than six years from the end of the fiscal year in which any transactions occurred, the first two years in an easily accessible place, a record of each such transaction (other than any transaction in which the person acting as broker is a person permitted to enter into a transaction with the investment company by §270.17a–10) setting forth the amount and source of the commission, fee or other remuneration received or to be received, the identity of the person acting as broker, the terms of the transaction, and the information or materials upon which the findings described in paragraph (b)(3) of this section were made.

[44 FR 37203, June 26, 1979, as amended at 58 FR 49921, Sept. 24, 1993; 66 FR 3759, Jan. 16, 2001; 68 FR 3154, Jan. 22, 2003; 69 FR 46389, Aug. 2, 2004]

§270.17f–1 Custody of securities with members of national securities exchanges.

(a) No registered management investment company shall place or maintain any of its securities or similar investments in the custody of a company which is a member of a national securities exchange as defined in the Securities Exchange Act of 1934 (whether or not such company trades in securities for its own account) except pursuant to a written contract which shall have been approved, or if executed before January 1, 1941, shall have been ratified not later than that date, by a majority of the board of directors of such investment company.

(b) The contract shall require, and the securities and investments shall be maintained in accordance with the following:

(1) The securities and similar investments held in such custody shall at all times be individually segregated from the securities and investments of any other person and marked in such manner as to clearly identify them as the property of such registered management company, both upon physical inspection thereof and upon examination of the books of the custodian. The physical segregation and marking of such securities and investments may be accomplished by putting them in separate containers bearing the name

of such registered management investment company or by attaching tags or labels to such securities and investments.

(2) The custodian shall have no power or authority to assign, hypothecate, pledge or otherwise to dispose of any such securities and investments, except pursuant to the direction of such registered management company and only for the account of such registered investment company.

(3) Such securities and investments shall be subject to no lien or charge of any kind in favor of the custodian or any persons claiming through the custodian.

(4) Such securities and investments shall be verified by actual examination at the end of each annual and semi-annual fiscal period by an independent public accountant retained by the investment company, and shall be examined by such accountant at least one other time, chosen by the accountant, during each fiscal year. A certificate of such accountant stating that an examination of such securities has been made, and describing the nature and extent of the examination, shall be attached to a completed Form N–17f–1 (17 CFR 274.219) and transmitted to the Commission promptly after each examination.

(5) Such securities and investments shall, at all times, be subject to inspection by the Commission through its employees or agents.

(6) The provisions of paragraphs (b) (1), (2) and (3) of this section shall not apply to securities and similar investments bought for or sold to such investment company by the company which is custodian until the securities have been reduced to the physical possession of the custodian and have been paid for by such investment company: *Provided*, That the company which is custodian shall take possession of such securities at the earliest practicable time. Nothing in this subparagraph shall be construed to relieve any company which is a member of a national securities exchange of any obligation under existing law or under the rules of any national securities exchange.

(c) A copy of any contract executed or ratified pursuant to paragraph (a) of this section shall be transmitted to the Commission promptly after execution or ratification unless it has been previously transmitted.

(d) Any contract executed or ratified pursuant to paragraph (a) of this section shall be ratified by the board of directors of the registered management investment company at least annually thereafter.

[Rule N–17F–1, 5 FR 4317, Oct. 31, 1940, as amended at 54 FR 32049, Aug. 4, 1989]

§ 270.17f–2 Custody of investments by registered management investment company.

(a) The securities and similar investments of a registered management investment company may be maintained in the custody of such company only in accordance with the provisions of this section. Investments maintained by such a company with a bank or other company whose functions and physical facilities are supervised by Federal or State authority under any arrangement whereunder the directors, officers, employees or agents of such company are authorized or permitted to withdraw such investments upon their mere receipt, are deemed to be in the custody of such company and may be so maintained only upon compliance with the provisions of this section.

(b) Except as provided in paragraph (c) of this section, all such securities and similar investments shall be deposited in the safekeeping of, or in a vault or other depository maintained by, a bank or other company whose functions and physical facilities are supervised by Federal or State authority. Investments so deposited shall be physically segregated at all times from those of any other person and shall be withdrawn only in connection with transactions of the character described in paragraph (c) of this section.

(c) The first sentence of paragraph (b) of this section shall not apply to securities on loan which are collateralized to the extent of their full market value, or to securities hypothecated, pledged, or placed in escrow for the account of such investment company in connection with a loan or other transaction authorized by specific resolution of its board of directors, or to securities in transit in connection with the sale, exchange, redemption, maturity or conversion, the exercise of warrants or rights, assents to changes in terms of the securities, or other transactions necessary or appropriate in the ordinary course of business relating to the management of securities.

(d) Except as otherwise provided by law, no person shall be authorized or permitted to have access to the securities and similar investments deposited in accordance with paragraph (b) of this section except pursuant to a resolution of the board of directors of such investment company. Each such resolution shall designate not more than five persons who shall be either officers or responsible employees of such company and shall provide that access to such investments shall be had only by two or more such persons jointly, at least one of whom shall be an officer; except that access to such investments shall be permitted (1) to properly authorized officers and employees of the bank or other company in whose safekeeping the investments are placed and (2) for the purpose of paragraph (f) of this section to the independent public accountant jointly with any two persons so designated or with such officer or employee of such bank or such other company. Such investments shall at all times be subject to inspection by the Commission through its authorized employees or agents accompanied, unless otherwise directed by order of the Commission, by one or more of the persons designated pursuant to this paragraph.

(e) Each person when depositing such securities or similar investments in or withdrawing them from the depository or when ordering their withdrawal and delivery from the safekeeping of the bank or other company, shall sign a notation in respect of such deposit, withdrawal or order which shall show (1) the date and time of the deposit, withdrawal or order, (2) the title and amount of the securities or other investments deposited, withdrawn or ordered to be withdrawn, and an identification thereof by certificate numbers or otherwise, (3) the manner of acquisition of the securities or similar investments deposited or the purpose for which they have been withdrawn, or ordered to be withdrawn, and (4) if withdrawn and delivered to another person the name of such person. Such notation shall be transmitted promptly to an officer or director of the investment company designated by its board of directors who shall not be a person designated for the purpose of paragraph (d) of this section. Such notation shall be on serially numbered forms and shall be preserved for at least one year.

(f) Such securities and similar investments shall be verified by actual examination by an independent public accountant retained by the investment company at least three times during each fiscal year, at least two of which shall be chosen by such accountant without prior notice to such company. A certificate of such accountant stating that an examination of such securities and investments has been made, and describing the nature and extent of the examination, shall be attached to a completed Form N–17f–2 (17 CFR 274.220) and transmitted to the Commission promptly after each examination.

[Rule N–17F–2, 12 FR 6717, Oct. 11, 1947, as amended at 54 FR 32049, Aug. 4, 1989]

§ 270.17f–3 Free cash accounts for investment companies with bank custodians.

No registered investment company having a bank custodian shall hold free cash except, upon resolution of its board or directors, a petty cash account may be maintained in an amount not to exceed $500: *Provided,* That such account is operated under the imprest system and is maintained subject to adequate controls approved by the board of directors over disbursements and reimbursements including, but not limited to fidelity bond coverage of persons having access to such funds.

(Sec. 17(f), 54 Stat. 815, 15 U.S.C. 80a–17(f), sec. 9, Pub. L. 91–547, 84 Stat. 1420)

[37 FR 9989, May 18, 1972]

§ 270.17f–4 Custody of investment company assets with a securities depository.

(a) *Custody arrangement with a securities depository.* A fund's custodian may place and maintain financial assets, corresponding to the fund's security entitlements, with a securities depository or intermediary custodian, if the custodian:

Securities and Exchange Commission § 270.17f–4

(1) Is at a minimum obligated to exercise due care in accordance with reasonable commercial standards in discharging its duty as a securities intermediary to obtain and thereafter maintain such financial assets;

(2) Is required to provide, promptly upon request by the fund, such reports as are available concerning the internal accounting controls and financial strength of the custodian; and

(3) Requires any intermediary custodian at a minimum to exercise due care in accordance with reasonable commercial standards in discharging its duty as a securities intermediary to obtain and thereafter maintain financial assets corresponding to the security entitlements of its entitlement holders.

(b) *Direct dealings with securities depository.* A fund may place and maintain financial assets, corresponding to the fund's security entitlements, directly with a securities depository, if:

(1) The fund's contract with the securities depository or the securities depository's written rules for its participants:

(i) Obligate the securities depository at a minimum to exercise due care in accordance with reasonable commercial standards in discharging its duty as a securities intermediary to obtain and thereafter maintain financial assets corresponding to the fund's security entitlements; and

(ii) Requires the securities depository to provide, promptly upon request by the fund, such reports as are available concerning the internal accounting controls and financial strength of the securities depository; and

(2) The fund has implemented internal control systems reasonably designed to prevent unauthorized officer's instructions (by providing at least for the form, content and means of giving, recording and reviewing all officer's instructions).

(c) *Definitions.* For purposes of this section the terms:

(1) *Clearing corporation, financial asset, securities intermediary, and security entitlement* have the same meanings as is attributed to those terms in § 8–102, § 8–103, and §§ 8–501 through 8–511 of the Uniform Commercial Code, 2002 Official Text and Comments, which are incorporated by reference in this section pursuant to 5 U.S.C. 552(a) and 1 CFR part 51. The Director of the Federal Register has approved this incorporation by reference in accordance with 5 U.S.C. 552(a) and 1 CFR part 51. You may obtain a copy of the Uniform Commercial Code from the National Conference of Commissioners on Uniform State Laws, 211 East Ontario Street, Suite 1300, Chicago, Il 60611. You may inspect a copy at the following addresses: Louis Loss Library, U.S. Securities and Exchange Commission, 100 F Street, NE., Washington, DC 20549, or at the National Archives and Records Administration (NARA). For information on the availability of this material at NARA, call 202–741–6030, or go to: *http://www.archives.gov/federal_register/code_of_federal_regulations/ibr_locations.html.*

(2) *Custodian* means a bank or other person authorized to hold assets for the fund under section 17(f) of the Act (15 U.S.C. 80a–17(f)) or Commission rules in this chapter, but does not include a fund itself, a foreign custodian whose use is governed by § 270.17f–5 or § 270.17f–7, or a vault, safe deposit box, or other repository for safekeeping maintained by a bank or other company whose functions and physical facilities are supervised by a federal or state authority if the fund maintains its own assets there in accordance with § 270.17f–2.

(3) *Fund* means an investment company registered under the Act and, where the context so requires with respect to a fund that is a unit investment trust or a face-amount certificate company, includes the fund's trustee.

(4) *Intermediary custodian* means any subcustodian that is a securities intermediary and is qualified to act as a custodian.

(5) *Officer's instruction* means a request or direction to a securities depository or its operator, or to a registered transfer agent, in the name of the fund by one or more persons authorized by the fund's board of directors (or by the fund's trustee, if the fund is a unit investment trust or a face-amount certificate company) to give the request or direction.

(6) *Securities depository* means a clearing corporation that is:

(i) Registered with the Commission as a clearing agency under section 17A

429

§ 270.17f-5

of the Securities Exchange Act of 1934 (15 U.S.C. 78q–1); or

(ii) A Federal Reserve Bank or other person authorized to operate the federal book entry system described in the regulations of the Department of Treasury codified at 31 CFR 357, Subpart B, or book-entry systems operated pursuant to comparable regulations of other federal agencies.

[68 FR 8442, Feb. 20, 2003, as amended at 69 FR 18803, Apr. 9, 2004; 73 FR 32228, June 5, 2008]

§ 270.17f-5 Custody of investment company assets outside the United States.

(a) *Definitions.* For purposes of this section:

(1) *Eligible Foreign Custodian* means an entity that is incorporated or organized under the laws of a country other than the United States and that is a Qualified Foreign Bank or a majority-owned direct or indirect subsidiary of a U.S. Bank or bank-holding company.

(2) *Foreign Assets* means any investments (including foreign currencies) for which the primary market is outside the United States, and any cash and cash equivalents that are reasonably necessary to effect the Fund's transactions in those investments.

(3) *Foreign Custody Manager* means a Fund's or a Registered Canadian Fund's board of directors or any person serving as the board's delegate under paragraphs (b) or (d) of this section.

(4) *Fund* means a management investment company registered under the Act (15 U.S.C. 80a) and incorporated or organized under the laws of the United States or of a state.

(5) *Qualified Foreign Bank* means a banking institution or trust company, incorporated or organized under the laws of a country other than the United States, that is regulated as such by the country's government or an agency of the country's government.

(6) *Registered Canadian Fund* means a management investment company incorporated or organized under the laws of Canada and registered under the Act pursuant to the conditions of § 270.7d–1.

(7) *U.S. Bank* means an entity that is:

(i) A banking institution organized under the laws of the United States;

(ii) A member bank of the Federal Reserve System;

(iii) Any other banking institution or trust company organized under the laws of any state or of the United States, whether incorporated or not, doing business under the laws of any state or of the United States, a substantial portion of the business of which consists of receiving deposits or exercising fiduciary powers similar to those permitted to national banks under the authority of the Comptroller of the Currency, and which is supervised and examined by state or federal authority having supervision over banks, and which is not operated for the purpose of evading the provisions of this section; or

(iv) A receiver, conservator, or other liquidating agent of any institution or firm included in paragraphs (a)(7)(i), (ii), or (iii) of this section.

(b) *Delegation.* A Fund's board of directors may delegate to the Fund's investment adviser or officers or to a U.S. Bank or to a Qualified Foreign Bank the responsibilities set forth in paragraphs (c)(1), (c)(2), or (c)(3) of this section, *provided that:*

(1) *Reasonable Reliance.* The board determines that it is reasonable to rely on the delegate to perform the delegated responsibilities;

(2) *Reporting.* The board requires the delegate to provide written reports notifying the board of the placement of Foreign Assets with a particular custodian and of any material change in the Fund's foreign custody arrangements, with the reports to be provided to the board at such times as the board deems reasonable and appropriate based on the circumstances of the Fund's arrangements; and

(3) *Exercise of Care.* The delegate agrees to exercise reasonable care, prudence and diligence such as a person having responsibility for the safekeeping of the Fund's Foreign Assets would exercise, or to adhere to a higher standard of care, in performing the delegated responsibilities.

(c) *Maintaining Assets with an Eligible Foreign Custodian.* A Fund or its Foreign Custody Manager may place and maintain the Fund's Foreign Assets in the care of an Eligible Foreign Custodian, *provided that:*

Securities and Exchange Commission § 270.17f–5

(1) *General Standard.* The Foreign Custody Manager determines that the Foreign Assets will be subject to reasonable care, based on the standards applicable to custodians in the relevant market, if maintained with the Eligible Foreign Custodian, after considering all factors relevant to the safekeeping of the Foreign Assets, including, without limitation:

(i) The Eligible Foreign Custodian's practices, procedures, and internal controls, including, but not limited to, the physical protections available for certificated securities (if applicable), the method of keeping custodial records, and the security and data protection practices;

(ii) Whether the Eligible Foreign Custodian has the requisite financial strength to provide reasonable care for Foreign Assets;

(iii) The Eligible Foreign Custodian's general reputation and standing; and

(iv) Whether the Fund will have jurisdiction over and be able to enforce judgments against the Eligible Foreign Custodian, such as by virtue of the existence of offices in the United States or consent to service of process in the United States.

(2) *Contract.* The arrangement with the Eligible Foreign Custodian is governed by a written contract that the Foreign Custody Manager has determined will provide reasonable care for Foreign Assets based on the standards specified in paragraph (c)(1) of this section.

(i) The contract must provide:

(A) For indemnification or insurance arrangements (or any combination) that will adequately protect the Fund against the risk of loss of Foreign Assets held in accordance with the contract;

(B) That the Foreign Assets will not be subject to any right, charge, security interest, lien or claim of any kind in favor of the Eligible Foreign Custodian or its creditors, except a claim of payment for their safe custody or administration or, in the case of cash deposits, liens or rights in favor of creditors of the custodian arising under bankruptcy, insolvency, or similar laws;

(C) That beneficial ownership of the Foreign Assets will be freely transferable without the payment of money or value other than for safe custody or administration;

(D) That adequate records will be maintained identifying the Foreign Assets as belonging to the Fund or as being held by a third party for the benefit of the Fund;

(E) That the Fund's independent public accountants will be given access to those records or confirmation of the contents of those records; and

(F) That the Fund will receive periodic reports with respect to the safekeeping of the Foreign Assets, including, but not limited to, notification of any transfer to or from the Fund's account or a third party account containing assets held for the benefit of the Fund.

(ii) The contract may contain, in lieu of any or all of the provisions specified in paragraph (c)(2)(i) of this section, other provisions that the Foreign Custody Manager determines will provide, in their entirety, the same or a greater level of care and protection for the Foreign Assets as the specified provisions, in their entirety.

(3)(i) *Monitoring the Foreign Custody Arrangements.* The Foreign Custody Manager has established a system to monitor the appropriateness of maintaining the Foreign Assets with a particular custodian under paragraph (c)(1) of this section, and to monitor performance of the contract under paragraph (c)(2) of this section.

(ii) If an arrangement with an Eligible Foreign Custodian no longer meets the requirements of this section, the Fund must withdraw the Foreign Assets from the Eligible Foreign Custodian as soon as reasonably practicable.

(d) *Registered Canadian Funds.* Any Registered Canadian Fund may place and maintain its Foreign Assets outside the United States in accordance with the requirements of this section, *provided*

(1) The Foreign Assets are placed in the care of an overseas branch of a U.S. Bank that has aggregate capital, surplus, and undivided profits of a specified amount, which must not be less than $500,000; and

§ 270.17f-6

(2) The Foreign Custody Manager is the Fund's board of directors, its investment adviser or officers, or a U.S. Bank.

NOTE TO § 270.17f–5: When a Fund's (or its custodian's) custody arrangement with an Eligible Securities Depository (as defined in § 270.17f–7) involves one or more Eligible Foreign Custodians through which assets are maintained with the Eligible Securities Depository, § 270.17f–5 will govern the Fund's (or its custodian's) use of each Eligible Foreign Custodian, while § 270.17f–7 will govern an Eligible Foreign Custodian's use of the Eligible Securities Depository.

[65 FR 25637, May 3, 2000]

§ 270.17f-6 Custody of investment company assets with Futures Commission Merchants and Commodity Clearing Organizations.

(a) A Fund may place and maintain cash, securities, and similar investments with a Futures Commission Merchant in amounts necessary to effect the Fund's transactions in Exchange-Traded Futures Contracts and Commodity Options, *Provided that:*

(1) The manner in which the Futures Commission Merchant maintains the Fund's assets shall be governed by a written contract, which provides that:

(i) The Futures Commission Merchant shall comply with the segregation requirements of section 4d(2) of the Commodity Exchange Act (7 U.S.C. 6d(2)) and the rules thereunder (17 CFR Chapter I) or, if applicable, the secured amount requirements of rule 30.7 under the Commodity Exchange Act (17 CFR 30.7);

(ii) The Futures Commission Merchant, as appropriate, to the Fund's transactions and in accordance with the Commodity Exchange Act (7 U.S.C. 1 through 25) and the rules and regulations thereunder (including 17 CFR part 30), may place and maintain the Fund's assets to effect the Fund's transactions with another Futures Commission Merchant, a Clearing Organization, a U.S. or Foreign Bank, or a member of a foreign board of trade, and shall obtain an acknowledgment, as required under rules 1.20(a) or 30.7(c) under the Commodity Exchange Act [17 CFR 1.20(a) or 30.7(c)], as applicable, that such assets are held on behalf of the Futures Commission Merchant's customers in accordance with the provisions of the Commodity Exchange Act; and

(iii) The Futures Commission Merchant shall promptly furnish copies of or extracts from the Futures Commission Merchant's records or such other information pertaining to the Fund's assets as the Commission through its employees or agents may request.

(2) Any gains on the Fund's transactions, other than de minimis amounts, may be maintained with the Futures Commission Merchant only until the next business day following receipt.

(3) If the custodial arrangement no longer meets the requirements of this section, the Fund shall withdraw its assets from the Futures Commission Merchant as soon as reasonably practicable.

(b) For purposes of this section:

(1) *Clearing Organization* means a clearing organization as defined in rule 1.3(d) under the Commodity Exchange Act (17 CFR 1.3(d)) and includes a clearing organization for a foreign board of trade.

(2) *Exchange-Traded Futures Contracts and Commodity Options* means commodity futures contracts, options on commodity futures contracts, and options on physical commodities traded on or subject to the rules of:

(i) Any contract market designated for trading such transactions under the Commodity Exchange Act and the rules thereunder; or

(ii) Any board of trade or exchange outside the United States, as contemplated in Part 30 under the Commodity Exchange Act.

(3) *Fund* means an investment company registered under the Act (15 U.S.C. 80a-1 et seq.).

(4) *Futures Commission Merchant* means any person that is registered as a futures commission merchant under the Commodity Exchange Act and that is not an affiliated person of the Fund or an affiliated person of such person.

(5) *U.S. or Foreign Bank* means a bank, as defined in section 2(a)(5) of the Act (15 U.S.C. 80a–2(a)(5)), or a banking institution or trust company that is incorporated or organized under the laws of a country other than the United States and that is regulated as such by

Securities and Exchange Commission § 270.17g–1

the country's government or an agency thereof.

[61 FR 66212, Dec. 17, 1996]

§ 270.17f–7 Custody of investment company assets with a foreign securities depository.

(a) *Custody arrangement with an eligible securities depository.* A Fund, including a Registered Canadian Fund, may place and maintain its Foreign Assets with an Eligible Securities Depository, *provided that:*

(1) *Risk-limiting safeguards.* The custody arrangement provides reasonable safeguards against the custody risks associated with maintaining assets with the Eligible Securities Depository, including:

(i) *Risk analysis and monitoring.* (A) The fund or its investment adviser has received from the Primary Custodian (or its agent) an analysis of the custody risks associated with maintaining assets with the Eligible Securities Depository; and

(B) The contract between the Fund and the Primary Custodian requires the Primary Custodian (or its agent) to monitor the custody risks associated with maintaining assets with the Eligible Securities Depository on a continuing basis, and promptly notify the Fund or its investment adviser of any material change in these risks.

(ii) *Exercise of care.* The contract between the Fund and the Primary Custodian states that the Primary Custodian will agree to exercise reasonable care, prudence, and diligence in performing the requirements of paragraphs (a)(1)(i)(A) and (B) of this section, or adhere to a higher standard of care.

(2) *Withdrawal of assets from eligible securities depository.* If a custody arrangement with an Eligible Securities Depository no longer meets the requirements of this section, the Fund's Foreign Assets must be withdrawn from the depository as soon as reasonably practicable.

(b) *Definitions.* The terms *Foreign Assets, Fund, Qualified Foreign Bank, Registered Canadian Fund,* and *U.S. Bank* have the same meanings as in § 270.17f–5. In addition:

(1) *Eligible Securities Depository* means a system for the central handling of securities as defined in § 270.17f–4 that:

(i) Acts as or operates a system for the central handling of securities or equivalent book-entries in the country where it is incorporated, or a transnational system for the central handling of securities or equivalent book-entries;

(ii) Is regulated by a foreign financial regulatory authority as defined under section 2(a)(50) of the Act (15 U.S.C. 80a–2(a)(50));

(iii) Holds assets for the custodian that participates in the system on behalf of the Fund under safekeeping conditions no less favorable than the conditions that apply to other participants;

(iv) Maintains records that identify the assets of each participant and segregate the system's own assets from the assets of participants;

(v) Provides periodic reports to its participants with respect to its safekeeping of assets, including notices of transfers to or from any participant's account; and

(vi) Is subject to periodic examination by regulatory authorities or independent accountants.

(2) *Primary Custodian* means a U.S. Bank or Qualified Foreign Bank that contracts directly with a Fund to provide custodial services related to maintaining the Fund's assets outside the United States.

NOTE TO § 270.17f–7: When a Fund's (or its custodian's) custody arrangement with an Eligible Securities Depository involves one or more Eligible Foreign Custodians (as defined in § 270.17f–5) through which assets are maintained with the Eligible Securities Depository, § 270.17f–5 will govern the Fund's (or its custodian's) use of each Eligible Foreign Custodian, while § 270.17f–7 will govern an Eligible Foreign Custodian's use of the Eligible Securities Depository.

[65 FR 25638, May 3, 2000]

§ 270.17g–1 Bonding of officers and employees of registered management investment companies.

(a) Each registered management investment company shall provide and maintain a bond which shall be issued by a reputable fidelity insurance company, authorized to do business in the place where the bond is issued, against

§ 270.17g–1

larceny and embezzlement, covering each officer and employee of the investment company, who may singly, or jointly with others, have access to securities or funds of the investment company, either directly or through authority to draw upon such funds or to direct generally the disposition of such securities, unless the officer or employee has such access solely through his position as an officer or employee of a bank (hereinafter referred to as "covered persons").

(b) The bond may be in the form of (1) an individual bond for each covered person or a schedule or blanket bond covering such persons, (2) a blanket bond which names the registered management investment company as the only insured (hereinafter referred to as "single insured bond") or (3) a bond which names the registered management investment company and one or more other parties as insureds (hereinafter referred to as a "joint insured bond"), such other insured parties being limited to (i) persons engaged in the management or distribution of the shares of the registered investment company, (ii) other registered investment companies which are managed and/or whose shares are distributed by the same persons (or affiliates of such persons), (iii) persons who are engaged in the management and/or distribution of shares of companies included in paragraph (b)(3)(i) of this section, (iv) affiliated persons of any registered management investment company named in the bond or of any person included in paragraph (b)(3)(i) or (b)(3)(iii) of this section who are engaged in the administration of any registered management investment company named as insured in the bond, and (v) any trust, pension, profit-sharing or other benefit plan for officers, directors or employees of persons named in the bond.

(c) A bond of the type described in paragraph (b)(1) or (b)(2) of this section shall provide that it shall not be cancelled, terminated or modified except after written notice shall have been given by the acting party to the affected party and to the Commission not less than sixty days prior to the effective date of cancellation, termination or modification. A joint insured bond described in paragraph (b)(3) of this section shall provide, that (1) it shall not be cancelled terminated or modified except after written notice shall have been given by the acting party to the affected party, and by the fidelity insurance company to all registered investment companies named as insureds and to the Commission, not less than sixty days prior to the effective date of cancellation, termination, or modification and (2) the fidelity insurance company shall furnish each registered management investment company named as an insured with (i) a copy of the bond and any amendment thereto promptly after the execution thereof, (ii) a copy of each formal filing of a claim under the bond by any other named insured promptly after the receipt thereof, and (iii) notification of the terms of the settlement of each such claim prior to the execution of the settlement.

(d) The bond shall be in such reasonable form and amount as a majority of the board of directors of the registered management investment company who are not "interested persons" of such investment company as defined by section 2(a)(19) of the Act shall approve as often as their fiduciary duties require, but not less than once every twelve months, with due consideration to all relevant factors including, but not limited to, the value of the aggregate assets of the registered management investment company to which any covered person may have access, the type and terms of the arrangements made for the custody and safekeeping of such assets, and the nature of the securities in the company's portfolio: *Provided, however,* That (1) the amount of a single insured bond shall be at least equal to an amount computed in accordance with the following schedule:

Amount of registered management investment company gross assets—at the end of the most recent fiscal quarter prior to date (in dollars)	Minimum amount of bond (in dollars)
Up to 500,000	50,000.
500,000 to 1,000,000	75,000.
1,000,000 to 2,500,000	100,000.
2,500,000 to 5,000,000	125,000.
5,000,000 to 7,500,000	150,000.
7,500,000 to 10,000,000	175,000.
10,000,000 to 15,000,000	200,000.
15,000,000 to 20,000,000	225,000.
20,000,000 to 25,000,000	250,000.
25,000,000 to 35,000,000	300,000.

Securities and Exchange Commission § 270.17g-1

Amount of registered management investment company gross assets—at the end of the most recent fiscal quarter prior to date (in dollars)	Minimum amount of bond (in dollars)
35,000,000 to 50,000,000	350,000.
50,000,000 to 75,000,000	400,000.
75,000,000, to 100,000,000	450,000.
100,000,000 to 150,000,000	525,000.
150,000,000 to 250,000,000	600,000.
250,000,000 to 500,000,000	750,000.
500,000,000 to 750,000,000	900,000.
750,000,000 to 1,000,000,000	1,000,000.
1,000,000,000 to 1,500,000,000	1,250,000.
1,500,000,000 to 2,000,000,000	1,500,000.
Over 2,000,000,000	1,500,000 plus 200,000 for each 500,000,000 of gross assets up to a maximum bond of 2,500,000.

(2) A joint insured bond shall be in an amount at least equal to the sum of (i) the total amount of coverage which each registered management investment company named as an insured would have been required to provide and maintain individually pursuant to the schedule hereinabove had each such registered management investment company not been named under a joint insured bond, plus (ii) the amount of each bond which each named insured other than a registered management investment company would have been required to provide and maintain pursuant to federal statutes or regulations had it not been named as an insured under a joint insured bond.

(e) No premium may be paid for any joint insured bond or any amendment thereto unless a majority of the board of directors of each registered management investment company named as an insured therein who are not "interested persons" of such company shall approve the portion of the premium to be paid by such company, taking all relevant factors into consideration including, but not limited to, the number of the other parties named as insured, the nature of the business activities of such other parties, the amount of the joint insured bond, and the amount of the premium for such bond, the ratable allocation of the premium among all parties named as insureds, and the extent to which the share of the premium allocated to the investment company is less than the premium such company would have had to pay if it had provided and maintained a single insured bond.

(f) Each registered management investment company named as an insured in a joint insured bond shall enter into an agreement with all of the other named insureds providing that in the event recovery is received under the bond as a result of a loss sustained by the registered management investment company and one or more other named insureds, the registered management investment company shall receive an equitable and proportionate share of the recovery, but at least equal to the amount which it would have received had it provided and maintained a single insured bond with the minimum coverage required by paragraph (d)(1) of this section.

(g) Each registered management investment company shall:

(1) File with the Commission (i) within 10 days after receipt of an executed bond of the type described in paragraph (b)(1) or (2) of this section or any amendment thereof, (a) a copy of the bond, (b) a copy of the resolution of a majority of the board of directors who are not "interested persons" of the registered management investment company approving the form and amount of the bond, and (c) a statement as to the period for which premiums have been paid; (ii) within 10 days after receipt of an executed joint insured bond, or any amendment thereof, (a) a copy of the bond, (b) a copy of the resolution of a majority of the board of directors who are not "interested persons" of the registered management investment company approving the amount, type, form and coverage of the bond and the portion of the premium to be paid by such company, (c) a statement showing the amount of the single insured bond which the investment company would have provided and maintained had it not been named as an insured under a joint insured bond, (d) a statement as to the period for which premiums have been paid, and (e) a copy of each agreement between the investment company and all of the other named insureds entered into pursuant to paragraph (f) of this section; and (iii) a copy of any amendment to the agreement entered into pursuant to paragraph (f) of this

§ 270.17j-1

section within 10 days after the execution of such amendment,

(2) File with the Commission, in writing, within five days after the making of any claim under the bond by the investment company, a statement of the nature and amount of the claim,

(3) File with the Commission, within five days of the receipt thereof, a copy of the terms of the settlement of any claim made under the bond by the investment company, and

(4) Notify by registered mail each member of the board of directors of the investment company at his last known residence address of (i) any cancellation, termination or modification of the bond, not less than forty-five days prior to the effective date of the cancellation or termination or modification, (ii) the filing and of the settlement of any claim under the bond by the investment company, at the time the filings required by paragraph (g) (2) and (3) of this section are made with the Commission, and (iii) the filing and of the proposed terms of settlement of any claim under the bond by any other named insured, within five days of the receipt of a notice from the fidelity insurance company.

(h) Each registered management investment company shall designate an officer thereof who shall make the filings and give the notices required by paragraph (g) of this section.

(i) Where the registered management investment company is an unincorporated company managed by a depositor, trustee or investment adviser, the terms "officer" and "employee" shall include, for the purposes of this rule, the officers and employees of the depositor, trustee, or investment adviser.

(j) Any joint insured bond provided and maintained by a registered management investment company and one or more other parties shall be a transaction exempt from the provisions of section 17(d) of the Act (15 U.S.C. 80a-17(d)) and the rules thereunder, if:

(1) The terms and provisions of the bond comply with the provisions of this section;

(2) The terms and provisions of any agreement required by paragraph (f) of this section comply with the provisions of that paragraph; and

(3) The board of directors of the investment company satisfies the fund governance standards defined in § 270.0-1(a)(7).

(k) At the next anniversary date of an existing fidelity bond, but not later than one year from the effective date of this rule, arrangements between registered management investment companies and fidelity insurance companies and arrangements between registered management investment companies and other parties named as insureds under joint insured bonds which would not permit compliance with the provisions of this rule shall be modified by the parties so as to effect such compliance.

[39 FR 10579, Mar. 21, 1974, as amended at 66 FR 3759, Jan. 16, 2001; 69 FR 46390, Aug. 2, 2004]

§ 270.17j-1 Personal investment activities of investment company personnel.

(a) *Definitions.* For purposes of this section:

(1) *Access person* means:

(i) Any Advisory Person of a Fund or of a Fund's investment adviser. If an investment adviser's primary business is advising Funds or other advisory clients, all of the investment adviser's directors, officers, and general partners are presumed to be Access Persons of any Fund advised by the investment adviser. All of a Fund's directors, officers, and general partners are presumed to be Access Persons of the Fund.

(ii) Any director, officer or general partner of a principal underwriter who, in the ordinary course of business, makes, participates in or obtains information regarding, the purchase or sale of Covered Securities by the Fund for which the principal underwriter acts, or whose functions or duties in the ordinary course of business relate to the making of any recommendation to the Fund regarding the purchase or sale of Covered Securities.

(2) *Advisory person* of a Fund or of a Fund's investment adviser means:

(i) Any director, officer, general partner or employee of the Fund or investment adviser (or of any company in a control relationship to the Fund or investment adviser) who, in connection

Securities and Exchange Commission § 270.17j–1

with his or her regular functions or duties, makes, participates in, or obtains information regarding, the purchase or sale of Covered Securities by a Fund, or whose functions relate to the making of any recommendations with respect to such purchases or sales; and

(ii) Any natural person in a control relationship to the Fund or investment adviser who obtains information concerning recommendations made to the Fund with regard to the purchase or sale of Covered Securities by the Fund.

(3) *Control* has the same meaning as in section 2(a)(9) of the Act [15 U.S.C. 80a–2(a)(9)].

(4) *Covered security* means a security as defined in section 2(a)(36) of the Act [15 U.S.C. 80a–2(a)(36)], except that it does not include:

(i) Direct obligations of the Government of the United States;

(ii) Bankers' acceptances, bank certificates of deposit, commercial paper and high quality short-term debt instruments, including repurchase agreements; and

(iii) Shares issued by open-end Funds.

(5) *Fund* means an investment company registered under the Investment Company Act.

(6) An *Initial public offering* means an offering of securities registered under the Securities Act of 1933 [15 U.S.C. 77a], the issuer of which, immediately before the registration, was not subject to the reporting requirements of sections 13 or 15(d) of the Securities Exchange Act of 1934 [15 U.S.C. 78m or 78o(d)].

(7) *Investment personnel* of a Fund or of a Fund's investment adviser means:

(i) Any employee of the Fund or investment adviser (or of any company in a control relationship to the Fund or investment adviser) who, in connection with his or her regular functions or duties, makes or participates in making recommendations regarding the purchase or sale of securities by the Fund.

(ii) Any natural person who controls the Fund or investment adviser and who obtains information concerning recommendations made to the Fund regarding the purchase or sale of securities by the Fund.

(8) A *Limited offering* means an offering that is exempt from registration under the Securities Act of 1933 pursuant to section 4(a)(2) or section 4(a)(5) [15 U.S.C. 77d(a)(2) or 77d(a)(5)] or pursuant to rule 504, or rule 506 [17 CFR 230.504 or 230.506] under the Securities Act of 1933.

(9) *Purchase or sale of a covered security* includes, among other things, the writing of an option to purchase or sell a Covered Security.

(10) *Security held or to be acquired* by a Fund means:

(i) Any Covered Security which, within the most recent 15 days:

(A) Is or has been held by the Fund; or

(B) Is being or has been considered by the Fund or its investment adviser for purchase by the Fund; and

(ii) Any option to purchase or sell, and any security convertible into or exchangeable for, a Covered Security described in paragraph (a)(10)(i) of this section.

(11) *Automatic investment plan* means a program in which regular periodic purchases (or withdrawals) are made automatically in (or from) investment accounts in accordance with a predetermined schedule and allocation. An Automatic Investment Plan includes a dividend reinvestment plan.

(b) *Unlawful actions.* It is unlawful for any affiliated person of or principal underwriter for a Fund, or any affiliated person of an investment adviser of or principal underwriter for a Fund, in connection with the purchase or sale, directly or indirectly, by the person of a Security Held or to be Acquired by the Fund:

(1) To employ any device, scheme or artifice to defraud the Fund;

(2) To make any untrue statement of a material fact to the Fund or omit to state a material fact necessary in order to make the statements made to the Fund, in light of the circumstances under which they are made, not misleading;

(3) To engage in any act, practice or course of business that operates or would operate as a fraud or deceit on the Fund; or

(4) To engage in any manipulative practice with respect to the Fund.

(c) *Code of Ethics*—(1) *Adoption and approval of Code of Ethics.* (i) Every Fund (other than a money market fund

§ 270.17j–1

or a Fund that does not invest in Covered Securities) and each investment adviser of and principal underwriter for the Fund, must adopt a written code of ethics containing provisions reasonably necessary to prevent its Access Persons from engaging in any conduct prohibited by paragraph (b) of this section.

(ii) The board of directors of a Fund, including a majority of directors who are not interested persons, must approve the code of ethics of the Fund, the code of ethics of each investment adviser and principal underwriter of the Fund, and any material changes to these codes. The board must base its approval of a code and any material changes to the code on a determination that the code contains provisions reasonably necessary to prevent Access Persons from engaging in any conduct prohibited by paragraph (b) of this section. Before approving a code of a Fund, investment adviser or principal underwriter or any amendment to the code, the board of directors must receive a certification from the Fund, investment adviser or principal underwriter that it has adopted procedures reasonably necessary to prevent Access Persons from violating the Fund's, investment adviser's, or principal underwriter's code of ethics. The Fund's board must approve the code of an investment adviser or principal underwriter before initially retaining the services of the investment adviser or principal underwriter. The Fund's board must approve a material change to a code no later than six months after adoption of the material change.

(iii) If a Fund is a unit investment trust, the Fund's principal underwriter or depositor must approve the Fund's code of ethics, as required by paragraph (c)(1)(ii) of this section. If the Fund has more than one principal underwriter or depositor, the principal underwriters and depositors may designate, in writing, which principal underwriter or depositor must conduct the approval required by paragraph (c)(1)(ii) of this section, if they obtain written consent from the designated principal underwriter or depositor.

(2) *Administration of Code of Ethics.* (i) The Fund, investment adviser and principal underwriter must use reasonable diligence and institute procedures reasonably necessary to prevent violations of its code of ethics.

(ii) No less frequently than annually, every Fund (other than a unit investment trust) and its investment advisers and principal underwriters must furnish to the Fund's board of directors, and the board of directors must consider, a written report that:

(A) Describes any issues arising under the code of ethics or procedures since the last report to the board of directors, including, but not limited to, information about material violations of the code or procedures and sanctions imposed in response to the material violations; and

(B) Certifies that the Fund, investment adviser or principal underwriter, as applicable, has adopted procedures reasonably necessary to prevent Access Persons from violating the code.

(3) *Exception for principal underwriters.* The requirements of paragraphs (c)(1) and (c)(2) of this section do not apply to any principal underwriter unless:

(i) The principal underwriter is an affiliated person of the Fund or of the Fund's investment adviser; or

(ii) An officer, director or general partner of the principal underwriter serves as an officer, director or general partner of the Fund or of the Fund's investment adviser.

(d) *Reporting requirements of access persons*—(1) *Reports required.* Unless excepted by paragraph (d)(2) of this section, every Access Person of a Fund (other than a money market fund or a Fund that does not invest in Covered Securities) and every Access Person of an investment adviser of or principal underwriter for the Fund, must report to that Fund, investment adviser or principal underwriter:

(i) *Initial holdings reports.* No later than 10 days after the person becomes an Access Person (which information must be current as of a date no more than 45 days prior to the date the person becomes an Access Person):

(A) The title, number of shares and principal amount of each Covered Security in which the Access Person had any direct or indirect beneficial ownership when the person became an Access Person;

Securities and Exchange Commission § 270.17j–1

(B) The name of any broker, dealer or bank with whom the Access Person maintained an account in which any securities were held for the direct or indirect benefit of the Access Person as of the date the person became an Access Person; and

(C) The date that the report is submitted by the Access Person.

(ii) *Quarterly transaction reports.* No later than 30 days after the end of a calendar quarter, the following information:

(A) With respect to any transaction during the quarter in a Covered Security in which the Access Person had any direct or indirect beneficial ownership:

(*1*) The date of the transaction, the title, the interest rate and maturity date (if applicable), the number of shares and the principal amount of each Covered Security involved;

(*2*) The nature of the transaction (i.e., purchase, sale or any other type of acquisition or disposition);

(*3*) The price of the Covered Security at which the transaction was effected;

(*4*) The name of the broker, dealer or bank with or through which the transaction was effected; and

(*5*) The date that the report is submitted by the Access Person.

(B) With respect to any account established by the Access Person in which any securities were held during the quarter for the direct or indirect benefit of the Access Person:

(*1*) The name of the broker, dealer or bank with whom the Access Person established the account;

(*2*) The date the account was established; and

(*3*) The date that the report is submitted by the Access Person.

(iii) *Annual Holdings Reports.* Annually, the following information (which information must be current as of a date no more than 45 days before the report is submitted):

(A) The title, number of shares and principal amount of each Covered Security in which the Access Person had any direct or indirect beneficial ownership;

(B) The name of any broker, dealer or bank with whom the Access Person maintains an account in which any securities are held for the direct or indirect benefit of the Access Person; and

(C) The date that the report is submitted by the Access Person.

(2) *Exceptions from reporting requirements.* (i) A person need not make a report under paragraph (d)(1) of this section with respect to transactions effected for, and Covered Securities held in, any account over which the person has no direct or indirect influence or control.

(ii) A director of a Fund who is not an "interested person" of the Fund within the meaning of section 2(a)(19) of the Act [15 U.S.C. 80a–2(a)(19)], and who would be required to make a report solely by reason of being a Fund director, need not make:

(A) An initial holdings report under paragraph (d)(1)(i) of this section and an annual holdings report under paragraph (d)(1)(iii) of this section; and

(B) A quarterly transaction report under paragraph (d)(1)(ii) of this section, unless the director knew or, in the ordinary course of fulfilling his or her official duties as a Fund director, should have known that during the 15-day period immediately before or after the director's transaction in a Covered Security, the Fund purchased or sold the Covered Security, or the Fund or its investment adviser considered purchasing or selling the Covered Security.

(iii) An Access Person to a Fund's principal underwriter need not make a report to the principal underwriter under paragraph (d)(1) of this section if:

(A) The principal underwriter is not an affiliated person of the Fund (unless the Fund is a unit investment trust) or any investment adviser of the Fund; and

(B) The principal underwriter has no officer, director or general partner who serves as an officer, director or general partner of the Fund or of any investment adviser of the Fund.

(iv) An Access Person to an investment adviser need not make a separate report to the investment adviser under paragraph (d)(1) of this section to the extent the information in the report would duplicate information required to be recorded under § 275.204–2(a)(13) of this chapter.

(v) An Access Person need not make a quarterly transaction report under paragraph (d)(1)(ii) of this section if the report would duplicate information contained in broker trade confirmations or account statements received by the Fund, investment adviser or principal underwriter with respect to the Access Person in the time period required by paragraph (d)(1)(ii), if all of the information required by that paragraph is contained in the broker trade confirmations or account statements, or in the records of the Fund, investment adviser or principal underwriter.

(vi) An Access Person need not make a quarterly transaction report under paragraph (d)(1)(ii) of this section with respect to transactions effected pursuant to an Automatic Investment Plan.

(3) *Review of reports.* Each Fund, investment adviser and principal underwriter to which reports are required to be made by paragraph (d)(1) of this section must institute procedures by which appropriate management or compliance personnel review these reports.

(4) *Notification of reporting obligation.* Each Fund, investment adviser and principal underwriter to which reports are required to be made by paragraph (d)(1) of this section must identify all Access Persons who are required to make these reports and must inform those Access Persons of their reporting obligation.

(5) *Beneficial ownership.* For purposes of this section, beneficial ownership is interpreted in the same manner as it would be under §240.16a–1(a)(2) of this chapter in determining whether a person is the beneficial owner of a security for purposes of section 16 of the Securities Exchange Act of 1934 [15 U.S.C. 78p] and the rules and regulations thereunder. Any report required by paragraph (d) of this section may contain a statement that the report will not be construed as an admission that the person making the report has any direct or indirect beneficial ownership in the Covered Security to which the report relates.

(e) *Pre-approval of investments in IPOs and limited offerings.* Investment Personnel of a Fund or its investment adviser must obtain approval from the Fund or the Fund's investment adviser before directly or indirectly acquiring beneficial ownership in any securities in an Initial Public Offering or in a Limited Offering.

(f) *Recordkeeping Requirements.* (1) Each Fund, investment adviser and principal underwriter that is required to adopt a code of ethics or to which reports are required to be made by Access Persons must, at its principal place of business, maintain records in the manner and to the extent set out in this paragraph (f), and must make these records available to the Commission or any representative of the Commission at any time and from time to time for reasonable periodic, special or other examination:

(A) A copy of each code of ethics for the organization that is in effect, or at any time within the past five years was in effect, must be maintained in an easily accessible place;

(B) A record of any violation of the code of ethics, and of any action taken as a result of the violation, must be maintained in an easily accessible place for at least five years after the end of the fiscal year in which the violation occurs;

(C) A copy of each report made by an Access Person as required by this section, including any information provided in lieu of the reports under paragraph (d)(2)(v) of this section, must be maintained for at least five years after the end of the fiscal year in which the report is made or the information is provided, the first two years in an easily accessible place;

(D) A record of all persons, currently or within the past five years, who are or were required to make reports under paragraph (d) of this section, or who are or were responsible for reviewing these reports, must be maintained in an easily accessible place; and

(E) A copy of each report required by paragraph (c)(2)(ii) of this section must be maintained for at least five years after the end of the fiscal year in which it is made, the first two years in an easily accessible place.

(2) A Fund or investment adviser must maintain a record of any decision, and the reasons supporting the decision, to approve the acquisition by investment personnel of securities under paragraph (e), for at least five

Securities and Exchange Commission §270.18f-1

years after the end of the fiscal year in which the approval is granted.

[64 FR 46834, Aug. 27, 1999; 65 FR 12943, Mar. 10, 2000, as amended at 69 FR 41707, July 9, 2004; 76 FR 81806, Dec. 29, 2011; 81 FR 83554, Nov. 21, 2016]

§270.18c-1 Exemption of privately held indebtedness.

The issuance or sale of more than one class of senior securities representing indebtedness by a small business investment company, licensed under the Small Business Investment Act of 1958, shall not be prohibited by section 18(c) so long as such small business investment company does not have outstanding any publicly held indebtedness, and all securities of any such class are (a) privately held by the Small Business Administration, or banks, insurance companies or other institutional investors, (b) not intended to be publicly distributed, and (c) not convertible into, exchangeable for, or accompanied by any option to acquire, any equity security.

[26 FR 11240, Nov. 29, 1961]

§270.18c-2 Exemptions of certain debentures issued by small business investment companies.

(a) The issuance or sale of any class of senior security representing indebtedness by a small business investment company licensed under the Small Business Investment Act of 1958 shall not be prohibited by section 18(c) of the Act provided such senior security representing indebtedness is (1) not convertible into, exchangeable for, or accompanied by an option to acquire any equity security; (2) fully guaranteed as to timely payment of all principal and interest by the Small Business Administration and backed by the full faith and credit of the United States; and (3) subordinated to any other debt securities not issued pursuant to this section or, if such security is not so subordinated, that such security, according to its own terms, will not be preferred over any other unsecured debt securities in the payment of principal and interest: *And further provided*, That all other debt securities then outstanding issued by such small business investment company were issued as permitted by §270.18c-1 or this section.

(b) Any security issued and sold as permitted by paragraph (a) of this section shall be deemed for purposes of §270.18c-1 to be privately held by the Small Business Administration and for purposes of §270.18c-1 shall not be deemed to be publicly held outstanding indebtedness.

(c) The issuance or sale of any security as permitted by paragraph (a) of this section shall not be deemed to be a sale to any person other than the Small Business Administration by any small business investment company licensed under the Small Business Investment Company Act of 1958 which is exempt from any provision of the Investment Company Act, if such exemption is conditioned on such company not offering or selling its securities to any person other than the Small Business Administration.

(Secs. 6(c), 38(a), 54 Stat. 800, 841, 15 U.S.C. 80a-6(c), 80a-37(a))

[37 FR 7590, Apr. 18, 1972]

§270.18f-1 Exemption from certain requirements of section 18(f)(1) (of the Act) for registered open-end investment companies which have the right to redeem in kind.

(a) A registered open-end investment company which has the right to redeem securities of which it is the issuer in assets other than cash may file with the Commission at any time a notification of election on Form N-18F-1 (§274.51 of this chapter) committing itself to pay in cash all requests for redemption by any shareholder of record, limited in amount with respect to each shareholder during any 90-day period to the lesser of

(1) $250,000 or

(2) 1 percent of the net asset value of such company at the beginning of such period.

(b) An election pursuant to paragraph (a) of this section:

(1) Shall be described in either the prospectus or the Statement of Additional Information, at the discretion of the investment company, and

(2) Shall be irrevocable while this §270.18f-1 is in effect unless the Commission by order upon application permits the withdrawal of such notification of election as being appropriate in

§ 270.18f-2

the public interest and consistent with the protection of investors.

(c) Upon making the election described in paragraph (a) of this section, an investment company shall be exempt from the requirements of section 18(f)(1) (of the Act) to the extent necessary for such company to effectuate redemptions in the manner set forth in such paragraph.

(Secs. 7, 10, and 19 of the Securities Act of 1933 (15 U.S.C. 77g, 77j, and 77s) and secs. 8, 30 and 38 of the Investment Company Act of 1940 (15 U.S.C. 80a-8, 80a-29 and 80a-37))

[36 FR 11919, June 23, 1971, as amended at 48 FR 37940, Aug. 22, 1983]

§ 270.18f-2 Fair and equitable treatment for holders of each class or series of stock of series investment companies.

(a) For purposes of this § 270.18f-2 a series company is a registered open-end investment company which, in accordance with the provisions of section 18(f)(2) of the Act, issues two or more classes or series of preferred or special stock each of which is preferred over all other classes or series in respect of assets specifically allocated to that class or series. Any matter required to be submitted by the provisions of the Act or of applicable State law, or otherwise, to the holders of the outstanding voting securities of a series company shall not be deemed to have been effectively acted upon less approved by the holders of a majority of the outstanding voting securities of each class or series of stock affected by such matter.

(b) For the purposes of paragraph (a) of this § 270.18f-2, a class or series of stock will be deemed to be affected by such a matter, unless (1) the interests of each class or series in the matter are substantially identical, or (2) the matter does not affect any interest of such class or series.

(c)(1) With respect to the submission of an investment advisory contract to the holders of the outstanding voting securities of a series company for the approval required by section 15(a) of the Act, such matter shall be deemed to be effectively acted upon with respect to any class or series of securities of such company if a majority of the outstanding voting securities of such class or series vote for the approval of such matter, notwithstanding (i) that such matter has not been approved by the holders of a majority of the outstanding voting securities of any other class or series affected by such matter, and (ii) that such matter has not been approved by the vote of a majority of the outstanding voting securities of such company, provided that if such a majority is required by State law or otherwise, such requirement shall apply.

(2) If any class or series of securities of a series company fails to approve an investment advisory contract in the manner required by paragraph (c)(1) of this section, the investment adviser of such company may continue to serve or act in such capacity for the period of time pending such required approval of such contract, of a new contract with the same or different adviser, or other definitive action: *Provided,* That the compensation received by such investment adviser during such period is equal to no more than its actual costs incurred in furnishing investment advisory services to such class or series or the amount it would have received under the advisory contract, whichever is less.

(d) With respect to the submission of a change in investment policy to the holders of the outstanding voting securities of a series company for the approval required by section 13 of the Act, such matter shall be deemed to have been effectively acted upon with respect to any class or series of such company if a majority of the outstanding voting securities of such class or series vote for the approval of such matter, notwithstanding (1) that such matter has not been approved by the holders of a majority of the outstanding voting securities of any other class or series affected by such matter, and (2) that such matter has not been approved by the vote of a majority of the outstanding voting securities of such company: *Provided,* That if such a majority is required by State law or otherwise, such requirement shall apply.

(e) The submission to shareholders of the selection of the independent public accountant of a series company required by section 32(a) (of the Act) shall be exempt from the separate voting requirements of paragraph (a) of this §270.18f-2.

(f) The submission to shareholders of a contract with a principal underwriter of a series company required by section 15(b) of the Act shall be exempt from the separate voting requirements of paragraph (a) of this §270.18f-2.

(g) The submission to shareholders of nominees for election as directors required by section 16(a) of the Act shall be exempt from the separate voting requirements of paragraph (a) of this §270.18f-2.

(h) For the purposes of this §270.18f-2 a "majority of the outstanding voting securities" of a class or series, (1) when used with respect to a matter required by any provision of the Act to be submitted to the outstanding voting securities of a series company, shall have the same meaning as a "majority of the outstanding voting securities of a company" as defined in section 2(a)(42) of the Act; and (2) when used with respect to any other matter required to be submitted to the outstanding voting securities of a series company, shall mean the lesser of (i) the minimum vote of the outstanding voting securities of a company required by applicable State law or other applicable requirement, or (ii) the minimum vote specified by paragraph (1) of this paragraph (h), unless State law requires approval of such matters by a specified percentage of the outstanding voting securities of a particular class or series, in which case, State law shall apply.

(Secs. 6(c), 13, 15(a), 15(b), 16(a), 18(f)(2), 32(a), 54 Stat. 800, 811, 812, 813, 817, 838, 841, 15 U.S.C. 80a-6(c), 80a-13, 80a-15(b), 80a-16(a), 80a-18(f)(2), 80a-31(a), 80a-37(a), Pub. L. 91-547, 84 Stat. 1421)

[37 FR 17386, Aug. 26, 1972]

§ 270.18f-3 Multiple class companies.

Notwithstanding sections 18(f)(1) and 18(i) of the Act (15 U.S.C. 80a-18(f)(1) and (i), respectively), a registered open-end management investment company or series or class thereof established in accordance with section 18(f)(2) of the Act (15 U.S.C. 80a-18(f)(2)) whose shares are registered on Form N-1A [§§ 239.15A and 274.11A of this chapter] ("company") may issue more than one class of voting stock, *provided* that:

(a) Each class:

(1)(i) Shall have a different arrangement for shareholder services or the distribution of securities or both, and shall pay all of the expenses of that arrangement;

(ii) May pay a different share of other expenses, not including advisory or custodial fees or other expenses related to the management of the company's assets, if these expenses are actually incurred in a different amount by that class, or if the class receives services of a different kind or to a different degree than other classes; and

(iii) May pay a different advisory fee to the extent that any difference in amount paid is the result of the application of the same performance fee provisions in the advisory contract of the company to the different investment performance of each class;

(2) Shall have exclusive voting rights on any matter submitted to shareholders that relates solely to its arrangement;

(3) Shall have separate voting rights on any matter submitted to shareholders in which the interests of one class differ from the interests of any other class; and

(4) Shall have in all other respects the same rights and obligations as each other class.

(b) Expenses may be waived or reimbursed by the company's adviser, underwriter, or any other provider of services to the company.

(c)(1) Income, realized gains and losses, unrealized appreciation and depreciation, and Fundwide Expenses shall be allocated based on one of the following methods (which method shall be applied on a consistent basis):

(i) To each class based on the net assets of that class in relation to the net assets of the company ("relative net assets");

(ii) To each class based on the Simultaneous Equations Method;

(iii) To each class based on the Settled Shares Method, *provided that* the company is a Daily Dividend Fund (such a company may allocate income and Fundwide Expenses based on the Settled Shares Method and realized

§ 270.18f-3

gains and losses and unrealized appreciation and depreciation based on relative net assets);

(iv) To each share without regard to class, *provided that* the company is a Daily Dividend Fund that maintains the same net asset value per share in each class; that the company has received undertakings from its adviser, underwriter, or any other provider of services to the company, agreeing to waive or reimburse the company for payments to such service provider by one or more classes, as allocated under paragraph (a)(1) of this section, to the extent necessary to assure that all classes of the company maintain the same net asset value per share; and that payments waived or reimbursed under such an undertaking may not be carried forward or recouped at a future date; or

(v) To each class based on any other appropriate method, *provided that* a majority of the directors of the company, and a majority of the directors who are not interested persons of the company, determine that the method is fair to the shareholders of each class and that the annualized rate of return of each class will generally differ from that of the other classes only by the expense differentials among the classes.

(2) For purposes of this section:

(i) *Daily Dividend Fund* means any company that has a policy of declaring distributions of net income daily, including any money market fund that operates in compliance with § 270.2a-7;

(ii) *Fundwide Expenses* means expenses of the company not allocated to a particular class under paragraph (a)(1) of this section;

(iii) The *Settled Shares Method* means allocating to each class based on relative net assets, excluding the value of subscriptions receivable; and

(iv) The *Simultaneous Equations Method* means the simultaneous allocation to each class of each day's income, realized gains and losses, unrealized appreciation and depreciation, and Fundwide Expenses and reallocation to each class of undistributed net investment income, undistributed realized gains or losses, and unrealized appreciation or depreciation, based on the operating results of the company, changes in ownership interests of each class, and expense differentials between the classes, so that the annualized rate of return of each class generally differs from that of the other classes only by the expense differentials among the classes.

(d) Any payments made under paragraph (a) of this section shall be made pursuant to a written plan setting forth the separate arrangement and expense allocation of each class, and any related conversion features or exchange privileges. Before the first issuance of a share of any class in reliance upon this section, and before any material amendment of a plan, a majority of the directors of the company, and a majority of the directors who are not interested persons of the company, shall find that the plan as proposed to be adopted or amended, including the expense allocation, is in the best interests of each class individually and the company as a whole; initial board approval of a plan under this paragraph (d) is not required, however, if the plan does not make any change in the arrangements and expense allocations previously approved by the board under an existing order of exemption. Before any vote on the plan, the directors shall request and evaluate, and any agreement relating to a class arrangement shall require the parties thereto to furnish, such information as may be reasonably necessary to evaluate the plan.

(e) The board of directors of the investment company satisfies the fund governance standards defined in § 270.0–1(a)(7).

(f) Nothing in this section prohibits a company from offering any class with:

(1) An exchange privilege providing that securities of the class may be exchanged for certain securities of another company; or

(2) A conversion feature providing that shares of one class of the company (the "purchase class") will be exchanged automatically for shares of another class of the company (the "target class") after a specified period of time, *provided that:*

(i) The conversion is effected on the basis of the relative net asset values of the two classes without the imposition of any sales load, fee, or other charge;

444

Securities and Exchange Commission § 270.18f–4

(ii) The expenses, including payments authorized under a plan adopted pursuant to § 270.12b–1 ("rule 12b–1 plan"), for the target class are not higher than the expenses, including payments authorized under a rule 12b–1 plan, for the purchase class; and

(iii) If the shareholders of the target class approve any increase in expenses allocated to the target class under paragraphs (a)(1)(i) and (a)(1)(ii) of this section, and the purchase class shareholders do not approve the increase, the company will establish a new target class for the purchase class on the same terms as applied to the target class before that increase.

(3) A conversion feature providing that shares of a class in which an investor is no longer eligible to participate may be converted to shares of a class in which that investor is eligible to participate, *provided that:*

(i) The investor is given prior notice of the proposed conversion; and

(ii) The conversion is effected on the basis of the relative net asset values of the two classes without the imposition of any sales load, fee, or other charge.

[60 FR 11885, Mar. 2, 1995, as amended at 62 FR 51765, Oct. 3, 1997; 66 FR 3759, Jan. 16, 2001; 69 FR 46390, Aug. 2, 2004; 79 FR 47967, Aug. 14, 2014]

§ 270.18f–4 Exemption from the requirements of section 18 and section 61 for certain senior securities transactions.

(a) *Definitions.* For purposes of this section:

Absolute VaR test means that the VaR of the fund's portfolio does not exceed 20% of the value of the fund's net assets, or in the case of a closed-end company that has issued to investors and has then outstanding shares of a class of senior security that is a stock, that the VaR of the fund's portfolio does not exceed 25% of the value of the fund's net assets.

Derivatives exposure means the sum of the gross notional amounts of the fund's derivatives transactions described in paragraph (1) of the definition of the term "derivatives transaction" of this section, and in the case of short sale borrowings, the value of the assets sold short. If a fund's derivatives transactions include reverse repurchase agreements or similar financing transactions under paragraph (d)(1)(ii) of this section, the fund's derivatives exposure also includes, for each transaction, the proceeds received but not yet repaid or returned, or for which the associated liability has not been extinguished, in connection with the transaction. In determining derivatives exposure a fund may convert the notional amount of interest rate derivatives to 10-year bond equivalents and delta adjust the notional amounts of options contracts and exclude any closed-out positions, if those positions were closed out with the same counterparty and result in no credit or market exposure to the fund.

Derivatives risk manager means an officer or officers of the fund's investment adviser responsible for administering the program and policies and procedures required by paragraph (c)(1) of this section, provided that the derivatives risk manager:

(1) May not be a portfolio manager of the fund, or if multiple officers serve as derivatives risk manager, may not have a majority composed of portfolio managers of the fund; and

(2) Must have relevant experience regarding the management of derivatives risk.

Derivatives risks means the risks associated with a fund's derivatives transactions or its use of derivatives transactions, including leverage, market, counterparty, liquidity, operational, and legal risks and any other risks the derivatives risk manager (or, in the case of a fund that is a limited derivatives user as described in paragraph (c)(4) of this section, the fund's investment adviser) deems material.

Derivatives transaction means:

(1) Any swap, security-based swap, futures contract, forward contract, option, any combination of the foregoing, or any similar instrument ("derivatives instrument"), under which a fund is or may be required to make any payment or delivery of cash or other assets during the life of the instrument or at maturity or early termination, whether as margin or settlement payment or otherwise;

(2) Any short sale borrowing; and

§ 270.18f–4

(3) If a fund relies on paragraph (d)(1)(ii) of this section, any reverse repurchase agreement or similar financing transaction.

Designated index means an unleveraged index that is approved by the derivatives risk manager for purposes of the relative VaR test and that reflects the markets or asset classes in which the fund invests and is not administered by an organization that is an affiliated person of the fund, its investment adviser, or principal underwriter, or created at the request of the fund or its investment adviser, unless the index is widely recognized and used. In the case of a blended index, none of the indexes that compose the blended index may be administered by an organization that is an affiliated person of the fund, its investment adviser, or principal underwriter, or created at the request of the fund or its investment adviser, unless the index is widely recognized and used.

Designated reference portfolio means a designated index or the fund's securities portfolio. Notwithstanding the first sentence of the definition of *designated index* of this section, if the fund's investment objective is to track the performance (including a leverage multiple or inverse multiple) of an unleveraged index, the fund must use that index as its designated reference portfolio.

Fund means a registered open-end or closed-end company or a business development company, including any separate series thereof, but does not include a registered open-end company that is regulated as a money market fund under § 270.2a–7.

Leveraged/inverse fund means a fund that seeks, directly or indirectly, to provide investment returns that correspond to the performance of a market index by a specified multiple ("leverage multiple"), or to provide investment returns that have an inverse relationship to the performance of a market index ("inverse multiple"), over a predetermined period of time.

Relative VaR test means that the VaR of the fund's portfolio does not exceed 200% of the VaR of the designated reference portfolio, or in the case of a closed-end company that has issued to investors and has then outstanding shares of a class of senior security that is a stock, that the VaR of the fund's portfolio does not exceed 250% of the VaR of the designated reference portfolio.

Securities portfolio means the fund's portfolio of securities and other investments, excluding any derivatives transactions, that is approved by the derivatives risk manager for purposes of the relative VaR test, provided that the fund's securities portfolio reflects the markets or asset classes in which the fund invests (*i.e.*, the markets or asset classes in which the fund invests directly through securities and other investments and indirectly through derivatives transactions).

Unfunded commitment agreement means a contract that is not a derivatives transaction, under which a fund commits, conditionally or unconditionally, to make a loan to a company or to invest equity in a company in the future, including by making a capital commitment to a private fund that can be drawn at the discretion of the fund's general partner.

Value-at-risk or *VaR* means an estimate of potential losses on an instrument or portfolio, expressed as a percentage of the value of the portfolio's assets (or net assets when computing a fund's VaR), over a specified time horizon and at a given confidence level, provided that any VaR model used by a fund for purposes of determining the fund's compliance with the relative VaR test or the absolute VaR test must:

(1) Take into account and incorporate all significant, identifiable market risk factors associated with a fund's investments, including, as applicable:

(i) Equity price risk, interest rate risk, credit spread risk, foreign currency risk and commodity price risk;

(ii) Material risks arising from the nonlinear price characteristics of a fund's investments, including options and positions with embedded optionality; and

(iii) The sensitivity of the market value of the fund's investments to changes in volatility;

(2) Use a 99% confidence level and a time horizon of 20 trading days; and

Securities and Exchange Commission § 270.18f–4

(3) Be based on at least three years of historical market data.

(b) *Derivatives transactions.* If a fund satisfies the conditions of paragraph (c) of this section, the fund may enter into derivatives transactions, notwithstanding the requirements of sections 18(a)(1), 18(c), 18(f)(1), and 61 of the Investment Company Act (15 U.S.C. 80a–18(a)(1), 80a–18(c), 80a–18(f)(1), and 80a–60), and derivatives transactions entered into by the fund in compliance with this section will not be considered for purposes of computing asset coverage, as defined in section 18(h) of the Investment Company Act (15 U.S.C. 80a–18(h)).

(c) *Conditions*—(1) *Derivatives risk management program.* The fund adopts and implements a written derivatives risk management program ("program"), which must include policies and procedures that are reasonably designed to manage the fund's derivatives risks and to reasonably segregate the functions associated with the program from the portfolio management of the fund. The program must include the following elements:

(i) *Risk identification and assessment.* The program must provide for the identification and assessment of the fund's derivatives risks. This assessment must take into account the fund's derivatives transactions and other investments.

(ii) *Risk guidelines.* The program must provide for the establishment, maintenance, and enforcement of investment, risk management, or related guidelines that provide for quantitative or otherwise measurable criteria, metrics, or thresholds of the fund's derivatives risks. These guidelines must specify levels of the given criterion, metric, or threshold that the fund does not normally expect to exceed, and measures to be taken if they are exceeded.

(iii) *Stress testing.* The program must provide for stress testing to evaluate potential losses to the fund's portfolio in response to extreme but plausible market changes or changes in market risk factors that would have a significant adverse effect on the fund's portfolio, taking into account correlations of market risk factors and resulting payments to derivatives counterparties. The frequency with which the stress testing under this paragraph is conducted must take into account the fund's strategy and investments and current market conditions, provided that these stress tests must be conducted no less frequently than weekly.

(iv) *Backtesting.* The program must provide for backtesting to be conducted no less frequently than weekly, of the results of the VaR calculation model used by the fund in connection with the relative VaR test or the absolute VaR test by comparing the fund's gain or loss that occurred on each business day during the backtesting period with the corresponding VaR calculation for that day, estimated over a one-trading day time horizon, and identifying as an exception any instance in which the fund experiences a loss exceeding the corresponding VaR calculation's estimated loss.

(v) *Internal reporting and escalation*—(A) *Internal reporting.* The program must identify the circumstances under which persons responsible for portfolio management will be informed regarding the operation of the program, including exceedances of the guidelines specified in paragraph (c)(1)(ii) of this section and the results of the stress tests specified in paragraph (c)(1)(iii) of this section.

(B) *Escalation of material risks.* The derivatives risk manager must inform in a timely manner persons responsible for portfolio management of the fund, and also directly inform the fund's board of directors as appropriate, of material risks arising from the fund's derivatives transactions, including risks identified by the fund's exceedance of a criterion, metric, or threshold provided for in the fund's risk guidelines established under paragraph (c)(1)(ii) of this section or by the stress testing described in paragraph (c)(1)(iii) of this section.

(vi) *Periodic review of the program.* The derivatives risk manager must review the program at least annually to evaluate the program's effectiveness and to reflect changes in risk over time. The periodic review must include a review of the VaR calculation model used by the fund under paragraph (c)(2) of this section (including the backtesting required by paragraph (c)(1)(iv) of this section) and any designated reference

447

portfolio to evaluate whether it remains appropriate.

(2) *Limit on fund leverage risk.* (i) The fund must comply with the relative VaR test unless the derivatives risk manager reasonably determines that a designated reference portfolio would not provide an appropriate reference portfolio for purposes of the relative VaR test, taking into account the fund's investments, investment objectives, and strategy. A fund that does not apply the relative VaR test must comply with the absolute VaR test.

(ii) The fund must determine its compliance with the applicable VaR test at least once each business day. If the fund determines that it is not in compliance with the applicable VaR test, the fund must come back into compliance promptly after such determination, in a manner that is in the best interests of the fund and its shareholders.

(iii) If the fund is not in compliance with the applicable VaR test within five business days:

(A) The derivatives risk manager must provide a written report to the fund's board of directors and explain how and by when (*i.e.*, number of business days) the derivatives risk manager reasonably expects that the fund will come back into compliance;

(B) The derivatives risk manager must analyze the circumstances that caused the fund to be out of compliance for more than five business days and update any program elements as appropriate to address those circumstances; and

(C) The derivatives risk manager must provide a written report within thirty calendar days of the exceedance to the fund's board of directors explaining how the fund came back into compliance and the results of the analysis and updates required under paragraph (c)(2)(iii)(B) of this section. If the fund remains out of compliance with the applicable VaR test at that time, the derivatives risk manager's written report must update the report previously provided under paragraph (c)(2)(iii)(A) of this section and the derivatives risk manager must update the board of directors on the fund's progress in coming back into compliance at regularly scheduled intervals at a frequency determined by the board.

(3) *Board oversight and reporting*—(i) *Approval of the derivatives risk manager.* A fund's board of directors, including a majority of directors who are not interested persons of the fund, must approve the designation of the derivatives risk manager.

(ii) *Reporting on program implementation and effectiveness.* On or before the implementation of the program, and at least annually thereafter, the derivatives risk manager must provide to the board of directors a written report providing a representation that the program is reasonably designed to manage the fund's derivatives risks and to incorporate the elements provided in paragraphs (c)(1)(i) through (vi) of this section. The representation may be based on the derivatives risk manager's reasonable belief after due inquiry. The written report must include the basis for the representation along with such information as may be reasonably necessary to evaluate the adequacy of the fund's program and, for reports following the program's initial implementation, the effectiveness of its implementation. The written report also must include, as applicable, the derivatives risk manager's basis for the approval of any designated reference portfolio or any change in the designated reference portfolio during the period covered by the report; or an explanation of the basis for the derivatives risk manager's determination that a designated reference portfolio would not provide an appropriate reference portfolio for purposes of the relative VaR test.

(iii) *Regular board reporting.* The derivatives risk manager must provide to the board of directors, at a frequency determined by the board, a written report regarding the derivatives risk manager's analysis of exceedances described in paragraph (c)(1)(ii) of this section, the results of the stress testing conducted under paragraph (c)(1)(iii) of this section, and the results of the backtesting conducted under paragraph (c)(1)(iv) of this section since the last report to the board. Each report under this paragraph must include such information as may be reasonably necessary for the board of

Securities and Exchange Commission § 270.18f-4

directors to evaluate the fund's response to exceedances and the results of the fund's stress testing.

(4) *Limited derivatives users.* (i) A fund is not required to adopt a program as prescribed in paragraph (c)(1) of this section, comply with the limit on fund leverage risk in paragraph (c)(2) of this section, or comply with the board oversight and reporting requirements as prescribed in paragraph (c)(3) of this section, if:

(A) The fund adopts and implements written policies and procedures reasonably designed to manage the fund's derivatives risk; and

(B) The fund's derivatives exposure does not exceed 10 percent of the fund's net assets, excluding, for this purpose, currency or interest rate derivatives that hedge currency or interest rate risks associated with one or more specific equity or fixed-income investments held by the fund (which must be foreign-currency-denominated in the case of currency derivatives), or the fund's borrowings, provided that the currency or interest rate derivatives are entered into and maintained by the fund for hedging purposes and that the notional amounts of such derivatives do not exceed the value of the hedged investments (or the par value thereof, in the case of fixed-income investments, or the principal amount, in the case of borrowing) by more than 10 percent.

(ii) If a fund's derivatives exposure exceeds 10 percent of its net assets, as calculated in accordance with paragraph (c)(4)(i)(B) of this section, and the fund is not in compliance with that paragraph within five business days, the fund's investment adviser must provide a written report to the fund's board of directors informing them whether the investment adviser intends either:

(A) To reduce the fund's derivatives exposure to less than 10 percent of the fund's net assets promptly, but within no more than thirty calendar days of the exceedance, in a manner that is in the best interests of the fund and its shareholders; or

(B) For the fund to establish a program as prescribed in paragraph (c)(1) of this section, comply with the limit on fund leverage risk in paragraph (c)(2) of this section, and comply with the board oversight and reporting requirements as prescribed in paragraph (c)(3) of this section, as soon as reasonably practicable.

(5) *Leveraged/inverse funds.* A leveraged/inverse fund that cannot comply with the limit on fund leverage risk in paragraph (c) of this section is not required to comply with the limit on fund leverage risk if, in addition to complying with all other applicable requirements of this section:

(i) As of October 28, 2020, the fund is in operation; has outstanding shares issued in one or more public offerings to investors; and discloses in its prospectus a leverage multiple or inverse multiple that exceeds 200% of the performance or the inverse of the performance of the underlying index;

(ii) The fund does not change the underlying market index or increase the level of leveraged or inverse market exposure the fund seeks, directly or indirectly, to provide; and

(iii) The fund discloses in its prospectus that it is not subject to the limit on fund leverage risk in paragraph (c)(2) of this section.

(6) *Recordkeeping*—(i) *Records to be maintained.* A fund must maintain a written record documenting, as applicable:

(A) The fund's written policies and procedures required by paragraph (c)(1) of this section, along with:

(*1*) The results of the fund's stress tests under paragraph (c)(1)(iii) of this section;

(*2*) The results of the backtesting conducted under paragraph (c)(1)(iv) of this section;

(*3*) Records documenting any internal reporting or escalation of material risks under paragraph (c)(1)(v)(B) of this section; and

(*4*) Records documenting the reviews conducted under paragraph (c)(1)(vi) of this section.

(B) Copies of any materials provided to the board of directors in connection with its approval of the designation of the derivatives risk manager, any written reports provided to the board of directors relating to the program, and any written reports provided to the board of directors under paragraphs (c)(2)(iii)(A) and (C) of this section.

(C) Any determination and/or action the fund made under paragraphs (c)(2)(i) and (ii) of this section, including a fund's determination of: The VaR of its portfolio; the VaR of the fund's designated reference portfolio, as applicable; the fund's VaR ratio (the value of the VaR of the fund's portfolio divided by the VaR of the designated reference portfolio), as applicable; and any updates to any VaR calculation models used by the fund and the basis for any material changes thereto.

(D) If applicable, the fund's written policies and procedures required by paragraph (c)(4) of this section, along with copies of any written reports provided to the board of directors under paragraph (c)(4)(ii) of this section.

(ii) *Retention periods.* (A) A fund must maintain a copy of the written policies and procedures that the fund adopted under paragraph (c)(1) or (4) of this section that are in effect, or at any time within the past five years were in effect, in an easily accessible place.

(B) A fund must maintain all records and materials that paragraphs (c)(6)(i)(A)(*1*) through (*4*) and (c)(6)(i)(B) through (D) of this section describe for a period of not less than five years (the first two years in an easily accessible place) following each determination, action, or review that these paragraphs describe.

(7) *Current reports.* A fund that experiences an event specified in the parts of Form N-RN [referenced in 17 CFR 274.223] titled "Relative VaR Test Breaches," "Absolute VaR Test Breaches," or "Compliance with VaR Test" must file with the Commission a report on Form N-RN within the period and according to the instructions specified in that form.

(d) *Reverse repurchase agreements.* (1) A fund may enter into reverse repurchase agreements or similar financing transactions, notwithstanding the requirements of sections 18(c) and 18(f)(1) of the Investment Company Act, if the fund:

(i) Complies with the asset coverage requirements of section 18, and combines the aggregate amount of indebtedness associated with all reverse repurchase agreements or similar financing transactions with the aggregate amount of any other senior securities representing indebtedness when calculating the asset coverage ratio; or

(ii) Treats all reverse repurchase agreements or similar financing transactions as derivatives transactions for all purposes under this section.

(2) A fund relying on paragraph (d) of this section must maintain a written record documenting whether the fund is relying on paragraph (d)(1)(i) or (ii) of this section for a period of not less than five years (the first two years in an easily accessible place) following the determination.

(e) *Unfunded commitment agreements.* (1) A fund may enter into an unfunded commitment agreement, notwithstanding the requirements of sections 18(a), 18(c), 18(f)(1), and 61 of the Investment Company Act, if the fund reasonably believes, at the time it enters into such agreement, that it will have sufficient cash and cash equivalents to meet its obligations with respect to all of its unfunded commitment agreements, in each case as they come due. In forming a reasonable belief, the fund must take into account its reasonable expectations with respect to other obligations (including any obligation with respect to senior securities or redemptions), and may not take into account cash that may become available from the sale or disposition of any investment at a price that deviates significantly from the market value of those investments, or from issuing additional equity. Unfunded commitment agreements entered into by the fund in compliance with this section will not be considered for purposes of computing asset coverage, as defined in section 18(h) of the Investment Company Act (15 U.S.C. 80a–18(h)).

(2) For each unfunded commitment agreement that a fund enters into under paragraph (e)(1) of this section, a fund must document the basis for its reasonable belief regarding the sufficiency of its cash and cash equivalents to meet its unfunded commitment agreement obligations, and maintain a record of this documentation for a period of not less than five years (the first two years in an easily accessible place) following the date that the fund entered into the agreement.

(f) *When issued, forward-settling, and non-standard settlement cycle securities transactions.* Notwithstanding the requirements of sections 18(a)(1), 18(c), 18(f)(1), and 61 of the Investment Company Act (15 U.S.C. 80a–18(a)(1), 80a018(c), 80a–18(f)(1), and 80a–60), a fund or registered open-end company that is regulated as a money market fund under § 270.2a–7 may invest in a security on a when-issued or forward-settling basis, or with a non-standard settlement cycle, and the transaction will be deemed not to involve a senior security, provided that: The fund intends to physically settle the transaction; and the transaction will settle within 35 days of its trade date.

[85 FR 83291, Dec. 21, 2020, as amended at 87 FR 22446, Apr. 15, 2022]

§ 270.19a–1 Written statement to accompany dividend payments by management companies.

(a) Every written statement made pursuant to section 19 by or on behalf of a management company shall be made on a separate paper and shall clearly indicate what portion of the payment per share is made from the following sources:

(1) Net income for the current or preceding fiscal year, or accumulated undistributed net income, or both, not including in either case profits or losses from the sale of securities or other properties.

(2) Accumulated undistributed net profits from the sale of securities or other properties (except that an open-end company may treat as a separate source its net profits from such sales during its current fiscal year).

(3) Paid-in surplus or other capital source.

To the extent that a payment is properly designated as being made from a source specified in paragraph (a) (1) or (2) of this section, it need not be designated as having been made from a source specified in this paragraph.

(b) If the payment is made in whole or in part from a source specified in paragraph (a)(2) of this section the written statement shall indicate, after giving effect to the part of such payment so specified, the deficit, if any, in the aggregate of (1) accumulated undistributed realized profits less losses on the sale of securities or other properties and (2) the net unrealized appreciation or depreciation of portfolio securities, all as of a date reasonably close to the end of the period as of which the dividend is paid. Any statement made pursuant to the preceding sentence shall specify the amount, if any, of such deficit which represents unrealized depreciation of portfolio securities.

(c) Accumulated undistributed net income and accumulated undistributed net profits from the sale of securities or other properties shall be determined, at the option of the company, either (1) from the date of the organization of the company, (2) from the date of a reorganization, as defined in clause (A) or (B) of section 2(a)(33) of the Act (54 Stat. 790; 15 U.S.C. 80a–2(a)(33)), (3) from the date as of which a write-down of portfolio securities was made in connection with a corporate readjustment, approved by stockholders, of the type known as "quasi- reorganization," or (4) from January 1, 1925, to the close of the period as of which the dividend is paid, without giving effect to such payment.

(d) For the purpose of this section, open-end companies which upon the sale of their shares allocate to undistributed income or other similar account that portion of the consideration received which represents the approximate per share amount of undistributed net income included in the sales price, and make a corresponding deduction from undistributed net income upon the purchase or redemption of shares, need not treat the amounts so allocated as paid-in surplus or other capital source.

(e) For the purpose of this section, the source or sources from which a dividend is paid shall be determined (or reasonably estimated) to the close of the period as of which it is paid without giving effect to such payment. If any such estimate is subsequently ascertained to be inaccurate in a significant amount, a correction thereof shall be made by a written statement pursuant to section 19(a) of the Act or in the first report to stockholders following discovery of the inaccuracy.

(f) Insofar as a written statement made pursuant to section 19(a) of the Act relates to a dividend on preferred stock paid for a period of less than a

§ 270.19b-1

year, a company may elect to indicate only that portion of the payment which is made from sources specified in paragraph (a)(1) of this section, and need not specify the sources from which the remainder was paid. Every company which in any fiscal year elects to make a statement pursuant to the preceding sentence shall transmit to the holders of such preferred stock, at a date reasonably near the end of the last dividend period in such fiscal year, a statement meeting the requirements of paragraph (a) of this section on an annual basis.

(g) The purpose of this section, in the light of which it shall be construed, is to afford security holders adequate disclosure of the sources from which dividend payments are made. Nothing in this section shall be construed to prohibit the inclusion in any written statement of additional information in explanation of the information required by this section. Nothing in this section shall be construed to permit a dividend payment in violation of any State law or to prevent compliance with any requirement of State law regarding dividends consistent with this rule.

CROSS REFERENCE: For interpretative release applicable to § 270.19a-1, see No. 71 in tabulation, part 271 of this chapter.

[Rule N-19-1, 6 FR 1114, Feb. 25, 1941. Redesignated at 36 FR 22901, Dec. 2, 1971, and amended at 38 FR 8593, Apr. 4, 1973]

§ 270.19b-1 Frequency of distribution of capital gains.

(a) No registered investment company which is a "regulated investment company" as defined in section 851 of the Internal Revenue Code of 1986 ("Code") shall distribute more than one capital gain dividend ("distribution"), as defined in section 852(b)(3)(C) of the Code, with respect to any one taxable year of the company, other than a distribution otherwise permitted by this rule or made pursuant to section 855 of the Code which is supplemental to the prior distribution with respect to the same taxable year of the company and which does not exceed 10% of the aggregate amount distributed for such taxable year.

(b) No registered investment company which is not a "regulated investment company" as defined in section 851 of the Code shall make more than one distribution of long-term capital gains, as defined in the Code, in any one taxable year of the company: *Provided,* That a unit investment trust may distribute capital gain dividends received from a "regulated investment company" within a reasonable time after receipt.

(c) The provisions of this rule shall not apply to a unit investment trust (hereinafter referred to as the "Trust") engaged exclusively in the business of investing in eligible trust securities (as defined in Rule 14a-3(b) (17 CFR 270.14a-3(b)) under this Act); *Provided,* That:

(1) The capital gain distribution is a result of—

(i) An issuer's calling or redeeming an eligible trust security held by the Trust,

(ii) The sale of an eligible trust security by the Trust to provide funds for redemption of Trust units when the amount received by the Trust for such sale exceeds the amount required to satisfy the redemption distribution,

(iii) The sale of an eligible trust security to maintain qualification of the Trust as a "regulated investment company" under section 851 of the Code,

(iv) Regular distributions of principal and prepayment of principal on eligible trust securities, or

(v) The sale of an eligible trust security in order to maintain the investment stability of the Trust; and

(2) Capital gains distributions are clearly described as such in a report to the unitholder which accompanies each such distribution.

(d) For purposes of paragraph (c) of this section, sales made to maintain the investment stability of the Trust means sales made to prevent deterioration of the value of the eligible trust securities held in the Trust portfolio when one or more of the following factors exist:

(1) A default in the payment of principal or interest on an eligible trust security;

(2) An action involving the issuer of an eligible trust security which adversely affects the ability of such

Securities and Exchange Commission § 270.22c-1

issuer to continue payment of principal or interest on its eligible trust securities; or

(3) A change in market, revenue or credit factors which adversely affects the ability of such issuer to continue payment of principal or interest on its eligible trust securities.

(e) If a registered investment company because of unforeseen circumstances in a particular taxable year proposes to make a distribution which would be prohibited by the provisions of this section, it may file a request with the Commission for authorization to make such a distribution. Such request shall comply with the requirements of § 270.0-2 of this chapter and shall set forth the pertinent facts and explain the circumstances which the company believes justify such distribution. The request shall be deemed granted unless the Commission within 15 days after receipt thereof shall deny such request as not being necessary or appropriate in the public interest or for the protection of investors and notify the company in writing of such denial.

(f) A registered investment company may make one additional distribution of long-term capital gains, as defined in the Code, with respect to any one taxable year of the company, which distribution is made, in whole or in part, for the purpose of not incurring any tax under section 4982 of the Code. Such additional distribution may be made prior or subsequent to any distribution otherwise permitted by paragraph (a) of this section.

(Secs. 6(c), 19(b) (15 U.S.C. 80a-19(b), and sec. 38(a)))

[36 FR 22901, Dec. 2, 1971, as amended at 44 FR 29647, May 22, 1979; 44 FR 40064, July 9, 1979; 52 FR 42428, Nov. 5, 1987]

§ 270.20a-1 Solicitation of proxies, consents and authorizations.

(a) No person shall solicit or permit the use of his or her name to solicit any proxy, consent, or authorization with respect to any security issued by a registered fund, except upon compliance with Regulation 14A (§ 240.14a-1 of this chapter), Schedule 14A (§ 240.14a-101 of this chapter), and all other rules and regulations adopted pursuant to section 14(a) of the Securities Exchange Act of 1934 that would be applicable to such solicitation if it were made in respect of a security registered pursuant to section 12 of the Securities Exchange Act of 1934. Unless the solicitation is made in respect of a security registered on a national securities exchange, none of the soliciting material need be filed with such exchange.

(b) If the solicitation is made by or on behalf of the management of the investment company, then the investment adviser or any prospective investment adviser and any affiliated person thereof as to whom information is required in the solicitation shall upon request of the investment company promptly transmit to the investment company all information necessary to enable the management of such company to comply with the rules and regulations applicable to such solicitation. If the solicitation is made by any person other than the management of the investment company, on behalf of and with the consent of the investment adviser or prospective investment adviser, then the investment adviser or prospective investment adviser and any affiliated person thereof as to whom information is required in the solicitation shall upon request of the person making the solicitation promptly transmit to such person all information necessary to enable such person to comply with the rules and regulations applicable to the solicitation.

Instruction. Registrants that have made a public offering of securities and that hold security holder votes for which proxies, consents, or authorizations are not being solicited pursuant to the requirements of this section should refer to section 14(c) of the Securities Exchange Act of 1934 (15 U.S.C. 78n(c)) and the information statement requirements set forth in the rules thereunder.

[25 FR 1865, Mar. 3, 1960, as amended at 37 FR 1472, Jan. 29, 1972; 52 FR 48985, Dec. 29, 1987; 57 FR 1102, Jan. 10, 1992; 59 FR 52700, Oct. 19, 1994; 87 FR 22446, Apr. 15, 2022]

§§ 270.20a-2—270.20a-4 [Reserved]

§ 270.22c-1 Pricing of redeemable securities for distribution, redemption and repurchase.

(a) No registered investment company issuing any redeemable security,

§ 270.22c–1

no person designated in such issuer's prospectus as authorized to consummate transactions in any such security, and no principal underwriter of, or dealer in, any such security shall sell, redeem, or repurchase any such security except at a price based on the current net asset value of such security which is next computed after receipt of a tender of such security for redemption or of an order to purchase or sell such security: *Provided,* That:

(1) This paragraph shall not prevent a sponsor of a unit investment trust (hereinafter referred to as the "Trust") engaged exclusively in the business of investing in eligible trust securities (as defined in Rule 14a–3(b) (17 CFR 270.14a–3(b))) from selling or repurchasing Trust units in a secondary market at a price based on the offering side evaluation of the eligible trust securities in the Trust's portfolio, determined at any time on the last business day of each week, effective for all sales made during the following week, if on the days that such sales or repurchases are made the sponsor receives a letter from a qualified evaluator stating, in its opinion, that:

(i) In the case of repurchases, the current bid price is not higher than the offering side evaluation, computed on the last business day of the previous week; and

(ii) In the case of resales, the offering side evaluation, computed as of the last business day of the previous week, is not more than one-half of one percent ($5.00 on a unit representing $1,000 principal amount of eligible trust securities) greater than the current offering price.

(2) This paragraph shall not prevent any registered investment company from adjusting the price of its redeemable securities sold pursuant to a merger, consolidation or purchase of substantially all of the assets of a company which meets the conditions specified in § 270.17a–8.

(3) Notwithstanding this paragraph (a), a registered open-end management investment company (but not a registered open-end management investment company that is regulated as a money market fund under § 270.2a–7 or an exchange-traded fund as defined in paragraph (a)(3)(v)(A) of this section) (a "fund") may use swing pricing to adjust its current net asset value per share to mitigate dilution of the value of its outstanding redeemable securities as a result of shareholder purchase or redemption activity, provided that it has established and implemented swing pricing policies and procedures in compliance with the paragraphs (a)(3)(i) through (v) of this section.

(i) The fund's swing pricing policies and procedures must:

(A) Provide that the fund must adjust its net asset value per share by a single swing factor or multiple factors that may vary based on the swing threshold(s) crossed once the level of net purchases into or net redemptions from such fund has exceeded the applicable swing threshold for the fund. In determining whether the fund's level of net purchases or net redemptions has exceeded the applicable swing threshold(s), the person(s) responsible for administering swing pricing shall be permitted to make such determination based on receipt of sufficient information about the fund investors' daily purchase and redemption activity ("investor flow") to allow the fund to reasonably estimate whether it has crossed the swing threshold(s) with high confidence, and shall exclude any purchases or redemptions that are made in kind and not in cash. This investor flow information may consist of individual, aggregated, or netted orders, and may include reasonable estimates where necessary.

(B) Specify the process for how the fund's swing threshold(s) shall be determined, considering:

(1) The size, frequency, and volatility of historical net purchases or net redemptions of fund shares during normal and stressed periods;

(2) The fund's investment strategy and the liquidity of the fund's portfolio investments;

(3) The fund's holdings of cash and cash equivalents, and borrowing arrangements and other funding sources; and

(4) The costs associated with transactions in the markets in which the fund invests.

(C) Specify the process for how the swing factor(s) shall be determined, which must include: The establishment

Securities and Exchange Commission § 270.22c–1

of an upper limit on the swing factor(s) used, which may not exceed two percent of net asset value per share; and the determination that the factor(s) used are reasonable in relationship to the costs discussed in this paragraph. In determining the swing factor(s) and the upper limit, the person(s) responsible for administering swing pricing may take into account only the near-term costs expected to be incurred by the fund as a result of net purchases or net redemptions that occur on the day the swing factor(s) is used, including spread costs, transaction fees and charges arising from asset purchases or asset sales resulting from those purchases or redemptions, and borrowing-related costs associated with satisfying redemptions.

(ii) The fund's board of directors, including a majority of directors who are not interested persons of the fund must:

(A) Approve the fund's swing pricing policies and procedures;

(B) Approve the fund's swing threshold(s) and the upper limit on the swing factor(s) used, and any changes to the swing threshold(s) or the upper limit on the swing factor(s) used;

(C) Designate the fund's investment adviser, officer, or officers responsible for administering the swing pricing policies and procedures ("person(s) responsible for administering swing pricing"). The administration of swing pricing must be reasonably segregated from portfolio management of the fund and may not include portfolio managers; and

(D) Review, no less frequently than annually, a written report prepared by the person(s) responsible for administering swing pricing that describes:

(*1*) Its review of the adequacy of the fund's swing pricing policies and procedures and the effectiveness of their implementation, including the impact on mitigating dilution;

(*2*) Any material changes to the fund's swing pricing policies and procedures since the date of the last report; and

(*3*) Its review and assessment of the fund's swing threshold(s), swing factor(s), and swing factor upper limit considering the requirements of paragraphs (a)(3)(i)(B) and (C) of this section, including the information and data supporting the determination of the swing threshold(s), swing factor(s), and swing factor upper limit.

(iii) The fund shall maintain the policies and procedures adopted by the fund under this paragraph (a)(3) that are in effect, or at any time within the past six years were in effect, in an easily accessible place, and shall maintain a written copy of the report provided to the board under paragraph (a)(3)(ii)(C) of this section for six years, the first two in an easily accessible place.

(iv) Any fund (a "feeder fund") that invests, pursuant to section 12(d)(1)(E) of the Act (15 U.S.C. 80a–12(d)(1)(E)), in another fund (a "master fund") may not use swing pricing to adjust the feeder fund's net asset value per share; however, a master fund may use swing pricing to adjust the master fund's net asset value per share, pursuant to the requirements set forth in this paragraph (a)(3).

(v) For purposes of this paragraph (a)(3):

(A) *Exchange-traded fund* means an open-end management investment company (or series or class thereof), the shares of which are listed and traded on a national securities exchange, and that has formed and operates under an exemptive order under the Act granted by the Commission or in reliance on an exemptive rule adopted by the Commission.

(B) *Swing factor* means the amount, expressed as a percentage of the fund's net asset value and determined pursuant to the fund's swing pricing policies and procedures, by which a fund adjusts its net asset value per share once a fund's applicable swing threshold has been exceeded.

(C) *Swing pricing* means the process of adjusting a fund's current net asset value per share to mitigate dilution of the value of its outstanding redeemable securities as a result of shareholder purchase and redemption activity, pursuant to the requirements set forth in this paragraph (a)(3).

(D) *Swing threshold* means an amount of net purchases or net redemptions, expressed as a percentage of the fund's net asset value, that triggers the application of swing pricing.

455

§ 270.22c-2

(E) *Transaction fees and charges* means brokerage commissions, custody fees, and any other charges, fees, and taxes associated with portfolio asset purchases and sales.

(b) For the purposes of this section,

(1) The current net asset value of any such security shall be computed no less frequently than once daily, Monday through Friday, at the specific time or times during the day that the board of directors of the investment company sets, in accordance with paragraph (d) of this section, except on:

(i) Days on which changes in the value of the investment company's portfolio securities will not materially affect the current net asset value of the investment company's redeemable securities;

(ii) Days during which no security is tendered for redemption and no order to purchase or sell such security is received by the investment company; or

(iii) Customary national business holidays described or listed in the prospectus and local and regional business holidays listed in the prospectus; and

(2) A "qualified evaluator" shall mean any evaluator which represents it is in a position to determine, on the basis of an informal evaluation of the eligible trust securities held in the Trust's portfolio, whether—

(i) The current bid price is higher than the offering side evaluation, computed on the last business day of the previous week, and

(ii) The offering side evaluation, computed as of the last business day of the previous week, is more than one-half of one percent ($5.00 on a unit representing $1,000 principal amount of eligible trust securities) greater than the current offering price.

(c) Notwithstanding the provisions above, any registered separate account offering variable annuity contracts, any person designated in such account's prospectus as authorized to consummate transactions in such contracts, and any principal underwriter of or dealer in such contracts shall be permitted to apply the initial purchase payment for any such contract at a price based on the current net asset value of such contract which is next computed:

(1) Not later than two business days after receipt of the order to purchase by the insurance company sponsoring the separate account ("insurer"), if the contract application and other information necessary for processing the order to purchase (collectively, "application") are complete upon receipt; or

(2) Not later than two business days after an application which is incomplete upon receipt by the insurer is made complete, *Provided*, That, if an incomplete application is not made complete within five business days after receipt,

(i) The prospective purchaser shall be informed of the reasons for the delay, and

(ii) The initial purchase payment shall be returned immediately and in full, unless the prospective purchaser specifically consents to the insurer retaining the purchase payment until the application is made complete.

(3) As used in this section:

(i) *Prospective Purchaser* shall mean either an individual contractowner or an individual participant in a group contract.

(ii) *Initial Purchase Payment* shall refer to the first purchase payment submitted to the insurer by, or on behalf of, a prospective purchaser.

(d) The board of directors shall initially set the time or times during the day that the current net asset value shall be computed, and shall make and approve such changes as the board deems necessary.

(Secs. 6(c), 22(c) and 38(a), 15 U.S.C. 80a-6(c), 80a-22(c) and 80a-37(a))

[44 FR 29647, May 22, 1979, as amended at 44 FR 48660, Aug. 20, 1979; 45 FR 12409, Feb. 26, 1980; 50 FR 7911, Feb. 27, 1985; 50 FR 24763, June 13, 1985; 50 FR 42682, Oct. 22, 1985; 58 FR 49922, Sept. 24, 1993; 81 FR 82137, Nov. 18, 2016; 87 FR 22446, Apr. 15, 2022]

§ 270.22c-2 Redemption fees for redeemable securities.

(a) *Redemption fee.* It is unlawful for any fund issuing redeemable securities, its principal underwriter, or any dealer in such securities, to redeem a redeemable security issued by the fund within seven calendar days after the security was purchased, unless it complies with the following requirements:

Securities and Exchange Commission

§ 270.22c-2

(1) *Board determination.* The fund's board of directors, including a majority of directors who are not interested persons of the fund, must either:

(i) Approve a redemption fee, in an amount (but no more than two percent of the value of shares redeemed) and on shares redeemed within a time period (but no less than seven calendar days), that in its judgment is necessary or appropriate to recoup for the fund the costs it may incur as a result of those redemptions or to otherwise eliminate or reduce so far as practicable any dilution of the value of the outstanding securities issued by the fund, the proceeds of which fee will be retained by the fund; or

(ii) Determine that imposition of a redemption fee is either not necessary or not appropriate.

(2) *Shareholder information.* With respect to each financial intermediary that submits orders, itself or through its agent, to purchase or redeem shares directly to the fund, its principal underwriter or transfer agent, or to a registered clearing agency, the fund (or on the fund's behalf, the principal underwriter or transfer agent) must either:

(i) Enter into a shareholder information agreement with the financial intermediary (or its agent); or

(ii) Prohibit the financial intermediary from purchasing in nominee name on behalf of other persons, securities issued by the fund. For purposes of this paragraph, "purchasing" does not include the automatic reinvestment of dividends.

(3) *Recordkeeping.* The fund must maintain a copy of the written agreement under paragraph (a)(2)(i) of this section that is in effect, or at any time within the past six years was in effect, in an easily accessible place.

(b) *Excepted funds.* The requirements of paragraph (a) of this section do not apply to the following funds, unless they elect to impose a redemption fee pursuant to paragraph (a)(1) of this section:

(1) Money market funds;

(2) Any fund that issues securities that are listed on a national securities exchange; and

(3) Any fund that affirmatively permits short-term trading of its securities, if its prospectus clearly and prominently discloses that the fund permits short-term trading of its securities and that such trading may result in additional costs for the fund.

(c) *Definitions.* For the purposes of this section:

(1) *Financial intermediary* means:

(i) Any broker, dealer, bank, or other person that holds securities issued by the fund, in nominee name;

(ii) A unit investment trust or fund that invests in the fund in reliance on section 12(d)(1)(E) of the Act (15 U.S.C. 80a–12(d)(1)(E)); and

(iii) In the case of a participant-directed employee benefit plan that owns the securities issued by the fund, a retirement plan's administrator under section 3(16)(A) of the Employee Retirement Income Security Act of 1974 (29 U.S.C. 1002(16)(A)) or any person that maintains the plan's participant records.

(iv) *Financial intermediary* does not include any person that the fund treats as an individual investor with respect to the fund's policies established for the purpose of eliminating or reducing any dilution of the value of the outstanding securities issued by the fund.

(2) *Fund* means an open-end management investment company that is registered or required to register under section 8 of the Act (15 U.S.C. 80a–8), and includes a separate series of such an investment company.

(3) *Money market fund* means an open-end management investment company that is registered under the Act and is regulated as a money market fund under § 270.2a–7.

(4) *Shareholder* includes a beneficial owner of securities held in nominee name, a participant in a participant-directed employee benefit plan, and a holder of interests in a fund or unit investment trust that has invested in the fund in reliance on section 12(d)(1)(E) of the Act. A shareholder does not include a fund investing pursuant to section 12(d)(1)(G) of the Act (15 U.S.C. 80a–12(d)(1)(G)), a trust established pursuant to section 529 of the Internal Revenue Code (26 U.S.C. 529), or a holder of an interest in such a trust.

(5) *Shareholder information agreement* means a written agreement under which a financial intermediary agrees to:

§ 270.22d-1

(i) Provide, promptly upon request by a fund, the Taxpayer Identification Number (or in the case of non U.S. shareholders, if the Taxpayer Identification Number is unavailable, the International Taxpayer Identification Number or other government issued identifier) of all shareholders who have purchased, redeemed, transferred, or exchanged fund shares held through an account with the financial intermediary, and the amount and dates of such shareholder purchases, redemptions, transfers, and exchanges;

(ii) Execute any instructions from the fund to restrict or prohibit further purchases or exchanges of fund shares by a shareholder who has been identified by the fund as having engaged in transactions of fund shares (directly or indirectly through the intermediary's account) that violate policies established by the fund for the purpose of eliminating or reducing any dilution of the value of the outstanding securities issued by the fund; and

(iii) Use best efforts to determine, promptly upon request of the fund, whether any specific person about whom it has received the identification and transaction information set forth in paragraph (c)(5)(i) of this section, is itself a financial intermediary ("indirect intermediary") and, upon further request by the fund:

(A) Provide (or arrange to have provided) the identification and transaction information set forth in paragraph (c)(5)(i) of this section regarding shareholders who hold an account with an indirect intermediary; or

(B) Restrict or prohibit the indirect intermediary from purchasing, in nominee name on behalf of other persons, securities issued by the fund.

[71 FR 58272, Oct. 3, 2006]

§ 270.22d-1 Exemption from section 22(d) to permit sales of redeemable securities at prices which reflect sales loads set pursuant to a schedule.

A registered investment company that is the issuer of redeemable securities, a principal underwriter of such securities or a dealer therein shall be exempt from the provisions of section 22(d) to the extent necessary to permit the sale of such securities at prices that reflect scheduled variations in, or elimination of, the sales load. These price schedules may offer such variations in or elimination of the sales load to particular classes of investors or transactions, *Provided,* That:

(a) The company, the principal underwriter and dealers in the company's shares apply any scheduled variation uniformly to all offerees in the class specified;

(b) The company furnishes to existing shareholders and prospective investors adequate information concerning any scheduled variation, as prescribed in applicable registration statement form requirements;

(c) Before making any new sales load variation available to purchasers of the company's shares, the company revises its prospectus and statement of additional information to describe that new variation; and

(d) The company advises existing shareholders of any new sales load variation within one year of the date when that variation is first made available to purchasers of the company's shares.

(Secs. 6(c) (15 U.S.C. 80a–6(c)) and 38(a) (15 U.S.C. 80a–37(a)))

[50 FR 7911, Feb. 27, 1985]

§ 270.22d-2 Exemption from section 22(d) for certain registered separate accounts.

A registered separate account, any principal underwriter for such account, any dealer in contracts or units of interest or participations in such contracts issued by such account and any insurance company maintaining such account shall, with respect to any variable annuity contracts, units, or participations therein issued by such account, be exempted from section 22(d) to the extent necessary to permit the sale of such contracts, units or participations by such persons at prices which reflect variations in the sales load or in any administrative charge or other deductions from the purchase payments; *Provided, however,* That (a) the prospectus discloses as precisely as possible the amount of the variations and the circumstances, if any, in which such variations shall be available or describes the basis for such variations and the manner in which entitlement shall be determined, and (b) any such

Securities and Exchange Commission § 270.22e-3

variations reflect differences in costs or services and are not unfairly discriminatory against any person.

(Secs. 6(c) (15 U.S.C. 80a–6(c)) and 38(a) (15 U.S.C. 80a–37(a)))

[40 FR 33970, Aug. 13, 1975. Redesignated at 50 FR 7911, Feb. 27, 1985]

§ 270.22e-1 Exemption from section 22(e) of the Act during annuity payment period of variable annuity contracts participating in certain registered separate accounts.

(a) A registered separate account, shall during the annuity payment period of variable annuity contracts participating in such account, be exempt from the provisions of section 22(e) of the Act prohibiting the suspension of the right of redemption or postponement of the date of payment or satisfaction upon redemption of any redeemable security, with respect to such contracts under which payments are being made based upon life contingencies.

(Sec. 6, 54 Stat. 800; 15 U.S.C. 80a–6)

[34 FR 12696, Aug. 5, 1969]

§ 270.22e-2 Pricing of redemption requests in accordance with Rule 22c-1.

An investment company shall not be deemed to have suspended the right of redemption if it prices a redemption request by computing the net asset value of the investment company's redeemable securities in accordance with the provisions of Rule 22c–1.

[50 FR 24764, June 13, 1985]

§ 270.22e-3 Exemption for liquidation of money market funds.

(a) *Exemption.* A registered open-end management investment company or series thereof ("fund") that is regulated as a money market fund under § 270.2a–7 is exempt from the requirements of section 22(e) of the Act (15 U.S.C. 80a–22(e)) if:

(1) The fund, at the end of a business day, has invested less than ten percent of its total assets in weekly liquid assets or, in the case of a fund that is a government money market fund, as defined in § 270.2a–7(a)(14) or a retail money market fund, as defined in § 270.2a–7(a)(21), the fund's price per share as computed for the purpose of distribution, redemption and repurchase, rounded to the nearest one percent, has deviated from the stable price established by the board of directors or the fund's board of directors, including a majority of directors who are not interested persons of the fund, determines that such a deviation is likely to occur;

(2) The fund's board of directors, including a majority of directors who are not interested persons of the fund, irrevocably has approved the liquidation of the fund; and

(3) The fund, prior to suspending redemptions, notifies the Commission of its decision to liquidate and suspend redemptions by electronic mail directed to the attention of the Director of the Division of Investment Management or the Director's designee.

(b) *Conduits.* Any registered investment company, or series thereof, that owns, pursuant to section 12(d)(1)(E) of the Act (15 U.S.C. 80a–12(d)(1)(E)), shares of a money market fund that has suspended redemptions of shares pursuant to paragraph (a) of this section also is exempt from the requirements of section 22(e) of the Act (15 U.S.C. 80a–22(e)). A registered investment company relying on the exemption provided in this paragraph must promptly notify the Commission that it has suspended redemptions in reliance on this section. Notification under this paragraph shall be made by electronic mail directed to the attention of the Director of the Division of Investment Management or the Director's designee.

(c) *Commission Orders.* For the protection of shareholders, the Commission may issue an order to rescind or modify the exemption provided by this section, after appropriate notice and opportunity for hearing in accordance with section 40 of the Act (15 U.S.C. 80a–39).

(d) *Definitions.* Each of the terms *business day, total assets,* and *weekly liquid assets* has the same meaning as defined in § 270.2a–7.

[75 FR 10117, Mar. 4, 2010, as amended at 79 FR 47967, Aug. 14, 2014; 87 FR 22446, Apr. 15, 2022]

§ 270.22e–4 Liquidity risk management programs.

(a) *Definitions.* For purposes of this section:

(1) *Acquisition (or acquire)* means any purchase or subsequent rollover.

(2) *Business day* means any day, other than Saturday, Sunday, or any customary business holiday.

(3) *Convertible to cash* means the ability to be sold, with the sale settled.

(4) *Exchange-traded fund* or *ETF* means an open-end management investment company (or series or class thereof), the shares of which are listed and traded on a national securities exchange, and that has formed and operates under an exemptive order under the Act granted by the Commission or in reliance on an exemptive rule adopted by the Commission.

(5) *Fund* means an open-end management investment company that is registered or required to register under section 8 of the Act (15 U.S.C. 80a–8) and includes a separate series of such an investment company, but does not include a registered open-end management investment company that is regulated as a money market fund under § 270.2a–7 or an In-Kind ETF.

(6) *Highly liquid investment* means any cash held by a fund and any investment that the fund reasonably expects to be convertible into cash in current market conditions in three business days or less without the conversion to cash significantly changing the market value of the investment, as determined pursuant to the provisions of paragraph (b)(1)(ii) of this section.

(7) *Highly liquid investment minimum* means the percentage of the fund's net assets that the fund invests in highly liquid investments that are assets pursuant to paragraph (b)(1)(iii) of this section.

(8) *Illiquid investment* means any investment that the fund reasonably expects cannot be sold or disposed of in current market conditions in seven calendar days or less without the sale or disposition significantly changing the market value of the investment, as determined pursuant to the provisions of paragraph (b)(1)(ii) of this section.

(9) *In-Kind Exchange Traded Fund* or *In-Kind ETF* means an ETF that meets redemptions through in-kind transfers of securities, positions, and assets other than a *de minimis* amount of cash and that publishes its portfolio holdings daily.

(10) *Less liquid investment* means any investment that the fund reasonably expects to be able to sell or dispose of in current market conditions in seven calendar days or less without the sale or disposition significantly changing the market value of the investment, as determined pursuant to the provisions of paragraph (b)(1)(ii) of this section, but where the sale or disposition is reasonably expected to settle in more than seven calendar days.

(11) *Liquidity risk* means the risk that the fund could not meet requests to redeem shares issued by the fund without significant dilution of remaining investors' interests in the fund.

(12) *Moderately liquid investment* means any investment that the fund reasonably expects to be convertible into cash in current market conditions in more than three calendar days but in seven calendar days or less, without the conversion to cash significantly changing the market value of the investment, as determined pursuant to the provisions of paragraph (b)(1)(ii) of this section.

(13) *Person(s) designated to administer the program* means the fund or In-Kind ETF's investment adviser, officer, or officers (which may not be solely portfolio managers of the fund or In-Kind ETF) responsible for administering the program and its policies and procedures pursuant to paragraph (b)(2)(ii) of this section.

(14) *Unit Investment Trust* or *UIT* means a unit investment trust as defined in section 4(2) of the Act (15 U.S.C. 80a–4).

(b) *Liquidity Risk Management Program.* Each fund and In-Kind ETF must adopt and implement a written liquidity risk management program ("program") that is reasonably designed to assess and manage its liquidity risk.

(1) *Required program elements.* The program must include policies and procedures reasonably designed to incorporate the following elements:

(i) *Assessment, management, and periodic review of liquidity risk.* Each fund and In-Kind ETF must assess, manage,

Securities and Exchange Commission

§ 270.22e-4

and periodically review (with such review occurring no less frequently than annually) its liquidity risk, which must include consideration of the following factors, as applicable:

(A) The fund or In-Kind ETF's investment strategy and liquidity of portfolio investments during both normal and reasonably foreseeable stressed conditions, including whether the investment strategy is appropriate for an open-end fund, the extent to which the strategy involves a relatively concentrated portfolio or large positions in particular issuers, and the use of borrowings for investment purposes and derivatives;

(B) Short-term and long-term cash flow projections during both normal and reasonably foreseeable stressed conditions;

(C) Holdings of cash and cash equivalents, as well as borrowing arrangements and other funding sources; and

(D) For an ETF:

(*1*) The relationship between the ETF's portfolio liquidity and the way in which, and the prices and spreads at which, ETF shares trade, including, the efficiency of the arbitrage function and the level of active participation by market participants (including authorized participants); and

(*2*) The effect of the composition of baskets on the overall liquidity of the ETF's portfolio.

(ii) *Classification.* Each fund must, using information obtained after reasonable inquiry and taking into account relevant market, trading, and investment-specific considerations, classify each of the fund's portfolio investments (including each of the fund's derivatives transactions) as a highly liquid investment, moderately liquid investment, less liquid investment, or illiquid investment. A fund must review its portfolio investments' classifications, at least monthly in connection with reporting the liquidity classification for each portfolio investment on Form N-PORT in accordance with § 270.30b1-9, and more frequently if changes in relevant market, trading, and investment-specific considerations are reasonably expected to materially affect one or more of its investments' classifications.

NOTE TO PARAGRAPH (b)(1)(ii)INTRODUCTORY TEXT: If an investment could be viewed as either a highly liquid investment or a moderately liquid investment, because the period to convert the investment to cash depends on the calendar or business day convention used, a fund should classify the investment as a highly liquid investment. For a discussion of considerations that may be relevant in classifying the liquidity of the fund's portfolio investments, see Investment Company Act Release No. IC-32315 (Oct. 13, 2016).

(A) The fund may generally classify and review its portfolio investments (including the fund's derivatives transactions) according to their asset class, provided, however, that the fund must separately classify and review any investment within an asset class if the fund or its adviser has information about any market, trading, or investment-specific considerations that are reasonably expected to significantly affect the liquidity characteristics of that investment as compared to the fund's other portfolio holdings within that asset class.

(B) In classifying and reviewing its portfolio investments or asset classes (as applicable), the fund must determine whether trading varying portions of a position in a particular portfolio investment or asset class, in sizes that the fund would reasonably anticipate trading, is reasonably expected to significantly affect its liquidity, and if so, the fund must take this determination into account when classifying the liquidity of that investment or asset class.

(C) For derivatives transactions that the fund has classified as moderately liquid investments, less liquid investments, and illiquid investments, identify the percentage of the fund's highly liquid investments that it has pledged as margin or collateral in connection with derivatives transactions in each of these classification categories.

NOTE TO PARAGRAPH (b)(1)(ii)(C): For purposes of calculating these percentages, a fund that has pledged highly liquid investments and non-highly liquid investments as margin or collateral in connection with derivatives transactions classified as moderately liquid, less liquid, or illiquid investments first should apply pledged assets that are highly liquid investments in connection

§ 270.22e–4

with these transactions, unless it has specifically identified non-highly liquid investments as margin or collateral in connection with such derivatives transactions.

(iii) *Highly liquid investment minimum.* (A) Any fund that does not primarily hold assets that are highly liquid investments must:

(*1*) Determine a highly liquid investment minimum, considering the factors specified in paragraphs (b)(1)(i)(A) through (D) of this section, as applicable (but considering those factors specified in paragraphs (b)(1)(i)(A) and (B) only as they apply during normal conditions, and during stressed conditions only to the extent they are reasonably foreseeable during the period until the next review of the highly liquid investment minimum). The highly liquid investment minimum determined pursuant to this paragraph may not be changed during any period of time that a fund's assets that are highly liquid investments are below the determined minimum without approval from the fund's board of directors, including a majority of directors who are not interested persons of the fund;

(*2*) Periodically review, no less frequently than annually, the highly liquid investment minimum; and

(*3*) Adopt and implement policies and procedures for responding to a shortfall of the fund's highly liquid investments below its highly liquid investment minimum, which must include requiring the person(s) designated to administer the program to report to the fund's board of directors no later than its next regularly scheduled meeting with a brief explanation of the causes of the shortfall, the extent of the shortfall, and any actions taken in response, and if the shortfall lasts more than 7 consecutive calendar days, must include requiring the person(s) designated to administer the program to report to the board within one business day thereafter with an explanation of how the fund plans to restore its minimum within a reasonable period of time.

(B) For purposes of determining whether a fund primarily holds assets that are highly liquid investments, a fund must exclude from its calculations the percentage of the fund's assets that are highly liquid investments that it has pledged as margin or collateral in connection with derivatives transactions that the fund has classified as moderately liquid investments, less liquid investments, and illiquid investments, as determined pursuant to paragraph (b)(1)(ii)(C) of this section.

(iv) *Illiquid investments.* No fund or In-Kind ETF may acquire any illiquid investment if, immediately after the acquisition, the fund or In-Kind ETF would have invested more than 15% of its net assets in illiquid investments that are assets. If a fund or In-Kind ETF holds more than 15% of its net assets in illiquid investments that are assets:

(A) It must cause the person(s) designated to administer the program to report such an occurrence to the fund's or In-Kind ETF's board of directors within one business day of the occurrence, with an explanation of the extent and causes of the occurrence, and how the fund or In-Kind ETF plans to bring its illiquid investments that are assets to or below 15% of its net assets within a reasonable period of time; and

(B) If the amount of the fund's or In-Kind ETF's illiquid investments that are assets is still above 15% of its net assets 30 days from the occurrence (and at each consecutive 30 day period thereafter), the fund or In-Kind ETF's board of directors, including a majority of directors who are not interested persons of the fund or In-Kind ETF, must assess whether the plan presented to it pursuant to paragraph (b)(1)(iv)(A) continues to be in the best interest of the fund or In-Kind ETF.

(v) *Redemptions in Kind.* A fund that engages in, or reserves the right to engage in, redemptions in kind and any In-Kind ETF must establish policies and procedures regarding how and when it will engage in such redemptions in kind.

(2) *Board oversight.* A fund or In-Kind ETF's board of directors, including a majority of directors who are not interested persons of the fund or In-Kind ETF, must:

(i) Initially approve the liquidity risk management program;

(ii) Approve the designation of the person(s) designated to administer the program; and

(iii) Review, no less frequently than annually, a written report prepared by the person(s) designated to administer the program that addresses the operation of the program and assesses its adequacy and effectiveness of implementation, including, if applicable, the operation of the highly liquid investment minimum, and any material changes to the program.

(3) *Recordkeeping.* The fund or In-Kind ETF must maintain:

(i) A written copy of the program and any associated policies and procedures adopted pursuant to paragraphs (b)(1) through (b)(2) of this section that are in effect, or at any time within the past five years were in effect, in an easily accessible place;

(ii) Copies of any materials provided to the board of directors in connection with its approval under paragraph (b)(2)(i) of this section, and materials provided to the board of directors under paragraph (b)(2)(iii) of this section, for at least five years after the end of the fiscal year in which the documents were provided, the first two years in an easily accessible place; and

(iii) If applicable, a written record of the policies and procedures related to how the highly liquid investment minimum, and any adjustments thereto, were determined, including assessment of the factors incorporated in paragraphs (b)(1)(iii)(A) through (B) of this section and any materials provided to the board pursuant to paragraph (b)(1)(iii)(A)(*3*) of this section, for a period of not less than five years (the first two years in an easily accessible place) following the determination of, and each change to, the highly liquid investment minimum.

(c) *UIT liquidity.* On or before the date of initial deposit of portfolio securities into a registered UIT, the UIT's principal underwriter or depositor must determine that the portion of the illiquid investments that the UIT holds or will hold at the date of deposit that are assets is consistent with the redeemable nature of the securities it issues, and must maintain a record of that determination for the life of the UIT and for five years thereafter.

[81 FR 82264, Nov. 18, 2016, as amended at 85 FR 83295, Dec. 21, 2020]

§ 270.23c-1 Repurchase of securities by closed-end companies.

(a) A registered closed-end company may purchase for cash a security of which it is the issuer, subject to the following conditions:

(1) If the security is a stock entitled to cumulative dividends, such dividends are not in arrears.

(2) If the security is a stock not entitled to cumulative dividends, at least 90 percent of the net income of the issuer for the last preceding fiscal year, determined in accordance with good accounting practice and not including profits or losses realized from the sale of securities or other properties, was distributed to its shareholders during such fiscal year or within 60 days after the close of such fiscal year.

(3) If the security to be purchased is junior to any class of outstanding security of the issuer representing indebtedness (except notes or other evidences of indebtedness held by a bank or other person, the issuance of which did not involve a public offering) all securities of such class shall have an asset coverage of at least 300 percent immediately after such purchase; and if the security to be purchased is junior to any class of outstanding senior security of the issuer which is a stock, all securities of such class shall have an asset coverage of at least 200 percent immediately after such purchase, and shall not be in arrears as to dividends.

(4) The seller of the security is not to the knowledge of the issuer an affiliated person of the issuer.

(5) Payment of the purchase price is accompanied or preceded by a written confirmation of the purchase.

(6) The purchase is made at a price not above the market value, if any, or the asset value of such security, whichever is lower, at the time of such purchase.

(7) The issuer discloses to the seller or, if the seller is acting through a broker, to the seller's broker, either prior to or at the time of purchase the approximate or estimated asset coverage per unit of the security to be purchased.

(8) No brokerage commission is paid by the issuer to any affiliated person of the issuer in connection with the purchase.

§ 270.23c-2

(9) The purchase is not made in a manner or on a basis which discriminates unfairly against any holders of the class of securities purchased.

(10) If the security is a stock, the issuer has, within the preceding six months, informed stockholders of its intention to purchase stock of such class by letter or report addressed to all the stockholders of such class.

(11) The issuer files with the Commission, as an exhibit to Form N-CSR (§ 249.331 and § 274.128), a copy of any written solicitation to purchase securities under this section sent or given during the period covered by the report by or on behalf of the issuer to 10 or more persons.

(b) Notwithstanding the conditions of paragraph (a) of this section, a closed-end company may purchase fractional interests in, or fractional rights to receive, any security of which it is the issuer.

(c) This rule does not apply to purchase of securities made pursuant to section 23(c)(1) or (2) of the Act (54 Stat. 825; 15 U.S.C. 80a-23). A registered closed-end company may file an application with the Commission for an order under section 23(c)(3) of the Act permitting the purchase of any security of which it is the issuer which does not meet the conditions of this rule and which is not to be made pursuant to section 23(c)(1) or (2) of the Act.

(d) This rule relates exclusively to the requirements of section 23(c) of the Act, and the provisions hereof shall not be construed to authorize any action which contravenes any other applicable law, statutory or otherwise, or the provision of any indenture or other instrument pursuant to which securities of the issuer were issued.

[Rule N-23C-1, 7 FR 10424, Dec. 15, 1942, as amended at 68 FR 64975, Nov. 17, 2003]

CROSS REFERENCE: For interpretative release applicable to § 270.23c-1, see No. 78 in tabulation, part 271 of this chapter.

§ 270.23c-2 Call and redemption of securities issued by registered closed-end companies.

(a) Notwithstanding the provisions of § 270.23c-1 (Rule N-23c-1), a registered closed-end investment company may call or redeem any securities of which it is the issuer, in accordance with the terms of such securities or the charter, indenture or other instrument pursuant to which such securities were issued: *Provided*, That, if less than all the outstanding securities of a class or series are to be called or redeemed the call or redemption shall be made by lot, on a pro rata basis, or in such other manner as will not discriminate unfairly against any holder of the securities of such class or series.

(b) A registered closed-end investment company which proposes to call or redeem any securities of which it is the issuer shall file with the Commission notice of its intention to call or redeem such securities at least 30 days prior to the date set for the call or redemption; *Provided, however*, That if notice of the call or the redemption is required to be published in a newspaper or otherwise, notice shall be given to the Commission at least 10 days in advance of the date of publication. Such notice shall be filed in triplicate and shall include (1) the title of the class of securities to be called or redeemed, (2) the date on which the securities are to be called or redeemed, (3) the applicable provisions of the governing instrument pursuant to which the securities are to be called or redeemed and, (4) if less than all the outstanding securities of a class or series are to be called or redeemed, the principal amount or number of shares and the basis upon which the securities to be called or redeemed are to be selected.

[Rule N-23C-2, 7 FR 6669, Aug. 25, 1942]

§ 270.23c-3 Repurchase offers by closed-end companies.

(a) *Definitions*. For purposes of this section:

(1) *Periodic interval* shall mean an interval of three, six, or twelve months.

(2) *Repurchase offer* shall mean an offer pursuant to this section by an investment company to repurchase common stock of which it is the issuer.

(3) *Repurchase offer amount* shall mean the amount of common stock that is the subject of a repurchase offer, expressed as a percentage of such stock outstanding on the repurchase request deadline, that an investment company offers to repurchase in a repurchase offer. The repurchase offer

Securities and Exchange Commission § 270.23c–3

amount shall not be less than five percent nor more than twenty-five percent of the common stock outstanding on a repurchase request deadline. Before each repurchase offer, the repurchase offer amount for that repurchase offer shall be determined by the directors of the company.

(4) *Repurchase payment deadline* with respect to a tender of common stock shall mean the date by which an investment company must pay securities holders for any stock repurchased. A repurchase payment deadline shall occur seven days after the repurchase pricing date applicable to such tender.

(5) *Repurchase pricing date* with respect to a tender of common stock shall mean the date on which an investment company determines the net asset value applicable to the repurchase of the securities. A repurchase pricing date shall occur no later than the fourteenth day after a repurchase request deadline, or the next business day if the fourteenth day is not a business day. In no event shall an investment company determine the net asset value applicable to the repurchase of the stock before the close of business on the repurchase request deadline.

(i) For an investment company making a repurchase offer pursuant to paragraph (b) of this section, the number of days between the repurchase request deadline and the repurchase pricing date for a repurchase offer shall be the maximum number specified by the company pursuant to paragraph (b)(2)(i)(D) of this section.

(ii) For an investment company making a repurchase offer pursuant to paragraph (c) of this section, the repurchase pricing date shall be such date as the company shall disclose to security holders in the notification pursuant to paragraph (b)(4) of this section with respect to such offer.

(iii) For purposes of paragraph (b)(1) of this section, a repurchase pricing date may be a date earlier than the date determined pursuant to paragraph (a)(5) (i) or (ii) of this section if, on or immediately following the repurchase request deadline, it appears that the use of an earlier repurchase pricing date is not likely to result in significant dilution of the net asset value of either stock that is tendered for repurchase or stock that is not tendered.

(6) *Repurchase request* shall mean the tender of common stock in response to a repurchase offer.

(7) *Repurchase request deadline* with respect to a repurchase offer shall mean the date by which an investment company must receive repurchase requests submitted by security holders in response to that offer or withdrawals or modifications of previously submitted repurchase requests. The first repurchase request deadline after the effective date of the registration statement for the common stock that is the subject of a repurchase offer, or after a shareholder vote adopting the fundamental policy specifying a company's periodic interval, whichever is later, shall occur no later than two periodic intervals thereafter.

(b) *Periodic repurchase offers.* A registered closed-end company or a business development company may repurchase common stock of which it is the issuer from the holders of the stock at periodic intervals, pursuant to repurchase offers made to all holders of the stock, *Provided* that:

(1) The company shall repurchase the stock for cash at the net asset value determined on the repurchase pricing date and shall pay the holders of the stock by the repurchase payment deadline except as provided in paragraph (b)(3) of this section. The company may deduct from the repurchase proceeds only a repurchase fee, not to exceed two percent of the proceeds, that is paid to the company and is reasonably intended to compensate the company for expenses directly related to the repurchase. A company may not condition a repurchase offer upon the tender of any minimum amount of shares.

(2)(i) The company shall repurchase the security pursuant to a fundamental policy, changeable only by a majority vote of the outstanding voting securities of the company, stating:

(A) That the company will make repurchase offers at periodic intervals pursuant to this section, as this section may be amended from time to time;

(B) The periodic intervals between repurchase request deadlines;

465

(C) The dates of repurchase request deadlines or the means of determining the repurchase request deadlines; and

(D) The maximum number of days between each repurchase request deadline and the next repurchase pricing date.

(ii) The company shall include a statement in its annual report to shareholders of the following:

(A) Its policy under paragraph (b)(2)(i) of this section; and

(B) With respect to repurchase offers by the company during the period covered by the annual report, the number of repurchase offers, the repurchase offer amount and the amount tendered in each repurchase offer, and the extent to which in any repurchase offer the company repurchased stock pursuant to the procedures in paragraph (b)(5) of this section.

(iii) A company shall be deemed to be making repurchase offers pursuant to a policy within paragraph (b)(2)(i) of this section if:

(A) The company makes repurchase offers to its security holders at periodic intervals and, before May 14, 1993, has disclosed in its registration statement its intention to make or consider making such repurchase offers; and

(B) The company's board of directors adopts a policy specifying the matters required by paragraph (b)(2)(i) of this section, and the periodic interval specified therein conforms generally to the frequency of the company's prior repurchase offers.

(3)(i) The company shall not suspend or postpone a repurchase offer except pursuant to a vote of a majority of the directors, including a majority of the directors who are not interested persons of the company, and only:

(A) If the repurchase would cause the company to lose its status as a regulated investment company under Subchapter M of the Internal Revenue Code [26 U.S.C. 851–860];

(B) If the repurchase would cause the stock that is the subject of the offer that is either listed on a national securities exchange or quoted in an inter-dealer quotation system of a national securities association to be neither listed on any national securities exchange nor quoted on any inter-dealer quotation system of a national securities association;

(C) For any period during which the New York Stock Exchange or any other market in which the securities owned by the company are principally traded is closed, other than customary week-end and holiday closings, or during which trading in such market is restricted;

(D) For any period during which an emergency exists as a result of which disposal by the company of securities owned by it is not reasonably practicable, or during which it is not reasonably practicable for the company fairly to determine the value of its net assets; or

(E) For such other periods as the Commission may by order permit for the protection of security holders of the company.

(ii) If a repurchase offer is suspended or postponed, the company shall provide notice to security holders of such suspension or postponement. If the company renews the repurchase offer, the company shall send a new notification to security holders satisfying the requirements of paragraph (b)(4) of this section.

(4)(i) No less than twenty-one and no more than forty-two days before each repurchase request deadline, the company shall send to each holder of record and to each beneficial owner of the stock that is the subject of the repurchase offer a notification providing the following information:

(A) A statement that the company is offering to repurchase its securities from security holders at net asset value;

(B) Any fees applicable to such repurchase;

(C) The repurchase offer amount;

(D) The dates of the repurchase request deadline, repurchase pricing date, and repurchase payment deadline, the risk of fluctuation in net asset value between the repurchase request deadline and the repurchase pricing date, and the possibility that the company may use an earlier repurchase pricing date pursuant to paragraph (a)(5)(iii) of this section;

(E) The procedures for security holders to tender their shares and the right of the security holders to withdraw or modify their tenders until the repurchase request deadline;

Securities and Exchange Commission § 270.23c–3

(F) The procedures under which the company may repurchase such shares on a pro rata basis pursuant to paragraph (b)(5) of this section;

(G) The circumstances in which the company may suspend or postpone a repurchase offer pursuant to paragraph (b)(3) of this section;

(H) The net asset value of the common stock computed no more than seven days before the date of the notification and the means by which security holders may ascertain the net asset value thereafter; and

(I) The market price, if any, of the common stock on the date on which such net asset value was computed, and the means by which security holders may ascertain the market price thereafter.

(ii) The company shall file three copies of the notification with the Commission within three business days after sending the notification to security holders. Those copies shall be accompanied by copies of Form N–23c–3 (§ 274.221 of this chapter) ("Notification of Repurchase Offer"). The format of the copies shall comply with the requirements for registration statements and reports under § 270.8b–12 of this chapter.

(iii) For purposes of sending a notification to a beneficial owner pursuant to paragraph (b)(4)(i) of this section, where the company knows that shares of common stock that is the subject of a repurchase offer are held of record by a broker, dealer, voting trustee, bank, association or other entity that exercises fiduciary powers in nominee name or otherwise, the company shall follow the procedures for transmitting materials to beneficial owners of securities that are set forth in § 240.14a–13 of this chapter.

(5) If security holders tender more than the repurchase offer amount, the company may repurchase an additional amount of stock not to exceed two percent of the common stock outstanding on the repurchase request deadline. If the company determines not to repurchase more than the repurchase offer amount, or if security holders tender stock in an amount exceeding the repurchase offer amount plus two percent of the common stock outstanding on the repurchase request deadline, the company shall repurchase the shares tendered on a pro rata basis; *Provided, however,* That this provision shall not prohibit the company from:

(i) Accepting all stock tendered by persons who own, beneficially or of record, an aggregate of not more than a specified number which is less than one hundred shares and who tender all of their stock, before prorating stock tendered by others; or

(ii) Accepting by lot stock tendered by security holders who tender all stock held by them and who, when tendering their stock, elect to have either all or none or at least a minimum amount or none accepted, if the company first accepts all stock tendered by security holders who do not so elect.

(6) The company shall permit tenders of stock for repurchase to be withdrawn or modified at any time until the repurchase request deadline but shall not permit tenders to be withdrawn or modified thereafter.

(7)(i) The current net asset value of the company's common stock shall be computed no less frequently than weekly on such day and at such specific time or times during the day that the board of directors of the company shall set.

(ii) The current net asset value of the company's common stock shall be computed daily on the five business days preceding a repurchase request deadline at such specific time or times during the day that the board of directors of the company shall set.

(iii) For purposes of section 23(b) [15 U.S.C. 80a–23(b)], the current net asset value applicable to a sale of common stock by the company shall be the net asset value next determined after receipt of an order to purchase such stock. During any period when the company is offering its common stock, the current net asset value of the common stock shall be computed no less frequently than once daily, Monday through Friday, at the specific time or times during the day that the board of directors of the company shall set, except on:

(A) Days on which changes in the value of the company's portfolio securities will not materially affect the current net asset value of the common stock;

(B) Days during which no order to purchase its common stock is received, other than days when the net asset value would otherwise be computed pursuant to paragraph (b)(7)(i) of this section; or

(C) Customary national, local, and regional business holidays described or listed in the prospectus.

(8) The board of directors of the investment company satisfies the fund governance standards defined in § 270.0–1(a)(7).

(9) Any senior security issued by the company or other indebtedness contracted by the company either shall mature by the next repurchase pricing date or shall provide for the redemption or call of such security or the repayment of such indebtedness by the company by the next repurchase pricing date, either in whole or in part, without penalty or premium, as necessary to permit the company to repurchase securities in such repurchase offer amount as the directors of the company shall determine in compliance with the asset coverage requirements of section 18 [15 U.S.C. 80a–18] or 61 [15 U.S.C. 80a–60], as applicable.

(10)(i) From the time a company sends a notification to shareholders pursuant to paragraph (b)(4) of this section until the repurchase pricing date, a percentage of the company's assets equal to at least 100 percent of the repurchase offer amount shall consist of assets that can be sold or disposed of in the ordinary course of business, at approximately the price at which the company has valued the investment, within a period equal to the period between a repurchase request deadline and the repurchase payment deadline, or of assets that mature by the next repurchase payment deadline.

(ii) In the event that the company's assets fail to comply with the requirements in paragraph (b)(10)(i) of this section, the board of directors shall cause the company to take such action as it deems appropriate to ensure compliance.

(iii) In supervising the company's operations and portfolio management by the investment adviser, the company's board of directors shall adopt written procedures reasonably designed, taking into account current market conditions and the company's investment objectives, to ensure that the company's portfolio assets are sufficiently liquid so that the company can comply with its fundamental policy on repurchases, and comply with the liquidity requirements of paragraph (b)(10)(i) of this section. The board of directors shall review the overall composition of the portfolio and make and approve such changes to the procedures as the board deems necessary.

(11) The company, or any underwriter for the company, shall comply, as if the company were an open-end company, with the provisions of section 24(b) [15 U.S.C. 80a–24(b)] and rules issued thereunder with respect to any advertisement, pamphlet, circular, form letter, or other sales literature addressed to or intended for distribution to prospective investors.

(c) *Discretionary repurchase offers.* A registered closed-end company or a business development company may repurchase common stock of which it is the issuer from the holders of the stock pursuant to a repurchase offer that is not made pursuant to a fundamental policy and that is made to all holders of the stock not earlier than two years after another offer pursuant to this paragraph (c) if the company complies with the requirements of paragraphs (b) (1), (3), (4), (5), (6), (7)(ii), (8), (10)(i), and (10)(ii) of this section.

(d) *Exemption from the definition of redeemable security.* A company that makes repurchase offers pursuant to paragraph (b) or (c) of this section shall not be deemed thereby to be an issuer of redeemable securities within section 2(a)(32) [15 U.S.C. 80a–2(a)(32)].

(e) *Registration of an indefinite amount of securities.* A company that makes repurchase offers pursuant to paragraph (b) of this section shall be deemed to have registered an indefinite amount of securities pursuant to Section 24(f) of the Act (15 U.S.C. 80a–24(f)) upon the effective date of its registration statement.

[58 FR 19343, Apr. 14, 1993; 58 FR 29695, May 21, 1993, as amended at 66 FR 3759, Jan. 16, 2001; 69 FR 46390, Aug. 2, 2004; 85 FR 33360, June 1, 2020]

Securities and Exchange Commission § 270.24e–1

§ 270.24b–1 Definitions.

(a) The term *form letter* as used in section 24(b) of the Act includes (1) one of a series of identical sales letters, and (2) any sales letter a substantial portion of which consists of a statement which is in essence identical with similar statements in sales letters sent to 25 or more persons within any period of 90 consecutive days.

(b) The term *distribution* as used in section 24(b) of the Act includes the distribution or redistribution to prospective investors of the content of any written sales literature, whether such distribution or redistribution is effected by means of written or oral representations or statements.

(c) The terms *rules and regulations* as used in section 24 (a) and (c) of the Act shall include the forms for registration of securities under the Securities Act of 1933 and the related instructions thereto.

(Sec. 19, 48 Stat. 85, as amended, sec. 319, 53 Stat. 1173; 15 U.S.C. 77s, 77sss)

[Rule N–24B–1, 6 FR 3020, June 21, 1941, as amended by 21 FR 1046, Feb. 15, 1956]

§ 270.24b–2 Filing copies of sales literature.

Copies of material filed with the Commission for the sole purpose of complying with section 24(b) of the Act (15 U.S.C. 80a–24(b)) either shall be accompanied by a letter of transmittal which makes appropriate references to said section or shall make such appropriate reference on the face of the material.

[70 FR 43570, July 27, 2005]

§ 270.24b–3 Sales literature deemed filed.

Any advertisement, pamphlet, circular, form letter or other sales literature addressed to or intended for distribution to prospective investors shall be deemed filed with the Commission for purposes of section 24(b) of the Act [15 U.S.C. 80a–24(b)] upon filing with a national securities association registered under section 15A of the Securities Exchange Act of 1934 [15 U.S.C. 78*o*] that has adopted rules providing standards for the investment company advertising practices of its members and has established and implemented procedures to review that advertising.

[53 FR 3880, Feb. 10, 1988]

§ 270.24b–4 Filing copies of covered investment fund research reports.

A covered investment fund research report, as defined in paragraph (c)(3) of § 230.139b of this chapter under the Securities Act of 1933 (15 U.S.C. 77a *et seq.*), of a covered investment fund registered as an investment company under the Act, shall not be subject to section 24(b) of the Act or the rules and regulations thereunder, except that such report shall be subject to such section and the rules and regulations thereunder to the extent that it is otherwise not subject to the content standards in the rules of any self-regulatory organization related to research reports, including those contained in the rules governing communications with the public regarding investment companies or substantially similar standards.

[83 FR 64222, Dec. 13, 2018]

§ 270.24e–1 Filing of certain prospectuses as post-effective amendments to registration statements under the Securities Act of 1933.

Section 24(e) of the Act requires that when a prospectus is revised so that it may be available for use in compliance with section 10(a)(3) of the Securities Act of 1933 for a period extending beyond the time when the previous prospectus would have ceased to be available for such use, such revised prospectus, in order to meet the requirements of section 10 of said Act, must be filed as an amendment to the registration statement under said Act and such amendment must have become effective prior to the use of the revised prospectus. Except as hereinabove provided, section 24(e) of the Act shall not be deemed to govern the times and conditions under which post-effective amendments shall be filed to registration statements under the Securities Act of 1933.

(Sec. 24, 54 Stat. 825, as amended; 15 U.S.C. 80a–24)

[20 FR 2856, Apr. 28, 1955, as amended at 62 FR 47938, Sept. 12, 1997]

§ 270.24f–2 Registration under the Securities Act of 1933 of certain investment company securities.

(a) *General.* Any face-amount certificate company, open-end management company, closed-end management company that makes periodic repurchase offers pursuant to § 270.23c–3(b), or unit investment trust ("issuer") that is deemed to have registered an indefinite amount of securities pursuant to Section 24(f) of the Act (15 U.S.C. 80a–24(f)) must not later than 90 days after the end of any fiscal year during which it has publicly offered such securities, file Form 24F–2 (17 CFR 274.24) with the Commission. Form 24F–2 must be prepared in accordance with the requirements of that form, and must be accompanied by the payment of a registration fee with respect to the securities sold during the fiscal year in reliance upon registration pursuant to section 24(f) of the Act calculated in the manner specified in section 24(f) of the Act and in the Form. An issuer that pays the registration fee more than 90 days after the end of its fiscal year must pay interest in the manner specified in section 24(f) of the Act and in Form 24F–2.

(b) *Issuer ceasing operations; mergers and other transactions.* For purposes of this section, if an issuer ceases operations, the date the issuer ceases operations will be deemed to be the end of its fiscal year. In the case of a liquidation, merger, or sale of all or substantially all of the assets ("merger") of the issuer, the issuer will be deemed to have ceased operations for the purposes of this section on the date the merger is consummated; *provided, however,* that in the case of a merger of an issuer or a series of an issuer ("Predecessor Issuer") with another issuer or a series of an issuer ("Successor Issuer"), the Predecessor Issuer will not be deemed to have ceased operations and the Successor issuer will assume the obligations, fees, and redemption credits of the Predecessor Issuer incurred pursuant to section 24(f) of the Act and § 270.24e–2 (as in effect prior to October 11, 1997; see 17 CFR part 240 to end, revised as of April 1, 1997) if the Successor Issuer:

(1) had no assets or liabilities, other than nominal assets or liabilities, and no operating history immediately prior to the merger;

(2) Acquired substantially all of the assets and assumed substantially all of the liabilities and obligations of the Predecessor Issuer; and

(3) The merger is not designed to result in the Predecessor Issuer merging with, or substantially all of its assets being acquired by, an issuer (or a series of an issuer) that would not meet the conditions of paragraph (b)(1) of this section.

(c) *Counting days.* To determine the date on which Form 24F–2 must be filed with the Commission under paragraph (a) of this section, the first day of the 90-day period is the first calendar day of the fiscal year following the fiscal year for which the Form is to be filed. If the last day of the 90-day period falls on a Saturday, Sunday, or federal holiday, the period ends on the first business day thereafter.

NOTE TO PARAGRAPH (c): For example, a Form 24F–2 for a fiscal year ending on June 30 must be filed no later than September 28. If September 28 falls on a Saturday, Sunday, the Form must be filed on the following Monday.

[62 FR 47938, Sept. 12, 1997, as amended at 85 FR 33360, June 1, 2020]

§ 270.26a–1 Payment of administrative fees to the depositor or principal underwriter of a unit investment trust; exemptive relief for separate accounts.

For purposes of section 26(a)(2)(C) of the Act, payment of a fee to the depositor of or a principal underwriter for a registered unit investment trust, or to any affiliated person or agent of such depositor or underwriter (collectively, "depositor"), for bookkeeping or other administrative services provided to the trust shall be allowed the custodian or trustee ("trustee") as an expense, provided that such fee is an amount not greater than the expenses, without profit:

(a) Actually paid by such depositor directly attributable to the services provided; and

Securities and Exchange Commission

§ 270.27d-1

(b) Increased by the services provided directly by such depositor, as determined in accordance with generally accepted accounting principles consistently applied.

[85 FR 26110, May 1, 2020]

§ 270.27c-1 [Reserved]

§ 270.27d-1 Reserve requirements for principal underwriters and depositors to carry out the obligations to refund charges required by section 27(d) and section 27(f) of the Act.

(a)(1) Every depositor of or principal underwriter for the issuer of a periodic payment plan certificate sold subject to section 27(d) or section 27(f) of the Act or both, shall deposit and maintain funds in a segregated trust account as a reserve and as security for the purpose of assuring the refund of charges required by sections 27(d) and 27(f) of the Act.

(2) The assets of such trust account may be held as cash or invested only in one or more of (i) government securities as defined in section 2(a)(16) of the Act (except equity securities) or (ii) negotiable certificates of deposit issued by a bank, as defined in section 2(a)(5) of the Act and having capital and surplus of at least $10 million: *Provided,* That no such investment may have a maturity of more than 5 years, no more than 50 percent of the assets may be invested in obligations having a maturity of more than 1 year, and certificates of deposit of a single issuer may not constitute more than 10 percent of the value of the assets in the account.

(3) Any income, gains, or losses from assets allocated to such account, whether or not realized, shall be credited to or charged against such account without regard to other income, gains, or losses of the depositor or principal underwriter.

(4) The assets of such trust account may be withdrawn only as permitted by paragraph (f) of this section and shall in no event be chargeable with liabilities arising out of any aspect of the business of the depositor or principal underwriter other than assuring the ability of the depositor or principal underwriter to refund the amounts required by such sections.

(b) For purposes of this section:

(1) "Excess sales load" on any payment is that portion of the sales load in excess of 15 percent of that payment.

(2) "Monthly payment" shall be the amount of the smallest monthly installment scheduled to be paid during the life of the plan. If payments are required or permitted to be made on a basis less frequently than monthly, an equivalent monthly payment shall be the amount determined by dividing the smallest minimum payment required or permitted in a payment period by the number of months included in such period.

(3) The assets in the segregated trust account shall be valued as follows: (i) With respect to securities for which market quotations are readily available, the market value of such securities; and (ii) with respect to other securities, fair value as determined in good faith by the depositor or principal underwriter.

(c) For every periodic payment plan certificate governed by section 27(d), the depositor or principal underwriter shall deposit into the segregated trust account not less than 45 percent of the excess sales load on each of the first six monthly payments or their equivalent.

(d) For all periodic payment plan certificates governed by section 27(d) which have not been surrendered in accordance with their terms, and for which the depositor or principal underwriter may be liable for the refund of any sales load, the depositor or principal underwriter shall maintain in the segregated trust account an amount equal to not less than 15% of the total refundable sales load on the payments made on those certificates. The depositor or principal underwriter shall also maintain in the segregated trust account such additional amounts as the Commission by order may require for the depositor or principal underwriter to carry out refund obligations pursuant to sections 27(d) and 27(f) of the Act.

(e) For every periodic payment plan certificate governed by section 27(f) of the Act, and for which the depositor or principal underwriter has no obligation to refund any excess sales load pursuant to section 27(d) of the Act, the depositor or principal underwriter shall deposit and maintain during the refund

§ 270.27d-2

period, at least the following amounts in the segregated trust account:

(1) For certificates that require monthly payments of $100 or less, 20 percent of the difference between the gross payments made and the net amount invested;

(2) For certificates that require monthly payments in excess of $100 and for single payment plan certificates, 30 percent of the difference between the gross payments made and the net amount invested;

(3) For certificates with respect to which the holder is entitled to receive the greater of the refund provided by section 27(f) (of the Act) or a refund of total payments and upon which a total of at least $1,000 has been paid, 100 percent of the difference between the gross payments made and net amount invested; and

(4) Such additional amounts as the Commission by order may require to carry out the obligation to refund charges pursuant to section 27(f) of the Act.

(f) Assets may be withdrawn from the segregated trust account by each depositor or principal underwriter:

(1) To refund excess sales load to a certificate holder exercising the right of surrender specified in section 27(d) of the Act; or

(2) To refund to a certificate holder exercising the right of withdrawal specified in section 27(f) of the Act the difference between the amount of his gross payments and the net amount invested; or

(3) For any other purpose: *Provided, however,* That such withdrawal shall not reduce the segregated trust account to an amount less than the sum of (i) 130 percent of the amount required to be maintained by paragraph (d) of this section, if any, and (ii) 100 percent of that amount required to be maintained by paragraph (e) of this section, if any.

(g) The minimum amounts required to be maintained by paragraphs (d) and (e) of this section shall be computed at least monthly. Any additional deposits required by paragraph (d) or (e) of this section shall be made immediately after such computation, and any withdrawals permitted by paragraph (f)(3) of this section may be made only at such time.

(h) Nothing in this section shall be construed to prohibit a depositor or principal underwriter, acting as such for two or more registered investment companies issuing periodic payment plan certificates, from combining in a single segregated trust account the reserves for such companies required by this section.

(i) The refunds required to be made to certificate holders pursuant to sections 27(d) and 27(f) (of the Act) shall be paid in cash not more than 7 days from the date the certificate is received in proper form by the custodian bank or such other paying agent as may be designated under the periodic payment plan.

(j) Each depositor or principal underwriter shall file with the Commission, within the appropriate period of time specified, an Accounting of Segregated Trust Account. Form N-27D-1 (§ 274.127d-1 of this chapter) is hereby prescribed as such accounting form.

[36 FR 13136, July 15, 1971, as amended at 40 FR 50712, Oct. 31, 1975]

§ 270.27d-2 [Reserved]

§ 270.27e-1 [Reserved]

§ 270.27f-1 [Reserved]

§ 270.27g-1 [Reserved]

§ 270.27h-1 [Reserved]

§ 270.27i-1 **Exemption from Section 27(i)(2)(A) of the Act during annuity payment period of variable annuity contracts participating in certain registered separate accounts.**

A registered separate account, and any depositor of or underwriter for such account, shall, during the annuity payment period of variable annuity contracts participating in such account, be exempt from the requirement of paragraph (1) of section 27(i)(2)(A) of the Act that a periodic payment plan certificate be a redeemable security.

[85 FR 26110, May 1, 2020]

Securities and Exchange Commission § 270.30a-3

§ 270.28b-1 Investment in loans partially or wholly guaranteed under the Servicemen's Readjustment Act of 1944, as amended.

(a) The term *qualified investments* as used in section 28(b) of the Investment Company Act of 1940 shall include:

(1) Any loan, any portion of which is guaranteed under Title III of the Servicemen's Readjustment Act of 1944, as amended, and which is secured by a first lien on real estate: *Provided,* The amount of the loan not so guaranteed does not exceed 66⅔ percent of the reasonable value of such real estate as determined by proper appraisal made by an appraiser designated by the Administrator of Veterans' Affairs;

(2) Any secondary loan the full amount of which is guaranteed under section 505(a) of Title III of the above mentioned act and which is secured by a second lien on real estate:

Provided, however, That any such loan shall be deemed a qualified investment only so long as (i) insurance policies are required to be procured and maintained in an amount sufficient to protect the security against the risks or hazards to which it may be subjected to the extent customary in the locality, and (ii) the loan shall remain guaranteed under Title III of the Servicemen's Readjustment Act of 1944, as amended, to the extent specified in paragraph (a) (1) or (2) of this section, as the case may be.

(b) Loans made pursuant to this section shall be valued at the original principal amount of the loan less all payments made thereon which have been applied to the reduction of such principal amount.

(Secs. 28(b), 38, 54 Stat. 832, 841; 15 U.S.C. 80a-28(b), 80a-38)

[Rule N-28B-1, 11 FR 6483, June 13, 1946]

§ 270.30a-1 Annual report for registered investment companies.

Every management investment company must file an annual report on Form N-CEN (§ 274.101 of this chapter) at least every twelve months and not more than seventy-five calendar days after the close of each fiscal year. Every unit investment trust must file an annual report on Form N-CEN (§ 274.101 of this chapter) at least every twelve months and not more than seventy-five calendar days after the close of each calendar year. A registered investment company that has filed a registration statement with the Commission registering its securities for the first time under the Securities Act of 1933 is relieved of this reporting obligation with respect to any reporting period or portion thereof prior to the date on which that registration statement becomes effective or is withdrawn.

[81 FR 82020, Nov. 18, 2016]

§ 270.30a-2 Certification of Form N-CSR.

(a) Each report filed on Form N-CSR (§§ 249.331 and 274.128 of this chapter) by a registered management investment company must include certifications in the form specified in Item 19(a)(3) of Form N-CSR, and such certifications must be filed as an exhibit to such report. Each principal executive and principal financial officer of the investment company, or persons performing similar functions, at the time of filing of the report must sign a certification.

(b) Each report on Form N-CSR filed by a registered management investment company under Section 13(a) or 15(d) of the Securities Exchange Act of 1934 (15 U.S.C. 78m(a) or 78o(d)) and that contains financial statements must be accompanied by the certifications required by Section 1350 of Chapter 63 of Title 18 of the United States Code (18 U.S.C. 1350) and such certifications must be furnished as an exhibit to such report as specified in Item 19(b) of Form N-CSR. Each principal executive and principal financial officer of the investment company (or equivalent thereof) must sign a certification. This requirement may be satisfied by a single certification signed by an investment company's principal executive and principal financial officers.

[87 FR 73141, Nov. 27, 2022]

§ 270.30a-3 Controls and procedures.

(a) Every registered management investment company, other than a small business investment company registered on Form N-5 (§§ 239.24 and 274.5

§ 270.30a–4

of this chapter), must maintain disclosure controls and procedures (as defined in paragraph (c) of this section) and internal control over financial reporting (as defined in paragraph (d) of this section).

(b) Each such registered management investment company's management must evaluate, with the participation of the company's principal executive and principal financial officers, or persons performing similar functions, the effectiveness of the company's disclosure controls and procedures, within the 90-day period prior to the filing date of each report on Form N-CSR (§§ 249.331 and 274.128 of this chapter).

(c) For purposes of this section, the term disclosure controls and procedures means controls and other procedures of a registered management investment company that are designed to ensure that information required to be disclosed by the investment company on Form N-CSR (§§ 249.331 and 274.128 of this chapter) is recorded, processed, summarized, and reported within the time periods specified in the Commission's rules and forms. Disclosure controls and procedures include, without limitation, controls and procedures designed to ensure that information required to be disclosed by an investment company in the reports that it files or submits on Form N-CSR is accumulated and communicated to the investment company's management, including its principal executive and principal financial officers, or persons performing similar functions, as appropriate to allow timely decisions regarding required disclosure.

(d) The term *internal control over financial reporting* is defined as a process designed by, or under the supervision of, the registered management investment company's principal executive and principal financial officers, or persons performing similar functions, and effected by the company's board of directors, management, and other personnel, to provide reasonable assurance regarding the reliability of financial reporting and the preparation of financial statements for external purposes in accordance with generally accepted accounting principles and includes those policies and procedures that:

(1) Pertain to the maintenance of records that in reasonable detail accurately and fairly reflect the transactions and dispositions of the assets of the investment company;

(2) Provide reasonable assurance that transactions are recorded as necessary to permit preparation of financial statements in accordance with generally accepted accounting principles, and that receipts and expenditures of the investment company are being made only in accordance with authorizations of management and directors of the investment company; and

(3) Provide reasonable assurance regarding prevention or timely detection of unauthorized acquisition, use, or disposition of the investment company's assets that could have a material effect on the financial statements.

[68 FR 36671, June 18, 2003, as amended at 69 FR 11264, Mar. 9, 2004; 81 FR 82021, Nov. 18, 2016]

§ 270.30a–4 Annual report for wholly-owned registered management investment company subsidiary of registered management investment company.

Notwithstanding the provisions of § 270.30a–1, a registered management investment company that is a wholly-owned subsidiary of a registered management investment company need not file an annual report on Form N–CEN if financial information with respect to that subsidiary is reported in the parent's annual report on Form N–CEN.

[81 FR 82021, Nov. 18, 2016]

§§ 270.30b1–1—270.b1–3 [Reserved]

§ 270.30b1–4 Report of proxy voting record.

Every registered management investment company, other than a small business investment company registered on Form N–5 (§§ 239.24 and 274.5 of this chapter), shall file an annual report on Form N–PX (§ 274.129 of this chapter) not later than August 31 of each year, containing the registrant's proxy voting record for the most recent twelve-month period ended June 30.

[68 FR 6581, Feb. 7, 2003]

EFFECTIVE DATE NOTE: At 87 FR 78809, Dec. 22, 2022, § 270.30b1–4 was amended by removing the phrase "Form N–PX (§ 274.129 of this

Securities and Exchange Commission

chapter)" and adding in its place "Form N–PX (§§ 249.326 and 274.129 of this chapter)", effective July 1, 2024.

§ 270.30b1–5 [Reserved]

§ 270.30b1–7 Monthly report for money market funds.

Every registered open-end management investment company, or series thereof, that is regulated as a money market fund under § 270.2a–7 must file with the Commission a monthly report of portfolio holdings on Form N–MFP (§ 274.201 of this chapter), current as of the last business day or any subsequent calendar day of the preceding month, no later than the fifth business day of each month.

[79 FR 47967, Aug. 14, 2014]

§ 270.30b1–8 Current report for money market funds.

Every registered open-end management investment company, or series thereof, that is regulated as a money market fund under § 270.2a–7, that experiences any of the events specified on Form N–CR (274.222 of this chapter), must file with the Commission a current report on Form N–CR within the period specified in that form.

[79 FR 47967, Aug. 14, 2014]

§ 270.30b1–9 Monthly report.

Each registered management investment company or exchange-traded fund organized as a unit investment trust, or series thereof, other than a registered open-end management investment company that is regulated as a money market fund under § 270.2a–7 or a small business investment company registered on Form N–5 (§§ 239.24 and 274.5 of this chapter), must file a monthly report of portfolio holdings on Form N–PORT (§ 274.150 of this chapter), current as of the last business day, or last calendar day, of the month. A registered investment company that has filed a registration statement with the Commission registering its securities for the first time under the Securities Act of 1933 is relieved of this reporting obligation with respect to any reporting period or portion thereof prior to the date on which that registration statement becomes effective or is withdrawn. Each registered investment company that is required to file reports on Form N–PORT must maintain in its records the information that is required to be included on Form N–PORT no later than 30 days after the end of each month. Such information shall be treated as a record under section 31(a)(1) of the Act [15 U.S.C. 80a–30(a)(1)] and § 270.31a–1(b) of this chapter subject to the requirements of § 270.31a–2(a)(2) of this chapter. Reports on Form N–PORT for each month in each fiscal quarter of a registered investment company must be filed with the Commission no later than 60 days after the end of such fiscal quarter.

§ 270.30b1–10

[84 FR 7987, Mar. 6, 2019]

§ 270.30b1–9(T) Temporary rule regarding monthly report.

(a) Until April 1, 2019, each registered management investment company subject to § 270.30b1–9 of this chapter must satisfy its reporting obligation under that section by maintaining in its records the information that is required to be included in Form N–PORT (§ 274.150 of this chapter).

(b) The information maintained in the registered management investment company's records under paragraph (a) of this section shall be treated as a record under section 31(a)(1) of the Act [15 U.S.C. 80a–30(a)(1)] and § 270.31a–1(b) of this chapter subject to the requirements of § 270.31a–2(a)(2) of this chapter.

(c) This section will expire and no longer be effective on March 31, 2026.

[82 FR 58739, Dec. 14, 2017]

EFFECTIVE DATE NOTE: At 82 FR 58739, Dec. 14, 2017, § 270.30b1–9(T) was added, effective Jan. 16, 2018, to Mar. 31, 2026.

§ 270.30b1–10 Current report for open-end and closed-end management investment companies.

Every registered open-end management investment company, or series thereof, and every registered closed-end management investment company, but not a fund that is regulated as a money market fund under § 270.2a–7, that experiences an event specified on Form N–RN, must file with the Commission a current report on Form N–

§ 270.30b2-1

RN within the period and according to the instructions specified in that form.

[85 FR 83295, Dec. 21, 2020]

§ 270.30b2-1 Filing of reports to stockholders.

(a) Every registered management investment company shall file a report on Form N-CSR (§§ 249.331 and 274.128 of this chapter) not later than 10 days after the transmission to stockholders of any report that is required to be transmitted to stockholders under § 270.30e-1.

(b) A registered investment company shall file with the Commission a copy of every periodic or interim report or similar communication containing financial statements that is transmitted by or on behalf of such registered investment company to any class of such company's security holders and that is not required to be filed with the Commission under paragraph (a) of this section. The filing shall be made not later than 10 days after the transmission to security holders.

[68 FR 5366, Feb. 3, 2003]

§ 270.30d-1 Filing of copies of reports to shareholders.

A registered management investment company, other than a small business investment company registered on Form N-5 (§§ 239.24 and 274.5 of this chapter), that is required to file annual and quarterly reports pursuant to section 13(a) or 15(d) of the Securities Exchange Act of 1934 (15 U.S.C. 78m(a) or 78o(d)) shall satisfy its requirement to file such reports by the filing, in accordance with the rules and procedures specified therefor, of reports on Form N-CSR (§§ 249.331 and 274.128 of this chapter). A registered unit investment trust or a small business investment company registered on Form N-5 that is required to file annual and quarterly reports pursuant to section 13(a) or 15(d) of the Securities Exchange Act of 1934 shall satisfy its requirement to file such reports by the filing, in accordance with the rules and procedures specified therefor, of reports on Form N-CEN (§§ 249.330 and 274.101 of this chapter).

[69 FR 11264, Mar. 9, 2004, as amended at 81 FR 82021, Nov. 18, 2016]

§ 270.30e-1 Reports to stockholders of management companies.

(a) Every registered management company shall transmit to each stockholder of record, at least semi-annually, a report containing the information required to be included in such reports by the company's registration statement form under the 1940 Act, except that the initial report of a newly registered company shall be made as of a date not later than the close of the fiscal year or half-year occurring on or after the date on which the company's notification of registration under the 1940 Act is filed with the Commission.

(b)(1) To satisfy its obligations under section 30(e) of the 1940 Act, an open-end management investment company registered on Form N-1A (§§ 239.15A and 274.11A of this chapter) also must:

(i) Make certain materials available on a website, as described under paragraph (b)(2) of this section; and

(ii) Deliver certain materials upon request, as described under paragraph (b)(3) of this section.

(2) The following website availability requirements are applicable to an open-end management investment company registered on Form N-1A (§§ 239.15A and 274.11A of this chapter).

(i) The company must make the disclosures required by Items 7 through 11 of Form N-CSR (§§ 249.331 and 274.128 of this chapter) publicly accessible, free of charge, at the website address specified at the beginning of the report to stockholders under paragraph (a) of this section, no later than 60 days after the end of the fiscal half-year or fiscal year of the company until 60 days after the end of the next fiscal half-year or fiscal year of the company, respectively. The company may satisfy the requirement in this paragraph (b)(2)(i) by making its most recent report on Form N-CSR publicly accessible, free of charge, at the specified website address for the time period that this paragraph (b)(2)(i) specifies.

(ii) Unless the company is a money market fund under § 270.2a-7, the company must make the company's complete portfolio holdings, if any, as of the close of the company's most recent first and third fiscal quarters, after the

Securities and Exchange Commission § 270.30e–1

date on which the company's registration statement became effective, presented in accordance with the schedules set forth in §§ 210.12–12 through 210.12–14 of this chapter (Regulation S–X), which need not be audited. The complete portfolio holdings required by this paragraph (b)(2)(ii) must be made publicly accessible, free of charge, at the website address specified at the beginning of the report to stockholders under paragraph (a) of this section, not later than 60 days after the close of the of the first and third fiscal quarters until 60 days after the end of the next first and third fiscal quarters of the company, respectively.

(iii) The website address relied upon for compliance with this section may not be the address of the Commission's electronic filing system.

(iv) The materials that are accessible in accordance with paragraph (b)(2)(i) or (ii) of this section must be presented on the website in a format, or formats, that are convenient for both reading online and printing on paper.

(v) Persons accessing the materials specified in paragraph (b)(2)(i) or (ii) of this section must be able to permanently retain, free of charge, an electronic version of such materials in a format, or formats, that meet the requirements of paragraph (b)(2)(iv) of this section.

(vi) The requirements set forth in paragraphs (b)(2)(i) through (v) of this section will be deemed to be met, notwithstanding the fact that the materials specified in paragraphs (b)(2)(i) and (ii) of this section are not available for a time in the manner required by paragraphs (b)(2)(i) through (v) of this section, provided that:

(A) The company has reasonable procedures in place to ensure that the specified materials are available in the manner required by paragraphs (b)(2)(i) through (v) of this section; and

(B) The company takes prompt action to ensure that the specified materials become available in the manner required by paragraphs (b)(2)(i) through (v) of this section, as soon as practicable following the earlier of the time at which it knows or reasonably should have known that the materials are not available in the manner required by paragraphs (b)(2)(i) through (v) of this section.

(vii) The materials specified in paragraph (b)(2)(i) or (ii) of this section may either be separately available for each series of a fund, or the materials may be grouped by the types of materials and/or by series, so long as the grouped information:

(A) Is presented in a format designed to communicate the information effectively;

(B) Clearly distinguishes the different types of materials and/or each series (as applicable); and

(C) Provides a means of easily locating the relevant information (including, for example, a table of contents that includes hyperlinks to the specific materials and series).

(3) The following requirements to deliver certain materials upon request are applicable to an open-end management investment company registered on Form N–1A (§§ 239.15A and 274.11A of this chapter).

(i) The company (or a financial intermediary through which shares of the company may be purchased or sold) must send, at no cost to the requestor and by U.S. first class mail or other reasonably prompt means, a paper copy of any of the materials specified in paragraph (b)(2)(i) or (ii) of this section, to any person requesting such a copy within three business days after receiving a request for a paper copy.

(ii) The company (or a financial intermediary through which shares of the company may be purchased or sold) must send, at no cost to the requestor, and by email or other reasonably prompt means, an electronic copy of any of the materials specified in paragraph (b)(2)(i) or (ii) of this section, to any person requesting such a copy within three business days after receiving a request for an electronic copy. The requirement to send an electronic copy of the requested materials may be satisfied by sending a direct link to the online location of the materials; provided that a current version of the materials is directly accessible through the link from the time that the email is sent through the date that is six months after the date that the email is sent and the email explains both how long the link will remain useable and

§ 270.30e–1

that, if recipients desire to retain a copy of the materials, they should access and save the materials.

(c) For registered management companies other than open-end management investment companies registered on Form N–1A, if any matter was submitted during the period covered by the shareholder report to a vote of shareholders, through the solicitation of proxies or otherwise, furnish the following information:

(1) The date of the meeting and whether it was an annual or special meeting.

(2) If the meeting involved the election of directors, the name of each director elected at the meeting and the name of each other director whose term of office as a director continued after the meeting.

(3) A brief description of each matter voted upon at the meeting and the number of votes cast for, against or withheld, as well as the number of abstentions and broker non-votes as to each such matter, including a separate tabulation with respect to each matter or nominee for office.

(i) *Instruction 1 to paragraph (c).* The solicitation of any authorization or consent (other than a proxy to vote at a shareholders' meeting) with respect to any matter shall be deemed a submission of such matter to a vote of shareholders within the meaning of this paragraph (c).

(ii) [Reserved]

(d) Each report shall be transmitted within 60 days after the close of the period for which such report is being made.

(e) The period of time within which any report prescribed by this rule shall be transmitted may be extended by the Commission upon written request showing good cause therefor. Section 270.0–5 shall not apply to such requests.

(f)(1) A company will be considered to have transmitted a report to shareholders who share an address if:

(i) The company transmits a report to the shared address;

(ii) The company addresses the report to the shareholders as a group (for example, "ABC Fund [or Corporation] Shareholders," "Jane Doe and Household," "The Smith Family") or to each of the shareholders individually (for example, "John Doe and Richard Jones"); and

(iii) The shareholders consent in writing to delivery of one report.

(2) The company need not obtain written consent from a shareholder under paragraph (f)(1)(iii) of this section if all of the following conditions are met:

(i) The shareholder has the same last name as the other shareholders, or the company reasonably believes that the shareholders are members of the same family;

(ii) The company has transmitted a notice to the shareholder at least 60 days before the company begins to rely on this section concerning transmission of reports to that shareholder. The notice must be a separate written statement and:

(A) State that only one report will be delivered to the shared address unless the company receives contrary instructions;

(B) Include a toll-free telephone number or be accompanied by a reply form that is pre-addressed with postage provided, that the shareholder can use to notify the company that he or she wishes to receive a separate report;

(C) State the duration of the consent;

(D) Explain how a shareholder can revoke consent;

(E) State that the company will begin sending individual copies to a shareholder within 30 days after the company receives revocation of the shareholder's consent; and

(F) Contain the following prominent statement, or similar clear and understandable statement, in bold-face type: "Important Notice Regarding Delivery of Shareholder Materials". This statement also must appear on the envelope in which the notice is delivered. Alternatively, if the notice is delivered separately from other communications to investors, this statement may appear either on the notice or on the envelope in which the notice is delivered;

NOTE TO PARAGRAPH (f)(2)(ii): The notice should be written in plain English. See § 230.421(d)(2) of this chapter for a discussion of plain English principles.

(iii) The company has not received the reply form or other notification indicating that the shareholder wishes to continue to receive an individual copy

Securities and Exchange Commission § 270.30e–3

of the report, within 60 days after the company sent the notice; and

(iv) The company transmits the report to a post office box or to a residential street address. The company can assume a street address is a residence unless it has information that indicates it is a business.

(3) At least once a year, the company must explain to shareholders who have consented under paragraph (f)(1)(iii) or paragraph (f)(2) of this section how they can revoke their consent. The explanation must be reasonably designed to reach these investors. If a shareholder, orally or in writing, revokes consent to delivery of one report to a shared address, the company must begin sending individual copies to that shareholder within 30 days after the company receives the revocation.

(4) For purposes of this section, *address* means a street address, a post office box number, an electronic mail address, a facsimile telephone number, or other similar destination to which paper or electronic documents are transmitted, unless otherwise provided in this section. If the company has reason to believe that the address is a street address of a multi-unit building, the address must include the unit number.

[46 FR 36126, July 14, 1981, as amended at 48 FR 37940, Aug. 22, 1983; 48 FR 44477, Sept. 29, 1983; 50 FR 26160, June 25, 1985; 57 FR 56836, Dec. 1, 1992; 59 FR 52760, Oct. 19, 1994; 61 FR 24657, May 15, 1996; 64 FR 62547, Nov. 16, 1999. Redesignated and amended at 66 FR 3759, Jan. 16, 2001; 87 FR 72847, Nov. 25, 2022]

§ 270.30e–2 **Reports to shareholders of unit investment trusts.**

(a) At least semiannually every registered unit investment trust substantially all the assets of which consist of securities issued by a management company must transmit to each shareholder of record (including record holders of periodic payment plan certificates), a report containing all the applicable information and financial statements or their equivalent, required by § 270.30d–1 to be included in reports of the management company for the same fiscal period. Each of these reports must be transmitted within the period allowed the management company by § 270.30e–1 for transmitting reports to its shareholders.

(b) Any report required by this section will be considered transmitted to a shareholder of record if the unit investment trust satisfies the conditions set forth in § 270.30e–1(f) with respect to that shareholder.

[64 FR 62547, Nov. 16, 1999. Redesignated and amended at 66 FR 3759, Jan. 16, 2001]

§ 270.30e–3 **Internet availability of reports to shareholders.**

(a) *General.* A Fund may satisfy its obligation to transmit a report required by § 270.30e–1 ("Report") to a shareholder of record if all of the conditions set forth in paragraphs (b) through (e) of this section are satisfied.

(b) *Availability of report to shareholders and other materials.* (1) The following materials are publicly accessible, free of charge, at the website address specified in the Notice from the date the Fund transmits the Report as required by § 270.30e–1 until the Fund next transmits a report required by § 270.30e–1 with respect to the Fund:

(i) *Current report to shareholders.* The Report.

(ii) *Prior report to shareholders.* Any report with respect to the Fund for the prior reporting period that was transmitted to shareholders of record pursuant to § 270.30e–1.

(iii) *Complete portfolio holdings from reports containing a summary schedule of investments.* If a report specified in paragraph (b)(1)(i) or (ii) of this section includes a summary schedule of investments (§ 210.12–12B of this chapter) in lieu of Schedule I—Investments in securities of unaffiliated issuers (§ 210.12–12 of this chapter), the Fund's complete portfolio holdings as of the close of the period covered by the report, presented in accordance with the schedules set forth in §§ 210.12–12 through 210.12–14 of Regulation S–X (§§ 210.12–12 through 210.12–14 of this chapter), which need not be audited.

(iv) *Portfolio holdings for most recent first and third fiscal quarters.* The Fund's complete portfolio holdings as of the close of the Fund's most recent first and third fiscal quarters, if any, after

§ 270.30e–3

the date on which the Fund's registration statement became effective, presented in accordance with the schedules set forth in §§ 210.12–12 through 210.12–14 of Regulation S–X [§§ 210.12–12 through 210.12–14 of this chapter], which need not be audited. The complete portfolio holdings required by this paragraph (b)(1)(iv) must be made publicly available not later than 60 days after the close of the fiscal quarter.

(2) The website address relied upon for compliance with this section may not be the address of the Commission's electronic filing system.

(3) The materials that are accessible in accordance with paragraph (b)(1) of this section must be presented on the website in a format, or formats, that are convenient for both reading online and printing on paper.

(4) Persons accessing the materials specified in paragraph (b)(1) of this section must be able to retain permanently, free of charge, an electronic version of such materials in a format, or formats, that meet the conditions of paragraph (b)(3) of this section.

(5) The conditions set forth in paragraphs (b)(1) through (4) of this section shall be deemed to be met, notwithstanding the fact that the materials specified in paragraph (b)(1) of this section are not available for a time in the manner required by paragraphs (b)(1) through (4) of this section, provided that:

(i) The Fund has reasonable procedures in place to ensure that the specified materials are available in the manner required by paragraphs (b)(1) through (4) of this section; and

(ii) The Fund takes prompt action to ensure that the specified documents become available in the manner required by paragraphs (b)(1) through (4) of this section, as soon as practicable following the earlier of the time at which it knows or reasonably should have known that the documents are not available in the manner required by paragraphs (b)(1) through (4) of this section.

(c) *Notice.* A paper notice ("Notice") meeting the conditions of this paragraph (c) must be sent to the shareholder within 70 days after the close of the period for which the Report is being made. The Notice may contain only the information specified by paragraphs (c)(1), (2), and (3) of this section, and may include pictures, logos, or similar design elements so long as the design is not misleading and the information is clear.

(1) The Notice must be written using plain English principles pursuant to paragraph (d) of this section and:

(i) Contain a prominent legend in bold-face type that states "[An] Important Report[s] to [Shareholders] of [Fund] [is/are] Now Available Online and In Print by Request." The Notice may also include information identifying the Fund, the Fund's sponsor (including any investment adviser or subadviser to the Fund), a variable annuity or variable life insurance contract or insurance company issuer thereof, or a financial intermediary through which shares of the Fund are held.

(ii) State that the Report contains important information about the Fund, including its portfolio holdings and financial statements. The statement may also include a brief listing of other types of information contained in the Report.

(iii) State that the Report is available at the website address specified in the Notice or, upon request, by mail, and encourage the shareholder to access and review the Report.

(iv) Include a website address where the Report and other materials specified in paragraph (b)(1) of this section are available. The website address must be specific enough to lead investors directly to the documents that are required to be accessible under paragraph (b)(1) of this section, rather than to the home page or a section of the website other than on which the documents are posted. The website may be a central site with prominent links to each document. In addition to the website address, the Notice may contain any other equivalent method or means to access the Report or other materials specified in paragraph (b)(1) of this section.

(v) Provide a toll-free (or collect) telephone number to contact the Fund or the shareholder's financial intermediary, and:

(A) Provide instructions describing how a shareholder may request a paper

Securities and Exchange Commission § 270.30e–3

or email copy of the Report and other materials specified in paragraph (b)(1) of this section at no charge, and an indication that the shareholder will not otherwise receive a paper or email copy;

(B) Explain that the shareholder can at any time elect to receive print reports in the future and provide instructions describing how a shareholder may make that election (*e.g.*, by contacting the Fund or by contacting the shareholder's financial intermediary); and

(C) If applicable, provide instructions describing how a shareholder can elect to receive shareholder reports or other documents and communications by electronic delivery.

(2) The Notice may include additional methods by which a shareholder can contact the Fund or the shareholder's financial intermediary (*e.g.*, by email or through a website), which may include any information needed to identify the shareholder.

(3) A Notice may include content from the Report if such content is set forth after the information required by paragraph (c)(1) of this section.

(4) The Notice may not be incorporated into, or combined with, another document, except that the Notice may incorporate or combine one or more other Notices.

(5) The Notice must be sent separately from other types of shareholder communications and may not accompany any other document or materials; provided, however, that the Notice may accompany:

(i) One or more other Notices;

(ii) A current Statutory Prospectus, Statement of Additional Information, or Notice of internet Availability of Proxy Materials under § 240.14a–16 of this chapter;

(iii) In the case of a Fund held in a separate account funding a variable annuity or variable life insurance contract, such contract or the Statutory Prospectus and Statement of Additional Information for such contract; or

(iv) The shareholder's account statement.

(6) A Notice required by this paragraph (c) will be considered transmitted to a shareholder of record if the conditions set forth in § 270.30e–1(f),

§ 240.14a–3(e), or § 240.14c–3(c) of this chapter are satisfied with respect to that shareholder.

(d) *Plain English requirements.* (1) To enhance the readability of the Notice, plain English principles must be used in the organization, language, and design of the Notice.

(2) The Notice must be drafted so that, at a minimum, it substantially complies with each of the following plain English writing principles:

(i) Short sentences;

(ii) Definite, concrete, everyday words;

(iii) Active voice;

(iv) Tabular presentation or bullet lists for complex material, whenever possible;

(v) No legal jargon or highly technical business terms; and

(vi) No multiple negatives.

(e) *Delivery of paper copy upon request.* A paper copy of any of the materials specified in paragraph (b)(1) of this section must be transmitted to any person requesting such a copy, at no cost to the requestor and by U.S. first class mail or other reasonably prompt means, within three business days after a request for a paper copy is received.

(f) *Investor elections to receive future reports in paper.* (1) This section may not be relied upon to transmit a Report to a shareholder if the shareholder has notified the Fund (or the shareholder's financial intermediary) that the shareholder wishes to receive paper copies of shareholder reports at any time after the Fund has first notified the shareholder of its intent to rely on the rule or provided a Notice to the shareholder.

(2) A shareholder who has notified the Fund (or the shareholder's financial intermediary) that the shareholder wishes to receive paper copies of shareholder reports with respect to a Fund will be deemed to have requested paper copies of shareholder reports with respect to:

(i) Any and all current and future Funds held through an account or accounts with:

(A) The Fund's transfer agent or principal underwriter or agent thereof for the same "group of related investment companies" as such term is defined in § 270.0–10; or

§ 270.30h–1

(B) A financial intermediary; and

(ii) Any and all Funds held currently and in the future in a separate account funding a variable annuity or variable life insurance contract.

(g) *Delivery of other documents.* This section may not be relied upon to transmit a copy of a Fund's currently effective Statutory Prospectus or Statement of Additional Information, or both, under the Securities Act of 1933 (15 U.S.C. 77a *et seq.*) as otherwise permitted by paragraph (d) of § 270.30e–1.

(h) *Definitions.* For purposes of this section:

(1) Fund means a management company registered on Form N–2 (§§ 239.14 and 274.11a of this chapter) or Form N–3 (§§ 239.17a and 274.11b of this chapter) and any separate series of the management company that is required to transmit a report to shareholders pursuant to 270.30e–1.

(2) Statement of Additional Information means the statement of additional information required by Part B of the applicable registration form.

(3) Statutory Prospectus means a prospectus that satisfies the requirements of section 10(a) of the Securities Act of 1933 (15 U.S.C. 77(j)(a)).

NOTE 1 TO § 270.30.E–3: For a discussion of how the conditions and requirements of this rule may apply in the context of investors holding Fund shares through financial intermediaries, see Investment Company Release No. 33115 (June 5, 2018).

[87 FR 72848, Nov. 25, 2022]

§ 270.30h–1 Applicability of section 16 of the Exchange Act to section 30(h).

(a) The filing of any statement prescribed under section 16(a) of the Securities Exchange Act of 1934 (15 U.S.C. 78p(a)) shall satisfy the corresponding requirements of section 30(h) of the Act (15 U.S.C. 80a–29(h)).

(b) The rules under section 16 of the Securities Exchange Act of 1934 (15 U.S.C. 78p) shall apply to any duty, liability or prohibition imposed with respect to a transaction involving any security of a registered closed-end company under section 30(h) of the Act (15 U.S.C. 80a–29(h)).

(c) No statements need be filed pursuant to section 30(h) of the Act (15 U.S.C. 80a–29(h)) by an affiliated person of an investment adviser in his or her capacity as such if such person is solely an employee, other than an officer, of such investment adviser.

[67 FR 43537, June 28, 2002]

§ 270.31a–1 Records to be maintained by registered investment companies, certain majority-owned subsidiaries thereof, and other persons having transactions with registered investment companies.

(a) Every registered investment company, and every underwriter, broker, dealer, or investment adviser which is a majority-owned subsidiary of such a company, shall maintain and keep current the accounts, books, and other documents relating to its business which constitute the record forming the basis for financial statements required to be filed pursuant to section 30 of the Investment Company Act of 1940 and of the auditor's certificates relating thereto.

(b) Every registered investment company shall maintain and keep current the following books, accounts, and other documents:

(1) Journals (or other records of original entry) containing an itemized daily record in detail of all purchases and sales of securities (including sales and redemptions of its own securities), all receipts and deliveries of securities (including certificate numbers if such detail is not recorded by custodian or transfer agent), all receipts and disbursements of cash and all other debits and credits. Such records shall show for each such transaction the name and quantity of securities, the unit and aggregate purchase or sale price, commission paid, the market on which effected, the trade date, the settlement date, and the name of the person through or from whom purchased or received or to whom sold or delivered. In the case of a money market fund, also identify the provider of any Demand Feature or Guarantee (as defined in § 270.2a–7(a)(9) or § 270.2a–7(a)(16) respectively) and give a brief description of the nature of the Demand Feature or Guarantee (e.g., unconditional demand feature, conditional demand feature, letter of credit, or bond insurance) and, in a subsidiary portfolio investment

Securities and Exchange Commission

§ 270.31a-1

record, provide the complete legal name and accounting and other information (including sufficient information to calculate coupons, accruals, maturities, puts, and calls) necessary to identify, value, and account for each investment.

(2) General and auxiliary ledgers (or other records) reflecting all assets, liability, reserve, capital, income and expense accounts, including:

(i) Separate ledger accounts (or other records) reflecting the following:

(*a*) Securities in transfer;
(*b*) Securities in physical possession;
(*c*) Securities borrowed and securities loaned;
(*d*) Monies borrowed and monies loaned (together with a record of the collateral therefor and substitutions in such collateral);
(*e*) Dividends and interest received;
(*f*) Dividends receivable and interest accrued.

INSTRUCTION. (a) and (b) of this subdivision shall be stated in terms of securities quantities only; (c) and (d) of this subdivision shall be stated in dollar amounts and securities quantities as appropriate; (e) and (f) of this subdivision shall be stated in dollar amounts only.

(ii) Separate ledger accounts (or other records) for each portfolio security, showing (as of trade dates) (*a*) the quantity and unit and aggregate price for each purchase, sale, receipt, and delivery of securities and commodities for such accounts, and (*b*) all other debits and credits for such accounts. Securities positions and money balances in such ledger accounts (or other records) shall be brought forward periodically but not less frequently than at the end of fiscal quarters. Any portfolio security, the salability of which is conditioned, shall be so noted. A memorandum record shall be available setting forth, with respect to each portfolio security account, the amount and declaration ex-dividend, and payment dates of each dividend declared thereon.

(iii) Separate ledger accounts (or other records) for each broker-dealer bank or other person with or through which transactions in portfolio securities are effected, showing each purchase or sale of securities with or through such persons, including details as to the date of the purchase or sale, the quantity and unit and aggregate price of such securities, and the commissions or other compensation paid to such persons. Purchases or sales effected during the same day at the same price may be aggregated.

(iv) Separate ledger accounts (or other records), which may be maintained by a transfer agent or registrar, showing for each shareholder of record of the investment company the number of shares of capital stock of the company held. In respect of share accumulation accounts (arising from periodic investment plans, dividend reinvestment plans, deposit of issued shares by the owner thereof, etc.), details shall be available as to the dates and number of shares of each accumulation, and except with respect to already issued shares deposited by the owner thereof, prices of each such accumulation.

(3) A securities record or ledger reflecting separately for each portfolio security as of trade date all "long" and "short" positions carried by the investment company for its own account and showing the location of all securities long and the off-setting position to all securities short. The record called for by this paragraph shall not be required in circumstances under which all portfolio securities are maintained by a bank or banks or a member or members of a national securities exchange as custodian under a custody agreement or as agent for such custodian.

(4) Corporate charters, certificates of incorporation or trust agreements, and by-laws, and minute books of stockholders' and directors' or trustees' meetings; and minute books of directors' or trustees' committee and advisory board or advisory committee meetings.

(5) A record of each brokerage order given by or in behalf of the investment company for, or in connection with, the purchase or sale of securities, whether executed or unexecuted. Such record shall include the name of the broker, the terms and conditions of the order and of any modification or cancellation thereof, the time of entry or cancellation, the price at which executed, and the time of receipt of report of execution. The record shall indicate the name of the person who placed the

§ 270.31a-1

order in behalf of the investment company.

(6) A record of all other portfolio purchases or sales showing details comparable to those prescribed in paragraph (b)(5) of this section.

(7) A record of all puts, calls, spreads, straddles, and other options in which the investment company has any direct or indirect interest or which the investment company has granted or guaranteed; and a record of any contractual commitments to purchase, sell, receive or deliver securities or other property (but not including open orders placed with broker-dealers for the purchase or sale of securities, which may be cancelled by the company on notices without penalty or cost of any kind); containing, at least, an identification of the security, the number of units involved, the option price, the date of maturity, the date of issuance, and the person to whom issued.

(8) A record of the proof of money balances in all ledger accounts (except shareholder accounts), in the form of trial balances. Such trial balances shall be prepared currently at least once a month.

(9) A record for each fiscal quarter, which shall be completed within ten days after the end of such quarter, showing specifically the basis or bases upon which the allocation of orders for the purchase and sale of portfolio securities to named brokers or dealers and the division of brokerage commissions or other compensation on such purchase and sale orders among named persons were made during such quarter. The record shall indicate the consideration given to (i) sales of shares of the investment company by brokers or dealers, (ii) the supplying of services or benefits by brokers or dealers to the investment company, its investment adviser or principal underwriter or any persons affiliated therewith, and (iii) any other considerations other than the technical qualifications of the brokers and dealers as such. The record shall show the nature of the services or benefits made available, and shall describe in detail the application of any general or specific formula or other determinant used in arriving at such allocation of purchase and sale orders and such division of brokerage commissions or other compensation. The record shall also include the identities of the persons responsible for the determination of such allocation and such division of brokerage commissions or other compensation.

(10) A record in the form of an appropriate memorandum identifying the person or persons, committees, or groups authorizing the purchase or sale of portfolio securities. Where an authorization is made by a committee or group, a record shall be kept of the names of its members who participated in the authorization. There shall be retained as part of the record required by this paragraph any memorandum, recommendation, or instruction supporting or authorizing the purchase or sale of portfolio securities. The requirements of this paragraph are applicable to the extent they are not met by compliance with the requirements of paragraph (b)(4) of this section.

(11) Files of all advisory material received from the investment adviser, any advisory board or advisory committee, or any other persons from whom the investment company accepts investment advice, other than material which is furnished solely through uniform publications distributed generally.

(12) The term "other records" as used in the expressions "journals (or other records of original entry)" and "ledger accounts (or other records)" shall be construed to include, where appropriate, copies of voucher checks, confirmations, or similar documents which reflect the information required by the applicable rule or rules in appropriate sequence and in permanent form, including similar records developed by the use of automatic data processing systems.

(c) Every underwriter, broker, or dealer which is a majority-owned subsidiary of a registered investment company shall maintain in the form prescribed therein such accounts, books and other documents as are required to be maintained by brokers and dealers by rule adopted under section 17 of the Securities Exchange Act of 1934.

Securities and Exchange Commission § 270.31a–2

(d) Every depositer of any registered investment company, and every principal underwriter for any registered investment company other than a closed-end investment company, shall maintain such accounts, books and other documents as are required to be maintained by brokers and dealers by rule adopted under section 17 of the Securities Exchange Act of 1934, to the extent such records are necessary or appropriate to record such person's transactions with such registered investment company.

(e) Every investment advisor which is a majority-owned subsidiary of a registered investment company shall maintain in the form prescribed therein such accounts, books and other documents as are required to be maintained by registered investment advisers by rule adopted under section 204 of the Investment Advisers Act of 1940.

(f) Every investment adviser not a majority-owned subsidiary of a registered investment company shall maintain such accounts, books and other documents as are required to be maintained by registered investment advisers by rule adopted under section 204 of the Investment Advisers Act of 1940, to the extent such records are necessary or appropriate to record such person's transactions with such registered investment company.

(Sec. 31, 54 Stat. 838; 15 U.S.C. 80a–30)

[27 FR 11993, Dec. 5, 1962, as amended at 61 FR 13983, Mar. 28, 1996; 62 FR 64986, Dec. 9, 1997; 79 FR 47968, Aug. 14, 2014; 80 FR 58155, Sept. 25, 2015]

§ 270.31a–2 **Records to be preserved by registered investment companies, certain majority-owned subsidiaries thereof, and other persons having transactions with registered investment companies.**

(a) Every registered investment company shall:

(1) Preserve permanently, the first two years in an easily accessible place, all books and records required to be made pursuant to paragraphs (1) through (4) of § 270.31a–1(b);

(2) Preserve for a period not less than six years from the end of the fiscal year in which any transactions occurred, the first two years in an easily accessible place, all books and records required to be made pursuant to paragraphs (b)(5) through (12) of § 270.31a–1 and all vouchers, memoranda, correspondence, checkbooks, bank statements, cancelled checks, cash reconciliations, cancelled stock certificates, and all schedules evidencing and supporting each computation of net asset value of the investment company shares, including schedules evidencing and supporting each computation of an adjustment to net asset value of the investment company shares based on swing pricing policies and procedures established and implemented pursuant to § 270.22c–1(a)(3), and other records required to be maintained by § 270.31a–1(a) and not enumerated in § 270.31a–1(b).

(3) Preserve for a period not less than 6 years from the end of the fiscal year last used, the first 2 years in an easily accessible place, any advertisement, pamphlet, circular, form letter or other sales literature addressed to or intended for distribution to prospective investors;

(4) Preserve for a period not less than six years, the first two years in an easily accessible place, any record of the initial determination that a director is not an interested person of the investment company, and each subsequent determination that the director is not an interested person of the investment company. These records must include any questionnaire and any other document used to determine that a director is not an interested person of the company;

(5) Preserve for a period not less than six years, the first two years in an easily accessible place, any materials used by the disinterested directors of an investment company to determine that a person who is acting as legal counsel to those directors is an independent legal counsel;

(6) Preserve for a period not less than six years, the first two years in an easily accessible place, any documents or other written information considered by the directors of the investment company pursuant to section 15(c) of the Act (15 U.S.C. 80a–15(c)) in approving the terms or renewal of a contract or agreement between the company and an investment adviser; and

§ 270.31a–2

(7) Preserve for a period not less than six years, the first two years in an easily accessible place, any shareholder report required by § 270.30e–1 (including any version posted on a website or otherwise provided electronically) that is not filed with the Commission in the exact form in which it was used.

(b) Every underwriter, broker, or dealer which is a majority-owned subsidiary of a registered investment company shall preserve for the periods prescribed therein such accounts, books and other documents as are required to be preserved by brokers and dealers by rule adopted under section 17 of the Securities Exchange Act of 1934.

(c) Every depositor of any registered investment company, and every principal underwriter for any registered investment company other than a closed-end company, shall preserve for a period of not less than six years such accounts, books and other documents as are required to be maintained by brokers and dealers by rule adopted under section 17 of the Securities Exchange Act of 1934, to the extent such records are necessary or appropriate to record such person's transactions with such registered investment company.

(d) Every investment adviser which is a majority-owned subsidiary of a registered investment company shall preserve for the periods prescribed therein such accounts, books and other documents as are required to be preserved by investment advisers by rule adopted under section 204 of the Investment Advisers Act of 1940.

(e) Every investment adviser not a majority-owned subsidiary of a registered investment company shall preserve for a period of not less than six years such accounts, books and other documents as are required to be maintained by registered investment advisers by rule adopted under section 204 of the Investment Advisers Act of 1940, to the extent such records are necessary or appropriate to record such person's transactions with such registered investment company.

(f) *Micrographic and electronic storage permitted*—(1) *General.* The records required to be maintained and preserved under this part may be maintained and preserved for the required time by, or on behalf of, an investment company on:

(i) Micrographic media, including microfilm, microfiche, or any similar medium; or

(ii) Electronic storage media, including any digital storage medium or system that meets the terms of this section.

(2) *General requirements.* The investment company, or person that maintains and preserves records on its behalf, must:

(i) Arrange and index the records in a way that permits easy location, access, and retrieval of any particular record;

(ii) Provide promptly any of the following that the Commission (by its examiners or other representatives) or the directors of the company may request:

(A) A legible, true, and complete copy of the record in the medium and format in which it is stored;

(B) A legible, true, and complete printout of the record; and

(C) Means to access, view, and print the records; and

(iii) Separately store, for the time required for preservation of the original record, a duplicate copy of the record on any medium allowed by this section.

(3) *Special requirements for electronic storage media.* In the case of records on electronic storage media, the investment company, or person that maintains and preserves records on its behalf, must establish and maintain procedures:

(i) To maintain and preserve the records, so as to reasonably safeguard them from loss, alteration, or destruction;

(ii) To limit access to the records to properly authorized personnel, the directors of the investment company, and the Commission (including its examiners and other representatives); and

(iii) To reasonably ensure that any reproduction of a non-electronic original record on electronic storage media is complete, true, and legible when retrieved.

(4) Notwithstanding the provisions of paragraphs (a) through (e) of this section, any record, book or other document may be destroyed in accordance with a plan previously submitted to

Securities and Exchange Commission § 270.32a–1

and approved by the Commission. A plan shall be deemed to have been approved by the Commission if notice to the contrary has not been received within 90 days after submission of the plan to the Commission.

[27 FR 11994, Dec. 5, 1962, as amended at 38 FR 7797, Mar. 26, 1973; 51 FR 42209, Nov. 24, 1986; 53 FR 3880, Feb. 10, 1988; 66 FR 3759, Jan. 16, 2001; 66 FR 29228, May 30, 2001; 69 FR 46390, Aug. 2, 2004; 81 FR 82138, Nov. 18, 2016; 87 FR 72850, Nov. 25, 2022]

§ 270.31a–3 Records prepared or maintained by other than person required to maintain and preserve them.

(a) If the records required to be maintained and preserved pursuant to the provisions of §§ 270.31a–1 and 270.31a–2 are prepared or maintained by others on behalf of the person required to maintain and preserve such records, the person required to maintain and preserve such records shall obtain from such other person an agreement in writing to the effect that such records are the property of the person required to maintain and preserve such records and will be surrendered promptly on request.

(b) In cases where a bank or member of a national securities exchange acts as custodian, transfer agent, or dividend disbursing agent, compliance with this section shall be considered to have been met if such bank or exchange member agrees in writing to make any records relating to such service available upon request and to preserve for the periods prescribed in § 270.31a–2 any such records as are required to be maintained by § 270.31a–1.

(Sec. 31, 54 Stat. 838; 15 U.S.C. 80a–30)

[27 FR 11994, Dec. 5, 1962]

§ 270.31a–4 Records to be maintained and preserved by registered investment companies relating to fair value determinations.

(a) *Appropriate documentation.* Every registered investment company shall maintain appropriate documentation to support fair value determinations made pursuant to § 270.2a–5 for at least six years from the time that the determination was made, the first two years in an easily accessible place.

(b) *Records when designating.* If the board of a registered investment company has designated performance of fair value determinations to a valuation designee under § 270.2a–5(b), in addition to the records required in paragraph (a) of this section, the registered investment company must maintain copies of:

(1) The reports and other information provided to the board as required under § 270.2a–5(b)(1) for at least six years after the end of the fiscal year in which the documents were provided to the board, the first two years in an easily accessible place; and

(2) A specified list of the investments or investment types whose fair value determination has been designated to the valuation designee to perform pursuant to § 270.2a–5(b) for a period beginning with the designation and ending at least six years after the end of the fiscal year in which the designation was terminated, in an easily accessible place until two years after such termination.

(c) *Party to maintain.* If the board of a registered investment company has designated performance of fair value determinations to its investment adviser under § 270.2a–5(b), such investment adviser shall maintain the records required by this section. If the investment adviser is not so designated, the fund shall maintain such records.

[86 FR 808, Jan. 6, 2021]

§ 270.32a–1 Exemption of certain companies from affiliation provisions of section 32(a).

A registered investment company shall be exempt from the provisions of paragraph (1) of section 32(a) of the Act (54 Stat. 838; 15 U.S.C. 80a–31), insofar as said paragraph requires that independent public accountants for such company be selected by a majority of certain members of the board of directors, if:

(a) Such company meets the conditions of paragraphs (1) to (8), inclusive, of section 10(d) of the Act (54 Stat. 807; 15 U.S.C. 80a–10); and

§ 270.32a-2

(b) Such accountants are selected by a majority of all the members of the board of directors.

[Rule N-32A-1, 6 FR 6631, Dec. 23, 1941, as amended at 87 FR 22446, Apr. 15, 2022]

§ 270.32a-2 Exemption for initial period from vote of security holders on independent public accountant for certain registered separate accounts.

(a) A registered separate account shall be exempt from the requirement under paragraph (2) of section 32(a) of the Act that selection of an independent public accountant shall have been submitted for ratification or rejection at the next succeeding annual meeting of security owners, subject to the following conditions:

(1) Such registered separate account qualifies for exemption from section 14(a) of the Act pursuant to § 270.14a-2, or is exempt therefrom by order of the Commission upon application; and

(2) The selection of such accountant shall be submitted for ratification or rejection to variable annuity contract owners at their first meeting after the effective date of the registration statement under the Securities Act of 1933, as amended (15 U.S.C. 77a *et seq.*), relating to contracts participating in such account: *Provided*, That such meeting shall take place within 1 year after such effective date, unless the time for the holding of such meeting shall be extended by the Commission upon written request showing good cause therefor.

(Sec. 6, 54 Stat. 800; 15 U.S.C. 80a-6)

[34 FR 12696, Aug. 5, 1969]

§ 270.32a-3 Exemption from provision of section 32(a)(1) regarding the time period during which a registered management investment company must select an independent public accountant.

(a) A registered management investment company ("company") organized in a jurisdiction that does not require it to hold regular annual meetings of its stockholders, and which does not hold a regular annual stockholders' meeting in a given fiscal year, shall be exempt in that fiscal year from the requirement of section 32(a)(1) of the Act (15 U.S.C. 80a-31(a)(1)) that the independent public accountant ("accountant") be selected at a board of directors meeting held within 30 days before or after the beginning of the fiscal year or before the annual meeting of stockholders in that year, *provided*, that such company is either:

(1) In a set of investment companies as defined in paragraph (b) of this section, if not all the members of such set have an identical fiscal year end and if such company selects an accountant at a board of directors meeting held within 90 days before or after the beginning of that fiscal year; or

(2) Not in a set of investment companies, or is in a set, each of whose members has the same fiscal year end, and if such company selects an accountant at a board of directors meeting held within 30 days before or 90 days after the beginning of that fiscal year.

(b) For purposes of this rule, "set of investment companies" means any two or more registered management investment companies that hold themselves out to investors as related companies for purposes of investment and investor services, and

(1) That have a common investment adviser or principal underwriter, or

(2) If the investment adviser or principal underwriter of one of the companies is an affiliated person as defined in section 2(a)(3)(C) of the Act (15 U.S.C. 80a-2(a)(3)(C)) of the investment adviser or principal underwriter of each of the other companies.

[54 FR 31332, July 28, 1989]

§ 270.32a-4 Independent audit committees.

A registered management investment company or a registered face-amount certificate company is exempt from the requirement of section 32(a)(2) of the Act (15 U.S.C. 80a-32(a)(2)) that the selection of the company's independent public accountant be submitted for ratification or rejection at the next succeeding annual meeting of shareholders, if:

(a) The company's board of directors has established a committee, composed solely of directors who are not interested persons of the company, that has responsibility for overseeing the fund's accounting and auditing processes ("audit committee");

Securities and Exchange Commission

(b) The company's board of directors has adopted a charter for the audit committee setting forth the committee's structure, duties, powers, and methods of operation or set forth such provisions in the fund's charter or bylaws; and

(c) The company maintains and preserves permanently in an easily accessible place a copy of the audit committee's charter and any modification to the charter.

[66 FR 3759, Jan. 16, 2001]

§ 270.34b-1 Sales literature deemed to be misleading.

Any advertisement, pamphlet, circular, form letter, or other sales literature addressed to or intended for distribution to prospective investors that is required to be filed with the Commission by section 24(b) of the Act [15 U.S.C. 80a-24(b)] (for purposes of paragraph (a) and (b) of this section, "sales literature") will have omitted to state a fact necessary in order to make the statements made therein not materially misleading unless the sales literature includes the information specified in paragraphs (a) and (b) of this section. Any registered investment company or business development company advertisement, pamphlet, circular, form letter, or other sales literature addressed to or intended for distribution to prospective investors in connection with a public offering (for purposes of paragraph (c) of this section, "sales literature") will have omitted to state a fact necessary in order to make the statements therein not materially misleading unless the sales literature includes the information specified in paragraph (c) of this section.

NOTE 1 TO § 270.34b-1 INTRODUCTORY TEXT: The fact that the sales literature includes the information specified in paragraphs (a) and (b) of this section does not relieve the investment company, underwriter, or dealer of any obligations with respect to the sales literature under the antifraud provisions of the Federal securities laws. For guidance about factors to be weighed in determining whether statements, representations, illustrations, and descriptions contained in investment company sales literature are misleading, see § 230.156 of this chapter.

§ 270.34b-1

(a) Sales literature for a money market fund shall contain the information required by paragraph (b)(4) of § 230.482 of this chapter, presented in the manner required by paragraph (b)(5) of § 230.482 of this chapter.

(b)(1) Except as provided in paragraph (b)(3) of this section:

(i) In any sales literature that contains performance data for an investment company, include the disclosure required by paragraph (b)(3) of § 230.482 of this chapter, presented in the manner required by paragraph (b)(5) of § 230.482 of this chapter.

(ii) In any sales literature for a money market fund:

(A) Accompany any quotation of yield or similar quotation purporting to demonstrate the income earned or distributions made by the money market fund with a quotation of current yield specified by paragraph (e)(1)(i) of § 230.482 of this chapter;

(B) Accompany any quotation of the money market fund's tax equivalent yield or tax equivalent effective yield with a quotation of current yield as specified in § 230.482(d)(1)(iii) of this chapter; and

(C) Accompany any quotation of the money market fund's total return with a quotation of the money market fund's current yield specified in paragraph (e)(1)(i) of § 230.482 of this chapter. Place the quotations of total return and current yield next to each other, in the same size print, and if there is a material difference between the quoted total return and the quoted current yield, include a statement that the yield quotation more closely reflects the current earnings of the money market fund than the total return quotation.

(iii) In any sales literature for an investment company other than a money market fund that contains performance data:

(A) Include the total return information required by paragraph (d)(3) of § 230.482 of this chapter;

(B) Accompany any quotation of performance adjusted to reflect the effect of taxes (not including a quotation of tax equivalent yield or other similar quotation purporting to demonstrate the tax equivalent yield earned or distributions made by the company) with

489

§ 270.35d–1

the quotations of total return specified by paragraph (d)(4) of § 230.482 of this chapter;

(C) If the sales literature (other than sales literature for a company that is permitted under § 270.35d–1(a)(4) to use a name suggesting that the company's distributions are exempt from federal income tax or from both federal and state income tax) represents or implies that the company is managed to limit or control the effect of taxes on company performance, include the quotations of total return specified by paragraph (d)(4) of § 230.482 of this chapter;

(D) Accompany any quotation of yield or similar quotation purporting to demonstrate the income earned or distributions made by the company with a quotation of current yield specified by paragraph (d)(1) of § 230.482 of this chapter; and

(E) Accompany any quotation of tax equivalent yield or other similar quotation purporting to demonstrate the tax equivalent yield earned or distributions made by the company with a quotation of tax equivalent yield specified in paragraph (d)(2) and current yield specified by paragraph (d)(1) of § 230.482 of this chapter.

(2) Any performance data included in sales literature under paragraphs (b)(1)(ii) or (iii) of this section must meet the currentness requirements of paragraph (g) of § 230.482 of this chapter.

(3) The requirements specified in paragraph (b)(1) of this section do not apply to any quarterly, semi-annual, or annual report to shareholders under Section 30 of the Act [15 U.S.C. 80a–29] containing performance data for a period commencing no earlier than the first day of the period covered by the report; nor do the requirements of paragraphs (d)(3)(ii), (d)(4)(ii), and (g) of § 230.482 of this chapter apply to any such periodic report containing any other performance data.

(c)(1) Except as provided in paragraph (c)(2) of this section:

(i) In any sales literature that contains fee and expense figures for a registered investment company or business development company, include the disclosure required by paragraph (i) of § 230.482 of this chapter.

(ii) Any fee and expense information included in sales literature must meet the timeliness requirements of paragraph (j) of § 230.482 of this chapter.

(2) The requirements specified in paragraph (c)(1) of this section do not apply to any quarterly, semi-annual, or annual report to shareholders under Section 30 of the Act [15 U.S.C. 80a–29] or to other reports pursuant to section 13 or section 15(d) of the Securities Exchange Act of 1934 (15 U.S.C. 79m or 78o(d)) containing fee and expense information; nor do the requirements of paragraphs (i) and (j) of § 230.482 of this chapter or paragraph (c)(3) of § 230.433 of this chapter apply to any such report containing fee and expense information.

NOTE: Sales literature (except that of a money market fund) containing a quotation of yield or tax equivalent yield must also contain the total return information. In the case of sales literature, the currentness provisions apply from the date of distribution and not the date of submission for publication.

[58 FR 19055, Apr. 12, 1993; 58 FR 21927, Apr. 26, 1993, as amended at 62 FR 64986, Dec. 9, 1997; 63 FR 13987, Mar. 23, 1998; 66 FR 9018, Feb. 5, 2001; 68 FR 57779, Oct. 6, 2003; 87 FR 72850, Nov. 25, 2022]

§ 270.35d–1 Investment company names.

(a) For purposes of section 35(d) of the Act (15 U.S.C. 80a–34(d)), a materially deceptive and misleading name of a Fund includes:

(1) *Names suggesting guarantee or approval by the United States government.* A name suggesting that the Fund or the securities issued by it are guaranteed, sponsored, recommended, or approved by the United States government or any United States government agency or instrumentality, including any name that uses the words "guaranteed" or "insured" or similar terms in conjunction with the words "United States" or "U.S. government."

(2) *Names suggesting investment in certain investments or industries.* A name suggesting that the Fund focuses its investments in a particular type of investment or investments, or in investments in a particular industry or group of industries, unless:

(i) The Fund has adopted a policy to invest, under normal circumstances, at

Securities and Exchange Commission § 270.38a–1

least 80% of the value of its Assets in the particular type of investments, or in investments in the particular industry or industries, suggested by the Fund's name; and

(ii) Either the policy described in paragraph (a)(2)(i) of this section is a fundamental policy under section 8(b)(3) of the Act (15 U.S.C. 80a–8(b)(3)), or the Fund has adopted a policy to provide the Fund's shareholders with at least 60 days prior notice of any change in the policy described in paragraph (a)(2)(i) of this section that meets the requirements of paragraph (c) of this section.

(3) *Names suggesting investment in certain countries or geographic regions.* A name suggesting that the Fund focuses its investments in a particular country or geographic region, unless:

(i) The Fund has adopted a policy to invest, under normal circumstances, at least 80% of the value of its Assets in investments that are tied economically to the particular country or geographic region suggested by its name;

(ii) The Fund discloses in its prospectus the specific criteria used by the Fund to select these investments; and

(iii) Either the policy described in paragraph (a)(3)(i) of this section is a fundamental policy under section 8(b)(3) of the Act (15 U.S.C. 80a–8(b)(3)), or the Fund has adopted a policy to provide the Fund's shareholders with at least 60 days prior notice of any change in the policy described in paragraph (a)(3)(i) of this section that meets the requirements of paragraph (c) of this section.

(4) *Tax-exempt Funds.* A name suggesting that the Fund's distributions are exempt from federal income tax or from both federal and state income tax, unless the Fund has adopted a fundamental policy under section 8(b)(3) of the Act (15 U.S.C. 80a–8(b)(3)):

(i) To invest, under normal circumstances, at least 80% of the value of its Assets in investments the income from which is exempt, as applicable, from federal income tax or from both federal and state income tax; or

(ii) To invest, under normal circumstances, its Assets so that at least 80% of the income that it distributes will be exempt, as applicable, from federal income tax or from both federal and state income tax.

(b) The requirements of paragraphs (a)(2) through (a)(4) of this section apply at the time a Fund invests its Assets, except that these requirements shall not apply to any unit investment trust (as defined in section 4(2) of the Act (15 U.S.C. 80a–4(2))) that has made an initial deposit of securities prior to July 31, 2002. If, subsequent to an investment, these requirements are no longer met, the Fund's future investments must be made in a manner that will bring the Fund into compliance with those paragraphs.

(c) A policy to provide a Fund's shareholders with notice of a change in a Fund's investment policy as described in paragraphs (a)(2)(ii) and (a)(3)(iii) of this section must provide that:

(1) The notice will be provided in plain English in a separate written document;

(2) The notice will contain the following prominent statement, or similar clear and understandable statement, in bold-face type: "Important Notice Regarding Change in Investment Policy"; and

(3) The statement contained in paragraph (c)(2) of this section also will appear on the envelope in which the notice is delivered or, if the notice is delivered separately from other communications to investors, that the statement will appear either on the notice or on the envelope in which the notice is delivered.

(d) For purposes of this section:

(1) *Fund* means a registered investment company and any series of the investment company.

(2) *Assets* means net assets, plus the amount of any borrowings for investment purposes.

[66 FR 8518, Feb. 1, 2001; 66 FR 14828, Mar. 14, 2001]

§ 270.38a–1 **Compliance procedures and practices of certain investment companies.**

(a) Each registered investment company and business development company ("fund") must:

(1) *Policies and procedures.* Adopt and implement written policies and procedures reasonably designed to prevent

§ 270.38a–1

violation of the Federal Securities Laws by the fund, including policies and procedures that provide for the oversight of compliance by each investment adviser, principal underwriter, administrator, and transfer agent of the fund;

(2) *Board approval.* Obtain the approval of the fund's board of directors, including a majority of directors who are not interested persons of the fund, of the fund's policies and procedures and those of each investment adviser, principal underwriter, administrator, and transfer agent of the fund, which approval must be based on a finding by the board that the policies and procedures are reasonably designed to prevent violation of the Federal Securities Laws by the fund, and by each investment adviser, principal underwriter, administrator, and transfer agent of the fund;

(3) *Annual review.* Review, no less frequently than annually, the adequacy of the policies and procedures of the fund and of each investment adviser, principal underwriter, administrator, and transfer agent and the effectiveness of their implementation;

(4) *Chief compliance officer.* Designate one individual responsible for administering the fund's policies and procedures adopted under paragraph (a)(1) of this section:

(i) Whose designation and compensation must be approved by the fund's board of directors, including a majority of the directors who are not interested persons of the fund;

(ii) Who may be removed from his or her responsibilities by action of (and only with the approval of) the fund's board of directors, including a majority of the directors who are not interested persons of the fund;

(iii) Who must, no less frequently than annually, provide a written report to the board that, at a minimum, addresses:

(A) The operation of the policies and procedures of the fund and each investment adviser, principal underwriter, administrator, and transfer agent of the fund, any material changes made to those policies and procedures since the date of the last report, and any material changes to the policies and procedures recommended as a result of the annual review conducted pursuant to paragraph (a)(3) of this section; and

(B) Each Material Compliance Matter that occurred since the date of the last report; and

(iv) Who must, no less frequently than annually, meet separately with the fund's independent directors.

(b) *Unit investment trusts.* If the fund is a unit investment trust, the fund's principal underwriter or depositor must approve the fund's policies and procedures and chief compliance officer, must receive all annual reports, and must approve the removal of the chief compliance officer from his or her responsibilities.

(c) *Undue influence prohibited.* No officer, director, or employee of the fund, its investment adviser, or principal underwriter, or any person acting under such person's direction may directly or indirectly take any action to coerce, manipulate, mislead, or fraudulently influence the fund's chief compliance officer in the performance of his or her duties under this section.

(d) *Recordkeeping.* The fund must maintain:

(1) A copy of the policies and procedures adopted by the fund under paragraph (a)(1) that are in effect, or at any time within the past five years were in effect, in an easily accessible place; and

(2) Copies of materials provided to the board of directors in connection with their approval under paragraph (a)(2) of this section, and written reports provided to the board of directors pursuant to paragraph (a)(4)(iii) of this section (or, if the fund is a unit investment trust, to the fund's principal underwriter or depositor, pursuant to paragraph (b) of this section) for at least five years after the end of the fiscal year in which the documents were provided, the first two years in an easily accessible place; and

(3) Any records documenting the fund's annual review pursuant to paragraph (a)(3) of this section for at least five years after the end of the fiscal year in which the annual review was conducted, the first two years in an easily accessible place.

(e) *Definitions.* For purposes of this section:

Securities and Exchange Commission § 270.57b–1

(1) *Federal Securities Laws* means the Securities Act of 1933 (15 U.S.C. 77a–aa), the Securities Exchange Act of 1934 (15 U.S.C. 78a–mm), the Sarbanes-Oxley Act of 2002 (Pub. L. 107–204, 116 Stat. 745 (2002)), the Investment Company Act of 1940 (15 U.S.C. 80a), the Investment Advisers Act of 1940 (15 U.S.C. 80b), Title V of the Gramm-Leach-Bliley Act (Pub. L. No. 106–102, 113 Stat. 1338 (1999), any rules adopted by the Commission under any of these statutes, the Bank Secrecy Act (31 U.S.C. 5311–5314; 5316–5332) as it applies to funds, and any rules adopted thereunder by the Commission or the Department of the Treasury.

(2) A *Material Compliance Matter* means any compliance matter about which the fund's board of directors would reasonably need to know to oversee fund compliance, and that involves, without limitation:

(i) A violation of the Federal securities laws by the fund, its investment adviser, principal underwriter, administrator or transfer agent (or officers, directors, employees or agents thereof),

(ii) A violation of the policies and procedures of the fund, its investment adviser, principal underwriter, administrator or transfer agent, or

(iii) A weakness in the design or implementation of the policies and procedures of the fund, its investment adviser, principal underwriter, administrator or transfer agent.

[68 FR 74729, Dec. 24, 2003]

§ 270.45a–1 Confidential treatment of names and addresses of dealers of registered investment company securities.

(a) Exhibits calling for the names and addresses of dealers to or through whom principal underwriters of registered investment companies are currently offering securities and which are required to be furnished with registration statements filed pursuant to section 8(b) of the Act (54 Stat. 804; 15 U.S.C. 80a–8), or periodic reports filed pursuant to section 30(a) or section 30(b)(1) of the Act (54 Stat. 836; 15 U.S.C. 80a–30), shall be the subject of confidential treatment and shall not be made available to the public, except that the Commission may by order make such exhibits available to the public if, after appropriate notice and opportunity for hearing, it finds that public disclosure of such material is necessary or appropriate in the public interest or for the protection of investors.

(b) The exhibits referred to in paragraph (a) of this section shall be filed in quadruplicate with the Commission at the time the registration statement or periodic report is filed. Such exhibits shall be enclosed in a separate envelope marked "Confidential Treatment" and addressed to the Chairman, Securities and Executive Commission, Washington, DC. Confidential treatment requests shall be submitted in paper only, whether or not the registrant is required to file in electronic format.

[Rule N–45A–1, 7 FR 197, Jan. 10, 1942, as amended at 20 FR 7036, Sept. 20, 1955; 58 FR 14860, Mar. 18, 1993]

§ 270.55a–1 Investment activities of business development companies.

Notwithstanding section 55(a) of the Act (15 U.S.C. 80a–54(a)), a business development company may acquire securities purchased in transactions not involving any public offering from an issuer, or from any person who is an officer or employee of the issuer, if the issuer meets the requirements of sections 2(a)(46)(A) and (B) of the Act (15 U.S.C. 80a–2(a)(46)(A) and (B)), but the issuer is not an eligible portfolio company because it does not meet the requirements of § 270.2a–46, and the business development company meets the requirements of paragraphs (i) and (ii) of section 55(a)(1)(B) of the Act (15 U.S.C. 80a–54(a)(1)(B)(i) and (ii)).

[71 FR 64092, Oct. 31, 2006]

§ 270.57b–1 Exemption for downstream affiliates of business development companies.

Notwithstanding subsection (b)(2) of section 57 of the Act, the provisions of subsection (a) of that section shall not apply to any person (a) solely because that person is directly or indirectly controlled by a business development company or (b) solely because that person is, within the meaning of section 2(a)(3) (C) or (D) of the Act [15 U.S.C.

§ 270.60a-1

80a-2(a)(3) (C) or (D)], an affiliated person of a person described in (a) of this section.

[46 FR 16674, Mar. 13, 1981]

§ 270.60a-1 Exemption for certain business development companies.

Section 12(d)(1) (A) and (C) of the Act shall not apply to the acquisition by a business development company of the securities of a small business investment company licensed to do business under the Small Business Investment Act of 1958 which is operated as a wholly-owned subsidiary of the business development company.

[46 FR 16674, Mar. 13, 1981]

PART 271—INTERPRETATIVE RELEASES RELATING TO THE INVESTMENT COMPANY ACT OF 1940 AND GENERAL RULES AND REGULATIONS THEREUNDER

AUTHORITY: 15 U.S.C. 80a et seq.

Subject	Release No.	Date	Fed. Reg. Vol. and Page
Statement of the Commission respecting distinctions between the reporting requirements of section 16(a) of the Securities Exchange Act of 1934 and section 30(f) of the Investment Company Act of 1940.	12	Nov. 16, 1940	11 FR 10991.
Letter of General Counsel relating to sections(b) and 26(c)	69	Feb. 19, 1941	Do.
Letter of the Director of the Investment Company Division relating to section 19 and Rule N-19-1 (17 CFR, 270.19a-1).	71	Feb. 21, 1941	Do.
Statement by the Commission relating to section 23(c)(3) and Rule N-23C-1 (17 CFR, 270.23c-1).	78	Mar. 4, 1941	Do.
Letter of General Counsel relating to section 22(d)	87	Mar. 14, 1941	11 FR 10992.
Letter of General Counsel relating to section 22(d)	89	Mar. 13, 1941	Do.
Letter of General Counsel relating to section 24(b)	150	June 20, 1941	Do.
Opinion of General Counsel relating to sections 8(b)(1) and 13(a)	167	July 23, 1941	11 FR 10993.
Letter of General Counsel relating to section 10(a)	214	Sept. 15, 1941	11 FR 10994.
Extract from letter of the Director of the Corporation Finance Division relating to sections 20 and 34(b).	446	Feb. 5, 1943	Do.
Excerpts from letters of the Director of the Corporation Finance Division relating to section 14 and Schedule 14A under Regulation X-14.	448	Feb. 17, 1943	Do.
Letter of the Director of the Corporation Finance Division relating to section 20 of the Investment Company Act of 1940 and to Rule X-14A-7 under the Securities Exchange Act of 1934 (17 CFR, 240.14a-7).	735	Jan. 3, 1945	11 FR 10995.
Statement of the Commission on the offering of common stock to the public at a per share price substantially in excess of the net asset value of the stock.	3187	Feb. 6, 1961	26 FR 1275.
Opinion of the Commission that "Equity Funding," "Secured Funding," or "Life Funding" constitutes an investment contract and when publicly offered is required to be registered under the Securities Act of 1933.	3480	May 22, 1962	27 FR 5190.
Statement of the Commission advising all registered investment companies to divest themselves of interest and securities acquired in contravention of the provisions of section 12(d)(3) of the Investment Company Act of 1940 within a reasonable period of time.	3542	Sept. 21, 1962	27 FR 9652.
Statement of the Commission advising any closed-end investment company contemplating repurchase of its own shares to consult with the Division of Corporate re nature of disclosure to be made to security holders.	3548	Oct. 3, 1962	27 FR 9987.
Opinion and statement of the Commission in regard to proper reporting of deferred income taxes arising from installment sales.	4426	Dec. 7, 1965	30 FR 15420.
Statement of the Commission to clarify the meaning of "beneficial ownership of securities" as relates to beneficial ownership of securities held by family members.	4483	Jan. 19, 1966	31 FR 1005.
Statement of the Commission setting the date of May 1, 1966 after which filings must reflect beneficial ownership of securities held by family members.	4516	Feb. 14, 1966	31 FR 3175.
Staff interpretative and no-action positions relating to property rights of an investment company and its investment adviser in the company's name and to the status of arrangement funding qualified Self-Employed Individual's Retirement Plans with life insurance contracts and investment company securities. The staff's comments do not purport to be an official expression of the Commission.	5510	Oct. 8, 1968	33 FR 15650.
Statement of the Director of the Commission's Division of Corporate Regulation re the filing of supplements to investment company prospectuses under the Securities Act of 1933 as a result of changes in stock exchange rules effective December 5, 1968 relating to "customer-directed give ups".	5554	Dec. 3, 1968	33 FR 18576.

Securities and Exchange Commission

Pt. 271

Subject	Release No.	Date	Fed. Reg. Vol. and Page
Interpretative positions of the Division of Corporate Regulation on questions relating to Rule 22c–1 which was adopted Oct. 16, 1968; text of questions and answers.	5569	Dec. 27, 1968	34 FR 382.
Statement of the Commission setting forth emergency procedures adopted by the Division of Corporate Regulation to expedite processing of registration statements, amendments, and proxy statements.	5632	Mar. 12, 1969	34 FR 5547.
Letter by Philip A. Loomis, Jr., General Counsel for the Commission, explaining obligations of mutual fund managements and brokers with respect to commissions on portfolio brokerage of mutual funds.	....	Nov. 10, 1969	34 FR 18543.
Commission's statement discussing restricted securities	5847	Oct. 21, 1969	35 FR 19989.
Commission's statement that disclosure requirements set forth in release of October 21, 1969 will be applied to lists of portfolio securities set forth not only in registration statements but also in reports to the Commission and to shareholders, in sales literature and in proxy statements.	6026	Apr. 13, 1970	35 FR 19991.
Publication of the Commission's guidelines re applicability of Federal securities law to offer and sale outside the U.S. of shares of registered open-end investment companies.	6082	June 23, 1970	36 FR 12103.
Statement of the Commission reminding reporting companies of obligation re Commission's rules to file reports on a timely basis.	6209	Oct. 15, 1970	35 FR 16733.
Commission's views relating to important questions re the accounting by registered investment companies for investment securities in their financial statements and in the periodic computations of net asset value for the purpose of pricing their shares.	6295	Dec. 23, 1970	35 FR 19986.
Publication of the Commission's procedure to be followed if requests are to be met for no action or interpretative letters and responses thereto to be made available for public use.	6330	Jan. 25, 1971	36 FR 2600.
First in a series of statements by the Commission alerting registered companies, their counsel, and other interested persons re certain changes made in the Investment Company Act of 1940 by Pub. L. 91–547 (1970 Act) such as approval of investment advisory contracts which should be considered in connection with 1971 annual meetings.	6336	Feb. 2, 1971	36 FR 2867.
The Commission's views on the purchase, redemption, or repurchase of fund shares.	6366	Mar. 5, 1971	36 FR 4978.
Second in a series of statements by the Commission calling attention to some important provisions of Pub. L. 91–547 (1970 Act) which in this case require companies that issue periodic payment plans and face-amount certificates to take certain actions.	6392	Mar. 19, 1971	36 FR 5840.
Third in a series of statements by the Commission on problems arising under Pub. L. 91–547 (1970 Act) re registration and regulation of insurance company separate accounts used as funding vehicles for certain employee stock bonus, pension and profit sharing plans.	6430	Apr. 2, 1971	36 FR 7897.
Publication by the Commission of certain important amendments relating to the repeal and modification of certain exemptions by the Investment Company Amendments Act of 1970 (Pub. L. 91–547) and to the pyramiding of investment companies and the regulation of fund holding companies under the same act.	6440	Apr. 6, 1971	36 FR 8729.
Commission's statement on amendments contained in Pub. L. 91–547 concerning policies of a registered investment company; ineligibility of certain persons to serve as employees of a registered company; legal standards for investment company reorganizations of unit investment trusts; and filing of certain legal documents with the Commission.	6506	May 5, 1971	36 FR 9130.
Commission's interpretative position relating to judiciary duty of Directors of a Registered Investment Company.	6480	May 10, 1971	36 FR 9627.
Commission's issuance of guidelines for additional disclosures for contractual plan prospectuses concerning new refund and election provisions of the Investment Company Amendments Act of 1970 (Pub. L. 91–547).	6568	June 11, 1971	36 FR 12164.
Commission's guidelines relating to checking accounts established by investment companies having bank custodians.	6863	Jan. 29, 1972	37 FR 1474.
Commission endorses the establishment by all publicly held companies of audit committees composed of outside directors.	7091	Apr. 5, 1972	37 FR 6850.
Commission's statement of factors to be considered in connection with investment company advisory contracts containing incentive arrangements.	7113	Apr. 19, 1972	37 FR 7690.
Applicability of Commission's policy statement on the future structure of securities markets to selection of brokers and payment of commissions by institutional managers.	7170	May 18, 1972	37 FR 9988.
Commission's statement and policy on misleading pro rata stock distributions to shareholders.	7204	June 9, 1972	37 FR 11559.
Commission's guidelines prepared by the Division of Corporate Regulation for use in preparing and filing registration statements for open-end and closed-end management investment companies on Forms S–4 and S–5.	7220	June 9, 1972	37 FR 12790.
Guidelines prepared by the Commission's Division of Corporate Regulation for use in preparation and filing of registration statements for both open-end and closed-end management investment companies on Form N–8B–1.	7221	June 9, 1972	37 FR 12790.

Subject	Release No.	Date	Fed. Reg. Vol. and Page
Commission's guidelines on independence of certifying accountants; example cases and Commission's conclusions.	7264	July 5, 1972	37 FR 14294.
Commission's decisions on advisory committee recommendations regarding commencement of enforcement proceedings and termination of staff investigations.	7390	Mar. 1, 1973	38 FR 5457.
Commission's interpretation of risk-sharing in pooling-of-interest accounting	7395	Oct. 5, 1972	37 FR 20937.
Amendment of previous interpretation (AS–130) of risk-sharing test in pooling-of-interest accounting.	7606	Jan. 18, 1973	38 FR 1734.
Commission expresses concern with failure of issuers to timely file periodic and current reports.	7856	July 10, 1973	38 FR 18366.
Commission's conclusion as to certain problems relating to the effect of treasury stock transaction on accounting for business combinations.	7955	Sept. 10, 1973	38 FR 24635.
Commission request for comments on Accounting Series Release No. 146	8025	Oct. 17, 1973	38 FR 28819.
Commission's statement on procedure to be followed upon issuance of a notice pursuant to Rule 0–5.	8236	Mar. 7, 1974	39 FR 8916.
Commission's statement of policy and interpretations	7955A	Apr. 12, 1974	39 FR 14588.
Commission's views on business combinations involving open-end investment companies.	8410	July 3, 1974	39 FR 26719.
Commission's guidelines for filings related to extractive reserves and natural gas supplies.	8433	July 22, 1974	39 FR 28520.
Commission's statement on two-tier real estate investment companies	8456	Sept. 5, 1974	39 FR 32129.
Division of Investment Management Regulation Interpretive Position Relating to Rule 22c–1.	8752	Apr. 24, 1975	40 FR 17986.
Commission's guidelines in Accounting Series Release No. 148	8819	June 13, 1975	40 FR 27441.
Commission's guidelines for filing of application for Order permitting registration of foreign investment companies.	8959	Oct. 2, 1975	40 FR 45424.
Commission's statements of investment policies of money market funds relating to industry concentration.	9011	Oct. 30, 1975	40 FR 54241.
Procedures for filing and processing registration statements and post-effective amendments filed by registered investment companies.	9426	Sept. 13, 1976	41 FR 39012. 41 FR 46851.
Valuation of debt instruments by money market funds and certain other open end investment companies.	9786	May 31, 1977	42 FR 28999.
Rescission of certain accounting series releases	9817	June 15, 1977	42 FR 33282.
Withdrawal of undertaking required of investment companies	9889	Aug. 12, 1977	42 FR 42196.
Disclosure of management remuneration	9900	Aug. 18, 1977	42 FR 43058; 42 FR 46047.
Bearing of distribution expenses by mutual funds	9915	Aug. 31, 1977	42 FR 44810.
Division of investment management interpretative position relating to rights offerings by closed-end investment companies below net asset value.	9932	Sept. 15, 1977	42 FR 47553.
Disclosure of management remuneration	10112	Feb. 6, 1978	43 FR 6060.
Sales load variation in special offerings to permit mutual fund shareholders to purchase additional shares.	10419	Oct. 4, 1978	43 FR 47492; 43 FR 52022.
Disclosure of management remuneration	10597	Feb. 22, 1979	44 FR 16368.
General statement of policy regarding exemptive provisions relating to annuity and insurance contracts.	10653	Apr. 5, 1979	44 FR 21629.
General statement of policy regarding securities trading practices of registered investment companies.	10666	Apr. 18, 1979	44 FR 25128.
Shareholder communications, shareholder participation in the corporate electoral process and corporate governance generally.	10860	Sept. 6, 1979	44 FR 53426.
Statement of staff position on pooled income funds	11016	Jan. 10, 1980	45 FR 3258.
Effect of credit controls on the operations of certain registered investment companies including money market refunds.	11088	Mar. 14, 1980	45 FR 17954.
Effective of the termination of credit controls on the operations of certain registered investment companies including money market funds.	11263	July 21, 1980	45 FR 49917.
Indemnification by investment companies	11330	Sept. 4, 1980	45 FR 62423; 45 FR 67082.
Issuance of "Retail Repurchase Agreements" by banks and savings and loan associations.	11958	Sept. 25, 1981	46 FR 48637.
Effect of revenue ruling 81–225 on issuers and holders of certain variable annuity contracts.	11960	Sept. 28, 1981	46 FR 48640.
Disclosure of management remuneration	12070	Dec. 3, 1981	46 FR 60421.
Statement of staff position on adoption of permanent notification forms for business development companies.	12274	Mar. 5, 1982	47 FR 10518.
Statement of staff position regarding securities trading practices of registered investment companies.	13005	Feb. 2, 1983	48 FR 5894.
Public statements by corporate representatives	13718	Jan. 13, 1984	49 FR 2469.
Statement of position of Commission's Division of Investment Management	14492	Apr. 30, 1985	50 FR 19339.
Statement of the Commission Regarding Disclosure Obligations of Companies Affected by the Government's Defense Contract Procurement Inquiry and Related Issues.	16509	Aug. 1, 1988	53 FR 29228.
Management's discussion and analysis of financial condition and results of operations; certain investment company disclosure.	16961	May 18, 1989	54 FR 22427.

Securities and Exchange Commission Pt. 274

Subject	Release No.	Date	Fed. Reg. Vol. and Page
Status under the Investment Company Act of 1940 of United States Branches or Agencies of Foreign Banks Issuing Securities;Interpretive Release.	17681	Aug. 17, 1990	55 FR 34551.
Ownership reports and trading by officers, directors and principal security holders.	18114	Apr. 26, 1991	56 FR 19928.
Use of electronic media for delivery purposes	21399	Oct. 6, 1995	60 FR 53467.
Use of electronic media for delivery purposes	21945	May 9, 1996	60 FR 24651.
Statement of the Commission Regarding Use of Internet Web Sites to Offer Securities, Solicit Securities Transactions or Advertise Investment Services Offshore.	23071	Mar. 23, 1998	63 FR 14813
Statement of the Commission Regarding Disclosure of Year 2000 Issues and Consequences by Public Companies, Investment Advisers, Investment Companies, and Municipal Securities Issuers.	23366	July 29, 1998	63 FR 41404.
Interpretive Matters Concerning Independent Directors of Investment Companies..	24083	Oct. 14, 1999	64 FR 59877.
Use of electronic media	24426	Apr. 28, 2000	65 FR 25857.
Commission Guidance on Mini-Tender Offers and Limited Partnership Tender Offers.	24564	July 24, 2000	65 FR 46588.
Exemption From Section 101(c)(1) of the Electronic Signatures in Global and National Commerce Act for Registered Investment Companies.	24582	July 27, 2000	65 FR 47284.
Application of the Electronic Signatures in Global and National Commerce Act to Record Retention Requirements Pertaining to Issuers.	25003	June 14, 2001	66 FR 33176.
Commission Guidance Regarding Prohibited Conduct in Connection with IPO Allocations.	26828	April 7, 2005	70 FR 19672.
Commission Guidance Regarding Accounting for Sales of Vaccines and Bioterror Countermeasures to the Federal Government for Placement Into the Pediatric Vaccine Stockpile or the Strategic National Stockpile.	27178	December 5, 2005	70 FR 73345
Commission Guidance on the Use of Company Web Sites	28351	August 1, 2008	73 FR 45874
Commission Guidance Regarding the Definition of the Terms "Spouse" and "Marriage" Following the Supreme Court's Decision in *United States* v. *Windsor*.	IC–31684	June 19, 2015	80 FR 37537
Commission Guidance Regarding Revenue Recognition for Bill-and-Hold Arrangements.	IC–32784	Aug. 18, 2017	82 FR 41148
Updates to Commission Guidance Regarding Accounting for Sales of Vaccines and Bioterror Countermeasures to the Federal Government for Placement into the Pediatric Vaccine Stockpile or the Strategic National Stockpile.	IC–32785	Aug. 18, 2017	82 FR 41151
Commission Guidance Regarding the Proxy Voting Responsibilities of Investment Advisers.	IC–33605	Aug. 21, 2019	84 FR 47426

PART 274—FORMS PRESCRIBED UNDER THE INVESTMENT COMPANY ACT OF 1940

Sec.
274.0–1 Availability of forms.

Subpart A—Registration Statements

274.5 Form N–5, for registration statement of small business investment company under the Securities Act of 1933 and the Investment Company Act of 1940.
274.10 Form N–8A, for notification of registration.
274.11 [Reserved]
274.11A Form N–1A, registration statement of open-end management investment companies.
274.11a–1 Form N–2, registration statement of closed end management investment companies.
274.11b Form N–3, registration statement of separate accounts organized as management investment companies.
274.11c Form N–4, registration statement of separate accounts organized as unit investment trusts.
274.11d Form N–6, registration statement of separate accounts organized as unit investment trusts that offer variable life insurance policies.
274.12 Form N–8B–2, registration statement of unit investment trusts which are currently issuing securities.
274.13 Form N–8B–3, registration statement of unincorporated management investment companies currently issuing periodic payment plan certificates.
274.14 Form N–8B–4, registration statements of face-amount certificate companies.
274.15 Form N–6F, notice of intent to elect to be subject to sections 55 through 65 of the Investment Company Act of 1940.
274.24 Form 24F–2, annual filing of securities sold pursuant to registration of certain investment company securities.
274.51 Form N–18F–1, for notification of election pursuant to § 270.18f–1 of this chapter.

§ 274.0–1

274.53 Form N–54A, notification of election to be subject to sections 55 through 65 of the Investment Company Act of 1940 filed pursuant to section 54(a) of the Act.
274.54 Form N–54C, notification of withdrawal of election to be subject to sections 55 through 65 of the Investment Company Act of 1940 filed pursuant to section 54(c) of the Investment Company Act of 1940.

Subpart B—Forms for Reports

§ 274.101 Form N–CEN, annual report of registered investment companies.
274.102–274.126 [Reserved]
274.127d–1 Form N–27D–1, accounting of segregated trust account.
274.128 Form N–CSR, certified shareholder report.
274.129 Form N–PX, annual report of proxy voting record of registered management investment company.
274.130 [Reserved]
274.150 Form N–PORT, Monthly portfolio holdings report.
274.200 Form N–17D–1, report filed by small business investment company (SBIC) registered under the Investment Company Act of 1940 and an affiliated bank, with respect to investments by the SBIC and the bank, submitted pursuant to paragraph (d)(3) of § 270.17d–1 of this chapter.

Subpart C—Forms for Other Statements

274.201 Form N–MFP, portfolio holdings of money market funds.
274.202 Form 3, initial statement of beneficial ownership of securities.
274.203 Form 4, statement of changes in beneficial ownership of securities.
274.218 Form N–8F, application for deregistration of certain registered investment companies.
274.219 Form N–17f–1, cover page for each certificate of accounting of securities and similar investments of a management investment company in the custody of a member of a national securities exchange, filed pursuant to rule 17f–1.
274.220 Form N–17f–2, cover page for each certificate of accounting of securities and similar investments in the custody of a registered management investment company, filed pursuant to rule 17f–2.
274.221 Form N–23c–3, Notification of repurchase offer.
274.222 Form N–CR, Current report of money market fund material events.
274.223 Form N–RN, Current report, open- and closed-end investment company reporting.

Subpart D—Forms for Exemptions

274.301 Notification of claim of exemption pursuant to Rule 6e–2 or Rule 6e–3(T) under the Investment Company Act.

Subpart E—Forms for Electronic Filing

274.401 [Reserved]
274.402 Form ID, uniform application for access codes to file on EDGAR.
274.403 Form SE, form for submission of paper format exhibits by electronic filers.
274.404 Form TH—Notification of reliance on temporary hardship exemption.

AUTHORITY: 15 U.S.C. 77f, 77g, 77h, 77j, 77s, 78c(b), 78*l*, 78m, 78n, 78*o*(d), 80a–8, 80a–24, 80a–26, 80a–29, and 80a–37 unless otherwise noted.

Section 274.128 is also issued under 15 U.S.C. 78j–1, 7202, 7233, 7241, 7264, and 7265; and 18 U.S.C. 1350.

EFFECTIVE DATE NOTE: At 87 FR 78809, Dec. 22, 2022, the general authority citation to part 274 was revised, effective July 1, 2024. For the convenience of the user, the revised text is set forth as follows:

AUTHORITY: 15 U.S.C. 77f, 77g, 77h, 77j, 77s, 78c(b), 78*l*, 78m, 78n, 78n–1, 78*o*(d), 80a–8, 80a–24, 80a–26, 80a–29, and sec. 939A, Pub. L. 111–203, 124 Stat. 1376, unless otherwise noted.

SOURCE: 33 FR 19003, Dec. 20, 1968, unless otherwise noted.

§ 274.0–1 Availability of forms.

(a) This part identifies and describes the forms prescribed for use under the Investment Company Act of 1940.

(b) Any person may obtain a copy of any form prescribed for use in this part by written request to the Securities and Exchange Commission, 100 F Street, NE., Washington, DC 20549. Any person may inspect the forms at this address and at the Commission's regional offices. (See § 200.11 of this chapter for the addresses of SEC regional offices)

[46 FR 17757, Mar. 20, 1981, as amended at 47 FR 26820, June 22, 1982; 59 FR 5946, Feb. 9, 1994; 73 FR 32228, June 5, 2008]

Securities and Exchange Commission § 274.11b

Subpart A—Registration Statements

§ 274.5 Form N-5, for registration statement of small business investment company under the Securities Act of 1933 and the Investment Company Act of 1940.

This form shall be used for the registration statement under both sections 6 and 7 of the Securities Act of 1933 (15 U.S.C. 77f, 77g) and section 8(b) of the Investment Company Act of 1940 (15 U.S.C. 80a–8(b)), by a small business investment company which is licensed as such under the Small Business Investment Act of 1958 or which has received preliminary approval of the Small Business Administration and has been notified by that Administration that it may submit a license application.

EDITORIAL NOTE: For FEDERAL REGISTER citations affecting Form N-5, see the List of CFR Sections Affected, which appears in the Finding Aids section of the printed volume and at *www.govinfo.gov*.

§ 274.10 Form N-8A, for notification of registration.

This form shall be used as the notification of registration filed with the Commission pursuant to section 8(a) of the Investment Company Act of 1940.

EDITORIAL NOTE: For FEDERAL REGISTER citations affecting Form N-8A, see the List of CFR Sections Affected, which appears in the Finding Aids section of the printed volume and at *www.govinfo.gov*.

§ 274.11 [Reserved]

§ 274.11A Form N-1A, registration statement of open-end management investment companies.

Form N-1A shall be used as the registration statement to be filed pursuant to section 8(b) of the Investment Company Act of 1940 by open-end management investment companies other than separate accounts of insurance companies or companies which issue periodic payment plan certificates or which are sponsors or depositors of companies issuing such certificates. This form shall be used for registration under the Securities Act of 1933 of the securities of all open-end management investment companies other than registered separate accounts of insurance companies. This form is not applicable for small business investment companies which register pursuant to §§ 293.24 and 274.5 of this chapter.

[48 FR 37940, Aug. 22, 1983, as amended at 59 FR 52701, Oct. 19, 1994]

EDITORIAL NOTE: For FEDERAL REGISTER citations affecting Form N-1A, see the List of CFR Sections Affected, which appears in the Finding Aids section of the printed volume and at *www.govinfo.gov*.

§ 274.11a-1 Form N-2, registration statement of closed end management investment companies.

This form shall be used as the registration statement to be filed pursuant to section 8(b) of the Investment Company Act of 1940 by closed end management investment companies other than companies which issue periodic payment plan certificates or which are sponsors or depositors of companies issuing such certificates. This form also shall be used for registration under the Securities Act of 1933 of the securities of all closed end management investment companies. This form is not applicable for small business investment companies which register pursuant to §§ 239.24 and 274.5 of this chapter.

[43 FR 39553, Sept. 5, 1978, as amended at 59 FR 52701, Oct. 19, 1994]

EDITORIAL NOTE: For FEDERAL REGISTER citations affecting Form N-2, see the List of CFR Sections Affected, which appears in the Finding Aids section of the printed volume and at *www.govinfo.gov*.

§ 274.11b Form N-3, registration statement of separate accounts organized as management investment companies.

Form N-3 shall be used as the registration statement to be filed pursuant to section 8(b) of the Investment Company Act of 1940 by separate accounts that offer variable annuity contracts to register as management investment companies. This form shall also be used for registration under the Securities Act of 1933 of the securities of such separate accounts (§ 239.17a of this chapter).

[50 FR 26161, June 25, 1985]

EDITORIAL NOTE: For FEDERAL REGISTER citations affecting Form N-3, see the List of CFR Sections Affected, which appears in the

§ 274.11c

Finding Aids section of the printed volume and at *www.govinfo.gov*.

§ 274.11c Form N-4, registration statement of separate accounts organized as unit investment trusts.

Form N-4 shall be used as the registration statement to be filed pursuant to section 8(b) of the Investment Company Act of 1940 by separate accounts that offer variable annuity contracts to register as unit investment trusts. This form shall also be used for registration under the Securities Act of 1933 of the securities of such separate accounts (§ 239.17b of this chapter).

[50 FR 26161, June 25, 1985]

EDITORIAL NOTE: For FEDERAL REGISTER citations affecting Form N-4, see the List of CFR Sections Affected, which appears in the Finding Aids section of the printed volume and at *www.govinfo.gov*.

§ 274.11d Form N-6, registration statement of separate accounts organized as unit investment trusts that offer variable life insurance policies.

Form N-6 shall be used as the registration statement to be filed pursuant to section 8(b) of the Investment Company Act of 1940 by separate accounts that offer variable life insurance policies to register as unit investment trusts. This form shall also be used for registration under the Securities Act of 1933 of the securities of such separate accounts (§ 239.17c of this chapter).

[67 FR 19870, Apr. 23, 2002]

EDITORIAL NOTE: For FEDERAL REGISTER citations affecting Form N-6, see the List of CFR Sections Affected, which appears in the Finding Aids section of the printed volume and at *www.govinfo.gov*.

§ 274.12 Form N-8B-2, registration statement of unit investment trusts that are currently issuing securities.

This form shall be used as the registration statement to be filed, pursuant to section 8(b) of the Investment Company Act of 1940, by unit investment trusts other than separate accounts that are currently issuing securities, including unit investment trusts that are issuers of periodic payment plan certificates.

[67 FR 19870, Apr. 23, 2002]

EDITORIAL NOTE: For FEDERAL REGISTER citations affecting Form N-8B-2, see the List of CFR Sections Affected, which appears in the Finding Aids section of the printed volume and at *www.govinfo.gov*.

§ 274.13 Form N-8B-3, registration statement of unincorporated management investment companies currently issuing periodic payment plan certificates.

(a) This form shall be used for registration statement to be filed, pursuant to section 8(b) of the Investment Company Act of 1940, by unincorporated management investment companies currently issuing periodic payment plan certificates.

EDITORIAL NOTE: For FEDERAL REGISTER citations affecting Form N-8B-3, see the List of CFR Sections Affected, which appears in the Finding Aids section of the printed volume and at *www.govinfo.gov*.

§ 274.14 Form N-8B-4, registration statements of face-amount certificate companies.

This form shall be used for registration statements of face-amount certificate companies registered under the Investment Company Act of 1940.

EDITORIAL NOTE: For FEDERAL REGISTER citations affecting Form N-8B-4, see the List of CFR Sections Affected, which appears in the Finding Aids section of the printed volume and at *www.govinfo.gov*.

§ 274.15 Form N-6F, notice of intent to elect to be subject to sections 55 through 65 of the Investment Company Act of 1940.

This form shall be used by a company that would be excluded from the definition of an investment company by section 3(c)(1) of the Investment Company Act of 1940 [15 U.S.C. 80a-3(c)(1)], except that at the time of filing it proposes to make a public offering of its securities as a business development company, to notify the Securities and Exchange Commission that the company intends in good faith to file, within 90 days, a notification of election to become subject to the provisions of sections 55 through 65 of the Investment Company Act of 1940 [15 U.S.C. 80a-54 through 64].

Securities and Exchange Commission

The text of the form is set forth in the appendix to this release.[1]

[47 FR 10520, Mar. 11, 1982]

EDITORIAL NOTE: For FEDERAL REGISTER citations affecting Form N-6F, see the List of CFR Sections Affected, which appears in the Finding Aids section of the printed volume and at www.govinfo.gov.

§ 274.24 Form 24F-2, annual filing of securities sold pursuant to registration of certain investment company securities.

Form 24F-2 shall be used as the annual report filed by face amount certificate companies, open-end management companies, and unit investment trusts pursuant to § 270.24f-2 of this chapter for reporting securities sold during the fiscal year.

[62 FR 47940, Sept. 12, 1997]

EDITORIAL NOTE: For FEDERAL REGISTER citations affecting Form 24F-2, see the List of CFR Sections Affected, which appears in the Finding Aids section of the printed volume and at www.govinfo.gov.

§ 274.51 Form N-18F-1, for notification of election pursuant to § 270.18f-1 of this chapter.

(a) This form shall be filed with the Commission in triplicate as the notification of election pursuant to § 270.18f-1 of this chapter by a registered open-end investment company to commit itself to pay in cash all redemptions requested by a shareholder of record as provided in said section.

[36 FR 11920, June 23, 1971 as amended at 36 FR 20504, Oct. 23, 1971; 39 FR 36003, Oct. 7, 1974; 59 FR 52701, Oct. 19, 1994]

EDITORIAL NOTE: For FEDERAL REGISTER citations affecting Form N-18F-1, see the List of CFR Sections Affected, which appears in the Finding Aids section of the printed volume and at www.govinfo.gov.

§ 274.53 Form N-54A, notification of election to be subject to sections 55 through 65 of the Investment Company Act of 1940 filed pursuant to section 54(a) of the Act.

This form shall be used pursuant to section 54(a) of the Investment Company Act of 1940 [15 U.S.C. 80a-53(a)] by a company of the type defined in sections 2(a)(48) (A) and (B) of the Investment Company Act of 1940 (15 U.S.C. 80a-2(a)(48) (A) and (B) to notify the Securities and Exchange Commission of its election to be subject to the provisions of sections 55 through 65 of said Act [15 U.S.C. 80a-54 through 64].

The text of the form is set forth in the appendix to this release.[2]

[47 FR 10520, Mar. 11, 1982]

EDITORIAL NOTE: For FEDERAL REGISTER citations affecting Form N-54A, see the List of CFR Sections Affected, which appears in the Finding Aids section of the printed volume and at www.govinfo.gov.

§ 274.54 Form N-54C, notification of withdrawal of election to be subject to sections 55 through 65 of the Investment Company Act of 1940 filed pursuant to section 54(c) of the Investment Company Act of 1940.

This form shall be used pursuant to section 54(c) of the Investment Company Act of 1940 [15 U.S.C. 80a-53(c)] by a business development company to file a notice of withdrawal of its election under section 54(a) of the Investment Company Act of 1940 [15 U.S.C. 80a-53(a)].

The text of the form is set forth in the appendix to this release.[3]

[47 FR 10520, Mar. 11, 1982]

EDITORIAL NOTE: For FEDERAL REGISTER citations affecting Form N-54C, see the List of CFR Sections Affected, which appears in the Finding Aids section of the printed volume and at www.govinfo.gov.

Subpart B—Forms for Reports

§ 274.101 Form N-CEN, annual report of registered investment companies.

This form shall be used by registered investment companies for annual reports to be filed pursuant to 17 CFR 270.30a-1.

[81 FR 82023, Nov. 18, 2016]

EDITORIAL NOTE: For FEDERAL REGISTER citations affecting Form N-CEN, see the List of CFR Sections Affected, which appears in

---

[1] A copy of Form N-6F accompanied this release as originally filed in the Office of the Federal Register.

[2] A copy of Form N-54A accompanied this release as originally filed in the Office of the Federal Register.

[3] A copy of Form N-54C accompanied this release as originally filed in the Office of the Federal Register.

§§ 274.102–274.126

the Finding Aids section of the printed volume and at *www.govinfo.gov*.

EDITORIAL NOTE: For FEDERAL REGISTER citations affecting Form N-SAR, see the List of CFR Sections Affected, which appears in the Finding Aids section of the printed volume and at *www.govinfo.gov*.

§§ 274.102–274.126 [Reserved]

§ 274.127d–1 Form N–27D–1 accounting of segregated trust account.

This form shall be completed and filed with the Commission as a report required by § 270.27d–1 of this chapter by each depositor or principal underwriter, within 15 days after the close of each quarter during the first 2 years after the effective date of § 270.27d–1 of this chapter, and thereafter this form shall be filed annually on or before January 31 of the following calendar year. Each investment company for which a segregated trust account is established shall be listed on the cover page. Two copies of the form, plus an additional copy for each registered investment company covered, shall be filed and the filing shall be signed by an authorized representative of the depositor or underwriter.

[36 FR 24056, Dec. 18, 1971]

EDITORIAL NOTE: For FEDERAL REGISTER citations affecting Form N–27D–1, see the List of CFR Sections Affected, which appears in the Finding Aids section of the printed volume and at *www.govinfo.gov*.

§ 274.128 Form N–CSR, certified shareholder report.

This form shall be used by registered management investment companies to file reports pursuant to § 270.30b2–1(a) of this chapter not later than 10 days after the transmission to stockholders of any report that is required to be transmitted to stockholders under § 270.30e–1 of this chapter.

[68 FR 5368, Feb. 3, 2003]

EDITORIAL NOTE: For FEDERAL REGISTER citations affecting Form N–CSR, see the List of CFR Sections Affected, which appears in the Finding Aids section of the printed volume and at *www.govinfo.gov*.

§ 274.129 Form N–PX, annual report of proxy voting record of registered management investment company.

This form shall be used by registered management investment companies, other than small business investment companies registered on Form N–5 (§§ 239.24 and 274.5 of this chapter), for annual reports to be filed not later than August 31 of each year, containing the company's proxy voting record for the most recent twelve-month period ended June 30, pursuant to section 30 of the Investment Company Act of 1940 and § 270.30b1–4 of this chapter.

[68 FR 6584, Feb. 7, 2003]

EDITORIAL NOTE: For FEDERAL REGISTER citations affecting Form N–PX, see the List of CFR Sections Affected, which appears in the Finding Aids section of the printed volume and at *www.govinfo.gov*.

EFFECTIVE DATE NOTE: At 87 FR 78811, Dec. 22, 2022, the heading for § 274.129 was revised July 1, 2024. For the convenience of the user, the revised text is set forth as follows:

§ 274.129 Form N–PX, annual report of proxy voting record.

§ 274.130 [Reserved]

§ 274.150 Form N–PORT, Monthly portfolio holdings report.

(a) Except as provided in paragraph (b) of this section, this form shall be used by registered management investment companies or exchange-traded funds organized as unit investment trusts, or series thereof, to file reports pursuant to § 270.30b1–9 of this chapter not later than 60 days after the end of each fiscal quarter.

(b) Form N–PORT shall not be filed by a registered open-end management investment company that is regulated as a money market fund under § 270.2a–7 of this chapter or a small business investment company registered on Form N–5 (§§ 239.24 and 274.5 of this chapter), or series thereof.

NOTE: The text of Form N–PORT will not appear in the *Code of Federal Regulations*.

[84 FR 7988, Mar. 6, 2019]

EDITORIAL NOTE: For FEDERAL REGISTER citations affecting Form N–PORT, see the List of CFR Sections Affected, which appears in the Finding Aids section of the printed volume and at *www.govinfo.gov*.

Securities and Exchange Commission

§ 274.200 Form N-17D-1, report filed by small business investment company (SBIC) registered under the Investment Company Act of 1940 and an affiliated bank, with respect to investments by the SBIC and the bank, submitted pursuant to paragraph (d)(3) of § 270.17d-1 of this chapter.

This form shall be filed pursuant to Rule 17d-2 (§ 270.17d-2 of this chapter) as the report required, under subparagraph (d)(3) of Rule 17d-1 (§ 270.17d-1(d)(3) of this chapter), to be filed, either jointly or separately, by a small business investment company (SBIC) licensed as such under the Small Business Investment Act of 1958, and by a bank which is an affiliated person of either the SBIC or of an affiliated person of the SBIC, with respect to investments in a small business concern by the SBIC and the bank.

EDITORIAL NOTE: For FEDERAL REGISTER citations affecting Form N-17D-1, see the List of CFR Sections Affected, which appears in the Finding Aids section of the printed volume and at *www.govinfo.gov*.

Subpart C—Forms for Other Statements

§ 274.201 Form N-MFP, portfolio holdings of money market funds.

This form shall be used by registered open-end management investment companies that are regulated as money market funds under § 270.2a-7 of this chapter to file reports pursuant to § 270.30b1-7 of this chapter no later than the fifth business day of each month.

[75 FR 10118, Mar. 4, 2010]

EDITORIAL NOTE: For FEDERAL REGISTER citations affecting Form N-MFP, see the List of CFR Sections Affected, which appears in the Finding Aids section of the printed volume and at *www.govinfo.gov*.

§ 274.202 Form 3, initial statement of beneficial ownership of securities.

This form shall be filed pursuant to § 270.30h-1 for initial statements of beneficial ownership of securities required to be filed pursuant to section 30(h) of the Investment Company Act of 1940 (15 U.S.C. 80a-29(h)). (Same as § 249.103 of this chapter.)

[67 FR 43537, June 28, 2002]

EDITORIAL NOTE: For FEDERAL REGISTER citations affecting Form 3, see the List of CFR Sections Affected, which appears in the Finding Aids section of the printed volume and at *www.govinfo.gov*.

§ 274.203 Form 4, statement of changes in beneficial ownership of securities.

This form shall be filed pursuant to § 270.30h-1 for statements of changes in beneficial ownership of securities required to be filed pursuant to section 30(h) of the Investment Company Act of 1940 (15 U.S.C. 80a-29(h)). (Same as § 249.104 of this chapter.)

[67 FR 43537, June 28, 2002]

EDITORIAL NOTE: For FEDERAL REGISTER citations affecting Form 4, see the List of CFR Sections Affected, which appears in the Finding Aids section of the printed volume and at *www.govinfo.gov*.

§ 274.218 Form N-8F, application for deregistration of certain registered investment companies.

This form must be used as the application for an order of the Commission in cases in which the applicant is a registered investment company that:

(a) Has sold substantially all of its assets to another registered investment company or merged into or consolidated with another registered investment company;

(b) Has distributed substantially all of its assets to its shareholders and has completed, or is in the process of, winding up its affairs;

(c) Qualifies for an exclusion from the definition of "investment company" under section 3(c)(1) (15 U.S.C. 80a-3(c)(1)) or section 3(c)(7) (15 U.S.C. 80a-3(c)(7)) of the Act; or

(d) Has become a business development company.

[64 FR 19471, Apr. 21, 1999]

EDITORIAL NOTE: For FEDERAL REGISTER citations affecting Form N-8F, see the List of CFR Sections Affected, which appears in the Finding Aids section of the printed volume and at *www.govinfo.gov*.

§ 274.219

§ 274.219 Form N–17f–1, cover page for each certificate of accounting of securities and similar investments of a management investment company in the custody of a member of a national securities exchange, filed pursuant to rule 17f–1.

[54 FR 32049, Aug. 4, 1989]

EDITORIAL NOTE: For FEDERAL REGISTER citations affecting Form N–17f–1, see the List of CFR Sections Affected, which appears in the Finding Aids section of the printed volume and at *www.govinfo.gov*.

§ 274.220 Form N–17f–2, cover page for each certificate of accounting of securities and similar investments in the custody of a registered management investment company, filed pursuant to rule 17f–2.

[54 FR 32049, Aug. 4, 1989]

EDITORIAL NOTE: For FEDERAL REGISTER citations affecting Form N–17f–2, see the List of CFR Sections Affected, which appears in the Finding Aids section of the printed volume and at *www.govinfo.gov*.

§ 274.221 Form N–23c–3, Notification of repurchase offer.

Form N–23c–3 shall be filed with copies of notifications of repurchase offers submitted to the Commission as required under rule 23c–3 (§ 270.23c–3 of this chapter).

[58 FR 19345, Apr. 14, 1993]

EDITORIAL NOTE: For FEDERAL REGISTER citations affecting Form N–23c–3, see the List of CFR Sections Affected, which appears in the Finding Aids section of the printed volume and at *www.govinfo.gov*.

§ 274.222 Form N–CR, Current report of money market fund material events.

This form shall be used by registered investment companies that are regulated as money market funds under § 270.2a–7 of this chapter to file current reports pursuant to § 270.30b1–8 of this chapter within the time periods specified in the form.

[79 FR 47973, Aug. 14, 2014]

EDITORIAL NOTE: For FEDERAL REGISTER citations affecting Form N–CR, see the List of CFR Sections Affected, which appears in the Finding Aids section of the printed volume and at *www.govinfo.gov*.

§ 274.223 Form N–RN, Current report, open- and closed-end investment company reporting.

This form shall be used by registered open-end management investment companies, or series thereof, and closed-end management investment companies, to file reports pursuant to § 270.18f–4(c)(7) and § 270.30b1–10 of this chapter.

[85 FR 83296, Dec. 21, 2020]

EDITORIAL NOTE: For FEDERAL REGISTER citations affecting Form N–RN, see the List of CFR Sections Affected, which appears in the Finding Aids section of the printed volume and at *www.govinfo.gov*.

Subpart D—Forms for Exemptions

AUTHORITY: Secs. 6(c), (15 U.S.C. 80a–6(c)), 6(e), (15 U.S.C. 80a–6(e)), 38(a), 15 U.S.C. 80a–37(a) of the Act.

§ 274.301 Notification of claim of exemption pursuant to Rule 6e–2 or Rule 6e–3(T) under the Investment Company Act.

This form shall be filed with the Commission as required by § 270.6e–2 or § 270.6e–3(T) of this chapter by each insurance company with respect to each separate account for which exemption is claimed pursuant to § 270.6e–2 or § 270.6e–3(T).

[49 FR 47228, Dec. 3, 1984]

EDITORIAL NOTE: For FEDERAL REGISTER citations affecting Form N–6EI–1, see the List of CFR Sections Affected, which appears in the Finding Aids section of the printed volume and at *www.govinfo.gov*.

Subpart E—Forms for Electronic Filing

SOURCE: 50 FR 40485, Oct. 4, 1985, unless otherwise noted.

§ 274.401 [Reserved]

§ 274.402 Form ID, uniform application for access codes to file on EDGAR.

Form ID must be filed by registrants, third party filers, or their agents, to request the following access codes to permit filing on EDGAR:

(a) Central Index Key (CIK)—uniquely identifies each filer, filing agent, and training agent.

Securities and Exchange Commission

(b) CIK Confirmation Code (CCC)—used in the header of a filing in conjunction with the CIK of the filer to ensure that the filing has been authorized by the filer.

(c) Password (PW)—allows a filer, filing agent or training agent to log on to the EDGAR system, submit filings, and change its CCC.

(d) Password Modification Authorization Code (PMAC)—allows a filer, filing agent or training agent to change its Password.

[69 FR 22711, Apr. 26, 2004, as amended at 86 FR 25805, May 11, 2021]

EDITORIAL NOTE: For FEDERAL REGISTER citations affecting Form ID, see the List of CFR Sections Affected, which appears in the Finding Aids section of the printed volume and at *www.govinfo.gov.*

§ 274.403 Form SE, form for submission of paper format exhibits by electronic filers.

This form shall be used by an electronic filer for the submission of any paper format document relating to an otherwise electronic filing, as provided in rule 311 of Regulation S-T (§ 232.311 of this chapter).

[58 FR 14861, Mar. 18, 1993]

EDITORIAL NOTE: For FEDERAL REGISTER citations affecting Form SE, see the List of CFR Sections Affected, which appears in the Finding Aids section of the printed volume and at *www.govinfo.gov.*

§ 274.404 Form TH—Notification of reliance on temporary hardship exemption.

Form TH shall be filed by any electronic filer who submits to the Commission, pursuant to a temporary hardship exemption, a document in paper format that otherwise would be required to be submitted electronically, as prescribed by rule 201(a) of Regulation S-T (§ 232.201(a) of this chapter).

[58 FR 14861, Mar. 18, 1993]

EDITORIAL NOTE: For FEDERAL REGISTER citations affecting Form TH, see the List of CFR Sections Affected, which appears in the Finding Aids section of the printed volume and at *www.govinfo.gov.*

PART 275—RULES AND REGULATIONS, INVESTMENT ADVISERS ACT OF 1940

Sec.
275.0-2 General procedures for serving nonresidents.
275.0-3 References to rules and regulations.
275.0-4 General requirements of papers and applications.
275.0-5 Procedure with respect to applications and other matters.
275.0-6 Incorporation by reference in applications.
275.0-7 Small entities under the Investment Advisers Act for purposes of the Regulatory Flexibility Act.
275.202(a)(1)-1 Certain transactions not deemed assignments.
275.202(a)(11)(G)-1 Family offices.
275.202(a)(30)-1 Foreign private advisers.
275.203-1 Application for investment adviser registration.
275.203-2 Withdrawal from investment adviser registration.
275.203-3 Hardship exemptions.
275.203(l)-1 Venture capital fund defined.
275.203(m)-1 Private fund adviser exemption.
275.203A-1 Eligibility for SEC registration; switching to or from SEC registration.
275.203A-2 Exemptions from prohibition on Commission registration.
275.203A-3 Definitions.
275.203A-4—203A-6 [Reserved]
275.204-1 Amendments to Form ADV
275.204-2 Books and records to be maintained by investment advisers.
275.204-3 Delivery of brochures and brochure supplements.
275.204-4 Reporting by exempt reporting advisers.
275.204-5 Delivery of Form CRS.
275.204(b)-1 Reporting by investment advisers to private funds.
275.204A-1 Investment adviser codes of ethics.
275.205-1 Definition of "investment performance" of an investment company and "investment record" of an appropriate index of securities prices.
275.205-2 Definition of "specified period" over which the asset value of the company or fund under management is averaged.
275.205-3 Exemption from the compensation prohibition of section 205(a)(1) for investment advisers.
275.206(3)-1 Exemption of investment advisers registered as broker-dealers in connection with the provision of certain investment advisory services.
275.206(3)-2 Agency cross transactions for advisory clients.
275.206(4)-1 Investment adviser marketing.

§ 275.0-2

275.206(4)-2 Custody of funds or securities of clients by investment advisers.
275.206(4)-3—275.206(4)-4 [Reserved]
275.206(4)-5 Political contributions by certain investment advisers.
275.206(4)-6 Proxy voting.
275.206(4)-7 Compliance procedures and practices.
275.206(4)-8 Pooled investment vehicles.
275.222-1 Definitions.
275.222-2 Definition of "client" for purposes of the national de mimimis standard.

AUTHORITY: 15 U.S.C. 80b-2(a)(11)(G), 80b-2(a)(11)(H), 80b-2(a)(17), 80b-3, 80b-4, 80b-4a, 80b-6(4), 80b-6a, and 80b-11, unless otherwise noted.

Section 275.203A-1 is also issued under 15 U.S.C. 80b-3a.

Section 275.203A-2 is also issued under 15 U.S.C. 80b-3a.

Section 275.203A-3 is also issued under 15 U.S.C. 80b-3a.

Section 275.204-1 is also issued under sec. 407 and 408, Pub. L. 111-203, 124 Stat. 1376.

Section 275.204-2 is also issued under 15 U.S.C. 80b-6.

Section 275.205-3 is also issued under 15 U.S.C. 80b-5(e).

Section 275.204-4 is also issued under sec. 407 and 408, Pub. L. 111-203, 124 Stat. 1376.

Section 275.204-5 is also issued under sec. 913, Public Law 111-203, sec. 124 Stat. 1827-28 (2010).

Section 275.211h-1 is also issued under sec. 913, Public Law 111-203, sec. 124 Stat. 1827-28 (2010).

§ 275.0-2 General procedures for serving non-residents.

(a) *General procedures for serving process, pleadings, or other papers on non-resident investment advisers, general partners and managing agents.* Under Forms ADV and ADV-NR [17 CFR 279.1 and 279.4], a person may serve process, pleadings, or other papers on a non-resident investment adviser, or on a non-resident general partner or non-resident managing agent of an investment adviser by serving any or all of its appointed agents:

(1) A person may serve a non-resident investment adviser, non-resident general partner, or non-resident managing agent by furnishing the Commission with one copy of the process, pleadings, or papers, for each named party, and one additional copy for the Commission's records.

(2) If process, pleadings, or other papers are served on the Commission as described in this section, the Secretary of the Commission (Secretary) will promptly forward a copy to each named party by registered or certified mail at that party's last address filed with the Commission.

(3) If the Secretary certifies that the Commission was served with process, pleadings, or other papers pursuant to paragraph (a)(1) of this section and forwarded these documents to a named party pursuant to paragraph (a)(2) of this section, this certification constitutes evidence of service upon that party.

(b) *Definitions.* For purposes of this section:

(1) *Managing agent* means any person, including a trustee, who directs or manages, or who participates in directing or managing, the affairs of any unincorporated organization or association other than a partnership.

(2) *Non-resident* means:

(i) An individual who resides in any place not subject to the jurisdiction of the United States;

(ii) A corporation that is incorporated in or that has its principal office and place of business in any place not subject to the jurisdiction of the United States; and

(iii) A partnership or other unincorporated organization or association that has its principal office and place of business in any place not subject to the jurisdiction of the United States.

(3) *Principal office and place of business* has the same meaning as in § 275.203A-3(c) of this chapter.

[65 FR 57448, Sept. 22, 2000]

§ 275.0-3 References to rules and regulations.

The term *rules and regulations* refers to all rules and regulations adopted by the Commission pursuant to the Act, including the forms for registration and reports and the accompanying instructions thereto.

[30 FR 4129, Mar. 30, 1965]

§ 275.0-4 General requirements of papers and applications.

(a) *Filings.* (1) All papers required to be filed with the Commission shall, unless otherwise provided by the rules and regulations, be delivered through the mails or otherwise to the Secretary

Securities and Exchange Commission

§ 275.0-4

of the Securities and Exchange Commission, Washington, DC 20549. Except as otherwise provided by the rules and regulations, such papers shall be deemed to have been filed with the Commission on the date when they are actually received by it.

(2) All filings required to be made electronically with the Investment Adviser Registration Depository ("IARD") shall, unless otherwise provided by the rules and regulations in this part, be deemed to have been filed with the Commission upon acceptance by the IARD. Filings required to be made through the IARD on a day that the IARD is closed shall be considered timely filed with the Commission if filed with the IARD no later than the following business day.

(3) Filings required to be made through the IARD during the period in December of each year that the IARD is not available for submission of filings shall be considered timely filed with the Commission if filed with the IARD no later than the following January 7.

NOTE TO PARAGRAPH (a)(3): Each year the IARD shuts down to filers for several days during the end of December to process renewals of state notice filings and registrations. During this period, advisers are not able to submit filings through the IARD. Check the Commission's Web site at *http://www.sec.gov/iard* for the dates of the annual IARD shutdown.

(b) *Formal specifications respecting applications.* Every application for an order under any provision of the Act, for which a form with instructions is not specifically prescribed, and every amendment to such application, shall be filed electronically pursuant to 17 CFR part 232 (Regulation S-T). Any filings made in paper, including filings made pursuant to a hardship exemption under Regulation S-T, shall be filed in quintuplicate. One copy shall be signed by the applicant, but the other four copies may have facsimile or typed signatures. Such applications shall be on paper no larger than 8½ x 11 inches in size. To the extent that the reduction of larger documents would render them illegible, those documents may be filed on paper larger than 8½ x 11 inches in size. The left margin should be at least 1½ inches wide and, if the application is bound, it should be bound on the left side. All typewritten or printed matter (including deficits in financial statements) should be set forth in black so as to permit photocopying.

(c) *Authorization respecting applications.* (1) Every application for an order under any provision of the Act, for which a form with instructions is not specifically prescribed and which is executed by a corporation, partnership, or other company and filed with the Commission, shall contain a concise statement of the applicable provisions of the articles of incorporation, bylaws, or similar documents, relating to the right of the person signing and filing such application to take such action on behalf of the applicant, and a statement that all such requirements have been complied with and that the person signing and filing the same is fully authorized to do so. If such authorization is dependent on resolutions of stockholders, directors, or other bodies, such resolutions shall be attached as an exhibit to, or the pertinent provisions thereof shall be quoted in, the application.

(2) If an amendment to any such application shall be filed, such amendment shall contain a similar statement or, in lieu thereof, shall state that the authorization described in the original application is applicable to the individual who signs such amendment and that such authorization still remains in effect.

(3) When any such application or amendment is signed by an agent or attorney, the power of attorney evidencing his authority to sign shall contain similar statements and shall be filed with the Commission.

(d) *Verification of applications and statements of fact.* Every application for an order under any provision of the Act, for which a form with instructions is not specifically prescribed, and every amendment to such application, and every statement of fact formally filed in support of, or in opposition to, any application or declaration shall be verified by the person executing the same. An instrument executed on behalf of a corporation shall be verified in substantially the following form, but suitable changes may be made in

507

§ 275.0–5

such form for other kinds of companies and for individuals:

The undersigned states that he or she has duly executed the attached dated , 20__, for and on behalf of (Name of company); that he or she is the (Title of officer) of such company; and that all action by stockholders, directors, and other bodies necessary to authorize the undersigned to execute and file such instrument has been taken. The undersigned further states that he or she is familiar with such instrument, and the contents thereof, and that the facts therein set forth are true to the best of his or her knowledge, information and belief.

(Signature)

(e) *Statement of grounds for application.* Each application should contain a brief statement of the reasons why the applicant is deemed to be entitled to the action requested with a reference to the provisions of the Act and of the rules and regulations under which application is made.

(f) *Name and address.* Every application shall contain the name and address of each applicant and the name and address of any person to whom any applicant wishes any question regarding the application to be directed.

(g) [Reserved]

(h) *Definition of application.* For purposes of this rule, an "application" means any application for an order of the Commission under the Act other than an application for registration as an investment adviser.

(i) The manually signed original (or in the case of duplicate originals, one duplicate original) of all registrations, applications, statements, reports, or other documents filed under the Investment Advisers Act of 1940, as amended, shall be numbered sequentially (in addition to any internal numbering which otherwise may be present) by handwritten, typed, printed, or other legible form of notation from the facing page of the document through the last page of that document and any exhibits or attachments thereto. Further, the total number of pages contained in a numbered original shall be set forth on the first page of the document.

[41 FR 39019, Sept. 14, 1976, as amended at 44 FR 4666, Jan. 23, 1979; 47 FR 58239, Dec. 30, 1982; 68 FR 42248, July 17, 2003; 76 FR 71877, Nov. 21, 2011; 87 FR 38976, June 30, 2022]

§ 275.0–5 Procedure with respect to applications and other matters.

The procedure hereinbelow set forth will be followed with respect to any proceeding initiated by the filing of an application, or upon the Commission's own motion, pursuant to any section of the Act or any rule or regulation thereunder, unless in the particular case a different procedure is provided:

(a) Notice of the initiation of the proceeding will be published in the FEDERAL REGISTER and will indicate the earliest date upon which an order disposing of the matter may be entered. The notice will also provide that any interested person may, within the period of time specified therein, submit to the Commission in writing any facts bearing upon the desirability of a hearing on the matter and may request that a hearing be held, stating his reasons therefor and the nature of his interest in the matter.

(b) An order disposing of the matter will be issued as of course following the expiration of the period of time referred to in paragraph (a) of this section, unless the Commission thereafter orders a hearing on the matter.

(c) The Commission will order a hearing on the matter, if it appears that a hearing is necessary or appropriate in the public interest or for the protection of investors, (1) upon the request of any interested person or (2) upon its own motion.

(d) *Definition of application.* For purposes of this rule, an "application" means any application for an order of the Commission under the Act other than an application for registration as an investment adviser.

[41 FR 39020, Sept. 14, 1976, as amended at 61 FR 49962, Sept. 24, 1996]

§ 275.0–6 Incorporation by reference in applications.

(a) *Exhibits.* Any document or part thereof, including any financial statement or part thereof, filed with the

Securities and Exchange Commission

§ 275.0-7

Commission pursuant to any Act administered by the Commission may be incorporated by reference as an exhibit to any application filed with the Commission by the same or any other person. If any modification has occurred in the text of any document incorporated by reference since the filing thereof, the registrant must file with the reference a statement containing the text of any such modification and the date thereof.

(b) *General.* Include an express statement clearly describing the specific location of the information you are incorporating by reference. The statement must identify the document where the information was originally filed or submitted and the location of the information within that document. The statement must be made at the particular place where the information is required, if applicable. Information must not be incorporated by reference in any case where such incorporation would render the disclosure incomplete, unclear, or confusing. For example, unless expressly permitted or required, disclosure must not be incorporated by reference from a second document if that second document incorporates information pertinent to such disclosure by reference to a third document.

(c) *Definition of Application.* For purposes of this rule, an "application" means any application for an order of the Commission under the Act other than an application for registration as an investment adviser.

[84 FR 12738, Apr. 2, 2019]

§ 275.0-7 Small entities under the Investment Advisers Act for purposes of the Regulatory Flexibility Act.

(a) For purposes of Commission rulemaking in accordance with the provisions of Chapter Six of the Administrative Procedure Act (5 U.S.C. 601 *et seq.*) and unless otherwise defined for purposes of a particular rulemaking proceeding, the term *small business* or *small organization* for purposes of the Investment Advisers Act of 1940 shall mean an investment adviser that:

(1) Has assets under management, as defined under Section 203A(a)(3) of the Act (15 U.S.C. 80b–3a(a)(2)) and reported on its annual updating amendment to Form ADV (17 CFR 279.1), of less than $25 million, or such higher amount as the Commission may by rule deem appropriate under Section 203A(a)(1)(A) of the Act (15 U.S.C. 80b–3a(a)(1)(A));

(2) Did not have total assets of $5 million or more on the last day of the most recent fiscal year; and

(3) Does not control, is not controlled by, and is not under common control with another investment adviser that has assets under management of $25 million or more (or such higher amount as the Commission may deem appropriate), or any person (other than a natural person) that had total assets of $5 million or more on the last day of the most recent fiscal year.

(b) For purposes of this section:

(1) *Control* means the power, directly or indirectly, to direct the management or policies of a person, whether through ownership of securities, by contract, or otherwise.

(i) A person is presumed to control a corporation if the person:

(A) Directly or indirectly has the right to vote 25 percent or more of a class of the corporation's voting securities; or

(B) Has the power to sell or direct the sale of 25 percent or more of a class of the corporation's voting securities.

(ii) A person is presumed to control a partnership if the person has the right to receive upon dissolution, or has contributed, 25 percent or more of the capital of the partnership.

(iii) A person is presumed to control a limited liability company (LLC) if the person:

(A) Directly or indirectly has the right to vote 25 percent or more of a class of the interests of the LLC;

(B) Has the right to receive upon dissolution, or has contributed, 25 percent or more of the capital of the LLC; or

(C) Is an elected manager of the LLC.

(iv) A person is presumed to control a trust if the person is a trustee or managing agent of the trust.

(2) *Total assets* means the total assets as shown on the balance sheet of the investment adviser or other person described above under paragraph (a)(3) of this section, or the balance sheet of the

§ 275.202(a)(1)-1

investment adviser or such other person with its subsidiaries consolidated, whichever is larger.

[63 FR 35515, June 30, 1998, as amended at 65 FR 57448, Sept. 22, 2000; 76 FR 43011, July 19, 2011]

§ 275.202(a)(1)-1 Certain transactions not deemed assignments.

A transaction which does not result in a change of actual control or management of an investment adviser is not an assignment for purposes of section 205(a)(2) of the Act.

[51 FR 32907, Sept. 17, 1986; 64 FR 2567, Jan. 15, 1999]

§ 275.202(a)(11)(G)-1 Family offices.

(a) *Exclusion.* A family office, as defined in this section, shall not be considered to be an investment adviser for purpose of the Act.

(b) *Family office.* A family office is a company (including its directors, partners, members, managers, trustees, and employees acting within the scope of their position or employment) that:

(1) Has no clients other than family clients; provided that if a person that is not a family client becomes a client of the family office as a result of the death of a family member or key employee or other involuntary transfer from a family member or key employee, that person shall be deemed to be a family client for purposes of this section for one year following the completion of the transfer of legal title to the assets resulting from the involuntary event;

(2) Is wholly owned by family clients and is exclusively controlled (directly or indirectly) by one or more family members and/or family entities; and

(3) Does not hold itself out to the public as an investment adviser.

(c) *Grandfathering.* A family office as defined in paragraph (a) of this section shall not exclude any person, who was not registered or required to be registered under the Act on January 1, 2010, solely because such person provides investment advice to, and was engaged before January 1, 2010 in providing investment advice to:

(1) Natural persons who, at the time of their applicable investment, are officers, directors, or employees of the family office who have invested with the family office before January 1, 2010 and are accredited investors, as defined in Regulation D under the Securities Act of 1933;

(2) Any company owned exclusively and controlled by one or more family members; or

(3) Any investment adviser registered under the Act that provides investment advice to the family office and who identifies investment opportunities to the family office, and invests in such transactions on substantially the same terms as the family office invests, but does not invest in other funds advised by the family office, and whose assets as to which the family office directly or indirectly provides investment advice represents, in the aggregate, not more than 5 percent of the value of the total assets as to which the family office provides investment advice; provided that a family office that would not be a family office but for this paragraph (c) shall be deemed to be an investment adviser for purposes of paragraphs (1), (2) and (4) of section 206 of the Act.

(d) *Definitions.* For purposes of this section:

(1) *Affiliated family office* means a family office wholly owned by family clients of another family office and that is controlled (directly or indirectly) by one or more family members of such other family office and/or family entities affiliated with such other family office and has no clients other than family clients of such other family office.

(2) *Control* means the power to exercise a controlling influence over the management or policies of a company, unless such power is solely the result of being an officer of such company.

(3) *Executive officer* means the president, any vice president in charge of a principal business unit, division or function (such as administration or finance), any other officer who performs a policy-making function, or any other person who performs similar policy-making functions, for the family office.

(4) *Family client* means:

(i) Any family member;

(ii) Any former family member;

(iii) Any key employee;

Securities and Exchange Commission § 275.202(a)(11)(G)–1

(iv) Any former key employee, provided that upon the end of such individual's employment by the family office, the former key employee shall not receive investment advice from the family office (or invest additional assets with a family office-advised trust, foundation or entity) other than with respect to assets advised (directly or indirectly) by the family office immediately prior to the end of such individual's employment, except that a former key employee shall be permitted to receive investment advice from the family office with respect to additional investments that the former key employee was contractually obligated to make, and that relate to a family-office advised investment existing, in each case prior to the time the person became a former key employee.

(v) Any non-profit organization, charitable foundation, charitable trust (including charitable lead trusts and charitable remainder trusts whose only current beneficiaries are other family clients and charitable or non-profit organizations), or other charitable organization, in each case for which all the funding such foundation, trust or organization holds came exclusively from one or more other family clients;

(vi) Any estate of a family member, former family member, key employee, or, subject to the condition contained in paragraph (d)(4)(iv) of this section, former key employee;

(vii) Any irrevocable trust in which one or more other family clients are the only current beneficiaries;

(viii) Any irrevocable trust funded exclusively by one or more other family clients in which other family clients and non-profit organizations, charitable foundations, charitable trusts, or other charitable organizations are the only current beneficiaries;

(ix) Any revocable trust of which one or more other family clients are the sole grantor;

(x) Any trust of which: Each trustee or other person authorized to make decisions with respect to the trust is a key employee; and each settlor or other person who has contributed assets to the trust is a key employee or the key employee's current and/or former spouse or spousal equivalent who, at the time of contribution, holds a joint, community property, or other similar shared ownership interest with the key employee; or

(xi) Any company wholly owned (directly or indirectly) exclusively by, and operated for the sole benefit of, one or more other family clients; provided that if any such entity is a pooled investment vehicle, it is excepted from the definition of "investment company" under the Investment Company Act of 1940.

(5) *Family entity* means any of the trusts, estates, companies or other entities set forth in paragraphs (d)(4)(v), (vi), (vii), (viii), (ix), or (xi) of this section, but excluding key employees and their trusts from the definition of family client solely for purposes of this definition.

(6) *Family member* means all lineal descendants (including by adoption, stepchildren, foster children, and individuals that were a minor when another family member became a legal guardian of that individual) of a common ancestor (who may be living or deceased), and such lineal descendants' spouses or spousal equivalents; provided that the common ancestor is no more than 10 generations removed from the youngest generation of family members.

(7) *Former family member* means a spouse, spousal equivalent, or stepchild that was a family member but is no longer a family member due to a divorce or other similar event.

(8) *Key employee* means any natural person (including any key employee's spouse or spouse equivalent who holds a joint, community property, or other similar shared ownership interest with that key employee) who is an executive officer, director, trustee, general partner, or person serving in a similar capacity of the family office or its affiliated family office or any employee of the family office or its affiliated family office (other than an employee performing solely clerical, secretarial, or administrative functions with regard to the family office) who, in connection with his or her regular functions or duties, participates in the investment activities of the family office or affiliated family office, provided that such employee has been performing such functions and duties for or on behalf of the

§ 275.202(a)(30)-1

family office or affiliated family office, or substantially similar functions or duties for or on behalf of another company, for at least 12 months.

(9) *Spousal equivalent* means a cohabitant occupying a relationship generally equivalent to that of a spouse.

[76 FR 37994, June 29, 2011, as amended at 81 FR 60457, Sept. 1, 2016]

§ 275.202(a)(30)-1 Foreign private advisers.

(a) *Client.* You may deem the following to be a single client for purposes of section 202(a)(30) of the Act (15 U.S.C. 80b-2(a)(30)):

(1) A natural person, and:

(i) Any minor child of the natural person;

(ii) Any relative, spouse, spousal equivalent, or relative of the spouse or of the spousal equivalent of the natural person who has the same principal residence;

(iii) All accounts of which the natural person and/or the persons referred to in this paragraph (a)(1) are the only primary beneficiaries; and

(iv) All trusts of which the natural person and/or the persons referred to in this paragraph (a)(1) are the only primary beneficiaries;

(2)(i) A corporation, general partnership, limited partnership, limited liability company, trust (other than a trust referred to in paragraph (a)(1)(iv) of this section), or other legal organization (any of which are referred to hereinafter as a "legal organization") to which you provide investment advice based on its investment objectives rather than the individual investment objectives of its shareholders, partners, limited partners, members, or beneficiaries (any of which are referred to hereinafter as an "owner"); and

(ii) Two or more legal organizations referred to in paragraph (a)(2)(i) of this section that have identical owners.

(b) *Special rules regarding clients.* For purposes of this section:

(1) You must count an owner as a client if you provide investment advisory services to the owner separate and apart from the investment advisory services you provide to the legal organization, provided, however, that the determination that an owner is a client will not affect the applicability of this section with regard to any other owner;

(2) You are not required to count an owner as a client solely because you, on behalf of the legal organization, offer, promote, or sell interests in the legal organization to the owner, or report periodically to the owners as a group solely with respect to the performance of or plans for the legal organization's assets or similar matters;

(3) A limited partnership or limited liability company is a client of any general partner, managing member or other person acting as investment adviser to the partnership or limited liability company;

(4) You are not required to count a private fund as a client if you count any investor, as that term is defined in paragraph (c)(2) of this section, in that private fund as an investor in the United States in that private fund; and

(5) You are not required to count a person as an investor, as that term is defined in paragraph (c)(2) of this section, in a private fund you advise if you count such person as a client in the United States.

NOTE TO PARAGRAPHS (a) AND (b): These paragraphs are a safe harbor and are not intended to specify the exclusive method for determining who may be deemed a single client for purposes of section 202(a)(30) of the Act (15 U.S.C. 80b-2(a)(30)).

(c) *Definitions.* For purposes of section 202(a)(30) of the Act (15 U.S.C. 80b-2(a)(30)):

(1) *Assets under management* means the regulatory assets under management as determined under Item 5.F of Form ADV (§ 279.1 of this chapter).

(2) *Investor* means:

(i) Any person who would be included in determining the number of beneficial owners of the outstanding securities of a private fund under section 3(c)(1) of the Investment Company Act of 1940 (15 U.S.C. 80a-3(c)(1)), or whether the outstanding securities of a private fund are owned exclusively by qualified purchasers under section 3(c)(7) of that Act (15 U.S.C. 80a-3(c)(7)); and

(ii) Any beneficial owner of any outstanding short-term paper, as defined in section 2(a)(38) of the Investment Company Act of 1940 (15 U.S.C. 80a-2(a)(38)), issued by the private fund.

Securities and Exchange Commission §275.203-1

NOTE TO PARAGRAPH (c)(2): You may treat as a single investor any person who is an investor in two or more private funds you advise.

(3) *In the United States* means with respect to:

(i) Any client or investor, any person who is a U.S. person as defined in §230.902(k) of this chapter, except that any discretionary account or similar account that is held for the benefit of a person in the United States by a dealer or other professional fiduciary is in the United States if the dealer or professional fiduciary is a related person, as defined in §275.206(4)-2(d)(7), of the investment adviser relying on this section and is not organized, incorporated, or (if an individual) resident in the United States.

NOTE TO PARAGRAPH (c)(3)(i): A person who is in the United States may be treated as not being in the United States if such person was not in the United States at the time of becoming a client or, in the case of an investor in a private fund, each time the investor acquires securities issued by the fund.

(ii) Any place of business, *in the United States*, as that term is defined in §230.902(l) of this chapter; and

(iii) The public, *in the United States*, as that term is defined in §230.902(l) of this chapter.

(4) *Place of business* has the same meaning as in §275.222-1(a).

(5) *Spousal equivalent* has the same meaning as in §275.202(a)(11)(G)-1(d)(9).

(d) *Holding out.* If you are relying on this section, you shall not be deemed to be holding yourself out generally to the public in the United States as an investment adviser, within the meaning of section 202(a)(30) of the Act (15 U.S.C. 80b-2(a)(30)), solely because you participate in a non-public offering in the United States of securities issued by a private fund under the Securities Act of 1933 (15 U.S.C. 77a).

[76 FR 39701, July 6, 2011]

§275.203-1 Application for investment adviser registration.

(a) *Form ADV.* (1) To apply for registration with the Commission as an investment adviser, you must complete Form ADV (17 CFR 279.1) by following the instructions in the form and you must file Part 1A of Form ADV, the firm brochure(s) required by Part 2A of Form ADV and Form CRS required by Part 3 of Form ADV electronically with the Investment Adviser Registration Depository (IARD) unless you have received a hardship exemption under §275.203-3. You are not required to file with the Commission the brochure supplements required by Part 2B of Form ADV.

NOTE 1 TO PARAGRAPH (a)(1): Information on how to file with the IARD is available on the Commission's website at *http://www.sec.gov/iard*. If you are not required to deliver a brochure or Form CRS to any clients, you are not required to prepare or file a brochure or Form CRS, as applicable, with the Commission. If you are not required to deliver a brochure supplement to any clients for any particular supervised person, you are not required to prepare a brochure supplement for that supervised person.

(2)(i) On or after June 30, 2020, the Commission will not accept any initial application for registration as an investment adviser that does not include a Form CRS that satisfies the requirements of Part 3 of Form ADV.

(ii) Beginning on May 1, 2020, any initial application for registration as an investment adviser filed prior to June 30, 2020, must include a Form CRS that satisfies the requirements of Part 3 of Form ADV by no later than June 30, 2020.

(b) *When filed.* Each Form ADV is considered filed with the Commission upon acceptance by the IARD.

(c) *Filing fees.* You must pay FINRA (the operator of the IARD) a filing fee. The Commission has approved the amount of the filing fee. No portion of the filing fee is refundable. Your completed application for registration will not be accepted by FINRA, and thus will not be considered filed with the Commission, until you have paid the filing fee.

(d) *Form ADV-NR*—(1) *General Requirements.* Each non-resident, as defined in 17 CFR 275.0-2(b)(2) (Rule 0-2(b)(2)), general partner or a non-resident managing agent, as defined in 17 CFR 275.0-2(b)(2) (Rule 0-2(b)(1)), of any investment adviser registered, or applying for registration with, the Commission must submit Form ADV-NR (17 CFR 279.4). Form ADV-NR must be completed in connection with the adviser's initial registration with the Commission. If a person becomes a

§ 275.203-2

non-resident general partner or a non-resident managing agent after the date the adviser files its initial registration with the Commission, the person must file Form ADV–NR with the Commission within 30 days of becoming a non-resident general partner or a non-resident managing agent. If a person serves as a general partner or managing agent for multiple advisers, they must submit a separate Form ADV–NR for each adviser.

(2) *When an amendment is required.* Each non-resident general partner or a non-resident managing agent of any investment adviser must amend its Form ADV–NR within 30 days whenever any information contained in the form becomes inaccurate by filing with the Commission a new Form ADV–NR.

(3) *Electronic filing.* Form ADV–NR (and any amendments to Form ADV–NR) must be filed electronically through the Investment Adviser Registration Depository (IARD), unless a hardship exemption under 17 CFR 275.203-3 (Rule 203-3) has been granted.

(4) *When filed.* Each Form ADV–NR is considered filed with the Commission upon acceptance by the IARD.

(5) *Filing fees.* No fee shall be assessed for filing Form ADV–NR through IARD.

(6) *Form ADV–NR is a report.* Each Form ADV–NR (and any amendment to Form ADV–NR) required to be filed under this rule is a "report" within the meaning of sections 204 and 207 of the Act.

[65 FR 57448, Sept. 22, 2000; 65 FR 81737, Dec. 27, 2000 as amended at 84 FR 33630, July 12, 2019; 87 FR 38977, June 30, 2022]

EDITORIAL NOTE: For FEDERAL REGISTER citations affecting Form ADV, see the List of CFR Sections Affected, which appears in the Finding Aids section of the printed volume and at www.govinfo.gov.

§ 275.203-2 Withdrawal from investment adviser registration.

(a) *Form ADV-W.* You must file Form ADV-W (17 CFR 279.2) to withdraw from investment adviser registration with the Commission (or to withdraw a pending registration application).

(b) *Electronic filing.* Once you have filed your Form ADV (17 CFR 279.1) (or any amendments to Form ADV) electronically with the Investment Adviser Registration Depository (IARD), any Form ADV-W you file must be filed with the IARD, unless you have received a hardship exemption under § 275.203-3.

(c) *Effective date—upon filing.* Each Form ADV-W filed under this section is effective upon acceptance by the IARD, provided however that your investment adviser registration will continue for a period of sixty days after acceptance solely for the purpose of commencing a proceeding under section 203(e) of the Act (15 U.S.C. 80b–3(e)).

(d) *Filing fees.* You do not have to pay a fee to file Form ADV-W through the IARD.

(e) *Form ADV-W is a report.* Each Form ADV-W required to be filed under this section is a "report" within the meaning of sections 204 and 207 of the Act (15 U.S.C. 80b–4 and 80b–7).

[65 FR 57449, Sept. 22, 2000]

§ 275.203-3 Hardship exemptions.

This section provides two "hardship exemptions" from the requirement to make Advisers Act filings electronically with the Investment Adviser Registration Depository (IARD).

(a) *Temporary hardship exemption*—(1) *Eligibility for exemption.* If you are registered or are registering with the Commission as an investment adviser and submit electronic filings on the Investment Adviser Registration Depository (IARD) system, but have unanticipated technical difficulties that prevent you from submitting a filing to the IARD system, you may request a temporary hardship exemption from the requirements of this chapter to file electronically.

(2) *Application procedures.* To request a temporary hardship exemption, you must:

(i) File Form ADV-H (17 CFR 279.3) in paper format with no later than one business day after the filing that is the subject of the ADV-H was due; and

(ii) Submit the filing that is the subject of the Form ADV-H in electronic format with the IARD no later than seven business days after the filing was due.

(3) *Effective date—upon filing.* The temporary hardship exemption will be granted when you file a completed Form ADV-H.

Securities and Exchange Commission § 275.203(l)–1

(b) *Continuing hardship exemption*—(1) *Eligibility for exemption.* If you are a "small business" (as described in paragraph (b)(5) of this section), you may apply for a continuing hardship exemption.

The period of the exemption may be no longer than one year after the date on which you apply for the exemption.

(2) *Application procedures.* To apply for a continuing hardship exemption, you must file Form ADV-H at least ten business days before a filing is due. The Commission will grant or deny your application within ten business days after you file Form ADV-H.

(3) *Effective date—upon approval.* You are not exempt from the electronic filing requirements until and unless the Commission approves your application. If the Commission approves your application, you may submit your filings to FINRA in paper format for the period of time for which the exemption is granted.

(4) *Criteria for exemption.* Your application will be granted only if you are able to demonstrate that the electronic filing requirements of this chapter are prohibitively burdensome or expensive.

(5) *Small business.* You are a "small business" for purposes of this section if you are required to answer Item 12 of Form ADV (17 CFR 279.1) and checked "no" to each question in Item 12 that you were required to answer.

NOTE TO PARAGRAPH (b): FINRA will charge you an additional fee covering its cost to convert to electronic format a filing made in reliance on a continuing hardship exemption.

[65 FR 57449, Sept. 22, 2000; 65 FR 81738, Dec. 27, 2000, as amended at 68 FR 42248, July 17, 2003; 73 FR 4694, Jan. 28, 2008]

§ 275.203(l)–1 Venture capital fund defined.

(a) *Venture capital fund defined.* For purposes of section 203(*l*) of the Act (15 U.S.C. 80b–3(*l*)), a venture capital fund is any entity described in subparagraph (A), (B), or (C) of section 203(b)(7) of the Act (15 U.S.C. 80b–3(b)(7)) (other than an entity that has elected to be regulated or is regulated as a business development company pursuant to section 54 of the Investment Company Act of 1940 (15 U.S.C. 80a–53)) or any entity described in subparagraph (A) or (B) of section 203(b)(8) of the Act (15 U.S.C. 80b–3(b)(8)) (other than an entity that has elected to be regulated or is regulated as a business development company pursuant to section 54 of the Investment Company Act of 1940 (15 U.S.C. 80a–53)) or any private fund that:

(1) Represents to investors and potential investors that it pursues a venture capital strategy;

(2) Immediately after the acquisition of any asset, other than qualifying investments or short-term holdings, holds no more than 20 percent of the amount of the fund's aggregate capital contributions and uncalled committed capital in assets (other than short-term holdings) that are not qualifying investments, valued at cost or fair value, consistently applied by the fund;

(3) Does not borrow, issue debt obligations, provide guarantees or otherwise incur leverage, in excess of 15 percent of the private fund's aggregate capital contributions and uncalled committed capital, and any such borrowing, indebtedness, guarantee or leverage is for a non-renewable term of no longer than 120 calendar days, except that any guarantee by the private fund of a qualifying portfolio company's obligations up to the amount of the value of the private fund's investment in the qualifying portfolio company is not subject to the 120 calendar day limit;

(4) Only issues securities the terms of which do not provide a holder with any right, except in extraordinary circumstances, to withdraw, redeem or require the repurchase of such securities but may entitle holders to receive distributions made to all holders pro rata; and

(5) Is not registered under section 8 of the Investment Company Act of 1940 (15 U.S.C. 80a–8), and has not elected to be treated as a business development company pursuant to section 54 of that Act (15 U.S.C. 80a–53).

(b) *Certain pre-existing venture capital funds.* For purposes of section 203(l) of the Act (15 U.S.C. 80b–3(l)) and in addition to any venture capital fund as set forth in paragraph (a) of this section, a venture capital fund also includes any private fund that:

(1) Has represented to investors and potential investors at the time of the offering of the private fund's securities

§ 275.203(m)-1

that it pursues a venture capital strategy;

(2) Prior to December 31, 2010, has sold securities to one or more investors that are not related persons, as defined in § 275.206(4)-2(d)(7), of any investment adviser of the private fund; and

(3) Does not sell any securities to (including accepting any committed capital from) any person after July 21, 2011.

(c) *Definitions.* For purposes of this section:

(1) *Committed capital* means any commitment pursuant to which a person is obligated to:

(i) Acquire an interest in the private fund; or

(ii) Make capital contributions to the private fund.

(2) *Equity security* has the same meaning as in section 3(a)(11) of the Securities Exchange Act of 1934 (15 U.S.C. 78c(a)(11)) and § 240.3a11-1 of this chapter.

(3) *Qualifying investment* means:

(i) An equity security issued by a qualifying portfolio company that has been acquired directly by the private fund from the qualifying portfolio company;

(ii) Any equity security issued by a qualifying portfolio company in exchange for an equity security issued by the qualifying portfolio company described in paragraph (c)(3)(i) of this section; or

(iii) Any equity security issued by a company of which a qualifying portfolio company is a majority-owned subsidiary, as defined in section 2(a)(24) of the Investment Company Act of 1940 (15 U.S.C. 80a-2(a)(24)), or a predecessor, and is acquired by the private fund in exchange for an *equity security* described in paragraph (c)(3)(i) or (c)(3)(ii) of this section.

(4) *Qualifying portfolio company* means any company that:

(i) At the time of any investment by the private fund, is not reporting or foreign traded and does not control, is not controlled by or under common control with another company, directly or indirectly, that is reporting or foreign traded;

(ii) Does not borrow or issue debt obligations in connection with the private fund's investment in such company and distribute to the private fund the proceeds of such borrowing or issuance in exchange for the private fund's investment; and

(iii) Is not an investment company, a private fund, an issuer that would be an investment company but for the exemption provided by § 270.3a-7 of this chapter, or a commodity pool.

(5) *Reporting or foreign traded* means, with respect to a company, being subject to the reporting requirements under section 13 or 15(d) of the Securities Exchange Act of 1934 (15 U.S.C. 78m or 78o(d)), or having a security listed or traded on any exchange or organized market operating in a foreign jurisdiction.

(6) *Short-term holdings* means cash and cash equivalents, as defined in § 270.2a51-1(b)(7)(i) of this chapter, U.S. Treasuries with a remaining maturity of 60 days or less, and shares of an open-end management investment company registered under section 8 of the Investment Company Act of 1940 (15 U.S.C. 80a-8) that is regulated as a money market fund under § 270.2a-7 of this chapter.

NOTE: For purposes of this section, an investment adviser may treat as a private fund any issuer formed under the laws of a jurisdiction other than the United States that has not offered or sold its securities in the United States or to U.S. persons in a manner inconsistent with being a private fund, provided that the adviser treats the issuer as a private fund under the Act (15 U.S.C. 80b) and the rules thereunder for all purposes.

[76 FR 39702, July 6, 2011, as amended at 83 FR 1302, Jan. 11, 2018; 85 FR 13741, Mar. 10, 2020]

§ 275.203(m)-1 Private fund adviser exemption.

(a) *United States investment advisers.* For purposes of section 203(m) of the Act (15 U.S.C. 80b-3(m)), an investment adviser with its principal office and place of business in the United States is exempt from the requirement to register under section 203 of the Act if the investment adviser:

(1) Acts solely as an investment adviser to one or more qualifying private funds; and

(2) Manages private fund assets of less than $150 million.

(b) *Non-United States investment advisers.* For purposes of section 203(m) of

Securities and Exchange Commission §275.203A–1

the Act (15 U.S.C. 80b–3(m)), an investment adviser with its principal office and place of business outside of the United States is exempt from the requirement to register under section 203 of the Act if:

(1) The investment adviser has no client that is a United States person except for one or more qualifying private funds; and

(2) All assets managed by the investment adviser at a place of business in the United States are solely attributable to private fund assets, the total value of which is less than $150 million.

(c) *Frequency of Calculations.* For purposes of this section, calculate private fund assets annually, in accordance with General Instruction 15 to Form ADV (§ 279.1 of this chapter).

(d) *Definitions.* For purposes of this section:

(1) *Assets under management* means the regulatory assets under management as determined under Item 5.F of Form ADV (§ 279.1 of this chapter), except the following shall be excluded from the definition of assets under management for purposes of this section:

(i) The regulatory assets under management attributable to a private fund that is an entity described in subparagraph (A), (B), or (C) of section 203(b)(7) of the Act (15 U.S.C. 80b– 3(b)(7)) (other than an entity that has elected to be regulated or is regulated as a business development company pursuant to section 54 of the Investment Company Act of 1940 (15 U.S.C. 80a–53)); and

(ii) The regulatory assets under management attributable to a private fund that is an entity described in subparagraph (A) or (B) of section 203(b)(8) of the Act (15 U.S.C. 80b–3(b)(8)) (other than an entity that has elected to be regulated or is regulated as a business development company pursuant to section 54 of the Investment Company Act of 1940 (15 U.S.C. 80a–53).

(2) *Place of business* has the same meaning as in § 275.222–1(a).

(3) *Principal office and place of business* of an investment adviser means the executive office of the investment adviser from which the officers, partners, or managers of the investment adviser direct, control, and coordinate the activities of the investment adviser.

(4) *Private fund assets* means the investment adviser's assets under management attributable to a qualifying private fund.

(5) *Qualifying private fund* means any private fund that is not registered under section 8 of the Investment Company Act of 1940 (15 U.S.C. 80a–8) and has not elected to be treated as a business development company pursuant to section 54 of that Act (15 U.S.C. 80a–53). For purposes of this section, an investment adviser may treat as a private fund an issuer that qualifies for an exclusion from the definition of an "investment company," as defined in section 3 of the Investment Company Act of 1940 (15 U.S.C. 80a–3), in addition to those provided by section 3(c)(1) or 3(c)(7) of that Act (15 U.S.C. 80a–3(c)(1) or 15 U.S.C. 80a–3(c)(7)), provided that the investment adviser treats the issuer as a private fund under the Act (15 U.S.C. 80b) and the rules thereunder for all purposes.

(6) *Related person* has the same meaning as in § 275.206(4)–2(d)(7).

(7) *United States* has the same meaning as in § 230.902(l) of this chapter.

(8) *United States person* means any person that is a U.S. person as defined in § 230.902(k) of this chapter, except that any discretionary account or similar account that is held for the benefit of a United States person by a dealer or other professional fiduciary is a United States person if the dealer or professional fiduciary is a related person of the investment adviser relying on this section and is not organized, incorporated, or (if an individual) resident in the United States.

NOTE TO PARAGRAPH (d)(8): A client will not be considered a United States person if the client was not a United States person at the time of becoming a client.

[76 FR 39703, July 6, 2011, as amended at 83 FR 1302, Jan. 11, 2018; 85 FR 13741, Mar. 10, 2020]

§ 275.203A–1 Eligibility for SEC registration; Switching to or from SEC registration.

(a) *Eligibility for SEC registration of mid-sized investment advisers.* If you are

§ 275.203A-2

an investment adviser described in section 203A(a)(2)(B) of the Act (15 U.S.C. 80b–3a(a)(2)(B)):

(1) *Threshold for SEC registration and registration buffer.* You may, but are not required to register with the Commission if you have assets under management of at least $100,000,000 but less than $110,000,000, and you need not withdraw your registration unless you have less than $90,000,000 of assets under management.

(2) *Exceptions.* This paragraph (a) does not apply if:

(i) You are an investment adviser to an investment company registered under the Investment Company Act of 1940 (15 U.S.C. 80a) or to a company which has elected to be a business development company pursuant to section 54 of the Investment Company Act of 1940 (15 U.S.C. 80a–54), and has not withdrawn the election; or

(ii) You are eligible for an exemption described in § 275.203A–2 of this chapter.

(b) *Switching to or from SEC registration*—(1) *State-registered advisers—switching to SEC registration.* If you are registered with a state securities authority, you must apply for registration with the Commission within 90 days of filing an annual updating amendment to your Form ADV reporting that you are eligible for SEC registration and are not relying on an exemption from registration under sections 203(l) or 203(m) of the Act (15 U.S.C. 80b–3(l), (m)).

(2) *SEC-registered advisers—switching to State registration.* If you are registered with the Commission and file an annual updating amendment to your Form ADV reporting that you are not eligible for SEC registration and are not relying on an exemption from registration under sections 203(l) or 203(m) of the Act (15 U.S.C. 80b–3(l), (m)), you must file Form ADV-W (17 CFR 279.2) to withdraw your SEC registration within 180 days of your fiscal year end (unless you then are eligible for SEC registration). During this period while you are registered with both the Commission and one or more state securities authorities, the Act and applicable State law will apply to your advisory activities.

[76 FR 43011, July 19, 2011]

§ 275.203A–2 Exemptions from prohibition on Commission registration.

The prohibition of section 203A(a) of the Act (15 U.S.C. 80b–3a(a)) does not apply to:

(a) *Pension consultants.* (1) An investment adviser that is a "pension consultant," as defined in this section, with respect to assets of plans having an aggregate value of at least $200,000,000.

(2) An investment adviser is a pension consultant, for purposes of paragraph (a) of this section, if the investment adviser provides investment advice to:

(i) Any employee benefit plan described in section 3(3) of the Employee Retirement Income Security Act of 1974 ("ERISA") [29 U.S.C. 1002(3)];

(ii) Any governmental plan described in section 3(32) of ERISA (29 U.S.C. 1002(32)); or

(iii) Any church plan described in section 3(33) of ERISA (29 U.S.C. 1002(33)).

(3) In determining the aggregate value of assets of plans, include only that portion of a plan's assets for which the investment adviser provided investment advice (including any advice with respect to the selection of an investment adviser to manage such assets). Determine the aggregate value of assets by cumulating the value of assets of plans with respect to which the investment adviser was last employed or retained by contract to provide investment advice during a 12-month period ended within 90 days of filing an annual updating amendment to Form ADV (17 CFR 279.1).

(b) *Investment advisers controlling, controlled by, or under common control with an investment adviser registered with the Commission.* An investment adviser that controls, is controlled by, or is under common control with, an investment adviser eligible to register, and registered with, the Commission ("registered adviser"), provided that the principal office and place of business of the investment adviser is the same as that of the registered adviser. For purposes of this paragraph, control means the power to direct or cause the direction of the management or policies of an investment adviser, whether through ownership of securities, by

Securities and Exchange Commission § 275.203A-2

contract, or otherwise. Any person that directly or indirectly has the right to vote 25 percent or more of the voting securities, or is entitled to 25 percent or more of the profits, of an investment adviser is presumed to control that investment adviser.

(c) *Investment advisers expecting to be eligible for Commission registration within 120 Days.* An investment adviser that:

(1) Immediately before it registers with the Commission, is not registered or required to be registered with the Commission or a state securities authority of any State and has a reasonable expectation that it would be eligible to register with the Commission within 120 days after the date the investment adviser's registration with the Commission becomes effective;

(2) Indicates on Schedule D of its Form ADV (17 CFR 279.1) that it will withdraw from registration with the Commission if, on the 120th day after the date the investment adviser's registration with the Commission becomes effective, the investment adviser would be prohibited by section 203A(a) of the Act (15 U.S.C. 80b–3a(a)) from registering with the Commission; and

(3) Notwithstanding § 275.203A–1(b)(2) of this chapter, files a completed Form ADV-W (17 CFR 279.2) withdrawing from registration with the Commission within 120 days after the date the investment adviser's registration with the Commission becomes effective.

(d) *Multi-state investment advisers.* An investment adviser that:

(1) Upon submission of its application for registration with the Commission, is required by the laws of 15 or more States to register as an investment adviser with the state securities authority in the respective States, and thereafter would, but for this section, be required by the laws of at least 15 States to register as an investment adviser with the state securities authority in the respective States;

(2) Elects to rely on paragraph (d) of this section by:

(i) Indicating on Schedule D of its Form ADV that the investment adviser has reviewed the applicable State and federal laws and has concluded that, in the case of an application for registration with the Commission, it is required by the laws of 15 or more States to register as an investment adviser with the state securities authorities in the respective States or, in the case of an amendment to Form ADV, it would be required by the laws of at least 15 States to register as an investment adviser with the state securities authorities in the respective States, within 90 days prior to the date of filing Form ADV; and

(ii) Undertaking on Schedule D of its Form ADV to withdraw from registration with the Commission if the adviser indicates on an annual updating amendment to Form ADV that the investment adviser would be required by the laws of fewer than 15 States to register as an investment adviser with the state securities authority in the respective States, and that the investment adviser would be prohibited by section 203A(a) of the Act (15 U.S.C. 80b–3a(a)) from registering with the Commission, by filing a completed Form ADV-W within 180 days of the adviser's fiscal year end (unless the adviser then is eligible for SEC registration); and

(3) Maintains in an easily accessible place a record of the States in which the investment adviser has determined it would, but for the exemption, be required to register for a period of not less than five years from the filing of a Form ADV that includes a representation that is based on such record.

(e) *Internet investment advisers.* (1) An investment adviser that:

(i) Provides investment advice to all of its clients exclusively through an interactive website, except that the investment adviser may provide investment advice to fewer than 15 clients through other means during the preceding twelve months;

(ii) Maintains, in an easily accessible place, for a period of not less than five years from the filing of a Form ADV that includes a representation that the adviser is eligible to register with the Commission under paragraph (e) of this section, a record demonstrating that it provides investment advice to its clients exclusively through an interactive website in accordance with the limits in paragraph (e)(1)(i) of this section; and

(iii) Does not control, is not controlled by, and is not under common

§ 275.203A-3

control with, another investment adviser that registers with the Commission under paragraph (b) of this section solely in reliance on the adviser registered under paragraph (e) of this section as its *registered adviser*.

(2) For purposes of paragraph (e) of this section, *interactive website* means a website in which computer software-based models or applications provide investment advice to clients based on personal information each client supplies through the website.

(3) An investment adviser may rely on the definition of *client* in § 275.202(a)(30)-1 in determining whether it provides investment advice to fewer than 15 clients under paragraph (e)(1)(i) of this section.

[62 FR 28133, May 22, 1997, as amended at 63 FR 39715, 39716, July 24, 1998; 65 FR 57450, Sept. 22, 2000; 67 FR 77625, Dec. 18, 2003; 76 FR 43012, July 19, 2011]

§ 275.203A-3 Definitions.

For purposes of section 203A of the Act (15 U.S.C. 80b-3a) and the rules thereunder:

(a)(1) *Investment adviser representative.* "Investment adviser representative" of an investment adviser means a supervised person of the investment adviser:

(i) Who has more than five clients who are natural persons (other than excepted persons described in paragraph (a)(3)(i) of this section); and

(ii) More than ten percent of whose clients are natural persons (other than excepted persons described in paragraph (a)(3)(i) of this section).

(2) Notwithstanding paragraph (a)(1) of this section, a supervised person is not an investment adviser representative if the supervised person:

(i) Does not on a regular basis solicit, meet with, or otherwise communicate with clients of the investment adviser; or

(ii) Provides only impersonal investment advice.

(3) For purposes of this section:

(i) "Excepted person" means a natural person who is a qualified client as described in § 275.205-3(d)(1).

(ii) "Impersonal investment advice" means investment advisory services provided by means of written material or oral statements that do not purport to meet the objectives or needs of specific individuals or accounts.

(4) Supervised persons may rely on the definition of "client" in § 275.202(a)(30)-1 to identify clients for purposes of paragraph (a)(1) of this section, except that supervised persons need not count clients that are not residents of the United States.

(b) *Place of business.* "Place of business" of an investment adviser representative means:

(1) An office at which the investment adviser representative regularly provides investment advisory services, solicits, meets with, or otherwise communicates with clients; and

(2) Any other location that is held out to the general public as a location at which the investment adviser representative provides investment advisory services, solicits, meets with, or otherwise communicates with clients.

(c) *Principal office and place of business.* "Principal office and place of business" of an investment adviser means the executive office of the investment adviser from which the officers, partners, or managers of the investment adviser direct, control, and coordinate the activities of the investment adviser.

(d) *Assets under management.* Determine "assets under management" by calculating the securities portfolios with respect to which an investment adviser provides continuous and regular supervisory or management services as reported on the investment adviser's Form ADV (17 CFR 279.1).

(e) *State securities authority.* "State securities authority" means the securities commissioner or commission (or any agency, office or officer performing like functions) of any State.

[62 FR 28134, May 22, 1997, as amended at 63 FR 39715, July 24, 1998; 69 FR 72088, Dec. 10, 2004; 76 FR 43012, July 19, 2011]

§§ 275.203A-4—275.203A-6 [Reserved]

§ 275.204-1 Amendments to Form ADV.

(a) *When amendment is required.* You must amend your Form ADV (17 CFR 279.1):

(1) Parts 1 and 2:

(i) At least annually, within 90 days of the end of your fiscal year; and

Securities and Exchange Commission § 275.204-2

(ii) More frequently, if required by the instructions to Form ADV.

(2) Part 3 at the frequency required by the instructions to Form ADV.

(b) *Electronic filing of amendments.* (1) Subject to paragraph (c) of this section, you must file all amendments to Part 1A, Part 2A, and Part 3 of Form ADV electronically with the IARD, unless you have received a continuing hardship exemption under § 275.203-3. You are not required to file with the Commission amendments to brochure supplements required by Part 2B of Form ADV.

(2) If you have received a continuing hardship exemption under § 275.203-3, you must, when you are required to amend your Form ADV, file a completed Part 1A, Part 2A and Part 3 of Form ADV on paper with the SEC by mailing it to FINRA.

(c) *Filing fees.* You must pay FINRA (the operator of the IARD) an initial filing fee when you first electronically file Part 1A of Form ADV. After you pay the initial filing fee, you must pay an annual filing fee each time you file your annual updating amendment. No portion of either fee is refundable. The Commission has approved the filing fees. Your amended Form ADV will not be accepted by FINRA, and thus will not be considered filed with the Commission, until you have paid the filing fee.

(d) *Amendments to Form ADV are reports.* Each amendment required to be filed under this section is a "report" within the meaning of sections 204 and 207 of the Act (15 U.S.C. 80b-4 and 80b-7).

(e) *Transition to Filing Form CRS.* If you are registered with the Commission or have an application for registration pending with the Commission prior to June 30, 2020, you must amend your Form ADV by electronically filing with IARD your initial Form CRS that satisfies the requirements of Part 3 of Form ADV (as amended effective September 30, 2019) beginning on May 1, 2020 and by no later than June 30, 2020.

NOTE 1 TO PARAGRAPHS (e): This note applies to paragraphs (a), (b), and (e) of this section. Information on how to file with the IARD is available on our website at *http://www.sec.gov/iard*. For the annual updating amendment: Summaries of material changes that are not included in the adviser's brochure must be filed with the Commission as an exhibit to Part 2A in the same electronic file; and if you are not required to prepare a brochure, a summary of material changes, an annual updating amendment to your brochure, or Form CRS you are not required to file them with the Commission. See the instructions for Part 2A and Part 3 of Form ADV.

[65 FR 57450, Sept. 22, 2000; 65 FR 81738, Dec. 27, 2000, as amended at 68 FR 42248, July 17, 2003; 73 FR 4694, Jan. 28, 2008; 75 FR 49267, Aug. 12, 2010; 76 FR 43013, July 19, 2011; 81 FR 60458, Sept. 1, 2016; 84 FR 33630, July 12, 2019]

§ 275.204-2 Books and records to be maintained by investment advisers.

(a) Every investment adviser registered or required to be registered under section 203 of the Act (15 U.S.C. 80b-3) shall make and keep true, accurate and current the following books and records relating to its investment advisory business;

(1) A journal or journals, including cash receipts and disbursements, records, and any other records of original entry forming the basis of entries in any ledger.

(2) General and auxiliary ledgers (or other comparable records) reflecting asset, liability, reserve, capital, income and expense accounts.

(3) A memorandum of each order given by the investment adviser for the purchase or sale of any security, of any instruction received by the investment adviser concerning the purchase, sale, receipt or delivery of a particular security, and of any modification or cancellation of any such order or instruction. Such memoranda shall show the terms and conditions of the order, instruction, modification or cancellation; shall identify the person connected with the investment adviser who recommended the transaction to the client and the person who placed such order; and shall show the account for which entered, the date of entry, and the bank, broker or dealer by or through whom executed where appropriate. Orders entered pursuant to the exercise of discretionary power shall be so designated.

(4) All check books, bank statements, cancelled checks and cash reconciliations of the investment adviser.

(5) All bills or statements (or copies thereof), paid or unpaid, relating to the business of the investment adviser as such.

(6) All trial balances, financial statements, and internal audit working papers relating to the business of such investment adviser.

(7) Originals of all written communications received and copies of all written communications sent by such investment adviser relating to:

(i) Any recommendation made or proposed to be made and any advice given or proposed to be given;

(ii) Any receipt, disbursement or delivery of funds or securities;

(iii) The placing or execution of any order to purchase or sell any security;

(iv) Predecessor performance (as defined in § 275.206(4)–1(e)(12) of this chapter) and the performance or rate of return of any or all managed accounts, portfolios (as defined in § 275.206(4)–1(e)(11) of this chapter), or securities recommendations; Provided, however:

(A) That the investment adviser shall not be required to keep any unsolicited market letters and other similar communications of general public distribution not prepared by or for the investment adviser; and

(B) That if the investment adviser sends any notice, circular, or other advertisement (as defined in § 275.206(4)–1(e)(1) of this chapter) offering any report, analysis, publication or other investment advisory service to more than ten persons, the investment adviser shall not be required to keep a record of the names and addresses of the persons to whom it was sent; except that if such notice, circular, or advertisement is distributed to persons named on any list, the investment adviser shall retain with the copy of such notice, circular, or advertisement a memorandum describing the list and the source thereof.

(8) A list or other record of all accounts in which the investment adviser is vested with any discretionary power with respect to the funds, securities or transactions of any client.

(9) All powers of attorney and other evidences of the granting of any discretionary authority by any client to the investment adviser, or copies thereof.

(10) All written agreements (or copies thereof) entered into by the investment adviser with any client or otherwise relating to the business of such investment adviser as such.

(11)(i) A copy of each

(A) Advertisement (as defined in § 275.206(4)–1(e)(1) of this chapter) that the investment adviser disseminates, directly or indirectly, except:

(*1*) For oral advertisements, the adviser may instead retain a copy of any written or recorded materials used by the adviser in connection with the oral advertisement; and

(*2*) For compensated oral testimonials and endorsements (as defined in § 275.206(4)–1(e)(17) and (5) of this chapter), the adviser may instead make and keep a record of the disclosures provided to clients or investors pursuant to § 275.206(4)–1(b)(1) of this chapter; and

(B) Notice, circular, newspaper article, investment letter, bulletin, or other communication that the investment adviser disseminates, directly or indirectly, to ten or more persons (other than persons associated with such investment adviser); and

(C) If such notice, circular, advertisement, newspaper article, investment letter, bulletin, or other communication recommends the purchase or sale of a specific security and does not state the reasons for such recommendation, a memorandum of the investment adviser indicating the reasons therefor; and

(ii) A copy of any questionnaire or survey used in the preparation of a third-party rating included or appearing in any advertisement in the event the adviser obtains a copy of the questionnaire or survey.

(12)(i) A copy of the investment adviser's code of ethics adopted and implemented pursuant to § 275.204A–1 that is in effect, or at any time within the past five years was in effect;

(ii) A record of any violation of the code of ethics, and of any action taken as a result of the violation; and

(iii) A record of all written acknowledgments as required by § 275.204A–1(a)(5) for each person who is currently, or within the past five years was, a supervised person of the investment adviser.

Securities and Exchange Commission § 275.204-2

(13)(i) A record of each report made by an access person as required by § 275.204A–1(b), including any information provided under paragraph (b)(3)(iii) of that section in lieu of such reports;

(ii) A record of the names of persons who are currently, or within the past five years were, access persons of the investment adviser; and

(iii) A record of any decision, and the reasons supporting the decision, to approve the acquisition of securities by access persons under § 275.204A–1(c), for at least five years after the end of the fiscal year in which the approval is granted.

(14)(i) A copy of each brochure, brochure supplement and Form CRS, and each amendment or revision to the brochure, brochure supplement and Form CRS, that satisfies the requirements of Part 2 or Part 3 of Form ADV, as applicable [17 CFR 279.1]; any summary of material changes that satisfies the requirements of Part 2 of Form ADV but is not contained in the brochure; and a record of the dates that each brochure, brochure supplement and Form CRS, each amendment or revision thereto, and each summary of material changes not contained in a brochure given to any client or to any prospective client who subsequently becomes a client.

(ii) Documentation describing the method used to compute managed assets for purposes of Item 4.E of Part 2A of Form ADV, if the method differs from the method used to compute regulatory assets under management in Item 5.F of Part 1A of Form ADV.

(iii) A memorandum describing any legal or disciplinary event listed in Item 9 of Part 2A or Item 3 of Part 2B (Disciplinary Information) and presumed to be material, if the event involved the investment adviser or any of its supervised persons and is not disclosed in the brochure or brochure supplement described in paragraph (a)(14)(i) of this section. The memorandum must explain the investment adviser's determination that the presumption of materiality is overcome, and must discuss the factors described in Item 9 of Part 2A of Form ADV or Item 3 of Part 2B of Form ADV.

(15)(i) If not included in the advertisement, a record of the disclosures provided to clients or investors pursuant to § 275.206(4)–1(b)(1)(ii) and (iii) of this chapter;

(ii) Documentation substantiating the adviser's reasonable basis for believing that a testimonial or endorsement (as defined in § 275.206(4)–1(e)(17) and (5) of this chapter) complies with § 275.206(4)–1 and that the third-party rating (as defined in § 275.206(4)–1(e)(18) of this chapter) complies with § 275.206(4)–1(c)(1) of this chapter; and

(iii) A record of the names of all persons who are an investment adviser's partners, officers, directors, or employees, or a person that controls, is controlled by, or is under common control with the investment adviser, or is a partner, officer, director or employee of such a person pursuant to § 275.206(4)–1(b)(4)(ii) of this chapter.

(16) All accounts, books, internal working papers, and any other records or documents that are necessary to form the basis for or demonstrate the calculation of any performance or rate of return of any or all managed accounts, portfolios (as defined in § 275.206(4)–1(e)(11) of this chapter), or securities recommendations presented in any notice, circular, advertisement (as defined in § 275.206(4)–1(e)(1) of this chapter), newspaper article, investment letter, bulletin, or other communication that the investment adviser disseminates, directly or indirectly, to any person (other than persons associated with such investment adviser), including copies of all information provided or offered pursuant to § 275.206(4)–1(d)(6) of this chapter; provided, however, that, with respect to the performance of managed accounts, the retention of all account statements, if they reflect all debits, credits, and other transactions in a client's or investor's account for the period of the statement, and all worksheets necessary to demonstrate the calculation of the performance or rate of return of all managed accounts shall be deemed to satisfy the requirements of this paragraph.

(17)(i) A copy of the investment adviser's policies and procedures formulated pursuant to § 275.206(4)–7(a) of this chapter that are in effect, or at any time within the past five years were in effect;

523

§ 275.204-2

(ii) Any records documenting the investment adviser's annual review of those policies and procedures conducted pursuant to § 275.206(4)-7(b) of this chapter;

(iii) A copy of any internal control report obtained or received pursuant to § 275.206(4)-2(a)(6)(ii).

(18)(i) Books and records that pertain to § 275.206(4)-5 containing a list or other record of:

(A) The names, titles and business and residence addresses of all covered associates of the investment adviser;

(B) All government entities to which the investment adviser provides or has provided investment advisory services, or which are or were investors in any covered investment pool to which the investment adviser provides or has provided investment advisory services, as applicable, in the past five years, but not prior to September 13, 2010;

(C) All direct or indirect contributions made by the investment adviser or any of its covered associates to an official of a government entity, or direct or indirect payments to a political party of a State or political subdivision thereof, or to a political action committee; and

(D) The name and business address of each regulated person to whom the investment adviser provides or agrees to provide, directly or indirectly, payment to solicit a government entity for investment advisory services on its behalf, in accordance with § 275.206(4)-5(a)(2).

(ii) Records relating to the contributions and payments referred to in paragraph (a)(18)(i)(C) of this section must be listed in chronological order and indicate:

(A) The name and title of each contributor;

(B) The name and title (including any city/county/State or other political subdivision) of each recipient of a contribution or payment;

(C) The amount and date of each contribution or payment; and

(D) Whether any such contribution was the subject of the exception for certain returned contributions pursuant to § 275.206(4)-5(b)(2).

(iii) An investment adviser is only required to make and keep current the records referred to in paragraphs

(a)(18)(i)(A) and (C) of this section if it provides investment advisory services to a government entity or a government entity is an investor in any covered investment pool to which the investment adviser provides investment advisory services.

(iv) For purposes of this section, the terms "contribution," "covered associate," "covered investment pool," "government entity," "official," "payment," "regulated person," and "solicit" have the same meanings as set forth in § 275.206(4)-5.

(19) A record of who the "intended audience" is pursuant to § 275.206(4)-1(d)(6) and (e)(10)(ii)(B) of this chapter.

(b) If an investment adviser subject to paragraph (a) of this section has custody or possession of securities or funds of any client, the records required to be made and kept under paragraph (a) of this section shall include:

(1) A journal or other record showing all purchases, sales, receipts and deliveries of securities (including certificate numbers) for such accounts and all other debits and credits to such accounts.

(2) A separate ledger account for each such client showing all purchases, sales, receipts and deliveries of securities, the date and price of each purchase and sale, and all debits and credits.

(3) Copies of confirmations of all transactions effected by or for the account of any such client.

(4) A record for each security in which any such client has a position, which record shall show the name of each such client having any interest in such security, the amount or interest of each such client, and the location of each such security.

(5) A memorandum describing the basis upon which you have determined that the presumption that any related person is not operationally independent under § 275.206(4)-2(d)(5) has been overcome.

(c)(1) Every investment adviser subject to paragraph (a) of this section who renders any investment supervisory or management service to any client shall, with respect to the portfolio being supervised or managed and to the extent that the information is reasonably available to or obtainable

Securities and Exchange Commission § 275.204-2

by the investment adviser, make and keep true, accurate and current:

(i) Records showing separately for each such client the securities purchased and sold, and the date, amount and price of each such purchase and sale.

(ii) For each security in which any such client has a current position, information from which the investment adviser can promptly furnish the name of each such client, and the current amount or interest of such client.

(2) Every investment adviser subject to paragraph (a) of this section that exercises voting authority with respect to client securities shall, with respect to those clients, make and retain the following:

(i) Copies of all policies and procedures required by § 275.206(4)-6.

(ii) A copy of each proxy statement that the investment adviser receives regarding client securities. An investment adviser may satisfy this requirement by relying on a third party to make and retain, on the investment adviser's behalf, a copy of a proxy statement (provided that the adviser has obtained an undertaking from the third party to provide a copy of the proxy statement promptly upon request) or may rely on obtaining a copy of a proxy statement from the Commission's Electronic Data Gathering, Analysis, and Retrieval (EDGAR) system.

(iii) A record of each vote cast by the investment adviser on behalf of a client. An investment adviser may satisfy this requirement by relying on a third party to make and retain, on the investment adviser's behalf, a record of the vote cast (provided that the adviser has obtained an undertaking from the third party to provide a copy of the record promptly upon request).

(iv) A copy of any document created by the adviser that was material to making a decision how to vote proxies on behalf of a client or that memorializes the basis for that decision.

(v) A copy of each written client request for information on how the adviser voted proxies on behalf of the client, and a copy of any written response by the investment adviser to any (written or oral) client request for information on how the adviser voted proxies on behalf of the requesting client.

(d) Any books or records required by this section may be maintained by the investment adviser in such manner that the identity of any client to whom such investment adviser renders investment supervisory services is indicated by numerical or alphabetical code or some similar designation.

(e)(1) All books and records required to be made under the provisions of paragraphs (a) to (c)(1)(i), inclusive, and (c)(2) of this section (except for books and records required to be made under the provisions of paragraphs (a)(11), (a)(12)(i), (a)(12)(iii), (a)(13)(ii), (a)(13)(iii), (a)(16), and (a)(17)(i) of this section), shall be maintained and preserved in an easily accessible place for a period of not less than five years from the end of the fiscal year during which the last entry was made on such record, the first two years in an appropriate office of the investment adviser.

(2) Partnership articles and any amendments thereto, articles of incorporation, charters, minute books, and stock certificate books of the investment adviser and of any predecessor, shall be maintained in the principal office of the investment adviser and preserved until at least three years after termination of the enterprise.

(3)(i) Books and records required to be made under the provisions of paragraphs (a)(11) and (a)(16) of this rule shall be maintained and preserved in an easily accessible place for a period of not less than five years, the first two years in an appropriate office of the investment adviser, from the end of the fiscal year during which the investment adviser last published or otherwise disseminated, directly or indirectly, the notice, circular, advertisement, newspaper article, investment letter, bulletin or other communication.

(ii) *Transition rule.* If you are an investment adviser that was, prior to July 21, 2011, exempt from registration under section 203(b)(3) of the Act (15 U.S.C. 80b–3(b)(3)), as in effect on July 20, 2011, paragraph (e)(3)(i) of this section does not require you to maintain or preserve books and records that would otherwise be required to be

§ 275.204-2

maintained or preserved under the provisions of paragraph (a)(16) of this section to the extent those books and records pertain to the performance or rate of return of such private fund (as defined in section 202(a)(29) of the Act (15 U.S.C. 80b–2(a)(29)), or other account you advise for any period ended prior to your registration, provided that you continue to preserve any books and records in your possession that pertain to the performance or rate of return of such private fund or other account for such period.

(f) An investment adviser subject to paragraph (a) of this section, before ceasing to conduct or discontinuing business as an investment adviser shall arrange for and be responsible for the preservation of the books and records required to be maintained and preserved under this section for the remainder of the period specified in this section, and shall notify the Commission in writing, at its principal office, Washington, D.C. 20549, of the exact address where such books and records will be maintained during such period.

(g) *Micrographic and electronic storage permitted*—(1) *General.* The records required to be maintained and preserved pursuant to this part may be maintained and preserved for the required time by an investment adviser on:

(i) Micrographic media, including microfilm, microfiche, or any similar medium; or

(ii) Electronic storage media, including any digital storage medium or system that meets the terms of this section.

(2) *General requirements.* The investment adviser must:

(i) Arrange and index the records in a way that permits easy location, access, and retrieval of any particular record;

(ii) Provide promptly any of the following that the Commission (by its examiners or other representatives) may request:

(A) A legible, true, and complete copy of the record in the medium and format in which it is stored;

(B) A legible, true, and complete printout of the record; and

(C) Means to access, view, and print the records; and

(iii) Separately store, for the time required for preservation of the original record, a duplicate copy of the record on any medium allowed by this section.

(3) *Special requirements for electronic storage media.* In the case of records on electronic storage media, the investment adviser must establish and maintain procedures:

(i) To maintain and preserve the records, so as to reasonably safeguard them from loss, alteration, or destruction;

(ii) To limit access to the records to properly authorized personnel and the Commission (including its examiners and other representatives); and

(iii) To reasonably ensure that any reproduction of a non-electronic original record on electronic storage media is complete, true, and legible when retrieved.

(h)(1) Any book or other record made, kept, maintained and preserved in compliance with §§ 240.17a–3 and 240.17a–4 of this chapter under the Securities Exchange Act of 1934, or with rules adopted by the Municipal Securities Rulemaking Board, which is substantially the same as the book or other record required to be made, kept, maintained and preserved under this section, shall be deemed to be made, kept, maintained and preserved in compliance with this section.

(2) A record made and kept pursuant to any provision of paragraph (a) of this section, which contains all the information required under any other provision of paragraph (a) of this section, need not be maintained in duplicate in order to meet the requirements of the other provision of paragraph (a) of this section.

(i) As used in this section the term "discretionary power" shall not include discretion as to the price at which or the time when a transaction is or is to be effected, if, before the order is given by the investment adviser, the client has directed or approved the purchase or sale of a definite amount of the particular security.

(j)(1) Except as provided in paragraph (j)(3) of this section, each non-resident investment adviser registered or applying for registration pursuant to section 203 of the Act shall keep, maintain and preserve, at a place within the United States designated in a notice from him as provided in paragraph (j)(2) of this

Securities and Exchange Commission

§ 275.204-2

section true, correct, complete and current copies of books and records which he is required to make, keep current, maintain or preserve pursuant to any provisions of any rule or regulation of the Commission adopted under the Act.

(2) Except as provided in paragraph (j)(3) of this section, each nonresident investment adviser subject to this paragraph (j) shall furnish to the Commission a written notice specifying the address of the place within the United States where the copies of the books and records required to be kept and preserved by him pursuant to paragraph (j)(1) of this section are located. Each non-resident investment adviser registered or applying for registration when this paragraph becomes effective shall file such notice within 30 days after such rule becomes effective. Each non-resident investment adviser who files an application for registration after this paragraph becomes effective shall file such notice with such application for registration.

(3) Notwithstanding the provisions of paragraphs (j)(1) and (2) of this section, a non-resident investment adviser need not keep or preserve within the United States copies of the books and records referred to in said paragraphs (j)(1) and (2), if:

(i) Such non-resident investment adviser files with the Commission, at the time or within the period provided by paragraph (j)(2) of this section, a written undertaking, in form acceptable to the Commission and signed by a duly authorized person, to furnish to the Commission, upon demand, at its principal office in Washington, DC, or at any Regional Office of the Commission designated in such demand, true, correct, complete and current copies of any or all of the books and records which he is required to make, keep current, maintain or preserve pursuant to any provision of any rule or regulation of the Commission adopted under the Act, or any part of such books and records which may be specified in such demand. Such undertaking shall be in substantially the following form:

The undersigned hereby undertakes to furnish at its own expense to the Securities and Exchange Commission at its principal office in Washington, DC or at any Regional Office of said Commission specified in a demand for copies of books and records made by or on behalf of said Commission, true, correct, complete and current copies of any or all, or any part, of the books and records which the undersigned is required to make, keep current or preserve pursuant to any provision of any rule or regulation of the Securities and Exchange Commission under the Investment Advisers Act of 1940. This undertaking shall be suspended during any period when the undersigned is making, keeping current, and preserving copies of all of said books and records at a place within the United States in compliance with Rule 204-2(j) under the Investment Advisers Act of 1940. This undertaking shall be binding upon the undersigned and the heirs, successors and assigns of the undersigned, and the written irrevocable consents and powers of attorney of the undersigned, its general partners and managing agents filed with the Securities and Exchange Commission shall extend to and cover any action to enforce same.

and

(ii) Such non-resident investment adviser furnishes to the Commission, at his own expense 14 days after written demand therefor forwarded to him by registered mail at his last address of record filed with the Commission and signed by the Secretary of the Commission or such person as the Commission may authorize to act in its behalf, true, correct, complete and current copies of any or all books and records which such investment adviser is required to make, keep current or preserve pursuant to any provision of any rule or regulation of the Commission adopted under the Act, or any part of such books and records which may be specified in said written demand. Such copies shall be furnished to the Commission at its principal office in Washington, DC, or at any Regional Office of the Commission which may be specified in said written demand.

(4) For purposes of this rule the term *non-resident investment adviser* shall have the meaning set out in § 275.0-2(d)(3) under the Act.

(k) Every investment adviser that registers under section 203 of the Act (15 U.S.C. 80b-3) after July 8, 1997 shall be required to preserve in accordance with this section the books and records the investment adviser had been required to maintain by the State in which the investment adviser had its principal office and place of business

§ 275.204-3

prior to registering with the Commission.

[26 FR 5002, June 6, 1961]

EDITORIAL NOTE: For FEDERAL REGISTER citations affecting § 275.204-2, see the List of CFR Sections Affected, which appears in the Finding Aids section of the printed volume and at *www.govinfo.gov.*

EFFECTIVE DATE NOTE: At 88 FR 13954, Mar. 6, 2023, § 275.204-2 was amended by revising paragraph (a)(7)(iii), effective May 5, 2023. For the convenience of the user, the revised text is set forth as follows:

§ 275.204-2 Books and records to be maintained by investment advisers.

(a) * * *

(7) * * *

(iii) The placing or execution of any order to purchase or sell any security; and, for any transaction that is subject to the requirements of § 240.15c6-2(a) of this chapter, each confirmation received, and any allocation and each affirmation sent or received, with a date and time stamp for each allocation and affirmation that indicates when the allocation and affirmation was sent or received;

*   *   *   *   *

§ 275.204-3 Delivery of brochures and brochure supplements.

(a) *General requirements.* If you are registered under the Act as an investment adviser, you must deliver a brochure and one or more brochure supplements to each client or prospective client that contains all information required by Part 2 of Form ADV [17 CFR 279.1].

(b) *Delivery requirements.* You (or a supervised person acting on your behalf) must:

(1) Deliver to a client or prospective client your current brochure before or at the time you enter into an investment advisory contract with that client.

(2) Deliver to each client, annually within 120 days after the end of your fiscal year and without charge, if there are material changes in your brochure since your last annual updating amendment:

(i) A current brochure, or

(ii) The summary of material changes to the brochure as required by Item 2 of Form ADV, Part 2A that offers to provide your current brochure without charge, accompanied by the Web site address (if available) and an e-mail address (if available) and telephone number by which a client may obtain the current brochure from you, and the Web site address for obtaining information about you through the Investment Adviser Public Disclosure (IAPD) system.

(3) Deliver to each client or prospective client a current brochure supplement for a supervised person before or at the time that supervised person begins to provide advisory services to the client; provided, however, that if investment advice for a client is provided by a team comprised of more than five supervised persons, a current brochure supplement need only be delivered to that client for the five supervised persons with the most significant responsibility for the day-to-day advice provided to that client. For purposes of this section, a supervised person will provide advisory services to a client if that supervised person will:

(i) Formulate investment advice for the client and have direct client contact; or

(ii) Make discretionary investment decisions for the client, even if the supervised person will have no direct client contact.

(4) Deliver the following to each client promptly after you create an amended brochure or brochure supplement, as applicable, if the amendment adds disclosure of an event, or materially revises information already disclosed about an event, in response to Item 9 of Part 2A of Form ADV or Item 3 of Part 2B of Form ADV (Disciplinary Information), respectively, (i) the amended brochure or brochure supplement, as applicable, along with a statement describing the material facts relating to the change in disciplinary information, or (ii) a statement describing the material facts relating to the change in disciplinary information.

(c) *Exceptions to delivery requirement.* (1) You are not required to deliver a brochure to a client:

(i) That is an investment company registered under the Investment Company Act of 1940 [15 U.S.C. 80a-1 to 80a-64] or a business development company as defined in that Act, provided that the advisory contract with that client meets the requirements of section 15(c) of that Act [15 U.S.C. 80a-15(c)]; or

Securities and Exchange Commission § 275.204-4

(ii) Who receives only impersonal investment advice for which you charge less than $500 per year.

(2) You are not required to deliver a brochure supplement to a client:

(i) To whom you are not required to deliver a brochure under subparagraph (c)(1) of this section;

(ii) Who receives only impersonal investment advice; or

(iii) Who is an officer, employee, or other person related to the adviser that would be a "qualified client" of your firm under § 275.205-3(d)(1)(iii).

(d) *Wrap fee program brochures.* (1) If you are a sponsor of a wrap fee program, then the brochure that paragraph (b) of this section requires you to deliver to a client or prospective client of the wrap fee program must be a wrap fee program brochure containing all the information required by Part 2A, Appendix 1 of Form ADV. Any additional information in a wrap fee program brochure must be limited to information applicable to wrap fee programs that you sponsor.

(2) You do not have to deliver a wrap fee program brochure if another sponsor of the wrap fee program delivers, to the client or prospective client of the wrap fee program, a wrap fee program brochure containing all the information required by Part 2A, Appendix 1 of Form ADV.

NOTE TO PARAGRAPH (d): A wrap fee program brochure does not take the place of any brochure supplements that you are required to deliver under paragraph (b) of this section.

(e) *Multiple brochures.* If you provide substantially different advisory services to different clients, you may provide them with different brochures, so long as each client receives all information about the services and fees that are applicable to that client. The brochure you deliver to a client may omit any information required by Part 2A of Form ADV if the information does not apply to the advisory services or fees that you will provide or charge, or that you propose to provide or charge, to that client.

(f) *Other disclosure obligations.* Delivering a brochure or brochure supplement in compliance with this section does not relieve you of any other disclosure obligations you have to your advisory clients or prospective clients under any federal or state laws or regulations.

(g) *Definitions.* For purposes of this section:

(1) *Impersonal investment advice* means investment advisory services that do not purport to meet the objectives or needs of specific individuals or accounts.

(2) *Current brochure* and *current brochure supplement* mean the most recent revision of the brochure or brochure supplement, including all amendments to date.

(3) *Sponsor* of a wrap fee program means an investment adviser that is compensated under a wrap fee program for sponsoring, organizing, or administering the program, or for selecting, or providing advice to clients regarding the selection of, other investment advisers in the program.

(4) *Supervised person* means any of your officers, partners or directors (or other persons occupying a similar status or performing similar functions) or employees, or any other person who provides investment advice on your behalf.

(5) *Wrap fee program* means an advisory program under which a specified fee or fees not based directly upon transactions in a client's account is charged for investment advisory services (which may include portfolio management or advice concerning the selection of other investment advisers) and the execution of client transactions.

[75 FR 49268, Aug. 12, 2010, as amended at 81 FR 60458, Oct. 31, 2016; 84 FR 33630, July 12, 2019; 87 FR 22447, Apr. 15, 2022]

§ 275.204-4 **Reporting by exempt reporting advisers.**

(a) *Exempt reporting advisers.* If you are an investment adviser relying on the exemption from registering with the Commission under section 203(l) or (m) of the Act (15 U.S.C. 80b-3(l) or 80b-3(m)), you must complete and file reports on Form ADV (17 CFR 279.1) by following the instructions in the Form, which specify the information that an exempt reporting adviser must provide.

(b) *Electronic filing.* You must file Form ADV electronically with the Investment Adviser Registration Depository (IARD) unless you have received a hardship exemption under paragraph (e) of this section.

NOTE TO PARAGRAPH (b): Information on how to file with the IARD is available on the Commission's Web site at *http://www.sec.gov/iard.*

(c) *When filed.* Each Form ADV is considered filed with the Commission upon acceptance by the IARD.

(d) *Filing fees.* You must pay FINRA (the operator of the IARD) a filing fee. The Commission has approved the amount of the filing fee. No portion of the filing fee is refundable. Your completed Form ADV will not be accepted by FINRA, and thus will not be considered·filed with the Commission, until you have paid the filing fee.

(e) *Temporary hardship exemption*—(1) *Eligibility for exemption.* If you have unanticipated technical difficulties that prevent submission of a filing to the IARD, you may request a temporary hardship exemption from the requirements of this chapter to file electronically.

(2) *Application procedures.* To request a temporary hardship exemption, you must:

(i) File Form ADV-H (17 CFR 279.3) in paper format no later than one business day after the filing that is the subject of the ADV-H was due; and

(ii) Submit the filing that is the subject of the Form ADV-H in electronic format with the IARD no later than seven business days after the filing was due.

(3) *Effective date—upon filing.* The temporary hardship exemption will be granted when you file a completed Form ADV-H.

(f) *Final report.* You must file a final report in accordance with instructions in Form ADV when:

(1) You cease operation as an investment adviser;

(2) You no longer meet the definition of exempt reporting adviser under paragraph (a); or

(3) You apply for registration with the Commission.

NOTE TO PARAGRAPH (f): You do not have to pay a filing fee to file a final report on Form ADV through the IARD.

[76 FR 43013, July 19, 2011]

§ 275.204–5 **Delivery of Form CRS.**

(a) *General requirements.* If you are registered under the Act as an investment adviser, you must deliver Form CRS, required by Part 3 of Form ADV [17 CFR 279.1], to each retail investor.

(b) *Delivery requirements.* You (or a supervised person acting on your behalf) must:

(1) Deliver to each retail investor your current Form CRS before or at the time you enter into an investment advisory contract with that retail investor.

(2) Deliver to each retail investor who is an existing client your current Form CRS before or at the time you:

(i) Open a new account that is different from the retail investor's existing account(s);

(ii) Recommend that the retail investor roll over assets from a retirement account into a new or existing account or investment; or

(iii) Recommend or provide a new investment advisory service or investment that does not necessarily involve the opening of a new account and would not be held in an existing account.

(3) Post the current Form CRS prominently on your website, if you have one, in a location and format that is easily accessible for retail investors.

(4) Communicate any changes made to Form CRS to each retail investor who is an existing client within 60 days after the amendments are required to be made and without charge. The communication can be made by delivering the amended Form CRS or by communicating the information through another disclosure that is delivered to the retail investor.

(5) Deliver a current Form CRS to each retail investor within 30 days upon request.

(c) *Other disclosure obligations.* Delivering Form CRS in compliance with this section does not relieve you of any other disclosure obligations you have to your retail investors under any Federal or State laws or regulations.

Securities and Exchange Commission § 275.204(b)–1

(d) *Definitions.* For purposes of this section:

(1) *Current Form CRS* means the most recent version of the Form CRS.

(2) *Retail investor* means a natural person, or the legal representative of such natural person, who seeks to receive or receives services primarily for personal, family or household purposes.

(3) *Supervised person* means any of your officers, partners or directors (or other persons occupying a similar status or performing similar functions) or employees, or any other person who provides investment advice on your behalf.

(e) *Transition rule.* (1) Within 30 days after the date by which you are first required by § 275.204–1(b) to electronically file your Form CRS with the Commission, you must deliver to each of your existing clients who is a retail investor your current Form CRS as required by Part 3 of Form ADV.

(2) As of the date by which you are first required to electronically file your Form CRS with the Commission, you must begin using your Form CRS as required by Part 3 of Form ADV to comply with the requirements of paragraph (b) of this section.

[84 FR 33631, July 12, 2019, as amended at 87 FR 22447, Apr. 15, 2022]

§ 275.204(b)–1 **Reporting by investment advisers to private funds.**

(a) *Reporting by investment advisers to private funds on Form PF.* If you are an investment adviser registered or required to be registered under section 203 of the Act (15 U.S.C. 80b–3), you act as an investment adviser to one or more private funds and, as of the end of your most recently completed fiscal year, you managed private fund assets of at least $150 million, you must complete and file a report on Form PF (17 CFR 279.9) by following the instructions in the Form, which specify the information that an investment adviser must provide. Your initial report on Form PF is due no later than the last day on which your next update would be timely in accordance with paragraph (e) if you had previously filed the Form; provided that you are not required to file Form PF with respect to any fiscal quarter or fiscal year ending prior to the date on which your registration becomes effective.

(b) *Electronic filing.* You must file Form PF electronically with the Form PF filing system on the Investment Adviser Registration Depository (IARD).

NOTE TO PARAGRAPH (b): Information on how to file Form PF is available on the Commission's Web site at *http://www.sec.gov/iard.*

(c) *When filed.* Each Form PF is considered filed with the Commission upon acceptance by the Form PF filing system.

(d) *Filing fees.* You must pay the operator of the Form PF filing system a filing fee as required by the instructions to Form PF. The Commission has approved the amount of the filing fee. No portion of the filing fee is refundable. Your completed Form PF will not be accepted by the operator of the Form PF filing system, and thus will not be considered filed with the Commission, until you have paid the filing fee.

(e) *Updates to Form PF.* You must file an updated Form PF:

(1) At least annually, no later than the date specified in the instructions to Form PF; and

(2) More frequently, if required by the instructions to Form PF. You must file all updated reports electronically with the Form PF filing system.

(f) *Temporary hardship exemption.* (1) If you have unanticipated technical difficulties that prevent you from submitting Form PF on a timely basis through the Form PF filing system, you may request a temporary hardship exemption from the requirements of this section to file electronically.

(2) To request a temporary hardship exemption, you must:

(i) Complete and file in paper format, in accordance with the instructions to Form PF, Item A of Section 1a and Section 5 of Form PF, checking the box in Section 1a indicating that you are requesting a temporary hardship exemption, no later than one business day after the electronic Form PF filing was due; and

(ii) Submit the filing that is the subject of the Form PF paper filing in electronic format with the Form PF filing system no later than seven business days after the filing was due.

§ 275.204A-1

(3) The temporary hardship exemption will be granted when you file Item A of Section 1a and Section 5 of Form PF, checking the box in Section 1a indicating that you are requesting a temporary hardship exemption.

(4) The hardship exemptions available under § 275.203-3 do not apply to Form PF.

(g) *Definitions.* For purposes of this section:

(1) *Assets under management* means the regulatory assets under management as determined under Item 5.F of Form ADV (§ 279.1 of this chapter).

(2) *Private fund assets* means the investment adviser's assets under management attributable to private funds.

[76 FR 71174, Nov. 16, 2011]

§ 275.204A-1 Investment adviser codes of ethics.

(a) *Adoption of code of ethics.* If you are an investment adviser registered or required to be registered under section 203 of the Act (15 U.S.C. 80b-3), you must establish, maintain and enforce a written code of ethics that, at a minimum, includes:

(1) A standard (or standards) of business conduct that you require of your supervised persons, which standard must reflect your fiduciary obligations and those of your supervised persons;

(2) Provisions requiring your supervised persons to comply with applicable Federal securities laws;

(3) Provisions that require all of your access persons to report, and you to review, their personal securities transactions and holdings periodically as provided below;

(4) Provisions requiring supervised persons to report any violations of your code of ethics promptly to your chief compliance officer or, provided your chief compliance officer also receives reports of all violations, to other persons you designate in your code of ethics; and

(5) Provisions requiring you to provide each of your supervised persons with a copy of your code of ethics and any amendments, and requiring your supervised persons to provide you with a written acknowledgment of their receipt of the code and any amendments.

(b) *Reporting requirements*—(1) *Holdings reports.* The code of ethics must require your access persons to submit to your chief compliance officer or other persons you designate in your code of ethics a report of the access person's current securities holdings that meets the following requirements:

(i) *Content of holdings reports.* Each holdings report must contain, at a minimum:

(A) The title and type of security, and as applicable the exchange ticker symbol or CUSIP number, number of shares, and principal amount of each reportable security in which the access person has any direct or indirect beneficial ownership;

(B) The name of any broker, dealer or bank with which the access person maintains an account in which any securities are held for the access person's direct or indirect benefit; and

(C) The date the access person submits the report.

(ii) *Timing of holdings reports.* Your access persons must each submit a holdings report:

(A) No later than 10 days after the person becomes an access person, and the information must be current as of a date no more than 45 days prior to the date the person becomes an access person.

(B) At least once each 12-month period thereafter on a date you select, and the information must be current as of a date no more than 45 days prior to the date the report was submitted.

(2) *Transaction reports.* The code of ethics must require access persons to submit to your chief compliance officer or other persons you designate in your code of ethics quarterly securities transactions reports that meet the following requirements:

(i) *Content of transaction reports.* Each transaction report must contain, at a minimum, the following information about each transaction involving a reportable security in which the access person had, or as a result of the transaction acquired, any direct or indirect beneficial ownership:

(A) The date of the transaction, the title, and as applicable the exchange ticker symbol or CUSIP number, interest rate and maturity date, number of shares, and principal amount of each reportable security involved;

Securities and Exchange Commission § 275.204A-1

(B) The nature of the transaction (i.e., purchase, sale or any other type of acquisition or disposition);

(C) The price of the security at which the transaction was effected;

(D) The name of the broker, dealer or bank with or through which the transaction was effected; and

(E) The date the access person submits the report.

(ii) *Timing of transaction reports.* Each access person must submit a transaction report no later than 30 days after the end of each calendar quarter, which report must cover, at a minimum, all transactions during the quarter.

(3) *Exceptions from reporting requirements.* Your code of ethics need not require an access person to submit:

(i) Any report with respect to securities held in accounts over which the access person had no direct or indirect influence or control;

(ii) A transaction report with respect to transactions effected pursuant to an automatic investment plan;

(iii) A transaction report if the report would duplicate information contained in broker trade confirmations or account statements that you hold in your records so long as you receive the confirmations or statements no later than 30 days after the end of the applicable calendar quarter.

(c) *Pre-approval of certain investments.* Your code of ethics must require your access persons to obtain your approval before they directly or indirectly acquire beneficial ownership in any security in an initial public offering or in a limited offering.

(d) *Small advisers.* If you have only one access person (i.e., yourself), you are not required to submit reports to yourself or to obtain your own approval for investments in any security in an initial public offering or in a limited offering, if you maintain records of all of your holdings and transactions that this section would otherwise require you to report.

(e) *Definitions.* For the purpose of this section:

(1) *Access person* means:

(i) Any of your supervised persons:

(A) Who has access to nonpublic information regarding any clients' purchase or sale of securities, or nonpublic information regarding the portfolio holdings of any reportable fund, or

(B) Who is involved in making securities recommendations to clients, or who has access to such recommendations that are nonpublic.

(ii) If providing investment advice is your primary business, all of your directors, officers and partners are presumed to be access persons.

(2) *Automatic investment plan* means a program in which regular periodic purchases (or withdrawals) are made automatically in (or from) investment accounts in accordance with a predetermined schedule and allocation. An automatic investment plan includes a dividend reinvestment plan.

(3) *Beneficial ownership* is interpreted in the same manner as it would be under § 240.16a-1(a)(2) of this chapter in determining whether a person has beneficial ownership of a security for purposes of section 16 of the Securities Exchange Act of 1934 (15 U.S.C. 78p) and the rules and regulations thereunder. Any report required by paragraph (b) of this section may contain a statement that the report will not be construed as an admission that the person making the report has any direct or indirect beneficial ownership in the security to which the report relates.

(4) *Federal securities laws* means the Securities Act of 1933 (15 U.S.C. 77a-aa), the Securities Exchange Act of 1934 (15 U.S.C. 78a-mm), the Sarbanes-Oxley Act of 2002 (Pub. L. 107-204, 116 Stat. 745 (2002)), the Investment Company Act of 1940 (15 U.S.C. 80a), the Investment Advisers Act of 1940 (15 U.S.C. 80b), title V of the Gramm-Leach-Bliley Act (Pub. L. 106-102, 113 Stat. 1338 (1999), any rules adopted by the Commission under any of these statutes, the Bank Secrecy Act (31 U.S.C. 5311–5314; 5316–5332) as it applies to funds and investment advisers, and any rules adopted thereunder by the Commission or the Department of the Treasury.

(5) *Fund* means an investment company registered under the Investment Company Act.

(6) *Initial public offering* means an offering of securities registered under the Securities Act of 1933 (15 U.S.C. 77a), the issuer of which, immediately before the registration, was not subject to the reporting requirements of sections 13

§ 275.205-1

or 15(d) of the Securities Exchange Act of 1934 (15 U.S.C. 78m or 78o(d)).

(7) *Limited offering* means an offering that is exempt from registration under the Securities Act of 1933 pursuant to section 4(a)(2) or section 4(a)(5) (15 U.S.C. 77d(a)(2) or 77d(a)(5)) or pursuant to §§ 230.504 or 230.506 of this chapter.

(8) *Purchase or sale of a security* includes, among other things, the writing of an option to purchase or sell a security.

(9) *Reportable fund* means:

(i) Any fund for which you serve as an investment adviser as defined in section 2(a)(20) of the Investment Company Act of 1940 (15 U.S.C. 80a-2(a)(20)) (i.e., in most cases you must be approved by the fund's board of directors before you can serve); or

(ii) Any fund whose investment adviser or principal underwriter controls you, is controlled by you, or is under common control with you. For purposes of this section, *control* has the same meaning as it does in section 2(a)(9) of the Investment Company Act of 1940 (15 U.S.C. 80a-2(a)(9)).

(10) *Reportable security* means a security as defined in section 202(a)(18) of the Act (15 U.S.C. 80b-2(a)(18)), except that it does not include:

(i) Direct obligations of the Government of the United States;

(ii) Bankers' acceptances, bank certificates of deposit, commercial paper and high quality short-term debt instruments, including repurchase agreements;

(iii) Shares issued by money market funds;

(iv) Shares issued by open-end funds other than reportable funds; and

(v) Shares issued by unit investment trusts that are invested exclusively in one or more open-end funds, none of which are reportable funds.

[69 FR 41708, July 9, 2004, as amended at 76 FR 81806, Dec. 29, 2011; 81 FR 83554, Nov. 21, 2016]

§ 275.205-1 Definition of "investment performance" of an investment company and "investment record" of an appropriate index of securities prices.

(a) *Investment performance* of an investment company for any period shall mean the sum of:

(1) The change in its net asset value per share during such period;

(2) The value of its cash distributions per share accumulated to the end of such period; and

(3) The value of capital gains taxes per share paid or payable on undistributed realized long-term capital gains accumulated to the end of such period; expressed as a percentage of its net asset value per share at the beginning of such period. For this purpose, the value of distributions per share of realized capital gains, of dividends per share paid from investment income and of capital gains taxes per share paid or payable on undistributed realized long-term capital gains shall be treated as reinvested in shares of the investment company at the net asset value per share in effect at the close of business on the record date for the payment of such distributions and dividends and the date on which provision is made for such taxes, after giving effect to such distributions, dividends and taxes.

(b) *Investment record* of an appropriate index of securities prices for any period shall mean the sum of:

(1) The change in the level of the index during such period; and

(2) The value, computed consistently with the index, of cash distributions made by companies whose securities comprise the index accumulated to the end of such period; expressed as a percentage of the index level at the beginning of such period. For this purpose cash distributions on the securities which comprise the index shall be treated as reinvested in the index at least as frequently as the end of each calendar quarter following the payment of the dividend.

Securities and Exchange Commission § 275.205-1

Exhibit I
[Method of computing the investment record of the Standard & Poor's 500 stock composite index for calendar 1971]

Quarterly ending—	Index value[1]	Quarterly dividend yield-composite index	
		Annual percent[2]	Quarterly percent[3] (¼ of annual)≤
Dec. 1970	92.15		
Mar. 1971	100.31	3.10	0.78
June 1971	99.70	3.11	.78
Sept. 1971	98.34	3.14	.79
Dec. 1971	102.09	3.01	.75

[1] Source: Standard & Poor's Trade and Securities Statistics, Jan. 1972, p. 33.
[2] Id. See Standard & Poor's Trade and Securities Statistics Security and Price Index Record—1970 Edition, p. 133 for explanation of quarterly dividend yield.
[3] Quarterly percentages have been founded to two decimal places.

Change in index value for 1971: 102.09 − 92.15 = 9.94.

Accumulated value of dividends for 1971:

$$\frac{\text{Quarter ending:}}{\text{Percent yield}} = \frac{\text{March}}{1.0078} \times \frac{\text{June}}{1.0079} \times \frac{\text{Sept.}}{1.0079} \times \frac{\text{Dec.}}{1.0075} - 1.00 = .0314$$

Aggregate value of dividends paid, assuming quarterly reinvestment and computed consistently with the index:
(Percent yield as computed above) × (ending index value) = Aggregate value of dividends paid
For 1971:

.0314 × 102.09 = 3.21

Investment record of Standard & Poor's 500 stock composite index assuming quarterly reinvestment dividends:

$$\frac{9.94 + 3.21}{92.15} = 14.27 \text{ percent}$$

The same method can be extended to cases where an investment company's fiscal quarters do not coincide with the fiscal quarters of the S & P dividend record or to instances where a "rolling period" is used for performance comparisons as indicated by the following example of the calculation of the investment record of the Standard & Poor's 500 Stock Composite Index for the 12 months ended November 1971:

Index value Nov. 30, 1971	93.99
Index value Nov. 30, 1970	87.20
Change in index value	6.79

Quarter ending—	Dividend yield		Rate for each month of quarter (¹⁄₁₂ of annual)≤
	Annual rate	¼ of annual	
Dec. 1970	3.41	0.85	0.28
Mar. 1971	3.10	.78	.26

Quarter ending—	Dividend yield		Rate for each month of quarter (¹⁄₁₂ of annual)≤
	Annual rate	¼ of annual	
June 1971	3.11	.78	.26
Sept. 1971	3.14	.79	.26
Dec. 1971	3.01	.75	.25

Accumulated value of dividends reinvested:
December = 1.0028
January-March = 1.0078
April-June = 1.0078
July-September = 1.0079
October-November = 1.0053 [4]
Dividend yield:

$(1.0028 \times 1.0078 \times 1.0078 \times 1.0079 \times 1.0053) - 1.00$
$= .0320$

Aggregate value of dividends paid computed consistently with the index:

.0320 × 93.99 = 3.01

Investment record of the Standard & Poor's 500 Stock Composite Index for the 12 months ended November 30, 1971:

$$\frac{6.79 + 3.01}{87.20} = 11.24 \text{ percent}$$

[4] The rate for October and November would be two-thirds of the yield for the quarter ended Sept. 30 (i.e. .667 × .79 = 5269) since the yield for the quarter ended Dec. 31 would not be available as of Nov. 30.

535

§ 275.205-1

17 CFR Ch. II (4-1-23 Edition)

Exhibit II

[Method of Computing the Investment Record of the New York Stock Exchange Composite Index for Calendar 1971]

(1)—Quarter ending	(2)—Index value [1]	(3)—Aggregate market value of shares listed on the NYSE as of end of quarter (billions of dollars) [2]	(4)—Quarterly value of estimated cash payments of shares listed on the NYSE (millions of dollars) [3]	(5)—Estimated yield [4] (quarterly percent)≤
Dec. 1970	50.23			
Mar. 1971	55.44	$709	$5,106	0.72
June 1971	55.09	710	4,961	.70
Sept. 1971	54.33	709	5,006	.71
Dec. 1971	56.43	742	5,183	.70

[1] Source: New York Stock Exchange Composite Index as reported daily by the New York Stock Exchange.
[2] Source: Monthly Review, New York Stock Exchange.
[3] Source: The Exchange, New York Stock Exchange magazine, May, Aug., Nov. 1971 and Feb. 1972 editions. Upon request the Statistics Division of the Research Department of the NYSE will make this figure available within 10 days of the end of each quarter.
[4] The ratio of column 4 to column 3.

Change in NYSE Composite Index value for 1971: 56.43 − 50.23 = 6.20.

Accumulated Value of Dividends of NYSE Composite Index for 1971:

$$\frac{\text{Quarter ending:}}{\text{Percent yield}} = \frac{\text{March}}{1.0072} \times \frac{\text{June}}{1.0070} \times \frac{\text{Sept.}}{1.0071} \times \frac{\text{Dec.}}{1.0070} - 1.00 = 0.0286$$

Aggregate value of dividends paid on NYSE Composite Index assuming quarterly reinvestment:
For 1971:

.0286 × 56.43 = 1.61

Investment record of the New York Stock Exchange Composite Index assuming quarterly reinvestment of dividends:

$$\frac{6.20 + 1.61}{50.23} = 15.55 \text{ percent}$$

The same method can be extended to cases where an investment company's fiscal quarters do not coincide with the fiscal quarters of the NYSE dividend record or to instances where a "rolling period" is used for performance comparisons as indicated by the following example of the calculation of the investment record of the NYSE Composite Index for the 12 months ended November 1971:

Index value Nov. 30, 1971	51.84
Index value Nov. 30, 1970	47.41
Change in index value	4.43

Quarter ending	Dividend yield quarterly percent	Rate for each month of quarter (1/12 of annual)≤
Dec. 1970	0.79	0.26
Mar. 1971	.72	.24
June 1971	.70	.23

Quarter ending	Dividend yield quarterly percent	Rate for each month of quarter (1/12 of annual)≤
Sept. 1971	.71	.24
Dec. 1971	.70	.23

Accumulated value of dividends reinvested:

December = 1.0026
January–March = 1.0072
April–June = 1.0070
July–September = 1.0071
October–November = 1.0047 [4]

Dividend yield:

(1.0026 × 1.0072 × 1.0070 × 1.0071 × 1.0047) − 1.00
= .0289

Aggregate value of dividends paid computed consistently with the index:

.0289 × 51.84 = 1.50

Investment record of the NYSE Composite Index for the 12 months ended November 30, 1971:

---

[4] The rate for October and November would be two thirds of the yield for the quarter ended September 30 (i.e. .667 × .71 = 4736), since the yield for the quarter ended December 31 would not be available as of November 30.

Securities and Exchange Commission § 275.205-3

$$\frac{4.43+1.50}{47.41} = 12.51 \text{ percent}$$

(Secs. 205, 211, 54 Stat. 852, 74 Stat. 887, 15 U.S.C. 80b–205, 80b–211; sec. 25, 84 Stat. 1432, 1433, Pub. L. 91–547)

[37 FR 17468, Aug. 29, 1972]

§ 275.205-2 Definition of "specified period" over which the asset value of the company or fund under management is averaged.

(a) For purposes of this rule:

(1) *Fulcrum fee* shall mean the fee which is paid or earned when the investment company's performance is equivalent to that of the index or other measure of performance.

(2) *Rolling period* shall mean a period consisting of a specified number of subperiods of definite length in which the most recent subperiod is substituted for the earliest subperiod as time passes.

(b) The specified period over which the asset value of the company or fund under management is averaged shall mean the period over which the investment performance of the company or fund and the investment record of an appropriate index of securities prices or such other measure of investment performance are computed.

(c) Notwithstanding paragraph (b) of this section, the specified period over which the asset value of the company or fund is averaged for the purpose of computing the fulcrum fee may differ from the period over which the asset value is averaged for computing the performance related portion of the fee, only if:

(1) The performance related portion of the fee is computed over a rolling period and the total fee is payable at the end of each subperiod of the rolling period; and

(2) The fulcrum fee is computed on the basis of the asset value averaged over the most recent subperiod or subperiods of the rolling period.

(Secs. 205, 106A, 211; 54 Stat. 852, 855; 84 Stat. 1433, 15 U.S.C. 80b–5, 80b–6a, 80b–11)

[37 FR 24896, Nov. 22, 1972]

§ 275.205-3 Exemption from the compensation prohibition of section 205(a)(1) for investment advisers.

(a) *General.* The provisions of section 205(a)(1) of the Act (15 U.S.C. 80b–5(a)(1)) will not be deemed to prohibit an investment adviser from entering into, performing, renewing or extending an investment advisory contract that provides for compensation to the investment adviser on the basis of a share of the capital gains upon, or the capital appreciation of, the funds, or any portion of the funds, of a client, *Provided,* That the client entering into the contract subject to this section is a qualified client, as defined in paragraph (d)(1) of this section.

(b) *Identification of the client.* In the case of a private investment company, as defined in paragraph (d)(3) of this section, an investment company registered under the Investment Company Act of 1940, or a business development company, as defined in section 202(a)(22) of the Act (15 U.S.C. 80b–2(a)(22)), each equity owner of any such company (except for the investment adviser entering into the contract and any other equity owners not charged a fee on the basis of a share of capital gains or capital appreciation) will be considered a client for purposes of paragraph (a) of this section.

(c) *Transition rules*—(1) *Registered investment advisers.* If a registered investment adviser entered into a contract and satisfied the conditions of this section that were in effect when the contract was entered into, the adviser will be considered to satisfy the conditions of this section; *Provided,* however, that if a natural person or company who was not a party to the contract becomes a party (including an equity owner of a private investment company advised by the adviser), the conditions of this section in effect at that time will apply with regard to that person or company.

(2) *Registered investment advisers that were previously not registered.* If an investment adviser was not required to register with the Commission pursuant to section 203 of the Act (15 U.S.C. 80b–3) and was not registered, section 205(a)(1) of the Act will not apply to an advisory contract entered into when the adviser was not required to register

§ 275.205-3

and was not registered, or to an account of an equity owner of a private investment company advised by the adviser if the account was established when the adviser was not required to register and was not registered; *Provided*, however, that section 205(a)(1) of the Act will apply with regard to a natural person or company who was not a party to the contract and becomes a party (including an equity owner of a private investment company advised by the adviser) when the adviser is required to register.

(3) *Certain transfers of interests.* Solely for purposes of paragraphs (c)(1) and (c)(2) of this section, a transfer of an equity ownership interest in a private investment company by gift or bequest, or pursuant to an agreement related to a legal separation or divorce, will not cause the transferee to "become a party" to the contract and will not cause section 205(a)(1) of the Act to apply to such transferee.

(d) *Definitions.* For the purposes of this section:

(1) The term *qualified client* means:

(i) A natural person who, or a company that, immediately after entering into the contract has, under the management of the investment adviser, at least the applicable dollar amount specified in the most recent order;

(ii) A natural person who, or a company that, the investment adviser entering into the contract (and any person acting on his behalf) reasonably believes, immediately prior to entering into the contract, either:

(A) Has a net worth (together, in the case of a natural person, with assets held jointly with a spouse) of more than the applicable dollar amount specified in the most recent order. For purposes of calculating a natural person's net worth:

(*1*) The person's primary residence must not be included as an asset;

(*2*) Indebtedness secured by the person's primary residence, up to the estimated fair market value of the primary residence at the time the investment advisory contract is entered into may not be included as a liability (except that if the amount of such indebtedness outstanding at the time of calculation exceeds the amount outstanding 60 days before such time, other than as a result of the acquisition of the primary residence, the amount of such excess must be included as a liability); and

(*3*) Indebtedness that is secured by the person's primary residence in excess of the estimated fair market value of the residence must be included as a liability; or

(B) Is a qualified purchaser as defined in section 2(a)(51)(A) of the Investment Company Act of 1940 (15 U.S.C. 80a–2(a)(51)(A)) at the time the contract is entered into; or

(iii) A natural person who immediately prior to entering into the contract is:

(A) An executive officer, director, trustee, general partner, or person serving in a similar capacity, of the investment adviser; or

(B) An employee of the investment adviser (other than an employee performing solely clerical, secretarial or administrative functions with regard to the investment adviser) who, in connection with his or her regular functions or duties, participates in the investment activities of such investment adviser, provided that such employee has been performing such functions and duties for or on behalf of the investment adviser, or substantially similar functions or duties for or on behalf of another company for at least 12 months.

(2) The term *company* has the same meaning as in section 202(a)(5) of the Act (15 U.S.C. 80b–2(a)(5)), but does not include a company that is required to be registered under the Investment Company Act of 1940 but is not registered.

(3) The term *private investment company* means a company that would be defined as an investment company under section 3(a) of the Investment Company Act of 1940 (15 U.S.C. 80a–3(a)) but for the exception provided from that definition by section 3(c)(1) of such Act (15 U.S.C. 80a–3(c)(1)).

(4) The term *executive officer* means the president, any vice president in charge of a principal business unit, division or function (such as sales, administration or finance), any other officer who performs a policy-making

function, or any other person who performs similar policy-making functions, for the investment adviser.

(5) The term *most recent order* means the most recently issued Commission order in accordance with paragraph (e) of this section and as published in the FEDERAL REGISTER.

(e) *Inflation adjustments.* Pursuant to section 205(e) of the Act, the dollar amounts referenced in paragraphs (d)(1)(i) and (d)(1)(ii)(A) of this section shall be adjusted, by order of the Commission, issued on or about May 1, 2026, and approximately every five years thereafter. The adjusted dollar amounts established in such orders shall be computed by:

(1) Dividing the year-end value of the Personal Consumption Expenditures Chain-Type Price Index (or any successor index thereto), as published by the United States Department of Commerce, for the calendar year preceding the calendar year in which the order is being issued, by the year-end value of such index (or successor) for the calendar year 1997;

(2) For the dollar amount in paragraph (d)(1)(i) of this section, multiplying $750,000 times the quotient obtained in paragraph (e)(1) of this section and rounding the product to the nearest multiple of $100,000; and

(3) For the dollar amount in paragraph (d)(1)(ii)(A) of this section, multiplying $1,500,000 times the quotient obtained in paragraph (e)(1) of this section and rounding the product to the nearest multiple of $100,000.

[63 FR 39027, July 21, 1998, as amended at 69 FR 72088, Dec. 10, 2004; 77 FR 10368, Feb. 22, 2012; 86 FR 62475, Nov. 10, 2021]

§ 275.206(3)-1 Exemption of investment advisers registered as broker-dealers in connection with the provision of certain investment advisory services.

(a) An investment adviser which is a broker or dealer registered pursuant to section 15 of the Securities Exchange Act of 1934 shall be exempt from section 206(3) in connection with any transaction in relation to which such broker or dealer is acting as an investment adviser solely (1) by means of publicly distributed written materials or publicly made oral statements; (2) by means of written materials or oral statements which do not purport to meet the objectives or needs of specific individuals or accounts; (3) through the issuance of statistical information containing no expressions of opinion as to the investment merits of a particular security; or (4) any combination of the foregoing services: *Provided, however,* That such materials and oral statements include a statement that if the purchaser of the advisory communication uses the services of the adviser in connection with a sale or purchase of a security which is a subject of such communication, the adviser may act as principal for its own account or as agent for another person.

(b) For the purpose of this Rule, publicly distributed written materials are those which are distributed to 35 or more persons who pay for such materials, and publicly made oral statements are those made simultaneously to 35 or more persons who pay for access to such statements.

NOTE: The requirement that the investment adviser disclose that it may act as principal or agent for another person in the sale or purchase of a security that is the subject of investment advice does not relieve the investment adviser of any disclosure obligation which, depending upon the nature of the relationship between the investment adviser and the client, may be imposed by subparagraphs (1) or (2) of section 206 or the other provisions of the federal securities laws.

[40 FR 38159, Aug. 27, 1975]

§ 275.206(3)-2 Agency cross transactions for advisory clients.

(a) An investment adviser, or a person registered as a broker-dealer under section 15 of the Securities Exchange Act of 1934 (15 U.S.C. 78o) and controlling, controlled by, or under common control with an investment adviser, shall be deemed in compliance with the provisions of sections 206(3) of the Act (15 U.S.C. 80b–6(3)) in effecting an agency cross transaction for an advisory client, if:

(1) The advisory client has executed a written consent prospectively authorizing the investment adviser, or any other person relying on this rule, to effect agency cross transactions for such advisory client, provided that such written consent is obtained after full

§ 275.206(4)-1

written disclosure that with respect to agency cross transactions the investment adviser or such other person will act as broker for, receive commissions from, and have a potentially conflicting division of loyalties and responsibilities regarding, both parties to such transactions;

(2) The investment adviser, or any other person relying on this rule, sends to each such client a written confirmation at or before the completion of each such transaction, which confirmation includes (i) a statement of the nature of such transaction, (ii) the date such transaction took place, (iii) an offer to furnish upon request, the time when such transaction took place, and (iv) the source and amount of any other remuneration received or to be received by the investment adviser and any other person relying on this rule in connection with the transaction, *Provided, however,* That if, in the case of a purchase, neither the investment adviser nor any other person relying on this rule was participating in a distribution, or in the case of a sale, neither the investment adviser nor any other person relying on this rule was participating in a tender offer, the written confirmation may state whether any other remuneration has been or will be received and that the source and amount of such other remuneration will be furnished upon written request of such customer;

(3) The investment adviser, or any other person relying in this rule, sends to each such client, at least annually, and with or as part of any written statement or summary of such account from the investment adviser or such other person, a written disclosure statement identifying the total number of such transactions during the period since the date of the last such statement or summary, and the total amount of all commissions or other remuneration received or to be received by the investment adviser or any other person relying on this rule in connection with such transactions during such period;

(4) Each written disclosure statement and confirmation required by this rule includes a conspicuous statement that the written consent referred to in paragraph (a)(1) of this section may be revoked at any time by written notice to the investment adviser, or to any other person relying on this rule, from the advisory client; and

(5) No such transaction is effected in which the same investment adviser or an investment adviser and any person controlling, controlled by or under common control with such investment adviser recommended the transaction to both any seller and any purchaser.

(b) For purposes of this rule the term *agency cross transaction for an advisory client* shall mean a transaction in which a person acts as an investment adviser in relation to a transaction in which such investment adviser, or any person controlling, controlled by, or under common control with such investment adviser, acts as broker for both such advisory client and for another person on the other side of the transaction.

(c) This rule shall not be construed as relieving in any way the investment adviser or another person relying on this rule from acting in the best interests of the advisory client, including fulfilling the duty with respect to the best price and execution for the particular transaction for the advisory client; nor shall it relieve such person or persons from any disclosure obligation which may be imposed by subparagraphs (1) or (2) of section 206 of the Act or by other applicable provisions of the federal securities laws.

[42 FR 29301 June 8, 1977, as amended at 48 FR 41379, Sept. 15, 1983; 62 FR 28135, May 22, 1997]

§ 275.206(4)-1 **Investment adviser marketing.**

As a means reasonably designed to prevent fraudulent, deceptive, or manipulative acts, practices, or courses of business within the meaning of section 206(4) of the Act (15 U.S.C. 80b-6(4)), it is unlawful for any investment adviser registered or required to be registered under section 203 of the Act (15 U.S.C. 80b-3), directly or indirectly, to disseminate any advertisement that violates any of paragraphs (a) through (d) of this section.

(a) *General prohibitions.* An advertisement may not:

(1) Include any untrue statement of a material fact, or omit to state a material fact necessary in order to make the statement made, in the light of the circumstances under which it was made, not misleading;
(2) Include a material statement of fact that the adviser does not have a reasonable basis for believing it will be able to substantiate upon demand by the Commission;
(3) Include information that would reasonably be likely to cause an untrue or misleading implication or inference to be drawn concerning a material fact relating to the investment adviser;
(4) Discuss any potential benefits to clients or investors connected with or resulting from the investment adviser's services or methods of operation without providing fair and balanced treatment of any material risks or material limitations associated with the potential benefits;
(5) Include a reference to specific investment advice provided by the investment adviser where such investment advice is not presented in a manner that is fair and balanced;
(6) Include or exclude performance results, or present performance time periods, in a manner that is not fair and balanced; or
(7) Otherwise be materially misleading.
(b) *Testimonials and endorsements.* An advertisement may not include any testimonial or endorsement, and an adviser may not provide compensation, directly or indirectly, for a testimonial or endorsement, unless the investment adviser complies with the conditions in paragraphs (b)(1) through (3) of this section, subject to the exemptions in paragraph (b)(4) of this section.
(1) *Required disclosures.* The investment adviser discloses, or reasonably believes that the person giving the testimonial or endorsement discloses, the following at the time the testimonial or endorsement is disseminated:
(i) Clearly and prominently:
(A) That the testimonial was given by a current client or investor, and the *endorsement* was given by a person other than a current client or investor, as applicable;

(B) That cash or non-cash compensation was provided for the *testimonial* or *endorsement,* if applicable; and
(C) A brief statement of any material conflicts of interest on the part of the person giving the testimonial or endorsement resulting from the investment adviser's relationship with such person;
(ii) The material terms of any compensation arrangement, including a description of the compensation provided or to be provided, directly or indirectly, to the person for the *testimonial* or *endorsement;* and
(iii) A description of any material conflicts of interest on the part of the person giving the *testimonial* or *endorsement* resulting from the investment adviser's relationship with such person and/or any compensation arrangement.
(2) *Adviser oversight and compliance.* The investment adviser must have:
(i) A reasonable basis for believing that the testimonial or endorsement complies with the requirements of this section; and
(ii) A written agreement with any person giving a testimonial or endorsement that describes the scope of the agreed-upon activities and the terms of compensation for those activities.
(3) *Disqualification.* An investment adviser may not compensate a person, directly or indirectly, for a testimonial or endorsement if the adviser knows, or in the exercise of reasonable care should know, that the person giving the testimonial or endorsement is an ineligible person at the time the testimonial or endorsement is disseminated. This paragraph shall not disqualify any person for any matter(s) that occurred prior to May 4, 2021, if such matter(s) would not have disqualified such person under §275.206(4)–3(a)(1)(ii) of this chapter, as in effect prior to May 4, 2021.
(4) *Exemptions.* (i) A testimonial or endorsement disseminated for no compensation or *de minimis compensation* is not required to comply with paragraphs (b)(2)(ii) and (3) of this section;
(ii) A testimonial or endorsement by the investment adviser's partners, officers, directors, or employees, or a person that controls, is controlled by, or

§ 275.206(4)–1

is under common control with the investment adviser, or is a partner, officer, director or employee of such a person is not required to comply with paragraphs (b)(1) and (2)(ii) of this section, provided that the affiliation between the investment adviser and such person is readily apparent to or is disclosed to the client or investor at the time the testimonial or endorsement is disseminated and the investment adviser documents such person's status at the time the testimonial or endorsement is disseminated;

(iii) A testimonial or endorsement by a broker or dealer registered with the Commission under section 15(b) of the Securities Exchange Act of 1934 (15 U.S.C. 78o(a)) is not required to comply with:

(A) Paragraph (b)(1) of this section if the testimonial or endorsement is a recommendation subject to § 240.151–1 of this chapter (Regulation Best Interest) under that Act;

(B) Paragraphs (b)(1)(ii) and (iii) of this section if the testimonial or endorsement is provided to a person that is not a retail customer (as that term is defined in § 240.151–1 of this chapter (Regulation Best Interest) under the Securities Exchange Act of 1934 (15 U.S.C. 78o(a)); and

(C) Paragraph (b)(3) of this section if the broker or dealer is not subject to statutory disqualification, as defined under section 3(a)(39) of that Act; and

(iv) A testimonial or endorsement by a person that is covered by rule 506(d) of Regulation D under the Securities Act of 1933 (§ 230.506(d) of this chapter) with respect to a rule 506 securities offering under the Securities Act of 1933 (§ 230.506 of this chapter) and whose involvement would not disqualify the offering under that rule is not required to comply with paragraph (b)(3) of this section.

(c) *Third-party ratings.* An advertisement may not include any third-party rating, unless the investment adviser:

(1) Has a reasonable basis for believing that any questionnaire or survey used in the preparation of the third-party rating is structured to make it equally easy for a participant to provide favorable and unfavorable responses, and is not designed or prepared to produce any predetermined result; and

(2) Clearly and prominently discloses, or the investment adviser reasonably believes that the third-party rating clearly and prominently discloses:

(i) The date on which the rating was given and the period of time upon which the rating was based;

(ii) The identity of the third party that created and tabulated the rating; and

(iii) If applicable, that compensation has been provided directly or indirectly by the adviser in connection with obtaining or using the third-party rating.

(d) *Performance.* An investment adviser may not include in any advertisement:

(1) Any presentation of gross performance, unless the advertisement also presents net performance:

(i) With at least equal prominence to, and in a format designed to facilitate comparison with, the gross performance; and

(ii) Calculated over the same time period, and using the same type of return and methodology, as the gross performance.

(2) Any performance results, of any portfolio or any composite aggregation of related portfolios, in each case other than any private fund, unless the advertisement includes performance results of the same portfolio or composite aggregation for one-, five-, and ten-year periods, each presented with equal prominence and ending on a date that is no less recent than the most recent calendar year-end; except that if the relevant portfolio did not exist for a particular prescribed period, then the life of the portfolio must be substituted for that period.

(3) Any statement, express or implied, that the calculation or presentation of performance results in the advertisement has been approved or reviewed by the Commission.

(4) Any related performance, unless it includes all related portfolios; provided that related performance may exclude any related portfolios if:

(i) The advertised performance results are not materially higher than if all related portfolios had been included; and

Securities and Exchange Commission § 275.206(4)-1

(ii) The exclusion of any related portfolio does not alter the presentation of any applicable time periods prescribed by paragraph (d)(2) of this section.

(5) Any extracted performance, unless the advertisement provides, or offers to provide promptly, the performance results of the total portfolio from which the performance was extracted.

(6) Any hypothetical performance unless the investment adviser:

(i) Adopts and implements policies and procedures reasonably designed to ensure that the hypothetical performance is relevant to the likely financial situation and investment objectives of the intended audience of the advertisement;

(ii) Provides sufficient information to enable the intended audience to understand the criteria used and assumptions made in calculating such hypothetical performance; and

(iii) Provides (or, if the intended audience is an investor in a private fund, provides, or offers to provide promptly) sufficient information to enable the intended audience to understand the risks and limitations of using such hypothetical performance in making investment decisions; Provided that the investment adviser need not comply with the other conditions on performance in paragraphs (d)(2), (4), and (5) of this section.

(7) Any predecessor performance unless:

(i) The person or persons who were primarily responsible for achieving the prior performance results manage accounts at the advertising adviser;

(ii) The accounts managed at the predecessor investment adviser are sufficiently similar to the accounts managed at the advertising investment adviser that the performance results would provide relevant information to clients or investors;

(iii) All accounts that were managed in a substantially similar manner are advertised unless the exclusion of any such account would not result in materially higher performance and the exclusion of any account does not alter the presentation of any applicable time periods prescribed in paragraph (d)(2) of this section; and

(iv) The advertisement clearly and prominently includes all relevant disclosures, including that the performance results were from accounts managed at another entity.

(e) *Definitions.* For purposes of this section:

(1) *Advertisement* means:

(i) Any direct or indirect communication an investment adviser makes to more than one person, or to one or more persons if the communication includes hypothetical performance, that offers the investment adviser's investment advisory services with regard to securities to prospective clients or investors in a private fund advised by the investment adviser or offers new investment advisory services with regard to securities to current clients or investors in a private fund advised by the investment adviser, but does not include:

(A) Extemporaneous, live, oral communications;

(B) Information contained in a statutory or regulatory notice, filing, or other required communication, provided that such information is reasonably designed to satisfy the requirements of such notice, filing, or other required communication; or

(C) A communication that includes hypothetical performance that is provided:

(*1*) In response to an unsolicited request for such information from a prospective or current client or investor in a private fund advised by the investment adviser; or

(*2*) To a prospective or current investor in a private fund advised by the investment adviser in a one-on-one communication; and

(ii) Any endorsement or testimonial for which an investment adviser provides compensation, directly or indirectly, but does not include any information contained in a statutory or regulatory notice, filing, or other required communication, provided that such information is reasonably designed to satisfy the requirements of such notice, filing, or other required communication.

(2) *De minimis compensation* means compensation paid to a person for providing a *testimonial* or *endorsement* of a total of $1,000 or less (or the equivalent value in non-cash compensation) during the preceding 12 months.

§ 275.206(4)-1

(3) A *disqualifying Commission action* means a Commission opinion or order barring, suspending, or prohibiting the person from acting in any capacity under the Federal securities laws.

(4) A *disqualifying event* is any of the following events that occurred within ten years prior to the person disseminating an endorsement or testimonial:

(i) A conviction by a court of competent jurisdiction within the United States of any felony or misdemeanor involving conduct described in paragraph (2)(A) through (D) of section 203(e) of the Act;

(ii) A conviction by a court of competent jurisdiction within the United States of engaging in, any of the conduct specified in paragraphs (1), (5), or (6) of section 203(e) of the Act;

(iii) The entry of any final order by any entity described in paragraph (9) of section 203(e) of the Act, or by the U.S. Commodity Futures Trading Commission or a self-regulatory organization (as defined in the Form ADV Glossary of Terms)), of the type described in paragraph (9) of section 203(e) of the Act;

(iv) The entry of an order, judgment or decree described in paragraph (4) of section 203(e) of the Act, and still in effect, by any court of competent jurisdiction within the United States; and

(v) A Commission order that a person cease and desist from committing or causing a violation or future violation of:

(A) Any scienter-based anti-fraud provision of the Federal securities laws, including without limitation section 17(a)(1) of the Securities Act of 1933 (15 U.S.C. 77q(a)(1)), section 10(b) of the Securities Exchange Act of 1934 (15 U.S.C. 78j(b)) and § 240.10b–5 of this chapter, section 15(c)(1) of the Securities Exchange Act of 1934 (15 U.S.C. 78o(c)(1)), and section 206(1) of the Investment Advisers Act of 1940 (15 U.S.C. 80b–6(1)), or any other rule or regulation thereunder; or

(B) Section 5 of the Securities Act of 1933 (15 U.S.C. 77e);

(vi) A disqualifying event does not include an event described in paragraphs (e)(4)(i) through (v) of this section with respect to a person that is also subject to:

(A) An order pursuant to section 9(c) of the Investment Company Act of 1940 (15 U.S.C. 80a–9) with respect to such event; or

(B) A Commission opinion or order with respect to such event that is not a disqualifying Commission action; provided that for each applicable type of order or opinion described in paragraphs (e)(4)(vi)(A) and (B) of this section:

(*1*) The person is in compliance with the terms of the order or opinion, including, but not limited to, the payment of disgorgement, prejudgment interest, civil or administrative penalties, and fines; and

(*2*) For a period of ten years following the date of each order or opinion, the advertisement containing the testimonial or endorsement must include a statement that the person providing the testimonial or endorsement is subject to a Commission order or opinion regarding one or more disciplinary action(s), and include the order or opinion or a link to the order or opinion on the Commission's website.

(5) *Endorsement* means any statement by a person other than a current client or investor in a private fund advised by the investment adviser that:

(i) Indicates approval, support, or recommendation of the investment adviser or its supervised persons or describes that person's experience with the investment adviser or its supervised persons;

(ii) Directly or indirectly solicits any current or prospective client or investor to be a client of, or an investor in a private fund advised by, the investment adviser; or

(iii) Refers any current or prospective client or investor to be a client of, or an investor in a private fund advised by, the investment adviser.

(6) *Extracted performance* means the performance results of a subset of investments extracted from a portfolio.

(7) *Gross performance* means the performance results of a portfolio (or portions of a *portfolio* that are included in extracted performance, if applicable) before the deduction of all fees and expenses that a client or investor has paid or would have paid in connection

Securities and Exchange Commission § 275.206(4)-1

with the investment adviser's investment advisory services to the relevant portfolio.

(8) *Hypothetical performance* means performance results that were not actually achieved by any portfolio of the investment adviser.

(i) Hypothetical performance includes, but is not limited to;

(A) Performance derived from model portfolios;

(B) Performance that is backtested by the application of a strategy to data from prior time periods when the strategy was not actually used during those time periods; and

(C) Targeted or projected performance returns with respect to any portfolio or to the investment advisory services with regard to securities offered in the advertisement, however:

(ii) Hypothetical performance does not include:

(A) An interactive analysis tool where a client or investor, or prospective client, or investor, uses the tool to produce simulations and statistical analyses that present the likelihood of various investment outcomes if certain investments are made or certain investment strategies or styles are undertaken, thereby serving as an additional resource to investors in the evaluation of the potential risks and returns of investment choices; provided that the investment adviser:

(*1*) Provides a description of the criteria and methodology used, including the investment analysis tool's limitations and key assumptions;

(*2*) Explains that the results may vary with each use and over time;

(*3*) If applicable, describes the universe of investments considered in the analysis, explains how the tool determines which investments to select, discloses if the tool favors certain investments and, if so, explains the reason for the selectivity, and states that other investments not considered may have characteristics similar or superior to those being analyzed; and

(*4*) Discloses that the tool generates outcomes that are hypothetical in nature; or

(B) Predecessor performance that is displayed in compliance with paragraph (d)(7) of this section.

(9) *Ineligible person* means a person who is subject to a disqualifying Commission action or is subject to any disqualifying event, and the following persons with respect to the ineligible person:

(i) Any employee, officer, or director of the ineligible person and any other individuals with similar status or functions within the scope of association with the ineligible person;

(ii) If the ineligible person is a partnership, all general partners; and

(iii) If the ineligible person is a limited liability company managed by elected managers, all elected managers.

(10) *Net performance* means the performance results of a portfolio (or portions of a portfolio that are included in extracted performance, if applicable) after the deduction of all fees and expenses that a client or investor has paid or would have paid in connection with the investment adviser's investment advisory services to the relevant portfolio, including, if applicable, advisory fees, advisory fees paid to underlying investment vehicles, and payments by the investment adviser for which the client or investor reimburses the investment adviser. For purposes of this rule, net performance:

(i) May reflect the exclusion of custodian fees paid to a bank or other third-party organization for safekeeping funds and securities; and/or

(ii) If using a model fee, must reflect one of the following:

(A) The deduction of a model fee when doing so would result in performance figures that are no higher than if the actual fee had been deducted; or

(B) The deduction of a model fee that is equal to the highest fee charged to the intended audience to whom the advertisement is disseminated.

(11) *Portfolio* means a group of investments managed by the investment adviser. A portfolio may be an account or a private fund and includes, but is not limited to, a portfolio for the account of the investment adviser or its advisory affiliate (as defined in the Form ADV Glossary of Terms).

(12) *Predecessor performance* means investment performance achieved by a group of investments consisting of an account or a private fund that was not

§ 275.206(4)-2

advised at all times during the period shown by the investment adviser advertising the performance.

(13) *Private fund* has the same meaning as in section 202(a)(29) of the Act.

(14) *Related performance* means the performance results of one or more related portfolios, either on a portfolio-by-portfolio basis or as a composite aggregation of all portfolios falling within stated criteria.

(15) *Related portfolio* means a portfolio with substantially similar investment policies, objectives, and strategies as those of the services being offered in the advertisement.

(16) *Supervised person* has the same meaning as in section 202(a)(25) of the Act.

(17) *Testimonial* means any statement by a current client or investor in a private fund advised by the investment adviser:

(i) About the client or investor's experience with the investment adviser or its supervised persons;

(ii) That directly or indirectly solicits any current or prospective client or investor to be a client of, or an investor in a private fund advised by, the investment adviser; or

(iii) That refers any current or prospective client or investor to be a client of, or an investor in a private fund advised by, the investment adviser.

(18) *Third-party rating* means a rating or ranking of an investment adviser provided by a person who is not a related person (as defined in the Form ADV Glossary of Terms), and such person provides such ratings or rankings in the ordinary course of its business.

[86 FR 13024, Mar. 5, 2021, as amended at 87 FR 22447, Apr. 15, 2022]

§ 275.206(4)-2 **Custody of funds or securities of clients by investment advisers.**

(a) *Safekeeping required.* If you are an investment adviser registered or required to be registered under section 203 of the Act (15 U.S.C. 80b-3), it is a fraudulent, deceptive, or manipulative act, practice or course of business within the meaning of section 206(4) of the *Act (15 U.S.C. 80b-6(4))* for you to have custody of client funds or securities unless:

(1) *Qualified custodian.* A qualified custodian maintains those funds and securities:

(i) In a separate account for each client under that client's name; or

(ii) In accounts that contain only your clients' funds and securities, under your name as agent or trustee for the clients.

(2) *Notice to clients.* If you open an account with a qualified custodian on your client's behalf, either under the client's name or under your name as agent, you notify the client in writing of the qualified custodian's name, address, and the manner in which the funds or securities are maintained, promptly when the account is opened and following any changes to this information. If you send account statements to a client to which you are required to provide this notice, include in the notification provided to that client and in any subsequent account statement you send that client a statement urging the client to compare the account statements from the custodian with those from the adviser.

(3) *Account statements to clients.* You have a reasonable basis, after due inquiry, for believing that the qualified custodian sends an account statement, at least quarterly, to each of your clients for which it maintains funds or securities, identifying the amount of funds and of each security in the account at the end of the period and setting forth all transactions in the account during that period.

(4) *Independent verification.* The client funds and securities of which you have custody are verified by actual examination at least once during each calendar year, except as provided below, by an independent public accountant, pursuant to a written agreement between you and the accountant, at a time that is chosen by the accountant without prior notice or announcement to you and that is irregular from year to year. The written agreement must provide for the first examination to occur within six months of becoming subject to this paragraph, except that, if you maintain client funds or securities pursuant to this section as a qualified custodian, the agreement must provide for the first examination to occur no later than six months after

Securities and Exchange Commission § 275.206(4)-2

obtaining the internal control report. The written agreement must require the accountant to:

(i) File a certificate on Form ADV-E (17 CFR 279.8) with the Commission within 120 days of the time chosen by the accountant in paragraph (a)(4) of this section, stating that it has examined the funds and securities and describing the nature and extent of the examination;

(ii) Upon finding any material discrepancies during the course of the examination, notify the Commission within one business day of the finding, by means of a facsimile transmission or electronic mail, followed by first class mail, directed to the attention of the Director of the Office of Compliance Inspections and Examinations; and

(iii) Upon resignation or dismissal from, or other termination of, the engagement, or upon removing itself or being removed from consideration for being reappointed, file within four business days Form ADV-E accompanied by a statement that includes:

(A) The date of such resignation, dismissal, removal, or other termination, and the name, address, and contact information of the accountant; and

(B) An explanation of any problems relating to examination scope or procedure that contributed to such resignation, dismissal, removal, or other termination.

(5) *Special rule for limited partnerships and limited liability companies.* If you or a related person is a general partner of a limited partnership (or managing member of a limited liability company, or hold a comparable position for another type of pooled investment vehicle), the account statements required under paragraph (a)(3) of this section must be sent to each limited partner (or member or other beneficial owner).

(6) *Investment advisers acting as qualified custodians.* If you maintain, or if you have custody because a related person maintains, client funds or securities pursuant to this section as a qualified custodian in connection with advisory services you provide to clients:

(i) The independent public accountant you retain to perform the independent verification required by paragraph (a)(4) of this section must be registered with, and subject to regular inspection as of the commencement of the professional engagement period, and as of each calendar year-end, by, the Public Company Accounting Oversight Board in accordance with its rules; and

(ii) You must obtain, or receive from your related person, within six months of becoming subject to this paragraph and thereafter no less frequently than once each calendar year a written internal control report prepared by an independent public accountant:

(A) The internal control report must include an opinion of an independent public accountant as to whether controls have been placed in operation as of a specific date, and are suitably designed and are operating effectively to meet control objectives relating to custodial services, including the safeguarding of funds and securities held by either you or a related person on behalf of your advisory clients, during the year;

(B) The independent public accountant must verify that the funds and securities are reconciled to a custodian other than you or your related person; and

(C) The independent public accountant must be registered with, and subject to regular inspection as of the commencement of the professional engagement period, and as of each calendar year-end, by, the Public Company Accounting Oversight Board in accordance with its rules.

(7) *Independent representatives.* A client may designate an independent representative to receive, on his behalf, notices and account statements as required under paragraphs (a)(2) and (a)(3) of this section.

(b) *Exceptions.* (1) *Shares of mutual funds.* With respect to shares of an open-end company as defined in section 5(a)(1) of the Investment Company Act of 1940 (15 U.S.C. 80a-5(a)(1)) ("mutual fund"), you may use the mutual fund's transfer agent in lieu of a qualified custodian for purposes of complying with paragraph (a) of this section.

(2) *Certain privately offered securities.* (i) You are not required to comply with paragraph (a)(1) of this section with respect to securities that are:

§ 275.206(4)-2

(A) Acquired from the issuer in a transaction or chain of transactions not involving any public offering;

(B) Uncertificated, and ownership thereof is recorded only on the books of the issuer or its transfer agent in the name of the client; and

(C) Transferable only with prior consent of the issuer or holders of the outstanding securities of the issuer.

(ii) Notwithstanding paragraph (b)(2)(i) of this section, the provisions of this paragraph (b)(2) are available with respect to securities held for the account of a limited partnership (or a limited liability company, or other type of pooled investment vehicle) only if the limited partnership is audited, and the audited financial statements are distributed, as described in paragraph (b)(4) of this section.

(3) *Fee deduction.* Notwithstanding paragraph (a)(4) of this section, you are not required to obtain an independent verification of client funds and securities maintained by a qualified custodian if:

(i) you have custody of the funds and securities solely as a consequence of your authority to make withdrawals from client accounts to pay your advisory fee; and

(ii) if the qualified custodian is a related person, you can rely on paragraph (b)(6) of this section.

(4) *Limited partnerships subject to annual audit.* You are not required to comply with paragraphs (a)(2) and (a)(3) of this section and you shall be deemed to have complied with paragraph (a)(4) of this section with respect to the account of a limited partnership (or limited liability company, or another type of pooled investment vehicle) that is subject to audit (as defined in rule 1–02(d) of Regulation S–X (17 CFR 210.1–02(d))):

(i) At least annually and distributes its audited financial statements prepared in accordance with generally accepted accounting principles to all limited partners (or members or other beneficial owners) within 120 days of the end of its fiscal year;

(ii) By an independent public accountant that is registered with, and subject to regular inspection as of the commencement of the professional engagement period, and as of each calendar year-end, by, the Public Company Accounting Oversight Board in accordance with its rules; and

(iii) Upon liquidation and distributes its audited financial statements prepared in accordance with generally accepted accounting principles to all limited partners (or members or other beneficial owners) promptly after the completion of such audit.

(5) *Registered investment companies.* You are not required to comply with this section (17 CFR 275.206(4)–2) with respect to the account of an investment company registered under the Investment Company Act of 1940 (15 U.S.C. 80a–1 to 80a–64).

(6) *Certain Related Persons.* Notwithstanding paragraph (a)(4) of this section, you are not required to obtain an independent verification of client funds and securities if:

(i) you have custody under this rule solely because a related person holds, directly or indirectly, client funds or securities, or has any authority to obtain possession of them, in connection with advisory services you provide to clients; and

(ii) your related person is operationally independent of you.

(c) *Delivery to Related Person.* Sending an account statement under paragraph (a)(5) of this section or distributing audited financial statements under paragraph (b)(4) of this section shall not satisfy the requirements of this section if such account statements or financial statements are sent solely to limited partners (or members or other beneficial owners) that themselves are limited partnerships (or limited liability companies, or another type of pooled investment vehicle) and are your related persons.

(d) *Definitions.* For the purposes of this section:

(1) *Control* means the power, directly or indirectly, to direct the management or policies of a person, whether through ownership of securities, by contract, or otherwise. Control includes:

(i) Each of your firm's officers, partners, or directors exercising executive responsibility (or persons having similar status or functions) is presumed to control your firm;

Securities and Exchange Commission § 275.206(4)–2

(ii) A person is presumed to control a corporation if the person:

(A) Directly or indirectly has the right to vote 25 percent or more of a class of the corporation's voting securities; or

(B) Has the power to sell or direct the sale of 25 percent or more of a class of the corporation's voting securities;

(iii) A person is presumed to control a partnership if the person has the right to receive upon dissolution, or has contributed, 25 percent or more of the capital of the partnership;

(iv) A person is presumed to control a limited liability company if the person:

(A) Directly or indirectly has the right to vote 25 percent or more of a class of the interests of the limited liability company;

(B) Has the right to receive upon dissolution, or has contributed, 25 percent or more of the capital of the limited liability company; or

(C) Is an elected manager of the limited liability company; or

(v) A person is presumed to control a trust if the person is a trustee or managing agent of the trust.

(2) *Custody* means holding, directly or indirectly, client funds or securities, or having any authority to obtain possession of them. You have custody if a related person holds, directly or indirectly, client funds or securities, or has any authority to obtain possession of them, in connection with advisory services you provide to clients. Custody includes:

(i) Possession of client funds or securities (but not of checks drawn by clients and made payable to third parties) unless you receive them inadvertently and you return them to the sender promptly but in any case within three business days of receiving them;

(ii) Any arrangement (including a general power of attorney) under which you are authorized or permitted to withdraw client funds or securities maintained with a custodian upon your instruction to the custodian; and

(iii) Any capacity (such as general partner of a limited partnership, managing member of a limited liability company or a comparable position for another type of pooled investment vehicle, or trustee of a trust) that gives you or your supervised person legal ownership of or access to client funds or securities.

(3) *Independent public accountant* means a public accountant that meets the standards of independence described in rule 2–01(b) and (c) of Regulation S–X (17 CFR 210.2–01(b) and (c)).

(4) *Independent representative* means a person that:

(i) Acts as agent for an advisory client, including in the case of a pooled investment vehicle, for limited partners of a limited partnership (or members of a limited liability company, or other beneficial owners of another type of pooled investment vehicle) and by law or contract is obliged to act in the best interest of the advisory client or the limited partners (or members, or other beneficial owners);

(ii) Does not control, is not controlled by, and is not under common control with you; and

(iii) Does not have, and has not had within the past two years, a material business relationship with you.

(5) *Operationally independent:* for purposes of paragraph (b)(6) of this section, a related person is presumed not to be operationally independent unless each of the following conditions is met and no other circumstances can reasonably be expected to compromise the operational independence of the related person: (i) Client assets in the custody of the related person are not subject to claims of the adviser's creditors; (ii) advisory personnel do not have custody or possession of, or direct or indirect access to client assets of which the related person has custody, or the power to control the disposition of such client assets to third parties for the benefit of the adviser or its related persons, or otherwise have the opportunity to misappropriate such client assets; (iii) advisory personnel and personnel of the related person who have access to advisory client assets are not under common supervision; and (iv) advisory personnel do not hold any position with the related person or share premises with the related person.

(6) *Qualified custodian* means:

(i) A bank as defined in section 202(a)(2) of the Advisers Act (15 U.S.C. 80b–2(a)(2)) or a savings association as defined in section 3(b)(1) of the Federal Deposit Insurance Act (12 U.S.C.

1813(b)(1)) that has deposits insured by the Federal Deposit Insurance Corporation under the Federal Deposit Insurance Act (12 U.S.C. 1811);

(ii) A broker-dealer registered under section 15(b)(1) of the Securities Exchange Act of 1934 (15 U.S.C. 78o(b)(1)), holding the client assets in customer accounts;

(iii) A futures commission merchant registered under section 4f(a) of the Commodity Exchange Act (7 U.S.C. 6f(a)), holding the client assets in customer accounts, but only with respect to clients' funds and security futures, or other securities incidental to transactions in contracts for the purchase or sale of a commodity for future delivery and options thereon; and

(iv) A foreign financial institution that customarily holds financial assets for its customers, provided that the foreign financial institution keeps the advisory clients' assets in customer accounts segregated from its proprietary assets.

(7) *Related person* means any person, directly or indirectly, controlling or controlled by you, and any person that is under common control with you.

[75 FR 1484, Jan. 11, 2010]

§§ 275.206(4)–(3)—275.206(4)–4 [Reserved]

§ 275.206(4)–5 Political contributions by certain investment advisers.

(a) *Prohibitions.* As a means reasonably designed to prevent fraudulent, deceptive or manipulative acts, practices, or courses of business within the meaning of section 206(4) of the Act (15 U.S.C. 80b–6(4)), it shall be unlawful:

(1) For any investment adviser registered (or required to be registered) with the Commission, or unregistered in reliance on the exemption available under section 203(b)(3) of the Advisers Act (15 U.S.C. 80b–3(b)(3)), or that is an exempt reporting adviser, as defined in section 275.204–4(a), to provide investment advisory services for compensation to a government entity within two years after a contribution to an official of the government entity is made by the investment adviser or any covered associate of the investment adviser (including a person who becomes a covered associate within two years after the contribution is made); and

(2) For any investment adviser registered (or required to be registered) with the Commission, or unregistered in reliance on the exemption available under section 203(b)(3) of the Advisers Act (15 U.S.C. 80b–3(b)(3)), or that is an exempt reporting adviser, or any of the investment adviser's covered associates:

(i) To provide or agree to provide, directly or indirectly, payment to any person to solicit a government entity for investment advisory services on behalf of such investment adviser unless such person is:

(A) A regulated person; or

(B) An executive officer, general partner, managing member (or, in each case, a person with a similar status or function), or employee of the investment adviser; and

(ii) To coordinate, or to solicit any person or political action committee to make, any:

(A) Contribution to an official of a government entity to which the investment adviser is providing or seeking to provide investment advisory services; or

(B) Payment to a political party of a State or locality where the investment adviser is providing or seeking to provide investment advisory services to a government entity.

(b) *Exceptions*—(1) *De minimis exception.* Paragraph (a)(1) of this section does not apply to contributions made by a covered associate, if a natural person, to officials for whom the covered associate *was* entitled to vote at the time of the contributions and which in the aggregate do not exceed $350 to any one official, per election, or to officials for whom the covered associate was not entitled to vote at the time of the contributions and which in the aggregate do not exceed $150 to any one official, per election.

(2) *Exception for certain new covered associates.* The prohibitions of paragraph (a)(1) of this section shall not apply to an investment adviser as a result of a contribution made by a natural person more than six months prior to becoming a covered associate of the investment adviser unless such person,

after becoming a covered associate, solicits clients on behalf of the investment adviser.

(3) *Exception for certain returned contributions.* (i) An investment adviser that is prohibited from providing investment advisory services for compensation pursuant to paragraph (a)(1) of this section as a result of a contribution made by a covered associate of the investment adviser is excepted from such prohibition, subject to paragraphs (b)(3)(ii) and (b)(3)(iii) of this section, upon satisfaction of the following requirements:

(A) The investment adviser must have discovered the contribution which resulted in the prohibition within four months of the date of such contribution;

(B) Such contribution must not have exceeded $350; and

(C) The contributor must obtain a return of the contribution within 60 calendar days of the date of discovery of such contribution by the investment adviser.

(ii) In any calendar year, an investment adviser that has reported on its annual updating amendment to Form ADV (17 CFR 279.1) that it has more than 50 employees is entitled to no more than three exceptions pursuant to paragraph (b)(3)(i) of this section, and an investment adviser that has reported on its annual updating amendment to Form ADV that it has 50 or fewer employees is entitled to no more than two exceptions pursuant to paragraph (b)(3)(i) of this section.

(iii) An investment adviser may not rely on the exception provided in paragraph (b)(3)(i) of this section more than once with respect to contributions by the same covered associate of the investment adviser regardless of the time period.

(c) *Prohibitions as applied to covered investment pools.* For purposes of this section, an investment adviser to a covered investment pool in which a government entity invests or is solicited to invest shall be treated as though that investment adviser were providing or seeking to provide investment advisory services directly to the government entity.

(d) *Further prohibition.* As a means reasonably designed to prevent fraudulent, deceptive or manipulative acts, practices, or courses of business within the meaning of section 206(4) of Advisers Act (15 U.S.C. 80b–6(4)), it shall be unlawful for any investment adviser registered (or required to be registered) with the Commission, or unregistered in reliance on the exemption available under section 203(b)(3) of the Advisers Act (15 U.S.C. 80b–3(b)(3)), or that is an exempt reporting adviser, or any of the investment adviser's covered associates to do anything indirectly which, if done directly, would result in a violation of this section.

(e) *Exemptions.* The Commission, upon application, may conditionally or unconditionally exempt an investment adviser from the prohibition under paragraph (a)(1) of this section. In determining whether to grant an exemption, the Commission will consider, among other factors:

(1) Whether the exemption is necessary or appropriate in the public interest and consistent with the protection of investors and the purposes fairly intended by the policy and provisions of the Advisers Act (15 U.S.C. 80b);

(2) Whether the investment adviser:

(i) Before the contribution resulting in the prohibition was made, adopted and implemented policies and procedures reasonably designed to prevent violations of this section; and

(ii) Prior to or at the time the contribution which resulted in such prohibition was made, had no actual knowledge of the contribution; and

(iii) After learning of the contribution:

(A) Has taken all available steps to cause the contributor involved in making the contribution which resulted in such prohibition to obtain a return of the contribution; and

(B) Has taken such other remedial or preventive measures as may be appropriate under the circumstances;

(3) Whether, at the time of the contribution, the contributor was a covered associate or otherwise an employee of the investment adviser, or was seeking such employment;

(4) The timing and amount of the contribution which resulted in the prohibition;

(5) The nature of the election (*e.g*, Federal, State or local); and

(6) The contributor's apparent intent or motive in making the contribution which resulted in the prohibition, as evidenced by the facts and circumstances surrounding such contribution.

(f) *Definitions.* For purposes of this section:

(1) *Contribution* means any gift, subscription, loan, advance, or deposit of money or anything of value made for:

(i) The purpose of influencing any election for Federal, State or local office;

(ii) Payment of debt incurred in connection with any such election; or

(iii) Transition or inaugural expenses of the successful candidate for State or local office.

(2) *Covered associate* of an investment adviser means:

(i) Any general partner, managing member or executive officer, or other individual with a similar status or function;

(ii) Any employee who solicits a government entity for the investment adviser and any person who supervises, directly or indirectly, such employee; and

(iii) Any political action committee controlled by the investment adviser or by any person described in paragraphs (f)(2)(i) and (f)(2)(ii) of this section.

(3) *Covered investment pool* means:

(i) An investment company registered under the Investment Company Act of 1940 (15 U.S.C. 80a) that is an investment option of a plan or program of a government entity; or

(ii) Any company that would be an investment company under section 3(a) of the Investment Company Act of 1940 (15 U.S.C. 80a–3(a)), but for the exclusion provided from that definition by either section 3(c)(1), section 3(c)(7) or section 3(c)(11) of that Act (15 U.S.C. 80a–3(c)(1), (c)(7) or (c)(11)).

(4) *Executive officer* of an investment adviser means:

(i) The president;

(ii) Any vice president in charge of a principal business unit, division or function (such as sales, administration or finance);

(iii) Any other officer of the investment adviser who performs a policy-making function; or

(iv) Any other person who performs similar policy-making functions for the investment adviser.

(5) *Government entity* means any State or political subdivision of a State, including:

(i) Any agency, authority, or instrumentality of the State or political subdivision;

(ii) A pool of assets sponsored or established by the State or political subdivision or any agency, authority or instrumentality thereof, including, but not limited to a "defined benefit plan" as defined in section 414(j) of the Internal Revenue Code (26 U.S.C. 414(j)), or a State general fund;

(iii) A plan or program of a government entity; and

(iv) Officers, agents, or employees of the State or political subdivision or any agency, authority or instrumentality thereof, acting in their official capacity.

(6) *Official* means any person (including any election committee for the person) who was, at the time of the contribution, an incumbent, candidate or successful candidate for elective office of a government entity, if the office:

(i) Is directly or indirectly responsible for, or can influence the outcome of, the hiring of an investment adviser by a government entity; or

(ii) Has authority to appoint any person who is directly or indirectly responsible for, or can influence the outcome of, the hiring of an investment adviser by a government entity.

(7) *Payment* means any gift, subscription, loan, advance, or deposit of money or anything of value.

(8) *Plan or program of a government entity* means any participant-directed investment program or plan sponsored or established by a State or political subdivision or any agency, authority or instrumentality thereof, including, but not limited to, a "qualified tuition plan" authorized by section 529 of the Internal Revenue Code (26 U.S.C. 529), a retirement plan authorized by section 403(b) or 457 of the Internal Revenue Code (26 U.S.C. 403(b) or 457), or any similar program or plan.

(9) *Regulated person* means:

Securities and Exchange Commission § 275.206(4)-7

(i) An investment adviser registered with the Commission that has not, and whose covered associates have not, within two years of soliciting a government entity:

(A) Made a contribution to an official of that government entity, other than as described in paragraph (b)(1) of this section; and

(B) Coordinated or solicited any person or political action committee to make any contribution or payment described in paragraphs (a)(2)(ii)(A) and (B) of this section;

(ii) A "broker," as defined in section 3(a)(4) of the Securities Exchange Act of 1934 (15 U.S.C. 78c(a)(4)) or a "dealer," as defined in section 3(a)(5) of that Act (15 U.S.C. 78c(a)(5)), that is registered with the Commission, and is a member of a national securities association registered under 15A of that Act (15 U.S.C. 78o-3), provided that:

(A) The rules of the association prohibit members from engaging in distribution or solicitation activities if certain political contributions have been made; and

(B) The Commission, by order, finds that such rules impose substantially equivalent or more stringent restrictions on broker-dealers than this section imposes on investment advisers and that such rules are consistent with the objectives of this section; and

(iii) A "municipal advisor" registered with the Commission under section 15B of the Exchange Act and subject to rules of the Municipal Securities Rulemaking Board, provided that:

(A) Such rules prohibit municipal advisors from engaging in distribution or solicitation activities if certain political contributions have been made; and

(B) The Commission, by order, finds that such rules impose substantially equivalent or more stringent restrictions on municipal advisors than this section imposes on investment advisers and that such rules are consistent with the objectives of this section.

(10) *Solicit* means:

(i) With respect to investment advisory services, to communicate, directly or indirectly, for the purpose of obtaining or retaining a client for, or referring a client to, an investment adviser; and

(ii) With respect to a contribution or payment, to communicate, directly or indirectly, for the purpose of obtaining or arranging a contribution or payment.

[75 FR 41069, July 14, 2010, as amended at 76 FR 43013, July 19, 2011; 77 FR 28477, May 15, 2012]

§ 275.206(4)-6 Proxy voting.

If you are an investment adviser registered or required to be registered under section 203 of the Act (15 U.S.C. 80b-3), it is a fraudulent, deceptive, or manipulative act, practice or course of business within the meaning of section 206(4) of the Act (15 U.S.C. 80b-6(4)), for you to exercise voting authority with respect to client securities, unless you:

(a) Adopt and implement written policies and procedures that are reasonably designed to ensure that you vote client securities in the best interest of clients, which procedures must include how you address material conflicts that may arise between your interests and those of your clients;

(b) Disclose to clients how they may obtain information from you about how you voted with respect to their securities; and

(c) Describe to clients your proxy voting policies and procedures and, upon request, furnish a copy of the policies and procedures to the requesting client.

[68 FR 6593, Feb. 7, 2003]

§ 275.206(4)-7 Compliance procedures and practices.

If you are an investment adviser registered or required to be registered under section 203 of the Investment Advisers Act of 1940 (15 U.S.C. 80b-3), it shall be unlawful within the meaning of section 206 of the Act (15 U.S.C. 80b-6) for you to provide investment advice to clients unless you:

(a) *Policies and procedures.* Adopt and implement written policies and procedures reasonably designed to prevent violation, by you and your supervised persons, of the Act and the rules that the Commission has adopted under the Act;

(b) *Annual review.* Review, no less frequently than annually, the adequacy of the policies and procedures established

§ 275.206(4)-8

pursuant to this section and the effectiveness of their implementation; and

(c) *Chief compliance officer.* Designate an individual (who is a supervised person) responsible for administering the policies and procedures that you adopt under paragraph (a) of this section.

[68 FR 74730, Dec. 24, 2003]

§ 275.206(4)-8 Pooled investment vehicles.

(a) *Prohibition.* It shall constitute a fraudulent, deceptive, or manipulative act, practice, or course of business within the meaning of section 206(4) of the Act (15 U.S.C. 80b-6(4)) for any investment adviser to a pooled investment vehicle to:

(1) Make any untrue statement of a material fact or to omit to state a material fact necessary to make the statements made, in the light of the circumstances under which they were made, not misleading, to any investor or prospective investor in the pooled investment vehicle; or

(2) Otherwise engage in any act, practice, or course of business that is fraudulent, deceptive, or manipulative with respect to any investor or prospective investor in the pooled investment vehicle.

(b) *Definition.* For purposes of this section "pooled investment vehicle" means any investment company as defined in section 3(a) of the Investment Company Act of 1940 (15 U.S.C. 80a-3(a)) or any company that would be an investment company under section 3(a) of that Act but for the exclusion provided from that definition by either section 3(c)(1) or section 3(c)(7) of that Act (15 U.S.C. 80a-3(c)(1) or (7)).

[72 FR 44761, Aug. 9, 2007]

§ 275.222-1 Definitions.

For purposes of section 222 (15 U.S.C. 80b-18a) of the Act:

(a) *Place of business.* "Place of business" of an investment adviser means:

(1) An office at which the investment adviser regularly provides investment advisory services, solicits, meets with, or otherwise communicates with clients; and

(2) Any other location that is held out to the general public as a location at which the investment adviser provides investment advisory services, solicits, meets with, or otherwise communicates with clients.

(b) *Principal office and place of business.* "Principal office and place of business" of an investment adviser means the executive office of the investment adviser from which the officers, partners, or managers of the investment adviser direct, control, and coordinate the activities of the investment adviser.

[62 FR 28135, May 22, 1997, as amended at 76 FR 43014, July 19, 2011]

§ 275.222-2 Definition of "client" for purposes of the national de minimis standard.

For purposes of section 222(d)(2) of the Act (15 U.S.C. 80b-18a(d)(2)), an investment adviser may rely upon the definition of "client" provided by §275.202(a)(30)-1, without giving regard to paragraph (b)(4) of that section.

[76 FR 43014, July 19, 2011]

PART 276—INTERPRETATIVE RELEASES RELATING TO THE INVESTMENT ADVISERS ACT OF 1940 AND GENERAL RULES AND REGULATIONS THEREUNDER

AUTHORITY: 15 U.S.C. 80b *et seq.*

Subject	Release No.	Date	Fed. Reg. Vol. and Page
Opinion of General Counsel relating to section 202(a)(11)(C) of the Investment Advisers Act of 1940.	2	Oct. 28, 1940	11 FR 10996.
Opinion of the General Counsel relating to the use of the name "investment counsel" under section 208(c) of the Investment Advisers Act of 1940.	8	Dec. 12, 1940	Do.

Securities and Exchange Commission

Pt. 276

Subject	Release No.	Date	Fed. Reg. Vol. and Page
Opinion of Director of Trading and Exchange Division, relating to section 206 of the Investment Advisers Act of 1940, section 17(a) of the Securities Act of 1933, and sections 10(b) and 15(c)(1) of the Securities Exchange Act of 1934.	40	Feb. 5, 1945	11 FR 10997.
Opinion of the General Counsel relating to the use of "hedge clauses" by brokers, dealers, investment advisers, and others.	58	Apr. 10, 1951	16 FR 3387.
Statement of the Commission to clarify the meaning of "beneficial ownership of securities" as relates to beneficial ownership of securities held by family members.	194	Jan. 25, 1966	31 FR 1005.
Statement of the Commission setting the date of May 1, 1966 after which filings must reflect beneficial ownership of securities held by family members.	196	Feb. 14, 1966	31 FR 3175.
Statement of the Commission describing nature of examination required to be made of all funds and securities held by an investment adviser and the content of related accountant's certificate.	201	June 1, 1966	31 FR 7821.
Publication of the Commission's procedure to be followed if requests are to be met for no action or interpretative letters and responses thereto to be made available for public use.	281	Jan. 25, 1971	36 FR 2600.
Commission's statement of factors to be considered in connection with investment company advisory contracts containing incentive arrangements.	315	Apr. 19, 1972	37 FR 7690.
Applicability of Commission's policy statement on the future structure of securities markets to selection of brokers and payment of commissions by institutional managers.	318	May 18, 1972	37 FR 9988.
Commission's decisions on advisory committee recommendations regarding commencement of enforcement proceedings and termination of staff investigations.	336	Mar. 1, 1973	38 FR 5457.
Commission's statement on obligations of underwriters with respect to discretionary accounts.	377	June 29, 1973	38 FR 17201.
Applicability of investment advisers act to certain publications	563	Jan. 10, 1977	42 FR 2953; 42 FR 8140.
Contingent advisory compensation arrangements	721	May 16, 1980	45 FR 34876.
Applicability of investment advisers act to financial planners, pension consultants, and other persons who provide investment advisory services as an integral component of other financially related services.	770	Aug. 13, 1981	46 FR 41771.
Statement of position of Commission's Division of Investment Management ..	969	Apr. 30, 1985	50 FR 19341.
Statement of staff interpretive position regarding certain rules and forms; uniform registration, disclolsure, and reporting requirements.	1000	Dec. 3, 1985	50 FR 49835.
Applicability of the investment Advisers Act to financial planners, pension consultants, and other persons who provide investment advisory services as a component of other financial services.	1092	Oct. 8, 1987	52 FR 38400.
Registration of Successors to Broker-Dealers and Investment Advisors	1357	Jan. 4, 1993	58 FR 11.
Use of electronic media for delivery purposes	1562	May 9, 1996	61 FR 24651.
Statement of the Commission Regarding Use of Internet Web Sites to Offer Securities, Solicit Securities Transactions or Advertise Investment Services Offshore.	1710	Mar. 23, 1998	63 FR 14814
Interpretation of Section 206(3) of the Investment Advisers Act of 1940	1732	July 17, 1998	63 FR 39508
Statement of the Commission Regarding Disclosure of Year 2000 Issues and Consequences by Public Companies, Investment Advisers, Investment Companies, and Municipal Securities Issuers.	1738	July 29, 1998	63 FR 41404
Release No. IA-2969		Dec. 30, 2009	75 FR 1494
Commission Guidance Regarding the Definition of the Terms "Spouse" and "Marriage" Following the Supreme Court's Decision in *United States* v. *Windsor.*	IA-4122	June 19, 2015	80 FR 37537
Commission Interpretation Regarding Standard of Conduct for Investment Advisers.	IA-5248	June 5, 2019	84 FR 33681
Commission Interpretation Regarding the Solely Incidental Prong of the Broker-Dealer Exclusion from the Definition of Investment Adviser.	IA-5249	June 5, 2019	84 FR 33689
Commission Guidance Regarding the Proxy Voting Responsibilities of Investment Advisers.	IA-5325	Aug. 21, 2019	84 FR 47427
Supplement to Commission Guidance Regarding the Proxy Voting Responsibilities of Investment Advisers.	IA-5547	Sept. 3, 2020	85 FR 55157
Supplement to Commission Guidance Regarding the Proxy Voting Responsibilities of Investment Advisers.	IA-6068	July 19, 2022	87 FR 43197

PART 279—FORMS PRESCRIBED UNDER THE INVESTMENT ADVISERS ACT OF 1940

Sec.
279.0–1 Availability of forms.
279.1 Form ADV, for application for registration of investment adviser and for amendments to such registration statement.
279.2 Form ADV-W, notice of withdrawal from registration as investment adviser.
279.3 Form ADV-H, application for a temporary or continuing hardship exemption.
279.4 Form ADV-NR, appointment of agent for service of process by non-resident general partner and non-resident managing agent of an investment adviser.
279.5–279.7 [Reserved]
279.8 Form ADV-E, cover page for certificate of accounting of securities and funds in possession or custody of an investment adviser.
279.9 Form PF, reporting by investment advisers to private funds.

AUTHORITY: The Investment Advisers Act of 1940, 15 U.S.C. 80b–1, *et seq.*, Pub. L. 111–203, 124 Stat. 1376.

SOURCE: 33 FR 19005, Dec. 20, 1968, unless otherwise noted.

§ 279.0–1 Availability of forms.

(a) This part identifies and describes the forms prescribed for use under the Investment Advisers Act of 1940.

(b) Any person may obtain a copy of any form prescribed for use in this part by written request to the Securities and Exchange Commission, 100 F Street, NE., Washington, DC 20549. Any person may inspect the forms at this address and at the Commission's regional offices. (See § 200.11 of this chapter for the addresses of SEC regional offices.)

[46 FR 17757, Mar. 20, 1981, as amended at 47 FR 26820, June 22, 1982; 59 FR 5946, Feb. 9, 1994; 73 FR 32229, June 5, 2008]

§ 279.1 Form ADV, for application for registration of investment adviser and for amendments to such registration statement.

This form shall be filed pursuant to Rule 203–1 (§ 275.203–1 of this chapter) as an application for registration of an investment adviser pursuant to sections 203(c) or 203(g) of the Investment Advisers Act of 1940, and also as an amendment to registration pursuant to Rule 204–1 (§ 275.204–1 of this chapter).

[44 FR 21008, Apr. 9, 1979]

EDITORIAL NOTE: For FEDERAL REGISTER citations affecting Form ADV, see the List of CFR Sections Affected, which appears in the Finding Aids section of the printed volume and at *www.govinfo.gov*.

§ 279.2 Form ADV-W, notice of withdrawal from registration as investment adviser.

This form shall be filed pursuant to Rule 203–2 (§ 275.203–2 of this chapter) by a registered investment adviser as a notice of withdrawal from registration as such under the Investment Advisers Act of 1940.

EDITORIAL NOTE: For FEDERAL REGISTER citations affecting Form ADV-W, see the List of CFR Sections Affected, which appears in the Finding Aids section of the printed volume and at *www.govinfo.gov*.

§ 279.3 Form ADV-H, application for a temporary or continuing hardship exemption.

An investment adviser must file this form under § 275.203–3 of this chapter to request a temporary hardship exemption or apply for a continuing hardship exemption.

[65 FR 57451, Sept. 22, 2000]

EDITORIAL NOTE: For FEDERAL REGISTER citations affecting Form ADV-H, see the List of CFR Sections Affected, which appears in the Finding Aids section of the printed volume and at *www.govinfo.gov*.

§ 279.4 Form ADV-NR, appointment of agent for service of process by non-resident general partner and non-resident managing agent of an investment adviser.

This form shall be filed and amended pursuant to § 275.203–1 of this chapter (Rule 203–1) as an appointment of agent for service of process by non-resident general partners and non-resident managing agents of an investment adviser pursuant to section 203 of the Investment Advisers Act of 1940.

[87 FR 38978, June 30, 2022]

EDITORIAL NOTE: For FEDERAL REGISTER citations affecting Form ADV-NR, see the List of CFR Sections Affected, which appears in the Finding Aids section of the printed volume and at *www.govinfo.gov*.

§§ 279.5–279.7 [Reserved]

§ 279.8 Form ADV-E, cover page for certificate of accounting of securities and funds in possession or custody of an investment adviser.

[54 FR 32049, Aug. 4, 1989]

EDITORIAL NOTE: For FEDERAL REGISTER citations affecting Form ADV-E, see the List of CFR Sections Affected, which appears in the Finding Aids section of the printed volume and at www.govinfo.gov.

§ 279.9 Form PF, reporting by investment advisers to private funds.

This form shall be filed pursuant to Rule 204(b)–1 (§ 275.204(b)–1 of this chapter) by certain investment advisers registered or required to register under section 203 of the Act (15 U.S.C. 80b–3) that act as an investment adviser to one or more private funds.

[76 FR 71175, Nov. 16, 2011]

EDITORIAL NOTE: For FEDERAL REGISTER citations affecting Form PF, see the List of CFR Sections Affected, which appears in the Finding Aids section of the printed volume and at www.govinfo.gov.

PART 281—INTERPRETATIVE RELEASES RELATING TO CORPORATE REORGANIZATIONS UNDER CHAPTER X OF THE BANKRUPTCY ACT

Subject	Release No.	Date	Fed. Reg. Vol. and Page
Letter of the Commission with respect to transmission to the Commission of all petitions, answers, orders, applications, reports and other papers filed under Chapter X of the Bankruptcy Act.	1	Sept. 26, 1938	11 FR 10997.
Statement by the Commission summarizing Chapter X of the Bankruptcy Act.	2	......do............	11 FR 10998.

PART 285—RULES AND REGULATIONS PURSUANT TO SECTION 15(a) OF THE BRETTON WOODS AGREEMENTS ACT

Sec.
285.1 Applicability of part.
285.2 Periodic reports.
285.3 Reports with respect to proposed distribution of primary obligations.
285.4 Preparation and filing of reports.
SCHEDULE A TO PART 285

AUTHORITY: Secs. 19, 23, 48 Stat. 85, as amended, 901, as amended, sec. 15, 63 Stat. 298; 15 U.S.C. 77i, 78w 22 U.S.C. 286k–1.

§ 285.1 Applicability of part.

This part (Regulation BW), prescribes the reports to be filed with the Securities and Exchange Commission by the International Bank for Reconstruction and Development pursuant to section 15(a) of the Bretton Woods Agreements Act.

[Reg. BW, 15 FR 281, Jan. 17, 1950]

§ 285.2 Periodic reports.

(a) Within 45 days after the end of each of its fiscal quarters, the Bank shall file with the Commission the following information:

(1) Information as to any purchases or sales by the Bank of its primary obligations during such quarter.

(2) Copies of the Bank's regular quarterly financial statements.

(3) Copies of any material modifications or amendments during such quarter of any exhibits (other than (i) constituent documents defining the rights of holders of securities of other issuers guaranteed by the Bank and (ii) loan and guaranty agreements to which the Bank is a party) previously filed with the Commission under any statute.

(b) Copies of each annual report of the Bank to its Board of Governors shall be filed with the Commission within 10 days after the submission of such report to the Board of Governors.

[20 FR 588, Jan. 27, 1955]

§ 285.3 Reports with respect to proposed distribution of primary obligations.

The Bank shall file with the Commission, on or prior to the date on which it sells any of its primary obligations

§ 285.4

in connection with a distribution of such obligations in the United States, a report containing the information and documents specified in Schedule A below. The term "sell" as used in this section and in Schedule A means the making of a completed sale or a firm commitment to sell.

[46 FR 48179, Oct. 1, 1981]

§ 285.4 Preparation and filing of reports.

(a) Every report required by this part shall be filed under cover of a letter of transmittal which shall state the nature of the report and indicate the particular rule and subdivision thereof pursuant to which the report is filed. At least the original of every such letter shall be signed on behalf of the Bank by a duly authorized officer thereof.

(b) Two copies of every report, including the letter of transmittal, exhibits and other papers and documents comprising a part of the report, shall be filed with the Commission.

(c) The report shall be in the English language. If any exhibit or other paper or document filed with the report is in a foreign language, it shall be accompanied by a translation into the English language.

(d) Reports pursuant to § 285.3 (Rule 3) may be filed in the form of a prospectus to the extent that such prospectus contains the information specified in Schedule A.

[Reg. BW, 15 FR 281, Jan. 17, 1950]

SCHEDULE A TO PART 285

This schedule specifies the information and documents to be furnished in a report pursuant to § 285.3 (Rule 3) with respect to a proposed distribution of primary obligations of the Bank. Information not available at the time of filing the report shall be filed as promptly thereafter as possible.

ITEM 1. *Description of obligations.* As to each issue of primary obligations of the Bank which is to be distributed, furnish the following information:

(a) The title and date of the issue.

(b) The interest rate and interest payment dates.

(c) The maturity date or if serial, the plan of serial maturities. If the maturity of the obligation may be accelerated, state the circumstances under which it may be so accelerated.

(d) A brief outline of (1) any redemption provisions and (2) any amortization, sinking fund or retirement provisions, stating the annual amount, if any, which the Bank will be under obligation to apply for the satisfaction of such provisions.

(e) If secured by any lien, the kind and priority thereof, and the nature of the property subject to the lien; if any other indebtedness is secured by an equal or prior lien on the same property, state the nature of such other liens.

(f) If any obligations issued or to be issued by the Bank will, as to the payment of interest or principal, rank prior to the obligations to be distributed, describe the nature and extent of such priority.

(g) Outline briefly any provisions of the governing instruments under which the terms of the obligations to be distributed may be amended or modified by the holders thereof or otherwise.

(h) Outline briefly any other material provisions of the governing instruments pertaining to the rights of the holders of the obligations to be distributed or pertaining to the duties of the Bank with respect thereto.

(i) The name and address of the fiscal or paying agent of the Bank, if any.

ITEM 2. *Distribution of obligations.* (a) Outline briefly the plan of distribution of the obligations and state the amount of the participation of each principal underwriter, if any.

(b) Describe any arrangements known to the Bank or to any principal underwriter named above designed to stabilize the market for the obligations for the account of the Bank or the principal underwriters as a group and indicate whether any transactions have already been effected to accomplish that purpose.

(c) Describe any arrangements for withholding commissions, or otherwise, to hold each underwriter or dealer responsible for the distribution of his participation.

ITEM 3. *Distribution spread.* The following information shall be given, in substantially the tabular form indicated, as to all obligations which are to be offered for cash (estimate, if necessary):

	Price to the public	Selling discounts and commissions	Proceeds to the Bank
Per			
Total			

ITEM 4. *Discounts and commissions to sub-underwriters and dealers.* State briefly the discounts and commissions to be allowed or paid to dealers. If any dealers are to act in the capacity of sub-underwriters and are to be allowed or paid any additional discounts or commissions for acting in such capacity,

Securities and Exchange Commission

a general statement to that effect will suffice, without giving the additional amounts so paid or to be so paid.

ITEM 5. *Other expenses of distribution.* Furnish a reasonably itemized statement of all expenses of the Bank in connection with the issuance and distribution of the obligations, except underwriters' or dealers' discounts and commissions.

Instructions: Insofar as practicable, the itemization shall include transfer agents' fees, cost of printing and engraving, and legal and accounting fees. The information may be given as subject to future contingencies. If the amounts of any items are not known, estimates, designated as such, shall be given.

ITEM 6. *Application of proceeds.* Make a reasonably itemized statement of the purposes, so far as determinable, for which the net proceeds to the Bank from the obligations are to be used, and state the approximate amount to be used for each such purpose.

ITEM 7. *Exhibits to be furnished.* The following documents shall be attached to or otherwise furnished as a part of the report:

(a) Copies of the constituent instruments defining the rights evidenced by the obligations.

(b) Copies of an opinion of counsel, in the English language, as to the legality of the obligations.

(c) Copies of all material contracts pertaining to the issuance or distribution of the obligations to which the Bank or any principal underwriter of the obligations is or is to be a party, except selling group agreements.

(d) Copies of any prospectus or other sales literature to be provided by the Bank or any of the principal underwriters for general use in connection with the initial distribution of the obligations to the public.

[Reg. BW, 15 FR 281, Jan. 17, 1950, as amended at 20 FR 588, Jan. 27, 1955]

PART 286—GENERAL RULES AND REGULATIONS PURSUANT TO SECTION 11(a) OF THE INTER-AMERICAN DEVELOPMENT BANK ACT

Sec.
286.1 Applicability of this part.
286.2 Periodic reports.
286.3 Reports with respect to proposed distribution of primary obligations.
286.4 Preparation and filing of reports.
SCHEDULE A TO PART 286

AUTHORITY: Secs. 3–9, 11, 12, 73 Stat. 299–301; 22 U.S.C. 283a–283i.

SOURCE: 25 FR 10452, Nov. 1, 1960, unless otherwise noted.

§ 286.1 Applicability of this part.

This part (Regulation IA) prescribes the reports to be filed with the Securities and Exchange Commission by the Inter-American Development Bank pursuant to section 11(a) of the Inter-American Development Bank Act.

§ 286.2 Periodic reports.

(a) Within 45 days after the end of each of its fiscal quarters, the Bank shall file with the Commission the following information:

(1) Information as to any purchases or sales by the Bank of its primary obligations during such quarter.

(2) Copies of the Bank's regular quarterly financial statement.

(3) Copies of any material modifications or amendments during such quarter of any exhibits (other than (i) constituent documents defining the rights of holders of securities of other issuers guaranteed by the Bank, and (ii) loans and guaranty agreements to which the Bank is a party) previously filed with the Commission under any statute.

(b) Copies of each annual report of the Bank to its Board of Governors shall be filed with the Commission within 10 days after the submission of such report to the Board of Governors.

§ 286.3 Reports with respect to proposed distribution of primary obligations.

The Bank shall file with the Commission, on or prior to the date on which it sells any of its primary obligations in connection with a distribution of such obligations in the United States, a report containing the information and documents specified in Schedule A below. The term "sell" as used in this section and in Schedule A means the making of a completed sale or a firm commitment to sell.

[46 FR 48179, Oct. 2, 1981]

§ 286.4 Preparation and filing of reports.

(a) Every report required by this part shall be filed under cover of a letter of transmittal which shall state the nature of the report and indicate the particular rule and subdivision thereof pursuant to which the report is filed.

At least the original of every such letter shall be signed on behalf of the Bank by a duly authorized officer thereof.

(b) Two copies of every report, including the letter of transmittal, exhibits and other papers and documents comprising a part of the report, shall be filed with the Commission.

(c) The report shall be in the English language. If any exhibit or other paper or document filed with the report is in a foreign language, it shall be accompanied by a translation into the English language.

(d) Reports pursuant to §286.3 may be filed in the form of a prospectus to the extent that such prospectus contains the information specified in Schedule A.

SCHEDULE A TO PART 286

This schedule specifies the information and documents to be furnished in a report pursuant to §286.3 with respect to a proposed distribution of primary obligations of the Bank. Information not available at the time of filing the report shall be filed as promptly thereafter as possible.

Item 1. Description of obligations

As to each issue of primary obligations of the Bank which is to be distributed, furnish the following information:

(a) The title and date of the issue.

(b) The interest rate and interest payment dates.

(c) The maturity date or, if serial, the plan of serial maturities. If the maturity of the obligation may be accelerated, state the circumstances under which it may be so accelerated.

(d) A brief outline of (1) any redemption provisions and (2) any amortization, sinking fund or retirement provisions, stating the annual amount, if any, which the Bank will be under obligation to apply for the satisfaction of such provisions.

(e) If secured by any lien, the kind and priority thereof, and the nature of the property subject to the lien; if any other indebtedness is secured by an equal or prior lien on the same property, state the nature of such other liens.

(f) If any obligations issued or to be issued by the Bank will, as the payment of interest or principal, rank prior to the obligations to be distributed, describe the nature and extent of such priority.

(g) Outline briefly any provisions of the governing instruments under which the terms of the obligations to be distributed may be amended or modified by the holders thereof or otherwise.

(h) Outline briefly any other material provisions of the governing instruments pertaining to the rights of the holders of the obligations to be distributed or pertaining to the duties of the Bank with respect thereto.

(i) The name and address[4] of the fiscal or paying agent of the Bank, if any.

Item 2. Distribution of obligations

(a) Outline briefly the plan of distribution of the obligations and state the amount of the participation of each principal underwriter, if any.

(b) Describe any arrangements known to the Bank or to any principal underwriter named above designed to stabilize the market for the obligations for the account of the Bank or the principal underwriters as a group and indicate whether any transactions have already been effected to accomplish that purpose.

(c) Describe any arrangements for withholding commissions, or otherwise, to hold each underwriter or dealer responsible for the distribution of his participation.

Item 3. Distribution spread

The following information shall be given, in substantially the tabular form indicated, as to all obligations which are to be offered for cash (estimate, if necessary):

	Price to the public	Selling discounts and commissions	Proceeds to the bank
Per unit			
Total			

Item 4. Discounts and commissions to sub-underwriters and dealers

State briefly the discounts and commissions to be allowed or paid to dealers. If any dealers are to act in the capacity of sub-underwriters and are to be allowed or paid any additional discounts or commissions for acting in such capacity, a general statement to that effect will suffice, without giving the additional amounts to be so paid.

Item 5. Other expenses of distribution

Furnish a reasonably itemized statement of all expenses of the Bank in connection with the issuance and distribution of the obligations, except underwriters' or dealers' discounts and commissions.

Instruction. Insofar as practicable, the itemization shall include transfer agents' fees, cost of printing and engraving, and legal and accounting fees. The information may be given as subject to future contingencies. If the amounts of any items are not known, estimates, designated as such, shall be given.

Securities and Exchange Commission

§ 287.4

Item 6. Application of proceeds

Make a reasonably itemized statement of the purposes, so far as determinable, for which the net proceeds to the Bank from the obligations are to be used, and state the approximate amount to be used for each such purpose.

Item 7. Exhibits to be furnished

The following documents shall be attached to or otherwise furnished as a part of the report:

(a) Copies of the constituent instruments defining the rights evidenced by the obligations.

(b) Copies of an opinion of counsel, in the English language, as to the legality of the obligations.

(c) Copies of all material contracts pertaining to the issuance or distributions of the obligations, to which the Bank or any principal underwriter of the obligations is or is to be a party, except selling group agreements.

(d) Copies of any prospectus or other sales literature to be provided by the Bank or any of the principal underwriters for general use in connection with the initial distribution of the obligations to the public.

PART 287—GENERAL RULES AND REGULATIONS PURSUANT TO SECTION 11(a) OF THE ASIAN DEVELOPMENT BANK ACT

Sec.
287.1 Applicability of this part.
287.2 Periodic reports.
287.3 Reports with respect to proposed distribution of primary obligations.
287.4 Preparation and filing of reports.
287.101 Schedule A—Information required in reports pursuant to § 287.3.

AUTHORITY: Sec. 11, 80 Stat. 73; 22 U.S.C. 285h.

SOURCE: AD1, 33 FR 259, Jan. 9, 1968, unless otherwise noted.

§ 287.1 Applicability of this part.

This part (Regulation AD) prescribes the reports to be filed with the Securities and Exchange Commission by the Asian Development Bank pursuant to section 11(a) of the Asian Development Bank Act.

§ 287.2 Periodic reports.

(a) Within 60 days after the end of each of its fiscal quarters, the Bank shall file with the Commission the following information:

(1) Information as to any purchases or sales by the Bank of its primary obligations during such quarter.

(2) Copies of the Bank's regular quarterly financial statement.

(3) Copies of any material modifications or amendments during such quarter of any exhibits (other than (i) constituent documents defining the rights of holders of securities of other issuers guaranteed by the Bank, and (ii) loans and guaranty agreements to which the Bank is a party) previously filed with the Commission under any statute.

(b) Copies of each annual report of the Bank to its Board of Governors shall be filed with the Commission within 10 days after the submission of such report to the Board of Governors.

§ 287.3 Reports with respect to proposed distribution of primary obligations.

The Bank shall file with the Commission, on or prior to the date on which it sells any of its primary obligations in connection with a distribution of such obligations in the United States, a report containing the information and documents specified in Schedule A below. The term "sell" as used in this section and in Schedule A means the making of a completed sale or a firm commitment to sell.

[46 FR 48179, Oct. 1, 1981]

§ 287.4 Preparation and filing of reports.

(a) Every report required by this regulation shall be filed under cover of a letter of transmittal which shall state the nature of the report and indicate the particular rule and subdivision thereof pursuant to which the report is filed. At least the original of every such letter shall be signed on behalf of the Bank by a duly authorized officer thereof.

(b) Two copies of every report, including the letter of transmittal, exhibits and other papers and documents comprising a part of the report, shall be filed with the Commission.

(c) The report shall be in the English language. If any exhibit or other paper or document filed with the report is in a foreign language, it shall be accompanied by a translation into the English language.

§ 287.101

(d) Reports pursuant to Rule 3 (17 CFR 287.3) may be filed in the form of a prospectus to the extent that such prospectus contains the information specified in Schedule A (17 CFR 287.101).

§ 287.101 Schedule A—Information required in reports pursuant to § 287.3.

This schedule specifies the information and documents to be furnished in a report pursuant to Rule 3 (17 CFR 287.3) with respect to a proposed distribution of primary obligations of the Bank. Information not available at the time of filing the report shall be filed as promptly thereafter as possible.

Item 1. Description of obligations. As to each issue of primary obligations of the Bank which is to be distributed, furnish the following information:

(a) The title and date of the issue.

(b) The interest rate and interest payment dates.

(c) The maturity date or, if serial, the plan of serial maturities. If the maturity of the obligation may be accelerated, state the circumstances under which it may be so accelerated.

(d) A brief outline of (1) any redemption provisions and (2) any amortization, sinking fund or retirement provisions, stating the annual amount, if any, which the Bank will be under obligation to apply for the satisfaction of such provisions.

(e) If secured by any lien, the kind and priority thereof, and the nature of the property subject to the lien; if any other indebtedness is secured by an equal or prior lien on the same property, state the nature of such other liens.

(f) If any obligations issued or to be issued by the Bank will, as to the payment of interest or principal, rank prior to the obligations to be distributed, describe the nature and extent of such priority.

(g) Outline briefly any provisions of the governing instruments under which the terms of the obligations to be distributed may be amended or modified by the holders thereof or otherwise.

(h) Outline briefly any other material provisions of the governing instruments pertaining to the rights of the holders of the obligations to be distributed or pertaining to the duties of the Bank with respect thereto.

(i) The name and address of the fiscal or paying agent of the Bank, if any.

Item 2. Distribution of obligations. (a) Outline briefly the plan of distribution of the obligations and state the amount of the participation of each principal underwriter, if any.

(b) Describe any arrangements known to the Bank or to any principal underwriter named above designed to stabilize the market for the obligations for the account of the Bank or the principal underwriters as a group and indicate whether any transactions have already been effected to accomplish that purpose.

(c) Describe any arrangements for withholding commissions, or otherwise, to hold each underwriter or dealer responsible for the distribution of his participation.

Item 3. Distribution spread. The following information shall be given, in substantially the tabular form indicated, as to all obligations which are to be offered for cash (estimate, if necessary):

	Price to the public	Selling discounts and commissions	Proceeds to the bank
Per unit	....	....	....
Total	....	....	....

Item 4. Discounts and commissions to subunderwriters and dealers. State briefly the discounts and commission to be allowed or paid to dealers. If any dealers are to act in the capacity of subunderwriters and are to be allowed or paid any additional discounts or commissions for action in such capacity, a general statement to that effect will suffice, without giving the additional amounts to be so paid.

Item 5. Other expenses of distribution. Furnish a reasonably itemized statement of all expenses of the Bank in connection with the issuance and distribution of the obligations, except underwriters' or dealers' discounts and commissions.

Instruction. Insofar as practicable, the itemization shall include transfer agents' fees, cost of printing and engraving, and legal and accounting fees. The information may be given as subject to future contingencies. If the amounts of any items are not known, estimates, designated as such, shall be given.

Item 6. Application of proceeds. Make a reasonably itemized statement of the purposes, so far as determinable, for which the net proceeds to the Bank from the obligations are to be used, and state the approximate amount to be used for each such purpose.

Item 7. Exhibits to be furnished. The following documents shall be attached to or otherwise furnished as a part of the report:

(a) Copies of the constituent instruments defining the rights evidenced by the obligations.

(b) Copies of an opinion of counsel, in the English language, as to the legality of the obligations.

(c) Copies of all material contracts pertaining to the issuance or distributions of the obligations, to which the Bank or any principal underwriter of the obligations is or is to be a party, except selling group agreements.

(d) Copies of any prospectus or other sales literature to be provided by the Bank or any of the principal underwriters for general use in connection with the initial distribution of the obligations to the public.

PART 288—GENERAL RULES AND REGULATIONS PURSUANT TO SECTION 9(a) OF THE AFRICAN DEVELOPMENT BANK ACT

Sec.
288.1 Applicability of this part.
288.2 Periodic reports.
288.3 Reports with respect to proposed distribution of primary obligations.
288.4 Preparation and filing of reports.
288.101 Schedule A. Information required in reports pursuant to § 288.3

AUTHORITY: Sec. 9(a), 95 Stat. 743, 22 U.S.C. 290i–9a; sec. 19(a), 48 Stat. 85, 15 U.S.C. 77s(a).

SOURCE: 50 FR 26191, June 25, 1985, unless otherwise noted.

§ 288.1 Applicability of this part.

This part (Regulation AFDB) prescribes the reports to be filed with the Securities and Exchange Commission by the African Development Bank pursuant to section 9(a) of the African Development Bank Act.

§ 288.2 Periodic reports.

(a) Within 60 days after the end of each of its fiscal quarters, the Bank shall file with the Commission the following information:

(1) Information as to any purchases or sales by the Bank of its primary obligations during such quarter;

(2) Two copies of the Bank's regular quarterly financial statement; and

(3) Two copies of any material modifications or amendments during such quarter of any exhibits (other than (i) constituent documents defining the rights of holders of securities of other issuers guaranteed by the Bank, and (ii) loans and guaranty agreements to which the Bank is a party) previously filed with the Commission under any statute.

(b) Two copies of each annual report of the Bank to its Board of Governors shall be filed with the Commission within 10 days after the submission of such report to the Board of Governors.

§ 288.3 Reports with respect to proposed distribution of primary obligations.

The Bank shall file with the Commission, on or prior to the date on which it sells any of its primary obligations in connection with a distribution of such obligations in the United States, a report containing the information and documents specified in Schedule A (17 CFR 288.101). The term "sell" as used in this section and in Schedule A means the making of a completed sale or a firm commitment to sell.

§ 288.4 Preparation and filing of reports.

(a) Every report required by this regulation shall be filed under cover of a letter of transmittal which shall state the nature of the report and indicate the particular rule and subdivision thereof pursuant to which the report is filed. At least the original of every such letter shall be signed on behalf of the Bank by a duly authorized officer thereof.

(b) Two copies of every report, including the letter of transmittal, exhibits and other papers and documents comprising a part of the report, shall be filed with the Commission.

(c) The report shall be in the English language. If any exhibit or other paper or document filed with the report is in a foreign language, it shall be accompanied by a translation into the English language.

(d) Reports pursuant to Rule 3 (17 CFR 288.3) may be filed in the form of prospectus to the extent that such prospectus contains the information specified in Schedule A (17 CFR 288.101).

§ 288.101 Schedule A. Information required in reports pursuant to § 288.3.

This schedule specifies the information and documents to be furnished in a report pursuant to Rule 3 (17 CFR 288.3) with respect to a proposed distribution of primary obligations of the Bank. Information not available at the time of filing the report shall be filed as promptly thereafter as possible.

§ 288.101

Item 1: Description of obligations.

As to each issue of primary obligations of the Bank which is to be distributed, furnish the following information:

(a) The title and date of the issue.

(b) The interest rate and interest payment dates.

(c) The maturity date or, if serial, the plan of serial maturities. If the maturity of the obligation may be accelerated, state the circumstances under which it may be so accelerated.

(d) A brief outline of (i) any redemption provisions and (ii) any amortization, sinking fund or retirement provisions, stating the annual amount, if any, which the Bank will be under obligation to apply for the satisfaction of such provisions.

(e) If secured by any lien, the kind and priority thereof, and the nature of the property subject to the lien; if any other indebtedness is secured by an equal or prior lien on the same property, state the nature of such other liens.

(f) If any obligations issued or to be issued by the Bank will, as to the payment of interest or principal, rank prior to the obligations to be distributed, describe the nature and extent of such priority.

(g) Outline briefly any provisions of the governing instruments under which the terms of the obligations to be distributed may be amended or modified by the holders thereof or otherwise.

(h) Outline briefly any other material provisions of the governing instruments pertaining to the rights of the holders of the obligations to be distributed or pertaining to the duties of the Bank with respect thereto.

(i) The name and address of the fiscal or paying agent of the Bank, if any.

Item 2. Distribution of obligations.

(a) Outline briefly the plan of distribution of the obligations and state the amount of the participation of each principal underwriter, if any.

(b) Describe any arrangements known to the Bank or to any principal underwriter named above designed to stabilize the market for the obligations for the acount of the Bank or the principal underwriters as a group and indicate whether any transactions have already been effected to accomplish that purpose.

(c) Describe any arrangements for withholding commissions, or otherwise, to hold each underwriter or dealer responsible for the distribution of his participation.

Item 3. Distribution spread.

The following information shall be given, in substantially the tabular form indicated, as to all obligations which are to be offered for cash (estimate, if necessary):

	Price to the public	Selling discounts and commissions	Proceeds to the bank
Per Unit	....	....	....
Total	....	....	....

Item 4. Discounts and commissions to sub-underwriters and dealers.

State briefly the discounts and commissions to be allowed or paid to dealers. If any dealers are to act in the capacity of sub-underwriters and are to be allowed or paid any additional discounts or commissions for acting in such capacity, a general statement to that effect will suffice, without giving the additional amounts to be so paid.

Item 5. Other expenses of the distribution.

Furnish a reasonably itemized statement of all expenses of the Bank in connection with the issuance and distribution of the obligations, except underwriters' or dealers' discounts and commissions.

Instruction. Insofar as practicable, the itemization shall include transfer agents' fees, cost of printing and engraving, and legal and accounting fees. The information may be given as subject to future contingencies. If the amounts of any items are not known, estimates, designated as such, shall be given.

Item 6. Application of proceeds.

Make a reasonable itemized statement of the purposes, so far as determinable, for which the net proceeds to the Bank from the obligations are to be used, and state the approximate amount to be used for each such purpose.

Item 7. Exhibits to be furnished.

The following documents shall be attached to or otherwise furnished as a part of the report:

(a) Copies of the constituent instruments defining the rights evidenced by the obligations.

(b) Copies of an opinion of counsel, in the English language, as to the legality of the obligations.

(c) Copies of all material contracts pertaining to the issuance or distributions of the obligations, to which the Bank or any principal underwriter of the obligations is or is to be a party, except selling group agreements.

(d) Copies of any prospectus or other sales literature to be provided by the Bank or any of the principal underwriters for general use in connection with the initial distribution of the obligations to the public.

PART 289—GENERAL RULES AND REGULATIONS PURSUANT TO SECTION 13(a) OF THE INTERNATIONAL FINANCE CORPORATION ACT

Sec.
289.1 Applicability of this part.
289.2 Periodic reports.
289.3 Reports with respect to proposed distribution of primary obligations.
289.4 Preparation and filing of reports.
289.101 Schedule A. Information required in reports pursuant to § 289.3.

AUTHORITY: 15 U.S.C. 77s(a); 22 U.S.C. 282m.

SOURCE: 56 FR 32079, July 15, 1991, unless otherwise noted.

§ 289.1 Applicability of this part.

This part (Regulation IFC) prescribes the reports to be filed with the Securities and Exchange Commission by the International Finance Corporation ("IFC") pursuant to section 13(a) of the International Finance Corporation Act.

§ 289.2 Periodic reports.

(a) Within 45 days after the end of each of its fiscal quarters the IFC shall file with the Commission the following information:

(1) Two copies of information as to any purchases or sales by the IFC of its primary obligations during such quarter;

(2) Two copies of the IFC's regular quarterly financial statement; and

(3) Two copies of any material modifications or amendments during such quarter of any exhibits (other than constituent documents defining the rights of holders of securities of other issuers guaranteed by the IFC, and loan and guaranty agreements to which the IFC is a party) previously filed with the Commission under any statute.

(b) Each annual report of the IFC to its Board of Governors shall be filed with the Commission within 10 days after the submission of such report to the Board of Governors.

§ 289.3 Reports with respect to proposed distribution of primary obligations.

The IFC shall file with the Commission, on or prior to the date on which it sells any of its primary obligations in connection with a distribution of such obligations in the United States, a report containing the information and documents specified in Schedule A of this part. The term "sell" as used in this section and in Schedule A of this Part means a completed sale, or a firm commitment to sell to an underwriter.

§ 289.4 Preparation and filing of reports.

(a) Every report required by this regulation shall be filed under cover of a letter of transmittal which shall state the nature of the report and indicate the particular rule and subdivision thereof pursuant to which the report is filed. At least the original of every such letter shall be signed on behalf of the IFC by a duly authorized officer thereof.

(b) Two copies of every report, including the letter of transmittal, exhibits and other papers and documents comprising a part of the report, shall be filed with the Commission.

(c) The report shall be in the English language. If any exhibit or other paper or document filed with the report is in a foreign language, it shall be accompanied by a translation into the English language.

(d) Reports pursuant to § 289.3 may be filed in the form of a prospectus to the extent that such prospectus contains the information specified in Schedule A of this Part.

§ 289.101 Schedule A. Information required in reports pursuant to § 289.3.

This schedule specifies the information and documents to be furnished in a report pursuant to § 289.3 with respect to a proposed distribution of primary obligations of the IFC. Information not available at the time of filing the report shall be filed as promptly thereafter as possible.

Item 1: Description of obligations.

As to each issue of primary obligations of the IFC that is to be distributed, furnish the following information:

(a) The title and date of the issue.

(b) The interest rate and interest payments dates.

§ 289.101

(c) The maturity date or, if serial, the plan of serial maturities. If the maturity of the obligation may be accelerated, state the circumstances under which it may be so accelerated.

(d) A brief outline of:

(i) Any redemption provisions, and

(ii) Any amortization, sinking fund or retirement provisions, stating the annual amount, if any, which the IFC will be under obligation to apply for the satisfaction of such provisions.

(e) If secured by any lien, the kind and priority thereof, and the nature of the property subject to the lien; if any other indebtedness is secured by an equal or prior lien on the same property, state the nature of such other liens.

(f) If any obligations issued or to be issued by the IFC will, as to the payment of interest and principal, rank prior to the obligations to be distributed, describe the nature and extent of such priority, to the extent known.

(g) Outline briefly any provisions of the governing instruments under which the terms of the obligations to be distributed may be amended or modified by the holder thereof or otherwise.

(h) Outline briefly any other material provisions of the governing instruments pertaining to the rights of the holders of the obligations to be distributed or pertaining to the duties of the IFC with respect thereto.

(i) The name and address of the fiscal or paying agent of the IFC, if any.

Item 2: Distribution of obligations.

(a) Outline briefly the plan of distribution of the obligations and state the amount of the participation of each principal underwriter, if any.

(b) Describe any arrangements known to the IFC or to any principal underwriter named above designed to stabilize the market for the obligations for the account of the IFC or the principal underwriters as a group and indicate whether any transactions have already been effected to accomplish that purpose.

(c) Describe any arrangements for withholding commissions, or otherwise, to hold each underwriter or dealer responsible for the distribution of his participation.

Item 3: Distribution spread.

The following information shall be given, in substantially the tabular form indicated, as to all primary obligations that are to be offered for cash (estimate, if necessary):

	Price to the public	Selling discounts & commissions	Proceeds to the IFC≤
Per Unit	___	___	___
Total	___	___	___

Item 4: Discounts and commissions to sub-underwriters and dealers.

State briefly the discounts and commissions to be allowed or paid to dealers. If any dealers are to act in the capacity of sub-underwriters and are to be allowed or paid any additional discounts or commissions for acting in such capacity, a general statement to that effect will suffice, without giving the additional amounts to be so paid.

Item 5: Other expenses of the distribution.

Furnish a reasonably itemized statement of all expenses of the IFC in connection with the issuance and distribution of the obligations, except underwriters' or dealers' discounts and commissions that are provided in Items 2, 3 and 4.

Instruction

Insofar as practicable, the itemization shall include transfer agents' fees, cost of printing and engraving, and legal and accounting fees. The information may be given as subject to future contingencies. If the amounts of any items are not known, estimates, designated as such, shall be given.

Item 6: Application of proceeds.

Make a reasonably itemized statement of the purposes, so far as determinable, for which the net proceeds to the IFC from the obligations are to be used, and state the approximate amount to be used for each such purpose.

Item 7: Exhibits to be furnished.

A copy of each of the following documents shall be attached to or otherwise furnished as a part of the report:

(a) Each constituent instrument defining the rights evidenced by the obligations.

(b) An opinion of counsel, written in the English language, as to the legality of the obligations.

Securities and Exchange Commission § 290.101

(c) Each material contract pertaining to the issuance or distribution of the obligations, to which the IFC or any principal underwriter of the obligations is or is to be party, except selling group agreements.

(d) Each prospectus or other sales literature to be provided by the IFC or any of the principal underwriters for general use in connection with the initial distribution of the obligations to the public.

PART 290—GENERAL RULES AND REGULATIONS PURSUANT TO SECTION 9(a) OF THE EUROPEAN BANK FOR RECONSTRUCTION AND DEVELOPMENT ACT

Sec.
290.1 Applicability of this part.
290.2 Periodic reports.
290.3 Reports with respect to proposed distribution of obligations.
290.4 Preparation and filing of reports.
290.101 Schedule A. Information required in reports pursuant to § 290.3.

AUTHORITY: 15 U.S.C. 77s(a); 22 U.S.C. 290l–9.

SOURCE: 56 FR 32082, July 15, 1991, unless otherwise noted.

§ 290.1 Applicability of this part.

This part (Regulation EBRD) prescribes the reports to be filed with the Securities and Exchange Commission by the European Bank for Reconstruction and Development ("EBRD") pursuant to section 9(a) of the European Bank for Reconstruction and Development Act.

§ 290.2 Periodic reports.

(a) Within 45 days after the end of each of its fiscal quarters the EBRD shall file with the Commission the following information:

(1) Two copies of information as to any purchases or sales by the EBRD of its primary obligations during such quarter;

(2) Two copies of the EBRD's regular quarterly financial statement; and

(3) Two copies of any material modifications or amendments during such quarter of any exhibits (other than constituent documents defining the rights of holders of securities of other issuers guaranteed by the EBRD, and loan guaranty agreements to which the EBRD is a party) previously filed with the Commission under any statute.

(b) Each annual report of the EBRD to its Board of Governors shall be filed with the Commission within 10 days after the submission of such report to the Board of Governors.

§ 290.3 Reports with respect to proposed distribution of obligations.

The EBRD shall file with the Commission, on or prior to the date on which it sells any of its primary obligations in connection with a distribution of such obligations in the United States, a report containing the information and documents specified in Schedule A of this part. The term "sell" as used in this section and in Schedule A of this part means a completed sale, or a firm committment to sell to an underwriter.

§ 290.4 Preparation and filing of reports.

(a) Every report required by this regulation shall be filed under cover of a letter of transmittal which shall state the nature of the report and indicate the particular rule and subdivision thereof pursuant to which the report is filed. At least the original of every such letter shall be signed on behalf of the EBRD by a duly authorized officer thereof.

(b) Two copies of every report, including the letter of transmittal, exhibits and other papers and documents comprising a part of the report, shall be filed with the Commission.

(c) The report shall be in the English language. If any exhibit or other paper or document filed with the report is in a foreign language, it shall be accompanied by a translation into the English language.

(d) Reports pursuant to § 290.3 may be filed in the form of a prospectus to the extent that such prospectus contains the information specified in Schedule A of this Part.

§ 290.101 Schedule A. Information required in reports pursuant to § 290.3.

This schedule specifies the information and documents to be furnished in a report pursuant to § 290.3 with respect

§ 290.101

to a proposed distribution of primary obligations of the EBRD. Information not available at the time of filing the report shall be filed as promptly thereafter as possible.

Item 1: Description of obligations.

As to each issue of primary obligations of the EBRD that is to be distributed, furnish the following information:

(a) The title and date of the issue.

(b) The interest rate and interest payment dates.

(c) The maturity date or, if serial, the plan of serial maturities. If the maturity of the obligation may be accelerated, state the circumstances under which it may be so accelerated.

(d) A brief outline of:

(i) Any redemption provisions and

(ii) Any amortization, sinking fund or retirement provisions, stating the annual amount, if any, which the EBRD will be under obligation to apply for the satisfaction of such provisions.

(e) If secured by any lien, the kind and priority thereof, and the nature of the property subject to the lien; if any other indebtedness is secured by an equal or prior lien on the same property, state the nature of such other liens.

(f) If any obligations issued or to be issued by the EBRD will, as to the payment of interest and principal, rank prior to the obligations to be distributed, describe the nature and extent of such priority, to the extent known.

(g) Outline briefly any provisions of the governing instruments under which the terms of the obligations to be distributed may be amended or modified by the holders thereof or otherwise.

(h) Outline briefly any other material provisions of the governing instruments pertaining to the rights of the holders of the obligations to be distributed or pertaining to the duties of the EBRD with respect thereto.

(i) The name and address of the fiscal or paying agent of the EBRD, if any.

Item 2: Distribution of obligations.

(a) Outline briefly the plan of distribution of obligations and state the amount of the participation of each principal underwriter, if any.

(b) Describe any arrangements known to the EBRD or to any principal underwriter named above designed to stabilize the market for the obligations for the account of the EBRD or the principal underwriters as a group and indicate whether any transactions have already been effected to accomplish that purpose.

(c) Describe any arrangements for withholding commissions, or otherwise, to hold each underwriter or dealer responsible for the distribution of his participation.

Item 3: Distribution spread.

The following information shall be given, in substantially the tabular form indicated, as to all primary obligations that are to be offered for cash (estimate, if necessary):

	Price to the public	Selling discounts & commissions	Proceeds to the EBRD≤
Per Unit	___	___	___
Total	___	___	___

Item 4: Discounts and commissions to sub-underwriters and dealers.

State briefly the discounts and commissions to be allowed or paid to dealers. If any dealers are to act in the capacity of sub-underwriters and are to be allowed or paid any additional discounts or commissions for acting in such capacity, a general statement to that effect will suffice, without giving the additional amounts to be so paid.

Item 5: Other expenses of the distribution.

Furnish a reasonably itemized statement of all expenses of the EBRD in connection with the issuance and distribution of the obligations, except underwriters' or dealers' discounts and commissions that are provided in Items 2, 3 and 4.

Instruction

Insofar as practicable, the itemization shall include transfer agents' fees, cost of printing and engraving, and legal and accounting fees. The information may be given as subject future contingencies. If the amounts of any items are not known, estimates, designated as such, shall be given.

Item 6: Application of proceeds.

Make a reasonably itemized statement of the purposes, so far as determinable, for which the net proceeds to the EBRD from the obligations are to be used, and state the approximate

Securities and Exchange Commission

amount to be used for each such purpose.

Item 7: Exhibits to be furnished.

A copy of each of the following documents shall be attached to or otherwise furnished as a part of the report:

(a) Each constituent instrument defining the rights evidenced by the obligations.

(b) An opinion of counsel, written in the English language, as to the legality of the obligations.

(c) Each material contract pertaining to the issuance or distribution of the obligations, to which the EBRD or any principal underwriter of the obligations is or is to be a party, except selling group agreements.

(d) Any prospectus or other sales literature to be provided by the EBRD or any of the principal underwriters for general use in connection with the initial distribution of the obligations to the public.

PART 300—RULES OF THE SECURITIES INVESTOR PROTECTION CORPORATION

ACCOUNTS OF "SEPARATE" CUSTOMERS OF SIPC MEMBERS

Sec.
300.100 General.
300.101 Individual accounts.
300.102 Accounts held by executors, administrators, guardians, etc.
300.103 Accounts held by a corporation, partnership or unincorporated association.
300.104 Trust accounts.
300.105 Joint accounts.

ACCOUNTS INTRODUCED BY OTHER BROKERS OR DEALERS

300.200 General.
300.201 Accounts introduced by same or different broker or dealer.

CLOSEOUT OR COMPLETION OF OPEN CONTRACTUAL COMMITMENTS

300.300 Definitions.
300.301 Contracts to be closed out or completed.
300.302 Mechanics of closeout or completion.
300.303 Report to trustee.
300.304 Retained rights of brokers or dealers.
300.305 Excluded contracts.
300.306 Completion or closeout pursuant to SIPC direction.
300.307 Completion with cash or securities of customer.

§ 300.100

300.400 Satisfaction of customer claims for standardized options.

RULES RELATING TO SATISFACTION OF A "CLAIM FOR CASH" OR A "CLAIM FOR SECURITIES"

300.500 General.
300.501 Claim for cash.
300.502 Claim for securities.
300.503 Voidable securities transactions.

RULES RELATING TO SUPPLEMENTAL REPORT ON SIPC MEMBERSHIP

300.600 Rules relating to supplemental report on SIPC membership.

AUTHORITY: 15 U.S.C. 78ccc.

SOURCE: 44 FR 5077, Jan. 25, 1979, unless otherwise noted.

NOTE: The numbers to the right of the decimal points correspond with the respective rule numbers of the rules of the Securities Investor Protection Corporation (hereinafter referred to as "SIPC").

EXPLANATORY NOTE: Pursuant to section 3(e)(2)(D) of the Securities Investor Protection Act of 1970 (hereinafter referred to as "the Act"), the Securities and Exchange Commission (hereinafter referred to as "the Commission") shall approve a proposed rule change submitted by the Securities Investor Protection Corporation if it finds that such proposed rule change is in the public interest and is consistent with the purposes of the Act, and any proposed rule change so approved shall be given force and effect as if promulgated by the Commission. The rules of this part 300 have been so approved.

ACCOUNTS OF "SEPARATE" CUSTOMERS OF SIPC MEMBERS

§ 300.100 General.

(a) For the purpose of sections 9(a)(2) and 16(12) of the Securities Investor Protection Act (hereinafter referred to as "the Act"), these rules will be applied in determining what accounts held by a person with a member of SIPC (hereinafter called a "member") are to be deemed accounts held in a capacity other than his individual capacity.

(b) Accounts held by a customer in different capacities, as specified by these rules, shall be deemed to be accounts of "separate" customers.

(c) A "person" as used in these rules includes, but is not limited to, an individual, a corporation, a partnership, an association, a joint stock company, a trust, an unincorporated organization,

§ 300.101

or a government or political subdivision thereof.

(d) The burden shall be upon the customer to establish each capacity in which he claims to hold accounts separate from his individual capacity.

§ 300.101 Individual accounts.

(a) Except as otherwise provided in these rules, all accounts held with a member by a person in his own name, and those which under these rules are deemed his individual accounts, shall be combined so as to constitute a single account of a separate customer.

(b) An account held with a member by an agent or nominee for another person as a principal or beneficial owner shall, except as otherwise provided in these rules, be deemed to be an individual account of such principal or beneficial owner.

§ 300.102 Accounts held by executors, administrators, guardians, etc.

(a) Accounts held with a member in the name of a decedent or in the name of his estate or in the name of the executor or administrator of the estate of the decedent shall be combined so as to constitute a single account of a separate customer.

(b) An account held with a member by a guardian, custodian, or conservator for the benefit of a ward or for the benefit of a minor under the Uniform Gifts to Minors Act or in a similar capacity shall be deemed to be held by such guardian, custodian, or conservator in a different capacity from any account or accounts maintained by such person in his individual capacity.

§ 300.103 Accounts held by a corporation, partnership or unincorporated association.

A corporation, partnership or unincorporated association holding an account with a member shall be deemed to be a separate customer distinct from the person or persons owning such corporation or comprising such partnership or unincorporated association if on the filing date it existed for a purpose other than primarily to obtain or increase protection under the Act.

§ 300.104 Trust accounts.

(a) A trust account held with a member shall be deemed a "qualifying trust account" if it is held on behalf of a valid and subsisting express trust created by a written instrument. No account held on behalf of a trust that on the filing date existed primarily to obtain or increase protection under the Act shall be deemed to be a qualifying trust account.

(b) A qualifying trust account held with a member shall be deemed held by a separate customer of the member, distinct from the trustee, the testator or his estate, the settlor, or any beneficiary of the trust.

(c) Any account held with a member on behalf of a trust which does not meet the requirements of paragraph (a) of this rule shall be deemed to be an individual account of the settlor of the trust on behalf of which the account is held.

§ 300.105 Joint accounts.

(a) A joint account shall be deemed to be a "qualifying joint account" if it is owned jointly, whether by the owners thereof as joint tenants with the right of survivorship, as tenants by the entirety or as tenants in common, or by husband and wife as community property, but only if each co-owner possesses authority to act with respect to the entire account.

(b) Subject to paragraph (c) of this rule, each qualifying joint account with a member shall be deemed held by one separate customer of the member.

(c) All qualifying joint accounts with a member owned by the same persons shall be deemed held by the same customer so that the maximum protection afforded to such accounts in the aggregate shall be the protection afforded to one separate customer of the member

(d) A joint account with a member which does not meet the requirements of paragraph (a) of this rule shall be deemed to be an individual or qualifying joint account of the co-owner or co-owners having the exclusive power to act with respect to it.

Securities and Exchange Commission

Accounts Introduced by Other Brokers or Dealers

§ 300.200 General.

A person having one or more accounts cleared by the member on a fully disclosed basis for one or more introducing brokers or dealers is a customer of the member and shall be protected with respect to such account or accounts without regard to the protection available for any other account or accounts he may have with the member.

§ 300.201 Accounts introduced by same or different broker or dealer.

All accounts of a person which are introduced by the same broker or dealer shall be combined and protected as the single account of a separate customer, unless such accounts are maintained in different capacities as specified in §§ 300.100 through 300.105; accounts introduced by different brokers or dealers shall be protected separately.

Closeout or Completion of Open Contractual Commitments

AUTHORITY: Sec. 3, 6(d), Pub. L. 91-598, 84 Stat. 1636 (15 U.S.C. 78ccc, 78fff(d)), as amended by secs. 3, 5, 9, Pub. L. 95-283, 92 Stat. 249.

SOURCE: Sections 300.300 through 300.307 appear at 44 FR 21211, Apr. 9, 1979, unless otherwise noted.

§ 300.300 Definitions.

For the purpose of these rules, adopted pursuant to section 8(e) of the Securities Investor Protection Act of 1970, as amended (hereinafter referred to as "the Act"):

(a) The term *failed to receive* shall mean a contractual commitment of the debtor made in the ordinary course of business to pay to another broker or dealer the contract price in cash upon receipt from such broker or dealer of securities purchased: *Provided*, That the respective obligations of the parties remained outstanding until the close of business on the filing date as defined in section 16(7) of the Act (hereinafter referred to as the "filing date").

(b) The term *failed to deliver* shall mean a contractual commitment of the debtor, made in the ordinary course of business, to deliver securities to another broker or dealer against receipt from such broker or dealer of the contract price in cash: *Provided*, That the respective obligations of the parties remained outstanding until the close of business on the filing date.

(c) The term *open contractual commitment* shall mean a failed to receive or a failed to deliver which had a settlement date prior to the filing date and the respective obligations of the parties remained outstanding on the filing date or had a settlement date which occurs on or within three business days subsequent to the filing date: *Provided, however*, That the term "open contractual commitment" shall not include any contractual commitment for which the security which is the subject of the trade had not been issued by the issuer as of the trade date.

(d) The term *customer* shall mean a person (other than a broker or dealer) in whose behalf a broker or dealer has executed a transaction out of which arose an open contractual commitment with the debtor, but shall not include any person to the extent that such person at the filing date (1) had a claim for property which by contract, agreement of understanding, or by operation of law, was a part of the capital of the broker or dealer who executed such transaction or was subordinated to the claims of creditors of such broker or dealer, or (2) had a relationship with the debtor which is specified in section 9(a)(4) of the Act.

[44 FR 21211, Apr. 9, 1979, as amended at 62 FR 10451, Mar. 7, 1997]

§ 300.301 Contracts to be closed out or completed.

An open contractual commitment shall be closed out or completed if:

(a) The open contractual commitment:

(1) Arises from a transaction in which a customer (as defined in § 300.300) of the other broker or dealer had an interest. For the purposes of this rule a customer is deemed to have an interest in a transaction if (i) the other broker was acting as agent for the customer or (ii) the other dealer was not a market maker in the security involved, to the extent such other dealer held a firm order from the customer and in connection therewith: In

§ 300.302

the case of a buy order, prior to executing such customer's order purchased as principal the same number of shares or purchased shares to accumulate the number of shares necessary to complete the order; or in the case of a sell order, prior to executing such customer's order sold the same number of shares or a portion thereof; and

(2)(i) Had a settlement date on or within 30 calendar days prior to the filing date and the respective obligations of the parties remained outstanding on the filing date or had a settlement date which occurs on or within three business days subsequent to the filing date; and

(ii) Had a trade date on or within three business days prior to such settlement date; and

(b) The other broker or dealer can establish to the satisfaction of the trustee through appropriate documentation that:

(1) In the case of a broker or dealer who maintains his records on a specific identification basis:

(i) The open contractual commitment arose out of a transaction in which his customer had such an interest, and

(ii) In the case of a failed to deliver of the debtor, as of the filing date such broker's or dealer's customer's interest had not been sold to such broker or dealer; or

(2) In the case of a broker or dealer who maintains his records other than on a specific identification basis, he has determined that a customer had such an interest in a manner consistent with that used by such broker or dealer prior to the filing date to allocate fails to receive and fails to deliver in computing the special reserve bank account requirement pursuant to the provisions of Rule 15c3–3 under the Securities Exchange Act of 1934 (17 CFR 240.15c3–3); or

(3) In the case of a broker or dealer not described in paragraph (b)(1) or (2) of this section, he has made the determination in a manner which the trustee finds to be fair and equitable.

[44 FR 21211, Apr. 9, 1979, as amended at 62 FR 10451, Mar. 7, 1997]

§ 300.302 Mechanics of closeout or completion.

(a) The closeout or completion of an open contractual commitment meeting the requirements of § 300.301 shall be effected only:

(1) By the buy-in or sell-out of the commitment by the other broker or dealer in accordance with the usual trade practices initiated by the other broker or dealer within or promptly upon the expiration of a period of 30 calendar days after settlement date; or

(2) At the option of the trustee by the delivery of securities against receipt of the contract price or payment of the contract price against the receipt of the securities at any time within 30 calendar days after settlement date unless the commitment previously has been bought-in or sold-out in accordance with paragraph (a)(1) of this section; or

(3) In the event of the refusal of the other broker or dealer to accept completion of an open contractual commitment in accordance with paragraph (a)(2) of this section, or the failure of the other broker or dealer to promptly buy-in or sell-out a commitment in accordance with paragraph (a)(1) of this section, or in the event of the failure of the other broker or dealer to provide the trustee with appropriate documentation as required by § 300.303, by delivery of securities against receipt of the contract price or payment of the contract price against receipt of securities, or the buy-in or sell-out of the commitment or cancellation of the commitment or otherwise, as may be appropriate, as the trustee in his discretion will most benefit the estate of the debtor.

(b) In the event of a close-out of an open contractual commitment pursuant to paragraph (a)(1) of this section, the money differences resulting from such close-out shall be payable by the other broker or dealer to the trustee or by the trustee to the other broker or dealer, whichever would be entitled to receive such difference under the usual trade practices: *Provided, however,* (1) That prior to the payment of any such money difference by the trustee to such other broker or dealer with respect to transactions executed by such other broker or dealer for any separate customer account, all open contractual commitments with respect to such account which meet the requirements of §300.301 must have been completed by delivery of securities against receipt of the contract price or by payment of the contract price against receipt of the securities in conformity with paragraph (a)(2) of this section, or by buy-in or sell-out in conformity with paragraph (a)(1) of this section, and (2) that the net amount so payable by the trustee to the other broker or dealer shall not exceed $40,000 with respect to any separate customer account.

§300.303 Report to trustee.

Promptly upon the expiration of 30 calendar days after the filing date, or if by the expiration of such 30-day period notice pursuant to section 8(a) of the Act of the commencement of proceedings has not been published, then as soon as practicable after publication of such notice, a broker or dealer who had executed transactions in securities out of which arose open contractual commitments with the debtor shall furnish to the trustee such information with respect to the buy-in, sell-out or other status of open contractual commitments as called for by Forms 300-A, B and C (§§ 301.300a–301.300c of this chapter) including appropriate supporting documentation and schedules.

§300.304 Retained rights of brokers or dealers.

(a) Nothing stated in these rules shall be construed to prejudice the right of a broker or dealer to any claim against the debtor's estate, or the right of the trustee to make any claim against a broker or dealer, with respect to a commitment of the debtor which was outstanding on the filing date, but (1) which is not described in §300.300(c), or (2) which, although described in §300.300(c), does not meet the requirements specified in §300.301 or was not closed out of completed in accordance with §300.302 or was not reported to the trustee in conformity with §300.303 or was not supported by appropriate documentation.

(b) Nothing stated in these rules shall be construed to prejudice the right of a broker or dealer to a claim against the debtor's estate for the amount by which the money difference due the broker or dealer upon a buy-in or sell-out may exceed the amount paid by the trustee to such broker or dealer.

§300.305 Excluded contracts.

Notwithstanding the fact that an open contractual commitment described in §300.300(c) meets the requirements of §300.301 and the other requirements of these rules, a court shall not be precluded from canceling such commitment, awarding damages, or granting such other remedy as it shall deem fair and equitable if, on application of the trustee or SIPC, it determines that such commitment was not entered into in the ordinary course of business or was entered into by the debtor, or the broker or dealer or his customer, for the purposes of creating a commitment in contemplation of a liquidation proceeding under the Act. Such a determination shall be made after notice and opportunity for hearing by the debtor, such broker or dealer, or such customer, and may be made before or after the delivery of securities or payment of the contract price or before or after any buy-in or sell-out of the open contractual commitment, or otherwise.

§300.306 Completion or closeout pursuant to SIPC direction.

In its discretion SIPC may, in order to prevent a substantial detrimental impact upon the finanical condition of one or more brokers or dealers, direct the closeout or completion of an open contractual commitment, irrespective of whether it is described in §300.300(c) or meets the requirements of §300.301 or has been reported in conformity with §300.303 or is supported by appropriate documentation. SIPC shall consult with the Securities and Exchange Commission before SIPC makes any determinations under this section.

§300.307 Completion with cash or securities of customer.

The trustee may, if authorized by the court, complete an open contractual commitment of the debtor, regardless of whether it is described in §300.300(c) or meets the requirements of §300.301 or has been reported to the trustee in conformity with §300.303, to the extent that such commitment is completed

§ 300.400 Satisfaction of customer claims for standardized options.

(a) For the purpose of sections 7(b)(1), 8 (b) and (d), and 16(11) of the Securities Investor Protection Act (hereinafter referred to as "the Act"), this rule will be applied in determining what a customer will receive in either (1) a liquidation proceeding pursuant to the Act or (2) a direct payment procedure pursuant to section 10 of the Act, in satisfaction of a claim based upon Standardized Options positions.

(b) As promptly as practicable after the initiation of a liquidation proceeding or a direct payment procedure under the Act, the trustee in a liquidation proceeding, or SIPC in a direct payment procedure, shall liquidate or cause to be liquidated, by sale or purchase, all Standardized Options positions held for the accounts of customers except to the extent that the trustee, with SIPC's consent, or SIPC as trustee, as the case may be, has arranged or is able promptly to arrange, a transfer of some or all of such positions to another SIPC member.

(c) A trustee in a liquidation proceeding, or SIPC in a direct payment procedure, shall calculate the dollar amount of all Standardized Options positions held for the account of a customer in accordance with section 16(11) of the Act, and credit or debit, as appropriate, the dollar amount so calculated to the account of such customer.

(d) Notwithstanding paragraph (b) of this section, neither the trustee in a liquidation proceeding nor SIPC in a direct payment procedure shall be required under this rule to liquidate any short position in Standardized Options covered by the deposit of (1) the underlying securities, in the case of a call option, or (2) treasury bills, in the case of a put option, by or on behalf of a customer with a bank or other depository. Any such positions that are not liquidated shall be excluded from the calculation provided for in paragraph (c) of this section.

(e) In no event will Standardized Options positions be delivered to or on behalf of customers in satisfaction of claims pursuant to section 7(b)(1) of the Act except to the extent that such positions have been transferred as provided in paragraph (b) of this section.

(f) In no event will Standardized Options be purchased for delivery to customers pursuant to section 8(d) of the Act.

(g) This rule shall not be construed as limiting or restricting in any way the exercise of any right of a broker or registered clearing agency to liquidate or cause the liquidation of Standardized Options Positions.

(h) As used in this rule the term *Standardized Options* means options traded on a national securities exchange, an automated quotation system of a registered securities association, or a foreign securities exchange, and any other option that is a security under section 16(14) of the Act, 15 U.S.C. 78lll(14), and is issued by a securities clearing agency registered under section 17A of the Securities Exchange Act of 1934, 15 U.S.C. 78q–1, or a foreign securities clearing agency.

[48 FR 49840, Oct. 28, 1983, as amended at 79 FR 2781, Jan. 16, 2014]

RULES RELATING TO SATISFACTION OF A "CLAIM FOR CASH" OR A "CLAIM FOR SECURITIES"

SOURCE: Sections 300.500 through 300.503 appear at 53 FR 10369, Mar. 31, 1988, unless otherwise noted.

§ 300.500 General.

These rules will be applied in determining whether a securities transaction gives rise to a "claim for cash" or a "claim for securities" on the filing date of either a liquidation proceeding pursuant to the Securities Investor Protection Act (hereinafter referred to as "the Act") or a direct payment procedure pursuant to section 10 of the Act.

§ 300.501 Claim for cash.

(a) Where a SIPC member ("Debtor") held securities in an account for a customer, the customer has a "claim for

Securities and Exchange Commission

§ 300.600

cash" with respect to any authorized securities sale:

(1) If the Debtor has sent written confirmation to the customer that the securities in question have been sold for or purchased from the customer's account; or

(2) Whether or not such a written confirmation has been sent, if the securities in question have become the subject of a completed or executory contract for sale for or purchase from the account.

(b) Where the Debtor held cash in an account for a customer, the customer has a "claim for cash", notwithstanding the fact that the customer has ordered securities purchased for the account, unless:

(1) The Debtor has sent written confirmation to the customer that the securities in question have been purchased for or sold to the customer's account; or

(2) Whether or not a written confirmation has been sent, if the securities in question have become the subject of a completed or executory contract for purchase for or sale to the account.

§ 300.502 Claim for securities.

(a) Where the Debtor held cash in an account for a customer, the customer has a "claim for securities" with respect to any authorized securities purchase:

(1) If the Debtor has sent written confirmation to the customer that the securities in question have been purchased for or sold to the customer's account; or

(2) Whether or not such a written confirmation has been sent, if the securities in question have become the subject of completed or executory contract for sale for or purchase from the account.

(b) Where the Debtor held securities in an account for a customer, the customer has a "claim for securities", notwithstanding the fact that the customer has ordered the securities sold for the account, unless:

(1) The Debtor has sent written confirmation to the customer that the securities in question have been sold for or purchased from the customer's account; or

(2) Whether or not written confirmation of the purchase has been sent, if the securities in question have become the subject of completed or executory contract for sale for or purchase form the account.

§ 300.503 Voidable securities transactions.

(a) Nothing in these Series 500 Rules shall be construed as limiting the rights of a trustee in a liquidation proceeding under the Act to avoid any securities transaction as fraudulent, preferential, or otherwise voidable under applicable law.

(b) Nothing in these Series 500 Rules shall be construed as limiting the right of the Securities Investor Protection Corporation, in a direct payment procedure under section 10 of the Act, to reject a claim for cash or a claim for securities if such claim arose out of a securities transaction which could have been avoided in a liquidation proceeding under the Act.

RULES RELATING TO SUPPLEMENTAL REPORT ON SIPC MEMBERSHIP

§ 300.600 Rules relating to supplemental report on SIPC membership.

(a)(1) *Who must file the supplemental report.* Except as provided in paragraph (a)(2) of this section, a broker or dealer must file with SIPC, within 60 days after the end of its fiscal year, a supplemental report on the status of its membership in SIPC (commonly referred to as the "Independent Accountants' Report on Applying Agreed-Upon Procedures") if a rule of the Securities and Exchange Commission (SEC) requires the broker or dealer to file audited financial statements annually.

(2) If the broker or dealer is a member of SIPC, the broker or dealer is not required to file the supplemental report for any year in which it reports $500,000 or less in total revenues in its annual audited statement of income filed with the SEC.

(b) *Requirements of the supplemental report.* The supplemental report must cover the SIPC Annual General Assessment Reconciliation Form (Form SIPC-7) or the Certification of Exclusion From Membership Form (Form SIPC-3) for each year for which an SEC

Rule requires audited financial statements to be filed. The supplemental report must include the following:

(1) A copy of the form filed or a schedule of assessment payments showing any overpayments applied and overpayments carried forward, including payment dates, amounts, and name of SIPC collection agent to whom mailed; or

(2) If exclusion from membership was claimed, a statement that the broker or dealer qualified for exclusion from membership under the Securities Investor Protection Act of 1970, as amended, and the date the Form SIPC-3 was filed with SIPC; and

(3) An independent public accountant's report. The independent public accountant, who must be independent in accordance with the provisions of 17 CFR 210.2–01, must be engaged to perform the following agreed-upon procedures in accordance with standards of the Public Company Accounting Oversight Board (PCAOB):

(i) Compare assessment payments made in accordance with the General Assessment Payment Form (Form SIPC-6) and applied to the General Assessment calculation on the Form SIPC-7 with respective cash disbursements record entries;

(ii) For all or any portion of a fiscal year, compare amounts reflected in the audited financial statements required by an SEC rule with amounts reported in the Form SIPC-7;

(iii) Compare adjustments reported in the Form SIPC-7 with supporting schedules and working papers supporting the adjustments;

(iv) Verify the arithmetical accuracy of the calculations reflected in the Form SIPC-7 and in the schedules and working papers supporting any adjustments; and

(v) Compare the amount of any overpayment applied with the Form SIPC-7 on which it was computed; or

(vi) If exclusion from membership is claimed, compare the income or loss reported in the audited financial statements required by an SEC rule with the Form SIPC-3.

[81 FR 14374, Mar. 17, 2016]

PART 301—FORMS, SECURITIES INVESTOR PROTECTION CORPORATION

Sec.
301.0-1 Availability of forms.

FORMS FOR CLOSEOUT OR COMPLETION OF OPEN CONTRACTUAL COMMITMENTS

301.300a Form 300-A, for summary of buy-ins or sell-outs of all open contractual commitments.
301.300b Form 300-B, for report of all fails to deliver.
301.300c Form 300-C, for report of all fails to receive.

AUTHORITY: Sec. 3, 84 Stat. 1636 (15 U.S.C. 78ccc), as amended by sec. 3, Pub. L. 95–283, 92 Stat. 249.

SOURCE: 44 FR 21213, Apr. 9, 1979, unless otherwise noted.

NOTE: Pursuant to section 3(e)(2)(D) of the Securities Investor Protection Act of 1970 (the "Act"), the Securities and Exchange Commission ("Commission") shall approve a proposed rule change submitted by the Securities Investor Protection Corporation ("SIPC") if the Commission finds the rule change is in the public interest and is consistent with the purposes of the Act. Any rule change so approved shall be given force and effect as if promulgated by the Commission. The forms described in this part have been so approved.

§ 301.0-1 Availability of forms.

The forms prescribed for use under the Securities Investor Protection Act of 1970, as amended, (the "Act") and under part 300 of this chapter are identified and described in this part. Copies of these forms may be obtained upon request to, as appropriate, the Securities Investor Protection Corporation ("SIPC") at 900 Seventeenth Street, NW., Washington, DC 20006, or the trustee appointed in a liquidation proceeding under section 5 of the Act.

FORMS FOR CLOSEOUT OR COMPLETION OF OPEN CONTRACTUAL COMMITMENTS

§ 301.300a Form 300-A, for summary of buy-ins or sell-outs of all open contractual commitments.

This form shall be filed as required by § 300.303 of this chapter with the trustee in a proceeding under section 5 of the Act by a broker-dealer who executed transactions out of which arose

Securities and Exchange Commission

open contractual commitments, as defined by §300.300(c) of this chapter, with the debtor in the proceeding. The form shall be used to summarize the buy-ins and sell-outs of those open contractual commitments and shall be accompanied by the forms described in §§ 301.300b and 301.300c.

EDITORIAL NOTE: For FEDERAL REGISTER citations affecting Form 300–A, see the List of CFR Sections Affected, which appears in the Finding Aids section of the printed volume and at *www.govinfo.gov*.

§ 301.300b Form 300–B, for report of all fails to deliver.

This form shall be filed as required by § 300.303 of this chapter with the trustee in a proceeding under section 5 of the Act by a broker-dealer who executed transactions out of which arose open contractual commitments, as defined by § 300.300(c) of this chapter, with the debtor in the proceeding. The form shall be used to report all the fails to deliver, as defined by § 300.300(b) of this chapter, that were open on the filing date, as well as any subsequent closeouts. This form shall accompany the form described in § 300.300a.

EDITORIAL NOTE: For FEDERAL REGISTER citations affecting Form 300–B, see the List of CFR Sections Affected, which appears in the Finding Aids section of the printed volume and at *www.govinfo.gov*.

§ 301.300c Form 300–C, for report of all fails to receive.

This form shall be filed as required by § 300.303 of this chapter with the trustee in a proceeding under section 5 of the Act by a broker-dealer who executed transactions out of which arose open contractual commitments, as defined by § 300.300(c) of this chapter, with the debtor in the proceeding. The form shall be used to report all the fails to receive, as defied by § 300.300(a) of this chapter, that were open on the filing date, as well as any subsequent closeouts. This form shall accompany the form described in § 300.300a.

EDITORIAL NOTE: For FEDERAL REGISTER citations affecting Form 300–C, see the List of CFR Sections Affected, which appears in the Finding Aids section of the printed volume and at *www.govinfo.gov*.

§ 302.100

PART 302—ORDERLY LIQUIDATION OF COVERED BROKERS OR DEALERS

Sec.
302.100 Definitions.
302.101 Appointment of receiver and trustee for covered broker or dealer.
302.102 Notice and application for protective decree for covered broker or dealer.
302.103 Bridge broker or dealer.
302.104 Claims of customers and other creditors of a covered broker or dealer.
302.105 Priorities for unsecured claims against a covered broker or dealer.
302.106 Administrative expenses of SIPC.
302.107 Qualified Financial Contracts.

AUTHORITY: 12 U.S.C. 5385(h).

SOURCE: 85 FR 53668, Oct. 30, 2020, unless otherwise noted.

§ 302.100 Definitions.

For purposes of §§ 302.100 through 302.107, the following terms shall have the following meanings:

(a) *Appointment date.* The term *appointment date* means the date of the appointment of the Corporation as receiver for a covered financial company that is a covered broker or dealer. This date shall constitute the *filing date* as that term is used in SIPA.

(b) *Bridge broker or dealer.* The term *bridge broker or dealer* means a new financial company organized by the Corporation in accordance with 12 U.S.C. 5390(h) for the purpose of resolving a covered broker or dealer.

(c) *Commission.* The term *Commission* means the Securities and Exchange Commission.

(d) *Covered broker or dealer.* The term *covered broker or dealer* means a covered financial company that is a qualified broker or dealer.

(e) *Customer.* The term *customer* of a covered broker or dealer shall have the same meaning as in 15 U.S.C. 78*lll*(2) *provided that* the references therein to *debtor* shall mean the covered broker or dealer.

(f) *Customer name securities.* The term *customer name securities* shall have the same meaning as in 15 U.S.C. 78*lll*(3) *provided that* the references therein to *debtor* shall mean the covered broker or dealer and the references therein to *filing date* shall mean the appointment date.

577

§ 302.101

(g) *Customer property.* The term *customer property* shall have the same meaning as in 15 U.S.C. 78*lll*(4) *provided that* the references therein to *debtor* shall mean the covered broker or dealer.

(h) *Net equity.* The term *net equity* shall have the same meaning as in 15 U.S.C. 78*lll*(11) *provided that* the references therein to *debtor* shall mean the covered broker or dealer and the references therein to *filing date* shall mean the appointment date.

(i) *Qualified broker or dealer.* The term *qualified broker or dealer* means a broker or dealer that (A) is registered with the Commission under Section 15(b) of the Securities Exchange Act of 1934 (15 U.S.C. 78o(b)); and (B) is a member of SIPC.

(j) *SIPA.* The term *SIPA* means the Securities Investor Protection Act of 1970, 15 U.S.C. 78aaa–*lll*.

(k) *SIPC.* The term *SIPC* means the Securities Investor Protection Corporation.

(l) *Corporation.* The term *Corporation* means the Federal Deposit Insurance Corporation.

(m) *Dodd-Frank Act.* The term *Dodd-Frank Act* means the Dodd-Frank Wall Street Reform and Consumer Protection Act, Public Law 111–203, 124 Stat. 1376, enacted July 21, 2010.

§ 302.101 Appointment of receiver and trustee for covered broker or dealer.

Upon the appointment of the Corporation as receiver for a covered broker or dealer, the Corporation shall appoint SIPC to act as trustee for the covered broker or dealer.

§ 302.102 Notice and application for protective decree for covered broker or dealer.

(a) SIPC and the Corporation, upon consultation with the Commission, shall jointly determine the terms of a notice and application for a protective decree that will be filed promptly with the Federal district court for the district within which the principal place of business of the covered broker or dealer is located; *provided that* if a case or proceeding under SIPA with respect to such covered broker or dealer is then pending, then such notice and application for a protective decree will be filed promptly with the Federal district court in which such case or proceeding under SIPA is pending. If such notice and application for a protective decree is filed on a date other than the appointment date, such filing shall be deemed to have occurred on the appointment date for the purposes of §§ 302.100 through 302.107.

(b) A notice and application for a protective decree may, among other things, provide for notice—

(1) Of the appointment of the Corporation as receiver and the appointment of SIPC as trustee for the covered broker or dealer; and

(2) That the provisions of Title II of the Dodd-Frank Act and any regulations promulgated thereunder may apply, including without limitation the following:

(i) Any existing case or proceeding with respect to a covered broker or dealer under the Bankruptcy Code or SIPA shall be dismissed effective as of the appointment date and no such case or proceeding may be commenced with respect to a covered broker or dealer at any time while the Corporation is receiver for such covered broker or dealer;

(ii) The revesting of assets in a covered broker or dealer to the extent that they have vested in any entity other than the covered broker or dealer as a result of any case or proceeding commenced with respect to the covered broker or dealer under the Bankruptcy Code, SIPA, or any similar provision of State liquidation or insolvency law applicable to the covered broker or dealer; *provided that* any such revesting shall not apply to assets held by the covered broker or dealer, including customer property, transferred prior to the appointment date pursuant to an order entered by the bankruptcy court presiding over the case or proceeding with respect to the covered broker or dealer;

(iii) The request of the Corporation as receiver for a stay in any judicial action or proceeding (other than actions dismissed in accordance with paragraph (b)(i) of this section) in which the covered broker or dealer is or becomes a party for a period of up to 90 days from the appointment date;

Securities and Exchange Commission § 302.103

(iv) Except as provided in paragraph (b)(v) of this section with respect to qualified financial contracts, no person may exercise any right or power to terminate, accelerate or declare a default under any contract to which the covered broker or dealer is a party (and no provision in any such contract providing for such default, termination or acceleration shall be enforceable), or to obtain possession of or exercise control over any property of the covered broker or dealer or affect any contractual rights of the covered broker or dealer without the consent of the Corporation as receiver of the covered broker or dealer upon consultation with SIPC during the 90-day period beginning from the appointment date; and

(v) The exercise of rights and the performance of obligations by parties to qualified financial contracts with the covered broker or dealer may be affected, stayed, or delayed pursuant to the provisions of Title II of the Dodd-Frank Act (including 12 U.S.C. 5390(c)) and the regulations promulgated thereunder.

§ 302.103 Bridge broker or dealer.

(a) The Corporation, as receiver for one or more covered brokers or dealers or in anticipation of being appointed receiver for one or more covered broker or dealers, may organize one or more bridge brokers or dealers with respect to a covered broker or dealer.

(b) If the Corporation establishes one or more bridge brokers or dealers with respect to a covered broker or dealer, then, subject to paragraph (d) of this section, the Corporation as receiver for such covered broker or dealer shall transfer all customer accounts and all associated customer name securities and customer property to such bridge brokers or dealers unless the Corporation determines, after consultation with the Commission and SIPC, that:

(1) The customer accounts, customer name securities, and customer property are likely to be promptly transferred to one or more qualified brokers or dealers such that the use of a bridge broker or dealer would not facilitate such transfer to one or more qualified brokers or dealers; or

(2) The transfer of such customer accounts to a bridge broker or dealer would materially interfere with the ability of the Corporation to avoid or mitigate serious adverse effects on financial stability or economic conditions in the United States.

(c) The Corporation, as receiver for such covered broker or dealer, also may transfer any other assets and liabilities of the covered broker or dealer (including non-customer accounts and any associated property and any assets and liabilities associated with any trust or custody business) to such bridge brokers or dealers as the Corporation may, in its discretion, determine to be appropriate in accordance with, and subject to the requirements of, 12 U.S.C. 5390(h), including 12 U.S.C. 5390(h)(1) and 5390(h)(5), and any regulations promulgated thereunder.

(d) In connection with customer accounts transferred to the bridge broker or dealer pursuant to paragraph (b) of this section, claims for net equity shall not be transferred but shall remain with the covered broker or dealer. Customer property transferred from the covered broker or dealer, along with advances from SIPC, shall be allocated to customer accounts at the bridge broker or dealer in accordance with § 302.104(a)(3). Such allocations initially may be based upon estimates, and such estimates may be based upon the books and records of the covered broker or dealer or any other information deemed relevant in the discretion of the Corporation, as receiver, in consultation with SIPC, as trustee. Such estimates may be adjusted from time to time as additional information becomes available. With respect to each account transferred to the bridge broker or dealer pursuant to paragraph (b) or (c) of this section, the bridge broker or dealer shall undertake the obligations of a broker or dealer only with respect to property transferred to and held by the bridge broker or dealer, and allocated to the account as provided in § 302.104(a)(3), including any customer property and any advances from SIPC. The bridge broker or dealer shall have no obligations with respect to any customer property or other property that is not transferred from the covered broker or dealer to the

§ 302.104

bridge broker or dealer. The transfer of customer property to such an account shall have no effect on calculation of the amount of the affected accountholder's net equity, but the value, as of the appointment date, of the customer property and advances from SIPC so transferred shall be deemed to satisfy any such claim, in whole or in part.

(e) The transfer of assets or liabilities held by a covered broker or dealer, including customer accounts and all associated customer name securities and customer property, assets and liabilities held by a covered broker or dealer for any non-customer creditor, and assets and liabilities associated with any trust or custody business, to a bridge broker or dealer, shall be effective without any consent, authorization, or approval of any person or entity, including but not limited to, any customer, contract party, governmental authority, or court.

(f) Any succession to or assumption by a bridge broker or dealer of rights, powers, authorities, or privileges of a covered broker or dealer shall be effective without any consent, authorization, or approval of any person or entity, including but not limited to, any customer, contract party, governmental authority, or court, and any such bridge broker or dealer shall upon its organization by the Corporation immediately and by operation of law—

(1) Be established and deemed registered with the Commission under the Securities Exchange Act of 1934;

(2) Be deemed to be a member of SIPC; and

(3) Succeed to any and all registrations and memberships of the covered broker or dealer with or in any self-regulatory organizations.

(g) Except as provided in paragraph (f) of this section, the bridge broker or dealer shall be subject to applicable Federal securities laws and all requirements with respect to being a member of a self-regulatory organization and shall operate in accordance with all such laws and requirements and in accordance with its articles of association; provided, however, that the Commission may, in its discretion, exempt the bridge broker or dealer from any such requirements if the Commission deems such exemption to be necessary or appropriate in the public interest or for the protection of investors.

(h) At the end of the term of existence of a bridge broker or dealer, any proceeds that remain after payment of all administrative expenses of such bridge broker or dealer and all other claims against such bridge broker or dealer shall be distributed to the receiver for the related covered broker or dealer.

§ 302.104 Claims of customers and other creditors of a covered broker or dealer.

(a) *Trustee's role.* (1) SIPC, as trustee for a covered broker or dealer, shall determine customer status, claims for net equity, claims for customer name securities, and whether property of the covered broker or dealer qualifies as customer property. SIPC, as trustee for a covered broker or dealer, shall make claims determinations in accordance with SIPA and with paragraph (a)(3) of this section, but such determinations, and any claims related thereto, shall be governed by the procedures set forth in paragraph (b) of this section.

(2) SIPC shall make advances in accordance with, and subject to the limitations imposed by, 15 U.S.C. 78fff-3. Where appropriate, SIPC shall make such advances by delivering cash or securities to the customer accounts established at the bridge broker or dealer.

(3) Customer property held by a covered broker or dealer shall be allocated as follows:

(i) First, to SIPC in repayment of advances made by SIPC pursuant to 12 U.S.C. 5385(f) and 15 U.S.C. 78fff-3(c)(1), to the extent such advances effected the release of securities which then were apportioned to customer property pursuant to 15 U.S.C. 78fff(d);

(ii) Second, to customers of such covered broker or dealer, or in the case that customer accounts are transferred to a bridge broker or dealer, then to such customer accounts at a bridge broker or dealer, who shall share ratably in such customer property on the basis and to the extent of their respective net equities;

(iii) Third, to SIPC as subrogee for the claims of customers; and

Securities and Exchange Commission

§ 302.104

(iv) Fourth, to SIPC in repayment of advances made by SIPC pursuant to 15 U.S.C. 78fff–3(c)(2).

(4) The determinations and advances made by SIPC as trustee for a covered broker or dealer under §§ 302.100 through 302.107 shall be made in a manner consistent with SIPC's customary practices under SIPA. The allocation of customer property, advances from SIPC, and delivery of customer name securities to each customer or to its customer account at a bridge broker or dealer, in partial or complete satisfaction of such customer's net equity claims as of the close of business on the appointment date, shall be in a manner, including form and timing, and in an amount at least as beneficial to such customer as would have been the case had the covered broker or dealer been liquidated under SIPA. Any claims related to determinations made by SIPC as trustee for a covered broker or dealer shall be governed by the procedures set forth in paragraph (b) of this section.

(b) *Receiver's role.* Any claim shall be determined in accordance with the procedures set forth in 12 U.S.C. 5390(a)(2)– (5) and the regulations promulgated by the Corporation thereunder, provided however, that—

(1) *Notice requirements.* The notice of the appointment of the Corporation as receiver for a covered broker or dealer shall also include notice of the appointment of SIPC as trustee. The Corporation as receiver shall coordinate with SIPC as trustee to post the notice on SIPC's public website in addition to the publication procedures set forth in 12 CFR 380.33.

(2) *Procedures for filing a claim.* The Corporation as receiver shall consult with SIPC, as trustee, regarding a claim form and filing instructions with respect to claims against the Corporation as receiver for a covered broker or dealer, and such information shall be provided on SIPC's public website in addition to the Corporation's public website. Any such claim form shall contain a provision permitting a claimant to claim status as a customer of the broker or dealer, if applicable.

(3) *Claims bar date.* The Corporation as receiver shall establish a claims bar date in accordance with 12 U.S.C. 5390(a)(2)(B)(i) and any regulations promulgated thereunder by which date creditors of a covered broker or dealer, including all customers of the covered broker or dealer, shall present their claims, together with proof. The claims bar date for a covered broker or dealer shall be the date following the expiration of the six-month period beginning on the date a notice to creditors to file their claims is first published in accordance with 12 U.S.C. 5390(a)(2)(B)(i) and any regulations promulgated thereunder. Any claim filed after the claims bar date shall be disallowed, and such disallowance shall be final, as provided by 12 U.S.C. 5390(a)(3)(C)(i) and any regulations promulgated thereunder, except that a claim filed after the claims bar date shall be considered by the receiver as provided by 12 U.S.C. 5390(a)(3)(C)(ii) and any regulations promulgated thereunder. In accordance with section 8(a)(3) of SIPA, 15 U.S.C. 78fff–2(a)(3), any claim for net equity filed more than sixty days after the date the notice to creditors to file claims is first published need not be paid or satisfied in whole or in part out of customer property and, to the extent such claim is paid by funds advanced by SIPC, it shall be satisfied in cash or securities, or both, as SIPC, as trustee, determines is most economical to the receivership estate.

(c) *Decision period.* The Corporation as receiver of a covered broker or dealer shall notify a claimant whether it allows or disallows the claim, or any portion of a claim or any claim of a security, preference, set-off, or priority, within the 180-day period set forth in 12 U.S.C. 5390(a)(3)(A) and any regulations promulgated thereunder (as such 180-day period may be extended by written agreement as provided therein) or within the 90-day period set forth in 12 U.S.C. 5390(a)(5)(B) and any regulations promulgated thereunder, whichever is applicable. In accordance with paragraph (a) of this section, the Corporation, as receiver, shall issue the notice required by this paragraph (c), which shall utilize the determination made by SIPC, as trustee, in a manner consistent with SIPC's customary practices in a liquidation under SIPA, with respect to any claim for net equity or customer name securities. The process

§ 302.105

established herein for the determination, within the 180-day period set forth in 12 U.S.C. 5390(a)(3)(A) and any regulations promulgated thereunder (as such 180-day period may be extended by written agreement as provided therein), of claims by customers of a covered broker or dealer for customer property or customer name securities shall constitute the exclusive process for the determination of such claims, and any procedure for expedited relief established pursuant to 12 U.S.C. 5390(a)(5) and any regulations promulgated thereunder shall be inapplicable to such claims.

(d) *Judicial review.* The claimant may seek a judicial determination of any claim disallowed, in whole or in part, by the Corporation as receiver, including any claim disallowed based upon any determination(s) of SIPC as trustee made pursuant to § 302.104(a), by the appropriate district or territorial court of the United States in accordance with 12 U.S.C. 5390(a)(4) or (5), whichever is applicable, and any regulations promulgated thereunder.

§ 302.105 Priorities for unsecured claims against a covered broker or dealer.

Allowed claims not satisfied pursuant to § 302.103(d), including allowed claims for net equity to the extent not satisfied after final allocation of customer property in accordance with § 302.104(a)(3), shall be paid in accordance with the order of priority set forth in 12 CFR 380.21 subject to the following adjustments:

(a) Administrative expenses of SIPC incurred in performing its responsibilities as trustee for a covered broker or dealer shall be included as administrative expenses of the receiver as defined in 12 CFR 380.22 and shall be paid *pro rata* with such expenses in accordance with 12 CFR 380.21(c).

(b) Amounts paid by the Corporation to customers or SIPC shall be included as amounts owed to the United States as defined in 12 CFR 380.23 and shall be paid *pro rata* with such amounts in accordance with 12 CFR 380.21(c).

(c) Amounts advanced by SIPC for the purpose of satisfying customer claims for net equity shall be paid following the payment of all amounts owed to the United States pursuant to 12 CFR 380.21(a)(3) but prior to the payment of any other class or priority of claims described in 12 CFR 380.21(a)(4) through (11).

§ 302.106 Administrative expenses of SIPC.

(a) In carrying out its responsibilities, SIPC, as trustee for a covered broker or dealer, may utilize the services of third parties, including private attorneys, accountants, consultants, advisors, outside experts, and other third party professionals. SIPC shall have an allowed claim for administrative expenses for any amounts paid by SIPC for such services to the extent that such services are available in the private sector, and utilization of such services is practicable, efficient, and cost effective. The term *administrative expenses of SIPC* includes the costs and expenses of such attorneys, accountants, consultants, advisors, outside experts, and other third party professionals, and other expenses that would be allowable to a third party trustee under 15 U.S.C. 78eee(b)(5)(A), including the costs and expenses of SIPC employees that would be allowable pursuant to 15 U.S.C. 78fff(e).

(b) The term *administrative expenses of SIPC* shall not include advances from SIPC to satisfy customer claims for net equity.

§ 302.107 Qualified Financial Contracts.

The rights and obligations of any party to a qualified financial contract to which a covered broker or dealer is a party shall be governed exclusively by 12 U.S.C. 5390, including the limitations and restrictions contained in 12 U.S.C. 5390(c)(10)(B), and any regulations promulgated thereunder.

PARTS 303–399 [RESERVED]

CHAPTER IV—DEPARTMENT OF THE TREASURY

SUBCHAPTER A—REGULATIONS UNDER SECTION 15C OF THE SECURITIES EXCHANGE ACT OF 1934

Part		Page
400	Rules of general application	585
401	Exemptions	591
402	Financial responsibility	596
403	Protection of customer securities and balances	620
404	Recordkeeping and preservation of records	628
405	Reports and audit	633
420	Large position reporting	638
449	Forms, Section 15C of the Securities Exchange Act of 1934	651

SUBCHAPTER B—REGULATIONS UNDER TITLE II OF THE GOVERNMENT SECURITIES ACT OF 1986

450	Custodial holdings of government securities by depository institutions	653
451–499	[Reserved]	

SUBCHAPTER A—REGULATIONS UNDER SECTION 15C OF THE SECURITIES EXCHANGE ACT OF 1934

PART 400—RULES OF GENERAL APPLICATION

Sec.
400.1 Scope of regulations.
400.2 Office responsible for regulations; filing of requests for exemptions, for interpretations, and of other materials.
400.3 Definitions.
400.4 Information concerning associated persons of financial institutions that are government securities brokers or dealers.
400.5 Amendments to application for registration and to notice of status as a government securities broker or dealer.
400.6 Notice of withdrawal from business as a government securities broker or dealer by a financial institution.

AUTHORITY: 15 U.S.C. 78o-5.

SOURCE: 52 FR 27926, July 24, 1987, unless otherwise noted.

§ 400.1 Scope of regulations.

(a) Title I of the Government Securities Act of 1986 (Pub. L. 99-571, 100 Stat. 3208) amends the Securities Exchange Act of 1934 (48 Stat. 881-905; 15 U.S.C. chapter 2B) ("Act") by adding section 15C, authorizing the Secretary of the Treasury to promulgate regulations concerning the financial responsibility, protection of customer securities and balances, recordkeeping and reporting of brokers and dealers in government securities. Those regulations constitute subchapter A of this chapter. Unless otherwise explicitly provided, all regulations in this subchapter apply to all government securities brokers or dealers, including registered brokers or dealers and financial institutions. Registered brokers or dealers include OTC derivatives dealers.

(b) Section 15C(a)(1)(A) of the Act (15 U.S.C. 78o-5(a)(1)(A)) requires all government securities brokers and government securities dealers, except those who are brokers or dealers registered pursuant to section 15 or section 15B of the Act or financial institutions, to register with the Securities and Exchange Commission ("Commission"). Regulations concerning registration are at § 240.15Ca2-1 et seq. of this title. The Commission is responsible for the interpretation of the definitions of government securities broker and government securities dealer and of the regulations at § 240.15Ca2-1 et seq.

(c) Section 15C(a)(1)(B)(i) of the Act (15 U.S.C. 78o-5(a)(1)(B)(i)) requires all government securities brokers or dealers that are also registered brokers or dealers to notify the Commission of their status as government securities brokers or dealers. Regulations concerning notice are at § 240.15Ca1-1 of this title.

(d) Section 15C(a)(1)(B)(i) of the Act also requires all government securities brokers or dealers that are financial institutions to notify the appropriate regulatory agency, as defined in section 3(a)(34)(G) of the Act (15 U.S.C. 78c(a)(34)(G)), of their status as government securities brokers or dealers. The form of notice, Form G-FIN, is at § 449.1 of this chapter. Forms are available from the appropriate regulatory agency.

(e) Section 104 of the Government Securities Act Amendments of 1993 (Pub. L. 103-202, 107 Stat. 2344) amended Section 15C of the Act (15 U.S.C. 78o-5) by adding a new subsection (f), authorizing the Secretary of the Treasury to adopt rules to require specified persons holding, maintaining or controlling a large position in to-be-issued or recently-issued Treasury securities to report such a position and make and keep records related to such a position. Part 420 of this subchapter contains the rules governing large position reporting.

[52 FR 27926, July 24, 1987, as amended at 61 FR 48348, Sept. 12, 1996; 71 FR 54410, Sept. 15, 2006]

§ 400.2 Office responsible for regulations; filing of requests for exemptions, for interpretations and of other materials.

(a) *Office responsible.* The regulations in this chapter are promulgated by the Assistant Secretary (Domestic Finance) pursuant to a delegation of authority from the Secretary of the

§ 400.2

Treasury. The office responsible for implementing the regulations, including interpretations and action on requests for exemption, classification, or modification, is the Office of the Commissioner, Bureau of the Fiscal Service.

(b)(1) *Exemptions and classifications.* Section 15C(a)(4) of the Act (15 U.S.C. 78o–5(a)(4)) authorizes the Secretary to exempt any government securities broker or dealer or class thereof, conditionally or unconditionally, from the requirements of registration or regulations promulgated under section 15C. In addition, section 15C(b)(3) of the Act (15 U.S.C. 78o–5(b)(3)) provides for classification, by the Secretary, of government securities brokers or dealers and authorizes the whole or partial exemption of classes from rules under section 15C or the application of different standards to different classes.

(2) *Interpretations.* Although the appropriate regulatory agencies, as defined in § 400.3, and the self-regulatory organizations, as defined in section 3(a)(26) of the Act (15 U.S.C. 78c(a)(26)), have enforcement responsibility under section 15C of the Act, Treasury is responsible for interpretation of section 15C(b) of the Act (15 U.S.C. 78o–5(b)) and related sections and for interpretation and amendment of the regulations under this chapter (with the exception of Forms G-FIN and G-FINW, §§ 449.1 and 449.2 of this chapter, which are the responsibility of the Board of Governors of the Federal Reserve System ["Board"]).

(c) *Requests for interpretations, exemptions, classifications.* (1) Interpretations under this chapter may be provided, at the discretion of the Department, to firms or individuals actually or potentially affected by the Act or regulations, or to their representatives.

(2) Exemptions and classifications under sections 15C (a), (b) and (d) of the Act (15 U.S.C. 78o–5 (a), (b), and (d)) and related sections and Treasury regulations thereunder may be provided at the discretion of the Department and after consultation with the SEC and the Board, to firms or individuals actually or potentially affected by the Act or regulations, or to their representatives.

(3) All requests for exemptions and classifications, and all requests for binding interpretations, shall be in writing, and shall conform to the following procedures.

(i) The names of the company or companies and all other persons involved shall be stated. Letters pertaining to unnamed companies or persons or hypothetical situations will not be answered.

(ii) The letter must contain a concise but complete statement of all material facts, a complete and accurate description of the entire transaction if the request is transactional (even though a request may apply to only a portion of a transaction), and a concise and unambiguous statement of the request, including precise statutory and regulatory citations.

(iii) The letter shall indicate why the writer believes a problem exists or interpretation is needed, the writer's opinion on the matter, and the basis for such opinion.

(iv) In addition to requests for confidential treatment under paragraph (c)(7)(ii) of this section, a person may request confidential treatment of information that is submitted as part of, or in support of, a request for interpretation, exemption, or classification. A separate request for confidential treatment and the basis for such request shall be submitted at the time the information for which confidential treatment is requested is submitted. The request for confidential treatment must specifically identify the information for which such confidential treatment is requested. To the extent practicable, the information should be segregated from information for which confidential treatment is not requested and should be clearly marked as confidential.

(v) Information designated as confidential in accordance with paragraph (c)(3)(iv) of this section shall not be disclosed to a person requesting such information other than in accordance with the procedures outlined in the Department's regulations published at 31 CFR 1.6.

(vi) An original and two copies of each request letter shall be submitted to the Office of the Commissioner, Government Securities Regulations Staff, Bureau of the Fiscal Service, 5th Floor, 401 14th Street SW., Washington, DC

20227. The envelope shall be marked "Government Securities Act Request." The letter shall indicate in the upper right hand corner of the first page the particular sections of the Act and of the regulations at issue.

(4) A written response by the Department to a request filed as stated in paragraph (c)(3) of this section shall be binding, with respect to the requester, on the Department, but shall cease to be binding if the facts are not as stated in the request or, prospectively, if the Department issues a superseding interpretation. In responding to such a request, the Department will, where appropriate, consult with and may obtain the formal concurrence of the appropriate regulatory agencies or their staffs. The Department understands that even if formal concurrence is not received the appropriate regulatory agencies and self-regulatory organizations will give appropriate deference to binding interpretations of the Department. The Department also expects the SEC staff to reflect such interpretations in responding, pursuant to the established procedures of the Commission, to no-action requests concerning rules the SEC enforces.

(5) The Department may decline to issue an interpretation for any reason and, in particular, may require that a requester make inquiry of its appropriate regulatory agency, the Commission or designated examining authority before the Department responds to a request.

(6) The Department will also provide informal oral and written advice, but such advice is not binding on the Department or on any other agency or organization.

(7)(i) Except as provided in paragraphs (c)(3)(iv) and (c)(7)(ii) of this section, every letter or other written communication requesting the Department to provide interpretive legal advice under the Act or to grant, deny or modify an exemption, classification or modification of the regulations, together with any written response thereto, shall be made available for inspection and copying as soon as practicable after the response has been sent or given to the person requesting it. These documents will be made available at the following location: Treasury Department Library, 1500 Pennsylvania Avenue NW., Annex, Room 1020, Washington, DC 20220.

(ii) Any person submitting a letter or communication may also simultaneously submit a request that the letter or communication and the Department's response be accorded confidential treatment for a specified period of time not to exceed 120 days from the date the response has been made or given to such person. The request shall state the basis upon which the request for confidential treatment has been made. If the Department determines that the request for confidential treatment should be denied, the requester will be given 30 days to withdraw either the request for confidential treatment or the letter or communication requesting an interpretation, classification, or exemption.

(d) *Effect of Commission interpretations.* Interpretations of the Commission and its staff (including no-action positions) and of the designated examining authorities, of any Commission regulation expressly adopted by reference in these regulations shall be of the same effect as if the regulation being interpreted were solely the Commission's regulation. However, in the event the Treasury has issued a formal interpretation on the subject, the Treasury understands that the Commission will give that interpretation appropriate deference, particularly with respect to both subsequent no-action positions and the continued validity of prior no-action positions.

[52 FR 27926, July 24, 1987, as amended at 53 FR 28984, Aug. 1, 1988; 72 FR 54410, Sept. 15, 2006; 79 FR 38454, July 8, 2014]

§ 400.3 Definitions.

Unless otherwise explicitly provided, in this subchapter and for the purposes of these regulations:

Act means the Securities Exchange Act of 1934 (48 Stat. 881, 15 U.S.C. chapter 2B, as amended);

Appropriate regulatory agency has the meaning set out in section 3(a)(34)(G) of the Act (15 U.S.C. 78c(a)(34)(G)), and, with respect to a financial institution for which an appropriate regulatory agency is not explicitly designated, the appropriate regulatory agency is the SEC;

§ 400.3

Associated person means a person other than a person whose functions are solely clerical or ministerial:

(1) Directly engaged in any of the following activities in either a supervisory or non-supervisory capacity:

(i) Underwriting, trading or sales of government securities;

(ii) Financial advisory or consultant services for issuers in connection with the issuance of government securities;

(iii) Research or investment advice, other than general economic information or advice, with respect to government securities in connection with the activities described in paragraphs (c)(1)(i) and (c)(1)(ii) of this section;

(iv) Activities other than those specifically mentioned which involve communication, directly or indirectly, with public investors in government securities in connection with the activities described in paragraphs (c)(1)(i) and (c)(1)(ii) of this section; or

(2) Directly engaged in the following activities in a supervisory capacity:

(i) Processing and clearance activities with respect to government securities;

(ii) Maintenance of records involving any of the activities described in paragraph (c)(1) of this section;

Provided, however,

(3) That in the case of a financial institution,

(i) Persons whose government securities functions: (A) Consist solely of carrying out the financial institution's activities in a fiduciary capacity and (B) are subject to examination by the appropriate regulatory agency for compliance with requirements applicable to activities by the financial institution in a fiduciary capacity, shall not be considered "associated persons";

(ii) Persons whose sole government securities activities are, without exercising any investment discretion and solely at the direction of customers, to receive and/or transmit customer orders to purchase or sell government securities, but who do not give investment advice or receive transaction-based compensation shall not be considered "associated persons"; and

(iii) Directors and senior officers of the financial institution who may from time to time set broad policy guidelines affecting the financial institution as a whole that are not directly related to the conduct of the financial institution's government securities business are not considered to be "directly engaged" in the activities described in this paragraph (c);

Board means the Board of Governors of the Federal Reserve System;

Branch or agency of a foreign bank means a Federal branch or Federal agency of a foreign bank or a State branch or State agency of a foreign bank as such terms are used in the International Banking Act of 1978, Pub. L. 95–369, 92 Stat. 607;

CFTC means the Commodity Futures Trading Commission;

Commission or *SEC* means the Securities and Exchange Commission;

Designated examining authority and *Examining Authority* mean (1) in the case of a registered government securities broker or dealer that belongs to only one self-regulatory organization, such self-regulatory organization, and (2) in the case of a registered government securities broker or dealer that belongs to more than one self-regulatory organization, the self-regulatory organization designated by the Commission pursuant to section 17(d) of the Act (15 U.S.C. 78q(d)) as the entity with responsibility for examining such registered government securities broker or dealer;

Fiduciary capacity includes trustee, executor, administrator, registrar, transfer agent, guardian, assignee, receiver, managing agent, and any other similar capacity involving the sole or shared exercise of discretion by a financial institution having fiduciary powers that is supervised by a Federal or state financial institution regulatory agency;

Financial institution has the meaning set out in section 3(a)(46) of the Act (15 U.S.C. 78c(a)(46)), and such term explicitly does not include a subsidiary or affiliate of an institution described in such section unless such subsidiary or affiliate is itself described in such section;

Government securities broker has the meaning set out in section 3(a)(43) of the Act (15 U.S.C. 78c(a)(43)), and explicitly includes not only registered government securities brokers, but

Department of the Treasury § 400.4

also registered brokers and financial institutions;

Government securities dealer has the meaning set out in section 3(a)(44) of the Act (15 U.S.C. 78c(a)(44)), and explicitly includes not only registered government securities dealers, but also registered dealers and financial institutions;

Government securities has the meaning set out in section 3(a)(42) of the Act (15 U.S.C. 78c(a)(42));

OTC derivatives dealer has the same meaning set out in 17 CFR 240.3b–12.

Registered broker or dealer means a broker or dealer registered pursuant to section 15 or section 15B of the Act (15 U.S.C. 78o, 78o–4)) but does not include a municipal securities dealer that is a bank or a separately identifiable department or division of a bank;

Registered government securities broker or dealer means a government securities broker or dealer registered pursuant to section 15C(a)(1)(A) of the Act (15 U.S.C. 78o–5(a)(1)(A));

Secretary means the Secretary of the Treasury; and

Treasury or *Department* means the Department of the Treasury, including in particular the Bureau of the Fiscal Service.

[52 FR 27926, July 24, 1987, as amended at 55 FR 6604, Feb. 26, 1990; 71 FR 54410, Sept. 15, 2006; 79 FR 38455, July 8, 2014]

§ 400.4 Information concerning associated persons of financial institutions that are government securities brokers or dealers.

(a) Every associated person of a financial institution that is a government securities broker or dealer that is not exempt pursuant to Part 401 of this chapter shall file with such financial institution a completed Form G-FIN-4 (§ 449.4 of this chapter) unless such person has on file with such financial institution a completed and current Form U-4 (promulgated by a self-regulatory organization) or Form MSD-4 (as required for associated persons of bank municipal securities dealers).

(b) To the extent any information furnished by an associated person pursuant to paragraph (a) of this section (including information on a Form U-4 or Form MSD-4) is or becomes materially inaccurate or incomplete, such associated person shall promptly furnish in writing to such financial institution, in a form acceptable to the appropriate regulatory agency for such financial institution, a statement correcting such information.

(c) For the purpose of verifying the information furnished by an associated person pursuant to paragraph (a) of this rule, every government securities broker or dealer that is a financial institution shall make inquiry of all other employers of such associated person during the immediately preceding three years concerning the accuracy and completeness of such information.

(d) Every government securities broker or dealer that is a financial institution not exempt from this section pursuant to Part 401 of this chapter shall:

(1) Promptly obtain and, within 10 days thereafter, file with the appropriate regulatory agency, in a form acceptable to such appropriate regulatory agency, the information required by paragraph (a) of this section (which shall consist of all Forms G-FIN-4 filed and a list of all associated persons who have filed Forms MSD-4 or U-4 with the financial institution since the last such filing, designating whether the associated person is serving in a supervisory or non-supervisory capacity) and by paragraph (b) of this section; and

(2) File with the appropriate regulatory agency within 30 days after the termination of the status of an individual as an associated person a Form G-FIN-5 (§ 449.4 of this chapter), unless—

(i) The financial institution is required to and has filed a Form U-5 or Form MSD-5 with respect to such person; or

(ii) The financial institution notifies the appropriate regulatory agency that the individual will remain in the financial institution's employment and the financial institution will continue to update the information about such individual as provided in paragraph (b) of this section and will file a Form G-FIN-5 within 30 days after the termination of such individual's employment with the financial institution.

(e) Every notice and form filed pursuant to this section shall constitute a

§ 400.5

"report" within the meaning of sections 15, 15C and 32(a) of the Act (15 U.S.C. 78o, 78o–5, 78ff(a)).

(Approved by the Office of Management and Budget under control number 1535–0089)

[52 FR 27926, July 24, 1987, as amended at 60 FR 11026, Mar. 1, 1995]

§ 400.5 Amendments to application for registration and to notice of status as a government securities broker or dealer.

(a)(1) If the information contained in any application for registration as a government securities broker or dealer (other than the statements required by § 240.15Ca2–2 of this title) or in any amendment thereto, becomes inaccurate for any reason, the registered government securities broker or dealer shall file within 30 days thereafter an amendment on Form BD (§ 249.501 of this title) correcting such information, in accordance with the instructions provided therein.

(2) If the information contained in any notice of status as a government securities broker or dealer filed by a registered broker or dealer, or in any amendment thereto, becomes inaccurate for any reason, the registered broker or dealer shall file within 30 days an amendment on Form BD (§ 249.501 of this title) correcting such information, in accordance with the instructions provided therein.

(b) If the information contained in any notice of status as a government securities broker or dealer filed by a financial institution, or any amendment thereto, becomes inaccurate for any reason, the financial institution shall file within 30 days an amendment on Form G-FIN (§ 449.1 of this chapter) correcting such information, in accordance with the instructions provided therein.

(c) Every amendment filed pursuant to this section shall constitute a "report" within the meaning of sections 15, 15C and 32(a) of the Act (15 U.S.C. 78o, 78o–5, 78ff(a)).

(Approved by the Office of Management and Budget under control number 1535–0089)

[52 FR 27926, July 24, 1987, as amended at 60 FR 11026, Mar. 1, 1995]

§ 400.6 Notice of withdrawal from business as a government securities broker or dealer by a financial institution.

(a) Whenever a financial institution that is a government securities broker or dealer that is not exempt from the notice requirements of section 15C(a)(1)(B)(i) of the Act (15 U.S.C. 78o–5(a)(1)(B)(i)) and of § 400.5 pursuant to part 401 of this chapter, ceases to act as a government securities broker or dealer, it shall file with the appropriate regulatory agency notice of such cessation on Form G-FINW (§ 449.2 of this chapter) in accordance with the instructions contained therein.

(b) Except as provided in paragraph (c) of this section, a notice that a financial institution has ceased to act as a government securities broker or dealer shall become effective for all purposes on the 60th day after the filing thereof with the appropriate regulatory agency or within such shorter period of time as the appropriate regulatory agency determines.

(c) If the notice described in paragraph (a) of this section is filed with the appropriate regulatory agency any time after the date of the issuance of a notice or order by the appropriate regulatory agency instituting proceedings pursuant to section 15C(c)(2)(A) of the Act (15 U.S.C. 78o–5(c)(2)(A)) to censure, suspend, limit, or bar from acting as a government securities broker or government securities dealer the entity filing such notice, or if the appropriate regulatory agency has instituted any action against the entity filing such notice pursuant to section 15C(2)(B) of the Act (15 U.S.C. § 78o–5(c)(2)(B)), the notice shall become effective pursuant to paragraph (b) of this section at such time and upon such terms and conditions as the appropriate regulatory agency deems necessary or appropriate in the public interest for the protection of investors.

(d) Every notice filed pursuant to this section shall constitute a "report" within the meaning of sections 15, 15C and 32(a) of the Act (15 U.S.C. 78o, 78o–5, 78ff(a)).

(Approved by the Office of Management and Budget under control number 1535–0089)

[52 FR 27926, July 24, 1987, as amended at 60 FR 18734, Apr. 13, 1995]

PART 401—EXEMPTIONS

Sec.
401.1 Exemption for organizations handling transactions in United States Savings Bonds.
401.2 Exemtion for depository institutions that submit tenders for the account of customers for purchase on original issue of United States Treasury securities.
401.3 Exemption for financial institutions that are engaged in limited government securities brokerage activities.
401.4 Exemption for financial institutions engaged in limited government securities dealer activities.
401.5 Exemption for corporate credit unions transacting limited government securities business with other credit unions.
401.6 Exemption for branches and agencies of foreign banks that deal solely with non-United States citizens resident offshore.
401.7 Exemption for certain foreign government securities brokers or dealers.

AUTHORITY: Sec. 101, Pub. L. 99-571, 100 Stat. 3209 (15 U.S.C. 78o-5(a)(4)).

SOURCE: 52 FR 27930, July 24, 1987, unless otherwise noted.

§ 401.1 Exemption for organizations handling transactions in United States Savings Bonds.

An organization that handles United States Savings Bond transactions, including a qualified issuing or paying agent or an organization that accommodates customers or employees by forwarding requested transactions to qualified issuing or paying agents or the Treasury and whose transactions in government securities are limited to these transactions and such other activities that are exempted by the regulations under this subchapter, shall be exempt from the provisions of section 15C (a), (b) and (d) of the Act (15 U.S.C. 78o-5 (a), (b), (d)) and the regulations of this subchapter. For the purposes of this section, the term "United States Savings Bond" means any savings-type security offered by the Treasury, including all series of United States Savings Bonds, United States Savings Notes and United States Savings Stamps.

§ 401.2 Exemption for depository institutions that submit tenders for the account of customers for purchase on original issue of United States Treasury securities.

(a) Subject to the requirements of paragraph (b) of this section, a depository institution that submits tenders or subscriptions for purchase on original issue of United States Treasury securities for the account of customers on a fully disclosed basis, whose transactions in government securities are limited to such transactions and such other activities as have been exempted by regulation under this subchapter shall be exempt from the provisions of section 15C (a), (b) and (d) of the Act (15 U.S.C. 78o-5 (a), (b), (d)) and the regulations of this subchapter.

(b) A depository institution that relies on the exemption contained in paragraph (a) of this section is required to comply with the regulations of part 450 of this chapter concerning custodial holdings of government securities.

(c) For the purposes of this section, "depository institution" has the meaning stated in clauses (i) through (vi) of section 19(b)(1)(A) of the Federal Reserve Act (12 U.S.C. 461(b)(1)(A)(i)–(vi)) and also includes a foreign bank, an agency or branch of a foreign bank and a commercial lending company owned or controlled by a foreign bank (as such terms are used in the International Banking Act of 1978, Pub. L. 95-369, 92 Stat. 607).

§ 401.3 Exemption for financial institutions that are engaged in limited government securities brokerage activities.

(a)(1) Subject to the requirements of paragraph (b) of this section, a financial institution shall be exempt from the provisions of sections 15C (a), (b), and (d) of the Act (15 U.S.C. 78o-5 (a), (b), (d)) and the regulations of this subchapter, unless it acts as a government securities broker by:

(i) Holding itself out as a government securities broker or interdealer broker; or

(ii) Actively soliciting purchases or sales of government securities on an agency basis;

§ 401.4

(2) Notwithstanding the provisions of paragraph (a)(1) of this section, a financial institution shall not be regarded as acting as a government securities broker within the meaning of this section if it:

(i) Effects fewer than 500 government securities brokerage transactions (other than transactions described in §§ 401.1 or 401.2) per year; or

(ii) Effects all such transactions (other than transactions described in §§ 401.1 or 401.2) pursuant to a contractual or other arrangement with one or more government securities brokers or dealers each of which has registered or filed notice pursuant to section 15C(a)(1) of the Act (15 U.S.C. 78o–5(a)(1)) (each referred to as the "transacting government securities broker or dealer") under which the transacting government securities broker or dealer will offer securities services on or off the premises of the financial institution, provided that:

(A) The transacting government securities broker or dealer is clearly identified to customers as the person performing the securities services;

(B) Financial institution employees perform only clerical and ministerial or order-taking functions in connection with government securities transactions unless such employees are associated persons (as defined in § 400.3 of this chapter) or registered representatives of the transacting government securities broker or dealer;

(C) Financial institution employees do not receive compensation for government securities activities other than clerical or ministerial functions unless such employees are associated persons (as defined in § 400.3 of this chapter) or registered representatives of the transacting government securities broker or dealer; and

(D) Such services are provided on a fully disclosed basis by the transacting government securities broker or dealer, i.e., the transacting government securities broker or dealer receives and maintains all required information concerning each customer, its trading and account.

(b)(1) A financial institution that relies on the exemption contained in paragraph (a) of this section is required to comply with the regulations of part 450 of this chapter concerning custodial holdings of government securities for customers.

(2) A branch or agency of a foreign bank that relies on the exemption contained in paragraph (a) of this section is in addition required to comply with § 403.5(e) of this chapter.

(c) For the purposes of this section "financial institution" includes an insured credit union, as defined in 12 U.S.C. 1752(7).

[52 FR 27930, July 24, 1987, as amended at 71 FR 54411, Sept. 15, 2006]

§ 401.4 Exemption for financial institutions engaged in limited government securities dealer activities.

(a) Subject to the requirements of paragraph (b) of this section, a financial institution shall be exempt from the provisions of sections 15C (a), (b), and (d) of the Act (15 U.S.C. 78o–5 (a), (b), (d)) and the regulations of this subchapter if its government securities dealer activities are limited to one or more of the following activities:

(1) Sales or purchases in a fiduciary capacity;

(2) The sale and subsequent repurchase and the purchase and subsequent resale of government securities pursuant to a repurchase or reverse repurchase agreement; and

(3) Such other activities as have been exempted by regulation under this subchapter.

(b)(1) A financial institution that relies on the exemption contained in paragraph (a) of this section is required to comply with:

(i) The regulations of part 450 of this chapter concerning custodial holdings of government securities for customers; and

(ii) Section 403.5(d) of this chapter concerning certain repurchase transactions with customers.

(2) A branch or agency of a foreign bank that relies on the exemption contained in paragraph (a) of this section is in addition required to comply with § 403.5(e) of this chapter.

(c) For the purposes of this section "financial institution" includes an insured credit union, as defined in 12 U.S.C. 1752(7).

Department of the Treasury

§ 401.5 Exemption for corporate credit unions transacting limited government securities business with other credit unions.

(a)(1) Subject to the requirements of paragraph (b) of this section, a corporate credit union shall be exempt from the provisions of section 15C (a), (b) and (d) of the Act (15 U.S.C. 78o-5 (a), (b), (d)) and the regulations thereunder if its government securities dealer activities are limited to the sale and subsequent repurchase and the purchase and subsequent resale, each pursuant to a repurchase or reverse repurchase agreement, of government securities to other credit unions and such other activities as have been exempted by regulation under this part.

(2) For the purposes of this section, "corporate credit union" means a credit union whose membership consists primarily of other credit unions and that is (i) a Federal credit union as defined in 12 U.S.C. 1752(1), (ii) an insured credit union as defined in 12 U.S.C. 1752(7), or (iii) a member of the National Credit Union Administration Central Liquidity Facility.

(b) A credit union that relies on the exemption contained in paragraph (a) of this section is required to comply with:

(1) The regulations of part 450 of this chapter concerning custodial holdings of government securities; and

(2) Section 403.5(d) concerning certain repurchase transactions with customers.

§ 401.6 Exemption for branches and agencies of foreign banks that deal solely with non-United States citizens resident offshore.

(a) Subject to the requirements of paragraph (b) of this section, a branch or agency of a foreign bank shall be exempt from the provisions of section 15C (a), (b), and (d) of the Act (15 U.S.C. 78o-5 (a), (b), (d)) and the regulations of this subchapter, if all the customers with or on behalf of whom it engages in government securities transactions are limited to foreign governments, agencies of foreign governments and other persons and entities who are not citizens of the United States and who reside or, in the case of a corporation, partnership or other entity, have their principal place of business, outside of the United States.

(b) A branch or agency that relies on the exemption contained in paragraph (a) of this section is required to comply with the regulations of part 450 of this chapter concerning custodial holdings of government securities.

§ 401.7 Exemption for certain foreign government securities brokers or dealers.

A government securities broker or dealer (excluding a branch or agency of a foreign bank) that is a non-U.S. resident shall be exempt from the provisions of sections 15C(a), (b), and (d) of the Act (15 U.S.C. 78o-5(a), (b) and (d)) and the regulations of this subchapter provided it complies with the provisions of 17 CFR 240.15a-6 (SEC Rule 15a-6) as modified in this section.

(a) For purposes of this section, *non-U.S. resident* means any person (including any U.S. person) engaged in business as a government securities broker or dealer entirely outside the U.S. that is not an office or branch of, or a natural person associated with, a registered broker or dealer, a registered government securities broker or dealer or a financial institution that has provided notice pursuant to § 400.1(d) of this chapter.

(b) Within § 240.15a-6 of this title, references to "security" and "securities" shall mean "government securities" as defined in § 400.3 of this chapter.

(c) Section 240.15a-6(a) of this title is modified to read as follows:

"(a) A foreign broker or dealer shall be exempt from the registration or notice requirements of section 15C(a)(1) of the Act to the extent that the foreign broker or dealer:"

(d) Paragraph 240.15a-6(a)(2)(iii) of this title is modified to read as follows:

"(iii) If the foreign broker or dealer has established a relationship with a registered broker or dealer for the purpose of compliance with paragraph (a)(3) of this rule, this relationship is disclosed in all research reports and all transactions with the foreign broker or dealer in securities discussed in the research reports are effected only through that registered broker or dealer, pursuant to the provisions of paragraph (a)(3); and"

§ 401.7

(e) Paragraph 240.15a-6(a)(3)(i)(B) of this title is modified to read as follows:

"(B) Provides its appropriate regulatory agency (upon request or pursuant to agreements reached between any foreign securities authority, including any foreign government as specified in section 3(a)(50) of the Act, and the Commission or the U.S. Government) with any information, documents, or records within the possession, custody, or control of the foreign broker or dealer, any testimony of foreign associated persons, and any assistance in taking the evidence of other persons, wherever located, that the appropriate regulatory agency requests and that relates to transactions under paragraph (a)(3) of this rule, except that if, after the foreign broker or dealer has exercised its best efforts to provide this information, including requesting the appropriate governmental body and, if legally necessary, its customers (with respect to customer information) to permit the foreign broker or dealer to provide this information to its appropriate regulatory agency, the foreign broker or dealer is prohibited from providing this information by applicable foreign law or regulations, then this paragraph (a)(3)(i)(B) shall not apply and the foreign broker or dealer will be subject to paragraph (c) of this rule;"

(f) Paragraphs 240.15a-6(a)(3)(iii)(A) (4), (5) and (6) of this title are modified to read as follows:

"(4) Maintaining required books and records relating to the transactions, including those required by § 404.1 of this title for registered brokers and dealers (excluding registered government securities brokers and dealers and noticed financial institutions), §§ 404.2 and 404.3 of this title for registered government securities brokers or dealers, and § 404.4 of this title for noticed financial institutions;

"(5) Complying with part 402 of this title with respect to the transactions; and

"(6) Receiving, delivering, and safeguarding funds and securities in connection with the transactions on behalf of the U.S. institutional investor or the major U.S. institutional investor in compliance with § 403.1 of this title for registered brokers and dealers (excluding registered government securities brokers and dealers and noticed financial institutions); §§ 403.2, 403.3, 403.4 and 403.6 of this title for registered government securities brokers and dealers, and § 403.5 of this title for noticed financial institutions."

(g) Paragraph 240.15a-6(a)(3)(iii)(C) of this title is modified to read as follows:

"(C) Has obtained from the foreign broker or dealer, with respect to each foreign associated person, the types of information specified in Rule 17a-3(a)(12) under the Act (17 CFR 240.17a-3(a)(12)), provided that the information required by paragraph (a)(12)(d) of that Rule shall include sanctions imposed by foreign securities authorities, exchanges, or associations, including, without limitation, those described in paragraph (a)(3)(ii)(B) of this rule. Notwithstanding the above, a registered broker or dealer that is a noticed financial institution shall comply with the provisions of paragraphs 404.4(a)(3)(i) (B) and (C) of this title, in lieu of Rule 17a-3(a)(12), provided that the information required by paragraphs 404.4(a)(3)(i) (B) and (C) of this title shall include sanctions imposed by foreign securities authorities, exchanges, or associations, including, without limitation, those described in (a)(3)(ii)(B) of this rule;"

(h) Paragraph 240.15a-6(a)(3)(iii)(D) of this title is modified to read as follows:

"(D) Has obtained from the foreign broker or dealer and each foreign associated person written consent to service of process for any civil action brought by or proceeding before its appropriate regulatory agency or a self-regulatory organization (as defined in section 3(a)(26) of the Act), providing that process may be served on them by service on the registered broker or dealer in the manner set forth on the registered broker's or dealer's current Form BD or other appropriate procedure as specified by the appropriate regulatory agency; and"

(i) Paragraph 240.15a-6(a)(3)(iii)(E) of this title is modified to read as follows:

"(E) Maintains a written record of the information and consents required by paragraphs (a)(3)(iii) (C) and (D) of this rule, and all records in connection with trading activities of the U.S. institutional investor or the major U.S. institutional investor involving the

Department of the Treasury § 401.7

foreign broker or dealer conducted under paragraph (a)(3) of this rule, in an office of the registered broker or dealer located in the United States (with respect to nonresident registered brokers or dealers, pursuant to Rule 17a-7(a) under the Act (17 CFR 240.17a-7(a)), provided that in Rule 17a-7(a) references to broker or dealer shall include government securities brokers or dealers, as those terms are defined in §§ 400.3 of this title), and makes these records available to the appropriate regulatory agency upon request; or"

(j) Paragraph 240.15a-6(a)(4)(i) of this title is modified to read as follows:

"(i) A registered broker or dealer, whether the registered broker or dealer is acting as principal for its own account or as agent for others, or a financial institution acting pursuant to §§ 401.3(a)(2)(ii) or 401.4(a)(1) of this title;"

(k) Paragraph 240.15a-6(b)(2) of this title is modified to read as follows:

"(2) The term *foreign associated person* shall mean any natural person domiciled outside the United States who is an associated person (a person associated with a government securities broker or a government securities dealer as defined in section 3(a)(45) of the Act) of the foreign broker or dealer and who participates in the solicitation of a U.S. institutional investor or a major U.S. institutional investor under paragraph (a)(3) of this rule."

(l) Paragraph 240.15a-6(b)(3) of this title is modified to read as follows:

"(3) The term "foreign broker or dealer" shall mean any non-U.S. resident person (including any U.S. person engaged in business as a broker or dealer entirely outside the United States, except as otherwise permitted by this rule) that is not an office or branch of, or a natural person associated with, a registered broker or dealer, whose securities activities, if conducted in the United States, would be described by the definition of "government securities broker" or "government securities dealer" in sections 3(a)(43) and 3(a)(44) of the Act."

(m) Paragraph 240.15a-6(b)(5) of this title is modified to read as follows:

"(5) Only for the purposes of this rule, the term "registered broker or dealer" shall mean a person that is registered with the Commission under section 15C(a)(2) of the Act or a broker or dealer or a financial institution who has provided notice to its appropriate regulatory agency under section 15C(a)(1)(B)(ii) of the Act."

(n) For the purposes of this section, § 240.15a-6(b) of this title shall include a new paragraph (8) to read as follows:

"(8) The term *registered government securities broker or dealer* has the meaning set out in § 400.3 of this title."

(o) For the purposes of this section, 240.15a-6(b) of this title shall include a new paragraph (9) to read as follows:

"(9) The term *noticed financial institution* means a financial institution as defined at § 400.3 of this title that has provided notice to its appropriate regulatory agency pursuant to § 400.1(d) of this title."

(p) For the purposes of this section, § 240.15a-6(b) of this title shall include a new paragraph (10) to read as follows:

"(10) The term *appropriate regulatory agency* has the meaning set out in § 400.3 of this title."

(q) Section 240.15a-6(c) of this title is modified to read as follows:

"(c) The Secretary of the Treasury, upon receiving notification from an appropriate regulatory agency that the laws or regulations of a foreign country have prohibited a foreign broker or dealer, or a class of foreign brokers or dealers, engaging in activities exempted by paragraph (a)(3) of this rule, from providing, in response to a request from an appropriate regulatory agency, information, documents, or records within its possession, custody, or control, testimony of foreign associated persons, or assistance in taking the evidence of other persons, wherever located, related to activities exempted by paragraph (a)(3) of this rule, may consider to be no longer applicable the exemption provided in paragraph (a)(3) of this rule with respect to the subsequent activities of the foreign broker or dealer or class of foreign brokers or dealers if the Secretary finds that continuation of the exemption is inconsistent with the public interest, the protection of investors and the purposes of the Government Securities Act."

(Approved by the Office of Management and Budget under control number 1535–0089)

[55 FR 27462, July 3, 1990; 55 FR 29293, July 18, 1990, as amended at 60 FR 11026, Mar. 1, 1995; 71 FR 54411, Sept. 15, 2006. Redesignated at 79 FR 38455, July 8, 2014]

PART 402—FINANCIAL RESPONSIBILITY

Sec.
402.1 Application of part to registered brokers and dealers and financial institutions; special rules for futures commission merchants and government securities interdealer brokers; effective date.
402.2 Capital requirements for registered government securities brokers and dealers.
402.2a Appendix A—Calculation of market risk haircut for purposes of §402.2(g)(2).
402.2b [Reserved]
402.2c Appendix C—Consolidated computations of liquid capital and total haircuts for certain subsidiaries and affiliates.
402.2d Appendix D—Modification of §240.15c3–1d of this title, relating to satisfactory subordination agreements, for purposes of §402.2.

AUTHORITY: 15 U.S.C. 78o–5(b)(1)(A), (b)(4), Pub. L. 111–203, 124 Stat. 1376.

SOURCE: 52 FR 27931, July 24, 1987, unless otherwise noted.

§ 402.1 Application of part to registered brokers and dealers and financial institutions; special rules for futures commission merchants and government securities interdealer brokers; effective date.

(a) *Application of part.* This part applies to all government securities brokers and dealers, except as otherwise provided herein.

(b) *Registered brokers or dealers.* This part does not apply to a registered broker or dealer (including an OTC derivatives dealer) that is subject to §240.15c3–1 of this title (SEC Rule 15c3–1).

(c) *Financial institutions.* This part does not apply to a government securities broker or dealer that is a financial institution and that is:

(1) Subject to the rules and regulations of its appropriate regulatory agency concerning capital requirements, or

(2) A branch or agency of a foreign bank subject to regulation, supervision, and examination by state or Federal authorities having regulatory or supervisory authority over commercial bank and trust companies.

(d) *Futures commission merchants.* A futures commission merchant subject to §1.17 of this title that is a government securities broker or dealer but is not a registered broker or dealer shall not be subject to the limitations of §402.2 but rather to the capital requirement of §1.17 or §240.15c3–1, except paragraph (e)(3) thereof, of this title, whichever is greater.

(e) *Government securities interdealer broker.* (1) A government securities interdealer broker, as defined in paragraph (e)(2) of this section, may, with the prior written consent of the Secretary, elect not to be subject to the limitations of §402.2 but rather to be subject to the requirements of §240.15c3–1 of this title (SEC Rule 15c3–1), except paragraphs (c)(2)(ix) and (e)(3) thereof, and paragraphs (e)(3) through (8) of this section by filing such election in writing with its designated examining authority. A government securities interdealer broker may not revoke such election without the written consent of its designated examining authority.

(2)(i) *Government securities interdealer broker* means an entity engaged exclusively in business as a broker that effects, on an initially fully disclosed or identified group basis, transactions in government securities for counterparties that are government securities brokers or dealers who have registered or given notice pursuant to section 15C(a)(1) of the Act (15 U.S.C. 78o–5(a)(1)), and that promptly transmits all funds and delivers all securities received in connection with its activities as a government securities interdealer broker and does not otherwise hold funds or securities for or owe money or securities to its counterparties and, except as provided in paragraph (e)(2)(ii) of this section, does not have or maintain any government securities in its proprietary or other accounts. For the purpose of this paragraph (e)(2)(i), "identified group basis" means that a counterparty has consented to the

Department of the Treasury § 402.1

identity of the specific group of entities from which the other counterparty is chosen.

(ii) A government securities interdealer broker may have or maintain government securities in its proprietary or other accounts only as a result of:

(A) Engaging in overnight reverse repurchase or securities borrowed transactions solely for the purpose of facilitating the process of clearing government securities transactions;

(B) Engaging in overnight repurchase or securities loaned transactions solely for the purpose of reducing its financing expense in connection with the clearance of government securities transactions;

(C) Subordinated loans subject to satisfactory subordination agreements pursuant to § 240.15c3–1(d) of this title;

(D) Collateral or depository requirements of a clearing corporation or association with which it participates in the clearance of government securities transactions; or

(E) The investment of its excess cash.

The maturities of any government securities held or maintained under paragraph (e)(2)(ii) (C), (D), or (E) of this section may not exceed one year.

(3) In order to qualify to operate under this paragraph (e), a government securities interdealer broker shall at all times have and maintain net capital, as defined in § 240.15c3–1(c)(2) of this title with the modifications of this paragraph (e), of not less than $1,000,000.

(4) For purposes of this paragraph (e), a government securities interdealer broker need not deduct loans to commercial banks for one business day of immediately available funds (commonly referred to as "sales of federal funds") held by the government securities interdealer broker in connection with the clearance of securities on the day the loan is made.

(5) For purposes of this paragraph (e), a government securities interdealer broker need not deduct net pair-off receivables and money differences until the close of business of the third business day following the day the funds are due and give-up receivables outstanding no more than 30 days from the billing date, which shall be no later than the last day of the month in which they arise, as otherwise would be required under § 240.15c3–1(c)(2)(iv)(B) of this title.

(6) For purposes of this paragraph (e), a government securities interdealer broker shall deduct from net worth ¼ of 1 percent of the contract value of each government securities failed-to-deliver contract which is outstanding 5 business days or longer. Such deduction shall be increased by any excess of the contract price of the failed-to-deliver contract over the market value of the underlying security.

(7) For purposes of this paragraph (e), a government securities interdealer broker may exclude from its aggregate indebtedness computation indebtedness adequately collateralized by government securities outstanding for not more than one business day and offset by government securities failed to deliver of the same issue and quantity. In no event may a government securities interdealer broker exclude any overnight bank loan attributable to the same government securities failed-to-deliver contract for more than one business day. A government securities interdealer broker need not deduct from net worth the amount by which the market value of securities failed to receive outstanding longer than thirty (30) calendar days exceeds the contract value of those failed to receive as required by § 240.15c3–1(c)(2)(iv)(E) of this title.

(8)(i) For purposes of this paragraph (e), a government securities interdealer broker shall deduct from net worth 5 percent of its net exposure to each counterparty.

(ii) *Net exposure.* For purposes of this paragraph (e), net exposure shall equal:

(A) The sum of the dollar amount of funds, debt instruments, other securities, and other inventory at risk, in the first instance, to the government securities interdealer broker in the event of the counterparty's default,

(B) Reduced, but not to less than zero, by the sum of:

(*1*) The dollar amount of funds, debt instruments, other securities, and other inventory at risk, in the first instance, to the counterparty in the event of the government securities interdealer broker's default;

597

§ 402.2

(2) The deductions taken from net worth for unsecured receivables, repurchase and reverse repurchase deficits, aged fails to deliver, and aged fails to receive arising from transactions with the counterparty;

(3) Demand deposits in the case where the counterparty is a commercial bank;

(4) Loans for one business day of immediately available funds (commonly referred to as "sales of federal funds") held by the government securities interdealer broker in connection with the clearance of securities on the day the loan is made in the case where the counterparty is a commercial bank;

(5) Custodial holdings of securities in the case where the counterparty is a clearing bank or clearing broker of the government securities interdealer broker; and

(6) Exposure to a counterparty due to holding marketable instruments subject to market risk haircuts under appendix A to this section (§ 402.2a) for which the counterparty is the obligor.

(9) On the application of the government securities interdealer broker, the designated examining authority may extend the periods of time in this paragraph (e) if it determines that the extension is warranted because of exceptional circumstances and that the government securities interdealer broker is acting in good faith.

(f) This part shall be effective July 25, 1987.

[52 FR 27931, July 24, 1987, as amended at 60 FR 11024, Mar. 1, 1995; 71 FR 54411, Sept. 15, 2006; 79 FR 38455, July 8, 2014]

§ 402.2 Capital requirements for registered government securities brokers and dealers.

(a) *General rule.* No government securities broker or dealer shall permit its liquid capital to be below an amount equal to 120 percent of total haircuts as defined in paragraph (g) of this section.

(b)(1) *Minimum liquid capital for brokers or dealers that carry customer accounts.* Notwithstanding the provisions of paragraph (a) of this section, a government securities broker or dealer that carries customer or broker or dealer accounts and receives or holds funds or securities for those persons within the meaning of § 240.15c3-1(a)(2)(i) of this title, shall have and maintain liquid capital in an amount not less than $250,000, after deducting total haircuts as defined in paragraph (g) of this section.

(2) *Minimum liquid capital for brokers or dealers that carry customer accounts, but do not generally hold customer funds or securities.* Notwithstanding the provisions of paragraphs (a) and (b)(1) of this section, a government securities broker or dealer that carries customer or broker or dealer accounts and is exempt from the provisions of § 240.15c3-3 of this title, as made applicable to government securities brokers and dealers by § 403.4 of this part, pursuant to paragraph (k)(2)(i) thereof (17 CFR 240.15c3-3(k)(2)(i)), shall have and maintain liquid capital in an amount not less than $100,000, after deducting total haircuts as defined in paragraph (g) of this section.

(c)(1) *Minimum liquid capital for introducing brokers that receive securities.* Notwithstanding the provisions of paragraphs (a) and (b) of this section, a government securities broker or dealer that introduces on a fully disclosed basis transactions and accounts of customers to another registered or noticed government securities broker or dealer but does not receive, directly or indirectly, funds from or for, or owe funds to, customers, and does not carry the accounts of, or for, customers shall have and maintain liquid capital in an amount not less than $50,000, after deducting total haircuts as defined in paragraph (g) of this section. A government securities broker or dealer operating pursuant to this paragraph (c)(1) may receive, but shall not hold customer or other broker or dealer securities.

(2) *Minimum liquid capital for introducing brokers that do not receive or handle customer funds or securities.* Notwithstanding the provisions of paragraphs (a), (b), and (c)(1) of this section, a government securities broker or dealer that does not receive, directly or indirectly, or hold funds or securities for, or owe funds or securities to, customers, and does not carry accounts of, or for, customers and that effects ten or fewer transactions in securities in

Department of the Treasury § 402.2

any one calendar year for its own investment account shall have and maintain liquid capital in an amount not less than $25,000, after deducting total haircuts as defined in paragraph (g) of this section.

(d) *Liquid capital.* "Liquid capital" means net capital as defined in § 240.15c3–1(c)(2) of this title with the following modifications:

(1) The percentages used to calculate the deductions for failed to deliver contracts required by § 240.15c3–1(c)(2)(ix) of this title when the underlying instrument is a Treasury market risk instrument as defined in paragraph (e) of this section are the appropriate net position haircut factors specified in paragraph (f)(2) of this section;

(2) The percentages used to calculate deductions required by § 240.15c3–1(c)(2)(iv)(B) of this title for securities that are Treasury market risk instruments are the appropriate net position haircut factors specified in paragraph (f)(2) of this section;

(3) The deduction required by § 240.15c3–1(c)(2)(iv)(F)(*3*)(*i*) of this title relating to repurchase agreement deficits shall be determined without reference to § 240.15c3–1(c)(2)(iv)(F)(*3*)(*i*)(*B*) or § 240.15c3–1(c)(2)(iv)(F)(*3*)(*i*)(*C*);

(4) The deductions from net worth required by §§ 240.15c3–1 (c)(2)(vi) and (c)(2)(viii) of this title and the adjustments to net worth set forth in § 240.15c3–1a and § 240.15c3–1b of this title (Appendices A and B to SEC Rule 15c3–1) are omitted;

(5) Net pair-off receivables and money differences need not be deducted as otherwise would be required under § 240.15c3–1(c)(2)(iv)(B) of this title until the close of business of the third business day following the day the funds are due;

(6) Give-up receivables outstanding no more than 30 days from the billing date, which shall be no later than the last day of the month in which they arise, need not be deducted as otherwise would be required under § 240.15c3–1(c)(2)(iv)(B) of this title;

(7) Loans to commercial banks for one business day of immediately available funds (commonly referred to as "sales of federal funds") held by the government securities broker or dealer in connection with the clearance of securities on the day the loan is made need not be deducted; and

(8) In determining net worth, all long and short positions in unlisted options that are Treasury market risk instruments shall be evaluated in the manner set forth in § 240.15c3–1(c)(2)(i)(B)(*1*) and not in the manner set forth in § 240.15c3–1(c)(2)(i)(B)(*2*) of this title.

(e) *Treasury market risk instruments.* (1) For purposes of this part, the term "Treasury market risk instrument" means the following dollar-denominated securities, debt instruments, and derivative instruments:

(i) Government securities, except equity securities and those mortgage-backed securities described in paragraph (e)(2) of this section;

(ii) Zero-coupon receipts or certificates based on marketable Treasury notes or bonds;

(iii) Marketable certificates of deposit of no more than one year to maturity;

(iv) Bankers acceptances;

(v) Commercial paper of no more than one year to maturity and which has only a minimal amount of credit risk as determined by the government securities broker or dealer pursuant to reasonably designed written policies and procedures the government securities broker or dealer establishes, maintains, and enforces to assess and monitor creditworthiness. These policies and procedures should result in creditworthiness assessments that typically are consistent with market data;

(vi) Securities, other than equity securities, issued by international organizations that have a statutory exemption from the registration requirements of the Securities Act of 1933 and the Securities Exchange Act of 1934 provided their changes in yield are closely correlated to the changes in yield of similar Treasury securities, including STRIPS;

(vii) Futures, forwards, and listed options on Treasury market risk instruments described in paragraphs (e)(1)(i)-(vi) of this section or on time deposits whose changes in yield are closely correlated with the Treasury market risk instruments described in paragraph (e)(1)(iii) of this section, settled on a cash or delivery basis;

599

§ 402.2

(viii) Options on those futures contracts described in paragraph (e)(1)(vii) of this section, settled on a cash or delivery basis; and

(ix) Unlisted options on marketable Treasury bills, notes or bonds.

(2) "Treasury market risk instrument" does not include mortgage-backed securities that do not pass through to each security holder on a pro rata basis a distribution based on the monthly payments and prepayments of principal and interest on the underlying pool of mortgage collateral less fees and expenses.

(f)(1) *Haircut categories.* For purposes of this part, the applicable categories within which non-zero-coupon and zero-coupon Treasury market risk instruments are classified are:

Category	Term or type for non-zero-coupon instruments	Term for zero-coupon instruments
A	Less than 45 days.	Less than 45 days.
B	At least 45 days but less than 135 days.	At least 45 days but less than 135 days.
C	At least 135 days but less than 9 months.	At least 135 days but less than 9 months.
D	At least 9 months but less than 1 year, 6 months.	At least 9 months but less than 1 year, 6 months.
E	At least 1 year, 6 months but less than 3 years, 6 months.	At least 1 year, 6 months but less than 3 years.
F	At least 3 years, 6 months but less than 7 years, 6 months.	At least 3 years but less than 5 years, 6 months.
G	At least 7 years, 6 months but less than 15 years.	At least 5 years, 6 months but less than 9 years.
H	15 years and over.	At least 9 years but less than 12 years.
I		At least 12 years but less than 21 years.
J		21 years and over.
MB	All fixed rate mortgage-backed securities that are Treasury market risk instruments.	
AR	All adjustable rate mortgage-backed securities that are Treasury market risk instruments.	

(2) *Haircut factors.* For purposes of this part, the applicable net position and offset haircut factors to be used in the calculation of the Treasury market risk haircut are as follows:

Category	Net position haircuts (percent)	Offsets (percent)
A	None	None
B	0.12	0.02
C	0.20	0.03
D	0.45	0.07
E	1.10	0.22
F	2.20	0.44
G	3.30	0.50
H	4.50	0.90
I	7.75	1.55
J	11.25	3.38
MB	3.30	0.66
AR	1.10	0.22

(3) *Category pair hedging disallowance haircut factors.* For purposes of this part, the applicable category pair hedging disallowance haircut factors to be used in the calculation of the Treasury market risk haircut are as follows:

Category	Percent disallowed					
	C	E	F	G	H	I	J	MB
B	30	40						
C		20	30					

Category	Percent disallowed							
	C	D	E	F	G	H	I	J	MB
D			20	30	40				
E				20	30	40			
F					20	30	40		30
G						20	30		30
H							20	40	40
I								40	

(g) *Total haircuts.* "Total haircuts" equals the sum of the credit risk haircut and the market risk haircut.

(1) *Credit risk haircut.* The "credit risk haircut" equals the sum of the total counterparty exposure haircut, the total concentration of credit haircut and the credit volatility haircut.

(i) *Net credit exposure.* For purposes of this part, net credit exposure shall equal:

(A) The sum of the dollar amount of funds, debt instruments, other securities, and other inventory at risk to the government securities broker or dealer in the event of the counterparty's default and the market value of purchased unlisted options written by the counterparty that are Treasury market risk instruments,

(B) Reduced, but not to less than zero, by the sum of:

Department of the Treasury § 402.2

(*1*) The dollar amount of funds, debt instruments, other securities, and other inventory at risk to the counterparty in the event of the government securities broker's or dealer's default and the market value of unlisted options written by the government securities broker or dealer and held by the counterparty that are Treasury market risk instruments;

(*2*) The deductions taken from net worth for unsecured receivables, repurchase and reverse repurchase agreement deficits, aged fails to deliver, and aged fails to receive arising from transactions with the counterparty;

(*3*) Demand deposits in the case where the counterparty is a commercial bank;

(*4*) Loans for one business day of immediately available funds (commonly referred to as "sales of federal funds") held by the government securities broker or dealer in connection with the clearance of securities on the day the loan is made in the case where the counterparty is a commercial bank;

(*5*) Custodial holdings of securities in the case where the counterparty is a clearing bank or clearing broker of the government securities broker or dealer; and

(*6*) Exposure to a counterparty due to holding marketable instruments subject to market risk haircuts under appendix A to this section (§ 402.2a) for which the counterparty is the obligor.

(ii) *Total counterparty exposure haircut.* The "total counterparty exposure haircut" equals the sum of the counterparty exposure haircuts taken for all counterparties except a Federal Reserve Bank, of the government securities broker or dealer. The "counterparty exposure haircut" equals the product of a counterparty exposure haircut factor of 5 percent and the net credit exposure to a single counterparty not in excess of 15 percent of the government securities broker's or dealer's liquid capital.

(iii) *Total concentration of credit haircut.* The "total concentration of credit haircut" equals the sum of the concentration of credit haircuts taken for all counterparties of the government securities broker or dealer. The "concentration of credit haircut" equals the product of a concentration of credit haircut factor of 25 percent and the amount by which the net credit exposure to a single counterparty is in excess of 15 percent of the government securities broker's or dealer's liquid capital.

(iv) *Credit volatility haircut.* The "credit volatility haircut" equals the product of a credit volatility haircut factor of 0.15 percent and the dollar amount of the larger of the gross long position or gross short position in those Treasury market risk instruments described in paragraphs (e)(1)(iii), (iv) and (v) of this section that have a term to maturity greater than 44 days, including futures and forwards thereon, settled on a cash or delivery basis, and futures and forwards on time deposits described in paragraph (e)(1)(vii) of this section, that have a term to maturity greater than 44 days, settled on a cash or delivery basis.

(2) *Market risk haircut.* The "market risk haircut" equals the sum of the Treasury market risk haircut and the other securities haircut, calculated in accordance with the provisions of appendix A of this section, § 402.2a.

(h) *Debt-equity requirements.* No government securities broker or dealer shall permit the total of outstanding principal amounts of its satisfactory subordination agreements as defined in § 240.15c3–1d of this title (appendix D to SEC Rule 15c3–1) modified as provided in appendix D to this section, § 402.2d, to exceed the allowable levels set forth in § 240.15c3–1(d) of this title.

(i) *Provisions relating to the withdrawal of equity capital*—(1) *Notice provisions.* No equity capital of the government securities broker or dealer or a subsidiary or affiliate consolidated pursuant to appendix C to this section, § 402.2c, may be withdrawn by action of a stockholder or partner, or by redemption or repurchase of shares of stock by any of the consolidated entities or through the payment of dividends or any similar distribution, nor may any unsecured advance or loan be made to a stockholder, partner, sole proprietor, employee or affiliate without providing written notice, given in accordance with paragraph (i)(1)(iv) of this section, when specified in paragraphs (i)(1) (i) and (ii) of this section:

§ 402.2

(i) Two business days prior to any withdrawals, advances or loans if those withdrawals, advances or loans on a net basis exceed in the aggregate in any 30 calendar day period, 30 percent of the government securities broker's or dealer's excess liquid capital. A government securities broker or dealer, in an emergency situation, may make withdrawals, advances or loans that on a net basis exceed 30 percent of the government securities broker's or dealer's excess liquid capital in any 30 calendar day period without giving the advance notice required by this paragraph, with the prior approval of its designated examining authority. When a government securities broker or dealer makes a withdrawal with the consent of its designated examining authority, it shall in any event comply with paragraph (i)(1)(ii) of this section; and

(ii) Two business days after any withdrawals, advances or loans if those withdrawals, advances or loans on a net basis exceed in the aggregate in any 30 calendar day period, 20 percent of the government securities broker's or dealer's excess liquid capital.

(iii) This paragraph (i)(1) of this section does not apply to:

(A) Securities or commodities transactions in the ordinary course of business between a government securities broker or dealer and an affiliate where the government securities broker or dealer makes payment to or on behalf of such affiliate for such transaction and then receives payment from such affiliate for the securities or commodities transaction within two business days from the date of the transaction; or

(B) Withdrawals, advances or loans which in the aggregate in any such 30 calendar day period, on a net basis, equal $500,000 or less.

(iv) Each required notice shall be effective when received by the Commission in Washington, DC, the regional or district office of the Commission for the area in which the government securities broker or dealer has its principal place of business, and the government securities broker's or dealer's designated examining authority.

(2) *Withdrawal limitations.* No equity capital of the government securities broker or dealer or a subsidiary or affiliate consolidated pursuant to appendix C to this section, § 402.2c, may be withdrawn by action of a stockholder or a partner, or by redemption or repurchase of shares of stock by any of the consolidated entities or through the payment of dividends or any similar distribution, nor may any unsecured advance or loan be made to a stockholder, partner, sole proprietor, employee or affiliate if, after giving effect thereto and to any other such withdrawals, advances or loans and any Payments of Payment Obligations (as defined in § 240.15c3–1d of this title, appendix D to SEC Rule 15c3–1, modified as provided in appendix D to this section, § 402.2d) under satisfactory subordination agreements which are scheduled to occur within 180 calendar days following such withdrawal, advance or loan, either:

(i) The ratio of liquid capital to total haircuts, determined as provided in § 402.2, would be less than 150 percent; or

(ii) Liquid capital minus total haircuts would be less than 120 percent of the minimum capital required by § 402.2(b) or § 402.2(c) as applicable; or

(iii) In the case of any government securities broker or dealer included in such consolidation, the total outstanding principal amounts of satisfactory subordination agreements of the government securities broker or dealer (other than such agreements which qualify as equity under § 240.15c3–1(d) of this title) would exceed 70% of the debt-equity total as defined in § 240.15c3–1(d).

(3) *Miscellaneous provisions.* (i) Excess liquid capital is that amount in excess of the amount required by the greater of § 402.2(a) or, §§ 402.2 (b) or (c), as applicable. For the purposes of paragraphs (i)(1) and (i)(2) of this section, a government securities broker or dealer may use the amount of excess liquid capital, liquid capital and total haircuts reported in its most recently required filed Form G–405 for the purposes of calculating the effect of a projected withdrawal, advance or loan relative to excess liquid capital or total haircuts. The government securities broker or dealer must assure itself that the excess liquid capital, liquid capital

Department of the Treasury

§ 402.2a

or the total haircuts reported on the most recently required filed Form G-405 have not materially changed since the time such report was filed.

(ii) The term equity capital includes capital contributions by partners, par or stated value of capital stock, paid-in capital in excess of par, retained earnings or other capital accounts. The term equity capital does not include securities in the securities accounts of partners and balances in limited partners' capital accounts in excess of their stated capital contributions.

(iii) Paragraphs (i)(1) and (i)(2) of this section shall not preclude a government securities broker or dealer from making required tax payments or preclude the payment to partners of reasonable compensation, and such payments shall not be included in the calculation of withdrawals, advances or loans for purposes of paragraphs (i)(1) and (i)(2) of this section.

(iv) For the purposes of this subsection (i), any transaction between a government securities broker or dealer and a stockholder, partner, sole proprietor, employee or affiliate that results in a diminution of the government securities broker's or dealer's liquid capital shall be deemed to be an advance or loan of liquid capital.

(j) *Modification of appendices to § 240.15c3-1 of this title.* For purposes of this section, appendix C to this section (§ 402.2c) is substituted for appendix C to Rule 15c3-1 (§ 240.15c3-1c of this title), and appendix D to Rule 15c3-1 (§ 240.15c3-1d of this title), relating to Satisfactory Subordination Agreements, is modified as provided in appendix D to this section (§ 402.2d).

(Approved by the Office of Management and Budget under control number 1535-0089)

[52 FR 27931, July 24, 1987, as amended at 53 FR 28984, Aug. 1, 1988; 60 FR 11024, Mar. 1, 1995; 79 FR 38455, July 8, 2014]

§ 402.2a Appendix A—Calculation of market risk haircut for purposes of § 402.2(g)(2).

The market risk haircut is the sum of the Treasury market risk haircut and the other securities haircut, calculated as follows.

(a) *Treasury market risk haircut.* The "Treasury market risk haircut" equals the sum of the total governments offset portion haircut, the total futures and options offset haircut, the total hedging disallowance haircut, and the residual net position haircut, calculated with respect to financings and positions in Treasury market risk instruments, except to the extent that a permissible election is made pursuant to paragraph (b)(1) of this section to include qualified positions in the calculation of the other securities haircut.

(1) *Total governments offset portion haircut.* The "total governments offset portion haircut" equals the sum of the governments offset portion haircuts calculated for each category in § 402.2(f)(1). The "governments offset portion haircuts" equal, for each category in § 402.2(f)(1), the product of the offset haircut factor for that category set out in § 402.2(f)(2) and the smaller of the absolute values of the gross long immediate position or gross short immediate position for that category. Schedules B and C in paragraph (c) of this section can be used to make this calculation.

(i)(A) The "gross long immediate position" for purposes of this part equals, for each category except categories MB and AR in § 402.2(f)(1), the sum of the market values of each long immediate position in Treasury market risk instruments with a term to maturity (or, in the case of a floating rate note, the time to the next scheduled interest rate adjustment or the term to maturity, whichever is less) corresponding to such category, the contract values of each reverse repurchase agreement with a term to maturity or time to the next scheduled interest rate adjustment, whichever is less, corresponding to that category, and the values of the cash collateral of each security borrowing with a term to maturity or time to next scheduled interest rate adjustment, whichever is less, corresponding to such category.

(B) In the case of category MB, the "gross long immediate position" equals the sum of the market values of all long immediate positions in fixed rate mortgage-backed securities which are Treasury market risk instruments.

(C) In the case of category AR, the "gross long immediate position" equals the sum of the market values of all long immediate positions in adjustable

§ 402.2a

rate mortgage-backed securities which are Treasury market risk instruments.

(ii)(A) The "gross short immediate position" for purposes of this section equals, for each category except categories MB and AR in § 402.2(f)(1), the sum of the market values of each short immediate position in Treasury market risk instruments with a term to maturity (or, in the case of a floating rate note, the time to the next scheduled interest rate adjustment or the term to maturity, whichever is less) corresponding to such category, and the values of funds received from each financing transaction (including repurchase agreements, securities lending secured by cash collateral, and term financings, but excluding subordinated debt which meets the requirements of § 240.15c3-1d of this title modified as provided in § 402.2d) with a term to maturity or time to the next scheduled interest rate adjustment, whichever is less, corresponding to that category.

(B) In the case of category MB, the "gross short immediate position" equals the sum of the market values of all short immediate positions in fixed rate mortgage-backed securities which are Treasury market risk instruments.

(C) In the case of category AR, the "gross short immediate position" equals the sum of the market values of all short immediate positions in adjustable rate mortgage-backed securities which are Treasury market risk instruments.

(iii) The term *long immediate position* in a Treasury market risk instrument means, for purposes of this part:

(A) The net long position in a Treasury market risk instrument as of the trade date, except when the settlement date, in the case of a Treasury market risk instrument except a mortgage-backed security, is scheduled more than five business days in the future, and, in the case of a mortgage-backed security, more than thirty calendar days in the future;

(B) The net long when-issued position in a marketable U.S. Treasury security between announcement and issue date;

(C) The net long when-issued position in a government agency or a government-sponsored agency debt security between release date and issue date; and

(D) The net long when-issued position in a security described in § 402.2(e)(1)(vi) between announcement date and issue date.

(iv) The term *short immediate position* on a Treasury market risk instrument means, for purposes of this part:

(A) The net short position in a Treasury market risk instrument as of the trade date, except when the settlement date, in the case of a Treasury market risk instrument except a mortgage-backed security, is scheduled more than five business days in the future, and, in the case of a mortgage-backed security, more than thirty calendar days in the future;

(B) The net short when-issued position in a marketable U.S. Treasury security between announcement and issue date;

(C) The net short when-issued position in a government agency or a government-sponsored agency debt security between release date and issue date; and

(D) The net short when-issued position in a security described in § 402.2(e)(1)(vi) between announcement date and issue date.

(2) *Net immediate position interim haircut.* The "net immediate position interim haircut" equals, for each category in § 402.2(f)(1), the product of the net position haircut factor for that category and the sum of the gross long immediate position and the gross short immediate position for that category. For purposes of this part, a gross long immediate position shall be a positive number and a gross short immediate position shall be a negative number. Schedules B and C in paragraph (c) of this section can be used to make this calculation.

(3) *Total futures and options offset haircut.* The "total futures and options offset haircut" equals the sum of the futures and options offset haircuts calculated for each category in § 402.2(f)(1). The "futures and options offset haircut" equals, for each category in § 402.2(f)(1), the product of a futures and options offset factor of 20 percent and the smaller of the absolute values of the positive and negative aggregate interim haircuts for that category.

Department of the Treasury § 402.2a

Schedule D in paragraph (c) of this section can be used to make this calculation.

(i) *Positive aggregate interim haircut.* The "positive aggregate interim haircut" equals, for each category in §402.2(f)(1), the sum of the positive net immediate position interim haircut (see paragraph (a)(2) of this section), the gross long futures and forward interim haircut, and the positive gross options interim haircut for that category. Schedule D in paragraph (c) of this section can be used to make this calculation.

(A) *Gross long futures and forward interim haircut.* The "gross long futures and forward interim haircut" equals, for each category in §402.2(f)(1), the sum of the interim haircuts on each long futures position and long forward position placed, in the case of a futures or forward contract which is a Treasury market risk instrument except those on mortgage-backed securities, in the category corresponding to the sum of the term to maturity of the contract and the term to maturity of the underlying instrument at the time of the maturity of the contract or, in the case of a futures or forward contract on Treasury market risk mortgage-backed securities, in the category corresponding to the type of Treasury market risk mortgage-backed security.

(*1*) For purposes of this part, the *interim haircut on each long futures position and each long forward position* is the product of the net position haircut factor for the category corresponding to, in the case of a futures or forward contract which is a Treasury market risk instrument except those on mortgage-backed securities, the maturity of the underlying instrument at the time of the maturity of the contract or, in the case of a futures or forward contract on Treasury market risk mortgage-backed securities, the type of Treasury market risk mortgage-backed security and the value of the long futures position or long forward position evaluated at the current market price for such contract.

(*2*) For purposes of this part, the gross long futures and forward interim haircut shall be a positive number.

(B) *Positive gross options interim haircut.* The "positive gross options interim haircut" equals, for each category in §402.2(f)(1), the sum of the interim haircuts on each purchased call and sold put placed in the category in which the underlying instrument would be placed.

(*1*) For purposes of this part, the "interim haircut on each purchased call and sold put" equals the lesser of the market value of the option or, (*i*) in the case of an option on a cash instrument, the product of the net position haircut factor for the category to which the underlying cash instrument corresponds and the market value of the underlying cash instrument or, (*ii*) in the case of an option on a futures contract, the interim haircut on the underlying futures contract.

(*2*) For purposes of this part, the positive gross options interim haircut is a positive number.

(ii) *Negative aggregate interim haircut.* The "negative aggregate interim haircut" equals, for each category in §402.2(f)(1), the sum of the negative net immediate position interim haircut (see paragraph (a)(2) of this section), the gross short futures and forward interim haircut, and the negative gross options interim haircut for that category. Schedule D in paragraph (c) of this section can be used to make this calculation.

(A) *Gross short futures and forward interim haircut.* The "gross short futures and forward interim haircut" equals, for each category in §402.2(f)(1), the sum of the interim haircuts on each short futures position and short forward position placed, in the case of a futures or forward contract which is a Treasury market risk instrument except those on mortgage-backed securities, in the category corresponding to the sum of the term to maturity of the contract and the term to maturity of the underlying instrument at the time of the maturity of the contract or, in the case of a futures or forward contract on Treasury market risk mortgage-backed securities, in the category corresponding to the type of Treasury market risk mortgage-backed security.

(*1*) For purposes of this part, the "interim haircut on each short futures position and each short forward position"

§ 402.2a

is the product of the net position haircut factor for the category corresponding to, in the case of a futures or forward contract which is a Treasury market risk instrument except those on mortgage-backed securities, the maturity of the underlying instrument at the time of the maturity of the contract or, in the case of a futures or forward contract on Treasury market risk mortgage-backed securities, the type of Treasury market risk mortgage-backed security and the value of the short futures position or short forward position evaluated at the current market price for such contract.

(2) For purposes of this part, the gross short futures and forward interim haircut is a negative number.

(B) *Negative gross options interim haircut.* The "negative gross options interim haircut" equals, for each category in § 402.2(f)(1), the sum of the interim haircuts on each sold call and purchased put placed in the category in which the underlying instrument would be placed.

(1) For purposes of this part, the "interim haircut on each sold call and purchased put" equals the lesser of the market value of the option or, (i) in the case of an option on a cash instrument, the product of the net position haircut factor for the category to which the underlying cash instrument corresponds and the market value of the underlying cash instrument or, (ii) in the case of an option on a futures contract, the interim haircut on the underlying futures contract.

(2) For purposes of this part, the negative gross options interim haircut is a negative number.

(4) *Total hedging disallowance haircut.* The "total hedging disallowance haircut" equals the sum of the hedging disallowance haircuts calculated pursuant to each netting of qualified netting interim haircuts. The "hedging disallowance haircut" equals the absolute value of the product of the applicable category pair hedging disallowance haircut factor specified in § 402.2(f)(3) and the smaller in absolute value of any two qualified netting interim haircuts, netted in accordance with the provisions of this paragraph. Schedule E in paragraph (c) of this section can be used to make this calculation.

(i) *Qualified netting interim haircut.* The term "qualified netting interim haircut" means a residual position interim haircut or a net residual position interim haircut.

(A) *Residual position interim haircut.* The "residual position interim haircut" equals, for each category in § 402.2(f)(1), the sum of the positive aggregate interim haircut and the negative aggregate interim haircut corresponding to the category, calculated in accordance with the provisions of paragraph (a)(3) of this section.

(B)(*1*) *Net residual position interim haircut.* The "net residual position interim haircut" equals, for any two categories between which netting is permitted, the sum of (i) the residual position interim haircuts calculated for those categories, in the case of the category of the larger in absolute value of the two residual position interim haircuts being netted, and (ii) zero, in the case of the category of the smaller in absolute value of the two residual position interim haircuts being netted.

(2) For the purposes of this paragraph (a)(4), netting is permitted only between categories for which a category pair hedging disallowance haircut factor has been specified in paragraph § 402.2(f)(3).

(ii) Net residual position interim haircuts shall be substituted for the residual position interim haircuts in the respective categories in which they have been placed and shall be considered as if they were residual position interim haircuts. New net residual position interim haircuts may continue to be calculated until for each category pair for which netting is permitted at least one of the two qualified netting interim haircuts is zero or both qualified netting interim haircuts are of the same sign.

(5) *Residual net position haircut.* The "residual net position haircut" equals the sum of the absolute values of all qualified netting interim haircuts remaining in each category after the completion of the calculation of permissible nettings described in paragraph (a)(4) of this section. Schedule E in paragraph (c) of this section can be used to make this calculation.

(b) *Other securities haircut.* The "other securities haircut" equals the sum of

Department of the Treasury

§ 402.2a

all deductions specified in § 240.15c3-1 (c)(2)(vi) and (c)(2)(viii) of this title and §§ 240.15c3-1a and 240.15c3-1b of this title for long and short positions in securities, futures contracts, forward contracts, options, and other inventory which are not Treasury market risk instruments as defined in § 402.2(e).

(1) A registered government securities broker or dealer may elect to exclude from its calculation of the Treasury market risk haircut and include in its calculation of the other securities haircut long and short positions in Treasury market risk instruments if such positions form part of a hedge against long and short positions in securities, futures contracts, forward contracts, or options which are not Treasury market risk instruments. Only the portion of the total position in a Treasury market risk instrument that forms part of such hedge may be excluded from the calculation of the Treasury market risk haircut and included in the calculation of the other securities haircut.

(2) For purposes of this paragraph (b), a gross long or short position in Treasury market risk instruments shall be considered part of a hedge if the inclusion of such position in the calculation of the other securities haircut would serve to reduce said haircut.

(3) For purposes of this paragraph (b) as it relates to § 240.15c3-1(c)(2)(vi)(M) ("undue concentration"), references to "10 percent of the 'net capital'" shall be understood to refer to 10 percent of the liquid capital and references to "Appendix (D) (17 CFR 240.15c3-1d)" shall be understood to refer to such section as modified by § 402.2d.

(c) *Schedules.* This paragraph sets forth schedules which may be used by government securities brokers or dealers in the calculation of total haircuts as required by this part 402. The appropriate regulatory agency or designated examining authority may specify other substantially similar forms required to be used by government securities brokers or dealers in the calculation of such haircuts.

SCHEDULE A—LIQUID CAPITAL REQUIREMENT, SUMMARY COMPUTATION
[In thousands of dollars]

1. Liquid capital[1] .... _____
2. Haircuts on security and financing positions including contractual commitments:
   a. Total governments offset portion haircut (Schedule C) .... _____
   b. Total futures and options offset haircut (Schedule D) .... _____
   c. Total hedging disallowance haircut (Schedule E) .... _____
   d. Residual net position haircut (Schedule E) .... _____
   e. Other securities haircut (use SEC factors) .... _____
3. Haircuts on credit exposure:
   a. Total counterparty exposure haircut .... _____
   b. Total concentration of credit haircut .... _____
   c. Credit volatility haircut .... _____
4. Total haircuts (sum of lines 2 a through e, 3 a, b, and c) .... _____
5. Capital-to-risk ratio (line 1 divided by line 4) .... _____

[1] Identical to the amount reported on line 3640 of the Report on Finances and Operations of Government Securities Brokers and Dealers, Form G-405.

§ 402.2a

17 CFR Ch. IV (4–1–23 Edition)

Schedule B

Calculation of Net Immediate Positions in Securities and Financings

Maturity Category 1/	Financings Long 2/ (+)	Financings Short 2/ (−)	Securities Positions Long (+)	Securities Positions Short (−)	Total Securities and Financing Positions (+)	Offset Portions (+)	Net Immediate Positions (+/−)	
0–45 days								A
45–135 days								B
135 days– 9 months								C
9–18 months								D
1.5–3.5 years (1.5–3 years)								E
3.5–7.5 years (3–5.5 years)								F
7.5–15 years (5.5–9 years)								G
15–30 years (9–12 years)								H
(12–21 years)								I
(21 years and over)								J
mortgage-backed adjustable rate								MB
mortgage-backed								AR
Column Number	1	2	3	4	5 (1+3)	6 (2+4)	7# (Note 1)	8# (5+6)

\# Carry forward (Column 7) to Schedule C.

Note 1: The offset portion (Column 7) is the smaller of Columns 5 and 6.

1/ The categories are designated in Sec. 402.2(f)(1). A category contains all securities with maturities greater than or equal to the lower of the designated maturities, but less than the higher. Maturity designations in parentheses refer to maturities of zero-coupon instruments to be placed in that category. In categories A, B, C, and D, zero-coupon instruments are to be treated in the same manner as all other instruments. A half year (.5) is always considered to be 6 months.

2/ Long financings are financings which provide securities to a broker or dealer; short financings are those which provide funds.

608

Department of the Treasury § 402.2a

Schedule C

Governments Offset Portion and Net Immediate Position Interim Haircuts Calculation

	Maturity Category 1/	Governments Offset Portion $ Amounts (+)	Factors	Haircuts (+)	Net Immediate Position $ Amounts (+/-)	Factors	Interim Haircuts (+/-)
A	0-45 days		None			None	
B	45-135 days		0.0002			0.0012	
C	135 days- 9 months		0.0003			0.0020	
D	9-18 months		0.0007			0.0045	
E	1.5-3.5 years (1.5-3 years)		0.0022			0.0110	
F	3.5-7.5 years (3-5.5 years)		0.0044			0.0220	
G	7.5-15 years (5.5-9 years)		0.0050			0.0330	
H	15-30 years (9-12 years)		0.0090			0.0450	
I	(12-21 years)		0.0155			0.0775	
J	(21 years and over)		0.0338			0.1125	
MB	mortgage-backed		0.0066			0.0330	
AR	adjustable rate mortgage-backed		0.0022			0.0110	

Total Governments Offset Portion Haircut $ _____

Column Number	7 (Note 1)	9	10# (7x9)	8 (Note 1)	11	12## (8x11)

\# Carry to Schedule A, line 2a
\## Carry forward to Schedule D (or Schedule E, if no forwards, futures, or options).
Note 1: From Schedule B.
1/ The categories are designated in Sec. 402.2(f)(1). A category contains all securities with maturities greater than or equal to the lower of the designated maturities, but less than the higher. Maturity designations in parentheses refer to maturities of zero-coupon instruments to be placed in the category. In categories A, B, C, and D, zero-coupon instruments are to be treated in the same manner as all other instruments. A half year (.5) is always considered to be 6 months.

§ 402.2a

17 CFR Ch. IV (4–1–23 Edition)

Schedule D
Consolidation of Net Immediate Position Interim Haircuts
with Gross Futures and Options Interim Haircuts
(In thousands of dollars)

Maturity Category 1/	Net Immediate Position Interim Haircuts (+/−)	Gross Interim Haircuts Futures & Forward (+) (−)	Options (+) (−)	Aggregate Interim Haircuts (+) (−)	Futures & Options Offset Portions 2/ (+)	Residual Position Interim Haircuts (+/−)
45–135 days						B
135 days– 9 months						C
9–18 months						D
1.5–3.5 years (1.5–3 years)						E
3.5–7.5 years (3–5.5 years)						F
7.5–15 years (5.5–9 years)						G
15–30 years (9–12 years)						H
(12–21 years)						I
(21 years and over)						J
MB mortgage-backed						MB
AR adjustable rate mortgage-backed						AR

Total Futures and Options Offset Portion: $ _____
Factor: x20%
Total Futures and Options Offset Haircut: $ _____ #

| Column Number | 12 (Note 1) | 13 | 14 | 15 | 16 | 17 | 18 | 19 (Note 2) | 20 ## (17+18) |

Carry to Schedule A, line 2b.
Carry forward to Schedule E.
Note 1: From Schedule C.
Note 2: Column 19 is the smaller of columns 17 and 18.

1/ The categories are designated in Sec. 402.2(f)(1). A category contains all securities with maturities greater than or equal to the lower of the designated maturities, but less than the higher. Maturity designations in parentheses refer to maturities of zero-coupon instruments to be placed in the category. In categories A, B, C, and D, zero-coupon instruments are to be treated in the same manner as all other instruments. A half year is always considered to be 6 months.
2/ The total futures and options haircut is calculated from the total of column 19.

610

Department of the Treasury

§ 402.2a

Schedule E

Calculation of Hedging Disallowance Haircuts when Netting Haircuts Across Categories 1/
(In thousands of dollars)

Maturity Category 2/	Residual Position Interim Haircuts (+/-)	20% Disallowance Hedging Disallowance Haircuts (+)	20% Disallowance Net Residual Position Interim Haircuts (+/-)	30% Disallowance Hedging Disallowance Haircuts (+)	30% Disallowance Net Residual Position Interim Haircuts (+/-)	40% Disallowance Hedging Disallowance Haircuts (+)	40% Disallowance Net Residual Position Interim Haircuts (+/-)	Hedging Disallowance Haircuts (+)	Qualified Netting Interim Haircuts (+)
B 45–135 days									
C 135 days–9 months									
D 9–18 months									
E 1.5–3.5 years (1.5–3 years)									
F 3.5–7.5 years (3–5.5 years)									
G 7.5–15 years (5.5–9 years)									
H 15–30 years (9–12 years)									
I (12–21 years)									
J (21 years and over)									
MB mortgage-backed adjustable rate									
AR mortgage-backed									

Total Hedging Disallowance Haircut: $ _____

Residual Net Position Haircut: $ _____

| Column Number | 20 (Note 1) | 21 | 22 (Note 2) | 23 | 24 (Note 2) | 25 | 26 (Note 2) | 27# (Note 3) | 28## |

\# Column 27 carries forward to Schedule A, line 2c.
\## Column 28 total carries forward to Schedule C, if no forwards, futures, or options). From Schedule D (or Schedule C, if no forwards, futures, or options).
Note 1: Net of two offsetting haircuts of paired maturity categories.
Note 2: For every entry in column 20 there should be an entry in either column 27 or 28 (but never both).
Note 3: See Sec. 402.2(f)(3) for category pair hedging disallowance haircut factors.
2/ The categories are designated in Sec. 402.2(f)(1). A category contains all securities with maturities greater than or equal to the lower of the designated maturities, but less than the higher. Maturity designations in parentheses refer to maturities of zero-coupon instruments to be placed in the category. In categories A, B, C, and D, zero-coupon instruments are to be treated in the same manner as all other instruments. A half year (.5) is always considered to be 6 months.

INSTRUCTIONS TO SCHEDULES A THROUGH E

Schedules A through E may be used by government securities brokers or dealers subject to 17 CFR 402 to determine the firm's capital-to-risk ratio. Section 402.2 provides that a government securities broker or dealer must meet the applicable minimum dollar liquid capital requirement and that the firm's ratio of liquid capital to risk (total haircuts) must be at least 1.2:1; liquid capital must exceed risk by at least 20 percent. Total haircuts is the risk measure used in the ratio; it is made up of measures of market risk and measures of credit risk. The market risk of a government securities broker's or dealer's positions is accounted for

611

§ 402.2a

through the Treasury market risk haircut and the other securities haircut. Credit risk is accounted for in the counterparty exposure, concentration of credit, and credit volatility haircuts and in the computation of liquid capital through the various deductions and charges.

Only positions in Treasury market risk instruments and financings may be used in the calculation of the Treasury market risk haircut. Treasury market risk instruments and financings are described in 17 CFR 402.2 and in the instructions to the schedule where they are to be first entered. All other types of financial instruments are to be included in the calculation of the other securities haircut. Calculation of the other securities haircut is based on the SEC's Rule 15c3–1 (17 CFR 240.15c3–1).

Treasury market risk instruments may be excluded from the calculation of the Treasury market risk haircut if they are included in the calculation of the other securities haircut as part of a hedge against long and short positions in securities, futures contracts, forward contracts, or options that are not Treasury market risk instruments. Only the portion of the total position in a Treasury market risk instrument that forms part of such a hedge may be excluded, and the result of this transfer of the Treasury market risk instruments must be a reduction in the other securities haircut.

The categories for classifying Treasury market risk instruments are designated in 17 CFR 402.2(f)(1). The categories, which are designated by a maturity range, contain all securities with remaining terms to maturity greater than or equal to the lower end of the range but less than the higher. A half year is always considered to be 6 months. In categories A through D, zero-coupon instruments are to be treated in the same manner as all other instruments. In categories E through J, the maturity designations in parentheses give the maturities of the zero-coupon instruments to be placed in that category. All mortgage-backed securities that are Treasury market risk instruments are to be placed in category MB or category AR, depending on whether they are backed by conventional or adjustable-rate mortgages.

All haircuts may be calculated to the nearest hundred dollars, unless such rounding would materially affect the liquid capital calculation.

Appendix A to the Preamble published with the temporary regulations for 17 CFR part 402 (52 FR 19669, May 26, 1987) contains an example of the capital calculation. It may also be used as an aid in completing these schedules.

Schedule A—Liquid Capital Requirement Summary Computation

Schedule A is used to determine the capital-to-risk ratio by comparing liquid capital to total haircuts. Schedule A will be the last schedule completed as many of the haircuts entered on Schedule A are calculated on Schedules B through E.

Line 1—Enter liquid capital, which is identical to the amount reported on line 3640 of the Report on Finances and Operations of Government Securities Brokers and Dealers, Form G–405.

Line 2—Haircuts on "Security and Financing Positions" including contractual commitments:

a. Enter the Total Governments Offset Portion Haircut from column 10 of Schedule C.

b. Enter the Total Futures and Options Offset Haircut from column 19 of Schedule D.

c. Enter the Total Hedging Disallowance Haircut as calculated in Schedule E, column 27.

d. Enter the Residual Net Position Haircut as given in column 28 of Schedule E.

e. Enter the other securities haircut as determined by applying the SEC haircut factors to securities, futures contracts, forward contracts, options and other inventory that are not Treasury market risk instruments as defined in 17 CFR 402.2(e). The other securities haircut is the sum of all applicable deductions as specified in 17 CFR 240.15c3–1 (c)(2)(vi) and (c)(2)(viii) and in 17 CFR 240.15c3–1a and 240.15c3–1b. Any position(s) in Treasury market risk instruments that have been excluded from the calculation of the Treasury market risk haircut because they are part of a hedge with these other instruments are to be included in the calculation of this haircut.

Line 3—Haircuts on credit exposure:

a. Enter the total counterparty exposure haircut which is the sum of the counterparty exposure haircut with each counterparty, except a Federal Reserve Bank. A counterparty exposure haircut is equal to 5 percent of the net credit exposure to a single counterparty which is not in excess of 15 percent of the government securities broker's or dealer's liquid capital. If the net credit exposure to a counterparty does exceed 15 percent of liquid capital, the excess will be used in calculating the total concentration of credit haircut on line 3b.

Net credit exposure equals the difference between the government securities broker's or dealer's credit exposure to a single counterparty and that counterparty's credit exposure to the government securities broker or dealer. The government securities broker's or dealer's credit exposure to a counterparty is equal to the sum of the dollar amount of funds, debt instruments, other securities, and other inventory at risk to the government securities broker or dealer in the event of the counterparty's default and the market value of purchased unlisted options that are Treasury market risk instruments and were written by the counterparty.

Department of the Treasury

§ 402.2a

It does not include, however, (1) the deduction taken from net worth for unsecured receivables, repurchase and reverse repurchase agreement deficits, aged fails to deliver, and aged fails to receive arising from transactions with the counterparty; (2) demand deposits in the case where the counterparty is a commercial bank; (3) loans of immediately available funds (commonly referred to as "sales of federal funds") held by the government securities broker or dealer in connection with the clearance of securities on the day the loan is made in the case where the counterparty is a commercial bank; (4) custodial holdings of securities in the case where the counterparty is a clearing bank or clearing broker of the government securities broker or dealer; or (5) credit exposure to the counterparty due to holding marketable instruments for which the counterparty is the obligor.

The counterparty's credit exposure to the government securities broker or dealer equals the dollar amount of funds, debt instruments, other securities, and other inventory at risk to the counterparty in the event of the government security broker's or dealer's default and any unlisted options written by the government securities broker or dealer and held by the counterparty.

b. Enter the total concentration of credit haircut which is the sum of all concentration of credit haircuts applied in cases where the net credit exposure (as defined above) to a single counterparty is in excess of 15 percent of the government securities broker's or dealer's liquid capital. The concentration of credit haircut is 25 percent of the amount of net credit exposure in excess of 15 percent of the government securities broker's or dealer's liquid capital.

c. Enter the credit volatility haircut which equals a factor of 0.15 percent applied to the larger of the gross long or gross short position in money market instruments qualifying as Treasury market risk instruments which mature in 45 days or more, in futures and forwards on these instruments that are settled on a cash or delivery basis, and in futures and forwards on time deposits described in § 402.2(e)(1)(vii), that mature in 45 days or more, settled on a cash or delivery basis. Money market instruments qualifying as Treasury market risk instruments are (1) marketable certificates of deposit with no more than one year to maturity, (2) bankers acceptances, and (3) commercial paper of no more than one year to maturity and which has only a minimal amount of credit risk as determined by the government securities broker or dealer pursuant to reasonably designed written policies and procedures the government securities broker or government securities dealer establishes, maintains, and enforces to assess and monitor creditworthiness. These policies and procedures should result in creditworthiness assessments that typically are consistent with market data.

Line 4—Enter total haircuts which is the sum of lines 2 a through e, and 3 a, b, and c.

Line 5—Enter the capital-to-risk ratio which is found by dividing line 1, "Liquid capital," by line 4, "Total haircuts." The capital-to-risk ratio must be at least equal to 1.2:1.

Schedule B—Calculation of Net Immediate Position in Securities and Financings

Schedule B is used to calculate the net immediate position in and offset portion of securities and financings. The results are then carried over to Schedule C for initial haircut calculations. Futures, forwards, and options which are Treasury market risk instruments are to be entered on Schedule D.

Positions in and financings on debt instruments other than mortgage-backed or adjustable rate mortgage-backed securities should be placed in the category corresponding to their remaining term to maturity. In the case of a floating rate note, however, the note should be placed in the category corresponding to the time to the next scheduled interest rate adjustment or remaining term to maturity, whichever is less.

Column 1—Under "Financings-Long" report in the appropriate category the contract value of reverse repurchase agreements and the value(s) of cash collateral on security borrowings. Financings so reported should be placed in the category corresponding to the remaining term to maturity or time to the next scheduled interest rate adjustment, whichever is less.

Column 2—Under "Financings-Short" report in the appropriate category as a negative number the values of funds received from financing transactions. Include repurchase agreements, securities lending secured by cash collateral, and term financings, but exclude subordinated debt which meets the requirements of 17 CFR 240.15c3-1d as modified by 17 CFR 402.2d. Financings so reported should be placed in the category corresponding to the remaining term to maturity or time to the next scheduled interest rate adjustment, whichever is less.

Columns 3 and 4—Report in the appropriate column by maturity or type of mortgage-backed security under "Securities Positions" the sum of the market values of immediate positions in Treasury market risk instruments. The net position in each individual Treasury market risk instrument is to be appropriately reported as a long (+) or short (−) position in summation with all other positions of the same category (long/short). Short positions are assigned a negative value. Treasury market risk instruments are defined in 17 CFR 402.2(e). Those to be reported in Schedule B are:

613

§ 402.2a

(1) Government securities as defined in 17 CFR 400.3 except equity securities and mortgage-backed securities which do not pass through to the security holder on a pro rata basis a distribution based on the monthly payments and prepayments of principal and interest on the underlying pool of mortgage collateral less fees and expenses;

(2) Zero-coupon receipts or certificates based on marketable Treasury notes or bonds;

(3) Marketable certificates of deposit of no more than one year to maturity;

(4) Bankers acceptances;

(5) Commercial paper of no more than one year to maturity and which has only a minimal amount of credit risk as determined by the government securities broker or dealer pursuant to reasonably designed written policies and procedures the government securities broker or dealer establishes, maintains, and enforces to assess and monitor creditworthiness. These policies and procedures should result in creditworthiness assessments that typically are consistent with market data; and

(6) Securities described in §402.2(e)(1)(vi).

Report all positions as of the trade date. If the settlement date is scheduled for more than five business days in the future (or, in the case of a mortgage-backed security, more than thirty calendar days in the future), then report the position as a forward contract on Schedule D. Also, under "Securities Positions" in the appropriate column and category, report any when-issued position in a marketable Treasury security between announcement and issue date, any when-issued position in a government agency or a government-sponsored agency debt security between release date and issue date, and any when-issued position in a security described in §402.2(e)(1)(vi) between announcement date and issue date.

Exclude positions in Treasury market risk instruments which form part of a hedge against long and short positions in securities, futures contracts, forward contracts, or options that are not Treasury market risk instruments and are to be included in the calculation of the other securities haircut. Only that portion of the total position in a Treasury market risk instrument that forms part of such a hedge may be excluded, and the inclusion of the Treasury market risk instruments must reduce the other securities haircut.

Column 5—Under "Total Securities and Financing Positions (+)" report in the appropriate category the sum of the long financings (column 1) and long securities positions (column 3).

Column 6—Under "Total Securities and Financing Positions (−)" report in the appropriate category the sum of the short financings (column 2) and short securities positions (column 4).

Column 7—Under "Offset Portions" report in the appropriate category the lesser of the absolute values of the positive (column 5) or negative (column 6) total securities and financing positions.

Column 8—Under "Net Immediate Positions" report in the appropriate category the sum, or net value, of the positive (column 5) and negative (column 6) total securities and financing positions.

Columns 7, "Offset Portions," and 8, "Net Immediate Positions," are to be carried to Schedule C.

Schedule C—Governments Offset Portion and Net Immediate Position Interim Haircuts Calculation

Schedule C is used to calculate the total governments offset portion haircut and net immediate position interim haircuts by applying offset and net position haircut factors to the offset portions and net immediate positions in Treasury market risk instruments and financings. The total governments offset portion haircut is then carried to Schedule A, and the net immediate position interim haircuts are carried to Schedule D or E.

Column 7—Transfer to column 7, "Governments Offset Portion—$ Amounts," column seven from Schedule B, "Offset Portions."

Column 9—These are the governments offset portion haircut factors given at 17 CFR 402.2(f)(2). They may be updated from time to time.

Column 10—Under "Governments Offset Portion—Haircuts" report in the appropriate category the product of the corresponding values in column 7, "$ Amounts," and in column 9, "Factors."

To determine the total governments offset portion haircut, sum the values under "Governments Offset Portion—Haircuts" in column 10, and enter this number in the appropriate space. Carry this value to Schedule A, line 2a, converting, if necessary, to thousands of dollars.

Column 8—Transfer to column 8, "Net Immediate Positions—$ Amounts," column eight from Schedule B, "Net Immediate Positions."

Column 11—These are the net immediate position haircut factors given at 17 CFR 402.2(f)(2). They may be updated from time to time.

Column 12—Under "Net Immediate Positions—Interim Haircuts" place in the appropriate category the product of the corresponding values in column 8, "$ Amounts," and in column 11, "Factors." A haircut on a short position remains negative.

Carry column 12 to Schedule D, or, if there are no futures, forwards, or options positions, to Schedule E.

Department of the Treasury

§ 402.2a

Schedule D—Consolidation of Net Immediate Position Interim Haircuts with Gross Futures and Options Interim Haircuts

Schedule D is used to enter haircuts on futures, forwards and options positions and to calculate the total futures and options offset haircut and the residual position interim haircuts as needed for Schedules A and E respectively. If there are no futures and options positions, it is not necessary to fill out Schedule D.

Report on Schedule D futures, forwards, and options which are Treasury market risk instruments as defined in § 402.2(e). These futures, forwards, and listed option contracts may be based on any of the Treasury market risk instruments described in the instructions to columns 3 and 4 on Schedule B or on time deposits whose changes in yield are closely correlated with marketable certificates of deposit which are Treasury market risk instruments, as described in § 402.2(e)(1)(vii). Options on Treasury market risk futures contracts and unlisted options on marketable Treasury bills, notes, and bonds are also to be included. Futures contracts may settle on a cash or delivery basis. Any of these contracts which are being included as part of a hedge in the calculation of the other securities haircut must be excluded from Schedule D.

Report as a forward contract any position for which the time between trade date and settlement date is more than five business days (30 calendar days for a mortgage-backed security). Any when-issued position in a marketable Treasury security established between announcement and issue date, any when-issued position in a government agency or a government-sponsored agency debt security established between release date and issue date, and any when-issued position in a security described in § 402.2(e)(1)(vi) between announcement date and issue date is reported in the appropriate category on Schedule B under "Securities Positions."

Column 12—Transfer to column 12, "Net Immediate Position Interim Haircuts," column 12 from Schedule C, "Net Immediate Positions—Interim Haircuts," converting, if necessary, to thousands of dollars.

Columns 13 and 14—Under "Gross Interim Haircuts—Futures and Forward" enter in the appropriate category the sum of the interim haircuts on the futures or forward positions belonging to that category. The interim haircut on a futures or forward position equals the product of the value of the position evaluated at the current market price for such contract and the net position haircut factor that corresponds to either the term to maturity of the underlying instrument or, for mortgage-backed securities, the type of security. The term to maturity of the underlying instrument is the term to maturity of the deliverable security at the time of the maturity of the futures or forward contract. The haircut on a futures or forward position on a non-mortgaged-backed instrument is to be entered in the category corresponding to the sum of the remaining time to maturity of the futures or forward contract and the maturity of the underlying instrument. Haircuts on futures and forwards on mortgage-backed securities are to be entered in the appropriate mortgage-backed securities category. The interim haircuts on long futures and forwards are positive (column 13), and on short futures and forwards, negative (column 14).

Columns 15 and 16—Under "Gross Interim Haircuts—Options" enter, in the category in which the instrument directly underlying the contract would be entered, the lesser of (1) the market value of the option or (2) the net immediate position interim haircut on the underlying cash instrument or gross futures interim haircut on the underlying futures contract. Note that in the case of an option on a futures contract the category in which the option contract is to be entered is the sum of the remaining time to maturity of the futures or forward contract and the maturity of the instrument underlying the futures or forward contract. The haircut factor used to determine the gross futures interim haircut is that factor corresponding to the term to maturity of the deliverable security at the time of the maturity of the futures or forward contract. Gross option haircuts on purchased calls and sold puts are positive, those on sold calls and purchased puts are negative.

Column 17—Under "Aggregate Interim Haircuts (+)" enter in the appropriate category, the sum of any positive net immediate position interim haircut (column 12) and the positive gross option (column 15) and gross futures and forward (column 13) interim haircuts for that category.

Column 18—Under "Aggregate Interim Haircuts (−)" enter in the appropriate category, the sum of any negative net immediate position interim haircut (column 12) and the negative gross option (column 16) and gross futures and forward (column 14) interim haircuts for that category.

Column 19—Under "Futures and Options Offset Portions" enter, in the appropriate category, the lesser of the absolute values of the positive and negative aggregate interim haircuts (columns 17 and 18) for that category.

The total futures and options offset portion is the sum of the values in column 19 under "Futures and Options Offset Portions."

The total futures and options offset haircut is the total futures and options offset portion multiplied by a factor of 20 percent and is carried to line 2b, Schedule A.

Column 20—Enter in the appropriate category under "Residual Position Interim

§ 402.2a

Haircuts" the sum, or net value, of the positive and negative aggregate interim haircuts. Carry this to column 20 on Schedule E.

Schedule E—Calculation of Hedging Disallowance Haircuts When Netting Haircuts Across Categories

Schedule E is used to calculate the hedging disallowance and residual net position haircuts which are then carried to Schedule A. The purpose of Schedule E is to hedge positions in different categories in order to reduce total haircuts. Netting the residual position interim haircuts reflects the risk reduction inherent in hedges between positions in different categories where the price volatility is reasonably well correlated.

Section 402.2(f)(3) of the rule specifies the hedging disallowance haircut factors for the category pairs. Netting of residual position interim haircuts is permitted only between any two categories for which a hedging disallowance haircut factor is specified. Hedging disallowance haircuts are similar to offset haircuts in that they are applied to the smaller of the two residual position interim haircuts and represent the portion of the hedge being "disallowed." A hedging disallowance haircut is determined each time two residual position interim haircuts are netted.

There are three levels of permissible netting corresponding to the three hedging disallowance haircut factors: The 20 percent, 30 percent, and 40 percent levels. It is not necessary to net all possible pairs at any one level. A greater reduction in total haircuts can sometimes be obtained by choosing not to net a pair at one level (e.g., the 20 percent level) so that one element of the pair can be netted against a third category at another level (e.g., the 30 percent level).

Column 20—Transfer column 20, "Residual Position Interim Haircuts," from Schedule D. If there are no futures or options positions, transfer instead column 12, "Net Immediate Positions—Interim Haircuts," from Schedule C.

Column 21—Use the matrix at 17 CFR 402.2(f)(3) to determine the categories from which the residual position interim haircuts may be paired at the 20 percent level. For each pair multiply the smaller of the absolute values of the two residual position interim haircuts by the hedging disallowance haircut factor of 20 percent, and, in the category of the smaller, enter the resulting hedging disallowance haircut.

Column 22—For each pair being netted at this level, enter under "Net Residual Position Interim Haircuts" (1) the sum, or net value, of the two residual position interim haircuts (and/or net residual position interim haircuts) in the category of the larger (in absolute value) of the two interim haircuts that were netted, and (2) a zero in the category of the smaller.

These net residual position interim haircuts replace the residual position interim haircuts (or net residual position interim haircuts) from which they were derived. Net residual position interim haircuts can in turn be used in any other allowable netting exactly as residual position interim haircuts would be. If further netting of that category at the same level is permissible and possible, it will be necessary to replace the net residual position interim haircut involved with a new (and smaller) net residual position interim haircut in column 22.

Since the net residual position interim haircut in any category containing a hedging disallowance haircut is zero, further netting with any such category is impossible.

After all netting has been completed for category pairs with a 20 percent hedging disallowance haircut factor, move on to column 23.

Column 23—Use the matrix at 17 CFR 402.2(f)(3) to determine the categories from which the residual position interim haircuts and/or net residual position interim haircuts may be paired at the 30 percent level. In each category, the newest (and smallest) net residual position interim haircut determined by netting at the 20 percent level replaces the old value and must be used in hedging in that category at higher levels. For each pair being netted, multiply the smaller of the absolute values of the two (net) residual position interim haircuts by the hedging disallowance haircut factor of 30 percent, and in the category of the smaller, enter the resulting hedging disallowance haircut.

Column 24—For each pair being netted at this level, enter under "Net Residual Position Interim Haircuts" (1) the sum, or net value, of the two residual position interim haircuts and/or net residual position interim haircuts in the category of the larger (in absolute value) of the two interim haircuts that were netted, and (2) a zero in the category of the smaller.

These net residual position interim haircuts replace the residual position interim haircuts (or net residual position interim haircuts) from which they were derived. Net residual position interim haircuts can in turn be used in any other allowable netting exactly as residual position interim haircuts would be. If further netting of that category at the same level is permissible and possible, it will be necessary to replace the net residual position interim haircut involved with a new (and smaller) net residual position interim haircut.

After all netting has been completed for category pairs with a 30 percent hedging disallowance haircut factor, continue to column 25.

Column 25—Use the matrix at 17 CFR 402.2(f)(3) to determine the categories from which the residual position interim haircuts and/or net residual position interim haircuts

Department of the Treasury

may be paired at the 40 percent level. In each category, any new net residual position interim haircut determined by netting at the 20 or 30 percent level replaces the old value and must be used in hedging with that category at the 40 percent level. For each pair being netted, multiply the smaller of the absolute values of the two (net) residual position interim haircuts by the hedging disallowance haircut factor of 40 percent and, in the category of the smaller, enter the resulting hedging disallowance haircut.

Column 26—For each pair being netted at this level, enter under "Net Residual Position Interim Haircuts" (1) the sum, or net value, of the two (net) residual position interim haircuts in the category of the larger (in absolute value) of the two interim haircuts that were netted, and (2) a zero in the category of the smaller. If further netting of that category at the same level is permissible and possible, it will be necessary to replace the net residual position interim haircut involved with a new (and smaller) net residual position interim haircut.

Column 27—When all possible (net) residual position interim haircuts have been netted, enter under "Hedging Disallowance Haircuts" all hedging disallowance haircuts calculated in the netting procedures, each in its appropriate category.

Enter under "Total Hedging Disallowance Haircut" the sum of all the hedging disallowance haircuts entered in column 27. Carry to Schedule A, line 2c.

Column 28—Under "Qualified Netting Interim Haircuts" enter in the appropriate category the absolute value of the haircut given under "Net Residual Position Interim Haircut" at the highest hedging disallowance factor used for that category (columns 26, 24, or 22). This value will also be the smallest of the net residual position interim haircuts in that category. If the position in a given category was not used in hedging then enter the absolute value of the residual position interim haircut from column 20.

Sum the qualified netting interim haircuts, enter this value under "Residual Net Position Haircut," and carry to Schedule A, line 2d.

[52 FR 27931, July 24, 1987, as amended at 53 FR 28985, Aug. 1, 1988; 71 FR 54411, Sept. 15, 2006; 79 FR 38455, July 8, 2014]

§ 402.2b [Reserved]

§ 402.2c Appendix C—Consolidated computations of liquid capital and total haircuts for certain subsidiaries and affiliates.

(a) *Consolidation.* (1) A government securities broker or dealer (the "parent broker or dealer"), in computing its liquid capital and total haircuts pursuant to § 402.2:

(i) Shall consolidate in a single computation of liquid capital the assets and liabilities of any subsidiary or affiliate for which the parent broker or dealer guarantees, endorses, or assumes directly or indirectly the obligations or liabilities if the parent broker or dealer has obtained the opinion of counsel described in paragraph (b) of this section with respect to such subsidiary or affiliate;

(ii) May not consolidate in a single computation of liquid capital the assets and liabilities of any subsidiary or affiliate for which the parent broker or dealer guarantees, endorses, or assumes directly or indirectly the obligations or liabilities if the parent broker or dealer has not obtained the opinion of counsel described in paragraph (b) of this section with respect to such subsidiary or affiliate, but in that event, the parent broker or dealer shall compute its total haircuts by adding the total haircuts of each such subsidiary or affiliate computed in accordance with the provisions of § 402.2 to the haircuts of the parent broker or dealer computed separately in accordance with the provisions of § 402.2; and

(iii) May consolidate in its computation of liquid capital the assets and liabilities of any majority owned and controlled subsidiary or affiliate for which the parent broker or dealer does not guarantee, endorse or assume directly or indirectly the obligations or liabilities if the parent broker or dealer has obtained the opinion of counsel described in paragraph (b) of this section with respect to such subsidiary or affiliate.

(2) With respect to any subsidiary or affiliate whose assets and liabilities are consolidated in the parent broker's or dealer's computation of liquid capital according to the provisions of paragraph (a)(1)(i) or (a)(1)(iii) of this section, the parent broker or dealer shall compute its haircuts in accordance with the provisions of § 402.2 as if the consolidated entity were one firm, or, in the alternative, shall add the total haircuts of each consolidated subsidiary or affiliate computed in accordance with the provisions of § 402.2 to the haircuts of the parent broker or

§ 402.2d

dealer computed separately in accordance with the provisions of § 402.2.

(b) *Required counsel opinion.* The opinion of counsel referred to in paragraph (a) of this section shall demonstrate to the satisfaction of the Commission, through the Designated Examining Authority, that net asset values, or the portion thereof related to the parent broker's or dealer's ownership interest in a majority owned and controlled subsidiary or affiliate, may be caused by the parent broker or dealer or an appointed trustee to be distributed to the parent broker or dealer within 30 calendar days. Such opinion shall also set forth the actions necessary to cause such a distribution to be made, identify the parties having the authority to take such actions, identify and describe the rights of other parties or classes of parties, including but not limited to customers, general creditors, subordinated lenders, minority shareholder employees, litigants and governmental or regulatory authorities, who may delay or prevent such a distribution and such other assurances as the Commission or the Designated Examining Authority by rule or interpretation may require. Such opinion shall be current and periodically renewed in connection with the parent broker's or dealer's annual audit pursuant to § 240.17a–5 of this title, as made applicable to government securities brokers or dealers by § 405.2 of this chapter, or upon any material change in circumstances.

(c) *Principles of consolidation.* The following minimum and non-exclusive requirements shall govern the consolidation of a subsidiary or affiliate in the computation of total liquid capital and total haircuts of a government securities broker or dealer pursuant to this section:

(1) The total liquid capital of the government securities broker or dealer shall be reduced by the estimated amount of any taxes reasonably anticipated to be incurred upon distribution of the assets of the subsidiary or affiliate.

(2) Liabilities of a consolidated subsidiary or affiliate that are subordinated to the claims of present and future creditors pursuant to a satisfactory subordination agreement shall not be added to consolidated net worth unless such subordination extends also to the claims of present or future creditors of the parent broker or dealer and all consolidated subsidiaries.

(3) Subordinated liabilities of a consolidated subsidiary or affiliate that are consolidated in accordance with paragraph (c)(2) of this section may not be prepaid, repaid or accelerated if any of the entities included in such consolidation would otherwise be unable to comply with the provision of § 240.15c3–1d of this title, as modified by § 402.2d.

(4) Each government securities broker or dealer included within the consolidation shall at all times be in compliance with the liquid capital or net capital requirement to which it is subject.

(d) *Certain Precluded Acts.* Even if consolidation is not required or allowed under paragraph (a) of this section, no parent broker or dealer shall guarantee, endorse or assume directly or indirectly any obligation or liability of a subsidiary or affiliate unless the obligation or liability is reflected in the parent broker's or dealer's computation of liquid capital.

§ 402.2d Appendix D—Modification of § 240.15c3–1d of this title, relating to satisfactory subordination agreements, for purposes of § 402.2.

Section 240.15c3–1d of this title shall apply to government securities brokers and dealers subject to the requirements of § 402.2 with the following modifications.

(a) References to "broker or dealer" include government securities brokers and dealers.

(b) References to "17 CFR 240.15c3–1" mean § 402.2.

(c) Section 240.15c3–1d(a)(2)(iii) is modified to read as follows:

"(iii) The term "Collateral Value" of any securities pledged to secure a secured demand note shall mean the market value of such securities after giving effect to the haircuts specified in § 402.2a of this title."

(d) References to "17 CFR 240.15c3–1d" mean that section as modified by this section.

(e) Section 240.15c3–1d(b)(6)(iii) is modified to read as follows:

"(iii) The secured demand note agreement may also provide that, in lieu of

Department of the Treasury § 402.2d

the procedures specified in the provisions required by paragraph (b)(6)(ii) of this section, the lender, with the prior written consent of the government securities broker or dealer and the Examining Authority for such broker or dealer, may reduce the unpaid principal amount of the secured demand note. After giving effect to such reduction, the liquid capital, as defined in § 402.2(d) of this title, of the government securities broker or dealer may not be less than 150% of the government securities broker's or dealer's total haircuts, as defined in § 402.2(g) of this title. No single secured demand note shall be permitted to be reduced by more than 15% of its original principal amount and after such reduction no excess collateral may be withdrawn. No Examining Authority shall consent to a reduction of the principal amount of a secured demand note if, after giving effect to such reduction, liquid capital after deducting total haircuts would be less than 120% of the minimum dollar amount required by § 402.2(b) or § 402.2(c) of this title as applicable."

(f) Section 240.15c3–1d(b)(7) is modified to read as follows:

"(7) A government securities broker or dealer at its option but not at the option of the lender may, if the subordination agreement so provides, make a Payment of all or any portion of the Payment Obligation thereunder prior to the scheduled maturity date of such Payment Obligation (hereinafter referred to as a "Prepayment"), but in no event may any Prepayment be made before the expiration of one year from the date such subordination agreement became effective. This restriction shall not apply to temporary subordination agreements which comply with the provisions of paragraph (c)(5) of this section. No Prepayment shall be made if, after giving effect thereto (and to all Payments of Payment Obligations under any other subordinated agreements then outstanding the maturities or accelerated maturities of which are scheduled to fall due within six months after the date such Prepayment is to occur pursuant to this provision or on or prior to the date on which the Payment Obligation in respect of such Prepayment is scheduled to mature disregarding this provision, whichever date is earlier) without reference to any projected profit or loss of the government securities broker or dealer, the liquid capital, as defined in § 402.2(d) of this title, of the government securities broker or dealer would be less than 150% of the government securities broker's or dealer's total haircuts, as defined in § 402.2(g) of this title. Notwithstanding the above, no Prepayment shall occur without the prior written approval of the Examining Authority for such government securities broker or dealer.".

(g) Section 240.15c3–1d(b)(8) is modified to read as follows:

"(i) The Payment Obligation of the government securities broker or dealer in respect of any subordination agreement shall be suspended and shall not mature if, after giving effect to Payment of such Payment Obligation (and to all Payments of Payment Obligations of such broker or dealer under any other subordination agreement(s) then outstanding which are scheduled to mature on or before such Payment Obligation), either the liquid capital, as defined in § 402.2(d) of this title, of the government securities broker or dealer would be less than 150% of the government securities broker's or dealer's total haircuts, as defined in § 402.2(g) of this title, or the government securities broker's or dealer's liquid capital after deducting total haircuts would be less than 120% of the minimum dollar amount required by § 402.2(b) or § 402.2(c) of this title, as applicable. The subordination agreement may provide that if the Payment Obligation of the government securities broker or dealer thereunder does not mature and is suspended as a result of the requirement of this paragraph (b)(8) for a period of not less than six months, the government securities broker or dealer shall thereupon commence the rapid and orderly liquidation of its business but the right of the lender to receive Payment, together with accrued interest or compensation, shall remain subordinate as required by the provisions of 17 CFR 240.15c3–1 and 240.15c3–1d.".

(h) Section 240.15c3–1d(b)(10)(ii)(B) is modified to read as follows:

"(B) The liquid capital, as defined in §402.2(d) of this title, of the government securities broker or dealer being less than 120% of total haircuts, as defined in §402.2(g) of this title, throughout a period of 15 consecutive business days, commencing on the day the broker or dealer first determines and notifies the Examining Authority for the government securities broker or dealer, or the Examining Authority or the Commission first determines and notifies the government securities broker or dealer of such fact;".

(i) Section 240.15c3–1d(c)(2) is modified to read as follows:

"(2) *Notice of Maturity or Accelerated Maturity.* Every government securities broker or dealer shall immediately notify the Examining Authority for such broker or dealer if, after giving effect to all Payments of Payment Obligations subordination agreements then outstanding which are then due or mature within the following six months without reference to any projected profit or loss of the broker or dealer, the liquid capital, as defined in §402.2(d) of this title, of such government securities broker or dealer would be less than 150% of total haircuts, as defined in §402.2(g) of this title.".

(j) Section 240.15c3–1d(c)(5)(i) is modified to read as follows:

"(i) For the purpose of enabling a government securities broker or dealer to participate as an underwriter of securities or other extraordinary activities in compliance with the capital requirements of §402.2 of this title, a government securities broker or dealer shall be permitted, on no more than three occasions in any 12 month period, to enter into a subordination agreement on a temporary basis which has a stated term of no more than 45 days from the date such subordination agreement became effective. This temporary relief shall not apply to a government securities broker or dealer if, within the preceding thirty calendar days, it has given notice pursuant to §405.3, or if immediately prior to entering into such subordination agreement, the liquid capital, as defined in §402.2(d) of this title, of such broker or dealer would be less than 150% of total haircuts, as defined in §402.2(g) of this title, or the amount of its then outstanding subordination agreements exceeds the limits specified in §240.15c3–1(d). Such temporary subordination agreement shall be subject to all other provisions of this appendix D.".

(k) Section 240.15c3–1d(c)(5)(ii)(A) is modified to read as follows:

"(A) After giving effect thereto (and to all Payments of Payment Obligations under any other subordinated agreements then outstanding the maturity or accelerated maturities of which are scheduled to fall due within six months after the date such prepayment is to occur pursuant to this provision or on or prior to the date on which the Payment Obligation in respect of such prepayment is scheduled to mature disregarding this provision, whichever date is earlier) without reference to any projected profit or loss of the government securities broker or dealer, the liquid capital, as defined in §402.2(d) of this title, of such broker or dealer, would be less than 180% of total haircuts, as defined in §402.2(g) of this title.".

[52 FR 27931, July 24, 1987, as amended at 59 FR 53731, Oct. 26, 1994]

PART 403—PROTECTION OF CUSTOMER SECURITIES AND BALANCES

Sec.
403.1 Application of part to registered brokers and dealers.
403.2 Hypothecation of customer securities.
403.3 Use of customers' free credit balances.
403.4 Customer protection—reserves and custody of securities.
403.5 Custody of securities held by financial institutions that are government securities brokers or dealers.
403.6 Compliance with part by futures commission merchants.
403.7 Effective dates.

AUTHORITY: Sec. 101, Pub. L. 99–571, 100 Stat. 3209; sec. 4(b), Pub. L. 101–432, 104 Stat. 963; sec. 102, sec. 106, Pub. L. 103–202, 107 Stat. 2344 (15 U.S.C. 78o–5(a)(5), (b)(1)(A), (b)(4)).

SOURCE: 52 FR 27947, July 24, 1987, unless otherwise noted.

§403.1 Application of part to registered brokers and dealers.

With respect to their activities in government securities, compliance by registered brokers or dealers with §240.8c–1 of this title (SEC Rule 8c–1),

Department of the Treasury

§ 403.4

as modified by § 403.2 (a), (b) and (c), with § 240.15c2–1 of this title (SEC Rule 15c2–1), with § 240.15c3–2 of this title (SEC Rule 15c3–2), as modified by § 403.3, and with § 240.15c3–3 of this title (SEC Rule 15c3–3), as modified by § 403.4 (a) through (d), (f)(2) through (3), (g) through (j), and (m), including provisions in those rules relating to OTC derivatives dealers, constitutes compliance with this part.

[71 FR 54411, Sept. 15, 2006]

§ 403.2 Hypothecation of customer securities.

Every registered government securities broker or dealer shall comply with the requirements of § 240.8c–1 of this title concerning hypothecation of customer securities with the following modifications:

(a) In § 240.8c–1(a), the words "no government securities broker or dealer" shall be substituted for the words "no member of a national securities exchange, and no broker or dealer who transacts a business in securities through the medium of such member."

(b) Section 240.8c–1(d) is modified to read as follows:

"(d) *Exemption for clearing liens.* The provisions of paragraphs (a)(2), (a)(3) and (f) of this section shall not apply to any lien or claim of a clearing bank, or the clearing corporation (or similar department or association) of a national securities exchange or a registered national securities association, for a loan made to acquire any securities subject to said lien and to be repaid on the same calendar day, which loan is incidental to the clearing of transactions in securities or loans through such bank, corporation, department or association; *provided, however,* that for the purpose of paragraph (a)(3) of this section, 'aggregate indebtedness of all customers in respect of securities carried for their accounts' shall not include indebtedness in respect of any securities subject to any lien or claim exempted by this paragraph."

(c) References to "member, broker or dealer" mean "government securities broker or dealer."

§ 403.3 Use of customers' free credit balances.

Every registered government securities broker or dealer shall comply with the requirement of § 240.15c3–2 of this title concerning the use of customer free credit balances. For purposes of this section, all references to "broker or dealer" in § 240.15c3–2 shall include government securities brokers and dealers.

§ 403.4 Customer protection—reserves and custody of securities.

Every registered government securities broker or dealer shall comply with the requirements of §§ 240.15c3–3 and 240.15c3–3a of this title (SEC Rule 15c3–3 and Exhibit A thereto), with the following modifications:

(a) References to "broker or dealer" include government securities brokers and dealers.

(b) "Fully paid securities," as defined in § 240.15c3–3(a)(3) of this title, includes all securities held by a government securities broker or a government securities dealer for the account of a customer who has made full payment for such securities.

(c) "Margin securities," as defined in § 240.15c3–3(a)(4) of this title, includes any securities for which a customer has not made full payment and for which the customer has received an extension of credit by a government securities broker or government securities dealer for a portion of the purchase price.

(d) "Excess margin securities," as defined in § 240.15c3–3(a)(5) of this title, includes margin securities carried for the account of a customer having a market value in excess of 140 percent of the total of the debit balances in the customer's account or accounts with the broker or dealer.

(e) For purposes of this section, § 240.15c3–3(b)(3)(iii)(A) of this title is modified to read as follows:

(A) Must provide to the lender upon the execution of the agreement, or by the close of the business day of the loan if the loan occurs subsequent to the execution of the agreement, collateral that fully secures the loan of securities, consisting exclusively of cash or United States Treasury bills or Treasury notes or an irrevocable letter of

§ 403.4

credit issued by a bank as defined in § 3(a)(6)(A)–(C) of the Act (15 U.S.C. 78c(a)(6)(A)–(C)) or such other collateral as the Secretary designates as permissible by order as consistent with the public interest, the protection of investors, and the purposes of the Act, after giving consideration to the collateral's liquidity,

(f)(1) For purposes of this section, § 240.15c3–3(b)(4)(i)(C) is modified to read as follows:

"(C) Advise the counterparty in the repurchase agreement that the Securities Investor Protection Act of 1970 will not provide protection to the counterparty with respect to the repurchase agreement."

(2) For purposes of this section, § 240.15c3–3(b)(4)(ii) is modified to read as follows:

"(ii) For purposes of this paragraph (4), securities are in the broker's or dealer's control only if they are in the control of the broker or dealer within the meaning of § 240.15c3–3(c)(1), (c)(3), (c)(5), (c)(6), or § 403.4(f) of this title."

(3) For purposes of this section, § 240.15c3–3(b)(4)(iv) is redesignated § 240.15c3–3(b)(4)(iv)(A) and paragraph (b)(4)(iv)(B) is added to read as follows:

"(B) A person that is a non-U.S. citizen residing outside of the United States or a foreign corporation, partnership, or trust may waive, but only in writing, the right to receive the confirmation required by paragraph (b)(4)(i)(B) of this section."

(g)(1) Securities under the control of a broker or dealer, as described in § 240.15c3–3(c) of this title, shall include securities maintained by a broker or dealer in an account at a depository institution, as defined in section 19(b)(A)(i)–(vi) of the Federal Reserve Act (12 U.S.C. 461(b)(1)(A)(i)–(vi)), which depository institution has a book-entry securities account at a Federal Reserve Bank through which it provides clearing services ("clearing bank"), provided the securities are maintained in a Segregated Account of the government securities broker or dealer. For purposes of this paragraph (f)(1) and paragraph (h) of this section, a Segregated Account is an account (other than a clearing account) of the government securities broker or dealer maintained on the books of a clearing bank pursuant to a written clearing agreement with such clearing bank which provides that:

(i) Such account is established for the purpose of segregating securities of counterparties or customers of such broker or dealer from proprietary securities of the broker or dealer;

(ii) The broker or dealer is entitled to direct the disposition of the securities; and

(iii) The clearing bank does not have, and will not assert, any claim or lien against such securities nor will the clearing bank grant any third party, including any Federal Reserve Bank, any interest in such securities so long as they are maintained in the segregated account.

(2) For purposes of this section, § 240.15c3–3(c)(2) of this title is redesignated as paragraph (c)(2)(i) and new paragraph (c)(2)(ii) is added to read as follows:

"(ii) Are carried for the account of any customer by a government securities broker or dealer in an account designated exclusively for customers of the government securities broker or dealer with a registered broker or dealer or another registered government securities broker or dealer (the "carrying broker or dealer") in compliance with instructions of the registered government securities broker or dealer to the carrying broker or dealer that the securities are to be maintained free of any charge, lien or claim of any kind in favor of the carrying broker or dealer or any persons claiming through such carrying broker or dealer; or".

(h) For the purposes of this section, § 240.15c3–3(d)(2) of this title is modified to read as follows:

"(2) Securities included on its books or records as failed to receive more than 30 calendar days, or in the case of mortgage-backed securities, more than 60 calendar days, then the government securities broker or government securities dealer shall, not later than the business day following the day on which such determination is made, take prompt steps to obtain possession or control of securities so failed to receive through a buy-in procedure or otherwise; or"

Department of the Treasury

(i) In addition to the notification required by § 240.15c3–3(i) of this title, whenever any government securities broker or dealer instructs its clearing bank to place securities in a Segregated Account (as defined in paragraph (f)(1) of this section), and the clearing bank refuses to do so as of the close of business on that day, the broker or dealer shall, in accordance with § 240.17a–11(f) of this title, give telegraphic notice of the notification by the clearing bank within 24 hours and within 48 hours of the telegraphic notice, file a report stating what steps are being taken to correct the situation.

(j) For purposes of this section, § 240.15c3–3(l) of this title is modified to read as follows:

"(1) *Delivery or disposition of securities.* Nothing stated in this section shall be construed as affecting the absolute right of a customer of a government securities broker or dealer, unless otherwise agreed in writing, in the normal course of business operations following demand made on the broker or dealer, to receive the physical delivery of certificates if the securities are issued in certificated form, or to direct a transfer of or otherwise to exercise control over any securities if they are:

"(1) Fully-paid securities to which the customer is entitled;

"(2) Margin securities upon full payment by such customer to the broker or dealer of the customer's indebtedness to the broker or dealer; or

"(3) Excess margin securities not reasonably required to collateralize such customer's indebtedness to the broker or dealer.".

(k) Except with respect to a government securities interdealer broker subject to the financial responsibility requirements of § 402.1(e) and a registered government securities broker or dealer that is a futures commission merchant registered with the CFTC, § 240.15c3–3(e)(3) is modified for purposes of this section to read as follows:

"(3) Computations necessary to determine the amount required to be deposited as specified in paragraph (e)(1) of this section shall be made weekly, as of the close of the last business day of the week, and the deposit so computed shall be made no later than 1 hour after the opening of banking business on the second following business day; provided, however, a government securities broker or dealer registered pursuant to section 15C(a)(1)(A) of the Act (15 U.S.C. 78o–5 (a)(1)(A)) which has a ratio of liquid capital to total haircuts (calculated in accordance with part 402 of this chapter) of 1.8 or greater and which carries aggregate customer funds (as defined in paragraph (a)(10) of this section), as computed at the last required computation pursuant to this section, not exceeding $1 million, may in the alternative make the computation monthly, as of the close of the last business day of the month, and, in such event, shall deposit not less than 105 percent of the amount so computed no later than 1 hour after the opening of banking business on the second following business day. If a registered government securities broker or dealer, computing on a monthly basis, has, at the time of any required computation, a ratio of liquid capital to total haircuts of less than 1.8, such broker or dealer shall thereafter compute weekly as aforesaid until four successive weekly computations are made, none of which were made at a time when its ratio of liquid capital to total haircuts was less than 1.8. Computations in addition to the computation required in this paragraph (3), may be made as of the close of any other business day, and the deposits so computed shall be made no later than 1 hour after the opening of banking business on the second following business day. The registered government securities broker or dealer shall make and maintain a record of each such computation made pursuant to this paragraph (3) or otherwise and preserve such record in accordance with § 240.17a–4.".

(l) Except with respect to a government securities interdealer broker subject to the financial responsibility requirements of § 402.1(e) and a registered government securities broker or dealer that is a futures commission merchant registered with the CFTC, Note E(5) of § 240.15c3–3a of this title is modified for purposes of this section to read as follows:

§ 403.5

"(5) Debit balances in margin accounts (other than omnibus accounts) shall be reduced by the amount by which any single customer's debit balance exceeds 25% (to the extent such amount is greater than $50,000) of the government securities broker's or dealer's liquid capital unless such broker or dealer can demonstrate that the debit balance is directly related to credit items in the Reserve Formula. Related accounts (e.g., the separate accounts of an individual, accounts under common control or subject to cross guarantees) shall be deemed to be a single customer's accounts for purposes of this provision.".

(m) For purposes of this section, the suspension of § 240.15c3–3(m) of this title (38 FR 12103, May 9, 1973) is no longer effective and the paragraph is modified to read as follows: "(m) If a government securities broker or government securities dealer executes a sell order of a customer (other than an order to execute a sale of securities which the seller does not own, which for the purposes of this paragraph shall mean that the customer placing the sell order has identified the sale as a short sale to the government securities broker or dealer) and if for any reason whatever the government securities broker or government securities dealer has not obtained possession of the government securities, other than mortgage-backed securities, from the customer within 30 calendar days, or in the case of mortgage-backed securities within 60 calendar days, after the settlement date, the government securities broker or government securities dealer shall immediately thereafter close the transaction with the customer by purchasing, or otherwise obtaining, securities of like kind and quantity. For purposes of this paragraph (m), the term "customer" shall not include a broker or dealer who maintains a special omnibus account with another broker or dealer in compliance with section 4(b) of Regulation T (12 CFR 220.4(b)).

(Approved by the Office of Management and Budget under control number 1535–0089)

[52 FR 27947, July 24, 1987, as amended at 53 FR 28986, Aug. 1, 1988; 59 FR 9406, Feb. 28, 1994; 60 FR 18734, Apr. 13, 1995; 69 FR 33259, June 14, 2004]

§ 403.5 Custody of securities held by financial institutions that are government securities brokers or dealers.

(a) A government securities broker or dealer that is a financial institution shall:

(1) Comply with part 450 with respect to all government securities held for the account of customers of the financial institution in its capacity as a fiduciary or custodian (unless otherwise exempt pursuant to § 450.3); and

(2) Comply with part 450 and with paragraphs (b), (c) and (d) of this section with respect to all fully paid and excess margin government securities held for customers of the financial institution in its capacity as government securities broker or dealer, and government securities that are the subject of a repurchase agreement between the financial institution and certain counterparties as described in paragraph (d) of this section.

(b) A financial institution shall not be in violation of the possession or control requirements of paragraphs (c) and (d) of this section if, solely as the result of normal business operations, temporary lags occur between the time when a security is first required to be in the financial institution's possession or control and the time when it is actually placed in possession or control, provided that the financial institution takes timely steps in good faith to establish prompt possession or control. In the event that a financial institution has accepted funds from a customer for the purchase of securities and the financial institution does not initiate the purchase of the specified securities by the close of the next business day after receipt of such customer's funds, the financial institution shall immediately deposit or redeposit the funds in an account belonging to such customer and send the customer notice of such deposit or redeposit.

Department of the Treasury

§ 403.5

(c)(1) On each business day a financial institution shall determine the quantity and issue of such securities, if any, that are required to be but are not in the financial institution's possession or control. As appropriate to bring such securities into possession or control, the financial institution shall:

(i) Promptly obtain the release of any lien, charge, or other encumbrance against such securities;

(ii) Promptly obtain the return of any securities loaned;

(iii) Take prompt steps to obtain possession or control of securities failed to receive for more than 30 calendar days, or in the case of mortgage-backed securities, for more than 60 calendar days; or

(iv) Take prompt steps to buy in securities as necessary to the extent any shortage of securities in possession or control cannot be resolved as required by any of the above procedures.

(2) The financial institution shall prepare and maintain a current and detailed description of the procedures and internal controls that it utilizes to comply with the possession or control requirements of this paragraph (c), which shall be made available upon request to its appropriate regulatory agency.

(3) Nothing stated in this section shall be construed as affecting the absolute right of a customer of a government securities broker or dealer, unless otherwise agreed in writing, in the normal course of business operations following demand made on the broker or dealer, to receive the physical delivery of certificates if the securities are issued in certificated form, or to direct a transfer of or otherwise to exercise control over any securities if they are:

(i) Fully-paid securities to which the customer is entitled;

(ii) Margin securities upon full payment by such customer to the broker or dealer of the customer's indebtedness to the broker or dealer; or

(iii) Excess margin securities not reasonably required to collateralize such customer's indebtedness to the broker or dealer.

(d)(1) A financial institution that retains custody of securities that are the subject of a repurchase agreement between the financial institution and a counterparty shall:

(i) Obtain the repurchase agreement in writing;

(ii) Confirm in writing the specific securities that are the subject of a repurchase transaction pursuant to such agreement at the end of the day of initiation of the transaction and at the end of any other day during which other securities are substituted if the substitution results in a change to issuer, maturity date, par amount or coupon rate specified in the previous confirmation;

(iii) Advise the counterparty in the repurchase agreement that the funds held by the financial institution pursuant to a repurchase transaction are not a deposit and therefore are not insured by the Federal Deposit Insurance Corporation, or the National Credit Union Share Insurance Fund, as applicable;

(iv) If the counterparty agrees to grant the financial institution the right to substitute securities, include in the written repurchase agreement the provision by which the financial institution retains the right to substitute securities;

(v) If the counterparty agrees to grant the financial institution the right to substitute securities, include in the written repurchase agreement the following disclosure statement, which must be prominently displayed in the written repurchase agreement immediately preceding the provision governing the right to substitution:

"REQUIRED DISCLOSURE

The [seller] is not permitted to substitute other securities for those subject to this agreement and therefore must keep the [buyer's] securities segregated at all times, unless in this agreement the [buyer] grants the [seller] the right to substitute other securities. If the [buyer] grants the right to substitute, this means that the [buyer's] securities will likely be commingled with the [seller's] own securities during the trading day. The [buyer] is advised that, during any trading day that the [buyer's] securities are commingled with the [seller's] securities, they may be subject to liens granted by the [seller] to third parties and may be used by the [seller] for deliveries on other securities transactions. Whenever the securities are commingled, the [seller's] ability to resegregate substitute securities for the [buyer] will be subject to the [seller's] ability to satisfy any lien or to obtain substitute securities."; and

(vi) Maintain possession or control of securities that are the subject of the agreement in accordance with §450.4(a) of this chapter, except when exercising its right of substitution in accordance with the provisions of the agreement and paragraph (d)(1)(iv) of this section.

(2)(i) A confirmation issued in accordance with paragraph (d)(1)(ii) of this section shall specify the issuer, maturity date, coupon rate, par amount and market value of the security and shall further identify a CUSIP or mortgage-backed security pool number, as appropriate, except that a CUSIP or a pool number is not required on the confirmation if it is identified in internal records of the broker or dealer that designate the specific security of the counterparty. For purposes of this paragraph (d)(2), the market value of any security that is the subject of the repurchase transaction shall be the most recently available bid price plus accrued interest, obtained by any reasonable and consistent methodology.

(ii) A person that is a non-U.S. citizen residing outside of the United States or a foreign corporation, partnership, or trust may waive, but only in writing, the right to receive the confirmation required by paragraph (d)(1)(ii) of this section.

(3) This paragraph (d) shall not apply to a repurchase agreement between the financial institution and a broker or dealer (including a government securities broker or dealer), a registered municipal securities dealer, or a director or principal officer of the financial institution or any person to the extent that his claim is explicitly subordinated to the claims of creditors of the financial institution.

(e)(1) A government securities broker or dealer that is a branch or agency of a foreign bank shall keep on deposit with an insured bank (as that term is defined in 12 U.S.C. 1813(h)) an amount equal to the amount that would be required to be set aside pursuant to §240.15c3–3(e)(1) of this title with respect to government securities of customers of such branch or agency that are citizens or residents of the United States. The amount required to be deposited pursuant to this §403.5(e)(1) may be reduced by the amount of assets pledged or deposited by the branch or agency pursuant to regulations promulgated by a Federal or State banking regulatory agency that are attributable to liabilities to customers which are included both in the calculation of the required pledge or deposit of assets and in the calculation of the amount to be set aside pursuant to §240.15c3–3(e)(1) of this title.

(2) The amount deposited in accordance with this section shall be pledged to the appropriate regulatory agency of the branch or agency making the deposit for the exclusive benefit of the customers to whom the credit balances are owed.

(3) For purposes of making the calculation pursuant to §240.15c3–3(e)(1) of this title, the terms "free credit balances," "other credit balances" and "credit balances" shall not include any funds placed in deposits or accounts enumerated at 12 CFR 204.2.

(4) For purposes of making the calculation pursuant to §240.15c3–3(e)(1) of this title, the formula set forth at §240.15c3–3a of this title shall be modified as follows:

(i) For purposes of this section, references to "securities account," "cash account," "margin account", or other customer accounts for purposes of this section shall not include any deposits or accounts enumerated at 12 CFR 204.2;

(ii) References to "security or "securities shall mean U.S. government securities;

(iii) References to net capital shall be inapplicable;

(iv) Item 2 is modified to read as follows:

"2. Monies borrowed by the branch or agency collateralized by securities carried for the account of customers. (See Note B.)";

(v) Item 4 is modified to read as follows:

"4. Customers' securities failed to receive only with respect to transactions for which payment has been received by and is under the control of the branch or agency. (See Note D.)";

Department of the Treasury § 403.5

(vi) Note B is modified to read as follows:

"NOTE B. Item 2 shall include the principal amount of Restricted Letters of Credit obtained by members of Options Clearing Corporation which are collateralized by customers' securities. Item 2 shall not include bank loans to customers in the ordinary course collateralized by the customers' U.S. government securities."; and

(vii) Note C is modified to read as follows:

"NOTE C. Item 3 shall include in addition to monies payable against customers' securities loaned the amount by which the market value of securities loaned exceeds the collateral value received from the lending of such securities. Item 3 shall exclude cash collateral received pursuant to a written securities lending agreement that complies fully with the supervisory guidelines of its appropriate regulatory agency that expressly govern securities lending practices.".

(5) Computations necessary to determine the amount required to be deposited as specified in paragraph (e)(1) of this section shall be made weekly, as of the close of the last business day of this week, and the deposit so computed shall be made no later than one hour after the opening of banking business on the second following business day.

(6) A government securities broker or dealer that is a branch or agency of a foreign bank shall make and maintain a record of each computation made pursuant to paragraph (e)(5) of this section and preserve each such record for a period of not less than three years, the first two years in an easily accessible place.

(f)(1) For purposes of this section, the terms "fully paid securities," "margin securities," and "excess margin securities" shall have the meanings described in § 403.4 (b), (c) and (d).

(2) For purposes of this section, the term "customer" shall include any person from whom or on whose behalf a financial institution that is a government securities broker or dealer has received or acquired or holds securities for the account of that person or funds resulting from transactions in securities for or with such person or that represent principal, interest, or other proceeds of such securities. The term shall not include a broker or dealer that is registered pursuant to section 15, 15B or 15C (a)(1)(A) of the Act (15 U.S.C. 78o, 78o–4, 78o–5(a)(1)(A)) or that has filed notice of its status as a government securities broker or dealer pursuant to section 15C(a)(1)(B) of the Act (15 U.S.C. 78o–5(a)(1)(B)) except with respect to securities maintained by such broker or dealer in a Segregated Account as defined in § 403.4(f)(1) and with respect to securities otherwise identified by such broker or dealer as customer securities for purposes of maintaining possession or control of such securities as required by this part. The term "customer" shall not include a director or principal officer of the financial institution or any other person to the extent that that person has a claim for property or funds, which by contract, agreement or understanding, or by operation of law, is part of the capital of the financial institution or is subordinated to the claims of creditors of the financial institution.

(g) If a financial institution executes a sell order of a customer (other than an order to execute a sale of securities which the seller does not own, which for the purposes of this paragraph shall mean that the customer placing the sell order has identified the sale as a short sale to the financial institution) and if for any reason whatever the financial institution has not obtained possession of the government securities, except mortgage-backed securities, from the customer within 30 calendar days, or in the case of mortgage-backed securities within 60 calendar days, after the settlement date, the financial institution shall immediately thereafter close the transaction with the customer by purchasing, or otherwise obtaining, securities of like kind and quantity.

(h) The appropriate regulatory agency of a financial institution that is a government securities broker or dealer may extend the period specified in paragraphs (c)(1)(iii) and (g) of this section on application of the financial institution for one or more limited periods commensurate with the circumstances, provided the appropriate regulatory agency is satisfied that the financial institution is acting in good faith in making the application and

§ 403.6

that exceptional circumstances warrant such action. Each appropriate regulatory agency should make and preserve for a period of not less than three years a record of each extension granted pursuant to this paragraph, which contains a summary of the justification for the granting of the extension.

(Approved by the Office of Management and Budget under control number 1535–0089)

[52 FR 27947, July 24, 1987, as amended at 53 FR 28986, Aug. 1, 1988; 55 FR 6604, Feb. 26, 1990; 59 FR 9406, Feb. 28, 1994; 60 FR 11026, Mar. 1, 1995]

§ 403.6 Compliance with part by futures commission merchants.

A registered government securities broker or dealer that is also a futures commission merchant registered with the CFTC shall comply with the provisions of this part with respect to all customer funds and securities except those that are incidental to the broker's or dealer's futures-related business, as defined in § 240.3a43–1(b) of this title. For purposes of the preceding sentence, the term "customer" shall have the meaning set forth in § 240.15c3–3(a)(1) of this title.

§ 403.7 Effective dates.

(a) *General.* Except as provided in paragraphs (b) through (e) of this section, this part shall be effective on the last business day in October 1987.

(b) *Confirmations.* The requirements of §§ 403.4 and 403.5(d) to describe the specific securities that are the subject of a repurchase transaction, including the market value of such securities, on a confirmation at the initiation of a repurchase transaction or on substitution of other securities shall be effective January 31, 1988.

(c) *Written repurchase agreements.* The requirement to obtain a repurchase agreement in writing with the provisions described in §§ 403.4 and 403.5(d) shall be effective October 31, 1987, in the case of new customers of a government securities broker or dealer and shall be effective January 31, 1988, in the case of existing customers of a government securities broker or dealer. For purposes of this paragraph, an "existing customer" of a government securities broker or dealer is any counterparty with whom the government securities broker or dealer has entered into a repurchase transaction on or after January 1, 1986, but before July 25, 1987. For purposes of this paragraph, a "new customer" of a government securities broker or dealer is any counterparty other than an existing customer.

[52 FR 27947, July 24, 1987, as amended at 53 FR 28986, Aug. 1, 1988; 79 FR 38456, July 8, 2014]

PART 404—RECORDKEEPING AND PRESERVATION OF RECORDS

Sec.
404.1 Application of part to registered brokers and dealers.
404.2 Records to be made and kept current by registered government securities brokers and dealers; records of non-resident registered government securities brokers and dealers.
404.3 Records to be preserved by registered government securities brokers and dealers.
404.4 Records to be made and preserved by government securities brokers and dealers that are financial institutions.
404.5 Securities counts by registered government securities brokers and dealers.

AUTHORITY: 15 U.S.C. 78o–5 (b)(1)(B), (b)(1)(C), (b)(2), (b)(4).

SOURCE: 52 FR 27952, July 24, 1987, unless otherwise noted.

§ 404.1 Application of part to registered brokers and dealers.

Compliance by a registered broker or dealer with § 240.17a–3 of this title (pertaining to records to be made), § 240.17a–4 of this title (pertaining to preservation of records), § 240.17a–13 of this title (pertaining to quarterly securities counts) and § 240.17a–7 of this title (pertaining to records of non-resident brokers or dealers), including provisions in those rules relating to OTC derivatives dealers, constitutes compliance with this part.

[71 FR 54411, Sept. 15, 2006]

§ 404.2 Records to be made and kept current by registered government securities brokers and dealers; records of non-resident registered government securities brokers and dealers.

(a) Every registered government securities broker or dealer shall comply

Department of the Treasury § 404.2

with the requirements of § 240.17a–3 of this title (SEC Rule 17a–3), with the following modifications:

(1) References to "broker or dealer" and "broker or dealer registered pursuant to Section 15 of the Act" include registered government securities brokers or dealers.

(2) References to §§ 240.17a–3, 240.17a–4, 240.17a–5, and 240.17a–13 mean such sections as modified by this part and part 405 of this chapter.

(3) (i) Except in the case of a government securities interdealer broker who is subject to the financial responsibility rules of § 402.1(e) of this chapter and a registered government securities broker or dealer that is a futures commission merchant registered with the CFTC, paragraph 240.17a–3(a)(11) is modified to read as follows:

"(11) A record of the proof of money balances of all ledger accounts in the form of trial balances, and a record of the computation of liquid capital and total haircuts, as of the trial date, determined as provided in § 402.2 of this title; *provided however,* that such computation need not be made by any registered government securities broker or dealer unconditionally exempt from part 402 of this title. Such trial balances and computations shall be prepared currently at least once a month.".

(ii) For a government securities interdealer broker who is subject to the financial responsibility rules of § 402.1(e) of this chapter, references to § 240.15c3–1 include modifications contained in § 402.1(e) of this chapter.

(4) Paragraph 240.17a–3(b)(1) is modified to read as follows:

"(1) This section shall not be deemed to require a government securities broker or dealer registered pursuant to section 15C(a)(1)(A) of the Act (15 U.S.C. 78o–5(a)(1)(A)) to make or keep such records of transactions cleared for such government securities broker or dealer as are customarily made and kept by a clearing broker or dealer pursuant to the requirements of §§ 240.17a–3 and 240.17a–4: *Provided,* that the clearing broker or dealer has and maintains net capital of not less than $250,000 (or, in the case of a clearing broker or dealer that is a registered government securities broker or dealer, liquid capital less total haircuts, determined as provided in § 402.2 of this title, of not less than $250,000) and is otherwise in compliance with § 240.15c3–1, § 402.2 of this title, or the capital rules of the exchange of which such clearing broker or dealer is a member if the members of such exchange are exempt from § 240.15c3–1 by paragraph (b)(2) thereof.".

(5) The undertaking in § 240.17a–3(b)(2) is modified to read as follows:

"The undersigned hereby undertakes to maintain and preserve on behalf of [registered government securities broker or dealer] the books and records required to be maintained by [registered government securities broker or dealer] pursuant to 17 CFR 404.2 and 404.3 and Rules 17a–3 and 17a–4 under the Securities Exchange Act of 1934 and to permit examination of such books and records at any time or from time to time during business hours by examiners or other representatives of the Securities and Exchange Commission, and to furnish to said Commission at its principal office in Washington, DC, or at any regional office of said Commission specified in a demand made by or on behalf of said Commission for copies of books and records, true, correct, complete, and current copies of any or all, or any part, of such books and records. This undertaking shall be binding upon the undersigned, and the successors and assigns of the undersigned.".

(6) Section 240.17a–3(c) is modified to read as follows:

"(c) This section shall not be deemed to require a government securities broker or dealer to make or keep such records as are required by paragraph (a) reflecting the sale and redemption of United States Savings Bonds, United States Savings Notes and United States Savings Stamps.".

(b) Every registered government securities broker or dealer shall comply with the requirements of § 240.17h–1T of this title (SEC Rule 17h–1T), with the following modifications:

(1) For the purposes of this section, references to "broker or dealer" and "broker or dealer registered with the Commission pursuant to Section 15 of the Act" mean registered government securities brokers or dealers.

(2) For the purposes of this section, references to §§ 240.17h–1T and 240.17h–2T of this title mean those sections as modified by §§ 404.2(b) and 405.5, respectively.

(3) For the purposes of this section, "associated person" has the meaning set out in Section 3(a)(18) of the Act (15 U.S.C. 78c(a)(18)), except that natural persons are excluded.

§ 404.2

(4) Paragraphs 240.17h–1T(a)(1)(iii) through (vi) of this title are modified to read as follows:

"(iii) A description of all material pending legal or arbitration proceedings involving a Material Associated Person or the registered government securities broker or dealer that are required to be disclosed, under generally accepted accounting principles on a consolidated basis, by the highest level holding company that is a Material Associated Person.

"(iv) Consolidated and consolidating balance sheets, prepared in accordance with generally accepted accounting principles, which may be unaudited and which shall include the notes to the financial statements, as of quarter-end for the registered government securities broker or dealer and its highest level holding company that is a Material Associated Person;

"(v) Quarterly consolidated and consolidating income statements and consolidated cash flow statements, prepared in accordance with generally accepted accounting principles, which may be unaudited and which shall include the notes to the financial statements, for the registered government securities broker or dealer and its highest level holding company that is a Material Associated Person;

NOTE 1 TO PARAGRAPH 240.17h–1T(a)(1)(v). Statements of comprehensive income (as defined in 17 CFR 210.1–02) must be included in place of income statements, if required by the applicable generally accepted accounting principles.

"(vi) The amount as of quarter-end, and at month-end if greater than quarter-end, of the aggregate long and short securities and commodities positions held by each Material Associated Person, including a separate listing of each single unhedged securities or commodities position, other than U.S. Treasury securities, that exceeds the Materiality Threshold at any month-end;"

(5) Paragraphs 240.17h–1T(a)(3) and (a)(4) of this title are modified to read as follows:

"(3) The information, reports and records required by the provisions of this section shall be maintained and preserved in accordance with the provisions of § 404.3 of this title and shall be kept for a period of not less than three years in an easily accessible place.

"(4) For the purposes of this section and § 405.5 of this title, the term "Materiality Threshold" shall mean the greater of:

"(i) $100 million; or

"(ii) 10 percent of the registered government securities broker's or dealer's liquid capital based on the most recently filed Form G–405 (or, in the case of futures commission merchants and interdealer brokers subject to the capital rules in §§ 402.1(d) and 402.1(e), respectively, tentative net capital based on the most recently filed Form X–17A–5) or 10 percent of the Material Associated Person's tangible net worth, whichever is greater."

(6) Paragraph 240.17h–1T(b) of this title is modified to read as follows:

"(b) *Special provisions with respect to Material Associated Persons subject to the supervision of certain domestic regulators.* A registered government securities broker or dealer shall be deemed to be in compliance with the recordkeeping requirements of paragraph (a)(1)(iii) through (x) of this section with respect to a Material Associated Person if: * * *"

(7) Paragraph 240.17h–1T(c) of this title is modified to read as follows:

"(c) *Special provisions with respect to Material Associated Persons subject to the supervision of a foreign financial regulatory authority.* A registered government securities broker or dealer shall be deemed to be in compliance with the recordkeeping requirements of paragraph (a)(1)(iii) through (x) of this section with respect to a Material Associated Person if such registered government securities broker or dealer maintains in accordance with the provisions of this section copies of the reports filed by such Material Associated Person with a Foreign Financial Regulatory Authority. The registered government securities broker or dealer shall maintain a copy of the original report and a copy translated into the English language. For the purposes of this section, the term Foreign Financial Regulatory Authority shall have the meaning set forth in section 3(a)(52) of the Act."

(8) Paragraph 240.17h–1T(d) of this title is modified to read as follows:

"(d) *Exemptions.* (1) The provisions of this section shall not apply to any registered government securities broker or dealer:

"(i) Which is exempt from the provisions of § 240.15c3–3 of this title, as made applicable by § 403.4, pursuant to paragraph (k)(2) of § 240.15c3–3 of this title; or

"(ii) If the registered government securities broker or dealer does not qualify for an exemption from the provisions of § 240.15c3–3 of this title, as made applicable by § 403.4, and such registered government securities broker or dealer does not hold funds or securities for, or owe money or securities to, customers and does not carry the accounts of, or for, customers; unless

"(iii) In the case of paragraphs (d)(1)(i) or (ii) of this section, the registered government securities broker or dealer maintains capital of at least $20,000,000, including debt

Department of the Treasury § 404.2

subordinated in accordance with Appendix D of § 240.15c3-1 of this title, as modified by Appendix D of § 402.2.

"(2) The provisions of this section shall not apply to any registered government securities broker or dealer which maintains capital of less than $250,000, including debt subordinated in accordance with Appendix D of § 240.15c3-1 of this title, as modified by Appendix D of § 402.2, even if the registered government securities broker or dealer holds funds or securities for, or owes money or securities to, customers or carries the accounts of, or for, customers.

"(3) The provisions of this section shall not apply to any registered government securities broker or dealer which has an associated person that is a registered broker or dealer, provided that:

"(i) The registered broker or dealer is subject to, and in compliance with, the provisions of § 240.17h–1T and § 240.17h–2T of this title, and

"(ii) All of the Material Associated Persons of the registered government securities broker or dealer are Material Associated Persons of the registered broker or dealer subject to § 240.17h–1T and § 240.17h–2T of this title.

"(4) In calculating capital for the purposes of this paragraph, a registered government securities broker or dealer shall include with its equity capital and subordinated debt the equity capital and subordinated debt of any other registered government securities brokers or dealers or registered brokers or dealers that are associated persons of such registered government securities broker or dealer, except that the equity capital and subordinated debt of registered brokers and dealers that are exempt from the provisions of § 240.15c3-3 of this title, pursuant to paragraph (k)(1) of § 240.15c3-3, shall not be included in the capital computation.

"(5) The Secretary may, upon written application by a Reporting Registered Government Securities Broker or Dealer, exempt from the provisions of this section, either unconditionally or on specified terms and conditions, any registered government securities brokers or dealers that are associated persons of such Reporting Registered Government Securities Broker or Dealer. The term "Reporting Registered Government Securities Broker or Dealer" shall mean any registered government securities broker or dealer that submits such application to the Secretary on behalf of its associated registered government securities brokers or dealers."

(9) Paragraph 240.17h–1T(g) of this title is modified to read as follows:

"(g) *Implementation schedule.* Every registered government securities broker or dealer subject to the requirements of this section shall maintain and preserve the information required by paragraphs (a)(1)(i), (ii), and (iii) of this section commencing June 30, 1995. Commencing September 30, 1995, the provisions of this section shall apply in their entirety."

(c)(1) Every non-resident government securities broker or dealer registered or applying for registration pursuant to Section 15C of the Act shall comply with § 240.17a–7 of this title, provided that:

(i) For the purposes of this section, references to "broker or dealer" and "broker or dealer registered or applying for registration pursuant to Section 15 of the Act" mean registered government securities brokers or dealers; and

(ii) For the purposes of this section, references to "any rule or regulation of the Commission" and "any rule or regulation of the Securities and Exchange Commission" mean any rule or regulation of the Secretary.

(2) For the purposes of this section, the term "non-resident government securities broker or dealer" means:

(i) In the case of an individual, one who resides in or has his principal place of business in any place not subject to the jurisdiction of the United States;

(ii) In the case of a corporation, one incorporated in or having its principal place of business in any place not subject to the jurisdiction of the United States; and

(iii) In the case of a partnership or other unincorporated organization or association, one having its principal place of business in any place not subject to the jurisdiction of the United States.

(d) *Effective date.* Paragraph (a) of this section shall be effective on October 31, 1987, *except that* registered government securities brokers and dealers are required to maintain the records specified in § 240.17a–3(a) (12), (13), (14) and (15) beginning July 25, 1987.

(Approved by the Office of Management and Budget under control number 1535–0089)

[52 FR 27952, July 24, 1987, as amended at 60 FR 11026, Mar. 1, 1995; 60 FR 20399, Apr. 26, 1995; 83 FR 66616, Dec. 27, 2018]

§ 404.3 Records to be preserved by registered government securities brokers and dealers.

(a) Every registered government securities broker or dealer, except a government securities interdealer broker subject to the financial responsibility rules of § 402.1(e) and a registered government securities broker or dealer that is also a futures commission merchant registered with the CFTC, shall comply with the requirements of § 240.17a–4 of this title (SEC Rule 17a–4), with the following modifications:

(1) References to "broker or dealer" and "broker and dealer registered pursuant to Section 15 of the Act" include registered government securities brokers or dealers.

(2) References to §§ 240.17a–3, .17a–4, and .17a–5 mean such sections as modified by this part and part 405 of this chapter.

(3) References to § 240.15c3–1, relating to net capital, and "Computation for Net Capital" thereunder mean § 402.2 of this chapter and the computation of the ratio of liquid capital to total haircuts required thereunder.

(4) References to § 240.15c3–3, relating to possession or control of customer securities and balances, mean § 403.4 of this chapter.

(5) References to Form X–17A–5 mean Form G–405 (§ 449.5 of this chapter).

(6) The computation described in § 240.17a–4(b)(8)(x) is not required.

(b) A government securities interdealer broker subject to the financial responsibility rules of § 402.1(e) and a registered government securities broker or dealer that is also a futures commission merchant registered with the CFTC, shall comply with the requirements of § 240.17a–4 of this title (SEC Rule 17a–4), with the following modifications:

(1) References to "broker or dealer" and "broker and dealer" include registered government securities brokers or dealers.

(2) References to §§ 240.17a–3, 240.17a–4, and 240.17a–5 mean such sections as modified by this part and part 405 of this chapter.

(3) With respect to a government securities interdealer broker subject to the financial responsibility rules of § 402.1(e) of this chapter, references to § 240.15c3–1, relating to net capital, and "Computation for Net Capital" thereunder include the modifications contained in § 402.1(e) of this chapter.

(4) References to § 240.15c3–3, relating to possession or control of customer securities and balances, mean § 403.4 of this chapter.

(c) This section shall be effective on July 25, 1987.

(Approved by the Office of Management and Budget under control number 1535–0089)

[52 FR 27952, July 24, 1987, as amended at 60 FR 11026, Mar. 1, 1995]

§ 404.4 Records to be made and preserved by government securities brokers and dealers that are financial institutions.

(a) *Records to be made and kept.* Every financial institution that is a government securities broker or dealer and that is not exempt from this part pursuant to part 401 of this chapter shall comply with the requirements of §§ 404.2 and 404.3 unless such financial institution:

(1) Is subject to 12 CFR part 12 (relating to national banks), 12 CFR part 208 (relating to state member banks of the Federal Reserve System) or 12 CFR part 344 (relating to state banks that are not members of the Federal Reserve System), or is a United States branch or agency of a foreign bank and complies with 12 CFR part 12 (for federally licensed branches and agencies of foreign banks) or 12 CFR part 208 (for uninsured state-licensed branches and agencies of foreign banks) or 12 CFR part 344 (for insured state licensed branches and agencies of foreign banks);

(2) Complies with the recordkeeping requirements of § 450.4(c), (d) and (f) of this chapter; and

(3) Makes and keeps current:

(i)(A) A securities record or ledger reflecting separately for each government security as of the settlement dates all "long" or "short" positions (including government securities that are the subjects of repurchase or reverse repurchase agreements) carried by such financial institution for its own account or for the account of its customers or others (except securities

Department of the Treasury

held in a fiduciary capacity) and showing the location of all government securities long and the offsetting position to all government securities short, including long security count differences and short security count differences classified by the date of the count and verification in which they were discovered, and in all cases the name or designation of the account in which each position is carried;

(B) A complete and current Form G-FIN-4 (§ 449.3 of this chapter) or Form U-4 (promulgated by a self-regulatory organization) or Form MSD-4 (as required for associated persons of bank municipal securities dealers) for each associated person as defined in § 400.3 of this chapter;

(C) A Form G-FIN-5 (§ 449.4 of this chapter) or Form U-5 (promulgated by a self-regulatory organization) or Form MSD-5 (as required for associated persons of bank municipal securities dealers) for each associated person whose association has been terminated as provided in § 400.4(d)(2) of this chapter; and

(D) A complete and current Form G-FIN (§ 449.1 of this chapter) and, if applicable, a Form G-FINW (§ 449.2 of this chapter).

(ii) For purposes of paragraph (a)(3)(i)(A) of this section, "safekeeping" may be shown as a location of any securities long as long as the financial institution complies with the requirements of part 450 of this chapter with respect to such securities.

(b) *Preservation of records.* (1) The records required by paragraph (a)(3)(i)(A) of this section shall be preserved for not less than six years, the first two years in an easily accessible place.

(2) The records required by paragraphs (a)(3)(i) (B) and (C) of this section shall be preserved for at least three years after the person who is the subject of the record has terminated his employment and any other association with the government securities broker or dealer function of the financial institution.

(3) The records required by paragraph (a)(3)(i)(D) of this section shall be preserved for at least three years after the financial institution has notified the appropriate regulatory agency that it has ceased to function as a government securities broker or dealer.

(c) *Effective date.* This section shall be effective on July 25, 1987, *except that* until October 31, 1987, a financial institution government securities broker or dealer is not required to make and keep current the securities position record required by paragraph (a)(3)(i)(A) of this section.

(Approved by the Office of Management and Budget under control number 1535–0089)

[52 FR 27952, July 24, 1987, as amended at 53 FR 28987, Aug. 1, 1988; 60 FR 11026, Mar. 1, 1995; 62 FR 7155, Feb. 18, 1997; 72 FR 54411, Sept. 15, 2006]

§ 404.5 Securities counts by registered government securities brokers and dealers.

(a) *Securities counts.* Every registered government securities broker or dealer shall comply with the requirements of § 240.17a–13 of this title (Commission Rule 17a–13), with the modification that references to "broker or dealer" and "broker and dealer registered pursuant to Section 15 of the Act" include registered government securities brokers or dealers.

(b) *Effective date.* This section shall be effective on October 31, 1987.

(Approved by the Office of Management and Budget under control number 1535–0089)

[52 FR 27952, July 24, 1987, as amended at 60 FR 11026, Mar. 1, 1995]

PART 405—REPORTS AND AUDIT

Sec.
405.1 Application of part to registered brokers and dealers and to financial institutions; transition rule.
405.2 Reports to be made by registered government securities brokers and dealers.
405.3 Notification provisions for certain registered government securities brokers and dealers.
405.4 Financial recordkeeping and reporting of currency and foreign transactions by registered government securities brokers and dealers.
405.5 Risk assessment reporting requirements for registered government securities brokers and dealers.

AUTHORITY: 15 U.S.C. 78o–5 (b)(1)(B), (b)(1)(C), (b)(2), (b)(4).

SOURCE: 52 FR 27954, July 24, 1987, unless otherwise noted.

§ 405.1 Application of part to registered brokers and dealers and to financial institutions; transition rule.

(a) Compliance by registered brokers or dealers with §§ 240.17a–5, 240.17a–8, and 240.17a–11 of this title (Commission Rules 17a–5, 17a–8 and 17a–11), including provisions of those rules relating to OTC derivatives dealers, constitutes compliance with this part.

(b) A government securities broker or dealer that is a financial institution and is subject to financial reporting rules of its appropriate regulatory agency is exempt from the provisions of §§ 405.2 and 405.3.

(c) This part shall be effective July 25, 1987, *Provided however,*

(1) That registered government securities brokers or dealers shall first be required to file the reports required by § 240.17a–5(a), by virtue of § 405.2, for the month and the quarter during which they were first required to comply with part 402 of this chapter other than the interim liquid capital requirements of § 402.1(f); but that

(2) For any quarter ending prior to the quarter during which they were first required to comply with part 402 of this chapter other than the interim liquid capital requirements of § 402.1(f), registered government securities brokers or dealers shall file with the designated examining authority for such registered broker or dealer, within 17 business days after the close of the quarter, an unaudited balance sheet (with appropriate notes) for such quarter, prepared in accordance with generally accepted accounting principles.

[52 FR 27954, July 24, 1987, as amended at 71 FR 54411, Sept. 15, 2006]

§ 405.2 Reports to be made by registered government securities brokers and dealers.

(a) Every registered government securities broker or dealer, except a government securities interdealer broker subject to the financial responsibility requirements of § 402.1(e) of this chapter and a government securities broker or dealer that is also a futures commission merchant registered with the CFTC, shall comply with the requirements of § 240.17a–5 of this title (SEC Rule 17a–5), with the following modifications:

(1) References to "broker or dealer" include registered government securities brokers and dealers.

(2) References to "rules of the Commission" or words of similar import include, where appropriate, the regulations contained in this subchapter.

(3) References to Form X–17A–5 mean Form G–405 (§ 449.5 of this chapter).

(4) For the purposes of § 240.17a–5(a)(4) of this title, the Commission may, on the terms and conditions stated in that subparagraph, declare effective a plan with respect to Form G–405, in which case, that plan shall be treated the same as a plan approved with respect to Form X–17A–5.

(5) References to "net capital" mean "liquid capital" as defined in § 402.2(d) of this chapter.

(6) References to § 240.15c3–1, relating to net capital, mean § 402.2 of this chapter.

(7) Paragraph 240.17a–5(c)(2)(ii) is modified to read as follows:

"(ii) A footnote containing a statement of the registered government securities broker's or dealer's liquid capital, total haircuts, and ratio of liquid capital to total haircuts, determined in accordance with § 402.2 of this title. Such statement shall include summary financial statements of subsidiaries consolidated pursuant to § 402.2c of this title, where material, and the effect thereof on the liquid capital, total haircuts and ratio of liquid capital to total haircuts of the registered government securities broker or dealer.".

(8) References to § 240.15c3–3 and the exhibits thereto, relating to possession or control of customer securities and reserve requirements, mean § 403.4 of this chapter.

(9) The reference to § 240.15b1–2 of this title, relating to financial statements to be filed upon registration, means § 240.15Ca2–2.

(10) The supplemental report described in § 240.17a–5(e)(4) of this title, concerning the Securities Investor Protection Act, is not required.

(11) The statement described in § 240.17a–5(f)(2) of this title shall be headed "Notice Pursuant to Section 405.2," and shall be filed within 30 days

Department of the Treasury § 405.3

following the effective date of registration as a government securities broker or dealer.

(12) References in § 240.17a–5(h)(2) of this title to § 240.17a–11 mean § 405.3(a) of this chapter.

(b) A government securities interdealer broker subject to the financial responsibility requirements of § 402.1(e) of this chapter shall comply with the requirements of § 240.17a–5 of this title (SEC Rule 17a–5), with the following modifications:

(1) References to "broker or dealer" include government securities interdealer brokers;

(2) References to "rules of the Commission" or words of similar import include, where appropriate, the regulations contained in this subchapter.

(3) References to "net capital" mean net capital calculated as provided in § 402.1(e) of this chapter.

(4) References to § 240.15c3–1, relating to net capital, include the modifications contained in § 402.1(e) of this chapter.

(5) References to § 240.15c3–3 and the exhibits thereto, relating to possession or control of customer securities and reserve requirements, mean § 403.4 of this chapter.

(6) The reference to § 240.15b1–2 of this title, relating to financial statements to be filed upon registration, means § 240.15Ca2–2.

(7) The supplemental report described in § 240.17a–5(e)(4) of this title, concerning the Securities Investor Protection Act, is not required.

(8) The statement described in § 240.17a–5(f)(2) of this title shall be headed "Notice Pursuant to Section 405.2" and shall be filed within 30 days following the effective date of registration as a government securities broker or dealer.

(9) References in § 240.17a–5(h)(2) of this title to § 240.17a–11 mean § 405.3(b) of this chapter.

(c) A registered government securities broker or dealer that is also a futures commission merchant registered with the CFTC shall comply with the requirements of § 240.17a–5 of this title (SEC Rule 17a–5), with the following modifications:

(1) References to "broker or dealer" include registered government securities brokers and dealers.

(2) References to "rules of the Commission" or words of similar import include, where appropriate, the regulations contained in this subchapter.

(3) References to § 240.15c3–3 and the exhibits thereto, relating to possession or control of customer securities and reserve requirements, mean § 403.4 of this chapter.

(4) The reference to § 240.15b1–2 of this title, relating to financial statements to be filed upon registration, means § 240.15Ca2–2.

(5) The supplemental report described in § 240.17a–5(e)(4) of this title, concerning the Securities Investor Protection Act, is not required.

(6) The statement described in § 240.17a–5(f)(2) of this title shall be headed "Notice Pursuant to § 405.2," and shall be filed within 30 days following the effective date of registration as a government securities broker or dealer.

(7) References in § 240.17a–5(h)(2) of this title to § 240.17a–11 mean § 405.3(c) of this chapter.

(Approved by the Office of Management and Budget under control number 1535–0089)

[52 FR 27954, July 24, 1987, as amended at 60 FR 11026, Mar. 1, 1995; 64 FR 1737, Jan. 12, 1999; 79 FR 38456, July 8, 2014]

§ 405.3 Notification provisions for certain registered government securities brokers and dealers.

(a) Every registered government securities broker or dealer, other than a government securities interdealer broker that is subject to the financial responsibility requirements of § 402.1(e) and a government securities broker or dealer that is also a futures commission merchant registered with the CFTC, shall comply with the requirements of § 240.17a–11 of this title (SEC Rule 17a–11), with the following modifications:

(1) References to "broker or dealer" include registered government securities brokers and dealers.

(2) References to § 240.15c3–1, relating to net capital, mean § 402.2 of this chapter.

(3) References to "net capital" mean "liquid capital" as defined in § 402.2 of this chapter.

§ 405.3

(4) References to § 240.17a–5, relating to reports and audit, mean § 405.2(a) of this chapter.

(5) Section 240.17a–11(c), for the purposes of this section, is modified to read as follows:

"(c) Every registered government securities broker or dealer shall send notice promptly (but within 24 hours) in accordance with paragraph (g) of this section if a computation made pursuant to the requirements of § 402.2 of this title shows, at any time during the month, that its liquid capital is less than 150 percent of total haircuts, determined in accordance with § 402.2 of this title, or that its capital after deducting total haircuts from liquid capital is less than 120 percent of the registered government securities broker or dealer's minimum capital requirement specified in § 402.2 (b) or (c) of this title as applicable."

(6) References to § 240.17a–3, relating to records, mean § 404.2 of this chapter.

(b) A government securities interdealer broker that is subject to the financial responsibility requirements of § 402.1(e) of this chapter shall comply with the requirements of § 240.17a–11 of this title (SEC Rule 17a–11), with the following modifications:

(1) References to "broker or dealer" include government securities interdealer brokers;

(2) References to § 240.15c3–1, relating to net capital, include the modifications contained in § 402.1(e) of this chapter.

(3) References to "net capital" mean net capital calculated as provided in § 402.1(e) of this chapter.

(4) References to § 240.17a–5, relating to reports and audit, mean § 405.2(b) of this chapter.

(5) References to § 240.17a–3, relating to records, mean § 404.2 of this chapter.

(c) A registered government securities broker or dealer that is also a futures commission merchant registered with the CFTC shall comply with the requirements of § 240.17a–11 of this title (SEC Rule 17a–11), with the following modifications:

(1) References to "broker or dealer" include government securities brokers and dealers.

(2) References to § 240.15c3–1, relating to net capital, mean either § 240.15c3–1 or § 1.17 of this title, depending on which computation results in the higher net capital requirement.

(3) References to "net capital" mean the higher of net capital calculated under § 240.15c3–1 or § 1.17 of this title.

(4) References to § 240.17a–5, relating to reports and audit, mean § 405.2(c) of this chapter.

(5) Section 240.17a–11(c) for the purposes of this section is modified to read as follows:

"(c) Every broker or dealer shall send notice promptly (but within 24 hours) after the occurrence of the events specified in paragraphs (c)(1), (c)(2), (c)(3), or (c)(4) of this section in accordance with paragraph (g) of this section:"

(6) A new paragraph 240.17a–11(c)(4) is added to read as follows:

"(4) If a computation made by a government securities broker or dealer that is not a registered broker or dealer but that is also a futures commission merchant registered with the Commodity Futures Trading Commission shows that:

"(i) The adjusted net capital of such entity is less than the greater of:

"(A) 150 percent of the appropriate minimum dollar amount required by § 1.17(a)(1)(i), or

"(B) 6 percent of the following amount: The customer funds required to be segregated pursuant to § 4d(2) of the Commodity Exchange Act and § 1.17 of this title, less the market value of commodity options purchased by option customers on or subject to the rules of a contract market, provided, however, the deduction for each option customer shall be limited to the amount of customer funds in such option customer's account; or

"(ii) At any point during the month, aggregate indebtedness is in excess of 1200 percent of net capital or total net capital is less than 120 percent of the minimum net capital required."

(7) References to § 240.17a–3, relating to records, mean § 404.2 of this chapter.

(Approved by the Office of Management and Budget under control number 1535–0089)

[52 FR 27954, July 24, 1987, as amended at 59 FR 53731, Oct. 26, 1994; 59 FR 55910, Nov. 9, 1994; 60 FR 18734, Apr. 13, 1995]

Department of the Treasury

§ 405.5

§ 405.4 Financial recordkeeping and reporting of currency and foreign transactions by registered government securities brokers and dealers.

Every registered government securities broker or dealer who is subject to the requirements of the Currency and Foreign Transactions Reporting Act of 1970 shall comply with the reporting, recordkeeping and record retention requirements of 31 CFR part 103. Where 31 CFR part 103 and § 404.3 of this chapter require the same records to be preserved for different periods of time, such records or reports shall be preserved for the longer period of time.

§ 405.5 Risk assessment reporting requirements for registered government securities brokers and dealers.

(a) Every registered government securities broker or dealer shall comply with the requirements of § 240.17h–2T of this title (SEC Rule 17h–2T), with the following modifications:

(1) For the purposes of this section, references to "broker or dealer" and "broker or dealer registered with the Commission pursuant to Section 15 of the Act" mean registered government securities brokers or dealers.

(2) For the purposes of this section, references to §§ 240.17h–1T and 240.17h–2T of this title mean those sections as modified by §§ 404.2(b) and 405.5, respectively.

(3) For the purposes of this section, "associated person" has the meaning set out in Section 3(a)(18) of the Act (15 U.S.C. 78c(a)(18)), except that natural persons are excluded.

(4) Paragraph 240.17h–2T(b) of this title is modified to read as follows:

"(b) *Exemptions.* (1) The provisions of this section shall not apply to any registered government securities broker or dealer:

"(i) Which is exempt from the provisions of § 240.15c3–3 of this title, as made applicable by § 403.4, pursuant to paragraph (k)(2) of § 240.15c3–3 of this title; or

"(ii) If the registered government securities broker or dealer does not qualify for exemption from the provisions of § 240.15c3–3 of this title, as made applicable by § 403.4, and such registered government securities broker or dealer does not hold funds or securities for, or owe money or securities to, customers and does not carry the accounts of, or for, customers; unless

"(iii) In the case of paragraphs (b)(1)(i) or (ii) of this section, the registered government securities broker or dealer maintains capital of at least $20,000,000, including debt subordinated in accordance with appendix D of § 240.15c3–1 of this title, as modified by appendix D of § 402.2.

"(2) The provisions of this section shall not apply to any registered government securities broker or dealer which maintains capital of less than $250,000, including debt subordinated in accordance with appendix D of § 240.15c3–1 of this title, as modified by appendix D of § 402.2, even if the registered government securities broker or dealer holds funds or securities for, or owes money or securities to, customers or carries the accounts of, or for, customers.

"(3) The provisions of this section shall not apply to any registered government securities broker or dealer which has an associated person that is a registered broker or dealer, provided that:

"(i) The registered broker or dealer is subject to, and in compliance with, the provisions of § 240.17h–1T and § 240.17h–2T of this title, and

"(ii) All of the Material Associated Persons of the registered government securities broker or dealer are Material Associated Persons of the registered broker or dealer subject to § 240.17h–1T and § 240.17h–2T of this title.

"(4) In calculating capital for the purposes of this paragraph, a registered government securities broker or dealer shall include with its equity capital and subordinated debt the equity capital and subordinated debt of any other registered government securities brokers or dealers or registered brokers or dealers that are associated persons of such registered government securities broker or dealer, except that the equity capital and subordinated debt of registered brokers and dealers that are exempt from the provisions of § 240.15c3–3 of this title, pursuant to paragraph (k)(1) of § 240.15c3–3, shall not be included in the capital computation.

"(5) The Secretary may, upon written application by a Reporting Registered Government Securities Broker or Dealer, exempt from the provisions of this section, either unconditionally or on specified terms and conditions, any registered government securities brokers or dealers that are associated persons of such Reporting Registered Government Securities Broker or Dealer. The term "Reporting Registered Government Securities Broker or Dealer" shall mean any registered government securities broker or dealer that submits such application to the Secretary on behalf of its associated registered government securities brokers or dealers."

(5) Paragraph 240.17h–2T(c) of this title is modified to read as follows:

"(c) *Special provisions with respect to Material Associated Persons subject to the supervision of certain domestic regulators.* A registered government securities broker or dealer shall be deemed to be in compliance with the reporting requirements of paragraph (a) of this section with respect to a Material Associated Person if such registered government securities broker or dealer files Items 1, 2, and 3 (in Part I) of Form 17–H in accordance with paragraph (a) of this section, provided that:

"(1) Such Material Associated Person is subject to examination by or the reporting requirements of a Federal banking agency and the registered government securities broker or dealer or such Material Associated Person furnishes in accordance with paragraph (a) of this section copies of reports filed by the Material Associated Person with the Federal banking agency pursuant to section 5211 of the Revised Statutes, section 9 of the Federal Reserve Act, section 7(a) of the Federal Deposit Insurance Act, section 10(b) of the Home Owners' Loan Act, or section 5 of the Bank Holding Company Act of 1956; or * * *"

(6) Paragraph 240.17h–2T(d) of this title is modified to read as follows:

"(d) *Special provisions with respect to Material Associated Persons subject to the supervision of a foreign financial regulatory authority.* A registered government securities broker or dealer shall be deemed to be in compliance with the reporting requirements of paragraph (a) of this section with respect to a Material Associated Person if such registered government securities broker or dealer furnishes, in accordance with the provisions of paragraph (a) of this section, Items 1, 2, and 3 (in Part I) of Form 17–H and copies of the reports filed by such Material Associated Person with a Foreign Financial Regulatory Authority. The registered government securities broker or dealer shall file a copy of the original Foreign Financial Regulatory report and a copy translated into the English language. For the purposes of this section, the term Foreign Financial Regulatory Authority shall have the meaning set forth in section 3(a)(52) of the Act."

(Approved by the Office of Management and Budget under control number 1535–0089)

[60 FR 20401, Apr. 26, 1995, as amended at 79 FR 38456, July 8, 2014]

PART 420—LARGE POSITION REPORTING

Sec.
420.1 Applicability.
420.2 Definitions.
420.3 Reporting.
420.4 Recordkeeping.
420.5 Applicability date.
APPENDIX A TO PART 420—SEPARATE REPORTING ENTITY
APPENDIX B TO PART 420—SAMPLE LARGE POSITION REPORT

AUTHORITY: 15 U.S.C. 78o-5(f).

SOURCE: 79 FR 73414, Dec. 10, 2014, unless otherwise noted.

§ 420.1 Applicability.

(a) This part is applicable to all persons that participate in the government securities market, including, but not limited to: Government securities brokers and dealers, depository institutions that exercise investment discretion, registered investment companies, registered investment advisers, pension funds, hedge funds, and insurance companies that may control a position in a recently-issued marketable Treasury bill, note, or bond as those terms are defined in § 420.2.

(b) Notwithstanding paragraph (a) of this section, Treasury requests that central banks (including U.S. Federal

Department of the Treasury § 420.3

Reserve Banks for their own account), foreign governments, and international monetary authorities voluntarily submit large position reports when they meet or exceed a reporting threshold.

§ 420.2 Definitions.

For the purposes of this part:

Aggregating entity means a single entity (*e.g.*, a parent company, affiliate, or organizational component) that is combined with other entities, as specified in the definition of "reporting entity" of this section, to form a reporting entity. In those cases where an entity has no affiliates, the aggregating entity is the same as the reporting entity.

Control means having the authority to exercise investment discretion over the purchase, sale, retention, or financing of specific Treasury securities.

Large position threshold means the minimum dollar par amount of the specified Treasury security that a reporting entity must control in order for the entity to be required to submit a large position report. It also means the minimum number of futures, options on futures, and exchange-traded options contracts for which the specified Treasury security is deliverable that the reporting entity must control in order for the entity to be required to submit a large position report. Treasury will announce the large position thresholds, which may vary with each notice of request to report large position information and with each specified Treasury security. Treasury may announce different thresholds for certain reporting criteria. Under no circumstances will a large position threshold be less than 10 percent of the amount outstanding of the specified Treasury security.

Recently-issued means:

(1) With respect to Treasury securities that are issued quarterly or more frequently, the three most recent issues of the security.

(2) With respect to Treasury securities that are issued less frequently than quarterly, the two most recent issues of the security.

(3) With respect to a reopened security, the entire issue of a reopened security (older and newer portions) based on the date the new portion of the reopened security is issued by Treasury (or for when-issued securities, the scheduled issue date).

(4) For all Treasury securities, a security announced to be issued or auctioned but unissued (when-issued), starting from the date of the issuance announcement. The most recent issue of the security is the one most recently announced.

(5) Treasury security issues other than those specified in paragraphs (1) and (2) of this definition, provided that such large position information is necessary and appropriate for monitoring the impact of concentrations of positions in Treasury securities.

Reporting entity means any corporation, partnership, person, or other entity and its affiliates, as further provided herein. For the purposes of this definition, an affiliate is any: Entity that is more than 50% owned, directly or indirectly, by the aggregating entity or by any other affiliate of the aggregating entity; person or entity that owns, directly or indirectly, more than 50% of the aggregating entity; person or entity that owns, directly or indirectly, more than 50% of any other affiliate of the aggregating entity; or entity, a majority of whose board of directors or a majority of whose general partners are directors or officers of the aggregating entity or any affiliate of the aggregating entity.

(1) Subject to the conditions prescribed in appendix A to this part, one aggregating entity, or a combination of aggregating entities, may be recognized as a separate reporting entity.

(2) Notwithstanding this definition, any persons or entities that intentionally act together with respect to the investing in, retention of, or financing of Treasury securities are considered, collectively, to be one reporting entity.

Reporting requirement means that an entity must file a large position report when it meets any one of eight criteria contained in appendix B to this part.

§ 420.3 Reporting.

(a) A reporting entity must file a large position report if it meets the reporting requirement as defined in § 420.2. Treasury will provide notice of the large position thresholds by issuing

§ 420.3

a public announcement and subsequently publishing the notice in the FEDERAL REGISTER. Such notice will identify the Treasury security issue(s) to be reported (including, where applicable, identifying the related STRIPS principal component); the date or dates for which the large position information must be reported; and the large position thresholds for that issue. A reporting entity is responsible for taking reasonable actions to be aware of such a notice.

(b) A reporting entity shall select one entity from among its aggregating entities (*i.e.*, the designated filing entity) as the entity designated to compile and file a report on behalf of the reporting entity. The designated filing entity shall be responsible for filing any large position reports in response to a notice issued by Treasury and for maintaining the additional records prescribed in § 420.4.

(c)(1) In response to a notice issued under paragraph (a) of this section requesting large position information, a reporting entity that controls an amount of the specified Treasury security that equals or exceeds one of the specified large position thresholds stated in the notice shall compile and report the amounts of the reporting entity's positions in the order specified, as follows:

(i) *Part I.* Positions in the Security Being Reported as of the Opening of Business on the Report Date, including positions:

(A) In book-entry accounts of the reporting entity;

(B) As collateral against borrowings of funds on general collateral finance repurchase agreements;

(C) As collateral against borrowings of funds on tri-party repurchase agreements;

(D) As collateral or margin to secure other contractual obligations of the reporting entity; and

(E) Otherwise available to the reporting entity.

(ii) *Part II.* Settlement Obligations Attributable to Outright Purchase and Sale Contracts Negotiated Prior to or on the Report Date (excluding settlement fails), including:

(A) Obligations to receive or deliver, on the report date, the security being reported attributable to contracts for cash settlement (T + 0);

(B) Obligations to receive or deliver, on the report date, the security being reported attributable to contracts for regular settlement (T + 1);

(C) Obligations to receive or deliver, on the report date, the security being reported attributable to contracts, including when-issued contracts, for forward settlement (T + n, n>1);

(D) Obligations to receive, on the report date, the security being reported attributable to Treasury auction awards; and

(E) Obligations to receive or deliver, on the report date, principal STRIPS derived from the security being reported attributable to contracts for cash settlement, regular settlement, when-issued settlement, and forward settlement.

(iii) *Part III.* Settlement Obligations Attributable to Delivery-versus-Payment Financing Contracts (including repurchase agreements and securities lending agreements) Negotiated Prior to or on the Report Date (excluding settlement fails), including:

(A) Obligations to receive or deliver, on the report date, the security being reported, and principal STRIPS derived from the security being reported, attributable to overnight agreements;

(B) Obligations to receive or deliver, on the report date, the security being reported, and principal STRIPS derived from the security being reported, attributable to term agreements due to open on, or due to close on, the report date; and

(C) Obligations to receive or deliver, on the report date, the security being reported, and principal STRIPS derived from the security being reported, attributable to open agreements due to open on, or due to close on, the report date.

(iv) *Part IV.* Settlement Fails from Days Prior to the Report Date (Legacy Obligations), including obligations to receive or deliver, on the report date, the security being reported, and principal STRIPS derived from the security being reported, arising out of settlement fails on days prior to the report date.

(v) *Part V.* Settlement Fails as of the Close of Business on the Report Date,

Department of the Treasury

§ 420.3

including obligations to receive or deliver, on the business day following the report date, the security being reported, and principal STRIPS derived from the security being reported, arising out of settlement fails on the report date.

(vi) *Part VI.* Positions in the Security Being Reported as of the Close of Business on the Report Date, including positions:

(A) In book-entry accounts of the reporting entity;

(B) As collateral against borrowings of funds on general collateral finance repurchase agreements;

(C) As collateral against borrowings of funds on tri-party repurchase agreements;

(D) As collateral or margin to secure other contractual obligations of the reporting entity; and

(E) Otherwise available to the reporting entity.

(vii) *Part VII.* Quantity of Continuing Delivery-versus-Payment Financing Contracts for the Security Being Reported, including the gross amount of security being reported borrowed or lent out on term delivery-versus-payment repurchase agreements opened before the report date and not due to close until after the report date, and on open delivery-versus-payment repurchase agreements opened before the report date and not closed on the report date.

(viii) *Part VIII.* Futures and Options Contracts, including:

(A)(*1*) Net position, as of the close of market on the business day prior to the report date, in futures, options on futures, and exchange-traded options contracts on which the security being reported is deliverable (report number of contracts); and

(*2*) Net position, as of the close of market on the report date, in futures, options on futures, and exchange-traded options contracts on which the security being reported is deliverable (report number of contracts).

(B)(*1*) Net position, as of the close of market on the business day prior to the report date, in over-the-counter options contracts on which the security being reported is deliverable (report notional amount of contracts regardless of option delta); and

(*2*) Net position, as of the close of market on the report date, in over-the-counter options contracts on which the security being reported is deliverable (report notional amount of contracts regardless of option delta).

(d) An illustration of a sample report is contained in appendix B of this part.

(e) Each of the components of Part I–Part VIII of paragraph (c)(1) of this section shall be reported as a positive number or zero. All reportable amounts should be reported in the order specified above and at par in millions of dollars, except futures, options on futures, and exchange-traded options contracts, which should be reported as the number of contracts. Over-the-counter options contracts should be reported as the notional dollar amount of contracts regardless of option delta.

(f) Each submitted large position report must include the following administrative information: Name of the reporting entity; address of the principal place of business; name and address of the designated filing entity; the Treasury security that is being reported; the CUSIP number for the security being reported; the report date or dates for which information is being reported; the date the report was submitted; name and telephone number of the person to contact regarding information reported; and name and position of the authorized individual submitting this report.

(1) Reporting entities have the option to identify the type(s) of business engaged in by the reporting entity and its aggregating entities with positions in the specified Treasury security by checking the appropriate box. The types of businesses include: Broker or dealer, government securities broker or dealer, municipal securities broker or dealer, futures commission merchant, bank holding company, non-bank holding company, bank, investment adviser, commodity pool operator, pension trustee, non-pension trustee, and insurance company. Reporting entities may select as many business types as applicable. If the reporting entity is engaged in a business that is not listed, it could select "other" and provide a description of its business with respect to positions in the specified Treasury security.

§ 420.4

(2) Reporting entities also have the option to identify their overall investment strategy with respect to positions in the specified Treasury security by checking the appropriate box. Active investment strategies include those that involve purchasing, selling, borrowing, lending, and financing positions in the security prior to maturity. Passive investment strategies include those that involve holding the security until maturity. A combination of active and passive strategies would involve applying the aforementioned active and passive strategies to all or a portion of a reporting entity's positions in the specified Treasury security. Reporting entities may select the most applicable investment strategy.

(g) The large position report must be signed by one of the following: The chief compliance officer; chief legal officer; chief financial officer; chief operating officer; chief executive officer; or managing partner or equivalent of the designated filing entity. The designated filing entity must also include in the report, immediately preceding the signature, a statement of certification as follows:

By signing below, I certify that the information contained in this report with regard to the designated filing entity is accurate and complete. Further, after reasonable inquiry and to the best of my knowledge and belief, I certify that: (i) The information contained in this report with regard to any other aggregating entities is accurate and complete; and (ii) the reporting entity, including all aggregating entities, is in compliance with the requirements of 17 CFR part 420.

(h) The report must be filed before noon Eastern Time on the fourth business day following issuance of a public announcement.

(i) A report to be filed pursuant to paragraph (c) of this section will be considered filed when received by Treasury or the Federal Reserve Bank of New York according to the instructions provided in the public announcement.

(j) A reporting entity that has filed a report pursuant to paragraph (c) of this section shall, at the request of Treasury, or the Federal Reserve Bank of New York at the direction of Treasury, timely provide any supplemental information pertaining to such report.

(Approved by the Office of Management and Budget under control number 1535–0089)

[79 FR 73414, Dec. 10, 2014, as amended at 83 FR 52768, Oct. 18, 2018]

§ 420.4 Recordkeeping.

(a) *Recordkeeping responsibility of aggregating entities.* Notwithstanding the provisions of paragraphs (b) and (c) of this section, an aggregating entity that controls a portion of its reporting entity's position in a recently-issued Treasury security, when such position of the reporting entity equals or exceeds $2 billion, shall be responsible for making and maintaining the records prescribed in this section.

(b) *Records to be made and preserved by entities that are subject to the recordkeeping provisions of the SEC, Treasury, or the appropriate regulatory agencies for financial institutions.* As an aggregating entity, compliance by a registered broker or dealer, registered government securities broker or dealer, noticed financial institution, depository institution that exercises investment discretion, registered investment adviser, or registered investment company with the applicable recordkeeping provisions of the SEC, Treasury, or the appropriate regulatory agencies for financial institutions shall constitute compliance with this section, provided that, if such entity is also the designated filing entity, it:

(1) Makes and keeps copies of all large position reports filed pursuant to this part;

(2) Makes and keeps supporting documents or schedules used to compute data for the large position reports filed pursuant to this part, including any certifications or schedules it receives from aggregating entities pertaining to their holdings of the reporting entity's position;

(3) Makes and keeps a chart showing the organizational entities that are aggregated (if applicable) in determining the reporting entity's position; and

(4) With respect to recordkeeping preservation requirements that contain more than one retention period, preserves records required by paragraphs (b)(1) through (3) of this section for the

Department of the Treasury

longest record retention period of applicable recordkeeping provisions.

(c) *Records to be made and preserved by other entities.* (1) An aggregating entity that is not subject to the provisions of paragraph (b) of this section shall make and preserve a journal, blotter, or other record of original entry containing an itemized record of all transactions that contribute to a reporting entity's position, including information showing the account for which such transactions were effected and the following information pertaining to the identification of each instrument: The type of security, the par amount, the CUSIP number, the trade date, the maturity date, the type of transaction (*e.g.*, a reverse repurchase agreement), and the name or other designation of the person from whom sold or purchased.

(2) If such aggregating entity is also the designated filing entity, then in addition it shall make and preserve the following records:

(i) Copies of all large position reports filed pursuant to this part;

(ii) Supporting documents or schedules used to compute data for the large position reports filed pursuant to this part, including any certifications or schedules it receives from aggregating entities pertaining to their holdings of the reporting entity's position; and

(iii) A chart showing the organizational entities that are aggregated (if applicable) in determining the reporting entity's position.

(3) With respect to the records required by paragraphs (c)(1) and (2) of this section, each such aggregating entity shall preserve such records for a period of not less than six years, the first two years in an easily accessible place. If an aggregating entity maintains its records at a location other than its principal place of business, the aggregating entity must maintain an index that states the location of the records, and such index must be easily accessible at all times.

(Approved by the Office of Management and Budget under control number 1535–0089)

§420.5 Applicability date.

The provisions of this part shall be first applicable beginning March 31, 1997.

APPENDIX A TO PART 420—SEPARATE REPORTING ENTITY

Subject to the following conditions, one or more aggregating entity(ies) (*e.g.*, parent, subsidiary, or organizational component) in a reporting entity, either separately or together with one or more other aggregating entity(ies), may be recognized as a separate reporting entity. All of the following conditions must be met for such entity(ies) to qualify for recognition as a separate reporting entity:

(1) Such entity(ies) must be prohibited by law or regulation from exchanging, or must have established written internal procedures designed to prevent the exchange of information related to transactions in Treasury securities with any other aggregating entity;

(2) Such entity(ies) must not be created for the purpose of circumventing these large position reporting rules;

(3) Decisions related to the purchase, sale or retention of Treasury securities must be made by employees of such entity(ies). Employees of such entity(ies) who make decisions to purchase or dispose of Treasury securities must not perform the same function for other aggregating entities; and

(4) The records of such entity(ies) related to the ownership, financing, purchase and sale of Treasury securities must be maintained by such entity(ies). Those records must be identifiable—separate and apart from similar records for other aggregating entities.

To obtain recognition as a separate reporting entity, each aggregating entity or group of aggregating entities must request such recognition from Treasury pursuant to the procedures outlined in §400.2(c) of this chapter. Such request must provide a description of the entity or group and its position within the reporting entity, and provide the following certification:

[Name of the entity(ies)] hereby certifies that to the best of its knowledge and belief it meets the conditions for a separate reporting entity as described in appendix A to 17 CFR part 420. The above named entity also certifies that it has established written policies or procedures, including ongoing compliance monitoring processes, that are designed to prevent the entity or group of entities from:

(1) Exchanging any of the following information with any other aggregating entity (a) positions that it holds or plans to trade in a Treasury security; (b) investment strategies that it plans to follow regarding Treasury securities; and (c) financing strategies that it plans to follow regarding Treasury securities, or

(2) In any way intentionally acting together with any other aggregating entity with respect to the purchase, sale, retention or financing of Treasury securities.

Pt. 420, App. B

The above-named entity agrees that it will promptly notify Treasury in writing when any of the information provided to obtain separate reporting entity status changes or when this certification is no longer valid.

Any entity, including any organizational component thereof, that previously has received recognition as a separate bidder in Treasury auctions from Treasury pursuant to 31 CFR part 356 is also recognized as a separate reporting entity without the need to request such status, provided such entity continues to be in compliance with the conditions set forth in appendix A to 31 CFR part 356.

APPENDIX B TO PART 420—SAMPLE LARGE POSITION REPORT

FORMULA FOR DETERMINING WHETHER TO SUBMIT A LARGE POSITION REPORT

(Report all components as a positive number or zero in millions of dollars at par value)

Department of the Treasury   **Pt. 420, App. B**

	Column A	Column B
	Quantity	
	Obligations to Receive	Obligations to Deliver

Part I. Positions in the Security Being Reported as of the Opening of Business on the Report Date

1. In book-entry accounts of the reporting entity

2. As collateral against borrowings of funds on general collateral finance repurchase agreements

3. As collateral against borrowings of funds on tri-party repurchase agreements

4. As collateral or margin to secure other contractual obligations of the reporting entity

5. Otherwise available to the reporting entity

Part II. Settlement Obligations Attributable to Outright Purchase and Sale Contracts Negotiated Prior to or on the Report Date (excluding settlement fails)

6. Obligations to receive or deliver, on the report date, the security being reported attributable to contracts for cash settlement (T+0)

7. Obligations to receive or deliver, on the report date, the security being reported attributable to contracts for regular settlement (T+1)

8. Obligations to receive or deliver, on the report date, the security being reported attributable to contracts, including when-issued contracts, for forward settlement (T+n, n>1)

Pt. 420, App. B   **17 CFR Ch. IV (4–1–23 Edition)**

	Obligations to Receive	Obligations to Deliver
9. Obligations to receive, on the report date, the security being reported attributable to Treasury auction awards		
10. Obligations to receive or deliver, on the report date, principal STRIPS derived from the security being reported attributable to contracts for cash settlement, regular settlement, when-issued settlement, and forward settlement		
Part III. Settlement Obligations Attributable to Delivery-versus-Payment Financing Contracts (including repurchase agreements and securities lending agreements) Negotiated Prior to or on the Report Date (excluding settlement fails)		
11. Obligations to receive or deliver, on the report date, the security being reported, and principal STRIPS derived from the security being reported, attributable to overnight agreements		
12. Obligations to receive or deliver, on the report date, the security being reported, and principal STRIPS derived from the security being reported, attributable to term agreements due to open on, or due to close on, the report date		
13. Obligations to receive or deliver, on the report date, the security being reported, and principal STRIPS derived from the security being reported, attributable to open agreements due to open on, or due to close on, the report date		
Part IV. Settlement Fails from Days Prior to the Report Date (Legacy Obligations)		
14. Obligations to receive or deliver, on the report date, the security being reported, and principal STRIPS derived from the security being reported, arising out of settlement fails on days prior to the report date		

Department of the Treasury   Pt. 420, App. B

Part V. Settlement Fails as of the Close of Business on the Report Date

	Quantity
15. Obligations to receive or deliver, on the business day following the report date, the security being reported, and principal STRIPS derived from the security being reported, arising out of settlement fails on the report date	

Part VI. Positions in the Security Being Reported as of the Close of Business on the Report Date

	Quantity
16. In book-entry accounts of the reporting entity	
17. As collateral against borrowings of funds on general collateral finance repurchase agreements	
18. As collateral against borrowings of funds on tri-party repurchase agreements	
19. As collateral or margin to secure other contractual obligations of the reporting entity	
20. Otherwise available to the reporting entity	

Part VII. Quantity of Continuing Delivery-versus-Payment Financing Contracts for the Security Being Reported

	Quantity Borrowed	Quantity Lent
21. Gross amount of security being reported borrowed or lent out on term delivery-versus-payment repurchase agreements opened before the report date and not due to close until after the report date, and on open delivery-versus-payment repurchase agreements opened before the report date and not closed on the report date		

647

Pt. 420, App. B   **17 CFR Ch. IV (4–1–23 Edition)**

	Quantity if Net Long	Quantity if Net Short

Part VIII. Futures and Options Contracts

22. a) Net position, as of the close of market on the business day prior to the report date, in futures, options on futures, and exchange-traded options contracts on which the security being reported is deliverable (report number of contracts)

   b) Net position, as of the close of market on the report date, in futures, options on futures, and exchange-traded options contracts on which the security being reported is deliverable (report number of contracts)

23. a) Net position, as of the close of market on the business day prior to the report date, in over-the-counter options contracts on which the security being reported is deliverable (report notional amount of contracts regardless of option delta)

   b) Net position, as of the close of market on the report date, in over-the-counter options contracts on which the security being reported is deliverable (report notional amount of contracts regardless of option delta)

A reporting entity must submit a large position report if it meets any one of the following criteria:

[ ] A. If the sum of column A in lines 1 through 5 and the gross amount lent in line 21 is greater than or equal to the announced large position threshold.
[ ] B. If the sum of column A in lines 16 through 20 and the gross amount lent in line 21 is greater than or equal to the announced large position threshold.
[ ] C. If the sum of column A in lines 6 through 14 is greater than or equal to the announced large position threshold.
[ ] D. If the sum of column B in lines 6 through 14 is greater than or equal to the announced large position threshold.
[ ] E. If column A in line 15 is greater than or equal to the announced large position threshold.
[ ] F. If column B in line 15 is greater than or equal to the announced large position threshold.
[ ] G. If line 22(a) or line 22(b) is greater than or equal to the announced futures, options on futures and exchange-traded options contract threshold.
[ ] H. If line 23(a) or line 23(b) is greater than or equal to the announced large position threshold.

Please specify which of the above criteria triggered the reporting requirement (check all that apply).

648

Department of the Treasury   **Pt. 420, App. B**

Administrative Information to be Provided in the Report

- Name of Reporting Entity:
- Address of Principal Place of Business:
- Name and Address of the Designated Filing Entity:
- Treasury Security Reported on:
- CUSIP Number:

- Date or Dates for which Information is Being Reported:
- Date Report Submitted:
- Name and Telephone Number of Person to Contact Regarding Information Reported:

Name and Position of Authorized Individual Submitting this Report (Chief Compliance Officer; Chief Legal Officer; Chief Financial Officer; Chief Operating Officer; Chief Executive Officer; or Managing Partner or Equivalent of the Designated Filing Entity Authorized to Sign Such Report on Behalf of the Entity):

(Optional) Identify the business(es) engaged in by the reporting entity and any of its aggregating entities with respect to the specified Treasury security (check all that apply).

[ ] A. Broker or Dealer
[ ] B. Government Securities Broker or Dealer
[ ] C. Municipal Securities Broker or Dealer
[ ] D. Futures Commission Merchant
[ ] E. Bank Holding Company
[ ] F. Non-Bank Holding Company
[ ] G. Bank
[ ] H. Investment Adviser
[ ] I. Commodity Pool Operator
[ ] J. Pension Trustee
[ ] K. Non-Pension Trustee
[ ] L. Insurance Company
[ ] M. Other (specify) _____

(Optional) Do you consider the reporting entity's overall investment strategy with respect to the specified Treasury security to be:

[ ] Active
[ ] Passive
[ ] Combination of Active and Passive

Statement of Certification: "By signing below, I certify that the information contained in this report with regard to the designated filing entity is accurate and complete. Further, after reasonable inquiry and to the best of my knowledge and belief, I certify that: (i) the information contained in this report with regard to any other aggregating entities is accurate and complete; and (ii) the reporting entity, including all aggregating entities, is in compliance with the requirements of 17 CFR Part 420."

Signature of Authorized Person:

PART 449—FORMS, SECTION 15C OF THE SECURITIES EXCHANGE ACT OF 1934

Sec.
449.1 Form G-FIN, notification by financial institutions of status as government securities broker or dealer pursuant to section 15C(a)(1)(B)(i) of the Securities Exchange Act of 1934.
449.2 Form G-FINW, notification by financial institutions of cessation of status as government securities broker or dealer pursuant to section 15C(a)(1)(B)(i) of the Securities Exchange Act of 1934 and §400.6 of this chapter.
449.3 Form G-FIN-4, notification by persons associated with financial institutions that are government securities brokers and dealers pursuant to section 15C(a)(1)(B)(i) of the Securities Exchange Act of 1934 and §400.4 of this chapter.
449.4 Form G-FIN-5, notification of termination of association with a financial institution that is a government securities broker or dealer pursuant to section 15C(a)(1)(B)(i) of the Securities Exchange Act of 1934 and §400.4 of this chapter.
449.5 Form G-405, information required of registered government securities brokers and dealers pursuant to section 15C of the Securities Exchange Act of 1934 and §§405.2 and 405.3 of this chapter.

AUTHORITY: 15 U.S.C. 78o-5(a), (b)(1)(B), (b)(4).

SOURCE: 52 FR 27956, July 24, 1987, unless otherwise noted.

§449.1 Form G-FIN, notification by financial institutions of status as government securities broker or dealer pursuant to section 15C(a)(1)(B)(i) of the Securities Exchange Act of 1934.

This form is to be used by financial institutions that are government securities brokers or dealers not exempt under part 401 of this chapter to notify their appropriate regulatory agency of their status. The form is promulgated by the Board of Governors of the Federal Reserve System and is available from the Board of Governors of the Federal Reserve System, the Comptroller of the Currency, the Federal Deposit Insurance Corporation, and the SEC.

[52 FR 27956, July 24, 1987, as amended at 79 FR 38456, July 8, 2014]

§449.2 Form G-FINW, notification by financial institutions of cessation of status as government securities broker or dealer pursuant to section 15C(a)(1)(B)(i) of the Securities Exchange Act of 1934 and §400.6 of this chapter.

This form is to be used by financial institutions that are government securities brokers or dealers to notify their appropriate regulatory agency that they have ceased to function as a government securities broker or dealer. The form is promulgated by the Board of Governors of the Federal Reserve System and is available from the Board of Governors of the Federal Reserve System, the Comptroller of the Currency, the Federal Deposit Insurance Corporation, and the SEC.

[52 FR 27956, July 24, 1987, as amended at 79 FR 38456, July 8, 2014]

§449.3 Form G-FIN-4, notification by persons associated with financial institutions that are government securities brokers and dealers pursuant to section 15C(a)(1)(B)(i) of the Securities Exchange Act of 1934 and §400.4 of this chapter.

This form is to be used by associated persons of financial institutions that are government securities brokers or dealers to provide certain information to the financial institution and the appropriate regulatory agency concerning employment, residence, and statutory disqualification. The form is promulgated by the Department of the Treasury and is available from the Board of Governors of the Federal Reserve System, the Comptroller of the Currency, the Federal Deposit Insurance Corporation, and the SEC.

[52 FR 27956, July 24, 1987, as amended at 79 FR 38456, July 8, 2014]

EDITORIAL NOTE: For FEDERAL REGISTER citations affecting Form G-FIN-4, see the List of CFR Sections Affected, which appears in the Finding Aids section of the printed volume and at www.govinfo.gov.

§ 449.4 Form G-FIN-5, notification of termination of association with a financial institution that is a government securities broker or dealer pursuant to section 15C(a)(1)(B)(i) of the Securities Exchange Act of 1934 and § 400.4 of this chapter.

This form is to be used by financial institutions that are government securities brokers or dealers to notify the appropriate regulatory agency of the fact that an associated person is no longer associated with the government securities broker or dealer function of the financial institution. The form is promulgated by the Department of the Treasury and is available from the Board of Governors of the Federal Reserve System, the Comptroller of the Currency, the Federal Deposit Insurance Corporation, and the SEC.

[52 FR 27956, July 24, 1987, as amended at 79 FR 38456, July 8, 2014]

§ 449.5 Form G–405, information required of registered government securities brokers and dealers pursuant to section 15C of the Securities Exchange Act of 1934 and §§ 405.2 and 405.3 of this chapter.

This form is to be used by registered government securities brokers and dealers to make the monthly, quarterly and annual financial reports required by part 405 of this chapter. The form is promulgated by the Department of the Treasury and is available from the SEC and the designated examining authorities.

EDITORIAL NOTE: For FEDERAL REGISTER citations affecting Form G–405, see the List of CFR Sections Affected, which appears in the Finding Aids section of the printed volume and at *www.govinfo.gov*.

SUBCHAPTER B—REGULATIONS UNDER TITLE II OF THE GOVERNMENT SECURITIES ACT OF 1986

PART 450—CUSTODIAL HOLDINGS OF GOVERNMENT SECURITIES BY DEPOSITORY INSTITUTIONS

Sec.
450.1 Scope of regulations; office responsible.
450.2 Definitions.
450.3 Exemption for holdings subject to fiduciary standards.
450.4 Custodial holdings of government securities.
450.5 Effective date.

AUTHORITY: Sec. 201, Pub. L. 99–571, 100 Stat. 3222–23 (31 U.S.C. 3121, 9110); Sec. 101, Pub. L. 99–571, 100 Stat. 3208 (15 U.S.C. 78o–5(b)(1)(A), (b)(4), (b)(5)(B)).

SOURCE: 52 FR 27957, July 24, 1987, unless otherwise noted.

§ 450.1 Scope of regulations; office responsible.

(a) This part applies to depository institutions that hold government securities as fiduciary, custodian, or otherwise for the account of a customer, and that are not government securities brokers or dealers, as defined in sections 3(a)(43) and 3(a)(44) of the Securities Exchange Act of 1934 (15 U.S.C. 78c(a)(43)–(44)). Depository institutions exempt under part 401 of this chapter from the requirements of Subchapter A of this chapter must comply with this part. Certain depository institutions that are government securities brokers or dealers must also comply with this part, as well as with additional requirements set forth in § 403.5.

(b) The regulations in this subchapter are promulgated by the Assistant Secretary (Domestic Finance) pursuant to a delegation of authority from the Secretary of the Treasury. The office responsible for the regulations is the Office of the Commissioner, Bureau of the Fiscal Service. Procedures for obtaining interpretations of the regulations are set forth at § 400.2.

[52 FR 27957, July 24, 1987, as amended at 53 FR 28987, Aug. 1, 1988; 79 FR 38456, July 8, 2014]

§ 450.2 Definitions.

For purposes of this subchapter:

(a) *Appropriate regulatory agency* has the meaning set out in section 3(a)(34)(G) of the Securities Exchange Act of 1934 (15 U.S.C. 78c(a)(34)(G)), except that the appropriate regulatory agency for—

(1) A Federal credit union as defined in 12 U.S.C. 1752(1) and an insured credit union as defined in 12 U.S.C. 1752(7) is the National Credit Union Administration; and

(2) Any depository institution for whom an appropriate regulatory agency is not explicitly specified by either section 3(a)(34)(G) or this paragraph, is the SEC;

(b) *Customer* includes, but is not limited to, the counterparty to a transaction pursuant to a repurchase agreement for whom the depository institution retains possession of the security sold subject to repurchase, but does not include a broker or dealer that is registered pursuant to section 15, 15B or 15C(a)(1)(A) of the Act (15 U.S.C. 78o, 78o–4, 78o–5(a)(1)(A)) or that has filed notice of its status as a government securities broker or dealer pursuant to section 15C(a)(1)(B) of the Act (15 U.S.C. 78o–5(a)(1)(B)) except as provided in § 450.4.

(c) *Depository institution* has the meaning stated in clauses (i) through (vi) of section 19(b)(1)(A) of the Federal Reserve Act (12 U.S.C. 461(b)(1)(A) (i)–(vi)) and also includes a foreign bank, an agency or branch of a foreign bank and a commercial lending company owned or controlled by a foreign bank (as such terms are defined in the International Banking Act of 1978, Pub. L. 95–369, 92 Stat. 607);

(d) *Fiduciary capacity* includes trustee, executor, administrator, registrar, transfer agent, guardian, assignee, receiver, managing agent, and any other similar capacity involving the sole or shared exercise of discretion by a depository institution having fiduciary powers that is supervised by a Federal or state financial institution regulatory agency; and

§ 450.3   17 CFR Ch. IV (4–1–23 Edition)

(e) *Government securities* means:

If . . .	Then . . .
(1)(i) A depository institution is a government securities broker or dealer as defined in sections 3(a)(43) and 3(a)(44) of the Securities Exchange Act of 1934 (15 U.S.C. 78c(a)(43)–(44)).	"Government securities" means those obligations described in subparagraphs (A), (B), (C), or (E) of section 3(a)(42) of the Securities Exchange Act of 1934 (15 U.S.C. 78c(a)(42)(A)–(C), (E)).
(ii) A depository institution is exempt under Part 401 of this chapter from the requirements of Subchapter A.	"Government securities" means those obligations described in subparagraphs (A), (B), (C), or (E) of section 3(a)(42) of the Securities Exchange Act of 1934 (15 U.S.C. 78c(a)(42)(A)–(C), (E)).
(2) A depository institution is not a government securities broker or dealer as defined in sections 3(a)(43) and 3(a)(44) of the Securities Exchange Act of 1934 (15 U.S.C. 78c(a)(43)–(44)).	"Government securities" means those obligations described in subparagraphs (A), (B), or (C) of section 3(a)(42) of the Securities Exchange Act of 1934 (15 U.S.C. 78c(a)(42)(A)–(C))

[52 FR 27957, July 24, 1987, as amended at 55 FR 6604, Feb. 26, 1990; 66 FR 28655, May 24, 2001; 66 FR 29888, June 1, 2001]

§ 450.3 Exemption for holdings subject to fiduciary standards.

(a) The Secretary has determined that the rules and standards of the Comptroller of the Currency, the Board of Governors of the Federal Reserve System, and the Federal Deposit Insurance Corporation governing the holding of government securities in a fiduciary capacity by depository institutions subject thereto are adequate. Accordingly, such depository institutions are exempt from this part with respect to their holdings of government securities in a fiduciary capacity and their holdings of government securities in a custodial capacity provided that:

(1) Such institution has adopted policies and procedures that would apply to such custodial holdings all the requirements imposed by its appropriate regulatory agency that are applicable to government securities held in a fiduciary capacity, and

(2) Such custodial holdings are subject to examination by the appropriate regulatory agency for compliance with such fiduciary requirements.

(b) The Secretary expects that each appropriate regulatory agency will notify the Department if it materially revises its rules and standards governing the holding of government securities in a fiduciary capacity.

[52 FR 27957, July 24, 1987, as amended at 70 FR 29446, May 23, 2005; 79 FR 38456, July 8, 2014]

§ 450.4 Custodial holdings of government securities.

Depository institutions that are subject to this part shall observe the following requirements with respect to their holdings of government securities for customer accounts:

(a)(1) Except as otherwise provided in this section, a depository institution shall maintain possession or control of all government securities held for the account of customers by segregating such securities from the assets of the depository institution and keeping them free of any lien, charge or claim of any third party granted or created by such depository institution.

(2)(i) Where customer securities are maintained by a depository institution at another depository institution, including but not limited to a correspondent bank or a trust company ("custodian institution"), the depository institution shall be in compliance with paragraph (a)(1) of this section if:

(A) The depository institution notifies the custodian institution that such securities are customer securities;

(B) The custodian institution maintains such securities in an account that is designated for customers of the depository institution and that does not contain proprietary securities of the depository institution; and

(C) The depository institution instructs the custodian institution to maintain such securities free of any lien, charge, or claim of any kind in favor of such custodian institution or any persons claiming through it.

Department of the Treasury § 450.4

(ii) To the extent that a custodian institution holds securities that have been identified as customer securities by a depository institution in accordance with paragraph (a)(2)(i) of this section, the custodian institution shall treat such securities as customer securities separate from any other securities held for the account of the depository institution.

(3)(i) Where securities that a depository institution is required, pursuant to this part 450, to keep free of all liens, charges, or other claims ("customer securities") are maintained by a depository institution at a Federal Reserve Bank, the depository institution shall be in compliance with paragraph (a)(1) of this section if any lien, charge or other claim of such Federal Reserve Bank or any person claiming through it against securities of the depository institution expressly excludes customer securities.

(ii) Notwithstanding paragraph (a)(3)(i) of this section, a depository institution described in that paragraph shall be in compliance with paragraph (a)(1) of this section if a Federal Reserve Bank retains a lien on securities received during the day that are subsequently determined to be customer securities, *provided that,*

(A) On that day, the depository institution:

(*1*) Because of extraordinary circumstances, at the end of that day either requests a discount window advance or is unable to eliminate an overdraft with its Federal Reserve Bank and the Federal Reserve Bank extends credit to the depository institution in order to assure the safety and soundness or liquidity of the depository institution; and

(*2*) After reasonable efforts, is unable to provide the Federal Reserve Bank with an adequate security interest in other collateral that is clearly identifiable as pledgeable by the depository institution sufficient to fully collateralize such extension of credit; and

(B) The depository institution diligently pursues with the Federal Reserve Bank the substitution of other collateral for securities determined to be customer securities; and

(C) The Federal Reserve Bank agrees that to the extent the lien extends to collateral of a value greater than the outstanding balance on the loan, customer securities will be the first collateral released from the lien.

(4)(i) To the extent that a depository institution holds securities that have been identified to such depository institution as customer securities by a government securities broker or dealer, or that the government securities broker or dealer has instructed the depository institution to place in a segregated account, in accordance with part 403 of subchapter A of this chapter, the depository institution shall treat such securities as customer securities separate from any other securities held for the account of the government securities broker or dealer and shall comply with all of the provisions of this section with respect to such customer securities, except as provided in paragraph (a)(4)(ii) of this section.

(ii) A clearing bank that provides clearing services for a government securities broker or dealer and that maintains a segregated account as described in § 403.4 of this chapter shall not be required to transfer securities to such account upon the instruction of the broker or dealer for whom such account is maintained if the clearing bank determines that such securities continue to be required as collateral for an extension of clearing credit to such dealer. Whenever a clearing bank does not segregate securities as of the close of business upon the instruction of such broker or dealer, it shall send a notification to the appropriate regulatory agency of the broker or dealer for whom such account is maintained. Such securities shall thereafter be segregated pursuant to the instruction of the broker or dealer as soon as they are no longer required by the clearing bank as collateral for the extension of clearing credit.

(5) A depository institution that is subject to part 403 is not required to maintain possession or control of margin securities as that term is defined in § 403.5(f)(1).

(6) Notwithstanding the requirement of paragraph (a)(1) to maintain possession or control of customer securities, a depository institution may lend such

§ 450.4

securities to a third party pursuant to the written agreement of the customer, if such loan of securities is carried out in full compliance with supervisory guidelines of its appropriate regulatory agency that expressly govern securities lending practices.

(b)(1) Except as otherwise provided in paragraph (b)(2) of this section, a depository institution shall issue a confirmation or a safekeeping receipt for each security held for a customer in accordance with this section with the exception of securities that are the subject of repurchase transactions which are subject to the requirements of § 403.5(d) of this chapter. The confirmation or safekeeping receipt shall identify the issuer, maturity date, par amount and coupon rate of the security being confirmed. The confirmation may be supplied to the customer in any manner that complies with applicable Federal banking regulations.

(2) A depository institution shall not be required to send the confirmation or safekeeping receipt required by paragraph (b)(1) of this section to a customer that is a non-U.S. citizen residing outside the United States or a foreign corporation, partnership, or trust, if such customer expressly waives in writing the right to receive such confirmation or safekeeping receipt.

(c) Records of government securities held for customers shall be maintained and shall be kept separate and distinct from other records of the depository institution. Such records shall:

(1) Provide a system for identifying each customer, and each government security (or the amount of each issue of a government security issued in book-entry form) held for the customer;

(2) Describe the customer's interest in the government security;

(3) Indicate all receipts and deliveries of government securities and all receipts and disbursements of cash by the depository institution in connection with such securities;

(4) Include a copy of the safekeeping receipt or a confirmation issued for each government security held; and

(5) Provide an adequate basis for audit of such information.

(d) Counts of government securities held for customers in both definitive and book-entry form shall be conducted at least annually and such counts shall be reconciled with customer account records.

(1) Counts of book-entry securities and of definitive securities held outside the possession of the depository institution shall be made by reconciliation of the records of the depository institution with those of any depository, depository institution, or Federal Reserve Bank on whose books the depository institution has securities accounts.

(2) The depository institution conducting the count shall also verify any such securities in transfer, in transit, pledged, loaned, borrowed, deposited, failed to receive, failed to deliver, subject to repurchase or reverse repurchase agreements or otherwise subject to the depository institution's control or direction that are not in its physical possession, where the securities have been in such status for longer than thirty days.

(3) The dates and results of such counts and reconciliations shall be documented with differences noted in a security count difference account not later than seven business days after the date of each required count and verification as provided in this paragraph (d).

(e) For purposes of this section, a depository institution shall treat a government securities broker or dealer as a customer with respect to securities maintained by such government securities broker or dealer in a Segregated Account as defined in § 403.4(f)(1) of this chapter and with respect to securities otherwise identified to the depository institution as customer securities for purposes of maintaining possession or control of such securities as required by part 403 of this chapter. The recordkeeping requirements of paragraph (c) of this section require the depository institution to treat such securities as customer securities separate from any other securities held for the account of the government securities broker or dealer, but do not require the depository institution to keep records identifying individual customers of the government securities broker or dealer.

(f) The records required by paragraphs (c) and (d)(3) of this section

Department of the Treasury

shall be preserved for not less than six years, the first two years in an easily accessible place.

(Approved by the Office of Management and Budget under control number 1535-0089)

[52 FR 27957, July 24, 1987, as amended at 60 FR 11026, Mar. 1, 1995]

§ 450.5 **Effective date.**

This part shall be effective October 31, 1987.

PARTS 451-499 [RESERVED]

FINDING AIDS

A list of CFR titles, subtitles, chapters, subchapters and parts and an alphabetical list of agencies publishing in the CFR are included in the CFR Index and Finding Aids volume to the Code of Federal Regulations which is published separately and revised annually.

Table of CFR Titles and Chapters
Alphabetical List of Agencies Appearing in the CFR
Table of OMB Control Numbers
List of CFR Sections Affected

Table of CFR Titles and Chapters
(Revised as of April 1, 2023)

Title 1—General Provisions

I Administrative Committee of the Federal Register (Parts 1—49)
II Office of the Federal Register (Parts 50—299)
III Administrative Conference of the United States (Parts 300—399)
IV Miscellaneous Agencies (Parts 400—599)
VI National Capital Planning Commission (Parts 600—699)

Title 2—Grants and Agreements

SUBTITLE A—OFFICE OF MANAGEMENT AND BUDGET GUIDANCE FOR GRANTS AND AGREEMENTS

I Office of Management and Budget Governmentwide Guidance for Grants and Agreements (Parts 2—199)
II Office of Management and Budget Guidance (Parts 200—299)

SUBTITLE B—FEDERAL AGENCY REGULATIONS FOR GRANTS AND AGREEMENTS

III Department of Health and Human Services (Parts 300—399)
IV Department of Agriculture (Parts 400—499)
VI Department of State (Parts 600—699)
VII Agency for International Development (Parts 700—799)
VIII Department of Veterans Affairs (Parts 800—899)
IX Department of Energy (Parts 900—999)
X Department of the Treasury (Parts 1000—1099)
XI Department of Defense (Parts 1100—1199)
XII Department of Transportation (Parts 1200—1299)
XIII Department of Commerce (Parts 1300—1399)
XIV Department of the Interior (Parts 1400—1499)
XV Environmental Protection Agency (Parts 1500—1599)
XVIII National Aeronautics and Space Administration (Parts 1800—1899)
XX United States Nuclear Regulatory Commission (Parts 2000—2099)
XXII Corporation for National and Community Service (Parts 2200—2299)
XXIII Social Security Administration (Parts 2300—2399)
XXIV Department of Housing and Urban Development (Parts 2400—2499)
XXV National Science Foundation (Parts 2500—2599)
XXVI National Archives and Records Administration (Parts 2600—2699)

Title 2—Grants and Agreements—Continued

Chap.
XXVII Small Business Administration (Parts 2700—2799)
XXVIII Department of Justice (Parts 2800—2899)
XXIX Department of Labor (Parts 2900—2999)
XXX Department of Homeland Security (Parts 3000—3099)
XXXI Institute of Museum and Library Services (Parts 3100—3199)
XXXII National Endowment for the Arts (Parts 3200—3299)
XXXIII National Endowment for the Humanities (Parts 3300—3399)
XXXIV Department of Education (Parts 3400—3499)
XXXV Export-Import Bank of the United States (Parts 3500—3599)
XXXVI Office of National Drug Control Policy, Executive Office of the President (Parts 3600—3699)
XXXVII Peace Corps (Parts 3700—3799)
LVIII Election Assistance Commission (Parts 5800—5899)
LIX Gulf Coast Ecosystem Restoration Council (Parts 5900—5999)
LX Federal Communications Commission (Parts 6000—6099)

Title 3—The President

I Executive Office of the President (Parts 100—199)

Title 4—Accounts

I Government Accountability Office (Parts 1—199)

Title 5—Administrative Personnel

I Office of Personnel Management (Parts 1—1199)
II Merit Systems Protection Board (Parts 1200—1299)
III Office of Management and Budget (Parts 1300—1399)
IV Office of Personnel Management and Office of the Director of National Intelligence (Parts 1400—1499)
V The International Organizations Employees Loyalty Board (Parts 1500—1599)
VI Federal Retirement Thrift Investment Board (Parts 1600—1699)
VIII Office of Special Counsel (Parts 1800—1899)
IX Appalachian Regional Commission (Parts 1900—1999)
XI Armed Forces Retirement Home (Parts 2100—2199)
XIV Federal Labor Relations Authority, General Counsel of the Federal Labor Relations Authority and Federal Service Impasses Panel (Parts 2400—2499)
XVI Office of Government Ethics (Parts 2600—2699)
XXI Department of the Treasury (Parts 3100—3199)
XXII Federal Deposit Insurance Corporation (Parts 3200—3299)
XXIII Department of Energy (Parts 3300—3399)
XXIV Federal Energy Regulatory Commission (Parts 3400—3499)
XXV Department of the Interior (Parts 3500—3599)

662

Title 5—Administrative Personnel—Continued

Chap.	
XXVI	Department of Defense (Parts 3600—3699)
XXVIII	Department of Justice (Parts 3800—3899)
XXIX	Federal Communications Commission (Parts 3900—3999)
XXX	Farm Credit System Insurance Corporation (Parts 4000—4099)
XXXI	Farm Credit Administration (Parts 4100—4199)
XXXIII	U.S. International Development Finance Corporation (Parts 4300—4399)
XXXIV	Securities and Exchange Commission (Parts 4400—4499)
XXXV	Office of Personnel Management (Parts 4500—4599)
XXXVI	Department of Homeland Security (Parts 4600—4699)
XXXVII	Federal Election Commission (Parts 4700—4799)
XL	Interstate Commerce Commission (Parts 5000—5099)
XLI	Commodity Futures Trading Commission (Parts 5100—5199)
XLII	Department of Labor (Parts 5200—5299)
XLIII	National Science Foundation (Parts 5300—5399)
XLV	Department of Health and Human Services (Parts 5500—5599)
XLVI	Postal Rate Commission (Parts 5600—5699)
XLVII	Federal Trade Commission (Parts 5700—5799)
XLVIII	Nuclear Regulatory Commission (Parts 5800—5899)
XLIX	Federal Labor Relations Authority (Parts 5900—5999)
L	Department of Transportation (Parts 6000—6099)
LII	Export-Import Bank of the United States (Parts 6200—6299)
LIII	Department of Education (Parts 6300—6399)
LIV	Environmental Protection Agency (Parts 6400—6499)
LV	National Endowment for the Arts (Parts 6500—6599)
LVI	National Endowment for the Humanities (Parts 6600—6699)
LVII	General Services Administration (Parts 6700—6799)
LVIII	Board of Governors of the Federal Reserve System (Parts 6800—6899)
LIX	National Aeronautics and Space Administration (Parts 6900—6999)
LX	United States Postal Service (Parts 7000—7099)
LXI	National Labor Relations Board (Parts 7100—7199)
LXII	Equal Employment Opportunity Commission (Parts 7200—7299)
LXIII	Inter-American Foundation (Parts 7300—7399)
LXIV	Merit Systems Protection Board (Parts 7400—7499)
LXV	Department of Housing and Urban Development (Parts 7500—7599)
LXVI	National Archives and Records Administration (Parts 7600—7699)
LXVII	Institute of Museum and Library Services (Parts 7700—7799)
LXVIII	Commission on Civil Rights (Parts 7800—7899)
LXIX	Tennessee Valley Authority (Parts 7900—7999)
LXX	Court Services and Offender Supervision Agency for the District of Columbia (Parts 8000—8099)
LXXI	Consumer Product Safety Commission (Parts 8100—8199)

Title 5—Administrative Personnel—Continued

Chap.

LXXIII	Department of Agriculture (Parts 8300—8399)
LXXIV	Federal Mine Safety and Health Review Commission (Parts 8400—8499)
LXXVI	Federal Retirement Thrift Investment Board (Parts 8600—8699)
LXXVII	Office of Management and Budget (Parts 8700—8799)
LXXX	Federal Housing Finance Agency (Parts 9000—9099)
LXXXIII	Special Inspector General for Afghanistan Reconstruction (Parts 9300—9399)
LXXXIV	Bureau of Consumer Financial Protection (Parts 9400—9499)
LXXXVI	National Credit Union Administration (Parts 9600—9699)
XCVII	Department of Homeland Security Human Resources Management System (Department of Homeland Security—Office of Personnel Management) (Parts 9700—9799)
XCVIII	Council of the Inspectors General on Integrity and Efficiency (Parts 9800—9899)
XCIX	Military Compensation and Retirement Modernization Commission (Parts 9900—9999)
C	National Council on Disability (Parts 10000—10049)
CI	National Mediation Board (Parts 10100—10199)
CII	U.S. Office of Special Counsel (Parts 10200—10299)
CIV	Office of the Intellectual Property Enforcement Coordinator (Part 10400—10499)

Title 6—Domestic Security

I	Department of Homeland Security, Office of the Secretary (Parts 1—199)
X	Privacy and Civil Liberties Oversight Board (Parts 1000—1099)

Title 7—Agriculture

SUBTITLE A—OFFICE OF THE SECRETARY OF AGRICULTURE (PARTS 0—26)

SUBTITLE B—REGULATIONS OF THE DEPARTMENT OF AGRICULTURE

I	Agricultural Marketing Service (Standards, Inspections, Marketing Practices), Department of Agriculture (Parts 27—209)
II	Food and Nutrition Service, Department of Agriculture (Parts 210—299)
III	Animal and Plant Health Inspection Service, Department of Agriculture (Parts 300—399)
IV	Federal Crop Insurance Corporation, Department of Agriculture (Parts 400—499)
V	Agricultural Research Service, Department of Agriculture (Parts 500—599)
VI	Natural Resources Conservation Service, Department of Agriculture (Parts 600—699)
VII	Farm Service Agency, Department of Agriculture (Parts 700—799)

Title 7—Agriculture—Continued

Chap.	
VIII	Agricultural Marketing Service (Federal Grain Inspection Service, Fair Trade Practices Program), Department of Agriculture (Parts 800—899)
IX	Agricultural Marketing Service (Marketing Agreements and Orders; Fruits, Vegetables, Nuts), Department of Agriculture (Parts 900—999)
X	Agricultural Marketing Service (Marketing Agreements and Orders; Milk), Department of Agriculture (Parts 1000—1199)
XI	Agricultural Marketing Service (Marketing Agreements and Orders; Miscellaneous Commodities), Department of Agriculture (Parts 1200—1299)
XIV	Commodity Credit Corporation, Department of Agriculture (Parts 1400—1499)
XV	Foreign Agricultural Service, Department of Agriculture (Parts 1500—1599)
XVI	[Reserved]
XVII	Rural Utilities Service, Department of Agriculture (Parts 1700—1799)
XVIII	Rural Housing Service, Rural Business-Cooperative Service, Rural Utilities Service, and Farm Service Agency, Department of Agriculture (Parts 1800—2099)
XX	[Reserved]
XXV	Office of Advocacy and Outreach, Department of Agriculture (Parts 2500—2599)
XXVI	Office of Inspector General, Department of Agriculture (Parts 2600—2699)
XXVII	Office of Information Resources Management, Department of Agriculture (Parts 2700—2799)
XXVIII	Office of Operations, Department of Agriculture (Parts 2800—2899)
XXIX	Office of Energy Policy and New Uses, Department of Agriculture (Parts 2900—2999)
XXX	Office of the Chief Financial Officer, Department of Agriculture (Parts 3000—3099)
XXXI	Office of Environmental Quality, Department of Agriculture (Parts 3100—3199)
XXXII	Office of Procurement and Property Management, Department of Agriculture (Parts 3200—3299)
XXXIII	Office of Transportation, Department of Agriculture (Parts 3300—3399)
XXXIV	National Institute of Food and Agriculture (Parts 3400—3499)
XXXV	Rural Housing Service, Department of Agriculture (Parts 3500—3599)
XXXVI	National Agricultural Statistics Service, Department of Agriculture (Parts 3600—3699)
XXXVII	Economic Research Service, Department of Agriculture (Parts 3700—3799)
XXXVIII	World Agricultural Outlook Board, Department of Agriculture (Parts 3800—3899)
XLI	[Reserved]

Title 7—Agriculture—Continued

Chap.
XLII Rural Business-Cooperative Service and Rural Utilities Service, Department of Agriculture (Parts 4200—4299)
L Rural Business-Cooperative Service, and Rural Utilities Service, Department of Agriculture (Parts 5000—5099)

Title 8—Aliens and Nationality

I Department of Homeland Security (Parts 1—499)
V Executive Office for Immigration Review, Department of Justice (Parts 1000—1399)

Title 9—Animals and Animal Products

I Animal and Plant Health Inspection Service, Department of Agriculture (Parts 1—199)
II Agricultural Marketing Service (Fair Trade Practices Program), Department of Agriculture (Parts 200—299)
III Food Safety and Inspection Service, Department of Agriculture (Parts 300—599)

Title 10—Energy

I Nuclear Regulatory Commission (Parts 0—199)
II Department of Energy (Parts 200—699)
III Department of Energy (Parts 700—999)
X Department of Energy (General Provisions) (Parts 1000—1099)
XIII Nuclear Waste Technical Review Board (Parts 1300—1399)
XVII Defense Nuclear Facilities Safety Board (Parts 1700—1799)
XVIII Northeast Interstate Low-Level Radioactive Waste Commission (Parts 1800—1899)

Title 11—Federal Elections

I Federal Election Commission (Parts 1—9099)
II Election Assistance Commission (Parts 9400—9499)

Title 12—Banks and Banking

I Comptroller of the Currency, Department of the Treasury (Parts 1—199)
II Federal Reserve System (Parts 200—299)
III Federal Deposit Insurance Corporation (Parts 300—399)
IV Export-Import Bank of the United States (Parts 400—499)
V [Reserved]
VI Farm Credit Administration (Parts 600—699)
VII National Credit Union Administration (Parts 700—799)
VIII Federal Financing Bank (Parts 800—899)
IX (Parts 900—999)[Reserved]

Title 12—Banks and Banking—Continued

Chap.
- X Consumer Financial Protection Bureau (Parts 1000—1099)
- XI Federal Financial Institutions Examination Council (Parts 1100—1199)
- XII Federal Housing Finance Agency (Parts 1200—1299)
- XIII Financial Stability Oversight Council (Parts 1300—1399)
- XIV Farm Credit System Insurance Corporation (Parts 1400—1499)
- XV Department of the Treasury (Parts 1500—1599)
- XVI Office of Financial Research, Department of the Treasury (Parts 1600—1699)
- XVII Office of Federal Housing Enterprise Oversight, Department of Housing and Urban Development (Parts 1700—1799)
- XVIII Community Development Financial Institutions Fund, Department of the Treasury (Parts 1800—1899)

Title 13—Business Credit and Assistance

- I Small Business Administration (Parts 1—199)
- III Economic Development Administration, Department of Commerce (Parts 300—399)
- IV Emergency Steel Guarantee Loan Board (Parts 400—499)
- V Emergency Oil and Gas Guaranteed Loan Board (Parts 500—599)

Title 14—Aeronautics and Space

- I Federal Aviation Administration, Department of Transportation (Parts 1—199)
- II Office of the Secretary, Department of Transportation (Aviation Proceedings) (Parts 200—399)
- III Commercial Space Transportation, Federal Aviation Administration, Department of Transportation (Parts 400—1199)
- V National Aeronautics and Space Administration (Parts 1200—1299)
- VI Air Transportation System Stabilization (Parts 1300—1399)

Title 15—Commerce and Foreign Trade

SUBTITLE A—OFFICE OF THE SECRETARY OF COMMERCE (PARTS 0—29)

SUBTITLE B—REGULATIONS RELATING TO COMMERCE AND FOREIGN TRADE

- I Bureau of the Census, Department of Commerce (Parts 30—199)
- II National Institute of Standards and Technology, Department of Commerce (Parts 200—299)
- III International Trade Administration, Department of Commerce (Parts 300—399)
- IV Foreign-Trade Zones Board, Department of Commerce (Parts 400—499)
- VII Bureau of Industry and Security, Department of Commerce (Parts 700—799)

Title 15—Commerce and Foreign Trade—Continued

Chap.

VIII — Bureau of Economic Analysis, Department of Commerce (Parts 800—899)

IX — National Oceanic and Atmospheric Administration, Department of Commerce (Parts 900—999)

XI — National Technical Information Service, Department of Commerce (Parts 1100—1199)

XIII — East-West Foreign Trade Board (Parts 1300—1399)

XIV — Minority Business Development Agency (Parts 1400—1499)

XV — Office of the Under-Secretary for Economic Affairs, Department of Commerce (Parts 1500—1599)

SUBTITLE C—REGULATIONS RELATING TO FOREIGN TRADE AGREEMENTS

XX — Office of the United States Trade Representative (Parts 2000—2099)

SUBTITLE D—REGULATIONS RELATING TO TELECOMMUNICATIONS AND INFORMATION

XXIII — National Telecommunications and Information Administration, Department of Commerce (Parts 2300—2399) [Reserved]

Title 16—Commercial Practices

I — Federal Trade Commission (Parts 0—999)

II — Consumer Product Safety Commission (Parts 1000—1799)

Title 17—Commodity and Securities Exchanges

I — Commodity Futures Trading Commission (Parts 1—199)

II — Securities and Exchange Commission (Parts 200—399)

IV — Department of the Treasury (Parts 400—499)

Title 18—Conservation of Power and Water Resources

I — Federal Energy Regulatory Commission, Department of Energy (Parts 1—399)

III — Delaware River Basin Commission (Parts 400—499)

VI — Water Resources Council (Parts 700—799)

VIII — Susquehanna River Basin Commission (Parts 800—899)

XIII — Tennessee Valley Authority (Parts 1300—1399)

Title 19—Customs Duties

I — U.S. Customs and Border Protection, Department of Homeland Security; Department of the Treasury (Parts 0—199)

II — United States International Trade Commission (Parts 200—299)

III — International Trade Administration, Department of Commerce (Parts 300—399)

IV — U.S. Immigration and Customs Enforcement, Department of Homeland Security (Parts 400—599) [Reserved]

Chap.

Title 20—Employees' Benefits

I Office of Workers' Compensation Programs, Department of Labor (Parts 1—199)
II Railroad Retirement Board (Parts 200—399)
III Social Security Administration (Parts 400—499)
IV Employees' Compensation Appeals Board, Department of Labor (Parts 500—599)
V Employment and Training Administration, Department of Labor (Parts 600—699)
VI Office of Workers' Compensation Programs, Department of Labor (Parts 700—799)
VII Benefits Review Board, Department of Labor (Parts 800—899)
VIII Joint Board for the Enrollment of Actuaries (Parts 900—999)
IX Office of the Assistant Secretary for Veterans' Employment and Training Service, Department of Labor (Parts 1000—1099)

Title 21—Food and Drugs

I Food and Drug Administration, Department of Health and Human Services (Parts 1—1299)
II Drug Enforcement Administration, Department of Justice (Parts 1300—1399)
III Office of National Drug Control Policy (Parts 1400—1499)

Title 22—Foreign Relations

I Department of State (Parts 1—199)
II Agency for International Development (Parts 200—299)
III Peace Corps (Parts 300—399)
IV International Joint Commission, United States and Canada (Parts 400—499)
V United States Agency for Global Media (Parts 500—599)
VII U.S. International Development Finance Corporation (Parts 700—799)
IX Foreign Service Grievance Board (Parts 900—999)
X Inter-American Foundation (Parts 1000—1099)
XI International Boundary and Water Commission, United States and Mexico, United States Section (Parts 1100—1199)
XII United States International Development Cooperation Agency (Parts 1200—1299)
XIII Millennium Challenge Corporation (Parts 1300—1399)
XIV Foreign Service Labor Relations Board; Federal Labor Relations Authority; General Counsel of the Federal Labor Relations Authority; and the Foreign Service Impasse Disputes Panel (Parts 1400—1499)
XV African Development Foundation (Parts 1500—1599)
XVI Japan-United States Friendship Commission (Parts 1600—1699)
XVII United States Institute of Peace (Parts 1700—1799)

Title 23—Highways

Chap.
I Federal Highway Administration, Department of Transportation (Parts 1—999)
II National Highway Traffic Safety Administration and Federal Highway Administration, Department of Transportation (Parts 1200—1299)
III National Highway Traffic Safety Administration, Department of Transportation (Parts 1300—1399)

Title 24—Housing and Urban Development

SUBTITLE A—OFFICE OF THE SECRETARY, DEPARTMENT OF HOUSING AND URBAN DEVELOPMENT (PARTS 0—99)

SUBTITLE B—REGULATIONS RELATING TO HOUSING AND URBAN DEVELOPMENT

I Office of Assistant Secretary for Equal Opportunity, Department of Housing and Urban Development (Parts 100—199)
II Office of Assistant Secretary for Housing-Federal Housing Commissioner, Department of Housing and Urban Development (Parts 200—299)
III Government National Mortgage Association, Department of Housing and Urban Development (Parts 300—399)
IV Office of Housing and Office of Multifamily Housing Assistance Restructuring, Department of Housing and Urban Development (Parts 400—499)
V Office of Assistant Secretary for Community Planning and Development, Department of Housing and Urban Development (Parts 500—599)
VI Office of Assistant Secretary for Community Planning and Development, Department of Housing and Urban Development (Parts 600—699) [Reserved]
VII Office of the Secretary, Department of Housing and Urban Development (Housing Assistance Programs and Public and Indian Housing Programs) (Parts 700—799)
VIII Office of the Assistant Secretary for Housing—Federal Housing Commissioner, Department of Housing and Urban Development (Section 8 Housing Assistance Programs, Section 202 Direct Loan Program, Section 202 Supportive Housing for the Elderly Program and Section 811 Supportive Housing for Persons With Disabilities Program) (Parts 800—899)
IX Office of Assistant Secretary for Public and Indian Housing, Department of Housing and Urban Development (Parts 900—1699)
X Office of Assistant Secretary for Housing—Federal Housing Commissioner, Department of Housing and Urban Development (Interstate Land Sales Registration Program) (Parts 1700—1799) [Reserved]
XII Office of Inspector General, Department of Housing and Urban Development (Parts 2000—2099)
XV Emergency Mortgage Insurance and Loan Programs, Department of Housing and Urban Development (Parts 2700—2799) [Reserved]

Title 24—Housing and Urban Development—Continued

Chap.

XX Office of Assistant Secretary for Housing—Federal Housing Commissioner, Department of Housing and Urban Development (Parts 3200—3899)

XXIV Board of Directors of the HOPE for Homeowners Program (Parts 4000—4099) [Reserved]

XXV Neighborhood Reinvestment Corporation (Parts 4100—4199)

Title 25—Indians

I Bureau of Indian Affairs, Department of the Interior (Parts 1—299)

II Indian Arts and Crafts Board, Department of the Interior (Parts 300—399)

III National Indian Gaming Commission, Department of the Interior (Parts 500—599)

IV Office of Navajo and Hopi Indian Relocation (Parts 700—899)

V Bureau of Indian Affairs, Department of the Interior, and Indian Health Service, Department of Health and Human Services (Part 900—999)

VI Office of the Assistant Secretary, Indian Affairs, Department of the Interior (Parts 1000—1199)

VII Office of the Special Trustee for American Indians, Department of the Interior (Parts 1200—1299)

Title 26—Internal Revenue

I Internal Revenue Service, Department of the Treasury (Parts 1—End)

Title 27—Alcohol, Tobacco Products and Firearms

I Alcohol and Tobacco Tax and Trade Bureau, Department of the Treasury (Parts 1—399)

II Bureau of Alcohol, Tobacco, Firearms, and Explosives, Department of Justice (Parts 400—799)

Title 28—Judicial Administration

I Department of Justice (Parts 0—299)

III Federal Prison Industries, Inc., Department of Justice (Parts 300—399)

V Bureau of Prisons, Department of Justice (Parts 500—599)

VI Offices of Independent Counsel, Department of Justice (Parts 600—699)

VII Office of Independent Counsel (Parts 700—799)

VIII Court Services and Offender Supervision Agency for the District of Columbia (Parts 800—899)

IX National Crime Prevention and Privacy Compact Council (Parts 900—999)

Title 28—Judicial Administration—Continued

Chap.

XI Department of Justice and Department of State (Parts 1100–1199)

Title 29—Labor

SUBTITLE A—OFFICE OF THE SECRETARY OF LABOR (PARTS 0–99)
SUBTITLE B—REGULATIONS RELATING TO LABOR

I National Labor Relations Board (Parts 100–199)
II Office of Labor-Management Standards, Department of Labor (Parts 200–299)
III National Railroad Adjustment Board (Parts 300–399)
IV Office of Labor-Management Standards, Department of Labor (Parts 400–499)
V Wage and Hour Division, Department of Labor (Parts 500–899)
IX Construction Industry Collective Bargaining Commission (Parts 900–999)
X National Mediation Board (Parts 1200–1299)
XII Federal Mediation and Conciliation Service (Parts 1400–1499)
XIV Equal Employment Opportunity Commission (Parts 1600–1699)
XVII Occupational Safety and Health Administration, Department of Labor (Parts 1900–1999)
XX Occupational Safety and Health Review Commission (Parts 2200–2499)
XXV Employee Benefits Security Administration, Department of Labor (Parts 2500–2599)
XXVII Federal Mine Safety and Health Review Commission (Parts 2700–2799)
XL Pension Benefit Guaranty Corporation (Parts 4000–4999)

Title 30—Mineral Resources

I Mine Safety and Health Administration, Department of Labor (Parts 1–199)
II Bureau of Safety and Environmental Enforcement, Department of the Interior (Parts 200–299)
IV Geological Survey, Department of the Interior (Parts 400–499)
V Bureau of Ocean Energy Management, Department of the Interior (Parts 500–599)
VII Office of Surface Mining Reclamation and Enforcement, Department of the Interior (Parts 700–999)
XII Office of Natural Resources Revenue, Department of the Interior (Parts 1200–1299)

Title 31—Money and Finance: Treasury

SUBTITLE A—OFFICE OF THE SECRETARY OF THE TREASURY (PARTS 0–50)
SUBTITLE B—REGULATIONS RELATING TO MONEY AND FINANCE

Title 31—Money and Finance: Treasury—Continued

Chap.

I	Monetary Offices, Department of the Treasury (Parts 51—199)
II	Fiscal Service, Department of the Treasury (Parts 200—399)
IV	Secret Service, Department of the Treasury (Parts 400—499)
V	Office of Foreign Assets Control, Department of the Treasury (Parts 500—599)
VI	Bureau of Engraving and Printing, Department of the Treasury (Parts 600—699)
VII	Federal Law Enforcement Training Center, Department of the Treasury (Parts 700—799)
VIII	Office of Investment Security, Department of the Treasury (Parts 800—899)
IX	Federal Claims Collection Standards (Department of the Treasury—Department of Justice) (Parts 900—999)
X	Financial Crimes Enforcement Network, Department of the Treasury (Parts 1000—1099)

Title 32—National Defense

SUBTITLE A—DEPARTMENT OF DEFENSE

I	Office of the Secretary of Defense (Parts 1—399)
V	Department of the Army (Parts 400—699)
VI	Department of the Navy (Parts 700—799)
VII	Department of the Air Force (Parts 800—1099)

SUBTITLE B—OTHER REGULATIONS RELATING TO NATIONAL DEFENSE

XII	Department of Defense, Defense Logistics Agency (Parts 1200—1299)
XVI	Selective Service System (Parts 1600—1699)
XVII	Office of the Director of National Intelligence (Parts 1700—1799)
XVIII	National Counterintelligence Center (Parts 1800—1899)
XIX	Central Intelligence Agency (Parts 1900—1999)
XX	Information Security Oversight Office, National Archives and Records Administration (Parts 2000—2099)
XXI	National Security Council (Parts 2100—2199)
XXIV	Office of Science and Technology Policy (Parts 2400—2499)
XXVII	Office for Micronesian Status Negotiations (Parts 2700—2799)
XXVIII	Office of the Vice President of the United States (Parts 2800—2899)

Title 33—Navigation and Navigable Waters

I	Coast Guard, Department of Homeland Security (Parts 1—199)
II	Corps of Engineers, Department of the Army, Department of Defense (Parts 200—399)
IV	Great Lakes St. Lawrence Seaway Development Corporation, Department of Transportation (Parts 400—499)

Chap.

Title 34—Education

SUBTITLE A—OFFICE OF THE SECRETARY, DEPARTMENT OF EDUCATION (PARTS 1—99)

SUBTITLE B—REGULATIONS OF THE OFFICES OF THE DEPARTMENT OF EDUCATION

I Office for Civil Rights, Department of Education (Parts 100—199)

II Office of Elementary and Secondary Education, Department of Education (Parts 200—299)

III Office of Special Education and Rehabilitative Services, Department of Education (Parts 300—399)

IV Office of Career, Technical, and Adult Education, Department of Education (Parts 400—499)

V Office of Bilingual Education and Minority Languages Affairs, Department of Education (Parts 500—599) [Reserved]

VI Office of Postsecondary Education, Department of Education (Parts 600—699)

VII Office of Educational Research and Improvement, Department of Education (Parts 700—799) [Reserved]

SUBTITLE C—REGULATIONS RELATING TO EDUCATION

XI [Reserved]

XII National Council on Disability (Parts 1200—1299)

Title 35 [Reserved]

Title 36—Parks, Forests, and Public Property

I National Park Service, Department of the Interior (Parts 1—199)

II Forest Service, Department of Agriculture (Parts 200—299)

III Corps of Engineers, Department of the Army (Parts 300—399)

IV American Battle Monuments Commission (Parts 400—499)

V Smithsonian Institution (Parts 500—599)

VI [Reserved]

VII Library of Congress (Parts 700—799)

VIII Advisory Council on Historic Preservation (Parts 800—899)

IX Pennsylvania Avenue Development Corporation (Parts 900—999)

X Presidio Trust (Parts 1000—1099)

XI Architectural and Transportation Barriers Compliance Board (Parts 1100—1199)

XII National Archives and Records Administration (Parts 1200—1299)

XV Oklahoma City National Memorial Trust (Parts 1500—1599)

XVI Morris K. Udall Scholarship and Excellence in National Environmental Policy Foundation (Parts 1600—1699)

Title 37—Patents, Trademarks, and Copyrights

I United States Patent and Trademark Office, Department of Commerce (Parts 1—199)

II U.S. Copyright Office, Library of Congress (Parts 200—299)

Title 37—Patents, Trademarks, and Copyrights—Continued

Chap.

III   Copyright Royalty Board, Library of Congress (Parts 300—399)

IV   National Institute of Standards and Technology, Department of Commerce (Parts 400—599)

Title 38—Pensions, Bonuses, and Veterans' Relief

I   Department of Veterans Affairs (Parts 0—199)

II   Armed Forces Retirement Home (Parts 200—299)

Title 39—Postal Service

I   United States Postal Service (Parts 1—999)

III   Postal Regulatory Commission (Parts 3000—3099)

Title 40—Protection of Environment

I   Environmental Protection Agency (Parts 1—1099)

IV   Environmental Protection Agency and Department of Justice (Parts 1400—1499)

V   Council on Environmental Quality (Parts 1500—1599)

VI   Chemical Safety and Hazard Investigation Board (Parts 1600—1699)

VII   Environmental Protection Agency and Department of Defense; Uniform National Discharge Standards for Vessels of the Armed Forces (Parts 1700—1799)

VIII   Gulf Coast Ecosystem Restoration Council (Parts 1800—1899)

IX   Federal Permitting Improvement Steering Council (Part 1900)

Title 41—Public Contracts and Property Management

SUBTITLE A—FEDERAL PROCUREMENT REGULATIONS SYSTEM [NOTE]

SUBTITLE B—OTHER PROVISIONS RELATING TO PUBLIC CONTRACTS

50   Public Contracts, Department of Labor (Parts 50–1—50–999)

51   Committee for Purchase From People Who Are Blind or Severely Disabled (Parts 51–1—51–99)

60   Office of Federal Contract Compliance Programs, Equal Employment Opportunity, Department of Labor (Parts 60–1—60–999)

61   Office of the Assistant Secretary for Veterans' Employment and Training Service, Department of Labor (Parts 61–1—61–999)

62—100   [Reserved]

SUBTITLE C—FEDERAL PROPERTY MANAGEMENT REGULATIONS SYSTEM

101   Federal Property Management Regulations (Parts 101–1—101–99)

102   Federal Management Regulation (Parts 102–1—102–299)

103—104   [Reserved]

105   General Services Administration (Parts 105–1—105–999)

Title 41—Public Contracts and Property Management—Continued

Chap.

109	Department of Energy Property Management Regulations (Parts 109-1—109-99)
114	Department of the Interior (Parts 114-1—114-99)
115	Environmental Protection Agency (Parts 115-1—115-99)
128	Department of Justice (Parts 128-1—128-99)
129—200	[Reserved]

SUBTITLE D—FEDERAL ACQUISITION SUPPLY CHAIN SECURITY

201	Federal Acquisition Security Council (Parts 201-1—201-99).

SUBTITLE E [RESERVED]

SUBTITLE F—FEDERAL TRAVEL REGULATION SYSTEM

300	General (Parts 300-1—300-99)
301	Temporary Duty (TDY) Travel Allowances (Parts 301-1—301-99)
302	Relocation Allowances (Parts 302-1—302-99)
303	Payment of Expenses Connected with the Death of Certain Employees (Part 303-1—303-99)
304	Payment of Travel Expenses from a Non-Federal Source (Parts 304-1—304-99)

Title 42—Public Health

I	Public Health Service, Department of Health and Human Services (Parts 1—199)
II—III	[Reserved]
IV	Centers for Medicare & Medicaid Services, Department of Health and Human Services (Parts 400—699)
V	Office of Inspector General-Health Care, Department of Health and Human Services (Parts 1000—1099)

Title 43—Public Lands: Interior

SUBTITLE A—OFFICE OF THE SECRETARY OF THE INTERIOR (PARTS 1—199)

SUBTITLE B—REGULATIONS RELATING TO PUBLIC LANDS

I	Bureau of Reclamation, Department of the Interior (Parts 400—999)
II	Bureau of Land Management, Department of the Interior (Parts 1000—9999)
III	Utah Reclamation Mitigation and Conservation Commission (Parts 10000—10099)

Title 44—Emergency Management and Assistance

I	Federal Emergency Management Agency, Department of Homeland Security (Parts 0—399)
IV	Department of Commerce and Department of Transportation (Parts 400—499)

Chap.	Title 45—Public Welfare
	SUBTITLE A—DEPARTMENT OF HEALTH AND HUMAN SERVICES (PARTS 1—199)
	SUBTITLE B—REGULATIONS RELATING TO PUBLIC WELFARE
II	Office of Family Assistance (Assistance Programs), Administration for Children and Families, Department of Health and Human Services (Parts 200—299)
III	Office of Child Support Enforcement (Child Support Enforcement Program), Administration for Children and Families, Department of Health and Human Services (Parts 300—399)
IV	Office of Refugee Resettlement, Administration for Children and Families, Department of Health and Human Services (Parts 400—499)
V	Foreign Claims Settlement Commission of the United States, Department of Justice (Parts 500—599)
VI	National Science Foundation (Parts 600—699)
VII	Commission on Civil Rights (Parts 700—799)
VIII	Office of Personnel Management (Parts 800—899)
IX	Denali Commission (Parts 900—999)
X	Office of Community Services, Administration for Children and Families, Department of Health and Human Services (Parts 1000—1099)
XI	National Foundation on the Arts and the Humanities (Parts 1100—1199)
XII	Corporation for National and Community Service (Parts 1200—1299)
XIII	Administration for Children and Families, Department of Health and Human Services (Parts 1300—1399)
XVI	Legal Services Corporation (Parts 1600—1699)
XVII	National Commission on Libraries and Information Science (Parts 1700—1799)
XVIII	Harry S. Truman Scholarship Foundation (Parts 1800—1899)
XXI	Commission of Fine Arts (Parts 2100—2199)
XXIII	Arctic Research Commission (Parts 2300—2399)
XXIV	James Madison Memorial Fellowship Foundation (Parts 2400—2499)
XXV	Corporation for National and Community Service (Parts 2500—2599)

Title 46—Shipping

I	Coast Guard, Department of Homeland Security (Parts 1—199)
II	Maritime Administration, Department of Transportation (Parts 200—399)
III	Coast Guard (Great Lakes Pilotage), Department of Homeland Security (Parts 400—499)
IV	Federal Maritime Commission (Parts 500—599)

Chap.

Title 47—Telecommunication

I Federal Communications Commission (Parts 0—199)
II Office of Science and Technology Policy and National Security Council (Parts 200—299)
III National Telecommunications and Information Administration, Department of Commerce (Parts 300—399)
IV National Telecommunications and Information Administration, Department of Commerce, and National Highway Traffic Safety Administration, Department of Transportation (Parts 400—499)
V The First Responder Network Authority (Parts 500—599)

Title 48—Federal Acquisition Regulations System

1 Federal Acquisition Regulation (Parts 1—99)
2 Defense Acquisition Regulations System, Department of Defense (Parts 200—299)
3 Department of Health and Human Services (Parts 300—399)
4 Department of Agriculture (Parts 400—499)
5 General Services Administration (Parts 500—599)
6 Department of State (Parts 600—699)
7 Agency for International Development (Parts 700—799)
8 Department of Veterans Affairs (Parts 800—899)
9 Department of Energy (Parts 900—999)
10 Department of the Treasury (Parts 1000—1099)
12 Department of Transportation (Parts 1200—1299)
13 Department of Commerce (Parts 1300—1399)
14 Department of the Interior (Parts 1400—1499)
15 Environmental Protection Agency (Parts 1500—1599)
16 Office of Personnel Management, Federal Employees Health Benefits Acquisition Regulation (Parts 1600—1699)
17 Office of Personnel Management (Parts 1700—1799)
18 National Aeronautics and Space Administration (Parts 1800—1899)
19 Broadcasting Board of Governors (Parts 1900—1999)
20 Nuclear Regulatory Commission (Parts 2000—2099)
21 Office of Personnel Management, Federal Employees Group Life Insurance Federal Acquisition Regulation (Parts 2100—2199)
23 Social Security Administration (Parts 2300—2399)
24 Department of Housing and Urban Development (Parts 2400—2499)
25 National Science Foundation (Parts 2500—2599)
28 Department of Justice (Parts 2800—2899)
29 Department of Labor (Parts 2900—2999)
30 Department of Homeland Security, Homeland Security Acquisition Regulation (HSAR) (Parts 3000—3099)
34 Department of Education Acquisition Regulation (Parts 3400—3499)

Title 48—Federal Acquisition Regulations System—Continued

Chap.

51	Department of the Army Acquisition Regulations (Parts 5100—5199) [Reserved]
52	Department of the Navy Acquisition Regulations (Parts 5200—5299)
53	Department of the Air Force Federal Acquisition Regulation Supplement (Parts 5300—5399) [Reserved]
54	Defense Logistics Agency, Department of Defense (Parts 5400—5499)
57	African Development Foundation (Parts 5700—5799)
61	Civilian Board of Contract Appeals, General Services Administration (Parts 6100—6199)
99	Cost Accounting Standards Board, Office of Federal Procurement Policy, Office of Management and Budget (Parts 9900—9999)

Title 49—Transportation

SUBTITLE A—OFFICE OF THE SECRETARY OF TRANSPORTATION (PARTS 1—99)

SUBTITLE B—OTHER REGULATIONS RELATING TO TRANSPORTATION

I	Pipeline and Hazardous Materials Safety Administration, Department of Transportation (Parts 100—199)
II	Federal Railroad Administration, Department of Transportation (Parts 200—299)
III	Federal Motor Carrier Safety Administration, Department of Transportation (Parts 300—399)
IV	Coast Guard, Department of Homeland Security (Parts 400—499)
V	National Highway Traffic Safety Administration, Department of Transportation (Parts 500—599)
VI	Federal Transit Administration, Department of Transportation (Parts 600—699)
VII	National Railroad Passenger Corporation (AMTRAK) (Parts 700—799)
VIII	National Transportation Safety Board (Parts 800—999)
X	Surface Transportation Board (Parts 1000—1399)
XI	Research and Innovative Technology Administration, Department of Transportation (Parts 1400—1499) [Reserved]
XII	Transportation Security Administration, Department of Homeland Security (Parts 1500—1699)

Title 50—Wildlife and Fisheries

I	United States Fish and Wildlife Service, Department of the Interior (Parts 1—199)
II	National Marine Fisheries Service, National Oceanic and Atmospheric Administration, Department of Commerce (Parts 200—299)
III	International Fishing and Related Activities (Parts 300—399)

Title 50—Wildlife and Fisheries—Continued

Chap.
- IV Joint Regulations (United States Fish and Wildlife Service, Department of the Interior and National Marine Fisheries Service, National Oceanic and Atmospheric Administration, Department of Commerce); Endangered Species Committee Regulations (Parts 400—499)
- V Marine Mammal Commission (Parts 500—599)
- VI Fishery Conservation and Management, National Oceanic and Atmospheric Administration, Department of Commerce (Parts 600—699)

Alphabetical List of Agencies Appearing in the CFR
(Revised as of April 1, 2023)

Agency	CFR Title, Subtitle or Chapter
Administrative Conference of the United States	1, III
Advisory Council on Historic Preservation	36, VIII
Advocacy and Outreach, Office of	7, XXV
Afghanistan Reconstruction, Special Inspector General for	5, LXXXIII
African Development Foundation	22, XV
Federal Acquisition Regulation	48, 57
Agency for International Development	2, VII; 22, II
Federal Acquisition Regulation	48, 7
Agricultural Marketing Service	7, I, VIII, IX, X, XI; 9, II
Agricultural Research Service	7, V
Agriculture, Department of	2, IV; 5, LXXIII
Advocacy and Outreach, Office of	7, XXV
Agricultural Marketing Service	7, I, VIII, IX, X, XI; 9, II
Agricultural Research Service	7, V
Animal and Plant Health Inspection Service	7, III; 9, I
Chief Financial Officer, Office of	7, XXX
Commodity Credit Corporation	7, XIV
Economic Research Service	7, XXXVII
Energy Policy and New Uses, Office of	2, IX; 7, XXIX
Environmental Quality, Office of	7, XXXI
Farm Service Agency	7, VII, XVIII
Federal Acquisition Regulation	48, 4
Federal Crop Insurance Corporation	7, IV
Food and Nutrition Service	7, II
Food Safety and Inspection Service	9, III
Foreign Agricultural Service	7, XV
Forest Service	36, II
Information Resources Management, Office of	7, XXVII
Inspector General, Office of	7, XXVI
National Agricultural Library	7, XLI
National Agricultural Statistics Service	7, XXXVI
National Institute of Food and Agriculture	7, XXXIV
Natural Resources Conservation Service	7, VI
Operations, Office of	7, XXVIII
Procurement and Property Management, Office of	7, XXXII
Rural Business-Cooperative Service	7, XVIII, XLII
Rural Development Administration	7, XLII
Rural Housing Service	7, XVIII, XXXV
Rural Utilities Service	7, XVII, XVIII, XLII
Secretary of Agriculture, Office of	7, Subtitle A
Transportation, Office of	7, XXXIII
World Agricultural Outlook Board	7, XXXVIII
Air Force, Department of	32, VII
Federal Acquisition Regulation Supplement	48, 53
Air Transportation Stabilization Board	14, VI
Alcohol and Tobacco Tax and Trade Bureau	27, I
Alcohol, Tobacco, Firearms, and Explosives, Bureau of	27, II
AMTRAK	49, VII
American Battle Monuments Commission	36, IV
American Indians, Office of the Special Trustee	25, VII
Animal and Plant Health Inspection Service	7, III; 9, I
Appalachian Regional Commission	5, IX
Architectural and Transportation Barriers Compliance Board	36, XI

Agency	CFR Title, Subtitle or Chapter
Arctic Research Commission	45, XXIII
Armed Forces Retirement Home	5, XI; 38, II
Army, Department of	32, V
Engineers, Corps of	33, II; 36, III
Federal Acquisition Regulation	48, 51
Benefits Review Board	20, VII
Bilingual Education and Minority Languages Affairs, Office of	34, V
Blind or Severely Disabled, Committee for Purchase from People Who Are	41, 51
Federal Acquisition Regulation	48, 19
Career, Technical, and Adult Education, Office of	34, IV
Census Bureau	15, I
Centers for Medicare & Medicaid Services	42, IV
Central Intelligence Agency	32, XIX
Chemical Safety and Hazard Investigation Board	40, VI
Chief Financial Officer, Office of	7, XXX
Child Support Enforcement, Office of	45, III
Children and Families, Administration for	45, II, III, IV, X, XIII
Civil Rights, Commission on	5, LXVIII; 45, VII
Civil Rights, Office for	34, I
Coast Guard	33, I; 46, I; 49, IV
Coast Guard (Great Lakes Pilotage)	46, III
Commerce, Department of	2, XIII; 44, IV; 50, VI
Census Bureau	15, I
Economic Affairs, Office of the Under-Secretary for	15, XV
Economic Analysis, Bureau of	15, VIII
Economic Development Administration	13, III
Emergency Management and Assistance	44, IV
Federal Acquisition Regulation	48, 13
Foreign-Trade Zones Board	15, IV
Industry and Security, Bureau of	15, VII
International Trade Administration	15, III; 19, III
National Institute of Standards and Technology	15, II; 37, IV
National Marine Fisheries Service	50, II, IV
National Oceanic and Atmospheric Administration	15, IX; 50, II, III, IV, VI
National Technical Information Service	15, XI
National Telecommunications and Information Administration	15, XXIII; 47, III, IV
National Weather Service	15, IX
Patent and Trademark Office, United States	37, I
Secretary of Commerce, Office of	15, Subtitle A
Commercial Space Transportation	14, III
Commodity Credit Corporation	7, XIV
Commodity Futures Trading Commission	5, XLI; 17, I
Community Planning and Development, Office of Assistant Secretary for	24, V, VI
Community Services, Office of	45, X
Comptroller of the Currency	12, I
Construction Industry Collective Bargaining Commission	29, IX
Consumer Financial Protection Bureau	5, LXXXIV; 12, X
Consumer Product Safety Commission	5, LXXI; 16, II
Copyright Royalty Board	37, III
Corporation for National and Community Service	2, XXII; 45, XII, XXV
Cost Accounting Standards Board	48, 99
Council on Environmental Quality	40, V
Council of the Inspectors General on Integrity and Efficiency	5, XCVIII
Court Services and Offender Supervision Agency for the District of Columbia	5, LXX; 28, VIII
Customs and Border Protection	19, I
Defense, Department of	2, XI; 5, XXVI; 32, Subtitle A; 40, VII
Advanced Research Projects Agency	32, I
Air Force Department	32, VII
Army Department	32, V; 33, II; 36, III; 48, 51
Defense Acquisition Regulations System	48, 2
Defense Intelligence Agency	32, I

682

Agency	CFR Title, Subtitle or Chapter
Defense Logistics Agency	32, I, XII; 48, 54
Engineers, Corps of	33, II; 36, III
National Imagery and Mapping Agency	32, I
Navy, Department of	32, VI; 48, 52
Secretary of Defense, Office of	2, XI; 32, I
Defense Contract Audit Agency	32, I
Defense Intelligence Agency	32, I
Defense Logistics Agency	32, XII; 48, 54
Defense Nuclear Facilities Safety Board	10, XVII
Delaware River Basin Commission	18, III
Denali Commission	45, IX
Disability, National Council on	5, C; 34, XII
District of Columbia, Court Services and Offender Supervision Agency for the	5, LXX; 28, VIII
Drug Enforcement Administration	21, II
East-West Foreign Trade Board	15, XIII
Economic Affairs, Office of the Under-Secretary for	15, XV
Economic Analysis, Bureau of	15, VIII
Economic Development Administration	13, III
Economic Research Service	7, XXXVII
Education, Department of	2, XXXIV; 5, LIII
Bilingual Education and Minority Languages Affairs, Office of	34, V
Career, Technical, and Adult Education, Office of	34, IV
Civil Rights, Office for	34, I
Educational Research and Improvement, Office of	34, VII
Elementary and Secondary Education, Office of	34, II
Federal Acquisition Regulation	48, 34
Postsecondary Education, Office of	34, VI
Secretary of Education, Office of	34, Subtitle A
Special Education and Rehabilitative Services, Office of	34, III
Educational Research and Improvement, Office of	34, VII
Election Assistance Commission	2, LVIII; 11, II
Elementary and Secondary Education, Office of	34, II
Emergency Oil and Gas Guaranteed Loan Board	13, V
Emergency Steel Guarantee Loan Board	13, IV
Employee Benefits Security Administration	29, XXV
Employees' Compensation Appeals Board	20, IV
Employees Loyalty Board	5, V
Employment and Training Administration	20, V
Employment Policy, National Commission for	1, IV
Employment Standards Administration	20, VI
Endangered Species Committee	50, IV
Energy, Department of	2, IX; 5, XXIII; 10, II, III, X
Federal Acquisition Regulation	48, 9
Federal Energy Regulatory Commission	5, XXIV; 18, I
Property Management Regulations	41, 109
Energy, Office of	7, XXIX
Engineers, Corps of	33, II; 36, III
Engraving and Printing, Bureau of	31, VI
Environmental Protection Agency	2, XV; 5, LIV; 40, I, IV, VII
Federal Acquisition Regulation	48, 15
Property Management Regulations	41, 115
Environmental Quality, Office of	7, XXXI
Equal Employment Opportunity Commission	5, LXII; 29, XIV
Equal Opportunity, Office of Assistant Secretary for	24, I
Executive Office of the President	3, I
Environmental Quality, Council on	40, V
Management and Budget, Office of	2, Subtitle A; 5, III, LXXVII; 14, VI; 48, 99
National Drug Control Policy, Office of	2, XXXVI; 21, III
National Security Council	32, XXI; 47, II
Presidential Documents	3
Science and Technology Policy, Office of	32, XXIV; 47, II
Trade Representative, Office of the United States	15, XX

683

Agency	CFR Title, Subtitle or Chapter
Export-Import Bank of the United States	2, XXXV; 5, LII; 12, IV
Family Assistance, Office of	45, II
Farm Credit Administration	5, XXXI; 12, VI
Farm Credit System Insurance Corporation	5, XXX; 12, XIV
Farm Service Agency	7, VII, XVIII
Federal Acquisition Regulation	48, 1
Federal Acquisition Security Council	41, 201
Federal Aviation Administration	14, I
Commercial Space Transportation	14, III
Federal Claims Collection Standards	31, IX
Federal Communications Commission	2, LX; 5, XXIX; 47, I
Federal Contract Compliance Programs, Office of	41, 60
Federal Crop Insurance Corporation	7, IV
Federal Deposit Insurance Corporation	5, XXII; 12, III
Federal Election Commission	5, XXXVII; 11, I
Federal Emergency Management Agency	44, I
Federal Employees Group Life Insurance Federal Acquisition Regulation	48, 21
Federal Employees Health Benefits Acquisition Regulation	48, 16
Federal Energy Regulatory Commission	5, XXIV; 18, I
Federal Financial Institutions Examination Council	12, XI
Federal Financing Bank	12, VIII
Federal Highway Administration	23, I, II
Federal Home Loan Mortgage Corporation	1, IV
Federal Housing Enterprise Oversight Office	12, XVII
Federal Housing Finance Agency	5, LXXX; 12, XII
Federal Labor Relations Authority	5, XIV, XLIX; 22, XIV
Federal Law Enforcement Training Center	31, VII
Federal Management Regulation	41, 102
Federal Maritime Commission	46, IV
Federal Mediation and Conciliation Service	29, XII
Federal Mine Safety and Health Review Commission	5, LXXIV; 29, XXVII
Federal Motor Carrier Safety Administration	49, III
Federal Permitting Improvement Steering Council	40, IX
Federal Prison Industries, Inc.	28, III
Federal Procurement Policy Office	48, 99
Federal Property Management Regulations	41, 101
Federal Railroad Administration	49, II
Federal Register, Administrative Committee of	1, I
Federal Register, Office of	1, II
Federal Reserve System	12, II
Board of Governors	5, LVIII
Federal Retirement Thrift Investment Board	5, VI, LXXVI
Federal Service Impasses Panel	5, XIV
Federal Trade Commission	5, XLVII; 16, I
Federal Transit Administration	49, VI
Federal Travel Regulation System	41, Subtitle F
Financial Crimes Enforcement Network	31, X
Financial Research Office	12, XVI
Financial Stability Oversight Council	12, XIII
Fine Arts, Commission of	45, XXI
Fiscal Service	31, II
Fish and Wildlife Service, United States	50, I, IV
Food and Drug Administration	21, I
Food and Nutrition Service	7, II
Food Safety and Inspection Service	9, III
Foreign Agricultural Service	7, XV
Foreign Assets Control, Office of	31, V
Foreign Claims Settlement Commission of the United States	45, V
Foreign Service Grievance Board	22, IX
Foreign Service Impasse Disputes Panel	22, XIV
Foreign Service Labor Relations Board	22, XIV
Foreign-Trade Zones Board	15, IV
Forest Service	36, II
General Services Administration	5, LVII; 41, 105
Contract Appeals, Board of	48, 61
Federal Acquisition Regulation	48, 5

Agency	CFR Title, Subtitle or Chapter
Federal Management Regulation	41, 102
Federal Property Management Regulations	41, 101
Federal Travel Regulation System	41, Subtitle F
General	41, 300
Payment From a Non-Federal Source for Travel Expenses	41, 304
Payment of Expenses Connected With the Death of Certain Employees	41, 303
Relocation Allowances	41, 302
Temporary Duty (TDY) Travel Allowances	41, 301
Geological Survey	30, IV
Government Accountability Office	4, I
Government Ethics, Office of	5, XVI
Government National Mortgage Association	24, III
Grain Inspection, Packers and Stockyards Administration	7, VIII; 9, II
Great Lakes St. Lawrence Seaway Development Corporation	33, IV
Gulf Coast Ecosystem Restoration Council	2, LIX; 40, VIII
Harry S. Truman Scholarship Foundation	45, XVIII
Health and Human Services, Department of	2, III; 5, XLV; 45, Subtitle A
Centers for Medicare & Medicaid Services	42, IV
Child Support Enforcement, Office of	45, III
Children and Families, Administration for	45, II, III, IV, X, XIII
Community Services, Office of	45, X
Family Assistance, Office of	45, II
Federal Acquisition Regulation	48, 3
Food and Drug Administration	21, I
Indian Health Service	25, V
Inspector General (Health Care), Office of	42, V
Public Health Service	42, I
Refugee Resettlement, Office of	45, IV
Homeland Security, Department of	2, XXX; 5, XXXVI; 6, I; 8, I
Coast Guard	33, I; 46, I; 49, IV
Coast Guard (Great Lakes Pilotage)	46, III
Customs and Border Protection	19, I
Federal Emergency Management Agency	44, I
Human Resources Management and Labor Relations Systems	5, XCVII
Immigration and Customs Enforcement Bureau	19, IV
Transportation Security Administration	49, XII
HOPE for Homeowners Program, Board of Directors of	24, XXIV
Housing and Urban Development, Department of	2, XXIV; 5, LXV; 24, Subtitle B
Community Planning and Development, Office of Assistant Secretary for	24, V, VI
Equal Opportunity, Office of Assistant Secretary for	24, I
Federal Acquisition Regulation	48, 24
Federal Housing Enterprise Oversight, Office of	12, XVII
Government National Mortgage Association	24, III
Housing—Federal Housing Commissioner, Office of Assistant Secretary for	24, II, VIII, X, XX
Housing, Office of, and Multifamily Housing Assistance Restructuring, Office of	24, IV
Inspector General, Office of	24, XII
Public and Indian Housing, Office of Assistant Secretary for	24, IX
Secretary, Office of	24, Subtitle A, VII
Housing—Federal Housing Commissioner, Office of Assistant Secretary for	24, II, VIII, X, XX
Housing, Office of, and Multifamily Housing Assistance Restructuring, Office of	24, IV
Immigration and Customs Enforcement Bureau	19, IV
Immigration Review, Executive Office for	8, V
Independent Counsel, Office of	28, VII
Independent Counsel, Offices of	28, VI
Indian Affairs, Bureau of	25, I, V
Indian Affairs, Office of the Assistant Secretary	25, VI
Indian Arts and Crafts Board	25, II

Agency	CFR Title, Subtitle or Chapter
Indian Health Service	25, V
Industry and Security, Bureau of	15, VII
Information Resources Management, Office of	7, XXVII
Information Security Oversight Office, National Archives and Records Administration	32, XX
Inspector General	
Agriculture Department	7, XXVI
Health and Human Services Department	42, V
Housing and Urban Development Department	24, XII, XV
Institute of Peace, United States	22, XVII
Intellectual Property Enforcement Coordinator, Office of	5, CIV
Inter-American Foundation	5, LXIII; 22, X
Interior, Department of	2, XIV
American Indians, Office of the Special Trustee	25, VII
Endangered Species Committee	50, IV
Federal Acquisition Regulation	48, 14
Federal Property Management Regulations System	41, 114
Fish and Wildlife Service, United States	50, I, IV
Geological Survey	30, IV
Indian Affairs, Bureau of	25, I, V
Indian Affairs, Office of the Assistant Secretary	25, VI
Indian Arts and Crafts Board	25, II
Land Management, Bureau of	43, II
National Indian Gaming Commission	25, III
National Park Service	36, I
Natural Resource Revenue, Office of	30, XII
Ocean Energy Management, Bureau of	30, V
Reclamation, Bureau of	43, I
Safety and Environmental Enforcement, Bureau of	30, II
Secretary of the Interior, Office of	2, XIV; 43, Subtitle A
Surface Mining Reclamation and Enforcement, Office of	30, VII
Internal Revenue Service	26, I
International Boundary and Water Commission, United States and Mexico, United States Section	22, XI
International Development, United States Agency for	22, II
Federal Acquisition Regulation	48, 7
International Development Cooperation Agency, United States	22, XII
International Development Finance Corporation, U.S.	5, XXXIII; 22, VII
International Joint Commission, United States and Canada	22, IV
International Organizations Employees Loyalty Board	5, V
International Trade Administration	15, III; 19, III
International Trade Commission, United States	19, II
Interstate Commerce Commission	5, XL
Investment Security, Office of	31, VIII
James Madison Memorial Fellowship Foundation	45, XXIV
Japan–United States Friendship Commission	22, XVI
Joint Board for the Enrollment of Actuaries	20, VIII
Justice, Department of	2, XXVIII; 5, XXVIII; 28, I, XI; 40, IV
Alcohol, Tobacco, Firearms, and Explosives, Bureau of	27, II
Drug Enforcement Administration	21, II
Federal Acquisition Regulation	48, 28
Federal Claims Collection Standards	31, IX
Federal Prison Industries, Inc.	28, III
Foreign Claims Settlement Commission of the United States	45, V
Immigration Review, Executive Office for	8, V
Independent Counsel, Offices of	28, VI
Prisons, Bureau of	28, V
Property Management Regulations	41, 128
Labor, Department of	2, XXIX; 5, XLII
Benefits Review Board	20, VII
Employee Benefits Security Administration	29, XXV
Employees' Compensation Appeals Board	20, IV
Employment and Training Administration	20, V
Federal Acquisition Regulation	48, 29

Agency	CFR Title, Subtitle or Chapter
Federal Contract Compliance Programs, Office of	41, 60
Federal Procurement Regulations System	41, 50
Labor-Management Standards, Office of	29, II, IV
Mine Safety and Health Administration	30, I
Occupational Safety and Health Administration	29, XVII
Public Contracts	41, 50
Secretary of Labor, Office of	29, Subtitle A
Veterans' Employment and Training Service, Office of the Assistant Secretary for	41, 61; 20, IX
Wage and Hour Division	29, V
Workers' Compensation Programs, Office of	20, I, VI
Labor-Management Standards, Office of	29, II, IV
Land Management, Bureau of	43, II
Legal Services Corporation	45, XVI
Libraries and Information Science, National Commission on	45, XVII
Library of Congress	36, VII
Copyright Royalty Board	37, III
U.S. Copyright Office	37, II
Management and Budget, Office of	5, III, LXXVII; 14, VI; 48, 99
Marine Mammal Commission	50, V
Maritime Administration	46, II
Merit Systems Protection Board	5, II, LXIV
Micronesian Status Negotiations, Office for	32, XXVII
Military Compensation and Retirement Modernization Commission	5, XCIX
Millennium Challenge Corporation	22, XIII
Mine Safety and Health Administration	30, I
Minority Business Development Agency	15, XIV
Miscellaneous Agencies	1, IV
Monetary Offices	31, I
Morris K. Udall Scholarship and Excellence in National Environmental Policy Foundation	36, XVI
Museum and Library Services, Institute of	2, XXXI
National Aeronautics and Space Administration	2, XVIII; 5, LIX; 14, V
Federal Acquisition Regulation	48, 18
National Agricultural Library	7, XLI
National Agricultural Statistics Service	7, XXXVI
National and Community Service, Corporation for	2, XXII; 45, XII, XXV
National Archives and Records Administration	2, XXVI; 5, LXVI; 36, XII
Information Security Oversight Office	32, XX
National Capital Planning Commission	1, IV, VI
National Counterintelligence Center	32, XVIII
National Credit Union Administration	5, LXXXVI; 12, VII
National Crime Prevention and Privacy Compact Council	28, IX
National Drug Control Policy, Office of	2, XXXVI; 21, III
National Endowment for the Arts	2, XXXII
National Endowment for the Humanities	2, XXXIII
National Foundation on the Arts and the Humanities	45, XI
National Geospatial-Intelligence Agency	32, I
National Highway Traffic Safety Administration	23, II, III; 47, VI; 49, V
National Imagery and Mapping Agency	32, I
National Indian Gaming Commission	25, III
National Institute of Food and Agriculture	7, XXXIV
National Institute of Standards and Technology	15, II; 37, IV
National Intelligence, Office of Director of	5, IV; 32, XVII
National Labor Relations Board	5, LXI; 29, I
National Marine Fisheries Service	50, II, IV
National Mediation Board	5, CI; 29, X
National Oceanic and Atmospheric Administration	15, IX; 50, II, III, IV, VI
National Park Service	36, I
National Railroad Adjustment Board	29, III
National Railroad Passenger Corporation (AMTRAK)	49, VII
National Science Foundation	2, XXV; 5, XLIII; 45, VI
Federal Acquisition Regulation	48, 25
National Security Council	32, XXI; 47, II

Agency	CFR Title, Subtitle or Chapter
National Technical Information Service	15, XI
National Telecommunications and Information Administration	15, XXIII; 47, III, IV, V
National Transportation Safety Board	49, VIII
Natural Resource Revenue, Office of	30, XII
Natural Resources Conservation Service	7, VI
Navajo and Hopi Indian Relocation, Office of	25, IV
Navy, Department of	32, VI
Federal Acquisition Regulation	48, 52
Neighborhood Reinvestment Corporation	24, XXV
Northeast Interstate Low-Level Radioactive Waste Commission	10, XVIII
Nuclear Regulatory Commission	2, XX; 5, XLVIII; 10, I
Federal Acquisition Regulation	48, 20
Occupational Safety and Health Administration	29, XVII
Occupational Safety and Health Review Commission	29, XX
Ocean Energy Management, Bureau of	30, V
Oklahoma City National Memorial Trust	36, XV
Operations Office	7, XXVIII
Patent and Trademark Office, United States	37, I
Payment From a Non-Federal Source for Travel Expenses	41, 304
Payment of Expenses Connected With the Death of Certain Employees	41, 303
Peace Corps	2, XXXVII; 22, III
Pennsylvania Avenue Development Corporation	36, IX
Pension Benefit Guaranty Corporation	29, XL
Personnel Management, Office of	5, I, IV, XXXV; 45, VIII
Federal Acquisition Regulation	48, 17
Federal Employees Group Life Insurance Federal Acquisition Regulation	48, 21
Federal Employees Health Benefits Acquisition Regulation	48, 16
Human Resources Management and Labor Relations Systems, Department of Homeland Security	5, XCVII
Pipeline and Hazardous Materials Safety Administration	49, I
Postal Regulatory Commission	5, XLVI; 39, III
Postal Service, United States	5, LX; 39, I
Postsecondary Education, Office of	34, VI
President's Commission on White House Fellowships	1, IV
Presidential Documents	3
Presidio Trust	36, X
Prisons, Bureau of	28, V
Privacy and Civil Liberties Oversight Board	6, X
Procurement and Property Management, Office of	7, XXXII
Public and Indian Housing, Office of Assistant Secretary for	24, IX
Public Contracts, Department of Labor	41, 50
Public Health Service	42, I
Railroad Retirement Board	20, II
Reclamation, Bureau of	43, I
Refugee Resettlement, Office of	45, IV
Relocation Allowances	41, 302
Research and Innovative Technology Administration	49, XI
Rural Business-Cooperative Service	7, XVIII, XLII, L
Rural Development Administration	7, XLII
Rural Housing Service	7, XVIII, XXXV, L
Rural Utilities Service	7, XVII, XVIII, XLII, L
Safety and Environmental Enforcement, Bureau of	30, II
Science and Technology Policy, Office of	32, XXIV; 47, II
Secret Service	31, IV
Securities and Exchange Commission	5, XXXIV; 17, II
Selective Service System	32, XVI
Small Business Administration	2, XXVII; 13, I
Smithsonian Institution	36, V
Social Security Administration	2, XXIII; 20, III; 48, 23
Soldiers' and Airmen's Home, United States	5, XI
Special Counsel, Office of	5, VIII
Special Education and Rehabilitative Services, Office of	34, III
State, Department of	2, VI; 22, I; 28, XI

Agency	CFR Title, Subtitle or Chapter
Federal Acquisition Regulation	48, 6
Surface Mining Reclamation and Enforcement, Office of	30, VII
Surface Transportation Board	49, X
Susquehanna River Basin Commission	18, VIII
Tennessee Valley Authority	5, LXIX; 18, XIII
Trade Representative, United States, Office of	15, XX
Transportation, Department of	2, XII; 5, L
Commercial Space Transportation	14, III
Emergency Management and Assistance	44, IV
Federal Acquisition Regulation	48, 12
Federal Aviation Administration	14, I
Federal Highway Administration	23, I, II
Federal Motor Carrier Safety Administration	49, III
Federal Railroad Administration	49, II
Federal Transit Administration	49, VI
Great Lakes St. Lawrence Seaway Development Corporation	33, IV
Maritime Administration	46, II
National Highway Traffic Safety Administration	23, II, III; 47, IV; 49, V
Pipeline and Hazardous Materials Safety Administration	49, I
Secretary of Transportation, Office of	14, II; 49, Subtitle A
Transportation Statistics Bureau	49, XI
Transportation, Office of	7, XXXIII
Transportation Security Administration	49, XII
Transportation Statistics Bureau	49, XI
Travel Allowances, Temporary Duty (TDY)	41, 301
Treasury, Department of the	2, X; 5, XXI; 12, XV; 17, IV; 31, IX
Alcohol and Tobacco Tax and Trade Bureau	27, I
Community Development Financial Institutions Fund	12, XVIII
Comptroller of the Currency	12, I
Customs and Border Protection	19, I
Engraving and Printing, Bureau of	31, VI
Federal Acquisition Regulation	48, 10
Federal Claims Collection Standards	31, IX
Federal Law Enforcement Training Center	31, VII
Financial Crimes Enforcement Network	31, X
Fiscal Service	31, II
Foreign Assets Control, Office of	31, V
Internal Revenue Service	26, I
Investment Security, Office of	31, VIII
Monetary Offices	31, I
Secret Service	31, IV
Secretary of the Treasury, Office of	31, Subtitle A
Truman, Harry S. Scholarship Foundation	45, XVIII
United States Agency for Global Media	22, V
United States and Canada, International Joint Commission	22, IV
United States and Mexico, International Boundary and Water Commission, United States Section	22, XI
U.S. Copyright Office	37, II
U.S. Office of Special Counsel	5, CII
Utah Reclamation Mitigation and Conservation Commission	43, III
Veterans Affairs, Department of	2, VIII; 38, I
Federal Acquisition Regulation	48, 8
Veterans' Employment and Training Service, Office of the Assistant Secretary for	41, 61; 20, IX
Vice President of the United States, Office of	32, XXVIII
Wage and Hour Division	29, V
Water Resources Council	18, VI
Workers' Compensation Programs, Office of	20, I, VII
World Agricultural Outlook Board	7, XXXVIII

Table of OMB Control Numbers

The OMB control numbers for chapter II of title 17 appear in § 200.800. For the convenience of the user, § 200.800 is reprinted below.

§ 200.800 OMB control numbers assigned pursuant to the Paperwork Reduction Act.

(a) *Purpose:* This subpart collects and displays the control numbers assigned to information collection requirements of the Commission by the Office of Management and Budget pursuant to the Paperwork Reduction Act of 1980, 44 U.S.C. 3500 *et seq.* This subpart displays current OMB control numbers for those information collection requirements of the Commission that are rules and regulations and codified in 17 CFR either in full text or incorporated by reference with the approval of the Director of the Office of the Federal Register.

(b) *Display.*

Information collection requirement	17 CFR part or section where identified and described	Current OMB control No.
Regulation S-X	Part 210	3235-0009
Regulation S-B	Part 228	3235-0417
Regulation S-K	Part 229	3235-0071
Rule 154	230.154	3235-0495
Rule 155	230.155	3235-0549
Rule 236	230.236	3235-0095
Rule 237	230.237	3235-0528
Regulation A	230.251 thru 230.263	3235-0286
Regulation C	230.400 thru 230.494	3235-0074
Rule 425	230.425	3235-0521
Rule 477	230.477	3235-0550
Rule 489	230.489	3235-0411
Rule 498	230.498	3235-0488
Rule 498A	230.498A	3235-0765
Regulation D	230.500 thru 230.508	3235-0076
Regulation E	230.601 thru 230.610a	3235-0232
Rule 604	230.604	3235-0232
Rule 605	230.605	3235-0232
Rule 609	230.609	3235-0233
Rule 701	230.701	3235-0522
Regulation S	230.901 thru 230.905	3235-0357
Regulation S-T	Part 232	3235-0424
Form SB-1	239.9	3235-0423
Form SB-2	239.10	3235-0418
Form S-1	239.11	3235-0065
Form S-2	239.12	3235-0072
Form S-3	239.13	3235-0073
Form N-2	239.14	3235-0026
Form N-1A	239.15A	3235-0307
Form S-6	239.16	3235-0184
Form S-8	239.16b	3235-0066
Form N-3	239.17a	3235-0316
Form N-4	239.17b	3235-0318
Form S-11	239.18	3235-0067
Form N-14	239.23	3235-0336
Form N-5	239.24	3235-0169
Form S-4	239.25	3235-0324
Form F-1	239.31	3235-0258
Form F-2	239.32	3235-0257
Form F-3	239.33	3235-0256
Form F-4	239.34	3235-0325
Form F-6	239.36	3235-0292
Form F-7	239.37	3235-0383
Form F-8	239.38	3235-0378
Form F-10	239.40	3235-0380

§ 200.800

17 CFR (4-1-23 Edition)

Information collection requirement	17 CFR part or section where identified and described	Current OMB control No.
Form F-80	239.41	3235-0404
Form F-X	239.42	3235-0379
Form F-N	239.43	3235-0411
Form ID	239.63	3235-0328
Form SE	239.64	3235-0327
Form TH	239.65	3235-0425
Form 1-A	239.90	3235-0286
Form 2-A	239.91	3235-0286
Form 144	239.144	3235-0101
Form 1-E	239.200	3235-0232
Form CB	239.800	3235-0518
Rule 6a-1	240.6a-1	3235-0017
Rule 6a-3	240.6a-3	3235-0021
Rule 6a-4	240.6a-4	3235-0554
Rule 6h-1	240.6h-1	3235-0555
Rule 8c-1	240.8c-1	3235-0514
Rule 9b-1	240.9b-1	3235-0480
Rule 10a-1	240.10a-1	3235-0475
Rule 10b-10	240.10b-10	3235-0444
Rule 10b-17	240.10b-17	3235-0476
Rule 10b-18	240.10b-18	3235-0474
Rule 10A-1	240.10A-1	3235-0468
Rule 11a1-1(T)	240.11a1-1(T)	3235-0478
Rule 12a-5	240.12a-5	3235-0079
Regulation 12B	240.12b-1 thru 240.12b-36	3235-0062
Rule 12d1-3	240.12d1-3	3235-0109
Rule 12d2-1	240.12d2-1	3235-0081
Rule 12d2-2	240.12d2-2	3235-0080
Rule 12f-1	240.12f-1	3235-0128
Rule 13a-16	240.13a-16	3235-0116
Regulation 13D/G	240.13d-1 thru 240.13d-7	3235-0145
Schedule 13D	240.13d-101	3235-0145
Schedule 13G	240.13d-102	3235-0145
Rule 13e-1	240.13e-1	3235-0305
Rule 13e-3	240.13e-3	3235-0007
Schedule 13E-3	240.13e-100	3235-0007
Schedule 13e-4F	240.13e-101	3235-0375
Regulation 14A	240.14a-1 thru 240.14a-12	3235-0059
Schedule 14A	240.14a-101	3235-0059
Regulation 14C	240.14c-1	3235-0057
Schedule 14C	240.14c-101	3235-0057
Regulation 14D	240.14d-1 thru 240.14d-9	3235-0102
Schedule TO	240.14d-100	3235-0515
Schedule 14D-1	240.14d-101	3235-0102
Schedule 14D-9	240.14d-101	3235-0102
Schedule 14D-1F	240.14d-102	3235-0376
Schedule 14D-9F	240.14d-103	3235-0382
Regulation 14E	240.14e-1 thru 240.14e-2	3235-0102
Rule 14f-1	240.14f-1	3235-0108
Rule 15a-4	240.15a-4	3235-0010
Rule 15a-6	240.15a-6	3235-0371
Rule 15b1-1	240.15b1-1	3235-0012
Rule 15b6-1(a)	240.15b6-1(a)	3235-0018
Rule 15c1-5	240.15c1-5	3235-0471
Rule 15c1-6	240.15c1-6	3235-0472
Rule 15c1-7	240.15c1-7	3235-0134
Rule 15c2-1	240.15c2-1	3235-0485
Rule 15c2-5	240.15c2-5	3235-0198
Rule 15c2-7	240.15c2-7	3235-0479
Rule 15c2-8	240.15c2-8	3235-0481
Rule 15c2-11	240.15c2-11	3235-0202
Rule 15c2-12	240.15c2-12	3235-0372
Rule 15c3-1	240.15c3-1	3235-0200
Rule 15c3-1(c)(13)	240.15c3-1(c)(13)	3235-0499
Appendix F to Rule 15c3-1	240.15c3-1f	3235-0496
Rule 15c3-3	240.15c3-3	3235-0078
Rule 15c3-4	240.15c3-4	3235-0497
Rule 15d-16	240.15d-16	3235-0116
Rule 15g-2	240.15g-2	3235-0434
Rule 15g-3	240.15g-3	3235-0392
Rule 15g-4	240.15g-4	3235-0393
Rule 15g-5	240.15g-5	3235-0394

OMB Control Numbers § 200.800

Information collection requirement	17 CFR part or section where identified and described	Current OMB control No.
Rule 15g–6	240.15g–6	3235–0395
Rule 15g–9	240.15g–9	3235–0385
Rule 15Aj–1	240.15Aj–1	3235–0044
Rule 15Ba2–1	240.15Ba2–1	3235–0083
Rule 15Ba2–5	240.15Ba2–5	3235–0088
Rule 15Bc3–1	240.15Bc3–1	3235–0087
Rule 17a–1	240.17a–1	3235–0208
Rule 17a–2	240.17a–2	3235–0201
Rule 17a–3	240.17a–3	3235–0033
Rule 17a–3(a)(16)	240.17a–3(a)(16)	3235–0508
Rule 17a–4	240.17a–4	3235–0279
Rule 17a–4(b)(10)	240.17a–4(b)(10)	3235–0506
Rule 17a–5	240.17a–5	3235–0123
Rule 17a–5(c)	240.17a–5(c)	3235–0199
Rule 17a–6	240.17a–6	3235–0489
Rule 17a–7	240.17a–7	3235–0131
Rule 17a–8	240.17a–8	3235–0092
Rule 17a–9T	240.17a–9T	3235–0524
Rule 17a–10	240.17a–10	3235–0122
Rule 17a–11	240.17a–11	3235–0085
Rule 17a–12	240.17a–12	3235–0498
Rule 17a–13	240.17a–13	3235–0035
Rule 17a–19	240.17a–19	3235–0133
Rule 17a–22	240.17a–22	3235–0196
Rule 17a–25	240.17a–25	3235–0540
Rule 17f–1(b)	240.17f–1(b)	3235–0032
Rule 17f–1(c)	240.17f–1(c)	3235–0037
Rule 17f–1(g)	240.17f–1(g)	3235–0290
Rule 17f–2(a)	240.17f–2(a)	3235–0034
Rule 17f–2(c)	240.17f–2(c)	3235–0029
Rule 17f–2(d)	240.17f–2(d)	3235–0028
Rule 17f–2(e)	240.17f–2(e)	3235–0031
Rule 17f–5	240.17f–5	3235–0269
Rule 17h–1T	240.17h–1T	3235–0410
Rule 17h–2T	240.17h–2T	3235–0410
Rule 17Ab2–1	240.17Ab2–1(a)	3235–0195
Rule 17Ac2–1	240.17Ac2–1	3235–0084
Rule 17Ad–2(c), (d), and (h)	240.17Ad–2(c), (d) and (h)	3235–0130
Rule 17Ad–3(b)	240.17Ad–3(b)	3235–0473
Rule 17Ad–4(b) and (c)	240.17Ad–4(b) and (c)	3235–0341
Rule 17Ad–6	240.17Ad–6	3235–0291
Rule 17Ad–7	240.17Ad–7	3235–0291
Rule 17Ad–10	240.17Ad–10	3235–0273
Rule 17Ad–11	240.17Ad–11	3235–0274
Rule 17Ad–13	240.17Ad–13	3235–0275
Rule 17Ad–15	240.17Ad–15	3235–0409
Rule 17Ad–16	240.17Ad–16	3235–0413
Rule 17Ad–17	240.17Ad–17	3235–0469
Rule 19b–1	240.19b–1	3235–0354
Rule 19b–4	240.19b–4	3235–0045
Rule 19b–4(e)	240.19b–4(e)	3235–0504
Rule 19b–5	240.19b–5	3235–0507
Rule 19b–7	240.19b–7	3235–0553
Rule 19d–1	240.19d–1(b) thru 240.19d–1(i)	3235–0206
Rule 19d–2	240.19d–2	3235–0205
Rule 19d–3	240.19d–3	3235–0204
Rule 19h–1	240.19h–1(a), (c) thru (e), and (g)	3235–0259
Rule 24b–1	240.24b–1	3235–0194
Rule 101	242.101	3235–0464
Rule 102	242.102	3235–0467
Rule 103	242.103	3235–0466
Rule 104	242.104	3235–0465
Rule 301	242.301	3235–0509
Rule 302	242.302	3235–0510
Rule 303	242.303	3235–0505
Rule 604	242.604	3235–0462
Rule 605	242.605	3235–0542
Rule 606	242.606	3235–0541
Rule 607	242.607	3235–0435
Rule 608	242.608	3235–0500
Rule 609	242.609	3235–0043
Rule 611	242.611	3235–0600

§ 200.800   17 CFR (4-1-23 Edition)

Information collection requirement	17 CFR part or section where identified and described	Current OMB control No.
Regulation S-P	Part 248	3235-0537
Form 1	249.1	3235-0017
Form 1-N	249.10	3235-0554
Form 25	249.25	3235-0080
Form 26	249.26	3235-0079
Form 3	249.103	3235-0104
Form 4	249.104	3235-0287
Form 5	249.105	3235-0362
Form 8-A	249.208a	3235-0056
Form 10	249.210	3235-0064
Form 10-SB	249.210b	3235-0419
Form 18	249.218	3235-0121
Form 20-F	249.220f	3235-0288
Form 40-F	249.240f	3235-0381
Form 6-K	249.306	3235-0116
Form 8-K	249.308	3235-0060
Form 10-Q	249.308a	3235-0070
Form 10-QSB	249.308b	3235-0416
Form 10-K	249.310	3235-0063
Form 10-KSB	249.310b	3235-0420
Form 11-K	249.311	3235-0082
Form 18-K	249.318	3235-0120
Form 12B-25	249.322	3235-0058
Form 15	249.323	3235-0167
Form 13F	249.325	3235-0006
Form SE	249.444	3235-0327
Form ID	249.446	3235-0328
Form DF	249.448	3235-0482
Form BD	249.501	3235-0012
Form BDW	249.501a	3235-0018
Form BD-N	249.501b	3235-0556
Form X-17A-5	249.617	3235-0123
Form X-17A-19	249.635	3235-0133
Form ATS	249.637	3235-0509
Form ATS-R	249.638	3235-0509
Form CRS	249.640	3235-0766
Form X-15AJ-1	249.802	3235-0044
Form X-15AJ-2	249.803	3235-0044
Form 19b-4	249.819	3235-0045
Form 19b-4(e)	249.820	3235-0504
Form Pilot	249.821	3235-0507
Form SIP	249.1001	3235-0043
Form MSD	249.1100	3235-0083
Form MSDW	249.1110	3235-0087
Form X-17F-1A	249.1200	3235-0037
Form TA-1	249b.100	3235-0084
Form TA-W	249b.101	3235-0151
Form TA-2	249b.102	3235-0337
Form CA-1	249b.200	3235-0195
Rule 7a-15 thru 7a-37	260.7a-15 thru 260.7a-37	3235-0132
Form T-1	269.1	3235-0110
Form T-2	269.2	3235-0111
Form T-3	269.3	3235-0105
Form T-4	269.4	3235-0107
Form ID	269.7	3235-0328
Form SE	269.8	3235-0327
Form T-6	269.9	3235-0391
Rule 0-1	270.0-1	3235-0531
Rule 2a-7	270.2a-7	3235-0268
Rule 2a19-1	270.2a19-1	3235-0332
Rule 3a-4	270.3a-4	3235-0459
Rule 6c-7	270.6c-7	3235-0276
Rule 6e-2	270.6e-2	3235-0177
Rule 7d-1	270.7d-1	3235-0311
Rule 7d-2	270.7d-2	3235-0527
Section 8(b) of the Investment Company Act of 1940	270.8b-1 thru 270.8b-32	3235-0176
Rule 10f-3	270.10f-3	3235-0226
Rule 11a-2	270.11a-2	3235-0272
Rule 11a-3	270.11a-3	3235-0358
Rule 12b-1	270.12b-1	3235-0212
Rule 17a-7	270.17a-7	3235-0214
Rule 17a-8	270.17a-8	3235-0235

OMB Control Numbers § 200.800

Information collection requirement	17 CFR part or section where identified and described	Current OMB control No.
Rule 17e–1	270.17e–1	3235–0217
Rule 17f–1	270.17f–1	3235–0222
Rule 17f–2	270.17f–2	3235–0223
Rule 17f–4	270.17f–4	3235–0225
Rule 17f–6	270.17f–6	3235–0447
Rule 17f–7	270.17f–7	3235–0529
Rule 17g–1(g)	270.17g–1(g)	3235–0213
Rule 17j–1	270.17j–1	3235–0224
Rule 18f–1	270.18f–1	3235–0211
Rule 18f–3	270.18f–3	3235–0441
Rule 19a–1	270.19a–1	3235–0216
Rule 20a–1	270.20a–1	3235–0158
Rule 22d–1	270.22d–1	3235–0310
Rule 23c–1	270.23c–1	3235–0260
Rule 23c–3	270.23c–3	3235–0422
Rule 27e–1	270.27e–1	3235–0545
Rule 30b2–1	270.30b2–1	3235–0220
Rule 30d–2	270.30d–2	3235–0494
Rule 30e–1	270.30e–1	3235–0025
Rule 30e–3	270.30e–3	3235–0758
Rule 31a–1	270.31a–1	3235–0178
Rule 31a–2	270.31a–2	3235–0179
Rule 32a–4	270.32a–4	3235–0530
Rule 34b–1	270.34b–1	3235–0346
Rule 35d–1	270.35d–1	3235–0548
Form N–5	274.5	3235–0169
Form N–8A	274.10	3235–0175
Form N–2	274.11a–1	3235–0026
Form N–3	274.11b	3235–0316
Form N–4	274.11c	3235–0318
Form N–8B–2	274.12	3235–0186
Form N–6F	274.15	3235–0238
Form 24F–2	274.24	3235–0456
Form N–18F–1	274.51	3235–0211
Form N–54A	274.53	3235–0237
Form N–54C	274.54	3235–0236
Form N–CEN	274.101	3235–0729
Form N–27E–1	274.127e–1	3235–0545
Form N–27F–1	274.127f–1	3235–0546
Form N–PORT	274.150	3235–0730
Form N–17D–1	274.200	3235–0229
Form N–23C–1	274.201	3235–0230
Form N–8F	274.218	3235–0157
Form N–17F–1	274.219	3235–0359
Form N–17F–2	274.220	3235–0360
Form N–23c–3	274.221	3235–0422
Form ID	274.402	3235–0328
Form SE	274.403	3235–0327
Rule 0–2	275.0–2	3235–0240
Rule 203–3	275.203–3	3235–0538
Rule 204–2	275.204–2	3235–0278
Rule 204–3	275.204–3	3235–0047
Rule 206(3)–2	275.206(3)–2	3235–0243
Rule 206(4)–2	275.206(4)–2	3235–0241
Rule 206(4)–3	275.206(4)–3	3235–0242
Rule 206(4)–4	275.206(4)–4	3235–0345
Form ADV	279.1	3235–0049
Schedule I to Form ADV	279.1	3235–0490
Form ADV–W	279.2	3235–0313
Form ADV–H	379.3	3235–0538
Form 4–R	279.4	3235–0240
Form 5–R	279.5	3235–0240
Form 6–R	279.6	3235–0240
Form 7–R	279.7	3235–0240
Form ADV–E	279.8	3235–0361

695

§ 200.800

[67 FR 14634, Mar. 27, 2002, as amended at 70 FR 37611, June 29, 2005; 76 FR 46616, Aug. 3, 2011; 77 FR 18684, Mar. 28, 2012; 80 FR 6902, Feb. 9, 2015; 82 FR 82009, Nov. 18, 2016; 83 FR 29203, June 22, 2018; 84 FR 33629, July 12, 2019; 85 FR 26092, May 1, 2020]

List of CFR Sections Affected

All changes in this volume of the Code of Federal Regulations (CFR) that were made by documents published in the FEDERAL REGISTER since January 1, 2018 are enumerated in the following list. Entries indicate the nature of the changes effected. Page numbers refer to FEDERAL REGISTER pages. The user should consult the entries for chapters, parts and subparts as well as sections for revisions.

For changes to this volume of the CFR prior to this listing, consult the annual edition of the monthly List of CFR Sections Affected (LSA). The LSA is available at *www.govinfo.gov*. For changes to this volume of the CFR prior to 2001, see the "List of CFR Sections Affected, 1949–1963, 1964–1972, 1973–1985, and 1986–2000" published in 11 separate volumes. The "List of CFR Sections Affected 1986–2000" is available at *www.govinfo.gov*.

2018

17 CFR

83 FR Page

Chapter II

242.101 (b)(1) revised 64222
242.105 (b)(1)(i)(C) and (ii) amended 58427
242.201 (a)(1), (2), (4) through (7), and (9) amended 58427
242.204 (g)(2) amended 58427
242.300 (f) introductory text, (2), and (3) revised; (k) added 38911
242.301 (a)(5), (b)(2)(i), (vii), (9)(i), (ii), (10) heading, (i) introductory text, and (ii) amended; (b)(2)(viii) added 38911
242.303 (a) introductory text and (2)(ii) amended; (a)(1)(v) added 38911
242.304 Added 38911
242.600 (b)(52) through (83) redesignated as (b)(56) through (87); (b)(49), (50), (51) redesignated as (b)(51), (52), and (53); (b)(1) through (48) redesignated as (b)(2) through (49); new (b)(1), (50), (54), and (55) added; new (b)(5)(i) amended; new (b)(20) and (49) revised 58427
242.602 (a)(5)(i) and (ii) amended 58427
242.605 (a)(2) preliminary note removed; (a)(2) introductory text added; (a)(2) amended 58427

17 CFR—Continued

83 FR Page

Chapter II—Continued

242.606 (a) and (b) revised 58427
242.611 (c) amended 58429
242.1000 Amended 58429
249 Interpretation 8166
249.210 Form 10 amended 32022
    Heading revised 50223
249.220f Form 20-F amended 40878, 50223, 66461
249.240f Form 40-F amended 40878, 50225
249.306 Form 6-K amended 40879
249.308a Form 10-Q amended 32022
249.310 Form 10-K amended 32022, 40880, 50225
249.311 Form 11-K amended 50225
249.312 Form 10-D amended 50226
249.322 Form 12b-25 amended 64222
249.331 Form N-CSR amended 29208
249.617 Form X-17A-5 amended ... 50226, 50227, 50228, 50230, 50231
249.640 Added 38913
    Form ATS-N amended 56257
249.1100 Form MSD amended 4139, 22193
249.1300 Form MA amended 22193
249.1310 Form MA-I amended 22193
249.2000 Form Funding Portal amended 22192
270 Interpretation 8342
270.8b-1 Revised 40880
270.8b-2 Introductory text revised 40880

697

17 CFR—Continued

83 FR Page

Chapter II—Continued
270.8b-33 Removed 40880
270.24b-4 Added 64222
270.30a-2 (d) removed 40880
270.30e-3 Added 29205
    (a) amended; (i) removed; eff. 1-1-22 29206
274 Interpretation 8342
274.5 Form N-5 amended 50232
274.11A Form N-1A amended 29206, 29207, 31876, 40880, 50232, 62454
274.11a-1 Form N-2 amended 29207, 50233
274.11b Form N-3 amended 29207, 29208, 50233
274.11c Form N-4 amended 29208, 50233
274.11d Form N-6 amended ... 29208, 50234
274.12 Form N-8B-2 amended 50234
274.128 Form N-CSR amended 29208
274.150 Form N-PORT amended 31876
274.402 Form ID amended 11639
275.203(l)-1 (a) introductory text revised 1302
275.203(m)-1 (d)(1) revised 1302

Chapter IV
404.2 (b)(4)(v) Note 1 added 66616
420.3 (a) amended; (h), (i), and (j) revised 52768
449.5 Form G-405 amended 66617, 66618

2019

17 CFR

84 FR Page

Chapter II
241 Authority citation added; interpretive release 47419
242 Compliance notification 18136
242.610T Added; eff. 4-22-19 through 12-29-23 5298
249 Authority citation amended 33630
249 Technical correction 13796
249.103 Form 3 amended 12728
249.104 Form 4 amended 12728
249.105 Form 5 amended 12728
249.208a Form 8-A amended 12728
249.210 Form 10 amended 12728
249.220f Form 20-F amended 12728
249.240f Form 40-F amended 12730
249.308 Form 8-K amended 12730
    Form 10-Q amended 12731
249.310 Form 10-K amended 12731
249.312 Form 10-D amended 12732, 39969
249.331 Form N-CSR amended 12738

17 CFR—Continued

84 FR Page

Chapter II—Continued
249.617—249.641 (Subpart G) Heading revised 68669
249.617 Revised 68669
    Form X-17A-5 amended 68669, 68671, 68721
249.641 Added 33630
255.1 (c) revised 35022
255.2 (r) revised 35022
    Revised 62237
255.3 (e)(5) through (13) redesignated as (e)(6) through (14); (b), (d)(3), (8), (9), new (e)(11), (12), and (14) revised; (d)(10) through (13) and new (e)(5) added 62239
255.4 Revised 62241
255.5 (b) and (c)(1) introductory text revised; (c)(4) added 62243
255.6 (e)(3) revised; (e)(4) and (6) removed; (e)(5) redesignated as new (e)(4) 62244
255.10 (d)(9)(iii) revised 35022
    (c)(7)(ii) and (8)(i)(A) revised 62244
255.11 (a)(6) revised 35022
    Regulation at 84 FR 35022 corrected 38115
    (c) revised 62244
255.12 Second (e)(2)(vi) redesignated as (e)(2)(vii) 62244
255.13 (a), (b)(3), (4), and (c) revised 62244
255.14 (a)(2)(ii)(B) revised 62245
255.20 (a), (b) introductory text, (c), (d), (e) introductory text, and (f)(2) revised; (g), (h), and (i) added 62245
255 Appendix A revised 62246
255 Appendix B removed 62248
255 Appendix Z added; eff. 1-1-20 through 12-31-20 62248
270 Technical correction 13796
    Authority citation amended 57234
270.0-4 Revised 12732
270.6c-11 Added 57234
270.8b-23 Removed 12732
270.8b-24 Removed 12732
270.8b-32 Removed 12732
270.30b1-9 Revised; interim 7987
271 Authority citation added; interpretive release 47426
274 Technical correction 13796
274.5 Form N-5 amended 12733, 39969
274.11A Form N-1A amended 12733, 39969, 57236
274.11a-1 Form N-2 amended 12734, 39969
274.11b Form N-3 amended ... 12735, 39969

List of CFR Sections Affected

17 CFR—Continued

84 FR Page

Chapter II—Continued
274.11c Form N-4 amended.... 12736, 39969
274.11d Form N-6 amended ... 12736, 39970
274.12 Form N-8B-2 amended 12737, 39970, 57237
274.101 Form N-CEN amended 57237
274.128 Form N-CSR amended 12738, 57237
274.150 Revised; Form N-PORT amended; interim 7988
Form N-PORT amended 57237
274.223 Form N-LIQUID amended; interim 7988
275 Authority citation amended 33630
275 Technical correction............... 13796
275.0-6 Revised............................. 12738
275.203-1 (a) revised 33630
275.204-1 (a) and (b) revised; (e) added... 33630
275.204-2 (a)(14)(i) revised 33630
275.204-5 Added 33631
276 Interpretive release 33681, 33689
276 Authority citation added; interpretive release 47427
279 Authority citation revised 33631
279.1 Form ADV amended............. 33631

2020

17 CFR

85 FR Page

Chapter II
241 Table amended........................ 10571
242.403 (b)(1) revised 75146
242.608 (a)(1), (8), and (b)(2) revised; (b)(1)(i) through (iv) added; (b)(3)(i) removed 65497
243.103 (a) revised........................... 33360
249 Technical correction............... 19884
249.220 Form 20-F amended 17242
249.220 Form 20-F amended 22007
249.220f Form 20-F amended 66142
249.240 Form 40-F amended 17242
249.308 Form 8-K amended............. 54072
249.310 Form 10-K amended 17242
249.310 Form 10-K amended 54073
249.330 Form N-CEN amended 83295
249.331 Form N-CSR amended 33394
249.480 Form CB amended 78230
249.1800—249.1801 (Subpart S) Removed 70948
255.6 (f) added............................... 46522
255.10 (c)(1), (3)(i), (8), (10) heading, (i), (11), and (d)(6) revised; (c)(15) through (18), and (d)(11) added....................................... 46523
255.10 Correction: amended........... 60356

17 CFR—Continued

85 FR Page

Chapter II—Continued
255.12 (b)(1)(ii), (4), (c)(1), (d), and (e) revised; (b)(5) added.............. 46527
255.13 (d) added 46528
255.14 (a)(2)(i), (ii)(C), and (c) revised; (a)(2)(iii) through (v), and (3) added 46528
255.20 (a), (d) heading, (1), and (e) introductory text revised 46529
255.20 Correction: instruction amended..................................... 60356
270 Authority citation amended 26101
270 Technical correction............... 28484
270.0-1 (e) introductory text and (2) revised 26101
270.0-5 (d) through (g) added; eff. 6-14-21 57107
270.6c-7 Introductory text revised; authority citation removed 26102
270.6c-8 (b) and (c) revised; authority citation removed 26102
270.6c-11 (c)(4) revised 83291
270.6e-2 Revised 26102
270.6e-3 Redesignated from 270.6e-3 (T) and revised 26105
270.6e-3(T) Redesignated as 270.6e-3 26105
270.8b-1 Amended........................ 26109
270.8b-2 (k) revised 54073
270.8b-11 (e) revised 78230
270.8b-16 (b)(2) and (4) revised; (e) added... 33360
270.11a-2 (c) and (d) revised; authority citation removed 26109
270.12d1-1 (a) revised 74005
270.12d1-2 Removed 74005
270.12d1-4 Added 74005
270.14a-2 Revised 26109
270.18f-4 Added............................. 83291
270.22e-4 (b)(1)(ii)(C) and (iii)(B) revised 83295
270.23c-3 (e) added; eff. 8-1-21 33360
270.24f-2emsp;(a) amended; eff. 8-1-21... 33360
270.26a-1 Revised 26110
270.26a-2 Removed 26110
270.27a-1 Removed 26110
270.27a-2 Removed 26110
270.27a-3 Removed 26110
270.27c-1 Removed 26110
270.27d-2 Removed 26110
270.27e-1 Removed 26110
270.27f-1 Removed 26110
270.27g-1 Removed 26110
270.27h-1 Removed 26110

17 CFR—Continued

85 FR Page

Chapter II—Continued
270.27i-1 Added.............................26110
270.30b1-10 Revised......................83295
274 Technical correction..............28484
274.11 Removed..........................26110
274.11a-1 Form N-2 amended.........33361, 54074, 83295
274.11b Form N-3 revised..............26110
274.11b Form N-3 amended............26204
274.11c Form N-4 revised..............26204
274.11c Correction: Form N-4 amended..................................29614
274.11d Correction: Form N-6 revised PG≤29614
274.11d Form N-6 amended 26309
274.24—Form 24f-2 amended.............33394
274.101 Form N-CEN amended 74007, 83295
274.127e-1 Removed.......................26309
274.127f-1 Removed 26309
274.128 Form N-CSR amended 33394
274.150 Form N-PORT amended..83295
274.223 Revised.............................83296
274.223 Form N-LIQUID amended..83297
274.302 Removed 26309
274.303 Removed 26309
275.203(l)-1 (a) introductory text revised 13741
275.203(m)-1 (d)(1) revised..............13741
276 Table amended........................55157
302 Added 53668

2021

17 CFR

86 FR Page

241 Policy statement 44604
242.105 (b)(1)(i)(C) and (ii) amended..18809
242.201 (a)(1) through (7), (9), (b)(1)(ii), and (3) amended..........18809
242.204 (g)(2) amended 18809
242.600 (b)(2) through (87) redesignated as (b)(3), (4), (6) through (15), (17), (18), (22) through (25), (27) through (58), (60) through (67), (69) through (77), (79) through (81), (84), and (86) through (100); new (b)(2), new (5), new (16), new (19), new (20) new (21), new (26), new (59), new (68), new (78), new (82), new (83), and new (85) added; new (b)(50) and new (70) revised..................18809
242.600 Correction: (b)(7)(i) amended..................................29196

17 CFR—Continued

86 FR Page

242.602 (a)(5)(i) and (ii) amended..18811
242.603 (b) revised..........................18811
242.611 (c) amended 18811
242.614 Added 18811
242.1000 Amended..........................18814
246 Determination........................71810
249 Authority citation amended..17541
249.220 Form 20-F amended.............2131
249.220f Form 20-F amended...3601, 70043
249.220f Form 20-F amended; interim...17541
249.240 Form 40-F amended.............2133
249.240f Form 40-F amended; interim...17541
249.240f Form 40-F amended 70044
249.308 Form 8-K amended.......2133, 3602
249.310 Form 10 amended 2134
249.310 Form 10-K amended....2134, 70044
249.310 Form 10-K amended; interim...17542
249.331 Form N-CSR amended; interim...17542
249.331 Form N-CSR amended 70044
249.446 Introductory text amended..25805
249.446 Form ID amended 25806
249.617 Correction: Form X-17A-5 amended..........................31116, 31117
249.1002 Added 18814
249.1900 Form SCI amended...........18825
249b.400 Form SD amended..............4715
259.602 Form ID amended 25806
269.7 Introductory text amended..25806
269.7 Form ID amended 25806
270.0-8 Revised; eff. 5-31-22.............70262
270.2a-5 Added 807
270.3a-9 Added 3602
270.31a-4 Added 808
274 Authority citation revised 70262
274.5 Form N-5 amended 3603
274.11a-1 Form N-2 amended...2134, 3603, 70262
274.11A Form N-1A 3603
274.11b Form N-3 amended..............3604
274.11c Form N-4 amended..............3604
274.11d Form N-6 amended..............3604
274.12 Form N-8B-2 amended..........3605
274.24 Form 24F-2 amended 70268
274.128 Form N-CSR amended; interim..................................17542, 70044
274.402 Introductory text amended..25806
274.402 Form ID amended 25806

700

List of CFR Sections Affected

17 CFR—Continued
86 FR Page

275.204-2 (a)(7)(iv), (11), (15), and (16) revised; (a)(19) added; eff. 5-4-21 13138
275.205-3 (d)(1)(i), (ii)(A) introductory text, and (e) introductory text revised; (d)(5) added 62475
275.206(4)-1 Revised; eff. 5-4-21 13139
275.206(4)-3 Removed; eff. 5-4-21 13142
279.1 Form ADV amended; eff. 5-4-21 13142

2022

17 CFR
87 FR Page

Chapter II
249.104 Form 4 amended 80431
249.105 Form 5 amended 80431
249.220f Form 20-F amended 35413, 73140, 80431
249.240f Form 40-F amended 35413, 73141
249.306 Form 6-K amended............. 35414
249.306—249.447 (Subpart D) Heading revised; eff. 7-1-24 78808
249.308a Form 10-Q amended........... 80432
249.310 Form 10-K amended 35414, 73141, 80432
249.311 Form 11-K amended 35414
249.325 Form 13F revised 38965
249.326 Added; eff. 7-1-24................ 78808
249.326 Form N-PX revised 78811
249.331 Form N-CSR amended 72857
249.444 Form SE amended 35412
249.480 Form CB amended 35414
249.617 Correction: Form X-17A-5 amended............................. 7934, 7935
269.8 Form SE amended 35412
270.0-2 (a) and (b) amended 38976
270.0-2 Correction: Instruction amended................................... 41060
270.0-4 (a)(1) amended; (b), (d), and (i) removed; (g) removed............ 38976
270.18f-4 (a) amended..................... 22446
270.20a-1 (a) amended..................... 22446
270.22c-1 (b)(1) amended 22446
270.22e-3 (a)(1) amended 22446
270.30a-2 (a) and (b) amended 72847
270.30a-2 Revised 73141
270.30e-1 (d) removed; (b) and (c) redesignated as (c) and new (d); new (b) added; new (c), new (d), and (f)(2)(ii)(F) revised............... 72847

17 CFR—Continued
87 FR Page

Chapter II—Continued
270.30e-3 Revised........................... 72848
270.30b1-4 Amended; eff. 7-1-24 78809
270.31a-2 (a)(5) and (6) amended; (a)(7) added 72850
270.32a-1 Introductory text amended................................... 22446
270.34b-1 Introductory text and (b)(3) revised; (c) added.............. 72850
274 Authority citation revised 73142, 78809
274.5 Form N-5 amended................ 22446
274.5 Form N-PX amended 22447
274.11A Form N-1A amended... 22446, 78809
274.11a-1 Form N-2 amended.......... 78809
274.11b Form N-3 amended 78810
274.11A Amended; Form N-1A amended................................... 72850
274.11a-1 Form N-2 amended.......... 22446
274.11b Form N-3 amended 22447
274.101 Form N-CEN amended 22447
274.128 Form N-CSR amended 72857, 73142
274.129 Heading revised; eff. 7-1-24... 78811
274.129 Form N-PX revised 78811
274.201 Form N-MFP amended....... 22447
274.403 Form SE amended 35412
275.203-1 (d) added 38977
275.204-2 (a)(15)(ii) amended 22447
275.204-3 (b) amended 22447
275.204-5 (e)(1) amended................. 22447
275.206(4)-1 (b)(2)(i) amended 22447
276 Table amended....................... 43197
279.1 Form ADV amended..... 22447, 38977
279.4 Revised 38978
279.4 Form ADV-NR amended 38978

2023

(Regulations published from January 1, 2023, through April 1, 2023)

17 CFR
88 FR Page

Chapter II
260.0-5 (c) revised 12209
275.204-2 (a)(7)(iii) revised; eff. 5-5-23... 13954

701